WORLDS TOGETHER,
WORLDS APART

Volume 1

NORTH POLAR REGION

ARCTIC OCEAN

NORTH AMERICA

ASIA

GREENLAND

North Pole ★
North Magnetic Pole

New Siberian Islands
Laptev Sea
East Siberian Sea
Severnaya Zemlya
Novaya Zemlya
Svalbard
Franz Josef Land
Baffin Bay
ARCTIC CIRCLE
Iceland

ARCTIC

QUEEN ELIZABETH ISLANDS

GREENLAND

Baffin Bay

Iceland

ARCTIC CIRCLE

NORTH AMERICA

ROCKY MOUNTAINS

Hudson Bay

Great Slave Lake
Lake Winnipeg
Lake Superior
Lake Michigan
L. Huron
L. Erie
L. Ontario

Island of Newfoundland
Gulf of St. Lawrence

NORTH PACIFIC OCEAN

Hawaii

TROPIC OF CANCER

GULF OF MEXICO

CENTRAL AMERICA

CARIBBEAN SEA

NORTH ATLANTIC OCEAN

MID-ATLANTIC RIDGE

EQUATOR

Amazon Basin

SOUTH AMERICA

ANDES

PERU-CHILE TRENCH

SOUTH PACIFIC OCEAN

POLYNESIA

Samoa Islands
Tahiti

TROPIC OF CAPRICORN

SOUTH ATLANTIC OCEAN

Falkland Islands

Cape Horn
Drake Passage

ANTARCTIC PENINSULA

WEDDELL SEA

ANTARCTIC CIRCLE

Marie Byrd Land

Ellsworth Land

ANTA

GLOBAL SATELLITE MOSAIC

The beauty and complexity of Earth's landscapes above and below the oceans is revealed with the Global Satellite Mosaic. The mosaic was developed for the National Geographic Society by NASA's Jet Propulsion Laboratory, using more than 500 satellite images from the National Oceanic and Atmospheric Administration. The cloud-free images show Earth in its natural colors as it would be seen from space. One can easily identify the world's major glaciers, deserts, mountain ranges, and rain forests. For example, follow the green ribbon of lush vegetation along the Nile into the stark, dry Sahara. The mountain ranges seem to rise off the map thanks to digital elevation databases from the Department of Defense. The deepest areas of the ocean realm are colored dark blue in contrast to the light blue areas highlighting continental shelves, submarine ridges, and underwater mountains.

BIOSPHERE

Thousands of satellite images are combined to show a picture of biological productivity. In the oceans, red, yellow, and green indicate waters rich in phytoplankton. On land, green areas show high-potential plant productivity. Tan areas suffer from productivity limitations due to aridity and temperature.

THE W
SATEL

OCEAN

20° 40° 60° 80° 100° 120° 140° 160° 180°

EUROPE

ASIA

SIBERIA

Arctic Circle

Franz Josef Land

North Land

BARENTS
SEA

Aral
Sea

Black Sea

Lake
Baikal

Kamchatka
Peninsula

AFRICA

ARABIAN
PENINSULA

INDIA

Plateau of Tibet

Arabian
Sea

BAY
OF
BENGAL

SOUTH
CHINA
SEA

Tropic of Cancer

PHILIPPINE SEA

NORTH

PACIFIC

OCEAN

MICRONESIA

Congo
Basin

Lake
Tanganyika

Lake
Malawi

INDONESIA

New Guinea

EQUATOR

0°

MELANESIA

Madagascar

AUSTRALIA

INDIAN

OCEAN

Kalahari
Desert

SOUTHWEST INDIAN RIDGE

Cape of Good Hope

SOUTHEAST INDIAN RIDGE

KERGUELEN
PLATEAU

Coral
Sea

Fiji
Islands

New Caledonia

TROPIC OF CAPRICORN

SOUTH
PACIFIC
OCEAN

20°

20°

Bass Strait

Tasmania

TASMAN
SEA

North Island

NEW
ZEALAND

South Island

40°

Wilkes
Land

TICA

20° 40° 60° 80° 100° 120° 140° 160° 180°

SOUTH POLAR
REGION

60°

Weddell
Sea

Queen Maud Land

Antarctic
Peninsula

ANTARCTICA

WEST

South Pole

EAST

Bellingshausen
Sea

ANTARCTICA

ANTARCTICA

Byrd Land

Ross
Ice
Shelf

Wilkes Land

Ross
Sea

180°

South
Magnetic Pole

ANTARCTIC CIRCLE

150°

120°

90°

60°

30°

0°

THE NEED FOR SATELLITES

The Global Satellite Mosaic along with the biosphere image (lower left) and the temperature image (lower right) provides an integrated view of our world. The way high elevations of the Himalaya and Tibet show up as a cold area (blue, temperature image) and as a plant-poor area (tan, biosphere image). Temperature, plant life, and landscape are interrelated. The need to understand the forces shaping environmental change has led to a space race among various countries. In 1997 alone some 85 rockets launched more than 140 satellites—mostly from China, Europe, Japan, Russia, and the United States. Some satellites provide vital communication links propelling economic development; other satellites supply data on patterns and trends associated with agricultural productivity, pollution monitoring, weather forecasting, and many other environmental concerns.

WINKEL TRIPEL PROJECTION, CENTRAL MERIDIAN 0°
SCALE 1:28,931,000
1 CENTIMETER = 389 KILOMETERS 1 INCH = 614 MILES AT THE EQUATOR

STATUTE MILES

ORLD
MAP

**SURFACE
TEMPERATURE**

Reddish colors vividly show average high temperatures on the two largest continents, Africa and Asia, from the Sahara to Central Asia. Latitude, mountains, and oceans influence land temperatures.

Political World

NORTH
POLAR
REGION

WINKEL TRIPEL PROJECTION, CENTRAL MERIDIAN 0°

KILOMETERS
0   500   1000 1500 2000 2500
0   500   1000   1500   2000   2500
STATUTE MILES

International boundaries and disputed territories, where scale permits, reflect de facto status at the time of publication.

SOUTH POLAR REGION

Azimuthal Equidistant Projection
⊕ Research station

FIFTH EDITION

WORLDS TOGETHER,

WORLDS APART

Volume 1: Beginnings through the Fifteenth Century

Robert **Tignor** · Jeremy **Adelman** · Peter **Brown** · Benjamin **Elman**

Xinru **Liu** · Holly **Pittman** · Brent **Shaw**

W. W. Norton & Company, Inc.

New York · London

W. W. Norton & Company has been independent since its founding in 1923, when William Warder Norton and Mary D. Herter Norton first published lectures delivered at the People's Institute, the adult education division of New York City's Cooper Union. The firm soon expanded its program beyond the Institute, publishing books by celebrated academics from America and abroad. By midcentury, the two major pillars of Norton's publishing program—trade books and college texts—were firmly established. In the 1950s, the Norton family transferred control of the company to its employees, and today—with a staff of four hundred and a comparable number of trade, college, and professional titles published each year— W. W. Norton & Company stands as the largest and oldest publishing house owned wholly by its employees.

Editor: Jon Durbin
Associate Editor: Scott Sugarmann
Project Editor: Jennifer Barnhardt
Editorial Assistant: Kelly Rafey
Managing Editor, College: Marian Johnson
Managing Editor, College Digital Media: Kim Yi
Production Manager: Andy Ensor
Media Editor: Laura Wilk
Associate Media Editor: Michelle Smith
Media Project Editor: Rachel Mayer
Assistant Media Editor: Chris Hillyer
Marketing Manager, History: Sarah England Bartley
Design Director: Rubina Yeh
Book Design: Jillian Burr
Photo Editor: Travis Carr
Permissions Manager: Megan Schindel
Permissions Associate: Elizabeth Trammell
Composition: Cenveo® Publisher Services
Illustrations: Mapping Specialists, Ltd.
Manufacturing: Quad Graphics—Versailles

Permission to use copyrighted material is included on page C-1.

The Library of Congress has cataloged the one-volume edition as follows:

Names: Tignor, Robert L., author.
Title: Worlds together, worlds apart : a history of the world from the
    beginnings of humankind to the present / Robert Tignor ... [and eleven
    others].
Description: Fifth edition. | New York : W. W. Norton & Company, [2018] |
    Includes bibliographical references and index.
Identifiers: LCCN 2017032085 | **ISBN 9780393624786 (hardcover)**
Subject: LCSH: World history—Textbooks. | World
    history—Examinations—Study guides. | Advanced placement programs
    (Education)—Examinations—Study guides
Classification: LCC D21 .T53 2018 | DDC 909—dc23 LC record available at https://lccn.loc.gov/2017032085

ISBN this edition: 978-0-393-62480-9 (pbk.)

W. W. Norton & Company, Inc., 500 Fifth Avenue, New York, NY 10110 0017
wwnorton.com

W. W. Norton & Company Ltd., 15 Carlisle Street, London W1D 3BS
1 2 3 4 5 6 7 8 9 0

CONTENTS IN BRIEF

CONTENTS

Chapter 1

BECOMING HUMAN 2

Chapter 2

RIVERS, CITIES, AND FIRST STATES, 3500–2000 BCE 42

Chapter 3

NOMADS, CHARIOTS, TERRITORIAL STATES, AND MICROSOCIETIES, 2000–1200 BCE **82**

Chapter 4

FIRST EMPIRES AND COMMON CULTURES IN AFRO-EURASIA, 1250–325 BCE 120

Pressures Leading to Upheaval and the Rise of Early Empires 122

Climate Change and Migrations 122

New Technologies 122

Administrative Innovations 123

Chapter 5
WORLDS TURNED INSIDE OUT, 1000–350 BCE 158

Chapter 6

SHRINKING THE AFRO-EURASIAN WORLD, 350 BCE–250 CE **198**

Chapter 8
THE RISE OF UNIVERSAL RELIGIONS, 300–600 CE 276

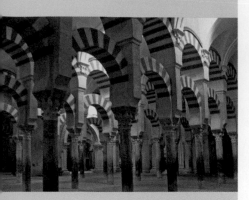

Chapter 9
NEW EMPIRES AND COMMON CULTURES, 600–1000 CE **316**

Chapter 10
BECOMING "THE WORLD," 1000–1300 CE **356**

Chapter 11

CRISES AND RECOVERY IN AFRO-EURASIA, 1300–1500   **402**

CURRENT TRENDS IN WORLD HISTORY

ANALYZING GLOBAL DEVELOPMENTS

PRIMARY SOURCES

MAPS

PREFACE

Worlds Together, Worlds Apart has set the standard for four editions for those who want to teach a globally integrated world history survey course. Just as the dynamic field of world history evolves, so, too, has *Worlds Together, Worlds Apart*. Building on the success of the first four editions, the Fifth Edition continues to offer a highly coherent, cutting-edge survey of the field built around world history stories of significance that make it possible for students to readily make connections and comparisons across time and place and make the teaching of the course more manageable for instructors (for example, the building of the Silk Road, the spread of the Black Death across Afro-Eurasia, the impact of New World silver on global trade, and alternative ways to organize societies during the rise of nineteenth-century capitalism). The Fifth Edition is the most accessible to date. Many of the chapters were substantially reorganized and streamlined to place greater emphasis on the main chapter ideas and amplify comparisons and connections—the book's greatest strength. The new edition will be the most relevant yet for students. They will find increased coverage on numerous topics, but in particular a topic students care a lot about: the environment's role in world history. The Fifth Edition pays considerable attention to the role of climate in producing radical changes in the lives of humans. For example, a long-term warming of the globe facilitated the domestication of plants and animals and led to an agricultural revolution and the emergence of settled societies. In the seventeenth century, the dramatic drop in global temperatures, now known as the Little Ice Age, produced political and social havoc and led to civil wars, population decline, and regime change all around the globe. These are the new focuses of Chapters 1 and 13. Indeed, all chapters have been substantially revised, not because they were inadequate when originally written, but because the recent studies of comparative and global historians have transformed our understanding of the history of the world.

The Fifth Edition is also the most interactive to date. Lead media author Alan Karras (University of California, Berkeley) has brought together an outstanding media team to develop the comprehensive ancillary package for the Fifth Edition, substantially increasing the learning and teaching support available to students and instructors.

- New **InQuizitive**, Norton's adaptive quizzing platform, uses interactive questions and guided feedback to support students' understanding of each chapter's focus questions.
- New **History Skills Tutorials** combine video and interactive activities to provide students with a framework for analyzing a variety of sources.
- New **Primary Source Exercises** in the Coursepack provide ready-made quizzes to assess students' ability to analyze images and documents tied to each chapter.
- New **Story Maps** break complex maps into a sequence of five annotated screens that focus on the story behind the geography.

Since work began on *Worlds Together, Worlds Apart*, world history has gained even more prominence in college classrooms and historical studies. Courses in the history of the world now abound, often replacing the standard surveys of European history and western civilization overviews. Graduate history students receive training in world history, and journals routinely publish studies in this field. A new generation of textbooks was needed to help students and instructors make sense of this vast, complex, and rapidly evolving field. We believe that *Worlds Together, Worlds Apart* remains the most current, cutting-edge, engaging, readable, interactive, and useful text available for all students of world history. We also believe that this text, one that has advanced the teaching of this field, could only have grown out of the highly collaborative effort of a team of scholars and teachers rather than the more typical single- or two-author efforts. Indeed, the idea to build each chapter around stories of world history significance and the execution of this model grew out of our monthly team meetings and our joint writing efforts during the development stage. As a team-driven text, *Worlds Together, Worlds Apart* also has the advantage of area experts to make sure the material is presented accurately, which is always a challenge for the single- or two-author texts, especially in world history. Finally, our book reads with a single voice, due to the extraordinary efforts of our general editor and leader, Robert Tignor, who with every edition makes the final major sweep through the text to make sure that the voice, style, and level of detail are consistent throughout. Building on these distinctive strengths, we have worked hard and thoughtfully to make the Fifth Edition of *Worlds Together, Worlds Apart* the best edition so far. While there are many exciting additions to the main text and support package, we have made every effort to remain true to our original vision.

OUR GUIDING PRINCIPLES

Five principles inform this book, guiding its framework and the organization of its individual chapters. The first is that **world history is global history**. There are many fine histories of the individual regions of the world, which we have endeavored to make good use of. But unlike the authors of many other so-called world histories, we have chosen not to deal with the great regions and cultures of the world as separate units, reserving individual chapters to East Asia, South Asia, Southwest Asia, Europe, Africa, and the Americas. Our goal is to place each of these regions in its largest geographical context. Accordingly, we have written chapters that are truly global in that most major regions of the world are discussed in each one. We achieved these globally integrated chapters by building each around a significant world history story or theme. There are a number of wonderful examples throughout the book: the peopling of the earth (Chapter 1), the building of the Silk Road (Chapter 6), the rise of universal religions (Chapters 8 and 9), the Black Death (Chapter 11), the Little Ice Age and its far-reaching impact on political systems globally as well as the effects of New World silver on the economies of the world (Chapter 13), alternative visions to nineteenth-century capitalism (Chapter 15), the rise of nation-states and empires (Chapter 16), and so on. It would be misleading, of course, to say that the context is the world, because none of these regions, even the most highly developed commercially, enjoyed

commercial or cultural contact with peoples all over the globe before Columbus's voyage to the Americas and later expeditions of the sixteenth century. But the peoples living in the Afro-Eurasian landmass, probably the single most important building block for our study, were deeply influenced by one another, as were the more scattered peoples living in the Americas and in Africa below the Sahara. Products, ideas, and persons traveled widely across the large land units of Eurasia, Africa, and the Americas. Indeed, Afro-Eurasia was not divided or thought of as divided into separate landmasses until recent times. It is in this sense that our world history is global.

The second principle informing this work is **the importance of chronology in framing world history**. Rather than telling the story of world history by analyzing separate geographical areas, we have elected to frame the chapters around significant world history themes and periods that transcended regional and cultural boundaries—moments or periods of meaningful change in the way that human beings organized their lives. Some of these changes were dramatic and affected many people. Environments changed; the earth became drier and warmer; humans learned to domesticate plants and animals; technological innovations in warfare, political organization, and commercial activities occurred; diseases crossed political and cultural borders, as did dramatic changes in the world's climate; and new religious and cultural beliefs spread far and wide. These changes swept across large landmasses, paying scant heed to preexisting cultural and geographical unity. They affected peoples living in widely dispersed societies, and they often led to radically varied cultural responses in different regions of the world. In other cases, changes occurred in only one locality while other places retained their traditions or took alternative routes. Chronology helps us understand the ways in which the world has, and has not, shared a common history.

The third principle is **historical and geographical balance**. Ours is not a history focused on the rise of the west. We seek to pay attention to the global histories of all peoples and not to privilege those developments that led directly into European history as if the rest of the history of the world was but a prelude to the rise of the West. We deal with peoples living outside Europe on their own terms and try to see world history from their perspective. Even more significantly, while we describe societies that obviously influenced Europe's historical development, we do so in a context very different from that which western historians have stressed. Rather than simply viewing these cultures in terms of their role in western development, we seek to understand them in their own right and to illuminate the ways they influenced other parts of the world. From our perspective, it is historically inaccurate to annex Mesopotamia and Egypt to the West because these territories lay well outside Europe and had a large influence on Africa, South Asia, and East Asia as well as on Europe. Indeed, our presentation of Europe in the period leading up to and including the founding of the Roman Empire is different from many of the standard treatments. The Europeans we describe are rather rough, wild-living, warring peoples living on the fringes of the settled parts of the world and looked down on by more politically stable communities. They hardly seem to be made of the stuff that will catapult Europeans to world leadership a millennium later—indeed, they were very different people from those who, as the result of myriad intervening and contingent events, founded the nineteenth- and twentieth-century empires whose ruins are still all around us.

Our fourth principle is **an emphasis on connections and what we call disconnections across societal and cultural boundaries**. World history is not the history of separate regions of the world at different periods of time. It is the history of the connections among peoples living often at great distances from one another, and it is also the history of the resistance of peoples living within and outside societies to connections that threatened to put them in subordinate positions or to rob them of their independence.

A stress on connections inevitably foregrounds those elements within societies that promoted long-distance ties. Merchants are important, as are military men and political potentates seeking to expand their polities. So are scholars and religious leaders, particularly those who believed that they had universalistic messages with which to convert others to their visions. Perhaps most important of all in premodern world history, certainly the most understudied, are the nomadic pastoral peoples, who were often the agents for the transmission of products, peoples, and ideas across long and harsh distances. They exploded onto the scene of settled societies at critical junctures, erasing old cultural and geographical barriers and producing new unities, as the Arabs did in the seventh century CE and the Mongols did in the thirteenth century. *Worlds Together, Worlds Apart* is not intended to convey the message that the history of the world is a story of increasing integration. What for one ruling group brought benefits in the form of increased workforces, material prosperity, and political stability often meant enslavement, political subordination, and loss of territory for other groups. The historian's task, then, is not only to represent the different experiences of increased connectedness, describing worlds that came together, but also to be attentive to the opposite trends, describing peoples and communities that remained apart.

The fifth and final principle is that **world history is a narrative of big themes and high-level comparisons**. *Worlds Together, Worlds Apart* is not a book of record. Indeed, in a work that tells the story of humankind from the beginnings of history to the present, the notion that no event or individual worthy of attention would be excluded is the height of folly. We have sought to offer clear themes and interpretations in order to synthesize the vast body of data that often overwhelms histories of the world. Our aspiration is to identify the main historical forces that have moved history, to highlight those monumental innovations that have changed the way humans lived, and to describe the creation and evolution of those bedrock institutions, many of which, of course, endure. In this regard, self-conscious cross-cultural comparisons of developments, institutions, and even founding figures receive attention to make students aware that some common institutions, such as slavery, did not have the same features in every society. But conversely, the seemingly diverse terms that were used, say, to describe learned and religious men in different parts of the world—monks in Europe, *ulama* in Islam, Brahmans in India, and scholar-gentries in China—often meant much the same thing in very different settings. We have constructed *Worlds Together, Worlds Apart* around big ideas, stories, and themes rather than filling the book with names and dates that encourage students only to memorize rather than understand world history concepts.

OUR MAJOR THEMES

The primary organizing framework of *Worlds Together, Worlds Apart*—one that runs through the chapters and connects the different parts of the narrative—is the theme of **interconnection and divergence**. While describing movements that facilitated global connectedness, this book also shows how different regions developed their own ways of handling or resisting connections and change. Throughout history, different regions and different population groups often stood apart from the rest of the world until touched by traders or explorers or missionaries or soldiers. Some of these regions welcomed global connections; others sought to change the nature of their connections with the outside world; and yet others resisted efforts to bring them into the larger world. All, however, were somehow affected by their experience of connection. Thus, the history of the world is not simply one of increasing globalization, in which all societies eventually join a common path to the present. Rather, it is a history of the ways in which, as people became linked, their experience of these global connections diverged.

Besides the central theme of interconnection and divergence, other themes also stand out in *Worlds Together, Worlds Apart*. First, the book discusses **how the recurring efforts of people to cross religious, political, and cultural borders brought the world together**. Merchants and educated men and women traded goods and ideas. Whole communities, in addition to select groups, moved to safer or more promising environments. **The transregional crossings of ideas, goods, and peoples produced transformations and conflicts**—a second important theme. Finally, the movement of ideas, peoples, products, climates, and germs over long distances upset the balance of power across the world and within individual societies. Such movements changed the relationship of different population groups with other peoples and areas of the world and led over time to dramatic shifts in the ascendancy of regions. **Changes in power arrangements within and between regions explain which parts of the world and regional groups benefited from integration and which resisted it.** These three themes (exchange and migration, conflict and resistance, and alterations in the balance of power) weave themselves through every chapter of this work. While we highlight major themes throughout, we tell the stories of the people caught in these currents of exchange, conflict, and changing power relations, paying particular attention to the role that gender and the environment play in shaping the evolution of societies. The history of the world is not a single, sweeping narrative. On the contrary, the last 5,000 years have produced multiple histories, moving along many paths and trajectories. Sometimes these histories merge, intertwining themselves in substantial ways. Sometimes they disentangle themselves and simply stand apart. Much of the time, however, they are simultaneously together and apart. In place of a single narrative, the usual one being the rise of the west, this book maps the many forks in the road that confronted the world's societies at different times and the surprising turns and unintended consequences that marked the choices that peoples and societies made, including the unanticipated and dramatic rise of the west in the nineteenth century. Formulated in this way, world history is the unfolding of many possible histories, and readers of this book should come away with a reinforced sense of the unpredictability of the past, the instability of the present, and the uncertainty of the future.

OVERVIEW OF VOLUME ONE

Volume One of *Worlds Together, Worlds Apart* deals with the period from the beginnings of human history through the Mongol invasions of the thirteenth century and the spread of the Black Death across Afro-Eurasia. It is divided into eleven chapters, each of which marks a distinct historical period. Hence, each chapter has an overarching theme or small set of themes that holds otherwise highly diverse material together.

Chapter 1, "Becoming Human," presents biological and cultural perspectives on the way that early hominins became truly human. This chapter incorporates much new research, largely the result of new techniques and methods employed by climatologists, biologists specializing in DNA analysis, linguists, and paleoanthropologists in the tradition of Mary and Louis Leakey. These scientists have transformed our understanding of the evolution of human beings. So much of this work is now being incorporated into the history profession and history courses that it has acquired its own name, big history. We believe that this chapter is important in establishing the global context of world history. We believe, too, that our chapter is unique in its focus on how hominins became humans—how early hominins became bipedal and how they developed complex cognitive processes such as language and artistic abilities. We have incorporated a new understanding of evolution, which now appears to have taken place not in a steady and gradual way as was once thought, but in punctuated bursts, often in response to major climate and environmental challenges. In addition, our findings about the evolution of hominins from *Austrolopithecus* to *Homo sapiens* are based on more precise information than was available in earlier editions. Research indicates that *Homo sapiens* originated in Africa, probably no more than 200,000 years ago. These early men and women walked out of the African landmass sometime between 100,000 and 50,000 years ago, gradually populating all regions of the world. What is significant in this story is that the different population groups around the world, the so-called races of humankind, have only recently broken off from one another. Also in this chapter, we emphasize the role of climate in human evolution; indeed, the first group of *Homo sapiens* nearly went extinct because of severe freezing temperatures, produced by an eruption of vast quantities of lava into the atmosphere. This critical phase in human evolution was followed almost immediately by a strong warming trend that occurred 10,000 years ago and that has remained with us ever since, despite some significant drops in global temperatures. This warming trend led humans to domesticate plants and animals and to found the first village settlements, beginning in Southwest Asia.

Chapter 2, "Rivers, Cities, and First States, 3500–2000 BCE," covers the period during which five of the great river basins experienced extraordinary breakthroughs in human activity. On the floodplains of the Tigris and Euphrates in Mesopotamia, the Nile in Egypt, the Indus Valley in modern-day northern India and Pakistan, and the Yellow and Yangzi Rivers in China, men and women mastered annual floods and became expert in seeding and cultivating foodstuffs. In these areas, populations became dense. River-basin cultures had much in common. They had highly developed hierarchical political, social, and cultural systems, priestly and bureaucratic classes, and organized religious and cultural systems. But they also differed greatly, and these differences were passed from generation to generation. The development of these major complex societies certainly is a turning point in world history. We include in this chapter an expanded discussion on the rise of city-states and provide a greater emphasis on the political aspects leading to the emergence of city-states.

Extensive climatic and technological changes serve as major turning points for **Chapter 3, "Nomads, Chariots, Territorial States, and Microsocieties, 2000–1200 BCE."** Drought, environmental degradation, and political instability brought the first river-basin societies to a crashing end around 2000 BCE. When aridity forced tribal and nomadic peoples living on the fringes of the settled populations to move closer to settled areas, they brought with them an insurmountable military advantage. They had become adept at yoking horses to war chariots and hence were in a position to subjugate and later intermarry with the peoples in the settled polities in the river basins. Around 2000 BCE, these peoples established new territorial kingdoms in Mesopotamia, Egypt, the Indus Valley, and China, which gave way a millennium later (1000 BCE) to even larger and more militarily and politically powerful states. The section on China features a major rewriting and reorganization of the Shang territorial states in East Asia with a new section on Shang writing. In the Americas, the Mediterranean, sub-Saharan Africa, and the Pacific worlds, microsocieties arose as an alternative form of a political system in which peoples lived in much smaller-scale societies that showcased their own unique and compelling features.

Chapter 4, "First Empires and Common Cultures in Afro-Eurasia, 1250–325 BCE," describes the different ways in which larger-scale societies grew and became unified. In the case of the world's first empires, the neo-Assyrian and Persian, political power was the main unifying element. Both states established different models that future empires would emulate. The Assyrians used brute force to intimidate and subjugate different groups within their societies and neighboring states. The Persians followed a pattern that relied less on coercion and more on tributary relationships, while reveling in cultural diversity.

The Zhou state in China offered yet a third way of political unity, basing its rule on the doctrine of the mandate of heaven, which legitimated its rulers' succession as long as they were able to maintain stability and order. Vedic society in South Asia offers a dramatically different model in which religion and culture rather than centralizing monarchies were the main unifying forces. Religion moves to the forefront of the narrative in other ways in this chapter. The birth of monotheism occurred in the Zoroastrian and Hebrew faiths and the beginnings of Buddhism. All three religions endure today.

The last millennium before the Common Era witnessed some of the most monumental developments in human history. In the six and a half centuries discussed in **Chapter 5, "Worlds Turned Inside Out, 1000–350 BCE,"** teachers and thinkers, rather than kings, priests, and warriors, came to the fore. Men like Confucius, the Buddha, Plato, and Aristotle, to name only the best known of this brilliant group, offered new insights into the natural world and provided new guidelines for how to govern justly and live ethically. Drawing on the work of sociologist Karl Jaspars, we call this era the Axial Age, during which Greek, Chinese, and South Asian thinkers elaborated political, religious, and philosophical ideas that informed the societies in which they lived and that have been central to the lives of these societies ever since. In this era, small scale societies, benefiting from more intimate relationships, took the place of the first great empires, now in decline. These highly individualistic cultures developed new strategies for political organization, even experimenting with a democratic polity. In Africa, the Bantu peoples spread across sub-Saharan Africa, and the Sudanic peoples of Meroe created a society that blended Egyptian and sub-Saharan influences. These were all dynamic hybrid societies building on existing knowledge. Equally dramatic transformations occurred in the Americas, where the Olmec and Chavin peoples were creating hierarchical societies of the like never before seen in their part of the world.

Chapter 6, "Shrinking the Afro-Eurasian World, 350 BCE–250 CE," describes three major forces that simultaneously integrated large segments of the Afro-Eurasian landmass culturally and economically. First, Alexander and his armies changed the political and cultural landscape of North Africa and Southwest and South Asia. Culturally, Alexander spread Hellenism through North Africa and Southwest and central Asia, making it the first cultural system to achieve a transregional scope. Second, it was in the post-Alexander world that long-distance trade was intensified and stabilized. For the first time, a trading network, known as the Silk Road, stretching from Palmyra in the west to central Asia in the east, came into being. This chapter incorporates new research on the origins of the Silk Road and its Afro-Eurasian political, commercial, and cultural importance. Despite the fact that the Silk Road was actually made up of many different roads and was not always accessible, and despite the fact that trade took place mainly over short distances, its reputation was well known to merchants, military adventurers, travelers, religious leaders, and political elites. Buddhism was the first religion to seize on the Silk Road's more formal existence as its followers moved quickly with the support of the Mauryan Empire to spread their ideas into central Asia. Finally, we witness the growth of a "silk road of the seas" as new technologies and bigger ships allowed for a dramatic expansion in maritime trade from South Asia all the way to Egypt and East Africa.

Chapter 7, "Han Dynasty China and Imperial Rome, 300 BCE–300 CE," builds on our comparison of the Neo-Assyrian and Persian Empires in Chapter 4 by comparing in great detail the Han dynasty and Roman Empire, the two political, economic, and cultural powerhouses that dominated much of the Afro-Eurasian landmass from 200 BCE to 200 CE. Both the Han dynasty and the Roman Empire ruled effectively in their own way, providing an instructive comparative case study. Both left their imprint on Afro-Eurasia; rulers for centuries afterward tried to revive these glorious imperial systems and use them as models of greatness. Only the Chinese were successful in restoring imperial rule and did so for more than two millennia. European efforts to re-create the Roman Empire, at least in western Europe, failed. This chapter also discusses the effect of state sponsorship on religion, as Christianity came into existence in the context of the late Roman Empire and Buddhism was introduced to China during the decline of the Han.

Out of the crumbling Roman Empire new political systems and a new religion emerged, the major topic of **Chapter 8, "The Rise of Universal Religions, 300–600 CE."** The Byzantine Empire, claiming to be the successor state to the Roman Empire, embraced Christianity as its state religion. The Tang rulers patronized Buddhism to such a degree that Confucian statesmen feared it had become the state religion. This chapter has new information on the Sogdians, a pastoral peoples who inhabited central Asia and were vital in spreading Buddhism and supporting Silk Road trade. Both Buddhism and Christianity enjoyed spectacular success in the politically fragmented post-Han era in China and in the feudal world of western Europe. These dynamic religions represent a decisive transformation in world history. Christianity enjoyed its eventual successes through state sponsorship via the Roman and Byzantine Empires and by providing spiritual comfort and hope during the chaotic years of Rome's decline. Buddhism grew through imperial sponsorship and significant changes to its fundamental beliefs, when adherents to the faith deified Buddha and created notions of an afterlife. In Africa, a wide range of significant developments and myriad cultural practices existed; yet large common cultures also arose. The Bantu peoples spread throughout the southern half of the landmass, spoke closely related languages, and developed similar political institutions based on the prestige of individuals of high achievement. In the Americas, the Olmecs established their own form of the city-state, while the Maya owed their success to a decentralized common culture built around a strong religious belief system and a series of spiritual centers.

In **Chapter 9, "New Empires and Common Cultures, 600–1000 CE,"** we see another world religion, Islam, explode with world-changing consequences in a relatively remote corner of the Arabian Peninsula. The rise of Islam provides a contrast to the way universalizing religions and political empires interacted. Islam and empire arose in a fashion quite different from Christianity and the Roman Empire. Christianity took over an already existing empire—the Roman—after suffering persecution at its hands for several centuries. In contrast, Islam created an empire almost at the moment of its emergence. There is much new scholarship on early Islam, the life of Muhammad, and the creation of the Quran, based mainly on the writings of non-Muslim observers and scholars. Although these texts are often critical of Muhammad and early Islam, they must be used (albeit very carefully) because of the dearth of information on the beginnings of Islam found in the few Muslim and Arabic sources that remain to us. We have added this important perspective to our discussion of the birth of Islam. By the time the Abbasid Empire came into being in the middle of the eighth century, Islamic armies, political leaders, and clerics exercised power over much of the Afro-Eurasian landmass from southern Spain, across North Africa, all the way to central Asia. The Tang Empire in China, however, served as a counterweight to Islam's power both politically and intellectually. Confucianism enjoyed a spectacular recovery in this period. With the Tang rulers, Confucianism slowed the spread of Buddhism and further reinforced China's development along different, more secular pathways. Japan and Korea also enter world history at this time as tributary states to Tang China and as hybrid cultures that mixed Chinese customs and practices with their own. The Christian world split in this period between the western Latin church and the eastern Byzantine church. Both branches of Christianity played a role in unifying societies, especially in western Europe, which lacked strong political rule at a time when all of Europe experienced a profound and disabling drop in temperature.

In the three centuries from 1000 to 1300 (**Chapter 10, "Becoming 'The World,' 1000–1300 CE"**), Afro-Eurasia experienced an unprecedented rise in prosperity and population that even spread into West and East Africa. Just as importantly, the world in this period divided into regional zones that are recognizable today. And trade grew rapidly.

A view of the major trading cities of this time demonstrates how commerce transformed cultures. Sub-Saharan Africa also underwent intense regional integration via the spread of the Mande-speaking peoples and the Mali Empire. The Americas witnessed their first empire in the form of the Chimu peoples in the Andes. This chapter ends with the Mongol conquests of the twelfth and thirteenth centuries, which brought massive destruction. The Mongol Empire, however, once in place, promoted long-distance commerce, scholarly exchange, and travel on an unprecedented scale. The Mongols brought Eurasia, North Africa, and many parts of sub-Saharan Africa into a new connectedness. The Mongol story also underscores the important role that nomads played throughout the history of the early world. Just as much of Europe had suffered through a drop in temperature in the ninth and tenth centuries, as described in Chapter 9, now a radical fall in temperature in combination with drought troubled the eastern Mediterranean and the Islamic world. Here the result was a steep decline in standards of living, leading to riots and political fragmentation. Even so, Islamic science flourished, and China became the most urbanized part of the world.

The Black Death brought Afro-Eurasia's prosperity and population growth to a catastrophic end, as discussed in **Chapter 11, "Crises and Recovery in Afro-Eurasia, 1300–1500."** The death and destruction of the fourteenth century saw traditional institutions give way, forcing peoples to rebuild their cultures. The political systems that came into being at this time and the intense religious experimentation that took place effected a sharp break with the past. The bubonic plague wiped out as much as two-thirds of the population in many of the densely settled locations of Afro-Eurasia. Societies once brought to their knees by the Mongols' depredations now suffered grievously from biological pathogens. In the face of one of humanity's grimmest periods, peoples and societies demonstrated tremendous resilience as they looked for new ways to rebuild their communities, some turning inward and others seeking inspiration, conquests, and riches elsewhere.

New dynasties emerged all across Afro-Eurasia. The Ming replaced the Mongol Yuan dynasty in China. A small band of Muslim warriors in Anatolia became sophisticated military tacticians and administrators and created an empire that would last as the Ottoman Empire until the end of World War I. New Muslim dynasts also took over South Asia (the Mughals) and the Iranian plateau (Safavids). Nor was Europe left behind, for here, too, new dynamic rulers came to the thrones in England, France, Spain, and Portugal, ready to project their power overseas. Volume One concludes on the eve of the Columbian Exchange, the moment when "old" worlds discovered "new" ones and a vast series of global interconnections and divergences commenced.

OVERVIEW OF VOLUME TWO

The organizational structure for Volume Two reaffirms the commitment to write a decentered, global history of the world. Christopher Columbus is not the starting point, as he is in so many modern world histories. Rather, we begin in the eleventh and twelfth centuries with two major developments in world history: the Mongols and the Black Death. The first, set forth in **Chapter 10, "Becoming 'The World,' 1000–1300 CE,"** describes a world that was divided for the first time into regions that are recognizable today. This world experienced rapid population growth, as is shown by a simple look at the major trading cities from Asia in the east to the Mediterranean in the west. Yet nomadic peoples remained a force, as revealed in the Mongol invasions of Afro-Eurasia.

Chapter 11, "Crises and Recovery in Afro-Eurasia, 1300–1500," describes how the Mongol warriors, through their conquests and the integration of the Afro-Eurasian world, unwittingly spread the bubonic plague, which brought death and depopulation to much of Afro-Eurasia. Both these stories set the stage for the modern world and are clear-cut turning points in world history. The primary agents of world connection described in this chapter were dynasts, soldiers, clerics, merchants, and adventurers who rebuilt the societies that disease and political collapse had destroyed.

The Mongols joined the two hemispheres, as we describe in **Chapter 12, "Contact, Commerce, and Colonization, 1450–1600,"** bringing the peoples and products of the Western Hemisphere into contact and conflict with Eurasia and Africa. It is the collision between the Eastern and Western Hemispheres that sets in motion modern world history and marks a distinct divide or turning point between the premodern and the modern. Here, too, disease and increasing trade linkages were vital. Unprepared for the advanced military technology and the disease pool of European and African peoples, the Amerindian population experienced a population decline even more devastating than that caused by the Black Death.

Europeans sailed across the Atlantic Ocean to find a more direct, less encumbered route to Asia and came upon lands, peoples, and products that they had not expected. One item, however, that they had sought in every part of the world and that they found in abundance in the Americas was precious metal. Although historians rightly emphasize the European intrusion into the Indian Ocean and their discovery of the Americas, we remind readers that the Europeans were not alone in expanding their influence through the oceans. The Ottomans made gains in the Red Sea and ventured into the Indian Ocean as rivals to the Portuguese.

In **Chapter 13, "Worlds Entangled, 1600–1750,"** we discuss how New World silver from Mexico and Peru became the major currency of global commerce, oiling the long-distance trading networks that had been revived after the Black Death. The effect of New World silver on the world economy was so great that it, even more than the Iberian explorations of the New World, brought the hemispheres together and marks the true genesis of modern world history. Sugar also linked the economies and political systems of western Europe, Africa, and the Americas and was a powerful force in a triangular trade centered on the Atlantic Ocean. This trade involved the shipment of vast numbers of African captives to the Americas, where they toiled as slaves on sugar, tobacco, cotton, and rice plantations.

For Europe and the rest of the world, the sudden dip in temperature in the seventeenth century, which historians now call the Little Ice Age, brought immense suffering not seen around the world since the Black Death. Wars broke out, and regimes were overthrown in China and Iran. Much of the new research into the Little Ice Age is based on a better understanding of the climate through the studies of climatologists, research that has transformed the way historians now look at the seventeenth century.

Chapter 14, "Cultures of Splendor and Power, 1500–1780," discusses the Ottoman scientists, Safavid and Mughal artists, Chinese literati, and European thinkers, whose notable achievements were rooted in their own cultures but tempered by awareness of the intellectual activities of others. In this chapter, we look closely at how culture is created as a historical process and describe how the massive increase in wealth during this period, growing out of global trade, led to one of the great periods of cultural flourishing in world history. In our discussion of Europe's scientific revolution, which got under way at the end of the sixteenth century and came to full fruition in the seventeenth century through the studies of Isaac Newton, we tackle the vexed question of why the scientific breakthrough occurred in Europe and not in China, India, and the Muslim world, which had been in the lead up to then. It was a turn to quantification that catapulted Europe ahead of the rest of the world, coupled with the fact that the Chinese had their exposure to European science through the Jesuits.

Around 1800, transformations reverberated outward from the Atlantic world and altered economic and political relationships in the rest of the world. In **Chapter 15, "Reordering the World, 1750–1850,"** we discuss how political revolutions in the Americas and Europe, new ideas about how to trade and organize labor, and a powerful rhetoric of freedom and universal rights underlay the beginning of "a great divide" between peoples of European descent and those who were not. These forces of laissez-faire capitalism, industrialization, the nation-state, and republicanism not only attracted diverse groups around the world; they also threatened groups that put forth alternative visions. Ideas of freedom, as manifested in trading relations, labor, and political activities, clashed with a traditional world based on inherited rights and statuses and further challenged the way men and women had lived in earlier times. These political, intellectual, and economic reorderings changed the way people around the world saw themselves and thus represent something quite novel in world history.

Much new comparative work has been done on the industrial revolution in the same way that historians have placed Europe's scientific revolution within a global context.

These new ways of envisioning the world did not go unchallenged, as **Chapter 16, "Alternative Visions of the Nineteenth Century,"** makes clear. Here, intense resistance to evolving modernity reflected the diversity of peoples and their hopes for the future. Wahabbism in Islam, the strongman movement in Africa, Indian resistance in America and Mexico, socialism and communism in Europe, the Taiping Rebellion in China, and the Indian mutiny in South Asia catapulted to historical prominence prophets and leaders whose visions often drew on earlier traditions and led these individuals to resist rapid change.

Chapter 17, "Nations and Empires, 1850–1914," discusses the political, economic, military, and ideological power that thrust Europe and North America to the fore of global events and led to an era of nationalism and modern imperialism, new forces in world history. Yet this period of seeming European supremacy was to prove short-lived. This chapter has new material on the Irish potato famine and an in-depth analysis of European colonialism.

As **Chapter 18, "An Unsettled World, 1890–1914,"** demonstrates, even before World War I shattered Europe's moral certitude, many groups at home (feminists, Marxists, and unfulfilled nationalists) and abroad (anticolonial nationalists) had raised a chorus of complaints about European and North American dominance. As in Chapter 14, we look at the processes by which specific cultural movements rose and reflected the concerns of individual societies. Yet here, too, syncretistic movements emerged in many cultures and reflected the sway of global imperialism, which by then had become a dominant force.

In keeping with our stress on the environment, this chapter discusses Teddy Roosevelt's promotion of the conservation of nature and other efforts by Europeans to be stewards of the earth. There is also a new environmentally oriented Current Trends in World History about the felt need for sustainable agricultural methods on the Russian steppe lands.

Chapter 19, "Of Masses and Visions of the Modern, 1910–1939," briefly covers World War I and then discusses how, from the end of World War I until World War II, different visions of being modern competed around the world. It is the development of modernism and its effects on multiple cultures that integrate the diverse developments discussed in this chapter. In the decades between the world wars, proponents of liberal democracy struggled to defend their views and often to impose their will on authoritarian rulers and anticolonial nationalists.

The chapter presents a number of revisionist views on the origins of World War I, the Armenian genocide, the Sykes-Picot agreement that was reached by Britain and France during World War I to partition the Ottoman Middle Eastern lands once the war was over, and the secularizing and modernizing ideas that animated Mustafa Kemal, later known as Ataturk, to create a new nation in Turkey.

Chapter 20, "The Three-World Order, 1940–1975," covers World War II and describes how new adversaries arose after the war. A three-world order came into being—the First World, led by the United States and extolling capitalism, the nation-state, and democratic government; the Second World, led by the Soviet Union and favoring authoritarian polities and economies; and the Third World, made up of former colonies seeking an independent status for themselves in world affairs. The rise of this three-world order dominated the second half of the twentieth century and constitutes another major theme of world history.

In **Chapter 21, "Globalization, 1970–2000,"** we explain that at the end of the cold war, the modern world, while clearly more unified than before, still had profound cultural differences and political divisions. At the beginning of the twenty-first century, capital, commodities, peoples, and ideas moved rapidly over long distances. But cultural tensions and political impasses continued to exist. The rise of this form of globalism represented a vital new element as humankind headed into a new century and millennium. This chapter contains an expanded discussion of the role of international and supranational financial organizations; the environmental crisis, brought on by the release of carbon emissions into the atmosphere and the resulting global warming; and the end of white rule in South Africa.

We close with the **Epilogue, "2001–The Present,"** which tracks developments since the turn of the millennium. These last few years have brought profound changes to the world order, yet we hope readers of *Worlds Together, Worlds Apart* will see more clearly how this most recent history is, in fact, entwined with trends of much longer duration that are the chief focus of this book.

We see the last half decade as pointing the peoples and countries of the world in more populist, ethnic nationalist, and violent directions. Britain's vote to withdraw from the European Union, known as Brexit; the election of Donald Trump to the American presidency; the rise of ethnic and religious consciousness in Turkey and India most notably and throughout the world in general; and the emergence of militant Islam in al-Qaeda and then in ISIS (the Islamic State in Iraq and Syria) all seem to us to be the consequence of various groups believing themselves to be disenfranchised and demanding to be heard.

MEDIA & PRINT ANCILLARIES

The Fifth Edition of *Worlds Together, Worlds Apart* is supported by an array of digital resources to help faculty meet their course goals—in the classroom and online—and activities for students to develop core skills in reading comprehension, historical analysis, and writing.

FOR STUDENTS

- **InQuizitive** (Shane Carter, Siobhan McGurk) is an adaptive quizzing tool that improves students' understanding of the themes and objectives of each chapter while honing their critical analysis skills with primary source, image, and map analysis questions. Students receive personalized quiz questions with detailed, guiding feedback on the topics in which they need the most help, while the engaging, gamelike elements motivate them as they learn.

- The **History Skills Tutorials** feature three modules—Images, Documents, and Maps—to support students' development of the key skills needed for the history course. These tutorials feature author videos modeling the analysis process, followed by interactive questions that will challenge students to apply what they have learned.

- The free and easy-to-use **Student Site** offers additional resources for students to use outside of class. Resources include interactive iMaps, author videos, and a comprehensive Online Reader featuring 100 additional sources.

- Free and included with new copies of the text, the **Norton Ebook Reader** provides an enhanced reading experience that works on all computers and mobile devices. Features include intuitive highlighting, note-taking, and book-marking, as well as pop-up definitions and enlargeable maps and images. Author videos are embedded throughout to create an engaging reading environment.

FOR INSTRUCTORS

- **Norton Coursepacks** allow instructors to bring strong assessment and lecture tools directly into their Learning Management System (LMS). Available at no cost to professors or students, Norton Coursepacks include chapter-based assignments, including Guided Reading Exercises, Primary Source Exercises, Chapter Review Quizzes, author videos, interactive iMaps, forum prompts, and more.

- **Story Maps** (Ruth Mostern) break complex maps into a sequence of five annotated screens that focus on the story behind the geography. Twelve maps, including two new maps, cover such topics as "The Silk Road," "The Spread of the Black Death," and "Population Growth and the Economy."

- The **Instructor's Manual** (Sharon Cohen) has everything instructors need to prepare lectures and classroom activities: lecture outlines, lecture ideas, classroom activities, and lists of recommended books, films, and Web sites.

- The **Test Bank** (Ryba Epstein, Derek O'Leary) contains approximately 1,400 multiple-choice, true/false, and essay questions. All test questions are now aligned with Bloom's Taxonomy for greater ease of assessment (available in print, PDF, Word, and Examview formats).

- **Lecture PowerPoints and Art PowerPoints** feature lecture outlines, key talking points, and the photographs and maps from the book to support in-class presentations.

ACKNOWLEDGMENTS

Worlds Together, Worlds Apart would never have happened without the full support of Princeton University. In a highly unusual move, and one for which we are truly grateful, the university helped underwrite this project with financial support from its 250th Anniversary Fund for undergraduate teaching and by allowing released time for the authors from campus commitments.

The history department's support of the effort over many years has been exceptional. Four chairs made funds and departmental support available, including the department's incomparable administrative talents. We would be remiss if we did not single out the department manager, Judith Hanson, who provided us with assistance whenever we needed it. We also thank Eileen Kane, who tracked down references and illustrations and merged changes into the manuscript. We also would like to thank Pamela Long, who made all of the complicated arrangements for ensuring that we were able to discuss matters in a leisurely and attractive setting. Sometimes that meant arranging for long-distance conference calls. She went even further and proofread the entire manuscript, finding errors that we had all overlooked.

We drew shamelessly on the expertise of the departmental faculty, and although it might be wise simply to include a roster of the Princeton history department, that would do an injustice to those of whom we took most advantage. So here they are: Mariana Candido, Robert Darnton, Sheldon Garon, Anthony Grafton, Molly Greene, David Howell, Harold James, William Jordan, Emmanuel Kreike, Michael Mahoney, Arno Mayer, Kenneth Mills, John Murrin, Susan Naquin, Willard Peterson, Theodore Rabb, Bhavani Raman, Stanley Stein, and Richard Turits. When necessary, we went outside the history department, getting help from Michael L. Bender, L. Carl Brown, Michael Cook, Norman Itzkowitz, Martin Kern, Thomas Leisten, Heath Lowry, and Peter Schaefer. Two departmental colleagues—Natalie Z. Davis and Elizabeth Lunbeck—were part of the original team but had to withdraw because of other commitments. Their contributions were vital, and we want to express our thanks to them. David Gordon, now at Bowdoin College, used portions of the text while teaching an undergraduate course at the University of Durban in South Africa and shared comments with us. Shamil Jeppie, like David Gordon a graduate of the Princeton history department, now teaching at the University of Cape Town in South Africa, read and commented on various chapters.

Beyond Princeton, we have also benefited from exceptionally gifted and giving colleagues who have assisted this book in many ways. Colleagues at Louisiana State

University, the University of North Carolina, the University of Pennsylvania, and the University of California at Los Angeles, where Suzanne Marchand, Michael Tsin, Holly Pittman, and Stephen Aron, respectively, are now teaching, pitched in whenever we turned to them. Especially helpful have been the contributions of Joyce Appleby, James Gelvin, Naomi Lamoreaux, and Gary Nash at UCLA; Michael Bernstein at Tulane University; and Maribel Dietz, John Henderson, Christine Kooi, David Lindenfeld, Reza Pirbhai, and Victor Stater at Louisiana State University. It goes without saying that none of these individuals bears any responsibility for factual or interpretive errors that the text may contain. Xinru Liu would like to thank her Indian mentor, Romila Thapar, who changed the way we think about Indian history.

The quality and range of reviews on this project were truly exceptional. The final version of the manuscript was greatly influenced by the thoughts and ideas of numerous instructors. We wish to particularly thank our consulting reviewers, who read multiple versions of the manuscript from start to finish.

First Edition Consultants

Hugh Clark, Ursinus College
Jonathan Lee, San Antonio College
Pamela McVay, Ursuline College
Tom Sanders, United States Naval Academy

Second Edition Consultants

Jonathan Lee, San Antonio College
Pamela McVay, Ursuline College
Steve Rapp, Georgia State University
Cliff Rosenberg, City University of New York

First Edition Reviewers

Lauren Benton, New Jersey Institute of Technology
Ida Blom, University of Bergon, Norway
Ricardo Duchesne, University of New Brunswick
Major Bradley T. Gericke, United States Military Academy
John Gillis, Rutgers University
David Kenley, Marshall University
John Kicza, Washington State University
Matthew Levinger, Lewis and Clark College
James Long, Colorado State University
Adam McKeown, Columbia University
Mark McLeod, University of Delaware
John Mears, Southern Methodist University
Michael Murdock, Brigham Young University
David Newberry, University of North Carolina, Chapel Hill

Tom Pearcy, Slippery Rock State University
Oliver B. Pollak, University of Nebraska, Omaha
Ken Pomeranz, University of California, Irvine
Major David L. Ruffley, United States Air Force Academy
William Schell, Murray State University
Major Deborah Schmitt, United States Air Force Academy
Sarah Shields, University of North Carolina, Chapel Hill
Mary Watrous-Schlesinger, Washington State University

Second Edition Reviewers

William Atwell, Hobart and William Smith Colleges
Susan Besse, City University of New York
Tithi Bhattacharya, Purdue University
Mauricio Borrerero, St. John's University
Charlie Briggs, Georgia Southern University
Antoinne Burton, University of Illinois, Urbana-Champaign
Jim Cameron, St. Francis Xavier University
Kathleen Comerford, Georgia Southern University
Duane Corpis, Georgia State University
Denise Davidson, Georgia State University
Ross Doughty, Ursinus College
Alison Fletcher, Kent State University
Phillip Gavitt, Saint Louis University
Brent Geary, Ohio University
Henda Gilli-Elewy, California State Polytechnic University, Pomona
Fritz Gumbach, John Jay College
William Hagen, University of California, Davis
Laura Hilton, Muskingum College
Jeff Johnson, Villanova University
David Kammerling-Smith, Eastern Illinois University
Jonathan Lee, San Antonio College
Dorothea Martin, Appalachian State University
Don McGuire, State University of New York, Buffalo
Pamela McVay, Ursuline College
Joel Migdal, University of Washington
Anthony Parent, Wake Forest University
Sandra Peacock, Georgia Southern University
David Pietz, Washington State University
Jared Poley, Georgia State University
John Quist, Shippensburg State University
Steve Rapp, Georgia State University
Paul Rodell, Georgia Southern University
Ariel Salzman, Queen's University
Bill Schell, Murray State University
Claire Schen, University at Buffalo
Jonathan Skaff, Shippensburg State University
David Smith, California State Polytechnic University, Pomona

Neva Specht, Appalachian State University
Ramya Sreeniva, State University of New York, Buffalo
Charles Stewart, University of Illinois, Urbana-Champaign
Rachel Stocking, Southern Illinois University, Carbondale
Heather Streets, Washington State University
Tim Teeter, Georgia Southern University
Charlie Wheeler, University of California, Irvine
Owen White, University of Delaware
James Wilson, Wake Forest University

Third Edition Reviewers

Henry Antkiewicz, Eastern Tennessee State University
Anthony Barbieri-Low, University of California, Santa Barbara
Andrea Becksvoort, University of Tennessee, Chattanooga
Hayden Bellonoit, United States Naval Academy
John Bloom, Shippensburg University
Kathryn Braund, Auburn University
Catherine Candy, University of New Orleans
Karen Carter, Brigham Young University
Stephen Chappell, James Madison University
Jessey Choo, University of Missouri, Kansas City
Timothy Coates, College of Charleston
Gregory Crider, Wingate University
Denise Davidson, Georgia State University
Jessica Davidson, James Madison University
Sal Diaz, Santa Rosa Junior College
Todd Dozier, Baton Rouge Community College
Richard Eaton, University of Arizona
Lee Farrow, Auburn University, Montgomery
Bei Gao, College of Charleston
Behrooz Ghamari-Tabrizi, University of Illinois, Urbana-Champaign
Steven Gish, Auburn University, Montgomery
Jeffrey Hamilton, Baylor University
Barry Hankins, Baylor University
Brian Harding, Mott Community College
Tim Henderson, Auburn University, Montgomery
Marjorie Hilton, University of Redlands
Richard Hines, Washington State University
Lisa Holliday, Appalachian State University
Jonathan Lee, San Antonio College
David Kalivas, University of Massachusetts, Lowell
Christopher Kelley, Miami University, Ohio
Kenneth Koons, Virginia Military Institute
Michael Kulikowski, Pennsylvania State University
Benjamin Lawrence, University of California, Davis
Lu Liu, University of Tennessee, Knoxville

David Longfellow, Baylor University
Harold Marcuse, University of California, Santa Barbara
Dorothea Martin, Appalachian State University
David Mayes, Sam Houston State University
James Mokhiber, University of New Orleans
Mark Munzinger, Radford College
David Murphree, Virginia Tech University
Joshua Nadel, North Carolina Central University
Wing Chung Ng, University of Texas, San Antonio
Robert Norrell, University of Tennessee, Knoxville
Chandrika Paul, Shippensburg University
Beth Pollard, San Diego State University
Timothy Pytell, California State University, San Bernardino
Stephen Rapp, professional historian
Alice Roberti, Santa Rosa Junior College
Aviel Roshwald, Georgetown University
James Sanders, Utah State University
Lynn Sargeant, California State University, Fullerton
William Schell, Murray State University
Michael Seth, James Madison University
Barry Stentiford, Grambling State University
Gabrielle Sutherland, Baylor University
Lisa Tran, California State University, Fullerton
Michael Vann, California State University, Sacramento
Peter Von Sivers, University of Utah
Andrew Wackerfuss, Georgetown University
Ted Weeks, Southern Illinois University, Carbondale
Angela White, Indiana University of Pennsylvania
Jennifer Williams, Nichols State University
Andrew Wise, State University of New York, Buffalo
Eloy Zarate, Pasadena City College
William Zogby, Mohawk Valley Community College

Fourth Edition Reviewers

Andrea Becksvoort, University of Tennessee, Chattanooga
Hayden Bellenoit, United States Naval Academy
Volker Benkert, Arizona State University
Gayle Brunelle, California State University, Fullerton
Jessica Clark, California State University, Chico
Brian Harding, Mott Community College
Emily Hill, Queen's University at Kingston
Laura Hilton, Muskingum University
Dennis Laumann, University of Memphis
Elaine MacKinnon, University of West Georgia
Ronald Mellor, University of California, Los Angeles
Carol Miller, Tallahassee Community College
Greg O'Malley, University of California, Santa Cruz
David Ortiz Jr., University of Arizona

Charles Parker, Saint Louis University
Juanjuan Peng, Georgia Southern University
Dana Rabin, University of Illinois, Urbana-Champaign
Matthew Rothwell, University of Southern Indiana
Teo Ruiz, University of California, Los Angeles
Jeffrey Shumway, Brigham Young University
Lisa Tran, California State University, Fullerton
Lela Urquhart, Georgia State University

Fifth Edition Reviewers

Andreas Agocs, University of the Pacific
Anthony Barbieri-Low, University of California, Santa Barbara
Michelle Benson-Saxton, University at Buffalo
Brett Berliner, Morgan State University
Carolyn Noelle Biltoft, Georgia State University
Edward Bond, Alabama A&M University
Gayle Brunelle, California State University, Fullerton
Grace Chee, West Los Angeles College
Stephen Colston, San Diego State University
Paula Devos, San Diego State University
Paul Hudson, Georgia Perimeter College
Alan Karras, University of California, Berkeley
Elaine MacKinnon, University of West Georgia
Harold Marcuse, University of California, Santa Barbara
Jeff McEwen, Chattanooga State Community College
Thomas McKenna, Concord University
Eva Moe, Modesto Junior College
Alice Pate, Kennesaw State University
Chandrika Paul, Shippensburg University
Jared Poley, Georgia State University
Dana Rabin, University of Illinois, Urbana-Champaign
Masako Racel, Kennesaw State University
Charles Reed, Elizabeth City State University
Alice Roberti, Santa Rosa Junior College
Steven Rowe, Chicago State University
Ariel Salzmann, Queen's University
Lynn Sargeant, California State University, Fullerton
Robert Saunders, Farmingdale State College
Sharlene Sayegh-Canada, California State University, Long Beach
Claire Schen, University at Buffalo
Jeffrey Shumway, Brigham Young University
Greg Smay, University of California, Berkeley
Margaret Stevens, Essex County College
Lisa Tran, California State University, Fullerton
Michael Vann, California State University, Sacramento
Theodore Weeks, Southern Illinois University
Krzysztof Ziarek, University of Buffalo

For the Fifth Edition, we also had a mix of new and returning authors who helped create the best support materials to accompany *Worlds Together, Worlds Apart*. Alan Karras served as the lead media author, directing the development of our ancillary author team. For their tremendous efforts, we would like to thank Sharon Cohen for authoring the Instructor's Manual, Ryba Epstein and Derek O'Leary for creating the test bank, and Shane Carter and Siobhan McGurk for developing InQuizitive.

For the Fifth Edition, we have some familiar and new friends at Norton to thank. Chief among them is Jon Durbin, who once again played a major role in bringing this edition to publication. Laura Wilk, our new media editor, has put together a fabulous package of support materials for students and instructors. Sarah England has put together a creative marketing plan for the book. Jillian Burr is responsible for the book's beautiful and effective design. Jennifer Barnhardt has done an amazingly efficient job as our project editor. Andy Ensor has shepherded the project through production beautifully. Kelly Rafey has done a masterful job compiling the manuscript with a special focus on photos, primary sources, and permissions. Michelle Smith and Chris Hillyer have done a fine job lending their support in strengthening the media support materials to meet the ever more complex classroom and assessment needs of instructors. Alice Vigliani did a spectacular job working on the manuscript, paying particular attention to our efforts to reorganize and streamline many of the chapters in both volumes. Janet Greenblatt did a superb job with the copyediting, turning the chapters around quickly to meet our schedule. A special shout-out goes to Debra Morton-Hoyt and her team of cover designers. *Worlds Together, Worlds Apart* has always been incredibly creative and distinctive looking, and the Fifth Edition covers are even more eye-catching and memorable than the first four editions. Bravo!

Finally, we must recognize that while this project often kept us apart from family members, their support held our personal worlds together.

ABOUT THE AUTHORS

ROBERT TIGNOR (*Ph.D. Yale University*) is professor emeritus and the Rosengarten Professor of Modern and Contemporary History at Princeton University and the three-time chair of the history department. With Gyan Prakash, he introduced Princeton's first course in world history nearly thirty years ago. Professor Tignor has taught graduate and undergraduate courses in African history and world history and written extensively on the history of twentieth-century Egypt, Nigeria, and Kenya. Besides his many research trips to Africa, Professor Tignor has taught at the University of Ibadan in Nigeria and the University of Nairobi in Kenya.

JEREMY ADELMAN (*D.Phil. Oxford University*) has lived and worked in seven countries and four continents. A graduate of the University of Toronto, he earned a master's degree in economic history at the London School of Economics (1985) and a doctorate in modern history at Oxford University (1989). He is the author or editor of ten books, including *Sovereignty and Revolution in the Iberian Atlantic* (2006) and *Worldly Philosopher: The Odyssey of Albert O. Hirschman* (2013), a chronicle of one of the twentieth century's most original thinkers. He has been awarded fellowships by the British Council, the Social Science and Humanities Research Council of Canada, the Guggenheim Memorial Foundation, and the American Council Learned Societies (the Frederick Burkhardt Fellowship). He is currently the Henry Charles Lea Professor of History and the director of the Global History Lab at Princeton University. His next book is called *Earth Hunger: Markets, Resources and the Need for Strangers*.

PETER BROWN (*B.A. Oxford University*) is the Rollins Professor of History emeritus at Princeton University. He previously taught at London University and the University of California, Berkeley. He has written on the rise of Christianity and the end of the Roman Empire. His works include *Augustine of Hippo*; *The World of Late Antiquity*; *The Cult of the Saints*; *Body and Society*; *The Rise of Western Christendom*; and *Poverty and Leadership in the Later Roman Empire*. His most recent book is *Treasure in Heaven*.

BENJAMIN ELMAN (*Ph.D. University of Pennsylvania*) is professor of East Asian studies and history at Princeton University. He has served as the chair of the Princeton East Asian Studies Department and as director of the East Asian Studies Program. He taught at the University of California, Los Angeles for over fifteen years, 1986–2002. His teaching and research fields include Chinese intellectual and cultural history, 1000–1900; the history of science in China, 1600–1930; the history of education in late imperial China; and Sino-Japanese cultural history, 1600–1850. He is the author of seven books, four of them translated into Chinese, Korean, or Japanese: *From Philosophy to Philology: Intellectual and Social Aspects of Change in Late Imperial China*; *Classicism, Politics, and Kinship: The Ch'angchou School of New Text Confucianism in Late Imperial China*; *A Cultural History of Civil Examinations in Late Imperial China*; *On Their Own Terms: Science in China, 1550–1900*; *A Cultural History of Modern Science in China*; *Civil Examinations and Meritocracy in Late Imperial China, 1400–1900*; and *Science in China, 1600–1900: Essays by Benjamin A. Elman*. He is the creator of Classical Historiography for Chinese History at http://libguides .princeton.edu/chinese-historiography, a bibliography and teaching Web site published since 1996.

ALAN KARRAS (*Ph.D. University of Pennsylvania*) is the Associate Director of International & Area Studies at the University of California, Berkeley, and has served as chair of the College Board's test development committee for world history and as co-chair of the College Board's commission on AP history course revisions. He studies the eighteenth-century Atlantic world and global interactions more broadly concerning illegal activities like smuggling and corruption.

XINRU LIU (*Ph.D. University of Pennsylvania*) is professor of early Indian history and world history at the College of New Jersey. She is associated with the Institute of World History and the Chinese Academy of Social Sciences. She is the author of *Ancient India and Ancient China, Trade and Religious Exchanges, AD 1–600*; *Silk and Religion, an Exploration of Material Life and the Thought of People, AD*

600–1200; *Connections across Eurasia: Transportation, Communication, and Cultural Exchange on the Silk Roads,* coauthored with Lynda Norene Shaffer; *A Social History of Ancient India* (in Chinese); and *The Silk Road in World History.* Professor Liu promotes South Asian studies and world history studies in both the United States and the People's Republic of China.

HOLLY PITTMAN (*Ph.D. Columbia University*) is professor of art history at the University of Pennsylvania, where she teaches art and archaeology of Mesopotamia and the Iranian Plateau. She also serves as curator in the Near East Section of the University of Pennsylvania Museum of Archaeology and Anthropology. Previously she served as a curator in the Ancient Near Eastern Art Department of the Metropolitan Museum of Art. She has written extensively on the art and culture of the Bronze Age in Southwest Asia and has participated in excavations in Cyprus, Turkey, Syria, Iraq, and Iran, where she currently works. Her research investigates works of art as media through which patterns of thought, cultural development, and historical interactions of ancient cultures of the Near East are reconstructed.

BRENT SHAW (*Ph.D. Cambridge University*) is the Andrew Fleming West Professor of Classics at Princeton University, where he has directed the Program in the Ancient World. He was previously at the University of Pennsylvania, where he chaired the Graduate Group in Ancient History. His principal areas of specialization as a Roman historian are Roman family history and demography, sectarian violence and conflict in Late Antiquity, and the regional history of Africa as part of the Roman Empire. His works include *Sacred Violence: African Christians and Sectarian Hatred in the Age of Augustine*; *Bringing in the Sheaves: Economy and Metaphor in the Roman World*; and *Spartacus and the Slave Wars*. He has also edited the papers of Sir Moses Finley, *Economy and Society in Ancient Greece*, and published in a variety of books and journals, including the *Journal of Roman Studies*, the *American Historical Review*, the *Journal of Early Christian Studies*, and *Past & Present*.

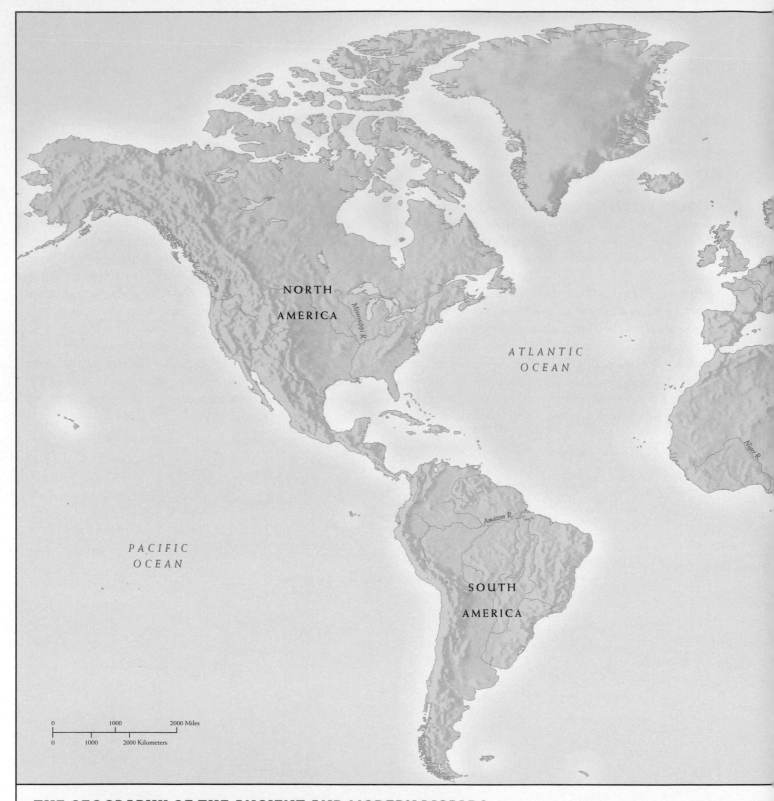

NORTH
AMERICA

Mississippi R.

ATLANTIC
OCEAN

PACIFIC
OCEAN

Amazon R.

SOUTH
AMERICA

Niger R.

| 0 | 1000 | 2000 Miles |
| 0 | 1000 | 2000 Kilometers |

THE GEOGRAPHY OF THE ANCIENT AND MODERN WORLDS

Today, we believe the world to be divided into continents, and most of us think that it was always so. Geographers usually identify six inhabited continents: Africa, North America, South America, Europe, Asia, and Australia. Inside these continents they locate a vast number of subcontinental units, such as East Asia, South Asia, Southeast Asia, the Middle East, North Africa, and sub-Saharan Africa. Yet this geographical understanding would have been completely alien to premodern men and women, who did not think that they inhabited continents bounded by large bodies of water. Lacking a firm command of the seas, they saw themselves living on contiguous landmasses, and they thought these territorial bodies were the main geographical units of their lives. Hence, in this volume we have chosen to use a set of geographical terms, the main one being Afro-Eurasia, that more accurately reflect the world that the premoderns believed that they inhabited.

The most interconnected and populous landmass of premodern times was Afro-Eurasia. The term Eurasia is widely used in general histories, but we think it is in its own ways inadequate. The preferred term from our perspective must be Afro-Eurasia, for the interconnected landmass of premodern and indeed much of modern times included large parts of Europe and Asia and significant regions in Africa. The major African territories that were regularly joined to Europe and Asia were Egypt, North Africa, and even parts of sub-Saharan Africa.

Only gradually and fitfully did the divisions of the world that we take for granted today take shape. The peoples inhabiting the northwestern part of the Afro-Eurasian landmass did not see themselves as European Christians, and hence as a distinctive cultural entity, until the Middle Ages drew to a close in the twelfth and thirteenth centuries. Islam did not arise and extend its influence throughout the middle zone of the Afro-Eurasian landmass until the eighth and ninth centuries. And, finally, the peoples living in what we today term the Indian subcontinent did not feel a strong sense of their own cultural and political unity until the Delhi Sultanate of the thirteenth and fourteenth centuries and the Mughal Empire, which emerged at the beginning of the sixteenth century, brought political unity to that vast region. As a result, we use the terms South Asia, Vedic society, and India in place of Indian subcontinent for the premodern part of our narrative, and we use Southwest Asia and North Africa to refer to what today is designated as the Middle East. In fact, it is only in the period from 1000 to 1300 that some of the major cultural areas that are familiar to us today truly crystallized.

WORLDS TOGETHER,
WORLDS APART

FIFTH EDITION

Becoming Human

- What are the various creation narratives identified in this chapter, in addition to that of human evolution? Explain how they differ.

- What major developments in hominin evolution resulted in the traits that make *Homo sapiens* "human"?

- What were the human ways of life and cultural developments from 200,000 to 12,000 years ago?

- In what varying ways did communities around the world shift to settled agriculture, and what was the significance of this shift for social organization?

In 2003, in a remote corner of the Ethiopian highlands of Africa, a team of evolutionary biologists came upon a remarkable cache of fossil remains lodged in volcanic rock. Identifying and reassembling these remains took six years, but the researchers eventually reconstructed one of the most revealing sets of human fossils ever found: a nearly complete skeleton of an adult male and the partial remains of another adult and a juvenile. By dating the volcanic rock, the team determined that the bones were about 160,000 years old. Although the skeletal remains were not identical to those of modern men and women (who are technically *Homo sapiens sapiens*, the sole surviving subspecies of *Homo sapiens*), they were close enough to form part of the family of modern humans. In short, the bones represented the oldest record of *Homo sapiens*. The fossil finds confirmed what earlier studies had suggested: *Homo sapiens*, or modern humans, originated in a small region of Africa about 200,000 years ago and migrated out of Africa less than 100,000 years ago. As the team leader proclaimed, "We are all Africans."

Not everyone agrees with the "Out of Africa" thesis, which contends that modern humans are all descendants of recent migrants out of Africa. Doubters claim that the world's "races" evolved separately in different regions for up to 1 million years after migrating out of Africa. These doubters argue that as the early descendants of modern men and women evolved in widely dispersed geographical settings, they took on diverse personality traits and distinctive physical appearances, with the result that they appear today as different "races." In this view, the story of humanity is about fundamental differences. But now it is becoming clear that all humans share a common heritage, and our differences are not genetic or crudely physical, but mainly cultural. We are also much newer than scholars once imagined.

As a species we have been living apart for a comparatively short amount of time, and as a result the world's "races" have much in common. Most of the common traits of human beings—the abilities to make tools, engage in family life, use language, and refine cognitive abilities—evolved over many millennia and crystallized on the eve of the exodus from Africa. Only with the advent of settled agriculture did significant cultural divergences occur, as artifacts such as tools, cooking devices, and storage containers reveal. The differences in humankind's cultures are less than 15,000 or 20,000 years old.

This chapter lays out the origins of humanity from its common source. It shows how many different **hominins** (erect two-footed mammals, represented today only by humans but in the past by many groups descended from the great apes) preceded modern humans and that humans came from only one—very recent—stock of migrants out of Africa. Fanning out across the world, our ancestors adapted to environmental constraints and opportunities. They created languages, families, and clan systems, often innovating to defend themselves against predators. One of the biggest breakthroughs was the domestication of animals and plants—the creation of agrarian settlements. With this development, humans could cease following food and begin producing it in their own backyards.

Before we begin our exploration, it will be useful to clarify two terms that occur frequently in this chapter's discussion: *evolution* and *modern humans*. **Evolution** is the process by which the different species of the world—its plants and animals—adapt in response to their often changing environments in ways that enable them to survive and increase in numbers. Biological evolution does not imply progress to higher and more exalted forms of life, only adaptation to environmental surroundings.

It was once thought that evolution is a gradual and steady process. The consensus now is that changes occur in punctuated bursts after long periods of stasis, or non-change. These transformative changes were often brought on, especially during early human development, by dramatic alterations in climate and by ruptures of the earth's crust caused by the movement of tectonic plates below the earth's surface. The heaving and decline of the earth's surface led to significant changes in climate and in animal and plant life.

Of even greater significance in causing radical climate variation were changes in the rotation of the earth around the sun. The twentieth-century breakthroughs of astronomers and climatologists have revealed that the earth does not move around the sun in a perfect oval. The earth's path around the sun is a wobbly one. When the earth tilts toward the sun, temperatures rise and rainfall is abundant. Conversely, when the earth moves away from the sun, temperatures plunge and aridity occurs. These phases tended to last 100,000 years.

Climate change has been dramatic and radical over time. For millions of years, glaciation reached all the way to the equator, while at other times the climate was so warm that dinosaurs flourished in Antarctica and ferns grew to spectacular heights in the Canadian Arctic. As we will see, throughout most of hominin existence these precursors to modern humans and *Homo sapiens* had to cope with a severely freezing and dry universe.

The term *modern humans* refers to members of the various *Homo sapiens* subspecies that evolved about 200,000 years ago. So when we say "modern" (and "recent"), we are speaking in relative terms; compared with the life of the universe and even the earliest hominins, the ancient creatures we call modern humans were indeed "modern." This chapter's discussion will show that as modern humans evolved in varying environments, they passed through successive waves of migration, adaptation, and innovation.

PRECURSORS TO MODERN HUMANS

To understand the origins of modern humans (*Homo sapiens*), we must consider what is common to all humans and what distinguishes them from one another. We must also come to terms with time. Though the hominins that evolved into modern humans lived millions of years ago, our tools for analyzing them are relatively new. What we now know about the origins of human existence and the evolution into modern humans would have been unimaginable a century ago.

Creation Narratives

For thousands of years, humans have constructed, out of their values and available evidence, narratives of how the world—and humans—came to be. These **creation narratives** have varied over time and across cultures. Only 350 years ago, English clerics claimed on the basis of biblical calculations and Christian tradition that the first day of creation was Sunday, October 23, 4004 BCE. One scholar even specified that creation happened at 9:00 A.M. on the morning of that day. Now we see things differently. The origin of the universe dates back some

PRIMARY SOURCE

A Hindu Creation Narrative

Around 1500 BCE, a migrant people settled in South Asia. These Vedic people sang hymns while making sacrifices to their gods, and the hymns were later collected in the Rig-Veda—the earliest Hindu sacred text. This hymn describes the creation of the universe by the gods' sacrifice ("oblation") of a creature—Purusha, or "Man." From Purusha's body come four different kinds of people: the Brahman, the Rajanya, the Vaishya, and the Shudra. They represent the forefathers of the four castes, or hereditary social classes, of India. (To compare this reading with a Mesoamerican creation narrative, see p. 32.)

Thousand-headed Purusha, thousand-eyed, thousand-footed—he, having pervaded the earth on all sides, extends ten fingers beyond it.

Purusha alone is all this—whatever has been and whatever is going to be. Further, he is the lord of immortality and also of what grows on account of food.

Such is his greatness; greater, indeed than this is Purusha. All creatures constitute but one-quarter of him, his three-quarters are the immortal in the heaven.

With his three-quarters did Purusha rise up; one-quarter of him again remains here. With it did he variously spread out on all sides over what eats and what eats not. . . . When the gods performed the sacrifice with Purusha as the oblation, then the spring was its clarified butter, the summer the sacrificial fuel, and the autumn the oblation.

The sacrificial victim, namely, Purusha born at the very beginning, they sprinkled with sacred water upon the sacrificial grass. With him as oblation, the gods performed the sacrifice, and also the Sādhyas [a class of semidivine beings] and the rishis [ancient seers].

From that wholly offered sacrificial oblation were born the verses and the sacred chants; from it were born the meters [*chandas*]; the sacrificial formula was born from it.

From it horses were born and also those animals who have double rows [i.e., upper and lower] of teeth; cows were born from it, from it were born goats and sheep.

When they divided Purusha, in how many different portions did they arrange him? What became of his mouth, what of his two arms? What were his two thighs and his two feet called?

His mouth became the brāhman; his two arms were made into the rājanya; his two thighs the vaishyas; from his two feet the shūdra was born.

The moon was born from the mind, from the eye the sun was born; from the mouth Indra and Agni, from the breath [*prāna*] the wind [*vāyu*] was born.

From the navel was the atmosphere created, from the head the heaven issued forth; from two feet was born the earth and the quarters (the cardinal directions) from the ear. Thus did they fashion the worlds.

QUESTIONS FOR ANALYSIS

- In early Vedic society the Brahman (priest) was the highest caste, and the Shudra (outsider/laborer) was the lowest. What parts of Purusha's body did these two castes come from, and what is the significance of each?
- According to this creation narrative, what other beings came into existence fully formed?

Source: *Sources of Indian Tradition*, vol. 1, *From the Beginning to 1800*, edited and revised by Ainslie T. Embree, 2nd ed. (Columbia University Press, 1988), pp. 18–19.

13.75 billion years, and hominins began to separate from apes some 6 or 7 million years ago. These discoveries have proved as mind-boggling to Hindus and Muslims as to Christians and Jews—all of whom believed, in different ways, in a creationist account of humanity's origins. The Judaic-Christian belief in creation was based on the first book of the Old Testament, Genesis, which portrayed God creating the universe from nothingness, all the plants and animals and the first set of human beings (Adam and Eve) over a period of seven days. This story became foundational for western societies and also for the Islamic world, which accepted the Old and New Testaments—though not the divinity of Jesus—as the word of God.

Modern discoveries about humanity's origins have also challenged other major cultural traditions, because no tradition conceived that creatures evolved into new kinds of life, that humans were related to apes, and that all of humanity originated in a remote corner of Africa. According to the Brahmanical Vedas and the Upanishads, which date to the seventh or sixth century BCE and remain fundamental to Hindu faith today, the world is millions, not billions, of years old. The Chinese do not appear to have their own creation story, and the Buddhists believe in a continuous reappearance of human and animal souls. (See Primary Source: A Hindu Creation Narrative; also see Primary Source: A Mesoamerican Creation Narrative, p. 32.)

Our knowledge of human origins has been the result of several remarkable scientific breakthroughs. Only recently have scholars been able to date fossil remains, to use biological research to understand the relationships among the world's early peoples, and to chart the evolution of climate change over long stretches of time.

The first major advance in the study of the time before written historical records occurred after World War II, and it involved the use of *radiocarbon dating*. All living things contain the radioactive isotope carbon-14 (^{14}C), which plants acquire directly from the atmosphere and animals acquire indirectly when they consume plants or other animals. When these living things die, the ^{14}C isotope begins to decay into a stable nonradioactive element, carbon-12 (^{12}C). Because the rate of decay is regular and measurable, it is possible to determine the age of fossils that leave organic remains for up to 40,000 years.

A second major dating technique, the *potassium-argon method*, also involves analysis of the changing chemical structure of objects over time. Scientists can calculate the age of nonliving objects by measuring the ratio of potassium to argon in them, since potassium decays into argon. This method allows scientists to calculate the age of objects up to a million years old. It also enables them to date the sediments in which researchers find fossils—as a gauge of the age of the fossils themselves.

DNA (deoxyribonucleic acid) analysis is a third crucial tool for unraveling the beginnings of modern humans. DNA, which determines biological inheritance, exists in two places within the cells of all living organisms—including the human body. *Nuclear DNA* occurs in the nucleus of every cell, where it controls most aspects of physical appearance and makeup. *Mitochondrial DNA* occurs outside the nucleus of cells and is located in mitochondria, structures used in converting the energy from food to a form that cells can use. Nuclear and mitochondrial DNA exists in males and females, but only mitochondrial DNA from females passes to their offspring: the female's egg cells carry her mitochondria with their DNA to the offspring, but sperm cells from males do not donate any mitochondrial DNA to the egg cell at fertilization. By examining mitochondrial DNA, researchers can measure the genetic relatedness and variation among living organisms—including human beings. Such analysis has enabled researchers to pinpoint human descent from an original African population to other, genetically related populations that lived approximately 100,000 years ago.

As this chapter demonstrates, the environment, especially climate, played a major role in the appearance of hominins and the eventual dominance of *Homo sapiens*. But how do we know so much about the world's climate going so far back in time? This brings us to the fourth of the scientific breakthroughs, known as *marine isotope stages*. By exploring the marine life, mainly pollen and plankton, deposited in deep-sea beds and measuring the levels of oxygen-16 (^{16}O) and oxygen-18 (^{18}O) isotopes in these life-forms, oceanographers and climatologists are able to determine the temperature of the world hundreds of thousands of years ago; and with reconstructions of the earth's orbital path around the sun, they have extended their knowledge of climate to billions of years, thus providing data on the cooling and warming cycles of the earth's climate.

Climatologists have probed the large ice sheets and glaciers in Greenland and elsewhere to obtain information on the earth's climate in the past and the prospects for the future. Crucially important in this endeavor were the investigations of a multinational team of European climatologists, whose drilling deep into the

Evolutionary Findings and Research Methods

Revisions in the time frame of the universe and human existence have occurred over a long period of time. Geologists made early breakthroughs in the eighteenth century when their research into the layers of the earth's surface revealed a world much older than biblical time implied. Evolutionary biologists, most notably Charles Darwin (1809–1882), concluded that all life had evolved over long periods from simple forms of matter. In the twentieth century, astronomers, evolutionary biologists, climatologists, and archaeologists (scholars of ancient cultures whose information comes mainly from nonliterary sources such as fossils, monuments, and artifacts) have employed sophisticated dating techniques to pinpoint the chronology of the universe's creation, the evolution of all forms of life on earth, and the decisive role that changes in climate have played in the evolution of living forms. (See Current Trends in World History: Determining the Age of Fossils and Sediments and Measuring Climate Change.) Understanding the sweep of human history, calculated in millions of years, requires us to revise our sense of time.

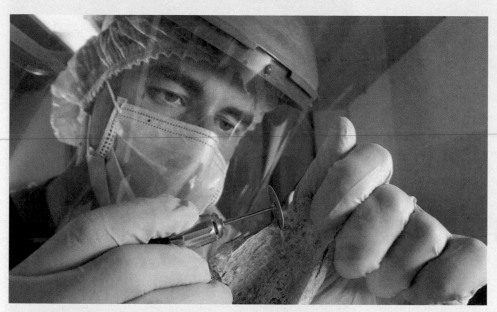

Neanderthal DNA Extraction. *This sample of fossilized Neanderthal bone will have its genetic material extracted and sequenced as part of the Neanderthal Genome Project.*

done for the last 16,000 years, created warmer and wetter conditions. A climate that was warmer and wetter facilitated the agricultural revolution and the rapid growth of the human population, as we observe in the text. Yet, in the twentieth and twenty-first centuries, the trapping of greenhouse gases in the earth's atmosphere has led to even higher degrees of temperature and now threatens the life of all species on earth.

QUESTIONS FOR ANALYSIS

- How has the study of prehistory changed since World War II? What are the consequences?
- How does the study of climate and environment relate to the origins of humans?

ice cores of Greenland revealed both the rapidity of climate change in the past and the crucial challenges encountered by plants and animals, including *Homo sapiens* and, before them, all hominins. Astronomical observations into the earth's varying orbital paths around the sun were additional and essential elements in charting the radical and rapid climate changes that have occurred over billions of years—for instance, when the earth's orbit around the sun, responding to the tilt of its axis and the gravitational pull of other planets, caused different distributions and intensities of light and major changes in temperature and rainfall. Moreover, when the earth's orbit took it away from the warming effects of the sun, freezing temperatures and aridity occurred. The earth's spinning more closely to the sun, as it has

Explore Further

Barham, Lawrence, and Peter Mitchell, *The First Africans: African Archaeology from the Earliest Toolmakers to Most Recent Foragers* (2008).

Barker, Graeme, *Agricultural Revolution in Prehistory: Why Did Foragers Become Farmers?* (2006).

Early Hominins and Adaptation

Not surprisingly, Charles Darwin predicted, though with little evidence, that Africa was the likely birthplace of humanity. In his *Descent of Man* (1871), he wrote, "In each great region of the world, the living mammals are closely related to the extinct species of the same region. It is therefore probable that Africa was formerly inhabited by extinct apes, closely allied to the gorilla and chimpanzee, and as these two species are man's closest allies, it is somewhat probable that our earliest progenitors lived on the African continent" (cited in Meredith, p. xvii). Of course,

evolution deniers appeared right away. Perhaps no one better expressed the skepticism and revulsion of this view that humanity owed its origins to apes than the wife of an English cleric, who wrote, "Let us hope that it is not true, but if it is true let us pray that it will not be widely known" (Meredith, p. xvii).

What was it like to be a hominin in the millions of years before the emergence of modern humans? An early clue came from a discovery made in 1924 at Taung, not far from the present-day city of Johannesburg, South Africa. Raymond Dart, a 29-year-old Australian anatomist teaching at the Witwatersrand University Medical School, happened upon a skull and bones that appeared to be partly human and partly ape. Believing the creature to be "an extinct race of apes intermediate between living anthropoids (apes) and man . . . a man-like ape," Dart labeled the creature the "Southern Ape of Africa," or *Australopithecus africanus* (Meredith, p. 61). This individual had a brain capacity of approximately 1 pint, or a little less than one-third that of a modern man and about the same as that of modern-day African apes. Yet, according to Dart, these **australopithecines** were different from other animals, for they walked on two legs.

Alas, Dart failed to convince most of the scholarly world. The fact that his British mentors, with whom he had studied, rejected his findings, claiming that Dart had not found a hominin precursor to humankind but a juvenile anthropoid, so disappointed Dart that he stopped his research in this area and plunged into a deep depression. Yet not all despaired. Robert Brown, a Scottish doctor with a keen interest in the origin of mammals, came to South Africa, entered Dart's laboratory, walked straight past Dart, knelt at the Taung skull, and exclaimed, "I am kneeling in adoration of our ancestor" (Meredith, p. 26). Brown went on to find other fossils and in 1946 copublished a book with Dart, *The South African Fossil Ape-Men: The Austrolopithenae*, asserting that "if one could be found alive today, I think it probable that most scientists would regard him as a primitive form of man" (Meredith, p. 32). This book persuaded even the most skeptical of Dart's and Brown's critics.

The fact that australopithecines survived at all for about 3 million years in a hostile environment is remarkable. But they did, and over the many million years of their existence in Africa, the australopithecines developed into more than six species. (A species is a group of animals or plants possessing one or more distinctive characteristics.) It is important to emphasize that these australopithecines were not humans but that they carried the genetic and biological material out of which modern humans would later emerge.

LUCY Luckily for researchers, australopithecines existed not only in southern Africa but in the north as well. In 1974, an archaeological team working at a site in present-day Ethiopia unearthed a relatively intact skeleton of a young adult female australopithecine in the valley of the Awash River. The researchers gave the skeleton a nickname, Lucy, based on the popular Beatles song "Lucy in the Sky with Diamonds."

Lucy was extraordinary. She stood a little over 3 feet tall, she walked upright, her skull contained a brain within the ape size range, and her jaw and teeth were humanlike. Her arms were long, hanging halfway from her hips to her knees, and her legs were short—suggesting that she was a skilled tree climber, might not have been two-footed at all times, and sometimes resorted to arms for locomotion, in the fashion of a modern baboon. Above all, Lucy's skeleton was very, very old—half a million years older than any other complete hominin skeleton

Fossil Bones of Lucy. *Archaeologist Donald Johanson discovered the fossilized bones of this young female in the Afar region of Ethiopia. They are believed to date from approximately 3.2 million years ago and provide evidence of some of the first hominins to appear in Africa. This find was of great importance because the bones were so fully and completely preserved.*

found up to that time. Lucy left the scholarly world with no doubt that human precursors were walking around as early as 3 million years ago. (See Table 1.1.)

ADAPTATION To survive, hominins had to adapt and evolve to keep pace with physical environments that underwent rapid and destabilizing change—for if they did not, they would die out. Many of the early hominin groups did just that. The places where researchers found early hominin remains in southern and eastern Africa were characterized by drastic changes in the earth's climate, with regions going from being heavily forested and well watered to being arid and desertlike and then back again. Survival required constant adaptation (the ability to alter behavior

TABLE 1.1 | Human Evolution

SPECIES	TIME
Orrorin tugenensis	6 MILLION YEARS AGO
Australopithecus anamensis	4.2 MILLION YEARS AGO
Australopithecus afarensis (INCLUDING LUCY)	3.4 MILLION YEARS AGO
Australopithecus africanus	3.0 MILLION YEARS AGO
Homo habilis (INCLUDING DEAR BOY)	2.5 MILLION YEARS AGO
Homo erectus and Homo ergaster (INCLUDING JAVA AND PEKING MAN)	2 MILLION YEARS AGO
Homo heidelbergensis (COMMON ANCESTOR OF NEANDERTHALS AND HOMO SAPIENS)	600,000 YEARS AGO
Homo neanderthalis	200,000 YEARS AGO
Homo sapiens	200,000 YEARS AGO
Homo sapiens sapiens (MODERN HUMANS)	35,000 YEARS AGO

and to innovate) and finding new ways of doing things. Some hominin groups were better at it than others. (See Map 1.1.)

In adapting, early hominins began to distinguish themselves from other mammals that were physically similar to themselves. It was not their hunting prowess that made the hominins stand out, because plenty of other species chased their prey with skill and dexterity. The major trait at this stage that gave early hominins a real advantage for survival was bipedalism: they became "two-footed" creatures that stood upright. At some point, the first hominins were able to remain upright and move about, leaving their arms and hands free for various useful tasks, such as carrying food over long distances. Once they ventured into open savannas (grassy plains with a few scattered trees), about 1.7 million years ago, hominins had a tremendous advantage. They were the only primates (an order of mammals consisting of humans, apes, and monkeys) to move consistently on two legs. Because they could move continuously and over great distances, they were able to migrate out of hostile environments and into more hospitable locations as needed.

Explaining why and how hominins began to walk on two legs is critical to understanding our human origins and how humans became differentiated from other animal groups. Along with the other primates, the first hominins enjoyed the advantages of being long-limbed, tree-loving animals with good vision and dexterous hands. Why did these primates, in contrast to their closest relatives (gorillas and chimpanzees), leave the shelter of trees and venture out into the open grasslands, where they were vulnerable to attack? The answer is not self-evident. Explaining

how and why some apes took these first steps also sheds light on why humanity's origins lie in Africa. Fifteen million years ago there were apes all over the world, so why did a small number of them evolve new traits in Africa?

ENVIRONMENTAL CHANGES Approximately 40 million years ago, the world endured its fourth great ice age, during which the earth's temperatures plunged and its continental ice sheets, polar ice sheets, and mountain glaciers increased. We know this because of the work of paleoclimatologists during the last several decades using measurements of ice cores and oxygen isotopes in the ocean to chart the often radical changes in the world's climate. This ice age lasted until 10,000 years ago. Like all ice ages, it had warming and cooling phases that lasted between 40,000 and 100,000 years each. Between 10 and 12 million years ago, the climate in Africa went through one such cooling and drying phase. To the east of Africa's Rift Valley, stretching from South Africa north to the Ethiopian highlands, the cooling and drying forced the forests to contract and the savannas to spread. It was in this region that some apes came down from the trees, stood up, and learned to walk, to run, and to live in savanna lands—thus becoming the precursors to humans and distinctive as a new species. Using two feet for locomotion augmented the means for obtaining food and avoiding predators and improved the chances of these creatures to survive in constantly changing environments.

In addition to being bipedal, hominins had another trait that helped them survive: opposable thumbs. This trait, shared with other primates, gave hominins great physical dexterity, enhancing their ability to explore and to alter materials found in nature—especially to create and use tools. They also used increased powers of observation and memory, what we call cognitive skills (such as problem solving and—much later—language), to gather wild berries and grains and to scavenge the meat and marrow of animals that had died of natural causes or as the prey of predators. All primates are good at these activities, but hominins excelled at them. Cognition was destined to become the basis for further developments and was another characteristic that separated hominins from their closest species.

The early hominins were highly social. They lived in bands of about twenty-five individuals, surviving by hunting small game and gathering wild plants. Not yet a match for large predators, they had to find safe hiding places. They also sought ecological niches where a diverse supply of wild grains and fruits and abundant wildlife ensured a secure, comfortable existence. In such locations, small hunting bands of twenty-five could swell through alliances with others to as many as 500 individuals. Hominins, like other primates, communicated through gestures, but they also may have developed an early form of spoken language that led (among other things) to the establishment of rules of conduct, customs, and identities.

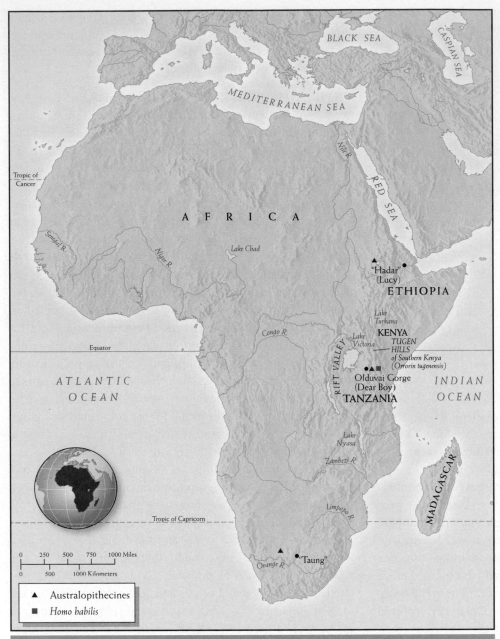

MEDITERRANEAN SEA

BLACK SEA

CASPIAN SEA

AFRICA

Nile R.

RED SEA

Tropic of Cancer

Senegal R.

Niger R.

Lake Chad

"Hadar"
(Lucy)
ETHIOPIA

Congo R.

Lake Turkana

KENYA
TUGEN
HILLS
of Southern Kenya
(Orrorin tugenensis)

Lake Victoria

RIFT VALLEY

Olduvai Gorge
(Dear Boy)
TANZANIA

INDIAN
OCEAN

Equator

ATLANTIC
OCEAN

Lake Nyasa

Zambezi R.

MADAGASCAR

Limpopo R.

Tropic of Capricorn

Orange R. "Taung"

| 0 | 250 | 500 | 750 | 1000 Miles |
| 0 | | 500 | 1000 Kilometers | |

▲ Australopithecines
■ Homo habilis

MAP 1.1 | Early Hominins

The earliest hominin species evolved in Africa millions of years ago.

- Judging from this map, what were the main geographical features of their environment?
- How did the changing environment of eastern and southern Africa shape the evolution of these modern human ancestors?
- What advantages did bipedalism give them?

As the environment changed over the millennia, these early hominins gradually altered in appearance. Over this 4-million-year period, their brains more than doubled in size; their foreheads became more elongated; their jaws became less massive; and they began to look much more like modern humans. Adaptation to environmental changes also created new skills and aptitudes, which expanded the ability to store and analyze information. With larger brains, hominins could form a mental map of their world—they could learn, remember what they learned, and convey these lessons to their neighbors and offspring. In this fashion, larger groups of hominins created communities with a shared understanding of their environment.

DIVERSITY We know that hominins were much older than we thought, but it turns out that they were also much more diverse. Consider some startling finds from South Africa and Kenya. In southern Kenya, researchers discovered bone remains, at least 6 million years old, of a chimpanzee-sized hominin (named *Orrorin tugenensis*) that walked upright on two feet. This discovery indicates that bipedalism must be millions of years older than we used to think. Moreover, these hominins' teeth indicate that they were closer to modern humans than to australopithecines. In their arms and hands, though, which show characteristics needed for tree climbing, the *Orrorin* hominins seemed more apelike than the australopithecines. So *Orrorin* hominins were still somewhat tied to an environment in the trees.

A spectacular discovery has recently come from South Africa. Far inside a cave near Johannesburg, researchers found more than 1,550 fossil remains, probably only a small fraction of the fossils still to be uncovered in the cave. Researchers were able to assemble a composite skeleton that revealed that the upper body parts resembled some of the early pre-*Homo* finds, while the hands (with curved fingers), palms, and wrists, the long legs, and the feet are close to those of modern humans. The species thus far has acquired the name *Homo naledi*, after

These early hominins lived in this manner for more than 4 million years, changing their way of life very little except for moving around the African landmass in their never-ending search for more favorable environments. Even so, their survival is surprising. There were not many of them, and they struggled in hostile environments surrounded by a diversity of large mammals, including predators such as lions.

Studying Climate Changes. *Paleoclimatologists at work on an ice cap in the Peruvian Andes. As members of a scientific team, they dug into the core of this ice cap for samples that would provide information on climate change over many millennia.*

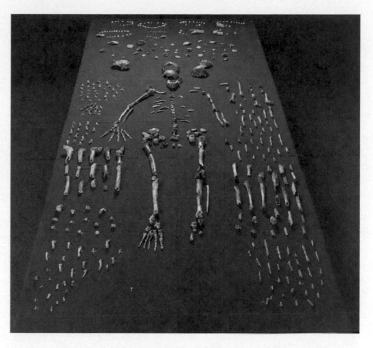

Fossil Remains of *Homo naledi.* *The bones found recently at a cave near Johannesburg, South Africa, and assembled at the Evolutionary Institute of the University of Witwatersrand in Johannesburg. The species has been named Homo naledi after the care where the bones were found. Notice the feet, hand, palm, and wrist bones and how like those of modern humans they are.*

the cave. Yet, given the small size of the brain, these creatures were probably part of the australopithecine group. The males were around 5 feet tall and weighed 100 pounds, while the females were shorter and lighter. Much research remains to be done, and as yet no date has been established for these fossils.

Homo Habilis and the Debate over Who the First Humans Were

One million years after Lucy, the first examples of creatures to whom the scholarly community gave the name *Homo*, or "true human," appeared. They, too, were bipedal, possessing a smooth walk based on upright posture. And they had an even more important advantage over other hominins, brains that were growing larger. Big brains are the site of innovation, learning and storing lessons so that humans can pass those lessons on to offspring, especially in the making of tools and the efficient use

Searching for Hominin Fossils. *Olorgasalie, in Kenya, has proved to be one of the most important archaeological sites for uncovering evidence of early hominin development. Rick Potts, a leader in the field, is shown here on-site. Among his discoveries were hand axes and indications that hominins in this area had learned to use fire.*

The Leakeys. *Louis and Mary Leakey were dedicated archaeologists whose work in East Africa established the area as one of the starting points of human development. Mary Leakey was among the most successful archaeologists studying hominins in Africa. Her finds, including the one in this photograph from Laetoli, Tanzania, highlight the activities of early men and women in Africa. The footprints, believed to be those of Australopithecus afarensis, date from 3.7 to 3 million years ago.*

Boy because the discovery meant so much to them and their research into hominins.

Other objects discovered with Dear Boy demonstrated that by this time early humans had begun to make tools for butchering animals and, possibly, for hunting and killing smaller animals. The tools were flaked stones with sharpened edges for cutting apart animal flesh and scooping out the marrow from bones. To mimic the slicing teeth of lions, leopards, and other carnivores, the Oldowans had devised these tools through careful chipping. Dear Boy and his companions had carried usable rocks to distant places, where they made their implements with special hammer stones—tools to make tools. Unlike other tool-using animals (for example, chimpanzees), early humans were now intentionally fashioning implements, not simply finding them when needed. Because the Leakeys believed that making and using tools represented a new stage in the evolution of human beings, they gave these creatures a new name: ***Homo habilis***, or "skillful man." By using the term *Homo* for them, the Leakeys implied that they were the first truly human creatures in the evolutionary scheme. According to the Leakeys, their toolmaking ability made them the forerunners, though very distant, of modern men and women.

of resources (and, we suspect, in defending themselves). British paleontologists Mary and Louis Leakey, who made astonishing fossil discoveries in the 1950s at Olduvai Gorge (part of the Great Rift Valley) in present-day northeastern Tanzania, identified these important traits. The Leakeys' finds are the most significant discoveries of early humans in Africa—in particular, an intact skull that was 1.8 million years old. The Leakeys nicknamed the creature whose skull they had unearthed Dear

Olduvai Gorge, Tanzania. *Olduvai Gorge is probably the most famous archaeological site containing hominin finds. Mary and Louis Leakey, convinced that early humans originated in Africa, discovered the fossil remains of Homo habilis ("skillful man") in this area between 1960 and 1963. They argued that these findings represent a direct link to Homo erectus.*

Skulls of Ancestors of *Homo sapiens.* *Shown here are seven skulls of ancestors of modern-day men and women, arranged to highlight brain growth over time. The skulls represent (left to right):* Adapis, *a lemur-like animal that lived 50 million years ago;* Proconsul, *a primate that lived about 23 million years ago;* Australopithecus africanus; Homo habilis; Homo erectus; Homo sapiens *from the Qafzeh site in Israel, about 90,000 years old; and* Cro-Magnon Homo sapiens sapiens *from France, about 22,000 years old.*

Although the term *Homo habilis* continues to be employed for these creatures, in many ways, especially in their brain size, they were not distinctly different from their australopithecan predecessors. In fact, just which of the many creatures warrant being seen as the world's first truly human beings turns on what traits are identified as most decisive in distinguishing bipedal apes from modern humans. If that trait is toolmaking, then *Homo habilis* is the first; if being entirely bipedal, then *Homo erectus* is the one; if having a truly large brain, then it might be *Homo sapiens* or their immediate predecessors.

Early Humans on the Move: *Homo Erectus*

Many different species of hominins flourished together in Africa between 2.5 and 1 million years ago. By 1 million years ago, however, many had died out. One surviving species, which emerged about 1.8 million years ago and was destined to remain in existence for more than a million years down to 200,000 years ago, had a large brain capacity and walked truly upright; in fact, its gait was remarkably similar to that of modern humans. Its gait gave it a capacity to run great distances because it had an endurance that no other primate possessed. Hence, this species gained the name **Homo erectus**, or "standing man." *Homo erectus* also enjoyed superior eye-hand coordination and used this skill to throw hand axes at herds of animals. In addition, it looked more human than earlier groups did, for it had lost much of its hair and had developed darker skin as protection from the sun's rays. Even though this species was more able to cope with environmental changes than other hominins had been, its story was not a predictable triumph. Only with the hindsight of millions of years can we understand the decisive advantage of intelligence over brawn—larger brains over larger teeth. Indeed, there were many more failures than successes in the gradual changes that led *Homo erectus* to be one of the few hominin species that would survive until the arrival of *Homo sapiens*.

INFANT CARE AND FAMILY DYNAMICS One of the traits that contributed to the survival of *Homo erectus* was the development of extended periods of caring for their young. Although their enlarged brain gave these hominins advantages over the rest of the animal world, it also brought one significant problem: their head was too large to pass through the female's pelvis at birth. Their pelvis was only big enough to deliver an infant with a cranial capacity that was about one-third an adult's size. As a result, offspring required a long period of protection by adults while they matured and their brain size tripled.

This difference from other species also affected family dynamics. For example, the long maturing process gave adult members of hunting and gathering bands time to train their children in those activities. In addition, maturation and brain growth required mothers to spend years breast-feeding and then preparing food for children after their weaning. To share the responsibilities of child rearing, mothers relied on other women (their own mothers, sisters, and friends) and girls (often their own daughters) to help in the nurturing and protecting, a process known as allomothering (literally, "other mothering").

USE OF FIRE *Homo erectus* began to make rudimentary attempts to control their environment by means of fire—another significant marker in the development of human culture. It is hard to tell from fossils when humans learned to use fire. The most reliable evidence comes from cave sites, less than 250,000 years old, where early humans apparently cooked some of their food. Less conservative estimates suggest that human mastery of fire occurred nearly 500,000 years ago. Fire provided heat, protection from wild animals, a gathering point for small communities, and, perhaps most important, a way to cook food. It was also symbolically powerful, for here was a source of energy that humans could extinguish and revive at will. Because they were able to boil, steam, and fry wild plants as well as otherwise indigestible foods (especially raw muscle fiber), early humans could expand their diets. Because cooked foods yield more energy than raw foods and because the brain, while only 2 percent of human body weight, uses between 20 and 25 percent of all the energy that humans take in, cooking was decisive in the evolution of brain size and functioning.

EARLY MIGRATIONS The populating of the world by hominins proceeded in waves. Around 1 or 2 million years ago, *Homo erectus* individuals migrated first into the lands of Southwest Asia. From there, they traveled along the Indian Ocean shoreline, moving into South Asia and Southeast Asia and later northward into what is now China. Their migration was a response in part to the environmental changes that were transforming the world. The Northern Hemisphere experienced thirty major cold phases during this period, marked by glaciers (huge sheets of ice) spreading over vast expanses of the northern parts of Eurasia and the Americas. The glaciers formed as a result of intense cold that froze much of the world's oceans, lowering them some 325 feet below present-day levels. So it was possible for the migrants to travel across land bridges into Southeast Asia and from East Asia to Japan, as well as from New Guinea to Australia. The last parts of the Afro-Eurasian landmass to be occupied were in Europe. The geological record indicates that ice mantles blanketed the areas of present-day Scotland, Ireland, Wales, Scandinavia, and the whole of northern Europe (including the areas of present-day Berlin, Warsaw, Moscow, and Kiev). Here, too, a lowered ocean level enabled human predecessors to cross by foot from areas in Europe into what is now England.

It is astonishing how far *Homo erectus* traveled. Discoveries of the bone remains of "Java Man" and "Peking Man" (named according to the places where archaeologists first unearthed their remains) confirmed early settlements of *Homo erectus* in Southeast and East Asia. The remains of Java Man, found in 1891 on the island of Java, turned out to be those of an early *Homo erectus* that had dispersed into Asia nearly 2 million years ago. Peking Man, found near Beijing in the 1920s, was a cave dweller, toolmaker, and hunter and gatherer who settled in the warmer climate in northern China perhaps 400,000 years ago. Peking Man's brain was larger than that of his Javan cousins, and there is evidence that he controlled fire and cooked meat in addition to hunting large animals. He made tools of vein quartz, quartz crystals, flint, and sandstone. A major innovation was the double-faced axe, a stone instrument whittled down to sharp edges on both sides to serve as a hand axe, a cleaver, a pick, and probably a weapon to hurl against foes or animals. Even so, these early predecessors lacked the intelligence, language skills, and ability to create culture that would distinguish the first modern humans from their hominin relatives.

Rather than seeing human evolution as a single, gradual development, increasingly scientists view our origins as shaped by a series of progressions and regressions as hominins adapted or failed to adapt and went extinct (died out). Several species existed simultaneously, but some were more suited to changing environmental conditions—and thus more likely to survive—than others. The early settlers of Afro-Eurasia from the *Homo erectus* group went extinct around 200,000 years ago. Yet we are not their immediate descendants. Although the existence of *Homo erectus* may have been necessary for the evolution into *Homo sapiens*, it was not, in itself, sufficient.

THE FIRST MODERN HUMANS

The first traces that we have of *Homo sapiens* come from two sites in modern-day Ethiopia and suggest that the first modern humans emerged sometime between 200,000 and 150,000 years ago. *Homo sapiens*, unlike other hominins, did not take long to become highly mobile, moving out of Africa sometime between 100,000 and 60,000 years ago. If we consider the 6 or 7 million years of hominin life as a single hour of our time today, then our own history (that of *Homo sapiens*) is slightly less than 2 minutes.

The early hominins could not form large communities, as they had limited communication skills. They could utter simple commands and communicate with hand signals, but complex linguistic expression eluded them. This achievement was one of the last in the evolutionary process of becoming human; it did not occur until between 100,000 and 50,000 years ago. Many scholars view it as the critical ingredient in distinguishing human beings from other animals. It is this skill that made **Homo sapiens** "sapiens," which is to say "wise" or "intelligent"— humans who could create culture. Creating language enabled humans to become modern humans.

Homo Sapiens's Precarious Beginnings and Migration

About 200,000 years ago, massive shifts in Africa's climate and environment again put huge pressures on all types of plants and animals, including hominins. Between 60,000 and 10,000 years ago, temperatures dropped, plummeting 40°F below present-day averages. A sheet of ice 2.5 miles thick blanketed northern Europe and North America. With much of the earth's water frozen in glaciers, the climate went dry. The Sahara and Kalahari Deserts expanded; Africa's large tropical rain forests became isolated pockets. Many plant and animal species died out all across Afro-Eurasia. Somehow *Homo sapiens* survived, causing one scholar to assert that humans are "children of the ice age" (Brooke, p. 56). To make matters worse for *Homo sapiens*, about 73,000 years ago, Mount Toba, in present-day Sumatra, erupted, spewing into the atmosphere an enormous quantity of volcanic ash, which created a global volcanic winter that lasted six full years. The hominin populations declined precipitously, and its new species, *Homo sapiens*, threatened to go extinct before it could get started. Only a few thousand survivors huddled together in what remained of the once-rich tropical rain forests of equatorial Africa—a fact that means that all 7 billion of us today descend from an incredibly small African core population. In these extremely cold and dry environments, what counted for survival was superior intelligence and extraordinary mobility, precisely the traits that *Homo sapiens* possessed in abundance.

The highlands of eastern Africa was one of the regions least affected by climate change, and it was there that this new bigger-brained, more dexterous, and more agile species of humans congregated. The *Homo sapiens* population rebounded from its environmental crisis more successfully than *Homo erectus*, and when members of the species began to move out of Africa and the two species encountered each other in the same places across the globe, *Homo sapiens* prevailed—in part because of their greater cognitive and language skills.

The *Homo sapiens* newcomers followed the trails blazed by earlier migrants from Africa. (See Map 1.2.) They frequently moved into the same areas as their genetic cousins, migrating by way of the Levant (the crescent-shaped area encompassing modern-day Lebanon, Israel, Palestine, Jordan, and Syria), into other parts of Southwest Asia and from there into central Asia—but not at this stage into Europe. They flourished and reproduced. By 30,000 years ago, the population of *Homo sapiens* had grown to about 300,000. Between 60,000 and 12,000 years ago, these modern humans were surging into areas tens of thousands of miles from the Rift Valley and the Ethiopian highlands of Africa (see Analyzing Global Developments: The Age of the Universe and Human Evolution). In the area of present-day China, they were thriving and creating distinct regional cultures. Consider Shandingdong Man, a *Homo sapiens* male whose fossil remains and relics date to about 18,000 years ago. His physical characteristics were closer to those of modern humans, and he had a similar brain size. His stone tools, which included choppers and scrapers for preparing food, were similar to those of the *Homo erectus* Peking Man. His bone needles, however, were the first stitching tools of their kind found in China, and they indicate the making of garments. Some of the needles measure a little over an inch in length and have small holes drilled in them. Shandingdong Man also buried his dead. In fact, a tomb of grave goods includes ornaments suggesting the development of aesthetic tastes and religious beliefs.

Homo sapiens populations were also migrating into the northeastern fringe of East Asia. In the frigid climate there, they learned to follow herds of large Siberian grazing animals. The bones and dung of mastodons, large-tusked mammals, made decent fuel and good building material. Pursuing their prey eastward as the herds sought pastures in the steppes (treeless grasslands) and marshes, these groups migrated across the ice

to Japan. Archaeologists have discovered a woolly mammoth fossil in the colder north of Japan, for example, and an elephant fossil in the warmer south. Elephants, in particular, roamed the warmer parts of inner Eurasia.

About 30,000 years ago, *Homo sapiens* began edging into the weedy landmass that linked Siberia and North America (which hominins had not populated). This thousand-mile-long land bridge, later called Beringia, must have seemed like an extension of familiar steppe-land terrain, and these individuals lived isolated lives there on a broad and (at the time) warm plain for 15,000 years before beginning to migrate into North America. The first migrations occurred around 15,000 years ago. During this period and later, modern humans poured eastward and southward into the uninhabited terrain of North America. The oldest known location of human settlement in the Americas is Broken Mammoth, a 14,000-year-old site in central Alaska. A final migration occurred about 8,000 years ago by boat, since by then the land bridge had disappeared under the sea. (See Table 1.2.)

Using their ability to adapt to new environments and to innovate, these expansionist migrants, who were the first discoverers of America, began to fill up the landmasses. They found ample prey in the herds of woolly mammoths, caribou, giant sloths (weighing nearly 3 tons), and 200-pound beavers. But the explorers could also themselves be prey, for they encountered saber-toothed tigers, long-legged eagles, and giant bears that moved faster than horses. The melting of the glaciers about 8,000 years ago and the resulting disappearance of

The Physical Evolution of Hominins. *Left to right, these three figures show the femur bones of Lucy (representing the hominin species* Australopithecus afarensis*), Orrorin tugenensis (one of the earliest of the hominins, who may have existed as many as 6 million years ago), and* Homo sapiens. Homo sapiens *has a larger femur bone and is bigger than Lucy but has the same bone structure.*

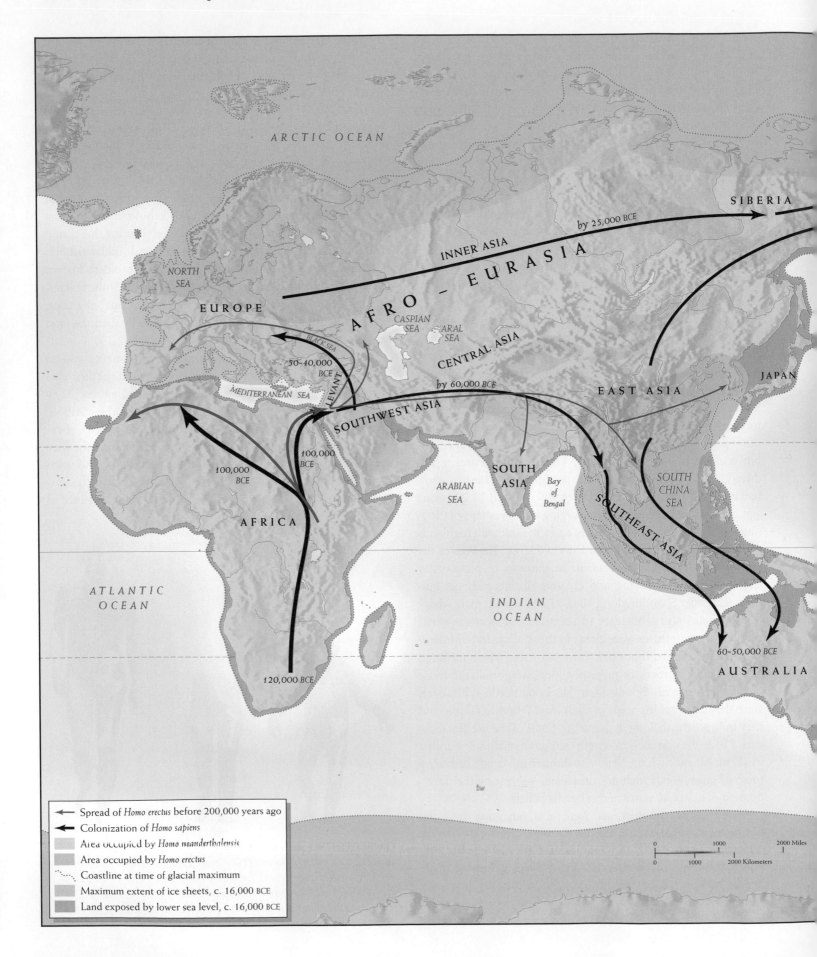

ARCTIC OCEAN

SIBERIA

by 25,000 BCE

INNER ASIA

NORTH SEA

EUROPE

A F R O – E U R A S I A

CASPIAN SEA

ARAL SEA

CENTRAL ASIA

EAST ASIA

JAPAN

BLACK SEA

50–40,000 BCE

MEDITERRANEAN SEA

LEVANT

by 60,000 BCE

SOUTHWEST ASIA

100,000 BCE

100,000 BCE

SOUTH ASIA

Bay of Bengal

ARABIAN SEA

SOUTH CHINA SEA

SOUTHEAST ASIA

AFRICA

ATLANTIC OCEAN

INDIAN OCEAN

60–50,000 BCE

120,000 BCE

AUSTRALIA

Spread of *Homo erectus* before 200,000 years ago
Colonization of *Homo sapiens*
Area occupied by *Homo neanderthalensis*
Area occupied by *Homo erectus*
Coastline at time of glacial maximum
Maximum extent of ice sheets, c. 16,000 BCE
Land exposed by lower sea level, c. 16,000 BCE

0   1000   2000 Miles
0   1000   2000 Kilometers

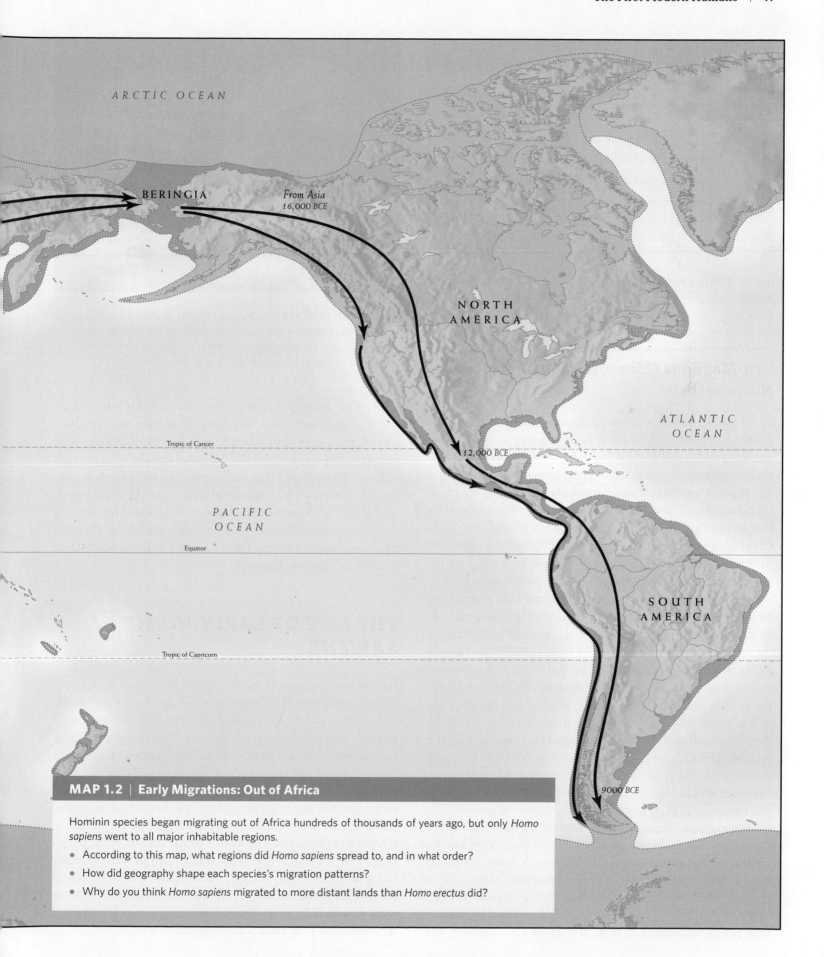

ARCTIC OCEAN

BERINGIA

From Asia
16,000 BCE

NORTH
AMERICA

ATLANTIC
OCEAN

Tropic of Cancer

12,000 BCE

PACIFIC
OCEAN

Equator

SOUTH
AMERICA

Tropic of Capricorn

9000 BCE

MAP 1.2 | Early Migrations: Out of Africa

Hominin species began migrating out of Africa hundreds of thousands of years ago, but only *Homo sapiens* went to all major inhabitable regions.

- According to this map, what regions did *Homo sapiens* spread to, and in what order?
- How did geography shape each species's migration patterns?
- Why do you think *Homo sapiens* migrated to more distant lands than *Homo erectus* did?

TABLE 1.2	*Migrations of Homo sapiens*
SPECIES	**TIME**
Homo erectus leaves Africa	c. 1.5 MILLION YEARS AGO
Homo sapiens leaves Africa	c. 100,000–60,000 YEARS AGO
Homo sapiens migrates into Asia	c. 60,000 YEARS AGO
migrates into Europe	c. 50,000–40,000 YEARS AGO
migrates into Australia	c. 40,000 YEARS AGO
migrates into the Americas	c. 14,000 YEARS AGO

Neanderthal (left) and Cro-Magnon (right) Skulls. *These two skulls show that Neanderthals had a large brain capacity and a larger head than modern humans. However, Neanderthals lost out to* Homo sapiens *in the struggle to survive as* Homo sapiens *spread across the globe.*

the land bridge eventually cut off the first Americans from their Afro-Eurasian origins. Thereafter, the Americas became a world apart from Afro-Eurasia.

Cro-Magnons (*Homo Sapiens*) Replace Neanderthals

Homo sapiens spread out and occupied habitats where earlier hominin migrants had dwelled. From the time they left Africa, they migrated over the whole globe. By 25,000 years ago, as DNA analysis reveals, all genetic cousins to *Homo sapiens* were extinct, leaving only modern humans' ancestors to populate the world. Neanderthals, members of an early wave of hominins from Africa, had settled in western Afro-Eurasia (ranging from present-day Uzbekistan and Iraq to Spain) perhaps 150,000 years ago. They were there well before *Homo sapiens*. Therein lies a tale, for scholars have had a long fascination with these hominins.

For a long time, many scholars believed that Neanderthals were the primary precursors of modern-day Europeans. We now know that this is not true. The first knowledge of Neanderthals came with the discovery in 1856 of a skull in the Neander Valley of present-day Germany (the *thal* or *tal* in their name is the German word for "valley"). Some authorities wondered if the skull represented the so-called missing link between apes and humans. Not only did Neanderthals have big brains, but they also used tools, buried their dead, hunted, and lived in rock-shelters and caves. To judge from their behavior, their brain structure was not as complex as that of modern humans, so their cognitive abilities were far more limited than those of *Homo sapiens*, especially in their perception and creation of symbols.

Neanderthals eventually gave way to Cro-Magnon peoples, a group of *Homo sapiens* named after fossil discoveries made in 1868 at a rock-shelter called Cro-Magnon in France. Although Neanderthal and Cro-Magnon communities overlapped in Europe for thousands of years and recent genetic evidence suggests that there was some interbreeding, the Neanderthals were not as well equipped to survive as the Cro-Magnons, who were truly modern humans. The Neanderthals' short arms and legs and bulky torso may have made them stronger than Cro-Magnon men and women, but the Neanderthals were awkward and clumsy. The Cro-Magnons had the advantages of physical dexterity and high intelligence; the latter attribute gave them cognitive skills, language abilities, and the capability of seeing their environment in symbolic ways that Neanderthals did not possess. Ultimately, the Neanderthals left only a small trace, somewhere between 1 and 4 percent in the gene pool that evolved into modern humanity.

THE LIFE OF EARLY *HOMO SAPIENS*

Having won out over *Homo erectus* and *Homo neanderthalensis*, *Homo sapiens* moved into favorable niches all over the world, endeavoring to find food, protect themselves from larger wild animals, and develop a group identity. The extreme cold that had gripped the earth starting 60 million years ago finally gave way around 60,000 years ago to a warming cycle that "has sheltered humanity ever since" (Brooke, p. 121). Humankind experienced a spurt in population growth as a result of the warm and stable climate that set in. The population grew from 7 million in 9000 BCE to 38 million in 3000 BCE to 252 million at the beginning of the Common Era. These human beings were intensely social and also highly artistic. Their creativity was expressed through language, painting, sculpture, and even music; in these ways as well as their hunting and gathering way of life, they set themselves off from their hominin predecessors.

The Age of the Universe and Human Evolution

Our universe is nearly 14 billion years old. Our sun, earth, and solar system appeared nearly 4.5 billion years ago, and the earliest life-forms on earth appeared 3.8 billion years ago. Hominins, however, only appeared on the scene about 7 million years ago, which represents not even 1 percent of the total time that the earth has existed. They were for a long time confined to the African landmass, learning to walk on two legs there, devising simple tools at first and perfecting their use over time. Africa remained the homeland for many different hominin groups for nearly 5 million years before *Homo erectus* ventured out of the continent, moving into central Asia, East Asia, Southeast Asia, and Europe though not into the Americas. There were probably other waves of hominin migrations out of Africa, but the most important of the migrations out of Africa occurred sometime between 100,000 and 60,000 years ago, when modern humans, *Homo sapiens*, left the continent and, with amazing rapidity, occupied all of the globe's landmasses. (See Map 1.2 to trace the migrations of *Homo erectus* and *Homo sapiens*.)

QUESTIONS FOR ANALYSIS

- How do we know the age of the universe and when and how hominins first appeared and their evolutionary patterns?
- Why are hominins and *Homo sapiens* so late in the evolutionary cycle, and why did *Homo sapiens* prevail over other hominins?
- In your opinion, which of the different families of hominins deserves the designation of the first humans—and why?
- Why are scientists disinclined to see a straight-line evolution from the earliest hominins to modern humans?

The Big Bang moment in the creation of the universe	13.75 BILLION YEARS AGO (BYA)
The formation of the sun, earth, and solar system	4.5 BYA
Earliest life-forms appear	3.8 BYA
Multicellular organisms appear	1.5 BYA
First hominins appear	7 MILLION YEARS AGO (MYA)
Australopithecus afarensis appears (including Lucy)	3.4 MYA
Homo habilis appears (including Dear Boy)	2.5 MYA
Homo erectus appears (including Java Man and Peking Man)	1.8 MYA
Homo erectus leaves Africa	1.5 MYA
Neanderthals appear	200,000 YEARS AGO
Homo sapiens appears	200,000 YEARS AGO
Homo sapiens leaves Africa	100,000–60,000 YEARS AGO
Homo sapiens migrates into Asia	60,000 YEARS AGO
Homo sapiens migrates into Europe	50,000–40,000 YEARS AGO
Homo sapiens migrates into Australia	40,000 YEARS AGO
Homo sapiens migrates into the Americas	14,000 YEARS AGO
Homo sapiens sapiens appears (modern humans)	35,000 YEARS AGO

<1% of earth's existence

Sources: Chris Scarre (ed.), *The Human Past: World Prehistory and the Development of Human Societies* (2005); Ian Tattersall, *Masters of the Planet: The Search for Our Human Origins* (Palgrave Macmillan, 2012).

Hunting and Gathering

Like their hominin predecessors, modern humans (*Homo sapiens*) were hunters and gatherers, though they were more advanced than earlier hominins because of their agility, their ability to move quickly into favorable locations, and their superior intelligence. Still, they subsisted as hunters and gatherers until around 12,000 years ago. They hunted animals, fished, and foraged for wild berries, nuts, fruit, and grains, rather than planting crops, vines, or trees. Even today, **hunting and gathering** societies endure, although only in the most marginal locations, mainly driven there by peoples living in settled societies. For example, researchers consider the present-day San peoples of southern Africa an isolated hunting and gathering remnant continuing their traditional mode of life. Modern scholars use the San to reveal how men and women must have lived hundreds of thousands of years ago. (See Primary Source: Problems in the Study of Hunters and Gatherers.) As late as 1500, hunters and gatherers occupied a third of the globe, including all of Australia, most of North America, and large tracts of South America, Africa, and North and Northeast Asia, and constituted as much as 15 percent of the world's population.

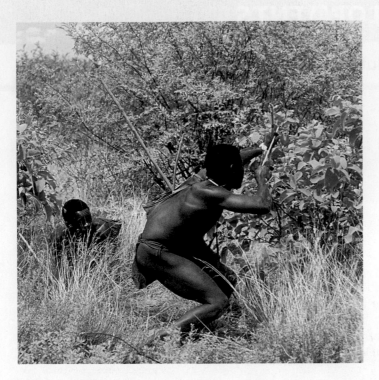

The San Hunters and Gatherers of Southern Africa. *The San, who live in the Kalahari Desert in present-day Botswana, continue to follow a hunting and gathering existence that has died out in many parts of the world. Hunting and gathering was the way that most humans lived for millennia.*

The fact that hominin men and women survived as hunters and gatherers for millions of years, that early *Homo sapiens* also lived this way, and that a few contemporary communities still forage for food suggests the powerful attractions of this way of life. Hunters and gatherers could find enough food in about 3 hours of foraging each day, thus affording time for other pursuits, such as relaxation, interaction, and friendly competitions with other members of their band. Scholars believe that these small bands were relatively egalitarian, and one scholar described foragers as "the original affluent society," producing much and wanting little (Sahlins, p. 85). Men specialized in hunting and women in gathering and child-rearing, but men and women contributed equally to the band's welfare. Scholars also believe that women made a larger contribution than men did and enjoyed high status because the dietary staples were cereals and fruits, whose harvesting and preparation were likely women's responsibility.

An extraordinary recent find of 10,000-year-old human fossil remains on the shore of Lake Turkana in Kenya provides an answer to a question that has intrigued researchers but had defied resolution for lack of evidence: Were human beings, living in what seventeenth- and eighteenth-century intellectuals termed a "state of nature," peace-loving individuals, or—like their closest relatives, the chimpanzees—were they violent beings capable of carrying out warlike raids against other hunter-gatherers? Researchers found that ten of the twelve

relatively intact skeletons had died violent deaths, and the partial remains of fifteen others suggested a massacre. Scholars at the site concluded that in this one and thus far only known incident, a group of hunter-gatherers were the victims of "inter-group violence" ("Inter-Group Violence," p. 394).

Cultural Forms

Despite the remorselessly nature-bound quality of life for early humans, the first *Homo sapiens* communities made an evolutionary breakthrough. They developed cultural forms that reflected a consciousness of self, a drive to survive, an appreciation of beauty, and an ability to manipulate information symbolically.

Few of the cultural achievements of early *Homo sapiens* communities have engaged modern-day observers more than their artistic endeavors. Accomplished drawings have come to light in many areas but have been most fully studied in Europe. The ability to draw enabled *Homo sapiens* peoples to understand their environment, to bond among their kin groups (groups related by blood ties), and to articulate important mythologies. Such behaviors gave individuals an adaptive advantage in surviving in extremely challenging circumstances.

"Look, Daddy, oxen!" That is what the daughter of Marcelino Sanz de Sauruola cried to her father as she looked up at the ceiling of a deep cave that he was exploring one summer afternoon on his property at Altamira, Spain. As he looked up, Sauruola could not believe what he saw. Arranged across the ceiling of the huge chamber were more than two dozen life-size figures of bison, horses, and wild bulls, all painted in vivid red, black, yellow, and brown. He did not think that anyone would believe these fabulous images were tens of thousands of years old, but he knew in his heart that they were. That was in 1879. Only in 1906 did the world accept that the Altamira paintings were the work of early humans and were at least 17,000 years old. Even today, with researchers having found more than 50,000 works of art by early humans in Europe, these paintings compel wonder and awe at the innate artistic abilities unique to humans. (See Primary Source: The Art of Chauvet Cave.)

The images were rendered on cave walls over a period of 25,000 years, and they changed very little during that long time. The earliest wall decorations are at least 41,000 years old. The subjects are most often large game—animals that early humans would have considered powerful symbols. The artists rendered these animals with a striking economy of line, frequently painted in such a way that the natural contours of the cave wall defined a bulging belly or an eye socket. Many appear more than once, suggesting that they are works from several occasions or by several artists. The remarkably few human images show naked females or dancing males. There are also many handprints made by blowing paint around a hand placed

Problems in the Study of Hunters and Gatherers

One of the challenges in studying the origins of humanity is that the evidence is incomplete. Archaeologists and anthropologists have to theorize on the basis of what they can lay their hands on. In the case of archaeologists, these include fossil records. In the case of anthropologists, their subjects are tribal peoples—such as the San of southern Africa—whose lifeways today may resemble those of their ancestors tens of thousands of years ago.

To date, the hunting way of life has been the most successful and persistent adaptation man has ever achieved.

. . . It is appropriate that anthropologists take stock of the much older way of life of the hunters. This is not simply a study of biological evolution, since zoologists have come to regard behavior as central to the adaptation and evolution of all species. The emergence of economic, social, and ideological forms are as much a part of human evolution as are the developments in human anatomy and physiology. . . .

. . . Ever since the origin of agriculture, . . . peoples have been steadily expanding at the expense of the hunters. Today the latter are often found in unattractive environments, in lands which are of no use to their neighbors and which pose difficult and dramatic problems of survival. The more favorable habitats have long ago been appropriated by peoples with stronger, more aggressive social systems.

. . . Taking hunters as they are found, anthropologists have naturally been led to the conclusion that their life (and by implication the life of our ancestors) was a constant struggle for survival.

At the dawn of agriculture 12,000 years ago, hunters covered most of the habitable globe, and appeared to be generally most successful in those areas which later supported the densest populations of agricultural peoples. By 1500 CE the area left to hunters had shrunk drastically and their distribution fell largely at the peripheries of the continents and in the inaccessible interiors. However, even at this late date, hunting peoples occupied all of Australia, most of western and northern North America, and large portions of South America and Africa. This situation rapidly changed with the era of colonial expansion, and by 1900, when serious ethnographic research got under way, much of this way of life had been destroyed. As a result, our notion of unacculturated hunter-gatherer life has been largely drawn from peoples no longer living in the optimum portion of their traditional range.

To mention a few examples, the Netsilik Eskimos, the Arunta, and the Kung Bushmen are now classic cases in ethnography. However, the majority of the precontact Eskimos, Australian aborigines, and Bushmen lived in much better environments. Two-thirds of the Eskimos, according to Laughlin, lived *south* of the Arctic circle, and the populations in the Australian and Kalahari deserts were but a fraction of the populations living in the well-watered regions of southeast Australia and the Cape Province of Africa. Thus, within a given region the "classic cases" may, in fact, be precisely the opposite: namely, the most isolated peoples who managed to avoid contact until the arrival of the ethnographers. In order to understand hunters better it may be more profitable to consider the few hunters in rich environments, since it is likely that these peoples will be more representative of the ecological conditions under which man evolved than are the dramatic and unusual cases that illustrate extreme environmental pressure. Such a perspective may better help us to understand the extraordinary persistence and success of the human adaptation.

Source: *Man the Hunter*, edited by Richard B. Lee, Irven DeVore, and Jill Nash (Chicago: Aldine Publishing, 1968), pp. 3, 5.

QUESTIONS FOR ANALYSIS

- Why is it important to study hunting and gathering communities?
- Why are the "classic cases" not necessarily the most representative of this early lifeway?

---

on the cave wall or by dipping hands in paint and then pressing them to the wall. There are even abstract symbols such as circles, wavy lines, and checkerboards; often these appear between different image forms, serving as artistic transitions in the caves. But they are accomplished with such consummate skill that one of the twentieth century's most celebrated painters, Pablo Picasso, is alleged to have exclaimed that the Ice Age artists left him little to do.

We can only speculate what the images meant to ancient humans. Scholars have rejected an initial explanation that they were decorative, for the deep caves were not the ancients' homes and had no natural light to render the images visible. Perhaps

The Art of Chauvet Cave

A spectacular discovery at Chauvet Cave, in southwestern France, in 1994 overturned all previous ideas about the development of prehistoric art. Dating to about 35,000 years ago (much older than the 20,000-year-old paintings from Lascaux, in southeastern France, or the 17,000-year-old paintings from Altamira, in northwestern Spain), they are the oldest prehistoric cave paintings known in Europe. The hundreds of representations found at Chauvet Cave are more detailed and more brilliant than the ones at Altamira and Lascaux. There are drawings of mammoths, musk oxen, horses, lions, bears, bison, and even rhinoceroses, as well as human palm prints (and footprints on the cave's floor) and "Venus" figures with exaggerated female genitalia—the latter apparently signifying a preoccupation with human fertility. These amazing engravings and paintings shocked scholars because they were produced only a few thousand years after the first modern humans appeared in Europe.

QUESTIONS FOR ANALYSIS

- These drawings show horses, a musk ox, and a rhinoceros. What characteristics of these animals might have inspired the early *Homo sapiens* artists, and why?
- What does their decision to portray certain animals but not others tell us?

Almost as soon as their first appearance in western Europe, modern humans seemed to have rapidly developed a sense, ability, and desire to portray other living beings in their environment. This brilliant drawing shows the detail in a depiction of horses' heads.

This image uses a doubling effect—drawing additional hindquarters and legs—to give the bison the appearance of motion and speed. The ability to portray dynamic movement was once thought to be a skill that humans developed much later.

the images had a social function, helping the early humans to define themselves as separate from other parts of nature. Among other interpretations is a theory that they were the work of powerful shamans, individuals believed to hold special powers to understand and control the mystifying forces of the cosmos.

Paintings were not the only form of artistic expression for early humans. Archaeologists also have unearthed small sculptures of animals shaped out of bone and stone that are even older than the paintings. Most famous are figurines of enormously fat and pregnant females. Statuettes like the so-called

Venus of Willendorf, found in Austria, demonstrate that successful reproduction was a very important theme. Among the most exquisite sculptures are those of animals carved in postures of movement or at rest.

The caves of early men and women also resounded to the strains of music. In 2008, archaeologists working in southwestern Germany discovered a hollowed-out bone flute with five openings that they dated to approximately 35,000 years ago, roughly the same time that humans began to occupy this region. When researchers put the flute to musical tests, they concluded that this seemingly primitive instrument was capable of making harmonic sounds comparable to those of modern-day flutes, no small achievement for these early humans, whose artistic prowess must have provided much enjoyment to listeners and viewers.

Only *Homo sapiens* had the cognitive abilities to produce the abundant sculptures and drawings of this era, thus leaving a permanent mark on the symbolic landscape of human development. Such visual expressions marked the dawn of human culture and a consciousness of men's and women's place in the world. Symbolic activity of this sort enabled humans to make sense of themselves, nature, and the relationship between humanity and nature.

Language

Few things set humans off from the rest of the animal world more starkly than their use of language, whose genesis and

Willendorf Venus. *This squat limestone statuette—only about 6 inches in height—was discovered in 1908 near the village of Willendorf, Austria, and dates back about 25,000 years. As one of the earliest representations of a female figure found in Europe, it is a famous icon of prehistoric art. The emphasis on the woman's breasts and reproductive organs—to the exclusion, for example, of her facial features— and the presence of a red ocher dye on her genitalia suggest the maker's concern with the woman's fertility and procreative functions.*

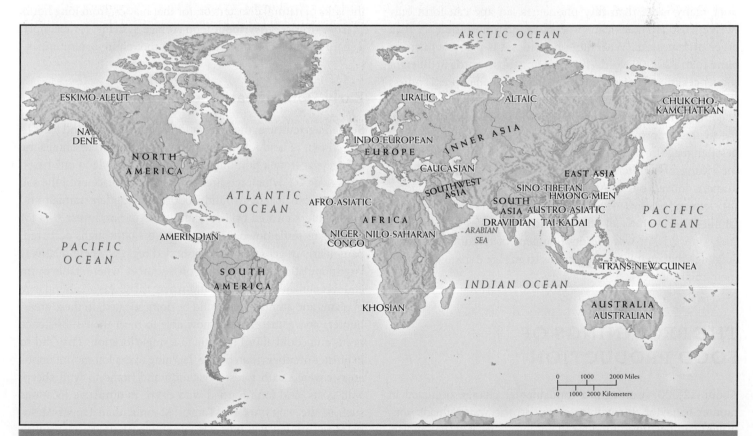

MAP 1.3 | Original Language Family Groups

The use of complex language developed around 80,000 years ago among *Homo sapiens* in Africa. As humans dispersed throughout the globe, numerous language families evolved from which all natural languages originate.

- How many different landmasses did language evolve on?
- On the basis of this map, what geographical features kept emerging language families distinct from one another?
- Why do you think separate languages emerged over time?

evolution spark heated controversies. Scholars do agree, however, that the cognitive abilities involved in language development marked an evolutionary milestone.

It is important to distinguish between meaningful vocal-utterance speech, possessed by many precursor hominins, and natural language (the use of sounds to make words that when strung together convey complex meaning to others), which is unique to modern humans. The development of language necessitated a large brain and complex cognitive skill to create word groups that would convey symbolic meaning. Verbal communication thus required an ability to think abstractly and to communicate abstractions. Language was a huge breakthrough, because individuals could teach words to offspring and neighbors and could use them to integrate communities for survival. Language also enhanced the ability to accumulate knowledge that could be transmitted across both space and time.

Biological research has demonstrated that humans can make and process many more primary and distinctive sounds, called phonemes, than other animals can. Whereas a human being can utter many more than fifty phonemes, an ape can form only twelve. Also, humans can process sounds more quickly than other primates can. With fifty phonemes it is possible to create more than 100,000 words; by arranging those words in different sequences in language (syntax), individuals can express endless subtle and complex meanings. Recent research suggests that use of complex languages occurred about 80,000 years ago and that the nearest approximation to humanity's proto-language (earliest language) existing today belongs to two African peoples, the !Kung of southern Africa and the Hadza of Tanzania. As humans moved out of Africa and dispersed around the globe, they expanded their original language into nineteen language families, from which all of the world's languages then evolved. (See Map 1.3.) It was the development of cultural forms and language that enabled *Homo sapiens* to engage dynamically with their environments.

THE BEGINNINGS OF FOOD PRODUCTION

About 12,000 years ago, a fundamental change occurred in human behavior. It involved a shift in the way humans controlled and produced food for themselves—what some scholars have called a revolution in agriculture and ecology. In this era of major change, some communities gradually stopped going out in search of wild grains and wild animals and learned instead the propagation of edible plants and the **domestication** (bringing under human control) of wild animals. In doing so, they also settled down in villages, expanding their numbers and gaining control over nature. Eight locations that scholars acknowledge

to be independent centers of this agricultural revolution were Southwest Asia, East Asia, Southeast Asia, the New Guinea highlands, sub-Saharan Africa, Andean South America, central Mexico, and the eastern United States. (See Map 1.4.)

Precisely what factors triggered the move to settled agriculture remains hotly contested. Undoubtedly, the significantly warmer temperatures and wetter climates made the move to settled agriculture easier. Population pressure was also a decisive factor, as hunting and gathering alone could not sustain growing foraging populations. The agricultural revolution shattered the population ceiling of natural food supplies and led to a vast population expansion, because men and women could now produce more calories per unit of land than in the past. But the changeover from foraging to settled agriculture did not occur quickly. It took many thousands of years for foragers to add farming and herding to their traditions of hunting and gathering and then eventually to rely entirely on farming and herding for their subsistence. To be sure, learning to control the environment and domesticate resources did not liberate humans from the risks of natural disasters or, for that matter, from long hours of labor drudgery. Without food storage systems, for example, a sharp drought could wipe out or uproot entire communities.

Early Domestication of Plants and Animals

Settled agriculture, the application of human labor and tools to a fixed plot of land for more than one growing cycle, entails the changeover from a hunting and gathering lifestyle to one based on agriculture, which requires staying in one place until the soil has been exhausted. Around 9000 BCE, abundant rainfall and mild winters created optimal conditions in Southwest Asia for humans to settle down. Here the first breakthroughs occurred, particularly in geographically bounded regions where relatively large populations were pressing on resources, where stable warm and wet climates abounded, and where there was an abundance of plants and animals that could be domesticated. In these areas, hunters and gatherers were now able to meet their subsistence needs and could afford to settle in a single location. They did so in greater numbers than before, learning to exploit mountainous areas covered with forest vegetation and home to wild sheep, wild goats, and long-horned wild oxen. In attractive locations such as the valleys of the Taurus Mountains in Upper Mesopotamia (present-day Iraq and Syria), the Anatolian plateau (in modern-day Turkey), and the hillsides of present-day northern Israel, early humans began to establish permanent settlements and to herd once-wild animals and cultivate once-wild grains.

The formation of these communities enabled humans to take risks, spurring agricultural innovation. With abundant wild game and edible plants, people could observe and experiment with the most adaptable plants and animals. For ages, people had been gathering grains by collecting seeds that fell freely from their stalks. At some point, observant collectors perceived that they could obtain larger harvests if they pulled grain seeds directly from plants. The process of plant domestication probably began when people noticed that certain edible plants retained their nutritious grains longer than others, so they collected these seeds and scattered them across fertile soils. When ripe, these plants produced bigger and hardier crops. People used most seeds for food but saved some for planting in the next growing cycle, to ensure a food supply for the next year. The gradual domestication of plants began in the southern Levant and spread from there into the rest of Southwest Asia. Even so, by 5,000 years ago, most of the major regions of the world had made agricultural breakthroughs. The result was that all of the basic crops that we consume today had been domesticated: wheat and barley in Southwest Asia; sorghum and yams in Africa; maize and potatoes in the Americas; and rice and millet in East Asia.

DOMESTICATION OF ANIMALS If dogs are a man's best friend, we are now beginning to learn how long and important that friendship has been. Dogs were the first animals to be domesticated (although in fact they may have adopted humans, rather than the other way around). At least 15,000 years ago in Central Asia, including Mongolia and Nepal, humans first domesticated gray wolves and made them an essential part of human society. These animals did more than comfort humans, however, for they provided a vital example of how to achieve the domestication of other animals. Moreover, dogs with herding instincts aided humans in controlling sheep once they had been domesticated.

Wild sheep and wild goats were the next animals to come under human control. This process took place in the central Zagros Mountains region in present-day western Iraq, where wild sheep and wild goats were abundant. A favored explanation is that hunters returned home with young wild sheep, which then grew up within the human community. They reproduced, and their offspring never returned to the wild. The animals accepted their dependence because the humans fed them. As it became clear that controlling animal reproduction was more reliable than hunting, domesticated herds became the primary source of protein in the early human diet. This shift probably happened first with the wild sheep living in herds on the mountain slopes.

When the number of animals under human control and living close to the settlement outstripped the supply of food needed to feed the human population, community members could move the animals to grassy steppes for grazing. This lifestyle, called **pastoralism** (the herding of domesticated animals), later became an important subsistence strategy that complemented settled farming. Pastoralists herded domesticated animals, moving them to new pastures on a seasonal basis.

Domestication. *This detail from a wall painting in the Tassili n'Ajjer mountain range in modern Algeria depicts early domestication of cattle and other animals.*

Goats, the other main domesticated animal of Southwest Asia, are smarter than sheep but more difficult to control. The pastoralists may have introduced goats into herds of sheep to better control herd movement. Pigs and cattle also came under human control at this time.

Pastoralists and Agriculturalists

Pastoralism, which involved the herding of sheep and goats but also cattle, appeared as a way of life around 5500 BCE, essentially at the same time that full-time farming appeared. The first pastoralists were closely affiliated with agricultural villages whose inhabitants grew grains, especially wheat and barley, which required large parcels of land. Pastoralists produced both meat and dairy products, as well as wool for textiles, and exchanged these products with the agriculturalists for grain, pottery, and other staples. In the Fertile Crescent, many extended families farmed and herded at the same time, growing crops in fertile flatlands and grazing their herds in the foothills and mountains nearby. These herders moved their livestock seasonally, usually pasturing their flocks in higher lands during summer and in valleys during winter. This movement over short distances is called transhumance and did not require herders to vacate their primary locations, which were generally in the mountain valleys.

A quite different form of pastoralism, often called nomadic pastoralism, also based on the herding of cattle and other livestock, came to flourish much later in other settings, notably

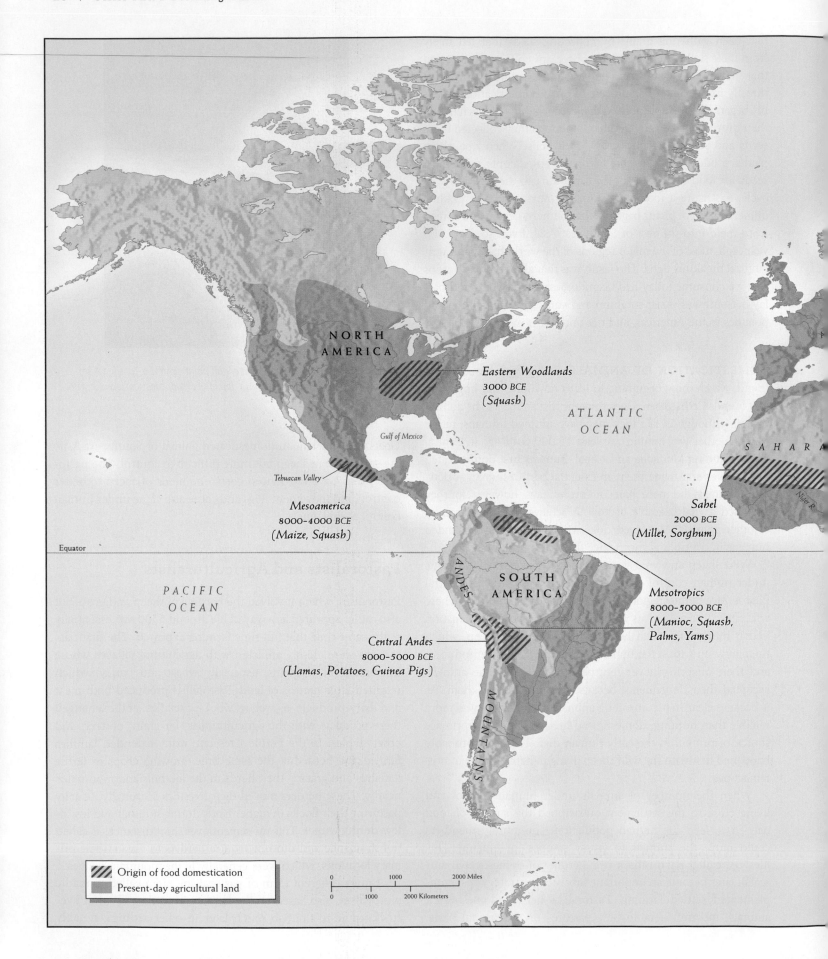

NORTH
AMERICA

Eastern Woodlands
3000 BCE
(Squash)

ATLANTIC
OCEAN

Gulf of Mexico

SAHARA

Tehuacan Valley

Mesoamerica
8000–4000 BCE
(Maize, Squash)

Sabel
2000 BCE
(Millet, Sorghum)

Niger R.

Equator

PACIFIC
OCEAN

ANDES

SOUTH
AMERICA

Mesotropics
8000–5000 BCE
(Manioc, Squash,
Palms, Yams)

Central Andes
8000–5000 BCE
(Llamas, Potatoes, Guinea Pigs)

MOUNTAINS

Origin of food domestication
Present-day agricultural land

0   1000   2000 Miles
0   1000   2000 Kilometers

MAP 1.4 | The Origins of Food Production

Agricultural production emerged in many regions at different times. The variety of patterns reflected local resources and conditions.

- How many different locations did agricultural production emerge in?
- Are there any common geographical features among these early food-producing areas?
- Why do you think agriculture emerged in certain areas and not in others?
- How did the domestication of plants and animals affect kinship systems, political organization, and social relations?

in the steppe lands north of the agricultural zone of southern Eurasia. This way of life was characterized by horse-riding herders of livestock. These herders often had no fixed home, unlike the transhumant herders of Southwest Asia, though they often returned to their traditional locations, but moved in response to the size and needs of their herds. The northern areas of the Eurasian landmass, stretching from present-day Ukraine across Siberia and Mongolia to the Pacific Ocean, became the preserve of these horse-riding pastoral peoples beginning in the second millennium BCE, living as they did in a region unable to support the extensive agriculture necessary for large settled populations.

The archaeological record indicates that full-fledged pastoralism crystallized on the steppe lands of northern Eurasia by 2000 BCE. By this time, the peoples living there had learned to yoke and ride animals, to milk them, and to use their hair for clothing, as well as to slaughter them for food. Of all the domesticated animals in the steppe lands, the horse became the most important. Because horses provided decisive advantages in transportation and warfare, they gained more value than other domesticated animals. Thus, horses soon became the measure of household wealth and prestige.

Historians know much less about these horse-riding pastoral peoples than about the agriculturalists and their transhumant cousins, as their numbers were small and they left fewer archaeological traces or historical records. Their role in world history, however, is as important as that of the settled societies. In Afro-Eurasia, they domesticated horses and developed weapons and techniques that at certain points in history enabled them to conquer sedentary societies. They also transmitted ideas, products, and people across long distances, maintaining the linkages that connected east and west. In spite of the low opinion that settled peoples usually had about nomadic pastoralists, often scorning them as uncivilized barbarians, their contribution to world history is now being acknowledged.

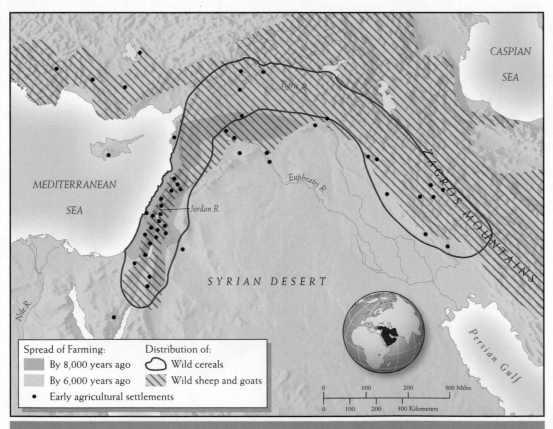

MAP 1.5 | The Birth of Farming in the Fertile Crescent

Agricultural production occurred in the Fertile Crescent starting roughly at 9000 BCE. Though the process was slow, farmers and herders domesticated a variety of plants and animals, which led to the rise of large-scale, permanent settlements.

- What does the map reveal about the environment and natural resources in the Fertile Crescent?
- Why was agriculture absent in the region of the southern Tigris and Euphrates Rivers during this period?
- What relationship existed between cereal cultivators and herders of goats and sheep?

EMERGENCE OF AGRICULTURE

Agricultural revolutions occurred worldwide between 9000 and 2000 BCE. They had much in common: the same factors of climatic change; increased knowledge about plants and animals; and the need for more efficient ways to feed, house, and promote the survival of larger numbers. These concerns led peoples in Afro-Eurasia and the Americas to see the advantages of cultivating plants and domesticating wildlife.

Some communities were independent innovators, developing agricultural techniques based on their specific environment, while others borrowed from the first innovators. The innovators were found in Southwest Asia, where control of water was decisive; the southern part of China in East Asia, where water controls and rice were critical; the Americas, which had the disadvantage of offering few animals that humans could domesticate; and Africa, where farmers just below the Sahara Desert in a region known as the Sahel innovated and then carried their skills to West Africa and the Ethiopian highlands. In contrast, the cultivators of western Europe were borrowers, learning from the first innovators of Southwest Asia. Even so, a broad array of patterns existed as humans settled down as farmers and herders.

Southwest Asia: Cereals and Mammals

The first agricultural revolution occurred in Southwest Asia in an area bounded by the Mediterranean Sea and the Zagros Mountains. Because of its rich soils and regular rainfall, this area played a leading role in the domestication of wild grasses and the taming of animals important to humans. Six large mammals—goats, sheep, pigs, cattle, camels, and horses—have been vital for meat, milk, skins (including hair), and transportation. Southwest Asians domesticated all of these except horses.

Around 9000 BCE, in the southern corridor of the Jordan River valley, humans began to domesticate the wild ancestors of barley and wheat. (See Map 1.5.) Various wild grasses were abundant in this region, and barley and wheat were the easiest to adapt to settled agriculture and the easiest to transport. Although the changeover from gathering wild cereals to regular cultivation took several centuries and saw failures as well as successes, by the end of the ninth millennium BCE, cultivators were selecting and storing seeds and then sowing them in prepared seedbeds. Moreover, in the valleys of the Zagros Mountains on the eastern side of the Fertile Crescent, similar experimentation was occurring with animals around the same time.

East Asia: Rice and Water

A revolution in food production also occurred among the coastal dwellers in East Asia, although under different circumstances. (See Map 1.6.) Throughout this region, the spread of lakes, marshes, and rivers created habitats

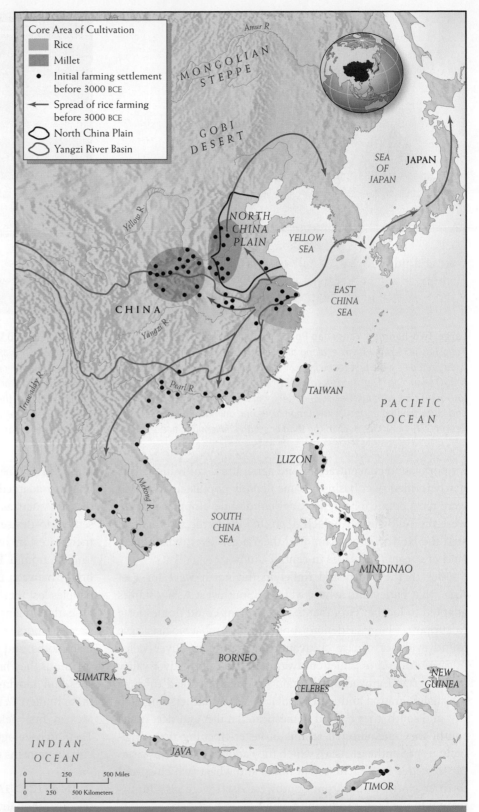

MAP 1.6 | The Spread of Farming in East Asia

Agricultural settlements appeared in East Asia later than they did in the Fertile Crescent.
- According to this map, where did early agricultural settlements appear in East Asia?
- What types of crops and animals were domesticated in East Asia?
- How did the physical features of these regions lend themselves to agricultural production?

Large Two-handled Yangshao Pot. *This pot comes from the village of Yangshao in Henan Province, along the Yellow River in Northwest China, where remains were first found in 1921 of a people who lived more than 6,000 years ago. The Yangshao people lived in small, rammed-earth fortresses and, without the use of pottery wheels, created fine white-, red-, and black-painted pottery with human faces and animal and geometric designs. This jar dates back to the third or second millennium BCE.*

Pottery in Banpo Village (c. 4800–4200 BCE). *This remarkable, intact village, one of the best-known ditch-enclosed settlements of Yangshao culture, provides us with clear evidence of a sophisticated agriculture based on millet and Chinese cabbage. One of China's first farming cultures, the people of Banpo interacted directly with other villages on the North China plain and were indirectly in contact with peoples from as far away as Southeast Asia.*

for population concentrations and agricultural cultivation. Two newly formed river basins became densely populated areas that were focal points for intensive agricultural development. These were the Yellow River, which deposited the fertile soil that created the North China plain, and the Yangzi River, which fed a land of streams and lakes in central China.

Rice in the south and millet in the north were for East Asia what barley and wheat were for Southwest Asia—staples adapted to local environments that humans could domesticate to support a large, sedentary population. Archaeologists have found evidence of rice cultivation in the Yangzi River valley in 6500 BCE and of millet cultivation in the Yellow River valley in 5500 BCE. Innovations in grain production spread through internal migration and wider contacts. When farmers migrated east and south, they carried domesticated millet and rice. In the south, they encountered strains of faster-ripening rice (originally from Southeast Asia), which they adopted. Rice was a staple in wetter South China, but millet and wheat (which spread to drier North China from Southwest Asia) were also fundamental to the food-producing revolution in East Asia.

The Americas: A Slower Transition to Agriculture

The shift to settled agriculture occurred more slowly in the Americas. When people crossed Beringia and trekked southward

through the Americas, they set off an ecological transformation but also adapted to unfamiliar habitats. The flora and fauna of the Americas were different enough to induce the early settlers to devise ways of living that distinguished them from their ancestors in Afro-Eurasia. Then, when the glaciers began to melt around 12,500 BCE and water began to cover the land bridge between East Asia and America, the Americas and their peoples lost their connections with Afro-Eurasia.

Early humans in America used chipped blades and pointed spears to pursue their prey, which included mastodons, woolly mammoths, and bison. In doing so, they extended the hunting traditions they had learned in Afro-Eurasia, establishing campsites and moving with their herds. Researchers have named these hunters "Clovis people" because a site near Clovis, New Mexico, first yielded their typical projectile point (arrowhead). Their archaeological sites, located all over North America, contain the remains of their weaponry.

CLIMATIC CHANGE AND ADAPTATION For many years, scientists thought that the Clovis communities had wiped out the large ice-age mammals they found in America. Recent research suggests, though, that climatic change destroyed the indigenous plants and trees—the feeding grounds of large mammals—and that abundant forage became scarce. The vast spruce forests that had fed the great mastodons, for instance, shrank into isolated pockets, leaving undernourished mastodons vulnerable to

"Long House." *The people who opened up the whole of central Europe to agriculture typically lived in communities of six to twelve "long houses." Although large in size (varying between 60 and 120 feet in length), long houses were built on simple principles: a framework of wooden beams and posts with walls made of mud and woven branches beneath a thatched roof. These dwellings probably sheltered large extended family or kinship units that cooperated to provide the hard work needed to carve out pioneer farming settlements along river valleys. This cutaway reconstruction of a long house shows the placement of wall timbers and internal support posts.*

human and animal predators until they vanished. The tall grass-land prairies gave way to areas with short grass; where short grass once flourished, cacti took over. As in Afro-Eurasia, the arrival of a long global warming cycle compelled those living in the Americas to adapt to different ecological niches and to create new subsistence strategies. Thus, in the woodland area of the present-day northeastern United States, hunters learned to trap smaller wild animals for food and furs. To supplement the protein from meat and fish, these people also dug for roots and gathered berries. What is important is that even as most communities adapted to the settled agricultural economy, they did not abandon basic survival strategies of hunting and gathering.

Food-producing changes in the Americas were different from those in Afro-Eurasia because the Americas did not undergo the sudden cluster of innovations that revolutionized agriculture in Southwest Asia and elsewhere. Tools ground from stone, rather than chipped implements, appeared in the Tehuacán Valley in present-day eastern central Mexico by 6700 BCE, and evidence of plant domestication there dates back to 5000 BCE. But villages, pottery making, and sustained population growth came later. For many early American inhabitants, the life of hunting, trapping, and fishing went on as it had for millennia.

On the coast of what is now Peru, people found food by fishing and by gathering shellfish from the Pacific. Archaeological remains include the remnants of fishnets, bags, baskets, and textile implements; gourds for carrying water; stone knives, choppers, and scrapers; and bone awls (long, pointed spikes often used for piercing) and thorn needles. Oddly enough, there

is no evidence of watercraft even though thousands of villages likely dotted the seashores and riverbanks of the Americas. Some communities made breakthroughs in the management of fire, which enabled them to manufacture pottery; others devised irrigation and water sluices in floodplains; and some even began to send their fish catches inland in return for agricultural produce.

DOMESTICATION OF PLANTS AND ANIMALS The earliest evidence of plant experimentation in Mesoamerica (the region now known as Mexico and Central America) dates from around 7000 BCE, and it went on for a long time. Maize (corn), squash, and beans (first found in what is now central Mexico) became dietary staples. The early settlers foraged small seeds of maize, peeled them from ears only a few inches long, and planted them. Maize offered real advantages because it was easy to store, relatively imperishable, nutritious, and easy to cultivate alongside other plants. Nonetheless, it took 5,000 years for farmers to complete its domestication. Over the years, farmers had to mix and breed different strains of maize for the crop to evolve from thin spikes of seeds to cobs rich with kernels, with a single plant yielding big, thick ears to feed a growing permanent population. (See Primary Source: A Mesoamerican Creation Myth.) Thus, the agricultural changes afoot in Mesoamerica were slow and late in maturing. The pace was even more gradual in South America, where early settlers clung to their hunting and gathering traditions.

Across the Americas, the settled, agrarian communities found that legumes (beans), grains (maize), and tubers (potatoes) complemented one another in keeping the soil fertile and offering a balanced diet. Unlike the Afro-Eurasians, however, the settlers did not use domesticated animals as an alternative source of protein. In only a few pockets of the Andean highlands is there evidence of the domestication of tiny guinea pigs, which may have been tasty but unfulfilling meals. Nor did people in the Americas tame animals that could protect villages (as dogs did in Afro-Eurasia) or carry heavy loads over long distances

Head of Maya Corn God. *Corn, or maize, was a revered crop in Mesoamerica, where people ritually prayed to their deities for good harvests. Notice the crown made not of precious metals and stones but of corn husks.*

PRIMARY SOURCE

A Mesoamerican Creation Narrative

There are very few extant texts from the indigenous peoples of the Americas before the time of European conquest and colonization. The Popol Vuh *is an extraordinary exception. Representing a whole body of mythological and historical narratives, it explained the elements of Maya cosmology and established the Maya right to rule by virtue of their descent from gods—although some scholars dispute this interpretation. (To compare this reading with a Hindu creation narrative, see p. 5.)*

Here, then, is the beginning of when it was decided to make man, and when what must enter into the flesh of man was sought.

And the Forefathers, the Creators and Makers, who were called Tepeu and Gucumatz said: "The time of dawn has come, let the work be finished, and let those who are to nourish and sustain us appear, the noble sons, the civilized vassals: let man appear, humanity, on the face of the earth." Thus they spoke.

They assembled, came together and held council in the darkness and in the night; then they sought and discussed, and here they reflected and thought. In this way their decisions came clearly to light and they found and discovered what must enter into the flesh of man.

It was just before the sun, the moon, and the stars appeared over the Creators and Makers.

From Paxil, from Cayalá, as they were called, came the yellow ears of corn and the white ears of corn.

These are the names of the animals which brought the food: *yac* [the mountain cat], *utiú* [the coyote], *quel* [a small parrot], and *hob* [the crow]. These four animals gave tidings of the yellow ears of corn and the white ears of corn, they told them that they should go to Paxil and they showed them the road to Paxil.

And thus they found the food, and this was what went into the flesh of created man, the made man; this was his blood; of this the blood of man was made. So the corn entered [into the formation of man] by the work of the Forefathers.

• • •

The animals showed them the road. And then grinding the yellow corn and the white corn, Xmucané made nine drinks, and from this food came the strength and the flesh, and with it they created the muscles and the strength of man. This the Forefathers did, Tepeu and Gucumatz, as they were called.

After that they began to talk about the creation and the making of our first mother and father; of yellow corn and of white corn they made their flesh; of corn meal dough they made the arms and the legs of man. Only dough of corn meal went into the flesh of our first fathers, the four men, who were created.

• • •

It is said that they only were made and formed, they had no mother, they had no father. They were only called men. They were not born of woman, nor were they begotten by the Creator nor by the Maker, nor by the Forefathers. Only by a miracle, by means of incantation were they created and made by the Creator, the Maker, the Forefathers, Tepeu and Gucumatz. And as they had the appearance of men, they were men; they talked, conversed, saw and heard, walked, grasped things; they were good and handsome men, and their figure was the figure of a man.

They were endowed with intelligence; they saw and instantly they could see far, they succeeded in seeing, they succeeded in knowing all that there is in the world. When they looked, instantly they saw all around them, and they contemplated in turn the arch of heaven and the round face of the earth.

The things hidden [in the distance] they saw all, without first having to move; at once they saw the world, and so, too, from where they were, they saw it.

Great was their wisdom; their sight reached to the forests, the rocks, the lakes, the seas, the mountains, and the valleys. In truth, they were admirable men, Balam-Quitzé, Balam-Acab, Mahucutah, and Iqui-Balam.

Then the Creator and the Maker asked them: "What do you think of your condition? Do you not see? Do you not hear? Are not your speech and manner of walking good? Look, then! Contemplate the world, look [and see] if the mountains and the valleys appear! Try, then, to see!" they said to [the four first men].

And immediately they [the four first men] began to see all that was in the world. Then they gave thanks to the Creator and the Maker: "We really give you thanks, two and three times!"

QUESTIONS FOR ANALYSIS

- From what material did the Creators make living creatures?
- Why do you think they chose this material?
- What commands did the Creator and the Maker convey to the first men? Why do you think this is significant?

Source: Popol Vuh: The Sacred Book of Ancient Quiché Maya. English version by Delia Goetz and Sylvanus G. Morley from the Spanish translation by Adrián Recinos (Norman: University of Oklahoma Press, 1950), pp. 165–67.

(as camels did in Afro-Eurasia). Although llamas could haul heavy loads, their patience and cooperation were limited. They were mainly useful for clothing.

Nonetheless, the domestication of plants and animals in the Americas, as well as the presence of villages and clans, suggests significant diversification and refinement of technique. At the same time, the centers of such activity were many, scattered, and more isolated than those in Afro-Eurasia—and thus more narrowly adapted to local geographical climatic conditions, with little exchange between communities. This fragmentation in migration and communication was a distinguishing force in the gradual pace of change in the Americas, and it contributed to their taking a path of development separate from Afro-Eurasia's.

Africa: The Race with the Sahara

Some societies, like those in Southwest Asia and East Asia, were innovators, while others, like those in Europe, were borrowers. What about Africa, where the story began? The evidence for settled agriculture in different regions there is uncertain. Most scholars think that the Sahel area (spanning the African landmass just south of the Sahara Desert) was most likely where hunters and gatherers became settled farmers and herders without any borrowing. In this area, an apparent move to settled agriculture, including the domestication of large herd animals, occurred two millennia before it did along the Mediterranean coast in North Africa. From this innovative heartland, Africans carried their agricultural breakthroughs across the landmass.

It was in the wetter and more temperate locations of the vast Sahel, particularly in mountainous areas and their foothills, that villages and towns developed. These regions were lush with grassland vegetation and teeming with animals. Before long, the inhabitants had made sorghum, a cereal grass, their principal food crop. Residents constructed stone dwellings, underground wells, and grain storage areas. In one such population center, fourteen circular houses faced each other to form a main thoroughfare, or street. Archaeological investigations have unearthed remarkable rock engravings and paintings, often one composed on top of another, filling the cave dwellings' walls. Many images portray in fascinating detail the changeover from hunting and gathering to pastoralism. Caves abound with pictures of cattle, which were a mainstay of these early men and women. The cave illustrations also depict daily activities of men and women living in conical huts, doing household chores, crushing grain on stone, and riding bareback on oxen (with women always sitting behind the men, potentially an early example of male superiority in some African societies).

The Sahel was colder and moister 10,000 years ago than it is today. As the world became warmer and the Sahara Desert expanded, around 4,000 years ago, this region's inhabitants had to disperse and take their agricultural and herding skills into other parts of Africa. (See Map 1.7.) Some went south to the tropical rain forests of West Africa, while others trekked eastward into the Ethiopian highlands. In their new environments, farmers searched for new crops to domesticate. The rain forests of West Africa yielded root crops, particularly the yam and cocoyam, both of which became the principal life-sustaining foodstuffs. The enset plant, similar to the banana, played the same role in the Ethiopian highlands. Thus, the beginnings of agriculture in Africa involved both innovation and diffusion.

Europe: Borrowing Agricultural Ideas

In some places, agricultural revolutions occurred through the borrowing of ideas from neighboring regions, rather than through innovation. Peoples living at the western fringe of Afro-Eurasia, in Europe, learned the techniques of settled agriculture through contact with other regions.

By 6000–5000 BCE, people in regions of Europe close to the societies of Southwest Asia, such as those living in what are modern-day Greece and the Balkans, abandoned their hunting and gathering lifeways to become settled agriculturists. (See Map 1.8.) Places like the Franchthi Cave, in Greece, reveal that around 6000 BCE, the inhabitants borrowed innovations from their neighbors in Southwest Asia, such as how to herd domesticated animals and to plant wheat and barley. From the Aegean and Greece, settled agriculture and domesticated animals expanded westward throughout Europe, accompanied by the development of settled communities.

The emergence of agriculture and village life occurred in Europe along two separate paths. The first and most rapid trajectory followed the northern rim of the Mediterranean Sea. Domestication of crops and animals moved westward, following the prevailing currents of the Mediterranean, from what is now Turkey through the islands of the Aegean Sea to mainland Greece, and from there to southern and central Italy and Sicily. Once the basic elements of domestication had arrived in the Mediterranean region, the speed and ease of seaborne communications aided astonishingly rapid changes. Almost overnight, hunting and gathering gave way to domesticated agriculture and herding.

The second trajectory took an overland route: from Anatolia, across northern Greece into the Balkans, then northwestward along the Danube River into the Hungarian plain, and from there farther north and west into the Rhine River valley in modern-day Germany. Change here likely resulted from the transmission of ideas rather than from population migrations, for community after community adopted domesticated plants and

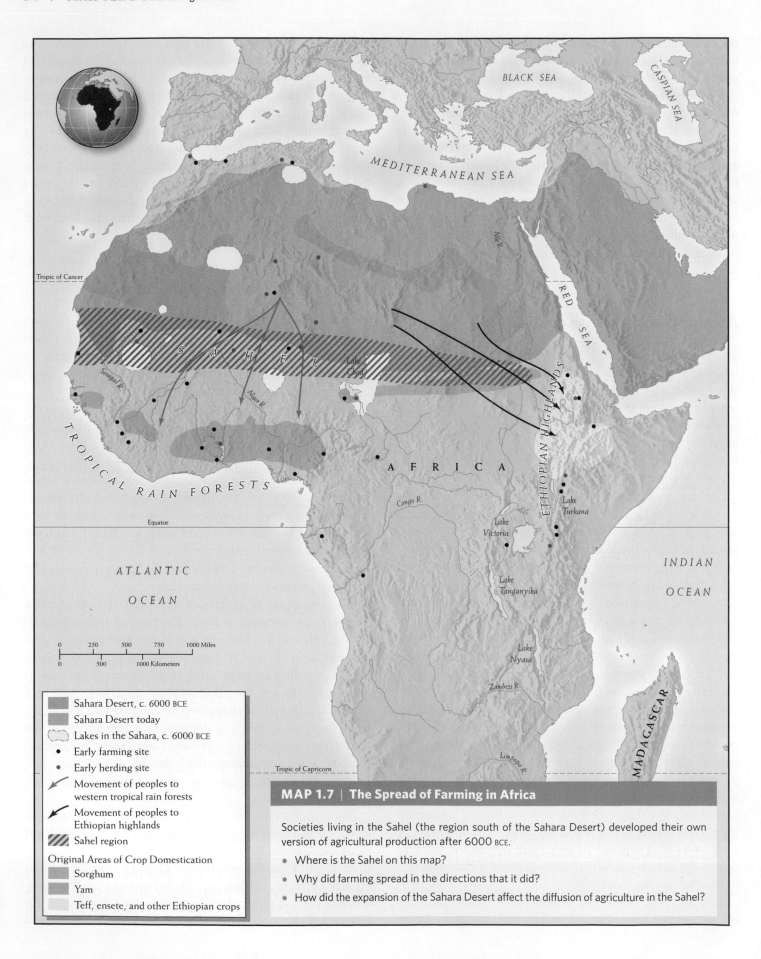

BLACK SEA

CASPIAN SEA

MEDITERRANEAN SEA

Nile R.

RED SEA

Tropic of Cancer

S A H E L

Lake Chad

Senegal R.

Niger R.

ETHIOPIAN HIGHLANDS

T R O P I C A L   R A I N   F O R E S T S

A F R I C A

Congo R.

Lake Turkana

Equator

ATLANTIC

OCEAN

Lake Victoria

Lake Tanganyika

INDIAN

OCEAN

| 0 | 250 | 500 | 750 | 1000 Miles |

| 0 | | 500 | 1000 Kilometers | |

Lake Nyasa

MADAGASCAR

Zambezi R.

Tropic of Capricorn

Limpopo R.

Legend:

- ▨ Sahara Desert, c. 6000 BCE
- ▨ Sahara Desert today
- ◌ Lakes in the Sahara, c. 6000 BCE
- • Early farming site
- • Early herding site
- ↙ Movement of peoples to western tropical rain forests
- ↙ Movement of peoples to Ethiopian highlands
- ▨ Sahel region

Original Areas of Crop Domestication
- Sorghum
- Yam
- Teff, ensete, and other Ethiopian crops

MAP 1.7 | The Spread of Farming in Africa

Societies living in the Sahel (the region south of the Sahara Desert) developed their own version of agricultural production after 6000 BCE.

- Where is the Sahel on this map?
- Why did farming spread in the directions that it did?
- How did the expansion of the Sahara Desert affect the diffusion of agriculture in the Sahel?

animals and the new mode of life. This route of agricultural development was slower than the Mediterranean route for two reasons. First, domesticated crops, or individuals who knew about them, had to travel by land, as there were few large rivers like the Danube. Second, it was necessary to find new groups of domesticated plants and animals that could flourish in the colder and more forested lands of central Europe. Agriculturalists here had to plant their crops in the spring and harvest in the autumn, rather than the other way around. Cattle rather than sheep became the dominant herd animals.

Not only did migrations introduce European hunters and gatherers to the agricultural revolution, but they also changed the DNA composition of the people. The original European population, arriving from Africa via Southwest Asia sometime between 40,000 and 30,000 years ago, were dark-skinned. Aided by a second wave of migrants arriving from the steppes of Russia beginning around 4500 BCE, these groups produced a population that was taller and lighter-skinned than the original population.

In Europe, the main cereal crops were wheat and barley, and the main herd animals were sheep, goats, and cattle—all of which had been domesticated in Southwest Asia. (Residents domesticated additional plants, such as olives, later.) These fundamental changes did not bring dramatic material progress, however. The typical settlement in Europe at this time consisted of a few dozen mud huts. These settlements, although few, often comprised large "long houses" built of timber and mud, designed to store produce and to shelter animals during the long winters. Some settlements had sixty to seventy huts—in rare cases, up to a hundred. Hunting, gathering, and fishing still supplemented the new settled agriculture and the herding of domesticated animals. The innovators were dynamic in blending the new ways with the old. Consider that around 6000 BCE, hunter-gatherers in southern France adopted the herding of domesticated sheep, but not the planting of domesticated crops—*that* would have conflicted with their preference for a life of hunting, which was a traditional part of their economy.

By about 5000–4000 BCE, communities living in areas around rivers and in the large plains had embraced the new food-producing economy. Elsewhere (notably in the rugged mountain lands that still predominate in Europe's landscape), hunting and foraging remained humans' primary way of subsisting. Thus, across Afro-Eurasia, humans changed and were changed by their environments. While hunting and gathering remained firmly entrenched as a way of life, certain areas with favorable climates and plants and animals that could be domesticated began to establish settled agricultural communities, which were able to support larger populations than hunting and gathering could sustain.

The Environmental Impact of the Agricultural Revolution and Herding

From the moment humans began to farm and herd on a large scale, they began to have a warming effect on the climate. The burning of forests, the cultivation of the major grain crops, and the amassing of large herds of domesticated animals caused methane and carbon dioxide (today called greenhouse gases) to escape from the earth and be trapped in the earth's atmosphere. As a result, cooling cycles that occurred as the earth tilted away from the sun were not as severe as they would have been. Of course, it was only in the last 200 years that these gases have caused the severe warming of the planet that threatens our planet's existence.

REVOLUTIONS IN SOCIAL ORGANIZATION

In addition to creating villages, the domestication of plants and animals brought changes in social organization, notably in gender relations. Men and women had been on an equal plane in hunting and gathering societies. Farming, herding, and settling down in villages brought radical changes in gender relations, elevating the status of men in their relationship with women.

Life in Villages

Agricultural villages were established near fields for accessible sowing and cultivating and near pastures for herding livestock. Villagers collaborated to clear fields, plant crops, and celebrate rituals in which they sang, danced, and sacrificed to nature and the spirit world for fertility, rain, and successful harvests. They produced stone tools to work the fields and clay and stone pots or woven baskets—and later on, pottery vessels—to collect and store the crops. As populations grew and lands yielded surplus food, some villagers became craftsworkers, devoting some of their time to producing pottery, baskets, textiles, or tools, which they could trade to farmers and pastoralists for food. Craft specialization and the buildup of surpluses contributed to early social stratification, as some people accumulated more land and wealth while others led the rituals and sacrifices.

Settling in villages also made possible the rise of the extended family as the principal social unit, eroding the influence of clusters of families and free-floating communities that had been the predominant social units among hunters and gatherers. Because successful families strove to accumulate wealth and power and

MAP 1.8 | The Spread of Agriculture in Europe

The spread of agricultural production into Europe after 7000 BCE represents geographical diffusion. Europeans borrowed agricultural techniques and technology from other groups, adapting those innovations to their own situations.

- Where did the ideas and techniques originate?
- Through what two pathways did agriculture spread across Europe?
- Did Europe's settled agricultural communities have different features from those that appeared in Southwest Asia, East Asia, and Africa?

to pass their successes on to offspring, the family also promoted social inequality and stratification.

The earliest dwelling places of the first settled communities were simple structures: circular pits with stones piled on top to form walls, with a cover stretched above that rested on

poles. Social structures were equally simple, being clan-like and based on birth relationships. With time, however, population growth enabled clans to expand. As the use of natural resources intensified, specialized tasks evolved and division of labor arose. Some community members procured and prepared food; others built terraces and defended the settlement. Later, residents built walls with stones or mud bricks and clamped them together with wooden fittings. Yet all were involved in securing food.

As construction techniques changed, houses changed from the traditional circular plan to a rectangular one. Because the rectangular shape does not exist in nature, it is a truly human mark on the landscape. This new shape reflected new attitudes and social behaviors: in rectangular houses, walls did more than support and protect—they also divided and separated. The introduction of interior walls meant that family members gained separate spaces, conferring privacy. Human relations would never again be as they had been in the relatively egalitarian arrangements of the mobile hunters and gatherers.

Although the food-producing changes were gradual and dispersed, a few communities stand out as pioneers in the long transition from hunting and gathering to agrarian and pastoral life. Around Wadi en-Natuf, located about 10 miles from present-day Jerusalem, a group of people known historically as Natufians began to dig sunken pit shelters and to chip stone tools around 12,500 BCE. Over the next two millennia, these bands stayed in one place, improving their toolmaking techniques, building circular shelters, and developing various ways to preserve and prepare food. They dwelled in solid structures, buried their dead, and harvested grains. Although they did not plant seeds and did not give up hunting, their increasing knowledge of wild plants paved the way for later breakthroughs.

It was only a matter of time before the full transition to settled agriculture and full-scale pastoralism took place. One of the best examples of this development occurred in central Anatolia (the area encompassing modern-day Turkey). The village of Çatal Höyük, a dense 32-acre honeycomb settlement that may have contained several thousand residents, featured rooms covered with wall paintings and sculptures of wild bulls, hunters, and pregnant women. This settlement, called by one scholar a precocious city, flourished from 7300 BCE to 6200 BCE. Its houses were constructed as rectangular boxes, the walls of one house being attached to four others. The village lacked lanes, and thus residents had to climb up on the roofs to enter their homes through trap doors.

Another example of village settlement occurred after 5500 BCE, when people moved into the river valley in Mesopotamia (in present-day Iraq) along the Tigris and Euphrates Rivers and small villages began to appear. The inhabitants collaborated to build simple irrigation systems to water their fields. Perhaps because of the increased demands for community work to maintain the irrigation systems, the communities in southern Mesopotamia became stratified, with some people having more power than others. We can see from the burial sites and myriad public buildings uncovered by archaeologists that for the first time, some people had higher status derived from birth rather than through the merits of their work. A class of people who had access to more luxury goods and who lived in bigger and better houses now became part of the social organization.

It is important to emphasize that changes arising from agriculture enabled larger numbers of people to live in denser concentrations, and the household with its dominant male replaced the small, relatively egalitarian band as the primary social unit.

Men, Women, and Evolving Gender Relations

The gradual transition to an agricultural way of life sharpened the differences in gender roles. For millions of years, biological differences—the fact that females give birth to offspring and that males do not—determined female and male behaviors and attitudes toward each other. But it is incorrect to think of these biologically based sexual relations as "gender" (social and cultural) relations. One can speak of the emergence of "gender" relations and roles only with the appearance of modern humans (*Homo sapiens*) and, perhaps, Neanderthals. Only when humans began to think in complex symbolic ways and give voice to these perceptions in a spoken language did well-defined gender categories of *man* and *woman* crystallize. As these cultural aspects of human life took shape, the distinction between "men" and "women," rather than between "males" and "females," arose. At that point, around 150,000 years ago, culture joined biology in governing human interactions. (See Primary Source: Mothering and Lactation.)

As human communities became larger, more hierarchical, and more powerful, the rough gender egalitarianism of hunting and gathering societies eroded. An enhanced human power over the environment did not bring equal power to everyone, and it is possible that women were the net losers of the agricultural revolution. Although their knowledge of wild plants had contributed to early settled agriculture, they did not necessarily benefit from that transition.

Advances in agrarian tools introduced a harsh working life that undermined women's traditional status as farmers. Men, no longer so involved in hunting and gathering, now took on the heavy work of yoking animals to plows. This left to women the backbreaking and repetitive tasks of planting, weeding, harvesting, and grinding the grain into flour. Thus, although agricultural innovations increased productivity, they also increased the drudgery of work, especially for women. Consider the evidence from fossils found in Abu Hureyra, Syria: damage to the vertebrae, osteoarthritis in the toes, and curved and arched

PRIMARY SOURCE

Mothering and Lactation

One of the dividing lines among all animals, humans included, involves child rearing and the division of labor between mothers and fathers. This text argues that lactation (milk production) became a major factor shaping the social roles of primate mothers.

"Is sex destiny?" When this question is posed, it's a safe bet that the underlying agenda has to do with what women *should* be doing. Should they be home caring for their children or off pursuing other interests? A comparative look at other creatures that (like humans) breed cooperatively and share responsibilities for rearing young with other group members reveals that sex *per se* is not the issue. Lactation is.

Caretakers of both sexes, wet-nurses, even "daycare"—none of these are uniquely human, nor particularly new. They are standard features of many cooperatively breeding species. As we saw, cooperative breeding is exquisitely well developed in insects such as honeybees and wasps. Shared provisioning is also common among birds such as acorn woodpeckers, bee-eaters, dunnocks, and scrub jays. Although cooperative breeding is uncommon among mammals generally, it is richly developed in species such as wolves, wild dogs, dwarf mongooses, elephants, tamarins, marmosets, and

humans. In all these animals, individuals other than the mother ("allomothers") help her provision or otherwise care for her young. Typically, allomothers will include the mother's mate (often but not necessarily the genetic progenitor). Individuals other than either parent ("alloparents") also help. These helpers are most often recruited from kin who are not yet ready to reproduce themselves, or from subordinates who do not currently—or may never have—better options. In the human case, the most important alloparents are often older, post-reproductive relatives who have already reproduced.

Among mammals, the trend toward having young who require costly long-term care began modestly enough. It probably began with an egg-laying brooding reptile that started to secrete something milklike. Such egg-layers gradually developed glands especially equipped for milk production. Only among mammals did one sex come to specialize in manufacturing custom-made baby formula, to provide something critical for infant

survival that the other sex could not. This peculiarity has had many ramifications, especially as infants became dependent for longer periods in the primate line.

The ante was upped substantially when primate mothers, instead of bearing litters, began focusing care on one baby at a time. These singletons were born mature enough to cling to their mother's fur, to be carried by her right from birth and for months thereafter. Whether or not this intimate and prolonged association is the mother's destiny, *sex* is not the issue. Lactation is.

QUESTIONS FOR ANALYSIS

- How does lactation affect mothers' child-rearing roles differently from fathers'?
- Why is the difference more marked among humans than among other species?

Source: Sarah Blaffer Hrdy, *Mother Nature: Maternal Instincts and How They Shape the Human Species* (New York: Ballantine Books, 2000), pp. 121–23.

---

femurs suggest that the work of bending over and kneeling in the fields took its toll on women farmers. These maladies do not usually appear among the bone remains of (male) hunters and gatherers.

The revolutions in social organizations sprang first of all from the domestication of plants and animals. These radical innovations permitted humans to settle down in villages and led to population increase. They also resulted in a differentiation of the roles of men and women. Power relations changed within households and communities, where the senior male figure became dominant in households and males dominated females in leadership positions. Where the agricultural transformation was most widespread and population densities grew,

marked inequalities appeared in the social and political realms. These inequalities affected gender relations, and patriarchy (the rule of senior males within households) began to spread around the globe.

CONCLUSION

Over thousands of generations, African hominins evolved from other primates into *Homo erectus* hominins, who migrated far from their native habitats to fill other landmasses. They did so in waves, responding to worldwide cycles of glaciation and melting. These human predecessors had some features in common with modern humans (*Homo sapiens*): they stood erect on two feet, made stone tools, lived in extended families, and, to a certain extent, communicated with one another (by means other than language).

What separated humans from other animal species was their ability to adapt to environmental change, to innovate, and to accumulate their breakthroughs in knowledge. *Homo sapiens* hominins, who had greater cognitive skills than earlier hominins, also emerged in Africa and migrated out of Africa between 100,000 and 60,000 years ago. Since *Homo sapiens* had greater adaptive and cognitive skills, members of this species were better prepared to face the elements when a cooling cycle returned and better able to understand the world around them and even to represent it symbolically through art and language. Eventually, they eclipsed their genetic cousins. Critical to their success was their use of language, which enabled them to engage in abstract, representational thought and to convey the lessons of experience to neighbors and descendants. As modern humans stored and shared knowledge, their adaptive abilities increased.

Although modern men and women shared an African heritage, these individuals adapted over many millennia to the environments they encountered as they began to fill the earth's corners. Some settled near lakes and took to fishing, while others roamed the northern steppes hunting large mammals. No matter where they went, their dependence on nature yielded broadly similar social and cultural structures. It took a powerful warming cycle for people ranging from Africa to the Americas to begin putting down their hunting weapons and start domesticating animals and plants.

The changeover to settled agriculture was not uniform worldwide, although there were some common features: one was the reliance on wood, stone, and natural fibers to make tools, shelter, and cultural items; another was increasing social hierarchies—especially an unequal status between men and women. As communities became more settled, though, the world's regions began to vary as humans learned to modify nature to fit their needs. The varieties of animals that they could domesticate, the wild plants that they learned to cultivate, and the differing climatic conditions and topography that they encountered shaped the ways in which people drifted apart in spite of their common origins.

One important commonality remained: there was a limit to the scale and complexity of settlements and communities. As a result, most people continued a life of moving in search of more reliable and plentiful amounts of food. Villages grew—but they did not become cities. Peoples moved across mountains or deserts to find fresh pastures for their animals, richer lands for their crops, or new waters where fish were spawning. The remains of rudimentary pottery, tools, and dwellings reflect worlds that were rural and dependent on the natural flow of fresh water and the natural fertility of soils. As we will see in Chapter 2, another round of technical advances was necessary before humans could further change their relationship to nature and create the foundations for complex societies.

Hunting. *This wall painting from Catal Huyuk (in present-day Turkey) depicts humans hunting a bull.*

TRACING THE GLOBAL STORYLINES

After You Read This Chapter

FOCUS ON: *What Makes Us Human*

- **Bipedalism** Hominins come down from the trees in Africa, become upright, and walk on two legs.

- **Big brains:** Ancestors to modern humans make tools and fire and acquire larger brains.

- **Cognitive skills:** *Homo sapiens* hominins develop the capacity for language and learn to communicate with one another, develop a sense of self, and produce art.

- **Village life:** People domesticate plants and animals and begin to live in more socially complex communities.

> Go to
> **INQUIZITIVE**
> to see what you
> know & learn
> what you've
> missed.

CHRONOLOGY

Africa	◆ First hominins appear at least **6 MYA** ◆ *Australopithecus africanus* hominin species appears **3 MYA**
	Homo habilis appears ◆ **2.5 MYA**
Afro-Eurasia	*Homo erectus* appears and migrates **2.5–1 MYA**
	Beginnings of Ice Age Across the Northern Hemisphere **2.5–1 MYA**
Europe and the Mediterranean	
Southwest and Inner and Central Eurasia	
East Asia	
The Americas	*millions of years ago **years ago

5 MYA   **1 MYA**

KEY TERMS

STUDY QUESTIONS

1. **Identify** the factors that influence human communities' creation narratives, and **explain** how some of these narratives differ.

2. **Discuss** how evolutionary biologists and archaeologists working in recent decades have transformed our understanding of human origins. What tools and discoveries led them to their conclusions?

3. **Describe** the evolutionary process through which *Homo sapiens* emerged and gained traits that made its members "human." Was it a linear progression? Why or why not?

4. **Analyze** the advantages that language and symbolic art gave *Homo sapiens* over other species. What can modern observers learn about early humans by studying their cultural forms?

5. **Describe** the ways of life and cultural developments of *Homo sapiens* while these humans were still hunter-gatherers. How did hunting and gathering shape the dynamics of early human communities?

6. **Evaluate** the advantages and disadvantages of agricultural production versus nomadic foraging. How were agricultural or pastoral communities different from those of hunters and gatherers?

7. **Define** pastoralism, and explain how varying types of pastoralists interacted with settled agricultural communities.

8. **Discuss** the varying ways that communities around the world shifted from hunting and gathering to settled agriculture. What did this shift mean for social organization?

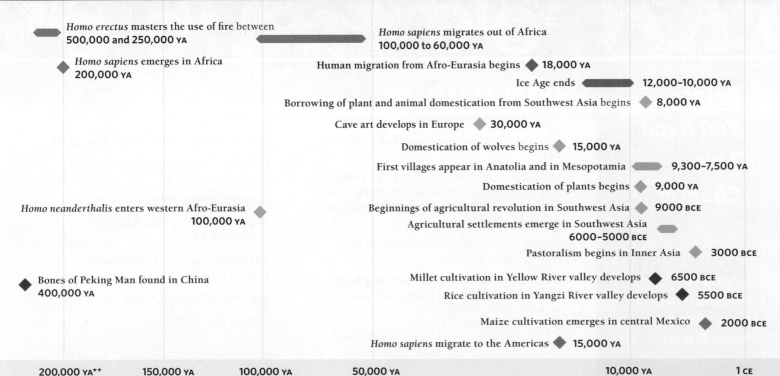

Homo erectus masters the use of fire between **500,000 and 250,000 YA**

Homo sapiens emerges in Africa **200,000 YA**

Homo neanderthalis enters western Afro-Eurasia **100,000 YA**

Bones of Peking Man found in China **400,000 YA**

Homo sapiens migrates out of Africa **100,000 to 60,000 YA**

Human migration from Afro-Eurasia begins ◆ **18,000 YA**

Ice Age ends ◀ **12,000–10,000 YA**

Borrowing of plant and animal domestication from Southwest Asia begins ◆ **8,000 YA**

Cave art develops in Europe ◆ **30,000 YA**

Domestication of wolves begins ◆ **15,000 YA**

First villages appear in Anatolia and in Mesopotamia ◀ **9,300–7,500 YA**

Domestication of plants begins ◆ **9,000 YA**

Beginnings of agricultural revolution in Southwest Asia ◆ **9000 BCE**

Agricultural settlements emerge in Southwest Asia **6000–5000 BCE**

Pastoralism begins in Inner Asia ◆ **3000 BCE**

Millet cultivation in Yellow River valley develops ◆ **6500 BCE**

Rice cultivation in Yangzi River valley develops ◆ **5500 BCE**

Maize cultivation emerges in central Mexico ◆ **2000 BCE**

Homo sapiens migrate to the Americas ◆ **15,000 YA**

| 200,000 YA** | 150,000 YA | 100,000 YA | 50,000 YA | | 10,000 YA | 1 CE |

2

Rivers, Cities, and First States, 3500–2000 BCE

FOCUS QUESTIONS

- In what areas did the world's earliest river-basin societies arise, and how were they alike and different?

- What religious, social, and political developments accompanied early urbanization from 3500 to 2000 BCE?

- Where did long-distance connections develop across Afro-Eurasia during this period, and what influences did they have on the early societies?

- How did early urbanization compare with the way of life in small villages and among pastoral nomads?

"The first city in human history" was Uruk (Van de Mieroop, 2004, p. 23). Located in southern Mesopotamia on a branch of the Euphrates River, its urban area encompassed 250 acres and was home to more than 10,000 people by the second half of the fourth millennium BCE. Flourishing between 3500 and 3100 BCE, Uruk boasted many large public structures and temples. One temple had stood there almost from the outset, erected to house and honor the city's patron deity. With a lime-plastered surface of niched mud-brick walls that formed stepped indentations, it perched high above the plain. In another sacred precinct, administrative buildings and temples adorned with elaborate facades stood in courtyards defined by tall columns. Colored stone cones arranged in elaborate geometric patterns covered parts of these buildings, making Uruk the "shining city" of King Gilgamesh.

Over the years, Uruk became an immense commercial and administrative center. A huge wall with seven massive gates surrounded the metropolis, and down the middle ran a canal carrying water from the Euphrates. On one side of the city were gardens, kilns, and textile workshops. On the other side was the temple quarter where priests lived, scribes kept records, and lu-gal ("the big man" in the Sumerian

Uruk. *A contemporary depiction of the sacred precinct of Uruk, the "shining city" of King Gilgamesh.*

language) conferred with the elders. As Uruk grew, many small industries became centralized in response to the increasing sophistication of construction and manufacturing. Potters, metalsmiths, stone bowl makers, and brickmakers all worked under the city administration.

As the first city in world history, Uruk marked a new phase in human development. Earlier humans had settled in small communities scattered over the landscape and lived close to nature; gradually, however, some communities attracted large populations and grew into cities. By living in their own constructed communities, inhabitants removed themselves from the natural world for the first time. Not only did these cities become focal points for trade; they also created institutions possessing economic, religious, and political power. Many city dwellers, though hardly the majority, no longer produced their own food, working instead in specialized professions.

Between 3500 and 2000 BCE, a handful of remarkable societies clustered in a few river basins on the Afro-Eurasian landmass. These regions, located along the banks or in the deltas of five rivers with regular annual floods (in Mesopotamia, northwest India, Egypt, northern China, and central China), became the heartlands for densely populated settlements with complex cultures. Here the world saw not only the birth of the first large cities but also the rise of territorial states. One of these settings (Mesopotamia) brought forth humankind's first writing system, and all laid the foundations for kingdoms radiating out of opulent cities. This chapter describes how each society evolved, and it explores their similarities and differences. It is important to note how exceptional these places were—and thus we cannot ignore the many smaller societies that prevailed elsewhere, far

from urbanizing locales. The Aegean, Anatolia, and western Europe as well as the Americas and sub-Saharan Africa serve as reminders that most of the world's people continued to dwell in small communities living in close proximity to the natural world and heavily dependent on it. They were far removed culturally from the monumental architecture and well-developed bureaucracies of the big new states.

SETTLEMENT, PASTORALISM, AND TRADE

Over many millennia, people had developed strategies to make the best of their environments. As populations expanded and sought out locations capable of supporting larger numbers, often it was reliable water sources that determined where and how people settled. Village dwellers gravitated toward predictable water supplies that enabled them to sow crops adequate to feed large populations. The story of the emergence of urban society is complex. In addition to having adequate water and a stable food supply, cities arose as a result of fundamental changes in economy, social organization, and political structures that required large, complex communities to function. Among these changes were conflict and warfare, causing people to coalese around and to submit to the authority of a leader, and large enough populations to require specialization of jobs and skills beyond the basic production of food.

While abundant rainfall was involved in the emergence of the world's first villages, the breakthroughs into big cities occurred in drier zones where large rivers formed beds of rich alluvial soils (created by deposits from rivers when in flood). With irrigation innovations, soils became arable. Equally important, a worldwide warming cycle caused growing seasons to expand. These environmental and technical shifts profoundly affected who lived where and how.

As rivers sliced through mountains, steppe lands (vast treeless grasslands), and deserts before reaching the sea, their waters carried topsoils and deposited them along their banks, creating large and highly fertile deltas. The combination of rich soils, water for irrigation, and availability of domesticated plants and animals made **river basins** (areas drained by a river, including all its tributaries) attractive for human habitation. Here, cultivators began to produce agricultural surpluses to feed the city dwellers.

Early Cities along River Basins

The material and social advances of the early cities occurred in a remarkably short period—from 3500 to 2000 BCE—in three locations: the basin of the Tigris and Euphrates Rivers in central Southwest Asia; the northern parts of the Nile River flowing toward the Mediterranean Sea; and the Indus River basin in northwestern South Asia. About a millennium later, a similar process began along the Yellow River in North China and the Yangzi River valley, laying the foundations for several cultures from which Chinese civilization evolved and flourished unbroken until this day. (See Map 2.1.)

In these regions, humans farmed and fed themselves by relying on intensive irrigation agriculture. Gathering in cities inhabited by rulers, administrators, priests, and craftworkers, the city dwellers changed how they related to their methods of organizing communities by worshipping new gods in new ways and by obeying divinely inspired monarchs and elaborate bureaucracies. They also transformed what and how they worshipped, praying to zoomorphic and anthropomorphic gods (taking the form and personality of animals and humans) who communicated through kings and priests living in palace complexes and temples. New technologies also appeared, ranging from the wheel for pottery production to metal and stoneworking for the creation of both luxury objects and utilitarian tools.

With cities came greater division of labor. Dense urban settlements enabled people to specialize in making goods for the consumption of others: weavers made textiles, potters made ceramics, and jewelers made precious ornaments. Soon these goods found additional uses in trade with outlying areas. And as trade expanded over longer distances, raw materials such as wood, metal, timber, and precious stones arrived in the cities. (See Map 2.2.) One of the most coveted metals was copper; easily smelted and shaped (not to mention shiny and alluring), it became the metal of choice for charms, sculptures, and valued commodities. When combined with arsenic or tin, copper hardens and becomes **bronze**, which was useful for

tools and weapons. Consequently, this period is often called the Bronze Age, though the term simplifies the breadth of the breakthroughs.

As people congregated in cities, new technologies appeared. The wheel, for example, served both as a tool for mass-producing pottery and as a key component of vehicles used for transportation. At first vehicles were heavy, using two or four solid wooden wheels drawn by oxen or onagers (Asian wild asses). Two other technologies, metallurgy and stoneworking, both developed in the surrounding highlands near the raw materials and provided luxury objects and utilitarian tools.

As the dynamic urban enclaves evolved, they made intellectual advances. One significant advance was the invention of writing systems, which enabled people to record and transmit sounds and words through visual signs. An unprecedented cultural breakthrough, the technology of writing used the symbolic storage of words and meanings to extend human communication and memory: scribes figured out ways to record oral compositions as written texts and, eventually, epics recounting life in these river settlements.

The emergence of cities as population centers created one of history's most durable worldwide distinctions: the **urban-rural divide**. Where cities appeared, at first alongside rivers, people adopted lifestyles based on specialized labor and the mass production of goods. In contrast, most people continued to cultivate the land or tend livestock, though they exchanged their grains and animal products for goods from the urban centers. The two ways of life were interdependent, and both worlds remained linked through family ties, trade, politics, and religion. Therefore, the new distinction never implied isolation, because the two lifeways supported each other.

Pastoral Nomadic Communities

Around 3500 BCE, Afro-Eurasia also witnessed the growth and spread of pastoral nomadic communities. The transhumant herder communities that had appeared in Southwest Asia around 5500 BCE (see Chapter 1) continued to be small and their settlements impermanent. They lacked substantial public buildings or infrastructure, but their seasonal moves were stable. Across the vast expanse of Afro-Eurasia's great mountains and its desert barriers, and from its steppe lands ranging across inner and central Eurasia to the Pacific Ocean, these transhumant herders lived alongside settled agrarian people, especially when occupying their lowland pastures. They traded meat and animal products for grains, pottery, and tools produced in the agrarian communities.

In the arid environments of inner and central Eurasia, transhumant herding and agrarian communities initially followed the same combination of herding animals and cultivating crops that had proved so successful in Southwest Asia. However, because

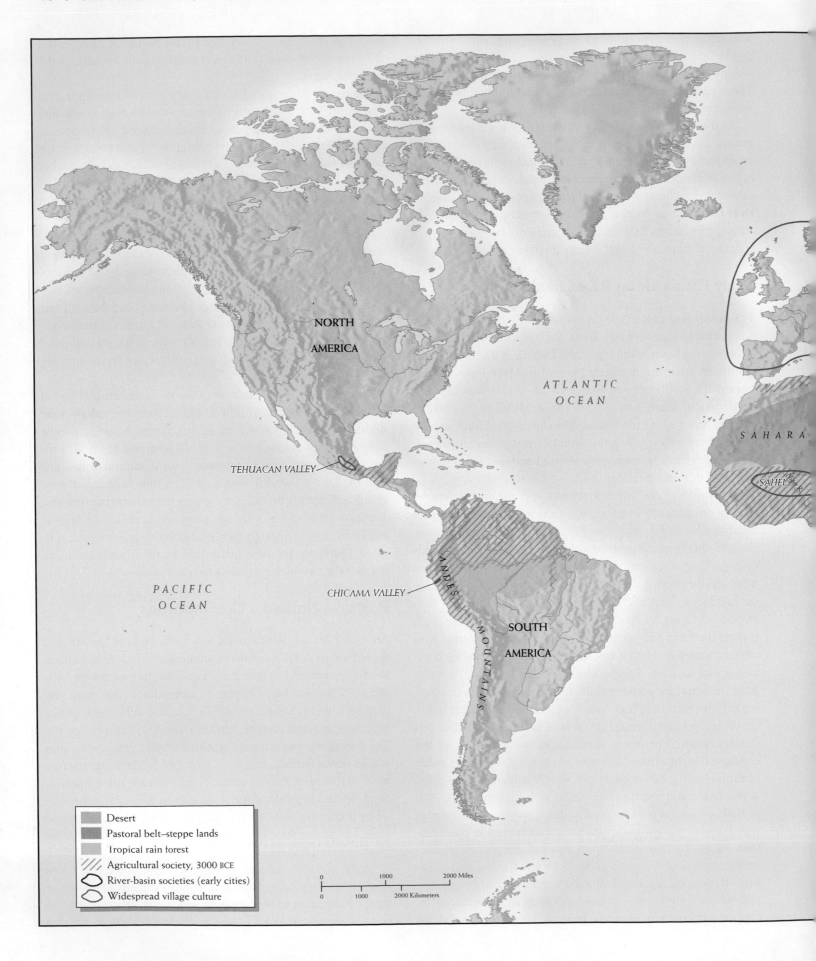

NORTH
AMERICA

ATLANTIC
OCEAN

SAHARA

TEHUACAN VALLEY

SAHEL

PACIFIC
OCEAN

CHICAMA VALLEY

ANDES MOUNTAINS

SOUTH
AMERICA

Desert
Pastoral belt–steppe lands
Tropical rain forest
Agricultural society, 3000 BCE
River-basin societies (early cities)
Widespread village culture

1000   2000 Miles
0   1000   2000 Kilometers

MAP 2.1 | The World in the Third Millennium BCE

Human societies became increasingly diversified as agricultural, urban, and pastoral nomadic communities expanded.

- In what different regions did pastoralism and river-basin societies emerge?

- Considering the geographical features highlighted on this map, why do you think cities appeared in the regions that they did?

- How did geographical and environmental factors promote interaction between nomadic pastoral and sedentary agricultural societies?

MAP 2.2 | Trade and Exchange in Southwest Asia and the Eastern Mediterranean—Third Millennium BCE

Extensive commercial networks linked the urban cores of Southwest Asia.

- Of the traded raw materials shown on the map, which ones were used for building materials and which ones for luxury items?
- Why were there more extensive trade connections between Mesopotamians and people to their northwest and east than with Egypt to the west?
- According to the map, in what ways did Mesopotamia become the crossroads of Afro-Eurasia?

the steppe environment could not support large-scale farming, these communities began to concentrate on animal breeding and herding. As secondary pursuits they continued to fish, hunt, and farm small plots in their winter pastures. Their economy centered on domesticated cattle, sheep, and horses. As their herds increased, these horse-riding nomads often had to move to new pastures, driving their herds across vast expanses of land. By the middle of the second millennium BCE, some had become full-scale nomadic pastoral communities, and they dominated the steppes. In these pastoral nomadic economies of the arid zones of central Eurasia, horses became crucial to survival. These nomadic and transhumant groups played a vital role in connecting cities and spreading ideas throughout Afro-Eurasia.

The Rise of Trade

When the earliest farming villages developed around 7000 BCE, trade patterns across Afro-Eurasia were already well established. Much of this trade was in exotic materials such as obsidian, a black volcanic glass that made superb chipped-stone tools. Although trade in nonessential items was obviously small, especially by the standards of later millennia, these trade goods provided vital links between different regions all across Afro-Eurasia.

Over thousands of years, trade increased. By the mid-third millennium BCE, flourishing communities populated the oases (fertile areas with water in the midst of arid regions) dotting the highlands of the Iranian plateau and the areas known today as northern Afghanistan and Turkmenistan. As these communities actively traded with their neighbors, trading stations at the borders facilitated exchanges among many partners. Here in these "borderlands," urbanites exchanged cultural information. Their caravans of pack animals—first donkeys and wild asses; much later, camels—transported goods through deserts and steppes and across mountain barriers. Stopping at oasis communities to exchange their wares for supplies, these caravans also carried ideas across Afro-Eurasia. In this way, people of the borderlands—along with the cities they connected—have played a vital role in world history.

BETWEEN THE TIGRIS AND EUPHRATES RIVERS: MESOPOTAMIA

The world's first complex society arose in Mesopotamia, from the Greek meaning "land between two rivers." Mesopotamia was a large landmass that included all of modern Iraq, eastern Syria, and southeastern Turkey. Here the Tigris and Euphrates Rivers flowed. From headwaters in the northwest, these wild and unpredictable rivers flowed to the mouth of the Persian Gulf. Providing water for irrigation, they also marked routes for transportation and communication by pack animal. Unpredictable waters can wipe out years of hard work, but when managed properly they can transform the landscape into verdant and productive fields. Here men and women, using abundant supplies of water and rich agricultural lands, established large cities and dramatically new cultural, political, and social institutions. By 3500 BCE, in a world where people had been living close to the land in small clans and settlements, a radical breakthrough occurred in this one place. Here the world's first complex society arose. Here the city and the river changed how people lived.

Tapping the Waters

Unless controlled by waterworks, the Tigris and Euphrates Rivers were profoundly unfavorable to cultivators, for the annual floods and low-water seasons came at the wrong times in the farming sequence. Floods occurred at the height of the growing season, when crops were most vulnerable. Low water levels occurred when crops required abundant irrigation. To prevent the river from overflowing during its flood stage, farmers built levees (barriers to the waters) along the banks and dug ditches and canals to drain away the floodwaters. Their solution was ingenious. Since the bed of the Euphrates is higher than that of the Tigris, and the Euphrates floods sometimes drained toward the Tigris, engineers devised extensive irrigation systems contoured to follow the downward sloping grade between the two

Early Mesopotamian Waterworks. *From the sixth millennium BCE, irrigation was necessary for successful farming in southern Mesopotamia. By the first millennium BCE, sophisticated feats of engineering allowed the Assyrians to redirect water through constructed aqueducts, like the one illustrated here on a relief from the palace of the Assyrian king Sennacherib at Nineveh (who will be discussed in Chapter 4).*

rivers. Under this scheme, the Euphrates served as the supply and the Tigris as the drain of the southern river basin. Storing and channeling water year after year required constant maintenance and innovation by a corps of engineers.

The Mesopotamian technological breakthrough was in irrigation, not in agrarian methods. Because the soils were fine, rich, and constantly replenished by the floodwaters' silt, soil tillage was light work. Farmers sowed a combination of wheat, millet, sesame, and barley (the basis for beer, a staple of their diet). Unforeseen, however, was the danger of planting every year, for by the third millennium the fertile soils had been destroyed by the constant accumulation of salts deposited through constant use.

Crossroads of Southwest Asia

Though its soil was rich and water was abundant, southern Mesopotamia had few other natural resources apart from mud, marsh reeds, spindly trees, and low-quality limestone that served as basic building materials. To obtain high-quality, dense wood, stone, metal, and other materials for constructing and embellishing their cities (notably their temples and palaces), Mesopotamians had to interact with the inhabitants of surrounding regions. Thus, long-distance trade was vitally important to the cities of southern Mesopotamia. In return for textiles, specialty foods, oils, and other commodities, they imported cedar wood from Lebanon, copper and stones from Oman, more copper from Turkey and Iran, and the precious blue gemstone called lapis lazuli, as well as the ever-useful tin, from faraway Afghanistan. Providing colorful stones, gold, and silver to elaborate the

ANALYZING GLOBAL DEVELOPMENTS

The Development of Writing

Agricultural surplus, and the urbanization and labor specialization that accompanied it, prompted the earliest development of writing and the profession of the scribes, whose job it was to write. Early forms of writing were employed for a variety of purposes, such as keeping financial and administrative records, recording the reigns of rulers, and documenting religious events and practices (calendars, rituals, and divinatory purposes). By the late third millennium BCE, some early societies (Mesopotamia and Egypt, in particular) used writing to produce literature, religious texts, and historical documents. Different types of writing developed in early societies, in part because each society developed writing for different purposes (see table):

- **Ideographic/logographic/pictographic systems:** symbols representing words (complex and cumbersome)
- **Logophonetic and logosyllabic systems:** symbols representing words, with a subset also representing sounds, usually syllables (fewer symbols)
- **Syllabic systems:** symbols representing syllables assembled to create words

- **Alphabetic systems:** letter symbols representing individual speech sounds assembled to create words

Scholars know more about early cultures whose writing has since been deciphered. Undeciphered scripts, such as the Indus Valley Script and Rongorongo, offer intrigue and promise to those who would attempt to decipher them.

QUESTIONS FOR ANALYSIS

- What is the relationship between writing and the development of the earliest river-basin societies? (See also Map 2.1.)
- To what extent does the type of society (river-basin, seafaring, and so on) seem to impact the development of writing in that region (date, type, purpose, and so on)?
- How has the decipherment, or lack thereof, of these scripts impacted scholars' understanding of the societies that produced them?

Name/Type of Society	Writing Form and Date of Emergence	Type of Writing and Purpose	Date and Means of Decipherment
Mesopotamia (Sumer)/ river-basin (Tigris-Euphrates)	Cuneiform, 3200 BCE	Transitions from about 1,000 pictographs to about 400 syllables (record keeping)	Deciphered in nineteenth century via Behistun/Beisitun inscription
Egypt (Old Kingdom)/ river-basin (Nile)	Hieroglyphs, 3100 BCE	Mixture of thousands of logograms and phonograms (religious)	Deciphered in early nineteenth century via trilingual Rosetta Stone
Harappan/river-basin (Indus)	Indus Valley Script, 2500 BCE	375–400 logographic signs (nomenclature and titleature)	Undeciphered
Minoan/Mycenaean Greece/seafaring microsociety	Phaistos Disk and Linear A (Minoan Crete); Linear B (Mycenaean, Crete and Greece); 1900 BCE–1300 BCE	Phaistos Disk (45 pictographic symbols in a spiral); Linear A (90 logographic-syllabic symbols); Linear B (roughly 75 syllabic symbols with some logographs) (record keeping)	Phaistos (undeciphered); Linear A (undeciphered); Linear B (deciphered in mid-twentieth century)
Shang Dynasty/river-basin (Yellow River)	Oracle bone script, 1400–1100 BCE	Thousands of characters (divinatory purposes)	Deciphered in early twentieth century
Maya/Central American rain forest	Maya glyphs, 250 BCE	Mixture of logograms (numeric glyphs), phonograms (around 85 phonetic glyphs), and hundreds of "emblem glyphs" (record of rulers and calendrical purposes)	Decipherment begun in twentieth century
Vikings/seafaring (Scandinavia)	Futhark (runic alphabet), 200 CE	24 alphabetic runes (ritual use or to identify owner or craftsperson)	Deciphered by Elder Futhark in nineteenth century
Inca/Andean highlands	Quipu, 3000? BCE	Knotted cords, essentially a tally system (record keeping)	Deciphered
Easter Island/seafaring microsociety	Rongorongo, 1500 CE	120 glyphs (calendrical or genealogical)	Undeciphered

Sources: Chris Scarre (ed.), *The Human Past: World Prehistory and the Development of Human Societies* (Thames and Hudson, 2005); Luigi Luca Cavalli-Sforza, *Genes, Peoples, and Languages*, translated by Mark Selestad from the original 1996 French publication (North Point Press, 2000).

temples and to embellish the elites, as well as useful copper and tin that when combined make bronze, this trade was fundamental to the development of the social and political hierarchy in Mesopotamia. Maintaining trading contacts was easy, given Mesopotamia's open boundaries on all sides. (In this crucial respect, Mesopotamia contrasted with Egypt, whose land was cut off by impassable deserts to the east and west, by the Nile River rapids to the south, and by the Mediterranean Sea to the north.) By 3000 BCE there was extensive interaction between southern Mesopotamia and the highlands of Anatolia, the forests of the Levant bordering the eastern Mediterranean, and the rich mountains and vast plateau of Iran. (See again Map 2.2.)

Mesopotamia also became a magnet for waves of newcomers from the deserts and the mountains and thus a crossroads for the peoples of Southwest Asia, the meeting grounds for distinct cultural and linguistic groups. Among the dominant groups were Sumerians, who concentrated in the south; Hurrians, who lived in the north; and Akkadians, who populated western and central Mesopotamia.

The World's First Cities

During the first half of the fourth millennium BCE, a demographic transformation occurred in the southern part of the Tigris-Euphrates River basin. This was an area stretching from present-day Baghdad to the Persian Gulf (usually referred to by scholars as Babylonia, even though a city in the location of Babylon did not emerge until the latter part of the third millennium BCE). The population here expanded as a result of the region's agricultural bounty, political advances, and the swelling ranks of Mesopotamians, who migrated from country villages to centers that eventually became cities. (A **city** is a large, well-defined urban area with a dense population.) Although this area was

relatively small, it possessed significant geographical diversity that served it well. To the west was an uninhabitable desert plateau. The farming lands and cities existed in the irrigated zones in the south, while beyond the river valley the mountainous regions to the north and east permitted the herding of livestock.

The earliest cities—Eridu, Nippur, and Uruk—developed over about 1,000 years, dominating the southern part of the floodplain by 3500 BCE. Here archaeologists have found buildings of mud brick marking successive layers of urban development. Consider Eridu, a village dating back to 6000 BCE. Home to the Sumerian water god, Ea, Eridu was a sacred site where temples piled up on top of one another for over 4,000 years. The final temple rose from a platform like a mountain, visible for miles in all directions, and was the home of the patron deity. The god's household was presided over by a coterie of priests, the most important of whom had substantial political powers.

As the temple grew skyward, the village expanded outward and became a city. Gods oversaw the sprawl. From their homes in temples located at the center of cities, they broadcast their powers through the priestly class. In return, urbanites provided finery, clothes, and enhanced lodgings for the gods and their priestly envoys. In Sumerian cosmology, humans were created solely to serve the gods, so the urban landscape reflected this fact: with a temple at the core, with goods and services flowing to the center, and with divine protection and justice flowing outward.

Some thirty-five cities with divine sanctuaries dotted the southern plain of Mesopotamia. Sumer glorified a way of life and a territory composed of politically equal city-states, each with a guardian deity and sanctuary supported by its inhabitants. (A **city-state** is a political organization based on the authority of a single, large city that controls the surrounding countryside.) Local communities in these urban hubs expressed homage to individual city gods and took pride in the temple, the god's home.

Layout of Eridu. *Over several millennia, temples of increasing size and complexity were built atop each other at Eridu, in southern Iraq. The culmination came with the elaborate structure of level VII.*

Because early Mesopotamian cities served as meeting places for peoples and their deities, they gained status as religious, political, and economic centers. Whether enormous (like Uruk and Nippur) or modest (like Ur and Abu Salabikh), all cities were spiritual, economic, and cultural homes for Mesopotamian subjects and places where considerable political power was exercised.

Simply making a city was not enough: it had to be made great. Urban design reflected the city's role as a wondrous place to pay homage to the gods and their human intermediary, the ruler figure. These early cities contained enormous spaces within their walls, with large houses separated by date palm plantations. The city limits also encompassed extensive sheepfolds (which became a frequent metaphor for the city). As populations grew, the Mesopotamian cities became denser and the houses smaller. Some urbanites established new suburbs, spilling out beyond old walls and creating neighborhoods in what used to be the countryside.

The typical layout of Mesopotamian cities reflected a common pattern: a central canal surrounded by neighborhoods of specialized occupational groups. The temple marked the city center, originally the supreme source of political authority, while the palace and other official buildings graced the periphery. In separate quarters for craft production, families passed down their trades across generations. In this sense, the landscape of the city mirrored the growing **social hierarchies** (distinctions between the privileged and the less privileged).

Gods and Temples

The worldview of the Sumerians and, later, the Akkadians included a belief in a group of gods that shaped their political institutions and controlled everything—including the weather, fertility, harvests, and the underworld. As depicted in the *Epic of Gilgamesh* (a second-millennium BCE composition based on oral tales about Gilgamesh, a historical but mythologized king of Uruk), the gods could give but could also take away—with searing droughts, unmerciful floods, and violent death. Gods, along with the natural forces they controlled, had to be revered and feared. Faithful subjects imagined their gods as immortal beings whose habits were capricious, contentious, and gloriously work free.

Each major god of the Sumerian pantheon (an officially recognized group of gods) dwelled in a lavish temple in a particular city, giving rise to each city's character, institutions, and relationships with its urban neighbors. Inside the temple was an altar displaying the god's image. Temples also featured statues of humans standing in perpetual worship and commemorating acts of piety and generosity carried out by the city's residents. By the end of the third millennium BCE, the temple's platform base had changed to a stepped platform called a *ziggurat*. On top of the temple tower stood the main temple. Surrounding the ziggurat were buildings that housed priests, officials, laborers, and servants—all bustling about to serve the city's god.

While the temple was the god's earthly residence, it was also the god's estate. As such, temples functioned like large households engaging in all sorts of productive and commercial activities. Their dependents cultivated cereals, fruits, and vegetables by using extensive irrigation. The temples owned vast flocks of sheep, goats, cows, and donkeys. Those located close to the river employed workers to collect reeds, to fish, and to hunt. Enormous labor forces were involved in maintaining this high level of production. Other temples operated huge workshops for manufacturing textiles and leather goods, employing

Ziggurat. *The first ziggurat of Mesopotamia, dedicated to the moon god Nanna, was built by the founder of the Neo-Sumerian dynasty, Ur-Nammu (2112–2095 BCE). Although temples had been raised on platforms since early times, the distinctive stepped form of the ziggurat was initially borrowed from the Iranian plateau. It became the most important sacred structure in Mesopotamia.*

craftworkers, metalworkers, masons, and stoneworkers. Yet temples also performed redistributive functions, returning some of their bounty to the city's residents, thereby enhancing the power of each patron god and his or her priests.

The Palace and Royal Power

Like the temples, royal palaces reflected the power of the ruling elite. The palace, as both an institution and a set of buildings, appeared around 2500 BCE—about two millennia later than the Mesopotamian temple. Palaces emerged as cities expanded and came into conflict with other cities. Disputes led to the emergence of another dominant political figure—the warrior chief, who was at first chosen because of military skills. Over time, however, these powers passed within families, leading to royal dynasties. A palace (or *e-gal*, "big house") was constructed on the outskirts of the city, in contrast to the founding temple, which stood at the center of the city. Like temples, palaces constituted significant landmarks of city life, upholding order and a sense of shared membership in city affairs. Over time, the palace became a source of power rivaling that of the temple, even though palaces were off limits to most citizens unless connected to the royal court.

Rulers tied their status to their gods through elaborate burial arrangements. The Royal Cemetery at Ur offers spectacular archaeological evidence of how Sumerian rulers dealt with death. Housed in a mud-brick structure, the royal burials held not only the primary remains but also the bodies of people who had been sacrificed—in one case, more than eighty men and women. Artifacts including huge vats for cooked food, bones of animals, drinking vessels, and musical instruments enable scholars to reconstruct the lifestyle of those who joined their masters in the graves. Honoring the royal dead by including their followers and possessions in their tombs reinforced the social hierarchies—including the vertical ties between humans and gods—that were the cornerstone of these early city-states.

Social Hierarchy and Families

Social hierarchies were an important part of the fabric of Sumerian city-states. Ruling groups secured their privileged access to economic and political resources by erecting systems of bureaucracies, priesthoods, and laws. Priests and bureaucrats served their rulers well, championing rules and norms that legitimized the political leadership. Mesopotamia's city-states at first had assemblies of elders and young men who made collective decisions for the community. At times, certain effective individuals took charge of emergencies, and over time these people acquired more durable political power. The social hierarchy set off the rulers from the ruled.

Occupations within the cities were highly specialized, and a Sumerian lexical list names some of the most important professions. The king and priest, at the top of the hierarchy in Sumer, do not appear on the list. First come bureaucrats (scribes and household accountants), supervisors, and craftworkers. The latter included cooks, jewelers, gardeners, potters, metalsmiths, and traders. The biggest group, which was at the bottom of the

The Royal Tombs of Ur. *The Royal Tombs of Ur, excavated in the 1930s, contained thousands of objects in gold, silver, lapis lazuli, and shell that were buried along with elites of the First Dynasty of Ur. In one grave, along with the skeletons of more than sixty members of a royal household, were musical instruments, including a large harp with a golden bull's head (left photo). Such instruments would have been played at the ritual meal associated with these fabulously rich burials. Pu-Abi, identified as a queen by the cylinder near her body, was buried in a separate chamber. She was interred in full regalia, including an elaborate headdress (right photo).*

hierarchy, comprised workers who were not slaves but who were dependent on their employers' households. Movement among economic classes was not impossible but, as in many traditional societies, it was rare. There were also independent merchants who risked long-distance trading ventures, hoping for a generous return on their investment.

The family and the household provided the fundamental structure for Sumerian society, and its organization reflected the balance between women and men, children and parents. The Sumerian family was hierarchical, so the senior male dominated as the patriarch. Most households were composed of a single extended family, all of whose members lived under the same roof. The family consisted of the husband and wife bound by a contract: she would provide children, preferably male, while he provided support and protection. Monogamy was the norm unless there was no son, in which case a second wife or a slave girl would bear male children to serve as the married couple's offspring. Adoption was another way to gain a male heir. Sons would inherit the family's property in equal shares, while daughters would receive dowries necessary for successful marriage into other families. Most women lived inside the contract of marriage, but a special class of women joined the temple staff as priestesses. By the second millennium BCE, they gained economic autonomy that included ownership of estates and productive enterprises. Even in this case, though, their fathers and brothers remained responsible for their well-being. The family hierarchy mirrored and also strengthened the social order.

First Writing and Early Texts

Mesopotamia was the birthplace of the first recorded words of history, inscribed to promote the power of the temples and kings in the expanding city-states. Small-scale hunter-gatherer societies and village-farming communities had developed rituals of oral celebrations based on collective memories transmitted by families across generations. But as societies grew larger and more complex and their members more anonymous, oral traditions provided inadequate "glue" to hold the centers together.

Those who wielded new writing tools were **scribes**; from the very beginning, they were at the top of the social ladder, under the major power brokers—the big man and the priests. As the writing of texts became more important to the social fabric of cities and facilitated information sharing across wider spans of distance and time, scribes consolidated their grip on the upper rungs of the social ladder.

Mesopotamians became the world's first record keepers and readers. The precursors to writing appeared in Mesopotamian societies when farming peoples and officials, who had been using clay tokens and images carved on stones to seal off storage areas, began to use them to convey messages. These images, when combined with numbers drawn on clay tablets, could record the distribution of goods and services.

In a flash of human genius, someone, probably in Uruk, understood that the marks (most were pictures of objects) could also represent words or sounds. Before long, scribes connected visual symbols with sounds, and sounds with meanings, and they discovered they could record messages by using symbols or signs to denote concepts. Such signs later came to represent syllables, the building blocks of words. (See Primary Source: The Origins of Writing According to the Sumerians.)

By impressing signs into wet clay with the cut end of a reed, scribes pioneered a form of wedge-shaped writing that we call *cuneiform;* it filled tablets with information that was intelligible to anyone who could decipher the signs, even in faraway locations or in future generations. At first, this Sumerian innovation was used exclusively to monitor and control economic transactions within the city-state: the distribution of sheep, goats, slaves, grain, rations, and textiles to supervisors or to the temple. Only hundreds of years later was the writing system used to transmit ideas through literature, historical records, and sacred texts. The result was a profound change in human experience, because representing symbols of spoken language facilitated an extension of communication and memory.

Much of what we know about Mesopotamia rests on our ability to decipher cuneiform script. By around 2400 BCE, texts began to describe the political makeup of southern Mesopotamia, giving details of its history and economy. Northern cities borrowed cuneiform to record economic transactions and political events, but in their own Semitic tongue. In fact, cuneiform's adaptability to different languages was a main reason its use spread widely.

As city life and literacy expanded, they gave rise not only to documents but also to written narratives, the stories of a "people" and their origins. One famous set of texts written around 2100 BCE, "The Temple Hymns," describes thirty-five divine sanctuaries. The magnificent Sumerian King List, composed around 2000 BCE, recounts the reigns of kings by dynasty, one city at a time. It narrates the fabulously long reigns of legendary kings before the so-called Great Flood, which, in turn, is one of many traditional stories that people transmitted orally for generations (and later evolved into the book of Genesis as part of the Bible's creation story). The Great Flood, a crucial event in Sumerian identity, explained Uruk's demise as the gods' doing. Flooding was the most riveting of natural forces in the lives of a river-basin people, and it helped shape the material and symbolic foundations of Mesopotamian societies.

The Origins of Writing According to the Sumerians

One Sumerian myth records the invention of writing by the lord of Kulaba, Enmerkar. He wanted to transmit complex messages across vast distances to the Land of Aratta, where his rival for the love of the goddess Inanna lived. Normally, messengers would memorize messages and responses and deliver them orally after making an arduous journey across the mountains. Enmerkar felt he could not trust his messenger's memory to deliver one particularly complicated message, so he invented writing in the form of cuneiform script.

His speech was substantial, and its contents extensive. The messenger, whose mouth was heavy, was not able to repeat it. Because the messenger, whose mouth was tired, was not able to repeat it, the lord of Kulaba patted some clay and wrote the message as if on a tablet. Formerly, the writing of messages on clay was not established. Now, under that sun and on that day, it was indeed so. The lord of Kulaba inscribed the message like a tablet. It was

Cuneiform version of the myth "Enmerkar and the Lord of Aratta."

just like that. The messenger was like a bird, flapping its wings; he raged forth like a wolf following a kid. He traversed five mountains, six mountains, seven mountains. He lifted his eyes as he approached Aratta. He stepped joyfully into the courtyard of Aratta, he made known the authority of his king. Openly he spoke out the words in his heart. The messenger transmitted the message to the lord of Aratta:

"Your father, my master, has sent me to you; the lord of Unug, the lord of Kulaba, has sent me to you." "What is it to me what your master has spoken? What is it to me what he has said?"

"This is what my master has spoken, this is what he has said. My king is like a huge *meš* tree, . . . son of Enlil; this tree has grown high, uniting heaven and earth; its crown reaches heaven, its trunk is set upon the earth. He who is made to shine forth in lordship and kingship, Enmerkar, the son of Utu, has given me a clay tablet. O lord of Aratta, after you have examined the clay tablet, after you have learned the content of the message, say whatever you will say to me, and I shall announce that message in the shrine E-ana as glad tidings to the scion of him with the glistening beard, whom his stalwart cow gave birth to in the mountains of the shining *me*, who was reared on the soil of Aratta, who was given suck at the udder of the good

cow, who is suited for office in Kulaba, the mountain of great *me*, to Enmerkar, the son of Utu; I shall repeat it in his *ĝipar*, fruitful as a flourishing *meš* tree, to my king, the lord of Kulaba."

After he had spoken thus to him, the lord of Aratta received his kiln-fired tablet from the messenger. The lord of Aratta looked at the tablet. The transmitted message was just nails, and his brow expressed anger. The lord of Aratta looked at his kiln-fired tablet. At that moment, the lord worthy of the crown of lordship, the son of Enlil, the god Iškur, thundering in heaven and earth, caused a raging storm, a great lion, in . . . He was making the mountains quake . . . , he was convulsing the mountain range . . . ; the awesome radiance . . . of his breast; he caused the mountain range to raise its voice in joy. (lines 500–551)

QUESTIONS FOR ANALYSIS

- What passages in this reading reveal the Sumerians' familiarity with pastoralism?

- What aspects of Sumerian history and geography does this mythical story preserve and transmit?

Source: J. A. Black, G. Cunningham, E. Fluckiger-Hawker, E. Robson, and G. Zólyomi, *The Electronic Text Corpus of Sumerian Literature* (Oxford, 1998–2006), www-etcsl.orient.ox.ac.uk/.

Cylinder Seal of Adda Carved from Green Stone. *Many people in Mesopotamia involved with administration and public life had one or more cylinder seals. Cylinder seals were carved with imagery and inscriptions and were impressed into clay tablets and other documents while they were still malleable in order to guarantee the authenticity of a transaction. The cylinder seal shown here carries the inscription of the scribe Adda. The imagery includes representations of important gods of the Akkadian pantheon. The sun god Shamash rises from between the mountains in the center. Ishtar as a warrior goddess stands to the left. To the right is Ea, the god of wisdom, who is associated with flowing water and fish. Behind him is the servant Usmu, whose double face allows him to see everything. At the far left is a god of hunting.*

Spreading Cities and the First Territorial States

Although no single state dominated the history of fourth- and third-millennium BCE Mesopotamia, a few stand out. The most powerful and influential were the Sumerian city-states of the Early Dynastic Age (2850–2334 BCE) and their successor, the Akkadian territorial state (2334–2193 BCE). While the city-states of southern Mesopotamia flourished and competed, giving rise to the land of Sumer, the rich agricultural zones to the north inhabited by the Hurrians also became urbanized. (See Map 2.3.) Beginning around 2600 BCE, northern cities were comparable in size to those in the south.

As Mesopotamia swelled with cities, it became unstable. The Sumerian city-states with expanding populations soon found themselves competing for agrarian lands, scarce water, and lucrative trade routes. And as pastoralists far and wide learned of the region's bounty, they journeyed in greater numbers to the cities, fueling urbanization and competition.

Cities also spawned rivalry and struggles for supremacy. In fact, the world's first great conqueror emerged from one of these cities, and by the end of his long reign he had united (by force) the independent Mesopotamian cities south of modern-day Baghdad. The legendary Sargon the Great (r. 2334–2279 BCE), king of Akkad, brought the era of competitive independent city-states to an end. His most remarkable achievement was unification of the southern cities through an alliance. Although this unity lasted only three generations, it represented the first multiethnic unification of urban centers—the **territorial state**. (A territorial state is a form of political organization that holds authority over a large population and landmass; its power extends over a wider area than that of city-states.) Just under a century after Sargon's death, foreign tribesmen from the Zagros Mountains conquered the capital city of Akkad, bringing an end to the Akkadian state. Its collapse in 2190 BCE fueled epic history

writing that depicted the struggles between city-state dwellers and those on the margins, who lived a simpler way of life.

The fall of Sargon's "empire" underscores a fundamental but often neglected reality of the ancient world: living side by side with the city-state dwellers were peoples who often did not enter the historical record except when they intruded on the lives of their more powerful, prosperous, and literate neighbors. The most obvious legacy of Sargon's dynasty was its sponsorship of monumental architecture, artworks, and literary works. These cultural achievements stood for centuries, inspiring generations of builders, architects, artists, and scribes. And by encouraging contact with distant neighbors, many of whom adopted aspects of Mesopotamian culture, the Akkadian kings increased the geographical reach of Mesopotamian influence.

Naram Sin. *This life-size head of a ruler cast of almost pure copper was found at Nineveh in northern Iraq in the destruction levels of the Assyrian Empire. The style and imagery of this sculptural masterpiece identify it as a ruler of the Old Akkadian dynasty. While sometimes identified as Sargon, it is most likely a portrait of his grandson, Naram Sin, who consolidated and transformed the Akkadian state. It must have stood for over 1,500 years in the courtyard of a temple at Nineveh before it was defaced by the Medes and Elamites, whose savage attack on Nineveh caused the Assyrian Empire to fall.*

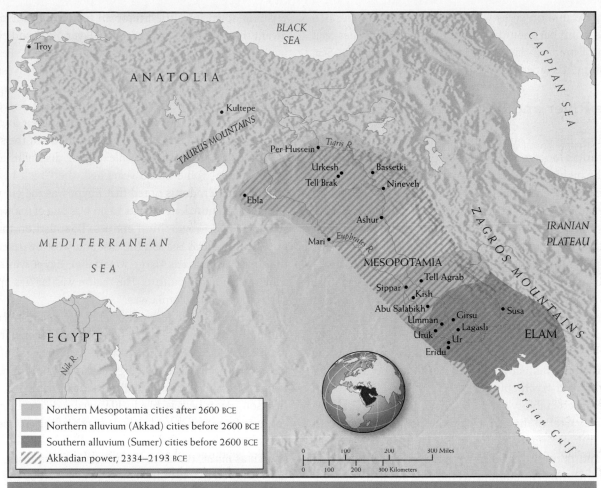

MAP 2.3 | The Spread of Cities in Mesopotamia and the Akkadian State, 2600–2200 BCE

Urbanization began in the southern alluvium of Mesopotamia and spread northward. Eventually, the region achieved unification under Akkadian power.

- According to this map, what were the natural boundaries of the Mesopotamian cities?
- How did proximity to the Zagros Mountains affect the new urban centers?
- How did the expansion northward reflect the continued influence of geographical and environmental factors on urbanization?

"THE GIFT OF THE NILE": EGYPT

While Mesopotamia led the way in creating city-states, Egypt went a step further, unifying a 600-mile-long landmass under a single ruler. Here, complex societies grew on the banks of the Nile River, and by the third millennium BCE, the Egyptian people had created a distinctive culture and a powerful, prosperous state. The earliest inhabitants along the banks of the Nile River were a mixed people. Some had migrated from the eastern and western deserts in Sinai and Libya as these areas grew barren from climate change. Others came from the Mediterranean. Equally important were peoples who trekked northward from Nubia and central Africa. Ancient Egypt was a melting pot where immigrants blended cultural practices and technologies.

Egypt had much in common with Mesopotamia. Like Mesopotamia, it had densely populated areas whose inhabitants depended on irrigation, gave their rulers immense authority, and created a complex social order. Like the Mesopotamians, they built monumental architecture. Tapping the Nile waters gave rise to agrarian wealth, commercial and devotional centers, early states, and new techniques of communication.

Yet the ancient Egyptian culture was profoundly distinct from its contemporaries in Mesopotamia. To understand its unique qualities, we must begin with geography. The environment and the natural boundaries of deserts, river rapids, and sea dominated the country and its inhabitants. The core area of ancient Egypt covered 386,560 square miles, of which only 11,720 square miles (7.5 million acres) were cultivable. Of this total, roughly 6 million acres were in the Nile delta—the rich alluvial land lying between the river's two main branches as it flows north of modern-day Cairo into the Mediterranean Sea. This environment shaped Egyptian society's unique culture.

The Nile River and Its Floodwaters

Understanding Egypt requires appreciating the pulses of the Nile. The world's longest river, it stretches 4,238 miles from its sources in the highlands of central Africa to its destination in the Mediterranean Sea. The Upper Nile is a sluggish river that cuts through the Sahara Desert. Rising out of central Africa and Ethiopia, its two main branches—the White and Blue Niles—meet at present-day Khartoum and then scour out a single riverbed 1,500 miles long to the Mediterranean. The annual floods gave the basin regular moisture and alluvial richness and gave rise to a society whose culture stretched along the navigable river and its carefully preserved banks. Away from the riverbanks, on both sides, lay a desert rich in raw materials but largely uninhabited. Egypt had no fertile hinterland like the sprawling plains of Mesopotamia. In a sense, Egypt was the most river focused of the river-basin cultures.

The Nile's predictability as the source of life and abundance shaped the character of the people and their culture. In contrast to the wild and uncertain Euphrates and Tigris Rivers, the Nile was gentle and bountiful, leading Egyptians to view the world as beneficent. During the summer as the Nile swelled, local villagers built earthen walls that divided the floodplain into basins. By trapping the floodwaters, these basins captured the rich silt

washing down from the Ethiopian highlands. Annual flooding meant that the land received a new layer of topsoil every year.

The light, fertile soils made planting simple. Peasants cast seeds into the alluvial soil and then had their livestock trample them to the proper depth. The never-failing sun, which the Egyptians worshipped, ensured an abundant harvest. In the early spring, when the Nile's waters were at their lowest and no crops were under cultivation, the sun dried out the soil.

The peculiarities of the Nile region distinguished it from Mesopotamia. Some 2,500 years ago, the Greek historian and geographer Herodotus noted that Egypt was the gift of the Nile and that the entire length of its basin was one of the world's most self-contained geographical entities. Bounded on the north by the Mediterranean Sea, on the east and west by deserts, and on the south by cataracts (large waterfalls), Egypt was destined to achieve a common culture. The region was far less open to outsiders than Mesopotamia was.

Like the other pioneering societies, Egypt created a common culture by balancing regional tensions and reconciling regional rivalries. Ancient Egyptian history is a struggle of opposing forces: the north, or Lower Egypt, versus the south, or Upper Egypt; the sand, the so-called red part of the earth, versus the rich soil, described as black; life versus death; heaven versus earth; order versus disorder. For Egypt's ruling groups—notably the kings—the primary task was to bring stability, or order, known as *ma'at*, out of these antagonistic impulses. The Egyptians believed that keeping chaos, personified by the desert and its marauders, at bay through attention to *ma'at* would allow all that was good and right to occur.

Nile Agriculture. *The Nile is fed by the Blue Nile, which has its source in the Ethiopian highlands, and the White Nile in southern Sudan. It rises and falls according to a regular pattern that was the basis for the ancient Egyptian agricultural cycle. Flooding the valley in August and September, the Nile then recedes, depositing a rich layer of silt in which the crops were planted in the fall and harvested in April and May.*

The Rise of the Egyptian State and Dynasties

Once the early Egyptians harnessed the Nile to agriculture, the area changed from being scarcely inhabited to socially complex. Whereas Mesopotamia developed gradually, Egypt seemed to grow overnight. It quickly became a powerhouse state, projecting its splendor along the full length of the river valley.

A king, called pharaoh, was at the center of Egyptian life. His primary responsibility was to ensure that the forces of nature, in particular the regular flooding of the Nile, continued without interruption. This task had more to do with appeasing the gods than with running a complex hydraulic system requiring considerable oversight. The king also had to protect his people from invaders from the eastern and western deserts as well as from Nubians on the southern borders and from the people of the sea on the north. These groups threatened Egypt with social chaos. As guarantors of the social and political order, the early kings depicted themselves as shepherds. In wall carvings, artists portrayed them carrying the crook and the flail, indicating their responsibility for the welfare of their flocks (the people) and of the land. Moreover, an elaborate bureaucracy organized labor and produced public works, sustaining both the king's vast holdings and general order throughout the realm.

The narrative of ancient Egyptian history follows its thirty-one dynasties, spanning three millennia from 3100 BCE down to its conquest by Alexander the Great in 332 BCE. (See Table 2.1.) Since the nineteenth century, however, scholars have recast the story around three periods of dynastic achievement: the Old Kingdom, the Middle Kingdom, and the New Kingdom. At the end of each era, cultural flourishing suffered a breakdown in central authority, known, respectively, as the First, Second, and Third Intermediate Periods.

Pharaohs, Rituals, Pyramids, and Cosmic Order

The Third Dynasty (2686–2613 BCE) launched the foundational period known as the Old Kingdom, the golden age of ancient Egypt. (See Map 2.4.) By the time this dynasty came to power, the basic institutions of the Egyptian state were in place, as were the ideology and ritual life that legitimized the dynastic rulers.

The pharaoh—king as god—presented himself to the population by means of impressive architectural spaces, and the priestly class performed rituals reinforcing his supreme status within the universe's natural order. The most important ceremony was the Sed festival, which renewed the king's vitality after he had ruled for thirty years. Although the festival focused on the king's well-being, its origins lay in ensuring the perpetual presence of water.

TABLE 2.1 | Dynasties of Ancient Egypt

PERIOD	TIME
Predynastic Period (dynasties I and II)	3100–2686 BCE
Old Kingdom (dynasties III–VI)	2686–2181 BCE
First Intermediate Period (dynasties VII–X)	2181–2055 BCE
Middle Kingdom (dynasties XI–XIII)	2055–1650 BCE
Second Intermediate Period (dynasties XIV–XVII)	1650–1550 BCE
New Kingdom (dynasties XVIII–XX)	1550–1069 BCE
Third Intermediate Period (dynasties XXI–XXV)	1069–747 BCE
Late Period (dynasties XXVI–XXXI)	747–332 BCE

Source: Compiled from Ian Shaw and Paul Nicholson, eds., *The Dictionary of Ancient Egypt* (1995), pp. 310–11.

King Djoser, the second king of the Third Dynasty, celebrated the Sed festival in his tomb complex at Saqqara. This magnificent complex, built of stone (rather than the mud brick of the temples and palaces of Mesopotamia), took shape during Djoser's reign. It began as a huge flat structure identical to earlier royal tombs. However, the architect, Imhotep, was not satisfied with the modest shape of earlier burial chambers. Through six renovations he transformed the structure into a step pyramid that ultimately rose some 200 feet above the plain, dominating the landscape like the later Mesopotamian ziggurats (see p. 52). This mountain-like structure stood at the center of an enormous walled precinct housing five courts, where the king performed rituals emphasizing the divinity of kingship and the unity of Upper and Lower Egypt. Pervasive at this pyramid were symbols stressing the unity of Upper and Lower Egypt, embodied in the entwined lotus and papyrus, representing each region. The step pyramid complex incorporated artistic and architectural forms that would characterize Egyptian culture for millennia.

The Egyptian cosmic order was one of inequality and stark hierarchy. Established at the time of creation, the universe was the king's responsibility to maintain for eternity. The belief that the king was destined to be a god after his death compelled him to behave like one: serene, orderly, merciful, and perfect. He always had to wear an expression of divine peace, not the angry snarl of mere human power.

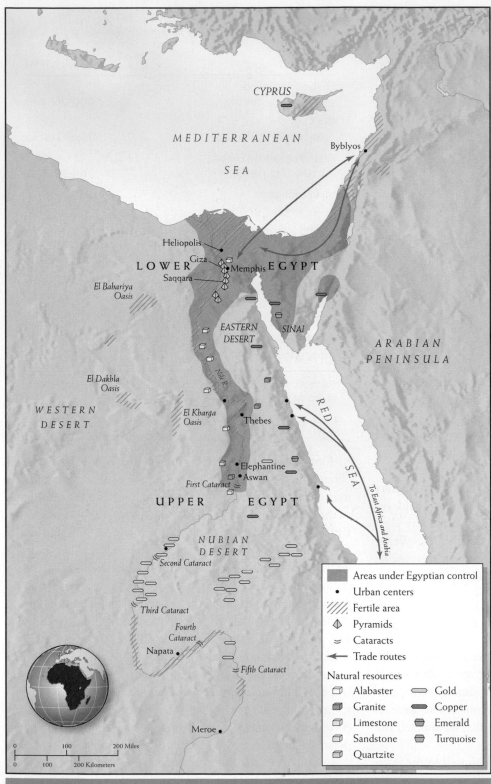

CYPRUS

MEDITERRANEAN

SEA

Byblyos

Heliopolis

LOWER Giza E G Y P T
        Memphis
Saqqara

El Babariya
Oasis

EASTERN   SINAI
DESERT

ARABIAN
PENINSULA

El Dakhla
Oasis

WESTERN
DESERT

El Kharga
Oasis   Thebes

RED

Elephantine
• Aswan
First Cataract

SEA

UPPER   EGYPT

To East Africa and Arabia

NUBIAN
DESERT

Second Cataract

Third Cataract

Fourth
Cataract

Napata

Fifth Cataract

Meroe •

0   100   200 Miles
0   100   200 Kilometers

Areas under Egyptian control
• Urban centers
Fertile area
⬦ Pyramids
⌣ Cataracts
← Trade routes
Natural resources
Alabaster   Gold
Granite   Copper
Limestone   Emerald
Sandstone   Turquoise
Quartzite

MAP 2.4 | Old Kingdom Egypt, 2686–2181 BCE

Old Kingdom Egyptian society reflected a strong influence from its unique geographical location.

- What geographical features contributed to Egypt's isolation from the outside world and the people's sense of their unity?
- What natural resource enabled the Egyptians to build the Great Pyramids?
- Based on the map, why do you think it was important for Upper and Lower Egypt to be united?

Pyramid building evolved rapidly from the step version of Djoser to the grand pyramids of the Fourth Dynasty (2613–2494 BCE). These kings erected their magnificent structures at Giza, just outside modern-day Cairo and not far from the early royal cemetery site of Saqqara. The pyramid of Khufu, rising 481 feet aboveground, is the largest stone structure in the world, and its corners are almost perfectly aligned to due north, west, south, and east. Khafra's pyramid, built by Khufu's son, though smaller, is even more alluring because it retains some of its original limestone casing and because it enjoys the protective presence of the Sphinx. Surrounding these royal tombs were those of high officials, almost all members of the royal family. The enormous amount of labor involved in constructing these monuments provides another measure of the degree of centralization and the surpluses in Egyptian society at this time. The labor force was made up of peasants and workers, who labored for the state at certain times of the year, as well as slaves brought from Nubia and captured Mediterranean peoples.

Through their majesty and architectural complexity, the Giza pyramids reflected the peak of Old Kingdom culture and the remarkable feats that its bureaucracy could accomplish. Construction of these monuments entailed the backbreaking work of quarrying the massive stones (some weighed over 2 tons), digging a canal so barges could bring them from the Nile to the base of the Giza plateau, building a harbor there, and then constructing sturdy brick ramps that could withstand the stones' weight as workers hauled them ever higher along the pyramids' faces. Most likely a permanent workforce of up to 21,000 laborers endured 10-hour workdays, 300 days a year, for approximately 14 years just to complete the great pyramid of Khufu.

The Pyramids of Giza. *The Pyramid Fields of Giza lie on the western side of the Nile just south of the modern city of Cairo. The Old Kingdom pharaohs built their eternal resting places there, surrounded by the smaller pyramids and bench tombs of their relatives and courtiers. The largest pyramid of Khufu is to the north. Khafra's is linked to the Nile by a causeway flanked by the famous Sphinx. The smallest is that of Menkaure, the penultimate king of the glorious Fourth Dynasty.*

Religion

Religion stood at the center of this ancient world, so all aspects of the culture reflected spiritual expression. Egyptians understood their world as inhabited by three groups: gods, kings, and the rest of humanity. Official records only showed representations of gods and kings.

CULTS OF THE GODS As in Mesopotamia, every region in Egypt had its resident god. Some gods, such as Amun (believed to be physically present in Thebes, the political center of Upper Egypt), came to transcend regional status because of the importance of their hometown. Over the centuries, the Egyptian gods evolved, combining often contradictory aspects into single deities represented by symbols: animals and human figures that often had animal as well as divine attributes. They included Horus, the hawk god; Osiris, the god of regeneration and the

Egyptian Gods. *Osiris (top) is the dying god who rules over the netherworld. Most frequently, he is depicted as a mummy wearing a white crown with plumes and holding the scepter across his chest. The god Horus (bottom), who was also rendered as Ra-Horakhty, is the falcon-headed Egyptian sky god. Horus is the earliest state god of Egypt and is always closely associated with the king. Horus is a member of the nine deities of Heliopolis and is the son of Osiris and Isis.*

underworld; Hathor, the goddess of childbirth and love; Ra, the sun god; and Amun, a creator considered to be the hidden god.

Official religious practices took place in the main temples, the heart of ceremonial events. The king and his agents cared for the gods in their temples, giving them respect, adoration, and thanks. In return the gods, embodied in sculptured images, maintained order and nurtured the king and—through him—all humanity. In this contractual relationship, the gods were passive and serene while the kings were active, a difference that reflected their unequal relationship. The practice of religious rituals and communication with the gods formed the cult, whose constant and correct performance was the foundation of Egyptian religion. Its goal was to preserve cosmic order fundamental to creation and prosperity.

One of the most enduring cults was that of the goddess Isis, who represented ideals of sisterhood and motherhood. According to Egyptian mythology, Isis, the wife of the murdered and dismembered Osiris, commanded her son, Horus, to reassemble all of the parts of Osiris so that he might reclaim his rightful place as king of Egypt, taken from him by his assassin, his evil brother Seth. Osiris was seen as the god of rebirth, while Isis was renowned for her medicinal skills and knowledge of magic. For millennia her principal place of worship was a magnificent temple on the island of Philae. Even as late as the fourth century CE, well after the Greeks and Romans had conquered Egypt at the end of the first millennium BCE, the people continued to pay homage to Isis at her Philae temple.

THE PRIESTHOOD Although the responsibility for upholding cults fell to the king, the actual tasks of upholding the cult—regulating rituals according to a cosmic calendar and mediating among gods, kings, and society—fell to one specialist class: the priesthood. Creating this class required elaborate rules for selecting and training the priests to project the organized power of spiritual authority. The fact that only the priests could enter the temple's inner sanctum demonstrated their exalted status. The god, embodied in the cult statue, left the temple only at great festivals. Even then the divine image remained hidden in a portable shrine. This arrangement ensured that priests monopolized communication between spiritual powers and their subjects—and that Egyptians understood their own subservience to the priesthood.

Although the priesthood helped unify the Egyptians and focused their attention on the central role of temple life, unofficial religion was equally important. Ordinary ancient Egyptians matched their elite rulers in faithfulness to the gods, but their distance from temple life caused them to find different ways to fulfill their religious needs and duties. Thus, they visited local shrines, just as those of higher status visited the temples. There they prayed, made requests, and left offerings to the gods.

MAGICAL POWERS Magic had a special importance for commoners, who believed that amulets (ornaments worn to bring good fortune and to protect against evil forces) held extraordinary powers—for example, preventing illness and guaranteeing safe childbirth. To deal with profound questions, commoners looked to omens and divination (a practice that residents of Mesopotamia and ancient China also used to predict and control future events). Like the elites, commoners attributed supernatural powers to animals. Chosen animals received special treatment in life and after death: for example, the Egyptians adored cats, whom they kept as pets and whose image they used to represent certain deities. Apis bulls, sacred to the god Ptah, merited special cemeteries and mourning rituals. Ibises, dogs, jackals, baboons, lizards, fish, snakes, crocodiles, and other beasts associated with deities enjoyed similar privileges. Spiritual expression was central to Egyptian culture at all levels, and religion helped shape the society's other cultural achievements, including the development of a written language.

Writing and Scribes

Egypt, like Mesopotamia, was a scribal culture. Egyptians often said that peasants toiled so that scribes could live in comfort; in other words, literacy sharpened the divisions between rural and urban worlds. Writing appeared in Egypt at the same time as it did in Mesopotamia, after 3500 BCE. By the middle of the third millennium BCE, literacy was well established among small circles of experts in Egypt and Mesopotamia. The fact that few individuals were literate heightened the scribes' social status. Although in both cultures writing emerged in response to economic needs, people soon grasped its utility for commemorative and religious purposes. As soon as literacy took hold, Mesopotamians and Egyptians were drafting historical records and literary compositions.

Both the early Mesopotamian and Egyptian scripts were complex. In fact, one feature of all writing systems is that over time they became simpler and more efficient at representing the full range of spoken utterances. Only when the first alphabet appeared (in Southwest Asia, to record Aramaic around 1500 BCE) did the potential for wider literacy surface. To judge from remaining records, it seems that more Egyptians than Mesopotamians were literate. Most high-ranking Egyptians were also trained as scribes working in the king's court, the army, or the priesthood. Some kings and members of the royal family learned to write as well.

Egyptians used two basic forms of writing throughout antiquity. *Hieroglyphs* (from the Greek for "sacred carving") served in temple, royal, or divine contexts. Hieroglyphs were derived from images that were sometimes identical to pictures seen in the tomb reliefs. In contrast, First Dynasty tombs yield records in a cursive script written with ink on papyrus, pottery, or other absorbent media. This *hieratic writing* was more common. Used

Egyptian Hieroglyphs and "Cursive Script." *The Egyptians wrote in two distinctive types of script. The more formal, the hieroglyphs, are based on pictorial images that carry values of either ideas (idiograms) or sounds (phonemes). All royal and funerary inscriptions, such as this funerary relief from the Old Kingdom (left), are rendered in hieroglyphic script. Daily documents, accountings, literary texts, and the like, were most often written in a cursive script called hieratic, which was written with ink on papyrus (right). The form of the cursive signs is based on the hieroglyphs but is more abstract and can be formed more quickly.*

for record keeping, it also found uses in letters and works of literature—including narrative fiction, manuals of instruction and philosophy, cult and religious hymns, love poems, medical and mathematical texts, collections of rituals, and mortuary books. By the sixth century BCE, this cursive script evolved into another script called *demotic* (from the Greek *demotika,* meaning "popular" or "in common use").

Becoming literate involved taking lessons from scribes, and these skills clustered in extended families. Most students started training when they were young, before entering the bureaucracy. After mastering the copying of standard texts in demotic cursive or hieroglyphs, students moved on to literary works. The upper classes prized the ability to read and write, regarding it as proof of high intellectual achievement. When they died, they had their student textbooks placed alongside their corpses as evidence of their talents. The literati produced texts mainly in temples, where these works were also preserved. Writing in hieroglyphs and transmitting texts continued without break in ancient Egypt for almost 3,000 years.

The Prosperity and Demise of Old Kingdom Egypt

The agrarian surpluses, urbanization, elaborate belief systems, population growth, and splendor that characterized Mesopotamian and Egyptian societies led to heightened standards of living and rising populations. Under pharaonic rule, Egypt enjoyed

spectacular prosperity. Its population grew at an unprecedented rate, swelling from 350,000 in 4000 BCE to 1 million in 2500 BCE and nearly 5 million by 1500 BCE.

As the Old Kingdom expanded without a uniting or dominating city, like those of Mesopotamia, the Egyptian state became more dispersed and the dynasties began to look increasingly outward. Expansion and decentralization eventually exposed the dynasties' weaknesses. The shakeup resulted not from external invasion or from bickering between rival city-states (as in Mesopotamia), but from feuding among elite political factions. More important, an extended drought that occurred across Afro-Eurasia profoundly strained Egypt's extensive irrigation system. As the Nile could no longer water the lands that fed the region's million inhabitants, images of great suffering filled the royal tombs' walls.

The long reign of Pepy II (2278–2184 BCE) marked the end of the Old Kingdom. Upon his death, royal power collapsed. (See Primary Source: The Admonitions of Ipuwer.) For the next hundred years, rivals jostled for the throne. Magnates, local people of influence, assumed hereditary control of the government in the provinces and treated lands previously controlled by the royal family as their personal property. And local leaders plunged into bloody regional struggles to keep the irrigation works functioning for their own communities. This so-called First Intermediate Period lasted roughly from 2181 to 2055 BCE, until the century-long drought ended. Although the Old Kingdom declined, it established institutions and beliefs that endured and were revived several centuries later.

The Admonitions of Ipuwer

To maintain power during a period of increasing drought, Pepy II (r. 2278–2184 BCE) gave many advantages and tax exemptions to provincial nobles. At the end of his long reign, no successors were capable of maintaining centralized power. The collapse of the central state was traumatic, and Egyptian society fell into chaos. A number of poignant texts written by prophets and wise men captured this situation. One of the most moving was the text known as the Ipuwer Papyrus, written by an Egyptian sage.

Behold, the fire has gone up on high, and its burning goes forth against the enemies of the land.

Behold, things have been done which have not happened for a long time past; the king has been deposed by the rabble.

Behold, he who was buried as a falcon [is devoid] of biers, and what the pyramid concealed has become empty.

Behold, it has befallen that the land has been deprived of the kingship by a few lawless men.

Behold, men have fallen into rebellion against the Uraeus, the [. . .] of Re, even she who makes the Two Lands content.

Behold, the secret of the land whose limits were unknown is divulged, and the Residence is thrown down in a moment.

Behold, Egypt is fallen to pouring of water, and he who poured water on the ground has carried off the strong man in misery.

Behold, the Serpent is taken from its hole, and the secrets of the Kings of Upper and Lower Egypt are divulged.

Behold, the Residence is afraid because of want, and [men go about] unopposed to stir up strife.

Behold, the land has knotted itself up with confederacies, and the coward takes the brave man's property.

Behold, the Serpent [. . .] the dead: he who could not make a sarcophagus for himself is now the possessor of a tomb.

Behold, the possessors of tombs are ejected on to the high ground, while he who could not make a coffin for himself is now [the possessor] of a treasury.

Behold, this has happened [to] men; he who could not build a room for himself is now a possessor of walls.

Behold, the magistrates of the land are driven out throughout the land: [. . .] are driven out from the palaces.

Behold, noble ladies are now on rafts, and magnates are in the labor establishment, while he who could not sleep even on walls is now the possessor of a bed.

Behold, the possessor of wealth now spends the night thirsty, while he who once begged his dregs for himself is now the possessor of overflowing bowls.

Behold, the possessors of robes are now in rags, while he who could not weave for himself is now a possessor of fine linen.

Behold, he who could not build a boat for himself is now the possessor of a fleet; their erstwhile owner looks at them, but they are not his.

Behold, he who had no shade is now the possessor of shade, while the erstwhile possessors of shade are now in the full blast of the storm.

Behold, he who was ignorant of the lyre is now the possessor of a harp, while he who never sang for himself now vaunts the Songstress-goddess.

QUESTIONS FOR ANALYSIS

- In this reading, the "Residence" is the palace and the "Two Lands" are Upper and Lower Egypt. Who do you think "he who was buried as a falcon" is?
- What were the effects of the collapse of Egypt's Old Kingdom?
- How can we use such a document as "The Admonitions of Ipuwer" to understand conditions in Egypt at this time?

Source: Translated by John A. Wilson in Ancient Near Eastern Texts Relating to the Old Testament, edited by J. B. Pritchard (Princeton: Princeton University Press, 1950), pp. 442–43.

THE INDUS RIVER VALLEY: A PARALLEL CULTURE

The Indus River valley, in South Asia, was yet another area in which large-scale cities emerged. Here they came to the fore later than in Mesopotamia and Egypt, in the third millennium BCE. We call the urban culture of the Indus area "Harappan" after the large site of Harappa that arose in the third millennium BCE on the banks of the Ravi River, a tributary of the Indus.

Developments in the Indus basin reflected an indigenous (local) tradition combined with strong influences from Iranian plateau peoples, as well as indirect influences from distant cities on the Tigris and Euphrates Rivers. Villages appeared before 5000 BCE on the Iranian plateau west of the Indus. By the early third millennium BCE, with changing river regimes, frontier villages began to spread eastward to the fertile banks of the Indus River and its tributaries. (See Map 2.5.) These river-basin settlements soon yielded agrarian surpluses that supported greater wealth, more trade with neighbors, and public works. In due course, urbanites of the Indus region and the Harappan peoples began to fortify their cities and to undertake public works similar in scale to those in Mesopotamia, but strikingly different in function.

The Indus Valley environment boasted many advantages—especially compared with the area near the Ganges River, the other great waterway of the South Asian landmass. The semi-tropical Indus Valley had plentiful water from melting snows in the Himalayas that ensured flourishing vegetation. Nor did the region suffer the yearly monsoon downpours that flooded the Ganges plain. The expansion of agriculture in the Indus basin depended on the river's annual floods to replenish the soil and avert droughts (as in Mesopotamia, Egypt, and China). From June to September, the rivers inundated the plain. Once the waters receded, farmers planted wheat and barley. They harvested crops the next spring as temperatures rose. At the same time, the villagers improved their tools of cultivation. Researchers have found evidence of furrows, probably made by plowing, that date to around 2600 BCE. The rise of the Harappan state along with increased agricultural production freed many inhabitants from producing food and enabled them to specialize in other activities.

In time, rural wealth produced urban splendor. More abundant harvests, now stored in large granaries, brought migrants into the area and supported expanding populations. By 2500 BCE, cities began to replace villages throughout the Indus River valley, and within a few generations, towering granaries marked the urban skyline. Harappa and Mohenjo Daro, the two largest cities, each covered a little less than half a square mile and may have housed 35,000 residents. Even more interesting is the smaller city of Dholavira, recently discovered. Its inhabitants quarried, transported, and worked stone, and its city builders erected large water reservoirs inside fortified city walls. As in Mesopotamia, such population densities were unprecedented departures from the more common agrarian villages or nomadic communities, which remained self-sufficient.

Harappan cities sprawled across a vast floodplain covering 500,000 square miles—two or three times the Mesopotamian

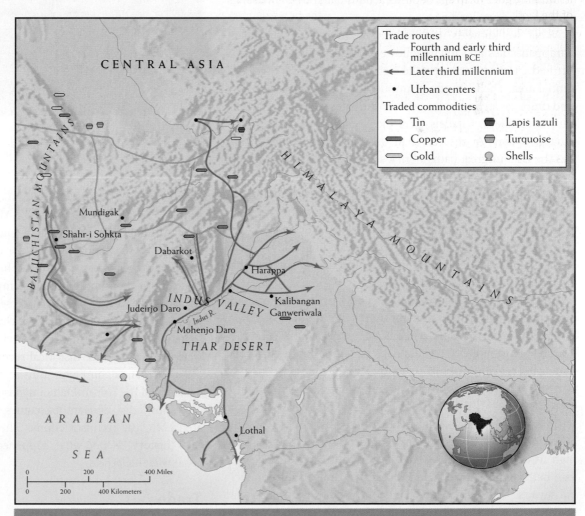

MAP 2.5 | The Indus River Valley in the Third Millennium BCE

Historians know less about the urban society of the Indus Valley in the third millennium BCE than they do about its contemporaries in Mesopotamia and Egypt. Still, archaeological evidence gives insight into this urban complex.

- Where were cities concentrated in the Indus Valley?
- How did the region's environment shape urban development?
- What functions do you think outposts such as Lothal played in Harappan society?

cultural zone. At the height of their development, the Harappan peoples reached the edge of the Indus ecological system and encountered the cultures of northern Afghanistan, the inhabitants of the desert frontier, the nomadic hunter-gatherers to the east, and the traders to the west. Moreover, because of the immense size of the Harappan cities' floodplain and the energy of their merchants, long-distance trade flourished and contributed greatly to the prosperity of this cultural zone.

Harappan City Life and Writing

We know less about Harappan culture than about other contemporary cultures of Afro-Eurasia because many of its remains lie buried under deep silt deposits accumulated over thousands of years of heavy flooding.

What we know is impressive nonetheless. The layout of Harappan cities and towns followed a well-planned pattern: a fortified citadel housing public facilities alongside a large residential area. The main street running through the city had covered drainage on both sides, with house gates and doors opening onto back alleys. Citadels were likely centers of political and ritual activities. At the center of the citadel of Mohenjo Daro was the famous great bath, a brick structure 39.3 feet by 23 feet and 9.8 feet deep. Flights of steps led to the bottom of the bath, while other stairs went up to a level of rooms surrounding it. The bath was sealed with mortar and bitumen (a sticky, tarlike form of petroleum), and its water came from a large well nearby. The water drained out through a channel leading to lower land. The location, size, and quality of the structure all suggest that the bath was for public bathing rituals.

The Harappans used brick extensively—in houses for notables, in city walls, and in underground water drainage systems. Workers used large ovens to manufacture the durable construction materials, which the Harappans laid so skillfully that basic structures remain intact to this day. While common construction materials were used throughout Harappan communities, the differences in the size of dwellings, particularly in urban settings, suggest that social distinctions existed. A well-built house of a more wealthy family could be two to three stories high. It contained at least one interior courtyard and had private bathrooms, showers, and toilets that drained into municipal sewers. More typical dwellings in the cities were one-room apartments with shared bathrooms. Houses in small towns and villages were made of less durable and less costly sun-baked bricks, which are used throughout southern Eurasia even today.

The peoples of the Indus Valley developed a system of writing made up of about 400 signs. However, because we do not know whether the language represented a script, it has been impossible to decipher it. Indeed, the signs might not represent spoken languages, but rather be a nonlinguistic symbol

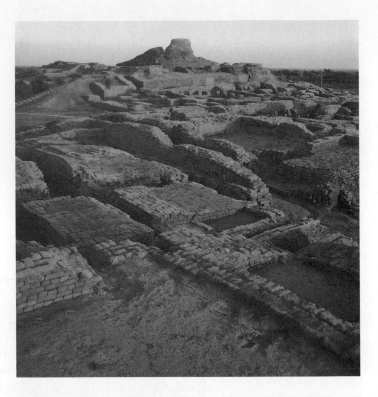

Mohenjo Daro. *Mohenjo Daro, the "mound of dead," is a large urban site of the Harappan culture. The view of the city demonstrates a neat layout of houses and civic facilities such as sewer draining.*

system. (See Primary Source: The Mystery of Harappan Writing.) Although a ten-glyph-long public inscription has been found at the Harappan site of the ancient city of Dholavira, nearly all of what remains of the Indus Valley script is to be found on a thousand or more stamp seals and small plaques excavated from the region. These seals and plaques may represent the names and titles of individuals rather than complete sentences. As of yet, there is no evidence that the Harappans were able to produce historical records such as the King Lists of Mesopotamia and Egypt, thus making it impossible to chart a history of the rise and fall of dynasties and kingdoms. Hence, our knowledge of Harappa comes exclusively from sketchy archaeological reconstructions. The sketchiness reminds us that "history" is not what happened but only *what we know about what happened.*

Trade

The Harappans engaged in trade along the Indus River, through the mountain passes to the Iranian plateau, and along the coast of the Arabian Sea as far as the Persian Gulf and Mesopotamia. They traded copper, flint, shells, and ivory, as well as pottery, flint blades, and jewelry created by their craftworkers, in exchange for gold, silver, gemstones, and textiles. Along with these goods came people bringing

PRIMARY SOURCE

The Mystery of Harappan Writing

No one has deciphered the writing system of the Harappan culture of the Indus Valley. The Indus script appeared on seals and tablets—and in a recently discovered site, on a board for public display. Although no one is sure which language it represents, some of its characteristics provide scholars with fuel for speculation.

As for verbal communication through writing, it needs to be understood that no one has as yet succeeded in deciphering the Harappan script and that this will remain an unlikely eventuality unless a bilingual inscription—in Harappan and a known form of writing—is found, that incorporates the names of people or places. The Harappan script may be a combination of logographic and syllabic signs: there are 375 to 400 signs, which rules out an alphabet (where one sign stands for one vowel or consonant) because alphabets usually have no more than thirty-six signs. Often Harappan bangles or metal tools are inscribed with just one sign. Harappan writing goes from right to left, as can be made out from close examination of overlapping signs scratched on pots. Short strokes indicate numbers, and numerals precede other signs, which could mean that in the Harappan language adjectives preceded the nouns they qualified. Certain signs, computer concordances reveal, tend to occur frequently at the end of inscriptions, which points to a language using a set of phonetic suffixes.

The Harappan language was probably agglutinative, or a language which added suffixes to an unchanging root. This feature is characteristic of the Dravidian language family rather than the Indo-Aryan languages. This, and the fact that the earliest Indo-Aryan text, the *Rigveda*, shows Dravidian influence (indicating that the early Indo-Aryans in the northwest had some contact with Dravidian speakers), make it likely that the language of the Harappans

was a Dravidian one. (Note, also, that Brahui, spoken in the hills of southern Baluchistan today, is a Dravidian language.)

The inscriptions on the seals being brief, on average five to six signs long, they probably gave little more than the owner's name and designation. Perhaps it was the pictorial (often solo animal) emblem, rendered with great skill, that indicated the lineage, ancestry, or social origins of the owner. There is no geographic pattern to the occurrence of the various seal animals (unicorn, bull, rhinoceros, antelope, tiger, or elephant), so the animal could not possibly have signified the place of origin of the seal owner. Perhaps it was this pictorial image that lent authority to any spoken message that accompanied a seal or an object stamped with one. It may be noted that so far it is Harappa and Mohenjo-daro—and mound E rather than the "citadel mound" AB at Harappa—that have yielded the evidence for the most intensive writing activity. These were probably centres of administration.

Harappan writing occurs on pots, seals, terracotta (stoneware) and shell bangles, copper tablets and tools, and ivory rods. Large numbers of scored goblets with pointed bases that occur at Harappa and Mohenjo-daro are important as they are one of the very few pottery forms that can occasionally carry seal impressions (as distinct from scratched signs)—their use remains a mystery. We get the impression that writing was for humdrum purposes. A striking exception to this is the occurrence of a huge "public" inscription that seems to have been set up on a street at Dholavira

in Kutch, with letters about 37 centimetres high cut out of stones and, R. S. Bisht suggests, fastened on a wooden board.

The most important point, however, is the enormous intellectual advance that the emergence of writing signifies. When we speak we utter sounds in one or another language using a series of sound sequences that carry specific meanings in that language. What writing does is to encode in visual form, that is, through a set of distinct symbols or signs, those sounds and sound sequences—thereby conveying meaning or information. Further, writing makes possible the storage of information or the maintenance of records for future reference. It makes communication at a distance possible. It requires of the writer knowledge of the signs and some amount of manual dexterity, and of the reader, knowledge of how the visual signs are vocalized and of course familiarity with the relevant language. Writing has been termed the most momentous invention human beings have ever made.

QUESTIONS FOR ANALYSIS

- Even though we cannot read Harappan script, why is the knowledge that the Harappans wrote in script important?
- Judging from the information above about Harappan writing, what language do you think the script most likely represents?

Source: Shereen Ratnagar, "The Mystery of Harappan Writing" from *Understanding Harappa Civilization in the Greater Indus Valley* (New Delhi: Tulika Publishers, 2001), pp. 60–62.

Harappan Seal Stamps. *The stamp seals of the Indus Valley culture are distinctive. Cut from the soft stone steatite and fired to a white color to make them hard, they have a rounded boss pierced for suspension on the back. The images carved on their surface are usually animals: elephants, tigers, and bulls. Occasionally, human figures, perhaps deities or rulers, are depicted seated on a platform or dancing or surrounded by animals. Many of the stamp seals have inscriptions across the top edge. The script of the Harappan people has not been deciphered, nor has its underlying language been identified.*

Harappan Gemstone Necklace. *Beadmakers perforated lapis lazuli and other semiprecious stones using a bow drill to make tiny holes for suspension.*

the major ideas and institutions of Harappan society to these surrounding cultures.

Some of the Harappan trading towns nestled in remote but strategically important places. Consider Lothal, a well-fortified port at the head of the Gulf of Khambhat (Cambay). Although distant from the center of Harappan society, it provided vital access to the sea and to valuable raw materials. Its many workshops processed precious stones, both local and foreign. Because the demand for gemstones was high in Mesopotamia, the Harappans knew that controlling their extraction and trade was essential to maintaining economic power. Carnelian, a precious red stone, was a local resource, but lapis lazuli had to come from what is now northern Afghanistan. So the Harappans built fortifications and settlements near its sources. Extending their frontier did not stop at gemstones, however. Because metals such as copper and silver also had strategic commercial importance, the Harappans established settlements near their copper mines as well.

The general uniformity in Harappan sites suggests a centralized and structured state. Unlike the Mesopotamians and the Egyptians, however, the Harappans apparently built neither palaces nor grand royal tombs nor impressive monumental

structures. The elites expressed their elaborate urban culture in ways that did not proclaim their high standing, with the exception, in some cases, of more substantial private homes. As a result, the Harappans were as unassuming as the Egyptians and Mesopotamians were boastful. This quality underscores the profound differences in ancient societies: they did not all value the same things, and they were not organized in the same ways. The advent of writing, urban culture, long-distance trade, and large cities did not always produce the same social hierarchies and the same ethos (a set of principles governing social and political relations). What the Indus River people show us is how much the urbanized parts of the world were diverging from one another, even as they borrowed from and imitated their neighbors.

THE YELLOW AND YANGZI RIVER BASINS: EAST ASIA

Like the Mesopotamians, Egyptians, and Harappans, East Asian peoples clustered in river basins. Their settlements along the Yellow River in the north and the Yangzi River in the south became the foundation of the future Chinese state. By 5000 BCE,

Living conditions and the environment played a key role in ancient Chinese society, just as they did in the river-basin cultures of Mesopotamia, Egypt, and Harappa. In the river basins of China, abundant food and widely dispersed communities encouraged the development of localized agrarian cultures. Complex cities would come later. Also contributing to their different development were a lack of easily domesticated animals and plants and an abundance of geographical barriers. Geography isolated China, for the Himalayan Mountains and the Taklamakan and Gobi Deserts prevented large-scale migrations between East Asia and central Asia and hindered the diffusion of cultural breakthroughs occurring elsewhere in Afro-Eurasia.

MAP 2.6 | River-Basin Peoples in East Asia, 5000–2000 BCE

Complex agricultural societies emerged in East Asia during the third millennium BCE.

- What were the regional cultures that flourished here during this time?
- What are the major geographical differences between the northern and southern regions of China in this period?
- Considering the geographical differences between the areas, how were these cultures different, and how were they similar?

From Yangshao to Longshan Culture

China's classical histories have claimed that China's cultural traditions originated in the Central Plains of the Yellow River basin and spread outward to less developed regions inside and even beyond mainland China. This location, seen by many as the birthplace of China's imperial traditions, was thought to have exercised a civilizing influence on these other communities. These histories place the beginnings of Chinese culture at the Xia dynasty, dating from 2200 BCE. Archaeological studies of river-basin environments in East Asia tell a different story, however. Whether or not the Xia existed as a historical dynasty, archaeological evidence suggests that our study of the Yellow River basin and Yangzi delta should begin earlier—in the two millennia from 4000 to 2000 BCE.

China in 4000 BCE was very different geographically and culturally from what it is today. A warmer and moister climate divided its vast landmass into quite distinctive and separate regions. The Shandong Peninsula was an island separated

both millet in the north and rice in the south were under widespread cultivation.

Yet in the following three millennia (when Mesopotamia, Egypt, and the Indus Valley were developing complex, city-based cultures), the Chinese moved slowly. China's great river-basin cultures did not arise until the second millennium BCE. (See Map 2.6.) Like the other regions' waterways, the Yellow and Yangzi Rivers had annual floods and extensive floodplains suitable for producing high agricultural yields and supporting dense populations. In China, however, the evolution of hydraulic works, big cities, priestly and bureaucratic classes, and a new writing system took longer.

Yangshao Bowl with Dancing Figures, c. 5000–1700 BCE. *The Yangshao, also referred to as the "painted pottery" culture, produced gray or red pottery painted with black geometric designs and occasionally with pictures of fish or human faces and figures. Because the potter's wheel was unknown at the time, the vessels were probably fashioned with strips of clay.*

from mainland China. Lakes abounded in southern Manchuria and southern Mongolia, and the Central Plains was a smaller area than it is today. Only after a long cycle of cooler and drier weather did these bodies of water dry up and the land-mass become a single geographical unit. According to recent archaeological research, at least eight distinct regional cultures appeared between 4000 and 2000 BCE, and only as these communities interacted did their institutions and ways of life come together to create a unified Chinese culture. Indeed, the main narrative of Chinese history from earliest times to the present is the spread of a people calling themselves the Han, along with their culture and institutions, from their original sites in the coastal northeast and northwest, moving in a westerly direction and imposing their lifeways on the other peoples and regions of what ultimately became China.

In addition to being geographically and culturally divided, China was never devoid of outside influences. Unlike the Americas, East Asia was not separated from the rest of Afro-Eurasia by great oceans. Some travelers did arrive via the ocean, but the nomadic and pastoralist steppe peoples of inner Asia (Mongolia, Manchuria, Tibet, and what is now western China) introduced important technologies, such as metal works. Nomads were drawn to the agricultural settlements (as they were in Mesopotamia), and they brought innovations, bronze, and other goods from the west. Through trade and migration, nomadic cultures and technologies filtered from the steppes to settled communities on the rivers.

TWO RIVER BASINS, TWO CULTURES The major divide in China was between the Yellow and Yangzi river basins. Not only did residents of these two regions rely on different crops—millet in the north and rice in the south—but they built their houses

differently, buried their dead in different ways, and produced distinctive pottery styles. The best known of these early cultures developed along the Yellow River and in the Central Plains area and is known as the Yangshao culture. Although it began on a small scale, in time it extended its influence northward to the present-day provinces of Qinghai and Gansu. Yangshao villages covered 10 to 14 acres and were composed of houses erected around a central square. Villagers had to move frequently because they practiced slash-and-burn agriculture. Once having exhausted the soil, residents picked up their belongings, moved to new lands, and constructed new villages. Their lives were difficult. Excavated cemeteries reveal that nearly 20 percent of the burials were of children fifteen years and younger; only a little more than half of those buried lived past the age of forty. Markings found on red pottery near the village of Yangshao, along the Yellow River, indicate that some residents were proficient in manipulating signs and symbols from as early as 5000 BCE. Yet writing, such as that developed by the Sumerians, did not appear until much later.

Around 3000 BCE, the Yangshao culture gave way to the Longshan culture, which had an even larger geographical scope and would provide some of the cultural foundations for the first strong states that emerged in the Central Plains. Longshan flourished from 3000 to 2000 BCE, having its center in Shandong Province. Although the Longshan way of life first took form in coastal and southern China, outside the Central Plains, it moved quickly into this hub of economic and political activity. Proof of its widespread cultural influence can be seen from the appearance of a unique style of black pottery, stretching all the way from Manchuria, in the north, through the Central Plains, to the coast and beyond to the island of Taiwan. Near the village of Longshan itself, in Shandong Province on the North China plain, for example, archaeologists discovered polished black pottery and a complete town wall formed by compacted earth. Such finds contrast with the simpler artifacts of the Yangshao sites. Furthermore, Longshan residents burned deer scapulas (shoulder blades) so that diviners could interpret the cracks that formed. This ritual probably gave rise to the inscribed oracle

Longshan Beaker, c. 2500 BCE. *Longshan has been called the "black pottery" culture, and its exquisite black pottery was not painted but rather decorated with rings, either raised or grooved. Longshan culture was more advanced than the Yangshao culture, and its distinctive pottery was likely formed on a potter's wheel.*

Oracle Bone Artifact. *The Shang dynasty use of oracle bones (such as the one shown here) may have grown out of the Jiahu or Longshanoid ritual of interpreting the cracks in burned deer scapulas.*

bones introduced later during the Shang dynasty (1600–1045 BCE), which diviners consulted for advice from ancestors when making important decisions.

The Longshan people likely migrated in waves from the peripheries of East Asia to the eastern China seashore. Their achievements, compared with those of the Yangshao, suggest marked development between 5000 and 2000 BCE. Several independent regional cultures in northern and southern China began to produce similar pottery and tools and to plant the same crops, probably reflecting contact. They did not yet produce city-states, but agriculture and small settlements flourished in the increasingly populated Yellow River valley.

Early Urban Life

Some of the hallmarks of early urban life are evident. For example, the Longshan buried their dead in cemeteries outside their villages. Of several thousand graves uncovered in southern Shanxi Province, the largest ones contain ritual pottery vessels, wooden musical instruments, copper bells, and painted murals. Shamans performed rituals using jade axes. Jade quarrying in

particular indicated technical sophistication, as skilled craftworkers incised jade tablets with powerful expressions of ritual and military authority. The recent discovery of a Longshan household whose members were scalped demonstrates the danger of organized violence. Attackers filled the water wells with five layers of human skeletons, some decapitated. Clearly, the villages' defensive walls were essential.

As communities became more centralized, contact between regions increased. Links between northern and southern China arose when peoples bearing the Longshan culture began to migrate along the East Asian coast to Taiwan and the Pearl River delta in the far south. Similarities in artifacts found along the coast and at Longshan sites in northern China, such as the form and decoration of pottery and jade items, also point to a shared sphere of culture and trade. (See Primary Source: Archaeological Evidence for Longshan Culture.)

Archaeologists also have found evidence of short-lived political organizations. Although they were nothing like the dynastic systems in Egypt, Mesopotamia, and the Indus Valley, they were wealthy—if localized—polities. They constituted what scholars call the era of Ten Thousand States (*Wan'guo*). One of them, the Liangzhu, has drawn particular interest for its remarkable jade objects and its sophisticated farmers, who grew rice and fruits. The Liangzhu domesticated water buffalo, pigs, dogs, and sheep. Archaeologists have discovered the remains of net sinkers, wooden floats, and wooden paddles, which demonstrate a familiarity with watercraft and fishing. Artisans produced a black pottery from soft paste thrown on a wheel, and like the Longshan, they created ritual objects from several varieties of jade. Animal masks and bird designs adorned many pieces, revealing a shared cosmology that informed the rituals of the Liangzhu elite.

In the late third millennium BCE, a long drought hit China (as it did Egypt, Mesopotamia, and the Indus Valley). (See Current Trends in World History: Climate Change at the End of the Third Millennium BCE in Egypt, Mesopotamia, and the Indus Valley.) Although the climate change limited progress and forced migrations to more dependable habitats, the Chinese recovered early in the second millennium BCE. They created elaborate agrarian systems along the Yellow and Yangzi Rivers that were similar to earlier irrigation systems along the Euphrates, Indus, and Nile. Extensive trading networks and a stratified social hierarchy emerged; like the other river-basin complexes of Asia and North Africa, China became a centralized polity. Here, too, a powerful monarchy eventually united the independent communities. But what developed in China was a social and political system that emphasized an idealized past and a tradition represented by sage-kings, which later ages emulated. In this and other ways, China diverged from the rest of Afro-Eurasia.

Archaeological Evidence for Longshan Culture

Over the course of a millennium, multiple cultures with strong similarities emerged in North and Northwest China. Some scholars argue that a single Longshan culture grew out of these close-knit groups. While these were not fully integrated spheres interacting with one another, the changes that Longshan represented were remarkable.

The spelling of Chinese names in the passages below are those that were employed by scholars before the present pinyin orthography was adopted. In modern orthography, Shantung, Honan, Shansi, Ch'i'-chia, and Lung-shan are written Shandong, Henan, Shanxi, Quijia, and Longshan, respectively.

Let us take a quick look at the kind of innovations that sprouted everywhere and that, because of the similarities of style, must be interrelated:

1. Archaeologically acceptable evidence of copper objects, mostly trinkets and small tools of no agricultural value, has been unearthed in Shantung, western Honan, southern Shansi, and Ch'i-chia from archaeological horizons comparable in age. The finds do not suffice to point to a major metal industry as yet, but in light of what happened later on one must regard the Lung-shan metallurgy as worthy of note. . . .

2. Industrially much more important is the extremely widespread use of potter's wheels for the manufacture of ceramics. There was tremendous variation in the pottery wares of the various Lung-shan cultures, but the overwhelming change from red to gray and the general decline of painted decoration must have been the result of a conscious choice on the part of the potters, who, armed with improved kilns and the wheel, must have represented a specialized profession in the Lung-shan society.

3. The stamped-earth construction technology and the construction of town walls using that technology are separate issues, but the town walls in Shantung, east Honan, north Honan, and west Honan indicate both the transmission of a technology and the rise of the necessity for defensive public works.

4. Related to the rise of defensive ramparts is the archaeological evidence of institutionalized violence. This takes two forms—evidence of raids or wars, such as the Chien-kou-ts'un finds of skulls and bodies in the water well; and burials of possible ritual victims relating to the construction of chiefly or royal monuments.

5. There are several manifestations of rituals, especially ones closely tied to persons of high political status. The first is the role of some animals and birds in ritual art, such as those found or identified recently in Liang-ch'eng, Shantung; the Liang-chu sites, in Kiangsu and Chekiang; and T'ao-ssu, Shansi.

6. The ts'ung tube, especially if associated with animals and birds, is a very distinctive ritual object manifesting a unique cosmology. Its discovery in Liang-chu on the coast and T'ao-ssu in the interior cannot be accidental; it indicates without question an interregional transmission of cosmology or even a spherewide substratum featuring that cosmology. If we include jade rings (pi) in this cosmological bag, the Ch'i-chia Culture also becomes involved.

7. The virtually universal occurrence of scapulimancy among the Lung-shan cultures is another manifestation of the spherewide communication or substratum of cosmology.

8. The archaeological evidence for violence and for ritual on an institutional basis almost inevitably means a society featuring sharp political and economic divisions, and that is exactly what we find in the mortuary remains of many of the Lung-shan cultures. We have already seen archaeological indications of social ranking in the mortuary remains of the Neolithic sites of the fifth and fourth centuries B.C. . . . These trends accelerated and further intensified in the Lung-shan cemeteries. Furthermore, as the Ch'eng-tzu (Shantung) and T'ao-ssu (Shansi) cemeteries show, the economic and political polarization appears to have taken place within the framework of the unilinear clans and lineages.

All of the above happenings are plainly indicated by archaeological evidence, but they do not point to a single Lung-shan culture. Instead, they indicate a series of interrelated changes in culture and society that took place within each of the regional cultures in the Chinese interaction sphere. From the point of view of each of the regional sequences, both the external interaction network and internal changes during a period of two thousand years were essential for its readiness, toward the end of the third millennium B.C., to step over the next threshold into the state society, urbanism, and civilization.

QUESTIONS FOR ANALYSIS

- What were the key features of Longshan culture?
- What does *scapulimancy* mean, and how widespread was its use?
- What does the evidence of violence reveal about Longshan society?

Source: Kwang-chih Chang, *The Archaeology of Ancient China,* 4th ed. (New Haven: Yale University Press, 1986), pp. 287–88.

MAP 2.7 | Settlements on the Margins: The Eastern Mediterranean and Europe, 5000–2000 BCE

Urban societies in Southwest Asia had profound influences on peripheral societies.

- What three peripheral worlds did the urban societies of Southwest Asia influence?
- In what ways did the spread of flint and copper tools and weapons transform Aegean and European societies?
- How did agriculture spread from Southwest Asia to these worlds?

LIFE OUTSIDE THE RIVER BASINS

In 3500 BCE, the vast majority of humans lived outside the complex cities that emerged in the river basins of Afro-Eurasia. Here, people continued to live as hunters and gatherers. Others lived in small farming-based villages or as pastoral nomads tending flocks. These communities existed beyond the reach of the great urban centers. Yet here, too—in the Aegean, Anatolia, Europe, and parts of China—small towns emerged, agriculture advanced, wars were fought, and trade existed; but these societies did not expand with the great leaps and bounds of the river-basin centers. (See Map 2.7.)

Many of the cultures outside the river basins—notably in the Aegean, Anatolia, and Europe—had a distinctive warrior-based

ethos, such that the top tiers of the social ladder held chiefs and military men in the highest regard rather than priests and scribes. This feature was especially evident in Europe and Anatolia, where weaponry rather than writing, palisades (defensive walls and turrets) rather than palaces, and conquest rather than commerce dominated everyday life. Here, too, the inhabitants moved beyond stone implements and hunting and gathering, but they remained more egalitarian than river-basin folk and did not evolve much beyond small societies led by chiefs.

Aegean Worlds

Contact with Egypt and Mesopotamia affected the Aegean worlds (that part of the Mediterranean Sea between the Greek

Climate Change at the End of the Third Millennium BCE in Egypt, Mesopotamia, and the Indus Valley

During the long third millennium BCE, the first urban centers in Egypt, Mesopotamia, Iran, central Asia, and South Asia flourished and grew in complexity and wealth in a wet and cool climate. This smooth development was sharply if not universally interrupted beginning around 2200 BCE. Both archaeological and written records agree that across Afro-Eurasia, most of the urban, rural, and pastoral societies underwent radical change. Those watered by major rivers were selectively destabilized, while the settled communities on the highland plateaus virtually disappeared. After a brief hiatus, some recovered, completely reorganized and using new technologies to manage agriculture and water. The causes of this radical change have been the focus of much interest.

After four decades of research by climate specialists working together with archaeologists, a consensus has emerged that climate change toward a warmer and drier environment contributed to this disruption. Whether this was caused solely by human activity, in particular agriculture

on a large scale, or was also related to cosmic causes, such as the rotation of the earth's axis away from the sun, is still a hotly debated topic. It was likely a combination of factors.

The urban centers dependent on the three major river systems in Egypt, Mesopotamia, and the Indus Valley all experienced disruption. In Egypt, the hieroglyphic inscriptions tell us that the Nile no longer flooded over its banks to replenish the fields with fresh soil and with water for crops. Social and political chaos followed for more than a century. In southern Mesopotamia, the deeply downcut rivers changed course, disrupting settlement patterns and taking fields out of cultivation. Other fields were poisoned by salts brought on through overcultivation and irrigation without periods of fallow. Fierce competition for water and land put pressure on the central authority. To the east and west, transhumant pastoralists, faced with shrinking pasture for their flocks, pressed in on the river valleys, disrupting the already challenged social and political structure of the densely urban centers.

In northern Mesopotamia, the responses to the challenges of aridity

were more varied. Some centers were able to weather the crisis by changing strategies of food production and distribution. Some fell victim to intraregional warfare, while others, on the rainfall margin, were abandoned. When the region was settled again, society was differently organized. Population did not drastically decrease, but rather it distributed across the landscape more evenly in smaller settlements that required less water and food. It appears that a similar solution was found by communities to the east on the Iranian plateau, where the inhabitants of the huge urban center of Shahr i Sokhta abruptly left the city and settled in small communities across the oasis landscape.

The solutions found by people living in the cities of the Indus Valley also varied. Some cities, like Harappa, saw their population decrease rapidly. It seems that the bed of the river shifted, threatening the settlement and its hinterland. Mohenjo Daro, on the other hand, continued to be occupied for another several centuries, although the large civic structures fell out of use, replaced by more modest structures. And to the south, on the Gujarat Peninsula, population and the number of

Peloponnese and Anatolia), but it did not transform them. Geography stood in the way of significant urban development on the mountainous islands, on the Anatolian plateau, and in Europe. Even though people from Anatolia, Greece, and the Levant had populated the Aegean islands in the sixth millennium BCE, their small villages endured for 2,000 years before becoming more complex.

On mainland Greece and on the Cycladic islands in the Aegean, fortified settlements housed local rulers who controlled a small area of agriculturally productive countryside. Metallurgy developed in both Crete and the Cyclades, southeast of mainland Greece. There is evidence of more formal administration and organization in some communities by 2500 BCE, but the norm was scattered settlements separated

by natural obstacles. Consider rocky and mountainous Crete, the largest island in the Aegean, where seafaring peoples occupied settlements sprinkled throughout its rugged interior. By the early third millennium BCE, Crete had made occasional contact with Egypt and the coastal towns of the Levant, encountering new ideas, technologies, and materials as foreigners arrived on its shores. People coming by ship from the coasts of Anatolia and the Levant, as well as from Egypt, traded stone vessels and other luxury objects for the island's abundant copper.

Lacking a rich agrarian base, most communities remained small at fewer than 100 inhabitants, and only a few grew over time. By the middle of the third millennium BCE, a more complex society was emerging in eastern Crete. During the second settlements increased. They abandoned wheat as a crop, instead cultivating a kind of drought-enduring millet that originated in West Africa. Apparently, conditions there became even more hospitable, allowing farming and fishing communities to flourish well into the second millennium BCE.

The evidence for this widespread phenomenon of climate change at the end of the third millennium BCE is complex and contradictory. This is not surprising, because every culture and each community naturally had an individual response to environmental and other challenges. Those with perennial sources of fresh water were less threatened than those in marginal zones, where only a slight decrease in rainfall could mean failed crops and herds. It is also important to note that certain types of social and political institutions were resilient and introduced innovations that allowed them to adapt, while others were too rigid or short-sighted to find local solutions. A feature of human culture is its remarkable ability to adapt rapidly. When faced with challenges, resilience, creativity, and ingenuity lead to cultural innovation and

Millet. *This hardy grain, cultivated for its resistance to drought, persists in the desert environment of present-day western Pakistan*

change. This is what we can see, even in our own times, during periods of environmental stress.

QUESTIONS FOR ANALYSIS

- What technological innovations resulted from the drought in the Indus Valley? Why?
- Imagine that the climate during the third millennium BCE had not changed. How do you think this might have affected the development of ancient Egypt?
- How has our understanding of global climate changed the way we study prehistory?

Explore Further

Behringer, Wolfgang, *A Cultural History of Climate* (2010).

Bell, Barbara, "The Dark Ages in Ancient History. 1. The First Dark Age in Egypt," *American Journal of Archaeology* 75 (January 1971): 1–26.

Weiss, Max, et al., "The Genesis and Collapse of Third Millennium North Mesopotamian Civilization," *Science* (New Series) 261 (August 20, 1993): 995–1004.

millennium BCE, Knossos, located in a rich agricultural plain, became the primary palace-town in an extended network of palaces. Evidence from burial sites suggests that some households belonged to an elite class, for they took gold jewelry and other exotic objects with them to their graves. Aegean elites did not reject the niceties of cultured life, but they knew that their power rested as much on their rugged landscape's resources as on self-defense and trade with others.

Anatolia

The highland plateau of Anatolia shows clear evidence of regional cultures focused on the control of trade routes and mining outposts. True cities did not develop here until the third millennium BCE, and even then they were not the sprawling population centers typical of the Mesopotamian plain. Instead, small communities emerged around fortified citadels housing local rulers who competed with one another. Two impressively fortified centers were Horoz Tepe and Alaça Hüyük, which have yielded more than a dozen graves—apparently royal—full of gold jewelry, ceremonial emblems, and elaborate weapons.

Another important site in Anatolia was Troy to the far west. It is legendary as the place of the famous war launched by the Greeks (the Achaeans) and recounted by Homer in the *Iliad*. Troy developed around 3000 BCE on the Mediterranean coast in a fertile plain. The settlement had monumental stone gateways, stone-paved ramps, and graves filled with gold and silver objects, vessels, and jewelry. Parallel grave goods on Crete, the Greek mainland, and as far away as Ur, in Mesopotamia, show that Troy participated in a trading system linking the Aegean and Southwest Asian worlds. At the same time, the peoples of Troy faced predatory neighbors and pirates who attacked from the sea—an observation that explains its impressive fortifications.

Europe: The Western Frontier

At the western reaches of the Afro-Eurasian landmass was a region featuring more temperate and also more frigid climates with smaller population densities. Its peoples—forerunners of present-day Europeans—began to make objects out of metal, formed permanent settlements, and started to create complex societies. Here, too, hierarchies replaced egalitarian ways. Yet, as in the Aegean worlds, population density and social complexity had limits.

More than in the Mediterranean or Anatolia, warfare dominated social development in Europe. Two contributing factors were the persistent fragmentation of the region's peoples and the type of agrarian development they pursued. The introduction of the plow and the clearing of woodlands expanded agriculture. Agrarian development here was not the result of city-states or dynasties organizing irrigation and settlement (as in Mesopotamia and Egypt), but rather the result of households and communities wielding axes for defense and for cutting down trees. Compared with the river-basin societies, Europe

was a wild frontier where violent conflicts over resources were common.

The gradual expansion of agricultural communities eventually reached a critical point. The growth of flint mining to an industrial level (as evident in the thousand shafts sunk at Krzemionki, in Poland, and the flint-mining complex of Grimes Graves, in England) indicates a social and economic transformation. Most important, mining output slashed the cost and increased the availability of raw materials needed to make tools for clearing forested lands and tilling them into arable fields. As agricultural communities proliferated, some became villages that dominated their regions. But nowhere did these societies create large cities and corresponding states.

By 3500 BCE, the more developed agrarian peoples had coalesced into large communities, constructing impressive monuments that remain visible today. In western Europe, large ceremonial centers shared the same model: enormous shaped stones, some weighing several tons each, set in common patterns—in alleyways, troughs, or circles—known as *megalithic* ("great stone") constructions. These daunting projects required cooperative planning and work. In the British Isles, where such developments occurred later, the famous megalithic complexes at Avebury and Stonehenge probably reached their highest stages of development just before 2000 BCE.

No matter how forbidding the ecology of Europe was in this period, in the centuries after 3000 BCE, culminating in new developments around 2000 BCE, the whole of the northern European plain came to share a common material culture based on agriculture, the herding of cattle for meat and milk, the use of the plow, and the use of wheeled vehicles and metal

Stonehenge. *This spectacular site, located in the Salisbury Plain in Wiltshire, in southwestern England, is one of several such megalithic structures found in the region. Constructed by many generations of builders, the arrangement of the large stone uprights enabled people to determine precise times in the year through the position of the sun. Events such as the spring and autumn equinoxes were connected with agricultural and religious activities.*

Corded Ware Pots. *Traded across northern Europe, this pottery is known for its ornamental grooves, made when twisted cords were pressed into the wet clay.*

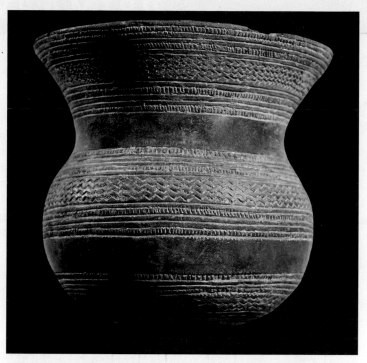

"Bell Beaker" Pottery. *Named for their characteristic inverted bell shape, these cups were carried across western Europe by tribes who primarily used the vessels to consume alcoholic beverages like beer or mead.*

tools and weapons, mainly of copper. The most characteristic objects associated with this shared culture were the Corded Ware pots—so-called from the cords used to impress lines on their surfaces. The fact that this new economy was found from areas we know today as Ukraine in the east to the Low Countries in the west is evidence of the much-improved communications that linked and united previous disparate and widely separated regions.

Increasing communication, exchange, and mobility among the European communities led to increasing wealth but also sparked organized warfare over frontier lands and valuable resources. In an ironic twist, the integration of local communities led to greater friction and produced regional social stratification. The violent men who now protected their communities received ceremonial burials complete with their own drinking cups and weapons. (See Primary Source: The Male Warrior Burials of Varna and Nett Down.) Archaeologists have found these warrior burials in a swath of European lands extending from present-day France and Switzerland to present-day central Russia. Because the agricultural communities were now producing surpluses that they could store, residents had to defend their land and resources from encroaching neighbors.

An aggressive culture was taking shape based on violent confrontations between adult males organized in "tribal" groups. War cultures arose in all western European societies, marked by the universal presence of a new drinking instrument, the "bell beaker"—so named by archaeologists because it resembled an inverted bell. Armed groups carried these cups across Europe, using them to swig beer and mead distilled from grains, honey, herbs, and nuts.

Warfare had the ironic effect of accentuating the borrowing among the region's competing peoples. After all, the violent struggles and emerging kinship groups fueled a massive demand for weapons, alcohol, and horses. Warrior elites borrowed from Anatolia the technique of combining copper with tin to produce harder-edged weapons made of the alloy bronze. Soon smiths were producing them in bulk—as evidenced by hoards of copper and bronze tools and weapons from the period found in central Europe. Traders used the rivers of central and northern Europe to exchange their prized metal products, creating one of the first commercial networks that covered the landmass.

The Americas

In certain places, including the Americas, environmental factors limited the size of human settlements. Here the techniques of food production and storage, transportation, and communication restricted the surpluses for feeding those who did not work the land. Thus, these communities did not grow in size and complexity. For example, in the Chicama Valley of Peru, which opens onto the Pacific Ocean, people still nestled in small coastal villages to fish, gather shellfish, hunt, and grow beans, chili peppers, and cotton (to make twined textiles, which they dyed with wild indigo). Around 3500 BCE, these fishermen abandoned their cane and adobe homes for sturdier houses, half underground, on streets lined with cobblestones.

The Male Warrior Burials of Varna and Nett Down

Burials of elite individuals across the region stretching from the Black Sea to the Atlantic reveal precious objects and weapons associated with a competitive warrior culture. At Varna, on the Black Sea coast of Bulgaria, the lifestyle of the "big men" associated with a farming village from around 4000 BCE came to light

in 1972 when a farmer driving a tractor uncovered an ancient cemetery. The burials at Varna may represent a powerful and well-connected settlement, since most other contemporary sites do not display such high levels of wealth. In the grave of a man who died at about age forty-five (pictured here), large pots

used for drinking and storage were found. More striking were the 990 gold objects: most were decorative devices sewn onto his clothing, but others included bracelets on both arms, a necklace, and a small gold-handled axe. The weapons buried with him—daggers, axes, spearheads, and points—were made of flint.

Another burial—from Nett Down in Wiltshire, England, and dating to around 2500 BCE—reveals a less developed culture. In this case, a small tomb cut into the chalk ground and covered with a small mound of earth contained a young male warrior. He was buried with the two most significant objects connected with his life: a bronze dagger and, by his hands, a large bell beaker. No gold or precious metal ornaments accompanied the man, who was clearly part of a poorer society than Varna's. As one scholar has remarked, "The grave neatly encapsulates the ideal male image of drinking and fighting."

QUESTIONS FOR ANALYSIS

- Most individual burials contain male bodies. What does this fact tell us about men's roles in these evolving patriarchal societies?

- When we compare these sites with those in Egypt and China, what can we learn about the importance of burying the dead across these societies?

Hundreds, if not thousands, of such villages dotted the seashores and riverbanks of the Americas. Some made the technological breakthroughs required to produce pottery; others devised irrigation systems and water sluices in floodplains (areas where rivers overflowed and deposited fertile soil). Some even began to send their fish catches inland in return for

agricultural produce. In the remains of these villages, archaeologists have recovered sacred spaces, fire-pit chambers, and tombs that reveal an elaborate religious life. These ceremonial structures highlighted communal devotion and homage to deities as well as rituals to celebrate birth, death, and the memory of ancestors.

In the Americas, the largest population center was in the valley of Tehuacán (near modern-day Mexico City). Here the domestication of corn created a subsistence base that enabled people to migrate from caves to a cluster of pit-house villages that supported a growing population. By 3500 BCE, the valley held nothing resembling a large city, although it teemed with inhabitants. People lived in clusters of interdependent villages, especially on the lakeshores: here was a case of high population density, but not urbanization.

Sub-Saharan Africa

The same pattern occurred in sub-Saharan Africa, where the population grew but did not concentrate in urban communities. About 12,000 years ago, when rainfall and temperatures increased, small encampments of hunting, gathering, and fishing communities congregated around the large lakes and rivers flowing through the region that would later become the Sahara Desert. Elephants, rhinoceroses, gazelles, antelopes, lions, and panthers roamed, posing a threat but also providing a source of food. Over the millennia, in the wetter and more temperate locations of this vast region—particularly the upland mountains and their foothills—permanent villages emerged.

As the Sahara region became drier, people moved to the desert's edges, to areas along the Niger River and the Sudan. Here they grew yams, oil palms (a tree whose fruit and seeds produce oil), and plantains (a fruit similar to bananas). In the savanna lands that stretched all the way from the Atlantic Ocean in West Africa to the Nile River basin in present-day Sudan, settlers grew grains such as millet and sorghum, which spread from their places of origin to areas along the lands surrounding the Niger River basin. Residents constructed stone dwellings and dug underground wells and food storage areas. As an increasing population strained resources, groups migrated south toward the Congo River and east toward Lake Nyanza, where they established new farms and villages. Although population centers were often hundreds or thousands of miles apart and were much smaller than the urban centers in Egypt and Mesopotamia, widespread use of the same pottery style, with rounded bottoms and wavy decorations, suggests that they maintained trading and cultural contacts. In these respects, sub-Saharan Africa matched the ways of life in Europe and the Americas.

CONCLUSION

Over the fourth and third millennia BCE, the world's social landscape changed in significant ways. In a few key locations, where giant rivers irrigated fertile lands, complex human cultures began to emerge. These areas experienced all the advantages and difficulties of expanding populations: occupational specialization; social hierarchy; rising standards of living; sophisticated systems of art and science; and centralized production and distribution of food, clothing, and other goods. Ceremonial sites and trading crossroads became cities that developed centralized religious and political systems. As scribes, priests, and rulers labored to keep complex societies together, the differences between countryfolk and city dwellers sharpened. In effect, urbanization was one of the many ways in which societies were becoming more complex and stratified. Social distinctions also affected the roles of men and women, as urban families began to differ from kinship groups in the countryside.

Although the river-basin cultures shared basic features, each one's evolution followed a distinctive path. Where there was a single river—the Nile or the Indus—the agrarian hinterlands that fed the cities lay along the banks of the mighty waterway. In these areas, cities were small; thus, the Egyptian and Harappan worlds enjoyed more political stability and less rivalry. In contrast, cities in the immense floodplain of the Tigris and Euphrates needed large hinterlands to sustain their populations. Because of their growing power and need for resources, Mesopotamian cities vied for preeminence, and their competition often became violent. (As we will see in Chapter 3, a similar pattern emerged after 1500 BCE in China, where the Yellow and Yangzi River environments facilitated the rapid expansion of Chinese settlements into cities.)

Cities stood at one end of the spectrum of social complexity. At the other end, in most areas of the world, people still lived in simple, egalitarian societies based on hunting, gathering, and basic agriculture—as in the Americas and sub-Saharan Africa. In between were worlds such as Anatolia, Europe, and large parts of China, where towns emerged and agriculture advanced—but not with the leaps and bounds of the great river-basin cultures. Beyond these frontiers, farmers and nomads survived as they had for many centuries. Some of them, as in the Aegean, forged warrior societies. Elsewhere, as in the borderlands between Mesopotamian city-states, people created thriving trading networks.

In spite of these global differences, changes in climate affected everyone and could slow or even reverse development. How—and whether—cultures adapted depended on local circumstances. As the next chapter will show, the human agents of change often came from the fringes of larger settlements and urban areas.

After You Read This Chapter

Go to InQuizitive to see what you know & learn what you've missed.

FOCUS ON: *Societies in the Great River Basins*

Mesopotamia
- Peoples living along the **Tigris** and **Euphrates Rivers** control floodwaters and refine irrigation techniques.
- Mesopotamians establish the world's first large cities, featuring powerful rulers, social hierarchies, and monumental architecture.
- Mesopotamia is the birthplace of writing.

Egypt
- Peoples of Egypt use **Nile River** waters to irrigate their lands and create a bountiful agriculture.
- Egyptian rulers known as pharaohs unify their territory, establish a powerful state, and develop a vibrant economy.
- Egyptians build magnificent burial chambers (pyramids) and worship a pantheon of gods.

Indus Valley
- South Asian peoples harness the **Indus River** and create cities like Harappa and Mohenjo Daro.

East Asia
- Peoples dwelling in the basins of the **Yellow** and the **Yangzi Rivers** control the waters' flow and expand agriculture.
- These people develop an elaborate culture, which scholars later label Yangshao and Longshan, respectively.

CHRONOLOGY

Southwest Asia and Egypt	Earliest Sumerian cities appear in Mesopotamia **3500 BCE** ◆
South Asia	
East Asia	◆ Yangshao culture thrives along Yellow River **5000 BCE**
Europe and the Mediterranean	
The Americas	Chicama Valley culture thrives on Pacific coast of South America **3500 BCE** ◆
	Tehuacan Valley in Mexico thrives **3500 BCE** ◆
	Dense village life along many lakes and rivers **3500 BCE** ◆
Inner and Central Asia	Spread of nomadic pastoralism begins **3500 BCE** ◆

5000 BCE   **4000 BCE**

KEY TERMS

STUDY QUESTIONS

1. **Explain** where and how the earliest river-basin societies arose; **compare and contrast** their characteristics.

2. **Describe** the religious, social, and political developments that accompanied urbanization from 3500 to 2000 BCE.

3. **Identify** shared characteristics among urbanites in Mesopotamia, the Indus Valley, and Egypt. What features distinguished each from the others?

4. **Describe** the long-distance connections that developed across Afro-Eurasia; **analyze** how these contacts with other people influenced each society.

5. **Define** pastoralism. **Compare** life in the cities of the river-basin societies with the lifeways in small villages and among pastoral nomads.

6. **Explain** East Asia's relative physical isolation from other Afro-Eurasian societies between 3500 and 2000 BCE. To what extent did this isolation shape social development in this region during this period?

7. **Contrast** the agricultural developments in East Asia with those taking place in Mesopotamia, Egypt, and the Indus Valley at about the same time (3500–2000 BCE).

8. **Describe** how cities in Mesopotamia, the Indus Valley, and Egypt differed from small village communities across the globe. Why did cities emerge in relatively few places between 3500 and 2000 BCE?

9. **Compare and contrast** the ways in which early writing emerged in the urban societies between 4000 and 2000 BCE. How did each use this new technology? How common was literacy?

10. **Identify** shared characteristics of settlements in northern Europe, Anatolia, the Aegean, the Americas, and Africa between 5000 and 2000 BCE. How did settlements in these regions differ from urban settlements in river basins?

First Dynasty emerges in Egypt **3100 BCE**

Sargon's Akkadian territorial state in Mesopotamia **2334–2103 BCE**

Old Kingdom Egypt **2649–2152 BCE**

Cities appear in Indus Valley **2500 BCE**

Longshan culture flourishes in Yellow River valley **5000–2000 BCE**

Fortified villages in the Aegean **2500 BCE**

Stonehenge constructed **2000 BCE**

3000 BCE   **2000 BCE**

Before You Read This Chapter

Go to INQUIZITIVE to see what you know & learn what you've missed.

GLOBAL STORYLINES

- Climate change and environmental degradation lead to the collapse of river-basin societies.

- Transhumant migrants (with their animal herds in need of pasturage) and pastoral nomads (with their horse-drawn chariots) interact, in both destructive and constructive ways, with settled agrarian societies.

- A fusion of migratory and settled agricultural peoples produces expanded territorial states—in Egypt, Southwest Asia, the Indus River valley, and Shang China—that supplant earlier river-basin societies.

- Microsocieties emerge in the South Pacific, the eastern Mediterranean, the northern frontier of Europe, and the Americas as a result of expanding populations and increased trade.

CHAPTER OUTLINE

Nomads, Chariots, Territorial States, and Microsocieties, 2000–1200 BCE

FOCUS QUESTIONS

- What were the effects of climate change on human settlement patterns in the second millennium BCE?

- In what ways did transhumant herders and pastoral nomads impact settled communities?

- How did territorial states form and interact with one another across Afro-Eurasia? In what ways were these varied processes alike and in what ways were they different?

- Where in the South Pacific, the Aegean, the northern frontier of Europe, and the early states of the Americas did microsocieties develop, and how did geographical factors affect their development?

Around 2200 BCE, the Old Kingdom of Egypt collapsed. Evidence for its ruin includes a history of numerous ineffective rulers, imprecise workmanship on pyramids, and many incomplete funerary and temple structures. Yet the collapse did not occur because of incompetent rulers or a decline in the arts and sciences. The Old Kingdom fell because of radical changes in climate—namely, a powerful warming and drying trend that blanketed Afro-Eurasia beginning around 2200 BCE. The Mesopotamians and Harappans were as hard hit as the Egyptians. In Egypt, the environmental disaster yielded a series of low Niles because the usual monsoon rains did not arrive to feed the river's upper regions, particularly the Blue Nile arising in the mountains of Ethiopia. (For the impact of climate change in the river-basin cultures, see the Current Trends in World History box, p. 74, in the previous chapter.)

Documents from this period reveal widespread suffering and despair. Indeed, people who had enjoyed prosperity and good government for centuries now lived in utter disbelief that the world had been turned upside down and that the wicked triumphed over the virtuous. Consider the following tomb inscription: "All of Egypt was dying of hunger to such a degree that everyone had come to eating his children." Or another: "The tribes of the desert have become Egyptians everywhere. . . . The plunderer is everywhere, and the servant takes what he finds" (Bell, pp. 9, 23).

Settled societies were not alone in their losses. Herders and pastoral nomads also felt the pinch. As these outsiders pressed upon permanent settlements in search of sustenance, the governing structures in Egypt, Mesopotamia, and the Indus Valley collapsed. The pioneering city-states may have created unprecedented differences between elites and commoners and between urbanites and rural folk, but everyone felt the effects of this disaster.

This chapter focuses on two related developments. The first is the effect of climate change on the peoples of Afro-Eurasia, the early consequences of which were decisively negative: famines occurred, followed by political and economic turmoil; the old order gave way; river-basin states in Egypt, Mesopotamia, and the Indus Valley collapsed. Herders and pastoral nomads, driven from grazing areas that were drying up, forced their way into the heartlands of these great states in pursuit of better-watered lands. Once there, they challenged the traditional ruling elites. They also brought with them an awesome new military weapon—the horse-drawn chariot, which is the second focus of this chapter. Chariots brought a type of warfare that would dominate the plains of Afro-Eurasia for half a millennium. The nomads' advantage proved only temporary, however. Soon the Egyptians, Mesopotamians, Chinese, and many others learned from these challengers: they assimilated some of the newcomers into their own societies and drove others away, adopting the invaders' most useful techniques, especially mastering the military uses of chariotry.

We must note that the rise of highly centralized polities does not tell the entire story of this period; thus, the chapter also examines worlds apart from the expanding centers of population and politics. Territorial states also emerged in Greece and the Aegean, where the newcomers who took power adopted local ways more completely. Other regions went through similar processes, but more slowly; they would not see state formation until later. In one fundamental way, the South Pacific, the Aegean, northern Europe, and the Americas were different from the lands stretching from North Africa to East Asia: because they were less densely populated, they experienced less competition for scarce resources. In these locales, **microsocieties** (small-scale, loosely interconnected communities) were the norm.

NOMADIC MOVEMENT, CLIMATE CHANGE, AND THE EMERGENCE OF TERRITORIAL STATES

As climate change spurred nomads and herders to bring new pressures and new technologies to settled communities, innovations in governance spurred the rise of larger, expansionist

territorial states. At the end of the third millennium BCE, drought and food shortages led to the overthrow of ruling elites throughout much of Afro-Eurasia. Walled cities could not defend their hinterlands. Trade routes lay open to predators, and pillaging became a lucrative enterprise. More immediately threatening were those herders living in close proximity to settled agriculturalists; these were the people whom we have called **transhumant herders.** (See Chapter 1 for the distinction between pastoral nomads and transhumant herders.) From the borderlands of the Iranian plateau and the Arabian Desert, herders advanced into the populated areas, searching for food and resources. Similar migrations occurred in the Indus River valley and the Yellow River valley. (See Map 3.1.)

Environmental changes compelled humans across Afro-Eurasia to adapt or perish. When and where the **pastoral nomads** and transhumant herders managed to adjust to the dry conditions, they prompted the rise of new, larger, and expansionist territorial states, from pharaonic Egypt and Mesopotamia to Vedic South Asia and Zhou China. Using chariots, the horse-mounted nomads introduced technologies that led to new forms of warfare, whose spread transformed the Afro-Eurasian world. Moreover, the new rulers' innovations in state building and governance enabled people to rebuild their communities and to flourish in the changed climate.

Climate Change and Migrations

Desperate for secure water sources and pastures, many transhumant herders and pastoralists migrated onto the highland plateaus bordering the inner Eurasian steppes. From there, some continued into the more populated river valleys and soon were competing with the farming communities over space and resources. They also streamed in from the western and southern deserts in Southwest Asia in modern-day inner Syria and Arabia.

These migrants settled in the agrarian heartlands of Mesopotamia, the Indus River valley, the highlands of Anatolia, Iran, China, and Europe. After the first wave of newcomers, more migrants arrived by foot or in wagons pulled by draft animals. Some sought temporary work; others settled permanently. They brought horses and new technologies that were useful in warfare. They brought new languages and religious practices but also created new pressures to feed, house, and clothe an ever-growing population.

HORSES AND CHARIOTS Although the hard riding pastoral nomads contributed much to settled societies (they linked cities in South Asia and China for the first time, enhanced trade, and maintained peace), they could not control what the elites whom they disrupted wrote about them. Those who lost power described the nomadic warriors as "barbaric," portraying them

War Chariots. Upper left: *A large vase typical of Mycenaean art on mainland Greece. The regular banding and presentation of scenes reflect a society that is more formally ordered and rigidly hierarchical than that on Minoan Crete. Note the presence of the horse-drawn chariot. Possessing this more elaborate means of transport and warfare characterized the warrior elites of Mycenaean society and linked them to developments over wide expanses of Afro-Eurasia at the time.* Bottom left: *This wooden chest covered with stucco and painted on all sides with images of the Egyptian pharaoh in his war chariot was found in the fabulously wealthy tomb of Tutankhamun in the Valley of the Kings, in Egypt. The war chariot was introduced into Egypt by the Hyksos. By the reign of Tutankhamun in the New Kingdom, depictions of the pharaoh single-handedly smiting the enemy from a war chariot drawn by two powerful horses were common.* Upper right: *The Shang fought with neighboring pastoral nomads from the central Asian steppes. To do this, they imported horses from central Asia and copied the chariots of nomads they had encountered. This gave Shang warriors devastating range and speed for further conquest.*

as cruel enemies of "civilization." Yet what we know of these nomads today suggests that they were anything but barbaric.

Perhaps the most vital breakthroughs that nomadic pastoralists transmitted to settled societies were the harnessing of horses and the invention of **chariots** (two-wheeled horse-drawn vehicles used in warfare but also in processions and races). On the vast steppe lands north of the Caucasus Mountains, during the late fourth millennium BCE, settled people had domesticated horses in their native habitat. Elsewhere, as on the northern steppes of what is now Russia, horses were a food source. Only during the late third millennium BCE did people harness them with cheek pieces and mouth bits, signaling their use for transportation. Parts of the horse harnesses, made from wood, bronze, and iron and found in tombs scattered across the steppe, revealed the evolution of headgear from simple mouth bits to full bridles with headpiece, mouthpiece, and reins.

Sometime around 2000 BCE, pastoral nomads beyond the Mesopotamian plain to the north in the mountains of the Caucasus joined the harnessed horse to the chariot. The invention of the chariot yoked to agile, speedy, and highly trained horses transformed warfare. Pastoralists lightened chariots so their warhorses could pull them faster. They were so light

that an empty one could be lifted by one hand. The chariots had spoked wheels made of special wood and bent into circular shapes, wheel covers, axles, and bearings—all produced by settled people. But there was even more adaptation: durable metal went into the chariot's moving parts, first bronze and later iron. A cluster of more than twenty settlements of steppe nomads, based in the area to the east of the Ural Mountains, led the way in making bronze weapons and chariot parts. Farther south, craftsmen residing in urban settlements fashioned true tin-bronze weapons and utensils, and communities imported horses and chariots from the steppe peoples.

The next innovation in the chariot was the use of iron. Initially, iron was a decorative and experimental metal, and all tools and weapons were bronze. Iron's hardness and flexibility, however, eventually made it more desirable for reinforcing moving parts and protecting wheels. Similarly, solid wood wheels that were prone to shatter gave way to spokes and hooped bronze (and later iron) rims. Thus, the horse chariots were the result

URAL MOUNTAINS

E U R A

BALTIC SEA

EUROPE

Volga R.

Dnieper R.

Dniester R.

HUNGARIAN PLAIN

Danube R.

O

BLACK SEA

R

ARAL SEA

Oxus R.

CENTRAL ASIA

Lake Balkas

CASPIAN SEA

A F

ANATOLIAN PLATEAU

Tigris R.

Euphrates R.

IRANIAN PLATEAU

PAMIR MTS.

HINDU KUSH MTS.

MEDITERRANEAN SEA

ZAGROS MTS.

SOUTHWEST ASIA

H I N.

Nile R.

Persian Gulf

Indus R.

SOUT

ARABIAN DESERT

RED SEA

ARABIAN SEA

Transhumant migrations
Spread of wheeled vehicles
Spread of war chariots
Dispersal of nomads
Pastoral nomads, c. 2000–1500 BCE

Southwest Asian societies
Zone of urbanization

0   500   1000 Miles

0   500   1000 Kilometers

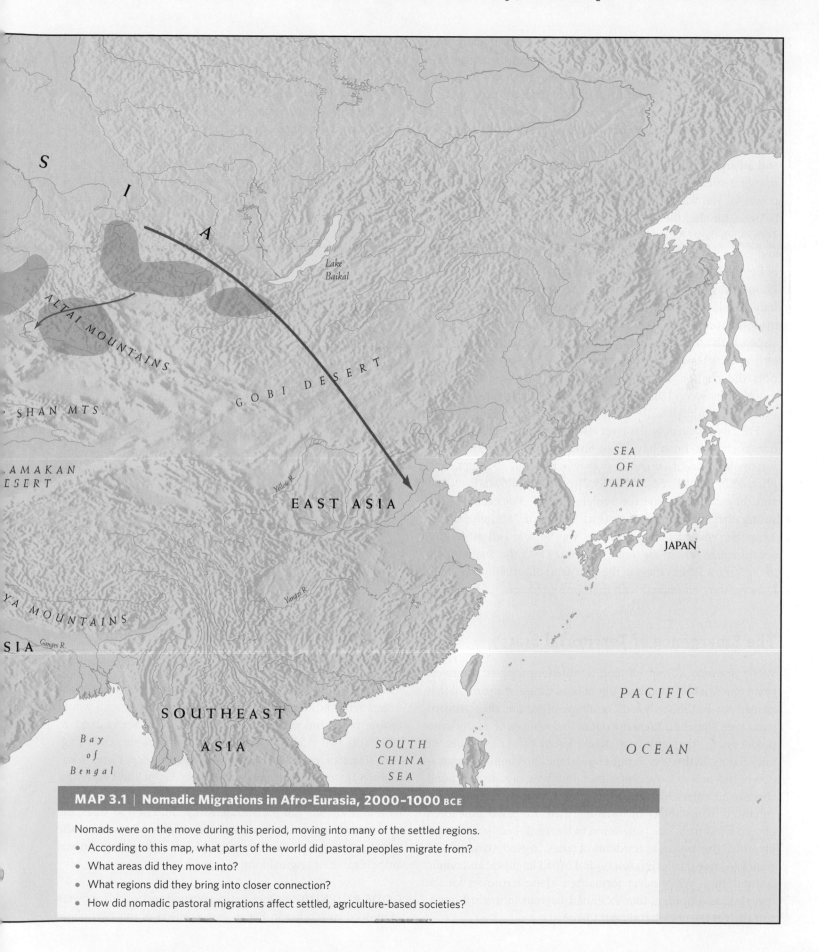

MAP 3.1 | Nomadic Migrations in Afro-Eurasia, 2000–1000 BCE

Nomads were on the move during this period, moving into many of the settled regions.

- According to this map, what parts of the world did pastoral peoples migrate from?
- What areas did they move into?
- What regions did they bring into closer connection?
- How did nomadic pastoral migrations affect settled, agriculture-based societies?

of a creative combination of innovations by both nomadic and agrarian peoples. These innovations—combining new engineering skills, metallurgy, and animal domestication—and their ultimate diffusion revolutionized the way humans made war.

The horse chariot slashed travel time between capitals and overturned the machinery of war. Slow-moving infantry now ceded to battalions of chariots. Each vehicle carried a driver and an archer and charged into battle with lethal precision and ravaging speed. In fact, the mobility, accuracy, and shooting power of warriors in horse-drawn chariots tilted the political balance, for after the nomads perfected this type of warfare (by 1600 BCE), they challenged the political systems of Mesopotamia and Egypt. Soon their innovations became central to the armies of Egypt, Assyria, Persia, the Vedic kings of South Asia, and the Zhou rulers in China, as well as to local nobles as far west as Italy, Gaul, and Spain. Only with the arrival of cheaper armor made of iron (after 1000 BCE) could foot soldiers (in China, armed with crossbows) recover their military importance. And only after states developed cavalry units of horse-mounted warriors did chariots lose their decisive military advantage. For much of the second millennium BCE, then, charioteer elites prevailed in Afro-Eurasia.

For city dwellers in the river basins, the first sight of horse-drawn chariots must have been terrifying, but they knew that war making had changed and they scrambled to adapt. The pharaohs in Egypt copied chariots from their Hyksos invaders, and they came to value the vehicles highly. For example, the young pharaoh Tutankhamun (r. c. 1336–1327 BCE) was a chariot archer who made sure that his war vehicle and other gear accompanied him in his tomb. A century later the Shang rulers of the Yellow River valley, in the heartland of agricultural China, likewise were entombed with their horse chariots.

The Emergence of Territorial States

While nomad and transhumant populations toppled the river-basin cities in Mesopotamia, Egypt, and China, the turmoil that ensued sowed the seeds for a new type of regime: the territorial state. (See Map 3.2.) Breaking out of the confines of its city-state predecessors, the territorial state exerted power over distant hinterlands. In this way, it represented the chief political innovation of this new era: the centralized kingdom, organized around charismatic rulers. The new rulers of these territorial states also enhanced their stability by devising rituals for passing the torch of command from one generation to the next. People no longer identified themselves as residents of cities; instead, they felt allegiance to large territories, rulers, and broad linguistic and ethnic communities. While never formalized, these territories for the first time had borders that extended beyond individual cities, and their residents felt a shared identity.

Territorial states differed from the city-states. The city-states of the river-basin societies, organized around the temple and palace, were autonomous polities (politically organized communities or states) without clearly defined hinterlands. In contrast, the new territorial states in Egypt and Mesopotamia based their authority on monarchs, widespread bureaucracies, elaborate legal codes, large territorial expanses, definable borders, and ambitions for continuous expansion. In China, the Shang state was beginning a process of centralization that would lead to the emergence of territorial dynastic states in the next millennium; in the Indus Valley, nomads brought the Harappan state to an end, preparing the way for the rise of a far-reaching Vedic cultural system.

THE TERRITORIAL STATE IN EGYPT

The first of the great territorial kingdoms of this era arose from the ashes of chaos in Egypt. There the pharaohs of the Middle Kingdom and, later, the New Kingdom reunified the river valley and expanded to the south and north. The long era of prosperity associated with the Old Kingdom had ended when drought brought catastrophe to the area. For several decades, the Nile did not overflow its banks, and Egyptian harvests withered. (See Analyzing Global Developments: Climate Change and the Collapse of River-Basin Societies.) As the pharaohs lost legitimacy and fell prey to feuding among rivals for the throne, regional notables replaced the authority of the centralized state. Egypt, which had been one of the most stable corners of Afro-Eurasia, would endure more than a century of tumult before a new order emerged.

Religion and Trade in Middle Kingdom Egypt (2055–1650 BCE)

Around 2050 BCE, after a century of drought, the Nile's floodwaters returned to normal. Crops grew again. But who would restore order and reunite the kingdom? From about 2061 to 1991 BCE, two rulers at Thebes (far south of the Old Kingdom's seat of power in Memphis), Mentuhotep I and Mentuhotep II, consolidated power in Upper Egypt and began new state-building activity. They ushered in a new phase of stability that historians call the Middle Kingdom. For 350 years, the new pharaonic line built on earlier foundations to increase the state's power and to develop religious and political institutions far beyond their original forms.

GODS AND KINGS Once again, spiritual and worldly powers reinforced each other in Egypt. Just as rulers of this new phase

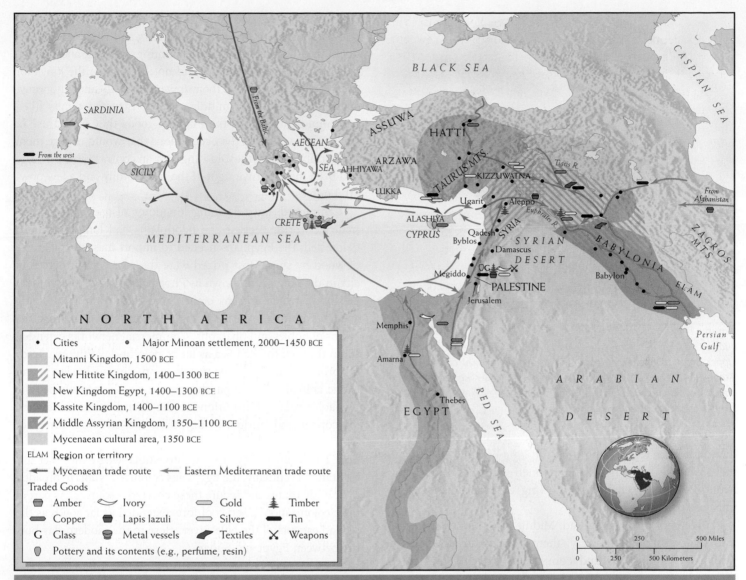

MAP 3.2 | Territorial States and Trade Routes in Southwest Asia, North Africa, and the Eastern Mediterranean, 1500–1350 BCE

Trade in many commodities brought the societies of the Mediterranean Sea and Southwest Asia into increasingly closer contact.

- What were the major trade routes and the major trading states in Southwest Asia, North Africa, and the eastern Mediterranean during this time?
- What were the major trade goods?
- Did trade enhance peaceful interactions among the territorial states?

came from the margins, so too did its gods. The Twelfth Dynasty (1985–1795 BCE), with its long list of kings, dominated the Middle Kingdom partly because its sacred order replaced the chaos that people believed had brought drought and despair. Amenemhet I (1985–1955 BCE) elevated a formerly insignificant god, Amun, to prominence. The king capitalized on the god's name, which means "hidden," to convey a sense of his own invisible omnipresence throughout the realm.

Because Amun's attributes of air and breath were largely hidden, believers in other gods were able to embrace his cult. Amun's cosmic power appealed to those in areas that had recently been impoverished. As the pharaoh elevated the cult of Amun, he unified the disparate parts of his kingdom, further empowering Amun—as well as the god's worldly sponsor, the pharaoh. In this way, Amun eclipsed all the other gods of Thebes. Merging with the formerly omnipotent sun god Re, the

Amun. *This sculpture of the head of the god Amun was carved from quartzite during the Eighteenth Dynasty, around 1335 BCE. At Thebes, in Upper Egypt, a huge temple complex was dedicated to the combined god Amun-Re. The powerful kings of the Middle and New Kingdoms each added a courtyard or a pylon, making this one of the largest religious structures in the ancient world.*

deity now was called Amun-Re: the king of the gods. Because the power of the gods was intertwined with that of the kings, Amun-Re's earthly champion (the king) enjoyed enhanced legitimacy as the supreme ruler.

While gods and kings allied, Middle Kingdom rulers tapped into their kingdom's bounty, their subjects' loyalty, and the work of untold slaves and commoners to build the largest, longest-lasting public works project ever undertaken. For more than 12,000 years, Egyptians and slaves toiled to erect monumental gates, enormous courtyards, and other structures in a massive temple complex at Thebes (present-day Luxor). Dedicated to Amun-Re, it demonstrated the glorious power of the pharaohs and the gods.

Unlike the spiritually perfect and remote rulers of the Old Kingdom, the Middle Kingdom rulers nurtured a cult of the pharaoh as the good shepherd, whose prime responsibility was to fulfill the needs of his human flock. By instituting charities, offering homage to gods at the palace to ensure regular floodwaters, and performing ceremonies to honor their own generosity, the pharaohs portrayed themselves as shepherds of their people. As a result, the cult of Amun-Re was both a tool of political power and a source of spiritual meaning for Egyptians.

MERCHANTS AND EXPANDING TRADE NETWORKS

Prosperity gave rise to an urban class of merchants and professionals who used their wealth and skills to carve out places for their own leisure and pastimes. Indoors they indulged in formal banquets with professional dancers and singers, and outdoors they honed their skills in hunting, fowling, and fishing. What was new was that they did not depend on the kings for such benefits. In a sign of their upward mobility and autonomy, some members of the middle class constructed tombs filled with representations of the material goods they would use in the afterlife as well as the occupations that would engage them for eternity. During the Old Kingdom, in contrast, this privilege had been the exclusive right of the royal family and a few powerful nobles.

Centralized and reforming kingdoms also expanded their trade networks. Because the floodplains had long since been deforested, the Egyptians needed to import massive quantities of wood by ship. Most prized were the cedars from Byblos (a city in the land soon known as Phoenicia, roughly present-day Lebanon), which artisans crafted into furniture for the living and coffins for the dead. Superb examples remain from the tombs of nobles and pharaohs. Commercial networks extended south through the Red Sea as far as present-day Ethiopia; traders brought back precious metals, ivory, livestock, slaves, and exotic animals such as panthers and monkeys to enhance the pharaoh's palace. Expeditions to the Sinai Peninsula searched for copper and turquoise. Egyptians looked south for gold, which they prized for personal and architectural ornamentation. To acquire it they crossed into Nubia, where they met stiff resistance; eventually, the Egyptians colonized Nubia to broaden their trade routes and secure these coveted resources. As part of their colonization, a series of forts extended as far south as the second cataract of the Nile River, close to the modern-day border between Egypt and Sudan.

Luxury Imports. *Crafted with lapis from the east and gold from the south, these amulets and other treasures from King Tut's tomb demonstrate the impact that trade had upon Egyptian religious and visual culture.*

Migrations and Expanding Frontiers in New Kingdom Egypt (1550–1069 BCE)

The success of the new commercial networks lured pastoral nomads searching for work. Later, chariot-driving Hyksos invaders from Southwest Asia attacked Egypt, setting in motion the events marking the break between what historians call the Middle and New Kingdoms of Egypt. The invaders brought down the rulers of the Middle Kingdom, but they also inspired a new generation of Egyptian rulers who created the New Kingdom and led the state to unparalleled levels of prosperity and territorial expansion.

HYKSOS INVADERS Sometime around 1640 BCE, a western Semitic-speaking people, whom the Egyptians called the **Hyksos** ("Rulers of Foreign Lands"), overthrew the unstable Thirteenth Dynasty. The Hyksos had mastered the art of horse chariots. Thundering into battle with their war chariots and their superior bronze axes and composite bows (made of wood, horn, and sinew), they easily defeated the pharaoh's foot soldiers. Yet the victors did not destroy the conquered land; instead, they ruled over it. Although they attempted to adopt Egyptian ways, they never succeeded in winning the Egyptians' acceptance. The Hyksos did settle down and ruled as the Fifteenth Dynasty, asserting control over the northern part of the country and transforming the Egyptian military force.

After a century of political conflict, an Egyptian who ruled the southern part of the country, Ahmosis (r. 1550–1525 BCE), successfully used the Hyksos weaponry—horse chariots—against the invaders themselves. This military success marked the beginning of the period known as the New Kingdom. The Egyptian rulers had learned an important lesson from the invasion: they had to monitor their frontiers vigilantly, for they could no longer rely on deserts as buffers. Ahmosis assembled large, mobile armies and drove the "foreigners" back. Diplomats followed in the armies' path, as the pharaoh initiated a strategy of interference in the affairs of small kingdoms in Southwest Asia. Such policies laid the groundwork for statecraft and an international diplomatic system that future Egyptian kings would use to dominate the eastern Mediterranean world.

The migrants and invaders from the west introduced new techniques that the Egyptians adopted to consolidate their power. These included bronze working (which the Egyptians had not perfected), an improved potter's wheel, and a vertical loom. In addition, South Asian animals such as humped zebu cattle, as well as vegetable and fruit crops, now appeared on the banks of the Nile for the first time.

Of course, the most significant innovations pertained to war: the horse and chariot, the composite bow, the scimitar (a sword with a curved blade), and other weapons from western Afro-Eurasia. These weapons transformed the Egyptian army from a standing infantry to a high-speed, mobile, and deadly fighting force. As Egyptian troops extended the military frontier as far south as the fourth cataract of the Nile River, the kingdom now stretched from the Mediterranean shores to Ethiopia.

EXPANDING FRONTIERS By the beginning of the New Kingdom, Egypt was projecting its interests outward: it defined itself as a superior, cosmopolitan society with an efficient bureaucracy run by competent and socially mobile individuals. For 100 years, Egypt expanded its control southward into Nubia, a source of gold, exotic raw materials, and labor. Historians identify this expansion most strongly with the reign of Egypt's most powerful woman ruler, Hatshepsut. She served as regent for her young son, Thutmosis III, who came to the throne in 1479 BCE. When he was seven years old, she proclaimed herself "king," ruling as co-regent until she died. During her reign, there was little military activity, but trade with the eastern Mediterranean and southward into Nubia flourished.

Thutmosis III (r. 1479–1425 BCE) launched another expansionist phase that lasted for 200 years. Spreading northeastward into Southwest Asia, under his rule the Egyptians collided with the Mitanni and the Hittite kingdoms. At the Battle of Megiddo

Hatshepsut. *The only powerful queen of Egyptian pharaonic history was Hatshepsut, seen here in a portrait head created during her reign. Because a woman on the throne of Egypt would offend the basic principles of order (ma'at), Hatshepsut usually portrayed herself as a man, especially late in her reign. This was reinforced by the use of male determinatives in the hieroglyphic renditions of her name.*

(1469 BCE), the first recorded chariot battle in history, Thutmosis III, whose army employed nearly 1,000 war chariots, defeated his adversaries and established an Egyptian presence in Palestine. Two centuries later, in 1274 BCE, Egypt's most notable pharaoh, Ramses II (r. 1279–1213 BCE), engaged in what historians regard as the greatest chariot battle in world history. More than 6,000 chariots fought to a draw on the plains of what is present-day Syria for control of the Fertile Crescent. Having evolved into a strong, expansionist territorial state, Egypt was now poised to engage in commercial, political, and cultural exchange with the rest of the region.

TERRITORIAL STATES IN SOUTHWEST ASIA

Climate change and invasions by migrants also transformed the societies of Southwest Asia, and new territorial kingdoms arose in Mesopotamia and Anatolia. Here, as in Egypt, the drought at the end of the third millennium BCE was devastating. Harvests shrank, the price of basic goods rose, and the social order broke down. In southern Mesopotamia, transhumant herders (not chariot-driving nomads, as in Egypt) invaded cities, seeking grazing lands to replace those swallowed up by expanding deserts. A millennium of intense cultivation, combined with severe drought, brought disastrous consequences: rich soil in the river basin was depleted of nutrients; salt water from the Persian Gulf seeped into the marshy deltas, contaminating the water table; and the main branch of the Euphrates River shifted to the west. Many cities lost access to their fertile hinterlands and withered away. Mesopotamia's center of political gravity shifted northward, away from the silted, marshy deltas of the southwestern heartland.

Transhumant herders may have been "foreigners" in the cities of Mesopotamia, but they were not strangers to them. Speaking a related Semitic language, they had always played an important role in Mesopotamian urban life and knew the culture of its city-states. These rural folk wintered in villages close to the river to water their animals, which grazed on fallow fields. In the scorching summer, they retreated to the cooler highlands. Their flocks provided wools for the vast textile industries of Mesopotamia, as well as leather, bones, and tendons for other crafted products. In return, the herders purchased crafted products and agricultural goods. They also paid taxes, served as warriors, and labored on public works projects. Yet despite being part of the urban fabric, they had few political rights within city-states.

Around 2000 BCE, **Amorites** ("westerners," as the Mesopotamian city dwellers called them) from the western desert joined allies from the Iranian plateau to bring down the Third Dynasty of Ur, which had controlled all of Mesopotamia and southwestern Iran for more than a century. These Amorites founded the Old Babylonian dynasty centered on the southern Mesopotamian city of Babylon, near modern Baghdad. Other territorial states arose in Mesopotamia in the centuries that followed, sometimes with one dominating the entire floodplain and sometimes with multiple powerful kingdoms vying for territory. As in Egypt, a century of political instability followed the demise of the old city-state models. Here, too, pastoralists played a role in the restoration of order, increasing the wealth of regions they conquered and helping the cultural realm to flourish. The Old Babylonian kingdom expanded trade and founded territorial states with dynastic ruling families and well-defined frontiers. As we will see, pastoralists also played a key role in the development of territorial kingdoms in Anatolia.

Mesopotamia: Power and Culture under the Amorites

Restored order and prosperity enabled the Amorite kings of Babylonia to nourish a vibrant intellectual and cultural milieu. Rulers commissioned public art and works projects and promoted institutions of learning. The court supported workshops for skilled artisans such as jewelers and sculptors, and it established schools for scribes, the transmitters of an expanding literary culture.

The Babylonians also reproduced and transmitted the cultural achievements of earlier Mesopotamia. To dispel their image as rustic foreigners and to demonstrate their familiarity with the region's core values, they studied the oral tales and written records of the earlier Sumerians and Akkadians. Scribes copied the ancient texts and preserved their traditions. Royal hymns portrayed the king as a legendary hero of quasi-divine status.

Heroic narratives about legendary founders, based on traditional stories about rulers of ancient Uruk, served to legitimize the new rulers. These great poems constituted the epic narratives of human—as opposed to godly—achievement. Written in the Old Babylonian dialect of the Semitic Akkadian language, they identified the history of a people with their king, and their wide circulation helped to unify the kingdom. The most famous was *The Epic of Gilgamesh* (see Primary Source: *The Epic of Gilgamesh*), one of the earliest surviving works of literature. This story, probably composed centuries earlier in the Sumerian language, narrated the heroism of Gilgamesh, the legendary king of early Uruk. Throughout the ages, scribes of royal courts preserved the tradition for future generations to venerate the idea of a benevolent king. *The Epic* stands out as an example of how the Mesopotamian kings continually invested in cultural production to explain important political relations, unify their people, and distinguish their subjects from those of other kingdoms.

Gilgamesh *This terra-cotta plaque in the Berlin Museum is one of the very few depictions of Gilgamesh (on the left wielding the knife) and his sidekick, Enkidu. It illustrates one of the episodes in their shared adventures, the killing of Humwawa, the monster of the Cedar Forest. The style of the plaque indicates that it was made during the Old Babylonian period, between 2000 and 1600 BCE.*

TRADE AND THE RISE OF A PRIVATE ECONOMY
Another feature of the territorial state in Mesopotamia was its shift away from economic activity dominated by the official and centralized city-state and toward independent private ventures. The new rulers designated private entrepreneurs rather than state bureaucrats to collect taxes. People paid taxes in the form of commodities such as grain, vegetables, and wool, which the entrepreneurs exchanged for silver. They, in turn, passed on the silver to the state after pocketing a percentage for their profit. This process generated more private activity and wealth as well as more revenues for the state.

Mesopotamia at this time was a crossroads for caravans leading east and west. When the region was peaceful and well governed, the trading community flourished. The ability to move exotic foodstuffs, valuable minerals, textiles, and luxury goods across Southwest Asia won Mesopotamian merchants and entrepreneurs a privileged position as they connected producers with distant consumers. Merchants also used sea routes for trade with the Indus Valley. Before 2000 BCE, mariners had charted the waters of the Red Sea, the Gulf of Aden, the Persian Gulf, and much of the Arabian Sea. Now, during the second millennium BCE, shipbuilders figured out how to construct larger vessels and to rig them with towering masts and woven sails—creating truly seaworthy craft that could carry bulkier loads. Of course, shipbuilding required wood (particularly cedar from Phoenicia) as well as wool and other fibers (from the pastoral hinterlands) for sails. Such reliance on imported materials reflected a growing regional economic specialization and an expanding sphere of interaction across western Afro-Eurasia.

Doing business in Mesopotamia was profitable but also risky. If harvests were poor, cultivators and merchants could not meet their tax obligations and thus incurred heavy debts. The frequency of such misfortune is evident from the many royal edicts that annulled certain debts as a gesture of tax relief. Moreover, traders and goods had to pass through lands where some hostile rulers refused to protect the caravans. Thus, taxes, duties, and bribes flowed out along the entire route. If goods reached their final destination, they yielded large profits; if disaster struck, investors and traders had nothing to show for their efforts. As a result, merchant households sought to lower their risks by formalizing commercial rules, establishing insurance schemes, and cultivating extended kinship networks in cities along trade routes to ensure strong commercial alliances and to gather intelligence. They also cemented their ties with local political authorities. Indeed, the merchants who dominated the ancient city of Assur, on the Tigris, pumped revenues into the coffers of the local kingdom in the hope that its wealthy dynasts would protect their interests.

MESOPOTAMIAN KINGSHIP The new rulers of Mesopotamia also changed the organization of the state and promoted a distinctive culture as well as expanding trade. Herders-turned-urbanite-rulers mixed their own nomadic social organization with that of the formerly dominant city-states to create the structures necessary to support much larger territorial states. The basic social organization of the Amorites, out of which the territorial states in Mesopotamia evolved, was tribal, dominated by a ruling chief, and clan based, claiming descent from a common ancestor. In time, chieftains drew on personal charisma and battlefield prowess to become kings; kings allied with the merchant class and nobility for bureaucratic and financial support, and kingship became hereditary.

The Epic of Gilgamesh

Gilgamesh, an early ruler of ancient Uruk, was the supreme hero of Mesopotamian legend. He was a successful ruler, boastful and vain, as well as a courageous adventurer and a devoted friend to his companion, Enkidu. The Gilgamesh epic, constructed in the early second millennium BCE from numerous stories, is the oldest piece of world literature. It portrays a tragic hero who is obsessed with glory and whose quest for immortality ends in failure. The following excerpt tells of his anguish on his fruitless journey to gain immortal life. He is speaking to an alewife (a woman who keeps an alehouse) as he continues to deny his humanity and the inevitability of death.

The alewife spoke to him, to Gilgamesh,
"If you are truly Gilgamesh, that struck
    down the Guardian,
Destroyed Humbaba, who lived in the Pine
    Forest,
Killed lions at the mountain passes,
Seized the Bull of Heaven who came down
    from the sky, struck him down,
Why are your cheeks wasted, your face
    dejected,
Your heart so wretched, your appearance
    worn out,
And grief in your innermost being?
Your face is like that of a long-distance
    traveler,
Your face is weathered by cold and
    heat . . .
Clad only in a lion skin you roam open
    country."
Gilgamesh spoke to her, to Siduri the
    alewife,
"How could my cheeks not be wasted, my
    face not dejected.

Nor my heart wretched, nor my appear-
    ance worn out,
Nor grief in my innermost being,
Nor my face like that of a long-distance
    traveler,
My friend whom I love so much, who
Experienced every hardship with me,
Enkidu, whom I love so much, who experi-
    enced every hardship with me—
The fate of mortals conquered him! Six
    days and seven nights I wept over him,
I did not allow him to be buried, until a
    worm fell out of his nose.
I was frightened and . . .
I am afraid of Death, and so I roam open
    country.
The words of my friend weigh upon me.
I roam open country for long distances;
    the words of my friend
Enkidu weigh upon me.
I roam open country on long journeys.
How, O how, could I stay silent, how O
    how could I keep quiet

My friend whom I love has turned
    to clay:
Enkidu my friend whom I love has turned
    to clay.
Am I not like him? Must I lie down too,
Never to rise, ever again?"

QUESTIONS FOR ANALYSIS

- What lines of the passage reveal how Gilgamesh feels about the death of Enkidu? Why does he feel that way?

- What does this passage tell us about human relationships and human nature during this period? What does it tell us about rulers and their relationship with their gods?

Source: Stephanie Dalley, *Myths from Mesopotamia: Creation, The Flood, Gilgamesh and Others* (New York: Oxford University Press, 1991), pp. 100–101.

Over the centuries, powerful Mesopotamian kings expanded their territories and subdued weaker neighbors, inducing them to pay tribute in luxury goods, raw materials, and manpower as part of a broad confederation of polities under the kings' protection. Control over military resources (access to metals for weaponry and, later, to herds of horses for pulling chariots) was necessary to gain dominance, but it was no guarantee of success. The ruler's charisma also mattered. Unlike the more institutionalized Egyptian leadership, Mesopotamian kingdoms could vacillate from strong to weak, depending on the ruler's personality.

The most famous Mesopotamian ruler of this period was Hammurapi (or Hammurabi, r. 1792–1750 BCE). Continuously struggling with powerful neighbors, he sought to centralize state authority and to create a new legal order. Using diplomatic and military skills to become the strongest king in Mesopotamia, he made Babylon his capital and declared himself "the king who made the four quarters of the earth obedient" (Frayne, vol. 4, p. 341). He implemented a new system to secure his power, appointing regional governors to manage outlying provinces and to deal with local elites.

Hammurapi's image as ruler mirrored that of the Egyptian pharaohs of the Middle Kingdom. The king was shepherd and patriarch of his people, responsible for proper preparation of the fields and irrigation canals and for his followers' well-being. Such an ideal recognized that being king was a delicate balancing act. While he had to curry favor among powerful merchants and elites, he also had to meet the needs of the poor and disadvantaged—in part to avoid a reputation for cruelty and in part to gain a key base of support should the elites become dissatisfied with his rule.

Hammurapi elevated this balancing act into an art form, encapsulated in a grand legal code—**Hammurapi's Code**. Much of the code itself was inscribed on a large stone stele, at the top of which was a portrait of Hammurapi himself, posing humbly before the sun god, Shamash, the patron of justice. Below came the laws, suggesting that they were handed down from the deity through a just, benevolent, and conquering ruler. The code began and concluded with the rhetoric of paternal justice. For example, he concluded by describing himself as "the shepherd who brings peace, whose scepter is just. My benevolent shade

Hammurapi's Code. *The inscription on the shaft of Hammurapi's Code is carved in a beautiful rendition of the cuneiform script. Because none of the laws on the code were recorded in the thousands of judicial texts of the period, it is uncertain if Hammurapi's Code presented actual laws or only norms for the proper behavior of Babylonian citizens.*

was spread over my city, I held the people of the lands of Sumer and Akkad safely on my lap" (Roth, p. 133).

In fact, Hammurapi's Code was a compilation of more than 300 edicts addressing crimes and their punishments. One theme rings loud and clear: governing public matters was man's work, and upholding a just order was the supreme charge of rulers. Whereas the gods' role in ordering the world was distant, the king was directly in command of ordering relations among people. Accordingly, the code elaborated in exhaustive detail the social rules that would ensure the kingdom's peace through its primary instrument—the family. The code outlined the rights and privileges of fathers, wives, and children. The father's duty was to treat his kin as the ruler would treat his subjects, with strict authority and care. Adultery, which represented the supreme violation of this moral code, was a female crime. Any woman found with a man who was not her husband would be bound and thrown into the river, and likewise her lover.

The code also divided the people in the Babylonian kingdom into three classes: free persons, dependents, and slaves. Each had an assigned value and distinct rights and responsibilities. In this way, Hammurapi's order stratified society while also pacifying the region. By the end of his reign, he had established Babylon as the single great power in Mesopotamia and had reduced competitor kingdoms to mere vassals. Following his death, his sons and successors struggled to maintain control over a shrinking domain for another 155 years in the face of internal rebellions and foreign invasions. In 1595 BCE, Babylon fell to the Hittite king Hattusilis I.

The era of Hammurapi and his successors was a high point in the intellectual life of Mesopotamia, setting the stage for the achievements of the first-millennium Assyrians and neo-Babylonians (see Chapter 4). In particular, mathematics and literature reached new heights, going far beyond what was needed for everyday applications. Religious life was also fundamentally altered. The city god of Babylon, Marduk, was raised to the level of a national god, becoming the primary cult of the land. It was Marduk who would confront Assur in the coming centuries in the struggle between north and south in the "land between two rivers."

THE KASSITE GOLDEN AGE The Kassites' origins are obscure, though they seem to have entered southern Mesopotamia from the Zagros Mountains and the Iranian plateau, at first encamping in small groups on the edges of cities and working as mercenaries in the Babylonian armies and as agricultural laborers. By 2000 BCE, they had integrated themselves into Babylonian society, becoming bureaucrats associated with the temple, and were destined to play a major role in the political and cultural history of Southwest Asia. Once entrenched, they were well placed to fill the power vacuum when the First Dynasty of Babylon fell. By 1475 BCE, Kassite rulers had reestablished order in the region. Over the next 350 years, they brought all of southern Mesopotamia under their control, creating one of the great territorial states within an emerging network of states from North Africa to Southwest Asia.

The Kassites presided over a golden age based on trade in such precious commodities as horses, chariots, and lapis lazuli, which they exchanged for gold, wood, and ivory. Like earlier immigrant communities to this ancient land, the Kassites absorbed the traditions and institutions of Mesopotamia. Even more than their predecessors, they strove to preserve the past and transmit its institutions to posterity. Although very little remains of their own language and customs (apart from their personal names), with thoroughness and dedication the Kassite scribes translated much of the older Sumerian literature into Akkadian. They revised and compiled texts into standard editions, from which scholars have recovered a Babylonian creation story called the Enuma Elish. In their determination to become even more Babylonian than the Babylonians, the Kassites saved a treasure trove of historical literature and cultural practices for later generations. During the subsequent period of the Community of Major Powers, the Kassites served as the crucial link between Egypt, Anatolia, and southwestern Iran.

Anatolia: The Old and New Hittite Kingdoms (1800–1200 BCE)

Chariot warriors known as the **Hittites** established territorial kingdoms in Anatolia, northwest of Mesopotamia. Anatolia (modern-day Turkey) was an overland crossroads that linked the Black and Mediterranean Seas. Like other plateaus of Afro-Eurasia, it had high tablelands, was easy to traverse, and was hospitable to large herding communities. Thus, during the third millennium BCE, Anatolia became home to numerous political systems run by indigenous elites. These societies combined pastoral lifeways, agriculture, and urban commercial centers. Before 2000 BCE, peoples speaking Indo-European languages began to enter the plateau, probably coming from the steppe lands north and west of the Black Sea. The newcomers lived in fortified settlements and often engaged in regional warfare, and their numbers grew. They also borrowed extensively from the cultural developments of Southwest Asian urban cultures, especially from Mesopotamia.

In the early second millennium BCE, the chariot warrior groups of Anatolia grew powerful on the commercial activity that passed through the region. Chief among them were the Hittites. Hittite lancers and archers rode chariots across vast expanses to plunder their neighbors and demand taxes and tribute. In the seventeenth century BCE, the Hittite leader Hattusilis I unified these chariot aristocracies, secured his base in

Anatolia, defeated the kingdom that controlled northern Syria, and then campaigned along the Euphrates River, even sacking Babylon in 1595 BCE.

Two centuries later, the Hittites enjoyed another period of political and military success. In 1274 BCE, they fought the Egyptians under the pharaoh Ramses II at the battle of Qadesh (in modern Syria), the largest and best-documented chariot battle of antiquity. Hittite control—spanning from Anatolia across the region between the Nile and Mesopotamia—was central to balancing power among the territorial states that grew up in the river valleys and was a factor in promoting diplomatic relations among the powers at this time.

As nomadic peoples combined with urban communities to create new territorial states in Egypt, Mesopotamia, and Anatolia, and as these states came into contact with one another through trade, they developed techniques of diplomacy that enabled states to resolve problems without having to go to war.

The Community of Major Powers (1400–1200 BCE)

Much of what we know of the Kassites and other states does not come from Mesopotamia and Anatolia, but from Egypt. Our knowledge is based on a remarkable cache of 350 letters found in the city of al-Amarna, briefly the capital of the Egyptian state under Akhenaten. Most are letters from the Egyptian king to his subordinates in the vassal states in Palestine, but others are from Akhenaten and his father to the Babylonian, Mitanni, Middle Assyrian, Kassite, and Hittite kings. Many are in Akkadian (used by Babylonian bureaucrats), which served as the diplomatic language of this era. The correspondence reveals a delicate balance of constantly shifting alliances among competing kings who were intent on maintaining their status and who knew that winning the loyalty of the small buffer kingdoms was crucial to political success. Powerful rulers referred to one another as brothers, suggesting not only a high degree of equality but also a desire to foster friendship among large states. Trade linked the regimes and was so vital to the economic and political well-being of rulers that if a commercial mission were plundered, the ruler of the area in which the robbery occurred assumed responsibility and offered compensation to the injured parties. Hence, between 1400 and 1200 BCE, the major territorial states of Southwest Asia and Egypt perfected instruments of international diplomacy that have stood the test of time and inspired later leaders. The result was that rulers used treaties and negotiations rather than the battlefield to settle differences. Moreover, each state knew its place in the political pecking order. It was an order that depended on constant communication—the foundation of what we now call diplomacy.

ANALYZING GLOBAL DEVELOPMENTS

Climate Change and the Collapse of River-Basin Societies

The three great river-basin societies discussed in Chapter 2 (Egypt, Mesopotamia, and the Indus Valley) collapsed at around the same time. The collapse in Egypt and Mesopotamia was almost simultaneous (roughly between 2200 and 2100 BCE). In contrast, while the collapse was delayed in the Indus Valley for approximately 200 years, when it came, it virtually wiped out the Harappan state and culture. At first historians focused on political, economic, and social causes, stressing bad rulers, nomadic incursions, political in-fighting, population migrations, and the decline of long-distance trade. In more recent times, however, a group of scientists—paleobiologists, climatologists, sedimentologists, and archaeologists—have studied these societies and found convincing evidence that a truly radical change in the climate—a 200-year-long drought spreading across the Afro-Eurasian landmass—was a powerful factor in the collapse of these cultures. But how can these researchers know so much about the climate 4,000 years ago? The following table assembles the evidence for their assertions, drawing on their scholarly studies of Egypt, Mesopotamia, and the Indus Valley.

QUESTIONS FOR ANALYSIS

- Why did more standard historical explanations for the collapse of the large river-basin societies precede the more recent emphasis on climate change?
- Few scholars, even those cited in this feature's source note, are willing to regard climate change as the overwhelming factor in the collapse of these river-basin societies. What do you think the reason is?
- After reading the source note, do you think that the evidence for climate change is convincing for all three societies? Which ones are the more persuasive, which the less convincing?

River-Basin Society	Date of Collapse	Climatological Evidence	Archaeological Evidence	Literary Evidence
Egypt	The Old Kingdom collapsed and ushered in a period a notable political instability, the First Intermediate Period (2184–2055 BCE).	Sedimentation studies reveal markedly lower Nile floods and an invasion of sand dunes into cultivated areas.	Much of the sacred sites of the Old Kingdom and their artwork are believed to have been destroyed in this period due to the political chaos.	An abundant literary record is full of tales of woe and poetry and stelae, calling attention to famine, starvation, low Nile floods, and even cannibalism.
Mesopotamia	The last effective ruler of the Kingdom of Akkad (2334–2193 BCE) was Naram Sin (r. 2254–2218 BCE).	Around 2100 BCE, inhabitants abruptly abandoned the Haabur drainage basin, whose soil samples reveal marked aridity as determined by the existence of fewer earthworm holes and wind-blown pellets.	Teil Leilan and other sites indicate that the large cities of this region began to shrink around 2200 BCE and were soon abandoned, remaining unoccupied for 300 years.	Later Ur III scribes described the influx of northern "barbarians" and noted the construction of a wall, known as the Repeller of the Amorites, to keep these northerners out.
Indus Valley and the Harappan society	Many of the Harappan peoples migrated eastward, beginning around 1900 BCE, leaving this region largely empty of people.	Hydroclimatic reconstructions show that precipitation began to decrease around 3000 BCE, reaching a low in 2000 BCE, at which point the Himalayan rivers stopped incising. Around 1700 BCE, the Ghaggar-Hakra River dried up.	Major Harappan urban sites began to shrink in size and lose their urban character between 1900 and 1700 BCE.	There is no literary source material because the Harappan script has still to be deciphered.

Sources: Barbara Bell, "The Dark Ages in Ancient History," American Journal of Archaeology, 75 (January 1971): 1–26; Max Weiss et al., "The Genesis and Collapse of Third Millennium North Mesopotamian Civilization," Science, New Series, 261 (August 20, 1993): 995–1004; H. M. Cullen et al., "Climate Change and the Collapse of the Akkadian Empire," Geology 28 (April 2000): 379–82; Liviu Giosan et al., "Fluvial Landscapes of the Harappan Civilization," Proceedings of the National Academy of Sciences, published online, May 29, 2012; and Karl W. Butzer, "Collapse, Environment, and Society," Proceedings of the National Academy of Sciences 109 (10): 3632–39, published online March 6, 2012. For a general overview of climate change and historical studies, consult Wolfgang Behringer, A Cultural History of Climate (2010).

Akhenaten. *The pharaoh Amenhotep IV changed his name to Akhenaten to reflect his deep devotion to Aten, the god of the sun disk. The art of the period of his reign, like his religion, challenged conventions. In it, the faces of the king and queen, as well as their bodies, were extremely elongated and distorted. Some scholars think that this distortion reflects a condition that the king himself suffered from.*

Formal treaties brought an end to military eruptions and replaced them with diplomatic contacts. In its more common form, diplomacy involved strategic marriages and the exchange of specialized personnel to reside at the court of foreign territorial states. Gifts also strengthened relations among the major powers and signaled a ruler's respect for his neighbors. Rulers had to acknowledge the gesture by reciprocating with gifts of equal value. The states even employed the practice of extradition, making it difficult for a criminal to flee from one territory and find safe haven in another.

The foundations of power were not always durable, however. Building the state system was ultimately the task of those at the bottom of the social pyramid, and the ruling classes' reliance on them for power and political authority was a weakness of these regimes. Commoners remained tied to the land, which sometimes belonged to communities or institutions, not individual families. They paid taxes to the state, performed labor required by the state for public works (such as irrigation or building projects), and served as foot soldiers. The collapse of the international age had many causes, but one factor was the disintegration of the social fabric as workers could not pay their taxes or fled their communities rather than fight in the rulers' armies.

NOMADS AND THE INDUS RIVER VALLEY

Territorial states emerged more slowly in the Indus River valley than they did in Egypt and Mesopotamia. Late in the third millennium BCE, drought ravaged the Indus River valley as it did other regions. By 1700 BCE, the population of the old Harappan heartland had plummeted. Here, too, around 1500 BCE, yet another group of nomadic peoples, calling themselves Aryans ("respected ones"), wandered out of their homelands in the steppes of Inner Eurasia. In contrast to Egypt, Anatolia, and Mesopotamia, these pastoral nomads were unable to establish large territorial states.

Crossing the northern highlands of central Asia through the Hindu Kush, they were a sight to behold. They descended into the fertile Indus River basin (see Map 3.3) with large flocks of cattle and horses. Their priests offered chants from the Rig Veda while sacrificing some of their livestock to their gods. Known collectively as the Veda ("knowledge"), these hymns served as the most sacred texts for the newcomers, who are known as the Vedic people. They also arrived with an extraordinary language, Sanskrit (perhaps prophetically labeled "perfectly made"). It is one of the earliest known Indo-European languages, having the same source as many of the European languages, including Greek, Latin, English, French, and German. (See Current Trends in World History: How Languages Spread: The Case of Nomadic Indo-European Languages.)

Like other nomads from the northern steppe, they brought domesticated animals—especially horses, which pulled their chariots and established their military superiority. Not only were the Vedic people superb horse charioteers, but they were also masters of copper and bronze metallurgy and wheel making. Their expertise in these areas enabled them to produce the very chariots that transported them into their new lands.

The Vedic peoples were deeply religious. They worshipped a host of natural and supernatural deities, the most powerful of which were the sky god and the gods that represented horses. They were confident that their chief god, Indra (the deity of war), was on their side. The Vedic people also brought elaborate rituals of worship, which set them apart from the indigenous populations. (See Primary Source: Vedic Hymns to the Chariot Race of the Gods.) But, as with many Afro-Eurasian migrations, the outsiders' arrival led to fusion as well as to conflict. While the native born peoples eventually adopted the newcomers' language, the newcomers themselves took up the techniques and rhythms of agrarian life.

The Vedic people used the Indus Valley as a staging area for migrations throughout the northern plain of South Asia. As

MAP 3.3 | Indo-European Migrations, Second Millennium BCE

One of the most important developments of the second millennium was the movement of Indo-European peoples.

- Where did the Indo-European migrations originate?
- Where did Indo-European migrations spread to during this time?
- How did widespread drought push or draw the migrants into more settled agricultural regions, such as the Indus Valley?

they mixed agrarian and pastoral ways and borrowed technologies (such as iron working) from farther west, their population expanded and they began to look for new resources. With horses, chariots, and iron tools and weapons, they marched south and east. By 1000 BCE, they reached the southern foothills of the Himalayas and began to settle in the Ganges River valley.

Five hundred years later, they had settlements as far south as the Deccan plateau.

Each wave of occupation involved violence, but the invaders did not simply dominate the indigenous peoples. Instead, the confrontations led them to embrace many of the ways of the vanquished. Although the Vedic people despised the local

Vedic Hymns to the Chariot Race of the Gods

There are no extant accounts of the Vedic people's chariot races and festivals, despite the centrality of these events to their culture. However, scholars have translated Vedic hymns praising the chariot races of gods. The following hymn portrays the Maruts—the storm gods under the direction of Indra—as skilled charioteers.

1. The Maruts charged with rain, endowed with fierce force, terrible like wild beasts, blazing in their strength, brilliant like fires, and impetuous, have uncovered the (rain-giving) cows by blowing away the cloud.

2. The [Maruts] with their rings appeared like the heavens with their stars, they shone wide like streams from clouds as soon as Rudra, the strong man, was born for you, O golden-breasted Maruts, in the bright lap of Prisni.

3. They wash their horses like racers in the courses, they hasten with the points of the reed on their quick steeds. O golden-jawed Maruts, violently shaking [your jaws], you go quick with your spotted deer, being friends of one mind.

4. Those Maruts have grown to feed all these beings, or, it may be, [they have come] hither for the sake of a friend, they who always bring quickening rain. They have spotted horses, their bounties cannot be taken away, they are like headlong charioteers on their ways.

5. O Maruts, wielding your brilliant spears, come hither on smooth roads with your fiery cows [clouds] whose udders are swelling; [come hither], being of one mind, like swans toward their nests, to enjoy the sweet offering.

6. O one-minded Maruts, come to our prayers, come to our libations like [Indra] praised by men! Fulfill [our prayer] like the udder of a barren cow, and make the prayer glorious by booty to the singer.

7. Grant us this strong horse for our chariot, a draught that rouses our prayers, from day to day, food to the singers, and to the poet in our homesteads luck, wisdom, inviolable and invincible strength.

8. When the gold-breasted Maruts harness the horses to their chariots, bounteous in wealth, then it is as if a cow in the folds poured out to her calf copious food, to every man who has offered libations.

QUESTIONS FOR ANALYSIS

- What parts of the hymn give clues about how the charioteers' horses looked and were cared for?
- How do the images relating rain-filled clouds to cows reflect the pastoral roots of the Vedic nomads?
- What kinds of gods were the Maruts, and what was their heavenly job when racing on horse chariots?

Source: Mandala II, Hymn 34, in "Vedic Hymns," translated by Hermann Oldenberg, in vol. 32 of *Sacred Books of the East*, edited by F. Max Müller (1897; reprint, New Delhi: Motilal Banarsidass, 1979), pp. 295–96.

rituals, they were in awe of the inhabitants' farming skills and knowledge of seasonal weather. These they adapted even as they continued to expand their territory. They built huts constructed from mud, bamboo, and reeds. They refined the already sophisticated production of beautiful carnelian stone beads, and they further aided commerce by devising standardized weights. In addition to raising domesticated animals, they sowed wheat and rye on the Indus plain, and they learned to plant rice in the marshy lands of the Ganges River valley. Later they mastered the use of plows with iron blades, an innovation that transformed the agrarian base of South Asia.

The turn to settled agriculture was a major shift for the pastoral Vedic people. After all, their staple foods had always been dairy products and meat, and they were used to measuring their wealth in livestock (horses were most valuable, and cows were more valuable than sheep). Moreover, because they could not breed their prized horses in South Asia's semitropical climate, they initiated a brisk import trade from central and Southwest Asia.

As the Vedic people adapted to their new environment and fanned out across uncharted agrarian frontiers, their initial political organization took a somewhat different course from those of Southwest Asia. Whereas competitive kingdoms dominated the landscape there, in South Asia competitive, balanced regimes were slower to emerge. The result was a slower process of political integration.

Indra with the Buddha. *The Vedic people worshipped their gods by sacrificing and burning cows and horses and by singing hymns and songs, but they never built temples or sculptured idols. Therefore, we do not know how they envisioned Indra and their other gods. However, when Buddhists started to make images of the Buddha in the early centuries CE, they also sculpted Indra and Brahma as attendants of the Buddha. Indra in Buddhist iconography evolved into Vajrapani, the Diamond Lord. In this plate, the one on the left holding a stick with diamond-shaped heads is Indra/Vajrapani.*

THE SHANG TERRITORIAL STATE IN EAST ASIA (1600–1045 BCE)

China's first major territorial state combined features of earlier Longshan culture with new technologies and religious practices. Climatic change affected East Asia much as it had central and Southwest Asia. Stories supposedly written on bamboo strips and later collected into what historians called the "Bamboo Annals" tell of a time before the Shang when the sun dimmed, frost and ice appeared in the summer, and a long drought followed heavy rainfall and flooding. Chinese lore says that during this era a mythological ruler, "Yu the Great," brought the rivers under control and founded the Xia dynasty. Also according to Chinese mythology, the first ruler of the Shang state defeated a Xia king and then offered to sacrifice himself so that the drought

would end. This leader, King Tang, survived to found the territorial state called Shang around 1600 BCE in northeastern China. (See Map 3.4.)

As in South Asia, the Shang political system gradually became more centralized from 1600 to 1200 BCE. Much like the territorial kingdoms of Southwest Asia, the Shang state did not have clearly established borders. To be sure, it faced threats—but not in the form of rival territorial states encroaching on its peripheries. Thus, it had little need for a strongly defended permanent capital, though its heartland was called Zhong Shang, or "center Shang." Its capital moved as its frontier expanded and contracted. This relative security is evident in the Shang kings' personalized style of rule, as they made regular trips around the country to meet, hunt, and conduct military campaigns with those who owed allegiance to them. Yet, like the territorial kingdoms of Southwest Asia, the Shang state had a ruling lineage (a line of male sovereigns descended from a common ancestor) that was eventually set down in a written record. (See Primary Source: Sima Qian on the Ruler's Mandate from Heaven to Rule.)

State Formation

The Shang built on the agricultural and river-basin village cultures of the Longshan peoples, who had set the stage for an increasingly centralized state, urban life, and a cohesive culture (see Chapter 2). As the population increased and the number of village conflicts grew, it became necessary to have larger and more central forms of control. The Shang political system emerged to play that governmental role.

Shang culture was built on four elements that the Longshan peoples had earlier introduced. These were a metal industry based on copper, pottery making, walled towns, and divination using animal bones. To these foundations the Shang leaders added hereditary rulers whose power derived from their relation to ancestors and gods, large-scale metallurgy, written records, tribute, and rituals that enabled them to commune with ancestors and foretell the future. By combining all of these elements, the Shang strengthened and brought into existence a wealthy and powerful elite, notable for its intellectual achievements and remarkable aesthetic sensibilities. It became the preeminent society in China during the second millennium BCE.

BRONZE METALLURGY Advanced Shang metalworking—the beginnings of which appeared in northwestern China at pre-Shang sites as early as 1800 BCE—was vital to the state. Metallurgical casting techniques were already in use at this time because copper and tin were available from the North China plain. (See Map 3.4.) Shang bronze work included weapons, fittings for chariots, and ritual vessels. Eventually, the new metallurgy technology gave the Shang unprecedented power over their neighbors.

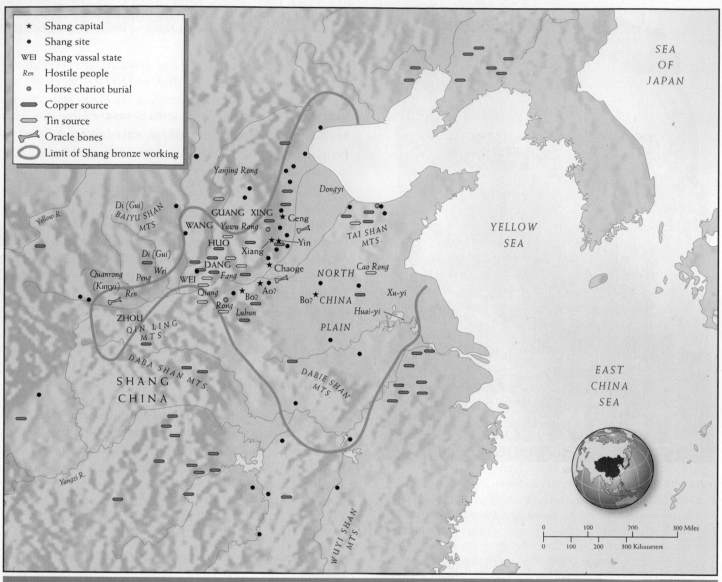

MAP 3.4 | Shang Dynasty in East Asia

The Shang state was one of the most important and powerful of the early Chinese dynasties.

- Based on this map, what raw materials were the most important to the Shang state?
- Why were there so many Shang capitals?
- Why were there no clear territorial boundaries for the Shang state?

Shang bronze-working techniques involved the use of hollow clay molds to hold the molten metal alloy, which, when removed after the liquid had cooled and solidified, produced firm bronze objects. The casting of modular components that artisans could assemble later promoted increased production and permitted the elite to make extravagant use of bronze vessels for burials. For example, archaeologists have unearthed a tomb at Anyang containing one enormous 1,925-pound bronze vessel; the Shang workshops had produced it in 1200 BCE. Another Anyang tomb from the same period contained 3,500 pounds of cast bronze.

The bronze industry of this period shows a high level not only of material culture (the physical objects produced) but also of cultural development and aesthetic sensibility. Artisans skilled in the production of bronze produced ewers, tureens, boxes, and all manner of weapons; decorated jade, stone, and ivory objects; and wove silk on special looms. The bronzes were of the highest quality, decorated as they were with geometric patterns and animal designs featuring elephants, rams, tigers, horses, and more. Because Shang metalworking required extensive mining, it necessitated a large labor force, efficient casting, and a reproducible

Sima Qian on the Ruler's Mandate from Heaven to Rule

Sima Qian was the first great historian in ancient China. He later had as much influence in East Asia as Herodotus, the first Greek historian, had in Greece and Rome. The excerpt below presents the transition from Xia ("Hsia") dynasty to Shang ("T'ang") dynasty as an example of the transfer of the ruler's heavenly mandate.

After Emperor K'ung-chia was enthroned, he delighted in following ghosts and spirits and engaging in licentious and disorderly actions. The prestige of the Hsia-hou Clan declined and the feudal lords rebelled against him.

Heaven sent down two dragons, a male and a female. K'ung-chia was not able to care for them and he lost the support of the Huan-lung (Dragon Raising) Clan. The Yao-t'ang Clan was already in decline, [but] among their descendants one Liu Lei learned the technique of taming dragons from the Huan-lung Clan and thus obtained service with K'ung-chia. K'ung-chia bestowed on him the *cognomen* Yü-lung (Dragon Tamer) and conferred on him the people descended from the Shih-wei [Clan]. The female dragon died and Liu Lei fed it to the Hsia-hou, the Hsia-hou sent [someone] to demand [more of it], and, fearing [that he would be punished], Liu Lei moved on.

When K'ung-chia passed away, his son Emperor Kao was enthroned. When Emperor Kao passed away his son Emperor Fa was enthroned. When Fa passed away, his son Emperor Lu-k'uei was enthroned. He was known as Chieh.

From K'ung-chia's time to the time of Emperor Chieh, the feudal lords had revolted many times against the Hsia. Chieh did not engage in virtuous [government] but in military power and [this] hurt the families of the hundred cognomens. The families of the hundred cognomens were not able to bear him.

Chieh then summoned T'ang and jailed him in Hsia-t'ai. After a while he freed him. T'ang cultivated his virtue and the feudal lords all submitted to T'ang. T'ang then led troops to attack Chieh of Hsia. Chieh fled to Ming-t'iao and subsequently was exiled and died there. Before he died he said to someone, "I regret failing to kill T'ang in Hsia-t'ai; that is what has brought me to this."

T'ang then ascended the throne of the Son of Heaven and received the world's homage in the Hsia's place. T'ang enfeoffed [made vassals or subjects] the descendants of the Hsia. In the Chou dynasty they were enfeoffed at Ch'i.

QUESTIONS FOR ANALYSIS

- What role did morality play in Sima Qian's description of the transfer of the Xia ruler's mandate from heaven to the Shang dynasty?
- How do the references to feuding illustrate the type of society that China had at this time?

Source: "The Hsia, Basic Annals" 2, in *The Grand Scribe's Records*, edited by William H. Nienhauser, Jr., translated by Tsai-fa Cheng, Zongli Lu, William H. Nienhauser, Jr., and Robert Reynolds, vol. 1 (Bloomington: Indiana University Press, 1994), pp. 37–38.

---

artistic style. Although the Shang state highly valued its artisans, it treated its copper miners as lowly tribute laborers.

By controlling access to tin and copper and to the production of bronze, the Shang rulers prevented their rivals from forging bronze weapons and thus increased their own power and legitimacy. With their superior weapons, Shang armies by 1300 BCE could easily destroy armies wielding wooden clubs and stone-tipped spears.

NONMILITARY USE OF CHARIOTS Chariots entered the Central Plains of China together with nomads from the north around 1200 BCE, more than 500 years after the Hittites had used these vehicles to dominate much of Southwest Asia. Although upper classes quickly assimilated them, chariots were not at first used extensively for military purposes and never achieved the military importance in China that they did elsewhere in Afro-Eurasia. The lesser use of chariots in the Shang era may have been because the large Shang infantry forces were able to awe their enemies by

sheer size and forged bronze weaponry. In Shang times, the chariots were used mostly for hunting and as a mark of high status, although Chinese chariots were much better built than those of their neighbors, having been improved by the addition of bronze fittings and harnesses. They were also larger than most of those in use in Egypt and Southwest Asia, accommodating three men standing in a box mounted on 18- or 26-spoke wheels. As symbols of power and wealth, chariots were often buried with their owners.

Rather than employ chariots to defend their borders against neighboring states and pastoral nomads on the central Asian steppes, the Shang created armies composed mainly of foot soldiers, armed with axes, spears, arrowheads, shields, and helmets, all made of bronze. These forces prevailed at first, but eventually they lost ground, and the Shang territorial domain shrank until the regime was unable to resist invasion, in 1045 BCE, from its western neighbor and former tributary, the Zhou, who may have employed chariots in overcoming the much larger Shang armies.

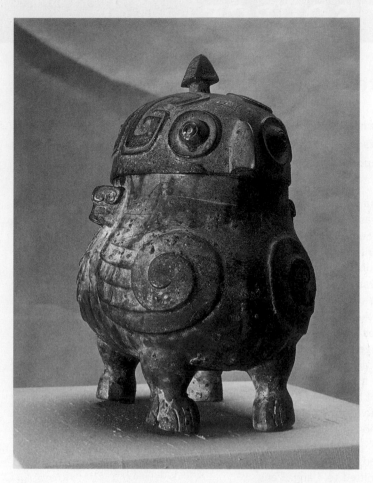

Bronze. *At the height of the Shang state, circa 1200 BCE, its rulers erected massive palaces at the capital of Yin, which required bronze foundries for its wine and food vessels. In these foundries, skilled workers produced bronze weapons and ritual objects and elaborate ceremonial drinking and eating vessels, like the one pictured.*

As a patchwork of regimes, East Asia did not rise to the level of military-diplomatic jostling seen in Southwest Asia. Other large states developed alongside the Shang. These included relatively urban and wealthy peoples in the southeast and more rustic peoples bordering the Shang. The latter traded with the former, whom they knew as the Fang—their label for those who lived in non-Shang areas. Other kingdoms in the south and southwest also had independent bronze industries, with casting technologies comparable to those of the Shang. Nonetheless, Shang metalworking and the incorporation of chariots enabled the Shang state to expand territorially and to dominate its neighbors.

Agriculture and Tribute

The Shang rulers understood the importance of agriculture for winning and maintaining power, so they did much to promote its development. In fact, the activities of local governors and the masses revolved around agriculture. The rulers controlled their own farms, which supplied food to the ruling family, craftworkers, and the army. New technologies led to increased food production. Farmers drained low-lying fields and cleared forested areas to expand the cultivation of millet, wheat, barley, and possibly rice. Their implements included stone plows, spades, and sickles. In addition, farmers cultivated silkworms and raised pigs, dogs, sheep, and oxen. To best use the land and increase production, they tracked the growing season. And to record the seasons, the Shang developed a twelve-month, 360-day lunar calendar; it contained leap months to maintain the proper relationship between months and seasons. The calendar also relieved fears about events such as solar and lunar eclipses by making them predictable.

As in other Afro-Eurasian states, the ruler's wealth and power depended on tribute from elites and allies. Elites supplied warriors and laborers, horses and cattle. Allies sent foodstuffs, soldiers, and workers and "assisted in the king's affairs"—perhaps by hunting, burning brush, or clearing land—in return for his help in defending against invaders and making predictions about the harvest. Commoners sent their tribute to the elites, who held the land as grants from the ruling family. Farmers transferred their surplus crops to the elite landholders (or to the ruler if they worked on his personal landholdings) on a regular schedule.

Tribute could also take the form of turtle shells and cattle scapulas (shoulder blades), which the Shang used for divination. Divining the future was a powerful way to legitimize the rulers' power—and then to justify the right to collect more tribute. By placing themselves symbolically and literally at the center of all exchanges, the Shang rulers reinforced their power over others.

Society and Ritual Practice

The advances in metalworking and agriculture gave the state the resources to create and sustain a complex society. The core organizing principle of Shang society was familial descent traced back many generations to a common male ancestor. Grandparents, parents, sons, and daughters lived and worked together and held property in common, but male family elders took precedence. Women from other patrilines married into the family and won honor when they became mothers, particularly of sons.

The death ritual, which involved sacrificing humans to accompany the deceased in the next life, also reflected the importance of family, male dominance, and social hierarchy. Members of the royal elite were often buried with full entourage, including wives, consorts, servants, chariots, horses, and drivers. The inclusion of personal slaves and servants indicates a belief that the familiar social hierarchy would continue in the afterlife. Modern Chinese historians have described the Shang as a "slave society," but the basis of its economy was not slave labor. Instead, the driving force

The Oracle Bone

About 3,000 years old, the oracle bone below dates from the Shang dynasty reign of King Wu Ding (c. 1200 BCE). Oracle bones enabled diviners to access the other world and provided the ruler with important information about the future. Shang kings often used divination to make political or military decisions and to predict the weather.

A partial translation of the left-hand side of this oracle bone reads:

[Preface:] Crack making on *gui-si* day, Que divined:

[Charge:] In the next ten days there will be no disaster.

[Prognostication:] The king, reading the cracks, said, "There will be no harm; there will perhaps be the coming of alarming news."

[Verification:] When it came to the fifth day, *ding-you*, there really was the coming of alarming news from the west. Zhi Guo, reporting, said, "The Du Fang [a border people] are besieging in our eastern borders and have harmed two settlements." The Gong-fang also raided the fields of our western borders.

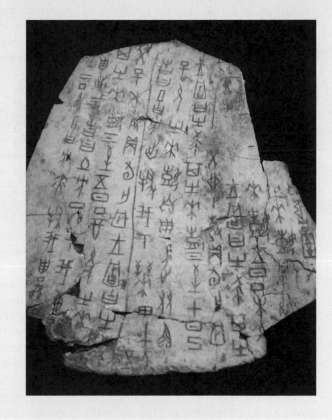

QUESTIONS FOR ANALYSIS

- What political or military decision do you think King Wu Ding might have made in response to the "alarming news"?
- Why did Shang kings rely on oracle bones?

Source: This translation follows, with slight modifications by Bryan W. Van Norden, David N. Keightley, *Sources of Shang History* (Berkeley: University of California Press, 1978), p. 44.

---

was the tribute labor (in particular, metalworking and farming) of the commoners who constituted most of society.

The Shang state was a full-fledged theocracy: it claimed that the ruler at the top of the hierarchy derived his authority through guidance from ancestors and gods. The Shang kings practiced ancestral worship, which was the major form of religious belief in China during this period. Ancestral worship involved performing rituals in which the rulers offered drink and food to their recently dead ancestors with the hope that they would intervene with their more powerful long-dead ancestors on behalf of the living. In finding ritual ways to communicate with ancestors and foretell the future, rulers relied on divination, much as did the rulers in Mesopotamia at this time. The technique involved diviners applying intense heat to the shoulder bones of cattle or to turtle shells and interpreting the cracks that appeared on these objects as auspicious or inauspicious signs from the ancestors regarding the plans and actions of rulers. (See Primary Source: The Oracle Bone.) On these bones scribes subsequently inscribed the queries asked of the ancestors to confirm the diviners' interpretations. Thus, Shang writing began as a dramatic ritual performance in which the living responded to their ancestors' oracular signs.

The **oracle bones** and tortoise shells also offer an invaluable window into the concerns and beliefs of the elite groups of these very distant cultures and often reveal to researchers how similar the worries and interests of these people were to our own concerns today. The questions that seem to have been put to diviners most frequently as they inspected bones and shells were about the weather (hardly surprising in communities so dependent on growing seasons and good harvests), about family health and well-being, and especially about the prospects of having male children, who would extend the family line.

How Languages Spread: The Case of Nomadic Indo-European Languages

Linguistics, or the study of language, is an important tool in world history. Language arose independently in a number of places around the world. All languages change with time, and their divergence from a mother tongue serves as a tool in determining at what point different languages, like German or French, separated from one another. Scholars call related tongues with a common origin "language families." Even though members of the same language family diverged over time, they all share grammatical features and root vocabularies.

Although there are more than 100 language families, a much smaller number have influenced vast geographical areas. For example, the *Altaic* languages spread from central Asia to Europe. The *Sino-Tibetan* language family includes Mandarin, the most widely spoken language in the world. The *Uralic* family, which includes Hungarian and Finnish, occurs mainly in Europe. The *Afro-Asiatic* language family contains several hundred languages spoken in North Africa, sub-Saharan Africa, and Southwest Asia, Semitic languages such as Hebrew and Arabic among them.

One language family that linguists have studied extensively, and the one with the largest number of speakers today, is *Indo-European*. It was identified by scholars who recognized similarities in grammar and vocabulary among classical Sanskrit, Persian, Greek, and Latin. Living languages in this family include English, Irish, German, Norwegian, Portuguese, French, Russian, Persian, Hindi, and Bengali. For the past 200 years, comparative linguists have sought to reconstruct Proto-Indo-European, the parent of all the languages in the family. They have drawn conclusions about its grammar, hypothesizing a highly inflected language with different endings on nouns and verbs according to their use. They have also made suggestions about its vocabulary. For example, after analyzing patterns of linguistic change, scholars have proposed that the basic Indo-European root that means "horse"—in Sanskrit, *a´sva*; Persian, *aspa*; Latin, *equus*; and Greek, *hippos (íppob)*—is *ekwo-.

Table 3.1 demonstrates the similarity of words in some of the major Indo-European languages. We have emphasized numbers, which are especially stable in language systems because people do not like to change the way they count. We have also provided the equivalents in two Semitic languages (Arabic and Hebrew) to show how different these basic words are in another language family (the Afro-Asiatic).

Attempts to locate the homeland of the original speakers of Proto-Indo-European involve mapping the reconstructed vocabulary onto a matching geography. For example, some of the vocabulary contains words for "snow," "mountain," and "swift river," as well as for animals that are not native to Europe, such as "lion," "monkey," and "elephant." Other words describe agricultural practices and farming tools that date back as far as 5000 BCE. Many linguists believe that nomadic and pastoral peoples of the Eurasian steppes took this language—along with their precious horses and chariots—as far as the borderlands of what is now Afghanistan and eastern Iran.

Migration is only one of the possible reasons that languages move and change over vast areas and periods of time. Other influential factors are invasions, climatic conditions, natural resources, and ways of life.

QUESTIONS FOR ANALYSIS

- What relationships does Table 3.1 suggest between the Semitic languages and the Indo-European languages?
- How does the study of linguistics enhance our understanding of human geography?

Explore Further

David W. Anthony, *The Horse, the Wheel, and Language: How Bronze-Age Riders from the Eurasian Steppes Shaped the Modern World* (2007).

Joseph T. Shipley, *The Origins of English Words: A Discursive Dictionary of Indo-European Roots* (2001).

In Shang theocracy, because the ruler was the head of a unified clergy and embodied both religious and political power, no independent priesthood emerged. Diviners and scribes were subordinate to the ruler and the royal pantheon of ancestors he represented. (Unlike in Mesopotamia and Egypt, rulers never entrusted diviners with independent action.) Ancestor worship sanctified Shang control and legitimized the rulers' lineage, ensuring that the ruling family kept all political and religious power.

Because the Shang gods were ancestral deities, the rulers were deified when they died and ranked in descending chronological order. The primary Shang deity was Di, the High God (Shangdi), who was the founding ancestor of the Shang ruling family. Still, Shang rulers when they became gods were thought to be closer to the world of humans than the supreme Egyptian and Mesopotamian gods, and they served to unite the world of the living with the world of the dead. Much as the Egyptians believed their pharaohs (supposedly born of human mothers and godlike fathers) ascended into heaven after their deaths, so the Shang believed their rulers moved into a parallel other world when they died.

TABLE 3.1 | Similarity of Words in Some Major Indo-European Languages

| | WORDS OF COMMON ORIGIN IN INDO-EUROPEAN LANGUAGES | | | | | | SEMITIC LANGUAGES | |
	SANSKRIT	HINDI	GREEK	LATIN	FRENCH	GERMAN	ARABIC	HEBREW
Numbers								
one	eka	ek	hen	unus	un	ein	wahid	ehad
two	dva	do	duo	duo	deux	zwei	ithnin	shnayim
three	tri	teen	treis	tres	trois	drei	Thalatha	shlasha
four	catur	chār	tessara	quattuor	quatre	vier	arba'a	arba'a
five	pañca	pānch	penta	quinque	cinq	fünf	khamsa	hamisha
ten	daśa	das	deka	decem	dix	zehn	ashra	asara
hundred	śata	sau	hekaton	centum	cent	hundert	mi'a	me'a
Other common words								
father	pitṛ	pitā	pater	pater	père	vater	abu	Aba
mother	mātṛ	mātā	mêter	mater	mère	mutter	umm	em
son	sūnu	betā	huios	filius	fils	sohn	ibn	ben
heart	hṛdaya	dil	kardia	cor	coeur	herz	qalb	lev
foot	pada	pair	pous	pes	pied	fuss	qadam	regel
god	deva	dev	theos	deus	dieu	gott	Allah	yahweh

Shang Writing

Once scribes and priests began etching their scripts on oracle bones for the Shang rulers, a predictable evolution took place. In the Shang archaic script of primary images (often called pictographs), the same characters were used for the same sounds in Chinese (such as "ma" for "horse" 馬 or "mother" 媽, which used the same basic graph for the sound of "ma" 馬 but also added the "radical" 女 meaning "female" to designate that the meaning of the graph was "mother"). Such phonetic compounds evolved into formal written graphs, which have endured to the present in East Asia. This graphic-based writing, which is based on stroke order for the graph and which combines sound and meaning, has set China (and later Japan, Korea, and Vietnam) apart from the societies in Mesopotamia and the Mediterranean that rely on syllable- and alphabet-based writing systems. (See Current Trends in World History: How Languages Spread: The Case of Nomadic Indo-European Languages.)

Although Shang scholars probably did not invent writing in East Asia, they perfected it. Evidence for writing in this era comes entirely from Shang oracle bones, which were central to the political and religious authority of the Shang. Other Asian written records may have been recorded on more perishable materials that have not survived. This possibly accidental preservation of Shang–Zhou oracle bones—but nothing else—may explain the major differences between ancient texts in China (primarily divinations on bones) and in Southwest Asian societies that impressed cuneiform on clay tables (primarily for economic transactions, literary and religious documents, and historical records). Compared with Mesopotamia and Egypt, the Shang transition from record keeping (for example, questions to ancestors, lineages of rulers, or economic transactions) to literature (for example, myths about the founding of the state) occurred more slowly. Shang rulers initially monopolized control over writing through their scribes, who positioned the ruling families at the top of the social and political hierarchy. And priests wrote on the oracle bones to address the otherworld and gain information about the future so that the ruling family could remain at the center of the political system.

As Shang China cultivated developments in agriculture, ornate bronze metalworking, and divinatory writing on oracle bones, the state continued to face waves of pastoral nomadic invaders, as seen in other parts of Afro-Eurasia, but on a much smaller scale. Hence, the Shang were influenced by the chariot culture that eventually filtered throughout East Asia; for the Shang, however, chariots served more for ceremonial purposes. Given that so many of the developments in Shang China bolstered the authority of the rulers and the aristocratic elite, it is perhaps not surprising that the chariot in China was initially more a marker of elite status than an effective tool for warfare, which it became under the succeeding Zhou dynasty.

MICROSOCIETIES IN THE SOUTH PACIFIC, THE AEGEAN, NORTHERN EUROPE, AND THE AMERICAS

As environmental circumstances drove pastoral nomads and transhumant herders toward settled agriculturalists, leading ultimately to the development of powerful and somewhat intertwined territorial states in Egypt, Southwest Asia, the Indus River valley, and Shang China, other pressures drove migrations across the South Pacific, the Aegean, the northern frontier of Europe, and the Americas. These migrations led to the development after 2000 BCE of microsocieties—small-scale, fragmented, and dispersed communities that had limited interactions with others.

The South Pacific (2500 BCE–400 CE)

As Afro-Eurasian populations grew and migration and trade brought cultures together, some peoples took to the waters in search of opportunities or refuge. By comparing the vocabularies and grammatical similarities of languages spoken today by the tribal peoples in Taiwan, the Philippines, and Indonesia, scholars can trace the ancient Austronesian-speaking peoples back to coastal South China in the fourth millennium BCE. A first wave of migrants reached the islands of Polynesia. A second wave from Taiwan around 2500 BCE again reached Polynesia and then went beyond into the South Pacific. By 2000 BCE, these peoples had replaced the earlier inhabitants of the East Asian coastal islands, the hunter-gatherers known as the Negritos, who had migrated south from the Asian landmass around 28,000 BCE, during an ice age when the coastal Pacific islands were connected to the Asian mainland.

SEAFARING SKILLS Using their remarkable double-outrigger canoes, which were 60 to 100 feet long and bore huge triangular sails, the early Austronesians crossed the Taiwan Straits and colonized key islands in the Pacific. Their vessels were much more advanced than the simple dugout canoes used in inland waterways. In good weather, double-outrigger canoes could cover more than 120 miles in a day. The invention of a stabilization device for deep-sea sailing sometime after 2500 BCE triggered further Austronesian expansion into the Pacific. By 400 CE, these nomads of the sea had reached most of the South Pacific except for Australia and New Zealand.

Their seafaring skills enabled the Austronesians to monopolize trade wherever they went (as the Phoenicians did during the first half of the first millennium BCE). Among their craftworkers were potters, who produced distinctive Lapita ware (bowls and vessels) on offshore islets or in coastal villages. Archaeological finds reveal that these canoe-building people also conducted interisland trade in New Guinea after 1600 BCE, reaching Fiji, Samoa, and Tonga according to the evidence from pottery fragments and the remains of domesticated animals.

ENVIRONMENT AND CULTURE Pottery, stone tools, and domesticated crops and pigs characterized Austronesian settlements throughout the coastal islands and in the South Pacific. These cultural markers reached the Philippines from Taiwan. By 2500 BCE, according to archaeologists, the same cultural features had spread to the islands of Java, Sumatra, Celebes, Borneo, and Timor. Austronesians arrived in Java and Sumatra in 2000 BCE; by 1600 BCE, they were in Australia and New Guinea, although they failed to penetrate the interior, where descendants of the indigenous peoples still live. The Austronesians then ventured farther eastward into the South Pacific, apparently arriving in Samoa and Fiji in 1200 BCE and on mainland Southeast Asia in 1000 BCE. (See Map 3.5.)

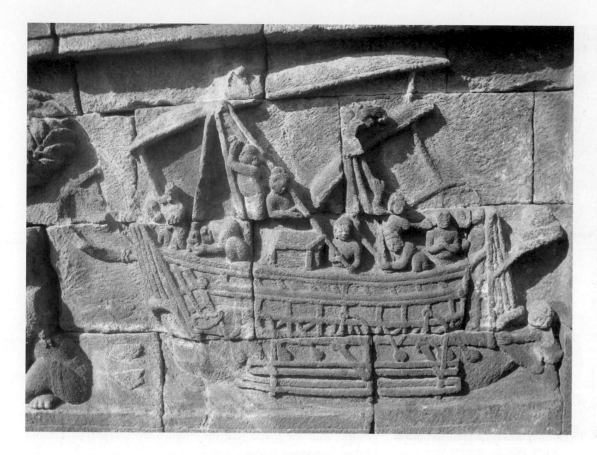

Austronesian Canoe. *Early Austronesians crossed the Taiwan Straits and colonized key islands in the Pacific using double-outrigger canoes from 60 to 100 feet long and equipped with triangular sails. In good weather, such canoes could cover more than 120 miles in a day.*

Equatorial lands in the South Pacific have a tropical or sub-tropical climate and, in many places, fertile soils containing nutrient-rich volcanic ash. In this environment, the Austronesians cultivated dry-land crops (yams and sweet potatoes), irrigated crops (more yams, which grew better in paddy fields or in rainy areas), and tree crops (breadfruit, bananas, and coconuts). In addition, colonized areas beyond the landmass, such as the islands of Indonesia, had labyrinthine coastlines rich in maritime resources, including coral reefs and mangrove swamps teeming with wildlife. Island hopping led the adventurers to encounter new food sources, but the shallow waters and reefs offered sufficient fish and shellfish for their needs.

In the South Pacific, the Polynesian descendants of the early Austronesians shared a common culture, language, technology, and store of domesticated plants and animals. These later seafarers came from many different island communities (hence the name *Polynesian,* "belonging to many islands"), and after they settled down, their numbers grew. Their crop surpluses allowed more densely populated communities to support craft specialists and soldiers. Most settlements boasted ceremonial buildings to promote local solidarity and forts to provide defense. On larger islands, communities often cooperated and organized workforces to enclose ponds for fish production and to build and maintain large irrigation works for agriculture. In terms of political structure, Polynesian communities ranged from tribal or village units to multi-island alliances that sometimes invaded other areas.

The Austronesians reached the Marquesas Islands in the central Pacific, strategically located for northern and southern exploration, around 200 CE. Over the next few centuries, some moved on to Easter Island to the south and Hawaii to the north. The immense 30-ton stone structures on Easter Island represent the monumental Polynesian architecture produced after their arrival. In separate migrations they traversed the Indian Ocean westward and arrived at the island of Madagascar by the sixth century CE. Along the way, they transmitted crops such as the banana to East Africa.

The expansion of East Asian peoples throughout the South Pacific and their trade back and forth did not, however, integrate the islands into a mainland-style culture. Expansion could not overcome the tendency of these microsocieties, dispersed across a huge ocean, toward fragmentation and isolation.

The Aegean World (2000–1200 BCE)

In the region around the Aegean Sea, the islands and the mainland of present-day Greece—in short, the island world of the eastern Mediterranean—initially resembled that of the South Pacific. No single power emerged before the second millennium BCE. Settled agrarian communities developed into local polities linked only by trade and culture. Fragmentation was the norm—in part because the landscape had no great river-basin systems or large common plain.

Seaborne Trade. *The size of the seaborne trade is revealed most spectacularly in the shipwrecks recovered by underwater archaeologists. One of these ships, sunk off the southern coast of Anatolia around 1325 BCE, was transporting 10 tons of copper in 354 oxhide-shaped ingots, as well as more than 100 amphorae (large, two-handled jars) containing all kinds of high-value commodities.*

As an unintended benefit of the lack of centralization, there was no single regime to collapse when the droughts arrived. Thus, in the second millennium BCE, peoples of the eastern Mediterranean did not struggle to recover lost grandeur. Rather, they enjoyed a remarkable though gradual development, making advances based on influences they absorbed from Southwest Asia, Egypt, and Europe. It was a time when residents of Aegean islands like Crete and Thera enjoyed extensive trade with the Greek mainland, Egypt, Anatolia, Syria, and Palestine. It was also a time of population movements from the Danube region and central Europe into the Mediterranean. Groups of these migrants settled in mainland Greece in the centuries after 1900 BCE; modern archaeologists have named them Mycenaeans after the famous palace at Mycenae, in the Greek Peloponnese, that dates to this era. Soon after settling in their new environment, the Mycenaeans turned to the sea to look for resources and interaction with their neighbors.

At the outset, the main influence on the Aegean world came from the east by sea. As the institutions and ideas that had developed in Southwest Asia moved westward, they found a ready reception along the coasts and on the islands of the Mediterranean. These innovations followed the sea currents, moving up the eastern seaboard of the Levant, then to the island of Cyprus and along the southern coast of Anatolia, and then westward to the islands of the Aegean Sea and to Crete. Trade was the main source of eastern influences, with vessels carrying cargoes from island to island and up and down the commercial centers along the coast. (See Map 3.6.)

The Mediterranean islands were important hubs that linked the mainland peoples of western Asia and Europe with the islanders. They also served as a springboard from which eastern influences shot northward into Europe. By 1500 BCE, the islands were booming. Trade centered on tin from the east and readily available copper, both essential for making bronze (the primary metal in tools and weapons). Islands located in the midst of the active sea-lanes flourished. Because Cyprus straddled the main sea-lane, it was a focal point of trade. It also had large reserves of copper ore, which started to generate intense activity around 2300 BCE. By 2000 BCE, harbors on the southern and eastern sides of the island were shipping and transshipping goods, along with copper ingots, as far west as Crete, east to the Euphrates River, and south to Egypt. So identified was this island with the metal that the English word *copper* is derived from the name Cyprus.

MINOAN CULTURE Crete, too, was an active trading node in the Mediterranean, with networks reaching as far east as Mesopotamia. Its culture reflected outside influences as well as local traditions. Around 2000 BCE, a large number of independent palace centers began to emerge on Crete, at Knossos and elsewhere. Scholars have named the people who built these elaborate centers the Minoans, after the legendary King Minos, who may have ruled Crete at this time. The Minoans sailed back and forth across the Mediterranean, and by 1600 BCE they were colonizing other Aegean islands as trading and mining centers. The Minoans' wealth soon became a magnet for the Mycenaeans, their mainland competitors, who took over Crete around 1400 BCE.

As the island communities traded with the peoples of Southwest Asia, they borrowed some ideas but also kept their own cultural traditions. In terms of borrowing, the monumental architecture of Southwest Asia found small-scale echoes in the Aegean world—notably in the palace complexes built on Crete between 1900 and 1600 BCE (the most impressive was at Knossos). Unlike in Mesopotamia or Egypt, however, microsocieties (small-scale insular communities) remained the norm for human organization on these Aegean islands.

Worship on the islands focused on a female deity, the Lady, but there are no traces of large temple complexes similar to those in Mesopotamia, Anatolia, and Egypt. Nor, apparently, was there any priestly class of the type that managed the temple

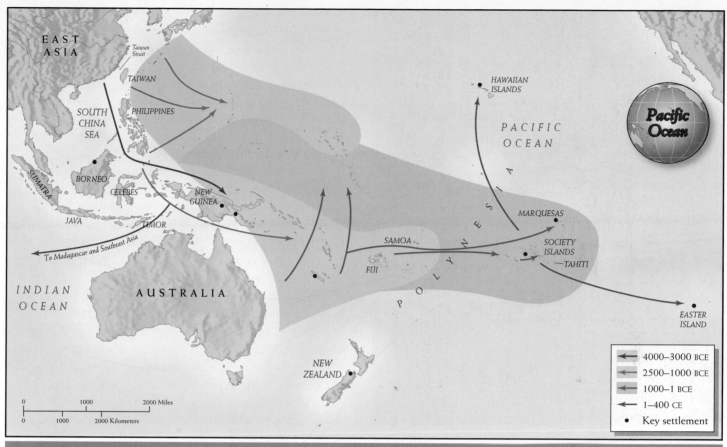

MAP 3.5 | Austronesian Migrations

The Pacific Ocean saw many migrations from East Asia.

- Where did the Austronesian migrants come from?
- What were the boundaries of their migration?
- Why, unlike other migratory people during the second millennium BCE, did Austronesian settlers in Polynesia become a world apart?

complexes of Southwest Asian societies. Moreover, it is unclear whether these island societies had full-time scribes.

There was significant regional diversity within this small Aegean world. On Thera, a small island to the north of Crete, archaeologists have uncovered a splendid trading city—one that was not centered on a major palace complex—in which private houses had bathrooms with toilets and running water and rooms decorated with exotic wall paintings. One painting depicted a flotilla of pleasure, trading, and naval vessels. On Crete, the large palace-centered communities controlled centrally organized societies of a high order of refinement. Confident in their wealth and power, the sprawling palaces had no fortifications and no natural defenses. They were light, airy, and open to their surrounding landscapes.

MYCENAEAN CULTURE The Mycenaean culture was more war oriented than that of the peaceful, seafaring Minoans. When

the Mycenaeans migrated to Greece from central Europe, they brought their Indo-European language, their horse chariots, and their metalworking skills. Their move was gradual, lasting from about 1850 to 1600 BCE, but ultimately they dominated the indigenous population. Known for their exceptional height, they maintained their dominance with their powerful weapon, the chariot, until 1200 BCE. Indeed, horse chariots were important in their mythology and cultural tradition. The battle chariots and festivities of chariot racing described in the epic poetry of Homer (which dates from after the collapse of Mycenaean societies) express memories of glorious chariot feats that echo Vedic legends from South Asia (see p. 98).

The Mycenaean material culture emphasized displays of weaponry, portraits of armed soldiers, and illustrations of violent conflicts. The main palace centers at Tiryns and Mycenae were the hulking fortresses of warlords surrounded by rough-hewn stone walls and strategically located atop large rock

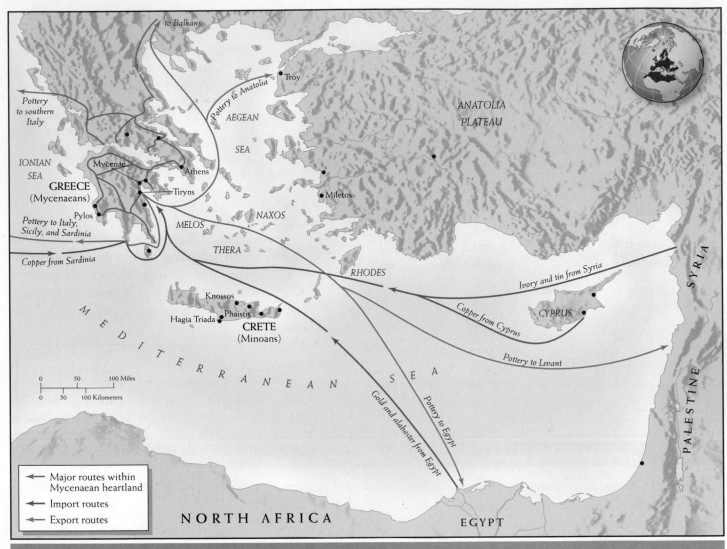

to Balkans

Pottery to southern Italy

Pottery to Anatolia

Troy

AEGEAN

SEA

ANATOLIA PLATEAU

IONIAN SEA

Mycenae

Athens

GREECE (Mycenaeans)

Tiryns

Pottery to Italy, Sicily, and Sardinia

Pylos

NAXOS

MELOS

Miletos

THERA

Copper from Sardinia

RHODES

M E D I T E R R A N E A N

Knossos

Phaistis

Hagia Triada

CRETE (Minoans)

Ivory and tin from Syria

S Y R I A

Copper from Cyprus

CYPRUS

Pottery to Levant

P A L E S T I N E

S E A

Gold and alabaster from Egypt

Pottery to Egypt

NORTH AFRICA

EGYPT

0   50   100 Miles
0   50   100 Kilometers

⟵ Major routes within Mycenaean heartland

⟵ Import routes

⟵ Export routes

MAP 3.6 | Trade in the Eastern Mediterranean World

Greece, Egypt, and Cyprus were trade hubs in the eastern Mediterranean.

- What were the major commodities that were traded in the eastern Mediterranean?
- Why did trade originally move from east to west?
- What role did geography play in the Mycenaeans' defeat of the Minoans?

outcroppings. The Mycenaeans amassed an amazing amount of wealth and carried some of it to their graves. Their tombs contain many gold vessels and decorations; most ostentatious were the gold masks. The many amber beads indicate that the warriors had contact with inhabitants of the coniferous forest regions in northern Europe.

Southwest Asian economic and political structures shaped the coastal sites where the Mycenaeans settled, such as Tiryns and Pylos. Massive stone fortresses and fortified palaces dominated these urban hubs. A preeminent ruler (*wanax*) stood atop a complex bureaucratic hierarchy; numerous subordinates aided him, including slaves. At the heart of the palace society

were scribes, who recorded the goods and services allotted to local farmers, shepherds, and metalworkers, among others. (See Primary Source: Linear A and B—Writing in the Early Mediterranean Worlds.)

Mycenaean expansion eventually overwhelmed the Minoans on Crete. The Mycenaeans also created colonies and trading settlements, reaching as far as Sicily and southern Italy. In this fashion, the trade and language of the early Greek speaking peoples created a veneer of unity linking the dispersed worlds of the Aegean Sea.

At the close of the second millennium BCE, the eastern Mediterranean faced internal and external convulsions that ended

Palace at Knossos. *An artist's reconstruction of the Minoan palace at Knossos, on Crete. This complex, the largest such center on the island, covered more than 6 acres and contained more than 1,300 rooms. Its main feature was a large, open-air central courtyard, around which were arranged the storage, archive, ritual, and ceremonial rooms. Rather than the complex cities that would emerge later, the urbanized centers on Crete were represented by these large complexes, similar to palace complexes in contemporary Levantine sites.*

the heyday of these microsocieties. Most notable was a series of migrations of peoples from central Europe who moved through southeastern Europe, Anatolia, and the eastern Mediterranean (see Chapter 4). The invasions, although often destructive, did not extinguish but rather reinforced the creative potential of

this frontier area. Following the upheaval at the close of the millennium, a new social order emerged that was destined to have an even greater brilliance and influence. Because theirs was a closed maritime world—in comparison with the wide-open Pacific—the Greek-speaking peoples around the Aegean quickly reasserted dominance in the eastern Mediterranean that the Austronesians did not match in Southeast Asia or Polynesia.

Europe—The Northern Frontier

The transition to settled agriculture and the raising of domesticated animals took longer in western Afro-Eurasia than in the rest of the landmass. Two millennia passed, from 5000 to 3000 BCE, before settled agriculture became the dominant economic form in Europe. In many areas, hunters and gatherers clung to their traditional ways. Even this frontier, however, saw occasional visits from peoples driving horse chariots during the second millennium.

Forbidding evergreen forests dominated the northern area of the far western stretches of Europe, and the area's sparse population was slow to implement the new ways. The first agricultural communities were frontier settlements where pioneers broke new land. Surrounded by hunting and foraging communities, these innovators lived hard lives in harsh environments, overcoming their isolation only by creating regional alliances. Such arrangements were too unstable to initiate or sustain long-distance trade. These were not fertile grounds for creating powerful kingdoms.

Aegean Fresco. *This is one of the more striking wall paintings, or frescoes, discovered by archaeologists in the 1970s and 1980s at Akrotiri, on the island of Thera (Santorini) in the Aegean Sea. Its brilliant colors, especially the blue of the sea, evoke the lively essence of Minoan life on the island. Note the houses of the wealthy along the port and the flotilla of ships that reflects the seaborne commerce that was beginning to flourish in the Mediterranean in this period.*

Mycenaean Sword. *The hilt and engraved gold pommel of a sword from the regal burials at the site of Mycenae. The presence of this weaponry, both depicted in the art of the period and preserved in artifacts buried with the dead, was typical of a violent society with a warrior elite. The riveted hilt and the bronze sword blade are of a kind found widely distributed in the Mediterranean, following the patterns of Mycenaean trade routes.*

gradually shifted from a primitive agriculture to an economy based on the herding of animals. In this zone, the exploitation of the horse fostered a highly mobile culture in which whole communities moved on horseback or by means of large wheeled wagons. Because these pastoral nomads regularly sought out the richer agricultural lands in central Europe, there was constant hostility between the two worlds.

These struggles among settlers, hunter-gatherers, and nomadic horse riders bred cultures with a strong warrior ethos. The fullest development of this mounted horse culture occurred in the centuries after 1000 BCE, when the steppe-land Scythian peoples engaged in rituals (such as drinking blood) that forged bonds of blood brotherhood among warriors and heightened their aggressive behavior. This rough-and-tumble frontier gave its people an appetite to borrow more effective means of waging war. Europeans desired the nomadic people's weaponry, and over time their dealings with the horsemen took the form of trade as well as warfare. The Europeans adopted horses and finer metalworking technologies from the Caucasus. Of course, such trade made their battles even more lethal. And while the connections between this frontier zone and other parts of the Afro-Eurasian world began to multiply, the frontier was still too dispersed and unruly to develop integrated kingdoms.

Recent fossil discoveries along the banks of the Tollense River, a narrow stream of water that flows through northern Germany toward the Baltic Sea, reveal that these societies were as ready to engage in deadly warfare as the empires already discussed in this chapter. Here, more than 4,000 warriors engaged in a territorial battle around 1200 BCE, using war clubs, spears, knives, and swords made of wood, flint, and the newly arrived and most deadly of the metals, bronze, with which warriors tipped their arrows. We know about this battle because archaeologists from the University of Griefswald and a nearby independent Department of Historical Preservation uncovered, lodged in swampy marshes, the skeletal remains of men who had died from battle wounds. The dig, which is ongoing and likely to provide more skeletons, so far has yielded the remains of 5 horses and 100 men. The scale of the battle astonished the researchers and prompted the codirector of the dig to assert that "there's nothing to compare to it [in this period in northern Europe]" (Curry, p. 1386). The battle brought together warriors from distant regions, and the fossils to this day represent the only nonwritten, archaeological record of the ancient worlds' most massive and lethal conflict. Even so, at a time when the

The early European cultivators adopted the techniques for controlling plants and animals that Southwest Asian peoples had developed. But rather than establishing large, hierarchical, and centralized societies, the Europeans used these techniques to create self-sufficient communities. They did not incorporate the other cultural and political features that characterized the societies of Egypt, Mesopotamia, and the eastern Mediterranean. Occasional innovations such as the working of metal (initially, copper), the manufacture of pottery, and the use of the plow had little impact on local conditions. Throughout this period, Europe was hardly a developed cultural center. Instead, it was a wild frontier.

Two significant changes affected the northern frontier: the domestication of the horse and the emergence of wheeled chariots and wagons, both achieved in the eastern steppe lands. Both became instruments of war, and both promoted adaptation to the grassy lands of inner and central Europe, where pasturing animals in large herds proved profitable. The success of this horse culture led to the creation of several new frontiers, including those of agriculturally self-sustaining communities.

The new agriculturalists faced constant challenges, not just within Europe but also to the east as they entered the rolling grasslands of central Eurasia. Their attempts to enter this zone usually met overpowering resistance by fierce men on horseback. The inhabitants of the steppe lands north of the Black Sea

PRIMARY SOURCE

Linear A and B—Writing in the Early Mediterranean Worlds

On the island of Crete and on the mainland of Greece, scribes working in the palace-centered societies kept records on clay tablets in two scripts that were linear. Linear A script, apparently written in Minoan, has not yet been deciphered. Linear B was deciphered in the 1950s and proved that, contrary to what almost all classical scholars had assumed, the Linear B tablets were the work of speakers of Mycenaean—an early form of Greek.

Massive numbers of these clay tablets have survived. Noting every detail of the goods and services that the palace bureaucracy managed, they contain lists short and long of persons or things—about as interesting as modern grocery lists. The following tablet from Pylos on the Greek mainland notes how much seed grain the bureaucrats were distributing to rural landholders who were dependent on the ruler.

This is a typical Linear B document inscribed on clay with linear marks representing syllables and signs. The clay tablet was stored in a palace archive. This tablet came from the excavated Mycenaean palace at Pylos, on the mainland of Greece.

The plot of Qelequhontas: this much seed: 276 l. of wheat

R. slave of the god, holds a lease: so much seed: 12 l. of wheat

W. the priest holds a lease: so much seed: 12 l. of wheat

Thuriatis, female slave of the god, dependant of P. the old man: so much seed: 108 l. of wheat

The plot of Admaos, so much seed: 216 l. of wheat. . . .

T. slave of the god, holds a lease: so much seed: 32 l. of wheat

The plot of A . . . eus, so much seed: 144 l. of wheat. . . .

The plot of T. slave of the god, holds a lease: 18 l. of wheat

The plot of R., so much seed: 138 l. of wheat. . . .

The plot of Aktaios, so much seed: 384 l. of wheat. . . .

This is an example of the earlier Linear A script, used to write the non-Greek language of the Minoans. Because evidence of the script has appeared only on the island of Crete, scholars believe that the Minoan palace elites were the sole users of the script (probably for keeping records). This example came from the small palace site at Hagia Triada.

QUESTIONS FOR ANALYSIS

- Notice that all the people identified in this passage are going to plant wheat. How does this underscore the blending of agriculture with war making in the aggressive Mycenaean society?

- What does this document suggest is the function of writing in these societies?

Source: M. Ventris and J. Chadwick, *Documents in Mycenaean Greek*, 2nd ed. (Cambridge: Cambridge University Press, 1973), doc. 116.

The Warrior Vase. *This detail from a large krater, discovered by Heinrich Schliemann in the Mycenae acropolis, depicts Mycenaean warriors in full armor ready to depart for battle. They wear helmets, cuirasses, greaves, and shields, with sacks of supplies hanging from their spears.*

Steppe Horse Culture. *This gold comb from the early fourth century BCE is decorated with a battle scene from a Scythian heroic epic and illustrates the fascination of these European peoples with horses, weapons, and warfare.*

rest of Afro-Eurasia was developing an interrelated network of large territorial states, Europe remained a land of war-making, small chieftainships.

Early States in the Americas

Across all the Americas, river valleys and coasts sheltered villages and towns drawing sustenance from the rich resources in their hinterlands. Hunting and gathering was still the main lifeway here. But without beasts of burden or domesticated animals to carry loads or plow fields, local communities produced limited surpluses. Local trade involved only luxuries and symbolic trade goods, such as shells, feathers, hides, and precious metals and gems.

In the Central Andes, however, archaeologists have found evidence of early state systems that transcended local communities to function as confederations, or alliances of towns. These were not as well integrated as many of the territorial states of Southwest Asia, the Indus Valley, and China; they were more like settlements in Europe and the eastern Mediterranean,

where towns traded basic goods and in some cases cooperated to resist aggressors.

The region's varied ecology promoted the development of such confederations. Along the arid coast of what is now Peru, fishermen harvested the currents teeming with large and small fish; this was a staple that, when dried, was hardly perishable and easy to transport. The rivers flowing down from the Andean mountains fanned out through the desert, often carving out basins suitable for agriculture. And where the mountains rose from the Pacific, rainfall and higher altitudes favored extensive pasturelands. Here roamed wild llamas and alpacas—difficult as beasts of burden, but valued for their wool in textile production. Such ecological diversity within a limited area promoted greater trade among subregions and towns. Indeed, the interchange of manioc (root of the cassava plant), chili peppers, dried fish, and wool gave rise to the commercial networks that could support political ones.

Communities on the coast, in the riverbeds, or in the mountain valleys were small but numerous. They took shape around central plazas, most of which had large platforms with special burial chambers for elders and persons of importance. Clusters of dwellings surrounded these centers. Much of what we know about political and economic transactions among these communities—as well as long-distance trade and statecraft—comes from the offerings and ornaments left in the burial chambers. Painted gourds, pottery, and fine textiles illustrate the increasing contact between cultures, often bound in alliances.

For instance, marriage between noble families could strengthen a pact or confederation.

One early site known as Aspero reveals how a local community evolved into a form of chiefship, with a political elite and diplomatic and trading ties with neighbors. Temples straddled the top of the central platform, and the large structure at the center boasted lavish ornamentation. Also, there is evidence that smaller communities around Aspero sent crops (fruits) and fish (anchovies) to Aspero as part of an intercommunity system of mutual dependence.

Not all politics among the valley peoples of Peru consisted of trade and diplomacy, however. In the Casma Valley, near the Pacific coast, a clay and stone architectural complex at Cerro Sechín has revealed a much larger sprawl of dwellings and plazas dating back to 1700 BCE. Around the community's central structure stood a wall composed of hundreds of massive stone tablets, carved with ornate etchings of warriors, battles, prisoners, executions, and human body parts. The warriors' clothing is simple and rustic, and the main weapon resembles a club. Clearly, warfare accompanied the first expressions of statecraft in the Americas.

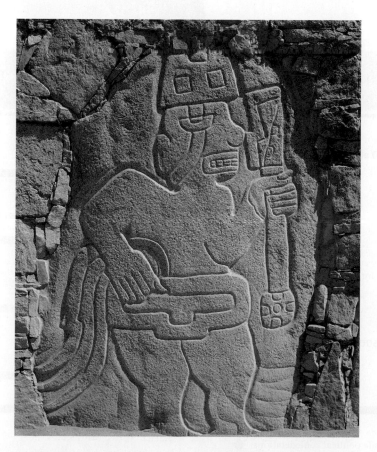

Cerro Sechín Artifact. *This stele of a warrior brandishing a club was discovered in the Casma Valley, in present-day Peru, and is a good example of the many striking stone sculptures found in this area.*

CONCLUSION

The second millennium BCE was an era of migrations, warfare, and kingdom building in Afro-Eurasia. Whereas river-basin societies had flourished in the fourth and third millennia BCE in Mesopotamia, Egypt, and the Indus Valley, now droughts and deserts shook the agrarian foundations of their economies. Old states crumbled; from the steppes and plateaus nomadic pastoralists and transhumant herders descended in search of food, grazing lands, and plunder. As transhumant herders pressed into the river-basin societies, the social and political fabric of these communities changed. Likewise, horse-riding nomads from steppe communities in inner Eurasia conquered and settled in the agrarian states, bringing key innovations. Foremost were the horse chariots, which became a military catalyst sparking the evolution from smaller states to large kingdoms encompassing crowded cities and vast hinterlands. The nomads and herders also adopted many of the settled peoples' beliefs and customs. On land and sea, migrating peoples created zones of long-distance trade that linked agrarian societies.

The Nile Delta, the basin of the Tigris and Euphrates Rivers, the Indus Valley, and the Yellow River basin were worlds apart before 2000 BCE. Now trade and conquest brought many of these societies into closer contact, especially those in Southwest Asia and the Nile River basin. Here, the interaction even led to an elaborate system of diplomatic relations. The first territorial states appeared in this millennium, composed of communities living under common laws and customs. An alliance of farmers and warriors united agrarian wealth and production with political power to create and defend extended territories. The new arrangements overshadowed the nomads' historic role as predators and enabled them to become military elites. Through taxes and drafted labor, villagers repaid their rulers for local security and state-run diplomacy.

The rhythms of state formation differed where regimes were not closely packed together. In East Asia, the absence of strong rivals allowed the emerging Shang dynasty to develop more gradually. Where landscapes had sharper divisions—as in the island archipelagos of the South China Sea or in northern Europe, the Aegean, and the South Pacific—small-scale, decentralized microsocieties emerged. This was true above all in the Americas, where the lack of wheeled vehicles and horses made long-distance communication much more challenging—and inhibited rulers' territorial ambitions. Here, too, microsocieties were the norm. But fragmentation is not the same as isolation. Even peoples on the fringes and the subjects of microsocieties were not entirely secluded from the increasing flow of technologies, languages, goods, and migrants.

After You Read This Chapter

Go to INQUIZITIVE to see what you know & learn what you've missed.

TRACING THE GLOBAL STORYLINES

FOCUS ON: *The Emergence of Territorial States*

Egypt and Southwest Asia

- Invasions by nomads and transhumant herders lead to the creation of larger territorial states: New Kingdom Egypt, Hittites, Babylonia, and Kassites.
- A centuries-long peaceful era, "The Community of Major Powers," emerges among the major states as the result of shrewd statecraft and diplomacy.

Indus River Valley

- Migratory Vedic peoples from the steppes of inner Eurasia use charioteer technology and rely on domesticated animals to spread out and begin integrating the northern half of South Asia.

Shang State (China)

- Shang dynasts promote improvements in metalworking, agriculture, and the development of writing, leading to the growth of China's first major state.

Microsocieties

- Substantial increases in population, migrations, and trade lead to the emergence of microsocieties among peoples in the South Pacific (Austronesians), the Aegean world (Minoans and Mycenaeans), the northern frontier of Europe, and the Americas.

CHRONOLOGY

	2500 BCE	2000 BCE	1500 BCE
Egypt and Southwest Asia	Middle Kingdom in Egypt **2055–1650 BCE**		Hammurapi's Babylonia **1792–1750 BCE**
South Asia		Vedic migration into Indus River valley begins **1500 BCE**	
East Asia			
The Mediterranean	Minoan culture in Aegean **2000–1600 BCE**		
South Pacific			
The Americas	Emergence of small-scale political confederations in Central Andes **1700 BCE**		

STUDY QUESTIONS

1. **Identify** the effects of climate change on human settlement patterns in the second millennium BCE.

2. **Explain** the impact of transhumant herders and pastoral nomads on settled communities.

3. **Analyze** the impact on Afro-Eurasia of the domestication of horses and the invention of the chariot. How did these developments affect both nomadic and settled peoples?

4. **Define** territorial state. **Compare and contrast** the ways in which territorial states formed across Afro-Eurasia and interacted with one another.

5. **Identify** the great territorial states of western Asia and North Africa during the second millennium BCE. **Describe** their relationships with one another. How did they pioneer international diplomacy?

6. **Describe** the Shang state in East Asia. How was it similar to and different from the territorial states of western Afro-Eurasia?

7. **Identify** where microsocieties developed in the South Pacific, the Aegean, northern Europe, and the Americas. **Analyze** how geographical factors affected the development of each.

8. **Explain** why early state structures were smaller and less integrated in Europe and the Central Andes than the territorial states that arose elsewhere. How similar and different were the early state structures in Europe and the Central Andes?

New Kingdom in Egypt **1550–1069 BCE**

Kassite rule in Mesopotamia **1475–1125 BCE**

Community of Major Powers **1400–1200 BCE**

Vedic migration into Ganges River valley begins **1000 BCE**

Shang State **1600–1046 BCE**

Mycenaean culture in Greece and Aegean **1850–1200 BCE**

Austronesian migrations **2500 BCE—500 CE**

1000 BCE   500 CE   1 CE

Before You Read This Chapter

Go to INQUIZITIVE to see what you know & learn what you've missed.

GLOBAL STORYLINES

- Climate change, migrations, technological advances, and administrative innovations contribute to the development of the world's first great empires.
- The Assyrian peoples of the Neo-Assyrian Empire and then the Persians employ two different approaches to consolidate and maintain empires in Southwest Asia.
- South Asia becomes more culturally integrated despite the absence of a strong, centralized political authority.
- East Asia under the Zhou state establishes loose political integration.

CHAPTER OUTLINE

4

First Empires and Common Cultures in Afro-Eurasia, 1250–325 BCE

FOCUS QUESTIONS

- What factors led to the rise of early empires and states in the centuries after 1200 BCE? What were the main characteristics of each?

- What are the similarities and differences in the ways empires formed, or did not form, in Southwest Asia, South Asia, and East Asia?

- What was the nature of the connection between empires and war, religion, and trade?

- How did the emergence of empires affect peoples on the peripheries? What types of relationships developed between these individuals and the empire?

Sennacherib—ruler of the Assyrian Empire early in the seventh century BCE—wrote that at the end of one successful campaign he took "200,150 people, great and small, male and female, horses, mules, asses, camels, and sheep without number." Those captives who resisted were dragged back to Assyria and forced to labor on Sennacherib's expanding, magnificent capital, Nineveh, and toiled on the immense irrigation works to open up new agricultural frontiers.

The booty that Sennacherib took away was unheard of in earlier ages. The immensity of his conquest highlights the arrival of a new era that involved states with even larger geographical, political, economic, and cultural ambitions and achievements. In fact, the prosperity and bounty of the first millennium BCE were the fruits of a wave of disorder across Afro-Eurasia that swept away almost all of the territorial states described in Chapter 3. As these states collapsed, their successors were replacements, not descendants.

The key factors shaping human development were warfare spurred by military innovation and radical climate change that drove many of the warrior/political leaders from the fringes of formerly powerful territorial states to the centers of power. Hybrid societies appeared in

Assyria, Persia, Vedic parts of South Asia, and Zhou China, where new imperial ideologies and religious beliefs were elaborated in support of the new states. Under the protection of fierce warriors, cities and hinterlands came together under a single ruler. Farming yields increased and populations grew. The expansion of territorial power by means of conquest led to the integration of increasingly larger states, some of which became the first empires. Also, on the fringes of formerly great empires, microsocieties—often in close contact with these states—arose and made significant contributions to human development. While seafaring peoples, moving down from the Danube River to the Black Sea, brought political upheaval to the peoples living in southeastern Europe, the Aegean, and the eastern Mediterranean, the Phoenicians provided Afro-Eurasia a simplified alphabet; the Israelites espoused a strict monotheism; and the Greek city-states came to the fore and began to challenge the power of the Persian Empire.

PRESSURES LEADING TO UPHEAVAL AND THE RISE OF EARLY EMPIRES

Although the new, bigger states built on the achievements of earlier complex societies, they also developed in response to new pressures. Four related pressures shaped the development of these early empires in the first millennium BCE: climate change, migrations, new technologies, and administrative innovations. Migrants driven by climate change mingled with settled peoples. Ambitious leaders used innovations in technology and administration to create new states that went on to conquer other kingdoms. Gradually, a new political organization came into being: the empire. An **empire** is a group of states or different ethnic groups brought together under a single sovereign power. With varying degrees and types of centralization, empires connected distant regions through common languages, unifying political systems, trade, and shared religious beliefs.

Climate Change and Migrations

Beginning around 1200 BCE, yet another prolonged drought gripped Afro-Eurasia, causing profound social upheavals and migrations and sweeping away most of the states that had been dominant up to that time. All across Afro-Eurasia, societies entered a two-century period of decline: artistic representation and large-scale construction diminished, urban centers ceased to exist, trading and shipping ebbed, and record keeping and

much else disappeared. Communities were smaller, technically simpler, impoverished, illiterate, and more violent.

Climate change and drought forced nomadic and seminomadic populations that had lived at the edge of settled societies out of their home territories and into the lands of the settled communities. Many of these nomadic peoples who had enjoyed rapid population growth now found themselves unable to support such large numbers, causing them to leave their homes in search of food and fertile land. (See Map 4.1.) Renewed migrations disrupted urban societies and destroyed the administrative centers of kings, priests, and dynasties, leaving the way open for new states to develop, but only after many centuries of turmoil and economic decline.

These migrations were usually violent. Invaders, moving out of loosely organized peripheral societies, assaulted the urban centers and territorial kingdoms of mainland Greece, Crete, Anatolia, Mesopotamia, and Egypt, causing the collapse of many of these once-powerful states. Marauders from the Mediterranean basin and the Syrian Desert upset the diplomatic relations and the elaborate system of international trade that had linked Southwest Asia and North Africa. In East Asia, nomads from the steppes of inner Eurasia tangled with the Shang authorities in the Yellow River valley and eventually overwhelmed the regime. In the Indus Valley of South Asia, waves of nomads pressed down from the northwest, lured by fertile lands to the south. Once there, they settled down and became an agrarian people.

New Technologies

Technological innovations were crucial in reconstructing communities that had been devastated by drought and violent population movements. Advances in the use of pack camels, seaworthy vessels, iron tools for cultivation, and iron weapons for warfare facilitated the rise of empires. The first-millennium empires in Southwest Asia were centralized and militarized states that used force to expand their boundaries, and here the role of changing technology was significant.

PACK CAMELS The camel became the chief overland agent of change during this period, helping to open up trade routes across the Syrian and Arabian Deserts. The fat stored in camels' humps allows them to survive long journeys and harsh desert conditions, and thick pads under their hoofs enable them to walk smoothly over sand. First to be domesticated was the one-humped camel called the *dromedary*, a camel native to the Sahara Desert. Other peoples, probably in central Asia, later domesticated the bigger, two-humped Bactrian camel. A stockier and hardier animal, it was better able than the dromedary to survive the scorching heat of northern Iran and the frozen

Camels. *Dromedary camels (left) are good draft animals for travel and domestic work in the deserts of Arabia, Afghanistan, and India. Two-hump camels (right) are much bigger than dromedary camels. They are more suited to the extreme dry and cold weather in Iran and central Asia.*

winters along the route from China that later became the Silk Road (so named because silk was a major product carried along this route).

NEW SHIPS New shipbuilding technologies had been developing rapidly since 1600 BCE and now were making a significant impact. Boats that had once been designed for limited transport on rivers and lakes and along shorelines could now be built stronger and bigger for sailing on seas. These new, truly seafaring ships boasted larger and better-reinforced hulls and stronger masts and rigging that allowed billowing sails to harness wind power effectively. These innovations, along with smaller ones in steering and ballast (among others), propelled bold mariners to venture out across large bodies of open water, such as the Mediterranean Sea.

IRON Although far more abundant than the tin and copper used to make bronze, iron is harder to extract from ore and to fabricate into useful shapes. (Iron is a malleable metal found almost everywhere in the world; it became the most important and widely used metal in world history from this time onward.) To make iron implements, metalworkers learned to apply intense heat to soften the ore and remove its impurities. Subsequently, they discovered that by adding carbon to the iron, they could make an early form of steel. When the technology to smelt and harden iron advanced, iron tools and weapons replaced those made of bronze. The ability to use iron was a staggering breakthrough that leaped across territorial and cultural borders.

Iron also promoted a revolutionary shift in agrarian techniques. Innovators learned to tip their plowshares with forged-iron edges that they could easily shape and resharpen. With the iron-tipped plow, cultivators could clear the dense jungle of the Ganges plain and till the topsoil to keep it weed free and to enhance its quality. Increasingly, farmers did not have to rely on floods to restore layers of rich soil to their fields. Instead, they could break the sod and turn it over to bring up fertile subsoils. The effects of this transformation drove the agrarian frontier far beyond the traditional floodplains of riverbank settings. Agricultural developments provided the technological basis for supporting larger, more integrated societies linked by roads and canals.

Administrative Innovations

Expansion of the first empires depended on military might, and control of expanded territories required new administrative techniques. With an army wielding the most advanced weapons and armor, the Neo-Assyrian king led annual campaigns to establish his control over the countryside. Deportations were another strategy to break resisters' unity, to provide slave labor in parts of the empire that needed workers and to integrate the realm. Throughout the 300 years of their rule, the Neo-Assyrian state (the name scholars employ for the third empire of the Assyrian peoples) constructed an infrastructure of roads, garrisons, and relay stations throughout the entire territory, making it easier to communicate and to move troops. Moreover, subject peoples were required to send tribute in the form of grains, animals, raw materials, and people in addition to precious goods such as gold and lapis lazuli, which was used to build imperial cities and to enrich the royal coffers. In later centuries, such innovations—well-equipped armies, deportation, road systems for transit and communication, and tribute—became common among empires. (See Current Trends in World History: Big Forces in Early Empires.)

NORTH SEA

BALTIC SEA

EUROPE

URAL MOUNTAINS

ARAL SEA

CASPIAN SEA

Dnieper R.

Dniester R.

Volga R.

Danube R.

BLACK SEA

CENT

MYCENAEANS
GREECE
AEGEAN SEA
Tiryns
Troy
ANATOLIA

CRETE

CYPRUS

MEDITERRANEAN SEA

SYRIAN DESERT

LEVANT

Tyre
Jericho
Jerusalem

HITTITES
NEO-ASSYRIANS
Nineveh
MITANNI
Ashur
MESOPOTAMIA
ELAMITES
Euphrates R.
Tigris R.
Babylon

IRANIAN PLATEAU

ZAGROS MTS.

SOUTHWEST ASIA

Persian Gulf

NORTH AFRICA

SAHARA

AFRICA

EGYPT
Amarna
Thebes
Nile R.

ARABIAN DESERT

ARABIAN PENINSULA

RED SEA

NUBIA

Sub-Saharan periphery:
Increased population
and gradual adoption
of agriculture

Niger R.

SUB – SAHARAN AFRICA

Congo R.

Lake Victoria

ATLANTIC OCEAN

Tropical woodlands:
Yams and palm nuts
cultivated

■ (dark shade)	Urban cores
■ (light shade)	Vedic settlement by 900 BCE
→	Population migration (Sea Peoples)
→	Nomadic incursions (pastoralists)
■	Destroyed site
•	City

MAP 4.1 | Afro-Eurasia, 1200 BCE—Urban Cores and Land and Sea Migrations

Nomadic incursions shattered the social and political status quo in Afro-Eurasia at this time. While destroying old polities, these migrations fostered a new social and political order in a variety of regions.

- Where did nomadic groups originate, and where did they migrate to?
- What is a major difference between the invasions of the Sea Peoples in this period versus pastoral invasions?
- Why do you think historians' knowledge of these nomadic incursions is limited and sketchy?

Conflict has always been a part of the human condition. But organized warfare with the use of "big force"—that is, large, well-disciplined armies—appears only with the formation of complex societies. The military units created in these complex societies became crucial vehicles for expanding the lands and peoples under the control of single states and broadcasting the influence of these states well beyond the territories that they controlled militarily. The field of comparative empires has become one of the hottest in world history because it allows for large-scale comparisons.

Evidence for intermittent conflict among the city-states of Sumer in the fourth millennium BCE and in Old Kingdom Egypt (2649–2152 BCE) shows that local populations were drafted into a common army when needed. Permanent forces, first recorded in the Old Akkadian period in the third millennium BCE, were used to forge unity, dominate trade routes, and repel threatening "barbarians." Over the next two millennia, across the full extent of Afro-Eurasia, the technologies and structure of war machines developed along similar paths, leading to large standing armies equipped with new and improved weapons, marked by continual innovation and new capabilities.

The earliest armies of Sumer were soldiers on foot arranged in a boxlike (*phalanx*) formation. The men wore protective leather capes and helmets and carried large shields to deflect spears and arrows. This mass-formation fighting of infantry that was enabled by uniform training, uniform armaments, and state provisioning became the norm for land forces in Egypt, Assyria, and, later, the Greek city-states. By the early second millennium BCE, horse-drawn chariots were added to the force, giving mobility and the potential of surprise to an ever-larger infantry force (see Chapter 3). Mounted cavalry was introduced late in the middle of the first millennium BCE in Assyria when fighting in mountainous terrain rendered the chariot impractical. Camels, long used as pack animals, were also used in warfare, primarily by Arab tribesmen conscripted into the Neo-Assyrian army. And elephants were one of the four components of the South Asian Vedic armies, combined with cavalry, infantry, and chariots into a highly effective fighting force.

Even before the rise of complex societies and large military forces, the weapons of warfare had been those of the hunter: bows and arrows, spears, and slings. Like these weapons, knives, daggers, axes, and maces were also incorporated into armies and were wielded by infantries in hand-to-hand combat. The compound bow, first used in warfare by the Sumerians, was refined by the Neo-Assyrians into a powerful projectile that could achieve an arc of more than 200 yards, raining destruction down on the opposing infantry. Although bronze was the most important metal for weapons, the introduction of iron toward the end of the second millennium BCE expanded the availability of metal for these state war machines. Because war was often conducted to acquire land, cities had to be conquered by force. Battering rams, first documented in Egypt, were added to mobile siege machines; towers supporting archers are pictured on the Neo-Assyrian stone sculptures. Levers and breaking bars as well as tunneling were used to undermine the integrity of the walls. And scaling ladders were thrown against the fortification for the final assault.

In China, the same elements of infantry, chariots, and archers were at the core of the army from as early as the Shang state. While their original goal was to capture prisoners needed for sacrifice to the ancestors, soon defensive forces were needed to protect them against their neighbors. The Zhou gradually defeated the Shang through their superior forces and more ingenious and agile tactics. A fundamental advance was made with the invention around 475 BCE of the crossbow, a far more

SOUTHWEST ASIA: CONTRASTING APPROACHES TO EMPIRE BUILDING

The Neo-Assyrians and Persians created markedly different empires. Although both empires were much larger than any that had preceded them, they adopted quite different policies and attitudes toward subject peoples. The Neo-Assyrian elites ruled with an iron fist, terrorizing the empire's subject peoples and often bringing vast numbers of defeated peoples back to the homeland as coerced agricultural and urban laborers. In contrast, the Persians sought to assimilate conquered peoples to their way of life and also embraced many of the practices of their subject populations. These radically different approaches to ruling may well have stemmed from the two groups' earlier institutions and values. The Neo-Assyrian state was the third in a long line of Assyrian states, having been preceded by the Old and Middle Assyrian Kingdoms. In other words, the Assyrian peoples had a long tradition of ruling others—a heritage that led them to regard those they conquered as inferiors. In contrast, the Persians had been nomadic peoples, roaming the Iranian powerful personal killing machine, and the torsion catapult, which threw both heavy projectiles and fiery masses onto the enemy. From the beginning, the techniques and technologies of war were rapidly shared across cultural boundaries as a natural result of adapting and improving on the achievements of the enemy. What mattered most for success was the ability to integrate and coordinate the increasing number of elements that went into a fighting force. The Persians learned at the hands of the Greeks that numbers and sheer firepower could not overcome agility, communication, and integration.

Toward the end of the second millennium BCE, new forms of force were appearing not just on land but also on the sea. The construction of ships for the purpose of conducting war on water—the world's first "battleships"—occurred over the course of the eighth century BCE in the eastern Mediterranean. These special ships were built mainly by the Phoenician and Greek city-states whose livelihood depended on commerce on the high seas. They were not designed like the slow-sailing bulky ships used for the transport of large cargoes but were sleek and slim—about 120 feet long and only 15 feet wide—with little room for anything other than the men rowing them. With up to 170 rowers, they were designed and constructed for speed and power. They had

Early Sumerian Infantry. *Dating back to 2400 BCE, this panel from the Syrian Temple of Ishtar illustrates the victorious homecoming of foot soldiers with battle-axes in hand.*

no purpose other than the deliberate sinking of other ships. At first, the rowers were arranged in ships with two banks (called *biremes* by the Greeks) and later with three (called *triremes*). They were armed with bronze "beaks," or rams, that were

used to cave in the sides of enemy ships. These ships were costly to construct, to man, to provision, and to command. As with the maintenance, training, and arming of large land forces, only relatively wealthy states and governments could afford to mount this kind of power on the high seas. The creation of large standing armies, innovations in weaponry like the crossbow, and the appearance of the first ever battleships transformed the nature of warfare during this period when the world's first empires emerged.

QUESTIONS FOR ANALYSIS

- In terms of using "big forces," what made some states or empires more successful than others?

- Why is it useful for historians to compare empires? What other ways could you compare empires (in addition to comparing big forces)?

Explore Further

Briant, Pierre. *From Cyrus to Alexander: A History of the Persian Empire* (2002).

Tanner, Harold M. *China: A History: From Neolithic Cultures through the Great Qing Empire (10,000 BCE–1799 CE)* (2009).

plateau, before creating their great empire. While they held on to many of their nomadic traditions, they were eager to adopt the practices of settled societies as they undertook to create what were novel to them: cities and imperial political institutions.

In one respect, however, the two empires were alike. They engaged in warfare not entirely for itself, but also to create huge and highly profitable trading networks. Their well-constructed roads were a boon to long-distance trade. They also relied on their control over distant territories to bring to their homeland building and decorative materials that were essential for embellishing their expanding and resplendent cities.

THE NEO-ASSYRIAN EMPIRE IN SOUTHWEST ASIA (911–612 BCE)

The story of the rise of empires begins in Southwest Asia with the Neo-Assyrian Empire, successor to the Old and Middle Assyrian Kingdoms of the second millennium. The Neo-Assyrian state was a military state par excellence, for all men could be called up for military service and all state offices were designated as military bodies, even if they had no military functions. The Assyrians perfected techniques of imperial rule that others imitated and that ultimately became standard in many ancient and modern empires. In particular, the Neo-Assyrian state revealed the raw military side of imperial rule: constant and harsh warfare, brutal exploitation of subjects, and an ideology that glorified imperial masters and justified the subjugation and harsh treatment of subjects.

In this regard the Assyrians were legendary for their ruthless efficiency and reliance on terror. They slaughtered their opponents and razed villages. Their taste for brutality knew few bounds. Not only did their warriors cut off ears, lips, and fingers, castrate and behead their enemies, flay the skins of the conquered, rape, and carry out mass executions, but they followed these brutal practices by displaying corpses, flayed skins, and the heads of those whom they had beheaded. Their obvious goal was to intimidate the yet-to-be-conquered communities. (In contrast, as we will see, the Persians, who took control of Southwest Asia after the Neo-Assyrians, balanced their multicultural empire through a combination of centralized administration and imperial ideology.)

Neo-Assyrian rulers had ambitions beyond governing their own people: they also wanted to subordinate peoples in distant lands and control those peoples' resources, trading cities, and trade routes. They succeeded by the mid-seventh century BCE with the conquest of Southwest Asia and parts of North Africa, including Egypt. (See Map 4.2.)

MAP 4.2 | The Neo-Assyrian Empire

The Neo-Assyrians built the first strong regional empire in Afro-Eurasia. In the process, they faced the challenge of promoting order and stability throughout their diverse realm.

- Where did the Neo-Assyrian Empire expand?
- Which parts of the empire were "the Land of Ashur" and which were "the Land under the Yoke of Ashur"?
- Why do you think expansion after 720 BCE led to the empire's destruction?

Expansion into an Empire

The heartland of Assyria cradled the ancient cities of Ashur and Nineveh on the upper reaches of the Tigris River. By the ninth century BCE, the Neo-Assyrian state had become strong enough to expand westward; by 824 BCE, it dominated the lands and peoples all the way to the Mediterranean, controlling trade and tribute from the entire area.

The Assyrian peoples had several advantages. First, their armies were hardened and disciplined professional troops led by officers who rose high in the ranks because of their merit, not their birth. In addition, they perfected the combined deployment of infantry and cavalry (horse-mounted warriors equipped with iron weapons) together with horse-drawn chariots armored with iron plates and carrying expert archers. The Assyrians were also skilled siege warriors, using iron to build massive wheeled siege towers and to cap their battering rams. No city walls could stand against them for long. Finally, the Neo-Assyrian armies were massive. At the height of their power in the ninth century BCE, the rulers sent 120,000 soldiers on the annual campaign to the west. (In contrast, Roman and Chinese armies would not reach this scale for another 500 years.)

Assyrian expansion provoked fierce but ultimately futile opposition, particularly from the small independent states in the west. Resisting populations were devastated—they were relocated through forced deportations, and their lands were annexed. The Neo-Assyrian state grew even more ambitious when a talented military leader usurped the throne. Tiglath Pileser III (r. 745–728 BCE) reorganized the Neo-Assyrian state to centralize power in royal hands and so prepared for a second phase of imperial expansion and consolidation. He took away the nobles' rights to own and inherit land and other wealth, and he replaced hereditary provincial governors with appointed officials whom the center of the empire controlled. He also reinstated aggressive, expansionary annual military campaigns. But the destruction and mass deportations carried out by his armies intensified the conquered peoples' hatred of the Assyrians.

Integration and Control of the Empire

Four defining features of the Neo-Assyrian Empire were (1) its unique imperial structure, (2) deportation and the forced labor of subjugated peoples, (3) a belief that empires worked, at least

Tiglath Pileser III. *The walls of the Neo-Assyrian palaces were lined with stone slabs carved with images of the victories of the king. This fragmentary slab from the palace of Tiglath Pileser III originally decorated the wall of his palace at Nimrud. It shows the inhabitants and their herds being forced to leave after the defeat of their town by the Assyrians. Below is Tiglath Pileser III, shaded by his royal umbrella, in his war chariot.*

for the imperialists, and (4) a rigid social hierarchy. While these features were hugely important to the success of the empire, they also contributed to its ultimate failure.

STRUCTURE OF THE EMPIRE The Neo-Assyrian rulers divided their empire into two parts and ruled them in different ways. The core, which the Assyrians called the "Land of Ashur," included the lands between the Zagros Mountains and the Euphrates River. The king's appointees governed these interior lands, whose inhabitants had to supply food for the temple of the national god Ashur, labor for the god's residence in the city of Ashur, and officials to carry out the state's business.

The other area, known as "the Land under the Yoke of Ashur," lay outside of Assyria proper. Its inhabitants were not considered Assyrians; rather, their local rulers held power as subjects of Assyria. Instead of supplying agricultural goods and labor, those men and women not subject to deportation had the burden of delivering massive amounts of tribute in the form of gold and silver. This wealth went directly to the king, who used it to pay for his extravagant court and ever-increasing military costs. After the reforms of Tiglath Pileser III, even more lands were incorporated into the Land of Ashur proper. While this eliminated the oppressive need for the inhabitants of these lands to pay tribute, the empire continued to harshly administer its programs of forced Assyrianization. (Many empires in later centuries, including the Persian, Roman, and even the modern-day British and French Empires, would use this strategy to overawe and ultimately compel subject peoples to accept the values of the conquerors.)

DEPORTATION AND FORCED LABOR In the empire's early years, the army comprised Assyrians who went to war on annual summer campaigns. Later, when campaigning became year-round, the army grew to several hundred thousand men mobilized to protect and extend the imperial holdings. These forces included not only Assyrians but also men from the conquered peoples. By the seventh century BCE, the Assyrians assigned different ethnic groups to specialized military functions: Phoenicians from the Levant provided ships and sailors for battle in the Mediterranean; Medes from the Iranian plateau served as the king's bodyguards; and charioteers from Israel subdued rebellious western provinces.

To accomplish its goals, the Neo-Assyrian state needed huge labor forces for agricultural work and for enormous building projects. Since so many Assyrians served in the army, the state recruited most agricultural and construction workers from conquered peoples. Over three centuries, the Neo-Assyrian state relocated more than 4 million people—a practice that not only supported its stupendous work projects but also undermined local resistance. It was these deportees who constructed a series of increasingly larger and more resplendent political capitals,

Capture of an Egyptian City. *This stone panel from the North Palace in Nineveh shows warriors scaling walls with ladders during Ashurbanipal's campaign against Egypt (mid-seventh century BCE).*

beginning with rebuilding the city of Kalhu (known today as Nimrud), a project that took fifteen years and glorified the state and its rulers. When completed, walls measuring 8 kilometers long enclosed an area of 900 acres, inside of which were the monarch's palace, numerous temples, and a ziggurat. Reliefs depicting battles and royal hunts decorated the main rooms in the palace. Not satisfied with Kalhu and the other capitals that these slave laborers constructed, one of Neo-Assyria's most powerful kings, Sennacherib (r. 704–681 BCE), made the city of Nineveh his political capital. More magnificent than the earlier capitals, Nineveh spread out over 1,800 acres and was surrounded by a 12-kilometer-long wall, inside of which were magnificent citadels and many public buildings, all decorated with images of state and royal power.

IDEOLOGY AND PROPAGANDA The Neo-Assyrian Empire put forth an imperial ideology to support and justify its system of expansion, exploitation, and inequality. (An ideology is the dominant set of ideas of a widespread culture or movement.) Even in the early stages of expansion, Neo-Assyrian inscriptions and art expressed a divinely determined destiny that drove the regime to expand westward toward the Mediterranean Sea. The national god Ashur had commanded all Assyrians to support the forcible growth of the empire, whose goal was to establish and maintain order and keep an ever-threatening cosmic chaos at bay. Only the god Ashur and his agent, the king, could bring universal order. The king conducted holy war to transform the known world into the well-regulated Land of Ashur, intensifying his campaign of terror and expansion with elaborate propaganda. This propaganda, based on a detailed historical record of countless military and political victories, proclaimed that

Assyria's triumph was inevitable. Its main focus was the nobles, whom the king and the empire relied on for support.

The rulers devised three mutually reinforcing types of propaganda. First, they used elaborate architectural complexes to stage ceremonial displays of pomp and power (as in Egypt and China). Second, they made sure that different types of texts glorified the king and the empire. These texts were recited at state occasions, inscribed on monuments, written on clay documents about the king's military campaigns and achievements, and buried at propitious places in public buildings, where only the eyes of Ashur could view them. (See Primary Source: The Banquet Stele of Assurnasirpal II.) Third, state officials placed images glorifying the king and the Assyrian army on palace walls. These images depicted the army's force, showing all who resisted being smashed into submission—their towns burned; their men killed, impaled on stakes, or flayed; and their women and children deported along with any male survivors.

The Annals of Ashurbanipal. *This baked clay cylinder carries a portion of the annals of Ashurbanipal. It was found at Nineveh along with thousands of other tablets preserved in his famous library. The annals of Ashurbanipal were detailed, almost novelistic accounts of his military and civic achievements. Unlike earlier annals, there is first-person discourse, indirect discourse, flashbacks, and lively descriptions of events and places.*

The Banquet Stele of Assurnasirpal II

Starting in the third millennium BCE, the rulers of Mesopotamia used architecture to signal their power to their subjects. When a change of dynasty or other reorganization of power occurred, rulers would build new palaces or even move their capital city. In the ninth century BCE, Assurnasirpal II established Neo-Assyria as an imperial power with the intention of expanding and consolidating its economic and political control of surrounding peoples. After moving the capital and building a new palace and royal precinct, he called all of the empire's peoples to a ten-day celebration. This remarkable event was commemorated by an inscribed stele (a stone pillar) that he erected next to the throne room.

(102) When Ashur-nasir-apli, king of Assyria, consecrated the joyful palace, the palace full of wisdom, in Kalach [and] invited inside Ashur, the great lord, and the gods of the entire land; 1,000 fat oxen, 1,000 calves [and] sheep of the stable, 14,000 . . . -sheep which belonged to the goddess Ishtar my mistress, 200 oxen which belonged to the goddess Ishtar my mistress, 1,000 . . . -sheep, 1,000 spring lambs, 500 *ayalu*-deer, 500 deer, 1,000 ducks [*iṣṣūrū rabûtu*], 500 ducks [*usū*], 500 geese, 1,000 wild geese, 1,000 *qaribu*-birds, 10,000 pigeons, 10,000 wild pigeons, 10,000 small birds, 10,000 fish, 10,000 jerboa, 10,000 eggs, 10,000 loaves of bread, 10,000 jugs of beer, 10,000 skins of wine, 10,000 containers of grain [and] sesame, 10,000 pots of hot . . . , 1,000 boxes of greens, 300 [containers of] oil, 300 [containers of] malt, 300 [containers of] mixed *raqqatu*-plants, 100 [containers of] *kudimmus*, 100 [containers of] . . . , 100 [containers of] parched barley, 100 [containers of] *ubuḥšennu*-grain, 100 [containers of] fine *billatu*, 100 [containers of] pomegranates,

100 [containers of] grapes, 100 [containers of] mixed *zamrus*, 100 [containers of] pistachios, 100 [containers of] . . . , 100 [containers of] *ionions*, 100 [containers of] garlic, 100 [containers of] *kunipḥus*, 100 *buncbes* of turnips, 100 [containers of] *ḥinḥinu*-seeds, 100 [containers of] *giddū*, 100 [containers of] honey, 100 [containers of] ghee, 100 [containers of] roasted *abšu*-seeds, 100 [containers of] roasted *šu'u*-seeds, 100 [containers of] *karkartu*-plants, 100 [containers of] *tiatu*-plants, 100 [containers of] mustard, 100 [containers of] milk, 100 [containers of] cheese, 100 bowls of *mīzu*-drink, 100 stuffed oxen, 10 homers of shelled *dukdu*-nuts, 10 homers of shelled pistachios, 10 homers of . . . , 10 homers of *ḥabbaququ*, 10 homers of dates, 10 homers of *titip*, 10 homers of cumin, 10 homers of *saḥūnu*, 10 homers of . . . , 10 homers of *andaḥšu*, 10 homers of *šišanibu*, 10 homers of *simberu*-fruit, 10 homers of *ḥašú*, 10 homers of fine oil, 10 homers of fine aromatics, 10 homers of . . . , 10 homers of *naṣṣabu*-gourds, 10 homers of *zinzimmu*-onions, 10 homers of olives; when I consecrated the palace of Kalach, 47,074 men [and] women who

were invited from every part of my land, 5,000 dignitaries [and] envoys of the people of the lands Suhu, Hindanu, Patinu, Hatti, Tyre, Sidon, Gurgumu, Malidu, Hubushkia, Gilzanu, Kumu, [and] Musasiru, 16,000 people of Kalach, [and] 1,500 *zarīqū* of my palace, all of them—altogether 69,574 [including] those summoned from all lands and the people of Kalach—for ten days I gave them food, I gave them drink, I had them bathed, I had them anointed. [Thus] did I honour them [and] send them back to their lands in peace and joy.

QUESTIONS FOR ANALYSIS

- What does the extensive list of food and drink listed in the text tell the reader about the size and geographical reach of the empire and the role of trade in it?

- What techniques, as reflected in the text of the Banquet Stele, did Assurnasirpal use to build loyalty among his subjects?

Source: Assyrian Royal Inscriptions, Part 2: From Tiglath-pileser I to Ashur-nasir-apli II, compiled and translated by Albert Kirk Grayson, vol. 2 of *Records of the Ancient Near East*, edited by Hans Goedicke (Wiesbaden: Otto Harrassowitz, 1976), pp. 175–76.

The commitment to record the regime's triumphal events was evident not only on palace walls but also in a uniquely Neo-Assyrian literary form called annals (historical records arranged year by year). Constituting a milestone in human history, these documents illustrate how communication and writing promoted the formation of organized states. Court scribes inscribed the annals on stone slabs as well as tablets and cylinders, detailing each campaign in the yearly report of the king's achievements. These written compositions, like the images, never gave any indication that the Assyrians did or could lose a battle.

SOCIAL STRUCTURE AND POPULATION The Assyrians' iron-fisted rule rested on a rigid social hierarchy. Alone at the top was the king, who as the sole agent of the god Ashur conducted war to expand the Land of Ashur. Below were the state's military elites, handsomely rewarded through gifts of land, silver, and exemptions from royal taxes. Over time, they became the noble class and intimates of the king, replacing the older landed elites who lost their resources after Tiglath Pileser III reorganized the empire's landholdings. Elites often controlled vast estates that included both the land and the local people who worked it. The throne and the elites owned the most populous part of the society, the peasantry, in which various categories of workers had differing privileges. Those who were enslaved because they could not pay their debts were allowed to marry nonslave partners, conduct financial transactions, and even own property with other slaves attached. In contrast, foreigners who were enslaved after being captured had no rights—they were forced to do hard manual labor on the state's monumental building projects. Those who were forcibly relocated were not slaves but became attached to the lands that they had to work. Families were small and lived on modest plots of land, where they raised vegetables and planted vineyards.

Women in Assyria were far more restricted than their counterparts in the earlier periods of Sumerian and Old Babylonian Mesopotamia (see Chapter 3). Under the Assyrians' patriarchal social system, women had almost no control over their lives. Because all inheritance passed through the male line, it was crucial that a man be certain of the paternity of the children borne by his wives. As a result, all interactions between men and women outside of the family were highly restricted. The Middle Assyrians introduced the practice of veiling in the thirteenth century BCE, requiring it of all respectable women. Indeed, prostitutes who serviced the men of the army and worked in the taverns were forbidden to wear the veil, so that their revealed faces and hair would signal their disreputable status. Any prostitute found wearing the veil would be dragged to the top of the city wall, stripped of her clothing, flogged, and perhaps even killed.

The queens of Neo-Assyria obeyed the same social norms, but their lives were more comfortable and varied than the commoners'. They lived in a separate part of the palace with servants who were either women slaves or eunuchs (castrated males). Though Assyrian queens rarely wielded genuine power, they enjoyed respect and recognition, especially in the role of mother of the king. In fact, a queen could serve as regent for her son if the king died while his heir was still a child. Such was the case of Sammuramat, who served as regent from 810 to 806 BCE, successfully ruling the empire until her son came of age.

The Instability of the Neo-Assyrian Empire

At their peak, the Assyrians controlled most of the lands stretching from the Zagros Mountains in the east to Egypt in the west. This was an awesome feat, but the empire was unstable. Assyrian commanders had to position occupying armies far and wide to keep subjects in line; and as the propaganda machine ramped up, so did discontent among the nobility. Once a successful rebellion challenged the Assyrian worldview of invincibility, the empire's fall was inevitable. Although successor states temporarily filled the Assyrian political vacuum, the three-millennium-long culture of Mesopotamia was dead. In 612 BCE, the Neo-Assyrian Empire collapsed when Nineveh was conquered.

THE PERSIAN EMPIRE IN SOUTHWEST ASIA (c. 560–331 BCE)

After a brief interlude of Neo-Babylonian rule, the Persians reasserted imperial power in Southwest Asia. They created a gentler form of imperial rule, based on persuasion and mutual benefit underpinned by raw military force. A nomadic group speaking an Indo-Iranian language, the Persians had arrived on the Iranian plateau from central Asia during the second millennium BCE and gradually spread to the plateau's southwestern part. These expert horsemen shot arrows with deadly accuracy while whirling on horseback in the midst of battle. After Cyrus the Great (r. 559–529 BCE) united the Persian tribes, his armies defeated the Lydians in southwestern Anatolia and took over their gold mines, land, and trading routes. He next overpowered the Greek city-states on the Aegean coast of Anatolia.

In building their immense empire, the Persians, whose ancestors were pastoralists and had no urban traditions to build on, adapted the ideologies and institutions of the Babylonians (see Chapter 3), the Assyrians, and the indigenous Elamites, modifying them to fit their own customs and political aims. This process gave rise to uniquely Persian institutions that undergirded the new empire, which would last until the arrival of Alexander the Great in 331 BCE.

The Integration of a Multicultural Empire

From their base on the Iranian plateau, over the next 200 years the Persian rulers developed an enormous empire that reached from the Indus Valley to northern Greece and from central Asia to the south of Egypt. (See Map 4.3.) Cyrus presented himself as a benevolent ruler who claimed to have liberated his subjects from the oppression of their own kings. He pointed to his victory in Babylon as a sign that the city's gods had turned against its king as a heretic. According to the cuneiform text known as the Cyrus cylinder, the Babylonians greeted him "with shining faces." At the same time, Cyrus released the Israelites from their fifty-year captivity in Babylon, to which they had been exiled

Cyrus the Great. *This great genius with four wings was preserved in the doorjamb of Gate R at the palace of Cyrus the Great at Pasargadae. When Cyrus forged the Persian Empire from Media, Assyria, Babylonia, and Egypt, there was no coherent imperial imagery to represent the new political entity. His court artists borrowed freely from the realms that he had brought into his empire. The image is a combination of features borrowed from Egypt (the headdress), Assyria (low-relief representation on a stone slab and the four wings), and Babylonia (the long garment).*

by the Neo-Babylonian king Nebuchadnezzar II about 587 BCE. They, too, considered him a savior who, having freed them on the orders of the Israelite god, allowed them to return to Jerusalem and rebuild their temple. Even the Greeks, who later defeated the Persians, saw Cyrus as a model ruler.

Following Cyrus's death on the battlefield, Darius I (r. 521–486 BCE) put the new empire on a solid footing. First he suppressed revolts across the lands, recording this feat on a monumental rock relief overhanging the road to his capital, Persepolis. (See Primary Source: Beisitun Inscription.) Then he conquered territories held by dozens of different ethnic groups, stretching from the Indus River in the east to the Aegean and Mediterranean Seas in the west, and from the Black, Caspian, and Aral Seas in the north to the Nile River in the south. To manage this huge domain, Darius introduced dynamic administrative systems that enabled the empire to flourish for another

two centuries. Its new bureaucracy combined central and local administration and made effective use of the strengths of local tradition, economy, and rule—rather than forcing Persian customs on subject people via rigid central control (as the Assyrians had done).

This empire was both centralized and multicultural. The Persians believed that all subject peoples were equal; the only requirement was to be loyal to the king and pay tribute—which was considered an honor, not a burden. Although local Persian administrators used local languages, Aramaic (a dialect of a Semitic language long spoken in Southwest Asia) became the empire's official language because many of its literate scribes came from Mesopotamia.

Darius understood that he could not expand the empire without reorganizing and centralizing. To bring the wealth of the provinces to the imperial center, he established a system of provinces, or **satrapies**, each ruled by a satrap (a governor) who was a relative or close associate of the king. The local bureaucrats and officials who administered the government worked under close monitoring by military officers, central tax collectors, and spies (the so-called eyes of the king), who enforced the satraps' loyalty. Further, Darius established a system of fixed taxation and formal tribute allocations. Moreover, he promoted trade throughout the empire by building roads, establishing a standardized currency including coinage, and introducing standard weights and measures. These strategies helped to integrate and centralize the empire's vast territories.

Zoroastrianism, Ideology, and Social Structure

Like the Assyrians, the Persians established their ideology of kingship and their social structure on religious foundations. They believed that the supreme god, Ahura Mazda, appointed the monarch as ruler over all peoples and lands of the earth and charged him with maintaining a perfect order from which all would benefit. Unlike their Mesopotamian neighbors, the Persians drew their religious ideas from their pastoral and tribal roots (which reflected the same traditions of warrior and priestly classes as those preserved in the Vedic texts of the Indus Valley; see Chapter 3).

Zoroaster (also known as Zarathustra), who most likely lived sometime after 1000 BCE in eastern Iran, was responsible for crystallizing the region's traditional beliefs into a formal religious system. The eastern tribes of the Iranian plateau spread the ideas of **Zoroastrianism** to the Iranian peoples living in the west, and Zoroastrianism ultimately became the religion of the entire empire. The main source for the teachings of Zoroaster is the Avesta, a collection of holy works initially transmitted orally by priests and then, according to legend, written down in the third century BCE.

MAP 4.3 | The Persian Empire, 550–479 BCE

Starting in the sixth century BCE, the Persians succeeded the Assyrians as rulers of the large regional empire of Southwest Asia. Compare the Persian Empire's territorial domains with those of the Neo-Assyrian Empire in Map 4.2.

- Geographically, how did the Persian Empire differ from the Neo-Assyrian state?
- Analyzing the map, how many Persian satrapies existed, and what role do you think they played in the success of the Persian Empire?
- How does geography help explain why the Greeks were able to defeat the Persians twice?

Zoroaster's teachings tried to wean the Iranian faithful away from their earlier animistic beliefs that led them to see all objects, alive and dead, as possessing life and vitality. In a radical change, Zoroaster promoted belief in the god Ahura Mazda, who had created the world and all that was good. (Though rare, monotheism also existed during this time in Judah—see p. 144; and it had briefly been the official religion of Egypt, when Akhenaten imposed worship of Aten, the sun—see Chapter 3.) The Persians came to believe that the universe was dualistic: Ahura Mazda was capable only of good, whereas his adversary, Ahriram, was deceitful and wicked. The Persians saw these two forces as engaging in a cosmic struggle for control of the universe.

Unlike the fatalistic religions of Mesopotamia, Zoroastrianism treated humans as capable of choosing between good and evil. Their choices had consequences: rewards or punishments in the afterlife. Strict rules of behavior determined the fate of each individual. For example, because animals were good, they deserved to be treated well. Intoxicants, widely used in tribal religions, were forbidden. Also, there were strict rules for treatment of the dead. For example, to prevent death from contaminating the sacred elements of earth, fire, and water, it was forbidden to bury, burn, or drown the deceased. Instead, people left corpses out for beasts and birds of prey to devour.

Persian kings enjoyed absolute authority. In return, they were expected to follow moral and political guidelines that reflected Zoroastrian notions of ethical behavior. As the embodiment of the positive virtues that made them fit to hold power, they were to display insight and the ability to distinguish right from wrong so that they could preserve justice and maintain social order.

PRIMARY SOURCE

Beisitun Inscription

To commemorate his consolidation of power over the Persian state, Darius I commissioned a pictorial relief of himself as victor high above the main road leading from Mesopotamia to Ecbatana (the modern city of Hamadan) in western Iran. The images are surrounded by a long text inscribed in three languages—Old Persian, Akkadian, and Elamite. This is the earliest Old Persian inscription; it is a version of cuneiform script that Darius devised especially for this occasion.

4.31–2. Saith Darius the King: These IX kings I took prisoner within these battles.

4.33–6. Saith Darius the King: These are the provinces which became rebellious. The Lie made them rebellious, so that these [men] deceived the people. Afterwards Ahuramazda put them into my hand; as was my desire, so I did unto them.

4.36–40. Saith Darius the King: Thou who shalt be king hereafter, protect thyself vigorously from the Lie; the man who shall be a Lie-follower, him do thou punish well, if thus thou shalt think, "May my country be secure!"

4.40–3. Saith Darius the King: This is what I did; by the favor of Ahuramazda, in one and the same year I did [it]. Thou who shalt hereafter read this inscription, let

that which has been done by me convince thee; do not thou think it a lie.

4.43–5. Saith Darius the King: I turn myself quickly to Ahuramazda, that this [is] true, not false, [which] I did in one and the same year. . . .

4.52–6. Saith Darius the King: Now let that which has been done by me convince thee; thus to the people impart, do not conceal it: if this record thou shalt not conceal, [but] tell it to the people, may Ahuramazda be a friend unto thee, and may family be unto thee in abundance, and may thou live long!

4.57–9. Saith Darius the King: If this record thou shalt conceal, [and] not tell it to the people, may Ahuramazda be a smiter unto thee, and may family not be to thee!

4.59–61. Saith Darius the King: This which I did, in one and the same year by the favor of Ahuramazda I did; Ahuramazda bore me aid, and the other gods who are.

4.61–7. Saith Darius the King: For this reason Ahuramazda bore aid, and the other gods who are, because I was not hostile, I was not a Lie-follower, I was not a doer of wrong—neither I nor my family. According to righteousness I conducted myself. Neither to the weak nor to the powerful did I do wrong. The man who cooperated with my house, him I rewarded well; whoso did injury, him I punished well.

4.67–9. Saith Darius the King: Thou who shalt be king hereafter, the man who shall be a Lie-follower or who shall be a doer of wrong—unto them do thou not be a friend, [but] punish them well.

4.69–72. Saith Darius the King: Thou who shalt hereafter behold this inscription which I have inscribed, or these sculptures, do thou not destroy them, [but] thence onward protect them; as long as thou shalt be in good strength!

Darius's Relief at Beisitun. *At Beisitun, high above the Royal Road through the Zagros Mountains, Darius carved a relief commemorating his victories over Gaumata (the false Smerdis) and nine rebel kings. The kings are roped together at the neck, and Gaumata lies under Darius's feet. Above the rebels is a winged disk, probably representing the god Ahura Mazda. Darius had his scribes develop a version of cuneiform script to represent Old Persian. In a trilingual inscription (Old Persian, Elamite, and Akkadian) he recorded this victory, which consolidated and expanded the empire founded by Cyrus. This inscription provided the key for deciphering Babylonian cuneiform.*

Source: Roland G. Kent, Old Persian: Grammar, Texts, Lexicon, *2nd rev. ed. (New Haven: American Oriental Society, 1953), pp. 131–32.*

QUESTION FOR ANALYSIS

- Throughout the millennia, local and imperial rulers on the Iranian plateau used rock reliefs such as the Beisitun inscription to project their power and to mark boundaries. Who would see these monuments, and what messages would they receive?

In addition, kings had to show physical superiority that matched their moral standing. They had to be expert horsemen and peerless in wielding bows and spears. These were qualities valued by all Persian nobles, who revered the virtues of their nomadic ancestors. As the ancient Greek historian Herodotus tells us, Persian boys were taught three things only: "to ride, to shoot with the bow, and to tell the truth."

The Persian social order included four diverse groups: a ruling class of priests, nobles, and warriors; an administrative and commercial class consisting of scribes, bureaucrats, and merchants; and two laboring groups of artisans and peasants. Each group had a well-defined role: priests maintained the ritual fire in temples; nobles administered the state by paying taxes and performing appropriate duties; warriors protected and expanded the empire; bureaucrats kept records; merchants secured goods from distant lands; artisans rendered raw materials into symbolic form; and peasants grew the crops and tended the flocks that fed the imperial machine.

Surrounding the king was the powerful Persian hereditary nobility. These men had vast landholdings and often served the king as satraps or advisers. Also close to the king were wealthy merchants who directed trade across the vast empire. In turn, the king was obligated to take his wives only from these families and to exempt these families from certain taxes. To consolidate his hold on the throne, Darius reduced the aristocrats' political power. By controlling all appointments, he essentially made the nobles his puppets, but he let them keep their high status in a society in which birth and royal favor counted for everything.

Royal gifts solidified the relations between king and nobles, reinforcing the king's place at the top of the political pyramid. In public ceremonies he presented gold vessels, elaborate textiles, and jewelry to reward each recipient's loyalty and demonstrate dependence on the crown. Any kind of failure would result in the withdrawal of royal favor. Should such failures be serious or treasonous, the offenders faced torture and death.

Public Works and Imperial Identity

The Persians undertook significant building projects that helped unify their empire and consolidate imperial identity. For example, they engaged in large-scale road building and constructed a system of rapid and dependable communication. The key element in the system was the Royal Road, which followed age-old trade routes some 1,600 miles from western Anatolia to the heart of the empire in southwestern Iran, continuing eastward across the northern Iranian plateau and into central Asia. Traders used the Royal Road, as did the Persian army; subjects took tribute to the king over this road, and royal couriers used the

Panel from the Palace of Darius. *The palace of Darius at Susa was elaborately decorated with glazed bricks. This panel shows human-headed winged lions in a heraldic seated posture. Above them is a winged disk with tendrils and a human bust. This symbol, which borrows from Assyrian and Egyptian imagery, is thought to represent the Zoroastrian god Ahura Mazda.*

road to carry messages to the satraps and imperial armies. As the Assyrians had done, the Persians placed way stations with fresh mounts and provisions along the route. Known routes and connections like these helped Babylonian merchants, such as the trading house of the Egibi family, based in Babylon itself, to conduct long-distance trade with regions like Media and Elam far to the east.

In addition to the Royal Road, the Persians devised other ways to connect the far reaches of the empire with its center. Darius oversaw the construction of a canal more than 50 miles long linking the Red Sea to the Nile River. The canal enabled merchants trading as far afield as the borders of India to reach the Mediterranean by sea. One of the Persians' most ingenious contributions was the invention of *qanats*, underground tunnels through which water flowed over long distances without evaporating or being contaminated. (Later adopted by many cultures, this type of system moves water under arid lands even today.) Laborers from the local populations toiled on these feats of engineering as part of their obligations as subjects of the empire.

Until Cyrus's time, the Persians had been pastoral nomads who lacked traditions of monumental architecture, visual arts, or written literature or history. But now multiple capitals at

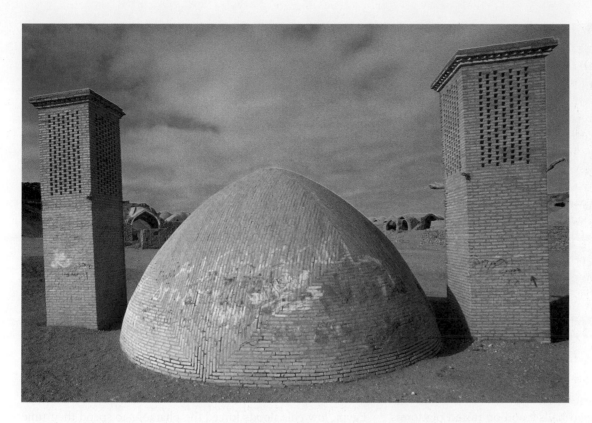

Persian Water-Moving Technique. *The Persians perfected the channeling of water over long distances through underground channels called qanats. This technique, an efficient way to move water without evaporation, is still used today in hot, arid regions. In this example near Yazd, in central Iran, the domed structure leading to the underground tunnel is flanked by two brick towers called "badgir," an ancient form of air conditioning that cools the water using wind (bad in Persian).*

Persepolis, Pasargadae, and Susa expressed a composite Persian imperial identity. Skilled craftworkers from all over the empire labored on the great cities, blending their distinct cultural influences into a new Persian architectural style. Beginning with Darius and his ceremonial capital at Persepolis, the Persians used monumental architecture with grand columned halls and huge open spaces to provide reception rooms for thousands of representatives bringing tribute from all over the empire and as a way to help integrate subject peoples by connecting them to one central, imperial authority. In the royal

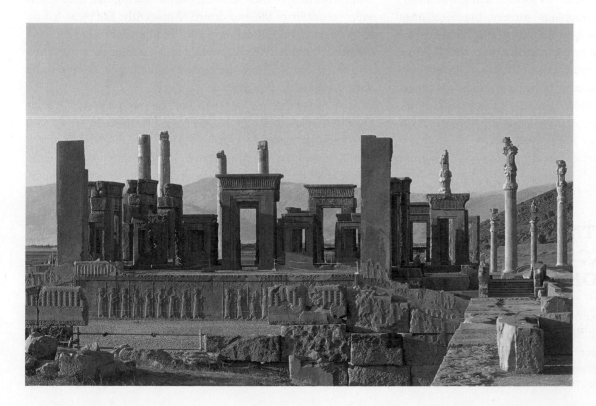

Persepolis. *In the highland valley of Fars, the homeland of the Persians, Darius and his successors built a capital city and ceremonial center at the site of Persepolis. On top of a huge platform, there were audience halls, a massive treasury, the harem, and residential spaces. The largest palace, called the Apadana, was constructed of mud brick. The roof was supported by enormous columns projecting the images of bulls.*

The King and His Courtiers. *Leading to the Apadana (the great palace) are two monumental staircases that are faced with low-relief representations of the king and his courtiers, as well as all of the delegations bringing tribute to the center of the empire. The lion attacking the bull is a symbolic rendering of the forces of nature. Above the central plane is the winged disk of Ahura Mazda and the human-headed lion griffins.*

palace, three of the columned halls stood on raised platforms accessed via processional stairways that were lined with elaborate images of subjects bringing gifts and tribute to the king. This highly refined program of visual propaganda showed the Persian Empire as a society of diverse but obedient peoples. The carvings on the great stairway of Persepolis offer a veritable ethnographic museum frozen in stone. Each group brings distinctive tribute—the Armenians present precious metal vessels, the Lydians from Anatolia carry gold armlets and bowls, the Egyptians offer exotic animals, and the Sogdians from central Asia lead proud horses. Thus, the Neo-Assyrians, and then later the Persians, fashioned their own brands of empire using a combination of military force, rigid political and social organization, and religious ideology to maintain successive control over Southwest Asia. (See Analyzing Global Developments: City-States to Empires: Growth in Scale: Mesopotamia.)

ENVIRONMENTAL CRISIS, ECONOMIC DECLINE, AND MIGRATION

The drought that descended on the Afro-Eurasian landmass in 1200 BCE caused grievous suffering on the lands bordering the eastern Mediterranean. The evidence gathered there leaves no doubt that climate change was a major underlying cause. In Egypt, low Nile floods forced the pharaohs to spend their time securing food supplies and repelling Libyans from the desert and Sea People marauders who were drawn toward a region known for its abundant resources. From Hattusas, the Hittite capital on the Anatolian plateau, kings dispatched envoys to the rulers of all of the major agricultural areas, pleading for grain shipments to save their starving people, noting that their needs were "a matter of life and death." Apparently, the pleas fell on deaf ears, for the Hittites were forced to move their capital from Anatolia to northern Syria, where food was more plentiful. Even this move did not save the empire, which soon collapsed, its capital burned to the ground.

The rise of the Neo-Assyrian state followed a period of aridity that lasted close to three centuries, from 1200 BCE to 900 BCE, and that made the rain-fed agriculture practiced in northern Mesopotamia, the homeland of the Assyrian people and the location of the Old and Middle Assyrian Kingdoms, precarious. The following text from an Assyrian chronicle, written in 1082 BCE, details an invasion of nomadic Aramean tribespeople and reveals how hazardous life was for the settled Assyrian people at that time: "[In King Tilgath-pileser I's 32nd year, a famine occurred so severe that] people ate one another's flesh. Aramean 'houses' plundered, seized the roads, and conquered and took [many fortified cities] of Assyria. [The people of Assyria fled] to the mountains . . . [to save their] lives. [The Arameans] took . . . their money and their property" (Radner, p. 68). It was only after this period of suffering had waned that the Neo-Assyrian state was able to rise and flourish.

The Mycenaeans were also hard hit, living in one of the marginal areas of the Greek mainland and dependent for their livelihood on exporting olives, wine, and timber. Diminished rains made it impossible for farmers there to export these products and led to the disintegration of their culture. As a result, the Greek mainland experienced a 400-year period of economic decline, vividly captured by the Athenian historian Thucydides, writing in the fifth century BCE. Looking back on a dismal past, he remembered a dark age, "when there was no commerce, when people did not have dealings with each other without fear either on land or sea, when they only cultivated enough of their own land to provide a living for themselves, and when they had no surpluses of goods" (*History of the Peloponnesian War*, 1.2.1).

The great trading cities of the Levant, and especially Ugarit, an important port city in what is today northern Syria, were destroyed in the tumultuous movement of peoples in the twelfth century BCE. In the remains of the destroyed palace, cuneiform tablets were found that report on the impending disaster in vivid detail. One of the tablets sent to the king warns of the arrival of the *hapiru*, one of the threatening nomad peoples, and asks the ruler to prepare 150 ships for defense. Another, earlier tablet sent by the king of Ugarit to the king of Alashia (Cyprus) describes the threat, saying, "behold, the enemy's ships came [here]; my cities were burned, and they did evil things to my country. . . . May my father know it: the seven ships of the enemy that came here inflicted much damage to us" (Astour, p. 255). All of the major centers of the coast and inland were burned to the ground, including Alalakh, Hamath, Qatna, and Kadesh. Many were never reoccupied.

IMPERIAL FRINGES IN WESTERN AFRO-EURASIA

The cultures that emerged on Afro-Eurasia's western edges were well beyond the reach of the Neo-Assyrian and Persian Empires. Although their powerful neighbors affected them, western peoples—such as the Sea Peoples, the Greeks, the Phoenicians, and the Israelites—retained their own languages, beliefs, and systems of rule. While their communities were smaller than those in Southwest Asia, each asserted power and had long-lasting influence disproportionate to its size. But here, too, as we will see, drought affected the entire region, causing marauders, originally inhabiting southern Europe, to pour out of their homelands in search of new, more favorable territories. They, along with drought conditions, undermined the Hittites, the Mycenaeans, and the Minoans on the island of Crete and even troubled the powerful New Kingdom state in Egypt. (See Map 4.4.)

Sea Peoples

New migrations brought violent change to long-established kingdoms and states in the Mediterranean and Southwest Asia. Among those feeling the effects of the drought that struck this area beginning around 1200 BCE were Indo-European-speaking peoples inhabiting the Danube River basin in central Europe. Previously, this area's dynamism had come from the outside, but two key factors reversed this trend: a rapid rise in population and the development of local natural resources, including metallurgy in a new metal, iron. By the end of the second millennium BCE, this surplus population, armed with its new iron weapons, moved in large groups back down the Danube into southeastern Europe, the Aegean, and the eastern Mediterranean. Advancing even into Southwest Asia, the invaders brought turmoil to the peoples living there. These huge movements weakened the power of empires and regimes in the region, increased the value of mobility as peoples vied for resources, and opened new frontiers for the development of smaller, more innovative communities.

The ultimate blow to the already weakened imperial states of the Aegean Sea and Southwest Asia came from the fringe in the form of armed invasions that caused the collapse of even the most highly developed societies in the region. The first to fall were the Hittites, who had once dominated the central lands of what is today Turkey. Once the invaders reached the Mediterranean, they mainly used boats for transport. These dynamic communities are sometimes known as the **Sea Peoples**. The Egyptians knew them as the Peleset, and only by marshaling all the resources of their land did the pharaohs manage to repel them. Outside Egypt, states and kingdoms suffered heavily from their ravages. The Sea Peoples settled along the southern coast of the Levant, where they later became known as the Philistines.

In the Mediterranean, the Sea Peoples' intrusion shook the social order of the Minoans on the island of Crete (see Chapter 3). Agricultural production declined, and as the palace-centered bureaucracies and priesthoods of the second millennium BCE vanished, more violent societies emerged that relied on the newcomers' iron weapons. This was the culture of warrior-heroes described in the *Iliad,* an epic poem about the Trojan War composed centuries after the events it relates. It was based on oral tales passed down and embellished for generations. (See Primary Source: War in Homer's *Iliad.*)

For the long-established kingdoms and states of Southwest Asia and the Mediterranean, these rapid transformations were destructive and traumatic. But they were also creative because they shattered traditional ways of doing things, wiping the social slate clean. In fact, violent change and the emergence of new powers at the margins were the first steps toward completely new patterns of human relations.

MAP 4.4 | The Mediterranean World, 1000-400 BCE

Peoples on the fringes of the great regional empires of Southwest Asia and North Africa had strong influences beyond their borders, despite their political marginalization. Though politically dwarfed by the Neo-Assyrian and Persian Empires, various groups in the Mediterranean basin displayed strong cultural and economic power.

- What were the borderland communities, and what did they trade?
- How far did their trading networks and settlement patterns extend?
- Why were such small communities able to flourish in terms of trade and settlement?

Legend:
- Greek homeland
- Area of Greek colonization
- Phoenician homeland
- Area of Phoenician settlement
- Area of Etruscan city-states
- Greek trade route
- Phoenician trade route
- Greek homeland city
- City founded by Greeks
- City founded by Phoenicians
- Etruscan city

Natural Resources
- Timber
- Grain
- Iron
- Copper
- Silver
- Gold

The Greeks

Among the different small-scale societies that emerged in Persia's shadow, the Greeks offer a good example of the energy and dynamism of these new communities. In areas of contact with the Persian Empire, Greek-speaking people in different cities sometimes cooperated with the Persians, even borrowing their ideas, but sometimes strongly resisted them.

In 499 BCE, some Greek city-states and others in the eastern Mediterranean revolted against the Persians, who claimed control over the Greek islands and mainland. During the struggle,

some Greek communities sided with the Persians and suffered condemnation by other Greeks for doing so. On the mainland, farther away from the contact zone, most Greek cities resisted the Persian king's authority. So, in 492 BCE, Darius sent his fleet to subdue Athens and Sparta on the mainland, but the ships were destroyed in a storm. Two years later, Darius and his vast army invaded mainland Greece but suffered a humiliating defeat at the hands of the much smaller force of Athenians at Marathon, near Athens. The Persians retreated and waited another decade before challenging their western foe again. Meanwhile, however, Athens was becoming a major sea power.

War in Homer's *Iliad*

The great epic poem called the Iliad—*about the war that took place at Ilium, a Greek name for the city of Troy—was attributed by the later Greeks to a poet named Homer. However, the written text is actually the result of generations of oral singers who composed different versions of this story in the ninth and eighth centuries BCE. The story takes place on the plains in front of Troy, and it focuses on a few prominent warriors—such as Achilles and Odysseus on the side of the Achaeans (the Greeks, also called Akhaians), and Hector and Paris (the son of Priam, king of Troy) on the Trojans' side. Historians debate the historical reality of the story, but almost all agree on the site of the ancient city it describes.*

The son of Priam wearing a gleaming breastplate
let fly through the lines but his sharp spear missed
and he hit Leucus instead, Odysseus' loyal comrade,
gouging his groin as the man hauled off a corpse—
it dropped from his hands and Leucus sprawled across it.
Enraged at his friend's death Odysseus sprang in fury,
helmed in fiery bronze he plowed through the front
and charging the enemy, glaring left and right
he hurled his spear—a glinting brazen streak—
and the Trojans gave ground, scattering back,
panicking there before his whirling shaft—
a direct hit! Odysseus struck Democoon,
. . . speared him straight through one temple
and out the other punched the sharp bronze point
and the dark came swirling thick across his eyes—
down he crashed, armor clanging against his chest.
And the Trojan front shrank back, glorious Hector too
as the Argives yelled and dragged away the corpses,
pushing on, breakneck on. But lord god Apollo,
gazing down now from the heights of Pergamus,
rose in outrage, crying down at the Trojans,

"Up and at them, you stallion-breaking Trojans!
Never give up your lust for war against these Argives!
What are their bodies made of, rock or iron to block
your tearing bronze? Stab them, slash their flesh!

• • •

Now a jagged rock struck Amarcineus's son
Diores against his right shin, beside the ankle.
Pirous son of Imbrasus winged it hard and true,
the Thracian chief who had sailed across from Aenus . . .
the ruthless rock striking the bones and tendons
crushed them to pulp—he landed flat on his back,
slamming the dust, both arms flung out to his comrades,
gasping out his life. Pirous who heaved the rock
came rushing in and speared him up the navel—
his bowels uncoiled, spilling loose on the ground
and the dark came swirling down across his eyes.
But Pirous—
Aetolian Thoas speared *him* as he swerved and sprang away,
the lancehead piercing his chest above the nipple
plunged deep in his lung, and Thoas, running up,

wrenched the heavy spear from the man's chest,
drew his blade, ripped him across the belly,
took his life but he could not strip his armor.
And now . . .
no man who waded into that work could scorn it any longer,
anyone still not speared or stabbed by tearing bronze
who whirled into the heart of all that slaughter—
not even if great Athena led him by the hand,
flicking away the weapons hailing down against him.
That day ranks of Trojans, ranks of Achaean fighters
sprawled there side-by-side, facedown in the dust.

QUESTIONS FOR ANALYSIS

- What do the style of combat and the weapons used in this period reveal about the larger society of the time?
- More important, what do the poet's words tell us about how violence connects gods, humans, social identity, and personal relationships?
- What can we surmise about the cultures from which these soldiers come?

Source: Homer, *The Iliad*, translated by Robert Fagles (New York: Viking, 1990), pp. 161–63.

Mycenaean Arms and Armor. *A Mycenaean vase that illustrates the central role of arms and war to the societies on mainland Greece in the period down to 1200 BCE. The men bear common suits of armor and weapons—helmets, corsets, spears, and shields—most likely supplied to them by the palace-centered organizations to which they belonged. Despite these advantages, they were not able to mount a successful defense against the land incursions that destroyed the Mycenaean palaces toward the end of the thirteenth century BCE.*

Under the leadership of Themistocles in the 480s BCE, Athens became a naval power whose strength was its fleet of triremes (battleships). This shift in power had a significant effect on the subsequent relationship between Greeks and Persians. When the two forces met again in 480 BCE, the Persians lost the pivotal naval battle at Salamis. A year later, they suffered a decisive

defeat on land and eventually lost the war. (But in a way that was typical of the intertwined relationships between the two cultures, Themistocles, the hero of Salamis, later finished his career in the service of the Persian king.)

Defeats of the Persian military changed the balance of power. For the next 150 years, Persia lost ground to the Greeks, who gradually regained territory in southeastern Europe and western Anatolia. That expanded territory and its governance would become in the fifth century BCE the root of Greek civil discord (see Chapter 5).

The Phoenicians

Certain peoples living on the borderlands of large empires, such as the Phoenicians, coexisted with and flourished under imperial rule, while maintaining some political and economic autonomy. Particularly successful were those on the western edges of the emerging Neo-Assyrian and later Persian Empires.

Living in the region of modern-day Lebanon were the Chanani (called Canaanites in the Bible). We know these entrepreneurial people by the name that the Greeks gave them—**Phoenicians** ("purple people")—because of an expensive purple dye that they manufactured and traded. A mixture of the local population and the more recently arrived Sea Peoples, these traders preferred opening up new markets and new ports to subduing frontiers. Their coastal cities were ideally situated to develop trade throughout the entire Mediterranean basin. Inland stood an extraordinary forest of massive cedars—perfect timber for making large, seaworthy craft and a highly desirable export to the treeless heartlands of Egypt and Mesopotamia.

The Sea Battle at Salamis. *A modern artist's reconstruction of the sea battle at Salamis in which the Greek ships led by Athens defeated a large invading fleet commanded by King Xerxes of Persia. The trireme—so-called because of its three banks of oars—was the state-of-the-art battleship of the time. Drawing on their long experience of sailing on the Mediterranean and using the fleet of triremes built under Themistocles, the Athenians gained a critical victory over the Persians and asserted ascendancy over the eastern Mediterranean.*

Innovations in shipbuilding and seafaring enabled the Phoenicians to sail as far west as present-day Morocco and Spain, carrying huge cargoes of such goods as timber, dyed cloth, glassware, wines, textiles, copper ingots, and carved ivory. Their trading colonies all around the southern and western rims of the Mediterranean (including Carthage in modern-day Tunisia on the North African coast) became major ports that shipped goods from interior regions throughout the Mediterranean—and that faced competition from Greek colonies in the western Mediterranean.

Although the Phoenicians are well known as sailors and merchants, they are better known for revolutionizing commerce and communication through their development of the **alphabet**. Introduced in the second millennium BCE in the western Levant, this new method of writing arrived in the west in 800 BCE, probably through Greek traders working in Phoenician centers. The alphabet allowed the educated to communicate directly with one another, dramatically reducing the need for professional scribes. Phoenician trade and their alphabet enabled this "fringe" group to exert influence far beyond the confines of their political borders.

The Israelites

To the south of the mountains of Lebanon, the homeland of the Phoenicians, another minor region extended to the borderlands of Egypt. In this narrow strip of land between the Mediterranean Sea to the west and the desert to the east, an important microsociety emerged, one that was to have an impact on world history that was out of proportion to its population and the geographical size of its homeland. The Israelites were less oriented to the Mediterranean and to seafaring than the Phoenicians. Their hybrid society mixed their local culture with social, economic, and religious forms commonly found across Southwest Asia and Egypt.

We do not know much that is certain about Israelite origins. Their own later stories emphasized beginnings in Mesopotamia to the east and origins of the patriarch Abraham from the city of Ur on the Euphrates River. Later stories also emphasized connections with Egypt to the west and the mass movement of a captive Israelite population out of Egypt under Moses. All that scholars can state with reasonable certainty is that material

PHÆNICIAN	ANCIENT GREEK	LATER GREEK	ENGLISH
⋈ X	A ΑΑΑ	A Α	A
9	₿ ℰ	B	B
⋀⋀	∧Γⲥ	Γ	G
⊿9	△▽ρ	△	D
∃	∃ℰℰE	E ϵ	E
⅂	⅂F		F
Z	⧖ Ⅰ	Z	Z
Ħ	θ ਖ		H
⊕	⊙⊗⊕◈□	Θ	Th
⌒	⟋⟨⟩	Ⅰ	I
⅄⅄	⅄ ⅄ Κ	Κ	K
⟨⟨	⟋⟍⟋⟍	∧	L
↯	⟋⟍⟋⟍⟋⟍⟋⟍	M	M
⟋⟍⟋⟍	⟋⟍⟋⟍⟋⟍	N	N
⟊⟊	⧧ ⟝	Ξ O	X
O	⊙◇□	O	O
⅂	⅂ ⌐	∏	P
⌄	Q		Q
⟨99	⟨99ρρρ	Ρ	R
⟋⟍⟋⟍ʍʍ	ΜʍⅯℰⲥ	Σ ⲥ	S
⅄⅄⅄	Ⅰ ⴕ	Τ	T

The Phoenician Alphabet. Top: *The first alphabet was written on clay tablets using the cuneiform script. It was developed by Phoenician traders who needed a script that was easy to learn so that they could record transactions without specially trained scribes. This tablet was found at the port town of Ugarit (Ras Shamra), in Syria, and is dated to the fourteenth century BCE.* Bottom: *The forms of the letters in the Phoenician alphabet of the first millennium BCE are based on signs used to represent the Aramaic language. These Phoenician letters were then borrowed by the ancient Greeks. Our alphabet is based on that used by the Romans, who borrowed their letter forms from the later Greek inscriptions.*

signs of a local regional culture began to emerge in the area of present-day Israel between 1200 and 1000 BCE, culminating with the emergence of a state in the form of a kingdom centered at Jerusalem under King David (r. c. 1000–960 BCE). The kingdom that David and his successor Solomon (r. c. 960–930 BCE) established around Jerusalem, centered on the great temple that Solomon built in the city, did not last long. Because of internal disputes, the kingdom fragmented immediately after Solomon's reign into a tiny northern kingdom, Israel, and a small southern one, Judah.

MONOTHEISM AND PROPHETS Within the microstate founded by David and Solomon, profound religious and cultural changes took place. A single great temple in Jerusalem now outranked all other shrines in the land. Especially among the educated upper classes linked to the temple, an absolute priority focused on one god, YHWH, over other regional deities. For a long time, however, this emphasis was relative, what modern scholars call *henotheism*: the ascendancy and power of one god over other spirits and deities that still exist. Gradually, however, there was a move to true **monotheism**: the acceptance of only one god to the exclusion of all others. The long transition to monotheism, however, did not take place without quarrels and resistance and was not in place until the seventh century BCE. A contentious process, the triumph of monotheism owed much to prophetic figures—freelance religious men of power who found themselves in opposition to the formal power of the kings and priests of the temple in Jerusalem.

The most ferocious of these prophets were men like Isaiah (c. 720s BCE), Ezra (c. 600s BCE), and Jeremiah (c. 590s BCE). They did not shrink from threatening divine annihilation for groups that opposed the new idea of one temple, one god, and one moral system to the exclusion of all others. On one occasion, the prophet Ezra thundered: "Whoever will not obey the law of your God and the law of the king, let judgment be rigorously executed upon him, be it death, banishment, confiscation of property, or imprisonment" (Ezra 7:26 New English Bible). The moral preaching, exhortations, and threats of these men marked the high point of a long and difficult battle to defeat the religious diversity to which many people were accustomed. But prevail they did. They were part of a movement to enforce belief in a single, all-powerful god and his strict social and moral codes that governed the daily lives of all members of the community. These laws came to be enshrined in the Torah, a series of books that encapsulated the laws governing all aspects of life, including family and marriage, food, clothing, sex, and worship. The whole of it was formulated as a "contract" between the Israelites and their one and only god. They alone were his people.

The monotheism of the Israelites was to have far-reaching and long-lasting historical consequences, in part because Jewish peoples scattered far and wide throughout Afro-Eurasia and in part because of its influence in Christianity and Islam.

FOUNDATIONS OF VEDIC CULTURE IN SOUTH ASIA (1500–600 BCE)

In South Asia, it was language and belief systems, rather than a unified political system enforced and enlarged by military conquest, that brought people together. People moved in greater numbers and covered longer distances in this period, and in doing so they created new mechanisms of integration. The Indo-European-speaking peoples (also known as Vedic peoples for the religious traditions they brought with them) who began to enter South Asia through the passes in the Hindu Kush Mountains in the middle of the second millennium BCE eventually occupied the whole of what are today Pakistan, Bangladesh, and northern India (see Chapter 3). Here their populations expanded and, together with the indigenous inhabitants, created a flourishing culture. Unlike societies in Mesopotamia and Egypt, the new rulers in this region did not have previous states on which to found their power.

Floods and earthquakes had weakened the earlier Harappan urban centers in the Indus River valley (see Chapter 2), and not only had its urban culture died out several centuries before the new people streamed in from the northwest, but rice farming had also suffered. In addition, the same drought conditions that had troubled the Egyptians, the Greeks, and the peoples of Southwest Asia also descended upon the Indus Valley. Thus, as the Vedic migrants moved into these new ecological zones, which did not support cattle herding, they had to master rice cultivation with little assistance from the original inhabitants. Even so, not only did the Vedic peoples become skilled rice farmers, but they also made cotton cultivation work in the wetter areas of the Ganges regions.

Social and Religious Culture

The men and women who migrated into the northern lands of South Asia were illiterate, chariot-riding, and cattle-keeping pastoral peoples who lacked experience of cities and urban life. They brought with them, however, much-beloved and elaborate rituals, mainly articulated in hymns, rhymes, and explanatory texts, called **Vedas** (Sanskrit for "wisdom" or "knowledge"), which they retained as they entered a radically different environment and which they relied on to provide a foundation for assimilating new ways. These hymns reflected their earlier lives on the plains of central Asia and were infused with images of animals and gods. In some of these Vedic poems, storms "gallop" across the heavens, and thunder sounds like the "neigh of horses." The rituals that the people brought with them involved sacrificing cattle, horses, and sheep to their gods and gathering together at festivities to sing hymns, make animal sacrifices, burn *ghee* (clarified butter) for the gods, and share banquets. Priests conducted these ceremonies, receiving payment in cows. The Vedas became sacred religious works and were eventually written down in Sanskrit.

The migrants encountered indigenous people who either lived in agricultural settlements or were herders like themselves. The newcomers allied themselves with some of the locals, who showed them how to live in their new environment. They made enemies of others, fighting with them for territory and dominance. In their interaction with peoples with different cultural practices and languages, the Vedic migrants kept their own language and religious rituals but also absorbed local words and deities. Allies and defeated enemies who became part of their society had to accept Vedic culture. By the middle of the first century BCE, the Vedic peoples covered all of what is now northern India, and their language and rituals had become dominant in their new land.

Material Culture

Initially, the material culture of Vedic society was rudimentary. Even chiefs and elite warriors enjoyed few luxuries. Early trade was based not on imported goods but on horses, which had to come in from the northwest beyond the Hindu Kush because local environmental factors prevented their successful breeding or training. The ruling elite never gave up its preoccupation with fine horses. To make their trade in these resplendent war mounts easier, they created a long-distance route across the North Indian plain that stretched from the Khyber Pass to the Lower Ganges. (See Map 4.5.) Symbolic of the continuing significance of the horse to the ruling elites of Vedic society was the *ashvamedha,* or horse sacrifice, later found in the period of the kings. In this ritual, the king's horse was consecrated and then allowed to roam for a year over land that then became the king's land. At the end of the year, the horse was sacrificed in a great ceremony.

As the Vedic people entered the fertile river basins, they gradually settled down as cultivators of the land and herders of animals. Their turn to agriculture could hardly have been easy, but they were aided by learning plowing from local farmers and gaining access to excellent iron ore. The iron plow was crucial for tilling the Ganges plain and transforming the Deccan plateau into croplands. In the drier Indus Valley to the north, the Vedic people grew wheat, barley, millet, and cotton; in the wet lowlands of the Ganges plain, they cultivated rice paddies. Farmers also toiled to produce tropical crops such as sugarcane and spices like pepper, ginger, and cinnamon. With these new crops, the Vedic people transformed a sparsely populated region into a crowded domain.

As farming became the dominant way of life and urban settlements stretched out across the region, trade blossomed via river and land routes. Trade between settlements developed as the agricultural surpluses grew; grain was transported to towns to feed them. Artisans pressed sugarcane into sugar in the cities, and merchants sold the finished product back to people in the agricultural villages.

Splintered States and Social Distinctions: Clans and Varna

The region's social and economic integration offered a stark contrast to its political fragmentation. In the process of fanning out from the Punjab (the region of the five tributaries of the Indus River) and settling in the plain between the Ganges and Yamuna Rivers, the Vedic peoples created small regional governments and chieftainships. And as much as they fought with the indigenous peoples, they fought even more fiercely among themselves. Such aggression reinforced the importance of warriors and elevated the worship of the gods of war (Indra) and fire (Agni). The elite warriors battled one another and the farmers for land and other resources, just as occurred in the Mycenaean societies, in the tribal societies of the Iranian plateau, and in Zhou China.

CLANS The chieftainships eventually became small states, nominally headed by rulers called kings, with inhabitants bound to one another through lines of descent from a common ancestor. Family descent or lineage was established through blood ties, through alliances by means of marriage, and through invented family relations. The earliest Vedic society had two main lineages: the lunar lineage and the solar lineage. Each had its own creation myth, ancestors, language, and rituals. The lineages included many clans (a clan is a social group comprising many households and claiming descent from a common ancestor) in which seniority determined one's power and importance. The Vedic peoples absorbed many local clans into their own lineages. Clans that adopted the Vedic culture became part of the lineage (through marriage or made-up ties) and were considered insiders. In contrast, clans that had other languages and rituals were considered to be uncivilized outsiders.

These two lineages became less important over time but were memorialized in the later *Mahabharata.* This epic poem relates the last phase of the lunar lineage, while the *Ramayana*—a Sanskrit epic poem like the *Mahabharata*—focuses on a hero of the solar lineage. Later rulers continued to draw on the memory of these two ancient lineages, legitimizing their regimes by claiming blood links with them. These kinship communities gradually formed into what were known as *mahajanapada,* or "great communities." Sixteen of these great communities were located in the Ganges River basin.

VARNA The Vedic peoples who spread across South Asia had originally been herding communities in which few social distinctions other than age and gender were important. As these peoples settled down, became farmers, and created state structures, their societies became more complex and hierarchical. In particular, the rise of settled agriculture after 1000 BCE led to a great divide between those who controlled the land and those who worked it. As these divisions developed, the Vedic peoples created a unique social system based on rigid distinctions of

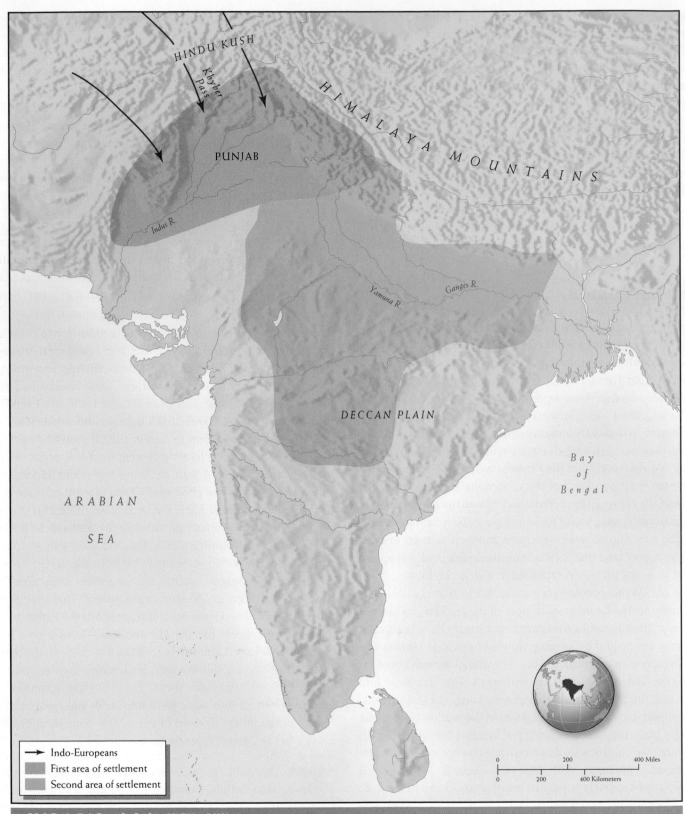

MAP 4.5 | South Asia, 1500–400 BCE

Indo-European peoples crossed over mountainous areas and entered northern South Asia, bringing with them their nomadic ways. They were, however, quick to learn settled agriculture from the local inhabitants.

- Where did the Indo-Europeans originally come from?
- What enabled Vedic culture to spread so rapidly?
- What kept it from spreading further?

status. These social divisions described the specific strata that carried out different social, political, and economic functions in South Asia. (See Chapter 5 for more discussion.)

In this earlier era, the Vedic peoples used the term **varna** to refer to these divisions and recognized four ranked social groups—Brahmans, Kshatriyas, Vaishyas, and Shudras. The Sanskrit word *varna* means "color." Vedic hymns claimed that the four *varnas* came from the dismembered body of Primeval Man, who had been sacrificed by the gods to create the universe. From Primeval Man's mouth came the Brahmans, or priests; his arms produced the Kshatriyas, or warriors; the thighs gave birth to the Vaishyas, or commoners; and from the feet emerged the lowly Shudras, or laborers and servants. This was the theory—no doubt biased toward the Brahmans, who composed the scriptures, and toward the Kshatriyas, the warriors and aristocratic ruling class, who supported the Brahmans. Even so, all the groups were believed to come from a single ancestry. In practice there were many local variations, and the four-group division was less a rigid system and more of a way to stratify an increasingly agricultural and settled world.

Those clan members who had been politically the most powerful and had led their communities into northern India claimed the status of Kshatriyas. It was they who controlled the land. Less powerful clan members who worked the land and tended livestock became Vaishyas. As rice production and labor-intensive paddy cultivation took hold, many households hired laborers and used slaves. These people came from outside the Vedic lineages and became the Shudras ("the small ones"). They constituted the lowest *varna*. The priests, or Brahmans, claimed the highest status, for they performed the rituals and understood the religious principles without which life was believed to be unsustainable. Only they were thought to be able to commune with the gods, a skill that many regarded as their most coveted talent. Some of these Brahmans functioned as priests for the chiefs, and some were sages who lived as ascetics (individuals who deny themselves comforts) in forests, where they discussed philosophical questions with their students. In addition, Brahmans and Kshatriyas reinforced each other's high status. Brahmans performed the sacrifices that converted warriors into kings, and kings reciprocated by paying fees and gifts to the Brahmans. The rest (Vaishyas and Shudras) were left with the tasks of ensuring the sustenance of the elite. (See Primary Source: Becoming a Brahman Priest.)

Of the many ways in which societies have stratified their members and accorded higher or lower statuses to individuals—mainly in the modern western world through class, race, and gender—the Vedic peoples overwhelmingly stressed birth. The three higher social groups (Brahmans, Kshatriyas, and Vaishyas) were twice born. The ritual of having undergone a second birth, which usually occurred at the age of twelve, set them off from the Shudras. Brahmans, who administered the rituals of second birth, were the least polluted of the social groups, followed by Kshatriyas and Vaishyas. Shudras, who did not undergo a second birth, were therefore considered the most polluted. A fifth social group later came into existence, even more polluted than the rest. This complex hierarchy so deeply connected with Vedic religion provided the primary unifying force for South Asian communities.

Unity through the Vedas and Upanishads

A Vedic culture, transmitted from generation to generation by the Brahman priests, unified what political rivalries had divided. Belief in Indra and other gods, a common language (Sanskrit), and shared cultural symbols linked the dispersed communities and gave Vedic peoples a collective identity. Sanskrit was a language carried by the Vedic people from central Asia into South Asia, where it was further refined. The Brahman priests used it to transmit the Vedas orally. By expressing the people's sacred knowledge in the beautiful rhythms and rhymes of Sanskrit, the Vedas effectively passed on their culture from one generation to the next.

The Vedas promoted cultural unity and pride through common ritual practices and support for hereditary *raja* states. As the priests of Vedic society, the Brahmans were responsible for memorizing every syllable and sound of the Vedic works. These included commentaries on sacred works from early nomadic times, as well as new rules and rituals explaining the settled, farming way of life. The main body of Vedic literature includes the four Vedas: Rig-Veda, Sama-Veda, Yajur-Veda, and Atharva-Veda. The Rig-Veda, the earliest text, is a collection of hymns praising the gods, including Indra (god of war), Agni (god of fire), and Varuna (god of water). Indra stands out as the most powerful and important, as he is the one who set the order of the universe and made life possible. The Sama-Veda is a textbook of songs for priests to perform when making ritual sacrifices; most of their stanzas also appear in the Rig-Veda. The Yajur-Veda is a prayer book for the priest who conducted rituals for chariot races, horse sacrifices, or the king's coronation. The Atharva-Veda includes charms and remedies; many address problems related to agriculture, a central aspect of life. Although the Vedic period left no impressive buildings and artifacts, it created a wealth of thinking about cosmology and human society. In this way, it laid the religious foundations for coming generations.

During the middle of the first millennium BCE, some thinkers (mostly Brahman ascetics dwelling in forests) felt that the Vedic rituals no longer provided satisfactory answers to the many questions of a rapidly changing society. The result was a collection of works known as the **Upanishads**, or "the supreme knowledge," which expanded the Vedic cultural system. Taking the form of dialogues between disciples and a sage, the

PRIMARY SOURCE

Becoming a Brahman Priest

When the Vedic people became farmers, many of them started to question the validity of sacrificing cows, the draft animals valued for their use in cultivation. Around the seventh century BCE, some thinkers abandoned Vedic rituals and chose to live simply in forests as they debated the meaning of life and the structure of the universe. Those sages were Brahman rishi, highly respected priests. However, not every one of the famous Brahmans was born a Brahman.

1. Satyakâma, the son of Gabâlâ, addressed his mother and said: 'I wish to become a Brahmakârin [religious student], mother. Of what family am I?'

2. She said to him: 'I do not know, my child, of what family thou art. In my youth when I had to move about much as a servant [waiting on the guests in my father's house] I conceived thee. I do not know of what family thou art. I am Gabâlâ by name, thou art Satyakâma [Philalethes]. Say that thou art Satyakâma Gâbâla.'

3. He going to Gautama Hâridrumata said to him, 'I wish to become a Brahmakârin with you, Sir. May I come to you, Sir?'

4. He said to him: 'Of what family are you, my friend?' He replied: 'I do not know, Sir, of what family I am. I asked my mother, and she answered: "In my youth when I had to move about much as a servant, I conceived thee. I do not know of what family thou art. I am Gabâlâ by name, thou art Satyakâma," I am therefore Satyakâma Gâbâla, Sir.'

5. He said to him: 'No one but a true Brâhmana would thus speak out. Go and fetch fuel, friend, I shall initiate you. You have not swerved from the truth.'

Having initiated him, he chose four hundred lean and weak cows, and said: 'Tend these friend.'

He drove them out and said to himself. 'I shall not return unless I bring back a thousand.' He dwelt a number of years [in the forest], until the cows became a thousand.

QUESTIONS FOR ANALYSIS

- Satyakama became a well-known Brahman teacher after his study. Judging from this story, was he born a Brahman?

- At that time, how did the rishis and their disciples survive in the forest areas when thinking and studying?

Source: The Upanishads, translated by F. Max Müller, vol. 1 of Sacred Books of the East, edited by F. Max Müller (1900; reprint, New Delhi: Motilal Banarsidass, 1981), pp. 60–61.

Upanishads explored questions of deep concern at that time. Out of these dialogues came a set of lessons that offered insights into the ideal social order, eventually becoming a canon to be shared beyond local communities. The Upanishads teach that people are not separate from one another but belong to an integrated cosmic universe called Brahma. While the physical world is always changing and is filled with chaos and illusion, *atman*, the eternal being, exists in all people and all creatures. Atman's presence in each living being makes all creatures part of a universal soul. While all living beings must die, the atman guarantees eternal life, ensuring that souls are reborn and transmigrate into new lives. This cycle continues with humans as they are reborn either as humans or as other living creatures, such as cows, insects, or plants.

These unique Vedic views of life and the universe were passed along as principles of faith, bringing spiritual unity to the northern half of South Asia. Unlike the societies of Southwest Asia and North Africa, here in the states of the Indus Valley and the Ganges plain the common Vedic culture—rather than larger political units—was the unifying bond.

THE EARLY ZHOU STATE IN EAST ASIA (1045–771 BCE)

Drought reshaped the political map of East Asia in much the same way that it altered power alignments in Southwest Asia. Here, too, a radical change in the climate was a major factor in the demise of the Shang state and the rise of a successor regime, the early Zhou state, also known as the Western Zhou. This state would be succeeded by the Eastern Zhou—in reality a time of turmoil, including the Warring States period (see Chapter 5).

East Asia's environmental crisis had its origins on the plains of central Asia and the steppe lands of Mongolia. In central Asia, the more arid conditions that were sweeping across the Afro-Eurasian landmass resulted in powerful hot and dry winds carrying immense quantities of dust onto the North China plain. The dust storms reduced the soil's ability to retain moisture and led to a sharp decline in soil fertility and reliable harvests. In Mongolia, steppe lands were like oases whenever rains were abundant, attracting large nomadic pastoralist populations.

Families expanded and herds increased during these periods. But when the climate changed, rains failed, and drought ensued, nomadic communities poured out of these regions in search of more favorable locations. Since many of these nomadic societies possessed military skills far superior to those of settled societies, their invasions proved devastating. Such was the case for the Han Chinese in the eighth century BCE as Mongol nomads inflicted severe damage on North Chinese communities.

One of the results of climate change in China was the replacement of the Shang state by the Zhou state. Zhou rulers claimed the "mandate of heaven" as one of the three allegedly original dynasties of Xia, Shang, and Zhou. The Zhou had been only a minor state during the height of Shang power, living in the valley of the Wei River; the two peoples traded and often were allies to fend off raiders from the northwest. Over time, the appearance of a dynamic leader, King Wu (literally, the "warrior king"), and the need to find more resources emboldened the Zhou to challenge the Shang for supremacy in North China. At a battle in 1045 BCE, the Zhou prevailed. Wu owed his success to an army of 45,000 troops and superior weaponry, including dagger axes, bronze armor, and 300 war chariots. These were small numbers by Southwest Asian standards, but overwhelming in East Asia. In addition, the Zhou state,

while unifying an area larger than that ruled over by the Shang, still governed a relatively small territory compared with the vast state that the later Qin and Han dynasties oversaw. In the centuries that followed, innovations in politics, agriculture, and social structure helped the Zhou to integrate their state and build a powerful tributary state. (See Map 4.6 and also Chapter 5.)

Integration through State Institutions and Agricultural Advances

When the Zhou took over from the Shang, their new state consisted of a patchwork of more than seventy small states, whose local rulers, however, accepted the overarching authority of the Zhou rulers as legitimate kings. To solidify their power, the Zhou copied the Shang's patrimonial state structure, centered on ancestor worship in which the rulers' power passed down through male ancestors reaching back to the gods. On such foundations the Zhou pioneered a dynastic principle; and though one dynasty succeeded another, the result was that the Chinese fostered one of the most long-lived dynastic systems in world history. Thirty-nine Zhou kings followed one after the other, mostly in an orderly father-to-son succession, over a span of eight centuries, and they in turn were succeeded by new "imperial" dynasties ruled by Qin and Han "emperors."

Even though the Zhou drew heavily on Shang precedents, their own innovations produced some of the most significant contributions to China's distinctive cultural and political development. Regarding all those whom they governed as a single people, the Zhou employed the term *Huaxia,* or "Chinese," when referring to their subjects. They also claimed that even though more than seventy states existed at this time, their territories were at heart unified. Thus, they named their lands *Zhongguo,* which at the time meant "the central states" but later came to be called the Middle Kingdom—a term that the Chinese used thereafter right down to present times to refer to their state, even as the territories under Qin and Han dynasts were extraordinarily larger. Moreover, the Zhou rulers of this Middle Kingdom, in addition to being required to rule justly, believed that they had a duty to extend their culture to "less civilized" peoples living in outlying regions.

Although smaller in size, the Zhou expanded their state in many similar ways to those in Southwest Asia. King Wu (r. 1049–1043 BCE) and his successors expanded north toward what is now Beijing and south toward the Yangzi River valley. (See Primary Source: Zhou Succession Story.) Seeking to retain the allegiance of the lords of older states and to gain the support of new lords, whom they appointed in annexed areas, Zhou rulers rewarded their political supporters with lands that they could pass on to their descendants. As the Zhou expanded their territory, their new lands often consisted of garrison towns where the Zhou lords lived surrounded by fields inhabited by local farmers. As under the Shang, Zhou regional lords were expected

Zhou Chariots. *After swearing allegiance to the Shang, the Zhou assembled superior military forces in the northwest, in part by emulating Shang chariots. The Zhou subsequently used their own chariots and archers to defeat the Shang in about 1045 BCE. The regional lords who owed allegiance to the Zhou ruler distinguished themselves in the aristocratic hierarchy by using chariots for travel and battle.*

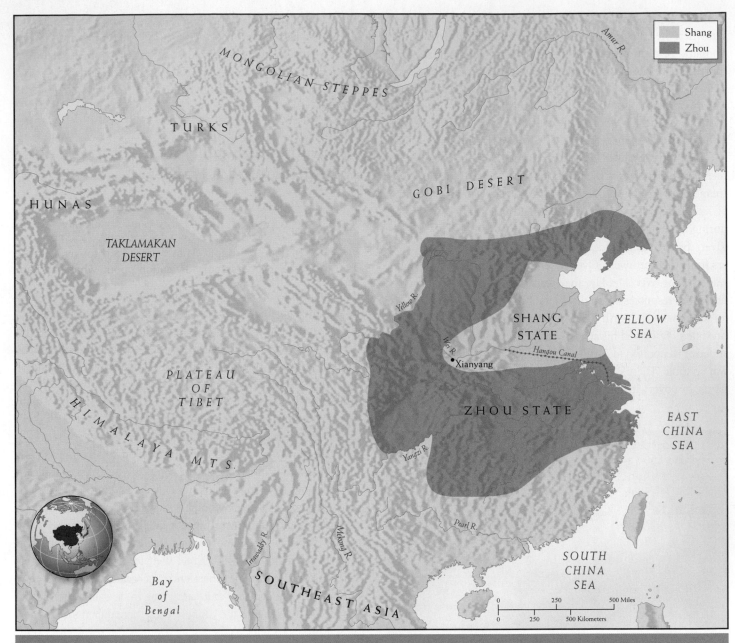

MAP 4.6 | The Zhou State, 2200–256 BCE

Toward the end of the second millennium BCE, the Zhou state supplanted the Shang state as the most powerful political force in East Asia. Using the map above, compare and contrast the territorial reach of the Zhou state with that of the Shang.

- In what direction did the Zhou state expand most dramatically?
- Why do you think this was the case?
- How did the Zhou integrate their geographically large and diverse state?

to supply military forces as needed, pay tribute, and appear at the imperial court to pledge their continuing allegiance.

TECHNOLOGICAL DEVELOPMENT What has been remarkable about China throughout history is how its integration progressed in small steps, not in a single triumphal bound. Zhou achievements likewise were incremental, rooted in a transformation of the countryside as both ruling elites and peasants began expanding the agrarian frontier inland. Wooden and, much later, iron plows enabled farmers to break the hard sod of lands beyond the river basins, and over time cultivators learned the practice of field rotation to prevent soil nutrients from being exhausted. A great advance occurred in the middle of the first millennium BCE as regional states organized local

PRIMARY SOURCE

Zhou Succession Story

Chinese lore often glamorized the early Zhou rulers as sage leaders such as Wu and the Duke of Zhou (Chou). The Shangshu (Classic of History) account, however, shows that the transition of power from the founder, Wu, to the Duke of Zhou was fraught with difficulty—as was often the case in early states. It reveals how the Duke of Zhou tried simultaneously to protect his reputation as adviser to Wu's young son and to preserve Zhou rule. This document also represents one of the first major efforts in Chinese history to provide a historical narrative of events.

After he had completed the conquest of the Shang people, in the second year, King Wu fell ill and was despondent. The two lords, the duke of Shao and Tai-kung Wang, said, "For the king's sake let us solemnly consult the tortoise oracle." But the duke of Chou [Wu's younger brother, named Tan] said, "We must not distress the ancestors, the former kings."

The duke of Chou then offered himself to the ancestors, constructing three altars within a single compound. . . . Then he made this announcement to the Great King, to King Chi, and to King Wen, his great grandfather, grandfather, and father, and the scribe copied down the words of his prayer on tablets:

"Your chief descendant So-and-so [Wu's personal name is tabooed] has met with a fearful disease and is violently ill. If you three kings are obliged to render to Heaven the life of an illustrious son, then substitute me, Tan, for So-and-so's person. I am good and compliant, clever and capable. I have much talent and much skill and can serve the spirits. . . ."

Then he divined with three tortoises, and all were auspicious. He opened the bamboo receptacles and consulted the documents, and they too indicated an auspicious answer. The duke of Chou said to the king, "According to the indications of the oracle, you will suffer no harm."

[King Wu said,] "I, the little child, have obtained a new life from the three kings. I shall plan for a distant end. I hope that they will think of me, the solitary man."

After the duke of Chou returned, he placed the tablets containing the prayer in a metal-bound casket. The next day the king began to recover.

[Later, Wu died and was succeeded by his infant son, Ch'eng. The duke of Chou acted as adviser and was slandered by Wu's younger brothers, whom he was eventually forced to punish.]

In the autumn, when a plentiful crop had ripened but had not yet been harvested, Heaven sent great thunder and lightning accompanied by wind. The grain was completely flattened and even large trees were uprooted. The people of the land were in great fear. The king and his high ministers donned their ceremonial caps and opened the documents of the metal-bound casket and thus discovered the record of how the duke of Chou had offered himself as a substitute for King Wu. . . . .

The king grasped the document and wept. "There is no need for us to make solemn divination about what has happened," he said. "In former times the duke of Chou toiled diligently for the royal house, but I, the youthful one, had no way of knowing it. Now Heaven has displayed its terror in order to make clear the virtue of the duke of Chou. I, the little child, will go in person to greet him, for the rites of our royal house approve such action."

When the king came out to the suburbs to meet the duke of Chou, Heaven sent down rain and reversed the wind, so that the grain all stood up once more. The two lords ordered the people of the land to right all the large trees that had been blown over and to earth them up. Then the year was plentiful. (*Chin t'eng.*)

QUESTIONS FOR ANALYSIS

- How does the passage demonstrate the Zhou's reliance on male ancestor worship?
- What do the direct speeches tell us about the place of divination in Zhou politics?

Source: Translated in Burton Watson, *Early Chinese Literature* (New York: Columbia University Press, 1962), pp. 35–36.

efforts to regulate the flow of the main rivers. They built long canals to promote communication and trade, and they dug impressive irrigation networks to convert arid lands into fertile belts. (Some of these systems remain in use today.) This slow agrarian revolution enabled the Chinese population to soar, reaching perhaps 20 million by the late Zhou era.

Under the Zhou, landowners and rulers organized the construction of dikes and irrigation systems to control the floodplain of the Yellow River and Wei River valley surrounding the capital at Xianyang (present-day Xi'an). For centuries, peasants labored over this floodplain and its tributaries—building dikes, digging canals, and raising levees as the waters flowed to the sea. When their work was done, the bottom of the floodplain was a latticework of rich, well-watered fields, with carefully manicured terraces rising in gradual steps to higher ground. This enormous undertaking was the work of many generations. Eventually, irrigation works grew to such a scale that they required management by the Zhou rulers, centered in the Wei River valley, and their skilled engineers. The engineers also designed canals that connected rivers and supported commerce and other internal exchanges. Tens of thousands of workers spent countless days digging these canals, paying tribute in the form of labor. As we have seen, other rulers in Afro-Eurasia also produced massive building works through forced labor.

Increasingly, the canals linked China's two breadbaskets: the wheat and millet fields in the north and the rice fields in the south. And as with the Yellow River in the north, engineers controlled the Yangzi River in the south. So wealthy was China that its influence even reached the distant steppe lands to the north and west. Nomads in mountainous areas or on the Zhou frontiers, who often fought with the Zhou ruler and his regional lords, now depended on trade with the fertile heartlands. In return for their pastoral produce the Zhou received textiles, metal tools and weapons, and luxury items. In these ways, the Zhou promoted greater unity within their territory and among the peoples living in and around it.

The "Mandate of Heaven" and Justification of Power

In addition to promoting a Chinese ethnic and political identity, the Zhou rulers introduced what was to prove one of East Asia's most enduring political doctrines—the concept of the **mandate of heaven**. They did so by asserting that their moral superiority justified taking over Shang wealth and territories and that heaven had imposed a moral mandate on them to replace the Shang and return good governance to the people. At first they presented the mandate of heaven as a religious compact between the Zhou people and their supreme god in heaven (literally, the "sky god"), but over time Zhou kings and the court detached the concept from the sky god and made it into a freestanding and fundamental Chinese political doctrine. The Zhou argued that since worldly affairs were supposed to align with those of the heavens, heavenly powers conferred legitimate rights to rule only on their chosen representative. In return, the ruler was duty-bound to uphold heaven's principles of harmony and honor. Any ruler who failed in this duty, who let instability creep into earthly affairs, or who let his people suffer would lose the mandate. Under this system, it was the prerogative of spiritual authority to withdraw support from any wayward ruler and to find another, more worthy one. In this way, the Zhou sky god legitimated regime change.

In using this creed, the Zhou rulers had to acknowledge that any group of rulers, even they themselves, could be ousted if they lost the mandate of heaven because of improper practices. In *The Classic of Poetry*, written in the Zhou period, King Wu intones this caution in an ode, saying "the mandate is not easy to keep"; and in another Zhou poem, we are told that "it is not easy to be king." Moreover, after the Zhou overturned the Shang line

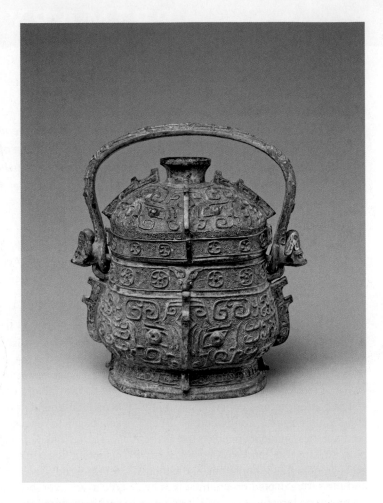

Zhou Wine Vessel. *Under the Zhou, bronze metallurgy depended on a large labor force. Many workers initially came from Shang labor groups, who were superior to the Zhou in technology. The use of bronze, such as for this wine vessel, exemplified dynastic continuity between the Shang and Zhou.*

of succession, rulers were no longer considered gods. From that point on, political legitimacy depended on ruling in accordance with the principles of good governance and upright behavior. Unlike the theocracies of Southwest Asia and the later emperors of Japan, China's rulers created a far-flung state, later an empire, based more on politics, military power, and morality than on religious legitimacy. This concept of the mandate of heaven would be used by later Chinese dynasties to justify their rule all the way down into the twentieth century, making it, along with the tradition of hereditary rule, one of the most important cultural characteristics developed during early Chinese history.

The early Zhou rulers contended that heaven favored their triumph because the last Shang rulers had been evil men whose policies brought pain to the people through waste and corruption. Thereafter, the mandate became a political tool. It was a compelling way to defend continuity of political institutions, if not rulers, in the name of preserving a natural order. It also helps explain why each change in power did not bring about an abrupt overhaul of political and cultural institutions.

A century after the Zhou had seized power, King Mu (r. 956–918 BCE) began a series of reforms that strengthened the powers of the state at a time when its authority was under severe challenge. In the years leading up to Mu's ascension to power, the Zhou had suffered many setbacks. The most ominous was the defeat of the Zhou armies in a battle against a large tributary neighbor on the state's southeastern border. Not only were the Zhou's famous six armies routed, but King Zhao was also killed. With the ruling house in obvious decline, poets began to compose satires that poked fun at it, and critics wondered whether the Zhou had lost the mandate of heaven. Mu turned first to the military, bringing in more competent leaders and reinvigorating the spirit of the forces. Next came the civil bureaucracy: he restructured the court and military by appointing officials, supervisors, and military captains who were not related to him, and he instituted a formal legal code. These changes created a need for bureaucratic records, including archives of appointments and legal verdicts. Increasingly, a pool of scribes and scholars joined the entourage of royal diviners, using their mastery of writing to find patrons at court and among regional powers. Through their powerful rhetoric, they tied many of the new changes to the early Zhou founding myth.

One of the duties and privileges of the ruler was to create a state calendar. This official document defined times for undertaking agricultural activities and celebrating rituals. But unexpected events such as solar eclipses or natural calamities threw into question the ruling house's mandate. Since rulers claimed that their authority came from heaven, the Zhou made great efforts to gain accurate knowledge of the stars and to perfect the astronomical system on which they based their calendar. Advances in astronomy and mathematics enabled Zhou astronomers to precisely calculate the length of a lunar month (29.53 days) and measure the length of the solar year (365.25 days). But a year of twelve lunar months is 354.36 days long. To resolve the discrepancy, the Zhou occasionally inserted a leap month. Scribes dated the reigns of rulers by days and years within a repeating sixty-year cycle.

Zhou legitimacy also derived indirectly from Shang material culture through the use of bronze ritual vessels, statues, ornaments, and weapons. As the Zhou emulated the Shang's large-scale production of ceremonial bronzes, they developed an extensive system of bronze metalworking that required a large force of tribute labor. Many of its members were Shang, who were sometimes forcibly transported to new Zhou towns to produce the bronze ritual objects, which were then sold and distributed across the lands, symbolizing Zhou legitimacy.

Social and Economic Controls

As the Chinese social order became more integrated, it also became more class based. Directly under the Zhou ruler and his royal ministers were the hereditary nobles, divided into five ranks.

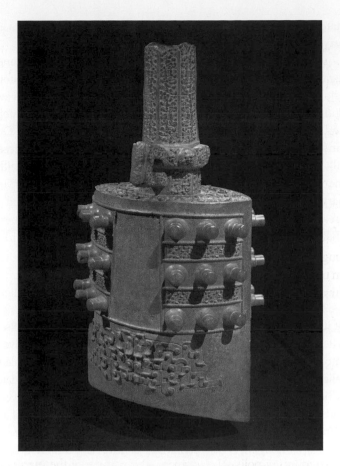

Yongzhong. *This Yongzhong, or ritual bell, from 550 BCE from the Eastern Zhou dynasty, demonstrating the skill that Chinese artisans from this period had in forging large pieces out of copper.*

These regional lords had landholdings of different sizes, but under the powerful tributary state they all owed allegiance to the Zhou ruler. They paid tribute and taxes and supplied warriors to fight in the Zhou army and laborers to clear land, drain fields, and do other work. They periodically appeared at court and took part in complex rituals to reaffirm their allegiance to the ruler. Below the regional lords were high officers at the Zhou court, as well as ministers and administrators who supervised the people's work. Aristocratic warriors stood at the bottom of the noble hierarchy.

Among commoners, an elaborate occupation-based hierarchy developed over time. Initially, most of the population worked as farmers on fields owned by great landholding families. Some commoners were artisans who produced valuable bronze ritual vessels or weavers who spun delicate silk textiles. The later occupation-based system, however, divided people more precisely by function: landholders who produced grain, growers of plants and fruit trees, woodsmen, breeders of cattle and chickens, artisans, merchants, weavers, servants, and those with no fixed occupation. The central government apparently controlled how each group did its work—for example, telling landholders what crops to plant, when to harvest, and when to irrigate. Although reports of these efforts may overstate the government's reach, the Chinese state played a major role in uniting the region's diverse peoples in ways that none of Afro-Eurasia's other great regimes did.

One important method of integration was the political and legal use of family structures. In their patrilineal society, the Zhou established strict hierarchies for both men and women. Both art and literature celebrated the son who honored his parents. Men and women had different roles in family and ceremonial life. On landholdings, men farmed and hunted, while women produced silk and other textiles and fashioned them into clothing. Wealth increasingly trumped gender and class distinctions, however. In particular, rich women high in the Zhou aristocracy enjoyed a greater range of actions than other women. And wealthy merchants in emerging cities challenged the authority of local lords.

Limits and Decline of Zhou Power

At its center, the Zhou state had great influence, but its power elsewhere was limited. Unlike Neo-Assyria and Persia, it never evolved into a regional power or became a territorial empire. The rulers relied instead on culture (its bronzes) and statecraft (the mandate of heaven) to maintain their leadership among competing powers and lesser principalities. Rather than having absolute control of an empire (like the Assyrians or Persians) or a primarily socioreligious unity (as among the Vedic peoples of South Asia), the Zhou state stood first among many regional economic and political allies.

The Zhou rulers governed a much larger territory than the Shang did, but it was not highly centralized. Instead, it expected regional lords (who in this regard resembled Persian satraps) to hold the provinces in line. Military campaigns continued to press into new lands or to defend Zhou holdings from enemies. Rulers attempted to keep neighbors and allies in line by giving them power, protecting them from aggression, and continuing the tried-and-true method of intermarriage between elite family members and local nobles. But their subordinates had more than autonomy. They also had genuine resources that they could turn against the rulers at opportune moments.

The power of the Zhou ruling house over its regional lords declined in the ninth and eighth centuries BCE. In response, the Zhou court at its impressive capital at Xianyang introduced ritual reforms with grandiose ceremonies featuring larger, standardized bronze vessels. Yet even this move could not reverse the regime's growing political weakness in dealing with its steppe neighbors and internal regional lords. For the most part, the Zhou court became a theatrical state, hoping that impressive rituals would conceal its lack of military might. Zhou rulers managed to cling to their authority until 771 BCE, when northern steppe invaders forced them to flee their western capital.

The Zhou state period, like the Shang, was later idealized by Chinese historians as a golden age of wise kings and officials. In fact, the Zhou model of government, culture, and society became the standard for later generations. Though the Mesopotamian and Persian superpowers were capable of greater expansion during this period, China was sowing the seeds of a more durable state.

CONCLUSION

Upheavals in the territorial states of Afro-Eurasia led to the emergence of more extensive political powers—in Mesopotamia, Persia, and China—during the first half of the first millennium BCE. For seven centuries, both the Neo-Assyrian Empire, based in Mesopotamia, and the Persian Empire, based in Iran, were superpowers whose reach continued to grow. These first empires expanded territorial states far beyond their "ethnic" or linguistic homelands and, in so doing, brought more extensive interactions and exchanges to parts of Afro-Eurasia. Driving these events were changes in climate, invasions by nomadic peoples, new weapons, trade, and new administrative strategies and institutions.

The Neo-Assyrian and Persian Empires differed in fundamental ways from the earlier city-states and territorial states of this area. The Assyrians and Persians created ideologies, political institutions, economic ties, and cultural ways that extended their power across vast regions. Indeed, their strong imperial institutions enabled them to exploit human and material resources at great distances from the imperial centers.

But there were other models of expansion that did not yield political empires, at least at first. In the Vedic world of the Indus Valley and Ganges plain, shared values and revered texts did not lead even to a single major state. The unparalleled degree of integration across northern South Asia was cultural and economic rather than political. Centuries would pass before a regime would layer a state over this shared cultural world.

In China as well, a core of cultural and political beliefs developed and set the stage for the creation of large-scale and fully formed empires under the Qin and Han dynasties (see Chapter 5). As in Persia and the Indus Valley and Ganges plain, shared ideas and values spanned a wide geographical area. But unlike in Vedic South Asia, a powerful political system began to emerge in China when the Zhou rulers began integrating diverse peoples and territories. Their rule did not last. Although the Zhou transformed China, they could not overcome the power of local nobles or fully protect the western frontier from nomadic attacks. The regime never developed military and fiscal powers as great as those of the Southwest Asian empires. Nevertheless, Zhou efforts did implant the foundations of a political and ruling culture that enabled later imperial rulers to achieve success. In the absence of an empire, political, economic, and cultural integration was achieved in East and South Asia by means of cultural "soft power."

Empire building did not occur everywhere. The majority of the world's people still lived in smaller political groupings. Even within Afro-Eurasia, some areas were completely untouched.

City-States to Empires: Growth in Scale: Mesopotamia

Dramatic developments in urban growth, agricultural production, military innovations, and governance in Southwest Asia in the first century BCE led to the emergence of the largest states known to that time, which we have called the first empires. Larger than either city-states or territorial states, empires represented a quantum leap in scale and size. In four distinct periods between 2900 and 350 BCE, this region was transformed from being governed by city-states, each covering less than 4 square miles with 30,000 people, to large-scale empires covering 3,000,000 square miles and governing 35,000,000 people. The Persian Empire (540–330 BCE) rivaled the Roman and Han empires in terms of its size and scale.

QUESTIONS FOR ANALYSIS

- By what scales of magnitude did each stage of empires increase? How much larger were the empires than the world's first states?
- When did the biggest leaps in development between stages occur?
- By what sort of mechanisms did these very large states come about?

State/Empire	Est. area (sq. miles)	Est. population	Notes
STAGE ONE: City States (2900–2100 BCE)			
Ur, Uruk, and Nipur	1–4	20–30,000 people	Uruk was the largest city-state for 2,000 years.
STAGE TWO: First Small Empire (c. 1800–1600 BCE)			
The Babylonian Empire	65,000	200,000 people	The city of Babylon was possibly the largest in the world, with 150,000 people.
STAGE THREE: First Large-Scale Empires (c. 910–540 BCE)			
The Neo-Assyrian Empire (c. 910–625 BCE)	540,000	15,000,000 people	Major cities included Kalhu, Nineveh, and Assur.
The Neo-Babylonian Empire (c. 625–540 BCE)	200,000	15,000,000 people	Babylon remained the largest city in the world, surrounded by 8–9 miles of walls.
STAGE FOUR: The Largest Empire of the Time (c. 540–330 BCE)			
The Persian Empire	3,000,000	35,000,000 people	The Persian Empire was the largest empire at the time (measured as a percentage of global population).

Sources: T. Boiy, *Late Achaemenid and Hellenistic Babylon* (Leuven, Belgium, Peters, 2004); Pierre Briant, *Histoire de l'empire perse* (Paris: Fayard, 1996); Amélie Kuhrt, *The Ancient Near East, 3000–330 BCE,* 2 vols. (London: Routledge, 1994–5); J. N. Postgate, *Early Mesopotamia: Society and Economy at the Dawn of History* (London/New York: Routledge, 1992); M. Roaf, *Cultural Atlas of Mesopotamia and the Ancient Near East* (New York: Facts on File, 1990); W. Scheidel, "The Dynamics of Ancient Empires," in Marc van de Mieroop, *A History of the Ancient Near East, ca. 3000–323,* 2nd ed. (Oxford: Blackwell, 2007); Marc van de Mieroop, *The Ancient Mesopotamian City* (Oxford: Clarendon Press, 1997).

And even where the Neo-Assyrian and Persian rulers, soldiers, and traders came into contact with certain groups, they did not necessarily crush or absorb them. For example, the nomadic peoples of the northern steppes and the southern desert locations throughout Afro-Eurasia continued to be autonomous. But fewer and fewer were untouched by the technological, cultural, and political pulses of empires.

The peoples living in Southwest Asia under Neo-Assyrian and Persian rulers, in the Vedic society of South Asia, and in the Zhou state of China made lasting contributions to the cultural and religious history of humanity. Yet peoples living in small-scale societies in close contact with larger states and empires also influenced Afro-Eurasian cultures. The Phoenicians traversed the whole of the Mediterranean basin and spread their simplified alphabet. From the land of the Israelites, a budding monotheism sprouted. Late Vedic South Asia spun out the concept of cyclic universal time in the form of reincarnation. And in late Zhou China, an ideal of statecraft and social order took shape. All evolved into powerful cultural forms that in time spread their influences far beyond their places of origin.

After You Read This Chapter

Go to InQuizitive to see what you know & learn what you've missed.

FOCUS ON: *First Empires and Smaller States*

Ancient Near East

- Neo-Assyrians use raw military power and massive population relocations to build and maintain the world's first empire.

- Persians rely on persuasion and tolerance to build a cosmopolitan empire.

Mediterranean World

- Greeks, Phoenicians, and Israelites show the advantages of small-scale states with innovations in writing, trading, and religious thought.

South Asia

- Vedic peoples build a unified common culture through religious and economic ties.

China

- Zhou rulers construct a powerful tributary state and legitimate their rule via the mandate of heaven doctrine (good governance together with upright behavior legitimates rule).

CHRONOLOGY

	1100 BCE	1000 BCE	900 BCE
Southwest Asia and Northern Africa			Neo-Assyrian Empire **911–612 BCE**
The Mediterranean			
South Asia	Vedic culture develops **1500–600 BCE**		
East Asia	Zhou state **1045–221 BCE**		

STUDY QUESTIONS

1. **Describe** how climate change, migrations, technological developments, and administrative innovations contributed to the rise of empires and states between 1250 and 325 BCE. **Identify** the main characteristics of each empire and state.

2. **Compare and contrast** the ways in which empires and states formed, or did not form, in Southwest Asia, South Asia, and East Asia.

3. **Analyze** the ways in which the Neo-Assyrian and Persian Empires consolidated their imperial control over vast territories. What role did religious and political innovations such as Zoroastrianism and satrapies play in that consolidation?

4. **Explain** how peoples on the peripheries were affected by the imperial powers. **Trace** the connections that developed between fringe societies and imperial powers, and **describe** the fringe societies' contributions to the cultural and religious history of humanity.

5. **Identify** the function of hereditary status, clans, and religious beliefs in Vedic society in South Asia during the first millennium BCE. To what extent did these beliefs and values maintain a culturally integrated and distinct world in the absence of political unity?

6. **Compare and contrast** the Zhou state to the regional empires in Western Afro-Eurasia at this time. What legacies did each leave? What role did the mandate of heaven play in the Zhou rulers' maintenance of power?

7. **Evaluate** the connection between empires and war, religion, and trade.

Persian Empire **560–330 BCE**

Phoenician and Greek colonization **800–500 BCE**

Greek/Persian battles **499–480 BCE**

800 BCE   700 BCE   600 BCE   500 BCE

Before You Read This Chapter

Go to INQUIZITIVE to see what you know & learn what you've missed.

GLOBAL STORYLINES

- A range of challenges—warfare, political upheaval, economic pressures, and social developments—transform the empires and states of Afro-Eurasia.

- "Second-generation" societies arise across Afro-Eurasia in a pivotal period sometimes called the Axial Age.

- Axial Age thinkers reshape peoples' views of the world and their place in it.

- Complex new societies develop in the Americas and sub-Saharan Africa.

CHAPTER OUTLINE

5

Worlds Turned Inside Out, 1000–350 BCE

FOCUS QUESTIONS

- What types of challenges did Afro-Eurasian empires and states face in the first millennium BCE? How were the solutions they devised alike and how were they different?

- Which teachers and prophets were the key thinkers of the Axial Age, and what were their distinctive ideas?

- In what ways did political and social transformations influence Axial Age thinkers across Afro-Eurasia (East Asia, South Asia, and the Mediterranean)?

- How did the political, cultural, and social developments across Afro-Eurasia compare with those occurring in the Americas and sub-Saharan Africa?

A struggle for power and territory gripped societies from China to Africa. It turned the sixth century BCE into an age of violent upheaval and resulted in profound societal and intellectual breakthroughs. In the midst of these changes, Master Kong Fuzi, of China, apparently instructed his disciples on how to govern, saying: "Guide them by edicts, keep them in line with punishments, and the people will stay out of trouble but will have no sense of shame. Guide them by virtue, keep them in line with the rites, and they will, besides having a sense of shame, reform themselves" (Confucius, *The Analects*, II, 3).

According to sources later gathered together, Master Kong, also known as Confucius, represented a new breed of influential leaders—teachers and thinkers, not kings, priests, or warriors. Instead of fighting wars of conquest, they conducted wars of ideas. At the same time, it was the convulsions around them—incessant warfare, population growth, and the emergence of new cities—that motivated the search for new insights and solutions. By viewing the world in new ways, they sought to lead society out of turbulence. Their arsenal: words. Their strategy: instruction. These teachers strove to instruct rulers on how to govern

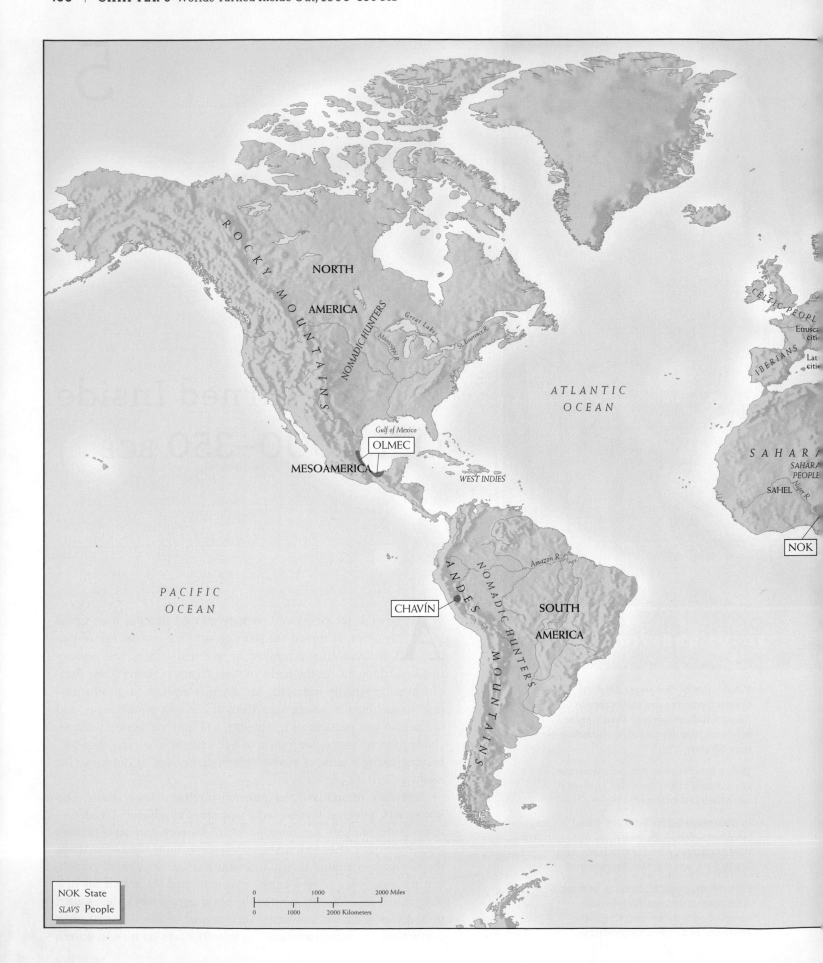

NORTH

AMERICA

ROCKY MOUNTAINS

NOMADIC HUNTERS

Great Lakes

Mississippi R.

St. Lawrence R.

CELTIC PEOPL

Etrusca
citi

IBERIANS

Lat
citi

ATLANTIC
OCEAN

Gulf of Mexico

OLMEC

MESOAMERICA

WEST INDIES

S A H A R A

SAHARA
PEOPLE

SAHEL

Niger R.

NOK

PACIFIC
OCEAN

Amazon R.

ANDES

NOMADIC HUNTERS

CHAVÍN

SOUTH

AMERICA

ANDES MOUNTAINS

NOK State

SLAVS People

0   1000   2000 Miles

0   1000   2000 Kilometers

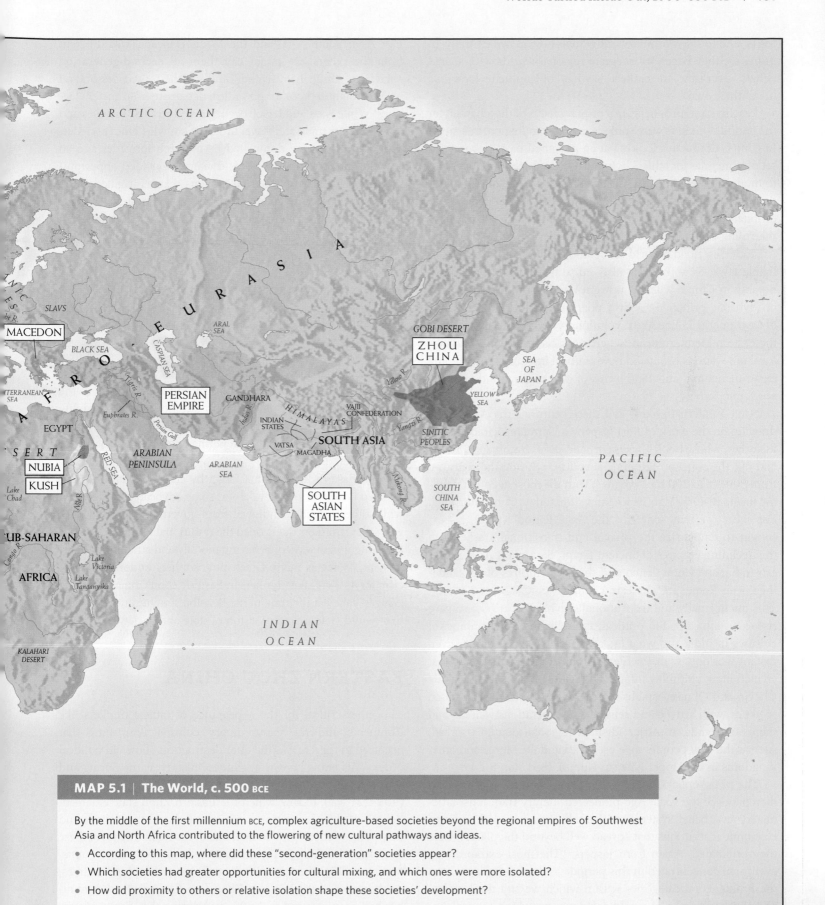

ARCTIC OCEAN

EURASIA

SLAVS

MACEDON

ARAL SEA

GOBI DESERT

ZHOU CHINA

BLACK SEA

CASPIAN SEA

SEA OF JAPAN

MEDITERRANEAN SEA

Tigris R.

PERSIAN EMPIRE

GANDHARA

Euphrates R.

EGYPT

Persian Gulf

Indus R.

HIMALAYAS

Yellow R.

YELLOW SEA

VAJII CONFEDERATION

INDIAN STATES

SOUTH ASIA

Yangzi R.

SINITIC PEOPLES

DESERT

NUBIA

KUSH

RED SEA

ARABIAN PENINSULA

ARABIAN SEA

VATSA

MAGADHA

Mekong R.

SOUTH CHINA SEA

PACIFIC OCEAN

Lake Chad

Nile R.

SOUTH ASIAN STATES

SUB-SAHARAN

Congo R.

Lake Victoria

AFRICA

Lake Tanganyika

INDIAN OCEAN

KALAHARI DESERT

MAP 5.1 | The World, c. 500 BCE

By the middle of the first millennium BCE, complex agriculture-based societies beyond the regional empires of Southwest Asia and North Africa contributed to the flowering of new cultural pathways and ideas.

- According to this map, where did these "second-generation" societies appear?
- Which societies had greater opportunities for cultural mixing, and which ones were more isolated?
- How did proximity to others or relative isolation shape these societies' development?

justly, and to show ordinary individuals how to live ethically. In doing so, they began to integrate regional worlds with shared beliefs. Over time, the earliest "sayings" of Confucius took on a life of their own.

Teachers and prophets are a primary focus of this chapter, for the period's thinkers were some of the most influential in history. In China, Confucius, looking at an imagined past, elaborated a set of principles for ethical living that has guided the Chinese up to modern times. In South Asia, Siddhartha Gautama (the Buddha) laid out social and spiritual tenets that challenged the traditional social hierarchy based on birth and with it the power of the ruling priests and warriors. In Greece, Socrates, Plato, and Aristotle described a world that conformed to natural and intelligible laws. New thinking also led to new institutions—most notably in China, where a powerful and populous state based on dynastic principles, a firm political ideology, and the rule of law emerged. Equally revolutionary were the city-states of the eastern Mediterranean, where political, economic, and cultural innovations produced new political institutions, including experiments in democratic forms of government, and vigorous economic activity.

Some modern thinkers call these centuries the **Axial Age**, drawing on the work of Karl Jaspers, a German sociologist and historian, whose book *The Origin and Goal of History* (1953) first laid out the concept. Jaspers claimed that during the centuries from 800 BCE to 200 BCE, "we meet with the most deep-cut dividing line in history. Man, as we know him today, came into being. For short, we may style this the Axial Period" (p. 1). Jaspers sought to emphasize the pivotal and transitional era between the declining empires of ancient Egypt, Southwest Asia, northern India, and Zhou China and the later empires of Alexander the Great, Rome, and the Han Chinese (see Chapters 6 and 7). This intellectually and institutionally dynamic period also gave rise to the ethical, philosophical, and religious underpinnings of cultures in India and what later became western Europe. Even distant worlds saw major breakthroughs in belief systems that created more culturally integrated regions. In Mesoamerica, the Chavín and Olmecs established the first complex, urban-based societies, with artistic and religious reverberations well beyond their homelands. In Africa, distinct regional identities spread, such as the Nok peoples in West Africa and the Meroe and other kingdoms in the Upper Nile (in Nubia). (See Map 5.1.)

The philosophers, theologians, poets, political leaders, and merchants of the Axial Age pioneered literary traditions, articulated new belief systems, and established new political and economic institutions that spread well beyond the places where they originated. Again from Jaspers: "The most extraordinary events are concentrated in this period. . . . In this age were born the fundamental categories within which we still think today, and the beginnings of world religions, by which we still live today, were created" (p. 2). Although each of the cultures—in

East Asia, South Asia, and the Mediterranean—was different from the others, we might call them all **second-generation societies**, simultaneously building on their predecessors yet with foresight representing a radical departure from ancient legacies. While wars and havoc occurred within their societies and long-distance trade and travel linked them with other societies, these centuries were dominated by a search for order and an appetite for new thinking. This dynamism yielded opportunities for the creation of cultural systems that reimagined entire regions integrated by more than trade or conquest, but also by common values and shared beliefs. The Axial Age involved powerful impulses for cultural integration.

ALTERNATIVE PATHWAYS AND IDEAS

New ideas by no means bred consensus. In fact, the age of great ideas witnessed magnificent disputes over what was best for humanity and over the very political and moral status of the individual. In Greece, philosophers questioned the possibility of gaining and transmitting true or reliable knowledge of the world. They began to doubt the permanence of the social order and pondered the relationship between humans and the cosmos. In Eastern Zhou China, beset by constant warfare, sages debated how best to restore order; some advocated engagement while others urged withdrawal from government. In the Ganges Valley, thinkers questioned the traditional Brahmanic rituals and sought new ways of behaving morally and attaining enlightenment. Whereas many Greek philosophers endorsed skepticism for its own sake, thinkers in Eastern Zhou China and in the Ganges Valley at the time of the Buddha sought ultimate truths that would yield a unitary vision of state and society.

EASTERN ZHOU CHINA

Altogether critical for the appearance of radical thinkers like Confucius and the extraordinary cultural flourishing that occurred in this era was the utter destruction of the old political order. This era is known in Chinese history as the Spring and Autumn period (722–481 BCE) and the Warring States period (403–221 BCE), during which the Eastern Zhou state emerged. Yet out of this destruction came new political institutions and new political ideologies. In fact, one of the main themes of these centuries in China was the dramatic reduction of political units. More than 10,000 such units allegedly existed during Xia times. At the onset of the Western Zhou (see Chapter 4), that number had been reduced to 1,200, and during the Warring States era only 7 remained, preparing the way for China's first truly

MAP 5.2 | Zhou China in the Warring States Period

The Warring States period witnessed a fracturing of the Zhou dynasty into a myriad of states.

- Find the Zhou capital of Luoyang on the map. Where was it located relative to the other key states?
- What about this map tells us why diplomacy was so important during this period?
- What does this map tell us about the relationships between "civilized" and "barbarian" peoples in East Asia?
- How do you think so many smaller polities could survive when they were surrounded first by seven and then by three even larger and more powerful states (Qin, Qi, and Chu)?

centralized imperial and dynastic state, the Qin. (See Map 5.2; for more on the Qin and Han Empires, see Chapter 7.) From the vantage point of the Qin and Han, these changes were epochal and created the conditions for the rise of the "Chinese empire."

China experienced levels of anarchic violence previously unseen for centuries. A chronicler of this era described over 500 battles between states and more than 100 civil wars within states all taking place within 260 years. Technological breakthroughs added to the political anarchy, for new smelting techniques that removed impurities from iron allowed stronger and more durable iron swords and armor to replace bronze weaponry all across China. Although Zhou rulers tried hard to monopolize iron production and stockpile weapons, the spread of cheaper and more lethal weaponry shifted influence from the central government to local authorities. In fact, the regional states became so powerful that they undertook large-scale projects, such as an early stage of the Grand Canal, that earlier had been feasible only for empires.

Qin Warriors. *Terra-cotta warriors were buried with the Qin emperor in the expectation that they would join in his military campaigns in the next life. For such battles the emperor was to have at his disposal over 8,000 soldiers, 130 chariots with 520 horses, and 150 cavalry horses to accompany his soul as he passed from this world to the next, intimidating his rivals along the way. These reproduced warriors and horses were quite modest in number, but they symbolically evoked the massive scale of the Qin armies aboveground. In the real world, the Qin mobilized millions of peasants in the northwest for their military campaigns and complemented them with hundreds of thousands of horses to produce the most devastating military force yet seen on earth before the famed Roman legions.*

Bronze Spearhead. *Although bronze weaponry gave way to stronger iron swords and armor during the Warring States period, stylized bronze spearheads were still prized by Zhou kings and regional lords.*

The wars and shifting political alliances of the seven large territorial states that dominated the Warring States period involved the mobilization of armies and resources on an unprecedented scale (far surpassing the Assyrian armies at the height of their power). The Qin state, which benefited from these achievements in warfare and ultimately replaced the Eastern Zhou state in 221 BCE, fielded armies that combined huge infantries in the tens of thousands with lethal cavalries and even more lethal legions of skilled archers using state-of-the-art crossbows. To ensure that the Qin war machine could match all threats, the preparation to defend the Chinese heartland even crossed into the otherworld. Some 7,000 artisans and workers prepared thousands of ornate, carefully made terra-cotta warriors and horses, which the Qin buried in precise military formations within the tomb of the first Qin emperor to help him in the expected wars he would face in the next life.

Overall, the conception of central power changed dramatically during this era, as royal appointees replaced hereditary officeholders. By the middle of the fourth century BCE, power was so concentrated in the major states' rulers that each began to call himself "king." Moreover, the Warring States formed coalitions if one of them became too strong. Despite the incessant warfare, scholars, soldiers, merchants, peasants, and artisans thrived in the midst of an expanding agrarian economy and interregional trade.

New Ideas and the Hundred Schools of Thought

Out of this extreme political and social turmoil came new visions that were to dominate Chinese thinking about man's and woman's place in society and provide the intellectual and philosophical underpinnings for the creation of the world's longest-lasting imperial system. Intense debates over how to achieve political stability and good governance led to the appearance of five canonical works that Confucius allegedly later compiled and edited. They were essential for making ancient Chinese the main language of the Han people and establishing the foundations of a classical Chinese education. They also contained many of the basic principles, credited to Confucius, for creating a stable political system and an integrated social order. These books were the *Shi Jing*, or *Book of Odes*; the *Li Ji*, or *Book of Rites*; the *Shu Jing*, or *Book of History*; the *Yi Ching*, or *Book of Changes*; and the *Chunqiu*, or *Spring and Autumn Annals*. They became Confucius's "five classics" under the Han.

The establishment of the Qin state in 221 BCE and the proclamation of an emperor (*huangdi*) in place of a king (*wang*) produced a succession of Chinese dynasties and emperors that, except for several periods of disunion, lasted for two millennia down to February 12, 1912, when China's last emperor abdicated in favor of the new Chinese Republic. Even more striking about the background to this chaotic starting point for imperial splendor is that it was often the losers among the political elites, seeking to replace their former advantages with status gained through new types of service, who sparked this intellectual creativity. Important teachers emerged in China's Axial Age, each with disciples. The most prominent of the "hundred masters" according to the Han state was **Confucius** (551–479 BCE); others either expanded on Confucian thought or, like the Qin, formulated opposing ideas about human nature and the role of government. Their philosophies constitute the Hundred Schools of Thought.

CONFUCIUS Han dynasty accounts show Confucius to be the product of his times. Born in the state of Lu at a time when Zhou power was crumbling, and at first a mere hanger-on at court, he looked back to earlier days of the Zhou dynasty for moral and political inspiration. Believing that the Zhou dynasty's founders had established ideals of good government and principled action, but seeing only division and war among rival states, he set out in search of an enlightened ruler, much as we will see the Buddha doing in South Asia. Confucius returned home in despair in 484 BCE. Though he died a discouraged man, his teachings, drawn from his unrivaled knowledge of the high traditions of Chinese thought, resonated in his own turbulent age and beyond to the Han.

Confucius's teachings stemmed foremost from his belief that human beings behave ethically, not to save their souls or gain a place in heaven as philosophers and priests elsewhere believed, but because it is in their human makeup to do so. Humanity's natural tendencies, if left alone, produce harmonious existence. Confucius saw the family, and notably filial piety (the duty of children to parents), as the foundation of proper ethical action, including loyalty to the state and rulers. His idea of modeling the state on the patriarchal family—that is, the ruler respecting heaven as if it were his father and protecting his subjects as if they were his children—became a bedrock principle of his thinking and the foundation of mainstream Chinese political thought. Although he regarded himself purely as a transmitter of ancient wisdom, later followers claimed that he had enunciated the major guidelines for Chinese thought and action. The first of his guidelines was respect for the pronouncements of scholar-teachers—persons of learning like himself. The second was a commitment to a broad education—one that befits a strong but benevolent state. The third was an insistence on providing training for all who are highly intelligent and willing to work, whether noble or humble in birth. This equal access to training for those willing and able offered a dramatic departure from earlier centuries, when only nobles were believed capable of ruling. Nonetheless, Confucius's distinctions between gentlemen-rulers and commoners continued to support a social hierarchy, although an individual's position in that hierarchy would ideally now rest on education rather than on birth.

Confucius's ethical teachings and cultural ideas were preserved by his followers in the *Analects*. In seeking to reclaim the lost ideals of the early Zhou, Confucius proposed a moral framework stressing correct performance of ritual (*li*) based on practices from an earlier, more enlightened age, humaneness (*ren*), responsibility, loyalty to the family (*xiao*), and perfection of moral character to become a "superior man" (*junzi*)—that is, a man defined by benevolence and goodness rather than by the pursuit of profit. A society of such superior men would not need coercive laws and punishment to achieve order.

MO DI One competing school of thought, later called Mohism, derived from the alleged teachings of Mozi, also known as Mo Di (c. 479–438 BCE). Recent studies have suggested that as a craftsman-builder he became for a time an articulate exponent of China's lower and middling classes. Extolling hard work and spurning what he regarded as distracting diversions such as music and philosophical ruminations, he favored a simple life and called on his followers to engage in useful and profitable occupations. He believed that each man should feel obligated to all other people, not just to his own family and friends. He emphasized practical concerns of good government: promoting social order, ensuring material benefits for its people, and supporting population growth. He opposed wars of conquest, arguing that they wasted life and resources and interfered with productivity and the fair distribution of wealth; but he recognized the need for strong urban defenses to keep out marauders. For at least two centuries, his utilitarian philosophy found many enthusiastic followers, and although his school of thought was soon superseded, his views of practical statecraft and efficient government remained a part of the classical canon, along with Legalism, or Statism, which emerged as the dominant credo of the Qin empire (discussed in Chapter 7).

LAOZI AND ZHUANGZI Another key philosophy was **Daoism**, which diverged sharply from that of Confucius and his followers by scorning rigid rituals and social hierarchies. Its ideas originated with a Master Lao (Laozi, "Old Master"), who—if he actually existed—may have been a contemporary of Confucius. His sayings were collected in *The Daodejing*, or *The Book of the Way and Its Power* (c. third century BCE), which in time became the subject of more commentaries and more translations than any other Chinese work. His book was then elaborated by Master Zhuang (Zhuangzi, c. 369–286 BCE). Daoism stressed the *dao*

Warring Ideas: Confucianism versus Daoism—On the Foundations of Government

Though both Confucians and Daoists viewed the world of political power as perilous, their competing teachings offered regional Chinese rulers a choice in political philosophies.

Confucius wanted to end the chaos of the times and restore order by promoting education, moral behavior, and the performance of ritual. He thought that cooperation rather than conflict, ethical behavior rather than reckless actions, merit rather than heredity, and concern with the welfare of others rather than self-aggrandizement should be the basis of society and government. Not as interventionist as other schools of thought, the Confucians opposed autocracy and appealed to the mandate of heaven as the "voice of the people." Not as laissez-faire as the Daoists, the Confucians prioritized strict ritual as a philosophy of behavior that would lead to cultural solidarity even in times of political chaos. The Daoists' rejoinder charged that the Confucians were, in effect, shutting the barn door after the horses had already escaped. A natural morality had once been the rule in small villages; a true morality was now the social exception, betrayed in practice by the moral hypocrisy of Confucian officials in the capital.

During the Qin dynasty, Confucius's call for moral rigor had little appeal to those in power. But some Han dynasty officials subsequently saw the attractions of his beliefs after they realized that a tyrannical government that punished its citizens harshly could be brought down by a peasant rebellion. In one exchange with a student, Confucius described the foundations of government:

> Zigong asked about government. The Master said, "Sufficient food, sufficient military force, the confidence of the people." Zigong said, "If one had, unavoidably, to dispense with one of these, which of them should go first?" The Master said, "Get rid of the military." Zigong said, "If one had, unavoidably, to dispense with one of the remaining two, which should go first?" The Master said, "Dispense with food: Since ancient times there has always been death, but without confidence a people cannot stand." (*Analects* 12.7)

Many individuals who sought power were drawn more to Daoism, whose teachings warned that overly assertive rulers could ruin the state. Thus, the *Daodejing* (*The Book of the Way and Its Power*), a famous Daoist work attributed to Master Lao (Laozi), argued that political and social intervention was futile and that long-term rule should be based on "doing nothing" (*wuwei*), that is, letting everything take its natural course without premeditated human intervention:

> If one desires to take the empire
> and act on it,
> I say that he will not succeed.
> The empire is a sacred vessel,
> That cannot be acted upon.
> In being acted upon, it is harmed;
> And in being grasped, it is lost.
> Thus the sage rejects the excessive,
> the extravagant,
>   the extreme.
> (*The Book of the Way and Its Power,* Vol. 1, p. 86)

QUESTIONS FOR ANALYSIS

- What elements of Confucius's teaching emphasized moral rigor and, when applied to government, would enable it to win "the confidence of the people"?
- Why did Confucius believe that a cruel tyrant could not remain in power for very long?
- Why did the Legalists find Daoism more appealing than Confucianism as a practical and moral philosophy?

Source: Sources of Chinese Tradition, 2nd ed., edited by William Theodore de Bary and Irene Bloom, Vol. 1 (New York: Columbia University Press, 1999) pg. 55–56, 86.

(the way) of nature and the cosmos: the best way to live is to follow the natural order of things. Its main principle was *wuwei,* "doing nothing": what matters is spontaneity, noninterference, and acceptance of the world as it is, rather than attempting to change it through politics and government. In Laozi's vision, the ruler who interferes least in the natural processes of change is the most successful. Zhuangzi focused on the enlightened individual living spontaneously and in harmony with nature, free of society's ethical rules and laws and viewing life and death simply as different stages of existence. (See Primary Source: Warring Ideas: Confucianism versus Daoism—On the Foundations of Government.)

XUNZI AND HAN FEI Legalism, or Statism, another view of how best to create an orderly life, grew out of the writings of Master Xun (Xunzi, 310–237 BCE) toward the end of the Warring States period. He believed that men and women are innately bad and therefore require moral education and authoritarian control. In the decades before the Qin victory over the Zhou, the Legalist thinker Han Fei (280–233 BCE) agreed that human nature is primarily evil. He imagined a state with a ruler who followed the Daoist principle of *wuwei*, detaching himself from everyday governance—but only after setting an unbending standard (strict laws, accompanied by harsh punishments) for judging his officials and people. For Han Fei, the establishment and uniform application of these laws would keep people's evil nature in check. As we will see in Chapter 7, the Qin state, before it became the dominant state in China, systematically followed the Legalist philosophy.

SCHOLARS AND THE STATE What emerged from all this activity was a foundational alliance of scholars and the state that ultimately became a vital feature of Chinese society through many centuries. Scholars became state functionaries dependent on the rulers' patronage. In return, rulers recognized the scholars' expertise in matters of punishment, ritual, astronomy, medicine, and divination. Philosophical deliberations focused on the need to maintain order and stability by preserving the state. (In contrast, philosophers and priests in Greece and South Asia did not exclusively serve the state or a particular ruler, so they freely speculated on a far broader range of issues.) The bonds that rulers forged with their scholarly elites distinguished governments in Warring States China from the other Afro-Eurasian political systems at this time.

The growing importance of statecraft and philosophical discourse promoted the use of writing. In fact, even though the Chinese script was not standardized until 221 BCE, its use in the philosophical debates raging across states and regions helped foster cultural unity at a time of intellectual pluralism (diversity of thinking). As scholar-diplomats and scribes debated the best methods for creating stable and harmonious societies, some 9,000 to 10,000 graphs or signs became required for writing. The elevated influence that scholar-bureaucrats enjoyed in these debates set China apart from other societies of this period. The ideas of Confucianism, Daoism, and Legalism provided them with a rationale for their crucial role in empire building.

Innovations in State Administration

Although the most durable new developments in China during this Axial Age occurred in the realm of ideas, important innovations also took place in politics and economics. In the political arena, the Spring and Autumn period saw regional rulers

enhance their ability to obtain natural resources, to recruit men for their armies, and to oversee conquered areas. This trend continued in the Warring States period, as elites in the major states created administrative districts with stewards, sheriffs, and judges and a system of registering peasant households to facilitate tax collection and army conscription. The officials were drawn from the *shi*, who under the Western Zhou had been knights but were now bureaucrats in direct service to the ruler. Confucius and other classical masters called them "gentlemen" or "superior men" (*junzi*) and considered them partners of the ruler in state affairs. Officials were paid in grain and sometimes received gifts of gold and silver, as well as titles and seals of office, from the ruler. Of all the ministers who sought to enhance the central government, none was more successful than Shang Yang of Qin. His reforms included a head tax, administrative districts for closer bureaucratic control of hinterlands, land distribution for individual households to farm, reward or punishment for military achievement or lack thereof, and a harsh penal code that applied equally to government officials and peasants.

Despite repeated conflict, China in this era was more centralized and effective than the other states in Afro-Eurasia. Its rulers were powerfully legitimized, soon to be called emperors, and under the Qin dynasty the populace was ready to accept a legal system developed in this earlier period (although in the end they resisted the Qin's repressive state power).

Shang Yang of Qin. *An important statesman of Qin during the Warring States period, Shang Yang introduced administrative reforms that enhanced the power of the central government.*

Innovations in Warfare

Along with administrative reform came reforms in military recruitment and warfare. One of the purposes of registering the rural population was to guarantee their military service. As a result, the most successful states in China, ruling over millions of people, boasted million-man armies by 221 BCE. (Contrast this with Athens, the most powerful city-state in the Mediterranean: with a population of 250,000, it could field an army of just 20,000 men. Only Rome, later to become a megastate, could ultimately match China's scale.)

In earlier battles, nobles had let fly their arrows from chariots while conscripted peasants fought beside them on the bloodstained ground. Now the Warring States relied on massed infantries of peasants bearing iron lances who fought fiercely and to the death, unconstrained by their relationships with nobles. War now involved huge state armies containing as many as 1 million commoners in the infantry, supported by 1,000 chariots and 10,000 bow-wielding cavalrymen. During the Spring and Autumn period, one state's entire army would face another state's; now, during the Warring States period, armies could divide into separate forces and wage several battles simultaneously.

Armies also boasted elite professional troops wearing heavy iron armor and helmets, brandishing iron weapons, and wielding the recently invented crossbow. The crossbow's tremendous power, range, and accuracy, with its ingenious trigger mechanism, enabled archers to easily kill lightly armored cavalrymen or charioteers at a distance. The technology of siege warfare also advanced in response to the growing presence of defensive walls along frontiers and around towns. Enemy armies used counterweighted siege ladders (the Chinese called them "cloud ladders") to scale urban walls or dug tunnels under the walls; defenders often pumped smoke into the tunnels to thwart the attackers. The rhythms of warfare also changed. Rather than lasting through an agricultural season, campaigns now stretched over a year or longer.

Economic, Social, and Cultural Changes

Rather than depressing the economy, incessant warfare spurred China's economic growth to remarkable heights. The agricultural revolution on the North China plain along the Yellow River led to rapid population growth, and the inhabitants of the Eastern Zhou reached approximately 20 million. Demographic changes also affected the environment. As more people required more fuel, deforestation—particularly on the North China plain—led to erosion of the fields. In addition, many animals were hunted to extinction; others, like the elephant, found their open range sharply curtailed. Many inhabitants migrated south

to domesticate the marshes, lakes, and rivers of the Yangzi River delta; here they created new arable frontiers, thus averting the ecological disaster that swept through northern China.

Eventually, such population pressures on arable land initiated a vicious and tragic economic cycle for Chinese peasants. The shortage of cultivable land eventually pushed agricultural technology, based largely on peasant manual labor, to its limits. Even though, during the late Zhou, peasants produced more rice and wheat than anyone else on earth, they also created families with an unprecedented number of mouths to feed. Peasants' standard of living declined even while farmers opened new frontiers by draining wetlands. When these frontiers reached their limits, Chinese families faced terrible food shortages and famines.

Commoners and elites alike tried to restore stability in their lives through religion, medicine, and statecraft. The elites' rites of divination to predict the future and medical recipes to heal the body found parallels in the commoners' use of ghost stories and astrological almanacs to understand the meaning of their lives and the significance of their deaths.

In the short term, economic changes began when peasants gained the right to own their land in exchange for taxes and military service. As their productivity increased along with

Chinese Calendar. *This Han-period calendar for 63 BCE is formed from sixteen slips of wood with handwritten characters; each begins with day one, day two, and so on; the calendar is to be read from right to left.*

Knife Coin. *Zhou dynasty coins, like the later Han coin shown here, were made of bronze and produced in a variety of shapes, some resembling spades and knives, depending on the region. Each of the Warring States had its own currency.*

Pendant. *Gender relations became more inflexible because of male-centered kinship groups. Relations between the sexes were increasingly ritualized and were marked by heavy moral and legal sanctions against any behavior that appeared to threaten the purity of powerful lineages. This pendant depicts two women who formed a close relationship with each other in the "inner chambers" of their homes.*

advances in agricultural technology and bronze and metal casting, trade in surplus grain, pottery, and ritual objects gave rise to an early market economy. Peasants continued to barter, but elites and rulers used minted coins. At the same time, social relations became more fluid as commoners gained power and aristocrats lost it; but gender relations became more rigid. Along with male domination within the family, relations between the sexes became increasingly constrained by sanctions against any behavior that appeared to threaten the purity of authoritarian male lineages.

Overall, despite the cycles of warfare and chaos—or perhaps because of them—many foundational beliefs, values, and philosophies for later dynasties sprang forth during the Spring and Autumn and Warring States periods. By the middle of the first millennium BCE, China's political activities and innovations were affecting larger numbers of people, spread over a much broader area, than comparable developments in South Asia and the Mediterranean.

THE NEW WORLDS OF SOUTH ASIA

The peoples of South Asia, like those in China, saw their world transformed, and although they, too, engaged in new thinking about just and stable political orders, they were not able to lay the foundations for a large-scale imperial state. In contrast to Chinese-scholar officials, who were theorizing about how to govern and organize their society, the Vedic peoples who settled in the Ganges Valley were assimilating earlier residents and forging their own political institutions, economic activities, and belief systems.

The heartland of South Asian developments in this period was the mid-Ganges plain, a roughly 70,000-square-mile area in the northeast of present-day India and the southern tip of Nepal. (See Map 5.3.) Waves of Vedic peoples migrated into

this region around 600 BCE, clearing land, establishing new cities and trade routes, expanding rice cultivation, and experimenting with new political forms. Abundant monsoon rains made the land suitable for rice farming, as opposed to the wheat and barley farming of the Indus Valley. Vedic migrants cleared the land by setting fire to the forests and using iron tools, fashioned from ore mined locally, to remove what was left of the jungle.

Whereas Chinese elites established a political ideology that legitimized centralized dynastic rule and established an overarching system of laws, the peoples of South Asia did not. Even so, there were many similarities to China. Like China, South Asian peoples had a dominant cultural ideology that they spread throughout the South Asian continent as Vedic groups migrated into new regions. Here, not only did they forge new political institutions and economic activities, but they also pioneered new ways of viewing the natural and supernatural worlds. In this turbulent environment, thinkers like the Buddha and Maharira fashioned an Axial Age in South Asia.

But in South Asia, the varna system became even more socially rigid through the creation of subcategories within the four *varnas* (Brahman priests, Kshatriya warriors, Vaishya commoners, and Shudra laborers; see Chapter 4). These were known as *jatis* groups (discussed shortly). The top of the social pyramid belonged to the Brahmans, a class of intellectuals and religious figures who presided over feasts and ceremonies and interpreted for the rest of South Asian society the meaning of the Vedic texts. Subordinate to the Brahmans but able to patronize them were the Kshatriyas, a warrior group.

The Rise of New Political Organizations

Two major kinds of states appeared in the Middle and Lower Ganges plain: those ruled by hereditary monarchs and those ruled by an elected elite, or oligarchies. The latter were the gana-sanghas, which in Sanskrit means "an assembly of people"—in this case, a ruling elite of a Kshatriya clan. As described in Chapter 4, the South Asian oligarchies were led by warriors and officials, collectively called the Kshatriya. Both the rulers of the kingdoms and citizens of the Kshatriya republics assumed the title *raja*, usually translated as "king," though in reality most *rajas* did not possess the powers associated with kings. They tended to be political higher-ups or tribal chiefs rather than founders of royal families. They owed their importance to military and administrative skills associated with their Kshatriya birth.

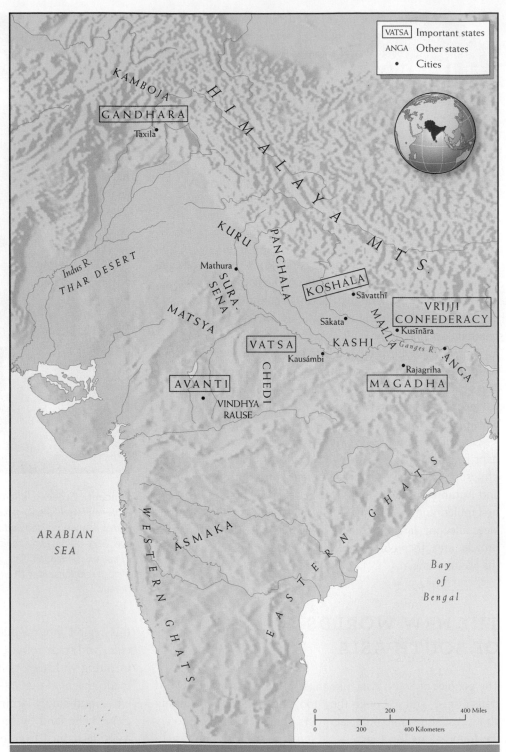

MAP 5.3 | Sixteen States in the Time of the Buddha in South Asia

South Asia underwent profound transformations in the first millennium BCE that reflected growing urbanization, increased commerce, and the emergence of two types of states: monarchies and oligarchies.

- Where did the new states and cities appear?
- What geographical and environmental features encouraged social and cultural integration?
- According to this map, what other regions had influence on South Asia, and where might South Asian culture spread?

Kshatriya oligarchs controlled the land and other resources and oversaw slaves and alien workers; in this regard, they did fulfill duties similar to those of hereditary kings. The political turmoil that these states created as they fought for preeminence was a fundamental factor leading to South Asia's Axial Age thinkers. Both the Buddha and Mahavira came from the lands of the gana-sanghas.

Evolution of the Caste System

In the kingdoms and oligarchic cities of northern India, a system of hierarchy, rigidly based on birth and occupation, evolved alongside the older *varnas*. Later, in the sixteenth century, when the Portuguese came into contact with South Asians, they called these social groupings castes—a term that has served ever since to describe and categorize the groupings representing social, political, and economic differences in South Asia. While the *varna* remained the primary basis for ranking the social order, its actual functioning came to depend on a wide range of occupational groups defined by birth. This expansion of the caste system to include professional groups and the hardening of the lines of divisions between social groups during this period remain a prominent feature in Indian society today.

The newer caste system emerged out of a booming agriculture that multiplied the number of professions and provided work for all manner of traders and artisans. Thus, as Vedic society became more complex, so did the caste system. Each of the occupational groups established its own sub-castes, called *jatis* (the Sanskrit word for "birth"); each of the *jatis* stressed kinship ties and created its own religious rituals. The occupational sub-castes were organized not only on the basis of profession but even by product. For example, a carpenter *jati* was more prestigious than a blacksmith *jati*, and farmers viewed leather tanners as literally untouchable. Social hierarchies layered cities as well as the countryside. In the emerging urban centers, traders were regarded as "purer" than artisans, while those making gold utensils had higher status than those making copper or iron products. Yet members of each group colluded to contain internal competition, and they closed ranks to preserve their status. Sub-castes monopolized skills and resources by banning intermarriage, thereby preventing other groups from accessing their knowledge. Even when outsiders joined the Vedic landowners' farming economy as laborers, tenants, or cultivators, sub-castes maintained their communal structure by restricting marriage to within the group.

Religion served to buttress the caste system and maintain hierarchies. Brahmanical texts invoked the principle of purity and pollution to rank castes and to hinder movement between castes. To fortify this deeply hierarchical order, occupations were made hereditary, and taboos were placed on intermarriage and interdining. These injunctions ensured that individuals did not move out of their inherited caste occupation. Nonetheless, a caste as a group could move upward over time by acquiring wealth and power and therefore claim a purer caste status than those *jatis* previously above them. South Asia's *varna* and *jatis* system, like political turmoil, was a factor in the emergence of thinkers like the Buddha, who was troubled by the social rigidity that such a deep-seated system of social stratification legitimized.

Brahman Recluse. *When Buddhists started to tell stories in sculptures and paintings, Brahmans were included when appropriate. This character in Gandharan Buddhist art probably represents a Brahman who lived as a recluse instead of as a priest. He is not shaved or dressed, but his expression is passionate.*

New Cities and an Expanding Economy

Supported by rice agriculture, cities began to emerge on the Ganges plain around 500 BCE and in turn became centers of commercial exchange and a robust intellectual life. Some, such as Shravasti (or Savatth) and Rajagriha, also thrived as artisanal centers. Others in the northwest, like Taxila (on the border between present-day Pakistan and Afghanistan), engaged in trade with Afghanistan and the Iranian plateau.

LIFE IN THE NEW CITIES These cities were dominated by new men and women—bankers, merchants, and scribes, whose occupations did not fit easily into the *varnas* and *jatis* and whose lifestyles often shocked nearby villagers. Precisely laid-out streets were crowded with vendors, and well-heeled residents employed elephants and horse-drawn chariots to move them about. Alleys leading from the main streets zigzagged between houses built with pebbles and clay. Although city expansion was often haphazard, civic authorities showed great interest in sanitation. The many squares dotting each city had garbage bins, and dirty water drained away in deep sink wells underground. Streets were graded so that rainfall would wash them clean. The important city of Shravasti may have contained as many as 200,000 inhabitants. Because most of these cities have been continuously inhabited, they have been difficult sites for archaeologists to explore. Taxila, located in the far northwest and destroyed in the fifth century CE, proved an exception: excavated in the twentieth century, it shed light on urban life in early South Asia. Taxila did not have the well-planned streets and water drainage of a center like Mohenjo Daro, an opulent Indus city (see Chapter 2); Taxila's building materials were simpler. But civic consciousness produced a hygienic and healthy urban environment. City officials arranged to have garbage taken out of town and dirty water routed to sink wells.

The new cities offered exciting opportunities for those who were adventurous. Rural householders who moved into them prospered by importing rice and sugarcane from villages to sell in the markets; they then transported manufactured goods such as sugar, salt, and utensils back to their villages. Those who already possessed capital became bankers who financed trade and industry. The less affluent turned to craftwork, fashioning textiles, tools such as needles, fine pottery, copper plates, ivory decorations, and gold and silver utensils. Other professions included physicians, launderers, barbers, cooks, tailors, and entertainers. The elaborate division of labor suggests a high degree of specialization and commercialization.

Coins came into use in these cities at about the same time as they appeared in Greece and China. Traders and bankers established municipal bodies that issued the coins and vouched for their worth. Made of silver, the coins had irregular shapes but specific weights, which determined their value; they also were stamped with symbols of authority.

UNEQUAL OPPORTUNITIES The new cities were melting pots of considerable social mobility—despite the rigid caste system. Yet the opportunities for social mobility did not ensure success for everyone. Many who lost their land and livelihood came in search of work, and some fared better than others. As a whole, city dwellers had more material wealth, but their lives were far more uncertain. In addition, urban life created a new social grouping: those who did the dirtiest jobs, such as removing garbage and sewage, and were therefore viewed as physically and ritually impure "untouchables." They were thought to be so polluting that a daughter of a decent householder was

Taxila. Left: *Taxila became the capital of Gandhara, a kingdom located in what is today northern Pakistan and eastern Afghanistan, at the time that it was occupied by the Persian Empire in the fifth century BCE. Dharmarajika was one of the most important monasteries. The walkway around the stupa, a moundlike structure containing Buddhist relics, was covered with glass tiles, and the stupa itself was decorated with jewels. Right: This corner of a stupa exhibits a variety of the architectural styles that prevailed in Gandharan art at its height. Both square and round columns are topped with Corinthian capitals. The right arch gate shows the style of Sanchi, the famous stupa in central India.*

expected to wash her eyes after seeing one. Even though their work kept the cities clean, they were forced to live in shanty-towns outside the city limits.

Some untouchables were dissatisfied with their fate. At a time when thinkers were questioning all types of authority, some of the outcastes joined dissident sects. As the turbulence in the new cities affected even the most abject of their inhabitants, they became receptive audiences for those challenging the Vedic rituals and Brahman priests.

Brahmans, Their Challengers, and New Beliefs

To the Brahmans, nothing about the cities seemed good, and their efforts to retain their superior status prompted new challenges to traditional beliefs. Indeed, as wise men looked at the urban life around them and the increasing levels of social violence, they decried what they saw. For Brahman priests, as the keepers of the Vedic religious rituals, mingling was a problem: castes mixing indiscriminately, they felt, polluted society. Moreover, lowborn persons grasped at higher status by acquiring wealth or skill. Even worse, as people learned to write, they threatened the Brahman priests' inherited monopoly of oral traditions. When an alphabetic script appeared around 600 BCE, it made sacred knowledge more accessible and thus undermined the Brahmans' ability to control the definition of right and wrong and the moral legitimacy of their order. Formerly, all of Vedic literature had been memorized, and only the brightest Brahmans could master the tradition.

Frightened by these conditions, Brahmans sought to strengthen their relationships with the *rajas* by establishing the idea of a king endowed with divine power. Kingship had been unnecessary in a long-ago golden age, according to Brahmanic scripts; a moral code and priests to uphold it were enough to keep things in order. Over time, though, the world deteriorated and the pure mixed with the impure, until many inhabitants spoke of "fish eating fish" to refer to the practice of individuals killing each other for wealth. According to Brahmanic writings, the gods then decided that people on earth needed a king to maintain order. The gods selected Manu ("Man"), but Manu did not want to accept the difficult job. To win his consent, the gods promised him one-tenth of the grain harvest, one-fiftieth of the cattle, one-quarter of the merits earned by the good behavior of his subjects, and the most beautiful woman in his domain. In this Brahmanic account, royal power has a divine origin: the gods chose the king and protected him. Moreover, priests and Vedic rituals were essential to royal power, since kingly authority was validated through religious ceremonies carried out by Brahman priests. Another Brahmanic account conveys this point, relating a story in which the priests themselves

magically create a king, whose "birth" wins divine celebration and approval. (See Primary Source: Warring Ideas: The Buddha versus the Brahmans—On the Origin of the King.)

This emphasis on divine kingship solved some problems but created new ones. The Brahmans' claim to moral authority caused resentment among the Kshatriyas—especially those in the oligarchic republics, whose leaders did not assert divine power. Merchants and artisans also chafed at the Brahmans' claims to superiority. Such resentments provoked challenges to the Brahmans' domination. Some thinkers in South Asia (like those in China and in the Greek cities experiencing similar upheavals around this time) believed that they were in an age of acute crisis because their culture's ancient harmony had been lost. And like many scholars and philosophers elsewhere in this Axial Age, a new group of South Asian scholars and religious leaders developed their own answers to questions about human existence.

DISSIDENT THINKERS Dissident South Asian thinkers challenged the Brahmans' worldview by refusing to recognize the gods that populated the Vedic world. Some of these rebels sprang from inside the Vedic tradition; though Brahmans, they rejected the idea that sacrificial rituals pleased the gods. To them, God was a universal concept, not a superhuman creature. Also, they felt that the many cows that priests slaughtered for ritual sacrifices could serve more practical uses, such as plowing the land and producing milk. Their discussions and teachings about the universe and life were later collected in the Upanishads (see Chapter 4).

Other dissidents came from outside the Vedic tradition. Consider the Buddha and Mahavira, who both came from the Middle Ganges region, where a pastoral economy and rituals of cattle sacrifice were nonexistent. Here people had never spoken Brahmanical Sanskrit and never had a Brahman caste in their communities. But they, too, challenged the Brahmans, though some adopted and developed ideas expressed in the Upanishads.

MAHAVIRA AND JAINISM Jainism and Buddhism were the two most influential schools outside the Vedic tradition that set themselves against the Brahmans. Vardhamana Mahavira (c. 540–468 BCE) popularized the doctrines of **Jainism**, which had emerged in the seventh century BCE. Born a Kshatriya in an oligarchic republic, Mahavira left home at age thirty to seek the truth about life; he spent twelve years as an ascetic (one who rejects material possessions and physical pleasures) wandering throughout the Ganges Valley before reaching enlightenment. He taught that the universe obeys its own everlasting rules and cannot be affected by any god or other supernatural being. He also believed that the purpose of life is to purify one's soul through asceticism and to attain a state of permanent bliss.

PRIMARY SOURCE

Warring Ideas: The Buddha versus the Brahmans—On the Origin of the King

THE ELECTION OF A KING

This passage is from one of the earliest Buddhist texts, Dialogues of the Buddha. *Here the Buddha explains to one of his disciples, Vāseṭṭha, how the state and king came into being. Early human beings were pure, but they became greedy and chaotic. As a result, they elected one person as king to maintain order. They rewarded the chosen one, called the Great Elect, with a share of their rice. (Note that in this account the people themselves choose the king. Unlike the Brahmanic account that follows, there is no mention of priests or gods.)*

When they had ceased rice appeared, ripening in open spaces, without powder, without husk, pure, fragrant and clean grained. Where we plucked and took away for the evening meal every evening, there next morning it had grown ripe again. Where we plucked and took away for the morning meal, there in the evening it had grown ripe again. There was no break visible. Enjoying this rice, feeding on it, nourished by it, we have so continued a long long while. But from evil and immoral customs becoming manifest among us, powder has enveloped the clean grain, husk too has enveloped the clean grain, and where we have reaped is no re-growth; a break has come, and the rice-stubble stands in clumps. Come now, let us divide off the rice fields and set boundaries thereto! And so they divided off the rice and set up boundaries round it.

Now some being, Vāseṭṭha, of greedy disposition, watching over his own plot, stole another plot and made use of it. They took him and holding him fast, said: Truly, good being, thou hast wrought evil in that, while watching thine own plot, thou hast stolen another plot and made use of it. See, good being, that thou do not such a thing again! Ay, sirs, he replied. And a second time he did so. And yet a third. And again they took him and admonished him. Some smote him with the hand, some with clods, some with sticks. With such a beginning, Vāseṭṭha, did stealing appear, and censure and lying and punishment became known.

Now those beings, Vāseṭṭha, gathered themselves together, and bewailed these things, saying: From our evil deeds, sirs, becoming manifest, inasmuch as stealing, censure, lying, punishment have become known, what if we were to select a certain being, who should be wrathful when indignation is right, who should censure that which should rightly be censured and should banish him who deserves to be banished? But we will give him in return a proportion of the rice.

Then, Vāseṭṭha, those beings went to the being among them who was the handsomest, the best favoured, the most attractive, the most capable and said to him: Come now, good being, be indignant at that whereat one should rightly be indignant, censure that which should rightly be censured, banish him who deserves to be banished. And we will contribute to thee a proportion of our rice.

And he consented, and did so, and they gave him a proportion of their rice.

Jainist religious doctrines emphasized asceticism over knowledge: strict self-denial enables one to avoid harming other creatures and thereby purify the soul. Moreover, the doctrine of *ahimsa* ("no hurt") held that every living creature has a soul. Killing even an ant would lead one to an unfavorable rebirth and further away from permanent bliss. Therefore, believers had to watch every step to avoid inadvertently becoming murderers.

Since land could not be cultivated without killing insects, the extreme nonviolence of Jainism excluded the peasants. Instead, it became a religion of traders and other city dwellers. Mahavira's followers originally transmitted his teachings orally; but a thousand years after his death, they wrote them down. The strictly nonviolent doctrine, though originally intended only for followers of Jainism, has profoundly affected the inhabitants of South Asia down to modern times.

BUDDHA AND BUDDHISM The most direct challenge to traditional Brahmanic thinking came from Siddhartha Gautama (c. 563–483 BCE), a contemporary of Mahavira and Confucius. Later called the **Buddha**, or the Enlightened One, Gautama not only objected to Brahmanic rituals and sacrifices but also denied their underlying cosmology (a branch of metaphysics devoted to understanding the order of the universe) and their preference for kingship that kept the priestly class in power. His Axial Age teachings provided the peoples of South Asia and elsewhere with alternatives to established social and religious traditions.

Gautama was born into a comfortable life, the son of a highly respected Kshatriya in a small oligarchic community nestled in the foothills of the Himalayas. Yet, at the age of twenty-nine, he walked away from everything, leaving behind a respected and loving father, a wife, and a few-days-old son. Family and friends wept

A KING SELECTED BY BRAHMANS AND ENDORSED BY GODS

Several stories about the beginning of monarchy are preserved in Brahmanic Hindu literature. The story of Prithu tells of the mutual dependence of the king and Brahman priests, who selected the king and guaranteed the gods' endorsement of him. Initially a king named Vena refused to worship gods, so the Brahmans killed him. Then they created a new king, Prithu, who followed all the rituals.

Afterwards (after the Brahmans killed the vicious king Vena who refused to worship gods) the Munis (Brahmans) beheld a great dust arise, and they said to the people who were nigh, "What is this?" and the people answered and said, "Now that the kingdom is without a king, the dishonest men have begun to seize the property of their neighbors. The great dust that you behold, excellent Munis, is raised by troops of clustering robbers, hastening to fall upon their prey." The sages, hearing this, consulted, and together rubbed the thigh of the king, who had left no offspring, to produce a son. From the thigh, thus rubbed came forth a being of the complexion of a charred stake, with flattened features, and of dwarfish stature. "What am I to do?" cried he eagerly to the Munis. "Sit down" (Nishida), said they; and thence his name was Nishada. His descendants, the inhabitants of the Vindhya mountain, are still called Nishadas, and are characterized by the exterior tokens of depravity. By this means the wickedness of Vena was expelled; those Nishadas being born of his sins, and carrying them away. The Brahmans then proceeded to rub the right arm of the king, from which friction was engendered the illustrious son of Vena, named Prithu, resplendent in person, as if the blazing deity of Fire had been manifested.

There then fell from the sky the primitive bow (of Mahadeva) named Ajagava, and celestial arrows, and panoply from heaven. At the birth of Prithu all living creatures rejoiced; and Vena, delivered by his being born from the hell named Put, ascended to the realms above. The seas and rivers, bringing jewels from their depths, and water to perform the ablutions of his installation, appeared. The great parent of all, Brahma, with the gods and the descendants of Angiras (the fires), and with all things animate or inanimate, assembled and performed the ceremony of consecrating the son of Vena. Beholding in his right hand the (mark of the) discus of Vishnu, Brahma recognized a portion of that divinity in Prithu, and was much pleased; for the mark of Vishnu's discus is visible in the hand of one who is born to be universal emperor (chakravarti). One whose power is invincible even by the gods.

QUESTIONS FOR ANALYSIS

- After the Vedic peoples migrated into the mid-Ganges plain, rice cultivation and feuding characterized their society. How does the Buddha's story about the election of the first king reflect this social history?
- How does the Brahmans' story underscore the role of the priests in upholding the monarchy? Why do you suppose the Brahman priests were so concerned that the king worship gods and follow traditional rituals?

Source: *Dialogues of the Buddha, Part III,* Vol. 4 of *Sacred Books of the Buddhists,* translated by T. W. Rhys David and C. A. F. Rhys David (London: Oxford University Press, 1921), pp. 87–88; *Vishnu Purana,* translated from Sanskrit by H. H. Wilson (1st ed. 1840, 3rd ed. Calcutta: Punthi Pustak, 1961), pp. 83–84.

as he donned a robe and shaved his head and beard to symbolize the ascetic life that he intended to pursue. (Ultimately, though, some relatives became eminent followers of his teaching.) Legend has it that he concluded that the life that he and most others were destined to live would consist of little more than endless episodes of suffering, beginning with the pain of childbirth, followed by aging, illness, disease, and death; afterward, reincarnated beings would experience more of the same. Yet he was no dropout or deserter, for he was full of faith that his search for nirvana—enlightenment and the absence of pain—would succeed.

Success eluded him for six years, however. At a fateful moment, he remembered a trance of ecstasy that he had experienced as a child and realized that this mystical moment showed him the way forward. Humans, he now understood, do not need to punish their bodies, for they have built-in capacities to achieve happiness and repose. The ascetics with whom he had lived had stressed depriving the body. But, in truth, *enlightenment* comes not through denial but by keeping a positive state of mind. Repose could be attained only by finding a middle ground between self-indulgence and self-denial.

The Buddha's wanderings and ascetic life led him to create a new credo, which his teachings expressed as the Four Noble Truths: (1) life, from birth to death, is full of suffering; (2) all sufferings are caused by desires; (3) the only way to rise above suffering is to renounce desire; and (4) only through adherence to the Rightful Eightfold Path can individuals rid themselves of desires and thus reach a state of contentment, or nirvana. The elements of the Eightfold Path represent wisdom (right views and right intentions), ethical behavior (right conduct, right speech, and right livelihood), and mental discipline (right effort, right thought, and right meditation). Because these principles were simple and clear, the Four Truths, as they became known, had a powerful appeal. The teachings of the Four Truths and the Eightfold Path combined represent the Buddhist *dharma*—the basic doctrine shared by Buddhists of all sects. This teaching also signified a dramatic shift in thinking about humanity and correct behavior. Like the teachings of Mahavira, the Buddha's doctrines left no space for deities to dictate human lives, a theme stressed in classical Brahmanic thinking. Buddha's logical explanation of human suffering and his guidelines for renouncing desire appealed to many people, for he set forth tenets by which his followers strove to live virtuously and to take some measure of control and responsibility for their own lives.

Like other dissident thinkers of this period, the Buddha delivered his message in a vernacular dialect of Sanskrit that all could understand. His many followers soon formed a community of monks called a *sangha* ("gathering"). The Buddha and his followers wandered from one city to another on the Ganges plain, where they found large audiences as well as the alms needed to sustain the expanding *sangha*. In fact, the Buddha's most influential patrons were urban merchants. And in struggles between oligarchs and kings, the Buddha sided with the oligarchs—reflecting his upbringing in an oligarchic republic. He inevitably aroused opposition from the Brahmans, who favored monarchical government. While the Buddha himself did not seek to erase the caste hierarchy, the *sangha* provided an escape from its oppressive aspects and the prestige that it afforded the Brahmans. Together with Jainism, Buddhism's challenge to Brahmanic thinking appealed particularly to the new urban residents of South Asia and to those who felt disadvantaged by prevailing Vedic hierarchies.

WARRING IDEAS IN THE MEDITERRANEAN WORLD

The first millennium BCE in the Mediterranean was a time of political, economic, and social changes, all of which stimulated new thinking and new political and economic institutions (just as in Eastern Zhou China and Vedic South Asia). (See Map 5.4.) The violent upheavals that tore through the borderland areas of the northern Levant, the coastal lands of Anatolia, the islands of the Aegean and Mediterranean Seas, and mainland Greece freed these peoples from the domination of Assyria and Persia. Now these borderland communities could explore new cultural ideas and create new social and political organizations. Thus, around 1000 BCE, these second-generation societies mixed the old and the new, developing innovative social and political methods of organization and exploring new Axial Age ideas.

Seafaring peoples from around the Mediterranean Sea basin—Phoenicians, Greeks, Cretans, Cypriots, Lydians, Etruscans, and many others—carried not just trade goods but also ideas about the virtues of self-sufficient cities whose inhabitants shared power more widely (even more democratically) than before. Inventions that proved valuable in one place, such as the use of money and the alphabet, spread rapidly, promoting unprecedented intercommunication between diverse communities. Part of the cost of this diversity was the extraordinary fragmentation of political states, most of which were much smaller than the large territorial states of Southwest Asia. A related downside was the frequency with which the new smaller competitive states engaged in armed conflicts with one another.

The Buddha's Footprints. *Before his followers came to regard Buddha as a god, they were reluctant to make an idol of him. The footprints are an early representation of Buddha. They were carved in a limestone panel in a first-century BCE stupa in India.*

A New World of City-States

New ways of thinking about the world burst forth in the ninth and eighth centuries BCE, as order returned to the eastern Mediterranean and the population rebounded. The peoples who clustered in more concentrated settlements at this time did not

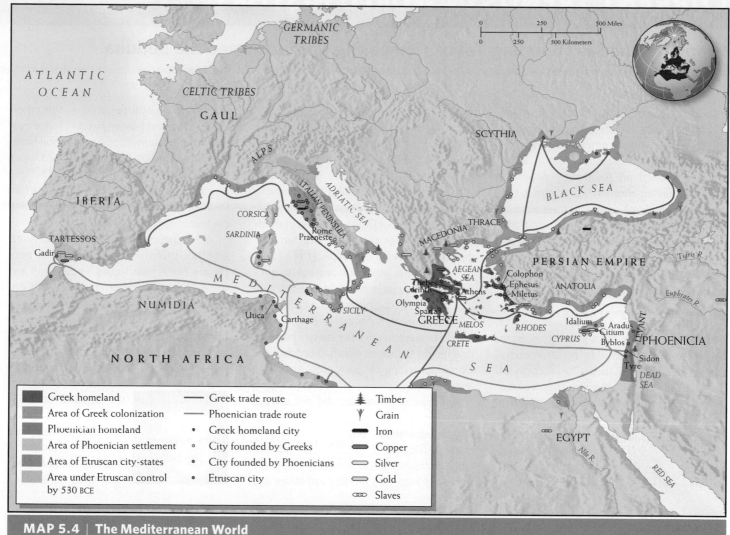

MAP 5.4 | The Mediterranean World

Phoenician and Greek city-states, as well as the colonies they founded, dotted the coastline of both the Mediterranean and Black Seas.

- What were the main goods traded in the Mediterranean world in this period?
- What areas did the Greeks and Phoenicians control, and what was their main settlement pattern?
- How do you think a small country like Phoenicia was able to extend its reach so dramatically?

revive the old palace and temple organizations of the Mycenae-ans and Minoans (see Chapter 3). Instead, they created something quite novel: city-states that were governed by their own citizens. They also unleashed powerful waves of cultural innovation and economic activity.

SELF-GOVERNMENT AND DEMOCRACY The self-governing city-state was a new political form that profoundly influenced the Mediterranean region. First found among the Phoenicians (see Chapter 4) and in their settlements, such as Carthage, but ultimately associated with the Greeks, these new urban communities had multiplied throughout the Mediterranean by the sixth century BCE. The new urban entity was known by the Phoenicians as a *qart*, by the Greeks as a *polis*, and by the Romans

as a *civitas*. Unlike the great urban centers in the Southwest Asian empires run by elite scribes, high priests, and monarchs, the Mediterranean city-states were governed by their citizens.

The new principles of rulership were revolutionary. Ordinary residents, or "citizens," of these cities—such as Carthage and Gadir (modern-day Cádiz in Spain) among the western Phoenicians; Athens, Thebes, Sparta, and Corinth among the Greeks; Rome and Praeneste among the early Latins—governed themselves and selected their leaders. Their self-government took various forms. One was rule by a popularly approved political head of the city, whom the Greeks called a *tyrannis* ("tyrant"). Another was rule by a few wealthy and powerful citizens—the *oligoi*, literally "the few" in Greek (hence "oligarchs" and "oligar-chies"). The most inclusive type of government involved all free

Prophets and the Founding Texts: Comparing Confucius and the Buddha

World history offers many opportunities to compare one society with another, and this chapter, with its emphasis on teachers, prophets, and intellectuals in what we have called an Axial Age, provides an unparalleled moment to contrast the lives and ideals of central figures whose teachings, spiritual movements, legal and political systems, and long-lasting traditions endured for centuries. In Confucianism and Buddhism, we find key leaders who inspired belief systems that honored them.

Confucius (551–479 BCE) was one of the ancient world's great innovators. Born in North China, he was posthumously remembered for elaborating a code of behavior that valued individual performance of traditional rituals and governmental morality based on correct social relationships, sincerity, and justice. Seeing division and war among rival states, he wished to restore order by promoting education, moral behavior, and the performance of ritual.

Over the centuries the method and substance of his teaching, with many revisions, became the mainstream value system of imperial China. His idea of modeling the state on the patriarchal family—that is, the ruler should respect the heaven as if it were his father and protect his subjects as if they were his children—became the foundation of Chinese political theory. Confucius wanted people to perform the rituals bequeathed by the early Zhou and to emulate the sages who had ordered the world according to principles of civility and culture.

Chinese philosophers did not always agree on how to interpret Confucius's ideas. Representing one school of Confucianists, Mencius (372–289 BCE) held that while recognizing the tendency of people to be led astray by worldly appetites and ambitions, he still believed in the inherent goodness of human nature. To recover that innate goodness required moral training. But according to Xunzi (310–237 BCE), Confucius saw humans as evil and lacking an innate moral sense. They therefore had to be controlled by education, ritual, and custom.

Nevertheless, both Mencius and Xunzi embraced Confucius's dictum that people are perfectible through education and the practice of proper conduct. All Confucians, whether pessimists or optimists, viewed moral cultivation through education as the heart of the civilizing process, and they ensured that his ideas remained a vital force throughout Chinese history.

The teachings of the **Buddha** (c. 563–483 BCE), like those of Confucius, had far-reaching influence. The two thinkers were roughly contemporary,

---

adult males in a city—in Greek, a *dēmokratia* ("democracy"). The wealthiest landowners often formed the power elite, but farmers, craftworkers, shopkeepers, merchants, soldiers, and traders ran the city's affairs, set priorities for development, and decided when to go to war.

These new cities became communities of adult male citizens, other free persons (including women, who could not vote or hold office), foreign immigrants, and large numbers of unfree persons (including slaves and people tied to the land who could not vote or fight for the polis). Those enjoying full citizenship rights—the adult freeborn males—in each community decided what tasks the city-state would undertake and what kind of government and laws it would adopt. Consequently, the cities differed markedly from one another. The competition among cities propelled competition among thinkers, with innovative ideas having a broader appeal and greater impact than ever before.

FAMILIES AS FOUNDATIONAL UNITS The small family unit was the most important social unit. In fact, the city-state was seen as a natural outgrowth of the household. Thus, the free adult male was entitled to engage in the city's public affairs. In contrast, adult women of free birth remained enclosed within the private world of the family and had no standing to debate policy in public, vote, or hold office. Women who did carry on intelligent conversations with men in public about public matters were criticized. Spartan women were a partial exception, and their unusual behavior—such as exercising in the nude in public (as did men) or holding property in their own right—evoked humor and hostility from men in the other Greek city-states.

COMPETITION AND ARMED WAR With no centralized governments to control residents' actions and thoughts, the city-states were freewheeling and competitive places, sometimes bloodily so. Their histories relate violent rivalries between individuals, social classes, and other groups. Among the larger Greek city-states, only Sparta avoided most of this internal strife, achieving greater calm through rigorous social discipline and military organization that cut off the city from many external influences. The Spartans rejected coined money and chattel slavery (discussed shortly), thereby avoiding the "corruption" of cities with more mercantile and both formulated their ideas in response to social chaos and degeneration. The Buddha presented a vision of society that challenged the Brahmanic order. Buddhism shaped the views of life and death and the scheme of time and space of the universe in South Asia. It also had a profound impact on peoples outside the region and even replaced Confucianism as the dominant religion in China for a few hundred years.

The Buddha offered a logical approach in the form of a unified system underlying the universe, instead of invoking divine intervention, to understand the universe and social life at a time of rapid political development. He believed that the universe and individual lives go through eternal cycles of birth, death, and rebirth, and he elaborated the concept of *karma* ("fate" or "action"), a universal principle of cause and effect. The birth of every living being, human or animal, reflects actions taken in his or her past lives. Karma embodies the

sins and merits of each individual, establishing his or her status in the current life. In turn, deeds in the current life affect that karma and thus determine suffering and happiness in the next life. Buddhist believers therefore focused on the consequences of their actions: through their own behavior, they could attain better future lives.

Confucianism and Buddhism, much like the Vedic, Brahmin, and Judaic faiths discussed in Chapter 4, emerged in times of great turmoil. All the faiths were first transmitted orally; later, adherents created a written record to spread them more widely. But Buddhism and Confucianism stand out in that they have founders whose identification with their belief systems remains their most defining characteristic: the Buddha as an enlightened one and Confucius as a sage. We will see this phenomenon again with the rise of Christianity (from the teachings of Jesus) and Islam (from

the teachings of Muhammad) as we continue our discussion of universalizing religions.

QUESTIONS FOR ANALYSIS

- What is the reward for good moral behavior for Confucius? For Buddha?
- What are the major similarities and differences between these two traditions?

Explore Further

Armstrong, Karen. *Buddha* (2001).

Schaberg, David. *A Patterned Past: Form and Thought in Early Chinese Historiography* (2002).

von Falkenhausen, Lothar. *Chinese Society in the Age of Confucius (1000–250 BC): The Archaeological Evidence* (2006).

interests. However successful it was as a military state, Sparta seemed to the other Greeks to be a very unusual polis.

Competition for honor and prestige shaped behavior in the city-states. This extreme competitive ethic found a benign outlet in organized sporting events. Almost from the moment that Greek city-states emerged, athletic contests sprang up—both as an essential part of each city's life and in centralized events in which all Greeks could participate. The greatest competitions were the Olympic Games, which began in 776 BCE at Olympia, in southern Greece.

The competitive spirit among communities took the destructive form of armed conflicts over borderlands, trade, valuable resources, religious shrines, and prestige. Wars were characteristic of city-state relations (as they were among states in Eastern Zhou China and Vedic South Asia during the same period). The incessant battles fueled new developments in military equipment, such as the heavy armor that gave its name to the hoplites, or infantrymen, and in tactics, such as the standard blocklike configuration (which the Greeks called a *phalanx*) in which the regular rank and file fought. These wars were so

destructive that they threatened to destabilize the city-states' world. The most famous conflict was the Peloponnesian War (431–404 BCE) between Athens and Sparta and their respective allies. It dragged on for decades, eating away the resources of the two great polities and their allies. Sparta finally won the war, but only at the cost of destroying its own traditional social culture. In the end, everyone lost.

Economic Innovations and Population Movement

Despite the destabilizing effects of warfare, city-states prospered, and economic innovations (the alphabet, coins, and the central marketplace) facilitated trade and exchange throughout the Mediterranean. As a result, the city-states enjoyed accelerated economic growth in the ninth and eighth centuries BCE. Even more spectacular was the speed with which they established colonies wherever they found resources and trade. The city-states' superior military technology, developed and tested

Hetaira. *The painting on this vase by the artist Oitos is of a "companion" woman—called by the Greeks a hetaira—putting on a sandal. Proper Greek women were protected and kept within their households; they were modest and always fully clothed. Women who were so bold as to be out in public, talking and otherwise associating with men—like the woman portrayed here—were deemed immoral. The artist therefore had no problem portraying this hetaira in the nude.*

Hoplites. *Most battles between Greek city-states took place on land between massed formations of infantrymen, or "hoplites" (from the Greek hoplon, meaning "shield"). Serving the community in this way defined one's right to citizenship, or membership in the city. Since hoplites wore the same armor and contributed equally to the battle line, the nature of hoplite warfare helped to define the democratic ethos of the individual citizen.*

in conflicts among themselves, enabled them to defeat local resistance. Moreover, through trade and colonization, the Mediterranean peoples acquired as slaves the inhabitants of frontier communities to the north. The slaves' labor further contributed to the city-states' wealth and growth.

FREE MARKETS AND MONEY-BASED ECONOMIES

Without a top-down bureaucratic and administrative structure, residents of the new cities devised other ways to run their affairs. They developed open trading markets and a system of money that enabled buyers and sellers to know the precise value of commodities so that exchanges were efficient. The Greek historian Herodotus, who journeyed widely in the mid-fifth century BCE, observed that the new city-states had at their center a marketplace (*agora*), a large open area where individuals bought and sold commodities. He found no such great open public commercial spaces in Egypt or Babylonia.

Soon most transactions required money rather than barter or gift exchange. Coins also bought services, perhaps at first to hire mercenary soldiers. In the absence of large bureaucracies, the Mediterranean cities relied on money to connect the producers and buyers of goods and services. By the late fifth century BCE, the Greek city-states were issuing a striking variety of coins, and other peoples, such as the Phoenicians, Etruscans, and Persians, were also using them. (During the same period, money developed independently and saw common use in Vedic South Asia and Eastern Zhou China.)

TRADE AND COLONIZATION The search for silver, iron, copper, and tin drove the first traders westward across the Mediterranean. By about 500 BCE, the Phoenicians, Greeks, and others from the eastern Mediterranean had planted new city-states around the shores of the western Mediterranean and the Black Sea. Once established, these colonial communities became independent, and they transformed the coastal world. City-based life became common from southern Spain and western Italy to the Crimea on the Black Sea.

With amazing speed, seaborne communications spread a Mediterranean-wide urban culture that bolstered the region's wealthy and powerful elites. Found among the local elites of Tartessos, in southern Iberia, the Gallic chiefs in southern France, and the Etruscan and Roman nobles of central Italy, the new aristocratic culture featured similar displays of wealth: richly decorated chariots, elaborate armor and weapons, high-class dining ware, elaborate houses, and public burials. Everywhere they took root, the city-state communities developed a culture founded on alphabetic scripts, market-based economies, and private property.

CHATTEL SLAVERY The explosion of buying and selling produced an ethos in which everything that the city dwellers

The Agora. *The agora, or central open marketplace, was one of the core defining features of Mediterranean city-states. At its center, each city had one of these open-air plazas, the heart of its commercial, religious, social, and political life. When a new city was founded, the agora was one of the first places that the colonists measured out. The large, rectangular, open area in this picture is the agora of the Greek colonial city of Cyrene (in modern-day Libya).*

needed, even human beings, acquired a monetary value. Treating men, women, and children as objects of commerce, to be bought and sold in markets, created a new form of slavery called chattel slavery. This commercial slavery spread quickly. Where dangerous and exhausting tasks such as mining required extra labor, the freeborn citizens purchased slave laborers. These slaves were mainly war captives. They were essential to all the new city-states, providing manual and technical labor and producing the agricultural surpluses that supported the urban population.

ENCOUNTERS WITH FRONTIER COMMUNITIES The forces that transformed the Mediterranean region's mosaic of urban communities and surrounding rural areas also affected those in northern and central Europe. Whether they wished it or not, diverse tribes and ethnic groups, such as the Celts and Germans in western Europe and the Scythians to the north of the Black Sea, who were living in nomadic bands, isolated settlements, and small villages became integrated into the expanding cities' networks of violence, conquest, and trade.

Mediterranean Coins. *From the sixth century BCE onward, money in the form of precious metal coins began spreading through the city-states of the Mediterranean, beginning with the Greek city-states in the western parts of what is today Turkey, then spreading to the other Greek poleis and beyond. On the left is the classic tetradrachm (four-drachma piece) coin of Athens with its owl of the goddess Athena; on the right is a silver coin of shekel weight produced by the city of Carthage, in the western Mediterranean.*

Increasingly drawn to the city-states' manufactured goods—money, wine, ornate clothing, weapons—these tribal peoples became an armed threat to the region's core societies. Seeking to acquire the desired commodities through force rather than trade, frontier peoples convulsed the settled urban societies in wavelike incursions between 2200 and 2000 BCE, 1200 and 1000 BCE, and 400 and 200 BCE. Called "barbarians" (the Greeks' mocking name for foreigners unable to speak their language), the invaders actually were not much different from the Phoenicians or Greeks—who themselves had sought new homes and a better future by migrating. In colonizing the Mediterranean, they, too, had dispossessed the original inhabitants. The Celts, Gauls, Germans, Scythians, and other northerners came to the Mediterranean first as conquerors. Later, when Mediterranean empires grew more powerful and could keep them at bay, they were imported as slaves. Regarding these outsiders as uncivilized, the Greeks and western Phoenicians seized and colonized their lands—and sold the captives as commodities in their marketplaces.

New Ideas

New ways of thinking about the world emerged from the competitive atmosphere that the Greek city-states fostered. In the absence of monarchical or priestly rule (as in the kingdoms of Southwest Asia), ideas were free to arise, circulate, and clash. Individuals argued publicly about the nature of the gods, the best state, what is good, and whether to wage war. There was no final authority to force the acceptance of any particular idea. New ideas emerged in areas that would become known as science and the arts, and professional thinkers proposed theories on human society and many other topics.

NATURALISTIC SCIENCE AND REALISTIC ART In this atmosphere, some daring thinkers developed novel ways of perceiving the cosmos and representing the environment. Rather than seeing everything as the handiwork of all-powerful deities, they took a naturalistic view of humans and their place in the universe. Artists increasingly represented humans, objects, and landscapes not in abstract or formal ways but in "natural" ways, as they appeared to the human eye. Even their portrayals of gods became more humanlike. Later, these objective and natural views of humans and nature turned into ideals, the highest of which was the unadorned human figure: the nude became the centerpiece of Greek art.

The public display of the uncovered human body, in both art and everyday life (notably in men's athletic training and competition), signaled the sharp break between the moral codes of the older, traditional societies of the East and those of the revolutionary cities of the Mediterranean. Vase painters such as Exekias signed their works and became known as individual artists.

Sculptors like Praxiteles also became famous. No less assertive were creative writers, such as the poets Archilochus and Sappho, who wrote lyrics exploring their own emotions—a clear manifestation of the new sense of the individual being freed from the restraints of an autocratic state or a controlling religious system.

NEW THINKING AND GREEK PHILOSOPHERS Armed with their own ideas and borrowed knowledge, thinkers in cities such as Miletus and Ephesus did not accept traditional explanations of how and why the universe works. Rather than focusing

The Human Form. *The human body as it appeared naturally, without any adornment, became the ideal set by Greek art. Even gods were portrayed in this nude human form. This statue by Praxiteles is of the god Hermes with the infant Dionysus. Such bold nude portraits of humans and gods were sometimes shocking to other peoples.*

PRIMARY SOURCE

Warring Ideas: Plato versus Aristotle—On Gaining Knowledge of the Essence of the World

Great debates raged among Greek thinkers during the fifth and fourth centuries BCE over the essence of the world and how humans can have knowledge of it. Rejecting the existence of creator gods and goddesses, they sought explanations elsewhere. Some looked to the material world (in primary substances like water), while others turned to abstractions.

The Greek philosopher and mathematician Pythagoras suggested that numbers are the basis of everything. Some later thinkers, notably Plato, took this argument further and argued that all existence—and therefore all human knowledge—is based on absolute concepts that are like numbers, existing independent of time and place. Each of them Plato called an *idea*, a word whose meanings in Greek include "shape," "form," and "appearance." In a number of Plato's dialogues, his teacher, Socrates, tries to explain this theory:

> **Socrates:** I am going to try to explain to you the theory of causes that I myself have thought out. . . . I assume that you admit the existence of absolutes like "beauty" and "good" and "size" and the rest. If you admit that these absolutes exist, then I can hope with their help to show you what causes are. . . . I remain obstinately committed . . . to the explanation that the one thing that causes a thing to be "beautiful," for example, is the existence in it of "the beautiful" or its sharing in "the beautiful"[;] . . . and so, is it not also the case that things that we call "big" are big because they share the idea of "bigness" and similarly that things that we call "small" are small because they share in the idea of "smallness"? [Socrates then dismisses the claim that in calling things "tall" or "small" we are simply describing them in relation to other things.]
>
> **Phaedo:** I believe that Socrates has persuaded us of these matters and that we have agreed that these different ideas do exist; and he has also persuaded us that the reason

why specific things in our world are named after these ideas is that they share in the existence of the specific idea. (*Phaedo* 99d–102b)

Still other thinkers drew on some of the first Greek philosophers of the sixth century BCE to argue that the basis of all existing things is, quite simply, other things. They rejected the proposal that all things we perceive with our senses are poor copies of permanent ideas of them that exist in a separate, unchangeable realm. Human knowledge, they argued, is in fact acquired through careful observation of existing things and through meticulous collection of data about them. Thus, in the following passage Aristotle rejects Plato's concept of ideas:

> As for the followers of Plato who claim that "ideas" (or "shapes") are the causes or origins of all things, this too is objectionable. First of all, in their struggle to find causes for things that exist in our world of sense perceptions, they simply introduce as many new things into the equation as they are attempting to explain[;] . . . so their "ideas" are as many . . . as the things whose causes they are seeking to explain and for which reason they were led to invent these ideas. They must do this because they must create an idea to match every substance that exists in our real everyday world . . . and also one in the realm of the eternal heavenly entities. Not one of the arguments by which they try to demonstrate that these ideas actually exist can demonstrate or prove their claim. From some of their arguments, indeed, no real conclusions follow. From other arguments

of theirs it only follows that there must be ideas of things for which they themselves hold no such ideas can exist. (*Metaphysics* 1.9, 990a–b)

In other works, Aristotle put forth his own views about how to gain reliable knowledge of the world:

> All teaching and learning by means of rational argument is based on our existing knowledge and observations; . . . and I think that we have reliable knowledge of each thing . . . when we think that we have found the cause because of which that thing exists—what is the cause of that thing and of nothing else, with the result that this thing or this fact cannot be other than it is. That this is real knowledge of something is very clear. . . . We know what we do by demonstration, by showing that it is true. By demonstration I mean an argument that produces real knowledge, . . . all of which is based on a knowledge and observation of facts and things. . . . But I also say that not all real knowledge can in fact be demonstrated or proved. (*Posterior Analytics* 1.1–3, 71a–72b)

QUESTIONS FOR ANALYSIS

- How do our modern attitudes toward what we know and how we know it reflect these two approaches?
- What might have provoked Plato and Aristotle to advance such different concepts of knowledge?
- Where else might such factors be linked to major developments of the time (for example, South or East Asia)?

Source: Plato, *Phaedo*, 99d–102b; Aristotle, *Metaphysics*, 1.9, 990a–b; *Posterior Analytics*, 1.1–3, 71a–72b. All translations are by Brent Shaw.

Axial Age Thinkers and Their Ideas

In the mid-twentieth century, the German philosopher Karl Jaspers coined the term *Axial Period* to describe the importance of ideas that originated in the first millennium BCE. These thinkers and their ideas are characterized as "axial" because (1) they were a pivot point, or axis, that seemed to turn the world in a new direction, (2) they occurred along an East-West axis stretching from the Mediterranean to East Asia, and (3) they are central to ethical thought even down to the present day. These Axial Age philosophers were both the product of, and a challenge to, the societies from which they came—in other words, they were spurred by complex social and political contexts to develop their new ideas, but these new ideas in many ways critiqued and offered alternatives to the status quo. The table presented here does not represent every Axial Age tradition, but is meant to draw into relief the relationship between the innovative thinker, his historical context, and the tenets of the new belief system.

QUESTIONS FOR ANALYSIS

- What connections, if any, do you see between the geopolitical situation of a society and the Axial Age philosophy that sprang from that region? In what ways does each philosopher support or challenge the status quo?

- Jaspers was particularly impressed that societies he understood as being disconnected from one another would develop philosophical ideas so similar. How might the temporal and geographical relationship of the philosophers listed in the table be explained? How does connectivity or disconnectivity impact the development of these ideas? What might account for similarities and differences in these Axial Age philosophies?

- What are the similarities and differences in how these philosophers' ideas were transmitted through time?

Thinker	Philosophy	Core Text	Historical Context	Central Tenet	Exemplary Sayings
Zoroaster, (1000–600 BCE)	Zoroastrianism	Avesta, the most sacred part of which is the Gathas, seventeen Middle Persian hymns purportedly written by Zoroaster himself	Southwest Asia, based in eastern Iranian nomadic culture, eventually becoming the central religion of the Persian Empire	**Dualistic ethical system**, a world order based on the cosmic struggle between Ahura Mazda, the god of light, and Angra Mainyu, the god of destruction. Humans must choose between good and evil with reward or retribution doled out in the afterlife.	**On dualism:** "There [are] . . . two spirits [present] in the primal [stage of one's existence], twins who have . . . [manifested themselves as] the two [kinds] of dreams, . . . thoughts and words, . . . [and] actions, the better and the evil." (30.3) **On rewards:** "Brilliant things . . . will be for the person who comes to the truthful one. But a long period of darkness, foul food, and the word "woe"—to such an existence your religious view will lead you, O deceitful ones, of your own actions." (31.20)
Ezekiel (6th century BCE) and Isaiah, among other Jewish writers and prophets	Judaism	The Hebrew Bible, whose second part, Nevi'im, contains the writings of the prophets	Southwest Asia, with origins in Mesopotamian tribal cultures, eventually spreading to the early empires of Egypt and the Levant	A strict monotheistic tradition that dictates that its followers are the chosen people and have entered a **covenant**, or contractual relationship, with their god	**On monotheism:** "I am the first and I am the last; besides me there is no god." (Isaiah 44:6) **On the covenant:** "[. . .] I will make a new covenant . . . not like the covenant which I made with their fathers . . . to bring them out of the land of Egypt, my covenant which they broke, though I was their husband, says the Lord." (Jeremiah 31:31-32)

Sources: H. Humbach and I. Ichaporia, *The Heritage of Zarathustra* (Heidelberg, 1994); Helmut Humbach "Gathas, i. Texts" *Encyclopedia Iranica* (2000) Vol. X, Fasc. 3, pp. 321-27; William W. Malandra, "Gathas, ii. Translations," *Encyclopedia Iranica* (2000) Vol. X, Fasc. 3, pp. 327-30; Thomas G. West and Grace Starry West, *Four Texts on Socrates* (Cornell, 1984); D.C. Lau's translation of Analects in *Norton Anthology of World Literature*, Vol. 1, edited by H. James (Norton, 2002), pp. 820-30; *The Dhammapada*, translated by Juan Mascaro (Penguin, 1973); *New Oxford Annotated Bible with Apocrypha*, Revised Standard Version (Oxford).

on gods, they looked to nature as constituting some fundamental substance (usually one of the traditional elements: earth, air or breath, fire, or water). Thales (c. 636–546 BCE) believed that water is the primal substance from which all other things are created.

As thinkers competed in offering persuasive and comprehensive explanations, theories became ever more radical. Men like Xenophanes (c. 570–480 BCE), from the city of Colophon, doubted the very existence of gods as they had been portrayed. Asserting instead that only one general divine aura suffuses all

Thinker	Philosophy	Core Text	Historical Context	Central Tenet	Exemplary Sayings
Buddha (c. 563–483 BCE)	Buddhism	Dhammapad, verse sayings of the Buddha, which were recorded in the third century BCE	India, as a challenge to Kshatriya oligarchy and the caste system of the Vedic society	An ethical system governed by the **Four Noble Truths**: 1. Life is suffering; 2. Suffering is rooted in attachment; 3. Escape suffering by escaping attachment; 4. Escape attachment via the **Eight-fold Path**	**On the Eight-fold Path**: "The best of the paths is the path of eight. The best of the truths, the four sayings. The best of states, freedom from passions. The best of men, the one who sees." (*Dhammapada*, 273) **On extremes**: "He who lives not for pleasures, and whose soul is in self-harmony, who eats and fasts with moderation, and has faith and the power of virtue—this man is not moved by temptations, as a great rock is not shaken by the wind." (8)
Confucius (551–479 BCE)	Confucianism	*Analects*, Confucius' dialogues with state leaders and students that were most likely recorded centuries later	China, during political turmoil toward the end of the Spring and Autumn period (722–481 BCE)	A code of moral behavior, as exemplified in the *junzi* (gentleman or superior man), centered on: 1. *ren* (benevolence), 2. *li* (proper ritual), 3. *xiao* (filial piety)	**On virtue**: "The rule of virtue can be compared to the Pole Star which commands the homage of the multitude of stars without leaving its place." (II.1) **On respect**: "Duke Ai asked: 'What must I do before the common people will look up to me?' Confucius answered: 'Raise the straight and set them over the crooked and the common people will look up to you.'" (II.19)
Socrates (469–399 BCE)	Greek philosophy	Dialogues recorded in the contemporary work of his students, especially Plato, and a collection of his sayings published later on	Greece, during a period of Greco-Persian conflict and inter-city-state wars	Ethical code that encourages self-discovery through knowledge, the recognition of the limits to one's own faculties, and the questioning of authority to find truth	**On self-discovery**: "The unexamined life is not worth living for a human being." (*Apology*, 38a) **On wisdom**: "I am wiser than this human being, for probably neither of us knows anything noble and good; but he supposes he knows something, when he does not know; while I, just as I do not know, do not even suppose that I do." (*Apology*, 21d).
Jesus (6/4 BCE–c. 30 CE)	Christianity	Sayings later known through canonical and noncanonical Christian Gospels, first put in writing in the late first century CE	Judea under Roman imperial rule, later spreads throughout the Indo-Mediterranean	God's personal relationship with humanity mediated by His son, Jesus, whose suffering expiates human sins and grants eternal life to believers	**On ethical thought**: "Blessed are you poor, for yours is the kingdom of God; Blessed are you that hunger now, for you shall be satisfied . . . Love your enemies, do good to those who hate you. . . . " (Luke 6:20-38) **On Judaism**: 'Love the Lord your God. . . .' This is the first . . . commandment. And the second is like it: 'Love your neighbor as yourself.' All the Law and the Prophets hang on these two commandments." (Matthew 22:37-40)

creation, he pointed out that each ethnic group in fact produced images of gods that resembled themselves: Ethiopians represented their gods with dark skins and broad noses, while Thracians depicted theirs as blue-eyed redheads. Such variation suggested that the gods existed only in the human imagination.

Some thinkers proposed that the real world has a physical, tangible basis. Among them was Democritus (c. 460–370 BCE), who claimed that everything comprises small and ultimately indivisible particles called *atoma* ("uncuttables"), or atoms. Even more radical were thinkers like Pythagoras, who undertook the study of numbers (although the famous Pythagorean theorem had already been discovered by Babylonian priests and mathematicians). Prefiguring the modern digital revolution, he held that a wide range of physical phenomena, like musical sounds, is in fact based in numbers.

The competition among ideas led to a more aggressive mode of public thinking. The Greeks called it *philosophia* ("love of wisdom") and the professional thinkers who were good at it *philosophoi* ("philosophers"). Some of the earliest recorded debates addressed the nature of the cosmos, the environment, and the physical elements of human existence. By the fifth century BCE, **Greek philosophers** were focusing on humans and their place in society. Finally, some thinkers tried to describe an ideal state possessing harmonious relationships and no corruption or political decline.

Socrates (469–399 BCE), a philosopher in Athens, stressed the importance of honor and integrity as opposed to wealth and power (just as Confucius had done in Eastern Zhou China and the Buddha in Vedic South Asia). Plato (427–347 BCE), a student of Socrates, presented Socrates's philosophy in a series of dialogues (much as Confucius's students had written down his thoughts). In *The Republic,* Plato envisioned a perfect city that philosopher-kings would rule. He thought that if humans could imitate this model city more closely, their polities would be less susceptible to the decline that was affecting the Greek city-states of his own day. This belief was an outgrowth of his more general theory of "ideas"—eternal and perfect models of abstract concepts and material objects that are imperfectly copied in the real world.

Plato's most famous pupil answered the same question differently. Deeply interested in the natural world, Aristotle (384–322 BCE) believed that by collecting all the facts one could about a given thing—no matter how imperfectly—and studying them closely, one could make deductions from these data about general patterns. This was in stark contrast to Plato's claim that everything a person observes is in fact only a flawed copy of the "real" thing that exists in a thought-world of abstract patterns accessible only by pure mental meditation—completely the opposite of Aristotle's method. Following his own method, Aristotle collected evidence from more than 150 Greek city-states, and in *The Politics* he proposed institutional responses and codes of moral conduct that would allow urban communities to function better. (See Primary Source: Warring Ideas: Plato versus Aristotle—On Gaining Knowledge of the Essence of the World.)

But neither Plato nor Aristotle was able to preserve the city-state as the ideal civilized society. During their own lifetimes the world of the independent city-state was to change dramatically as new forms of bigger states became dominant. This competition of ideas raged on for centuries, with the new ideas of these Mediterranean Axial Age thinkers at times fueling the aspirations of the city-states and at other times challenging them. (See Analyzing Global Developments: Axial Age Thinkers and Their Ideas.)

CHAVÍN AND OLMEC CULTURES IN THE AMERICAS

Although peoples living in the Americas during what we have termed the Axial Age in Eurasia, North Africa, and the Mediterranean did not have immense cities, elaborate written texts, domesticated animals, and the other ingredients that underlay the radical new ideas of this era elsewhere, political and intellectual leaders among the Chavín peoples of the Andes and the Olmecs of Mesoamerica provided answers to many of the same questions that were perplexing Eurasians, North Africans, and the peoples of the Mediterranean. Their insights also left a profound imprint on their communities and on future generations. Of course, because we do not have the impressive documentary record that exists for the other regions we have discussed, our knowledge of their beliefs has to be based primarily on archaeological remains.

The Chavín in the Andes

In a world of extreme localization and diversity, the steep mountainsides and deep fertile valleys of the Andes Mountains became the home of a distinctive people called the **Chavín**. (See Map 5.5.) In what is now northern Peru, farmers and pastoralists began to share a common belief system around 1400 BCE. With time, their artistic influence and spiritual principles touched a broad expanse of Andean folk. Like the peoples of South Asia, the Chavín were united by culture and faith more than by any political structure.

The Chavín peoples literally organized their societies vertically. Communities and households spread their trading systems up the mountainsides: valley floors yielded tropical and subtropical produce; the mountains supported maize and other crops; and in the highlands, potatoes became a staple and llamas produced wool and dung (as fertilizer and fuel) and, eventually, served as beasts of burden. Llamas could not transport humans, however, so the Chavín migratory and political reach remained limited. No empire would emerge in the Andes for another millennium.

The ecological diversity of the Chavín societies enabled them to find all necessities close at hand, but they did undertake some long-distance trade—mainly in dyes and precious stones, such as obsidian. By 900 BCE, the Chavín were erecting elaborate stone carvings, using advanced techniques to weave fine cotton textiles, and making gold, silver, and copper metal goods. Scholars have found evidence that by 400 BCE, trade in painted textiles, ceramics, and gold objects spanned the Pacific coast, the Andean highlands, and the watershed eastward to the tropical rain forests of the Amazon basin.

What unified the fragmented Chavín communities in a common culture was a shared artistic tradition reflecting devotion to

MAP 5.5 | The Chavín and Olmec Worlds

The Chavín people and the Olmecs had a strong impact on early cultural integration, the Chavín in the Andes and the Olmecs in Mesoamerica.

- According to this map, how did the Olmecs influence people living beyond their heartland?
- What factors limited the extent of Chavín and Olmec influence?
- Why do you think the Chavín and Olmecs never developed a politically unified regional empire?
- What elements held the Chavín people together? What elements held the Olmec people together?

powerful deities. Their spiritual capital was the central temple complex of Chavín de Huántar, in modern Peru's northeastern highlands. The temple boasted a U-shaped platform whose opening to the east surrounded a sunken, circular plaza; from its passageways and underground galleries, priests could make dramatic entrances during ceremonies. The priests took hallucinogenic drugs, which believers felt enabled them to become jaguars—the region's most dangerous predator—and to commune with the supernatural. Pilgrims brought tribute to Chavín de Huántar, where they worshipped and feasted together.

The Chavín drew on influences from as far away as the Amazon and the Pacific coast as they created devotional cults that revered wild animals as representatives of spiritual forces. Carved stone jaguars, serpents, and hawks, baring their large fangs and claws to remind believers of nature's powers, dominated the spiritual landscape. The "Smiling God" at Chavín de Huántar, El Lanzón, shaped from a slab of white granite 15 feet high, had a human form but a fanged, catlike face, hair of writhing snakes, feet ending with talons, and hands bristling with claws. This supernatural image dominated an awe-inspiring stage: dimly lit

El Lanzón. *The Chavín excelled at elaborate stone carvings with complex images of their deities. This image of El Lanzón is a good example. At the center of one of the Chavín peoples' greatest temples is a massive gallery with a giant monument in the middle, etched with images of snakes, felines, and humans combined into one hybrid supernatural form. Observe the hands and feet with claws and the eyebrows that turn into serpents. The rendering on the right makes it easier to see the details on the actual object.*

from above so that his face would glow from the reflection of polished mirrors, the god stood over a canal, and the vibrations and deep rumbling sounds of the rushing water below conveyed a sense of spiritual forces. Though they borrowed from neighbors and refined existing sculptural techniques, the Chavín created the first great art style of the Andes. Their cult gave way around 400 BCE to local cultural heirs, but some elements of it survived in successor religions adopted by stronger states to the south.

The Olmecs in Mesoamerica

Further to the north, in Mesoamerica, the first complex society emerged around 1500 BCE between the highland plateaus of central Mexico and the Gulf Coast around modern-day Veracruz. The **Olmecs** are an example of a first-generation community that created new political and economic institutions while contemplating profound questions about the nature of humanity and the world beyond.

The culture of the Olmecs, a name meaning "inhabitants in the land of rubber"—one of their staples—sprang up from local village roots. The region's peoples formed a loose confederation of villages scattered from the coast to the highlands, mainly nestling in river valleys and along the shores of swampy lakes. Their residents traded with one another, shared a common language, and worshipped the same gods. Around 1500 BCE, the residents of hundreds of hamlets began to develop a single

common culture and to spread their beliefs, artistic achievements, and social structure far beyond their heartland.

At the core of Olmec culture were its decentralized villages, which housed hundreds—possibly thousands—of households apiece. In these settlements, productive subsistence farmers cultivated most of the foodstuffs their communities needed (especially maize, beans, squash, and cacao), while shipping lightweight products, including ceramics and precious goods (such as jade, obsidian, or quetzal feathers, used to create masks and ritual figurines), to other villages. Most of the precious objects were for religious purposes rather than everyday consumption. Despite their dispersed social landscape, the Olmec peoples created shared belief systems, a single language, and a priestly class who ensured that villagers followed highly ritualized practices.

CITIES AS SACRED CENTERS The Olmecs' primary cities, including San Lorenzo, La Venta, and Tres Zapotes, were not large compared with the urban centers of Afro-Eurasia, but they were religious and secular hubs. They were built around specialized buildings that featured massive earthen mounds, platforms, palaces, and capacious plazas.

The rulers of San Lorenzo, for instance, constructed a city of terraces and ridges on a plateau high above the Chiquito River. Their vassals used baskets to haul more than 2.3 million cubic feet of soil to lay out the enormous central platform, two football fields in length, upon which palaces and workshops rose. All around the courtyards and paths were massive stone monuments—colossal heads, jaguar sculptures, and basalt thrones—as well as clusters of large wooden busts. These vast sculpture gardens depicted the human rulers and deities to whom the Olmecs paid homage and offered sacrifice. Artificial lagoons and channels crisscrossed the precinct. Beneath these mounds archaeologists have found axes, knives of sharpened obsidian, other tools, and simple yet breathtaking figurines made most often of jade, buried as tokens for those who dwelled in the supernatural world. San Lorenzo was not a capital city with rulers and laws that controlled territorial domains. Rather, it was a devotional center whose monumental architecture and art had widespread influence reaching as far as the Olmec hinterlands.

Paying homage to their gods and rulers was part of the Olmecs' daily life. While devotional activity occurred on lakeshores, in caves, on mountaintops, and in other natural settings, it occurred above all in the primary cities. In La Venta, huge pits (one was 13 feet deep and 75 feet wide) contained massive offerings of hundreds of tons of serpentine carved blocks. Olmec art speaks to the powerful influence of devotion on creativity. (See Primary Source: Olmec Art as Ideology.) Many images featured representations of natural and supernatural entities—not just snakes, jaguars, and crocodiles, but also certain humans called shamans, whose powers supposedly enabled them to commune with the supernatural and to transform themselves wholly or partly into beasts (also evident in images at Chavín sites). A common figurine is the "were-jaguar," a being that was part man, part animal. Shamans representing jaguars invoked the Olmec rain god, a jaguarlike being, to bring rainfall and secure the land's fertility. Indeed, the Olmecs' ceremonial life revolved around agricultural and rainfall cycles. Evidence of a shared iconography throughout the heartland suggests an integrated culture that transcended ecological niches.

CITIES AS ATHLETIC HUBS The Olmecs' major cities were not just devotional centers but also athletic hubs, where victorious teams paid homage to their deities. Intricate ball courts had room on the sidelines for fans to applaud and jeer at the sweating contestants, who struggled to bounce hard rubber balls off parallel sidewalls and their bodies and into a goal. Noble players, bearing helmets and heavy padding, could touch the 6-pound rubber ball only with their elbows, hips, knees, and buttocks, and they were honored when they knocked the ball through the stationary stone hoop. Massive sculptures of helmeted heads carved out of volcanic basalt suggest monuments to famous ballplayers. At La Venta, a huge mosaic made out of greenstone served as an elegant ball court; at its center was a portal that was thought to open into the otherworld. Olmec archaeological sites are filled with the remains of game equipment and trophies, some of which were entombed with dead rulers so they could play ball with the gods in the otherworld.

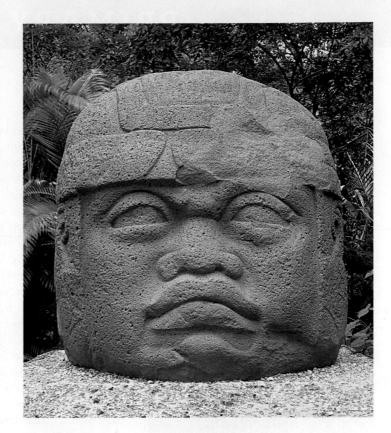

Olmec Head. *At La Venta, in the Mexican state of Tabasco, four colossal heads rest on the ground, remnants of a field of monumental figures that once ornamented this Olmec site. Nine feet high and weighing up to 20 tons, the heads are the source of much speculation. Carved from single boulders, they are thought to be portraits of great kings or legendary ballplayers. Each head bears distinctive elements in homage to its subject.*

Ritual ball games, for all their entertainment value, were integral to Olmec devotional culture. It was in honor of the powerful rain god that players struggled to win.

What added to the thrill of the ball courts was that they were dangerous places associated with water and agricultural fertility, for an equally important aspect of devotional culture was human sacrifice. Indeed, it is likely that athletics and sacrifice were blended in the same rituals. Many monuments depict a victorious and costumed ballplayer (sporting a jaguar headdress or a feathered serpent helmet) atop a defeated, bound human, though scholars are not sure whether the losers were literally executed. Rainmaking rites did include human sacrifice, which involved executing and dismembering captives. At El Manatí, offering sites alongside a spring and a boggy lakeshore have yielded the bones of children slaughtered for the gods. Across the Olmecs' artistic landscape are representations of human victims fed to the gods and to the rulers who embodied them.

MAN, NATURE, AND TIME The Olmec cosmology assumed a relationship between the natural and supernatural worlds.

Olmec Art as Ideology

Olmec ideology emphasized ties between the natural, supernatural, and human worlds. It also sought to influence and possibly convert the Olmecs' neighbors. Known primarily for their monumental architecture and artwork, Olmec craftworkers also made portable objects and miniature figures that unified their belief systems and could be transported over long distances to expand the spiritual frontier of Olmec belief throughout Mesoamerica.

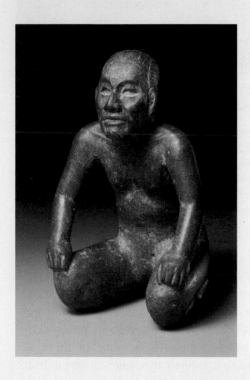

One beautiful example of these surviving portable spiritual icons is called "Kneeling Lord." It combines many of the basic elements of Olmec belief into a single beautiful stone figurine. At about 7 inches tall and 4 inches wide and made of durable stone (and not ceramic), it was the ideal portable artifact for spreading a complex mythology and style far and wide. The figurine fit into a carrier's hand. The lord's pose is stable, with his hands resting on his knees, filling the work with a compact confidence. The viewer can almost sense the softness of muscle and fat, while at the same time noting the sharp contours of the human skeleton underneath. Note in particular the delicacy of the Lord's collarbones. The sagging chest and paunch suggest an older man, a mature lord.

If many Olmec carvings represent fierce rulers or supernatural beings, this lord is special because he reveals shamanistic powers, the power to commune between the natural world and the spiritual world. Shamanism presumes that specially chosen people can communicate between the spirits of ancestors and the forces that control the natural world and living humans. The shaman does so by traveling between these worlds in trances, often flying or floating back and forth as animals—often jaguars, eagles, or bears.

Kneeling Lord is remarkable because the lord's body is in transition from or to being a toad. The figure's scalp is split. Two flaps of hair hang off the back of his head. Beneath the scalp is carved the image of a molting toad, a small reptile shedding its skin. Some have speculated that the toad secretions yield the hallucinogens to bring on the trance to transport the lord to supernatural worlds. Others have noted that the toad is shedding its skin to represent the renewal of life, a representation of the cyclic continuity of the figurine's royal inheritance: he connects ancestors to descendants. This was a useful way to represent the legitimacy—and spiritual necessity—of dynastic continuity, which tells us why the Olmecs were so effective at building a complex political and cultural system in Mesoamerica.

This is a powerful image, one meant to drive home the authority of Olmec rulers to their subjects and neighbors.

QUESTIONS FOR ANALYSIS

- What wild beings do the carvings on figurines such as this represent? What characteristics of each one would have led the Olmecs to use them as symbols?
- What do the symbols reveal about spiritual and political aspects of Olmec society?

Olmec culture was saturated with belief in the power of supernatural forces and with tales of shamans controlling the supernatural. But the Olmecs were hardly a simple, superstitious folk; in fact, their conviction that the supernatural pervades the natural world drove them to systematically observe the natural world so that they could discover godly meanings. There was no hard-and-fast line between "faith" and "science." The way that rulers reckoned time reflects this belief system, for they were convinced that the gods defined calendric passages—thus the seasons and crucial rainfall patterns. Priests, charting celestial movements, devised a complex calendar that marked the passage of seasons and generations. Indeed, the Olmecs' ceremonial life—from ball games to human sacrifice to calendars—was focused on agricultural and rainfall cycles. As in China and Mesopotamia, a cultural flowering encouraged priests and scholars to study and accurately chart the rhythms of the terrestrial and celestial worlds.

A WORLD OF SOCIAL DISTINCTIONS Unlike many simple and egalitarian agrarian cultures, the Olmecs developed an elaborate cultural system with tiered social ranks, not greatly dissimilar from South Asia's caste system and producing, by American standards of the time, a remarkable cohesion. Daily labor kept Olmecs busy. The vast majority worked the fertile

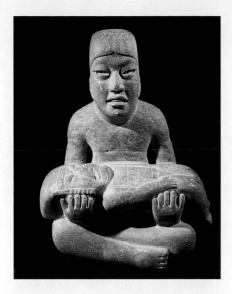

The Las Limas Monument. *The were-jaguar was an important figure in the pantheon of Olmec deities. This sculpture represents a youth holding a limp were-jaguar baby. We do not know what these figures represent exactly—most likely they refer to spiritual journeys. Some have argued that this monument harkens to child sacrifice.*

lands as part of household units, with children and parents toiling in the fields with wooden tools, fishing in streams with nets, and hunting turtles and other small animals. Most Olmecs had to juggle the needs of their immediate families, their village neighbors, and the taxes imposed by rulers.

The priestly class, raised and trained in the palaces at La Venta, San Lorenzo, and Tres Zapotes, directed the exchanges of sacred ritual objects among farming communities. Because these exchanges involved immense resources, the wealthy ruling families had to be involved—an association that buttressed their claim to be the descendants of divine ancestors. At the same time, by controlling trade in precious secular goods, they added to their fortunes. As ruling families blurred the line between the everyday and the religious, they legitimized their power and gained access to vast resources.

Alongside the priestly elite, a secular one emerged composed of chieftains who supervised agrarian transactions, oversaw artisans, and accepted villagers' tribute. They set up workshops, managed by foremen, where craftworkers created pots, painted, sculpted, and wove. Some of their work featured stones and gems imported from surrounding villages. The highest-ranking chieftains commanded villages scattered over the approximate area of a territorial state (such as current-day Veracruz, in Mexico).

Ultimately, the Olmecs' influence radiated well beyond their heartland through trade. As their arts expanded, so did their demand for imported obsidian and jade, seashells, plumes, and other precious goods. The Olmecs themselves exported rubber (made by combining different latexes from trees and vines into a tough but pliable material—just right for a playing ball!), cacao, pottery, ceramics, figurines, jaguar pelts, and crocodile skins all throughout Mesoamerica. Importing and exporting were probably in the hands of a merchant class, about which scholars know little. The Olmecs also conveyed their belief system to neighbors—if not to convert them, at least to influence them and reinforce a sense of superiority. Without an urge to

conquer or colonize, the Olmecs nonetheless shaped the social development of much of Mesoamerica.

THE LOSS OF CENTERS The breakdown of the Olmec culture around the middle of the first millennium is shrouded in mystery. The decline was abrupt in some centers and drawn out in others. At La Venta, the altars and massive basalt heads were defaced and buried, indicating a dramatic shift. Yet there is little evidence of a spasm of war, a peasant uprising, a population shift, or conflict within the ruling classes. Indeed, in many parts of the heartland, the religious centers that had been the hubs of the Olmec world were abandoned but not destroyed.

Apparently the machinery for drawing resources into Olmec capitals eventually failed. As the bonds between rulers and subjects weakened, so did the exchange of ritual objects that had enlivened the Olmec centers and made them magnets for obedience and piety. Although Olmec hierarchies collapsed, much of the Olmec hinterland remained heavily populated and productive. While it lasted, the Olmec combination of an integrated structure, a complex hierarchical structure, and urban-centered devotional practice offered a degree of cohesion unprecedented in the Americas and in many respects similar to the integration that dynastic China would soon enjoy. What was left of the Olmec heritage passed on to other Mesoamericans—especially those of the central plateaus and the tropical lowlands of the Yucatán Peninsula.

SUDANIC, NOK, AND MEROE CULTURES IN SUB-SAHARAN AFRICA

In Africa, too, widespread common cultures emerged in this era in a number of favorable locations. Yet to understand these communities, it is essential first to describe the climate and geography of Africa because these forces played a critical role in cultural formation. Climatically, Africa's most significant historical development at this time was the continued drying up of the northern and central landmass and the sprawl of the great Sahara Desert as its primary geographical and population barrier. (See Map 5.6.) Large areas that had once supported abundant plant and animal life, including human settlements, now became sparsely populated. As a result, the African peoples began to coalesce in a few locations. Most important was the Nile Valley, which may have held more than half of the entire population at this time.

The Four Zones

Climatic change divided Africa from the equator northward to the Sahara Desert into four zones. The first zone was the Sahara

MAP 5.6 | Africa, 500 BCE

The first millennium BCE was a period of cultural, economic, and political integration for North and sub-Saharan Africa.

- According to this map, what effect did the Mediterranean colonies have on Africa?
- What main factor integrated Kush, Nubia, and Egypt?
- Does the map reveal a relationship between the rise of Sudanic culture and the spread of ironworking? If so, what is it?

In time, some of Africa's great commercial cities, like Timbuktu, would arise here; but in the first millennium BCE, no city of great size made an appearance.

The next zone was the Sudanic savanna, an area of high grasslands stretching from present-day Senegal along the Atlantic Ocean in the west to the Nile River and the Red Sea in the east. Many of West Africa's kingdoms later emerged there because the area was free of the tsetse fly, which was as lethal to animals as to humans, killing off cattle, horses, and goats. The fourth zone comprised the western and central African rain forests, a sparsely populated region characterized by small-scale societies.

Although there was contact across the Sahara, Africa below the Sahara differed markedly from North Africa, Egypt, and Eurasia. It did not develop plow agriculture; instead, its farmers depended on hoes. Also, except in densely populated regions, land was held communally and never carried as much value as labor. African peoples could always move into new locations. They had more difficulty finding workers to turn the soil.

Distinctive and widespread common cultures that would characterize certain parts of sub-Saharan Africa from 1000 CE onward were only beginning to emerge during the first millennium BCE. In the savanna, millet and sorghum were the primary food crops; in the rain forests, yams and other root crops predominated. Relatively large populations inhabited the Sudanic savanna, the sole area for which substantial historical records exist. Here, in fact, a way of life that we can call Sudanic began to crystallize.

These Sudanic peoples were not completely dependent on their feet to get around (in contrast to their counterparts in the Americas). They had domesticated several animals, including cattle and goats, and even possessed small horses. Although

itself, which never completely emptied out despite its extreme heat and aridity. Its oases supported pastoral peoples, like the ancestors of the modern Tuareg tribal communities, who raised livestock and promoted contact between the northern and western parts of the landmass. South of the Sahara was the Sahel, literally the "coast" (Arabic *sahil*) of the great ocean of sand.

their communities were scattered widely across Africa, they had much in common. For example, they all possessed a cosmology dominated by a high god, political organizations led by sacred kings, and burial customs of interring servants alongside dead rulers to serve them in the afterlife—all highly similar to the practices existing in pharaonic Egypt, Mesopotamia, and China before the Common Era. These peoples were skilled cultivators and weavers of cotton, which they had domesticated. Archaeologists and historians used to believe that the Sudanic peoples borrowed their institutions, notably their sacred kingships, from their Egyptian neighbors; but linguistic evidence and their burial customs indicate that the Sudanic communities developed these practices independently.

Nubia: Between Sudanic Africa and Pharaonic Egypt

One of the most highly developed locations of common culture in sub-Saharan Africa was Nubia, a region lying between the first Nile cataract (a large waterfall) and the last (near where the Blue and White Niles come together). From at least the fourth millennium BCE onward, peoples in this region had contact with both the northern and southern parts of the African landmass. It was one of the few parts of sub-Saharan Africa known to the outside world. The Greek poet Homer described its inhabitants as "the remotest nation, the most just of men; the favorites of the gods."

In the second and first millennia BCE, complex societies formed and developed into states in Nubia. The first of the important Nubian states was Kush. It flourished between 1700 and 1500 BCE between the first and third cataracts and had its capital at Kerma. Because of its close proximity to Egypt, it adopted many Egyptian cultural and political practices, even though it was under constant pressure from the northern powerhouse. Its successor states had to move farther south, up the Nile, to keep free from the powerful Egyptians; the kingdom's capitals were repeatedly uprooted and relocated upriver.

Nubia was Egypt's corridor to sub-Saharan Africa; a source of ivory, gold, and slaves; and an area that Egyptian monarchs wanted to dominate. The Egyptians called the region Kush, the name that later historians gave to the various regimes that flourished there. To the Egyptians, Kush was a land and the Kushites a people to be exploited. It was not a location that the Egyptians wished to reside in. Their chroniclers best described the Egyptian view of the territory and the people, referring to it repeatedly as "miserable Kush." The best known of the Egyptian conquerors was Ramses II, who left his imprint on Nubian culture with his magnificent monuments at Abu Simbel. Historians have long stressed such connections with Egypt, but only recently have scholars determined just how deeply the Nubian peoples were influenced by the cultures of sub-Saharan Africa.

Building on the foundations of earlier kings that had ruled Nubia, the **Meroe** kingdom arose in the fourth century BCE and flourished until 300 CE. Its rulers were influenced by the pharaonic culture, adapting hieroglyphs, erecting pyramids in which to bury their rulers, viewing their kings as divine, and worshipping the Egyptian god Amun. Meroe soon became a thriving center of production and commerce. Its residents were especially skilled in iron smelting and the manufacture of textiles, and their products circulated widely throughout Africa. The capital city itself covered a square mile; at its center was a royal complex surrounded by a wall 300 yards long and half again as wide. The city featured monumental and highly decorated buildings that were constructed, according to local custom, not of stone but of mud bricks.

However, Meroe was equally a part of the Sudanic savanna lifeway—as evidenced by the distinctiveness of the language and the determination of its inhabitants to retain political autonomy from Egypt, including, if necessary, moving farther south out of the orbit of Egypt and more into the orbit of Sudanic political systems. Although they called their kings pharaohs, the influential leaders of Meroe selected them from among the many members of the royal family, attempting to ensure that their rulers were men of proven talents. In addition, the Nubian states had close commercial contact with other merchants and commercial hubs in Sudanic Africa.

West African Kingdoms

Meroe was not the only sacred kingship in the Sudanic savanna lands. Similar polities thrived in West Africa, among peoples living in the Senegal River basin and among the Mande peoples living inland around the western branch of the Niger River. They established settlements at such places as Jenne and Gao, which eventually became large trading centers. Here, artisans smelted iron ore and wove textiles, and merchants engaged in long-distance trade.

Even more spectacular was the Nok culture, which arose in the sixth century BCE in an area that is today the geographical center of Nigeria. Though slightly south of the savanna lands of West Africa, the area was (and still is) in regular contact with that region. At Taruga, near the present-day village of Nok, early iron smelting occurred in 600 BCE. Taruga may well have been the first place in western Africa where iron ores were smelted. Undeniably, ironworking was significant for the Nok peoples, who moved from using stone materials directly to iron, bypassing bronze and copper that were so essential in the societies in Eurasia, Egypt, and North Africa. They made iron axes and hoes, iron knives and spears, and luxury items for trade. This region in West Africa was also home to the Bantu-speaking peoples destined to play a major role in the history of the landmass.

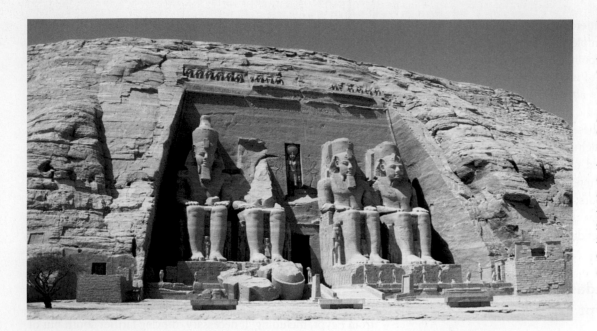

The Temple of Ramses II.
The temple of Ramses II at Abu Simbel was constructed during the reign of Ramses II between 1304 and 1237 BCE. It was cut out of the rock and featured four colossal statues of the king, each of which was 65 feet high. When the Aswan High Dam was built in the 1960s, the monument had to be cut into large stone slabs and moved to higher ground so that it would not be submerged under the waters of Lake Nasser, which the High Dam formed.

Around 300 BCE, small Bantu groups began to migrate southward into the equatorial rain forests, where they cleared land for farming; from there, some moved on to southern Africa. (See Chapter 8 for a discussion of the Bantu peoples.)

Nok has achieved its historical fame not for its iron-smelting prowess but for its magnificent terra-cotta figurines, discovered in the 1940s in the tin-mining region of central Nigeria. These naturalistic figures, whose features bear a striking resemblance to those of the region's modern inhabitants, date to at least 500 BCE. They were altarpieces for a cult associated with the land's fertility. Placed next to new lands that were coming into cultivation, they were believed to bless the soil and enhance its productivity. (See Primary Source: Reconstructing the History of Preliterate African Peoples.)

Although most sub-Saharan African communities lived in small-scale dispersed communities, in several locations, notably Nubia and West Africa, larger, common cultures based on shared beliefs and political institutions arose. The ability of these societies to produce more food and sustain larger settled communities ultimately caused the sub-Saharan population to triple in this period. As in the Americas, these lifeways proved durable.

CONCLUSION

Afro-Eurasia's great river-basin areas were still important in the first millennium BCE, but their time as centers of world cultures was passing. Now they yielded some of their leadership to regions that had been on the fringes, giving way to a generation of cultural and intellectual flourishing in search of alternative, new orders. Within the territorial states in China, the kingdoms

and oligarchies in urbanizing South Asia, and the city-states in the Mediterranean world, great social and intellectual dynamism occurred.

During this Axial Age across much of Afro-Eurasia, influential thinkers came to the fore with perspectives quite different from those of the river-basin civilizations. In China, the political instability of the Warring States period propelled scholars such as Confucius to engage in political debate, where they stressed respect for social hierarchy. In South Asia, dissident thinkers challenged the Brahmanic spiritual and political order, and the Buddha articulated a religious belief system that was much less hierarchical than its Vedic predecessor. The Mediterranean Greek philosophers offered new views about nature, their political world, and human relations and values—all based on secular rather than religious ideas.

Even where contact with other societies was less intense, innovation occurred. In the Americas, the Olmecs developed a worldview in which mortals had to appease angry gods through human sacrifice and elaborate temples where many peoples could pay homage to the same deities. In sub-Saharan Africa, settled pockets devised complex cultural foundations for community life. The Mediterranean and Egyptian cultures continued to expand their influence up the Nile through Nubia and into sub-Saharan Africa. A spectacular example of sub-Saharan and Egyptian synthesis was the culture of Meroe. And in West Africa, the Nok peoples promoted interregional trade and cultural contact as they expanded their horizons.

As the world was coalescing into culturally distinct regions, all the ideas newly forged in Afro-Eurasia, the Americas, and sub-Saharan Africa would endure. No matter where they were created, they had a continuing impact on the societies that followed.

Reconstructing the History of Preliterate African Peoples

Traditionally, historians have relied on written records and thus have had difficulty reconstructing the history of preliterate societies. Sources that now aid in understanding preliterate African groups include art, pottery, linguistic analysis, oral traditions, and many other elements. Here are two such vital historical sources.

The first is Nok terra-cottas. Discovered in the central region of modern-day Nigeria, the figurines probably were created in the Common Era but are part of a vibrant culture that dates back to the fifth century BCE.

The second source, Kush burial pyramids, comes from the sub-Saharan kingdom of Meroe, by no means a preliterate society but one that has many important nonwritten sources. Meroe flourished for nearly a millennium from around the fourth century BCE to the fourth century CE. Its predecessor kingdoms, referred to as the kingdoms of Kush, were located between the first and third Nile cataracts. The first kingdom of Kush existed between 1700 and 1500 BCE. A second powerful Kushitic state arose around 1000 BCE, and its most dynamic dynasty even overpowered Egypt, creating Egypt's "black pharaohs" dynasty, Egypt's Twenty-fifth Dynasty. Later, when Egyptian power was again ascendant, the peoples of Nubia moved even farther south to establish

Nok Figurine

the kingdom of Meroe. Although Meroe continued to be deeply influenced by the culture and political forms of Egypt, its peoples spoke a different language from the Egyptians, a Nilo-Saharan language.

Nubia's close contact with Egypt led to profound and obvious influences—for example, the use of the term *pharaoh* to refer to the king, borrowed religious beliefs, and the use of hieroglyphs. Like

the Egyptians, the Kushitic and Meroitic peoples buried their kings in pyramids and wrote texts on the walls of these burial chambers about what constituted an orderly and good life. The Meroitic peoples had a powerful priestly class, like the ancient Egyptians, but they retreated up the Nile to be independent of Egyptian rule. Scholars with the same archaeological and linguistic training as students of ancient Egypt (known as Egyptologists) have studied the Nubian cultures, but their studies have taken place more recently than those of ancient Egypt and have not yet yielded as much information.

QUESTIONS FOR ANALYSIS

- How do the Nok terra-cottas help scholars understand the very ancient culture of West Africa?
- Do they provide insight into the artistic abilities of the people living in this region?
- What can they tell us about how people dressed and how they looked?
- Can you see the Egyptian influence in the photograph of the Kush burial pyramids?

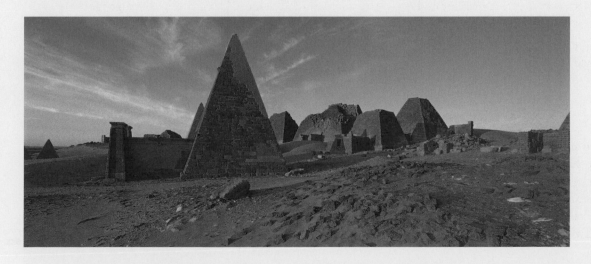

Burial Pyramids. *Dated between 300 BCE and 300 CE, these tombs are located in the royal necropolis of the ancient kingdom of Kush.*

After You Read This Chapter

Go to inQuizitive to see what you know & learn what you've missed.

FOCUS ON: *Innovative Societies*

China

- A multistate system emerges from warfare, revolutionizing society and thought.

- Confucius and Master Lao outline new ideals of governing and living.

South Asia

- Small monarchies and urban oligarchies emerge after the Vedic peoples' migrations and rule over societies organized around the varna and jatis system.

- Dissident thinkers such as Mahavira and the Buddha challenge Brahman priests and the varna and jatis system.

The Mediterranean World

- Independent city-states emerge from social destruction and facilitate revolutionary principles in rulership, commerce, and thought.

- Thinkers such as Socrates, Plato, and Aristotle challenge conventions and encourage public discourse about the role of the individual in society and the way the universe works.

The Americas

- Chavín peoples and the Olmecs produce increasingly hierarchical societies and connect villages via trade.

- Large-scale common cultures emerge.

Sub-Saharan Africa

- Expansion of the Sahara Desert and population migrations cause people to coalesce in a few locations.

- Early signs of a common culture appear across the Sudanic savanna.

CHRONOLOGY

The Americas		
Sub-Saharan Africa		
South Asia		
The Mediterranean		
East Asia		

KEY TERMS

STUDY QUESTIONS

1. **Describe** the challenges that Afro-Eurasian empires and states faced in the first millennium BCE. **Analyze** the similarities and differences among the solutions they devised.

2. **Compare and contrast** Confucius in China, the Buddha in South Asia, and the Greek philosophers Socrates, Plato, and Aristotle. What were the defining qualities of each one's ideas?

3. **Explain** the "war of ideas" that occurred during the first millennium BCE in China. How did Confucianism and Daoism influence political developments during the Warring States period?

4. **Analyze** the impact of commerce and urbanization on the Brahman order in South Asia in the first millennium BCE. Why were urban audiences receptive to Buddhist and other challenges to Brahman concepts?

5. **Describe** the political and economic innovations in the Mediterranean world in the first millennium BCE. What impact did these ideas have on peoples living on the periphery of that world?

6. **Explore** the ways in which the great Axial Age thinkers in East Asia, South Asia, and the Mediterranean world altered the societies in which they lived, and **identify** the political and cultural transformations that motivated these individuals to develop their ideas.

7. **Explain** the broad cultural features that characterized Olmec and Chavín societies in the Americas in the first millennium BCE. To what extent did each cultural group leave an imprint on its region?

8. **Compare and contrast** the main institutions and belief systems of societies of the Americas and sub-Sahara Africa with those of cultures across Eurasia, Egypt, and North Africa.

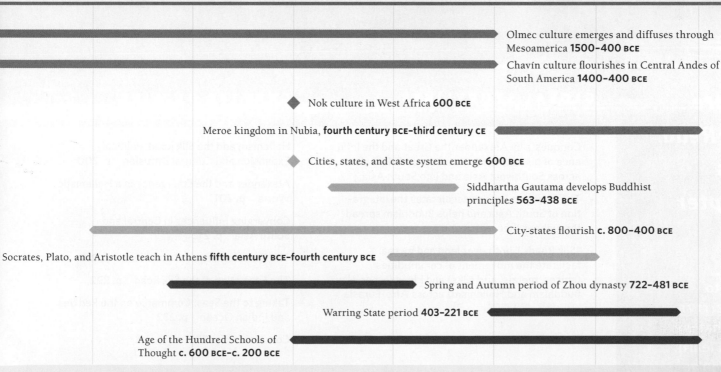

Olmec culture emerges and diffuses through Mesoamerica **1500–400 BCE**

Chavín culture flourishes in Central Andes of South America **1400–400 BCE**

Nok culture in West Africa **600 BCE**

Meroe kingdom in Nubia, **fourth century BCE–third century CE**

Cities, states, and caste system emerge **600 BCE**

Siddhartha Gautama develops Buddhist principles **563–438 BCE**

City-states flourish **c. 800–400 BCE**

Socrates, Plato, and Aristotle teach in Athens **fifth century BCE–fourth century BCE**

Spring and Autumn period of Zhou dynasty **722–481 BCE**

Warring State period **403–221 BCE**

Age of the Hundred Schools of Thought **c. 600 BCE–c. 200 BCE**

500 BCE   **300 BCE**

Before You Read This Chapter

Go to INQUIZITIVE to see what you know & learn what you've missed.

GLOBAL STORYLINES

- Conquests by Alexander the Great and the influence of his successor states spread Hellenism across Southwest Asia and into South Asia.

- The Mauryan Empire accelerates the integration of South Asia and helps Buddhism spread throughout that region and beyond.

- "Silk Roads," both over land and by sea, facilitate the movement of commodities (spices, metals, and silks) and ideas (especially Buddhism and Hellenism) across Afro-Eurasia.

CHAPTER OUTLINE

6

Shrinking the Afro-Eurasian World, 350 BCE–250 CE

FOCUS QUESTIONS

- What was Hellenism, and in what ways did it have an impact across Afro-Eurasia?

- How did Alexander's incursion in central and South Asia promote political changes in those areas, and what were those changes?

- Into what areas did Buddhism spread during this period, and what forces influenced its spread?

- Where did the early "Silk Road" develop, and how important were these trade routes in connecting areas of Afro-Eurasia?

In the blistering August heat of 324 BCE, at a town on the Euphrates River that the Greeks called Opis (not far from modern Baghdad), Alexander the Great's crack Macedonian troops declared that they had had enough. They had been fighting far from their homeland for more than a decade. They had marched eastward from the Mediterranean, forded wide rivers, traversed great deserts, trudged over high mountain passes, and slogged through rain-drenched forests. Along the way they had defeated massive armies, including those armed with fearsome war elephants. Some had taken wives from the cities and tribes they vanquished, so the army had become a giant swarm of ethnically mixed families. This was an army like no other. It did more than just defeat neighbors and rivals—it forcefully connected entire worlds, bringing together diverse peoples and lands.

Conquering in the name of building a new world, however, was not what the soldiers had bargained for. They loved their leader, but many thought he had gone too far. They had lost companions and grown weary of war. Some had mutinied at a tributary of the Indus, halting Alexander's advance into South Asia. Now they threatened to desert him altogether. Summoning up their courage, they voiced these resentments to their supreme commander. Alexander's response was immediate and inspired. In persuading his troops not to desert him, he evoked the astounding military triumphs and historic achievement they had accomplished: establishing his personal rule from Macedonia to the Indus Valley. This far-reaching political vision came to a sudden end with Alexander's death a year later, when he was thirty-two years old. Even in his short lifetime, though, he set in motion political, cultural, and economic forces that would transform Afro-Eurasia.

During this period, two broad cultural movements came to link diverse populations across wide expanses of the Afro-Eurasian landmass: Hellenism and Buddhism. They constitute the central subject of this chapter. In both cases, new empires and broad trade routes created the circuits through which—and beyond which—new cultures flowed. Imperial conquests and long-distance trade laid the foundations for widespread cultural systems that were far more enduring than the empires themselves. Alexander's armies forged only a fleeting political regime, though an enormous one, extending all the way from the Greek homeland to northern India, enabling a Greek-infused culture that we call Hellenism to stretch over the regions of conquests and beyond. Although this movement did not eradicate local cultures, it provoked profound shifts in them. In the process, many of the world's regions, from China to Africa, became more integrated.

One region where Hellenism had a profound impact was South Asia, where it initiated a process of gradual political integration and religious change. The result: an equally powerful cultural movement, Buddhism, spread outward from its founding in South Asia to become the world's most expansive religious system (see Chapter 5 for a discussion of this Axial Age religion). It, too, had a political agent: the Mauryan dynasty of South Asia, indirectly influenced by Alexander's triumphs, whose powerful armies and legions of magistrates and monks spread the religion of the Buddha throughout South Asia, laying the groundwork for its expansion beyond. Dynastic empires, therefore, created the political latticework and institutions through which cultural influences grew and extended like vines spreading into regions far from their roots.

HELLENISM AND THE SILK ROAD: POLITICAL EXPANSION AND CULTURAL DIFFUSION

Alexander's bloody campaigns made for legendary drama. But from a long-term perspective, their cultural effects were more dramatic. His armies transformed Afro-Eurasia, promoting the establishment of culturally Greek-oriented communities across the region. For at least five centuries after Alexander's short-lived rule, Hellenistic culture reverberated from Rome in the west all the way to the Ganges in the east.

Hellenism—a term derived from the Greeks' name for themselves, *Hellēnes*—was a new phenomenon. It involved the process by which the individual cultures of the Greek city-states gave way to a uniform culture stressing the common identity of all who embraced Greek ways. This culture had common features of language, art, architecture, drama, politics, philosophy, and much more, to which anyone anywhere in the Afro-Eurasian world could have access. By diffusing well beyond its homeland, it brought worlds together: its influence spread from Greece to all shores of the Mediterranean, into parts of sub-Saharan Africa, across Southwest Asia, and through the Iranian plateau into central and South Asia. It even had echoes in China. Like "Americanization" in the modern world, Hellenism took the attractive elements of one culture—its language, its music, its modes of dress and entertainment—and made these parts of a new global culture.

Alexander not only conquered but also laid the foundations for state systems and introduced institutional stability for trading systems. Instead of plundering, governments under his rule promoted trade. With their fear of attack reduced, cities could thrive. In effect, major commercial arteries replaced the early passageways that had carried small bands of traders. Hellenistic traders and travelers benefited from the emergence of the **Silk Road**, a series of routes arising from conflicts and realliances between central Asian nomadic groups such as the Sogdians, the Xiongnu, and the Yuezhi and agrarian China. For nearly a thousand years, the Silk Road was the primary commercial network linking East Asia and the Mediterranean world. These trade routes extended over 5,000 miles and took their collective name from the huge quantities of precious silk that passed along them.

We cannot make sense of Alexander and the Hellenistic cultural movement or the spread of Buddhism without acknowledging the important ways in which distinct parts of the Afro-Eurasian world were already in contact. Alexander's conquests did not take arbitrary pathways; rather, earlier long-distance trade and cross-cultural exchanges had laid the trails for them. Similarly, Buddhism spread along preexisting trade routes. Slowly a new idea took hold: common cultures and shared commodities could integrate the Afro-Eurasian world. Merchants joined with monks and administrators in connecting widespread parts of Afro-Eurasia, enabling busy sea-lanes and the Silk Road to flourish. Merely a few centuries after the conquests of Alexander and Mauryan kings, the world looked very different in the realms their armies had traversed.

ALEXANDER AND THE EMERGENCE OF A HELLENISTIC WORLD

The armed campaigns of a minor Greek people, the Macedonians, and their leader, Alexander the Great (356–323 BCE), began a drive for empire into Asia and North Africa that ultimately spread a Hellenistic culture throughout the conquered lands. (See Map 6.1.) Alexander's novel use of new kinds of armed forces in a series of lightning attacks on the Persian Empire further undermined barriers that separated the Mediterranean world from the rest of Southwest Asia. The massive transfers of wealth and power resulting from his conquests transformed the Mediterranean into a more unified world of economic and cultural exchange.

Conquests of Alexander the Great

Historians and biographers have filled libraries with books about Alexander the Great, yet he still remains one of the most intriguing figures in world history. Alexander came from the frontier state of Macedonia to the north of Greece and commanded a highly mobile force armed with advanced military technologies that had developed during the incessant warfare among Greek city-states (see Chapter 5).

Under Alexander's predecessors—especially his father, Philip II—Macedonia had become a large ethnic and territorial state. Philip had unified Macedonia and then gone on to conquer neighboring states. Importantly, Macedonia boasted gold mines that could finance his new military technology and a disciplined, full-time army. The costs of heavily armored infantry in closely arrayed phalanxes, allied with large-scale shock cavalry formations, were supported not just from the mines' substantial income but also from the enormous profits of a slave trade that passed directly through Macedonia. By the early 330s BCE, Philip had crushed the Greek city-states to the south, including Athens. After Philip's assassination, his son Alexander used this new military machine in a series of daring attacks on the apparently invincible power of the Persian Empire and its king, Darius III.

Like many other successful conquerors, Alexander owed much of his success to a readiness to take risks. In his initial forays into Southwest Asia, he outpaced and outflanked his adversaries, repeatedly taking them by surprise. Through these rapid assaults he brought under the rule of his Greek-speaking elites all the lands of the former Persian Empire, which extended from Egypt and the shores of the Mediterranean to the interior of what is now Afghanistan, and as far as the Indus River valley

Battle of Issus. *Mosaic of the Battle of Issus between Alexander the Great of Macedonia and Darius, the king of Persia (found as a wall decoration in a house at Pompeii, in southern Italy). Alexander is the bareheaded figure to the far left; Darius is the figure to the right, gesturing with his right hand. The men represent two different types of warfare. On horseback, Alexander leads the cavalry-based shock forces of the Macedonian Greeks, while Darius directs his army from a chariot in the style of the great kings of Southwest Asia.*

even farther to the east. (See Primary Source: Clash of Empires: The Battle of Gaugamela.)

The result of this violent rampage was hardly an empire, given that Alexander did not live long enough to establish institutions to hold the distant lands together. But his military campaigns continued a process that the Persians had already set in motion of smashing barriers that had separated peoples on the eastern and western ends of Afro-Eurasia. The conqueror saw himself as a new universal figure, a bridge connecting distant cultures. He demonstrated this vision in his choice of Roxana, the daughter of a chief from Bactria (present-day Afghanistan), as a wife.

Alexander's conquests exposed Syria, Palestine, Egypt, and Mesopotamia to the commodities of the Mediterranean, to money-based economies (both Philip and Alexander issued gold coins to pay for their invasions), and to cultural ideas associated with the Greek city-states. Alexander founded dozens of new cities named after himself, the most famous of which was Alexandria in Egypt.

One of Alexander's most significant acts involved seizing the accumulated wealth that the Persian kings stored in their immense palaces, especially at Persepolis, and dispersing it into the money economies of the Mediterranean city-states. This massive redistribution of wealth (like the post-Columbian exploitation of the Americas; see Chapters 12 and 13) fueled a widespread economic expansion in the Mediterranean and beyond.

NORTH SEA

GERMANIC
PEOPLES

BALTIC PEOPLES

C
E
L
T
I
C

CELTIC PEOPLES

GAULS

Ebro R.

Massilia

Rome

SARDINIA

SICILY

Syracuse

Carthage

CARTHAGE

MEDITERRANEAN
SEA

CONQUESTS
OF
ALEXANDER
THE GREAT,
323 BCE

GREEK
CITY-
STATES

Pella

MACEDONIA

Delphi

Athens

Corinth

Sparta

RHODES

GREEK
CITY-
STATES

Byzantium

Troy

Gordium

Sardis

CYPRUS

BLACK SEA

S C Y T H I A N S

GREEK
CITY-
STATES

Sinope

Ancyra

CAUCASIAN
PEOPLES

CASPIAN
SEA

S T E P P

ARAL
SEA

Samark

Bukhara

Merv

Aï Khanoum

B

Antioch

SYRIA

Tyre

PALESTINE
Jerusalem
JUDEA

Alexandria

Memphis

Siwa
Oasis

EGYPT
PTOLEMAIC
EMPIRE

Nile R.

MESOPOTAMIA

Tigris R.

Euphrates R.

Gaugamela

Seleucia

Babylon

Susa

Ecbatana

SELEUCID EMPIRE

Persepolis

Persian Gulf

AFGH

Herat

Kandah

A R A B S

KUSH

Meroe

Axum

RED SEA

ARABIAN
PENINSULA

ARABIA

SAHARA DESERT

SAHARAN
PEOPLES

SUB-SAHARAN

AFRICA

NOK

Niger R.

Congo R.

ATLANTIC

OCEAN

B
A
N
T
U
S

INDIAN

MADAGASCAR

KALAHARI
DESERT

0   500   1000 Miles

0   500   1000 Kilometers

MAP 6.1 | Afro-Eurasia in 250 BCE

Alexander of Macedonia did not live long enough to create one large politically unified empire, but his conquests integrated various Afro-Eurasian worlds culturally and economically. Trace the pathways that Alexander followed on his conquests.

- What were the names and locations of the Hellenistic successor states? What did these states have in common?
- Which states on the map did Greeks *not* rule? How did the spread of Hellenism affect them?

Legend:
- → Campaigns of Alexander the Great
- ☐ Conquests of Alexander the Great
- Qin Empire
- Greek City-State
- Carthage
- Area of Roman control
- Macedonia
- Ptolmaic Empire
- Seleucid Empire
- Graeco-Bactria
- Mauryan Empire
- Empire of Xiongnu

PRIMARY SOURCE

Clash of Empires: The Battle of Gaugamela

The following passage, taken from the Greek historian Arrian, delineates the makeup of Darius's army as it prepared to confront Alexander and his forces in 331 BCE. In describing the size of the army—much larger than that of the largest Greek city-state, Athens—Arrian mentions the various ethnic groups of the Persian Empire that contributed troops. Contingents came from lands as far-flung as Bactria (near modern-day Afghanistan), Scythia (the broad area stretching from Ukraine to Kazakhstan), Armenia, Cappadocia (in east-central Turkey), and Caria (in southwestern Turkey), as well as from lands close to the Red Sea.

Darius's army was so large because it had been reinforced with Sogdians, with Bactrians, and with Indian peoples from the borderlands of Bactria, all under the command of Bessus, the satrap [i.e., the regional governor] of Bactria. There were also units of the Sakai—who were part of the Scythians who are found in Asia. They owed no loyalty to Bessus, but were still allies of Darius. These soldiers were mounted bowmen commanded by one Mauaces. The Arachotoi and the hillmen from India were commanded by Barsaentes, the satrap of Arachosia. The Areioi were commanded by their satrap, Satibarzanes; the Parthians, the Hyrcanians, and Tapeiroi, all cavalrymen, were commanded by Phrataphernes. The Medes, to whom were attached the Kadousioi, the Albanoi, and Sakesinai, were commanded by Atropates the Mede. All the units from the lands near the Red Sea were commanded by Orontobates, Ariobarzanes, and Orxines. The Ouxioi and Sousianoi were commanded by Oxathres, son of Aboultius. The men from Babylon, to whom were attached the Siracenioi and Carians, were commanded by Boupares—these Carians had been resettled in the empire by a mass transfer of their people. The Armenians were commanded by Orontes and Mithraustes; the Cappadocians, by Ariaces. The Syrians from Hollow Syria [i.e., the Bekáa Valley in modern Lebanon] and from Mesopotamia were commanded by Mazaeus. The total number of men in the army of Darius was reported to be 40,000 cavalry, 1,000,000 infantry, 200 scythed chariots [i.e., war chariots with blades mounted on both ends of the axle], and some war elephants—the Indians who came from this side of the Indus River had about fifteen of them.

QUESTIONS FOR ANALYSIS

- How many ethnic groups can you identify in this passage?
- What does Darius's command of so many ethnic loyalties tell us about the nature of the Persian Empire?
- How do you think Alexander was able to defeat such a large and talented army?

Source: Arrian, *The Anabasis of Alexander*, 3.8; translated by Brent Shaw.

Alexander's Successors and the Territorial Kingdoms

Alexander died in Babylon at age thirty-two, struck down by overconsumption of alcohol and other excesses that matched his larger-than-life personality and reflected the war culture of Macedonian warriors. His death in 323 BCE brought on the collapse of the regime he had personally held together. The conquered lands fragmented into large territories over which his generals squabbled for control.

Alexander's generals, his successors—Seleucus, Ptolemy, Antigonus, Lysimachus, and others—did not think of themselves as citizens, even very important ones, of a Greek city-state, but rather modeled themselves on the regional rulers they had defeated. As these men installed kingdoms in the eastern Mediterranean and Southwest and central Asia, they not only introduced Alexander's style of absolute rulership but also unified large blocks of territory under single, powerful rulers.

One effect of powerful families controlling whole kingdoms was that a few women could now hold great power, an unthinkable prospect in the democracies of the city-states. Queens in Macedonia, Syria, and Egypt—whether independent or as co-regents with their husbands—established new public roles for women. For example, Berenice of Egypt (c. 320–280 BCE) was the first in a series of powerful royal women who helped rule the kingdom of the Nile, a line that ended with the most famous of them all, Cleopatra, in the 30s BCE.

Three large territorial states stood out in the new Hellenistic world: the Seleucid Empire (the dynasty established by Seleucus), stretching from Syria to present-day Afghanistan; Macedonia, ruled by the Antigonids (the dynasty established by Antigonus); and Egypt, ruled by the Ptolemies (the dynasty established by Ptolemy). In areas between these larger states, middle-sized kingdoms emerged. The old city-states of the Mediterranean, such as Athens and Corinth, still thrived, but now they functioned in a world dominated by much larger power blocs. On mainland Greece, larger confederations of previously independent city-states formed.

In general, political states coalesced into larger units that displayed a uniformity unknown in the governments of the earlier city-states. Competition in war remained an unceasing fact of life, but the wars between the kingdoms of Alexander's successors were broader in scope and more complex in organization than ever before. At the same time, their relative parity in strength meant a near-constant state of war between the new kings that never achieved very much. After all, every large state had access to essentially the same advanced military technology: rulers went into the marketplace and acquired the highly trained soldiers, mercenaries, generals, and military advisers required to run their armies. After battles that killed tens of thousands and severely injured and wounded hundreds of thousands more, the three major kingdoms—and even the minor ones—remained largely unchanged.

The great powers therefore settled into a centuries-long game of watching one another and balancing threats with alliances. What emerged was a fierce competition that dominated international relations, in which diplomacy and treaty making sometimes replaced actual fighting. This was an equilibrium reminiscent of the first age of international interstate relations in the second millennium BCE (see Chapter 3). Long periods of peace began to grace the intervals between the new kingdoms' violent and destructive wars.

Hellenistic Culture

Just as broad uniformity in politics and war trumped the small size and diversity of the old city-state, so the individual city-state cultures now gave way to a homogenized Hellenistic culture. Following the existing commercial networks, this uniform Greek culture spread rapidly through the entire Mediterranean basin and into Southwest Asia. It was an alluring package, and ruling elites in all regions that encountered it fell under its powerful spell.

Hellenistic culture included philosophical and political thinking, secular disciplines ranging from history to biology, popular entertainment in theaters, competitive public games, and art for art's sake in all kinds of media. No other society at the time had such a complete package of high culture—hence its widespread appeal and diffusion. Archaeologists have found a Greek-style gymnasium and theater in the town of Aï Khanoum in modern Afghanistan and adaptations of Greek sculptures made at the

Berenice. *Portrait head of Berenice, wife and consort of Ptolemy I, the first Macedonian king of Egypt after its conquest by Alexander the Great. Berenice was one of the women who, as queens of huge empires, wielded power and commanded wealth in their own right.*

order of the Indian king Chandragupta, of the Mauryan Empire (discussed shortly). We also know of Carthaginians in North Africa who became "Greek" philosophers, and Gallic and Berber chieftains from the far west of France and North Africa had fine Greek-style drinking vessels buried with them.

COMMON LANGUAGE The core element of Hellenism was a common language known as *Koine,* or "common," Greek. Replacing the city-states' numerous dialects with an everyday form that people anywhere could understand, **Koine Greek** quickly became the international language of its day.

Most peoples who came into contact with Hellenistic culture accepted the benefits that it afforded in expanding a network of communication and exchange. Peoples in Egypt, Judea, Syria, Sicily, and even Afghanistan, who all had distinct languages and cultures, could now communicate more easily with one another and enjoy the same dramatic comedies and new forms of art and sculpture. Despite pockets of resistance, the Hellenizing movement was remarkably successful in spreading a shared Greek culture throughout the Mediterranean world and into Southwest Asia.

COSMOPOLITAN CITIES Individuals were no longer citizens of a particular city (*polis*); instead they were the first **cosmopolitans**—that is, citizens (*polites*) belonging to the whole world (*cosmos*). The new political style was relentlessly cosmopolitan, radiating out of cities not just into nearby hinterlands but also to distant (and often rivalrous) cities. Much as Athens

PRIMARY SOURCE

The Cosmopolitan City of Alexandria

According to legend, Alexander selected the site of Alexandria and named the city after himself. As a result of his personal influence and its strategic location, Alexandria attracted an immense and diverse immigrant population from the entire Mediterranean world. In the following description, the Greek geographer Strabo—writing later during the time of the Roman Empire—emphasizes the city's function as an enormous entrepôt for trade and commerce across Afro-Eurasia. (Entrepôts are transshipment centers where seafaring vessels unload their cargoes and then send them elsewhere, by sea or by land.)

As for the Great Harbor at Alexandria, it is not only wonderfully well closed in and protected by artificial levees and by nature, it is also so deep that even the largest ships can be moored right at the stairs along its quayside. This Great Harbor is divided up into several minor harbors. . . . Even more exports are handled than imports. Anyone who might happen to be at Alexandria and at Dichaiarchia [the large Italian port on the Bay of Naples] would easily see for himself that the cargo ships sailing from here are bigger and more heavily laden. . . . The city itself is crisscrossed by streets that are wide enough for riding horses and driving chariots, and intersected by two main roads very much broader than the others. Its streets and avenues cut across each other at right angles.

The city also boasts exceedingly beautiful public parks and its royal quarters take up a quarter, perhaps even a third of the whole city. . . . In earlier times, not even twenty ships would dare to go as far as the Arabian Gulf and manage to get a look outside its straits. But now large fleets of ships are sent out as far as India and to the furthest lands of the Ethiopians, from which the most valuable cargoes are brought to Egypt and then sent out again to other regions of the world. Double charges are collected on these shipments—both when they come in and when they go out—and the duties are especially high on luxury goods . . . for Alexandria alone does not just receive trade goods of this kind from all over the world, but it also furnishes supplies to the whole of the world outside.

Source: Strabo, *Geography,* 17.1.6, 7, 8, 13; translated by Brent Shaw.

QUESTIONS FOR ANALYSIS

- According to this passage, what features of the site made Alexandria well suited as a center for sea trade and a destination for immigrants?
- By Strabo's time, Alexandria was the second-largest city in the Mediterranean, surpassed only by Rome. How does this passage reflect the role of trade in its development?
- The passage indicates that Alexandria exported more than it imported. In what way does this indicate the city's role as a cosmopolitan entrepôt?

had been the model city of the age of the Greek city-state, Alexandria in Egypt became exemplary in the new age. Whereas the city-states of the fifth century BCE, such as Athens, Sparta, and Corinth, had zealously maintained an exclusive civic identity, Alexandria was a multiethnic city built from scratch by immigrants, who rapidly totaled half a million as they streamed in from all over the Mediterranean and Southwest Asia seeking new opportunities. Members of its dynamic population, representing dozens of Greek and non-Greek peoples, communicated in the common language that supplanted their original dialects. Soon a new urban culture emerged to meet the needs of so diverse a population. (See Primary Source: The Cosmopolitan City of Alexandria.)

The culture of the Hellenistic movement took the place of local art forms. In the previous city-state world, comic playwrights had written plays for their individual cities and local

cultures, highlighting familiar languages, foibles, problems, and politicians. In contrast, entertainment in the more widely connected world had to appeal to bigger audiences and a greater variety of people. Plays were now staged in any city touched by Greek influence, and they were understood in any environment. Distinctive regional humor and local characters gave way to dramas populated by stock characters of standard sitcoms that any audience could identify with: the greedy miser, the old crone, the jilted lover, the golden-hearted whore, the boastful soldier, the befuddled father, the cheated husband, the rebellious son. At performances throughout the Mediterranean basin, laughter would be just as loud in Syracuse, on the island of Sicily, as in Scythopolis, in the Jordan Valley of Judea.

Kingdoms and states by now had become so enormous that individuals could relate to political style only through the personality of kings or rulers and their families. Rulership was

The Theater at Syracuse.
The great theater in the city-state of Syracuse, in Sicily, was considerably refurbished and enlarged under the Hellenistic kings. It could seat 15,000 to 20,000 persons. Here the people of Syracuse attended plays written by playwrights who lived on the far side of their world, but whose works they could understand as if the characters were from their own neighborhood. In the common culture of the Hellenistic period, plays deliberately featured typecast characters and situations, thereby broadening their audience.

personality, and personality and style united large numbers of subjects. For example, Demetrius Poliorcetes, the ruler of Macedonia, wore high-platform shoes and heavy makeup, and he decorated his elaborate, flowing cape with images of the sun, the stars, and the planets. In the presence of a powerful and solitary sun king like Demetrius, ordinary individuals felt small, inconsequential, and isolated. In response, an obsessive cult of the self arose, as Hellenistic religion and philosophy increasingly focused on the individual and his or her place in the larger world.

PHILOSOPHY AND RELIGION Growing concern with the individual self found expression in many new philosophical schools that proposed a range of ideas, including living a "natural" life (Cynicism), living a life of detachment (Epicureanism), and living according to laws governing the cosmos (Stoicism). Consider the Athenian philosopher Diogenes (c. 412–323 BCE), an early proponent of the Cynic school of philosophy. He sought self-sufficiency and freedom from society's laws and customs, rejecting cultural norms as human-made inventions not in tune with nature and therefore false. He masturbated in public to "relieve himself" (it was, after all, a "natural need"), as well as to show disdain for what he considered the city's artificial sexual mores. He lived with no clothing in a wooden barrel in the public square, or *agora*, of Athens, with his female companion in her own barrel beside him. Other teachers also rejected the values of the city-state, although with more finesse and less contentiousness than Diogenes. Nonetheless, all recognized the need for a new orientation now that

the world of the city-state, with its face-to-face relationships, had vanished.

The teacher Epicurus (c. 341–279 BCE), founder of a school in Athens that he called The Garden, likewise emphasized the self. He envisioned an ideal community centered on The Garden and stressed the importance of sensation, saying that pleasurable sensations were good and painful sensations were bad. Epicurus taught his students to pursue a life of contemplation and ask themselves, "What is the good life?" Known as Epicureans, his followers struggled to develop a sense of "not caring" (*ataraxia*) about worries—like threats to personal health or the challenges of coping with excessive wealth—in order to find peace of mind. In Epicurus's cult, none of the social statuses of the old city-state had more value than any other: women, slaves, and others in the underclass were equally welcome in The Garden.

Epicurus and his new ideas acquired followers throughout the Mediterranean, but they were hardly alone. Unrestrained by the controls of any one city-state, other cults and schools of philosophy emerged. Of these, Stoicism was perhaps the most widespread. A man named Zeno (c. 334–262 BCE), from the island of Cyprus, initiated it, and other cosmopolitan figures across the Hellenistic world—from Babylon in Mesopotamia to Sinope on the Black Sea—developed its beliefs. Their mission was to help individuals understand their place in the cosmos. Zeno put forth his ideas in the Stoa Poikil, a decorated and roofed colonnade that opened onto the central marketplace in Athens and gave his followers their name. For the Stoics, everything was grounded in nature itself, which they saw as the

The Painted Stoa. *An artist's reconstruction of the Stoa Poikilē, or "Painted Stoa," in the city-state of Athens of the fourth century BCE. In the manner of a modern-day strip mall, this business and administrative center ran along the northern side of the agora, or central business and marketplace of the city. Philosophers and their students would hang out at the Stoa, lounging in the shaded areas under the colonnade as they debated the ideas flowing into Athens from all over the Hellenistic world. Although not visible here, the painted wall decoration behind the columns (from which the Stoa received its name) depicts the Battle of Marathon.*

ultimate, permanent world. They regarded cities and kingdoms as human-made things, important but transient. Being in tune with nature and living a good life required understanding the rules of the natural order and being in control of one's passions and thus indifferent to pleasure and pain.

Greek colonial control of other lands transformed long-established religions, and then re-exported them throughout the Mediterranean. The Greeks in Egypt drew on the indigenous cult of Osiris and his consort, Isis (formerly a vital element in pharaonic temple rituals; see Chapter 2), to fashion a new narrative about Osiris's death and rebirth that represented personal salvation from death. Isis became a supreme goddess whose "excellencies" or "supreme virtues" encompassed the powers of dozens of other Mediterranean gods and goddesses. Believers experienced personal revelations and out-of-body experiences (*exstasis*, "ecstasy"). A ritual of dipping in water (*baptizein*, "to baptize") marked the transition of believers, "born again" into lives devoted to a "personal savior" who delivered an understanding of a new life by direct revelation. These new beliefs, like the worship of Isis, emphasized the spiritual concerns of humans as individuals, rather than the collective worries of towns or cities. Other Hellenistic adaptations from earlier Greek

cults, like the ecstatic worship of the god Dionysus, now seen as having made long journeys from the Mediterranean to India, similarly focused on the salvation of the individual as they spread throughout the Hellenistic world.

Plantation Slavery and Money-Based Economies

Ironically, philosophical and religious innovations focused on the self were accompanied by the rise of plantation slavery—the ultimate devaluing of an individual—as an engine of the Hellenistic economy. Indeed, the main economic innovation that accompanied unification of the Mediterranean world was the use of large numbers of slaves in agricultural production—especially in Italy, Sicily, and North African regions close to Carthage. After all, Alexander's conquests and Rome's political rise had produced unprecedented wealth for a small elite. These men and women used their riches to acquire huge tracts of land and to purchase slaves (either kidnapped individuals or conquered peoples) on a scale and with a degree of managerial organization never seen before.

The circulation of money reinforced the effects of forced labor. With more cash in the economy, wealthy landowners, urban elites, and merchants could more easily do business. The increasing use of Greek-style coins to pay for goods and services (in place of barter) promoted the importation of commodities such as wine from elsewhere in the Mediterranean. As coined money became even more available, it led to even more commercial exchanges. The forced transfer of precious metals to the Mediterranean from Southwest Asia by Alexander's conquests was so large that it actually caused the price of gold to fall. In the west, Carthage now began to mint its own coins—at first mainly in gold, but later in other metals. Rome moved to a money economy at the same time. By the 270s and 260s BCE, the Romans were issuing coins on a large scale under the pressures of their first war with Carthage (264–241 BCE). By the end of the third century BCE, even borderland peoples such as the Gauls had begun to mint coins, imitating the galloping-horse images found on Macedonia's gold coins. So, too, did kingdoms in North Africa, where the coins of Kings Massinissa and Syphax bore the same Macedonian royal imagery. By the end of this period, inhabitants of the entire Mediterranean basin and surrounding lands were using coins to buy and sell all manner of commodities.

To pay for the goods that satisfied their newly acquired tastes, Celtic chieftains in the regions encompassing modern-day France began selling their own people in the expanding slave markets of the Mediterranean. Slavery and slave trading also became central to the economies of the Iberian Peninsula—especially in the hinterlands of large river valleys like the Ebro, where local elites founded urban centers imitating Greek styles.

Roman Slaves. *One of the most profitable occupations for peoples living beyond the northwestern frontiers of the Roman Empire, in what was called Germania, was providing bodies for sale to Roman merchants. In this relief, we see chained German prisoners whose fate was to become slaves in the empire. This stone picture supported columns in front of the headquarters of the Roman fortress at Mainz-Kästrich.*

The slave plantations, wholly devoted to producing surplus crops for profit, became one of the forces driving a new Mediterranean economy. The estates created vast wealth for their owners—though at a heavy price to others, as reliance on slave labor now left the free peasants who used to work the fields with no option but to move into overcrowded cities, where employment was hard to find. The sudden importation of so many slaves to work in harsh conditions also had unanticipated outcomes. Between 135 and 70 BCE, authorities on Sicily and in southern Italy faced several massive slave uprisings, the largest and most dangerous of them led by the slave gladiator Spartacus in the late 70s BCE. These were among the greatest slave wars in world history. The superior military force of the Roman state prevailed in all three wars, and the rebels were finally defeated. But the political repercussions of the wars had a fundamental impact in the subsequent political crises that transformed the Roman state.

Early Roman Coin. *Coins like this one were the standard means by which the state paid its expenditures; they later were widely used in ordinary commercial dealings. This coin features the prow of a ship with an "evil eye" decoration and armed beak for ramming other ships. The legend ROMA at the bottom signals that Rome is a state with the power and autonomy to have its own money.*

Conflicting Responses: Adaptation and Resistance to Hellenism

The new high Greek culture spread far and wide, although it was not fully accepted everywhere in the Mediterranean. Its appeal to elites was obvious. The well educated and wealthy could use a mastery of the common language to enhance their status and enable them to move into more attractive places. To other groups, however, less enamored of Greek ways and more steeped in local traditions, Hellenism produced resentment, even armed resistance.

ELITES AND ADAPTATION The appeal of high Greek culture to elites in widely dispersed communities along the major communication routes became almost irresistible. Elites sought to enhance their position by adopting Hellenistic culture, the only culture that had standing above the level of local values. Syrian, Jewish, and Egyptian elites in the eastern Mediterranean adopted this attitude, as well as Roman, Carthaginian, and African elites in the western Mediterranean. Early Roman high culture was itself a form of Greek culture. Secular plays, philosophy, poetry, competitive games, art, and the writing of history followed, all based on Greek forms or local imitations. North African kings similarly decked themselves out in Greek dress, built Greek-style theaters, imported Greek philosophers, and wrote history. Now they, too, had "culture."

The Hellenistic influences penetrated into sub-Saharan Africa, where the kingdom of Meroe (see Chapter 5), already influenced by pharaonic forms, now absorbed characteristics of Greek culture as well. It is not surprising that Greek influences were extensive at Meroe, because continuous interaction with the Egyptians also exposed its people to the world of the Mediterranean. Both Meroe and its rival, Axum, located in the Ethiopian highlands, used Greek steles, inscribed stone pillars, to boast of their military exploits. Moreover, the Greek historian Herodotus mentions that "of all the gods the men who live in this place [Meroe] worship only Zeus and Dionysius. These [gods] they especially honor. They have an oracle of Zeus and go to war whenever the god commands them to do so through his prophecies" (*Histories*, 2.29). The rulers of Meroe, understanding the advantages of the Greek language, employed Greek scribes to record their accomplishments on the walls of Greek-Egyptian temples. In this way, Meroe developed a remarkable mix of Greek, Egyptian, and African cultural and political elements.

THE JEWS: RESISTANCE AND REVOLT Not every community succumbed to the allure of Hellenism. The Jews in Judea, squeezed between Egypt and the superstates of Mesopotamia, offer a striking case of resistance to its universalizing forces. The Jews had a long schooling in surviving and resisting foreign rule, having been conquered by the Assyrians and the Babylonians (see Chapter 4). After the Persians defeated Babylon, a royal edict of restoration issued by the Persian monarch Cyrus led to the integration of Judea—now a province—into the Persian Empire. As the Jews who had once been forced to move to Babylon returned to Judea, the process of rebuilding Jerusalem began.

All this rebuilding of Jewish society occurred under the administration of another great Southwest Asian empire—that of the Persian Empire, which tolerated local customs and beliefs. It took Alexander's lightning defeat of the Persian Empire in the 330s BCE to introduce a shocking new openness to the cultural innovations of the Mediterranean world.

While some parts of the Jewish ruling elite began to adopt Greek ways—to wear Greek clothing, to introduce the culture of the gymnasium with its cult of male nudity, to produce images of gods as art—others rejected the push. Those who spurned assimilation rebelled against the common elements of Hellenism—its language, music, gymnasia, nudity, public art, and secularism—as being deeply immoral and threatening to their beliefs. Ultimately, this resistance led to a full-scale armed revolt, headed up by the family of the Maccabees, in 167 BCE, provoked when Syrian overlords, the Seleucids, forbade certain core rituals of Judaism (like circumcision) and entered the innermost sanctuary of the Jews' temple, "the Holy of Holies," and desecrated the altar by burning/sacrificing something that Jews regarded as profane.

Though the Maccabees succeeded in establishing an independent Jewish state centered on the temple in Jerusalem, they did not entirely overcome the impact of the new universal culture. By the beginning of the first century BCE, descendants of the Maccabees were calling themselves kings, minting coins with Greek legends, and presiding over a largely secular kingdom. Moreover, a huge Jewish society in the Hellenistic city of Alexandria, in Egypt, embraced the new culture. Scholars there produced a Bible in *Koine* Greek, and historians (such as Jason of Cyrene) and philosophers (such as Philo of Alexandria) wrote in Greek, imitating Greek models.

THE ROMANS: ASSIMILATION AND DEBATE Other cities were less reluctant than Jerusalem to follow Hellenistic ways. Early on, the Romans saw the Greek model as offering opportunities to increase their own importance. In the 330s and 320s BCE, when Alexander was uniting the eastern Mediterranean, a city-state on the Tiber River in central Italy took the first critical military actions to unify Italy; eventually, it would bring together the rest of the Mediterranean and parts of Southwest Asia. Rather than beginning as a kingdom like Macedonia, Rome went from being a city-state to flourishing as a large territorial state. During this transformation, it adopted significant elements of Hellenistic culture: Greek-style temples, elaborately decorated Greek-style pottery and paintings, and an alphabet based on that of the Greeks.

Many elite Romans saw immersion in Greek culture and language as a way to appear to the rest of the world as "civilized," while others did not accept this notion without resistance, worry, and debate. Consider the conservative Roman senator Cato the Elder (234–149 BCE), who struggled with the tensions that these changes involved. Although he was devoted to the Roman past, the Latin language, and the ideal of small-scale Roman peasant farmers and their families, he embraced many Hellenistic influences. He wrote a standard manual for the new economy of slave plantation agriculture, invested in shipping and trading, learned Greek rhetoric (both speaking and writing the language), added the genre of history to Latin literature, and much more. Indeed, Cato blended an extreme devotion to tradition, manifested in his public statements, with bold innovations in most aspects of his daily life.

CARTHAGE AND EXPANDED COMMERCE In contrast to Rome, which assimilated Greek ways to elevate its status in the Mediterranean world, cities that were prosperous and already well integrated into the world economy welcomed Hellenistic culture because it facilitated communication and exchange. When these influences reached the great city of Carthage (in the area of present-day Tunisia), its residents adopted them with less internal conflict than at Rome.

Carthaginian culture (or Punic culture, to use the Romans' name for the people with whom they would soon be at war; see Chapter 7) took on important elements of Hellenistic culture. For example, some Carthaginians went to Athens to become philosophers. Also, the design of their sanctuaries, temples, and other public buildings reveals a marriage of styles: Greek-style pediments and columns mixed with Punic designs and measurements, along with local North African motifs and structures added to the mix. The splendid jewelry that Phoenician women adorned themselves with reflected styles from Egypt, such as ornate necklaces of gold and earrings of lapis lazuli, but coinage and innovative ideas on political theory and warfare came from the Greek city-states.

Not only did Carthaginian merchants trade with other Phoenician colonies in the western Mediterranean, but the city's ruling families took control over western Sicily and Sardinia as well. Remains of pottery and other materials demonstrate that the Carthaginians' trading contacts extended far beyond other Phoenician settlements to towns of the Etruscans and Romans in Italy, to the Greek trading city of Massilia (modern Marseilles) in southern France, and to Athens in the eastern Mediterranean. In addition, the Carthaginians expanded their commercial interests into the Atlantic, moving north along the coast of Iberia and south along the coast of West Africa which the commander Hanno explored and colonized. Pushing their influence even farther, they established a trading post at the island of Mogador,

Aerial View of Punic Carthage. Carthage was located on a promontory in the Bay of Tunis. In the bottom left of this artist's reconstruction is a rectangular area of water and above it a circular-shaped one. These were the two major harbors of Carthage—the rectangular one was the commercial port and the circular one was the military harbor. Above these harbors are the main market square and the high central point, named the Byrsa. A 20-mile long wall protected the city on the land and on the coasts, as depicted on the bottom right of this fresco.

more than 600 miles down the Atlantic coast of Africa. Profoundly shaped by Alexander's conquests, Hellenism spread even farther across Afro-Eurasia under Alexander's successors.

CONVERGING INFLUENCES IN CENTRAL AND SOUTH ASIA

During this period, imperial expansion of the Mauryan kingdom in South Asia helped to spread new influences, such as Hellenism and Buddhism, across the region. In addition to the Mauryan armies that carried Greek and Buddhist practices into distant lands, merchants, travelers, and nomadic groups were also active in promoting these two great cultural movements.

The Hindu Kush mountains in what we know today as Afghanistan are formidable but not impenetrable. The passes between the high plateau of Iran to the west and the towering ranges of Tibet to the east are pinched like the narrow neck of an hourglass—but they offer the shortest route through the mountains. By crossing these passes, Alexander's armies expanded the routes between the eastern and western portions of Afro-Eurasia, fashioned a land bridge that has remained open to this day, and brought about massive political and cultural changes in central and South Asia.

These routes and states created opportunities for unprecedented cross-cultural exchange that eventually remapped entire regions. Conquerors moved from west to east (like Alexander), from east to west (like the Mauryans and later nomads from central Asia), and from north to south, through the mountains and into the rich plains of the Indus and Ganges River valleys. At the same time, South Asian trade and religious influences moved northward toward routes running west to east along what became known as the Silk Road.

The Bolan Pass. *The formidable Bolan Pass separated India from the highland of Baluchistan. It was both an artery for transportation and a strategic military position.*

Influences from the Mauryan Empire

Alexander's brief occupation of the Indus Valley (327–325 BCE) paved the way for one of the largest empires in South Asian history, the Mauryan Empire. Before the arrival of Alexander's forces, South Asia had been a conglomerate of small warring states. Its political instability came to an abrupt halt when, in 321 BCE, an ambitious young man named Chandragupta Mori, inspired by Alexander, ascended the throne of the Magadha kingdom and launched a series of successful military expeditions in what is now northern India.

THE REGIME OF CHANDRAGUPTA The Magadha kingdom, located on the Lower Ganges plain, had great strategic advantages over other states. For one thing, it contained rich iron ores and fertile rice paddies. Moreover, on the northeast Deccan plateau, ample woods supported herds of elephants, the mainstay of the potent Magadha mobile military forces. The Mori family, or Mauryans, did not start out as a distinguished ruling family, but economic strength and military skill elevated them over their rivals. Alexander's retreat created a momentary political vacuum that gave the Mauryans an opportunity to extend the dynasty's claims to northwestern regions of South Asia that had previously been controlled by the Persian Empire.

Chandragupta's **Mauryan Empire** constituted South Asia's first empire and served as a model for later Indian empire builders. The contemporary Greek world knew this empire as "India," stretching from the Indus River eastward. Indeed, the Mauryan regime began to etch out the territorial contours of what would become, many centuries later, modern India.

Chandragupta (r. 321–297 BCE), though of lowly origins, probably from the Vaishya caste, grew up in the Punjab region observing Alexander and his forces and aspiring to be an equally powerful military and political leader. When Alexander withdrew his forces from northern India, Chandragupta inserted himself into the political vacuum created by the Greek withdrawal. After supplanting the Nanda monarchy in Magadha, he used his military resources to reach westward beyond the Ganges plain into "Five Rivers," the area around the upper stream of the Indus where four tributaries join it. Here he pushed up to the border with the Seleucid kingdom, the largest successor kingdom of Alexander's empire, based in Mesopotamia. Its king, Seleucus Nicator, fretted about his neighbor's challenge and invaded Mauryan territory—only to face Chandragupta's impregnable defenses.

Soon thereafter, a treaty between the two powers gave a large portion of Afghanistan to the Mauryan Empire. Yet, even after being incorporated into the Mauryan Empire, this territory remained Greek-speaking for centuries, and some garrison towns developed into genuine Greek-style city-states. The treaty yielded a round of gift exchanges and diplomacy. One of the daughters of Seleucus went to the Mauryan court at Pataliputra, accompanied by a group of Greek women. Seleucus also sent an ambassador, Megasthenes, to Chandragupta's court. In return, the Mauryans sent Seleucus many South Asian valuables, including hundreds of elephants, which the Greeks soon learned to use in battles.

The Seleucid ambassador Megasthenes gathered his observations while at the Mauryan court into a book titled *Indica*, from which much information about the Mauryan Empire has been learned. The book depicted a well-ordered and highly stratified society divided into seven groups: philosophers, farmers, soldiers, herdsmen, artisans, magistrates, and councillors. People respected the boundaries between groups and honored rituals that reinforced their identities: members of different groups did not intermarry or even eat together. Megasthenes also noted the ways in which rulers integrated the region—for example, with extensive roads connecting major cities. These arteries were lined with trees and were provided with stone mileage markers. If these roads helped traders, they also enabled the ruler's troops to march around his dominions. According to Megasthenes, soldiers were a profession separate from the rest of the population. This surprised the Greek observer, who was more accustomed to the idea of the military closely integrated into civil society. Mauryan troops did not work when there was no war. They constituted a standing force of immense proportions, ready to obey their commander. This military force was huge, boasting cavalry divisions of mounted horses, war elephants, and scores of infantry.

THE REGIME OF AŚOKA The Mauryan Empire reached its height during the reign of the third king, Aśoka (r. 268–231 BCE),

Chandragupta's grandson. Aśoka's lands comprised almost all of South Asia; only the southern tip of the peninsula remained outside his control. In 261 BCE, Aśoka waged the dynasty's last campaign: the conquest of Kalinga, a kingdom on the eastern coast of the South Asian peninsula by the Bay of Bengal. It was a gruesome and despicable operation. The Mauryan army triumphed, but at a high price: about 100,000 soldiers died in battle, many more perished in its aftermath, and some 150,000 people endured forcible relocation. Aśoka himself, when he learned of the devastation, was shocked and appalled at his army's brutality. Overcome by remorse, he vowed to cease inflicting pain on his people and pledged to follow the peaceful doctrines of Buddhism. While in this state of guilt, he issued a famous edict renouncing brutal ways.

Although his grandfather, Chandragupta, was a Jain, and his father an Ajavika, an ascetic sect that arose at the same time as Jainism and Buddhism, Aśoka was a faithful follower and patron of Buddhism. In fact, the Kalinga campaign deepened his devotion to Buddhism, which informed his edict on peace. (See Primary Source: Aśoka's Kalinga Edict.) Following the conquest of Kalinga, Aśoka claimed that henceforth his conquests would only be religious conquests. All over his domain he built stupas, or dome monuments, marking the burial sites of relics of the Buddha.

In his Kalinga edict, Aśoka proclaimed his intention to rule according to the Indian concept of *dhamma* (a vernacular form of the Sanskrit word *dharma*), a term widely known in the empire and understood to mean tolerance of others, obedience to the natural order of things, and respect for all of earth's life-forms. *Dhamma* was to apply to everyone, including the priestly Brahmans, Buddhists, members of other religious sects, and even Greeks. It became an all-encompassing moral code that all religious sects in South Asia accepted. With *dhamma* as a unifying symbol, Aśoka required all people, whatever their religious practices and cultural customs, to consider themselves his subjects, to respect him as their father, and to conform to his moral code—starting with the precept that people of different religions or sects should get along with one another. He also praised the benefits of agrarian progress and banned large-scale cattle sacrifice as detrimental to agriculture. Meanwhile, he warned the "forest people," the hunters and gatherers living beyond the reach of government, to avoid making trouble and to be wary of his anger.

To disseminate the ideals of *dhamma*, Aśoka regularly issued decrees, which he had chiseled on stone pillars and boulders in every corner of his domain, selecting locations where people were likely to congregate and where they could hear the words as read to them by the few who were literate. Occasionally, he also issued edicts to explain his Buddhist faith. All were inscribed in local languages. While most of his decrees were in dialects of Sanskrit, those proclaimed in northwestern regions were in Greek or in Aramaic, the administrative script

Aśoka's Kalinga Edict

After the Kalinga war, Aśoka issued an edict to express his regret at the miseries it had caused his people. From this edict, we can tell that Aśoka ruled a country of many different cultures and religions.

Beloved of the Gods, is that those who dwell there, whether brahmans, *śramanas*, or those of other sects, or householders who show obedience to their superiors, obedience to mother and father, obedience to their teachers and behave well and devotedly towards their friends, acquaintances, colleagues, relatives, slaves, and servants; all suffer violence, murder, and separation from their loved ones. Even those who are fortunate to have escaped, and whose love is undiminished [by the brutalizing effect of war], suffer from the misfortunes of their friends, acquaintances, colleagues, and relatives. This participation of all men in suffering weighs heavily on the mind of the Beloved of the Gods. Except among the Greeks, there is no land where the religious orders of brahmans and *śramanas* are not to be found, and there is no land anywhere where men do not support one sect or another. Today if a hundredth or a thousandth part of those people who were killed or died or were deported when Kalinga was annexed were to suffer similarly, it would weigh heavily on the mind of the Beloved of the Gods.

The Beloved of the Gods believes that one who does wrong should be forgiven as far as it is possible to forgive him. And the Beloved of the Gods conciliates the forest tribes of his empire, but he warns them that he has power even in his remorse, and he asks them to repent, lest they be killed. For the Beloved of the Gods wishes that all beings should be unharmed, self-controlled, calm in mind, and gentle.

The Beloved of the Gods considers victory by *Dhamma* to be the foremost victory. And moreover the Beloved of the Gods has gained this victory on all his frontiers to a distance of six hundred *yojanas* [i.e., about 1,500 miles], where reigns the Greek king named Antiochus, and beyond the realm of that Antiochus in the lands of the four kings named Ptolemy, Antigonus, Magas, and Alexander; and in the south over the Colas and Pāndyas as far as Ceylon. Likewise here in the imperial territories among the Greeks and the Kambojas, Nābhakas and Nābhapanktis, Bhojas and Pitinikas, Andhras and Pārindas, everywhere the people follow the Beloved of the Gods' instructions in *Dhamma*. Even where the envoys of the Beloved of the Gods have not gone, people hear of his conduct according to *Dhamma*, his precepts and his instruction in *Dhamma*, and they follow *Dhamma* and will continue to follow it.

What is obtained by this is victory everywhere, and everywhere victory is pleasant. This pleasure has been obtained through victory by *Dhamma*—yet it is but a slight pleasure, for the Beloved of the Gods only looks upon that as important in its results which pertains to the next world.

This inscription of *Dhamma* has been engraved so that any sons or great grandsons that I may have should not think of gaining new conquests, and in whatever victories they may gain should be satisfied with patience and light punishment. They should only consider conquest by *Dhamma* to be a true conquest, and delight in *Dhamma* should be their whole delight, for this is of value in both this world and the next.

QUESTIONS FOR ANALYSIS

- Why would Aśoka refer to himself as "the Beloved of the Gods"? Whose gods might he be referring to?
- Aśoka was a follower of Buddhism, which held that mortals passed through cycles of life, death, and rebirth. What parts of this passage reflect that belief?
- Aśoka promises to rule his people with *dhamma* (*dharma* in Sanskrit). Whereas Buddhist doctrine considers *dharma* to encompass religious teachings that guided the Buddha's followers, Aśoka's *dhamma* refers to a general moral standard that applied to all religious and ethnic communities—Buddhists or not. Why do you suppose he emphasizes this broader meaning?

Source: Romila Thapar, Aśoka and the Decline of the Maurya, 2nd ed. (Delhi: Oxford University Press, 1973), pp. 255–57.

of old Persia. Aśoka's legal pronouncements helped legitimize the Greek-speaking population that had arrived with Alexander and now resided in Greek-style towns.

One of these inscribed pillars provides a sense of the ideology that Aśoka promoted and the meaning of the term *dhamma* that he wanted all to live by. "There is no gift comparable to the gift of dhamma, the praise of dhamma, the sharing of dhamma, the fellowship of dhamma. This is good behavior toward slaves and servants, obedience to mother and father, generosity toward friends, acquaintances and relatives, and toward brahmans, and

Stupa and Pillar at Sarnath. *King Aśoka had stupas built across his domain, each holding relics of the Buddha. The stupa at Sarnath at the Deer Garden (left), is one of the few that has remained standing since Aśoka's time, and marks the place where the Buddha delivered his first sermon. Also in the Deer Garden stands this edict pillar (right). Aśoka had his policies carved on grand pillars like this one, capped by majestic sculptures of animals. This pillar capital has been established as the national emblem of the Indian Republic since its independence.*

abstention from killing human beings. . . . By doing so, there is gain in this world and in the next there is infinite merit" (Keay, pp. 94–95).

The works of art during Aśoka's reign celebrated the copious cultural and economic exchanges among Greeks, Persians, and Indians. The most famous of these works is the edict pillar that Aśoka erected in Sarnath at the Deer Garden, where the Buddha gave his first sermon. Atop the pillar, four lions sat facing four directions. Beneath the four lions were four wheels representing universal rule; they were separated by a bull, a horse, elephants, and another lion. The majestic images of lions, animals not found in the Ganges plain, represented an Indian version of the Persian royal symbol. Its artistic technique displayed Greek influence in a vivid, animated style.

Aśoka hoped that *dhamma* would function as a unifying ideology, binding together an immense landmass and diverse people. The Mauryan Empire at its height encompassed 3 million square miles, including all of what is today Pakistan, much

of what is Afghanistan, the southeastern part of Iran, and the whole of the Indian subcontinent except for the lands at the southern tip. Its extraordinarily diverse geography consisted of jungles, mountains, deserts, and floodplains, and its equally disparate population of 50 to 60 million inhabitants was made up of pastoralists, farmers, forest dwellers, merchants, artisans, and religious leaders. Yet his empire, which had an elaborate administrative structure that stretched all the way from the capital at Pataliputra into small villages, did not last long after Aśoka's death in 231 BCE. The proliferation of Buddhism made possible by Aśoka's adoption and wholehearted sponsorship of the faith, however, was a lasting impact of his reign.

The Seleucid Empire and Greek Influences

Hellenistic influences shaped politics and culture in the regimes that succeeded direct Greek control in central Asia.

Building Roads: Early Highways for Communication, Trade, and Control

World historians have become fascinated with the history of roads because they provide insight into the way nations and empires functioned, and they allow us to study transnational forces that cross borders, such as trade, migration, and the spread of ideas. Indeed, reliable communications and regular trade were among the most important forces that enabled the great regions of the world to be linked. If rivers and seas offered natural waterways to meet this demand, roads were the human-made answer that enabled soldiers, traders, and travelers to cross great stretches of land or go around high mountain ranges more quickly. Road building required huge financial and labor resources. Only empires had the incentives and resources to build large-scale roads and the networks that fed into them; these roads would aid in the empire's rule over its domain and in gathering the revenue that came from transregional trade.

The Persian (Achaemenid) Empire was the largest state in the Afro-Eurasian world, which necessitated efficient communications over vast distances and terrain that was varied and forbidding. The problems were overcome by the construction of many "great" or "royal" roads across the empire to connect the royal capitals where the king resided from time to time. One of the best-known great roads connected the far western coast at Sardis in Asia Minor (present-day Turkey) with the heartland of the Persian Empire around Susa (southern Iran) in the east, more than 1,700 miles away. The great roads featured way stations, supply depots, relays of horses and other pack animals, and state personnel, all to enable the local governors, or satraps, of the emperor to dispatch men and missions to the King of Kings.

If the royal Persian road communications system was a marvel of its age, the roads of the Roman Empire are rightly renowned for their extent and quality of construction. At its height, the empire boasted about 250,000 miles of roads; about 55,000 miles were of the formal stone-paved quality that most impresses us today. They were formally called "public roads" and were open to travel by anyone. Provincial, city, and municipal officials were in charge of upkeep. High standards of construction were imposed for the main paved highways—land was leveled and roadbeds were built up of layers of hard-packed sand and gravel, with careful gradients that allowed for drainage. The top layer was paved with heavy flagstones that provided long life.

It is easy to underestimate the amount of hard work and engineering required to construct the roadbeds, drainage, and bridges. The work and materials required to construct one major road in Italy, the Via Appia (the "Appian Way"), would be several times that required to build the great pyramids in Egypt. The major roads were marked with milestones that informed the traveler about the distance from the point of departure or to the next major town (5,000 or so of these have survived). The English word *mile* comes from the Roman *milia passuum* (slightly less than our mile in length). The system of roads allowed the Roman state to maintain a public relay service called the *cursus publicus,* along which imperial officials and units of the army, as well as information, could move efficiently and predictably from one part of the empire to another.

One of the singular achievements of the Qin dynasty was the building of a road

Alexander's military thrust into Asia had reached as far as the Punjab. There he defeated several rulers of Gandhara in 326 BCE. In the course of this campaign he planted many garrison towns—especially in eastern Iran, northern Afghanistan, and the Punjab, where he needed to protect his easternmost territorial acquisition. These towns were originally stations for soldiers, but they soon became centers of Hellenistic culture. Many of these outposts, such as those at Ghazni, Kandahar, Kapisi, and Bactra (modern Balkh), displayed the characteristic features of a Greek city-state: a colonnaded main street lined by temples to patron gods or goddesses, a theater, a gymnasium for education, an administrative center, a marketplace. After Alexander's death, Seleucus Nicator (358–281 BCE), ruler of the Hellenistic successor state in this area, built more of these Greek garrison towns. Seleucus, who also controlled Mesopotamia, Syria, and Persia, named sixteen cities "Antioch" after his father, five "Laodicea" after his mother, nine "Seleucia" after himself, three "Apamea" after his wife Apama, and one "Stratonicea" after another wife.

Even while the garrison towns founded by Alexander and Nicator remained and grew into Hellenistic centers, most of the Greek invaders integrated themselves into the local societies. Once the soldiers realized they would be spending their lives far from their homeland, they married local women and started families. Bringing Hellenistic customs to the local populations, they established institutions familiar to them from the Greek city-states. *Koine* Greek was the official language; but because local women used their own languages in daily life, subsequent generations were bilingual. For centuries the traditional Greek institutions—especially Greek language and writing—survived system to create sufficient infrastructure to unify its far-flung empire. The Qin network of roads connected the capital at Xianyang to every part of the country. The Qin used peasants, soldiers, and some slaves as forced laborers to build new roads and widen existing ones, so that troops could move quickly and easily to put down revolts anywhere in the empire.

Inca Road System. *This extraordinarily advanced transportation network provided the Incas access to over 1 million square miles of territory. Pictured here is the famous Inca Trail to Machu Picchu, which winds through the Andes Mountains.*

These roads were expanded under the succeeding Han dynasty to facilitate travel not only for the military, but also for merchants and commoners.

The road system of Qin and Han China paralleled the Persian royal roads and the Roman road network in scale and magnitude. By 100 BCE, many roads were wide, surfaced with stone, and lined with trees; steep mountains were traversed by stone-paved stairways with broad treads and low steps. By the end of the sixth century CE, the internal road network, not counting the Silk Road from the Han and Tang capital of Chang'an to central Asia, had grown to encompass some 25,000 miles.

Similarly, the Inca (Tawantinsuyu) in the Americas were able to connect the far-flung parts of their large empire in the Andean highlands by the construction of a complex network of roads based on two great north-south trunk roads that ran parallel to the Pacific coast from modern Ecuador to modern Argentina. The backbone of the system, called the Qahpag Ñan, or Beautiful Road, was 3,700 miles long. The two big highways knit together an immense system of about 25,000 miles of roads. Traversing some of the most difficult mountainous terrain on the planet, the Inca roads had to vary considerably in size and design to function, punctuated with stone bridges and impressive hanging bridges constructed of rope that bridged deep canyons. This ingeniously engineered system of travel ways enabled the Inca—like other world empires—to control an empire of daunting geographical disparity.

QUESTIONS FOR ANALYSIS

- What political and geographical motives did empires have to build road systems?
- What sort of people benefited most from these road systems? Who actually built the roads?

Explore Further

Liu, Xinru. *The Silk Road in World History* (2010).

Wood, Francis. *The Silk Road: Two Thousand Years in the Heart of Asia* (2004).

many political changes and much cultural assimilation, providing a common basis of engagement in a long zone stretching from the Mediterranean to South Asia.

The Kingdom of Bactria and the Yavana Kings

Hellenistic influences were even more pronounced in the Seleucid successor regimes of central Asia in the late third century BCE. The Seleucid state had taken over the entirety of the former Persian Empire, including its central Asian and South Asian territory. The Hellenistic kingdom of **Bactria** broke away from the Seleucids around 200 BCE to establish a strong state that included the Gandhara region in modern Pakistan. As Mauryan power receded from the northwestern part of India, the Bactrian rulers extended their conquests into this area. Because the cities that the Bactrian Greeks founded included many Indian residents, they have been called "Indo-Greek." Those in Gandhara incorporated familiar features of the Greek city-state, but inhabitants still revered Indian patron gods and goddesses.

Hellenistic Bactria served as a bridge between South Asia and the Greek world of the Mediterranean. Among the goods that the Bactrians sent west were elephants, which were vital to the Greek armies there. Not only did the Bactrian Greeks revive the cities in India left by Alexander, but they also founded new Hellenistic cities in the Gandhara region. The Greek king Demetrius, who invaded India around 200 BCE, entrusted the extension of his empire in the northern region of India to his generals, many of whom became independent rulers after his

Elephant Cavalry. *As shown by this terra-cotta statuette from 200 BCE, elephant cavalry was an important component of the Greek military. In their exchanges with India, Hellenistic states requested numerous elephants for their armies.*

Three Coins. Top: *Wearing an elephant cap, Demetrius of Bactria titled himself the king of Indians as well as Greeks. On the other side of the coin is Hercules. Middle: The king Menander is remembered by Buddhists for his curiosity about their theology. His image appears on one side of the coin with a Greek legend of his name and title. On the other side, Athena is surrounded by Kharoshthi script, an Indian type of writing. Bottom: The Scythian king Maues used Greek to assert his position as "King of Kings" on one side of his coin. On the other side, the goddess Nike is surrounded by Kharoshthi letters.*

death. Sanskrit literature refers to these Greek rulers as the Yavana kings—a word derived from "Ionia," a region whose name applied to all those who spoke Greek or came from the Mediterranean.

Aï Khanoun, on the Oxus River (now the Amu) in present-day Afghanistan, was the site of an administrative center, possibly the capital of the Bactrian state. The Greek-style architecture and inscriptions indicate that the original residents were soldiers from Greece. Following the typical pattern, they married local women and established the basic institutions of a Greek city-state. Aï Khanoum's characteristic Greek structures included a palace complex, a gymnasium, a theater, an arsenal, several temples, and elite residences. Featuring marble columns with Corinthian capitals, the palace contained an administrative section, storage rooms, and a library. A main road divided the city into lower and higher parts, with the main religious buildings located in the lower city. Though far from Greece, the elite Greek residents read poetry and philosophy and staged Greek dramas in the theater. Grape cultivation supported a wine festival associated with the god Dionysus. The remains of various statues indicate that the residents not only revered the Greek deity Athena and the demigod Heracles but also paid homage to the Zoroastrian religion.

Perhaps the most adept ruler at mingling Greek and Indian influences was Menander, the best-known Yavana city-state king of the mid-second century BCE. Using images and legends on coins to promote both traditions among his subjects, Menander claimed legitimacy as an Indian ruler who also cultivated Greek cultural forms. The face of one of his coins bore his regal image surrounded by the Greek words *Basileus Sōtēr Menandros* ("King, Savior, Menander"). The reverse side featured the Greek goddess Athena and the king's title in the local Prakrit language. Menander's curiosity about Buddhism led him to invite the Buddhist sage Nagasena to the court for discussions. The meeting resulted in the publication of a Buddhist literary work,

PRIMARY SOURCE

Sâgala: The City of the Gods

The Indo-Greek king Menander was a famous patron of Buddhism, as described in the Questions of King Milinda. *The book, written in Pāli, a northwestern dialect of Sanskrit, begins with a description of the kingdom of Milinda (Menander) located in the country of Yonakas, the Pāli name for Greeks. This kingdom, according to the following passage, is a center of prosperous trade and people of many creeds, with a city called Sâgala whose glory rivals that of "the city of the gods."*

Thus hath it been handed down by tradition—There is in the country of the Yonakas a great centre of trade, a city that is called Sâgala, situated in a delightful country well watered and hilly, abounding in parks and gardens and groves and lakes and tanks, a paradise of rivers and mountains and woods. Wise architects have laid it out, and its people know of no oppression, since all their enemies and adversaries have been put down. Brave is its defence, with many and various strong towers and ramparts, with superb gates and entrance archways; and with the royal citadel in its midst, white walled and deeply moated. Well laid out are its streets, squares, cross roads, and market places. Well displayed are the innumerable sorts of costly merchandise with which its shops are filled. It is richly adorned with hundreds of almshalls of various kinds; and splendid with hundreds of thousands of magnificent mansions, which rise aloft like the mountain peaks of the Himâlayas. Its streets are filled with elephants, horses, carriages, and foot-passengers, frequented by groups of handsome men and beautiful women, and crowded by men of all sorts and conditions, Brahmans, nobles, artificers, and servants. They resound with cries of welcome to the teachers of every creed, and the city is the resort of the leading men of each of the differing sects. Shops are there for the sale of Benares muslin, of Kotumbara stuffs and of other cloths of various kinds; and sweet odours are exhaled from the bazaars, where all sorts of flowers and perfumes are tastefully set out. Jewels are there in plenty, such as men's hearts desire, and guilds of traders in all sorts of finery display their goods in the bazaars that face all quarters of the sky. So full is the city of money, and of gold and silver ware, of copper and stone ware, that it is a very mine of dazzling treasures. And there is laid up there much store of property and corn and things of value in warehouses—foods and drinks of every sort, syrups and sweetmeats of every kind. In wealth it rivals Uttara-kuru, and in glory it is as Âlakamandâ, the city of the gods.

QUESTIONS FOR ANALYSIS

- The city Sâgala is in the country of the Yonakas, that of the Greeks. Judging from the references to elephants, horses, and the Himalayas, where approximately would it have been located?
- What kinds of people lived there?
- Why do you suppose Buddhist ideas found easy acceptance there?

Source: The Questions of King Milinda, translated by T. W. Rhys Davis (1890; reprint, Delhi: Motilal Banarsidass, 1975), pp. 2–3.

Milindapanha, or *Questions of King Menander*. Menander's effort to blend Greek and Indian influences persisted long after the Hellenistic regimes collapsed and enabled travelers and merchants of many different backgrounds and religions to communicate and trade around the rim of the Indian Ocean.

THE TRANSFORMATION OF BUDDHISM

During this time of political and social change, South Asia also experienced upheavals in the religious sphere as Hellenism and other influences transformed Buddhism. Impressed by Hellenistic thought, South Asian peoples sought to blend its principles with their own ethical and religious traditions. Begun among the Yavana (that is, Greek) city-states in the northwest, where Buddhism's sway was most pronounced, Buddhism rapidly spread to other regions that were experiencing the same currents of change. (See Primary Source: Sâgala: The City of the Gods.) In addition to Hellenism, other layers of influence came together in South Asia through increased seafaring and interactions with nomadic peoples. This cultural fusion profoundly changed and enriched Buddhism. For example, the Yavana king Menander's discussion with Nagasena as seen in *Milindapanha* helped the Buddhist community in India to embrace the idea that Buddha was a god. Nonetheless, the transformation of Buddhism into a religion with Hellenistic influences and with wide-ranging support in other states was far from complete when Menander died around 130 BCE. (See Chapter 8 for Buddhism's further development.)

India as a Spiritual Crossroads

Hellenism was not the sole cultural movement to affect other cultures. Nomadic peoples and new seafarers added another layer of cultural change (a fuller discussion of these two groups follows shortly). The latter's mastery of the monsoon trade winds opened the Indian Ocean to commerce and made India the hub for long-distance ocean traders and travelers. Many land and sea routes now seemed to converge on India, rendering the region a melting pot of ideas and institutions. From the mixing of the influences of Hellenism, nomadism, and seafaring, a profoundly transformed and wealthier form of Buddhism emerged. Under the influence of nomadic groups, the Buddhist *sangha* grew so rich through India's commercial prosperity that monks began to live in elegant monastic complexes. The center of each was a stupa decorated with sculptures depicting the Buddha's life and teachings. Such monasteries provided generously for the monks, furnishing them with halls where they gathered and worshipped and rooms where they meditated and slept. And Buddhist monasteries were also open to the public as places for worship.

The New Buddhism: The Mahayana School

The mixing of new ways—nomadic, Hellenistic, Persian, and Mesopotamian—with traditional Buddhism produced a spectacular spiritual and religious synthesis: **Mahayana Buddhism**. For at least a hundred years, Buddhist scholars had debated whether the Buddha was a god or a wise human being. The Mahayana Buddhists resolved this dispute in the first two centuries of the Common Era with a ringing affirmation: the Buddha was indeed a deity. Yet Mahayana Buddhism was worldly and accommodating, a spiritual pluralism that positioned Indian believers as a cosmopolitan people—welcoming contacts with peoples from other parts of Afro-Eurasia and laying the spiritual foundations for a region that had become a crossroads of world cultures.

As Buddhism adapted to external impulses, Mahayana Buddhism appealed especially to foreigners and immigrants who traded or settled in India. It made the Buddha easier to understand. The Buddha's preaching had stressed life's suffering and the renunciation of desire to end suffering and achieve nirvana. This was a tough road to a better life. As we saw in Chapter 5, those who did not believe in reincarnation found it difficult to understand the appeal of nirvana. Newcomers such as migrants or traders saw no attraction in a belief that life consists of painful cycles of birth, growth, death, and rebirth. This sharp dichotomy between a real world of hardship and the Buddha's abstract one of nirvana gave way to the Mahayana Buddhists' vision that **bodhisattvas**, enlightened demigods ready to reach nirvana, delayed doing so to help others attain it. They prepared "Buddha-lands"—spiritual halfway points—to welcome deceased devotees not yet ready to release desires and enter nirvana. In this fashion the universe of the afterlife in Mahayana Buddhism was colorful and pleasant, presenting an array of alternatives to the harsh real existence of worldly living. With its bodhisattvas, Mahayana ("Great Vehicle") Buddhism enabled all individuals—the poor and powerless as well as the rich and powerful—to move from a life of suffering into a happy existence.

The new Buddhist brokers—the bodhisattvas—were effective instruments for helping all classes find their way to heaven. One of these bodhisattvas, Avalokiteshvara, proclaimed his willingness to stay in this world to guide people out of trouble—especially

Buddhist Cave Temple at Ajanta. *Buddhists excavated cave temples along the trade routes between ports on the west coast of India and places inland. Paintings and sculptures from Ajanta became the models of Buddhist art in central Asia and China.*

those who traveled in caravans and had the misfortune of running into murderous robbers, or those who had to navigate unwieldy ships through violent storms. As Avalokiteshvara guided and protected the living more than he appeased the dead, lay followers, especially traveling merchants, invoked him constantly and spread his cult along trade routes.

New Images of Buddha in Literature and Art

Just as Buddhism absorbed outside influences and became more appealing, it also inspired literary and artistic works that diverse peoples could embrace. A new genre of literature dealing with the Buddha and the bodhisattvas emerged. Buddhist texts written in Sanskrit disseminated the life of the Buddha and his message far and wide, reaching the far corners of Asia. Aśvaghosa (c. 80–150 CE), a great Buddhist thinker and the first known Sanskrit writer, wrote a biography of the Buddha. This work set the Buddha's life story within the commercial urban environment of the Kushan Empire (instead of in the rural Shakya republic in the Himalaya foothills, where he had actually lived). Aśvaghosa said that the Buddha was born as a prince into a life of extreme luxury and only became aware of human suffering after experiencing heavenly revelations. To escape his mundane life, the young prince left home in the middle of the night, riding on a white horse. This largely fictive version of the Buddha's life story spread rapidly throughout India and beyond, introducing the Buddha and his teachings to many potential converts.

The colorful images of Sanskrit Buddhist texts of the first centuries CE gave rise to a large repertoire of Buddhist sculptural art and drama. On Buddhist stupas and shrines, artisans carved scenes of the Buddha's life, figures of bodhisattvas, and statues of patrons and donors. Buddhist sculptures from the northern Kushan territory, fashioned from gray schist rock, are called **Gandharan art**. Those from the central region of India, created mainly from local red sandstone, are called Mathuran art. Gandharan Buddhist art shows strong Greek and Roman influences, whereas the Mathuran style evolved from the carved idols of South Asian folk gods and goddesses. In addition, the story of the Buddha celebrated the horse, an important nomadic cultural symbol.

Despite their stylistic differences, the schools shared themes and cultural elements. Inspired by Hellenistic art and religious tradition, both took the bold step of sculpting the Buddha and

Buddhas. *The bronze Buddha on the left often strikes viewers as a Christlike figure. Greco-Roman influence on the iconography of Buddha was probably responsible for the Gandharan-style attire and facial expression of Buddhas and bodhisattvas. The Mathuran Buddha of Gupta times, shown on the right, is more refined than the Buddhas of the Kushan era. The robe is so transparent that the artist must have had very fine silk in mind when sculpting it.*

*P*eriplus Maris Erythraei, or *Periplus of the Red Sea*, was a first-century BCE handbook that offered advice to merchants traveling and trading along two major, connected routes: one that scaled the African coast from the Red Sea ports of Egypt and the other that traveled eastward to India in the Arabian Sea. A shrewd trader, keen observer, and experienced navigator, the author catalogued the navigable routes, listed marketable goods at each port, and even recorded anthropological insights on the inhabitants of the far-flung regions he encountered.

The author's voyage began in the Red Sea port of Berenice and moved southward to the tribal countries of modern-day Sudan and Eritrea. To the east, he found the placid waters of the Gulf of Aden and the frankincense of the Arabian coast. Though Indian products like rice and ghee were widely sold in Arabian market towns, the Indian port of Barygaza remained the most sought-after port of the time, despite its rugged coast, uneven sea bottom, and tidal waves. An important node in the Afro-Eurasian trade network, Barygaza proved to be a curious mix of the exotic and the familiar in the author's eyes, with its vendors hawking everything from Chinese silks to old Greek coins. Pragmatic in tone, the *Periplus* and its display of economic opportunity cannot help but dazzle even modern readers. The following table gives an overview of a few important ports in the *Periplus*, as well as a taste of the ancient world.

QUESTIONS FOR ANALYSIS

- What do the author's highly specific descriptions of imports and exports suggest about the types of goods that were traded along this route? What might these commodities imply about the socioeconomic status of the Greek trader and the status of the consumers of the goods that moved along these routes?

- What are some apparent patterns or commonalities in the goods that these market towns imported? In the goods that they exported? What goods exported at some of these ports were imported at other ports listed in the *PME*'s itinerary? What does that suggest about the nature of trade along this overseas route?

- What other specific types of evidence might help you interpret the nature of the trade that took place on these overseas routes? In what ways might that evidence complete, or even add complexity to, the snapshot of trade offered by a periplus such as this one for Red Sea trade?

Source: Lionel Casson, *The* Periplus Maris Erythraei: *Text with Introduction, Translation, and Commentary* (1989).

---

bodhisattvas in realistic human, rather than symbolic, form (such as a bodhi tree, which symbolizes Buddha's enlightenment). Though the Buddha wore no decorations because he had cut off all links to the world, bodhisattvas were dressed as princes because they were still in this world, generously helping others. What was important was bringing the symbolic world of Buddhism closer to the people.

Buddhist art reflected a spiritual system that appealed to people of diverse cultural backgrounds. Consider the clothes of the patron figures. For male and female figures alike, the garments were simple and well adapted to tropical climates. Those indigenous to the semitropical land had nude upper bodies and a wrapping like the modern *dhoti,* or loincloth, on their lower bodies. Jewelry adorned their headdresses and bodies. By contrast, the nomadic patron figures wore traditional cone-shaped leather hats, knee length robes, trousers, and boots. Figures with Greek clothing demonstrate continuing Hellenistic influence, and those wearing Roman togas reveal imperial Rome's influence. The jumble of clothing styles illustrates that Buddhist devotees could share a faith while retaining their ethnic or regional differences.

THE FORMATION OF THE SILK ROAD

In the first century BCE, trade routes stretching from China to central Asia and westward had merged into one big intertwined series of routes that came to be called the Silk Road. The first use of the term by modern Europeans occurred when a German traveler and geographer, Baron Ferdinand von Richthofen, entered the term on a map in 1877. But Ammanus Marcellinus, a fourth-century CE Roman soldier and historian, had used the term "The Great Silk Road" in the twenty-third book of his *The History* (Kuzima, p. 2). Those living along the Silk Road in earlier centuries called it "the road to Samarkand" or whatever city travelers were bound for on the northern or southern routes around the Taklamakan Desert. Most of the trade was small, took place over short distances, and involved barter. Traders traveled only segments of the route, passing their goods on to others who took them farther along the road and, in turn, passed them on again. The Silk Road owed much to earlier overland routes through which merchants exchanged frankincense and

	Port	Exports	Imports	Gifts for Rulers
Southern Arabia	Muza (Section 24 of the text)	Myrrh, white marble, stacte (sweet spice for ancient Hebrew incense)	Purple cloth; Arab-sleeved clothing, with no adornment, with checks, or interwoven with gold thread; herbs cyperus and saffron; blankets, with traditional local adornment or none; girdles with shaded stripes; ungent; money, considerable amount; wine; grain	Horses, pack mules, expensive clothing, goldware, embossed silverware, copperware
East Africa	Opone (Section 13)	Cinnamon, frankincense, cassia (Chinese cinnamon), better-quality slaves, tortoise shell	Grain, rice, ghee, sesame oil, *monache* and *sagmatogene* (India cotton cloth), girdles, Indian cane sugar	
Persia	Omana, Apologos (Section 36)	Purple cloth; native clothing; slaves; wine; dates; *madarate* (local sewn boats); pearls, in quantity but inferior to Indian	Copper, teakwood beams, saplings, logs of sissoo (rosewood), ebony, frankincense from Kane	
Western India	Barygaza (Sections 14, 47–8)	Grain, rice, ghee, sesame oil, *monache* and *sagmatogene* (Indian cotton cloth), girdles, cane sugar, onyx, agate, molochinon (?), nard, costus, bedellium, ivory, lykion, Chinese [silk] cloth, long pepper	Italian, Laodicean, and Arabian wine; copper, tin, lead; coral, peridot; printed and plain clothing; multicolored girdles, 18 inches wide; storax, yellow sweet clover; raw glass; Roman money, gold and silver, which commands an exchange at some profit against the local currency; inexpensive ungent	Slave musicians, beautiful girls for concubinage, precious silverware, fine wine, expensive clothing with no adornment, choice ungent
Eastern India	Ganges (Sections 63–4)	Malabathron; Gangetic nard; pearls; cotton garments of the very finest quality, the so-called Gangetic; *kaltis* (gold coins); finest tortoise shell; silk floss; yarn		

myrrh from the Arabian Peninsula for copper, tin, iron, gemstones, and textiles. Even so, silk was its most expensive and prized commodity and hence deserving of its present name.

The Silk Road, in addition, was a route through which Buddhists, Zoroastrianists, Syrian Christians, and later on Muslims spread their religions eastward, translating their scriptures and modifying their beliefs as believers moved from one culture to another. Nor was the Silk Road a straight and paved road like the Appian Way in the Roman Empire. It was not human made but entirely natural, traversing mountain passes, valleys, and desert oases—and only mapped for the first time in the twentieth century. Often, it was no more than footpaths. Travelers wishing to journey through remote regions were compelled to hire guides. There is no documentary evidence of direct traffic between China and the Roman Empire; the often-stated remark that the Romans exchanged gold for Chinese silk is a falsehood. Even so, the Silk Road did transform cultures in east and west by bringing into contact "a dazzling array of peoples, languages, and cultural cross currents" (Hansen, p. 5). The oases of Kucha, located on the northern route around the Taklamakan Desert, served as the major entry point for Buddhist teachings to enter China. The first written evidence of the Silk Road comes from Zhang Qian (d. 113 BCE), a Chinese traveler to central Asia during the Han dynasty.

In the opinion of the scholar who has carried out the most recent study of the Silk Road (Hansen, p. 235), "The Silk Road was one of the least traveled routes in human history. . . . Yet, the Silk Road changed history, largely because the people who managed to traverse part or all of the Silk Road planted their cultures like seeds of exotic species to distant lands." (See Map 6.2.)

A New Middle Ground

The expansion of commerce between the Mediterranean and Asia reinforced a frenetic rise in commercial activity within each region. Over land and across the seas, traders loaded textiles, spices, and precious metals onto the backs of camels and into the holds of oceangoing vessels destined for distant markets. The effects of long-distance exchanges altered the political geography of Afro-Eurasia. Egypt and Mesopotamia faded as sources of innovation and knowledge, becoming instead crossroads for peoples on either side of them. The former borderlands emerged as new imperial centers.

NORTH SEA

ROMAN
EMPIRE

SCYTHIANS

URAL MTS.

BLACK SEA

ARAL
SEA

CASPIAN
SEA

from the west
to India and China:

Rome

ANATOLIA

Oxus R.

Merv

Bu

Athens

Antioch

PARTHIAN
EMPIRE

Carthage

Dura Europos

IRANIAN
PLATEAU

MEDITERRANEAN   SEA

Palmyra

Euphrates R.

Tigris R.

ZAGROS MTS.

from India
to the west:
A/D

Alexandria

Petra

Persepolis

Persian Gulf

EGYPT

NABATAEAN
KINGDOM

Myos
Hormos

ARABIAN

from Arabia
to India:

SAHARA   DESERT

Berenice

DESERT

from Arabia,
Ethiopia and East Africa
to the west:
I ○ ⚬⚬⚬ ● LF

from Arabia
and Ethiopia
to India and Chi
I

Nile R.

NUBIA

Meroe

ARABI

RED SEA

ARABIAN
STATES

AXUMITE
KINGDOM

from the west
to India and Southeast
Asia:
○ G □LT

Lake
Victoria

INDIAN

Bhapta

MADAGASCAR

Legend

Symbol	Description
——	Silk Road
——	Incense trade route
——	Other trade routes
SCYTHS	Nomad group
——	Boundary of empires, states, and kingdoms
⌐⌐⌐⌐	Defensive wall, forerunner of later Great Wall
•	Port/trading town
⬭	Buddhist heartland
←	Spread of Buddhism
○	Buddhist centers
⬠	Buddhist rock-carved temples
▲	Sacred Buddhist mountains

Traded Goods

A/D	Aromatics and drugs	○	Jewelry and cut gems
Cu	Copper	▬	Laquerware
●	Coral	LF	Luxury foods
◢	Everyday textiles	LT	Luxury textiles
◣	Fine cotton/garments	●	Peacocks
◈	Furs	○	Pearls
●	Fine stone and metal vessels	◣	Silk
G	Glassware	⚬⚬⚬	Slaves
⬠	Gems	S	Spices
□	Gold	▮	Statuary
Y	Grain	Sn	Tin
H	Horses	●	Tortoiseshell
I	Incense	🍇	Wine
○	Ivory	🌲	Wood

0   500   1000 Miles
0   500   1000 Kilometers

EASTERN SCYTHS

Lake Baikal

from Central Asia to the
west via China and
Silk Road towns:
H ⧗

from Central Asian
nomads to China:
H ⧗

XIONGNU

GOBI DESERT

Lake Balkas

WUSUN

from Ferghana
to China:
H

TIAN SHAN MTS.

KUCHA

Turfan

Jade
Gates
Pass

Dunhuang

Datong

from China to
Central Asia
(Xiongnu) as
bribes:

Kashgar

TAKLAMAKAN
DESERT

Loulan

PAMIR
MTS.

LF

Khotan   Niya

WESTERN REGIONS
PROTECTORATE

Yellow R.

SEA
OF
JAPAN

KOREA

JAPAN

...ra

SHAN
...PIRE

Taxila

HIMALAYA MTS.

Chang'an   Luoyang

HAN
EMPIRE
c. 150 CE

Yangzi R.

Mathura

Ganges R.

Buddhist
Heartland

...barikon

Tamluk

from China to
India and the west:

Barygaza

BAY OF BENGAL

...m India
...Arabia
...Ethiopia:

SOUTH
CHINA
SEA

PACIFIC

OCEAN

Mekong R.

...A

from India to
Southeast Asia:

from India to
the west:
A/D
S ● LF

from Southeast Asia
to India and the west:
Cu ⬢ □ S Sn ● LF

OCEAN

INDONESIA

Bali

AUSTRALIAN
ABORIGINES

MAP 6.2 | Afro-Eurasian Trade, c. 150 CE

During the period covered in this chapter, trade increasingly brought Afro-Eurasian worlds together. This map highlights important commercial linkages among societies.

- Where did mariners develop ocean-based commercial links?
- Compare this map with Map 6.3, and identify areas where the migrations of nomadic groups contributed to the creation of trade routes. How did trade facilitate the spread of Buddhism during this time?

Jiaohe City *Ruins of Jiaohe city in Turfan. Jiaohe was the administrative center of Turfan area during the Tang Dynasty. The prickly green shrubs, called "camel thorns" by local people, were the main fodder for camels on the desert routes. The center of the city was a Buddhist shrine.*

What we now call the Middle East literally became a commercial middle ground between the Mediterranean and India.

East Asia, principally China, finally connected with the Mediterranean via central and South Asia. Through China, whose traders penetrated Bali and other Indonesian islands, connections developed with Japan, Korea, and Southeast Asia. But China remained politically and culturally a mysterious land to those from the Mediterranean. Although Alexander had marched as far east as the Indus Valley, the Himalayas and Pamir Mountains kept the Chinese insulated. Yet products made of silk—a word derived from *Sēres,* the Greek and Roman name for the people of northwestern China—revealed to the Greeks and Romans that an advanced society lay far to the east.

Nomads, Frontiers, and Trade Routes

The horse-riding nomads of Inner Eurasia were vital intermediaries in long-distance trade. As pioneers in a slow but powerful transformation of Afro-Eurasian trade in the second millennium BCE, they responded to the drying out of their homelands by sending out conquering armies that linked entire regions and facilitated trade and interactions between distant communities (see Chapter 3). Moreover, interacting with other populations had another advantage for the nomads. Because of their movements from place to place, they were exposed to—and acquired resistance to—a greater variety of microbes than settled peoples did. Their relative immunity to disease made them ideal agents for linking distant settled communities. Finally, even more important were the ways in which nomads raced into political vacuums and installed new regimes that would link northwest China and the Iranian plateau. (See Map 6.3.)

First to feel the impact of the nomads was the Seleucid state in Iran. Having lost control of Bactria, it now came under relentless pressure from nomadic peoples living on the steppes to the north. The first to prey on them were the horse-riding Parthians, who wiped out the Greek kingdoms in Iran. The Parthians then extended their power all the way to the Mediterranean, where they would ultimately face the forces of the Roman Empire.

THE PARTHIANS The Parthian people had moved south from present-day Turkmenistan and settled in the region comprising the modern states of Iraq and Iran. Unlike the Persians before them, the Parthians had a social order founded on nomadic pastoralism and a war capability based on technical advances in mounted horseback warfare. Reliance on horses made their style of fighting highly mobile and ideal for warfare on arid plains and deserts. They perfected the so-called Parthian shot: the arrow shot from a bow with great accuracy at long distance and from horseback at a gallop. On the flat, open plains of Iran and Iraq, the Parthians had a decisive advantage over slow-moving, cumbersome mass infantry formations that had been developed for war in the Mediterranean. Eventually, the expansionist states of Parthia and Rome became archenemies: they confronted each other in Mesopotamia for nearly four centuries. In spite of the conflicts between Romans and Parthians, Hellenistic caravan cities on the Roman Empire's eastern frontier continued to trade with the east, and Greek remained the

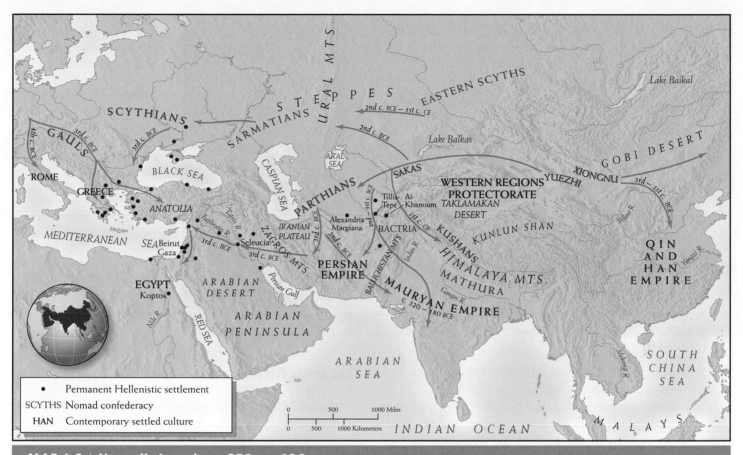

MAP 6.3 | Nomadic Invasions, 350 BCE–100 CE

Interaction between nomadic and settled societies was a major engine of change in Afro-Eurasia in the first millennium BCE.

- According to the map, where did most of the nomadic and settled societies come from? What were the two primary destinations of nomadic peoples?
- How did this interaction shape cross-cultural processes (the spread and diffusion of goods, peoples, and ideas)?

essential language for commercial activities from the eastern shore of the Mediterranean all the way to Afghanistan.

In the second century BCE, a vast nomadic tribal confederacy called the Xiongnu became dominant in the East Asian steppe lands. While consolidating their power, the Xiongnu drove many other pastoral groups, including the Yuezhi, out of their homelands. Meanwhile, the Parthians, who had supplanted the Greek Seleucids in Iran, entered the Indus Valley from the northwest, through the mountain passes of Baluchistan.

THE KUSHANS Though first defeated by the Xiongnu around 130 BCE, the Yuezhi appeared as a political force around 50 CE. Led by their chief, the Yuezhi unified the region's tribes and established the Kushan dynasty in Afghanistan and the Indus River basin. The Kushans' empire embraced a large and diverse territory and was critical in the formation of the Silk Road.

Like the Parthians, the Kushans had been an illiterate people, but they adopted Greek as their official language. The face of the second Kushan king to rule South Asia, Wima Kadphises,

is featured on a gold coin surrounded by Greek legends. The reverse side shows the Hindu god Shiva with his cow. Until the end of the Kushan Empire in the early third century CE, Greek letters continued to appear on Kushan coins. Their rulers kept alive the influence of Hellenism in an area strategically located on the Silk Road, even though by this time few fluent speakers of Greek were left in the population. Mediterranean traders arriving in the Kushan markets to purchase silks from China, as well as Indian gemstones and spices, conducted their transactions in Greek. The coins they used—struck to Roman weight standards (themselves derived from Greek coinage) and inscribed in Greek—served their needs perfectly.

The many peoples living under Kushan rule shared important cultural traits. They preferred Hellenistic or pseudo-Hellenistic architecture, favoring columns, and they reveled in Greek music and dance. We can recognize many of their musical instruments, such as the lyre (a small version of the harp), the flute, cymbals, drums, and the xylophone. In their carvings, grape and grape-leaf motifs celebrated wine's intoxicating pleasure.

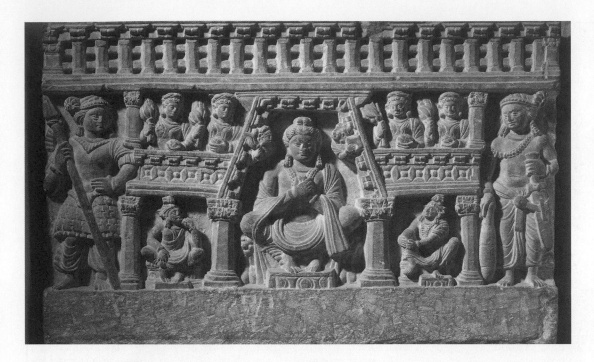

Bodhisattva Maitreya *This bas relief portrays a seated bodhisattva, a person within Mahayana Buddhism who possesses the capacity to achieve nirvana but delays doing so in order to help others cope with worldly suffering. The bodhisattva is flanked on either side by his assistants and women paying homage to him, all of whom are framed by columns capped with Corinthian-inspired capitals. This relief is representative of the spread and blending of iconography and ideology that took place under the Kushan dynasty.*

The monasteries also welcomed traders bringing incense and jewels to decorate bodhisattvas and stupas.

The Kushans also courted the local population by patronizing local religious cults. In Bactria, where they encountered the shrines of many different gods, the Kushan kings had their coins cast with images of various deities. They also donated generously to shrines of Zoroastrian, Vedic, and Buddhist cults. Around Kushan political centers, religious shrines mushroomed and sculptural works reached a high artistic level. Kushan kings also built royal dynastic shrines, beside which they placed statues of themselves as patrons of the local deities. Governors and generals followed their example of patronizing local religions, as did traders, artisans, and other city dwellers. Wealth flowed into religious institutions, especially Buddhist monasteries. Under the Kushans, Buddhist monasteries were cosmopolitan organizations where Greco-Roman, Indic, and steppe nomadic cultures blended together.

Although these diverse nomadic groups did not undermine local cultural traditions or the Hellenistic heritage, they introduced a powerful new ingredient: the culture of the warhorse. The proud Kushans carried their horse-riding skills into India and, in spite of the hot climate, continued to wear their trademark cone-shaped leather hats, knee-length robes, trousers, and boots. Since the time of the Vedic invaders (see Chapter 3), horses had been valued imports into the region, and under the Kushans they became the most prestigious status symbol of the ruling elite. At the same time, the Kushans began consuming exotic goods that arrived from as far east as China and as far west as the Mediterranean. Their rule also stabilized the trading routes through central Asia that stretched from the steppes in the east to the Parthian Empire in the west. This territory would become a major segment of the Silk Road.

Caravan Cities and the Incense Trade

A new kind of commercial hub emerged within and on the edge of the deserts of Southwest Asia: the **caravan city**. Established at strategic locations such as oases, these cities became locations where vast trading groups assembled before beginning their arduous journeys. Some caravan cities originating as Greek garrison towns became centers of Hellenistic culture, displaying such staples of the Greek city-state as public theaters. Even those founded by Arab traders had a Hellenistic tinge, as local traders often admired Greek culture and had frequent commercial interactions with the Mediterranean world. They wrote in Greek, sometimes speaking it in addition to their native tongues.

Caravan cities were among the most spectacular and resplendent urban centers of this era. They often emerged at the end points of major trade arteries. One such end point for traders was at the extreme southwestern tip of the Arabian Peninsula, in the area of present-day Yemen. The area was a wonder of its own, a vivid patch of green at the end of 1,200 miles of desert. Its prosperity was in part due to its role as a major gathering place—both for long-distance spice traders heading north through the Arabian Desert and for sailors whose ships traveled the Red and Arabian Seas and later crossed the Indian Ocean. (See again Map 6.2.)

The southern Arabian Peninsula had long been famous for its frankincense and myrrh, products that the Greeks and Romans used to make perfume and incense. They reached their buyers via an overland route sometimes called the Incense or Spice Road. The Sabaeans of southern Arabia became fabulously wealthy from these sales and from the Indian Ocean spice trade. The traders who transported the spices and fragrances to the Mediterranean were another Arabic-speaking people: the

Nabataeans, sheepherders who eked out a living in the Sinai Desert and the northwestern Arabian Peninsula.

Because the Greeks and later the Romans needed large quantities of incense to burn in worshipping their gods, the trade passing through this region was extremely lucrative. But the camel caravans had a difficult journey through the rock ravines stretching across desert regions. The Nabataean herders, however, had learned to cut cisterns out of solid stone to catch rainwater and to create cave shelters, and they profited by supplying water and food to the travelers. In one of these valleys the Nabataeans built their capital—a city called Petra, or "Rock City" ("rock" in Greek is *petros*)—which displayed abundant Greek influences. Many of the houses and shrines were cut directly out of the steep rock cliffs. Their colonnaded facades and tombs, constructed for common people as well as nobles, projected Hellenistic motifs. (See Primary Source: The Caravan City of Petra.) Most striking was a vast theater. The entire structure—the stage platform, orchestra, and forty-five rows of seats—was carved out of the sandstone terrain and could accommodate an audience of 6,000 to 10,000 people. Actors performed plays at first in Greek and later in Latin.

Petra's power and wealth lasted from the mid-second century BCE to the early second century CE. Greek persisted as the common language among Petran merchants seeking to maintain their trading ties. The caravan traders, the ruling elite of the rock city, controlled the supply of spices and fragrances from Arabia and India to the ever-expanding Roman Empire.

Nabataean traders based in Petra traveled throughout the eastern Mediterranean, erecting temples wherever they established trading communities.

The Western End of the Silk Road: Palmyra

Just as trading hubs proliferated in central Asia, similar commercial cities thrived in Southwest Asia as well. They soon overshadowed the older political or religious capitals. With Petra's decline during the Roman period, another settlement became the most important caravan city at the western end of the Silk Road: Palmyra. Rich citizens of Rome relied on the Palmyran traders to procure luxury goods for them, importing Chinese silks for women's clothing and incense for religious rituals, as well as gemstones, pearls, and many other precious items.

Administered by the chiefs of local tribes, Palmyra had considerable autonomy even under formal Roman control. Although the Palmyrans used a Semitic dialect in daily life, for state affairs and business they used Greek. Their merchants had learned Greek when the region came under Seleucid rule, and it remained useful when doing business with caravans from afar, long after the political influences of Hellenism had waned. Palmyran traders handled many kinds of textiles, including cotton from India and cashmere wool from Kashmir or the nearby central Asian highlands. The many silk textiles discovered at this site were products of Han China (see Chapter 7), indicating that the Silk Road had

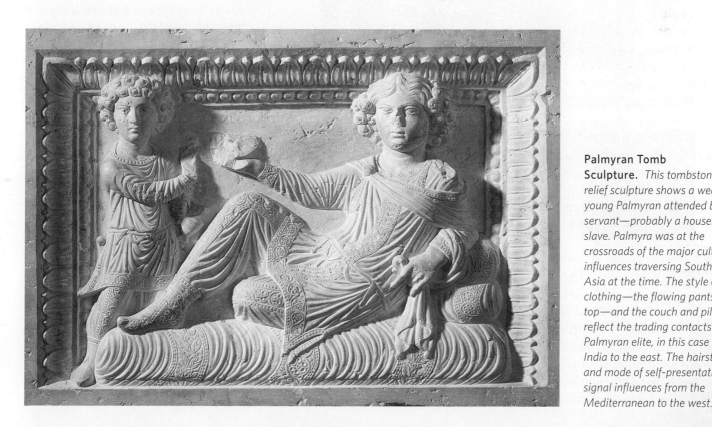

Palmyran Tomb Sculpture. *This tombstone relief sculpture shows a wealthy young Palmyran attended by a servant—probably a household slave. Palmyra was at the crossroads of the major cultural influences traversing Southwest Asia at the time. The style of the clothing—the flowing pants and top—and the couch and pillows reflect the trading contacts of the Palmyran elite, in this case with India to the east. The hairstyle and mode of self-presentation signal influences from the Mediterranean to the west.*

The Caravan City of Petra

Petra was a city cut out of the pink rock cliffs in the valley between the Dead Sea and the Red Sea. The Nabataeans built the city to host traders from west and east; from here, caravans headed out to trading centers in the Mediterranean and on the Iranian plateau. Petra's good fortune ran out under the Roman Empire when the silk trade favored another caravan city, Palmyra. Yet even today the rock structure of the city shining in the sun is an imposing sight, as this account by a modern traveler makes vividly clear.

When one descends into the valley from the surrounding heights towards the place where the river has cut for itself a passage between the dark-red rocks, one seems to be gazing at some large and fantastic excrescence—a piece of reddish-mauve raw flesh set between the gold of the desert and the green of the hills. It is a most extraordinary sight, which becomes even more extraordinary when the cavalcade slowly descends into the river valley, and the rocky walls of the ever-narrowing gorge tower up to the right and left, speckled with red, orange, mauve, grey, and green layers. Wild and beautiful they are, with their contrasts of light and shade; the light blinding, the shadows black. And there is seldom even anything to remind the visitor that this gorge served for centuries as a main road, trodden by camels, mules, and horses, and that along it rode Bedouin merchants who must have felt like ourselves its horror and its mystic fascination. Yet suddenly one may be confronted with the façade of a tomb-tower with dog-tooth design, or with an altar set high up on one of the vertical walls, bearing a greeting or prayer to some god, inscribed in the Nabataean tongue. Our caravan advanced slowly along the gorge, until an unexpected bend disclosed to us an apparition sparkling pinky-orange in the sun, which must once have been the front of a temple or tomb. Elegant columns joined by fascinating pediments and arches form the frames of the niches in which its statues stand. All this rose up before us dressed in a garb of classicism yet in a style new and unexpected even by those well acquainted with antiquity. It was as though the magnificent scenery of some Hellenistic theatre had appeared, . . . chiselled in the rock.

Petra. *This beautiful building, known as El-Khaznah, or the Treasury, is located at Petra. The wealth created by the region's long-distance trade is manifest in the magnificent buildings at the center of the city. Both the face of the building and its interior are cut out of the sandstone rock that forms the cliffs surrounding Petra.*

Source: M. Rostovtzeff, *Caravan Cities* (Oxford: Clarendon Press, 1932), pp. 42–43.

QUESTIONS FOR ANALYSIS

- What features in the description of Petra and the monuments in and around the city suggest that it hosted a variety of cultures with different art forms?
- Imagine being part of a caravan arriving in bustling Petra via the route described here. What feelings would the atmosphere evoke in you?

Silk Texts. *Before the invention of paper, silk was widely used as writing material because it was more mobile and durable than bamboo or wood for correspondence, maps, illustrations, and important texts included as funerary objects in the tombs of aristocrats. The Mawangdui silk texts shown here are from a Hunan tomb that was closed in 168 BCE and opened in 1973.*

reached the Mediterranean by the first century CE. While the local leaders retained some of the exquisite silks for themselves, most were headed to wealthier consumers in the Mediterranean. The Romans not only purchased silk cloth but also had it woven to order in eastern Mediterranean cities such as Beirut and Gaza. Silk yarns and dyes have also been found at Palmyra.

This lucrative trade enabled the Palmyrans to build a splendid marble city in the desert. A colonnade, theater, senate house, agora, and major temples formed the metropolitan area. The Palmyrans worshipped many deities, both local and Greek, but seemed most concerned about their own afterlife. Like Petra, Palmyra had a cemetery as big as its residential area, with marble sculptures on the tombs depicting city life. Many tombs showed the master or the master and his wife reclining on Greek-style couches, holding drinking goblets. The clothes on those statues appear more Iranian than Greek: robes with wide stripes and hems bearing exquisite designs. Sculptures of camel caravans and horses tell us that the deceased were caravan traders in this world who anticipated continuing their rewarding occupation in the afterlife.

Palmyra rapidly became a commercial powerhouse. The city not only provided supplies and financial services to passing caravans but also hosted self-contained trading communities—complexes of hostels, storage houses, offices, and temples.

Palmyra achieved its golden age at the same time that the Silk Road constituted the major artery for silk and other luxuries traveling from China to the eastern rim of the Indian Ocean. Some of the goods went across the Iranian plateau, reaching the Mediterranean via Syria's desert routes. Another artery went through Afghanistan, the Indus, and the western coast of India, then across the Indian Ocean to the Red Sea.

Reaching China along the Silk Road

China was the ultimate end and beginning point of the Silk Road. Its flourishing commerce owed much to the fact that Chinese silks were the most sought-after commodity in long-distance trade. As thousands of precious silk bales made their way to Indian, central Asian, and Mediterranean markets, silk became the ultimate prestige commodity of the regions' ruling classes. But the exchange between eastern and western portions of the Silk Road was always mediated by Persian, Xiongnu, Kushan, and other intermediaries at the great oases and trading centers that grew up in central Asia. Local communities took profitable advantage of the silk trade from China based on their increased knowledge and contacts.

THE SILK ECONOMY Not only was silk China's most valuable export, but it also served as a tool in diplomacy with the nomadic kingdoms on China's western frontiers and in funding the Chinese armies. The country's rulers used silk to pay off neighboring nomads and borderlanders, buying both horses and peaceful borders with the fabric. During the Zhou dynasty, it served as a precious medium of exchange and trade.

Silk has always been prized as a material for clothing; as a filament made by spinning the protein fibers extracted from the cocoons of silkworms, it is smooth yet strong. Whereas cloth spun from hemp, flax, and other fibers tends to be rough, silk looks and feels rich. Moreover, it is cool against the skin in hot summers and warm in the winter. Silk also has immense tensile strength, being useful for bows, lute strings, and fishing lines. Artisans even spun it into a tight fabric to make light body armor or light bags for transporting liquids (particularly useful for traders crossing arid expanses). Before the Chinese invented paper, silk was a popular writing material that was more durable than bamboo or wood. Brush writing on silk was the medium of choice for correspondence, maps, and illustrations, and important texts written on silk often joined other funerary objects in the tombs of aristocratic lords and wealthy individuals.

As the long-distance silk trade grew, commerce within China also expanded. Because of reforms in the Warring States period, economic life in China after 300 BCE centered increasingly on independent farmers producing commercial crops for the marketplaces along land routes as well as rivers, canals, and lakes. As this market economy grew, merchants organized themselves into influential family lineages and occupational guilds. Now power shifted away from agrarian elites and into the hands of urban financiers and traders. The latter benefited from the improvement in roads and waterways, which eased the transportation of grain, hides, horses, and silk from the villages to the new towns and cities. Bronze coins of various sizes and shapes (such as the spade-shaped money of several semiautonomous Warring States; see photo in Chapter 5), as well as cloth and silk used in barter, also spurred long-distance trade. By the second century BCE, wealthy merchants were ennobled as local magnates and wore clothing that marked their official status. As commerce further expanded, regional lords opened local customs offices along land routes and waterways to extract a share of the money and products for themselves.

THE EXPANSION OF TRADE Though China still had little intellectual interaction with the rest of Afro-Eurasia, its commercial exchanges skyrocketed due to the Silk Road trade. Silk was only the first of many Chinese commodities that reached the world beyond the Taklamakan Desert. China also became an export center for lacquer, hemp, and linen. From Sichuan came iron, steel, flint, hard stone, silver, and animals, while jade came from the northwest. At the same time, China was importing Mediterranean, Indian, and central Asian commodities.

Han imperial powers extended a wall westward designed to keep northern nomads out of China proper to protect the trade routes and set up garrisons at oases at the rim of Taklamakan Desert. Even so, the oasis towns could not compare to the caravan cities of Petra and Palmyra. Internal, interregional trade predominated, and it fed into the Silk Road through decentralized networks. Most cities in the landlocked north were administrative centers where farmers and traders gathered under the regional states' political and military protection. The larger cities had gates that closed between sunset and sunrise; during the night, mounted soldiers patrolled the streets. Newer towns along the southeastern seacoast still looked upriver to trade with inland agrarian communities, which also produced silk for export. Facilitating oceanic trade did become more of a concern for the state during this period. For example, merchant ships now enjoyed the protection of military boats able to cover 75 miles in a day and carry fifty soldiers and supplies for a three-month voyage. It would not be until later, during the sixth and seventh centuries CE, that China would become the site of massive trading centers.

The Spread of Buddhism along the Trade Routes

Traders were not the only individuals who traversed Afro-Eurasian trade arteries. Monks also traveled these roads to spread the word of new religions. While Christians would later take advantage of these trade routes to spread their faith (see Chapter 8), Buddhism was the chief expansionist faith in this period. The Buddha was no longer just a sage departed to the state of nirvana; he was also a god whom people could worship like any Greek deity.

Under Kushan patronage during the first centuries CE, Buddhism reached out from India to China and central Asia, following the Silk Road. Monks from the Kushan Empire accompanied traders to Luoyang, the eastern capital of the Han Empire. There they translated Buddhist texts into Chinese and other languages, aided by Chinese converts who were also traders. Nevertheless, Buddhist ideas took several centuries to gain acceptance and only after a new wave of nomadic migrations.

Buddhism fared less well when it followed the commercial arteries westward. Although Buddhists did gain some followers in the Parthian Empire, the religion never became established on the Iranian plateau and made no further headway toward the Mediterranean. The main barrier was Zoroastrianism, which had been a state religion in the Persian Empire during the fifth and fourth centuries BCE (see Chapter 4); by the time Buddhism began to spread, Zoroastrianism had long been established in Iran. Iranian Hellenism had done little to weaken the power of Zoroastrianism, whose adherents formed city-based religious communities affiliated primarily with traders. These Zoroastrian traders continued to adhere to their own faith while traveling along the Silk Road and therefore did nothing to help Buddhism spread westward.

TAKING TO THE SEAS: COMMERCE ON THE RED SEA AND INDIAN OCEAN

Using new navigational techniques and larger ships, seafarers eventually expanded the transport of Silk Road commodities via the Red Sea and the Indian Ocean. Although land routes were the tried-and-true avenues for migrants, traders, and wayfarers, they carried only what could be borne on the backs of humans and animals. Travel on them was slow, and they were vulnerable to marauders. With time, some risk takers found ways of traversing waterways—eventually on an unprecedented scale and with an ease unimaginable to earlier merchants. These risk takers were Arabs, from the commercial middle ground of the Afro-Eurasian trading system.

Arab traders had long carried such spices as frankincense and myrrh to the Egyptians, who used them in religious and funerary rites, and later to the Greeks and Romans. Metals such as copper, tin, and iron passed along overland routes from Anatolia, as did gold, silver, and chlorite from the Iranian plateau. Ivory and other goods from the northern part of India passed through Taxila (the capital of Gandhara) and the Hindu Kush Mountains into Persia as early as the sixth century BCE. Following the expansion of the Hellenistic world, however, ships increasingly conducted long-distance trade. They sailed down the Red Sea and across the Indian Ocean as they carried goods between the tip of the Arabian Peninsula and the ports of the Indian landmass.

Arab seafarers led the way into the Indian Ocean, forging links that joined East Africa, the eastern Mediterranean, and the Arabian Peninsula with India, Southeast Asia, and East Asia. Such voyages involved longer stays at sea and were far more dangerous than sailing in the Mediterranean. Yet by the first century CE, Arab and Indian sailors were transporting Chinese silks, central Asian furs, and fragrances from Himalayan trees across the Indian Ocean. The city of Alexandria in Egypt soon emerged as a key transit point between the Mediterranean Sea and the Indian Ocean. Boats carried Mediterranean exports of olives and olive oil, wine, drinking vessels, glassware, linen and wool textiles, and red coral up the Nile, stopping at Koptos and other port cities, from which camel caravans took the goods to the Red Sea ports of Myos Hormos and Berenice. For centuries, Mediterranean merchants had considered the Arabian Peninsula to be the end of the Spice Road. But after Alexander's expedition and the establishment of colonies between Egypt and Afghanistan, they began to value the wealth and opportunities that lay along the shores of the Indian Ocean.

Arab sailors who ventured into the Indian Ocean benefited from new navigational techniques, especially celestial bearings (using the position of the stars to determine the position of the ship and the direction to sail). They used large ships called *dhows*, whose triangular sails were rigged to easily capture the wind; these forerunners of modern cargo vessels were capable of long hauls in rough waters. Beginning about 120 BCE, mariners came to understand the seasonal rain-filled monsoon winds, which blow from the southwest between October and April and then from the northeast between April and October—knowledge that propelled the maritime trade connecting the Mediterranean with the Indian Ocean.

Mariners accumulated the new sailing knowledge in books—each called a ***periplus*** ("sailing around")—in which sea captains recorded the landing spots and ports between their destinations, as well as their precious cargoes. By now, the revolution in navigational techniques and knowledge had dramatically reduced the cost of long-distance shipping and multiplied the ports of call around large bodies of water. Some historians have argued that there were now two Silk Roads: one by land and one by sea.

CONCLUSION

Alexander's conquests were awesome in their scale and brilliant in their execution. But his empire was as transitory as it was huge. Though it crumbled upon his death, it had effects more profound than those of any military or political regime that preceded it. Alexander's armies ushered in an age of thinking and practices that transformed Greek achievements into a common culture—Hellenism—whose influences, both direct and indirect, touched far-flung societies for centuries thereafter.

Hellenism offered a common language, both literally and figuratively, that linked culture, institutions, and trade. However, many Greek-speaking peoples and their descendants in parts of Southwest and central Asia integrated local cultural practices with their own ways, creating diverse and rich cultures. Thus, the influences of culture flowed both ways. The economic story is equally complex. In many respects, Alexander and his successors followed pathways established by previous kingdoms and empires. If anything, Alexander's successors helped strengthen and expand the existing trade routes and centers of commercial activity, which ultimately led to the creation of the Silk Road.

Although the effects of this Hellenistic age lasted longer than most cultural systems and had a wider appeal than previous philosophical and spiritual ideas, they did not sweep away everything before them. Some, like the Jewish people of Judea, fought against Hellenism with all their might. Others, like the Romans and Carthaginians, took from the new common culture what they liked and discarded the rest.

Of all those exposed to Hellenistic thinking, the South Asian peoples produced the most varied responses because they represented a multitude of cultures. The immediate successor to Alexander's military was the Mauryan Empire, which established its dominion over almost all of South Asia and even some of central Asia for close to a century and a half. Once Mauryan control receded, South Asia was opened up more decisively than before to currents moving swiftly across Afro-Eurasia, including the institutions and cultures of steppe nomads, seafarers, and Hellenists. The most telling South Asian responses occurred in the realm of spiritual and ethical norms, where Buddhist doctrines evolved toward a full-fledged world religious system.

Greater political integration helped fashion highways for commerce and enabled the spread of Buddhism. Nomads, like the Kushans, left their steppe lands and exchanged wares across great distances. As they found greater opportunities for business, their trade routes shifted farther south, radiating out of the oases of central Asia. Eventually, merchants, rather than the trading nomads, seized the opportunities provided by new technologies, especially in sailing and navigation, and by thriving caravan cities. Commercial exchanges along the Silk Road and new sea-lanes connected ports and caravan cities across distant parts of Afro-Eurasia. These commercial arteries created new social classes, produced new urban settings, supported powerful new polities, and transported Hellenism and Buddhism well beyond their points of origin.

After You Read This Chapter

Go to INQUIZITIVE to see what you know & learn what you've missed.

FOCUS ON: *Forces that Unify Afro-Eurasia*

The Mediterranean World

- The spread of Hellenism around the Mediterranean via Alexander's conquests leads to a common language, cosmopolitan cities, new types of philosophy and religion, plantation slavery, and money-based economies.

Central and South Asia

- Alexander's withdrawal from the Indus Valley leads to the creation of the Mauryan Empire, which integrates the northern half of India.

- The Seleucid and Bactrian kingdoms further solidify the spread of Hellenism into central Asia.

Transformation of Buddhism

- The combined influences of Hellenism, nomadism, and Indian Ocean seafaring transform Buddhism into a world religion.

Formation of the Silk Road

- Nomadic warriors from central Asia complete the final links of the overland Silk Road, strengthening the ties that joined peoples across Afro-Eurasia.

- Overland traders carry spices, transport precious metals, and convey Buddhist thought along the Silk Road into China.

- Seafaring traders use new navigation techniques and larger ships called *dhows* to expand the transport of Silk Road commodities to the Mediterranean world via the Indian Ocean.

CHRONOLOGY

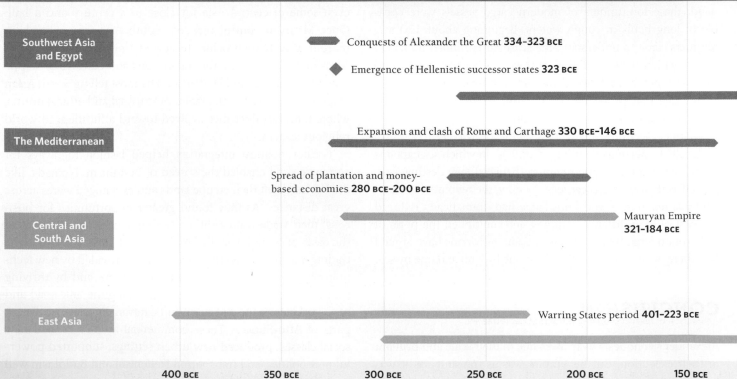

Southwest Asia and Egypt

Conquests of Alexander the Great **334–323 BCE**

Emergence of Hellenistic successor states **323 BCE**

The Mediterranean

Expansion and clash of Rome and Carthage **330 BCE–146 BCE**

Spread of plantation and money-based economies **280 BCE–200 BCE**

Central and South Asia

Mauryan Empire **321–184 BCE**

East Asia

Warring States period **401–223 BCE**

| 400 BCE | 350 BCE | 300 BCE | 250 BCE | 200 BCE | 150 BCE |

1. **Describe** Hellenism, and **explain** its influence on various Afro-Eurasian societies. What aspects of Hellenistic culture held broad appeal for diverse groups?

2. **Analyze** the impact of Alexander's conquest on political structures in central and South Asia. **Explain** how his military pursuits brought together diverse worlds.

3. **Compare and contrast** Judean, Roman, and Carthaginian responses to Hellenistic influences. How receptive was each society to Greek cultural influence?

4. **Analyze** the ways in which the Mauryan Empire brought continuity and change to South Asia. What role did *dhamma* play in Aśoka's uniting of South Asia?

5. **Explain** how South Asia became a melting pot for the intellectual, political, and economic currents sweeping across Afro-Eurasia at this time. How did this development affect Buddhist doctrine?

6. **Identify** the areas into which Buddhism spread, and **assess** the role of interregional contacts in promoting its expansion across a variety of cultures.

7. **Explore** the extent to which early long-distance trade routes, notably the Silk Road, connected certain societies during this period. **Identify** the routes and the societies involved. What role did caravan cities and, later, the Kushans play in the development of these routes?

8. **Explain** how art, architecture, and other forms of material culture in Afro-Eurasian societies reflected broader patterns of cultural, political, and economic integration during this period.

Parthian State **240 BCE–224 CE**

Kushan State **first–third centuries**

Transformation of Buddhism begins **first century**

Growth of market economy **third–first centuries** BCE

| 100 BCE | 50 BCE | 1 CE | 50 CE | 100 CE | 150 CE | 200 CE | 250 CE |

Before You Read This Chapter

Go to
INQUIZITIVE
to see what you
know & learn
what you've
missed.

GLOBAL STORYLINES

- Flourishing at roughly the same times, Han China and the Roman Empire become powerful and enduring "globalizing empires."
- The Han dynasty, building on Qin foundations, establishes a bureaucratic imperial model and social order in East Asia.
- The Roman Empire becomes a Mediterranean superpower exerting far-reaching political, legal, economic, and cultural influence.

CHAPTER OUTLINE

Han Dynasty China and Imperial Rome, 300 BCE–300 CE

FOCUS QUESTIONS

- What features of the Han dynasty and the Roman Empire made them globalizing empires?

- What political, social, economic, and cultural elements characterized the development of the Han dynasty from its beginnings through the third century CE?

- What were the steps in the process of Rome transitioning from a minor city-state to a dominating Mediterranean power?

- How were Han China and imperial Rome similar and different in terms of political authority, economic activity, cultural developments, and military expansion?

In third-century BCE China, the Eastern Zhou state of Qin absorbed the remaining Warring States (see Chapter 5) and set the stage for the epic Han dynasty. The chief minister of the Qin state, Li Si, urged his king to dispense with niceties and seize opportunities: a man who aimed at great achievements must exploit the advantages offered to him. By combining his fearsome armies and his own personal virtues, the king could sweep away his rivals as if dusting ashes from a kitchen hearth—he could eliminate them all. In this way he could establish a truly imperial rule and unify the entire world. "This is the one moment in ten thousand ages," Li Si whispered. The king listened carefully. He followed the advice. He laid the foundations for a mighty empire.

The Qin Empire was an important transitional empire, but it was not meant to endure, and it collapsed in 207 BCE. The Han Empire took its place, becoming one of the most successful dynasties in Chinese history. Following the Qin model, the Han defeated other regional groups and established the first long-lasting Chinese empire. Subjects of the Han basked in a society whose landholding elites, free farmers, trained artisans, itinerant traders, and urban merchants were building a society that, unlike the allegedly cruel Qin state, would emulate the statecraft ideals of antiquity.

At the other end of Afro-Eurasia, another great state, imperial Rome, also met its rivals in war, emerged victorious, and consolidated its power into a vast empire. The Romans achieved this feat by using violent force on a scale hitherto unseen in their part of the globe. The result was a state of huge size, astonishingly unified and stable. Living in the Roman Empire in the mid-70s CE, Pliny the Elder, a man of middle rank, wrote glowingly about the unity of the imperial state. In his eyes, all the benefits that flowed from its extensive reach derived from the boundless greatness of a peace that joined diverse peoples under one benevolent emperor.

The Han and the Roman states were not novel in that they found new ways to plow resources into big armies and civil bureaucracies or in the reasons that rulers gave to justify their rulership. Instead, they were novel in being the first truly **globalizing empires**, eclipsing the other states that we have studied in terms of geographical size, population size, and—especially—their efforts to incorporate their neighbors and those they conquered as subjects of the same empire. They laid out the political and cultural boundaries of regions that we now recognize as "China" and "Christendom," although those boundaries also included many non-Christians for Rome and hordes of non-Chinese for the Han Empire. Nowadays, the boundaries of both bear remarkable resemblances to those defined by these two empires at their peak. In addition, these states transcended the limits of previous territorial kingdoms and the first empires by deploying resources and reasons of state in new ways. They concentrated military power in professionalized military elites that owed allegiance above all to the state, not to its ruler. They modernized tax collecting to support large-scale killing machines—that is, armies. They wrote laws and codes for their subjects. And they promoted the idea that the state should support schooling, the arts, architecture, and a learned society as ways to bring peace and prosperity. Ever since, we have come to associate the ideal of empire with these two founders at either end of Afro-Eurasia.

Just as we see these empires as models for world history, we must understand how they were built—for they did not emerge as the inevitable consequences of destiny. They were crafted of a delicate mixture of coercion, coaxing, and convincing—and not just to prove that empires were exalted and enjoyed benefits that faraway neighbors did not. They actually had to deliver on these promises in order to endure. These were no short-lasting conquerings, like Alexander the Great's. They had the institutional muscle to outlive any particular ruler.

HAN CHINA AND IMPERIAL ROME: HOW GLOBALIZING EMPIRES WERE BUILT

Afro-Eurasia had seen empires come and go, emerging out of territorial kingdoms to exercise their power over neighboring states as clients, often demanding tribute in return for protection. The Romans and the Han took imperial expansion to the next level: not content to exercise influence over neighbors, they wanted to incorporate them fully into their realm. What distinguished these two from their predecessors was their commitment to integrating conquered neighbors and rivals into their worlds—by extending laws, offering systems of representation, exporting belief systems, colonizing lands, and promoting trade within and beyond the empires. In effect, subject peoples became members of empires, not just the vanquished. Those who resisted not only waved away the benefits of living under an imperial mantle but also became the targets of awesome and relentless armies.

Empire and Cultural Identity

The existence of these two vast imperial states meant that at least one out of every two human beings in Afro-Eurasia now fell directly under the control of China or Rome, thus shaping the destiny and identity of the countless millions living under their imperial umbrellas.

To be "Han Chinese" meant that elites shared a common written language based on the Confucian classics, which qualified them for public office. It also meant that commoners from all walks of life shared the elites' belief system based on ancestor worship, ritual practices stressing appropriate decorum and dress for each social level, and a view that the Han as an agrarian-based empire was a small-scale model of the entire cosmos. Those who lived beyond the realm of the Han were considered uncivilized.

What it meant to be "Roman" changed over time as Rome's imperial reach expanded. In the fifth century BCE, being Roman meant being a citizen of the city of Rome, speaking Latin (the regional language of central Italy), and eating and dressing like Latin-speaking people. By the late second century BCE, however, the concept of citizenship expanded to include not only citizens of the city but also anyone who had formal membership in the larger territorial state that the Romans were building. By the beginning of the third century CE, even this bigger view was no longer true. Now being Roman meant simply being a subject of the Roman emperors. This identity became so deeply rooted that when the western parts of the empire disintegrated two centuries later, the inhabitants of the surviving eastern parts—who had no connection with Rome, did not speak Latin, and did not dress or eat like the original Romans—still considered themselves "Romans" in this broader sense.

Patterns of Imperial Expansion

Despite their similarities, the empires reflected different patterns of development, different types of public servants, and different ideals for the best kind of government. For example, whereas the civilian magistrate and the bureaucrat were typical of the Han Empire, the citizen, the soldier, and the military governor stood for the Roman Empire. In China, dynastic empires fashioned themselves according to the models of past empires. The Chinese treated imperial culture as an ideal descended from the past that had to be emulated in the present. By contrast, Rome began as a collectively ruled city-state and pursued a pragmatic road to domination of its world as if creating something anew. Only by a long, sometimes violent process of trial and error did the Romans achieve a political system of one-man rule by emperors. Nonetheless, they, like the Chinese, were strongly traditional. They also idealized their ancestors. But what characterized Roman expansion and empire building was a process of continual experimentation, innovation, and adaptation.

Both new empires united huge landmasses and extraordinarily diverse populations. While both China and Rome participated in Silk Road exchange, both economies were primarily agrarian based; yet in China, free peasants worked the land, while huge enslaved populations worked the fields of the Roman Empire. At its height, the scale of the Han dynasty was unprecedented for East Asia. A land survey by the imperial government in 2 CE revealed a registered population of 12,233,062 households, or around 58 million people. These households paid taxes, provided military recruits, and supplied laborers for public works. At this time, the Han Empire covered some 3 million square miles in China proper and, for a while, another 1 million square miles in central Asia. The Roman Empire governed an area and a population as great as those of Han China.

Both empires left indelible legacies; following their collapses, both survived as models. Successor states in the Mediterranean sought to become the Second Rome, and after the Han dynasty fell, the Chinese people always identified themselves and their language simply as "Han." Both empires raised life to a new level of bureaucratic and military complexity and offered a common identity on a grander scale than ever before. It was a vision that would never be lost.

THE HAN DYNASTY (206 BCE–220 CE)

The Han dynasty oversaw an unprecedented period of peace and prosperity. Although exponents of the Han dynasty boasted of the regime's imperial uniqueness, in reality it owed much to its predecessor, the Qin state. Indeed, the Qin contributed vital elements of political unity and economic growth to its more powerful successor regime. (See Map 7.1.) Together, the Qin and Han created the political, social, economic, and cultural foundations that would characterize imperial China thereafter.

A Crucial Forerunner: The Qin Dynasty (221–207 BCE)

Although it lasted only fourteen years, the Qin dynasty integrated much of China and made important administrative and economic innovations. The Qin were but one of many militaristic regimes during the Warring States period, though in many ways it was the most warlike of them. What enabled the Qin to prevail over rivals was not its taste for violence, but a decision to expand southwestward from its base in the Wei valley into the Sichuan region, a vast area twice the size of its home territory and remarkable for rich mineral resources and fertile soils. There, in the fourth century, a full century before the Qin became all-powerful, its leaders used a dynamic merchant class and an expanding silk trade to spur economic growth. Its myriad public works turned the region into the rice bowl of China. By the time that King Zheng ascended the throne at the age of fourteen in 247 BCE, the Qin were prepared to defeat the remaining Warring States and unify an empire that covered roughly two-thirds of modern China. It did so between 230 and 221 BCE, ending one of the most violent periods in Chinese history.

With the help of able ministers and generals and a large conscripted army composed mainly of peasant farmers, as well as a system of taxation that financed all-out war, King Zheng assumed the mandate of heaven from the Zhou and unified the states into a centralized empire. Having accomplished this feat, he declared himself **Shi Huangdi**, or "First August Emperor," in 221 BCE (much as Rome's first emperor also called himself Augustus). In this instance, Zheng harkened back to China's mythical emperors of great antiquity. He took the title of emperor (*di*), a term that had meant "ancestral ruler" in Shang and Zhou, to exalt his dynasty over that of the Zhou and the rulers of the Warring States, all of whom had called themselves kings (*wang*). To further consolidate his power, he forced the defeated rulers and their families to move to Xianyang, the Qin

MAP 7.1 | East Asia, 206 BCE–220 CE

Both the Qin and the Han dynasties consolidated much of East Asia into one large regional empire.

- According to the map, what physical features imposed a limit to this territorial expansion?
- Why was the defensive wall so long, and why was it placed facing north?
- What impact did the pastoral Xiongnu have on each empire's effort to consolidate a large territorial state?
- According to your reading, why did the Han expand their influence farther west than the Qin?

capital—where, under his watchful eye, they would be unable to gather rebel armies.

ADMINISTRATION AND CONTROL The First August Emperor parceled out the territory of his massive state into thirty-six provinces, or **commanderies** (*jun*), which he subdivided into counties (*xian*). Each commandery had a civilian and a military governor answering to an imperial inspector. These reforms provided China with a centralized bureaucracy and a hereditary emperor that later dynasties, including the Han, inherited. Crucial to this administrative strategy was the requirement that regional and local officials answer directly to the emperor, and he could dismiss them at will. Moreover, he made sure that civilian governors did not serve in their home areas—a calculated move that prevented them from building up power for themselves.

By providing the basis for taxation and conscription, the new system ensured that all able-bodied males would serve in the army and work on public projects, building border walls, imperial roads, canals, and huge palaces in the capital. These practices imposed a social order that had been lacking. To further unify the varied systems surviving from the Warring States period, the Qin emperor established standard weights and measures as well as a standard currency. The Qin extended China's boundaries in the northeast to the Korean Peninsula, in the south to present-day Vietnam, and in the west into central Asia. Li Si subscribed to the Warring States principles of Legalism. This philosophy valued written law codes, administrative regulations, and inflexible punishments more highly than rituals and ethics (which the Confucians emphasized) or spontaneity and the natural order (which the Daoists stressed). Determined to bring order to a turbulent world, Li Si made sure that strict laws and regulations, as well as harsh punishments, were applied to everyone regardless of rank or wealth. Punishments included beheading, mutilation by cutting off a person's nose or foot, tattooing, shaving off a person's beard or hair, hard labor, and loss of office and rank. After registering people in groups of five and ten, officials made them all responsible for one another—and subject to punishment for any crime that any one of them might commit.

The Qin also improved communications systems. They constructed roads radiating out from their capital to all parts of the empire. These immense thoroughfares had lanes to accommodate vehicles, pedestrians, animals, and soldiers. Their thick embankments of soil bristled with reinforcing metal poles and pine trees to check erosion. Officials required vehicles to have a standard axle length so that all wheels would fit in the same dirt ruts. Still, the dust and stench were nearly unbearable as travelers journeyed along the hundreds of miles from local towns and villages to the capital and back. After several days of travel, merchants would be lucky if their wares and goods survived undamaged.

Intellectual Censorship. *This seventeenth-century painting depicts the infamous "Burning of the Books and Burying of the Scholars" edict. As luck would have it, even the state-approved texts were destroyed a mere six years later, during the fall of the dynasty and sack of the capital.*

Just as crucial was the Qin effort to standardize writing. Banning regional variants in written characters, the Qin required scribes and ministers throughout the empire to adopt the "small seal script," a revised form of writing that resembled the pictographic forms carved on ancient Shang oracle bones (see Chapter 3). Its simpler characters evolved into the less complicated style of bureaucratic writing known as "clerical script" that was prominent during the Han dynasty.

The Qin then used this standard type of writing to disseminate their vision of the state. Standardization also eliminated troublesome ideas that might disturb the new imperial unity. In 213 BCE, a Qin decree ordered officials to confiscate and burn all books in private possession, except for technical works on medicine, divination, and agriculture. In addition, the court prosecuted teachers who used outlawed classical books, including some Confucian works that troublemakers could cite to criticize the Qin regime. Education and learning were now under the exclusive control of state officials. (See Primary Source: A Qin Legal Document: Memorial on the Burning of Books.)

ECONOMIC AND SOCIAL CHANGES The agrarian empire of the Qin yielded wealth that the state could tax, and increased tax revenues meant more resources for imposing order. The government issued rules on working the fields, taxed farming

Qin Coin. *After centuries of distinctive regional currencies, the Qin created this standardized bronze coin as part of its general unification policy.*

Small Seal Script. *Under the Qin, the "large seal" script of the Zhou dynasty was unified and simplified to produce a style of calligraphy still used today.*

PRIMARY SOURCE

A Qin Legal Document: Memorial on the Burning of Books

When the first Qin emperor came to power, his minister, Li Si, devised a policy to enhance state power through a unified political ideology. Any traditions of learning that differed from the Qin orthodoxy were targets for elimination. The most serious threat to Qin power came from the Five Classics (said to have been compiled by Confucius), which stressed moral rectitude, personal character, and political responsibility while holding office. Such texts were an affront to imperial power, Li thought, so he called for their destruction and the execution of scholars who defended them in public.

In earlier times the empire disintegrated and fell into disorder, and no one was capable of unifying it. Thereupon the various feudal lords rose to power. In their discourses they all praised the past in order to disparage the present and embellished empty words to confuse the truth. Everyone cherished his own favorite school of learning and criticized what had been instituted by the authorities. But at present Your Majesty possesses a unified empire, has regulated the distinctions of black and white, and has firmly established for yourself a position of sole supremacy. And yet these independent schools, joining with each other, criticize the codes of laws and instructions. Hearing of the promulgation of a decree, they criticize it, each from the standpoint of his own school. At home they disapprove of it in their hearts; going out they criticize it in the thoroughfare. They seek a reputation by discrediting their sovereign; they appear superior by expressing contrary views, and they lead the lowly multitude in the spreading of slander. If such license is not prohibited, the sovereign power will decline above and partisan factions will form below. It would be well to prohibit this.

Your servant suggests that all books in the imperial archives, save the memoirs of Qin, be burned. All persons in the empire, except members of the Academy of Learned Scholars, in possession of the *Classic of Odes, the Classic of Documents*, and discourses of the hundred philosophers should take them to the local governors and have them indiscriminately burned. Those who dare to talk to each other about the *Odes* and *Documents* should be executed and their bodies exposed in the marketplace. Anyone referring to the past to criticize the present should, together with all members of his family, be put to death. Officials who fail to report cases that have come under their attention are equally guilty. After thirty days from the time of issuing the decree, those who have not destroyed their books are to be branded and sent to build the Great Wall. Books not to be destroyed will be those on medicine and pharmacy, divination by the turtle and milfoil, and agriculture and arboriculture. People wishing to pursue learning should take the officials as their teachers.

QUESTIONS FOR ANALYSIS

- According to Li Si, how would the burning of classic texts help the Qin emperor keep "a unified empire" and "sole supremacy"?
- What types of books were still acceptable? Why would the first Qin emperor want to keep these practical works alive?

Source: *Sources of Chinese Tradition*, vol. 1, *From Earliest Times to 1600*, compiled by William Theodore de Bary and Irene Bloom, 2nd ed. (New York: Columbia University Press, 1999), pp. 209–10.

households, and conscripted laborers to build irrigation systems and canals so that even more land could come under cultivation. Unlike the Greek city-states and the Roman Empire, which relied on slave labor for many large-scale tasks in city and countryside, the Qin and the Han dynasties relied much more on free farmers and conscripted their able-bodied sons into their huge armies. Free to work their own land, and paying only a small portion of their crops in taxes, peasant families were the economic bedrock of the Chinese empire.

Agricultural surpluses fueled long-distance commerce—the source of even more wealth and revenues. A class of merchants turned China's cities into dynamic regional market centers. Merchants peddled foodstuffs as well as weapons, metals, horses, dogs, hides, furs, silk, and salt—all produced in different regions and transported on the improved road system. Taxed both in transit and in the market at a higher rate than foodstuffs, these trade goods yielded even more revenue for the imperial government.

NOMADS AND THE QIN ALONG THE NORTHERN FRONTIER Both the Qin dynasty and, later, the Han dynasty grappled with the need to expand and defend their borders. After the Qin united the Warring States into an empire, it started looking beyond to the north and west, where it encountered nomadic warrior peoples—especially the proud Xiongnu discussed in Chapter 5, who dominated the steppes to the north and west of China.

Relations between nomadic peoples and the settled Chinese teetered in a precarious balance until 215 BCE, when the Qin Empire pushed north into the middle of the Yellow River basin, seizing pasturelands from the Xiongnu and opening the region up for settlement. Qin officials built roads into these areas and employed conscripts and criminals to create a massive defensive wall, forerunner of the "Great Wall" constructed more than a millennium later. In 211 BCE, the Qin settled 30,000 colonists in the steppe lands of Inner Eurasia.

THE QIN DEBACLE Despite its military power, the Qin dynasty collapsed quickly. Its rule weighed heavily on taxpayers, and its constant warfare consumed massive tax revenues and huge numbers of laborers. When desperate conscripted workers mutinied in 209 BCE, they found allies in descendants of Warring States nobles, local military leaders, and influential merchants. The rebels swept up thousands of supporters with their call to arms against the "tyrannical" Qin. Shortly after the First Emperor died in 210 BCE, even the educated elite joined former lords and regional vassals in revolt. The second Qin emperor committed suicide early in 207 BCE, and his weak successor surrendered to the leader of the Han forces later that year. The resurgent Xiongnu confederacy also reconquered their old pasturelands as the Qin dynasty fell.

The civil war that followed opened the way for the formation of the Western Han dynasty. An unheralded commoner and former policeman named Liu Bang (r. 206–195 BCE) declared himself prince of his home area of Pei before he was exiled to the state of Han by a powerful adversary. In 202 BCE, Liu proclaimed himself the first Han dynasty emperor. Emphasizing his peasant origins, Liu demonstrated his initial disdain for intellectuals by urinating into the hat of a court scholar. But he quickly learned that power would be better served through good manners. Confucian scholars loyal to the Han soon were busy justifying Liu Bang's victory by depicting his Qin predecessors as cruel dynasts and ruthless despots. The scholar Jia Yi (c. 200–168 BCE) rhetorically claimed that the Qin fell "because the ruler lacked moral values." (See Primary Source: Jia Yi on "The Faults of the Qin.") Under the cover of receiving the mandate of heaven, the Han portrayed the Qin as evil; yet at the same time they adopted the Qin's bureaucratic system. In reality—as we can see from a cache of pre-imperial Qin penal codes and administrative ordinances, which were written on some 1,000 bamboo slips for a single tomb circa 230 BCE—Qin laws originally were no crueler than those of the Han until the Confucian moralization of legal judgments (discussed shortly) took shape much later in the Han dynasty.

Beginnings of the Han Dynasty

The Han dynasty, which lasted 400 years, became China's formative empire. (See Map 7.2.) Its armies swelled with some

Qin Archer and Crossbow. *This kneeling archer in the bottom photo was discovered in the tomb of the First Emperor. Notice his breastplate. The wooden bow he was holding has disintegrated, but a replica appears in the top photo. The bronze arrowhead and trigger mechanism in this reproduction were found with the terra-cotta army.*

50,000 crossbowmen who brandished mass-produced weapons made from bronze and iron. Armed with the crossbow, foot soldiers and mounted archers extended Han imperial lands in all directions. Following the Qin practice, the Han also relied on a huge conscripted labor force for special projects such as building canals, roads, and defensive walls.

The first part of the Han dynastic cycle, later known as the Western (or Former) Han dynasty (206 BCE–9 CE), brought economic prosperity and the expansion of empire. This was especially the case under **Emperor Wu**, or Wudi, who presided over one of the longest and most eventful reigns in Chinese history (r. 140–87 BCE). Although he was known as the "Martial Emperor" because of the state's many military campaigns, Emperor Wu rarely inspected his military units and never led them in battle. As a ruler, he endeavored to cultivate the Daoist principle of *wuwei* ("letting things be"—a policy of laissez-faire), striving to remain aloof from day-to-day activities and permitting the empire to function on its own as if it did not require intervention. Still, he used a stringent penal code to eliminate powerful officials who got in his way. In a single year, his court

PRIMARY SOURCE

Jia Yi on "The Faults of the Qin"

After the Qin dynasty disintegrated, Confucians sought to explain the fall of so strong a military power that had unified China just fourteen years before. Jia Yi tied the dynasty's collapse to its autocratic rule and mean-spirited policies. Rather than blame the imperial system itself, Jia blamed the immorality of the Qin penal code and the first Qin emperor's totalitarian policies for his loss of the mandate of heaven. If the Qin had ruled according to Confucian teachings and ritual guidelines, Jia contended, the dynasty would have endured.

[Later] when the First Emperor ascended [the throne] he flourished and furthered the accomplishments of the six generations before him. Brandishing his long whip, he drove the world before him; destroying the feudal lords, he swallowed up the domains of the two Zhou dynasties. He reached the pinnacle of power and ordered all in the Six Directions, whipping the rest of the world into submission and thus spreading his might through the Four Seas. . . . He then abolished the ways of ancient sage kings and put to the torch the writings of the Hundred Schools in an attempt to keep the people in ignorance. He demolished the walls of major cities and put to death men of fame and talent, collected all the arms of the realm at Xianyang and had the spears and arrowheads melted down to form twelve huge statues in human form—all with the aim of weakening his people. Then he . . . posted capable generals and expert bowmen at important passes and placed trusted officials and well-trained soldiers in strategic array to challenge all who passed. With the empire thus pacified, the First Emperor believed that, with the capital secure within the pass and prosperous cities stretching for ten thousand *li*, he had indeed created an imperial structure to be enjoyed by his royal descendants for ten thousand generations to come.

Even after the death of the First Emperor, his reputation continued to sway the people. Chen She was a man who grew up in humble circumstances in a hut with broken pots for windows and ropes as door hinges and was a mere hired field hand and roving conscript of mediocre talent. He could neither equal the worth of Confucius and Mozi nor match the wealth of Tao Zhu or Yi Dun, yet, even stumbling as he did amidst the ranks of common soldiers and shuffling through the fields, he called forth a tired motley crowd and a mob of several hundred to turn upon the Qin. Cutting down trees to make weapons, and hoisting their flags on garden poles, they had the whole world come to them like gathering clouds, with people bringing their own food and following them like shadows. These men of courage from the East rose together, and in the end they defeated and extinguished the House of Qin.

. . . Qin, from a tiny base, had become a great power, ruling the land and receiving homage from all quarters for a hundred-odd years. Yet after they had unified the land and secured themselves within the pass, a single common rustic could nevertheless challenge this empire and cause its ancestral temples to topple and its ruler to die at the hand of others, a laughingstock in the eyes of all. Why? Because the ruler lacked humaneness and rightness; because preserving power differs fundamentally from seizing power.

QUESTIONS FOR ANALYSIS

- According to the reading, what specific steps did the Qin emperor take that were mean-spirited and autocratic?
- What details in this reading help you to imagine the peasant rebellion? What did the peasants use for weapons? What was their typical dwelling like?
- Why would Jia Yi want to preserve imperial government after the Qin had been so cruel?

Source: Sources of Chinese Tradition, vol. 1, *From Earliest Times to 1600*, compiled by William Theodore de Bary and Irene Bloom, 2nd ed. (New York: Columbia University Press, 1999), pp. 229–30.

system prosecuted over a thousand such cases. A usurper tried to introduce land reforms and took power from 9 to 23 CE, but he lost control to a coalition of landowners and peasants who restored the Han dynasty to power. Thereafter, the Han reconsolidated the somewhat later empire as the Eastern (or Later) Han dynasty (25–220 CE) and moved the capital slightly eastward from Chang'an to Luoyang on the North China plain.

Out of the experience of the Han, the Chinese produced a political narrative known as the dynastic cycle. In this scheme, influential families would vie for supremacy. Upon gaining power, they legitimated their authority by claiming to be the heirs of previous grand dynasts and by preserving or revitalizing the ancestors' virtuous governing ways. As a consequence, the Chinese empire was, in the minds of the Chinese at least,

MAP 7.2 | *Pax Sinica*: The Han Empire in the First Century BCE

Agriculture, commerce, and industry flourished in East Asia under Han rule.

- According to the map, what were the main commodities that passed among the empire's regions?
- What type of administrative infrastructure integrated the vast domain?
- What Han policies contributed to this period of peace and prosperity?

different from all other empires. Other empires, such as the Roman or the Persian, rose and fell. Though dynasties rose and fell, the Chinese empire itself did not, since heaven would grant its mandate to anyone who could keep the empire going. Indeed, the imperial continuity established by the Han was extraordinarily long-lasting, enduring more than 2,000 years, until 1911.

Foundations of Han Power

The Han and Roman Empires relied on political institutions, ideological supports, and control of economic assets to maintain power. Yet they differed in their use of civil bureaucracy, the military, and ideologies to ensure their subjects' consent. Undergirding

Emperor Wu. *This idealized representation of Emperor Wu (156–87 BCE, r. 141–87 BCE) welcoming a man of letters was one of a series of seventeenth-century silk paintings of Chinese emperors.*

the Han Empire was the tight-knit alliance between the imperial family and the new elite—the scholar-gentry class—who shared a determination to impose order on the Chinese population.

POWER AND ADMINISTRATION Although the first Han emperors had no choice but to compromise with the aristocratic groups who had helped overthrow the Qin, in time the Han created the most highly centralized bureaucracy in the world, far more centralized than that of the Roman Empire. No fewer than 23,500 individuals staffed the central and local governments. That structure became the source of the Han's enduring power. As under the Qin, the bureaucracy touched everyone because all males had to register, pay taxes, and serve in the military.

The Han court also moved quickly to tighten its grip on regional administration. First it removed powerful princes, crushed rebellions, and took over the areas controlled by regional lords. According to arrangements instituted in 106 BCE by Emperor Wu, the empire consisted of thirteen provinces under imperial inspectors. A civilian official and a commandant for military affairs shared the work of administering each commandery. These men shouldered immense responsibilities, far exceeding those of their counterparts in the Roman Empire. The commanderies covered vast lands inhabited by countless ethnic groups totaling millions of people. These officials, like their Roman equivalents, had to maintain political stability and ensure the efficient collection of taxes. However, given the immense numbers under their jurisdiction and the heavy duties they bore, in many respects the local administrative staff was inadequate to the tasks facing them.

Government schools that promoted the scholar-official ideal became fertile sources for recruiting local officials. Emperor Wu founded a college for classical scholars in 136 BCE and soon expanded it into the **Imperial University**. By the second century CE, it boasted 30,000 students and faculty, dwarfing the number of students in even the very largest Roman training schools. Not only did students study the classics, but Han scholars also were naturalists and inventors. They made important medical discoveries, dealing with rational diagnoses of the body's functions and the role of wind and temperature in transmitting diseases. They also invented the magnetic compass and developed high-quality paper, which replaced silk, wood, and bamboo strips as media for communicating laws, ideas, rituals, and technical knowledge. Increasingly, even local elites encouraged their sons to master the classical teachings of Confucianism. This practice not only guaranteed a future entry into the ruling class but also planted the Confucian classics at the heart of the imperial state and society.

Early Han legal materials that survive from Zhangjiashan Tomb no. 247 (c. 186 BCE) show quite clearly the evolution of law in Han China beyond the purely legalistic Qin code. The chief concern of the new Han legal thinking was that it must conform with the ideals of Confucianized officials who were appointed to serve in local prefectures. This entailed pursuing order and harmony through the stipulation and regulation of interpersonal relationships. Once in power, Confucian officials such as Dong Zhongshu increasingly opposed the Qin model for enumerating each subject's obligations to the state. (See Primary Source: Han Legal Philosophy from Dong Zhongshu.) The Qin had enforced such obligations through clearly prescribed rewards and punishments. For Confucians, an effective law stipulated not just one's political obligations, but also one's obligations to others, which were determined by the nature of their social or familial relationships.

CONFUCIAN IDEOLOGY AND LEGITIMATE RULE Confucian thought slowly became the ideological buttress of the Han Empire. Under Emperor Wu, the people's welfare was deemed the essential purpose of legitimate rule. (See Primary Source: Dong Zhongshu on Responsibilities of Han Rulership.) When the scholar-official Jia Yi wrote that "the state, the ruler, and the officials all depend on the people for their mandate," he was underscoring "the primacy of the people" in affirming the mandate of heaven. However, such principles did *not* imply that the people actually chose their own leaders, as in the Greek city-states (see Chapter 5). The people's only power was the ability to revolt against rulers who did not promote general well-being.

By 50 BCE, the *Analects* containing Confucius's sayings was widely disseminated, and three Confucian ideals reigned as

Han Legal Philosophy from Dong Zhongshu

The Qin legal system was considered brutal in its application of uniform punishments against criminals. Scholars claimed that the Qin punished all equally, regardless of the accused's motive or social status. Under the Han emperor Wu, Dong Zhongshu devised an ingenious way to humanize the Han penal code by using Confucian philosophy, so that jurists could consider the litigant's social status and personal motives behind allegedly criminal behavior. In essence, Dong as a Confucian argued that the spirit of the law took precedence over its letter when true justice was the goal.

At the time, there were those who questioned the verdict saying: "A had no son. On the side of the road, he picked up the child B and raised him as his own son. When B grew up, he committed the crime of murder. The contents of the accusation [against B] included [the fact that] A had concealed B [after the crime]. What should be the judgment regarding A?"

Tung Chung-shu passed judgment saying: "A had no son. He restored [B] to life and raised him [as his own son]. Although B was not A's natural son, who would think of seeing [B] as anyone but [A's] son? The *Poetry* [*Classic*] says: 'The mulberry-tree caterpillar has little ones, but the wasp raises them.' According to the intent of the *Annals*, a father must cover up for his son. A accordingly concealed B. The verdict: A does not deserve to be punished."

QUESTIONS FOR ANALYSIS

- Mulberry-tree caterpillars are silkworms. What does the use of this example in a classic text indicate about the importance of that creature to Chinese culture?
- Why would the Han penal code exonerate a stepfather for harboring his son even though the son had committed a serious crime?

Source: Pan Ku, *Han-shu* 3:1714 *(chüan 30)*; quoted in Benjamin A. Elman, *Classicism, Politics, and Kinship: The Ch'ang-chou School of New Text Confucianism in Late Imperial China* (Berkeley: University of California Press, 1990), p. 262.

---

the official doctrine of the Han Empire: honoring tradition, respecting the lessons of history, and acknowledging the emperor's responsibility to heaven. Scholars such as Dong now used Confucius's words to tutor the princes. By embracing such political ideals, the Han rulers established an empire based on the mandate of heaven and crafted a careful balance in which the officials provided a counterweight to the emperor's autocratic strength. Of course, when the interests of the court and the bureaucracy clashed, the emperor's will was paramount.

The New Social Order and the Economy

Part of the Han leaders' genius was their ability to win the support of diverse social groups that had been squabbling for centuries. The basis for their success was their ability to organize daily life, create a stable social order, promote economic growth, and foster a state-centered religion. They let aristocratic Qin survivors reacquire some of their former power and urged enterprising peasants who had worked the nobles' lands to become local leaders in the countryside. Successful merchants won permission to extend their influence in cities, and in local areas scholars found themselves in the role of masters when their lords were removed.

Out of a massive agrarian base flowed a steady stream of tax revenues and labor for military forces and public works. The Han court also drew revenues from state-owned imperial lands, mining, and mints; tribute from outlying domains; household taxes on the nobility; and surplus grains from wealthy merchants. Emperor Wu established state monopolies in salt, iron, and wine to fund his expensive military campaigns. His policies promoted silk and iron production—especially iron weapons and everyday tools—and controlled profiteering through price controls. He also minted standardized copper coins and imposed stiff penalties for counterfeiting.

Wuzhu Coin. *This copper coin was issued by Emperor Xuandi during the Western Han dynasty, 73–49 BCE. Wuzhu, which means "five grains," refers to the weight of the coin (1 wuzhu = 5 grains = 4 grams). The wuzhu was in circulation until 621 CE.*

Dong Zhongshu on Responsibilities of Han Rulership

Early Han dynasty officials sought to enhance the government's legitimacy by adding to the Legalist defense of an autocratic state a Confucian view of the ruler as the moral and cosmological foundation of government and laws. Thus, the philosopher Dong Zhongshu offered a new theory to legitimize the Han dynasty, while criticizing the Qin's mismanagement of government. Under the guidance of Confucian officials, Dong argued, the imperial system would nourish the people and promote upright officials who would maintain the Han dynasty's mandate to govern, rather than ruling through fear and intimidation.

He who rules the people is the foundation of the state. Now in administering the state, nothing is more important for transforming [the people] than reverence for the foundation.... What do I mean by the foundation? Heaven, Earth, and humankind are the foundation of all living things. Heaven engenders all living things, Earth nourishes them, and humankind completes them. With filial and brotherly love, Heaven engenders them; with food and clothing, Earth nourishes them; and with rites and music, humankind completes them. These three assist one another just as the hands and feet join to complete the body. None can be dispensed with because without filial and brotherly love, people lack the means to live; without food and clothing, people lack the means to be nourished; and without rites and music, people lack the means to become complete. If all three are lost, people become like deer, each person following his own desires and each family practicing its own customs. Fathers will not be able to order their sons, and rulers will not be able to order their ministers. Although possessing inner and outer walls, [the ruler's city] will become known as "an empty settlement." Under such circumstances, the ruler will lie down with a clod of earth for his pillow. Although no one endangers him, he will naturally be endangered; although no one destroys him, he will naturally be destroyed. This is called "spontaneous punishment." When it arrives, even if he is hidden in a stone vault or barricaded in a narrow pass, the ruler will not be able to avoid "spontaneous punishment."

One who is an enlightened master and worthy ruler believes such things. For this reason he respectfully and carefully attends to the three foundations. He reverently enacts the suburban sacrifice, dutifully serves his ancestors, manifests filial and brotherly love, encourages filial conduct, and serves the foundation of Heaven in this way. He takes up the plough handle to till the soil, plucks the mulberry leaves and nourishes the silkworms, reclaims the wilds, plants grain, opens new lands to provide sufficient food and clothing, and serves the foundation of Earth in this way. He establishes academies and schools in towns and villages to teach filial piety, brotherly love, reverence, and humility, enlightens [the people] with education, moves [them] with rites and music, and serves the foundation of humanity in this way.

If these three foundations are all served, the people will resemble sons and brothers who do not dare usurp authority, while the ruler will resemble fathers and mothers. He will not rely on favors to demonstrate his love for his people nor severe measures to prompt them to act. ... [W]hen the ruler relies on virtue to administer the state, it is sweeter than honey or sugar and firmer than glue or lacquer. This is why sages and worthies exert themselves to revere the foundation and do not dare depart from it.

QUESTIONS FOR ANALYSIS

- Count the number of times the following words appear in this reading: *fathers, sons, brothers, filial conduct.* What do these words tell us about Han officials' view of the proper relationship between rulers and subjects?
- How does this reading reflect the gender ideology of Han China?
- Why was the emperor so important in Dong Zhongshu's vision of Han political culture after the fall of the Qin? Was the law code actually made more humane in practice?

Source: Sources of Chinese Tradition, vol. 1, *From Earliest Times to 1600*, compiled by William Theodore de Bary and Irene Bloom, 2nd ed. (New York: Columbia University Press, 1999), pp. 299–300.

Laid out in an orderly grid, Han cities—particularly capitals—reflected their political functions. Bustling markets served as public areas. Carriages transported rich families up and down wide avenues (and they paid a lot for the privilege: keeping a horse required as much grain as a family of six would consume). Court palaces became forbidden inner cities, off-limits to all but those in the imperial lineage or the government. Monumental architecture in China announced the palaces and tombs of rulers rather than the sites of mass entertainment, like the Colosseum in Rome.

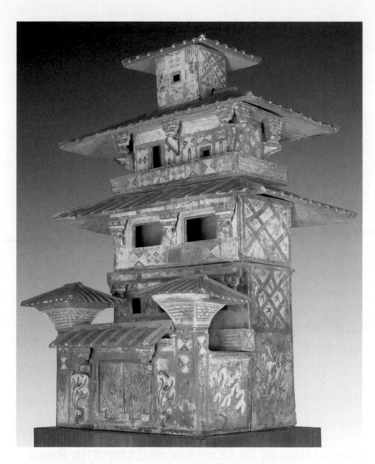

Model of a Han House. *Elite families in Chang'an and other Han cities typically lived in two-story houses with carved crossbeams and rafters and enclosed courtyards. The floors were covered with embroidered cushions, wool rugs, and mats for sitting. Screens were used for privacy. Women and children were cloistered in the inner quarters.*

DOMESTIC LIFE Daily life in Han China included new luxuries for the elite and reinforced traditional ideas about gender. Wealthy families took pride in their several-story homes displaying richly carved crossbeams and rafters. They cushioned their floors with embroidered pillows, wool rugs, and mats. Fine embroideries hung as drapes, and screens in the rooms secured privacy. Families also sharply distinguished gender roles to increase the authority of the father figure. Women and children stayed cloistered in inner quarters, preserving the sense that the family patriarch's role was to protect mothers, wives, and children from a harsh society. But this did not deprive women from following careers of their own.

Ban Zhao, the younger sister of the historian Ban Gu (32–92 CE), serves as an example of an elite woman whose talents reached outside the home. She became the first female Chinese historian and lived relatively unconstrained. After marrying a local resident, Cao Shishu, at the age of fourteen, she was called Madame Cao at court. Subsequently, she completed her elder brother's *History of the Former Han Dynasty* when he was imprisoned and executed. In addition to completing the first full dynastic history in China, Ban

Zhao wrote *Lessons for Women,* in which she described the status of elite women and presented the ideal woman in light of her virtue, her type of work, and the words she spoke and wrote. Elite women, often literate, like Ban Zhao, enjoyed respect as teachers and managers within the family while their husbands served as officials away from home. Women who were commoners led less protected lives. Many worked in the fields, and some joined troupes of entertainers to sing and dance for food at open markets.

Silk was abundant and available to all classes, though in winter only the rich wrapped themselves in furs while everyone else stayed warm in woolens and ferret skins. The rich also wore distinctive slippers inlaid with leather or lined with silk. No longer were wine and meat reserved only for festivals, leading critics to decry the debauches of the well-to-do. In the cooked-meat stalls of the markets, those who could afford them pushed and shoved to buy their piglets, dog cutlets, or chopped liver. These tasty foods came to the dinner tables of the wealthy on vessels fashioned with silver inlay or golden handles.

Entertainment for those who could afford it included performing animals, tiger fights, and foreign dancing girls. Some gambled, betting for high stakes at *liubo,* a board game that involved shaking bamboo sticks out of a cup. Live music was popular at private homes, and rich families kept their own orchestras, complete with bells and drums. Although events like these had occurred during the Zhou dynasty, they had marked only public ritual occasions.

SOCIAL HIERARCHY At the base of Han society was a free peasantry—farmers who owned and tilled their own land. The Han court upheld an agrarian ideal by honoring the peasants' productive labors, while subjecting merchants to a range of controls (including regulations on luxury consumption) and belittling them for not doing physical labor. Confucians and Daoists supported this hierarchy. Confucians envisioned scholar-officials as working hard for the ruler to enhance a moral economy in which profiteering by greedy merchants would be minimal.

In reality, however, the first century of Han rule perpetuated powerful elites. At the apex were the imperial clan and nobles, followed, in order, by high-ranking officials and scholars, great merchants and manufacturers, and a regionally based class of local magnates. Below these elites, lesser clerks, medium and small landowners, free farmers, artisans, small merchants, poor tenant farmers, and hired laborers eked out a living. The more destitute became government slaves and relied on the state for food and clothing. At the bottom was a thin layer of convicts and private slaves.

Between 100 BCE and 200 CE, scholar-officials linked the imperial center with local society. At first, their political clout and prestige complemented the power of landlords and large clans, but over time their autonomy grew as they gained wealth by acquiring private property. Following the fall of the Han, they emerged as the dominant aristocratic clans.

Han Entertainment. *Han entertainment included dancing, particularly by foreign girls (top left), and acrobatics, for which the Chinese remain famous today (bottom). Music was often played at the homes of rich families, who kept their own orchestras, complete with bells and drums. Musical events became so popular, for both the entertainers (note the face in the Han statue on the top right) and the entertained, that performances ceased being only somber ritual occasions.*

In the long run, the imperial court's struggle to limit the power of local lords and magnates failed. Rulers had to rely on local officials to enforce their rule, but those officials could rarely stand up to the powerful men they were supposed to be governing. And when central rule proved too onerous for local elites, they always had the option of rebelling. Local uprisings against the Han that began in 99 BCE forced the court to relax its measures and left landlords and local magnates as dominant powers in the provinces. Below these privileged groups, powerless agrarian groups turned to Daoist religious organizations that crystallized into potent cells of dissent.

RELIGION AND OMENS Under Emperor Wu, Confucianism took on religious overtones. Dong Zhongshu, Wu's chief minister, advocated a more activist Confucius. One treatise portrayed him not as a humble teacher but as an uncrowned monarch and even as a demigod and a giver of laws, which differed from the more sober portrait of Confucius in the *Analects*.

Classical learning also informed popular religion. In the early Han world dominated by social elites, religion linked scholars and officials to the peasantry. Although classical learning remained the preserve of the Confucians at court, many local communities practiced forms of a remarkably dynamic popular Chinese religion.

Imperial cults, magic, and sorcery reinforced the court's interest in astronomical omens—such as the appearance of a supernova, solar halos, meteors, and lunar and solar eclipses. Unpredictable celestial events, as well as earthquakes and famines, were taken as signs of the emperor's lack of virtue, and powerful ministers exploited them to intimidate their ruler. A cluster of calamities, prodigies, and heavenly omens usually meant that the emperor had lost the mandate of heaven. At the same time, people of high and low social position alike took witchcraft very seriously, believing that its practitioners could manipulate natural events and interfere with the will of heaven. Religion in many forms, from philosophy to witchcraft, was an essential feature of Han society from the elite to the poorer classes.

Expansion of the Empire and the Silk Road

Empires seldom stand on shared political and cultural beliefs alone. More often, they survive by force. The Han Chinese were no exception to the general rule. Like their Roman counterparts, they created a ruthless military machine that was effective at expanding their borders and enforcing stability around the borderlands. Peace was good for business, specifically for creating stable conditions that allowed the safe transit of goods over the Silk Road.

Emperor Wu did much to transform the military forces. Following the Qin precedent, he again made military service compulsory. The number of men under arms was stunning: some 100,000 crack troops in the Imperial Guard were stationed in the capital, and more than a million were in the standing army. In contrast, the armies of Athens, the largest of the Greek city-states, rarely exceeded 20,000 men; even the Roman field armies rarely exceeded 30,000, and the full standing army of the empire reached only 250,000 or so. The Han created armies on an entirely different scale.

EXPANDING BORDERS Han forces were particularly active along the borders. During the reign of Emperor Wu, Han control extended from southeastern China to northern Vietnam. China also extended its influence into Korea when pro-Han Koreans appealed for Han help against rulers in their internal squabbles. After Emperor Wu's expeditionary force defeated the Korean king, four Han commanderies sprang up in northern Korea. Incursions into Sichuan and the southwestern border areas were less successful, as both mountainous terrain and malaria hampered the Han armies. Nevertheless, a commandery took root in southern Sichuan in 135 BCE, and soon it opened trading routes to Southeast Asia.

Mighty as this empire was, expansion invariably renewed conflicts along more extended borders. The Han's most serious military threat came from nomadic peoples in the north, especially the Xiongnu. The Han inherited from the Qin a symbiotic relationship with these proud, horse-riding nomads from outside the frontier's defensive wall. Merchants of the Han Empire brought silk cloth and thread, bronze mirrors, and lacquerware to the nomadic chiefs, exchanging them for furs, horses, and cattle.

At first, the Han suffered humiliating defeats at the hands of the Xiongnu. But as the regime grew more powerful, the tables turned. Under Emperor Wu, the Han launched offensive campaigns across the northern steppe to drive back the raiders. Between 129 and 124 BCE, they repelled several Xiongnu invasions. In subsequent campaigns, Han forces penetrated deep into Xiongnu territory, reaching as far as the northern Mongolian steppe. Eventually, the Han armies split the Xiongnu tribes. The southern tribes surrendered, but the northern ones moved westward—toward the Mediterranean, where they eventually threatened the eastern flank of the Roman Empire.

THE CHINESE PEACE: TRADE, OASES, AND THE SILK ROAD The retreat of the Xiongnu (and other nomadic peoples) introduced a glorious period of peace and prosperity. Now China achieved a *Pax Sinica* ("Chinese Peace," 149–87 BCE) that was much like the *Pax Romana* (25 BCE–235 CE) in the west. Long-distance trade flourished, cities ballooned, standards of living rose, and the population surged. As a result of their military campaigns, Emperor Wu and his successors became monarchs enjoying tribute from distant vassal states. Normally, the Han did not intervene in the domestic policy of such states unless they rebelled. Instead, the Han relied on trade and markets to induce their vassals to work within the tribute system and become prosperous satellite states.

Although clashes occurred between the nomadic Xiongnu and the settled Chinese, more often relations in the borderlands produced benefits for both sides. After all, Han expansion coincided with the flourishing of the Silk Road, where Xiongnu nomads were key middlemen. When the Xiongnu were no longer a threat to the north, Emperor Wu expanded westward. By 100 BCE, he had extended the northern defensive wall from the Tianshan Mountains to the Gobi Desert. Along the wall stood signal beacons for sending emergency messages, and its gates opened periodically for trading fairs. The westernmost gate was called the Jade Gate, since jade from the Taklamakan

Desert passed through it. Wu also built garrison cities at oases to protect the trade routes; farthest west was Dunhuang, which later become a culturally diverse center of Buddhist thought and activity.

It was expensive to maintain a strong military force in such a remote and barren country, so Wu established military and farming settlements in the semidesert region. The state even encouraged soldiers to bring their families to settle on the frontier. As warfare in these territories was relatively infrequent, soldiers could spend time digging wells, building canals, and reclaiming wastelands. Soon after its military power expanded beyond the Jade Gate, the Han government set up a similar system of oases on the rim of the Taklamakan Desert. With irrigation, oasis agriculture attracted many more settlers. Traders now could find food for themselves and fodder for their animals as the Xiongnu fled westward. Trade routes passing through deserts and oases now were safer and more reliable than the steppe routes, which they gradually replaced. These new desert routes would flourish for another century, until fierce Tibetan tribes challenged the distant Han frontiers.

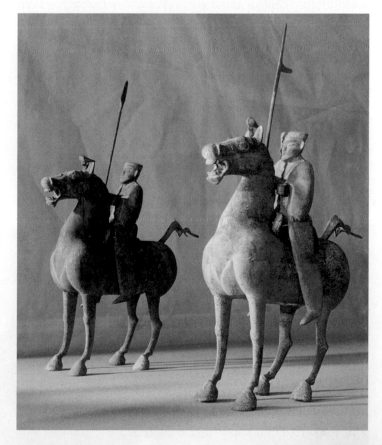

Bronze Horsemen. *Two bronze horsemen holding Chi-halberds from the Later Han dynasty, circa second century CE. These statues were excavated in 1969 in Gansu along the Silk Road. Note the size and strength of these Ferghana horses from central Asia.*

The Jade Gate. *Through the Jade Gate, the most significant pass on the Silk Road, foods, fruits, and religions of the "western regions" were introduced into central China during the Han dynasty. Chinese inventions, such as paper during the Later Han and then the compass and gunpowder, traveled in the opposite direction.*

THE HAN EMPIRE AND DEFORESTATION Both the Han and the Roman Empires had significant, if unintended, impacts on the environment. Han peoples deforested vast expanses of China proper, while Rome was an early and powerful polluter of the earth's atmosphere (discussed shortly). As the Han peoples moved southward and later westward, filling up empty spaces and driving elephants, rhinoceroses, and other animals into extinction, the farming communities cleared immense tracts of land of shrubs and forests to prepare for farming. The Han admired trees. They were especially fond of oak, pine, ash, and elm, and their artists celebrated them in paintings. But farmers hated forests. China's grand environmental narrative has been the clearing of old-growth forests that had originally covered the greater part of the territory of China. Trees prevent erosion, and one of the results of the massive deforestation campaigns during the Han period in the regions surrounding the Yellow River was massive runoffs of soil into the Yellow River. In fact, the Yellow River owes its name to the immense quantities of mud that it absorbed from surrounding farmlands. This sediment raised the level of the river above the surrounding plain in many places. In spite of villagers' efforts to build levees along the river's banks, severe flooding occurred, threatening crops, destroying villages, and even undermining the legitimacy of ruling dynasties. During most of the Han Empire, a break in the levees took place every

sixteen years. The highest concentration of flooding was between 66 BCE and 34 CE, when severe floods occurred every nine years. Like many empires, the Han's expansion was based on an expanded agriculture and brisk trade, but expansion came at a major environmental price: deforestation, flooding, and the destruction of the habitats of many plants and animals.

Social Convulsions, a Usurper, and the Later Han Dynasty

The immense burden of military expenses and the tax pressures that they inflicted ultimately were more than the Han Empire could bear. Emperor Wu's dramatic military expansions required the stationing of soldiers in garrisons from central Asia to the Pacific and from Korea to Vietnam. But further conquests failed to bolster the state's coffers, and supporting the huge expenses of maintaining a gigantic army exhausted the imperial treasury. Wu raised taxes, which put a strain on small landholders and peasants—the bedrock of the empire. The strain continued after his death, and by the end of the first century BCE, the Chinese empire was drained financially.

During this epoch, large segments of the population suffered a dramatic economic blow, as natural disasters led to crop

Yellow River Flooding. *The Yellow River, a dangerous and wild body of water, frequently flooded and, during high floods, cut out new channels. This photo from September 1919 shows workers preparing for flood conditions, a practice that went back several millennia.*

failures. These worsened the plight of poor farmers, for their taxes were based not on their crop yield but on the size of their holdings. Unable to pay their taxes, many free peasants had to sell their land to large landholders; they then became tenant farmers and sometimes slaves. As local landlords rebuilt their power and their landholdings, they accumulated even more wealth, which enabled them to obtain classical educations and pursue careers as government officials. As a burgeoning population faced land shortages in the countryside, the social fabric of Han society finally tore apart. In desperation, the dispossessed peasants rebelled.

This crisis enabled Wang Mang (r. 9–23 CE), a former Han minister and regent to a child emperor, to take over the throne and establish a new dynasty. He believed that the Han had lost the mandate of heaven. He enacted reforms to help the poor and fostered economic activity by confiscating gold from wealthy landowners and merchants. His words seemed to favor the redistribution of excess land equitably based on the Confucian ideal of an ancient "well-field" land system: all families would work their own parcels and share in cultivating a communal plot whose crops would become tax surplus for the state. His idealistic reforms failed miserably.

NATURAL DISASTERS AND REBELLION Wang Mang succumbed to a violent upheaval by peasants and large landholders against central authority. Bad luck also played a part. Up to 5 million Chinese lived along the great northern plain south of the Yellow River, whose course—unluckily for Wang—changed soon after he assumed power. In 11 CE, the river broke through its dikes. Rather than bending northward on the Central Plain, it flowed due southward toward the Yellow Sea.

This demographic catastrophe plunged the northern part of China into famine and banditry; it would repeat itself several more times in Chinese history. Each time the river changed course from north to south and then back again, "China's Sorrow," as the river was called, unleashed tremendous floods that caused mass death and vast migrations. Peasant impoverishment and revolt followed with chilling regularity. Researchers estimate that the floods of 11 CE affected some 28 million Chinese, or nearly half the total population.

Wang Mang's reforming regime was utterly unable to cope with a cataclysm of such magnitude. Rebellious peasants, led by Daoist clerics, used the disaster as a pretext to march on Wang's capital at Chang'an. The peasants painted their foreheads red and called themselves Red Eyebrows in imitation of demon warriors, and their leaders spoke to them through inspired religious mediums. By 23 CE, they had overthrown Wang Mang. Wang's enemies attributed the natural disaster to the emperor's unbridled misuse of power. They created a history of legitimate Han dynastic power that Wang Mang had illegitimately overturned, and soon Wang became the model of the evil usurper.

THE LATER (EASTERN) HAN DYNASTY After Wang Mang's fall, problems of social, political, and economic inequalities fatally weakened the power of the emperor and the court. As a result, the Eastern (or Later) Han dynasty (25–220 CE), with its capital at Luoyang on the North China plain, followed a hands-off economic policy, under which large landowners and merchants amassed more wealth and more property. Decentralizing the regime was also good for local business and long-distance trade, as the Silk Road continued to flourish. Chinese silk became popular as far away as the Roman Empire. In return, China received glass, jade, horses, precious stones, tortoiseshells, and fabrics.

By the second century CE, landed elites were enjoying the fruits of their success in manipulating the Later Han tax system. It granted them so many land and labor exemptions that the government never again firmly controlled its human and agricultural resources as Emperor Wu had. As the court focused on the new capital in Luoyang, local power fell into the hands of great aristocratic families, who acquired even more privately owned land and forced free peasants to become their rent-paying tenants.

Such prosperity bred greater social inequity and a new source of turmoil. Pressure grew on tenants to pay high rents, on the remaining free peasants to pay most of the taxes, and on poor migrant workers to serve as laborers. As the Later Han state's power weakened, its ritual tasks became more formalized. The simmering tensions between landholders and peasants boiled over in a full-scale rebellion in 184 CE. Popular religious groups, such as the Red Eyebrows, championed new ideas among commoners and elites. Confucius was no longer an exemplary figure: the new models were a mythical Yellow Emperor, extolled as the inventor of traditional Chinese writing and medicine, and the Daoist sage Master Laozi, the voice of naturalness and spontaneity. Laozi was now treated as a god. Although scholars scorned folk cults and magical practices, both commoners and local magnates in rural communities kept these beliefs alive.

At this propitious moment, Buddhist clerics from central Asia arrived in northern China preaching personal enlightenment for the elite and millenarian salvation for the masses. (A millenarian movement is a broad, popular upheaval calling for the restoration of a bygone moral age, often led by charismatic spiritual prophets.) Their message received a warm welcome from an increasingly hostile population. Yet the most powerful challenge to the Later Han came not from the Buddhists but from the Daoists. As Daoist masters challenged Confucian ritual conformity, they advanced their ideas in the name of a divine order that would redeem all people, not just elites. Officials, along with other political outcasts, headed strong dissident groups and eventually formed local movements. Under their leadership, religious groups such as the Yellow Turbans—so called because

Jade Burial Shroud. *Shown here is the jade burial suit of Princess Tou Wan, late second century BCE.*

they wrapped yellow scarves around their heads—championed Daoist millenarian movements across the empire.

Proclaiming the Daoist millenarian belief in a future "Great Peace," the Yellow Turbans demanded fairer treatment by the Han state and equal distribution of all farmlands. As agrarian conditions got worse, a widespread famine ensued. It was a catastrophe that, in the rebels' view, demonstrated the emperor's loss of the mandate of heaven. The economy disintegrated when people refused to pay taxes and provide forced labor, and internal wars engulfed the dynasty. After the 180s CE, three competing states replaced the Han: the Wei in the northwest, the Shu in the southwest, and the Wu in the south. A unified empire would not return until three centuries later.

THE ROMAN EMPIRE (c. 300 BCE–c. 300 CE)

The other large empire of the time flexed its muscle at the other end of Afro-Eurasia. There, in a centuries-long process, Rome became a great power, ruling 60 to 70 million subjects. The Roman Empire at its height encompassed lands from the highlands of what is now Scotland to the lower reaches of the Nile River in modern-day Egypt and part of Sudan and from the borders of the Inner Eurasian steppe in Ukraine and the Caucasus to the Atlantic shores of North Africa. (See Map 7.3.) It was comparable in size to Han dynasty China.

Whereas the Han Empire dominated an enormous and unbroken landmass, the Roman Empire dominated lands around the Mediterranean Sea. Like Han China, though, the Romans acquired command over their world through violent military expansion. By the first century CE, almost unceasing wars against their neighbors had enabled the Romans to forge an unparalleled number of ethnic groups and minor states into

a single, large political state. (See Analyzing Global Developments: Great Empires Compared.) This achievement was so striking that the Jewish historian and general Josephus, writing in the 90s CE, saw the empire as the unchallengeable work of God on earth. We can easily see how the Latin word that the Romans used to designate command over their subjects—*imperium*—became the source for the English words *empire* and *imperialism*.

Foundations of the Roman Empire

The emergence of Rome as a world-dominating power was a surprise. Although the Romans might have looked to the Persians or to Alexander the Great for imperial models, they did not. And unlike the Han, they had no great direct imperial ancestors. Down to the 350s BCE, the Romans were just one of a number of Latin-speaking communities in Latium, a region in the center of the Italian Peninsula. Although Rome was one of the largest urban centers there, it was still only a city-state that had to ally with other towns for self-defense. However, Rome soon began an extraordinary phase of military and territorial expansion, and by 265 BCE it had taken control of most of the Peninsula. At least three factors contributed to this achievement: a migration of foreign peoples and the Romans' own military and political innovations. These factors came into play more or less in chronological order. The first step, at the beginning of the fourth century BCE, was an armed intervention of external peoples from the north who cleared the way for Roman expansion; then the Romans themselves began a series of military conquests that rolled over the Italian Peninsula by the mid-third century BCE. In the final step, beginning in the late third and second centuries BCE, the Romans initiated a series of political and organizational innovations that allowed them to consolidate their conquests into a new whole.

POPULATION MOVEMENTS Between 450 and 250 BCE, migrations from northern and central Europe brought large numbers of Celts to settle in lands around the Mediterranean Sea. They convulsed the northern rim of the Mediterranean, staging armed forays into lands from what is now Spain in the west to present-day Turkey in the east.

One of these migrations involved dozens of Gallic peoples from the region of the Alps and beyond in a series of violent incursions into northern Italy that ultimately—around 390 BCE—led to the seizure of Rome. The important result for the Romans was not their city's capture, but the permanent dislocation that the invaders inflicted on the city-states of the Etruscans, who until then had dominated the Italian Peninsula. The Etruscans survived and, with great effort, drove the invading Gauls back northward. But the Etruscan cities never recovered their ability to dominate other peoples in Italy, including the Romans.

Thus, the Gallic migrations removed one of the most formidable roadblocks to Roman expansion in Italy.

MILITARY INSTITUTIONS AND THE WAR ETHOS

Rome's unparalleled expansion could not have occurred without the unique military and political institutions that it developed. Basically, the Romans were more successful and more efficient in killing other humans than any other people in their part of the world. They achieved unassailable military power by organizing the communities that they conquered in Italy into a system that generated huge reservoirs of manpower for their army. This development began between 340 and 335 BCE, when the Romans faced a concerted attack by other Latin city-states. By then, the other Latins were viewing Rome not as an ally in a system of mutual defense but as a growing threat to their own independence. After overcoming the nearby Latins, the Romans charged onward to defeat one community after another in Italy. Their main demand of all defeated enemies was to provide men for the Roman army every year. The result was a snowball-like accumulation of military manpower.

By 265 BCE, Rome controlled the Italian Peninsula. It next entered into three great **Punic Wars** with the Carthaginians, the major power centered in the northern parts of present-day Tunisia. The First Punic War (264–241 BCE) was a prolonged naval battle over the island of Sicily. With their victory, the Romans acquired a dominant position in the western Mediterranean. The Second Punic War (218–201 BCE), however, revealed the real strength and might of Roman arms. The Carthaginian general Hannibal realized that if his troops were to have any hope of victory, they would have to attack the Italian Peninsula itself.

The new Roman military system, however, made a Roman victory almost certain. Whereas the Carthaginians' resources were those of a large city-state, by this time Rome was more like a modern nation-state drafting manpower from a huge population. After the heroic feat of crossing the Pyrenees and the Alps with his war elephants, Hannibal entered Italy with a force of only about 20,000 soldiers. In contrast, Rome could draw on reserves of more than 750,000 men. With those numbers, Roman commanders could afford to lose battles—which they proceeded to do, suffering casualties of about 60,000 to 80,000 dead in three great encounters with the Carthaginian general—and still win the war. They finally did so in 201 BCE. In the end, not even a strategic and tactical genius like Hannibal could prevail against the Roman military system. In a final war of extermination, waged between 149 and 146 BCE, the Romans used their overwhelming advantage in manpower, ships, and other resources to bring the five-centuries-long hegemony of Carthage to an end.

In addition to their overwhelming advantage in manpower, the Romans cultivated an unusual war ethos. A heightened sense of honor drove Roman men to push themselves into battle again and again and never to accept defeat. They were educated to imitate the example of soldiers such as Marcus Sergius. Wounded twenty-three times in battle, Sergius was crippled in both hands and both feet. In the war with Hannibal he lost one hand but continued to serve, using a false right hand made out of iron. He was twice taken prisoner by Hannibal, each time escaping despite being kept in chains. Going into action four times with his artificial hand tied to the stump of his arm, Sergius helped to rescue major Roman cities from Carthaginian sieges—and twice the horse that he was riding was cut out

War Elephants. *There are no contemporary illustrations of the elephants that Hannibal brought when he invaded Italy. Hannibal was influenced by the Hellenistic armies in the east who had borrowed the idea of war elephants, and the elephants themselves, from Indian rulers. This painting, by Giulio Romano, an artist from the school of the Renaissance painter Raphael, highlights the terrifying aspect of the elephants at the battle of Zama in 202 BCE, and reduces the human warriors to bit players. In fact, the elephants were not decisive in the winning of any major battle in Italy in the Second Roman-Carthaginian War. Hannibal won them all by superior generalship.*

ATLANTIC OCEAN

NORTH SEA

BALTIC SEA

BRITANNIA

Londinium ⊙

GERMANIA INFERIOR

GERMANI

GALLIA LUGDUNENSIS

BELGICA

Rhine R.

AGRI DECUMATES

IUTHUN

GALLIA AQUITANIA

GERMANIA SUPERIOR

RAETIA

NORICUM

Danube R.

PANNONIA

GALLIA NARBONENSIS

PYRENEES

TARRACONENSIS

ITALIA

ITALIAN PENINSULA

ADRIATIC SEA

DALMATIA

LUSITANIA

CORSICA

Rome ⊙
Ostia

Herculaneum
Pompeii

⊙ Corduba

SARDINIA

BAETIA

MAURETANIA TINGITANA

MAURETANIA CAESARIENSIS

MEDITERRANEAN

SICILY

Carthage ⊙

Syracusa ⊙

NUMIDIA

AFRICA

MEDITERRANEAN

GAETULI

NORTH AFRICA

GARAMANTES

→	Mediterranean Sea current
	Roman expansion to 201 BCE
	Roman expansion, 201–100 BCE
	Roman expansion, 100–44 BCE
	Roman expansion, 44 BCE–14 CE
	Roman expansion, 14–96 CE
	Roman expansion, 96–106 CE
GALLIA	Roman province
AGRI	Roman region
⊙	Roman provincial capital

0 · · · 250 · · · 500 Miles
0 · · · 250 · · · 500 Kilometers

MAP 7.3 | Roman Expansion to 120 CE

Roman expansion continued for several centuries before reaching its peak in the second century CE.

- According to the map, what were the first provinces to fall under Rome's power? What were the last two?
- Why did the Romans not expand their empire farther into eastern Europe or Southwest Asia?
- What were the geographical limits to Rome's expansion?

Empires, Allies, and Frontiers

Both the Han and the Roman Empires faced threats on their frontiers and used allies as well as their own military prowess to counter such threats. Keeping good relations with frontier allies was essential to the statecraft of empires. It could also yield important intelligence for rulers in capitals.

THE HAN

Consider how the Han dealt with their enemies, the Xiongnu. Emperor Wu sent a special envoy to the Yuezhi, whom he thought would be willing to ally with him against the Xiongnu. His emissary was Zhang Qian, who had volunteered to undertake the journey into the dangerous steppe. In 139 BCE, Zhang set out with a group of 100 people; one was a former slave from the steppe, Ganfu, who guided the travelers and used his bow to kill wild animals when they ran out of food. Aware of the envoy's purpose, the Xiongnu chief detained the group when they tried to pass through his territory. The Xiongnu kept Zhang Qian for ten years, during which time he married a Xiongnu woman and had children. Zhang learned much of steppe life and

geography, but he did not forget his mission; together with Ganfu, he eventually managed to escape. At last they reached the Yuezhi camp on the northern bank of the Oxus River.

Unfortunately, Zhang Qian did not succeed in enlisting the support of the Yuezhi. Their surviving leaders had little inclination to return to the steppe to again battle the fierce Xiongnu, especially as they could see before them the fertile Bactrian plain dotted with Hellenistic cities (see Chapter 6). Zhang Qian accompanied the Yuezhi court in touring the land of Bactria. After spending a year in futile negotiations with the Yuezhi leaders, Zhang set out for home, bearing much information about the cultures and products of Bactria and regions beyond, including India and Persia. He finally reached Chang'an, the Han capital, thirteen years after beginning his expedition. Although he had failed in his diplomatic mission, Zhang had collected invaluable information for Wudi about the frontier areas in central Asia.

THE ROMANS

The Romans also had to deal with their frontiers. To the north they contended with peoples whom they called "barbarians," and to the east they confronted the

powerful kingdoms of the Parthians and the Sasanians. They also had occasional contacts with kingdoms far to the east. For example, in the reign of Augustus (r. 27 BCE–14 CE) an embassy came from Poros, a king in India. In a letter that his ambassadors carried, Poros described himself as the king over 600 other kings, and he offered any help that the emperor Augustus might want of him. With the letter came gifts carried by eight slaves, naked except for their scented loincloths: a "freak," a number of large snakes, a huge turtle, and a partridge larger than a vulture.

More important than statecraft were exchanges along the Silk Road that brought news, rumors, and impressions of distant empires. The Chinese were the source of the most expensive item in the Roman Empire: the highly valued commodity silk. But in Roman eyes, the Chinese were still very remote and unknown. As Pliny the Elder wrote, "Though mild in character, the Chinese still resemble wild animals in that they shun the company of the rest of human-kind, and wait for trade to come to them." Although connected, the two empires that so dominated their own worlds were still worlds apart.

Far more important and transformative for the Roman Empire were the constant migrations of people to the north—mainly

from under him. Such men set a high standard of commitment to war. What also propelled Roman soldiers was an unusual regime of training and discipline, in which minor infractions of duty were punishable by death (in Greek armies, by contrast, misconduct merely drew fines). Disobedience by a whole unit led to a savage mass punishment, called "decimation," in which every tenth man was arbitrarily selected and executed. For men like Sergius, marching out to war in annual spring campaigns in the month dedicated to Mars (still called March today), the Roman god of war, had an almost biological rhythm.

With an unrelenting drive to war, the Romans continued to draft, train, and field extraordinary numbers of men for combat. Soldiers, conscripted at age seventeen or eighteen, could expect

to serve for up to ten years at a time. With so many young men devoted to war for such long spans of time, a war ethos became deeply embedded in the ideals of every generation. After 200 BCE, the Romans unleashed this successful war machine on the kingdoms of the eastern Mediterranean—with devastating results. In one year, 146 BCE, the Romans achieved the final extermination of what was left of Carthage in the west—killing all its adult males and selling all its women and children into slavery—and the parallel obliteration of the great Greek city-state of Corinth in the east. Their monopoly of power over the entire Mediterranean basin was now unchallenged.

Roman military forces served under men who knew they could win not just glory and territory for the state, but also those coming out of the western Eurasian steppe, such as the Alans and the Huns. Their movements in turn prompted the movement into the empire by Germanic and other ethnic groups farther west along the Rhine and Danube. The empire had constant contact with these peoples over the whole of its existence. They were already migrating into the empire in groups large and small. The Romans' "barbarians" therefore developed means to communicate with one another, a common "frontier culture" that negotiated the differences among them. This frontier culture was a mixture of commercial dealings and military values. Because the majority of the Roman army was stationed in this northern frontier zone, the area became intensely militarized, and army service became a high value for both the Romans and the "barbarians" in the region. Although the intensity of commercial exchanges in this zone included the pastoral products of nomads, the conditions of violence in and beyond the frontier zone encouraged a trade in human captives or slaves as well.

Zhang Qian. *This painting shows Zhang Qian crossing the Yellow River during his journey to the Yuezhi. Although he failed to forge an alliance for Emperor Wu, he returned home with valuable information about frontier areas of central Asia.*

QUESTIONS FOR ANALYSIS

- Compare and contrast the ways in which the Hans and Romans dealt with enemies on the fringes of their respective empires.
- What makes frontier zones useful for the study of world history?

Explore Further

Loewe, Michael. *The Government of Qin and Han Empires: 221 BCE–220 CE* (2006).

Wells, Peter S. *The Barbarians Speak: How the Conquered Peoples Shaped Roman Europe* (1999).

enormous rewards for themselves. They were talented men driven by burning ambition, from, in the 200s BCE, Scipio Africanus, the conqueror of Carthage (a man who claimed that he personally communicated with the gods), to Julius Caesar, the great general of the 50s BCE. A man of prodigious abilities, the greatest orator of his age, and a writer of boundless persuasion, Julius Caesar (100–44 BCE) allegedly could dictate seven letters simultaneously while attending to other duties. He was also a mass killer who kept an exact body count: he knew that he had killed precisely 1,192,000 of the enemy in his wars. And that number did not include his fellow citizens, whose murders during civil wars he refused to acknowledge or add to the total. The eight-year-long cycle of his wars in Gaul (modern-day France and the Rhine valley) was one of the most murderous of his expeditions. By Caesar's own estimation, his army killed more than 1 million Gauls and enslaved another million. The western Afro-Eurasian world had never witnessed war on this scale; it had no equal anywhere, except in China.

POLITICAL INSTITUTIONS AND INTERNAL CONFLICT The conquest of the Mediterranean placed unprecedented power and wealth in the hands of a few men in the Roman social elite. The rush of battlefield successes had kept Romans and their Italian allies preoccupied with the demands of army service overseas. Once this process of territorial expansion slowed, social and political problems that had been lying dormant began to resurface.

Following the traditional date of its foundation in 509 BCE, the Romans had lived in a state that they called the "public thing," or **res publica** (hence, the modern word *republic*). In this state, policy and rules of behavior issued from the Senate—a body of permanent members, 300 to 600 of Rome's most powerful and wealthy citizens—and from popular assemblies of the citizens. Every year the citizens elected the officials of state, principally two consuls who held power for a year and commanded the armies. In addition, the people annually elected ten men who, as tribunes of the plebs ("the common people"), had the special task of protecting their interests against those of the rich and the powerful. In severe political crises, the Romans sometimes chose one man to hold absolute power over the state; his words, or *dicta,* were law—so he was called a *dictator.* (Under a similar device in China, centrally designated overlords were charged with stabilizing unruly provinces.) Ordinarily, the dictator could hold those powers for no longer than six months. The problems with using these institutions, originally devised for a city-state, to rule a Mediterranean-sized empire became glaringly apparent by the second century BCE.

Rome's power elite exploited the wealth from its Mediterranean conquests to acquire huge tracts of land in Italy and Sicily, and then they imported enormous numbers of slaves from all around the Mediterranean to work them. This process drove the free citizen farmers, the backbone of the army, off their lands and into the cities. The result was a severe agrarian and recruiting crisis. In 133 and 123–121 BCE, two tribunes, the brothers Tiberius and Gaius Gracchus, tried—much as Wang Mang would in China more than a century later—to address these inequalities. The Gracchus brothers attempted to institute land reforms guaranteeing to all of Rome's poor citizens a basic amount of land that would qualify them for army service. But political enemies assassinated both men. Thereafter, poor Roman citizens looked not to state institutions but to army commanders, to whom they gave their loyalty and support, to provide them with land and a decent income. These generals became increasingly powerful and started to compete with one another, ignoring the Senate and the traditional rules of politics. As generals sought control of the state and their supporters took sides, a long series of civil wars began in 90 BCE. The tremendous resources built up during the conquest of the Mediterranean were now turned inward by the Romans on themselves. These civil wars, lasting down to the late 30s BCE, threatened to tear the empire to pieces from the inside.

Emperors, Authoritarian Rule, and Administration

It is ironic that the most warlike of all ancient Mediterranean states was responsible for creating the most pervasive and long-lasting peace of its time—the *Pax Romana* ("Roman Peace"; 25 BCE–235 CE). Worn out by half a century of savage civil wars, by the 30s BCE the Romans, including their warlike governing

Roman Farmers and Soldiers. *In the late Republic, most Roman soldiers came from rural Italy, where small farms were being absorbed into the landholdings of the wealthy and powerful. In the empire, soldiers were recruited from rural provincial regions. They sometimes worked small fields of their own and sometimes worked the lands of the wealthy—like the domain in the Roman province of Africa (in modern-day Tunisia) that is depicted in this mosaic.*

elite, were ready to change their values. They were now prepared to embrace the virtues of peace. But political stability came at a price: authoritarian one-man rule. Peace depended on the power of one man who possessed enough authority to enforce an orderly competition among Roman aristocrats. Ultimately, Julius Caesar's adopted son, Octavian (63 BCE–14 CE), would reunite the fractured empire and emerge as undisputed master of the Roman world.

Octavian concentrated immense wealth and the most important official titles and positions of power in his own hands. To signal the transition to a new political order in which he alone would control the army, the provinces, and the political processes in Rome, he assumed a new name, **Augustus** ("the Revered One"—much as the founder of the Qin dynasty in China, King Zheng, assumed the new name of Shi Huangdi (First August Emperor). He also assumed a series of titles: *imperator,* or "commander in chief" (compare the English word *emperor*); *princeps,* or "first man" (whence the English *prince*); and *caesar* (pronounced "kaisar" in Latin and the source of the words *tsar* in Russian and *kaiser* in German). Augustus became the first of dozens of men who, over the next five centuries, were to rule over Rome's vast dominions as emperors.

Rome's subjects tended to see these emperors as heroic or semidivine beings in life and to think of the good ones as becoming gods on their death. This propensity to deify good emperors prompted the Emperor Vespasian's famous deathbed joke: "Dear me, I think I'm turning into a god!" Yet emperors were always careful to present themselves as civil rulers whose power ultimately depended on the consent of Roman citizens and the might of the army. They contrasted themselves with the image of "king," or absolute tyrannical ruler, whom the Romans for centuries had learned to detest. The emperors' powers were nevertheless immense. Moreover, many of them deployed their powers arbitrarily and whimsically, exciting a profound fear of emperors in general. One such emperor was Caligula (r. 37–41 CE), who presented himself as a living god on earth, engaged in casual incest with his sister, and kept books filled with the names of persons he wanted to kill. His violent behavior was so erratic that people thought he suffered from serious mental disorders; those who feared him called him a living monster.

Being a Roman emperor was a high-wire act that required finesse and talent, and few succeeded at it. Of the twenty-two emperors who held power in the most stable period of Roman history (between the first Roman emperor, Augustus, and the early third century CE), fifteen met their end by murder or suicide. As powerful as he might be, no individual emperor alone could govern an empire of such great size and population, encompassing a multitude of languages and cultures. He needed institutions and competent people to help him. In terms of sheer power, the most important institution was the army.

So the emperors systematically transformed the army into a full-time professional force. Men now entered the imperial army not as citizen volunteers but as paid experts who signed up for life and swore loyalty to the emperor and his family. And it was part of the emperor's image to present himself as a victorious battlefield commander, inflicting defeat on the "barbarians" who threatened the empire's frontiers. Such a warrior emperor was a "good" emperor.

For most emperors, however, governance was largely a daily chore of listening to complaints, answering petitions, deciding court cases, and hearing reports from civil administrators and military commanders. By the second century CE, the empire encompassed more than forty provinces, or administrative units; as in Han China, each had a governor appointed or approved by the emperor. In turn, these governors depended on lower-ranking officials. Compared with the Chinese imperial state, however, which had its ranks of senior and junior officials, the Roman empire of this period was relatively understaffed in terms of central government officials. The emperor and his provincial governors had to depend very much on local help, sometimes aided by elite slaves and freedmen (former slaves) serving as government bureaucrats. With these few full-time assistants and an entourage of friends and acquaintances, the governor was expected to guarantee peace and collect taxes for his province. For many essential tasks, though, especially the collection of imperial taxes, even these helpers were insufficient. Thus, the state had to rely on private companies, a measure that set up a tension between the profit motives of the publicans (the men in the companies that took up government contracts) and expectations of fair government among the empire's subjects.

Julius Caesar. *This full-size statue represents Caesar as a high-ranking Roman army commander and conveys some of the power and influence that a charismatic military and political leader like Caesar had over both soldiers and citizen voters. Caesar belonged to a generation of Roman politicians who were immensely attentive to their public image.*

Symbols of Roman Power.
Imperial power was conveyed to the people through highly symbolic public art. In this relief from the Sant'Omobono, archaeological site in Rome, which dates to the third century BCE, the winged figures to the left and right of the military shield represent the idea of victory; the eagle on the shield, holding lightning bolts in its claws, represents brute power; and the garland at the top of the shield represents the wealth and rewards of empire. These symbols of power have been adopted by many modern states in the western world.

AN EMPIRE OF LAW The sometimes arbitrary power of the emperors was balanced by a more uniform system of laws and courts than had ever been seen in the Mediterranean world. The numerous laws enunciated by emperors, the Senate, and other imperial officials were commented on and developed by many generations of jurists—private legal experts whose authority in interpreting the law strongly affected its practice. One of them, named Gaius (c. 150), produced the first known law textbook for the Roman law school at Beirut. Often the biggest event that any town experienced was the annual appearance of the Roman governor to hear important court cases in the local town forum. Even if courts and judges were often thought to be biased and corrupt, they nevertheless offered greater access to more persons than ever before. These courts arbitrated everything from small thefts and property disputes to serious matters like assault and homicide. From histories of the time and novels, we know that everyday people—like a Jewish woman named Babatha in the province of Arabia and peasant farmers in the province of Africa—expected that they would have fair access to the courts and to the rule of law. A Christian missionary named Paul, facing a capital charge of sedition before the governor of Judea, could appeal to be heard by the Roman emperor and have his appeal respected.

Town and City Life

Above all, the emperor counted on local elites to see him as a presence that guaranteed the stability of their world and their personal well-being. Because of the conditions of peace and the unusual concentration of wealth that imperial unity generated,

core areas of the empire—central Italy, southern Spain, northern Africa, and the western parts of present-day Turkey—had surprising densities of urban settlements.

MUNICIPALITIES Inasmuch as these towns imitated Roman forms of government, they provided the backbone of local

A Roman Town. *Roman towns featured many of the standard elements of modern towns and cities. Streets and avenues crossed at right angles; streets were paved, sidewalks run between streets and houses. The houses were often several stories high and had wide windows and open balconies. All these elements can be seen in this street from Herculaneum, nicely preserved by the pyroclastic flow that ran down the slopes of nearby Mount Vesuvius when its volcano erupted in August of 79 CE, burying the town and its inhabitants.*

A Roman Municipal Charter. *This bronze tablet inscribed in Latin is part of a group of six bronze tablets discovered in 1981 at the Roman town of Irni, near modern Molino del Postero, in southern Spain. Charters like this one, set up for public display in the forum or central open area of the town, displayed regulations for the conduct of public life in a Roman town, from rules governing family inheritance and property transfers to the election of town officials and definitions of their powers and duties. (For some of these rules, see Primary Source: Municipal Charter of a Roman Town.)*

administration for the empire. (See Primary Source: Municipal Charter of a Roman Town.) This system of municipalities would become a permanent legacy of Roman government to the western world. Some of our best records of how these towns operated come from Spain, which later flourished as a colonial power that exported Roman forms of municipal life to the Americas. Remarkable physical records of such towns come from Pompeii and Herculaneum, in southern Italy. Both towns were almost perfectly preserved by the ash and debris that buried them following the explosion of a nearby volcano, Mount Vesuvius, in 79 CE.

Towns often were walled, and inside those walls the streets and avenues ran at right angles. A large, open-air, rectangular area called the *forum* dominated the town center. Around it clustered the main public buildings: the markets, the main temples of principal gods and goddesses, and the building that housed city administrators. Residential areas featured regular blocks of houses, usually roofed with bright red tiles, close together and fronting on the streets. Larger towns like Ostia, the port city of Rome, contained large apartment blocks that were not much different from the four- and five-story buildings in any modern city. In the smaller towns, sanitary and nutritional standards were reasonably good. Human skeletons discovered at Herculaneum in the 1970s revealed people in good health, with much better teeth than many people have today—a difference we can explain largely by the lack of sugar in their diet.

ROME The imperial metropolis of Rome was another matter. With well over a million inhabitants, it was an almost grotesque

exaggeration of everything good and bad in Roman city life. (The only other urban centers of comparable size at the time were Xianyang and Chang'an—the Qin and Han capitals, respectively—each with a population of between 300,000 and 500,000.) Rome's inhabitants were privileged, because there

Aqueduct. *The Romans built aqueducts to transport to Rome the huge amounts of water needed for the city's population of over a million. The idea soon spread to the provinces, where these structures were built to bring water to Roman-style cities developing in the peripheral regions of Roman rule. This aqueduct at Segovia, in modern Spain, is one of the best preserved.*

Municipal Charter of a Roman Town

Town governments in the Roman Empire followed standard rules and regulations that developed during the Roman conquest of Italy. In 1981, detailed copies of some of these regulations came to light in southern Spain at Molino del Postero (called Irni in Roman times). The Roman governor of Spain in 81 CE had the rules incised on ten plates of bronze for public display in the town's forum. By following these and other rules, the residents of a Spanish community learned how to govern themselves as the Romans did. (A Roman municipal charter appears on the previous page.)

XIX ON AEDILES: The aediles [the two town business managers] . . . are to have the right and power of managing the grain supply, the sacred buildings, the sacred and holy places, the town and its roads and neighborhoods, the drains and sewers, the baths, the marketplace, and of checking weights and measures; and also of setting a night watch if the need arises.

XX CONCERNING THE RIGHT AND POWER OF QUAESTORS: The quaestors [the two town financial officers] . . . are to have the right and power of collecting, spending, storing, administering, and managing the common funds of the municipality at the discretion of the duumviri [the two town mayors]. And they are allowed to have the public slaves belonging to the municipality to help them.

XXI HOW ROMAN CITIZENSHIP IS ACQUIRED IN THE MUNICIPALITY: When those who are senators, decurions [town councillors], or conscripted town councillors who have been or are chosen as town magistrates according to the terms of this law, have completed their term of office, they are to become Roman citizens, along with their parents and wives and any children who have been born out of legal marriages and who are in the power of their parents, and likewise grandsons and granddaughters born to a son. . . .

XXVIII CONCERNING THE FREEING OF SLAVES BEFORE THE MAYORS: If any citizen of the municipality of Flavian Irni . . . in the presence of a duumvir [mayor] of that municipality in charge of the administration of justice sets free his male or female slave from slavery into freedom or orders him or her to be free . . . then any male slave who has been manumitted or ordered to be free in this way is to be free, any female slave who has been manumitted or ordered to be free in this way is also to be free. . . . Someone who is under twenty years of age may manumit his or her slave only if the number of town councillors necessary for decrees passed under this law to be valid decides that the grounds for said manumission are proper.

QUESTIONS FOR ANALYSIS

- What were some of the titles of civil servants in a typical Roman town or municipality?
- According to this charter, what different types of people were part of the normal social structure?
- In what ways could certain inhabitants of towns such as Irni become Roman citizens?
- Why would making small towns uniform in design and function be important to the Roman Empire?

Source: J. González, "*The Lex Irnitana*: A New Copy of the Flavian Municipal Law," *Journal of Roman Studies* 76 (1986): 147–243; translated by Brent Shaw.

the emperor's power and state's wealth guaranteed them a basic food supply. Thirteen huge and vastly expensive aqueducts provided a dependable daily supply of water, sometimes flowing in from great distances. Most adult citizens regularly received a free, basic amount of wheat (and, later, olive oil and pork). But living conditions were often appalling, with people jammed into ramshackle high rise apartments that threatened to collapse on their renters or go up in flames. And people living in Rome constantly complained of crime and violence. Even worse was the lack of sanitary conditions—despite the sewage and drainage works that were wonders of their time. Rome was disease-ridden; its inhabitants died from infection at a fearsome rate—malarial infections were particularly bad—so the city required a substantial input of immigrants every year just to maintain its population.

MASS ENTERTAINMENT Every self-respecting Roman town had at least two major entertainment venues. One was an adoption from Hellenistic culture: a theater devoted to plays, dances, and other popular events. The other was a Roman innovation that combined two of these horseshoe-shaped theaters into a single, more elaborate structure called an amphitheater. A much larger seating capacity than in a regular theater surrounded the oval performance area at its center. The emperors Vespasian and

North African Amphitheater. *This huge amphitheater is in the remains of the Roman city of Thysdrus, in North Africa (the town of El Jem in modern-day Tunisia). The wealth of the Africans under the empire enabled them to build colossal entertainment venues that competed with the one at Rome in scale and grandeur.*

Roman Gladiators. *In this brilliant mosaic from Rome, we see two gladiators at the end of a full combat in which Astacius has killed Astivus. The Greek letter theta, or "th" (the circle with crossbar through it), beside the names of Astivus and Rodan indicates that these men are dead— thanatos being the Greek word for "death."*

Titus completed the Flavian Amphitheater in Rome and dedicated it in 80 CE. It is the vast structure that we know today as the Colosseum, after the colossal statue of the emperor Nero that used to stand beside it. It was a state-of-the-art facility whose floor area, the arena, could handle elaborate hunts of exotic wild animals such as giraffes and elephants. The arena could also be flooded to stage naval battles between hostile fleets, much to the delight of the audience, or it could provide a venue for a Roman invention, gladiatorial games. In these expensive public entertainments, heavily armed and well-trained men— most of them slaves and prisoners of war, but sometimes free men who volunteered—fought each other, wounding or killing for the enjoyment of the huge crowds of appreciative spectators.

Westerners tend to think of these structures for public entertainment as ordinary and normal. Seen from a contemporary Chinese perspective, however, they were strange and unusual. Among the Han, local elites and the imperial family created gigantic palace complexes complete with hunting parks to impress and amuse themselves, not the general public. In contrast, the public entertainment facilities of a Roman town reflected attitudes that stressed the importance of citizens in town life.

Social and Gender Relations

Even more significant than political forums and game venues were the personal relations that linked the rich and powerful with the mass of average citizens. Men and women of wealth and high social status acted as patrons, protecting and supporting dependents or "clients" from the lower classes. From the emperor at the top to the local municipal man at the bottom, these relationships were reinforced by generous distributions of food and entertainment from wealthy men to their people. The bonds between these groups in each city found formal expression in legal definitions of patrons' responsibilities to clients; at the same time, this informal social code raised expectations that the wealthy would be public benefactors. For example, a senator, Pliny the Younger, constructed for his hometown a public library and a bathhouse; supported a teacher of Latin; and established a fund to support the sons and daughters of former slaves. The emperors at the very top were no different. Augustus documented the scale of his gifts to the Roman people in his autobiography, gifts that exceeded hundreds of millions of sesterces (a small silver or bronze coin) in expenditures from his own pocket. A later emperor, Trajan, established a social scheme for feeding the children of poor Roman citizens in Italy—a benefaction that he advertised on coins and in pictures on arches in various towns in Italy.

The essence of Roman civil society, though, involved the formal relationships governed by Rome's laws and courts. By the last century BCE, the Roman state's complex legal system featured not only a rich body of written law but also institutions for settling legal disputes and a growing number of highly educated men who specialized in interpreting the law. The apparatus of Roman law eventually appeared in every town and city of the empire, creating a deeply entrenched civil culture. It is no surprise that this legal infrastructure persisted long after the empire's political and military institutions had disappeared.

Municipal charters and civil laws—as well as secular philosophers and, later, Christian writers—placed the family at the very foundation of the Roman social order.

PRIMARY SOURCE

Birthday Invitation of Claudia Severa

The ability to write in Latin became so widespread under the Roman Empire that even its frontier areas could boast basic literacy. Excavations of a Roman army base at Vindolanda, in northern England, have unearthed a cache of documents written on thin sheets of wood. These reveal the normal use of Latin writing for everyday activities late in the first century CE. Officers' wives were just as skilled in writing as the men. One of these elite women, Claudia Severa, sent a letter inviting a good friend (whom she addresses affectionately as "sister") to her birthday party. The elegant handwriting on several documents is almost certainly that of Claudia herself. The second letter is her friend's reply.

[Address on the outside:] To Sulpicia Lepidina, wife of Cerialis, from Severa.
[Claudia Severa to her Lepidina, Greetings!]

My sister, I am sending an invitation to you to attend my birthday festivities on the third day before the Ides of September [September 11 in our calendar]—just to make sure that you come to visit us. Your presence will make the day all the more enjoyable for me. Please convey my greetings to your Cerialis [i.e., Lepidina's husband]. My Aelius and our little son send him their warmest greetings.

I await your arrival, my sister.

I bid you goodbye, my sister, my dearest soul. Be well.

[Sulpicia Lepidina to Claudia Severa] Greeting.

Just as I had told you, my sister, and had promised that I would ask your Brocchus [i.e., Claudia Severa's husband, Aelius Brocchus] for permission to come to visit you, he replied to me that I was, of course, always most welcome to come. . . . [I shall try] to come to you by whatever way I can, for there are certain things that we must do . . . on which matter you will receive a letter from me so that you will know what I am going to do. . . .

Farewell, my sister, my dearest and most-desired soul . . .

QUESTIONS FOR ANALYSIS

- What does the writing of letters in Latin at this far edge of the empire tell us about Roman culture?
- Sulpicia mentions asking Claudia's husband for permission to visit Claudia. Why would she do this? Do you think it indicates that the women's husbands were of different military rank, or that Sulpicia was merely following Roman social customs for women—or both? Or something else?
- What does the very existence of these letters tell us about Roman women?

Source: Alan K. Bowman and J. David Thomas, with contributions by J. N. Adams, *The Vindolanda Writing-Tablets (Tabulae Vindolandenses II)* (London: British Museum Press, 1994), nos. 291 and 292, pp. 256–62. Translated by Brent Shaw.

The authoritarian *paterfamilias* ("father of the family") headed the family. Legally speaking, he had nearly total power over his dependents, including his wife, children, grandchildren, and the slaves whom he owned. Imperial society heightened the importance of the basic family unit of mother, father, and children in the urban centers. As in Han dynasty China, the Roman state regularly undertook a census, rigorously counting the empire's inhabitants and assessing their property for tax purposes—a process that underscored the family as the core unit of society.

This system might seem to place women under the domineering rule of fathers and husbands. That is certainly the picture presented in the repressive laws that Roman men drafted and in the histories that Roman men wrote. But compared with women in most Greek city-states, Roman women, even those of only modest wealth and status, had much greater freedom of action and much greater control of their own wealth and property. (See Primary Source: Birthday Invitation of Claudia Severa.) Thus, Terentia, the wife of the Republican senator Cicero (and a woman reminiscent of Ban Zhao, the female Han historian discussed earlier), bought and sold properties on her own, made decisions regarding her family and wealth without consulting her husband (much to his chagrin—he later divorced her), and apparently fared well following her separation from Cicero. Her behavior was normal for a woman of her status: she was well educated, literate, well connected, and in control of her own life—despite what the laws and ideas of Roman males might suggest. The daily lives of ordinary women that we know of from papyrus documents found in the Roman province of Egypt, for example, show them buying, selling, renting, and leasing with no sign that the legal constraints subjecting them to male control had any significant effect on their dealings.

Economy and New Scales of Production

Rome achieved staggering transformations in the production of agricultural, manufactured, and mined goods. Public and private demand for metals, for example, led the Romans to mine massive quantities of lead, silver, and copper in Spain. Evidence from Mediterranean shipwrecks similarly indicates a seaborne trade on an unprecedented scale. The area of land surveyed and cultivated rose steadily throughout this period, as Romans reached into arid lands on the periphery of the Sahara Desert to the south and opened up heavily forested regions in present-day France and Germany to the north. (See Map 7.4.)

The Romans also built an unprecedented number of roads to connect far-flung parts of their empire. Although many roads did not have the high-quality flagstone paving and excellent drainage exhibited by highways in Italy, such as the Via Appia, most were systematically marked by milestones (for the first time in this part of the world) so that travelers would know their precise location and the distance to the next town. Also for the first time, complex land maps and itineraries specified all major roads and distances between towns. Adding to the roads' significance was their deliberate coordination with Mediterranean sea routes to support the smooth and safe flow of traffic, commerce, and ideas on land and at sea.

The mines produced copper, tin, silver, and gold—out of which the Roman state produced the most massive coinage known in the western world before early modern times. Coinage facilitated the exchange of commodities and services, which now carried standard values. Throughout the Roman Empire, from small towns on the edge of the Sahara Desert to army towns along the northern frontiers, people appraised, purchased, and sold goods in coin denominations. Taxes were assessed and hired laborers were paid in coin. The economy in its leading sectors functioned more efficiently because of the production of coins on an immense scale (paralleled only by the coinage output of Han dynasty China and its successors).

Roman mining, as well as other sizable operations, relied on chattel slaves—human beings purchased as private property. The massive concentration of wealth and slaves at the center of the Roman world led to the first large-scale commercial plantation agriculture, along with the first technical handbooks on how to run such operations for profit. (It also led to dramatic slave rebellions, such as the Sicilian Revolt of 135–132 BCE and the Spartacus uprising of 73–71 BCE, although the latter began among slaves in a school for gladiators.) These estates specialized in products destined for the big urban markets: wheat, grapes, and olives, as well as cattle and sheep. Such developments

rested on a bedrock belief that private property and its ownership were sacrosanct. In fact, the Roman senator Cicero argued that the defense and enjoyment of private property constituted basic reasons for the existence of the state. (See Primary Source: Cicero on the Role of the Roman State.) Roman law more clearly defined and more strictly enforced the rights of the private owner than any previous legal system had done. The extension of private ownership of land and other property to regions having little or no prior knowledge of it—Egypt in the east, Spain in the west, the lands of western Europe—was one of the most enduring effects of the Roman Empire.

ROME THE POLLUTER Sometimes the size of empires must be measured in terms of side effects. The Roman Empire required huge resources, a need fulfilled through extensive mining. The result was a pollution on a scale never previously witnessed and which can be traced everywhere in the environment. The copper mines at Phaedo, in southern Jordan in the Roman province of Arabia, offer as good an example as any. The effects of pollution on the local population are clearly traceable in spite of the fact that this area was a truly fragile and marginal economy. They can even be seen on a global scale. Ice core samples taken from the Mediterranean Sea and the ice sheets of Greenland reveal concentrations of isotopes of copper and lead whose levels peaked in the first centuries CE, clearly the result of airborne pollutants produced by the colossal Roman mining operations. Other signs of pollution have also been found in lake sediments in Sweden, dated again to the first centuries CE. Although pollution from mining and metal production occurred in other territories, such as Song dynasty China, the Roman Empire seems to have been the world's first global polluter.

Roman Roads. *Like Qin and Han China, the Roman Empire was characterized by large-scale road building, which began as early as the late fourth century BCE. Roads eventually connected most land areas and larger urban centers in the empire, considerably easing ordinary travel as well as trade and commerce. Here we see part of the Via Appia, the great highway that connected Rome with the southern parts of Italy.*

Legend:
- ⊙ Important provincial capital
- • Roman trading cities
- 〰 Defense works
- 〰 African fortification
- — Main Roman road
- – – – Sea-lane
- ■ Legionary base
- ⚓ Naval base
- Roman territory under *Pax Romana*
- Territory occupied after 106 BCE

Traded items
- 🪙 Metals
- Ɏ Grain
- 🍷 Wine
- 〰 Oil
- 🐟 Fish
- ⬭ Slaves
- ▯ Marble
- ⬮ Ceramics
- ⬯ Amber

MAP 7.4 | *Pax Romana*: The Roman Empire in the Second Century CE

The Roman Empire enjoyed remarkable peace and prosperity in the second century CE. Economic production increased, and Roman culture expanded throughout the realm.

- According to the map, what commodities were traded most widely?
- With what groups did Romans trade beyond their empire, and for what commodity in particular?
- How did the *Pax Romana* promote the spread of Christianity?

Religious Cults and the Rise of Christianity

The world of gods, spirits, and demons that characterized earlier periods remained hugely important. But if there was any religion of empire, it was **Christianity**. Its foundations lay in a direct confrontation with Roman imperial authority: the trial of Yeshua ben Yosef (Joshua son of Joseph). He preached the new doctrines of what was originally a sect of Judaism, and we know him today by the Greek form of his name, Jesus. A Roman governor, Pontius Pilatus, tried Jesus in a typical Roman provincial trial; he was found guilty of sedition and executed, along with two bandits, by a standard Roman penalty—crucifixion.

We know of Jesus only after his death. No reference to him survives from his own lifetime. Two years after the crucifixion, Paul of Tarsus, a Jew and a Roman citizen from southeastern Anatolia, claimed to have seen Jesus in full glory outside the city of Damascus. Paul and the communities to whom he preached between 40 and 60 CE were the first to call Yeshua "Jesus." They also referred to him as "the Christ" (*ho Christos*) or the Anointed One (that is, the Messiah) and thought of him as a god.

Paul had not been one of Jesus's original disciples. Only much later did four of those men—Matthew, Mark, Luke, and John—write about his life and record his sayings in accounts that came to be called the Gospels. (That early English word

PRIMARY SOURCE

Cicero on the Role of the Roman State

Whereas Greek thinkers debated ethics and morals, the role of the good life, and the nature of the universe, Romans deliberated more about the nature of government and the role of the state. This focus reflects their pragmatic attitudes and their possession of a huge empire. In the following passage, Marcus Tullius Cicero, one of the leading Roman politicians from the 60s to the 40s BCE, *discusses how any man who holds public office in the Roman state has a duty to defend the state's main function.*

That man who undertakes responsibility for public office in the state must make it his first priority to see that every person can continue to hold what is his and that no inroads are made into the goods or property of private persons by the state. It was a bad policy when Philippus, when he was tribune of the plebs [about 104 BCE], proposed an agrarian reform law. When his law was defeated, he took the defeat well and was moderate in his response. In the debates themselves, however, he tried to curry popular favor and acted in a bad way when he said, "In our community there are not more than two thousand men who have real property."

That speech ought to be condemned outright for attempting to advocate equality of property holdings. What policy could be more dangerous? It was for this very reason—that each person should be able to keep his own property—that

states and local governments were founded. Although it was by the leadership of nature herself that men gathered together in communities, it was for the hope of keeping their own property that they sought the protection of states....

Some men want to become known as popular politicians and for this reason they engage in making revolutionary proposals about land, with the result that owners are driven from their homes and money lent out by creditors is simply given free to the borrowers with no need for repayment. Such men are shaking the very foundations of the state. First of all, they are destroying that goodwill and sense of trust which can no longer exist when money is simply taken from some people and given to others [by the state]. And then they take away fairness, which is totally destroyed if each person is not permitted to keep what is his own. For,

as I have already said, it is the peculiar function of the state and of local government to make sure that each person should be able to keep his own things freely and without any worry.

QUESTIONS FOR ANALYSIS

- According to Cicero, what is the main function of the Roman state and the main reason men "sought the protection of states"?
- How does the protection of private property rights affect the claims that citizens had on their rulers?
- And how does this differ from the role of the state in contemporaneous Han dynasty China?

Source: De Officiis (On Duties), 2.21.73, 22.78; translated by Brent Shaw.

---

comes from the original Greek *Evangeliai*, meaning "Good News.") The Gospels all sought to tell the world not what Jesus had said, but who he had been. They served as answers to the question that Jesus reportedly asked his disciples a few months before he died: "Who do people say that I am?" (Mark 8:27).

Jesus's preachings could not have been more Jewish. He taught that God is the father of his people—sinners who are always liable to fall away. But God is like a good shepherd to them. Scrambling down dangerous ravines, the good shepherd seeks those who have gone astray, joyfully carrying home on his shoulders even a single lost lamb (see John 10:1–18). We have already met the image of the great king as shepherd of his people in both Egypt and Mesopotamia (see Chapter 3). With Jesus, this ancient image took on a new, personal closeness. Not a distant monarch but a preacher, Jesus had set out on God's behalf to gather a new, small flock. Jesus's teachings (like those

of the Buddha) comforted people who lived at a distance from power, such as scholars, merchants, and farmers.

Through the preaching of Paul in Greek and the textual portraits painted in the Gospels, also in Greek, this image of Jesus rapidly spread beyond Palestine (where Jesus had preached only to Jews and only in the local language, Aramaic) and entered the religious bloodstream of the Mediterranean. Core elements of Jesus's message, such as the special responsibilities of the well-off for the poor and the promised eventual empowerment of "the meek," appealed to huge numbers of ordinary persons in the wider Mediterranean world. But it was the apostle Paul who was especially responsible for reshaping this message for a wider audience. While Jesus directed his teachings to villagers and peasants, Paul's writing and preaching dealt with a world strongly divided by ethnic identity and gender, between the super wealthy at the top and the completely rightless slaves

Great Empires Compared: The Han, the Roman, and the British Empires after World War I

The Roman and Han Empires were the most powerful and extensive empires that the world had known at the time, and because of their grandeur and accomplishments, they remained part of the European and Chinese historical traditions. Even the British imperialists, who, as the following table demonstrates, ruled over much larger populations than the Romans and the Han Chinese, though with lesser military forces, often compared their empire to that of the Romans. We have added the Qing Empire at its height at the end of the nineteenth century because it rivaled the British Empire in so many respects.

QUESTIONS FOR ANALYSIS

- If you compare the modern-day British Empire with the empires of the Romans and the Han Chinese, what differences stand out in terms of land area and total population? How can we explain some of these differences?
- Can you explain why the Han Empire and the Qing Empire had much larger armies than the Roman and British Empires?
- What does the population data on cities suggest about the place of cities in early world history versus modern world history?

Maximum Land Area	
Roman Empire	970,000 square miles, mainly land based
Han Empire	4,000,000 square miles, mainly land based
British Empire	1,800,000 square miles, largely sea borne
Qing Empire	3,500,000 square miles, largely land based

Total Population	
Roman Empire	c. 60,000,000 (c. one-quarter of the Afro-Eurasian population)
Han Empire	c. 59,000,000 (c. one-quarter of the Afro-Eurasian population)
British Empire	459,307,735 (c. one-quarter of the world's population)
Qing Empire	450,000,000 (c. one-quarter of the world's population)

Size of the Military Forces	
Roman Empire	400,000
Han Empire	1,000,000
British Empire	330,000
Qing Empire	1,000,000

Largest Cities	
ROMAN EMPIRE	
Rome	1,100,000
Alexandria	600,000
Carthage	400,000
Athens	300,000
Antioch	250,000
HAN EMPIRE	
Chang'an City	1,000,000
Luoyang City	400,000
BRITISH EMPIRE IN 1920	
London	7,488,000
Calcutta	1,328,000
Bombay	1,176,000
Glasgow	1,052,000
Birmingham	922,000
Cairo	791,000
QING EMPIRE IN 1910	
Beijing	1,100,000
Guangzhou	739,000
Yangzhou	567,300
Shanghai	444,318

Sources: Ping-Ti Ho, *Studies on the Population of China, 1368–1953* (Cambridge, MA: Harvard University Press, 1959); Susan Naquin, *Peking: Temples and City Life, 1400–1900* (Berkeley: University of California Press, 2000); Tim Cornelland and John Matthews, *Atlas of the Roman World* (New York: Checkmark Books, 1982); Greg Woolf, *Rome: An Empire's Story* (New York: Oxford University Press, 2012).

at the bottom. Facing this disparity, Paul promised that "there is neither Jew nor Greek, neither slave nor free, neither male nor female, since you are all one in Jesus Christ" (in his letter to the Galatians 3:28). The new inclusive message immediately appealed to the diverse town and city dwellers of the empire.

Just half a century after Jesus's crucifixion, the followers of Jesus saw in his life not the wanderings of a Jewish charismatic and teacher but a moment of head-on conflict between "God" and "the world." (A charismatic is a person who uses his personal strengths or virtues, often laced with a divine aura, to command followers.) Thus, the preaching that his followers brought to confront this world was no longer the preaching of a man. It was the message of a divine being—who, for thirty years half a century before, had moved (largely unrecognized) among human beings. Jesus's followers formed a church: a permanent gathering committed to the charge of leaders chosen by God and by their fellow believers. For these leaders and their followers, death—death for Jesus—was the hallmark of their faith. In dying, they witnessed for the faith. Indeed, the defining experience for Christians was that of the Roman trial and the idea of "witnessing" to God. The Greek word *martus* means "a witness in a trial." From this came the English term *martyr* and the concept of martyrdom.

At first, persecutions of Christians were sporadic responses to local concerns. Not until the emperor Decius, in the mid-third century CE, did the state direct an empire-wide attack on Christians. And that attempt failed. Decius died within the year, and Christians interpreted their persecutor's death as evidence

Coin Hoard. *The use of coins for a wide spectrum of economic exchanges became common in the Roman Empire. Looking at the batches buried for safekeeping gives us an idea of the range of coins in circulation at any one time. This coin hoard was found near Didcot in Oxfordshire, England. Buried about 165 CE, it contained about 125 gold coins minted between the 50s and 160s CE and represents the equivalent of about eleven years' pay for a Roman soldier. Gold coins were used for expensive transactions or to store wealth. Most ordinary purchases or payments were made with silver or brass coins.*

of the hand of God in human affairs. By the last decades of the third century CE, Christian communities of various kinds, reflecting the different strands of their movement through the Mediterranean as well as the local cultures in which they settled, were present in every society in the empire. (For more detail on the rise and spread of Christianity, see Chapter 8.)

The Limits of Empire

The empire labeled outsiders as those whom it excluded, and a crucial part of this process was the exercise of force in extending its borders. (See Map 7.5.) The limitations of Roman force determined who belonged in the empire and was subject to it and who was outside it and therefore excluded. To the west the Romans pushed their authority to the shores of the Atlantic Ocean, and to the south they drove it to the edges of the Sahara Desert. In both cases, there was little more useful land available to dominate. Roman power was blocked, however, in the east by the Parthians and then the Sasanians and in the west by the Goths and other German peoples. (See Current Trends in World History: Empires, Allies, and Frontiers.)

THE PARTHIANS AND SASANIANS On Rome's eastern frontiers, powerful Romans such as Marcus Crassus in the mid-50s BCE and Mark Antony in the early 30s BCE wished to imitate the achievements of Alexander the Great and conquer the arid lands lying east of Judea and Syria. But they failed miserably, stopped by the Parthian Empire and their successors, the Sasanian Empire (see Chapter 6 for a full discussion of the Parthians and Chapter 8 for more on the Sasanians). The Sasanians expanded the technical advances in mounted horseback warfare that the Parthians had used so successfully in open-desert warfare against the slow-moving Roman mass infantry formations. King Shapur I (Shabuhr), their greatest monarch, exploited the weaknesses of the Roman Empire in the mid-third century CE, even capturing the Roman emperor Valerian. As successful as Parthians and Sasanians were in fighting the Romans, however, they could never challenge the Romans' sway over Mediterranean lands. Their decentralized political structure limited their coordination and resources, and their horse-mounted warfare was ill suited to fight around the more rocky and hilly environments of the Mediterranean world.

GERMAN AND GOTHIC "BARBARIANS" In the lands across the Rhine and Danube, to the north, environmental conditions largely determined the limits of empire. The long and harsh winters, but excellent soil and growing conditions, produced hardy populations clustered densely across vast distances. These illiterate, kin-based agricultural societies had changed little since the first millennium BCE. And because their warrior elites

MAP 7.5 | Population of Roman World in 362 CE

Roman frontiers at the northern and eastern limits of the empire were persistent sources of anxiety and concern for imperial leaders. While not as densely populated as the heart of the Roman Empire, these regions contained large population centers as well.

- Name some of the major groups of peoples that lived just beyond Roman rule in the areas of eastern Europe and Southwest Asia.
- What were the geographical limits of the Roman Empire?
- According to your reading, why were Roman armies never able to subdue these neighboring peoples?

still engaged in armed competition, war and violence tended to characterize their connections with the Roman Empire.

As the empire fixed its northern frontiers along the Rhine and Danube Rivers, two factors determined its relationship with the Germans and Goths on the rivers' other side. First, these small societies had only one big commodity for which the empire was willing to pay big money: human bodies. So the slave trade out of the land across the Rhine and Danube became immense: gold, silver, coins, wine, arms, and other luxury items flowed across the rivers in one direction in exchange for slaves in the other. Second, their wars were unremitting, as every emperor faced the expectation of dealing harshly with the "barbarians." These connections, involving arms and violence, were to enmesh the Romans ever more tightly with the tribal societies to the north.

One of the main ways in which peoples beyond the northern frontier related to the empire was by military service. They were frequently found serving in "ethnic units" that were attached to the Roman army. As internal conflicts within the Roman Empire increased, there was more frequent recourse to the use of "barbarians" as soldiers and officers who served in its armed forces. The truly vast areas of the western Eurasian steppelands harbored horse-mounted mobile populations, most of whom were dependent on the herding of animals for their sustenance. Groups known variously as Alans and Sarmatians, or more generally as Scythians or Goths, were involved in internal conflicts that pushed some of them to the edge of the empire and then across the Danube into the empire itself. These armed migrations became increasingly difficult for the empire to control. The effects for the peoples in the contact zone were often worse: caught in violent conflicts between enemies pressing in from the north and the heavy defenses of the empire to the south, not a few of them simply went out of existence.

While the Han Empire had fallen by 300 CE, the Roman Empire would continue to exist politically for nearly two more centuries, during which its history would become intertwined with the rise of Christianity, one of the world's universalizing religions.

CONCLUSION

China and Rome both constructed empires of unprecedented scale and duration, yet they differed in fundamental ways. Starting out with a less numerous and less dense population than China, Rome relied on slaves and "barbarian" immigrants to expand and diversify its workforce. While less than 1 percent of the Chinese population were slaves, more than 10 percent were slaves in the Roman Empire. The lifeblood of the Chinese rural economy was a huge population of free peasant farmers; this enormous labor pool, together with a remarkable bureaucracy, enabled the Han to achieve great political stability. In contrast, the millions of peasant farmers who formed the backbone of rural society in the Roman Empire were much more loosely integrated into the state structure. They never unified to revolt against their government and overthrow it, as did the mass peasant movements of Later Han China. By comparison with their counterparts in China, the peasants in the Roman Empire were not as well connected in their proximity or density or as united in purpose. Here, too, the Mediterranean environment accented separation and difference.

By Chinese standards, the Roman Empire was relatively fragmented and underadministered. Moreover, philosophy and religion never underpinned the Roman state in the way that Confucianism buttressed the dynasties of China. Both empires, however, benefited from the spread of a uniform language and imperial culture. The process was more comprehensive in China, which possessed a single language that the elites used, a literary language based on classical Chinese, than in Rome, whose empire spanned a two-language world: Latin in the western

Soldier versus Barbarian. *On the frontiers of the Roman Empire, the legionary soldiers faced the non-Roman "barbarians" from the lands beyond. In this piece of a stone-carved picture from the northwestern frontier, we see a civilized and disciplined Roman soldier, to the left, facing a German "barbarian"—hair uncut and unkempt, without formal armor, his house a thatched hut. Frontier realities were never so clear-cut, of course. Roman soldiers, often recruited from the "barbarian" peoples, were a lot more like them than was convenient to admit, and the "barbarians" were influenced by and closer to Roman cultural models than this picture indicates.*

Mediterranean, Greek in the east. Both states fostered a common imperial culture across all levels of society. Once entrenched, these cultures and languages lasted well after the end of empire.

Differences in human resources, languages, and ideas led the Roman and Han states to evolve in unique ways. In both states, however, the faith of outsiders—Christians or Buddhists—eclipsed the classical and secular traditions that grounded the state's foundational ideals. Transmission of these new faiths benefited from expanded communications networks. The new religions added to the cultural mix that succeeded the Roman Empire and the Han dynasty.

At their height, both states surpassed their forebears by translating unprecedented military power into the fullest form of state-based organization. Each state's complex organization involved the systematic control, counting, and taxing of its population. In both cases, the general increase of the population, the growth of huge cities, and the success of long-distance trade contributed to the new scales of magnitude, making these world's first two globalizing empires. The Han would not be superseded in East Asia as the model empire until the Tang dynasty in the seventh century CE. In western Afro-Eurasia, the Roman Empire would not be surpassed in scale or intensity of development until the rise of powerful European nation-states more than a millennium later.

After You Read This Chapter

FOCUS ON: *Comparing the Two Empires*

- Han China and imperial Rome assimilate diverse peoples to their ways and regard outsiders as uncivilized.

- Both empires develop professional military elites, codify laws, and value the role of the state (not just the ruler) in supporting their societies.

- Both empires serve as models for successor states in their regions.

- The empires differ in their ideals and the officials they value: Han China values civilian bureaucrats and magistrates; Rome values soldiers and military governors.

Go to INQUIZITIVE to see what you know & learn what you've missed.

CHRONOLOGY

East Asia		Qin Empire **221–207 BCE**	
		Emperor Wu expands Han Empire **140–87 BCE**	
The Mediterranean	Rome eliminates Carthage (Punic Wars) **265–146 BCE**	Roman state expands through Italian peninsula **350–265 BCE**	

400 BCE	300 BCE	200 BCE	100 BCE

KEY TERMS

STUDY QUESTIONS

1. **Identify** the features that made Han China and imperial Rome globalizing empires.

2. **Describe** the development of the Han dynasty—in terms of political, social, economic, and cultural elements—from its beginnings through the third century CE.

3. **Explain** the influence of Confucian ideas during the Han dynasty. How did these ideas shape political and social hierarchies during this period?

4. **Discuss** the impact of Xiongnu pastoralists on imperial policies of the Qin and Han dynasties. How did each dynasty counter the threat of nomadic incursions into its territorial heartlands?

5. **Explain** the process through which the Roman city-state created a vast empire in the Mediterranean world. How did Roman attitudes toward military service influence the empire's growth?

6. **Analyze** the social and legal hierarchies that governed Roman urban life. In what ways did Christianity challenge these hierarchies? To what extent did residents enjoy personal autonomy?

7. **Identify** the political features that were central to the Roman *res publica*.

8. **Compare and contrast** Han China and imperial Rome in terms of their respective political authority, economic activity, cultural developments, and military expansion.

9. **Explain** the concepts of *Pax Sinica* and *Pax Romana*. How did Han and Roman leaders promote long periods of peace and prosperity in eastern and western Afro-Eurasia, respectively?

10. **Compare and contrast** the methods through which Han and Roman leaders enlisted their subjects' support. What emphasis did each state place on ideology, civil bureaucracy, and military organization?

11. **Compare and contrast** Roman strategies for promoting stability along its borders with those of the Han dynasty. How different were the threats that each empire faced from borderland peoples?

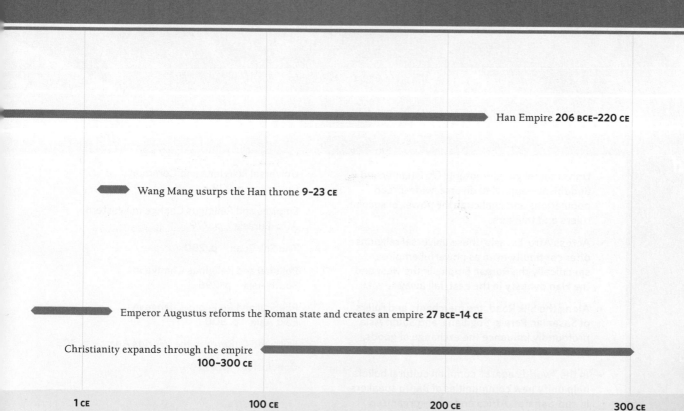

Han Empire **206 BCE–220 CE**

Wang Mang usurps the Han throne **9–23 CE**

Emperor Augustus reforms the Roman state and creates an empire **27 BCE–14 CE**

Christianity expands through the empire **100–300 CE**

| 1 CE | 100 CE | 200 CE | 300 CE |

Before You Read This Chapter

Go to
INQUIZITIVE
to see what you
know & learn
what you've
missed.

GLOBAL STORYLINES

- Universal religions—notably Christianity and Buddhism—appeal to diverse, widespread populations and challenge the power of secular rulers and thinkers.

- Across Afro-Eurasia, these universal religions offer continuity even as powerful empires, specifically the Roman Empire in the west and the Han dynasty in the east, fall away.

- Along the Silk Road, the merchants and rulers of Sasanian Persia, Sogdiana, and South Asia profoundly influence the exchange of goods, people, and ideas between east and west.

- In the "worlds apart," common cultural beliefs help unify new communities of Bantu speakers in sub-Saharan Africa and newly organized polities in Mesoamerica.

CHAPTER OUTLINE

8

The Rise of Universal Religions, 300–600 CE

FOCUS QUESTIONS

- What characteristics made Christianity and Buddhism universal religions, and why did they have such wide appeal in Afro-Eurasia?

- What was the nature of the relationship between empires and universal religions across Afro-Eurasia during this period?

- To what extent did connections between political unity and religious development influence sub-Saharan Africa and Mesoamerica in the fourth to sixth century CE?

- How did the unifying political and cultural developments in sub-Saharan Africa and Mesoamerica compare with those occurring in Afro-Eurasia during this period?

Around 180 CE, a humble group of seven men and five women stood trial before the provincial governor at Carthage. They claimed to be Christians, and their crime was refusal to worship the gods of the Roman Empire. The governor was unimpressed; his god was "the protecting spirit of our lord the emperor." One Christian retorted that his god was also an emperor, but that he could not be seen, for he stood "above all kings and all nations." There was an unbridgeable gap between the governor and the Christians. So the governor read out a death sentence, ordering their immediate execution. "Thanks be to God!" cried the Christians, and straightaway they were beheaded.

As the centuries unfolded, the tables would turn dramatically. Old ideas of the supremacy of an emperor-lord gave way to those of the Lord God as emperor. Previously, the impulse toward universalism—that is to say, bringing everyone under the sway of a single ruler or a single religion—had come from ambitious empire builders, such as Alexander the Great and the Roman emperors. Now, for the first time, religious leaders became the agents of spreading, or universalizing, these spiritual messages and worked to convert humanity to their belief systems.

This period, which witnessed the bonding of religions to universal aspirations, spread religious tenets across the Afro-Eurasian landmass and gave religions, notably Christianity and Buddhism, a universalistic message and widespread appeal to diverse peoples and cultures. In this era, spiritual and religious fervor, while it triggered new divides in the world, became an even more powerful force of integration than political ambitions. This advent of universal religions as global shapers of unity was anything but simple. It built on the expansive reach of the Roman and Han Empires while at the same time reshaping the institutions of these states. It also profited from the closer commercial and intellectual connections between east and west. This chapter tells the story of how Christianity and Buddhism became universal faiths that changed world history forever.

UNIVERSAL RELIGIONS AND COMMON CULTURES

From 300 to 600 CE, the entire Afro-Eurasian landmass experienced a surge of religious ferment. In the west, Christianity became the state faith of the Roman Empire. In India, Vedic religion (Brahmanism) evolved into a more formal spiritual system called Hinduism. In northern India, central Asia, and even China, Buddhism—originally a code of ethics—became a religion. Across much of the world, spiritual concerns integrated scattered communities into shared faiths.

Two faiths in particular aspired to universality in this era—Christianity and Buddhism. They were to be joined by Islam several centuries later. What made them **universal religions** in comparison with, say, Judaism, Hinduism, and traditional African religious beliefs was that they were not tied to a locality. Hinduism was the belief system of the peoples of South Asia; Judaism was tied to a specific ethnicity; and traditional African religious beliefs varied from people to people. In contrast, Christianity and Buddhism appealed to diverse populations (men and women, freeborn and slaves, rich and poor) and proved adaptable as they moved from one cultural and geographical area to another. They were promoted by energetic and charismatic missionizing agents, and despite their many and insistent demands, they provided a deep sense of community to their converts. Christianity and (to a lesser extent) Buddhism also benefited from the support of powerful empires. Even as the Roman Empire and the Han dynasty began to crumble, these universalizing traditions continued to flourish.

The new spirituality blossomed inside and also outside the empires. In western Europe, Christianity continued to expand alongside a decaying Roman state. In the eastern Mediterranean, it inspired a revived Roman *imperium* at Byzantium. In India, Hinduism and Buddhism vied for cultural preeminence; in central Asia and China, Buddhism flourished as the old polities

foundered. These religions crossed over political and cultural barriers and appealed to a wide variety of ethnic groups because of the ecumenical nature of their spiritual messages.

The peoples living in sub-Saharan Africa and the Americas, too, reached beyond their local communities, creating common cultures across wider geographical areas. As in Eurasia and North Africa, political and cultural transformations undergirded the emergence of these common belief systems. (See Map 8.1.) In Africa, the Bantu-speaking peoples, residing in the southeastern corner of present-day Nigeria, began to spread their way of life throughout the entire southern half of the landmass. Similarly, across the Atlantic Ocean, the Mayas established political and cultural institutions over a large portion of Mesoamerica and laid the foundations of a common culture.

Across Afro-Eurasia, universal religions were on the move. (See Map 8.2.) Religious leaders carrying written texts (books, scrolls, or tablets of wood or palm leaf) often traveled widely.

Xuanzang. *This painting c. 900 CE, which survives in the caves of Dunhuang along the Silk Road, portrays the Chinese pilgrim Xuanzang accompanied by a tiger on his epic travels to South Asia to collect important Buddhist scriptures.*

Christian Martyrs. *The Christian martyr Perpetua (left) came to be represented as an upper-class Roman matron with carefully covered hair. Set in a circle of bright blue, in the golden dome of a church, she looks out from a distant, peaceful Heaven. The detail from a mosaic found in a Roman circus in North Africa (right) shows a criminal tied to a stake and being pushed on a little cart toward a lunging leopard. Christian martyrs were treated much the same as criminals: they were executed—exposed to animals without even the "privilege" of suffering at the hands of a human executioner.*

Christians from Persia went to China. Buddhists journeyed from South Asia to Afghanistan and used the caravan routes of central Asia to reach China. In 643 CE, the Chinese Buddhist Xuanzang brought back to Chang'an (then the world's largest city) an entire library of Buddhist scriptures—527 boxes of writings and 192 birchbark tablets—that he had collected on a pilgrimage to Buddhist holy sites in South Asia. He lodged them in the Great Wild Goose Pagoda and immediately began to translate every line into Chinese. Here was the "truth" of Buddhism for Xuanzang, similar to the way we accept information we find in a modern science textbook, and as exciting a revelation when they reached distant China as when Buddhist thinkers had elaborated them in northern India, more than 5,000 miles away. Some Chinese Buddhists at that time referred to India as the "Central Kingdom." In this way, voyages, translations, and pilgrimages like that of Xuanzang remapped the spiritual landscape of the world.

EMPIRES AND RELIGIOUS CHANGE IN WESTERN AFRO-EURASIA

By the fourth century CE in western Afro-Eurasia, the Roman Empire was hardly the political and military juggernaut it had been 300 years earlier. Surrounded by peoples who coveted its wealth while resisting its power, Rome was fragmenting. Yet its endurance was a boon to the new religious ferment, which took hold in its rapidly changing political institutions. Although so-called barbarians eventually overran the western parts of the empire, in many ways those areas still felt "Roman." They looked to the new faith of Christianity to maintain continuity with the past, eventually founding a central church in Rome to rule the remnants of the empire.

The Rise and Spread of Christianity

Ironically, the most crucial change ever to befall the Roman Empire had little to do with distant frontier wars. Instead, it grew from a religious war fought, from the bottom up, in the peaceful and tightly administered towns that were the nerve centers of the Roman Mediterranean.

Christianity's rise owed much to the willingness of people to die for their beliefs, since this new faith experienced periods of savage persecution. Without the appearance of **martyrs**, Christianity would not have gained such a determined following or enjoyed such widespread support. Martyrs were people whom the Roman authorities executed for persisting in their Christian beliefs instead of submitting to traditional rituals or beliefs. Many of them were remarkable witnesses to their faith.

In 203 CE, a well-to-do mother in her early twenties, Vibia Perpetua, faced a horrible punishment for refusing to sacrifice to the Roman gods. Denied the benefit of a human executioner, she and her companions were condemned to face wild beasts in the amphitheater of Carthage. The amphitheater is still there, north of modern Tunis. It is a mean, small place—not a gigantic stadium. The condemned and the spectators would have had eye contact with one another throughout the fatal encounter. The remembered heroism of women martyrs, like Perpetua, balanced the increasingly all-male leadership—bishops and clergy—that was rising as the Christian church became institutionalized.

As Christianity and other new religious ideas gained followings in the Roman Empire, they transformed the way

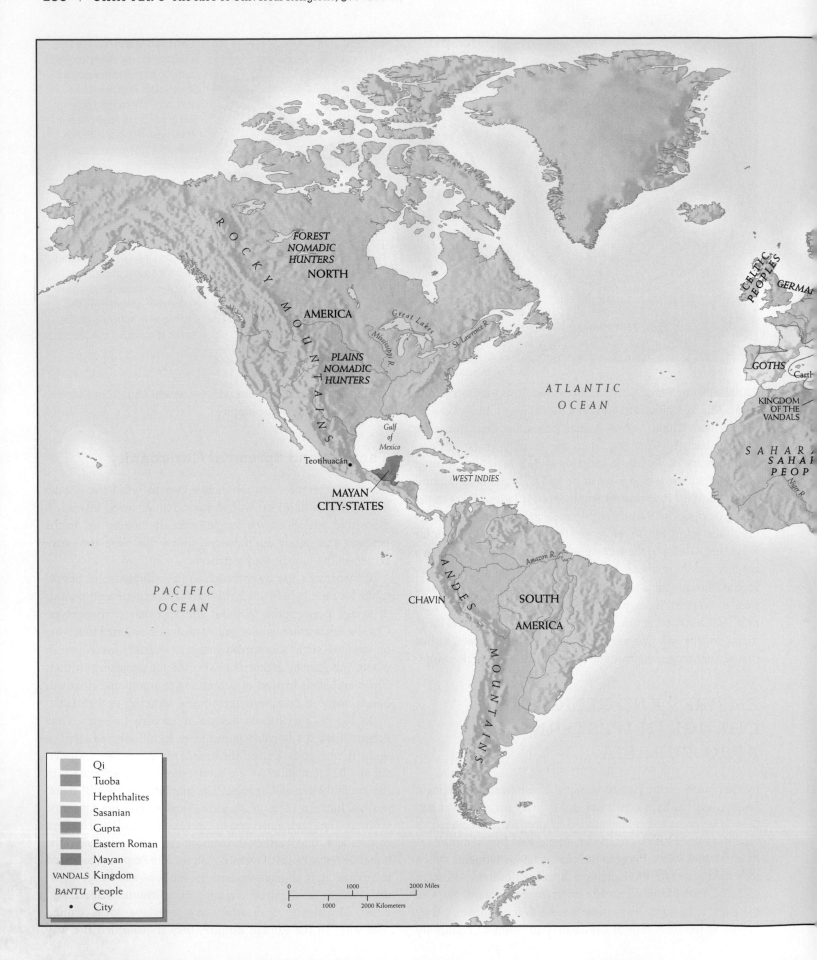

FOREST
NOMADIC
HUNTERS

NORTH

AMERICA

Great Lakes

St. Lawrence R.

Mississippi R.

R O C K Y   M O U N T A I N S

PLAINS
NOMADIC
HUNTERS

Gulf of Mexico

ATLANTIC OCEAN

Teotihuacán

WEST INDIES

MAYAN CITY-STATES

PACIFIC OCEAN

CHAVIN

A N D E S   M O U N T A I N S

Amazon R.

SOUTH

AMERICA

CELTIC PEOPLES

GERMAN

GOTHS

Carth

KINGDOM OF THE VANDALS

S A H A R
SAHAR
PEOP

Niger R.

	Qi
	Tuoba
	Hephthalites
	Sasanian
	Gupta
	Eastern Roman
	Mayan
VANDALS	Kingdom
BANTU	People
•	City

0   1000   2000 Miles

0   1000   2000 Kilometers

MAP 8.1 | Empires and Common Cultures from 300 to 600 CE

The period 300–600 CE was a time of tumultuous political change.

- Comparing this map with Map 6.2, which polities are new? Which polities have disappeared? Which ones have expanded or contracted?

- What historical factors were driving these changes in the political landscape?

MAP 8.2 | The Spread of Universal Religions in Afro-Eurasia, 300–600 CE

The spread of universal religions and the shifting political landscape were intimately connected.

- Using Map 8.1, identify the major polities in Afro-Eurasia during this era. How did these political configurations differ from those in the era covered in Chapter 7?
- Compare and contrast Map 8.1 with Map 8.2. Where did Hinduism, Buddhism, and Christianity emerge, and where did they spread?
- How did the rise and fall of empires affect the expansion of universal religions?

people viewed their existence. Believing now implied that an important "other" world loomed beyond the world of physical matter. Feeling contact with it gave worshippers a sense of worth; it guided them in this life, and they anticipated someday meeting their guides and spiritual friends there. No longer were the gods local powers to be placated by archaic rituals in sacred places. Many became omnipresent figures whom mortals could touch through loving attachment. As ordinary mortals now could hope to meet these divine beings

in another, happier world, the sense of an afterlife glowed more brightly.

Above all, gods now expected to be obeyed; and it was on the issue of obedience to God, rather than to a human ruler, that the Christians sparked a Mediterranean-wide debate on the nature of religion. Like the Jews, the Christians possessed divinely inspired scriptures that told them what to believe and do, even when those actions went against the empire's laws. (See Analyzing Global Developments: One God,

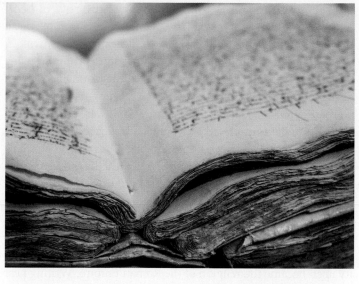

Scroll and Codex. *Constructed from carefully joined sheets of parchment, the Torah scroll (on the left) is still used in modern synagogues as it was in the ancient world. The Christian Scriptures, however, took on an alternate yet no less labor-intensive form: the codex, or bound book. On the right is a view of a codex from the foot of the book's spine, showing how the pages are folded into groups, or signatures, which are then stitched together onto the spine.*

Two Communities: Comparing the Structures of Christianity and Judaism, 600 CE.)

In their emphasis on texts, the Christians were moving with the times. Around 300 CE, a revolution in book production took place. The scroll that all ancient readers had used (and that survives in the Torah scrolls of Jewish synagogues) gave way to the codex: separate pages bound together as a book (just like the book that you now have in your hands). Christians spoke of their scriptures as "a divine codex." Bound in a compact volume or set of volumes, this was the definitive code of God's law that outlined proper belief and behavior.

CONSTANTINE: FROM CONVERSION TO CREED Crucial in spurring Christianity's expansion was the transformative experience of a man named Constantine (c. 280–337 CE). Born near the Danubian frontier, he belonged to a class of professional soldiers whose careers took them far from the Mediterranean. His troops proclaimed him emperor after the death of his father, the emperor Constantius. It was a time of political confusion when several claimants fought for power. In 312 CE, Constantine's armies closed in on Rome in his first bid to rule the Mediterranean heartlands.

Like earlier Roman emperors, Constantine looked for signs from the gods. Before the decisive battle for Rome, which took place for control of a strategic bridge, he supposedly had a dream in which he saw an emblem bearing the words "In this sign conquer." He was told to place this mysterious sign on his soldiers' shields. It took the form of an X (the Greek letter chi, representing a "ch" sound) placed over P (the Greek letter rho, or "r")—the first two letters of the Greek *christos*, a title for Jesus, meaning "anointed one." In the ensuing battle, the rival troops were routed and the rival emperor was pushed off the bridge and drowned. Thereafter, Constantine's visionary sign became known all over the Roman world.

The persecuted Christian church was the beneficiary of Constantine's vision, as he soon issued a proclamation exalting the work of Christian bishops and giving them significant tax exemptions and, most important, showered the favors of the Roman emperor on this religious group. The edict's effects were long-lasting, for it would be through the institutions and over the roads of the Roman Empire that Christianity would spread.

By the time Constantine embraced Christianity, it had already made considerable progress within the Roman Empire. At the outset, it was only one of many different new sects competing for attention within the empire. It prevailed in the face of stiff competition and episodes of intense persecution from the imperial authorities largely because of the universalistic aspects of its message, the charisma of its holy men and women, the sacred aura surrounding its scriptural literature, and the fit that existed between its doctrines and popular preexisting religious beliefs and practices. The new religion made few distinctions. It appealed alike to rich and poor, city dwellers and peasants, slave and free, young and old, men and women.

In 325 CE, hoping to bring unity to the diversity of belief within Christian communities, Constantine summoned all the Christian bishops to a council at Nicaea (modern Iznik in western Turkey). Though their religion has since produced many denominations, all Christians still regard the Council of Nicaea as the foundational moment when their faith was summed up in a **creed** (from the Latin *credo,* "I believe"). It was a statement of religious belief formulated in technical, philosophical terms. It asked believers to balance three separate Gods in one supreme being—God "the father," "the son," and "the holy spirit." Also at Nicaea the bishops agreed to hold Easter, the day on which Christians celebrate Christ's resurrection from the tomb, on the same day in every church of the Christian world.

Constantine's legacy to the Christian church was monumental. His conversion had happened in such a way that Christianity itself became the religion of the Roman Empire. Writing near the end of Constantine's reign, an elderly bishop in Palestine named Eusebius presented a vision of the new Christian Roman Empire that would have surprised the martyrs of Carthage, who had willingly died rather than recognize any "empire of this world." (See Primary Source: Eusebius: In Praise of "One Unity and Concord.") From the time of Constantine onward, many Christians around the eastern Mediterranean believed that Christianity, empire, and culture had merged into a new unity.

CHRISTIANITY IN THE CITIES AND BEYOND After 312 CE, the large churches built in every major city, many with imperial funding, signaled Christianity's growing strength. These gigantic meeting halls often accommodated over a thousand worshippers. Called *basilicas* (from the Greek *basileus,* "king"), the solemn halls were modeled on Roman law court buildings. And unlike ancient temples, which housed the gods deep inside while the people worshipped outdoors, the basilicas were open to all. Those who entered found a vast space shimmering with the light of oil lamps playing on shining marble and mosaics. Rich silk hangings, swaying between rows of columns, increased the sense of mystery and directed the eye to the far end of the building—a semicircular apse furnished with particular splendor. Worshippers had come into a different world. This was heaven on earth.

And it was a very orderly heaven. The bishop and priests sat under the dome of the apse, which represented the dome of heaven. The bishop had a special throne, or *cathedra* (the Latin word for both a teacher's seat and a governor's throne). Low marble screens and especially vivid floor mosaics marked off the holy space around the bishop and clergy. (The church at Verona, in Italy, even had under-floor heating in this area!) Ordinary worshippers would stand, as a gesture of respect, while the bishop sat and preached.

The Conversion of Constantine. *In this painting, the seventeenth-century artist Rubens uses "period" details for historical accuracy: the XP (the first letters of the name of Christ in Greek) in the sky; beneath them, the "dragon" standard of the Roman cavalry of the year 312 CE (the standard came from China and passed to Rome via the cavalry nomads of central Asia); beside the dragon, the eagle of the traditional Roman standard.*

PRIMARY SOURCE

Eusebius: In Praise of "One Unity and Concord"

Eusebius (c. 263–339?) believed that the Roman Empire owed its success to divine providence. He viewed the birth of Christ during the rule of the emperor Augustus as no coincidence: it showed God's choice to come to earth at a time when the preaching of his message could coincide with a blessed era of peace and unity in the Roman world. Christianity had ridden to its favored position on the providential tide of a unified world empire. The excerpt below is from a speech commemorating thirty years of Constantine's rule.

Now formerly all the peoples of the earth were divided, and the whole human race cut up into provinces and tribal and local governments, states ruled by despots or by mobs. Because of this continuous battles and wars, with their attendant devastations and enslavements, gave them no respite in countryside or city. . . .

But now two great powers—the Roman Empire, which became a monarchy at that time, and the teaching of Christ—proceeding as if from a single starting point, at once tamed and reconciled all to friendship. Thus each blossomed at the same time and place as the other. For while the power of our Savior destroyed the multiple rule and polytheism of the demons [the old gods] and heralded the one kingdom of God to Greeks and barbarians and all men to the furthest end of the earth, the Roman Empire, now that the causes of manifold governments had been abolished, subdued the visible governments of, in order to merge the entire race into one unity and concord. . . .

Moreover, as One God and one knowledge of this God is heralded to all, one empire has waxed strong among men, and the entire race of mankind has been re-directed into peace and friendship as all acknowledged each other as brothers. . . . All at once, as if sons and daughters of one father, the One God, and children of one mother, true religion, they greeted and received each other peaceably, so that from that time the whole inhabited world differed in no way from a single well-ordered and related household. It became possible for anyone who pleased to make a journey and to leave home for wherever he might wish with all ease. Thus some from the East moved freely to the West, while others went from here [the East] back there, as easily as if traveling to their native lands.

QUESTIONS FOR ANALYSIS

- The elderly Eusebius was a bishop in Palestine, and as a younger man he had witnessed the persecution of Christians. Can you find evidence of this background in his praise of Constantine as the first Christian emperor, who fostered "one unity and concord" among "the whole human race"?

- Being patriarchal, Roman society highly valued the family unit. What lines in the excerpt reflect this outlook?

- What elements in the history of Christianity would have led Eusebius to emphasize its role as a unifying force in the Roman world?

Source: Eusebius, *Tricennial Oration* 16.2–7 [Jubilee Oration on the Thirtieth Year of the Reign of Constantine, delivered on July 25, 336 CE], translated by H. L. Drake in *In Praise of Constantine: A Historical Study and New Translation of Eusebius' Tricennial Orations* (Berkeley: University of California Press, 1976), pp. 119–21.

Such churches became the new urban public forums, ringed with spacious courtyards where the city's poor would gather. In return for the tax exemptions that Constantine had granted them, the bishops were responsible for the metropolitan poor, becoming in effect their governors. Bishops also became judges, as Constantine turned their arbitration process for disputes between Christians into a kind of small claims court.

It was by such means—offering the poor shelter, quick justice, and moments of unearthly splendor in grand basilicas—that bishops throughout the Roman world secured a position that would last until modern times. And in their basilicas, "Rome" lived on for centuries after the empire had disappeared.

Christianity also spread into the hinterlands of Africa and Southwest Asia, and these efforts required the breaking of language barriers. After around 300 CE, the Christian clergy in Egypt replaced hieroglyphs—which only a few temple priests could read—with a more accessible script based on Greek letters: it is known today as Coptic. (See Primary Source: The Earliest Known Christian Hymn with Musical Score.) With this innovation the Christian clergy brought the countryside and its local languages closer to the towns, and the towns closer to the countryside.

A similar pattern unfolded in Nubia and Ethiopia, as each developed its own scripts and language under Christian influence. And in the crucial corridor that joined Antioch to

Mesopotamia, Syriac, an offshoot of the ancient Semitic language Aramaic, became a major Christian language. Christianity also spread farther north, to Georgia in the Caucasus and to Armenia. Christian clergy created the written languages that are still used in those regions.

The "Fall" of Rome in the West

Despite the vigorous spread of Christianity, the Roman world soon began to fall apart. (See Map 8.3.) After 400 CE, the western European provinces went their own way, as the presence of "barbarian" peoples and large Roman armies and cities along the Rhine and Danube had blurred the boundary between Roman and non-Roman worlds.

WHO WERE THE BARBARIANS? The so-called barbarian invasions of the late fourth and fifth centuries CE were simply a more violent and chaotic form of a steady immigration of young fighting men from the frontiers of the empire. Today the term *barbarian* implies uncultivated or savage, but its core meaning is "foreigner" (with overtones of inferiority). Inhabitants of the western provinces had become used to non-Roman soldiers from across the frontiers, and for them *barbarian* was synonymous with "soldier." Soldiers could be destructive, but

Basilica Interior. *The interior of a basilica was dominated by rows of ancient marble columns and was filled with light from upper windows, so that the eye was led directly to the apse of the church, where the bishop and clergy would sit under a dome, close to the altar.*

nobody feared that the presence of barbarians fighting in armies on Roman territory would bring the end of Roman culture.

THE GOTHS The popular image of bloodthirsty barbarian hordes streaming into the empire bears little resemblance to reality. In fact, it was the Romans' need for soldiers that drew the barbarians in. The process reached a crisis point when Gothic tribes, no strangers to Roman influence, petitioned the emperor Valens (r. 365–378 CE) to let them immigrate into the empire. Desperate for manpower, Valens encouraged their entrance. But the Roman authorities failed to feed their guests. It was a lethal combination of famine and anger at the breakdown of supplies—not innate bloodlust—that turned the Goths against Valens. When he marched against them on the flat plains outside Adrianople (located close to present-day Turkey's borders with Greece and Bulgaria) in the hot August of 378 CE, he was not seeking to halt a barbarian invasion. He was planning to teach a lesson in obedience to his new recruits. But the Goths had brought cavalry from the steppes, and its thunderous charge proved decisive. Valens and a large part of the Roman army of the east vanished in a cloud of red dust, trampled to death by the men and horses they had hoped to hire.

In 406 CE, barbarian invasions followed a similar pattern. The barbarians did not truly invade but were sucked into the crumbling empire by its own civil wars. These internal wars had long been a feature of Roman society, but the state could not survive this bout, as it was constantly being fed by too many barbarian recruits.

In the last analysis, the barbarians did not destroy the empire. They were only the last straw. The "fall" of the empire in western Europe was the result of a long process of overextension. Rome could never be as strong along its frontiers as it was around the Mediterranean, because those frontiers were too far away. Despite the famous Roman roads, travel time between the Rhine border and Rome was more than thirty days. Lacking the vast network of canals that enabled Chinese emperors to move goods and soldiers by water, Roman power could survive in the north only at the cost of constant effort and high taxes. But after 400 CE, the western emperors could no longer raise enough taxes to maintain control of the northern provinces, and invaders simply moved into the vacuum.

In 418 CE, the Goths settled in southwest Gaul as a kind of local militia to fill the absence left by the contracting Roman authority. Ruled by their own king, who kept his military in order, they suppressed the peasants' revolts that were occurring with alarming frequency. Though never as savage or widespread as the uprisings that had undermined the Han dynasty in China, they created a mood of emergency. Now the Roman landowners of Gaul and elsewhere anxiously allied themselves with the new military leaders rather than face social revolution and the raids of even more dangerous armies. The Goths came as Christian allies of the aristocracy, not as enemies of Rome.

THE HUNS Romans and non-Romans also drew together because both suddenly confronted a common enemy. As happened many times in the history of Afro-Eurasia, a nomad confederation—in this case, that of the Huns—threatened the edge of western Europe. For twenty chilling years, a single king, Attila (434–453 CE), imposed himself as sole ruler of all the Hunnish tribes. He was a harsh overlord who frightened the Germanic peoples even more than he frightened the Romans. The Romans had walls to hide behind—Hadrian's Wall, town walls, villa walls, city walls. In the open plains north of the Danube, however, the Hunnish cavalry found only scattered villages and open fields, whose harvests they plundered on a regular basis.

Attila intended to be a "real" emperor. Having adopted (perhaps from the Chinese empire) the notion of a "mandate of heaven"—in his case, a divine right to rule the tribes of the north—he fashioned the first opposing empire that Rome ever had to face in northern Europe. Its traces remain in the archaeology of Ukraine, Hungary, and central Europe. Spectacular jewelry of a Hunnish style, often bearing dragon motifs originating in China, reveals a true warrior aristocracy. Rather than selling his people's services to Rome, Attila extracted thousands of pounds of gold coins from the Roman emperors in tribute. With Roman gold, he could dominate the barbarian world. The result: the Roman Empire in the west vanished only twenty years after his death. In 476 CE, the last Roman emperor of the west, a young boy named Romulus Augustulus (namesake of both Rome's founder and, as "Mini-Augustus," its first emperor), resigned to make way for a so-called barbarian king in Italy.

CONTINUITY THROUGH THE CHURCH Now the political unity of the Roman Empire in the west gave way to a sense of continued unity through the church. The Catholic Church (*Catholic* meaning "universal," centered in the bishops' authority) became the one institution to which all Christians in western Europe, Romans and non-Romans alike, felt that they belonged. Rome became for them the spiritual capital of the west. As a result, the bishops of Rome emerged as "popes" (*papa* originally meant "grand old man"—a revered figure of authority) and became symbols of the unity of the church in western Europe. Other bishops appealed to their judgment. Moreover, the customs observed by Christians in Rome were presented as required of all western Christians. The city of Rome itself became a holy city, and pilgrims in the thousands came every year to the tomb of Saint Peter and of the many other Christian martyrs. The splendid basilica churches in Rome, many of which dated from the time of Constantine

in the fourth century CE, became centers of a lively tourist trade. What we call the papacy—the claim of the bishop of Rome to act as the head of the Catholic Church—developed over the following centuries, starting from the need of the former subjects of the Roman Empire in western Europe to have a center to which they could still look for inspiration and guidance.

Continuity of Rome in the East: Byzantium

Elsewhere the Roman Empire was alive and well. From the borders of Greece to the borders of modern Iraq, and from the Danube River to Egypt and the borders of Saudi Arabia, the empire survived undamaged. Rich and self-confident, it saw itself as a more fortunate version of Old Rome.

Whatever we call it—whether by its modern name of **Byzantium** or simply the surviving empire of Rome—this was a highly centralized empire. The new Roman Empire of the east now had its own Rome. In 324 CE, a year before he assembled the Christian bishops at Nicaea, Constantine decided to build a grandiose city on the European side of the Bosporus—the waterway that separates Europe from Asia. He chose the site of the ancient Greek city of Byzantium and called it by his own name—"Constantine's City," or Constantinople. All roads led to Constantinople. All decisions were made in the great palace. Gold from taxes and grain to feed the city arrived regularly. In fact, the speed of sea travel in the eastern Mediterranean facilitated this centralization. As long as emperors of Constantinople controlled the sea-lanes, they controlled the heart of their empire. Constantinople was soon seen as "New Rome."

Constantinople grew explosively, becoming an even bigger and better Rome. It was one of the most spectacularly successful cities in Afro-Eurasia, soon boasting a population of over half a million and 4,000 new palaces. Every year, more than 20,000 tons of grain arrived from Egypt, unloaded on a dockside over a mile long. A gigantic hippodrome echoing Rome's Circus Maximus straddled the city's central ridge, flanking an imperial palace whose opulent, enclosed spaces stretched down to the busy shore. As in Rome, the emperor would sit in his imperial box, witnessing chariot races as rival teams careered around the stadium. The Hippodrome also featured displays of eastern imperial might, as ambassadors came from as far away as central Asia, northern India, and Nubia.

Constantinople had the resources of a world capital. Long after their western colleagues had been declared bankrupt, its emperors had a yearly budget of 8.5 million gold pieces. No other state west of China had tax revenues so gigantic. It was a predominantly Greek city whose residents were proud to live under Roman law, a circumstance that made them "Romans."

The Earliest Known Christian Hymn with Musical Score

Egypt was one of the most important areas for the early development of Christianity. It had close proximity to Palestine and a large Jewish population, some of whom were ready to embrace the message of Jesus and his followers. In fact, it has been widely believed that the apostle Mark, a writer of one of the four books of the New Testament, made his way to Egypt a little more than a decade after the death of Jesus. Once Christianity became established in Egypt, Egyptian clerics and laypersons provided intellectual leadership in the great debates that were at the heart of the evolution of Christianity during this critical period of its emergence: Was Jesus a god or simply a saintly man? What books were deserving of inclusion in the scriptures that ultimately became the New Testament, and which ones should be excluded? What should the power of the clergy be, and should an individual's own faith and personal revelation be more highly valued than clerical rulings? What role should women play in church affairs? Were they to be subordinated to men, or were their spiritual inspirations to be greatly valued?

In addition, the two types of monastic orders that ultimately came to prominence in Europe—ermetic monasticism, or a monk living alone, and cenobitic monasticism, or monks living together in a monastery—had their origins in Egypt in the third and fourth centuries CE. Although Christianity gave way to Islam as the religion of most Egyptians following the Arab conquest in the seventh century CE, Coptic Christians remained an important element in Egyptian society throughout the centuries. They constitute about 10 percent of Egypt's total population today.

It should therefore come as no surprise that to date the earliest Christian hymn with accompanying score known to the scholarly world was discovered in an Egyptian village, Behnasa, approximately 100 miles south of Cairo. The discovery took place in 1922, but the most authoritative study of the hymn has only recently appeared. The hymn was written in Greek on the back of a papyrus documenting grain deliveries from the city of Oxyrhynchus, hence its scholarly designation as Oxyrhynchus 1786. Oxyrhynchus was a thriving metropolis and the capital of a province in Upper Egypt. Toward the end of the third century CE, the date of the papyrus, the city was home to between 15,000 and 30,000 inhabitants, including Egyptians, Greeks, Romans, Jews, and others, of whom more than 10,000 had converted to Christianity.

The lyrics of the hymn were written in Greek, the primary cultural language of Egypt at that time. It bore unmistakable Greek musical influences, for Greek music

Oxyrhynchus 1786. *A fragment of the Oxyrhynchus hymn. The lyrics, written in ancient Greek, are placed underneath their corresponding musical notes, represented by letters of the Ionian alphabet, along with a set of additional signs that indicated rhythm.*

This was the Constantinople to which the future emperor Justinian came, as a young man from an obscure Balkan village, to seek his fortune. When he became emperor in 527 CE, he considered himself the successor of a long line of forceful Roman emperors—and he was determined to outdo them.

Most important, Justinian reformed the Roman laws. Within six years, a commission of lawyers had created the *Digest*: a volume of 800,000 words that condensed the contents of 1,528 Latin law books. Its companion volume was the *Institutes*, a teacher's manual for schools of Roman law. These works were the foundation of what later ages came to know as "Roman law,"

followed in both eastern and western Europe for more than a millennium.

Reflecting the marriage of Christianity with empire was the Hagia Sophia, a basilica at one end of the Hippodrome. Constructed on the spot where the city's old basilica church was destroyed during a riot, Hagia Sophia ("Holy Wisdom") must have astounded those who first entered it. The nave was twice the span of the former basilica—230 feet wide— and the new church was more than twice as high. The largest church built by Constantine, the basilica of Saint Peter in Rome, would have reached only as high as its lower galleries.

dominated the ancient Mediterranean world then. Professional musicians took part in nearly every festive and ceremonial occasion. Yet, the hymn itself reflected the emerging Christian theology, stressing the intensely debated Trinitarian view that God was three persons in one: Father, Son, and Holy Ghost. Scholars do not know whether the music was performed in private gatherings or in church services; but in its final phrases of praise to God, "the sole giver of all good things," and its amens, it constituted a doxology, or praise hymn to God.

What follows are the translated words to the five lines of the hymn as set to music.

Source: Charles H. Cosgrove, *An Ancient Christian Hymn with Musical Notation* (Tubingen, Germany: Mohr Siebeck, 2011).

QUESTIONS FOR ANALYSIS

- Why was Egypt so vital an arena for the growth of Christianity?
- Why was the hymn written in Greek and its musical composition based on Greek musical traditions?
- In what ways does the hymn offer insight into the theology of Christianity at this time?
- Can you play the hymn (or get someone to play it for you) and sing the words? What feelings does it evoke? You can also listen to it online by searching "Oxyrhynchus Hymn."
- This is the only Primary Source reading in the text that features music. How does music enable us to understand a society and its values in ways that more traditional sources do not?

Above all, the solemn straight lines of the traditional Christian basilica were transformed. Great cliffs of stone, sheathed in multicolored marble and supported on gigantic columns of green and purple granite, rose to a dreamlike height. Audaciously curved semicircular niches placed at every corner made the entire building seem to dance. And a spectacular dome lined with gleaming gold mosaics floated almost 200 feet above it all.

In later centuries, Greek and non-Greek Christians of the east called Hagia Sophia "the eye of the civilized world." It represented the flowing together of Christianity and imperial culture that, for another 1,000 years, would mark the eastern Roman Empire centered on Constantinople.

Unfortunately, Justinian had the misfortune of ruling an empire at the edge of Asia when Asia itself was changing dramatically. To begin with, the contact between east and west was intensifying. The most unexpected reminder of this was a sudden onslaught of the bubonic plague—the grim gift of the Indian Ocean trade routes. One-third of the population of Constantinople died within weeks. Justinian himself survived, but thereafter he ruled an empire whose heartland was decimated. The great plague of 541–544 CE, not the "barbarian" invasions,

MAP 8.3 | Western Afro-Eurasia: War, Immigration, and Settlement in the Roman World, 375–450 CE

Invasions and migrations brought about the reconstitution of the Roman Empire at this time.

- Using the map, identify the people who migrated to or invaded the Roman Empire. Where were they from, and where did they go? How did they reshape the political landscape of western Afro-Eurasia?

- Considering these effects, was the Roman depiction of these groups as "barbarians" a fair assessment?

brought about the real end of the ancient world. Studies of climate change also seem to show that a period of substantial rainfall, which had favored agriculture in the eastern empire, gave way to drier weather, which proved fatal to the villages of Southwest Asia on which the prosperity of the eastern Roman Empire had depended. In these regions, nature was no longer on the side of the "Roman" empire. Nonetheless, Justinian's contributions—to the law, to Christianity, to the maintenance of imperial order—helped Byzantium last for nearly a millennium after Rome in the west had fallen away.

THE SILK ROAD

Although exchange along the Silk Road had been taking place for centuries (see Chapter 6), the sharing of knowledge between the Mediterranean and China began in earnest during this period. Wending their way across its difficult terrains, a steady parade of merchants, scholars, and travelers transmitted commodities, technologies, and ideas between the Mediterranean worlds and China and across the Himalayas into northern India, exploiting the commercial routes of the Silk Road. Ideas, including the

Justinian and Theodora. *These portraits face each other on either side of the altar in the apse of the Church of San Vitale, at Ravenna, Italy. Both Justinian and Theodora are shown presenting lavish gifts. Left: As emperor, Justinian heads the procession. On his left are the clergy; on his right are guards with Constantine's XP symbol on their shields and his lay advisers. Thus, both church and state line up behind their leader, the emperor. Right: Theodora is more secluded. She is surrounded by ladies with veiled heads and by beardless eunuchs. The curtain is pulled back to enable Theodora to place her gift on the altar.*

beliefs of universal religions described in this chapter, traveled along with goods on these routes.

The great oasis cities of central Asia played a crucial role in the effective functioning of the Silk Road system. While the Sasanians controlled Merv in the west, nomadic rulers became the overlords of Sogdiana and Tukharistan and extracted tribute from the cities of Samarkand and Panjikent in the east. The tribal confederacies in this region maintained the links

The Hagia Sophia. *After the conquest of Constantinople by the Muslim Ottomans in 1453, the Hagia Sophia was made into a mosque by having minarets (slender, high towers) added to each corner. Otherwise, it looks exactly as it did in the days of Justinian. In modern times, it became the model for the domed mosques that appear all over the Islamic world.*

between west and east by patrolling the Silk Road between Iran and China. They also joined north to south as they passed through the mountains of Afghanistan into the plains of northern India. As a result, central Asia between 300 and 600 CE was the hub of a vibrant system of religious and cultural contacts covering the whole of Afro-Eurasia. (See Map 8.4.)

Sasanian Persia (224–651 CE)

Another reminder of growing interconnectedness was an escalating rivalry for territorial control. Justinian's empire had struggled with a formidable eastern rival for the control of Southwest Asia. Beginning at the Euphrates River and stretching for eighty days of slow travel across the modern territories of Iraq, Iran, Afghanistan, and much of central Asia, the Sasanian Empire of Persia encompassed all the land routes of western Asia.

As we saw in Chapter 7, the Sasanians had replaced the Parthians as rulers of the Iranian plateau and Mesopotamia. Westerners called this domain the empire of Persia, but its precise title is more revealing of the Sasanians' universalistic aspirations: the Sasanian ruler called himself the "King of Kings of Eran and An-Eran"—"of the Iranian and non-Iranian lands." The ancient, irrigated fields of what is modern Iraq became the economic heart of this empire. These irrigation systems of the Upper Tigris and Euphrates Rivers were greatly expanded and developed under the aegis of the later Sasanian monarchs. The capital of the empire, Ctesiphon, arose where the two rivers come closest to each other, only 20 miles south of modern Baghdad.

MAP 8.4 | Southwest Asia, 300–600 CE

Southwest Asia remained the crossroads of Afro-Eurasia in a variety of ways. Trade goods flowing between west and east passed through this region, as did universal religions. The question mark in eastern Africa indicates scholars' uncertainty about the origination of the plague.

- Using your finger, trace the principal trade routes and maritime routes. What were the areas of major religious influence? What was the relationship between trade routes and the areas of major religious influence?

- Then point out each area of religious influence. How did religious geography correspond to political geography?

- How was Southwest Asia affected by other regions, such as sub-Saharan Africa and central Asia, and how did it shape developments in these regions?

Symbolizing the king's presence was a 110-foot-high vaulted arch decorated with rows of smaller, window-like arches, called the Great Arch of Khusro after Justinian's rival, Khusro I Anoshirwan (Khusro of the Righteous Soul; 501–579 CE). As his name implied, Khusro Anoshirwan exemplified the model ruler: strong and just. His image in the east as an ideal monarch was as glorious as that of Justinian in the west as an ideal Christian Roman emperor. For both Persians and Arab Muslims of later ages, the Arch of Khusro was as awe-inspiring as Justinian's Hagia Sophia was to Christians.

As Khusro's reign unfolded, it became obvious that the Sasanian Empire was more than the equal of the Mediterranean empire of Rome, for it controlled the trade crossroads of Afro-Eurasia and posed a military threat to Byzantium. (See Current Trends in World History: Religious Conflict in Imperial Borderlands.) But control of trade was only part of the story. Christian forces also met their match in the form of

Iranian armored cavalry, a fighting machine adapted from years of competition with the nomads of central Asia. These fearless Persian horsemen fought covered from head to foot in flexible armor (small plates of iron sewn onto leather) and chain mail, riding "blood-sweating horses" draped in thickly padded cloth. Their lethal swords were light and flexible owing to steelmaking techniques imported from northern India. With such cavalry, Khusro sacked Antioch in 540 CE. The campaign was a warning, at the height of Justinian's glory, that Mesopotamia could reach out once again to conquer eastern Mediterranean shores.

Under Khusro II the confrontation between Persia and Rome escalated into the greatest war that had been seen for centuries. Between 604 and 628 CE, Persian forces conquered Egypt and Syria and even reached Constantinople. But Khusro II finally fell to the Byzantine emperor Heraclius in a series of brilliant campaigns in northern Mesopotamia. Never had either

Religious Conflict in Imperial Borderlands

World historians often study borderland areas because it is in these zones where they can see most clearly the effects of cultural interaction. One example is the borderlands of the Sasanian Empire, which through the Persian Gulf reached out to control the trade on the Indian Ocean. This effort brought Persians into conflict with Roman merchants, who strove to reach India from the Red Sea. As a result, the entire region bounded by present-day Ethiopia (at the western end of the Red Sea), Yemen (in southern Arabia), and the Persian Gulf became a field of conflict between the Roman and Sasanian Empires.

Their clash took religious as well as commercial and political form. Both Axum (modern-day Ethiopia) and Himyar (modern-day Yemen) had embraced monotheism, expressed in the worship of a Most High God known as al-Rahmānā (the Merciful One). In Axum, this monotheism was Christian: Christ was the protector of its kings, and the Cross of Christ was their talisman in battle. In contrast, the leaders of Himyar and the southern coast of Arabia were Jewish, and they dismissed Jesus as a crucified sorcerer.

The kings of Axum occupied the African side of the southern end of the Red Sea, looking down from the foothills of the well-watered and populous mountains of Ethiopia. Their formidable warrior-kingdom stretched as far as the Nile to the northwest, south into equatorial Africa, and eastward across the Red Sea to southern Arabia and Yemen. Axum's rulers, who became Christian around 340 CE, celebrated their victories on gigantic granite obelisks; they were monuments to a God that was very much a god of battles.

Faced by the aggressive Christian kingdom of Axum, the Sasanians reached out to support the kings of Himyar, who since 380 CE had been Jewish. Thus two monotheisms faced each other across the narrow southern opening of the Red Sea. Each was associated with a rich and aggressive kingdom. Each was backed by a Great Power—Axum by Christian Rome and Himyar by the Persians.

Between 522 and 530 CE, a Jewish king of Himyar popularly known as Dhu-Nuwas (the Man with the Forelock) drove the Ethiopian Christian garrisons out of southern Arabia. He turned churches into synagogues (just as, in the Christian empire far to the north, many synagogues had been turned into churches). In 523 CE, the Christians of the oasis city of Najran were ordered to become Jewish. Those who refused to do so, Dhu-Nuwas burned on pyres of brushwood piled into a deep trench.

Swept by these rivalries, the Arabian Peninsula was no longer a world apart, shut off from "civilization" by its cruel deserts and by its inhabitants' nomadic lifestyle. Far from it. Arabia had become a giant soundboard that amplified claims about the pros and cons of Judaism and Christianity, argued over with unusual intensity for an entire century. The "non-aligned" Arabs of the intermediate regions (between southern Arabia and Mesopotamia) still worshipped their ancestral tribal gods. But they had heard much, of late, about Jews and Christians, Romans and Persians. Arab tribes around Yathrib (modern Medina) adopted Judaism and remained in touch with the rabbis of Galilee along the caravan routes of northern Arabia. Here was a new kind

Crossing Boundaries. *This Iranian rock relief of a Roman king paying obeisance to a Sasanian ruler is an instance of cross-cultural interchange*

of borderland between empires and between religions. In fact, it would be from this borderland that a new religion and a new prophet would emerge. His name was Muhammad.

QUESTIONS FOR ANALYSIS

- How did the geographical features of the Arabian Peninsula shape its religious development?
- What about borderlands makes them useful locations of analysis for world historians?

Explore Further

Fowden, Garth, *Empire to Commonwealth: The Consequences of Monotheism in Late Antiquity* (1993).

Yarshater, Ehsan, *Encyclopedia Iranica* (1982+).

The Great Arch. *For a Persian king-of-kings, the prime symbol of royal majesty was the great arch marking the entrance gate of his palace. Here, in a Southwest Asian tradition that reached back for millennia, the king would appear to his subjects to deliver judgment. This building was associated with Khusro I, who came to be remembered as an ideal ruler.*

empire reached so far into the heart of the other, and the effort exhausted both. For that reason, both fell easily to an Arab invasion only a few years later (see Chapter 9).

In their confrontations with Rome, Khusro I and Khusro II had the benefit of several factors. Culturally, Southwest Asia was already more united than its political boundaries implied. The political frontier cut across an exuberant common zone where Syriac was the main language and Christianity was making inroads. The Sasanians themselves were devout Zoroastrians, but they were forbearing rulers. Indeed, Jews and Christians enjoyed a tolerance in Mesopotamia that no Christian emperor had extended to non-Christians within the Roman Empire. Protected by the King of Kings, the rabbis of Mesopotamia compiled the monumental Babylonian Talmud at a time when their western peers, in Roman Palestine, were feeling cramped under the Christian state.

Christians flourished in the Sasanian Empire, establishing dynamic communities in northern Mesopotamia, at the head of the Persian Gulf, and along the trade routes of central Asia. Named by their enemies "Nestorian" Christians after Nestorius, a bishop of Constantinople, these members of the "Church of the East" exploited Sasanian trade and diplomacy to spread their faith more widely. As Nestorian merchants passed along the Silk Road, they settled numerous communities and even established monasteries and a church in Chang'an, China. Others operating out of the Persian Gulf founded colonies on the west coast of southern India. Although they were Nestorian Christians, these colonists asserted a special claim for themselves as having been converted by Thomas the Apostle, the companion of Jesus. The Christians of this part of India are still called Saint Thomas Christians.

Christianity and Judaism were not the only phenomena that interested the Sasanian court. It also embraced offerings from northern India, including the *Pancantantra* stories (moral tales played out in a legendary kingdom of the animals), polo, and

the game of chess. In this regard, Khusro's was truly an empire of crossroads, where the cultures of central Asia and India met that of the eastern Mediterranean.

The Sogdians as Lords of the Silk Road

Sogdians in the oasis cities of Samarkand and Panjikent served as human links between the two ends of Afro-Eurasia. Their religion was a blend of Zoroastrian and Mesopotamian beliefs, touched with Brahmanic influences, although they also played a critical role in transmitting Christianity and Buddhism into East Asia and later on Islam as well. Their language was the common tongue of the early Silk Road, and their shaggy camels bore the commodities that passed through their entrepôts (transportation centers). Moreover, their splendid mansions (excavated at Panjikent) show strong influences from the warrior aristocracy culture of Iran. The palace walls display gripping frescoes of armored riders, reflecting the revolutionary change to cavalry warfare from Rome to China. The Sogdians were known as merchants as far away as China. To the Chinese, they were persons "with honey on their tongues and gum on their fingers"—to sweet-talk money out of others' pockets and to catch every stray coin. Their commercial skills enabled them to become the richest country in central Asia, building large houses and decorating the walls of their homes with elaborate paintings. (See Primary Source: A Letter from a Sogdian Merchant Chief.)

The Sogdian city of Panjikent, 30 miles east of Samarkand in present-day Tajikistan, is one of the most important archaeological sites from this period. Built in the fifth century CE, it achieved the zenith of its population and wealth in the seventh century, at which time its residents numbered between 5,000 and 7,000. A walled city, it had several streets, alleyways, bazaars, and temples, one with an altar and another with a statue of the god Shiva. Many caravans bound for China set out from the city or rested in it before journeying on to China. The great Arab geographer and traveler Ibn Hawqal, writing in a later period (977 CE), observed the remains of a now less-well-to-do place, describing "the ruin of a giant building that could house up to two hundred travelers and their animals, with food for all and rooms to sleep as well" (Hansen, p. 122).

Simurgh. *This legendary dog-headed bird of Persian mythology, as shown on this seventh-century silver plate from Sasanian Persia, was a favored motif on textiles, sculptures, paintings, and architecture from the Byzantine Empire to Tang China.*

A Letter from a Sogdian Merchant Chief

Perhaps the clearest demonstration of how the Sogdians linked the ends of Afro-Eurasia is a document discovered in western China. In 313 CE (during a period of upheaval following the fall of the Han dynasty), a Sogdian merchant chief wrote a letter from China to his partner in Samarkand, his homeland some 2,000 miles to the west. He describes a state of civil war made more violent by invading barbarian armies. He also describes the "business as usual" attitude of traders. The letter never reached Samarkand, however. It was among several Sogdian letters in a mailbag found in one of the guard posts of the Great Wall of China.

And sirs, it is three years since a Sogdian came from "inside" [i.e., from China]. And now no one comes from there so that I might write to you about the Sogdians who went inside, how they fared and which countries they reached. And, sirs, the last emperor, so they say, fled from Luoyang because of the famine and fire was set to his palace and to the city, and the palace was burnt and the city [destroyed]. Luoyang is no more, Ye is no more! And sirs, we do not know whether the remaining Chinese were able to expel the Huns [from] Chany'an, from China, or whether they took the country beyond. . . .

And from Dunhuang up to Jincheng . . . to sell, linen cloth is going [selling well?], and whoever has made cloth or woolen cloth. . . .

And, sirs, as for us, whoever dwells in the region from Ji[ncheng] up to Dunhuang, we only survive so long as the . . . lives, and we are without family, old and on the point of death. . . .

Moreover, four years ago, I sent another man named Artikhu-vandak. When the caravan left Guzang, Wakhushakk . . . was there, and when they reached Luoyang . . . the Indians and the Sogdians there had all died of starvation.

QUESTIONS FOR ANALYSIS

- What does the letter elucidate about the difficulties and dangers of trade along the Silk Road?
- What does it reveal about the fall of Luoyang—and about the way news traveled over long distances at this time?
- The letter seems to imply that cloth is in high demand in northern areas of China. How might this indicate the effects of civil war and invasions disrupting local agriculture and trade?

Source: Annette L. Juliano and Judith A. Lerner (eds.), *Monks and Merchants: Silk Road Treasures from Northwest China Gansu and Ningxia, 4th–7th Century* (New York: Harry N. Abrams with the Asia Society, 2001), p. 49.

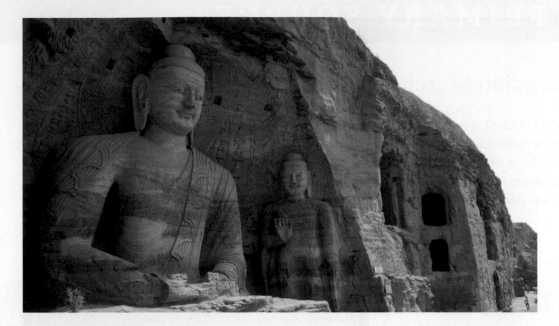

Yungang Buddha. *This is one of the five giant statues of the Buddha in Yungang, created under the emperors of the Northern Wei, a dynasty built by nomads who invaded and occupied northern China. Sitting at the foothills of the Great Wall, the Buddhas marked the eastern destination of the central Asian Silk Road.*

Through the Sogdians, products from western Asia and North Africa found their way to the eastern end of the landmass. Carefully packed for the long trek on jostling camel caravans, goods displaying Persian motifs—such as the legendary and mythical simurgh bird (a massive winged creature in the shape of a bird) and prancing rams with fluttering ribbons—rode side by side with Roman glass from Mediterranean cities. Along with Sasanian silver coins and gold pieces minted in Constantinople, these exotic products found eager buyers as far to the east as China and Japan.

Buddhism on the Silk Road

Unstable political systems did not hinder the flow of ideas or commodities. Instead, the civil wars marking the end of the Han Empire rendered China more open to the cultures of its far western regions. South of the Hindu Kush Mountains, in northern India, nomadic groups made the roads into central Asia safe to travel, enabling Buddhism to spread northward and eastward via the mountainous corridor of Afghanistan into China. (See Map 8.5.) Buddhist monks were the primary missionary agents, the bearers of a universal message who traveled across the roads of central Asia, carrying holy books, offering salvation to commoners, and establishing themselves more securely in host communities than did armies, diplomats, or merchants. Starting at Bamiyan, a valley of the Hindu Kush—where two gigantic statues of the Buddha, 121 and 180 feet in height, were hewn from the stone face of the cliff during the fourth and fifth centuries CE (and stood there for 2,500 years until dynamited by the Taliban in 2001)—travelers found welcoming cave monasteries at oases all along the way from the

Taklamakan Desert to northern China. They also encountered five huge Buddhas carved from cliffs in Yungang. While those at Bamiyan stood tall with royal majesty, the Buddhas of Yungang sat in postures of meditation. Surrounding the Buddhas, over fifty caves sheltered more than 50,000 statues representing Buddhist deities and patrons. The Yungang Buddhas, seated just inside the Great Wall, welcomed travelers to the market in China and marked the eastern end of the central Asian Silk Road system.

The Bamiyan and Yungang Buddhas, placed more than 2,500 miles apart, are a reminder that by now religious ideas were creating world empires of the mind. Religions such as early Christianity and Buddhism saw themselves as transcending kingdoms of this world: they were bringing a universal message contained in holy scriptures. And they enjoyed greater reach than the ponderous empires that *were* of this world—whether Roman or Chinese. Religion traveled light and traveled faster than did armies.

POLITICAL AND RELIGIOUS CHANGE IN SOUTH ASIA

South Asia, especially the area of modern India, also enjoyed a surge of religious enthusiasm during the Gupta dynasty, the largest political entity in South Asia from the early fourth to the mid-sixth century CE. (See again Map 8.5.) Its kings facilitated commercial and cultural exchange, much as the Roman Empire had done in the west. Chandragupta (r. c. 320–335 CE), calling himself "King of Kings, Great King," and his son expanded the Gupta territory to the entire northern Indian plain and made a long expedition to southern India. In these areas,

MAP 8.5 | Buddhist Landscapes, 300–600 CE

Buddhism spread from its heartland in northern India to central and East Asia at this time.

- Using your finger, trace the red lines of trade routes and then the red arrows showing the spread of Buddhism.
- According to the map, what role did increasingly extensive trade routes play in pushing this movement?
- What was the relationship between Buddhist centers and rock-carved temples, trade routes, and the spread of this universal faith?
- How did the travels of Xuanzang symbolize growing connections between East and South Asia?

the development of Hinduism out of the *varna*-bound Vedic Brahmanic religion and the spread of Buddhism continued the unification of a diverse region and the many different peoples who lived there.

The Hindu Transformation

During this period, the ancient Brahmanic Vedic religion also spread widely and became the dominant religion of South

A Gold Coin of Chandragupta II. *The Gupta dynasty, based in the Middle and Lower Ganges plains, was known for its promotion of indigenous Indian culture. Here, Chandragupta II, the most famous king of the dynasty, is shown riding a horse in the style of the invaders from the central Asian steppes.*

Asia. Because Buddhism and Jainism (see Chapter 5) had many devotees in cities and commercial communities, conservative Brahmans turned their attention to rural India and refashioned their religion, bringing it in accord with rural life and agrarian values. As a result of these changes, the Brahmanic religion emerged as the dominant faith in Indian society in the form of what we today call **Hinduism**. (*Hinduism* is a modern word coined from *Hindu*, the people who live in Hind, the Arabic word for India.)

In the religion's new, more accessible form, believers became vegetarians, forsaking the animal sacrifices that had been important to their earlier rituals. They abandoned long-held customs associated with pastoralists and nomads and even absorbed Buddhist and Jain practices as they identified themselves with agrarian culture. Their new rituals were linked to self-sacrifice—denying themselves meat rather than offering up slaughtered animals to the gods, as they had done previously. Three major deities—Brahma, Vishnu, and Siva—formed a trinity representing the three phases of the universe—birth, existence, and destruction, respectively—and the three expressions of the eternal self, or *atma*.

Vishnu, who embodied the present, was the most popular of the three deities. Believers thought he revealed himself to the world in various avatars, or incarnations. One of these was Krishna, the dark-skinned cattle herder and charioteer of the ancient hero Arjuna in the epic poem *Mahabharata*, who also became a religious teacher to Arjuna. A central part of this epic revolves around the final battle between two warring confederations of Vedic tribes. Arjuna, the best warrior of one of these confederations, holds back from the fray, unwilling to fight against his enemies because many of them are his cousins. At a crucial moment on the battlefield, Krishna intervenes, commanding him to slay his foes—even those related to him. Krishna reminds Arjuna that he belongs to the Kshatriyas, the warrior caste that has been put on earth to govern and to fight against the community's enemies. In the early rendition of this tale, the episode takes up little space. But by the Gupta period, the story had become a lengthy poem, *The Bhagavad Gita*, or "Song of the God." In this form it prescribed religious and ethical precepts, or *dharma*, for people in all

walks of life and became part of the authoritative literature of Hindu spirituality.

Hindus also adopted the deities of other religions, even regarding the Buddha as an avatar of Vishnu. Thus, the Hindu world of gods became larger and more accessible than the Vedic one, enabling more believers to share a single faith. Hindus did not wish to approach the gods only through sacrificial rituals at which Brahmans alone could officiate. They preferred to devote their passion and faith to an individual form of each of the great gods. For example, women, especially widows, tended to worship Krishna and kept a small idol of him in the home. This practice, which stressed personal devotion to gods, was called *bhakti*. It attracted Hindus of all social strata, while the body of mythological literature wove the deities into an intriguing heavenly order presided over by the trinity of Brahma, Vishnu, and Siva as universal gods. Hindu temples and Buddhist monasteries also developed into centers of education, with both communities learning from each other.

The poetry during the reign of Chandragupta, a generous patron of the arts, also expressed the widespread religious yearnings and popular sentiments of the age. Kalidasa, a prolific poet and playwright, for instance, worked with the motifs and episodes from two early epics, *Mahabharata* and *Ramayana* (see Chapter 4), to address new problems and to extol new virtues. In his and others' hands, what had once been lyric dramas and narrative poems written to provide entertainment now served as collective memories of the past and underscored religious precepts of ideal behavior. The heroes and deeds that the poets praised served as models for kings and their subjects.

Hindu Statue. *This huge statue of a three-headed god, located in a cave on a small island near Mumbai (Bombay), represents the monotheistic theology of Hinduism. Brahma, the creator, Vishnu, the keeper, and Siva, the destroyer, are all from one* atma, *the single soul of the universe.*

Because these epics were intended to become part of the religious literature, they were rendered in classical Sanskrit.

These works preserve stories from ancient times and offer insights into those eras. Consider the original *Mahabharata* epic, which told of a king who left his court for an attractive woman of a forest society. In Kalidasa's account, what had been a saga of love and suffering became a morality play about holding to strict religious precepts. The main character, Sakuntala, portrayed as a shy girl who had been adopted by a forest holy man but who had neglected her religious duties, was made to suffer punishments and to live out her life in great misery. The moral of Kalidasa's story was that misfortune comes from failing to follow Brahmanical religious rules.

While Hinduism achieved a more popular appeal than the old Vedic Brahmanism, it was still tied to the old *varna* hierarchical system—a connection that limited its appeal outside South Asia and meant that it did not achieve the universal successes or even ambitions of Christianity and Buddhism.

The Transformation of the Buddha

During the Gupta period, two main schools of Buddhism acquired universal features. Initially regarded as a contemplative ascetic (someone who chooses a simple, hard life of self-denial), the Buddha now came to be worshipped as a god.

The doctrines of both schools—the Mahayana (Greater Vehicle school) and the school of elders, the Hinayana (Lesser Vehicle school)—became quite different from what the Buddha had preached centuries earlier. As we saw in Chapter 5, the historical Buddha was a sage who was believed to enter nirvana, ending the pain of consciousness. In the earliest Buddhist doctrine, the Buddha was not regarded as a god nor seen as having supernatural powers. But by 200 CE, a crucial transformation had occurred: his followers started to view the Buddha as a god (see Chapter 6). Mahayana (Greater Vehicle) Buddhism also extended worship to the many bodhisattvas who bridged the gulf between the Buddha's perfection and the world's sadly imperfect peoples.

Some Buddhists fully accepted the Buddha as god but could not accept the divinity of bodhisattvas; these adherents belonged to the more monkish school of old-fashioned Hinayana (Lesser Vehicle) Buddhism, later called Theraveda in Ceylon and Southeast Asia. They rejected the Sanskrit authoritative scripture on the supernatural power of bodhisattvas and remained loyal to the early Buddhist texts, which were probably based on the words of the Buddha himself. Hinayana temples barred all colorful idols of the bodhisattvas and other heavenly beings; only images of the Buddha were permitted.

It was especially in the Mahayana school that Buddhism became a universal religion, whose adherents worshipped divinities rather than recognizing them merely as great men.

Spreading along the Silk Road, this new religion with claims to universality that rivaled those of Christianity eventually appealed to peoples all over East Asia.

Culture and Ideology Instead of an Empire

Unlike China and Rome, India did not have a centralized empire that could establish a code of laws and an overarching administration. What emerged to unify South and even large parts of Southeast Asia was a distinctive form of cultural synthesis, based on Hindu spiritual beliefs and articulated in the Sanskrit language. Recently, scholars have called this cultural synthesis, which prevailed for a full millennium (300 to 1300 CE), the **Sanskrit cosmopolis**. Spearheading this development were priests and intellectuals, well versed in the Sanskrit language and literary and religious texts. As they carried Sanskrit far and wide, it stepped beyond religious scriptures and became the public language of politics. Kings and emperors used it to express the ideals of royal power and responsibility. Rulers issued inscriptions in it, recording their genealogies and their prestigious acts. Poets celebrated ruling dynasties and recorded important moments in the language. Although local languages retained their prominence in day-to-day administration and everyday life, kings delivered their speeches and issued their edicts in Sanskrit.

THE CODE OF MANU The emergence of Sanskrit as the common language of the elites in South and Southeast Asian

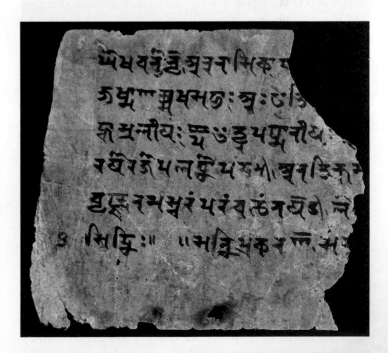

Sanskrit. *The widespread and enduring nature of this language is demonstrated in this thirteenth-century Sanskritic manuscript of Mongolian origin.*

societies also facilitated the spread of Brahmanism. Possessing an unparalleled knowledge of the language, Brahmans circulated their ideals on morality and society in Sanskritic texts, the most influential of which was the **Code of Manu**. This document is a discourse given by a sage, Manu, to a gathering of wise men seeking answers on how to organize their communities after a series of floods has brought the people to their knees. The text lays out a set of laws designed to address the problems of assimilating strangers into expanding towns and refining the caste order as the agricultural frontier expanded. In Hindu mythology, Manu ("Human") was the father of the human race, and the Laws of Manu were held to apply to all persons, no matter where they lived. Kingdoms might come and go, but the "true" order of society, summed up in the Laws of Manu, remained the same everywhere.

Above all, the Code of Manu offered guidance for living within the caste system, whose origins lay centuries earlier. (See Primary Source: The Laws of Manu: Castes and Occupations.) The laws prescribed that every person had to marry within his or her caste and follow the caste's profession and dietary rules in order to perpetuate its status. Thus, social and religious pressure, not government coercion, kept all individuals in orderly social groups. Though seemingly rigid, the Laws of

Caste System. *The dazzlingly diverse population of India, as depicted in this palace scene from a Gupta dynasty cave painting, depended on the ancient caste system to lend it law and order.*

Manu offered a way to cope with a constantly changing Indian society. In providing mechanisms for absorbing new groups into the caste system, it propelled Hinduism into every aspect of life, far beyond the boundaries of imperial control.

INTERNAL COLONIZATION Behind these developments was a remarkable movement of internal colonization, as settlers from northern India pushed southward into lands formerly outside the domain of the Brahmans. In these territories, Brahmans encountered Buddhists and competed with them to win followers. The mixing of these two groups and the intertwining of their ideas and institutions ultimately created a common "Indic" culture organized around a shared vocabulary addressing concepts such as the nature of the universe and the cyclic pattern of life and death. Much of this mixing of ideas took place in schools, universities, and monasteries. The Buddhists already possessed large monasteries, such as Nalanda in northeast India, where 10,000 residential faculty and students assembled, and more than 100 smaller establishments in southeast India housing at least 10,000 monks. In these settings, Buddhist teachers debated subjects like theology, theories about the universe, mathematics, logic, and botany. In response, the Brahmans established schools, called *maths*, where similar high intellectual topics were discussed and where Buddhist and Brahmanic Hindu ideas were fused.

The resulting Indic cultural unity covered around 1 million square miles (an area as great as the extent of the Roman Empire) and a highly diverse population. Although India was not one polity like China and did not adhere to one religious system as in the Christian Roman Empire and in medieval western Europe, it was developing a distinctive culture based on the intertwining of two shared, accessible, and to varying degrees universalizing religious traditions that sought to project their beliefs to new populations.

POLITICAL AND RELIGIOUS CHANGE IN EAST ASIA

With the fall of the Han dynasty, China experienced a period of political disunity and a surge of new religious and cultural influences. In the first century CE, Han China had been the largest state in the world, with as great a population as the Roman Empire had at its height. Its emperor ruled an area more than twice the size of the Roman Empire, extracted an annual income of millions of pounds of rice and bolts of cloth, and conscripted millions of workers whose families paid tribute through their labor. Later Chinese regarded the end of the Han Empire as a disaster just as great as western Europeans regarded the end of the Roman Empire. In post-Han China, new influences arrived

PRIMARY SOURCE

The Laws of Manu: Castes and Occupations

Brahmans compiled the Laws of Manu during the first or second century CE, when the Kushans from the northern steppes ruled over much of South Asia. It was a time of constant social upheaval. Among the many law codes that appeared throughout Indian history, that of Manu (father of the human race) holds the most authority among Hindus because it is the most comprehensive. It describes the origins of the four castes and clearly designates the occupations that provide members of each with their livelihood.

87. But in order to protect this universe He, the most resplendent one, assigned separate (duties and) occupations to those who sprang from his mouth, arms, thighs, and feet.

88. To Brâhmanas he assigned teaching and studying (the Veda), sacrificing for their own benefit and for others, giving and accepting (of alms).

89. The Kshatriya he commanded to protect the people, to bestow gifts, to offer sacrifices, to study (the Veda), and to abstain from attaching himself to sensual pleasures;

90. The Vaisya to tend cattle, to bestow gifts, to offer sacrifices, to study (the Veda), to trade, to lend money, and to cultivate land.

91. One occupation only the lord prescribed to the Sûdra, to serve meekly even these (other) three castes.

QUESTIONS FOR ANALYSIS

- According to Hindu belief, the four castes sprang from "the mouth, arms, thighs, and feet" of "the most resplendent one." In what ways is it significant that the Brahman caste sprang from the mouth?
- What caste do soldiers belong to? What caste do farmers and merchants belong to? Which caste do you suppose represents the majority of the population?
- How are the different caste statuses reflected in the jobs that their members can take?

Source: The Laws of Manu, I.87–91; translated by G. Bühler, vol. 25 of The Sacred Books of the East (Oxford: Clarendon Press, 1886), p. 24.

---

via the Silk Road through contact with nomadic peoples and the proselytizing of Buddhist monks; at the same time, new forms of Daoism responded to a changing society.

The Wei Dynasty in Northern China

After the fall of the Han in 220 CE, several small kingdoms—at times as many as sixteen of them—competed for the remembered glories of a large empire. Civil wars raged for roughly three centuries, a time called the Six Dynasties period, when no single state was able to conquer more than half of China's territory.

The most successful regime was that of the Tuoba, a people originally from Inner Mongolia. In 386 CE, the Tuoba founded the Northern Wei dynasty, which lasted one and a half centuries and administered part of the Han territory. These "barbarian" rulers from northern China maintained many of their preconquest forms of state and society. Because they had lived for generations within the Chinese orbit as tributary states, they were "civilized" by imperial standards. They even maintained many Chinese traditions of statecraft and court life: they taxed land and labor on the basis of a census, conferred official ranks and titles, practiced court rituals, preserved historical archives, and promoted classical learning and the use of classical Chinese for record keeping and political discourse. Though they were nomadic warriors, they adapted their large standing armies to city-based military technology, which required dikes, fortifications, canals, and walls. Following the Qin and Han precedent, they drafted huge numbers of workers to complete such enormous projects as rebuilding a capital city at Luoyang.

Among the challenges facing the Northern Wei rulers was the need to consolidate authority over their own highly competitive nomadic people. One strategy, which they pursued with little success for nearly a century, was to make their own government more "Chinese." Under Emperor Xiaomen (r. 471–499 CE), for example, the Tuoba royal family adopted the Chinese family name of Yuan and required all court officials to speak Chinese and wear Chinese clothing. However, the Tuoba warrior families resisted these policies. They blatantly spoke their native tongue, shaved most of their head and tied the remaining hair in a pigtail, and continued wearing loose-fitting pants and shirts more typical of the warrior on horseback rather than the flowing gowns of urbane Han Chinese civilians riding in carts or walking the streets.

One God, Two Communities: Comparing the Structures of Christianity and Judaism, 600 CE

Christianity emerged from Judaism in the first and second centuries CE and continues to share the same God and many of the same scriptures to this very day. Yet, despite these fundamental commonalities, what arose were two distinct religious communities, each with its own notions of God in relation to humanity. The following diagrams illustrate the major impact that the Christian and Jewish understanding of the same God had on the structures of their early religious institutions and their ability to grow and become universalizing.

Looking at the diagram, Judaism's institutional structure is flatter and simpler, while Christianity's is more hierarchical. One would think the more direct connection to God found in Judaism, with rabbis being the primary teachers of the Torah and overseeing most of the responsibilities at the synagogue, would make it more appealing and universalizing than Christianity, with its hierarchical structure composed of bishops, priests, monks, and nuns—but this was not the case.

QUESTIONS FOR ANALYSIS

- The diagram suggests that the people of Israel had a direct connection to God. What does the diagram suggest about the relationship of Christians to the same God? Why is this relationship important in understanding the structures of the two religions and their universalizing appeal?

- Martyrs, like Perpetua (discussed in the chapter), played a big role in both Christianity and Judaism (for example, rabbis resisting Rome c. 100 CE). Where would you place martyrs on this diagram, and why? What role might martyrdom have played in the universalizing appeal of Christianity as opposed to Judaism?

- Based on your reading, what were the origins of the hierarchical structure of Christianity, and why would it actually aid in the growth of the religion?

At the same time, the Wei rulers sought stronger relationships with the Han Chinese families of Luoyang that had not fled south. The Wei offered them more political power as officials in the Wei bureaucracy and more land. A key figure in this effort was the Dowager Empress Fang (regent 476–490 CE). As widows, such dowagers often held power over their young emperor sons and controlled their own property, or dower. Her most substantial initiative involved progressive land reforms: all young men—whether Han or Wei—who agreed to cultivate the land would receive two allotments, one at age eleven and one at fifteen, which they could pass on to their heirs. After age seventy, they would no longer have to pay taxes on it. But even this plan failed to bridge the cultural divides between the "civilized" Han Chinese of Luoyang and the "barbarian" Tuoba Wei because the latter showed no interest in farming.

The boldest attempt to unify northern China came under Emperor Xiaomen, who rebuilt the old Han imperial capital of Luoyang based on classical architectural models dating from the Han dynasty (see Chapter 7) and made it the seat of his government. To gain political legitimacy with the Han, members of the Wei court supported Buddhist temples and monumental cave sites in an appeal to their Tuoba roots while also honoring Confucian traditions dating to the ancient Zhou period. Emperor Xiaomen's untimely death cut short his efforts to unify the north, however. Several decades of intense fighting among military rulers followed, leading ultimately to the downfall of the Northern Wei dynasty.

Changing Daoist Traditions

Daoism, a popular Chinese religion under the Han and a challenge to the Confucian state and its scholar-officials (see Chapter 7), lost its political edge and adapted to the new realities during this period of disunity. Two new traditions of Daoist thought flourished in this era of self-doubt. The first was organized, community oriented, and involved heavenly masters who as mortals guided local religious groups or parishes. Followers sought salvation through virtue, confession, and liturgical ceremonies. Through ecstatic initiation rites, often achieved via an "external alchemy," including the use of hallucinatory drugs, a new Daoist clergy also brought believers into contact with the divine.

A second Daoist tradition was more individualistic. In the Yangzi delta, personal expressions of religious faith emerged. For example, Ge Hong (283–343 CE) sought to reconcile Confucian classical learning with Daoist religious beliefs in the occult and magical. He focused on "internal alchemy"—the use of trance and meditation to control human physiology. Through such mental and physical exertions, an adept, both as believer and practitioner, believed that the soul could accumulate enough religious merit to prolong his life. A recommended set of nine body postures involved full chest breathing combined with extensive stretching to facilitate the healthy flow of Qi, the life force circulating throughout the body. Adepts complemented this extension of life via trance and physiological control by taking elixirs, boiling exquisite teas as medical beverages, and knowing the specific effects of herbs and minerals.

Buddhism in China

Buddhism's universalist message appealed to many people living in the fragmented Chinese empire. By the third and fourth centuries CE, travelers from central Asia who had converted to Buddhism had become frequent visitors in the streets and temples of the competing capitals: Chang'an, Luoyang, and Nanjing. (See Primary Source: The Art of Religious Fervor in China: The Pagoda.)

Spreading the increasingly universalizing faith required intermediaries, endowed with texts or codes, to convey its message. Kumarajiva (344–413 CE), a renowned Buddhist scholar and missionary, was the right man, in the right place, at the right time to spread Buddhism in China—where it already coexisted with other faiths. He was a bearer of exotic holy books (not unlike the Christian missionaries of the Roman Empire), and his influence on Chinese Buddhist thought was critical. Kumarajiva produced the first understandable translations of Buddhist texts from Sanskrit into Chinese, and he also clarified Buddhist terms and philosophical concepts. A polyglot, he was fluent in Kuchean, Chinese, Sanskrit, Gandari, and most likely Agneau and Sogdian. Although of Indian descent, Kumarajiva was born in the important Silk Road oasis city of Kucha, an entry point of Buddhist thoughts into China, because his father had migrated there to pursue Buddhist studies. The city of Kucha was a place of great wealth and religiosity. Its high city walls had three enclosures, and it boasted more than 1,000 pagodas and temples. The city's inhabitants lived luxuriously from the Silk Road trade.

The Chinese emperor brought Kumarajiva to Chang'an, the capital of China, and put him in charge of a translation bureau. Kumarajiva's legacy in China was that he and his disciples established a Mahayana branch known as **Madhyamika (Middle Way) Buddhism**, which used irony and paradox to show that reason is limited. For example, they contended that all reality is transient because nothing remains unchanged over time. They sought enlightenment by means of transcendental visions and spurned experiences in the material world of sights and sounds.

Kumarajiva represented the beginning of a profound cultural shift. After 300 CE, Buddhism began to expand in northwestern China, taking advantage of imperial disintegration and the decline of Daoism and state-sponsored Confucian classical learning. The Buddhists stressed devotional acts, such as daily prayers and mantras, which included seated meditations in solitude requiring mind and breath control, and they had faith in the saving power of the Buddha and the saintly bodhisattvas, who postponed their own salvation for the sake of others. They even encouraged the Chinese to join a new class—the clergy. The idea that persons could be defined by faith rather than kinship was not new in Chinese society (see Chapter 7), but it had special appeal in a time of unprecedented crisis. In the south, the immigrants from the north found that membership in the Buddhist clergy and monastic orders offered a way to restore their lost prestige.

Even more important, in the northern states—now part-Chinese, part-"barbarian"—Buddhism provided legitimacy. With Buddhists holding prominent positions in government, medicine, and astronomy, the Wei ruling houses could espouse a philosophy that was just as legitimate as that of the Han

The Art of Religious Fervor in China: The Pagoda

Religious fervor changed the visual environment of China. For example, the decorations on pottery and metal objects from this time show strong central Asian and Sasanian influences, transmitted primarily through Buddhism. The impact on architecture was even more striking. In India, Buddhists had adapted a form of dome-shaped tombs (called stupas) into shrines for housing relics of the Buddha. Now, in China, huge pagodas represented an attempt—mostly in wood—to imitate the stone and brick stupas of India. Regarded by Koreans and Japanese (and later by westerners) as quintessentially Chinese, the pagoda was in fact a distant echo, on Chinese soil, of northern Indian Buddhism. Similarly, the complexes of cave temples at Longmen and Yungang reflect Indian and central Asian influences. In these ways, a universal religion created common artistic themes that stretched from central Asia to East Asia.

One site that featured the work of central Asian artisans was the oasis city of Dunhuang. Located along the Silk Road, it contained a number of cave temples. Starting in 400 CE, they were adorned with paintings and statues, and between the fifth and eighth centuries CE, hundreds of them were decorated with wall paintings. Some illustrated Buddhist legends; others depicted scenes of paradise. The caves were sealed in 1035 to save them from raids by Tibetans, and they have survived to this day. In 1900, the cave housing the great Buddhist library at Dunhuang was found unopened. The dry climate had preserved thousands of manuscripts, including Buddhist texts and works of popular literature.

QUESTIONS FOR ANALYSIS

- What do the architectural links from India to China, Japan, and Korea tell us about Buddhism?
- Why do you suppose the Dunhuang caves are essential to our understanding of Chinese Buddhism at this time?

The Western Pure Land. *This mural painting of the Western Pure Land (a place where enlightenment is achieved) is from Dunhuang, close to the eastern end of the Silk Road. The facial features of the celestial beings and the art style are more Chinese than Indian. Lazulite blue, a pigment made from lapis lazuli from Badakhshan, Afghanistan, is the dominant color here, as it is on all the cave art along the central Asian Silk Road.*

Pagoda on Mount Song. *This is probably the earliest pagoda in China. The solid stone structure shows the influence of pagodas in the eastern part of India, such as the one in Mahabodhi Temple, in Bodhgaya.*

Amitabha. *This exquisite tapestry is an illustration for the Amitabha Sutra, the "Sutra of the Western Pure Land." Since the text was translated into Chinese by Kumarajiva in the fourth century CE, Amitabha has been one of the most popular bodhisattvas in China. A devotee who invokes the name of Amitabha ten times before death would be saved to this Western Pure Land, where the Seven Treasures decorated the quiet landscape.*

Chinese. As a Tuoba who ruled at the height of the Northern Wei, Emperor Xuanwu, for instance, was an avid Buddhist who made Mahayana Buddhism the state religion during his reign.

Buddhism, unlike Christianity, was not a universalizing religion that sought to be the same in all places and at all times. On the contrary, as the expression of a cosmic truth as timeless but varied as the world itself, Buddhism showed a high level of adaptability, easily absorbing as its own the gods and the wisdom of every country it touched, making it a different kind of universalizing religion.

By 400 CE, China had more than 1,700 Buddhist monasteries and about 80,000 monks and nuns. By contrast, in 600 CE (after two centuries of monastic growth), Gaul and Italy—the two richest regions of western Europe—had, altogether, only 320 Christian monasteries, many with fewer than thirty monks. Yet, in the two ends of Afro-Eurasia, the principal bearers of the new religions were monks. Set apart from "worldly" affairs in their refuges, they enjoyed the pious support of royal courts and warriors, whose lifestyles differed sharply from their own. It would be through their devoted faith in the divine and the support of secular rulers that these two universalizing religions would continue to grow, flourish, and revitalize themselves.

FAITH AND CULTURES IN THE WORLDS APART

In most areas of sub-Saharan Africa and the Americas, it was not easy for ideas, institutions, peoples, and commodities to circulate broadly. Thus, we do not see the development of universalizing faiths. Rather, belief systems and their deities remained local.

This is not to say that sub-Saharan Africa and the Americas lacked the elements for creating communities of faith. Africans and Americans alike had prophetic figures who, they believed, communicated with deities and brought to humankind divinely prescribed rules of behavior. Moreover, peoples in both regions honored beliefs and rules that were passed down orally from generation to generation. These spiritual traditions guided behavior, established social customs, and determined people's fates. In fact, relationships with deities and spirits governed the calendar of rituals across these regions.

Bantus of Sub-Saharan Africa

Today, most of Africa south of the equator is home to peoples who speak some variant of more than 400 Bantu languages. Early Bantu history is shrouded in mystery. At present, scholars using oral traditions and linguistic evidence can trace the narrative of these peoples no further back than 1000 CE.

The first Bantu speakers lived in the southeastern part of modern Nigeria, where about 4,000 or 5,000 years ago they likely shifted from hunting, gathering, and fishing to practicing settled agriculture. The areas they spread into, being tropical rain forest, demanded an immense amount of work. To ready a new acre for cultivation required removing some 600 tons of moist vegetation, and the migrants brought to the task only simple tools (mainly machetes and billhooks). In fact, their most effective technique was controlled burning. Moreover, the African equatorial forests were almost totally devoid of food plants. So these peoples made do with woodland plants such as yams and mushrooms, as well as palm oils and kernels. Yet the difficulties in preparing the land for settled agriculture did not keep the Bantus from being the most expansionist of African peoples (see Map 8.6).

BANTU MIGRATIONS Following riverbeds and elephant trails, Bantu migrants traveled out of West Africa in two great waves. One group moved across the Congo forest region to East Africa, aided by their knowledge of iron smelting, which enabled them to use iron tools for agriculture. Because their new habitats supported a mixed economy of animal husbandry and sedentary agriculture, this group became relatively prosperous. The second wave of migrants moved southward through the rain forests in present-day Congo, eventually reaching the Kalahari Desert. They were not so fortunate, for they entered a tsetse fly–infested environment that brought sleeping sickness to humans and wiped out animals. The result was that these communities were limited to subsistence farming. They learned to use iron later than those who had moved to the Congo region in the east.

Precisely when the **Bantu migrations** began is unclear, but once under way, the travelers moved with extraordinary rapidity. Genetic and linguistic evidence reveals that they swept all else before them, absorbing most of the hunting and gathering populations who originally inhabited these areas.

What enabled the Bantus to prevail and then to prosper was their skill as settled agriculturalists. They knew how to cultivate the soil, and they adapted their farming techniques to widely different environments. They thrived equally well in the tropical rain forests of the Congo River basin, the high grasslands around Lake Nyanza (former Lake Victoria), and the highlands of Kenya, even though they had to grow different crops in each location.

For the Bantu of the rain forests of central Africa (the western Bantu), the introduction of the banana plant was decisive. The banana plant originated in tropical South and Southeast Asia and spread rapidly into many regions. Linguistic evidence suggests that it first arrived in the Upper Nile region and then traveled into the rest of Africa with small groups migrating from one favorable location to another; the earliest proof of its presence is a record from the East African coast dating to 525 CE. When it

MAP 8.6 | Bantu Migrations

The migration of Bantu speakers throughout much of sub-Saharan Africa in the first millennium CE dramatically altered the cultural landscape.

- According to the map, where did the Bantu speakers originate? Where did they migrate to?
- What skills did they have that enabled them to dominate the peoples already living there?
- Did the Bantu migrations create a common culture below the Sahara Desert during this time?

reached the equatorial rain forests, its adaptability to local conditions was unmatched. Not only did it provide more nutrients than the yam crop, but it better withstood heavy rainfalls. In addition, banana plantings required the clearing of fewer trees than yam cultivation and created an environment free of the *Anopheles* mosquito, the insect that carries malaria. Exploiting the benefits of banana cultivation, the western Bantu expanded into the equatorial rain forests of central Africa—perhaps as early as 500 CE, certainly by 1000 CE.

BANTU CULTURES, EAST AND WEST Did these peoples create a common Bantu culture? Clearly, they could not establish the same political, social, and cultural institutions in widely different ecological zones. In the Great Lakes area of the East African savanna lands, where communication was relatively easy, the Bantu speakers developed centralized polities whose kings ruled

Instructions to a Young Man in West Africa

The words that were traditionally spoken to young men coming of age in the Cameroons in West Africa (an area where the Bantus likely originated) reflect the importance that families attached to being a strong and enterprising individual.

The grandfather gave an ivory bracelet and said:
"This elephant which I put on your arm, become a man of crowds,
a hero in war, a man with women
rich in children, and in many objects of wealth
prosper within the family, and be famous throughout the villages."

The grandmother gave a charm of success as a belt and said:
"Father, you who are becoming a man
Let toughness and fame be with you as this sap of the
[*Baillonella toxisperma*] tree is glued to this thread.
Become dominant, *a great man,*
a hero in war, who surpasses strangers and visitors;
prosper, Have us named!"

QUESTIONS FOR ANALYSIS

- Think about the Bantu speakers' environment. Why would a bracelet made from elephant tusk carry special meaning?
- How do the words and gifts (typically charms) offered reflect a belief that spirits inhabited the natural world?
- According to the chapter text, why did the sub-Saharan peoples organize themselves around "big men" rather than kings or other sorts of rulers?
- Have you ever had or attended a coming-of-age ceremony? Were certain words or gifts significant? Have you ever owned any good-luck charms? What were (or are) they?

Source: Jan Vansina, Paths in the Rainforests: Toward a History of Political Tradition in Equatorial Africa (Madison: University of Wisconsin Press, 1990), pp. 73–74.

by divine right. Mostly, however, they moved into heavily forested areas similar to those they had left in southeastern Nigeria. These locations supported a way of life that remained fundamentally unaltered for perhaps a millennium and a half, withstanding the later impact of the Atlantic slave trade and withering only under European colonialism in the twentieth century.

The western Bantu-speaking communities of the lower Congo River rain forests formed small-scale societies based on family and clan connections. They organized themselves socially and politically into age-groups, the most important of which were the ruling elders. Within these age-based networks, individuals who demonstrated talent in warfare, commerce, and politics provided leadership.

Age grading tended to impose certain rights and duties on different social groups based mainly on their age. Many such societies established three age grades for males and two for females. Males moved from (1) being children and learning male roles from older men, to (2) acquiring warrior status, when they defended the community, raided for livestock, and acquired new lands for the community, and then (3) becoming the politically ruling age grade—the elders. Females' age grades consisted of childhood and marriage. Bonds among those who belonged to the same age grade were powerful, and movement from one to the next was marked by meaningful and well-remembered rituals.

Lacking chiefs and kings, the loosely organized Bantu societies rallied around individuals of talent—so-called big men—whose abilities attracted followers and thereby promoted territorial expansion. Their courage, military valor, and wisdom won them many supporters, but rarely did their high positions pass along to offspring or relatives. Invariably, other dynamic individuals arose to compete for power. In the rain forest, land was abundant but labor was in short supply. Thus, individuals who could attract a large community of followers, marry many women, and sire many children could lead their bands into new locations and establish dominant communities.

Although dispersed, these rain forest communities embraced a common worldview. They believed that the natural world was inhabited by spirits, many of whom were their own heroic ancestors. These spiritual beings intervened in mortals' lives and required constant appeasement. Diviners helped men and women understand the spirits' ways, and charms warded off the misfortune that aggrieved spirits might wish to inflict. Diviners and charms also protected against the injuries that living beings—witches and sorcerers—could inflict. In fact, much of the misfortune that occurred in the Bantu world was attributed to these malevolent forces. The Bantus believed that their big men could control such forces and use them to punish opponents and reward friends. These beliefs survived unchallenged for well over a millennium. (See Primary Source: Instructions to a Young Man in West Africa.)

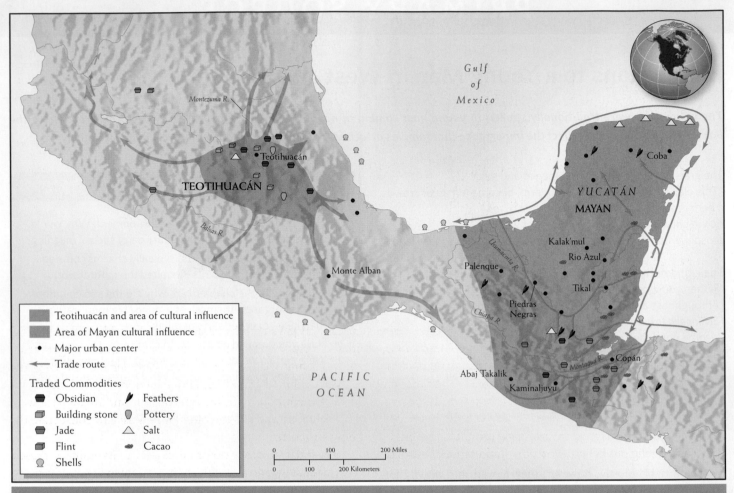

MAP 8.7 | Mesoamerican Worlds, 200–700 CE

At this time, two groups dominated Mesoamerica: one was located at the city of Teotihuacán, in the center, and the other, the Mayas, was in the south.

- What commodities did these cultures trade? Look at the symbols for Traded Commodities in the map key, and find them all on the map.
- Judging by what you see, how did each group create a common culture in surrounding regions?
- To what extent do you believe the people of the Teotihuacán and Maya worlds influenced each other?

The Bantu migrations ultimately filled up more than half the African landmass and introduced settled agriculture throughout its southern part. They spread a political and social order based on family and clan structures that allowed considerable leeway for individual achievement, and they maintained an intense relationship to the world of nature that they believed, for good or ill, was dominated by supernatural forces. Although the Bantu migrations did not lead to the widespread and powerful political and cultural unities that brought large segments of Afro-Eurasian peoples together in this period, the Bantu peoples created similar cultural forms and political systems based mainly on age grading and the role of big men that resulted in an overarching commonality among peoples living in widely dispersed communities over vast areas.

Mesoamericans

As in sub-Saharan Africa, the process of settlement and expansion in Mesoamerica differed from that in the large empires of Afro-Eurasia. Mesoamerica had no integrating artery of a giant river and its floodplain, and so it lacked the extensive resources that a state could harness for monumental ambitions. Given these circumstances, what Mesoamericans achieved was truly remarkable.

In the case of Teotihuacán, the first major community to emerge since the Olmecs (see Chapter 5), we see the growth of a city-state that ruled over a large, mountainous valley in the area of present-day Mexico. (See Map 8.7.) While it did not evolve into a territorial state, it traded and warred with neighboring peoples and created a smaller-scale common culture. In the

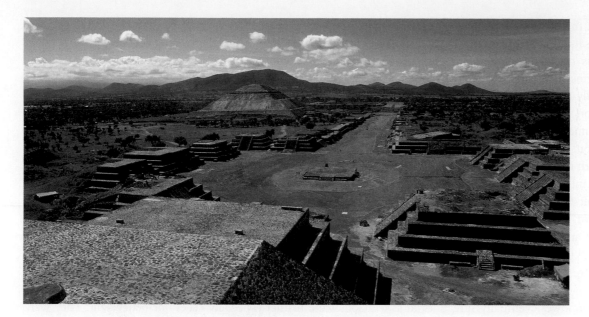

Teotihuacán. *The ruins of Teotihuacán convey the importance of monumental architecture to Aztec culture. In the foreground is the Plaza of the Moon, leading to the Street of the Dead, with the Pyramid of the Sun to the left. These massive structures were meant to confirm the importance of spiritual affairs in urban life.*

case of the Mayas, in contrast, we witness the emergence of a common culture that ruled over large stretches of Mesoamerica under a series of kingdoms built around ritual centers rather than cities. The Mayas aggressively engaged in warfare and trade, expanding their borders through tributary relationships. The extraordinary feature of Maya society was that its people were defined not by a great ruler or a great capital city, but by their shared religious beliefs, worldview, and sense of purpose.

TEOTIHUACÁN Around 300 BCE, people in the central plateau and the southeastern districts of Mesoamerica where the dispersed villages of Olmec culture had risen and fallen (see Chapter 5) began to gather in larger settlements. Soon, political and social integration led to city-states. Teotihuacán, in the heart of the fertile valley of central Mexico, arose around the first century CE to become the largest center of the Americas before the emergence of the Aztecs a millennium later.

Fertile land and ample water from the valley's marshes and lakes fostered high agricultural productivity despite the inhabitants' technologically rustic methods of cultivation. The local food supply sustained a metropolis of between 100,000 and 200,000 residents, living in more than 2,000 apartment compounds lining the city's streets. At one corner rose the massive pyramids of the sun and the moon—the focus of spiritual life for the city dwellers. Marking the city's center was the huge royal compound, or Ciudadela; the grandeur and refinement of its stepped stone pyramid, the Temple of the Feathered Serpent, were famous throughout Mesoamerica.

The feathered serpent was the anchor for their spiritual lives. It was a symbol of fertility, a deity that governed reproduction and life, often bearing powerful maternal features—despite the fearsome (to our eyes) appearance of the

fangs and jaws and the snakes that invariably writhed in the deity's grip. Its temple was the core of a much larger structure. From it radiated the awesome promenade known as the Street of the Dead, which culminated in the hulking Pyramid of the Moon. Here foreign warriors and dignitaries were mutilated, sacrificed, and often buried alive to consecrate the holy structure.

Teotihuacán was a powerful city-state. Its military muscle was imposing. After overwhelming or annexing its rivals, by 300 CE Teotihuacán controlled the entire basin of the Valley of Mexico. It dominated its neighbors and demanded gifts, tribute, and humans for ritual sacrifice. Its massive public architecture displayed art that commemorated decisive battles, defeated neighbors, and captured fighters.

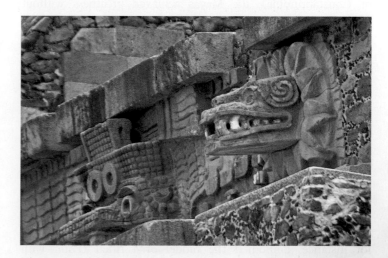

Quetzalcoatl. *The artisans of Teotihuacán decorated the sides of their monumental buildings with sculptures. Here, feathered serpents, denoting the god Quetzalcoatl, burst from the sides of a wall to stare menacingly at passersby.*

Beyond the basin, though, the city's political influence was limited. Far more important was its cultural and economic diffusion, for Teotihuacán's merchants traded throughout Mesoamerica. Ceramics, ornaments of marine shells, and all sorts of decorative and valued objects (especially of green obsidian) made by Teotihuacáno artisans traveled on the backs of porters for exchange far and wide. At the same time, Teotihuacán imported pottery, feathers, and other goods from distant lowlands.

This kind of expansion left much of the political and cultural independence of neighbors intact, with only the threat of force keeping them in check. But for some unknown reason, that threat apparently waned, for late in the fifth century CE, the city fell. Invaders burned it and smashed the carved figurines of the central temples and palaces, targeting Teotihuacán's institutional and spiritual core.

THE MAYAS Teotihuacán's power eventually spread as far as the Caribbean region of the Yucatán and its interior. Here the Maya people arose and flourished from about 250 CE to their zenith in the eighth century. The Mayas have been a never-ending mystery to historians and archaeologists. They lived in an inhospitable region—hot, infertile, lacking navigable river systems, and vulnerable to hurricanes. Still, their communities, grouped into large settlements, conducted long-distance trade and produced stunning scientific and mathematical innovations. The Mayas were also great artists and builders, and it is largely from the remains of their prodigious constructions that scholars know much about them. Like the earlier Olmecs, the Mayas accomplished magnificent feats only to collapse, leaving their centers deserted for centuries and entire provinces utterly depopulated.

In contrast to the inhabitants of Teotihuacán (or Chang'an or Constantinople), the Mayas achieved greatness without founding a single great central metropolis. Instead, they established hundreds, possibly thousands, of agrarian villages scattered across present-day southern Mexico to western El Salvador. In this region of diverse ecological zones, people shared the same Mayan language. Villages were also linked through tribute payments, chiefly from lesser settlements to sacred towns. At their peak, the Mayas may have numbered as many as 10 million—a figure that qualifies them as a "big" culture. Bigness in a cultural system without big cities made them unique.

MAYA POLITICAL AND SOCIAL STRUCTURE The Mayas established a variety of kingdoms around major hubs and their hinterlands. Palenque, Copán, and Piedras Negras, for instance, embodied the model of a ritual center with hinterlands (similar in some respects to Mesopotamian city-states surrounded by transhumant societies; see Chapter 3). Such hubs were politically independent but culturally and economically interconnected. Some larger polities, such as Tikal and Kalak'mul, became sprawling centers with dependent provinces. Ambitious rulers in these larger states frequently engaged in hostilities with one another.

Thus, a single culture encompassed about a dozen kingdoms that shared many features. Each was highly stratified, displaying an elaborate class structure. At the center was a shamanistic king who legitimated his position by extolling his lineage, which reached back to a founding father and, ultimately, the gods. While there was a vast pantheon of gods and each subregion had its own patron, there were some common features. There was a creator god and there were deities for rain, maize, war, and the sun—as well as for bees and midwifery. The importance of reproduction is evident, but the creation of humans was only one act in an eternal cycle of births, deaths, and renewals that constituted the entire population of the cosmos. Gods were neither especially cruel nor benevolent. They were just very busy with the work, or dance, that sustained the axis connecting the underworld and the skies. What humans had to worry about was making sure that the gods got the attention and reverence they needed.

This was the job of Maya rulers. Kings sponsored elaborate public rituals to reinforce their divine heritages, including ornate processions down their cities' main boulevards to pay homage to gods and their descendants, the rulers. Lords and their wives performed ritual blood sacrifice to feed their ancestors. Though there may have been a powerful priestly elite, the pillars of these societies were their scribes, legal experts, military advisers, and skilled artisans.

Most of the Maya people remained tied to the land, which could sustain a high population only through dispersed settlements. In much of the region, the soil was poor and quickly exhausted. Limited water also prevented large-scale agriculture, as major rivers or irrigation systems were lacking. Mayas therefore employed a combination of adaptations to the ecology. Where possible, they created terraces and drained fields for intensive cultivation. But in much of the region they relied on slash-and-burn agriculture, which pushed the arable frontier farther into the dense jungle. The result: a subsistence economy of diversified agrarian production. Villagers cultivated maize, beans, and squash, rotating them to prevent the depletion of soil nutrients. Where possible, farmers supplemented these staples with root crops such as sweet potato and cassava. Cotton was the basic fiber used for robes, dresses, and blouses; it frequently grew amid rows of other crops as part of a diversified mix.

MAYA WRITING, MATHEMATICS, AND ARCHITECTURE Commerce connected the dispersed Maya villages, as did a common set of beliefs, codes, and values. Villagers spoke

Palenque. *Deep in the Lacandon jungle lies the ruin of the Maya city of Palenque. Its pyramid, on the left, overlooks the site; on the right, the Tower of the Palace shadows a magnificent courtyard where religious figures and nobles gathered. There is no mistaking how a city like Palenque could command its hinterland with religious authority.*

dialects of roughly the same language. Writing developed very early, though the Maya script was deciphered only recently. The advent of writing created an important caste of scribes who were vital to the society's integration. Rulers rewarded them with great titles and honors, as well as material comforts, for writing grand epics about dynasties and their founders, major battles, marriages, deaths, and sacrifices. Such writings taught generations of Maya subjects that they shared common histories, beliefs, and gods—always associated with the narratives of ruling families.

The combination of writings and performances created a historic memory to serve rulers' power and to venerate the gods whose patronage they required. The best-known surviving text is the *Popol Vuh*, a "Book of Community." It narrates one community's creation myth, extolling its founders (twin heroes) and trials and tribulations—wars, natural disasters, human ingenuity—that enabled a royal genealogy to rule the Quiché kingdom. It begins with the gods' creation of the earth, in this case the work of three water-dwelling plumed serpents. And it ends with the elaboration of rituals to which the kingdom's tribes must subscribe if they are to avoid losing their way, which had occurred several times throughout their history. One must note, however, that Maya "written" texts like the *Popol Vuh* comprise narratives recited to later Spanish sources; they are not texts inscribed in the Classical Maya era.

The Mayas also were skilled mathematicians, devising a calendar and studying astronomy. They charted regular celestial movements with amazing accuracy and marked the passage of time by precise lunar and solar cycles. Keen readers of the stars, the Mayas could map heavenly motions onto their sacred calendars and rigorously observe their rituals at the proper times.

Indeed, the movement of the stars and the chronology of the calendar governed annual ritual cycles. Each change in the cycle had particular rituals, dances, performances, and offerings, including the offering of human blood to honor the gods with life's sustenance. The most sacred blood was drawn from ears, tongues, and the foreskins of penises, to open pathways to the gods through which "donors" could hear, speak, and participate in heavenly reproduction.

Here, then, was a world characterized by political divisions and often crippling warfare, but with common religious and cultural features. A common faith provided a powerful human resource that rulers could exploit. Cities reflected a ruler's ability to summon his subjects to contribute to the kingdom's greatness. Plazas, ball courts, terraces, and palaces sprouted out from neighborhoods in an early form of urban sprawl. Activity revolved around grand royal palaces and massive ball courts, where competing teams treated enthusiastic audiences to contests that were more religious ritual than game (see discussion of Olmec ball courts in Chapter 5). Moreover, rulers exhorted their people to build not just outward but upward.

The Mayas excelled at building skyscrapers. In Tikal, for instance, surviving buildings include six steep and massive funerary pyramids featuring thick masonry walls and vaulted ceilings and chambers; the tallest temple soars above the treetops, more than 220 feet high (40 feet higher than Justinian's Hagia Sophia). Embellishing the outsides are giant carvings and paintings, and deep within lie the crypts of royal family members. For example, the famous Bonampak site (in current-day southern Mexico) has a magnificent Temple of the Murals with the finest examples of Classical Maya painting. These depict a series of events in precise detail—from an

Wood Tablet. *This detail of a wood-carved tablet from a temple in the city of Tikal (c. 741 CE) is a fine example of the ornate form of scribal activity, which combined images and portraits with glyphs that tell a narrative.*

POP	UO	ZIP	ZOTZ	TZEC
XUL	YAXKIN	MOL	CHEN	YAX
ZAC	CEH	MAC	KANKIN	MUAN
PAX	KAYAB	CUMHU	uayeb	

Maya Pictograms. *The Mayas were famous for keeping records of time with an elaborate calendar. Different pictograms represent the months of the year. All literate Mayas would have recognized this index.*

orchestra performing, to nobles discussing current affairs, to captured warriors being prepared for human sacrifice. The artwork dates from 790 CE. This kind of artwork likely adorned other Maya centers as well.

MAYA BLOODLETTING AND WARFARE The elites were obsessed with blood, for spilling it was a way to honor dynastic lineages as well as gods. This rite led to chronic warfare, especially among rival dynasties, the goal of which was to capture victims for the bloody rituals. Rulers also would shed their own blood at intervals set by the calendar. Royal wives drew blood from their tongues; men had their penises perforated by a stingray spine or sharpened bone. Such bloodletting was reserved for those of noble descent, with the aid of elaborately adorned and sanctified instruments; carvings and paintings portray blood cascading from rulers' mutilated bodies.

The spiral of warfare doomed the Mayas, especially after devastating confrontations between Tikal and Kalak'mul during the fourth through seventh centuries CE. With each outbreak, rulers drafted larger armies and sacrificed greater numbers of captives, and their resolve fueled the carnage. Crops perished. People fled. Food supplies dwindled. After centuries of misery, it must have seemed as if the gods themselves were abandoning the Maya people.

As warfare engulfed the fractured Maya communities and ruling households collapsed, entire states fell. The cycle of violence destroyed the cultural underpinnings of elite rule that had held the Maya world together. There was no single catastrophic event, no great defeat by a rival power. The Maya people simply abandoned their spiritual centers, and cities became ghost towns. As populations declined, jungles overtook temples. Eventually, the hallmark of Maya unity—the ability to read a shared script—vanished.

The two Mesoamerican societies described here—Teotihuacán and the Mayas—were quite different from the dispersed and politically segregated Bantu communities that spread out over much of the African continent south of the Sahara. Enjoying unifying political systems and widespread and accepted cultural beliefs and institutions, these Mesoamerican communities were more akin to imperial China, the Gupta dynasty in South Asia, and the Byzantine Empire. Even so, they hardly represented the majority of the peoples who inhabited the Americas and who lived, like the Bantu peoples, in widely dispersed and politically unified communities. Yet, like sub-Saharan Africa, vibrant religious traditions thrived in these two Mesoamerican societies and served more to reinforce the political and social situations from which they arose rather than to spread a universal message far beyond their original context.

CONCLUSION

The breakdown of two imperial systems—Rome around the Mediterranean and Han China in East Asia—introduced an era in which religion and shared culture rather than military conquest and political institutions linked large areas of Afro-Eurasia.

The Roman Empire gave way to a new religious unity, first represented by Christian dissenters and then co-opted by the emperor Constantine. In western Europe, the sense of unity unlimited by imperial frontiers gave rise to a universal, or "Catholic," church—the "true" Christian religion that believers felt all peoples should share. In the eastern Mediterranean, where the Roman Empire survived, Christianity and empire coalesced to reinforce the feeling that true religion, high culture, and empire went hand in hand. Christians here held that beliefs about God and Jesus found their most correct expression within the Eastern Roman Empire and in its capital, Constantinople.

Similarly, in East Asia, the weakening of the Han dynasty enabled Buddhism to dominate Chinese culture. Without a unified state in China, Confucian officials lost their influence, while Buddhist priests and monks enjoyed patronage from regional rulers, local warriors, and commoners. In India, too, a political vacuum allowed the unfolding of a new culture: the Brahman elites exploited population movements beyond the reach of traditional rulers as they established ritual forms for daily life on every level of society, while melding together aspects of their own Vedic faith with those of Buddhism to create a new Hindu synthesis.

Not all regions felt the spread of universalizing religions, however. In most of sub-Saharan Africa, belief systems were much more localized. The same pattern emerged in the Americas, where long-distance transportation was harder and language systems had not yielded texts to share with nonbelievers. But spiritual life was no less profound. Here it was the strong sense of a shared worldview, a shared sense of purpose, and a shared sense of faith that enabled common cultures to develop. Indeed, the Bantus and Mayas became large-scale common cultures—but ruled at the local level.

Thus, the period 300–600 CE saw the emergence of three great cultural units in Afro-Eurasia, each defined in religious terms: Christianity in the Mediterranean and Southwest Asia, Hinduism in South Asia, and Buddhism in East Asia. They illustrated the ways in which peoples were converging under larger religious tents, while also becoming more distinct. Universalizing religions, whether Christian or Buddhist, and universal codes of behavior, such as the Brahmanic Laws of Manu, gave people a new way to define themselves and their loyalties.

But the pattern would soon change. As we will see, empire would return to East Asia in the form of the mighty Tang dynasty. And the zone stretching from Morocco to central Asia would find itself united in a gigantic imperial system fashioned by followers of the Prophet Muhammad.

After You Read This Chapter

Go to **inQUIZITIVE** to see what you know & learn what you've missed.

TRACING THE GLOBAL STORYLINES

FOCUS ON: *Religions and Regions*

Western and Eastern Europe and Southwest Asia

- Christianity moves from a minority, persecuted faith to a state religion in the Roman Empire.

- The Sasanian state in Iran provides fertile ground for a tolerant mixture of Zoroastrianism, Nestorian Christianity, Judaism, Buddhism, and Brahmanic religion.

South Asia and East Asia

- Brahmanism, or Hinduism, becomes the dominant religion among the Vedic peoples of South Asia.

- Buddhism spreads out of South Asia along the Silk Road through central Asia and into East Asia.

Sub-Saharan Africa and Mesoamerica

- Large parts of Africa and the Americas develop common cultures based on religious beliefs shared by large, widely dispersed groups.

CHRONOLOGY

The Mediterranean and Southwest Asia	Sasanian Empire flourishes in Iran and Mesopotamia **third–sixth century CE**			
	Emperor Constantine legalizes Christianity in Roman Empire **313 CE**			
Central Asia	Buddhism spreads through central Asia **third–sixth century CE**			
South Asia	Sogdian merchant communities dominate Silk Road trade through central Asia **fourth–sixth centuries CE**			
	Transformation of Brahmanism to Hinduism begins **300 CE**			
	Gupta Empire **320–550 CE**			
East Asia				
Sub-Saharan Africa	Bantu migrations from western Africa to south, central, and east **1000 BCE–nineteenth century**			
Mesoamerica	Maya culture dominates Yucatán Peninsula and surrounding area **third–ninth century CE**			

1 CE	100 CE	200 CE	300 CE	400 CE

STUDY QUESTIONS

1. **Identify** the characteristics of a universal religion, and **explain** why Christianity and Buddhism had such wide appeal in Afro-Eurasia.

2. **Describe** the connections between the growing power of Christianity and the political reconfiguration of the Roman Empire. What was the appeal of Christianity in the Roman Empire?

3. **Analyze** the Sasanian Empire's role in facilitating the spread of universal religions and the development of common cultures in Afro-Eurasia. How did the empire's geographical location support this cross-cultural dissemination?

4. **Explain** the role of Sogdians and other central Asian peoples in the dispersion of universal religions. How did they influence East Asian societies in particular?

5. **Describe** how Brahmanism (Vedic religion) evolved into Hinduism during this era. What factors contributed to this development?

6. **Identify** key changes in Buddhist thought and practice in South Asia at this time. How did these refinements aid the spread of this religious outlook beyond its homeland?

7. **Explain** the role of written texts in universalizing religion. How did these texts reshape social attitudes toward spiritual behavior and identity?

8. **Analyze** the ways in which political decentralization affected the growing popularity of Buddhist and other religious ideas in East Asia. To what extent did they challenge Confucian ideas on social and political organization?

9. **Discuss** the extent to which universal religions brought worlds together and pushed them apart. How did religion create new cultural boundaries and rivalries in Afro-Eurasia? **Characterize** the nature of the relationship between empires and universal religions during this period.

10. **Explore** the extent to which connections between political unity and religious development influenced sub-Saharan Africa and Mesoamerica in the fourth to sixth centuries BCE.

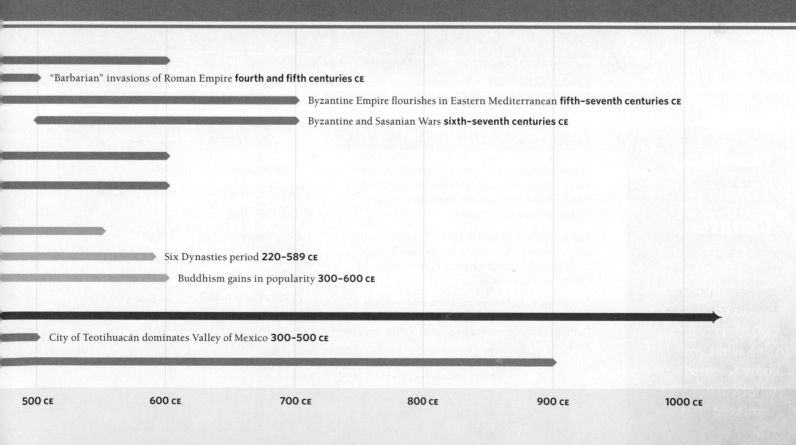

"Barbarian" invasions of Roman Empire **fourth and fifth centuries** CE

Byzantine Empire flourishes in Eastern Mediterranean **fifth–seventh centuries** CE

Byzantine and Sasanian Wars **sixth–seventh centuries** CE

Six Dynasties period **220–589** CE

Buddhism gains in popularity **300–600** CE

City of Teotihuacán dominates Valley of Mexico **300–500** CE

| 500 CE | 600 CE | 700 CE | 800 CE | 900 CE | 1000 CE |

Before You Read This Chapter

Go to INQUIZITIVE to see what you know & learn what you've missed.

GLOBAL STORYLINES

- The universalizing religion of Islam, based on the message of the prophet Muhammad, originates on the Arabian Peninsula and spreads rapidly across Afro-Eurasia.

- The expanding Tang dynasty in East Asia consolidates its bureaucracy, struggles with religious pluralism, and extends its influence into central and East Asia.

- Christianity splits over religious and political differences, leading to a divide between Roman Catholicism in the west and Greek Orthodoxy in the east.

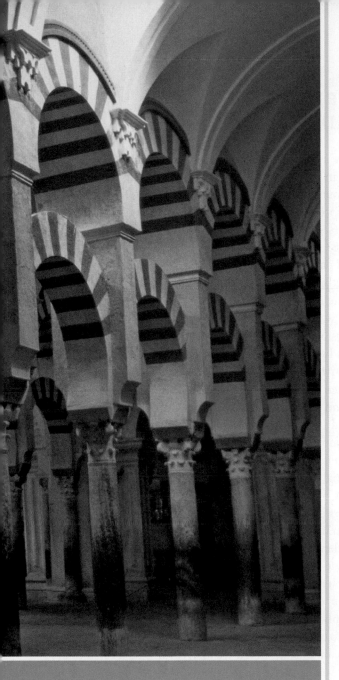

9

New Empires and Common Cultures, 600–1000 CE

FOCUS QUESTIONS

- Why did a universal religion arise in the Arabian Peninsula at the beginning of the seventh century CE, and how do its origins compare with those of other religions covered in this book (Judaism, Buddhism, and Christianity)?

- How and where did Islam, Buddhism, and Christianity spread in the period 600–1000 CE?

- What were the organizational structures of the Abbasids, Tang China, and Christendom?

- What were the forces of opposition and change within the Islamic, Tang, and Christian worlds?

- In what ways did the interactions between religion, empire, and commercial exchange affect developments across Afro-Eurasia during this period?

In 754 CE, the Muslim caliph (ruler) al-Mansur decided to relocate his capital city. Islam was barely a century old, yet it was flourishing under its second dynasty, the Abbasids. Al-Mansur wanted to relocate power away from Damascus (the capital of Islam's first dynasty) to the Abbasids' home region on the Iranian plateau to signal its new dawn. After traveling the length of the Tigris and Euphrates Rivers in search of a perfect site, the caliph decided to build his capital near an unimposing village called Baghdad.

He had good reasons for this selection. The site lay between Mesopotamia's two great rivers at the juncture of the canals that linked them. It was also a powerful symbolic location: close to the ancient capital of the Sasanian Empire, Ctesiphon, where the Arch of Khusro was still standing. It was also the site of earlier Sumerian and Babylonian power. By building at Baghdad, al-Mansur could reaffirm Mesopotamia's centrality in the world and exalt the universalist ambitions of Islam. Within five years of laying the first brick, towering walls surrounded what soon became known as the "round city," so named because of the way in which the different segments radiated out from the administrative and religious center.

Al-Mansur's choice had enduring effects. As the new capital of Islam, Baghdad also became a vital crossroads for commerce. Overnight, the city exploded into a bustling world entrepôt. Chinese goods arrived by land and sea; commodities from Inner Eurasia flowed in over the Silk Road; and cargo-laden camel caravans wound across Baghdad's western desert, linking the capital with Syria, Egypt, North Africa, and southern Spain. In effect, the unity that the Abbasids imposed from Baghdad intensified the movement of peoples, ideas, innovations, and commodities.

Baghdad's eminence and prosperity reflected its role as the center of the Islamic world. Yet, while Islam was gaining ground in central Afro-Eurasia, Chinese might was surging in East Asia—powerfully under the Tang—and Christianity was striving to extend its domains and add to its converts. Unquestionably, however, the two imperial powerhouses of this period were Islam and Tang China, and they are the focus of this chapter.

RELIGION AND EMPIRE

How religion and empire connect can vary in important ways. For example, as we will see in this chapter, Islam and Tang China were manifestly different worlds. The Islamic state had a universalizing religious mission: to bring humankind under the authority of the religion espoused by the Prophet Muhammad. In contrast, the Tang had no such grandiose religious aspirations, and while the ruling elite supported religious pluralism within China, they did not use Buddhism to expand their control into areas outside China. Instead, the Tang rulers expected that their neighbors would emulate Chinese institutions and pay tribute as symbols of respect to the greatness of the Tang Empire. With Islam's warriors, traders, and scholars crossing to Europe, Chinese influences taking deeper root in East Asia, and Christendom extending itself across Europe, religion, empire, and commercial exchange once again intertwined to serve as the social foundation across much of Afro-Eurasia.

Given the surge of religious energy across Afro-Eurasia, it was perhaps only a matter of time before a prophetic figure would arise among the Arabs. Christianity and Buddhism were laying claim to universal truths, spreading their faiths across wide geographical areas outside their places of origin, and competing groups now had to speak the language of universal religion. Only the Tang dynasty resisted the universalizing faiths, as Confucianism and Daoism withstood the upsurge of Chinese Buddhism—revealing that China would follow a different path by maintaining past traditions. In the seventh century CE, Arab peoples would become the makers of their own universal faith, which would join and jostle with predecessors in Afro-Eurasia.

THE ORIGINS AND SPREAD OF ISLAM

Islam began inside Arabia. Despite its remoteness and sparse population, in the sixth century CE, Arabia was feeling the effects of exciting outside currents: long-distance trade, imperial politics, and especially religious debate. As early as the the fourth century CE (see Current Trends in World History on p. 293 of Chapter 8), inhabitants in the state of Himyar (present-day Yemen) had embraced Judaism, only to see their territory conquered by Ethiopian Christians in 525 CE. In addition to establishing a state in the southeastern tip of the Arabian Peninsula, Christianity was making deep inroads into Arab societies, sending out missionaries eastward into southwestern Asia, where many Arabs lived. They established a notably strong following in northern Arabia. Also, commodities from Egypt, Syria, and Iraq circulated in local Arabian markets, and Arabs joined in the Byzantine and Sasanian military and civil bureaucracies. Thus, while one of the world's most universalizing faiths would be born in a remote region of Southwest Asia, Islam was quickly in a position to take advantage of the dynamic trade routes and to adapt imperial political institutions in Southwest Asia, the Iranian Plateau, and North Africa as it spread its faith and shaped its political empire.

Mecca, in the Hijaz (the western region of the Arabian Peninsula, bordering the Red Sea), was not an imposing place. A pre-Islamic poet wrote that its "winter and summer are equally intolerable. No waters flow . . . [and there is] not a blade of grass on which to rest the eye; no, nor hunting. [Here there are] only merchants, the most despicable of professions" (Peters, p. 23). Hardly more than a village of simple mud huts, Mecca's inhabitants sustained themselves less as traders than as caretakers of a revered sanctuary called the Kaaba. They regarded this collection of unmortared rocks piled on top of one another as the dwelling place of deities, whom the polytheistic Meccans worshipped. It was in this remote region that one of the world's major prophets was born, and the universalizing faith he founded soon spread from Arabia through the trade routes stretching across Southwest Asia and North Africa.

A Vision, a Text

In the early life of Muhammad, little suggested that momentous events would soon occur. Born in Mecca around 570 CE into a well-respected tribal family, he enjoyed only moderate success as a trader. Then came a revelation, which would convert this broker of commodities into a proselytizer of a new faith. In 610 CE, while Muhammad was on a month-long spiritual retreat

Mecca. *At the great mosque at Mecca, which many consider the most sacred site in Islam, hundreds of thousands of worshippers gather for Friday prayers. Many are performing their religious duty to go on a pilgrimage to the holy places in the Arabian Peninsula.*

in a cave near Mecca, he believed that God came to him in a vision and commanded him to recite these words:

> Recite in the Name of the Lord who createth,
>
> Createth man from a clot
>
> Recite: And thy Lord is the most Bounteous who teacheth by the pen
>
> Teacheth man that which he knew not.

Further revelations followed. The early ones were like the first: short, powerful, emphasizing a single, all-powerful God (Allah), and full of instructions for Muhammad's fellow Meccans to carry this message to nonbelievers. The words were eminently memorable, an important feature in an oral culture where poetry recitation was the highest art form. Muhammad's early preaching had a clear message. He urged his small band of followers to act righteously, to set aside false deities, to submit themselves to the one and only true God, and to care for the less fortunate—for the Day of Judgment was imminent. Muhammad's most insistent message was the oneness of God, a belief that has remained central to the Islamic faith ever since.

These teachings, compiled into an authoritative version after the Prophet's death, constituted the foundational text of Islam: the Quran. Its 114 chapters, known as suras, occur in descending order of length; the longest has 300 verses and the shortest, a mere 3. Accepted as the very word of God, they were believed to flow without flaw through God's perfect instrument, the Prophet Muhammad. (See Primary Source: The Quran: Two Suras in Praise of God.) Like the Jewish Torah, the Christian Bible, and other foundational texts, this one proclaimed the tenets of a new

faith to unite a people and to expand its spiritual frontiers. Its message already had universalist elements, though how far it was to be extended, whether just to the tribal peoples living in the Arabian Peninsula or well beyond, was not at all clear at first.

Muhammad believed that he was a prophet in the tradition of Moses, other Hebrew prophets, and Jesus and that he communicated with the same God that they did. As we have seen, Christian and Jewish communities existed in the Arabian Peninsula at this time. The city of Yathrib (later called Medina) held a substantial Jewish community. Just how deeply Muhammad understood the tenets of Judaism and Christianity is difficult to determine, but his professed indebtedness to their tradition is a part of Islamic belief.

The Move to Medina

In 622 CE, Muhammad and a small group of followers, opposed by Mecca's leaders because of their radical religious tenets and their challenge to the ruling elite's authority, escaped to Medina. Known as the *hijra* ("breaking off of relations" or "departure"), the perilous 200-mile journey yielded a new form of communal unity: the *umma* ("band of the faithful"). So significant was this moment that Muslims date the beginning of the Muslim era from this year.

Medina thus became the birthplace of a new faith called Islam ("submission"—in this case, to the will of God) and a new community called Muslims ("those who submit"). The city of Medina had been facing tribal and religious tensions, and by inviting Muhammad and his followers to take up residence there, its elders hoped that his leadership and charisma would

The Quran: Two Suras in Praise of God

These two suras from the Quran are relatively short, but they convey some of the essence of Muhammad's message. The Quran opens with a sura known as the fatiha ("of the opening"), which in its powerfully prayerlike quality lends itself to frequent recitation. Sura 87, "The Most High," provides a deeper insight into the nature of humanity's relationship with God.

THE FATIHA

In the name of God the beneficent, the merciful.
Praise be to God, Lord of the worlds,
The beneficent, the merciful.
Owner of the day of judgement,
You (alone) do we worship. You (alone) do we ask for help.
Show us the straight path,
The path of those whom You have favored; not the (path) of those who earn Your anger nor of those who go astray.

(1.1–1.7)

THE MOST HIGH

In the name of God the beneficent, the merciful.
Praise the name of your Lord the most high,
Who creates, then disposes;
Who measures, then guides;
Who brings forth the pasturage,
Then turns it to russet stubble.
We shall make you read (O Muhammad) so that you shall not forget
Except that which God wills. He knows the disclosed and that which still is hidden;
And We shall ease your way to the state of ease.
Therefore remind (men), for of use is the reminder.
He who fears will heed,
But the most wretched will flout it,
He who will be flung to the great fire
In which he will neither die nor live.
He is successful who grows,
And remembers the name of his Lord, so prays.
But you prefer the life of the world
Although the hereafter is better and more lasting.
This is in the former scrolls,
The scrolls of Abraham and Moses.

(87.1–87.19)

QUESTIONS FOR ANALYSIS

- What themes do these passages reveal about Islam's view of the relationship between God and mortals?
- Do you find any similarities to the tenets of Judaism and Christianity as you have encountered them in this book?

Source: "Sura I," and "Sura 87," *The Norton Anthology of World Religions: Islam,* ed. Jane Dammen McAuliffe, trans. Marmaduke Pickthall (New York: W. W. Norton & Company, 2015), pp. 86, 119–120.

---

bring peace and unity to their city. Early in his stay, Muhammad promulgated a document, the Constitution of Medina, requiring the community's people to refer all disputes to God and him. Now the residents were expected to replace traditional family, clan, and tribal affiliations with loyalty to Muhammad as the one and true Prophet of God. From Medina the faithful broadcast their faith and their mission, at first mainly by military means, to the recalcitrants of Mecca and then to all of Arabia and then later to the entire world. In this way, Islam joined Christianity in seeking to bring the whole known world under its authority.

Over time, the core practices and beliefs of every Muslim would crystallize as the **five pillars of Islam**. Muslims were expected to (1) *adhere to and repeat* the phrase that there is no God but God and that Muhammad was His Prophet; (2) *pray* five times daily facing Mecca; (3) *fast* from sunup until sundown during the month of Ramadan; (4) *make a pilgrimage* to Mecca at least once in a lifetime if their personal resources permitted; and (5) *pay alms* in the form of taxation that would alleviate the hardships of the poor. These clear-cut expectations gave the imperial system that would soon develop a doctrinal and legal structure and a broad appeal to diverse populations.

Difficulties in Documentation

Few data can be gleaned about Muhammad and the evolution of Islam from Arabic-Muslim sources known to have been written in the seventh century CE. Non-Muslim sources, especially Christian and Jewish texts, while often unsympathetic to Muhammad and early Islam, are nonetheless more abundant and contain useful data on the Prophet and the early messages of Islam. Questions have been raised based on these sources about Muhammad's birth place, his relationship to the most powerful of the Quraysh clans during his stay in Mecca, even the date of his death. A number of non-Muslim sources, for example, contend that the Prophet did not die, as Muslim tradition holds, in 632 CE, but was alive in 634 CE, leading a military campaign into Palestine. Many of these sources, as well as the Quran itself, stress the eschatological content of Muhammad's preachings and the actions of his early followers, arguing (1) that Muhammad believed that the hour of judgment was near and (2) that it was only later, during the middle of the Umayyad period in the eighth century CE, that Islam lost its end-of-the-world emphasis and settled into a long-term religious and political system.

The only Muslim source that we have on Muhammad and early Islam is the Quran itself, which, according to Muslim tradition, was compiled, with variations, during the caliphate of Uthman (r. 644–655). Once again, recent scholarship has questioned this claim, suggesting a later date, sometime in the early eighth century CE, for the standardization of the Quran. Some scholars even contend that the text by then had additions and redactions to Muhammad's message. The Quran, in fact, is singularly quiet on some of the most important events in Muhammad's life. It mentions Muhammad's name only four times. Nor do the struggles with the Quraysh in Mecca or his flight to Medina appear. Instead, scholars are dependent on biographies of Muhammad, one of the first of which was compiled by Ibn Ishaq (704–767 CE), a work not available to present scholarship but used by later Muslim authorities, notably Ibn Hisham (d. 833 CE), who wrote *The Life of Muhammad*, and Islam's most illustrious historian, Muhammad Ibn al-Jarir al-Tabari (838–925 CE). Although these two later works come from the ninth and tenth centuries CE, Muslim tradition ever since has held these sources to be reliable on Muhammad's early life and the evolution of Islam after the death of the Prophet.

Muhammad's Successors and the Expanding *Dar al-Islam*

In 632 CE, in his early sixties, the Prophet is believed to have passed away. Islam might have withered without its leader, but the movement remained vibrant thanks to the energy of the early followers—especially Muhammad's first four successors, the "rightly guided caliphs." The Arabic word *khalīfa* means "successor," and in this context it referred to Muhammad's successors as political rulers over Muslim peoples and the expanding state. Their breakthrough was to institutionalize the new faith. They set the new religion on the pathway to imperial greatness and linked religious uprightness with territorial expansion, empire building, and an appeal to all peoples.

Now Islam's expansive spiritual force galvanized its political authority. But what kind of polity would this be? Driven by religious fervor and a desire to acquire the wealth of conquered territories, Muslim soldiers embarked on military conquests and sought to found a far-reaching territorial empire. This expansion of the Islamic state was one aspect of the struggle that they called *jihad*. From the outset, Muslim religious and political leaders divided the world into two units: the *dar al-Islam* (or the world of Islam) and the *dar al-harb* (the world of warfare), seeking nothing less than world dominion. Within fifteen years, Muslim soldiers had grasped Syria, Egypt, and Iraq—centerpieces of the former Byzantine and Sasanian Empires that now became pillars undergirding an even larger Islamic empire. Mastery of desert warfare and inspired military leadership yielded these astonishing exploits, as did the exhaustion of the Byzantine and Sasanian Empires after generations of warfare.

The Byzantines saved the core of their empire by pulling back to the highlands of Anatolia, where they had readily defensible frontiers. In contrast, the Sasanians gambled all on a final effort: they hurled their remaining military resources against the Muslim armies, only to be crushed. Having lost Iraq and unable to defend the Iranian plateau, the Sasanian Empire passed out of existence. The result: Islam acquired political foundations within a generation of its birth.

The Battle of Badr. *This image depicts the battle of Badr, which took place in 624 CE and marked the beginning of Muhammad's reconquest of Mecca from his new base in the city of Medina.*

Creating an empire and stabilizing it were two different things. We have seen some come and go, such as Alexander's. Others had more stamina. How would Islam fare? A political vacuum opened in the new and growing Islamic empire with the assassination of Ali, the last of the "rightly guided caliphs." Ali, an early convert to Islam, was a fierce leader in the early battles for expansion. The Umayyads, a branch of the Quraysh, laid claim to Ali's legacy. Having been governors of the province of Syria under Ali, this first dynasty moved the core of Islam out of Arabia to the Syrian city of Damascus. They also introduced a hereditary monarchy to resolve leadership disputes. These adaptable, cosmopolitan traders ruled from Damascus until the Abbasids overthrew them in 750 CE.

The Abbasid Revolution

As the Umayyad dynasts spread Islam beyond Arabia, some peoples resented the rulers' high-handed ways. In particular, they believed that their continuing discrimination despite their conversion to Islam was humiliating and unfair. The Arab conquerors enslaved large numbers of non-Arabs in the course of their conquests. These slaves could only lose their servile status through manumission. Even so, the non-Arab freedpeople found that they, too, were still regarded as lesser persons in spite of living in Arab households and becoming Muslims, so dominant were ethnic Arabs within a still Arab-dominated Islamic world. This situation existed even though the Arabs totaled about 250,000 to 300,000 during the Umayyad era, while non-Arab populations were 100 times as populous, totaling between 25 and 30 million. The area where protest against Arab domination reached a crescendo was in the east, notably in Khurasan, where most of the Arab conquerors did not live separate from the local populations in garrison cities (as was commonplace elsewhere) but were in close contact and intermarried local, ethnically different women. One of the early leaders of Iranian protest movements in this region was Abu Muslim, whose message about Islam was that it was a universal religion, open equally to all groups. He stated: "I am a man from among the Muslims, and I do not trace my descent to any group to the exclusion of any other. . . . My only ancestry is Islam" (Hoyland, p. 206).

Even though opponents assassinated Abu Muslim, they did not silence his message. A coalition of dissidents emerged under a movement harkening back to Abbas ibn al-Muttalid (566–653 CE), an uncle of the Prophet, hence called the Abbasid movement and claiming descent from the Prophet. Soon disgruntled provincial authorities and their military allies, as well as non-Arab converts, joined the movement. After amassing a sizable military force, the Abbasid coalition trounced the Umayyad ruler in 750 CE. Thereafter, the center of the caliphate shifted to Iraq (at Baghdad; recall the opening anecdote about al-Mansur), signifying the eastward sprawl of the faith and its empire. It

also represented a success for non-Arab groups within Islam without eliminating Arab influence at the dynasty's center—the capital, Baghdad, in Arabic-speaking Iraq. This process changed the nature of the emerging empire. For as the political center of Islam moved out of Arabia to Syria (at Damascus) and then with the Abbasids to Baghdad, ethnic and geographical diversity replaced what had been ethnic purity. Thus, even as the universalizing religion strove to create a common spiritual world, it became more diverse within its political dimensions.

Not only did the Abbasids open Islam to Persian peoples, but they also embraced Greek and Hellenistic learning, Indian science, and Chinese innovations. In this fashion, Islam, drawing its original impetus from the teachings and actions of a prophetic figure, followed the trajectory of Christianity and Buddhism and became a faith with a universalist message and appeal. It owed much of its success to its ability to merge the contributions of vastly different geographical and intellectual territories into a rich yet unified culture. (See Map 9.1.)

THE CALIPHATE An early challenge for the Abbasid rulers was to determine how traditional, or "Arab," they could be and still rule so vast an empire. They chose to keep the bedrock political institution of the early Islamic state—the **caliphate** (the line of political leaders reaching back to Muhammad). Signifying both the political and spiritual head of the Islamic community, this institution had arisen as the successor to Muhammad's shining leadership. Although the caliphs exercised political and spiritual authority over the Muslim community, they did not inherit Muhammad's prophetic powers. Nor were they authorities in religious doctrine. That power was reserved for religious scholars, called *ulama*; some of these men were schooled in Islamic law, others were experts in Quranic interpretation, and still others were religious thinkers.

Abbasid rule reflected borrowed practices from successful predecessors. The caliphs' leadership style was a mixture of Persian absolute authority and the royal seclusion of the Byzantine emperors who lived in palaces far removed from their subjects. As the empire expanded, it became increasingly decentralized politically, enabling wily regional governors and competing caliphates in Spain and Egypt to grab power. The political result was an Islamic world shot through with multiple centers of power, nominally led by a weakened Abbasid caliphate. Even as Islam's political center diffused, though, its spiritual center remained fixed in Mecca, where many of the faithful gathered to circle the kaaba and to reaffirm their devotion to Islam as part of their pilgrimage obligation.

THE ARMY The Abbasids, like all rulers, relied on force to integrate their empire. For imperial Islam (as for the Romans), exercising military power required marshaling warriors and soldiers from across Afro-Eurasia.

How "Arab" should the Muslim armies be? In the early stages, leaders had conscripted military forces from local Arab populations, creating citizen armies. But as Arab populations settled down in garrison cities, the Abbasid rulers turned to professional soldiers from the empire's peripheries. Now they recruited from Turkish-speaking communities in central Asia and from the non-Arab, Berber-speaking peoples of North and West Africa. Their reliance on foreign—that is, non-Arab—military personnel represented a major shift in the Islamic world. Not only did the change infuse the empire with dynamic new populations, but soon these groups gained political authority (just as the "barbarians" had done in the last centuries of the Roman Empire; see Chapters 6 and 8). Having begun as an Arab state and then incorporated strong Persian influence, the Islamic empire now embraced Turkish elements from the pastoral belts of central Asia.

ISLAMIC LAW (THE *SHARIA*) AND THEOLOGY In the Abbasid period, not just the caliphate but also Islamic law took shape. The *sharia* stands as the crucial foundation of Islam. It covers all aspects of practical and spiritual life, providing legal principles for marriage contracts, trade regulations, and religious prescriptions such as prayer, pilgrimage rites, and ritual fasting. It reflects the work of generations of religious scholars, rather than soldiers, courtiers, and bureaucrats. And it has remained vital throughout the Muslim world, independent of empires, to the present day.

Early Muslim communities prepared the ground for the *sharia,* endeavoring (guided by the Quran) to handle legal matters in ways that they thought Muhammad would have wanted. However, because the Quran mainly addressed family concerns, religious beliefs, and social relations (such as marriage, divorce, inheritance, dietary restrictions, and treatment of women) but not other legal questions, local judges exercised their own judgment where the Quran was silent. The most influential early legal scholar was an eighth-century CE Palestinian-born Arab, al-Shafi'i, who wanted to make the empire's laws entirely Islamic. He insisted that Muhammad's laws as laid out in the Quran, in addition to his sayings and actions as written in later reports (*hadith*), provided all the legal guidance that Islamic judges needed.

The triumph of scholars such as al-Shafi'i was deeply significant: it placed the *ulama,* the Muslim scholars, at the heart of Islam. *Ulama,* not princes and kings, became the lawmakers, insisting that the caliphs could not define religious law. Only the scholarly class could interpret the Quran and determine which *hadith* were authentic. The *ulama*'s ascendance opened a sharp division within Islam: between the secular realm of the caliphs and the religious sphere of judges, experts on Islamic jurisprudence, teachers, and holy men.

GENDER IN EARLY ISLAM Pre-Islamic Arabia was one of the last regions in Southwest Asia where patriarchy had not triumphed. Instead, men still married into women's families and moved to those families' locations, as was common in tribal communities. Some women engaged in a variety of occupations and even, if they became wealthy, married more than one husband. But contact with the rest of Southwest Asia, where men's power over women prevailed, was already altering women's status in the Arabian Peninsula before the birth of Muhammad.

Muhammad's relations with women reflected these changes. As a young man, he married a woman fifteen years his senior—Khadija, an independent trader—and took no other wives before she died. It was Khadija to whom he went in fear following his first revelations. She wrapped him in a blanket and assured him of his sanity. She was also his first convert. Later in life, however, he took younger wives, some of whom were widows of his companions, and insisted on their veiling (partly as a sign of their modesty and privacy). He married his favorite wife, Aisha, when she was only nine or ten years old. An important figure in early Islam, she was the daughter of Abu Bakr, who became the first caliph after Muhammad's death. She became a major source for collecting Muhammad's sayings.

Khadija. *The importance of women to the founding of Islam is apparent in this Ottoman miniature, which depicts Khadija (left) bearing witness to Gabriel (center) as he conveys God's will to Muhammad (right). Both wife and prophet are veiled in accordance with hadiths promoting female modesty and prohibiting representations of Muhammad, respectively.*

By the time Islam reached Southwest Asia and North Africa, where strict gender rules and women's subordinate status were entrenched, the new faith was adopting a patriarchal outlook. Muslim men could divorce freely; women could not. A man could take four wives and numerous concubines; a woman could have only one husband. Well-to-do women, always veiled, lived secluded from male society. Still, the Quran did offer women some protections. Men had to treat each wife with respect if they took more than one. Women could inherit property (although only half of what a man inherited). Infanticide was taboo. Marriage dowries went directly to the bride rather than to her guardian, indicating women's independent legal standing. And while a woman's adultery drew harsh punishment, its proof required eyewitness testimony. The result was a legal system that reinforced men's dominance over women but empowered magistrates to oversee the definition of male honor and proper behavior.

The Blossoming of Abbasid Culture

The arts flourished during the Abbasid period, a blossoming that left its imprint throughout society. Within a century, Arabic had superseded Greek as the Muslim world's preferred language for poetry, literature, medicine, science, and philosophy. Like Greek, it spread beyond native speakers to become the language of the educated classes.

Arabic scholarship now made significant contributions, including the preservation and extension of Greek and Roman thought and the transmission of Greek and Latin treatises to Europe. Scholars at Baghdad translated the principal works of Aristotle; essays by Plato's followers; works by Hippocrates, Ptolemy, and Archimedes; and the medical treatises of Galen, using these works to extend their understanding of the natural world. To house such manuscripts, patrons of the arts and sciences—including the caliphs—opened magnificent libraries.

The Muslim world absorbed scientific breakthroughs from China and other areas, incorporated the use of paper from China, adopted siege warfare from China and Byzantium, and applied

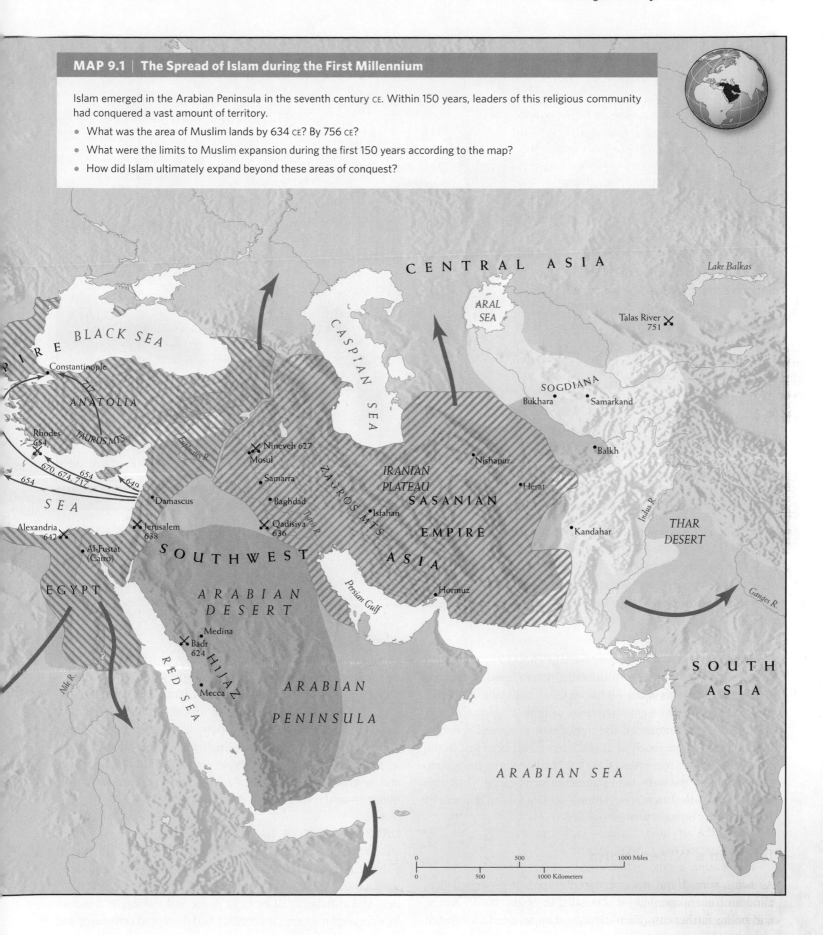

MAP 9.1 | The Spread of Islam during the First Millennium

Islam emerged in the Arabian Peninsula in the seventh century CE. Within 150 years, leaders of this religious community had conquered a vast amount of territory.

- What was the area of Muslim lands by 634 CE? By 756 CE?
- What were the limits to Muslim expansion during the first 150 years according to the map?
- How did Islam ultimately expand beyond these areas of conquest?

CENTRAL ASIA

Lake Balkas

BLACK SEA

ARAL SEA

Talas River 751

CASPIAN SEA

SOGDIANA

Constantinople

Bukhara • Samarkand

ANATOLIA

TAURUS MTS.

Rhodes 654

Euphrates R.

Nineveh 627

Mosul

Nishapur

Balkh

670, 674, 717

654

654

Samarra

649

IRANIAN PLATEAU

Herat

SEA

Damascus

Baghdad

ZAGROS MTS.

SASANIAN

Indus R.

THAR DESERT

Alexandria 642

Jerusalem 638

Qadisiya 636

Isfahan

Tigris R.

EMPIRE

Kandahar

Al-Fustat (Cairo)

SOUTHWEST

ASIA

EGYPT

ARABIAN DESERT

Persian Gulf

Hormuz

Ganges R.

Medina

SOUTH ASIA

Nile R.

Badr 624

HIJAZ

ARABIAN

RED SEA

Mecca

PENINSULA

ARABIAN SEA

0   500   1000 Miles
0   500   1000 Kilometers

MAP 9.2 | Political Fragmentation in the Islamic World, 750–1000 CE

By 1000 CE, the Islamic world was politically fractured and decentralized. The Abbasid caliphs still reigned in Baghdad, but they wielded very limited political authority. Looking at the map, first point to Baghdad and then point out all the areas under Abbasid control.

- What are the regions where major Islamic powers emerged?
- What areas were Sunni versus Shiite?
- Why were the Abbasids unable to sustain political unity in the Islamic world?

knowledge of plants from the ancient Greeks. From Indian sources, scholars borrowed a numbering system based on the concept of zero and units of ten—what we today call Arabic numerals. Arab mathematicians were pioneers in arithmetic, geometry, and algebra, and they expanded the frontiers of plane and spherical trigonometry. Since much of Greek science had been lost in the west and later was reintroduced via the Muslim world, the Islamic contribution to the west was of immense significance. Thus, this intense borrowing, translating, storing, adding to, and diffusing of written works brought worlds together.

Islam in a Wider World

As Islam spread and became decentralized, it generated dazzling and often competitive dynasties in Spain, North Africa, and points farther east. Each dynastic state revealed the Muslim

talent for achieving high levels of artistry far from its heartland. As more peoples came under the roof provided by the Quran, they invigorated a broad world of Islamic learning and science. But growing diversity led to a problem: Islam's political structures could not hold its widely dispersed believers under a single regime. Although its political system shared many legal elements (especially those controlled by Islamic texts and its enforcers), in terms of secular power Islam was deeply divided—and remains so to this day. (See Map 9.2.)

DAZZLING CITIES IN SPAIN One extraordinary Muslim state arose in Spain under Abd al-Rahman III, also known as al-Nasir li-din Allah (the Victorious; r. 912–961 CE), the successor ruler of a Muslim kingdom founded there over a century earlier. Abd al-Rahman III brought peace and stability to a violent frontier region where civil conflict had disrupted commerce and

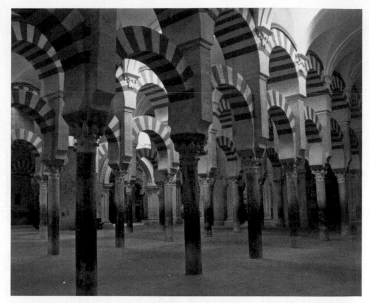

The Great Mosque of Cordoba. *The great mosque of Cordoba was built in the eighth century CE by the Umayyad ruler Abd al-Rahman I and added to by other Muslim rulers, including al-Hakim II (who succeeded Abd al-Rahman III), considered by many historians to have been the most powerful and effective of the Spanish Umayyad caliphs.*

intellectual exchange. His evenhanded governance promoted amicable relations among Muslims, Christians, and Jews, and his diplomatic relations with Christian potentates as far away as France, Germany, and Scandinavia generated prosperity across western Europe and North Africa. He expanded and beautified the capital city of Cordoba, and his successor made the Great Mosque of Cordoba one of Spain's most stunning sites.

The Great Mosque of Cordoba, known in Spanish as la Mezquita, is the oldest standing Muslim building on the Iberian Peninsula. It is a stirring tribute to the architectural brilliance and religious zeal of Iberia's Muslims. Conceived of in 785 CE by the Umayyad ruler Abd al-Rahman I, it was finished within a year of the laying of the foundations. Abd al-Rahman I commanded that it be built in the form of a perfect square. Its most striking features were alternating red and white arches, made of jasper, onyx, marble, and granite and fashioned from materials from the Roman temple and other buildings in the vicinity. These huge double arches hoisted the ceiling to 40 feet and filled the interior with light and cooling breezes. Around the doors and across the walls, Arabic calligraphy proclaimed Muhammad's message and asserted the superiority of Arabic as God's chosen language.

A CENTRAL ASIAN GALAXY OF TALENT The other end of the Islamic empire, 8,000 miles east of Spain, enjoyed an equally spectacular cultural flowering. In a territory where Greek culture had once sparkled and where Sogdians had become leading intellectuals, Islam was now the dominant faith and the source of intellectual ferment.

The Abbasid rulers in Baghdad delighted in surrounding themselves with learned men from this region. They promoted and collected Arabic translations of Persian, Greek, and Sanskrit manuscripts, and they encouraged central Asian scholars to enhance their learning by moving to Baghdad. One of their protégés, the Islamic cleric al-Bukhari (d. 870 CE), was Islam's most dedicated collector of *hadith,* which provided vital knowledge about the Prophet's life.

Others made notable contributions to science and mathematics. Al-Khwarizmi (c. 780–850 CE) modified Indian digits into Arabic numerals and wrote the first book on algebra. The renowned Abbasid philosopher al-Farabi (d. 950 CE), from a Turkish military family, also made his way to Baghdad, where he studied eastern Christian teachings. Although he considered himself a Muslim, he thought good societies would succeed only if their rulers implemented political tenets espoused in Plato's *Republic.* He championed a virtuous "first chief" to rule over an Islamic commonwealth in the same way that Plato had favored a philosopher-king.

In the eleventh century, the Abbasid caliphate began to decline, devastated by climatic change (see Chapter 10) and weakened from overextension and the influx of outsider groups (the same problems the Roman Empire had faced). Scholars no longer trekked to the court at Baghdad. Yet the region's intellectual vitality remained strong, for young men of learning found patrons among local rulers. Consider Ibn Sina, known in the west as Avicenna (980–1037 CE). He grew to adulthood in Bukhara, practiced medicine in the courts of various Islamic rulers, and spent his later life in central Persia. Schooled in the Quran, Arabic secular literature, philosophy, geometry, and Indian and Euclidean mathematics, Ibn Sina was a master of many disciplines. His *Canon of Medicine* stood as the standard medical text in both Southwest Asia and Europe for centuries.

Ibn Sina. *Ibn Sina was a versatile scholar, most famous for his* Canon *of Medicine.*

TRADE AND ISLAM IN SUB-SAHARAN AFRICA Islam also crossed the Sahara Desert and penetrated well into Africa, carried by traders and scholars (see Map 9.3); there merchants exchanged weapons and textiles for gold, salt, and slaves. Trade did more than join West Africa to North Africa. It also generated prodigious wealth, which allowed centralized political kingdoms to develop. The most celebrated was Ghana, which lay at the terminus of North Africa's major trading routes. (See Primary Source: Ghana as Seen by a Muslim Observer in the Eleventh Century.)

Seafaring Muslim traders carried Islam into East Africa via the Indian Ocean. There is evidence of a small eighth-century CE Islamic trading community at Lamu, along the northern coast of present-day Kenya; and by the mid-ninth century CE, other coastal trading communities had sprung up. They all exported ivory and, possibly, slaves. On the island of Pate, off the coast of Kenya, the inhabitants of Shanga constructed the region's first mosque. This simple structure was replaced 200 years later by a mosque capable of holding all adult members of the community when they gathered for Friday prayers. By the tenth century, the East African coast featured a mixed African-Arab culture. The region's evolving Bantu language absorbed Arabic words and before long gained a new name, Swahili (derived from the Arabic plural of the word meaning "coast"). In sub-Saharan Africa as in North Africa and Asia, Islam promoted trade and elevated the status of merchants, who were themselves important agents for spreading their faith.

Opposition within Islam: Shiism and the Rise of the Fatimids

Islam's whirlwind rise generated internal tensions from the start. It is hardly surprising that a religion that extolled territorial conquests and created a large empire in its first decades would also spawn dissident religious movements that challenged the existing imperial structures. Muslims shared a reverence for a basic text and a single God, but often they had little else in common. Religious and political divisions only grew deeper as Islam spread into new corners of Afro-Eurasia. Once the charismatic Prophet died, believers disagreed over who should take his place and how to preserve authority. Strains associated with selecting the first four caliphs after Muhammad's death left a legacy of protest; to this day, they represent the greatest challenge facing Islam's efforts to create a unified culture.

SUNNIS AND SHIITES The most powerful opposition movement arose in North Africa, lower Iraq, and the Iranian plateau. The questions that fueled disagreements were who should succeed the Prophet, how the succession should take place, and who should lead Islam's expansion into the wider world. The vast majority of Muslims today are **Sunnis** (from the Arabic word meaning "tradition"). They accept that the political succession to the Prophet through the four rightly guided caliphs and then to the Umayyad and Abbasid dynasties was the correct one. Dissidents, such as the Shiites, contest this version.

Shiites ("members of the party of Ali"), among the earliest dissidents, felt that the proper successors should have been Ali, who had married the Prophet's daughter Fatima, and his descendants. Ali was one of the early converts to Islam and one of the band of Meccans who had migrated with the Prophet

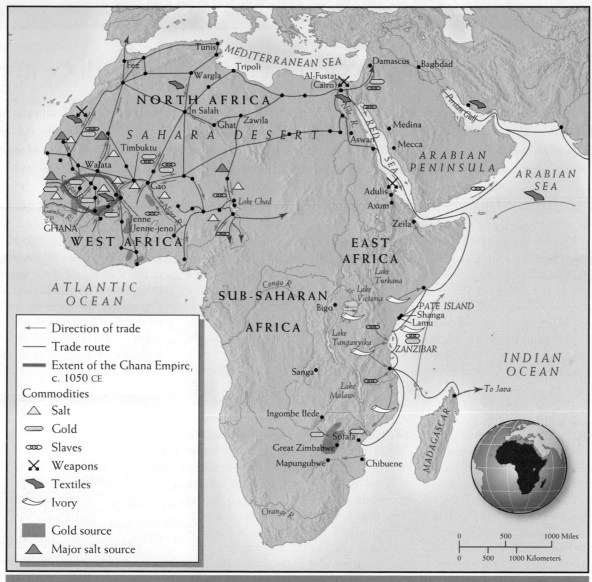

MAP 9.3 | Islam and Trade in Sub-Saharan Africa, 700–1000 CE

Islamic merchants and scholars, not Islamic armies, carried Islam into sub-Saharan Africa.

- Trace the trade routes in Africa, being sure to follow the correct direction of trade.
- According to the map key and icons, what commodities were Islamic merchants seeking below the Sahara?
- How did trade and commerce lead to the geographical expansion of the Islamic faith?

to Medina. The fourth of the rightly guided caliphs, he ruled over the Muslim community from 656 to 661 CE, dying at the hands of an assassin who struck him down as he was praying in a mosque in Kufa, Iraq. Shiites believe that Ali's descendants, whom they call *imams,* have religious and prophetic power as well as political authority—and thus should enjoy spiritual primacy.

Shiism appealed to groups whom the Umayyads and Abbasids had excluded from power; it became Islam's most potent dissident force and created a permanent divide within

Islam. Shiism was well established in the first century of Islam's existence. Over time the Sunnis and Shiites diverged even more than the early political disputes would have indicated. Both groups had their own versions of the *sharia,* their own collections of *hadith,* and their own theological tenets.

FATIMIDS After 300 years of struggling, the Shiites finally seized power. Repressed in Iraq and Iran, Shiite activists made their way to North Africa, where they joined with dissident Berber groups to topple several rulers. In 909 CE, a Shiite religious and

Ghana as Seen by a Muslim Observer in the Eleventh Century

The following excerpt is from an eleventh-century manuscript written by a Muslim serving under the Umayyads in Spain. Its author, Abdullah Abu Ubayd al-Bakri, produced a massive general geography and history of the known world, as did many Muslim scholars of the period. This manuscript has special value because it provides information about West Africa, a region in which the Spanish rulers had great interest and into which Islam had been spreading for several centuries.

Ghana is the title of the king of the people. The name of the country is Aoukar. The ruler who governs the people at the present time—the year 460 AH (after the Hijra and 1067-68 CE)—is called Tenkamein. He came to the throne in 455 AH. His predecessor, who was named Beci, began his reign at the age of 85. He was a prince worthy of great praise as much for his personal conduct as for his zeal in the pursuit of justice and his friendship to Muslims. . . .

Ghana is composed of two towns situated in a plain. The one inhabited by Muslims is large and contains twelve mosques, in which the congregants celebrate the Friday prayer. All of these mosques have their imams, their muezzins, and their salaried readers. The city possesses judges and men of great erudition. . . . The city where the king resides is six miles away and carries the name el-Ghaba, meaning "the forest." The territory separating these two locations is covered with dwellings, constructed out of rocks and the wood of the acacia tree. The dwelling of the king consists of a chateau and several surrounding huts, all of which are enclosed by a wall-like structure. In the ruler's town, close to the royal tribunal, is a mosque where Muslims come when they have business with the ruler in order to carry out their prayers. . . . The royal interpreters are chosen from the Muslim population, as was the state treasurer and the majority of the state ministers. . . .

The opening of a royal meeting is announced by the noise of a drum, which they call a *deba*, and which is formed from a long piece of dug-out wood. Upon hearing the drumming, the inhabitants assemble. When the king's coreligionists [people of the same religion] appear before him, they genuflect and throw dust on their heads. Such is the way in which they salute their sovereign. The Muslims show their respect for the king by clapping their hands. The religion of the peoples is paganism and fetishism. . . . The land of Ghana is not healthy and has few people. Travelers who pass through the area during the height of the agricultural season are rarely able to avoid becoming sick. When the grains are at their fullest and are ready for harvesting is the time when mortality affects visitors.

The best gold in the land comes from Ghiarou, a town located eighteen days' journey from the capital. All of the gold found in the mines of the empire belongs to the sovereign, but the sovereign allows the people to take gold dust. Without this precaution, the gold would become so abundant that it would lose much of its value. . . . It is claimed that the king owns a piece of gold as large as an enormous rock.

QUESTIONS FOR ANALYSIS

- From this excerpt, how much can you learn about the kingdom of Ghana? Try drawing a sketch of the region based on the description in the second paragraph.
- What influence did Islam have in the empire? What aspects of the excerpt reveal the extent of Islam's acceptance?
- What elements of Ghana most interested the author?

Source: Abou-Obeïd-el-Bekri, *Description de l'Afrique septentrionale*, revised and corrected edition, translated by [William] Mac Guckin de Slane (Paris: A. Maisonneuve, 1965), pp. 327–31; translated from the French by Robert Tignor.

military leader, Abu Abdallah, overthrew the Sunni ruler there. Thus began the Fatimid regime.

After conquering Egypt in 969 CE, the Fatimids set themselves against the Abbasid caliphs of Baghdad, refusing to acknowledge their legitimacy and claiming to speak for the whole Islamic world. The Fatimid rulers established their capital in a new city that arose alongside al-Fustat, the old Umayyad capital. They called this place al-Qahira (or Cairo), "the Victorious," and promoted its beauty. Early on they founded a place of worship and learning, Al-Azhar Mosque, which attracted scholars from all over Afro-Eurasia and spread Islamic learning outward; they also built other elegant mosques and centers of learning. The Fatimid regime lasted until the late twelfth century, though its rulers made little headway in persuading the Egyptian population to embrace their Shiite beliefs. Most of the population remained Sunnis.

By 1000 CE, Islam, which had originated as a radical religious revolt in a small corner of the Arabian Peninsula, had grown into

Djinguereber Mosque. *This grand mosque was built in Timbuktu, Mali, at the height of the kingdom's power. Built by Mansa Musa in the fourteenth century, the mosque speaks to the depth and importance of Islam's roots in the Malian kingdom.*

Al-Azhar Mosque. *The mosque of al-Azhar is Cairo's most important ancient mosque. Built in the tenth century by the Fatimid conquerors and rulers of Egypt, it quickly became a leading center for worship and learning, frequented by Muslim clerics and admired in Europe.*

a vast political and religious empire. It had become the dominant political and cultural force in the middle regions of Afro-Eurasia. Like its rival in this part of the world, Christianity, it aspired to universality. But unlike Christianity, it was linked from its outset to political power. Muhammad and his early followers created an empire to facilitate the expansion of their faith, while their Christian counterparts inherited an empire when Constantine embraced their faith. A vision of a world under the jurisdiction of Muslim caliphs, adhering to the dictates of the *sharia,* drove Muslim armies, merchants, and scholars to territories thousands of miles away from Mecca and Medina. Yet the impulse to expand ran out of energy at the fringes of Islam's reach, creating political fragmentation within the Muslim world and leaving much of western Europe and China untouched. But it also had important internal consequences: Muslims were no longer the minority within their own lands, owing to the conversion of Christians, Jews, and other populations under Muslim emperors.

THE TANG STATE

The short-lived Sui dynasty (589–618 CE) and the more durable Tang dynasty (618–907 CE) expanded the territory that they controlled into central and East Asia, thus paralleling Islam's explosion out of Arabia and throughout Afro-Eurasia. Once again the landmass had two centers of power, as Islam replaced the Roman Empire in counterbalancing the power and wealth of China.

This bipolar world differed significantly from that of the Roman and Han Empires: in the centuries since their waning, Eurasian and African worlds had drawn much closer through trade, conversion, and regular political contacts. Now the two

powerhouses competed for dominance in central Asia, sharing influences and even mobile populations that weaved back and forth across porous borders between them.

China was both a recipient of foreign influences and a source of influences on its neighbors. It was becoming the hub of East Asian integration. Like the Umayyads and the Abbasids, the Tang dynasty, recovering the territory and confidence of the Han Empire, promoted a cosmopolitan culture. Under its rule, Buddhism, medicine, and mathematics from India gave China's chief cities an international flavor. Buddhist monks from Bactria; Greeks, Armenians, and Jews from Constantinople; Muslim envoys from Samarkand and Persia; Vietnamese tributary missions from Annam; nomadic chieftains from the Siberian plains; officials and students from Korea; and monkish visitors from Japan all rubbed elbows in the streets of two of China's largest cities, Chang'an and Luoyang. Ideas also traveled eastward—notably to Korea and Japan, where Daoism and Buddhism made inroads. Similarly, Chinese statecraft, as expressed through the Confucian classics, struck the early Koreans and Japanese as the best model for their own state building.

Territorial Expansion under the Tang Dynasty

China had faced a long period of political fragmentation (see Chapter 8) before Tang rulers restored Han models of empire building. Their claims that an imperial system could outperform small states found a receptive audience in a populace fatigued by internal chaos. The Tang dynasty expanded China's boundaries and reestablished its dominance in central and East Asia.

Green Revolutions in the Islamic World and Tang China, 300–600 CE

World historians often focus on the more famous Columbian Exchange to talk about how the sharing of foods between regions of the world created revolutions in diet. The Afro-Eurasian world underwent a food revolution of its own between 300 and 600 CE. New crops, especially food crops, leaped across political and cultural borders during this period, offering expanding populations more diverse and nutritious diets and the ability to feed increased numbers. Such was true of the Islamic world and Tang China in the eighth century CE. Now, however, it was India that replaced Mesopotamia as the source of a dazzling array of new cultigens. Most of them originated in Southeast Asia, made their way to India, and dispersed throughout the Muslim world and into China. These crops included new strains of rice, taro, sour oranges, lemons, limes, and most likely coconut palm trees, sugarcane, bananas, plantains, and mangoes. Sorghum and possibly cotton and watermelons arrived from Africa. Only the eggplant was indigenous to India. Although these staples spread quickly to East Asia, their westward movement was slower. Not until the Muslim conquest of Sindh in northern India in 711 CE did territories to the west fully discover the crop innovations pioneered in Southeast Asia.

India fascinated the Arabs, and they exploited its agricultural offerings to the hilt. Soon a revolution in crops and diet swept through the Muslim world. Sorghum supplanted millet and the other grains of antiquity because it was hardier, had higher yields, and required a shorter growing season. Citrus trees added flavor to the diet and provided refreshing drinks during the summer heat. Increased cotton cultivation led to a greater demand for textiles.

For over 300 years, farmers from northwest India to Spain, Morocco, and West Africa made impressive use of the new crops. They increased agricultural output, slashed fallow periods, and grew as many as three crops on lands that formerly had yielded one. (See Map 9.4.) As a result, farmers could feed larger communities; even as cities grew, the countryside became more densely populated and even more productive.

The same agricultural revolution that was sweeping through South Asia and the Muslim world also took East Asia by storm. China received the same crops that Muslim cultivators were carrying westward. Rice was critical. New varieties entered from the south, and groups migrating from the north (after the collapse of the Han Empire) eagerly took them up. Soon Chinese farmers became the world's most intensive wet-field rice

cultivators. Early- and late-ripening seeds supported two or three plantings a year. Champa rice, introduced from central Vietnam, was especially popular for its drought resistance and rapid ripening.

Because rice needs ample water, Chinese hydraulic engineers went into the fields to design water-lifting devices, which peasant farmers used to construct hillside rice paddies. They also dug more canals, linking rivers and lakes (see Map 9.5) and even drained swamps, alleviating the malaria that had long troubled the region. Their efforts yielded a booming and constantly moving rice frontier.

QUESTIONS FOR ANALYSIS

- Historians think of the eighteenth century as having produced an agricultural revolution. Are we justified in using the same term for this earlier period?
- How did the new crops change diets and contribute to population growth?

Explore Further

Watson, Andrew. *Agricultural Innovation in the Early Islamic World: The Diffusion of Crops and Farming Techniques, 700–1100* (1983).

A sudden change in the course of the Yellow River (not the first such environmental calamity; see Chapter 7) caused extensive flooding on the North China plain and set the stage for the emergence of the Tang dynasty at the expense of the Sui. (See Map 9.5 for a view of the extent of the Sui dynasty.) Revolts ensued as the population faced starvation. Li Yuan, the governor of a province under the Sui dynasty, marched on Chang'an and took the throne for himself in 618 CE. He promptly established the Tang dynasty and began building a strong central government by doubling the number of government offices. By 624 CE, the initial steps of establishing the Tang dynasty were complete. But the fruits of these gains slipped into the hands

of Li Yuan's ambitious son Li Shimin, who forced his father to abdicate and took the throne in 627 CE.

With a large and professionally trained army capable of defending far-flung frontiers and squelching rebellious populations, the Tang built a military organization of aristocratic cavalry and peasant soldiers. The cavalry regularly clashed on the northern steppes with encroaching nomadic peoples, who also fought on horseback; at its height the Tang military had some 700,000 horses. At the same time, between 1 and 2 million peasant soldiers garrisoned the south and toiled on public works projects.

Much like the Islamic forces, the Tang's frontier armies increasingly relied on pastoral nomadic soldiers from the Inner

MAP 9.4 | Agricultural Diffusion in the First Millennium

The second half of the first millennium saw a revolution in agriculture throughout Afro-Eurasia. Agriculturalists across the landmass increasingly cultivated similar crops.

- Where did most of the cultigens originate? In what direction and where did most of them flow?
- What role did the spread of Islam and the growth of Islamic empires (see Map 9.1) play in the process?

Eurasian steppe. Notable were the Uighurs, Turkish-speaking peoples who had moved into western China and by 750 CE constituted the empire's most potent military force. These hard-riding and hard-drinking warriors galvanized fearsome cavalries, fired longbows at distant range, and wielded steel swords and knives in hand-to-hand combat. The Tang military also pushed the state into Tibet, the Red River valley in northern Vietnam, Manchuria, and Bohai (near the Korean peninusla).

By 650 CE, as Islamic armies were moving toward central Asia, the Tang were already the region's new colossus. At its height, Tang armies controlled more than 4 million square miles of territory—an area as large as the entire, by now politically

fragmented, Islamic world in the ninth and tenth centuries. The Tang benefited from South China's rich farmlands, brought under peasant cultivation by draining swamps, building an intricate network of canals and channels, and connecting lakes and rivers to the rice lands. The state thereby was able to collect taxes from roughly 10 million families, representing 57 million individuals. Taxes that took the form of agricultural labor propelled the expansion of cultivated frontiers throughout the south.

In spite of the Abbasid Empire's precocious spread, China in 750 CE was the most powerful, most advanced, and best administered empire in the world. (See Map 9.6.) Korea and Japan recognized its superiority in every material aspect of life.

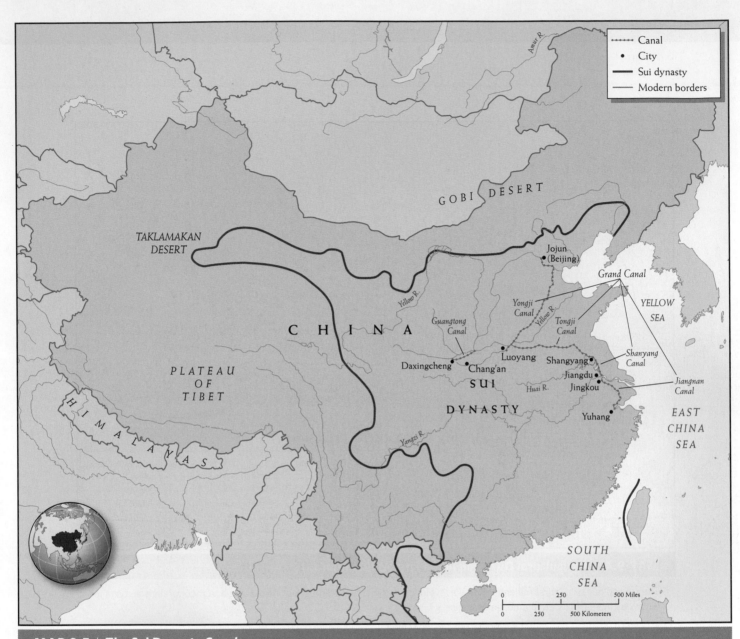

MAP 9.5 | The Sui Dynasty Canals

China, like the Islamic world, experienced a population explosion during this period.

- Where are the Sui dynasty canals on the map and the two areas showing population concentration?
- Why do you think the population concentrations are located along the canals?
- What other roles might the canals have played in addition to fostering population growth in this period within China?

Muslims were among the people who arrived at Chang'an to pay homage. Persians, Armenians, and Turks brought tribute and merchandise via the busy arteries of the Silk Road or by sea, and other travelers and traders came from Southeast Asia, Korea, and Japan. This network of routes was rarely traversed the entire length by a single person, however. It was more a chain of entrepôts than an early version of an interstate.

The peak of Chinese power occurred just as the Abbasids were expanding into Tang portions of central Asia. Rival Muslim forces drove the Tang from Turkistan in 751 CE at the Battle of Talas River, and their success emboldened groups such as the Sogdians and Tibetans to challenge the Tang in the west. As a result, the Tang gradually retreated into the old heartlands along the Yellow and Yangzi Rivers. They even saw their capital fall

MAP 9.6 | The Tang State in East Asia, 750 CE

The Tang dynasty, at its territorial peak in 750 CE, controlled a state that extended from central Asia to the East China Sea.

- What foreign areas are under Tang control? What areas were heavily influenced by Tang government and culture?
- How can we tell from the map that China was undergoing an economic revolution during the Tang period?
- How did the Tang maintain order and stability in such a large, dynamic realm?

to invading Tibetans and Sogdians. Thereafter, misrule, court intrigues, economic exploitation, and popular rebellions weakened the empire, even though it held on for over a century more until northern invaders toppled it in 907 CE.

Organizing an Empire

The Tang Empire, a worthy successor to the Han, ranks as one of China's great dynastic polities. Although its rulers emulated the Han in many ways (for example, by compiling a legal code based on the Han's), they also introduced new institutions.

The heart of the Tang state was the magnificent capital city of Chang'an, the population of which reached 1 million, half of

whom lived within its impressive city walls and half on the outside. The outer walls enclosed an immense area, 6 miles along an east-west axis and 5 miles from north to south. Internal security arrangements made it one of the safest urban locales for its age. Its more than 100 quarters were separated from each other by interior walls with gates that were closed at night, after which no one was permitted on the streets, which were patrolled by horsemen, until the gates reopened in the morning. As befitted a city that was in the western region of China and in close contact with central Asia, Chang'an had a large foreign population, estimated at one-third of its total, and a diverse religious life. Zoroastrian fires burned as worshippers sacrificed animals and chanted temple hymns. Nestorian Christians from Syria found a welcoming community, and not to be outdone, the Buddhists boasted that they had ninety-one of their own temples in Chang'an in 722 CE.

CONFUCIAN ADMINISTRATORS The fruits of agriculture and the day-to-day control of the Tang Empire required an efficient and loyal civil service. Whereas a shared spiritual commitment to Islam held together the multilingual, multiethnic, and even multireligious Islamic empire, the Tang found other ways to integrate remote territories and diverse groups. Their efforts, building on past practice, produced an empire-wide political culture based on Confucian teachings and classically educated elites.

Chinese integration began at the top. Entry into the ruling group required knowledge of Confucian ideas and all of the commentaries on the Confucian classics. It also required skill in the intricate classical Chinese language, in which this literature was written. A deep familiarity with these texts was as crucial in forging a Chinese cultural and political solidarity as understanding the Quran and the *sharia* was for the Abbasid state or the New Testament for Christian Europe and the Byzantine Empire.

Reinforcing the Tang state were the world's first fully written **civil service examinations**. These examinations, which tested literary skills and the Confucian classics, were the primary route to the top echelons of power and the ultimate means of uniting the Chinese state. Candidates for office, whom local elites recommended, gathered in the capital triennially to take qualifying exams. They had been trained since the age of three in the classics and histories, either by their families—especially mothers—or in Buddhist temple schools. Most failed the grueling competition, but those who were successful underwent further trials to evaluate their character and determine the level of their appointments. New officials were selected from the pool of graduates on the basis of social conduct, eloquence, skill in calligraphy and mathematics, and legal knowledge. (See Primary Source: The Pressures of Maintaining Empire by Examination.) When Emperor Li Shimin observed the new officials obediently parading out of the examination hall, he slyly noted, "The heroes of the empire are all in my pocket!" (Miyazaki, p. 13). Overall, the civil service system gave rise in China to the perennial belief in the value of a classically trained meritocracy (rule by persons of talent), which has lasted into modern times.

Having assumed the mandate of heaven (see Chapter 4), the Tang rulers and their supporters sought to establish a code of moral values for the whole empire. Building on Han dynasty models, they expanded the state school in the capital into an empire-wide series of select schools that accepted only fully literate candidates for the civil examinations. They also allowed the use of Daoist classics as texts for the exams, believing that the early Daoists represented another important stream of ancient wisdom. Ultimately, the Tang amalgamated this range of texts, codes, and tests into a common intellectual and moral credo for the governing classes.

Although official careers were in theory open to anyone of proven talent, in practice they were closed to certain groups. Despite Empress Wu's prominence (see next page), women

Christianity in China. *As subjects of the largest Christian church of the ninth century CE, Nestorian priests made a lasting impression on the Tang Empire, including this mural of their Palm Sunday procession in Xinjiang, China.*

Tang Official. *Tang officials were selected through competitive civil examinations in order to limit the power of Buddhist and Daoist clerics. This painted clay figure of a Tang official circa 717 CE was excavated in 1972.*

PRIMARY SOURCE

The Pressures of Maintaining Empire by Examination

Young and old competed equally in the Tang examination halls. The rituals of success were alluring to youths, while the tortures of failure weighed heavily on older competitors still seeking an elusive degree. For all, the tensions of seeing the posted list of successful candidates—following years of preparation for young boys and even more years of defeat for old men—were intensely personal responses to success or failure. The few who passed would look back on that day with relief and pride.

In the Southern Court they posted the list. (The Southern Court was where the Board of Rites ran the administration and accepted documents. All prescribed forms together with the stipulations for each [degree] category were usually publicized here.) The wall for hanging the list was by the eastern wall of the Southern Court. In a separate building a screen was erected which stood over ten feet tall, and it was surrounded with a fence. Before dawn they took the list from the Northern Court to the Southern Court where it was hung for display.

In the sixth year of Yuanhe [811 CE] a student at the University, Guo Dongli, broke through the thorn hedge. (The thorn hedge was below the fence. There was another outside the main gate of the Southern Court.) He then ripped up the ornamental list [*wenbang*]. It was because of this that afterwards they often came out of the gateway of the Department [of State Affairs] with a mock list. The real list was displayed a little later.

QUESTIONS FOR ANALYSIS

- Why were the stakes so high in the civil examinations? What happened to those who failed?
- Was the Tang civil examination system an open system that tested talent—that is, a meritocracy?
- Can you relate to the candidates' anxiety in terms of your own experiences—for example, waiting for college acceptance letters or your year-end grade point average?

Source: Wang Dingbao (870–940 CE), quoted in Oliver J. Moore, *Rituals of Recruitment in Tang China* (Leiden: Brill, 2004), p. 175.

were not permitted to serve, nor were sons of merchants, nor those who could not afford a classical education. Over time, Tang civil examinations forced aristocrats to compete with commoner southern families, whose growing wealth gave them access to educational resources that made them the equals of the old elites. Through examinations, this new elite eventually outdistanced the sons of the northern aristocracy in the Tang government by out-studying them.

The system underscored education as the primary avenue for success. Even impoverished families sought the best classical education they could afford for their sons. Although few succeeded in the civil examinations, many boys and even some girls learned the fundamentals of reading and writing. Classically literate mothers, for example, helped educate their sons. In fact, the Buddhists played a crucial role in extending education across society: as part of their charitable mission, their temple schools introduced many children to primers based on classical texts. Buddhist monks would never admit that many in their own ranks had initially hoped to become Confucian officials,

but in reality quite a few entered the clergy only after not qualifying for or failing the civil examinations.

CHINA'S FEMALE EMPEROR Not all Tang power brokers were men. The wives and mothers of emperors also wielded influence in the court—usually behind the scenes, but sometimes publicly. The most striking example is the Empress Wu, who dominated the court in the late seventh and early eighth centuries CE. Usually vilified in Chinese accounts, she deftly exploited the examination system to check the power of aristocratic families and consolidated courtly authority by creating groups of loyal bureaucrats, who in turn preserved loyalty to the dynasty at the local level.

Born into a noble family, Wu Zhao played music and mastered the Chinese classics as a young girl. By age thirteen, because she was witty, intelligent, and beautiful, she was recruited to Li Shimin's court and became his favorite concubine. She also fell in love with his son. When Li Shimin died, his son assumed power and became the Emperor Gaozong. Wu became the

Empress Wu. *When she seized power in her own right as Empress Wu, Wu Zhao became the first and only female ruler in Chinese history.*

new emperor's favorite concubine and gave birth to the sons he required to succeed him. As the mother of the future emperor, Wu enjoyed heightened political power. Subsequently, she took the place of Gaozong's Empress Wang by accusing her of killing Wu's newborn daughter. Gaozong believed Wu and married her.

After Gaozong suffered a stroke, Wu Zhao became administrator of the court, a position equal to the emperor's. She allegedly created a reign of terror via her secret police, who spied on her opposition and eliminated those who stood in her way. Following her husband's death in 684 CE, she expanded the military and recruited her ministers from civil examination candidates to oppose her enemies at court. After deposing two of her sons as emperors, she made herself emperor of a fifteen-year new dynasty (r. 690–705 CE), the "Zhou dynasty," the only female ruler in Chinese history.

Wu ordered scholars to write biographies of famous women, and she empowered her mother's clan by assigning high political posts to her relatives. Later, she moved the capital from Chang'an to Luoyang, She elevated Buddhism over Daoism as the favored state religion, invited the most gifted Buddhist scholars to her capital at Luoyang, built Buddhist temples, and subsidized spectacular cave sculptures. In fact, Chinese Buddhism achieved its highest officially sponsored development in this period.

EUNUCHS Tang rulers protected themselves, their possessions, and especially their women, with loyal and well-compensated men, many of whom were **eunuchs** (surgically castrated as youths and thus sexually impotent). By the late eighth century CE, more than 4,500 eunuchs were entrenched in the Tang Empire's institutions, wielding significant power not only within the imperial household but also at court and beyond.

The Chief Eunuch controlled the military. Through him, the military power of court eunuchs extended to every province and garrison station in the empire, forming an all-encompassing network. In effect, the eunuch bureaucracy mediated between the emperor and the provincial governments.

Under Emperor Xianzong (r. 806–820 CE), eunuchs acted as a third pillar of the government, working alongside the official bureaucracy and the imperial court. By establishing clear career patterns for eunuchs that paralleled those in the civil service, Xianzong sparked a striking rise in their levels of literacy and their cultural attainments. And yet, they remained the rivals of most officials. By 838 CE, the delicate balance of power between throne, eunuchs, and civil officials had evaporated. Eunuchs became an unruly political force in late Tang politics, and their competition for influence produced political instability.

An Economic Revolution

In Tang China, just as in the Abbasid caliphate, political stability fueled remarkable economic achievements. Highlighting China's success were rising agricultural production based on an egalitarian land allotment system, an increasingly fine handicrafts industry, a diverse commodity market, and a dynamic urban life.

The earlier short-lived Sui dynasty had started this economic progress by building canals, especially the Grand Canal, reunifying the north and south (see again Map 9.5). The Tang continued by centering their efforts on the Grand Canal and the Yangzi River, which flows from west to east. These waterways aided communication and transport throughout the empire and helped raise living standards. The south grew richer, largely through the backbreaking labor of immigrants from the north. Fertile land along the Yangzi became China's new granary, and areas south of the Yangzi became its demographic center. (See Current Trends in World History: Green Revolutions in the Islamic World and Tang China, 300–600 CE.)

Chinese merchants took advantage of the Silk Road to trade indirectly with India and the Islamic world; but when rebellions in northwest China and the rise of Islam in central Asia jeopardized the land route, the "silk road by sea" became the avenue of choice. Via such local exchanges from all over Asia and Africa, merchant ships arrived in South China ports bearing intoxicating cargoes of spices, medicines, and jewelry traded for Chinese silks and porcelain (see again Map 9.6). Chang'an became the richest city in the world, with its million or so residents including foreigners of every description. Rather than long-distance trade, what really drove the economic boom in the oasis states was the Tang and Islamic military presence. The integration between China and central Asia brought not only safety but also new customers.

In the large cities of the Yangzi delta, bronze, pottery, and clothing workshops proliferated. Their reputations spread far and wide for the elegance of their wares, which included rich brocades (silk fabrics), fine paper, intricately printed woodblocks,

The Tang Court. Left: *This tenth-century painting of elegant ladies of the Tang imperial court enjoying a feast and music tells us a great deal about the aesthetic tastes of elite women in this era. It also shows the secluded "inner quarters," where court ladies passed their daily lives far from the hurly-burly of imperial politics.* Right: *Castrated males, known as eunuchs, guarded the harem and protected the royal family of Tang emperors. By the late eighth century CE, eunuchs were fully integrated into the government and wielded a great deal of military and political power.*

unique Iron casts, and exquisite porcelains. Art collectors all across Afro-Eurasia especially valued Tang "tricolor pottery," fired up to 900°C (1,652°F) and metallurgically decorated with brilliant hues of yellow, green, white, brown, and blue. Meanwhile, Chinese artisans transformed locally grown cotton into highest-quality clothing. The textile industry prospered as painting and dyeing technology improved, and superb silk products generated significant tax revenue. Such Chinese luxuries dominated the localized networks that connected to Southwest Asia, Europe, and Africa via the Silk Road and the Indian Ocean. (See Analyzing Global Developments: Islam and the Silk Trade: Adapting Religion to Opulence.)

Accommodating World Religions

The early Tang emperors tolerated remarkable religious diversity. Nestorian Christianity, Zoroastrianism, and Manichaeanism (a radical Christian sect) had entered China from Persia during the time of the Sasanian Empire. Islam came later. These spiritual impulses—together with Buddhism and the indigenous teachings of Daoism and Confucianism—spread throughout the Tang Empire and at first were widely used to enhance state power.

THE GROWTH OF BUDDHISM Buddhism, in particular, thrived under Tang rule. Initially, Emperor Li Shimin distrusted

Buddhist monks because they avoided serving the government and paying taxes. Yet after Buddhism gained acceptance as one of the "three ways" of learning—joining Daoism and Confucianism—Li endowed huge monasteries, sent emissaries to India to collect texts and relics, and commissioned Buddhist paintings and statuary. Caves along the Silk Road, such as those at Dunhuang, provided ideal venues for monks to paint the inside walls where religious rites and meditation took place. Soon the caves boasted bright color paintings and massive statues of the Buddha and the bodhisattvas.

ANTI-BUDDHIST CAMPAIGNS By the mid-ninth century CE, the proliferation and growing influence of hundreds of thousands of Buddhist monks and nuns threatened China's Confucian and Daoist leaders. They attacked Buddhism, arguing that its values conflicted with native traditions.

One of the boldest attacks came from the Confucian scholar-official Han Yu, who represented the rising literati from the south. His memorial against Buddhism, in 819 CE, protested the emperor's plan to bring a relic of the Buddha to the capital for exhibition. Striking a note that would have been inconceivable under the early Tang's cosmopolitanism, Han Yu attacked Buddhism as a foreign doctrine of barbarian peoples who were different in language, culture, and knowledge. These objections earned him exile to the malaria-infested southern province of Guangdong.

Yet, two decades later the state began suppressing Buddhist monasteries and confiscating their wealth, fearing that religious

One of the Four Sacred Mountains. *This monastery on Mount Song is famous because in 527 CE, an Indian priest named Bodhidharma arrived there to initiate the Zen school of Buddhism in China.*

loyalties would undermine political ones. Increasingly intolerant Confucian scholar-administrators argued that the Buddhist monastic establishment threatened the imperial order. They claimed that members of the unmarried clergy were conspiring to destroy the state, the family, and the body.

Piecemeal measures against the monastic orders gave way in the 840s CE to open persecution. Emperor Wuzong, for instance, closed more than 4,600 monasteries and destroyed 40,000 temples and shrines. More than 260,000 Buddhist monks and nuns endured a forced return to secular life, after which the state parceled out monastery lands to taxpaying landlords and peasant farmers. To expunge the cultural impact of Buddhism, classically trained literati revived ancient prose styles and the teachings of Confucius and his followers. Linking classical scholarship, ancient literature, and Confucian morality, they constructed a cultural fortress that reversed the early Buddhist successes in China.

Ultimately, the Tang era represented the triumph of homegrown ideologies (Confucianism and Daoism) over a foreign universalizing religion (Buddhism). In addition, by permanently breaking apart huge monastic holdings, the Tang made sure that no religion would rival its power. Successor dynasties continued to keep religious establishments weak and fragmented, although Confucianism maintained a more prominent role within society as the basis of the ruling classes' ideology and as a quasi-religious belief system for a wider portion of the population. As a result, within China persistent religious pluralism remained, even including Buddhism, which continued to be important in the face of dynastic persecution.

The Fall of Tang China

China's deteriorating economic conditions in the ninth century CE led to peasant uprisings, some even led by unsuccessful examination candidates. These revolts eventually brought down the dynasty. Power-hungry eunuchs also contributed to the demise of the Tang, as did pressures from Muslim incursions into the western regions of the Tang Empire and Sogdian and Tibetan pressures in the northwest. By the tenth century CE, China had fragmented into regional states and entered a new but much shorter era of decentralization. The Song dynasty that emerged in 960 CE could not unify the Tang territories, and even the Mongols, invading steppe peoples, were able to restore the glory of the Han and Tang Empires only for a century.

EARLY KOREA AND JAPAN

Chinese influence, both direct and indirect, had reached into Korea for more than a millennium and later into Japan—but not without local resistance and the flourishing of entirely indigenous and independent political and religious developments. (See Map 9.7.) Here, too, religion contributed to the strengthening of the political power of elites, and lively commercial exchanges brought new prosperity to large segments of the population. The decline of Tang power in central Asia after 750 CE caused its rulers and merchants to look toward Southeast Asia and other parts of East Asia, including the lands of the Yellow

Sea and the Sea of Japan. Buddhism also spread into these territories, bringing a more flexible and less distinctly Chinese influence, although Confucianism also proved well tailored to the needs of Japan, Korea, and Vietnam.

Early Korea

By the fourth century CE, three independent states had emerged on the Korean Peninsula. Chinese influence had increasingly penetrated the peninsula and had become a decisive element in Korean history from at least the third century BCE. Korea remained divided into "Three Kingdoms" until 668 CE, when one of these states, Silla, led a movement to prevent Chinese domination, gaining control over the entire peninsula and unifying it.

UNIFICATION UNDER THE SILLA Unification enabled the Koreans to establish an autonomous government. Their opposition to the Chinese did not deter them from modeling their government on the Tang imperial state. The Silla rulers dispatched annual emissaries bearing tribute payments to the Chinese capital and regularly sent students and monks. As a result, literary Chinese became the written language of Korean elites—not their vernacular (just as Latin did among diverse populations in medieval Europe). Chinese influence especially convinced the Silla state to organize its court and the bureaucracy and to build its capital city of Kumsong in imitation of the Tang capital of Chang'an.

In spite of Chinese influences, the loyalty of most non-Chinese Koreans was to their kinship groups. These early Koreans believed that birth, not displays of learned achievement, should be the source of influence in religious and political life. Korean holy men and women (known today as shamans) interceded with gods, demons, and ancestral spirits and remained prominent in local village life.

Silla's fortunes were entwined with the Tang's to such an extent that once the Tang declined, Silla also began to fragment. But Silla never established a full-blown Tang-style government. That would happen later under the Koryo dynasty (935–1392 CE).

THE KORYO DYNASTY The Koryo dynasty (from which the country's modern name derives) began to construct a new cultural identity by enacting a bureaucratic system, which replaced the archaic tribal system that the Silla had maintained. The Koryo went beyond earlier Silla reforms and fully used Tang-style civil service examinations for selecting semi-official military elites who would govern at court and in the provinces. The heirs of Wang Kon, who founded the dynasty, consolidated control over the peninsula and strengthened its political and economic foundations by following the Tang's bureaucratic and land allotment systems.

During this period, Korea, like Tang China itself, suffered continual harassment from northern tribes such as the Khitan.

To escape the realities of this troubled period, Koryo artisans anxiously carved wooden printing blocks drawn from the Buddhist literary works as an offering to the Buddha to protect them from invading enemies—but in vain. The Korean royal family at the time was under siege, and they hoped that the woodblocks would elicit a change in fortune. The scriptures were hidden away in a single temple and when rediscovered represented the most comprehensive and intact version of Buddhist literature written in the Chinese script.

Early Japan

Like Korea, Japan also felt China's influences, and it responded by thwarting some of these influences and accommodating others simultaneously. But Japan enjoyed added autonomy: it was an archipelago of islands, separated from the mainland although internally fragmented. In the mid-third century CE, a warlike group arrived by sea from Korea and imposed their military and social power on southern Japan. These conquerors—known as the "Tomb Culture" because of their elevated burial sites—unified Japan by extolling their imperial ancestors and maintaining their social hierarchy. They also introduced a belief in the power of female shamans, who married into the imperial clans and became rulers of early Japanese kinship groups.

Chinese dynastic records describe the early Japanese, with whom imperial China had contact in this period, as a "dwarf" people who maintained a rice and fishing economy. Japanese farmers also mastered Chinese-style sericulture: the production of raw silk by raising silkworms.

The Yamato Emperors and Shinto Origins of the Japanese Sacred Identity

In time, the complex aristocratic society that developed within the Tomb Culture gave rise to a Japanese state on the Yamato plain in the region now known as Nara, south of Osaka. Becoming the ruling faction in this area, the Yamato clan incorporated native Japanese as well as Korean migrants. Clan leaders also elevated their own belief system that featured ancestor worship into a national religion known as Shinto. (Shinto means "the way of the deities.") Shinto beliefs derived from the early Japanese groups and held that after death a person's soul (or spirit) became a Shinto *kami,* or local deity, provided that it was nourished and purified through proper rituals and festivals. Before the imperial Yamato clan became dominant, each clan had its own ancestral deities; but after 500 CE, all Japanese increasingly worshipped the Yamato ancestors, whose origins went back to the fourth-century CE Tomb Culture. Other regional ancestral deities were later subordinated to the Yamato deities, who

Islam and the Silk Trade: Adapting Religion to Opulence

The Silk Road emerged from the localized industries and commercial networks of the Han, Kushan, Parthian, and Roman Empires in the first century BCE. The greatest volume of trade along this network took place over short distances, from one oasis to the next. It was not until centuries later, after the collapse of these states, that the golden age of Afro-Eurasian trade arose with new, powerful players. Tang China inherited the Han monopoly on silk production, while the Byzantine Empire utilized its Roman resources to develop its own silk weaving industry. Yet, a major threat to these monopolies appeared in the seventh century CE, when the first Islamic empire, the Umayyad Caliphate (661–750 CE), built a vast, state-run textile industry to exert influence over its newly conquered cities. Not only did the establishment of textile factories throughout the empire keep the working classes in line, but the luxury textiles produced were incentives for the elite of newly conquered territories (many of which were wealthy and were more sophisticated than the Arab tent culture of early Islamic caliphs) to submit to Muslim rule.

Tensions arose between this opulent lifestyle and the Muslim way of life, which forbade its adherents from wearing silk. The political, social, and religious authority that the Islamic silk trade lent the caliphate, however, was crucial to its unity and longevity. What's more, the Islamic silk industry was rapidly expanding, with no limits in sight, unlike Byzantine and Tang silk, which were restricted by their respective emperors. And so this textile-centered culture proliferated in an unbridled fashion, eventually infiltrating even religious rituals. The Abbasid Caliphate (750–1258 CE) became one of the wealthiest medieval states, and its capital, Baghdad, the most cosmopolitan. To illustrate the sheer extent of the impact that the Islamic silk trade had on the values of its people, the following table is a record of the goods that Caliph Harun al-Rashid, upon whom several *Arabian Nights* stories are based, left behind upon his death in 809 CE.

Source: Xinru Liu, *The Silk Road in World History* (New York: Oxford University Press, 2010).

QUESTIONS FOR ANALYSIS

- Looking back at Map 6.3 and assuming that the exports of each region remained relatively constant throughout the history of the Silk Road, with which cities and empires did the Abbasid Empire conduct most of its trade? The least? What might account for these differences?

- What can this table tell us about the values and activities of a caliph circa 800 CE? What, if anything, does the inventory reveal about the values and activities of the non-elite or working classes?

- What kind of evidence from contemporary Tang China or western Christendom would allow you to draw comparable conclusions to arguments that can be constructed from al-Rashid's inventory?

Textiles: Silk Items	
4,000	silk cloaks, lined with sable and mink
1,500	silk carpets
100	silk rugs
1,000	silk cushions and pillows
1,000	cushions with silk brocade
1,000	inscribed silk cushions
1,000	silk curtains
300	silk brocade curtains
Everyday Textile Items	
4,000	small tents with their accessories
150	marquees (large tents)

claimed direct lineage from the primary Shinto deity Amaterasu, the sun goddess and creator of the sacred islands of Japan.

PRINCE SHOTOKU AND THE TAIKA POLITICAL REFORMS After 587 CE, the Soga kinship group—originally from Korea but by 500 CE a minor branch of the Yamato imperial family—became Japan's leading family and controlled the Japanese court through intermarriage. Soon, they were attributing their cultural innovations to their own Prince Shotoku (574–622 CE), a direct descendant of the Soga and thus of the Yamato imperial family as well.

Contemporary Japanese scribes claimed that Prince Shotoku, rather than Korean immigrants, introduced Buddhism to Japan and that his illustrious reign sparked Japan's rise as an exceptional island kingdom. Shotoku promoted both Buddhism and Confucianism, thus enabling Japan, like its neighbor China, to be accommodating to numerous religions. Although earlier Korean immigrants had laid the groundwork for the growth of these views, Shotoku was credited with introducing these faiths into the native religious culture, Shinto. The prince also had ties with several Buddhist temples modeled on Tang pagodas and halls; one of these, in Nara (Japan's first imperial capital),

Luxury Textile Items	
4,000	embroidered robes
500	pieces of velvet
1,000	Armenian carpets
300	carpets from Maysan (present-day east Iraq)
1,000	carpets from Darabjird (present-day Darab, Iran)
500	carpets from Tabaristan (southern coast of the Caspian sea)
1,000	cushions from Tabaristan

Fine Cotton Items and Garments	
2,000	drawers of various kinds
4,000	turbans
1,000	hoods
1,000	capes of various kinds
5,000	kerchiefs of different kinds
10,000	caftans (long robes)
4,000	curtains
4,000	pairs of socks

Fur and Leather Items	
4,000	boots lined with sable and mink
4,000	special saddles
30,000	common saddles
1,000	belts

Metal Goods	
500,000	dinars (cash)
2,000	brass objects of various kinds
10,000	decorated swords
50,000	swords for the guards and pages (ghulam)
150,000	lances
100,000	bows
1,000	special suits of armor
10,000	helmets
20,000	breast plates
150,000	shields
300	stoves

Aromatics and Drugs	
100,000	mithqals of musk (1 mithqual = 4.25 grams)
100,000	mithqals of ambergris (musky perfume ingredient)
	Many kinds of perfume
1,000	baskets of India aloes

Jewelry and Cut Gems	
	Jewels valued by jewelers at 4 million dinars
1,000	jeweled rings

Fine Stone and Metal Vessels	
1,000	precious porcelain vessels, now called Chinaware
1,000	ewers

is Horyuji Temple, the oldest surviving wooden structure in the world. Its frescoes include figures derived from the art of Iran and central Asia. They are a reminder that within two centuries, Buddhism had dispersed its visual culture along the full length of the Silk Road—from Afghanistan to China and then on to Korea and the island kingdom of Japan.

Political integration under Prince Shotoku did not mean political stability, however. In 645 CE, the Nakatomi clan seized the throne and eliminated the Soga and their allies. Via inter-marriage with imperial kin, the Nakatomi became the new spokesmen for the Yamato tradition. Thereafter, Nakatomi no Kamatari (614–669 CE) enacted a series of reforms, known as the Taika Reforms, which reflected Confucian principles of government allegedly enunciated by Shotoku. These reforms enhanced the power of the ruler, no longer portrayed simply as an ancestral kinship group leader but now depicted as an exalted "emperor" (tenno) who ruled by the mandate of heaven, as in China, and exercised absolute authority.

MAHAYANA BUDDHISM AND THE SANCTITY OF THE JAPANESE STATE Religious influences continued to flow into Japan, contributing to spiritual pluralism while bolstering

Legend:

- Extent of Silla power, 670–935 CE
- Extent of Nara state by 600 CE
- ⊙ Capital
- • City
- ⛩ Buddhist temple
- ✪ Shinto shrine
- ▲ Holy mountain
- Bohai

MAP 9.7 | Borderlands: Korea and Japan, 600–1000 CE

The Tang dynasty held great power over the emerging Korean and Japanese states, although it never directly ruled either region.

- Based on the map, what connections do you see between Korea and Japan and the Tang Empire?
- To what extent did Korea and Japan adopt Tang customs during this period?

the Yamato rulers. Although Prince Shotoku and later Japanese emperors turned to Confucian models for government, they also dabbled in occult arts and Daoist purification rituals. In addition, the Taika edicts promoted Buddhism as the state religion of Japan. Although the imperial family continued to support native Shinto traditions, association with Buddhism gave the Japanese state extra status by lending it the prestige of a universal religion whose appeal stretched to Korea, China, and India.

State-sponsored spiritual diversity led native Shinto cults to formalize a creed of their own. Indeed, the introduction of

Creation Myth. *Tsukioka Yoshitoshi (1839–1892) depicted Japan's creation myth in* Amaterasu Appearing from the Cave. *To lure Amaterasu, the goddess of the sun, out so that light would return to the world, the other gods performed a ribald dance.*

Confucianism and Buddhism motivated Shinto adherents to assemble their diverse religious practices into a well-organized belief system to compete for followers. Shinto priests now collected ancient liturgies, and Shinto rituals (such as purification rites to ward off demons and impurities) gained recognition in the official Department of Religion.

Although the Japanese welcomed the Buddhist faith, they did not fully accept the traditional Buddhist view that the state was merely a vehicle to propagate moral and social justice for the ruler and his subjects. Instead, the Japanese saw their emperor (the embodiment of the state) as an object of worship, a sacred ruler, one in a line of luminous Shinto gods, a supreme *kami*—a divine force in his own right. Thus, Buddhism as imported from China and Korea changed in Japan to serve the interests of the state (much as Christianity served the interests of European monarchs and Islam served Islamic dynasties).

THE EMERGENCE OF EUROPEAN CHRISTENDOM

European historians previously labeled the period discussed in this chapter as the Dark Ages. In their opinion, cultural, political, and economic decline followed the fall of the Roman Empire. More recently, however, historians have marshaled evidence of significant advances in every avenue of human endeavor. Their findings have resulted in a new name for this period in European history—Late Antiquity, a label that stresses both political and cultural continuities between Rome and its successor states and new dynamic institutions.

Few revisions go unchallenged, however. Environmental historians have brought back the label "Dark Ages," arguing that the period was indeed a dark one, the result of a colder and drier climate. Agricultural production declined, famines occurred year after year, and infectious diseases spread across Afro-Eurasia. This harsher climate between 400 and 900 CE caused dying and morbidity on a large scale. There is much evidence for this assertion other than that assembled by climatologists. To begin with, a plague swept across Afro-Eurasia and decimated the Byzantine Empire during the reign of Justinian. Even more important is evidence that drought in the Arabian Peninsula led Arab tribal peoples, carrying the banner of Islam, to pour out of their severely affected lands in search of better lands and a better life, as other nomadic groups had done.

In these bleak times, Christianity provided a crucial source of unity in much the same fashion that Abbasid Islam and Tang China offered to those who sheltered under their imperial umbrellas. In the fifth century CE, the mighty Roman military machine gave way to a multitude of warrior leaders whose principal allegiances were local affiliations. Although the political ideal of the Roman Empire cast a vast shadow over western Europeans, the inheritor of the mantle of Rome was a spiritual institution—the Roman Catholic Church—whose powerful head, the pope, was based in Rome and whose universalizing agents—missionaries and monks—carried its message far and wide. (See Map 9.8.) In eastern Europe and Byzantium, a form of Christianity known as Greek Orthodoxy prevailed. Thus, the realm of Christendom, made up of Western Roman Catholicism and Greek Orthodoxy, dominated all of Europe, except for parts of the Iberian Peninsula and parts of Asia, and served to unify the lives of millions.

Charlemagne's Fledgling Empire

Far removed from the old centers of high culture, Charlemagne (r. 768–814 CE), king of the Franks in northern Europe, expanded his western European kingdom through constant warfare and plunder. In 802 CE, Harun al-Rashid, the ruler of Baghdad, sent

Prince Shotoku Taishi. *Shotoku was instrumental in the establishment of Buddhism in Japan, although his actual historical role was overstated. Left: In this hanging scroll painting from the early fourteenth century, he is idealized as a sixteen-year-old son, holding an incense censer and praying for the recovery of his sick father, the Emperor Yomei (r. 585–587 CE). Right: The main hall of the Horyuji Temple in Nara, Japan.*

the gift of an elephant to Charlemagne. The elephant caused a sensation among the Franks, who saw the gift as an acknowledgment of Charlemagne's power. In fact, Harun often sent rare beasts to distant rulers as a gracious reminder of his own formidable power. In his eyes, Charlemagne's "empire" was a minor principality.

This was an empire that Charlemagne ruled for over forty years, often traveling 2,000 miles a year on campaigns of plunder and conquest. He ultimately controlled much of western Europe, which was a significant accomplishment; yet compared with the Islamic world's rulers, he was a political lightweight. His empire had a population of less than 15 million; he rarely commanded armies larger than 5,000; and he had a rudimentary tax system. At a time when the palace quarters of the caliph at Baghdad covered nearly 250 acres, Charlemagne's palace at Aachen was merely 330 by 655 feet. Baghdad itself was almost 40 square miles in area, whereas there was no "town" outside the palace at Aachen. It was little more than a large country house set in open countryside, close to the Ardennes woods, where Charlemagne and his Franks loved to hunt wild boar on horseback.

He and his men were representatives of the warrior class that dominated post-Roman western Europe. For a time, Roman rule had imposed an alien way of life in this rough world. After that empire faded, however, war became once again the duty and joy of the aristocrat. Buoyed up by their chieftains' mead—a heavy beer made with honey, "yellow, sweet and ensnaring"—young men eagerly followed their lords into battle "among the war horses and the blood-stained armor" (Aneirin, ll. 102, 840).

And although the Franks vigorously engaged in trade, that trade was based on war. In fact, Europe's principal export at this time was Europeans, and the massive sale of prisoners of war financed the Frankish empire. From Venice, which grew rich from its role as middleman, captives were sent as slaves across the sea to Alexandria, Tunis, and southern Spain. The main victims of this trade were Slavic-speaking peoples, tribal hunters and cultivators from eastern Europe. It is this trade that gave us our modern term *slave* (from *Slav*) for persons bought and sold as items of merchandise.

Yet this seemingly uncivilized and inhospitable zone offered fertile ground for Christianity to sink down roots. Although its worldwide expansion did not occur for centuries, its spiritual conquest of European peoples established institutions and fired enthusiasms that would later drive believers to carry its message to faraway lands.

Christianity in Western Europe

Charlemagne's empire was unquestionably primitive when compared with the Islamic empire or the Tang Empire of China. What made it significant was its location. Far removed from the old centers of high culture, it was a political system of the borderlands. It featured an expansionist Christianity that drew energy from its rough frontier mentality. Indeed, Christianity now entered a world profoundly different from the Mediterranean cities in which it had taken form.

AUGUSTINE AND THE UNIVERSAL CATHOLIC CHURCH
Christians of the west felt that theirs was the one truly universal religion. (See Primary Source: Christendom on the Edge: A View of Empire in Ireland.) Their goal was to bring rival groups into a single "catholic" church that was replacing a political unity lost in western Europe when the Roman Empire fell.

MAP 9.8 | Christendom, 600–1000 CE

The end of the first millennium saw much of Europe divided between two versions of Christianity, each with different traditions.

- Locate Rome and Constantinople on the map, the two seats of power in Christianity.
- According to the map, what were the two major regions where Christianity held sway?
- In what directions did Latin Christianity and Orthodox Christianity spread?
- Why do you suppose the Catholic Church, based in Rome, was successful in expanding to the west, but not to the east?
- Why do you suppose Orthodox Christianity, based in Constantinople, expanded into eastern Europe, but not into the west?

As far back as 410 CE, reacting to the Goths' sack of Rome, the Christian bishop Augustine of Hippo (a seaport in modern Algeria) had laid down the outlines of this belief. His book *The City of God* assured contemporary Christians that the barbarian takeover happening around them was not the end of the world. The "city of God" would take earthly shape in the form of the Catholic Church, and the Catholic Church was not just for Romans—it was for all times and for all peoples, "in a wide world which has always been inhabited by many differing peoples, that have so many different customs and languages, so many different forms of organization and so many languages, and who have had so many different religions"

Charlemagne's Palace and Chapel. *Though not large by Byzantine or Islamic standards, Charlemagne's palace and chapel were heavy with symbolic meaning. A royal hall for banqueting in Frankish, "barbarian" style was linked by a covered walkway to the imperial domed chapel, which was meant to look like a miniature version of the Hagia Sophia of Constantinople. Outside the chapel was a courtyard, like the one outside the shrine of Saint Peter at Rome.*

(Augustine, 14.1). Only one organization would bring them all to paradise: the Catholic Church.

Several developments gave rise to this attitude. First, the arrival of Christianity in northern Europe had provoked a cultural revolution. Preliterate societies now encountered a sacred text—the Bible—in a language that seemed utterly strange. Latin had become a sacred language, and books themselves were vehicles of the holy. The bound codex (see Chapter 8), which had replaced the clumsy scroll, was still a messy object. It had no divisions between words, no punctuation, no paragraphs, no chapter headings. Readers who knew Latin as a spoken language could understand the script. But Irishmen, Saxons, and Franks could not, for they had never spoken Latin; hence the care lavished in the newly Christian north on the Latin scriptures. The few parchment texts that circulated there were carefully prepared with words separated, sentences correctly punctuated and introduced by uppercase letters, and chapter headings provided. They were far more like this textbook than anything available to Romans at the height of the empire.

Second, those who produced the Bibles were starkly different from ordinary men and women. They were monks and nuns. Christian **monasticism** had originated in Egypt, but it suited the missionary tendencies of Christianity in northern Europe particularly well. (The words *monastic* and *monk* come from the Greek *monos*, "alone": a man or a woman who chooses to live alone, without the support of marriage or family.) Monasticism

placed small groups of men and women in the middle of societies with which they had nothing in common. It appealed to a deep sense that the very men and women who had little in common with "normal" people were best suited to mediate between believers and God. Laypersons (common believers, not clergy) gave gifts to the monasteries and offered them protection. In return, they gained the prayers of monks and nuns and the reassurance that although they themselves were warriors and men of blood, the monks' and nuns' intercessions would keep them from going to hell. Payment for human sin, the atoning power of Jesus's crucifixion, and the efficacy of monastic prayers were significant theological emphases for Roman Catholics.

MONKS, NUNS, AND POPES With the spread of monasticism, Christianity in the west took a decisive turn. In Muslim (as in Jewish) societies, religious leaders emphasized what they had in common with those around them: many Islamic

Celtic Bible. *Unlike the simple codex of early Christian times, the Bible came to be presented in Ireland and elsewhere in the northern world as a magical book. Its pages were filled with mysterious, intricate patterns, which imitated on parchment the jewelry and treasure for which early medieval warlords yearned.*

PRIMARY SOURCE

Christendom on the Edge: A View of Empire in Ireland

A young Christian Briton of Roman citizenship who lived near Hadrian's Wall experienced the pull of Christianity around 400 CE. Captured by Irish slave raiders as a teenager, Patricius spent six years herding pigs on the Atlantic coast of Mayo. He escaped but years later returned to convert his former captors to Christianity. He believed that in making the fierce Irish Christians, he also made them "Romans." He thus brought Christianity to the Atlantic edge of the known world. Patricius is remembered today as Saint Patrick.

16 But after I reached Ireland, well, I pastured the flocks every day. . . . I would even stay in the forests and on the mountain and would wake to pray before dawn in all weathers, snow, frost, rain. . . .

17 And it was in fact there that one night while asleep I heard a voice saying to me: 'You do well to fast, since you will soon be going to your home country;' and again, very shortly after, I heard this prophecy: 'See, your ship is ready.' And it was not near at hand but was perhaps two hundred miles away, and I had never been there and did not know a living soul there. And then I soon ran away and abandoned the man with whom I had been for six years . . . till I reached the ship.

23 And again a few years later I was in Britain with my kinsfolk. . . . And it was there that I saw one night in a vision a man coming as it were from Ireland . . . with countless letters, and he gave me one of them, and I read the heading of the letter, 'The Voice of the Irish,' and as I read these opening words aloud, I imagined at that very instant that I heard the voice of those who were beside the forest of Foclut which is near the western sea; and thus they cried, as though with one voice: 'We beg you, holy boy, to come and walk again among us.'

QUESTIONS FOR ANALYSIS

- What does this passage reveal about life in the Celtic worlds?
- How many voices or visions does Patricius experience in this passage? What other religious figure in this chapter also had a vision or a revelation?
- Based on your reading, how do St. Patrick's spiritual experiences compare with those of rulers and priests in the older Christian communities of Rome and Constantinople?

Source: *St. Patrick: His Writings and Muirchu's Life*, edited and translated by A. B. E. Hood (London: Phillimore, 1978), pp. 41, 44–46, 50.

---

scholars, theologians, and mystics were married men just like the public, even merchants and courtiers. In the Christian west, the opposite was true: warrior societies honored small groups of men and women (the monks and nuns) who were utterly unlike themselves: unmarried, unfit for warfare, and intensely literate in an incomprehensible tongue. Even their hair looked different. Unlike warriors, these men were close-shaven; by contrast, the Orthodox clergy of the Eastern Roman Empire grew long, silvery beards (signifying wisdom and maturity; not, as in the west, the warrior's masculine strength). Catholic monks and priests shaved their heads as well.

The Catholic Church of northern Europe owed its missionary zeal to the same principles that explained the spread of Buddhism: it was a religion of monks, whose communities represented an otherworldly alternative to the warrior societies of the time. By 800 CE, most regions of northern Europe held great monasteries, many of which were far larger than the local villages. Supported by thousands of serfs, donated by kings and local warlords, the monasteries became powerhouses of prayer that kept the regions safe. Northern Christianity also gained new ties to an old center: the city of Rome. The Christian bishop of Rome had always enjoyed much prestige. But being only one bishop among many, he often took second place to his peers in Alexandria, Antioch, and Constantinople. Though people spoke of him with respect as pope, many others shared that title.

By 800 CE, this picture had changed. As believers looked down from the distant north, they saw only one pope left in western Europe: Rome's pope. The papacy as we know it arose because of the fervor with which the Catholic Church of western Europe united behind one symbolic center, represented by the popes at Rome and the desire of new Christians in northern borderlands to find a religious leader for their hopes.

Charlemagne recognized this desire very well. In 800 CE, he went out of his way to celebrate Christmas Day by visiting the shrine of Saint Peter at Rome. There, Pope Leo III acclaimed him as the new "emperor" of the west. The ceremony ratified the aspirations of an age. A "modern" Rome—inhabited by popes, famous for shrines of the martyrs, and protected by a "modern" Christian monarch from the north—was what Charlemagne's subjects wanted.

Vikings and Christendom

Vikings from Scandinavia exposed the weakness of Charlemagne's Christian empire. When Harun's elephant died in 813 CE, one year before Charlemagne himself, the Franks viewed the elephant's death as an omen of coming disasters. The great beast keeled over when his handlers marched him out to confront a Viking army from Denmark. In the next half-century, Charlemagne's empire of borderland peoples met its match on the widest border of all: that between the European landmass and the mighty Atlantic. (See Map 9.9.)

The Vikings' motives were announced in their name, which derives from the Old Norse *vik*, "to be on the warpath." The **Vikings** sought to loot the now-wealthy Franks and replace them as the dominant warrior class of northern Europe. It was their turn to extract plunder and to sell droves of slaves across the water. They succeeded because of a deadly technological advantage: ships of unparalleled sophistication, developed by Scandinavian sailors in the Baltic Sea and the long fjords of Norway. Light and agile, with a shallow draft, they could penetrate far up the rivers of northern Europe and even be carried overland from one river system to another. Under sail, the same boats could tackle open water and cross the unexplored wastes of the North Atlantic.

In the ninth century CE, the Vikings set their ships on both courses. They emptied northern Europe of its treasure, sacking

the great monasteries along the coasts of Ireland and Britain and overlooking the Rhine and the Seine—rivers that led into the heart of Charlemagne's empire. At the same time, Norwegian adventurers colonized the uninhabited island of Iceland, and then Greenland. By 982 CE, they had even reached North America and established a settlement at L'Anse aux Meadows on the Labrador coast. Recent aerial reconnaissance suggests a second Viking settlement in North America roughly 300 miles south of L'Anse aux Meadows. Viking goods have been found as far west as the Inuit settlements of Baffin Island to the north of Hudson Bay, carried there along trading routes by Native Americans.

The consequences of this spectacular reach across the ocean to America were short-lived, but the penetration of eastern Europe had lasting effects. Supremely well equipped to traverse long river systems, the Vikings sailed east along the Baltic and then turned south, edging up the rivers that cross the watershed of central Russia. Here the Dnieper, the Don, and the Volga begin to flow south into the Black Sea and the Caspian. By opening this link between the Baltic and what is now Kiev in modern Ukraine, the Vikings created an avenue of commerce that linked Scandinavia and the Baltic directly to Constantinople and Baghdad. And they added yet more slaves: Muslim geographers bluntly called this route "The Highway of the Slaves."

On reaching the Black Sea, the Vikings made straight for Constantinople. In 860 CE, more than 200 Viking longships gathered ominously in the straits of the Bosporus, beneath the walls of Constantinople. What they found was not Charlemagne's rustic Aachen, but a proud city with a population exceeding 100,000 surrounded by well-engineered late Roman walls.

The Vikings had come up against a state hardened by battle. For two centuries the empire of "East Rome," centered in Constantinople, had held Islamic armies at bay. From 640 to 840 CE, they faced almost yearly campaigns launched by the Islamic

The Coronation of Charlemagne. *This is how the coronation of Charlemagne at Rome in 800 CE was remembered in medieval western Europe. This painting stresses the fact that it was the pope who placed the crown on Charlemagne's head, thereby claiming him as a ruler set up by the Catholic Church for the Catholic Church. But in 800 CE, contemporaries saw the pope as recognizing the fact that Charlemagne had already deserved to be emperor. The rise of the papacy to greater prominence and power in later medieval Europe caused this significant "re-remembering" of the event.*

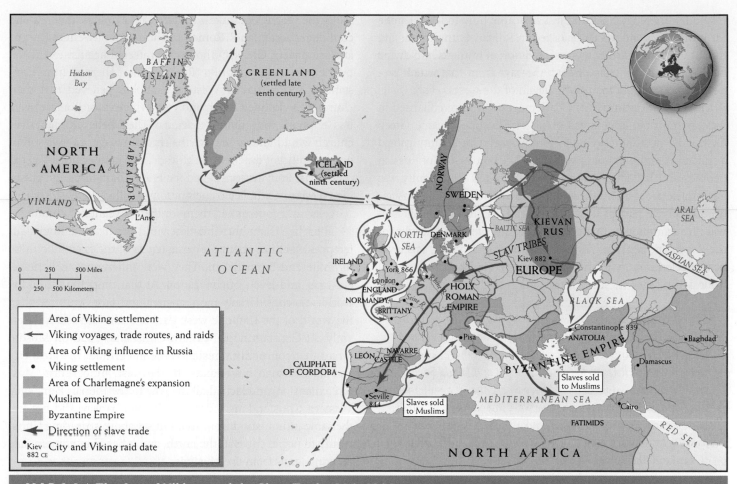

MAP 9.9 | The Age of Vikings and the Slave Trade, 800–1000 CE

Vikings from Scandinavia dramatically altered the history of Christendom.

- In what directions did the Vikings carry out their voyages, trade routes, and raids?
- What were the geographical limits of the Viking explorations in each direction?
- In what direction did the slave trade move, and what role did the Vikings and the Holy Roman emperors play in expanding the slave trade?

empire of Damascus and Baghdad, powerhouses that grew to be ten times greater than their own. For years on end, Muslim armies and navies came within striking distance of Constantinople. Each time they failed, outmaneuvered by highly professional generals and blocked by a skillfully constructed line of fortresses that controlled the roads across Anatolia. The Christian empire of East Rome fought the caliphs of Baghdad to a draw. The Viking fleet was even less suited to assault Constantinople, as the empire of "East Rome" had a deadly technological advantage in naval warfare: Greek fire, a combination of petroleum and potassium that, when sprayed from siphons, would explode in a great sheet of flame on the water. A previous emperor had used it to destroy the Muslim fleet as it lay at anchor within sight of Constantinople. Now, a century and a half later, the experience and weaponry of East Rome were too much for the Vikings, and their raid was a spectacular failure.

Despite their inability to take Byzantium, the Vikings asserted an enduring influence through their forays across the North Atlantic, their brutal interactions with Christian communities in northern Europe, and their expansion into eastern Europe, especially the slave trade they facilitated there.

Greek Orthodox Christianity in the East

In the long run, the sense of having outlasted so many military emergencies bolstered the morale of East Roman Christianity and led to its unexpected flowering. Not just Constantinople but Justinian's glorious church, the Hagia Sophia—its heart—had survived. That great building and the solemn Greek liturgy that reverberated within its domed spaces symbolized the branch of Christianity that dominated the east: **Greek Orthodoxy**. Greek

Orthodox theology held that Jesus became human less to atone for humanity's sins, as emphasized in Roman Catholicism, and more to facilitate *theosis*, a transformation of humans into divine beings. This was a truly distinct message from that which predominated in the Roman Catholicism of the west.

In the tenth century, as Charlemagne's empire collapsed in western Europe, large areas of eastern Europe became Greek Orthodox, not Catholic. As a result, Greek Christianity gained a spiritual empire in Southwest Asia. The conversion of Russian peoples and Balkan Slavs to Greek Orthodox Christianity was a complex process. It reflected a deep admiration for Constantinople on the part of Russians, Bulgarians, and other Slavs. It was an admiration as intense as that of any western Catholic for the Roman popes. This admiration amounted to awe, as shown by the famous story of the conversion to Greek Christianity of the rulers of Kiev (descendants of Vikings):

> The envoys reported[,]. . . "We went among the Germans [the Catholic Franks] and we saw them performing many ceremonies in their churches; but we beheld no glory there. Then we went to Greece [in fact, to Constantinople and Hagia Sophia], and the Greeks led us to the edifices where they worship their God, and we knew not whether we were in heaven or on earth. For on earth there is no such splendor or such beauty, and we are at a loss to describe it. . . . [W]e can not forget that beauty. (Cross and Sherbowitz-Westor, p. 111)

By the year 1000, there were two Christianities: the new and confident "borderland" **Roman Catholicism** of western Europe and an ancient Greek Orthodoxy, protected against extinction by the iron framework of a "Roman" state inherited from Constantine and Justinian. Western Catholics believed that their church was destined to expand everywhere. East Romans were less euphoric but more tenacious. They believed that their church would forever survive the regular ravages of invasion. It was a significant difference in attitude, and neither side liked the other. East Romans considered the Franks barbarous and grasping; Western Catholics contemptuously called the East Romans "Greeks" and condemned them for their "Byzantine" cunning.

Thus, like Islam, the Christian world was divided. But its differences were not about the basic tenets of the faith, like those of Shiite and Sunni Islam. They were differences in heritage, customs, and levels of civilization. At that time, the Orthodox world was considerably more ancient and more cultured than the world of the Catholic west. And it dealt with Islam differently. At Constantinople, eastern Christianity held off Muslim forces that constantly threatened the integrity of the great city and its Christian hinterlands. In the west, by contrast, Muslim expansionism reached all the way to the Iberian Peninsula. Western Christendom, led by the Roman papacy, did not feel the same intimidation from Islam. It set about spreading Christianity to pagan tribes in the north, and it began to contemplate retaking lands from the Muslims.

Monasticism. Left: *The great monasteries of the age of Charlemagne, such as the St. Gallen Monastery, were like Roman legionary settlements. Placed on the frontiers of Germany, they were vast stone buildings, around which entire towns would gather. Their libraries, the largest in Europe, were filled with parchment volumes, carefully written out and often lavishly decorated in a "northern," Celtic style.* Right: *Monasticism was also about the lonely search for God at the very end of the world, which took place in these Irish monasteries on the Atlantic coast. The cells, made of loose stones piled in round domes, are called "beehives."*

Oseberg Ship. *The Viking ship was a triumph of design. It could be rowed up the great rivers of Europe, and at the same time, its sail could take it across the Atlantic.*

CONCLUSION

The period 600–1000 CE saw heightened movement across cultural boundaries as well as an insistence on the distinctiveness of individual societies. Commodities, technological innovations, ideas, merchants, adventurers, and scholars traveled from one end of Afro-Eurasia to the other and up and down coastal Africa. Spreading religion into new frontiers accompanied this mercantile activity. The proximity of the period's two powerhouses—Abbasid Islam and Tang China—facilitated the dynamic movement.

Despite the intermixing of peoples, ideas, and goods across Afro-Eurasia, new political and cultural boundaries were developing that would split this landmass in ways it could never have imagined. The most important dividing force was religion, as Islam challenged and slowed the spread of Christianity and as Buddhism challenged the ruling elite of Tang China. As a consequence, Afro-Eurasia's major cultural zones began to compete in terms of religious and cultural doctrines. The Islamic Abbasid Empire pushed back the borders of the Tang Empire. But the conflict grew particularly intense between the Islamic and Christian worlds, where the clash involved faith as well as frontiers.

The Tang Empire revived Confucianism, insisting on its political and moral primacy as the foundation of a new imperial order, and it embraced the classical written language as another unifying element. By doing so, the Tang counteracted universalizing foreign religions—notably Buddhism but also Islam—spreading into the Chinese state. The same adaptive strategies influenced new systems on the Korean Peninsula and in Japan.

In some circumstances, faith followed empire and relied on rulers' support or tolerance to spread the word. This was the

Jelling Stone. *Carved on the side of this great stone, Christ appears to be almost swallowed up in an intricate pattern of lines. For the Vikings, complicated interweaving like serpents or twisted gold jewelry was a sign of majesty: hence, in this, the first Christian monument in Denmark, Christ is part of an ancient pattern of carving, which brought good luck and victory to the king.*

case especially in East Asia. At the opposite extreme, empire followed faith—as in the case of Islam, whose believers endeavored to spread their empire in every conceivable direction. The Islamic empire and its successors represented a new force: expanding political power backed by one God whose instructions were to spread his message. In the worlds of Christianity, a common faith absorbed elements of a common culture (shared books, a language for learned classes). But in the west, political rulers never overcame inhabitants' intense allegiance to local authority.

While universalizing religions expanded and common cultures grew, debate raged within each religion over foundational principles. In spite of the diffusion of basic texts in "official" languages, regional variations of Christianity, Islam, and Buddhism proliferated as each belief system spread. The period from 600 to 1000 CE demonstrated that religion, reinforced by prosperity and imperial resources, could bring peoples together in unprecedented ways. But it could also, as the next chapter will illustrate, drive them apart in bloodcurdling confrontations.

After You Read This Chapter

Go to
INQUIZITIVE
to see what you know & learn what you've missed.

FOCUS ON: *Faith and Empire*

The Islamic Empire

- Warriors from the Arabian Peninsula defeat Byzantine and Sasanian armies and establish an Islamic empire stretching from Morocco to South Asia.

- The Abbasid state takes over from the Umayyads, crystallizes the main Islamic institutions of the caliphate and Islamic law, and promotes cultural achievements in religion, philosophy, and science.

- Disputes over Muhammad's succession lead to a deep and enduring split between Sunnis and Shiites.

Tang China

- The Tang dynasty dominates East Asia and exerts a strong influence on Korea and Japan.

- Tang rulers balance Confucian and Daoist ideals with Buddhist thought and practice.

- A common written language and shared philosophy, rather than a universalist religion, integrate the Chinese state.

Christian Europe

- Monks, nuns, and Rome-based popes spread Christianity throughout western Europe.

- Constantinople-based Greek Orthodoxy survives the spread of Islam.

CHRONOLOGY

	600 CE	700 CE
The Islamic World	Life of Muhammad **570–632 CE** / Umayyad caliphate **661–750 CE**	
East Asia	Prince Shotoku initiates reforms in Japan **574–622 CE**	
Europe	Arab armies conquer much of Byzantine Empire but the empire survives **632–661 CE**	

STUDY QUESTIONS

1. **Describe** the origins and basic beliefs of Islam, including Muhammad, the Quran, and the five pillars of Islam. To what extent does this tradition fit the model for a universal religion?

2. **Analyze** the successes and failures of Islamic leaders in creating one large empire to govern Islamic communities. What opponents challenged this goal? How did the empire's expansion require a balancing act between political powers (such as the caliphate) and religious authority (such as the *ulama* and *sharia* law)?

3. **Evaluate** the impact of the spread of Islam on Afro-Asian societies. How did the large Islamic empire shape the movement of peoples, ideas, innovations, and commodities?

4. **Describe** the Tang dynasty's attempts to restore political unity to East Asia. What roles did the army, civil service examinations, and eunuchs play in Tang political organization? How did Tang leaders react to the growth of universal religions within their realm?

5. **Explain** how the Tang interacted with foreign ideas (including Zoroastrianism, Christianity, and Buddhism) and influenced other polities (as in Korea and Japan).

6. **Describe** the state structure that emerged in Korea and Japan during this era. How did other developments in Afro-Eurasia, such as the spread of universal religions, shape these new states?

7. **Identify** some of the distinctive features of Christendom in western, northern, and eastern Europe.

8. **Compare and contrast** the spread of Islam, Buddhism, and Christianity. What was the geographical range of each religious community? How did each religion gain new converts?

9. **Examine** the similarities and differences between the organizational structures of the Abbasids, Tang China, and Christendom.

10. **Compare and contrast** the forces of opposition and change within the Islamic, Tang, and Christian worlds.

11. **Analyze** the Vikings' impact on world history during this era, both in Europe and beyond. How did they shape developments in the Christian world especially?

12. **Explore** the ways in which the interaction between religion, empire, and commercial exchange affected developments across Afro-Eurasia during this period.

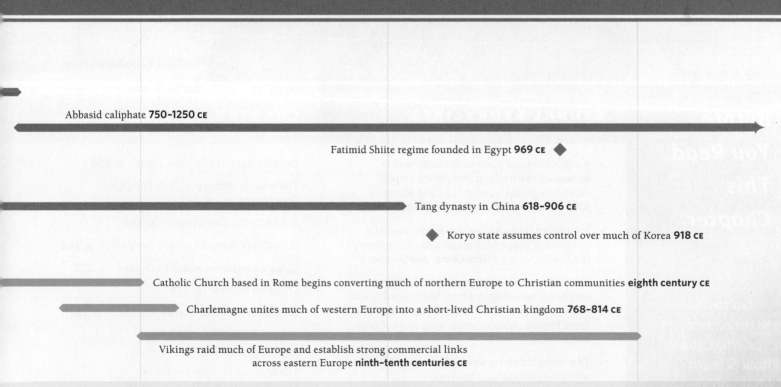

Abbasid caliphate **750–1250 CE**

Fatimid Shiite regime founded in Egypt **969 CE**

Tang dynasty in China **618–906 CE**

Koryo state assumes control over much of Korea **918 CE**

Catholic Church based in Rome begins converting much of northern Europe to Christian communities **eighth century CE**

Charlemagne unites much of western Europe into a short-lived Christian kingdom **768–814 CE**

Vikings raid much of Europe and establish strong commercial links across eastern Europe **ninth–tenth centuries CE**

800 CE　　　　**900 CE**　　　　**1000 CE**

tagaza

GITINIA

sudam

tenbuch

ciutatdomelh

Before You Read This Chapter

Go to INQUIZITIVE to see what you know & learn what you've missed.

GLOBAL STORYLINES

- Advances in maritime technology lead to increased sea trade, transforming coastal cities into global trading hubs and elevating Afro-Eurasian trade to unprecedented levels.

- Intensified trade and religious and linguistic integration shape four major cultural "spheres": the Islamic world, India, China, and Europe.

- Sub-Saharan Africa is drawn into Eurasian exchange, resulting in a true Afro-Eurasia–wide network. Meanwhile, the Americas experience more limited political, economic, and cultural integration.

- The Mongol Empire integrates many of the world's major cultural spheres.

CHAPTER OUTLINE

10

Becoming "The World," 1000–1300 CE

FOCUS QUESTIONS

- What technological advances occurred during this period, especially in ship design and navigation, and how did they facilitate the expansion of Afro-Eurasian trade?

- What types of social and political forces shaped the Islamic world, India, China, and Europe at this time? To what degree did these forces integrate cultures and geographical areas?

- How did sub-Saharan Africa compare with the Americas in terms of internal integration and external interactions?

- In what ways did the Mongol Empire influence peoples and places within Afro-Eurasia?

In the late 1270s, two Christian monks, Bar Sāwmā and Markōs, voyaged into the heart of Islam. They were not Europeans. They were Uighurs, a Turkish people of central Asia, many of whom had converted to Christianity centuries earlier. Sent by the mighty Mongol ruler Kubilai Khan as he prepared to become the first formally recognized emperor of China's Yuan dynasty, the monks were supposed to worship at the temple in Jerusalem. But the Great Khan also had political ambitions. He was eager to conquer Jerusalem, held by the Muslims. Accordingly, he dispatched the monks as agents to make alliances with Christian kings in the area and to gather intelligence about his potential enemy in Palestine.

By 1280, conflict and conquest had transformed many parts of the world. But friction was simply one manifestation of cultures brushing up against one another. More important was trade. Indeed, Bar Sāwmā and Markōs lingered at the magnificent trading hub of Kashgar in what is now western China, where caravan routes converged in a market for jade, exotic spices, and precious silks. Later, at Baghdad, the monks parted ways. Bar Sāwmā visited Constantinople (where the king gave him gold and silver), Rome (where he met with the pope at the shrine of Saint Peter), and Paris (where he saw that city's vibrant university) before deciding to return to China, where the Christians of the east awaited his reports. In the end, neither monk ever returned. Yet their voyages exemplified the criss-crossing of people, money, and goods along the trade routes and sea-lanes that connected the world's regions. For just as religious conflict was a hallmark of this age, so was a surge in trade, migration, and global exchange.

The period brought to a climax many centuries of human development, and it ushered in a new, very long cycle of cultural interaction from which emerge three interrelated themes. First, trade was shifting from land-based routes to sea-based routes. Coastal trading cities began to dramatically expand. Second, intensified trade and linguistic and religious integration generated the world's four major cultural "spheres," whose inhabitants were linked by shared institutions and beliefs: the Islamic world, India, China, and Europe. Not all cultures turned into "spheres," though. In the Americas and sub-Saharan Africa, there was not the same impulse to integrate regions, which remained more fragmented but thrived nonetheless. Third, the rise of the Mongol Empire represented the peak in the long history of ties and tensions between settled and mobile peoples. From China to Persia and as far as eastern Europe, the Mongols ruled over much land in the world's major cultural spheres. Each of these three themes contributes to an understanding of how Afro-Eurasia became a "world" unified through trade, migration, and even religious conflict.

DEVELOPMENT OF MARITIME TRADE

Innovations at Sea

By the tenth century CE, sea routes were eclipsing land networks for long-distance trade. Improved navigational aids, refinements in shipbuilding, better mapmaking, and new legal arrangements and accounting practices made shipping easier and slashed the costs of seaborne trade. The numbers testify to the maritime revolution: while a porter could carry about 10 pounds over long distances, and animal-drawn wagons could move 100 pounds over small distances, the Arab dhows plying the Indian Ocean were capable of transporting up to 5 tons of cargo. (Dhows are ships with triangle-shaped sails, called lateens, that allow the best use of the monsoon trade winds on the Arabian Sea and the Indian Ocean.) As a result, some coastal ports, like Mogadishu in eastern Africa, became vast transshipment centers for a thriving trade across the Indian Ocean.

A new navigational instrument spurred this boom: the needle compass. This Chinese invention initially identified promising locations for houses and tombs, but eleventh-century sailors from Guangzhou (anglicized as Canton) used it to find their way on the high seas. The device spread rapidly. Not only did it allow sailing under cloudy skies, but it also improved mapmaking. And it made all the oceans, including the Atlantic, easier to navigate.

Dhow. This modern dhow in the harbor of Zanzibar displays the characteristic triangle sail. The triangle sail can make good use of the trade wind monsoon and thus has guided dhows on the Arabian Sea since ancient times.

Antique Chinese Compass. *Chinese sailors from Canton started to use needle compasses in the eleventh century. By the thirteenth century, needle compasses were widely used on ships in the Indian Ocean and were starting to appear in the Mediterranean.*

Now shipping became less dangerous. Navigators relied on lateen-rigged dhows between the Indian Ocean and the Red Sea, heavy junks in the South China Sea, and Atlantic "cogs," which linked Genoa to locations as distant as the Azores and Iceland. They also enjoyed the protection of political authorities, such as the Song dynasts in China, in guiding the trading fleets in and out of harbors. The Fatimid caliphate in Egypt, for instance, profited from maritime trade and defended merchant fleets from pirates. Armed convoys of ships escorted commercial fleets and regularized the ocean traffic. The system soon spread to North Africa and southern Spain. Most of these shipping firms were family based, and they sent young men of the family, sometimes servants or slaves, to work in India. Wives in Cairo could expect gifts from their husbands to arrive with the fleet.

Changes in navigation ushered in the demise of overland routes. Silk Road merchants eventually gave up using camel trains, caravansaries (inns for travelers), and oasis hubs as they switched to the sea-lanes. The shift took centuries, but overland routes and camels were no match for multiple-masted cargo ships.

Global Commercial Hubs

Long-distance trade spawned the growth of commercial cities. (See Map 10.1.) These cosmopolitan **entrepôts** served as transshipment centers where ships could drop anchor and merchants could find lodging, exchange commodities, and replenish supplies. Their locations between borders or in ports enabled merchants to link diverse peoples commercially. Beginning in the late tenth century CE, regional centers became major anchorages of the maritime trade: in the west, the Egyptian port cities of Alexandria and Cairo; in the east, the Chinese city of Quanzhou; in the Malaysian Archipelago, the city of Melaka; and near the tip of the Indian Peninsula, the port of Kollam (often anglicized as Quilon). These hubs thrived under the political stability of dynasts who recognized that the free-for-all of trade and market life would generate wealth for them through taxes collected on cargoes.

Cairo and Alexandria were the Mediterranean's main maritime commercial centers. Cairo was home to numerous Muslim and Jewish trading firms, and Alexandria was their lookout post on the Mediterranean. It was through Alexandria that Europeans acquired silks from China and Spanish silks headed to eastern Mediterranean markets along with olive oil, glassware, flax, corals, and metals. Gemstones and aromatic perfumes poured in from India. Also changing hands were minerals and chemicals for dyeing or tanning and raw materials such as timber and bamboo. The real novelties were paper and books. Hand-copied Bibles, Talmuds, Qurans, legal and moral works, grammars in various languages, and Arabic books became the first best-sellers of the Mediterranean.

The Islamic legal system prevalent in Egypt promoted a favorable business environment. Legal specialists got around the rule that might have brought commerce to a halt—the *sharia's* (see Chapter 9) prohibition against earning interest on loans. With the clerics' blessing, Muslim traders formed partnerships between those who had capital to lend and those who needed money to expand their businesses: owners of capital entrusted their money or commodities to agents who, after completing their work, returned the investment and a share of the profits to the owners—and kept the rest as their reward. The English word *risk* derives from the Arabic *rizq,* the extra allowance paid to merchants in lieu of interest.

In China, the Song government set up offices of Seafaring Affairs in three major ports: Canton, Quanzhou, and an area near present-day Shanghai in the Yangzi Delta. In return for a portion of the taxes, these offices registered cargoes, sailors, and traders, while guards kept a keen eye on the traffic. Arabs, Persians, Jews, and Indians, as well as Chinese, traded at Quanzhou, and some stayed on to manage their businesses. Perhaps as many as 100,000 Muslims lived there during the Song dynasty. A mosque from this period is still standing. Hindu traders living in Quanzhou worshipped in a Buddhist shrine where statues of Hindu deities stood alongside those of Buddhist gods.

Because of its strategic location and proximity to Malayan tropical produce, Melaka became a key cosmopolitan city.

MAP 10.1 | Afro-Eurasian Trade, 1000–1300

During the early second millennium, Afro-Eurasian merchants increasingly turned to the Indian Ocean to transport their goods.

- Locate the global hubs of Kollam, Alexandria, Cairo, Melaka, and Quanzhou on this map.
- What regions do each of these global hubs represent?
- Based on the map, why would sea travel have been preferable to overland travel?
- According to the text, what revolutions in maritime travel facilitated this development?

During peak season, Southeast Asian ports teemed with colorfully dressed Indian, Javanese, and Chinese merchants and sailors selling their goods, purchasing return cargo, and waiting for the winds to change so they could reach their next destination. Local artisans hawked batik handicrafts, and money-grubbing traders converged from all over Asia to flood the markets with their merchandise and to search for pungent herbs, aromatic spices, and agrarian staples to ship out.

In the tenth century CE, South India likewise supported a nerve center of maritime trade. Many Muslim traders settled in Malabar, on the southwest coast of the Indian Peninsula, and Kollam became a cosmopolitan hub. Dhows delivered goods from the Red Sea and Africa. Chinese junks unloaded silks and

porcelain and picked up passengers and commodities for East Asian markets. Muslim traders shipped horses from Arab countries to India and the southeast islands, where kings viewed them as symbols of royalty. There was even trade in elephants and cattle from tropical countries, though most goods were spices, perfumes, and textiles. Personal relationships were key. When striking a deal with a local merchant, a Chinese trader would mention his Indian neighbor in Quanzhou and that family's residence in Kollam.

Global commercial hubs relied on friendship and family to keep their businesses thriving across religious and regional divides. Whether in India, Melaka, China, or Egypt, each bustling port teemed with a cosmopolitan mix of peoples,

Mazu. *As much as sailors used compasses, they could still appeal for divine help—as these Quanzhou sailors did in seeking protection at the shrine of Mazu, the goddess of seafarers. According to legend, before assuming godhood Mazu had performed many miracles. Her temple became prominent after 1123, when Quanzhou's governor survived a storm at sea while returning from Korea. After that, sailors and their families burned incense for the goddess and prayed for her aid in keeping them safe at sea.*

goods, and ideas that flowed through the growing maritime networks, thanks to improved ships and better navigational tools.

THE ISLAMIC WORLD IN A TIME OF POLITICAL FRAGMENTATION

While the number of Muslim traders began to increase in commercial hubs from the Mediterranean to the South China Sea, it was not until the ninth and tenth centuries CE that Muslims became a majority within their own Abbasid Empire (see Chapter 9). From the outset, Muslim rulers and clerics dealt with large non-Muslim populations, even as these groups were converting to Islam. Rulers accorded non-Muslims religious toleration as long as the non-Muslims accepted Islam's political dominion. Jewish, Christian, and Zoroastrian communities were free to choose their own religious leaders and to settle internal disputes in their own religious courts. They did, however, have to pay a special tax, the *jizya*, and defer to their rulers. While tolerant, Islam was an expansionist, universalizing faith. Intense proselytizing—especially by Sufi merchants—carried the sacred word to new frontiers and, in the process, reinforced the spread of Islamic institutions that supported commercial exchange. (See Primary Source: The Merchants of Egypt.)

Environmental Challenges and Fragmentation

Whereas western Europe experienced a climatic dark age between 500 and 900 CE (see Chapter 9), severe conditions—freezing temperatures and lack of rainfall—afflicted the eastern Mediterranean and the Islamic lands of Mesopotamia, the Iranian plateau, and the steppe region of central Asia in the late eleventh and early twelfth centuries. The Nile's low water levels devastated Egypt, the breadbasket for much of the area. No less than one-quarter of the summer floods that normally brought sediment-enriching deposits to Egypt's soils and guaranteed abundant harvests were utter failures in this period. Turkish nomadic pastoralists poured out of the steppe lands of central Asia, driven by drought, in search of better lands, wreaking political and economic havoc everywhere they invaded.

The Seljuk Turks entered the Iranian plateau in 1029, bringing an end to the magnificent cultural flourishing of the first half of the eleventh century (see Chapter 9). Seljuk warriors invaded Baghdad in 1055, establishing a nomadic state in Mesopotamia over a once powerful Abbasid state that now lacked the resources to defend its lands and its peoples, weakened by famines and pestilence. The invaders destroyed institutions of learning and public libraries and looted the region's antiquities. Nor was the Byzantine Empire spared.

PRIMARY SOURCE

The Merchants of Egypt

The most comprehensive collection of eleventh- and twelfth-century commercial materials from the Islamic world comes from a repository, known as a geniza, connected to the Jewish synagogue in Cairo. (It was the custom of the Jewish community to preserve, in a special storeroom, all texts that mention God.) These papers, a rich source of information about the Jewish community in Egypt at that time, touch on all manner of activities: cultural, religious, judicial, political, and commercial. The following letter is addressed to Joseph ibn 'Awkal, one of Egypt's leading merchants in the eleventh century.

Dear and beloved elder and leader, may God prolong your life, never take away your rank, and increase his favors and benefactions to you.

I inform you, my elder, that I have arrived safely. I have written you a letter before, but have seen no answer. Happy preoccupations—I hope. In that letter I provided you with all the necessary information.

I loaded nine pieces of antimony (kohl), five in baskets and four in complete pieces, on the boat of Ibn Jubār—may God keep it; these are for you personally, sent by Mūsā Ibn al-Majjānī. On this boat, I have in partnership with you—may God keep you—a load of cast copper, a basket with (copper) fragments, and two pieces of antimony. I hope God will grant their safe arrival. Kindly take delivery of everything, my lord.

I have also sent with Banāna a camel load for you from Ibn al-Majjānī and a camel load for me in partnership with you—may God keep you. He also carries another partnership of mine, namely, with 'Ammār Ibn Yijū, four small jugs (of oil).

With Abū Zayd I have a shipload of tin in partnership with Salāma al-Mahdawī. Your share in this partnership with him is fifty pounds. I also have seventeen small jugs of s[oap]. I hope they arrive safely. They belong to a man [called . . .] r b. Salmūn, who entrusted them to me at his own risk. Also a bundle of hammered copper, belonging to [a Muslim] man from the Maghreb, called Abū Bakr Ibn Rizq Allah. Two other bundles, on one is written Abraham, on the other M[. . .]. I agreed with the shipowner that he would transport the goods to their destination. I wish my brother Abū Nasr—may God preserve him—to take care of all the goods and carry them to his place until I shall arrive, if God wills.

Please sell the tin for me at whatever price God may grant and leave its "purse" (the money received for it) until my arrival. I am ready to travel, but must stay until I can unload the tar and oil from the ships.

Please take care of this matter and take from him the price of five skins (filled with oil). The account is with Salāma.

Al-Sabbāgh of Tripoli has bribed Bu 'l-'Al ā the agent, and I shall unload my goods soon.

Kindest regards to your noble self and to my master [. . . and] Abu 'l-Fadl, may God keep them.

QUESTIONS FOR ANALYSIS

- List all the different kinds of commodities that the letter talks about.
- How many different people are named as owners, partners, dealers, and agents?
- What does the letter reveal about the ties among merchants and about how they conducted their business?

Source: Letters of Medieval Jewish Traders, translated with introductions and notes by S. D. Goitein (Princeton, NJ: Princeton University Press, 1973), pp. 85–87.

Constantinople, once with a population of 1 million, saw its numbers dwindle to 200,000 by the late eleventh century; yet it was still Europe's largest city.

Political Divisions

These environmental challenges also caused Islam's political institutions to fragment just when it appeared that Shiism would be the vehicle for uniting the Islamic world. The Fatimid Shiites had established their authority over Egypt and much of North Africa (see Chapter 9), and the Abbasid state in Baghdad was controlled by a Shiite family, the Buyids. Each group created universities, in Cairo and Baghdad, respectively, ensuring that leading centers of higher learning were Shiite. But divisions also sapped Shiism, as Sunni Muslims began to challenge Shiite power and establish their own strongholds. In Baghdad, the Buyid family surrendered to a group of Sunni strongmen in 1055. A century later, the last of the Shiite Fatimid rulers gave way to a new Sunni regime in Egypt (see Map 10.2).

The new strongmen were mainly Turks. Their people had been migrating into the Islamic heartland from the Asian

10.2 | Islam between 900 and 1200

The Muslim world experienced political disintegration in the first centuries of the second millennium.

- According to the map key, what were the two major types of Muslim states in this period and what were the two major empires?
- What were the sources of instability in this period according to the map?
- As Islam continued to expand in this period, what challenges did it face?

steppes since the eighth century CE, bringing superior military skills and an intense devotion to Sunni Islam. Once established in Baghdad, they founded outposts in Syria and Palestine and then moved into Anatolia after defeating Byzantine forces in 1071. But this Turkish state also crumbled, as tribesmen quarreled for preeminence.

By the thirteenth century, the Islamic heartland had fractured into three regions. In the east (central Asia, Iran, and eastern Iraq), the remnants of the old Abbasid state persevered. Caliphs succeeded one another, still claiming to speak for all of Islam yet deferring to their Turkish military commanders. In the core of the Islamic world—Egypt, Syria, and the Arabian Peninsula—where Arabic was the primary tongue, military men of non-Arab origin held the reins of power. Farther west in North Africa, Arab rulers prevailed, but the influence of Berbers, some from the northern Sahara, was extensive. Islam was a vibrant faith, but its political systems were splintered.

The Spread of Sufism

Even in the face of political splintering, Islam's spread was facilitated by a popular form of the religion, highly mystical and communal, called **Sufism**. The term *Sufi* comes from the Arabic word for wool (*suf*), which many of the early mystics wrapped themselves in to mark their penitence. Seeking closer union with God, they also performed ecstatic rituals, such as repeating over and over again the name of God. In time, groups of devotees gathered to read aloud the Quran and other religious tracts. Sufi mystics' desire to experience God's love found ready expression in poetry. Most admired of Islam's mystic poets was Jalal al-Din Rumi (1207–1273), spiritual founder of the Mevlevi Sufi order that became famous for the ceremonial dancing of its whirling devotees, known as dervishes.

Although many *ulama* (scholars) despised the Sufis and loathed their seeming lack of theological rigor, the movement

Dervishes. *Today, the whirling dance of dervishes is a tourist attraction, as shown in this picture from the Jerash Cultural Festival in Jordan. Though Sufis in the early second millennium were not this neatly dressed, the whirling dance was an important means of reaching union with God.*

spread with astonishing speed and offered a unifying force within Islam. Sufism's emotional content and strong social bonds, sustained in Sufi brotherhoods, added to its appeal. Sufi missionaries carried the universalizing faith to India, to Southeast Asia, across the Sahara Desert, and to many other distant regions. It was from these brotherhoods that Islam became truly a religion of the people. As trade increased and more converts appeared in the Islamic lands, urban and peasant populations came to understand the faith practiced by the political, commercial, and scholarly upper classes even while they remained attached to their Sufi brotherhood ways. Over time, Islam became even more accommodating, embracing Persian literature, Turkish ruling skills, and Arabic-language contributions in law, religion, literature, and science.

What Was Islam?

Buoyed by Arab dhows on the high seas and carried on the backs of camels following commercial networks, Islam had been transformed from Muhammad's original goal of creating a religion for Arab peoples. By 1300, its influence spanned Afro-Eurasia and enjoyed multitudes of non-Arab converts. (See Map 10.3.) It attracted urbanites and rural peasants alike, as well as its original audience of desert nomads. Its extraordinary universal appeal generated an intense Islamic cultural flowering around 1000 CE.

Some people worried about the preservation of Islam's true nature as, for example, Arabic ceased to be the language of many Islamic believers. True, the devout read and recited the Quran in its original tongue, as the religion mandated. But Persian was now the language of Muslim philosophy and art, and Turkish

was the language of law and administration. Moreover, Jerusalem and Baghdad no longer stood alone as Islamic cultural capitals. Other cities, housing universities and other centers of learning, promoted alternative versions of Islam. In fact, some of the most dynamic thought came from Islam's fringes.

At the same time, diversity fostered cultural blossoming in all fields of high learning. Indicative of the prominence of the Islamic faith and the Arabic language in thought was the legendary Ibn Rushd (1126–1198). Known as Averroës in the west, where scholars pored over his writings, he wrestled with the same theological issues that troubled western scholars. Steeped in the writings of Aristotle, Ibn Rushd became Islam's most thoroughgoing advocate for the use of reason in understanding the universe. His knowledge of Aristotle was so great that it influenced the thinking of the Christian world's leading philosopher and theologian, Thomas Aquinas (1225–1274). Above all, Ibn Rushd believed that faith and reason could be compatible. He also argued for a social hierarchy in which learned men would command influence akin to Confucian scholars in China or Greek philosophers in Athens. Ibn Rushd believed that the proper forms of reasoning had to be entrusted to the educated class—in the case of Islam, the *ulama*—who would serve the common people.

Equally powerful works appeared in Persian, which by now was expressing the most sophisticated ideas of culture and religion. Best representing the new Persian ethnic pride was Abu al-Qasim Firdawsi (920–1020), a devout Muslim who believed in the importance of pre-Islamic Sasanian traditions. In the epic poem *Shah Namah,* or *Book of Kings,* he celebrated the origins of Persian culture and narrated the history of the Iranian highland peoples from the dawn of time to the Muslim conquest. As part of his effort to extol a pure Persian culture, Firdawsi attempted to compose his entire poem in Persian, unblemished by other languages and even avoiding Arabic words.

The Islamic world's achievements in science were truly remarkable. Its scholars were at the pinnacle of scientific knowledge throughout the world in this era. In truth, the "Islamic sciences"—law, study of the Quran, traditions of the Prophet (*hadith*), theology, poetry, and the Arabic language—held primacy among the learned classes. In contrast, "foreign sciences" (later called the natural sciences in Europe) were held in lower esteem. Even so, Ibn al-Shatir (1304–1375), working on his own in Damascus, produced non-Ptolemaic models of the universe that later researchers noted were mathematically equivalent to those of Copernicus. Even earlier, the Maragha school of astronomers (1259 and later) in western Iran had produced a non-Ptolemaic model of the planets. Some historians of science believe that Copernicus must have seen an Arabic manuscript written by a thirteenth-century Persian astronomer that contained a table of the movements of the planets. In addition,

MAP 10.3 | Islamic and Hindu States and the Byzantine Empire between 1200 and 1300

Islam continued to expand after the thirteenth century.

- Where were its largest and most important gains according to the map?
- How did other religions fare under Islamic rule in this period?
- How was Islam able to continue to expand in this period?

scholars in the Islamic world produced works in medicine, optics, and mathematics as well as astronomy that were in advance of the achievements of Greek and Roman scholars.

By the fourteenth century, Islam had achieved what early converts would have considered unthinkable. No longer a religion of a minority of peoples living among Christian, Zoroastrian, and Jewish communities, it had become the people's faith. The agents of conversion were mainly Sufi saints and Sufi brotherhoods—not the *ulama,* whose exhortations had little impact on common people. The Sufis had carried their faith far and wide to North African Berbers, to Anatolian villagers, and to West African animists who believed that things in nature have souls. Ibn Rushd worried about the growing appeal of what he considered an "irrational" piety. But his message failed, because he did not appreciate that Islam's expansionist powers rested on its appeal to common folk. While the *sharia* was the core of Islam for the educated and scholarly classes, Sufism spoke to ordinary men and women.

During this period, Islam became one of the four cultural spheres that would play a major role in world history. Islam became the majority religion of most of the inhabitants of Southwest Asia and North Africa, Arabic became the everyday language for most people, and the Turks began to establish themselves as the dominant rulership force, ultimately creating the Ottoman Empire, which would last into the twentieth century. The Islamic world became integral in transregional trade and the creation and maintenance of knowledge.

INDIA AS A CULTURAL MOSAIC

Trade and migration affected India, just as it did the rest of Asia and Africa. As in the case of Islam, India's growing cultural interconnections and increasing prosperity produced little political integration. Under the canopy of Hinduism it remained a cultural mosaic; Islamic faith now joined others to make the region even more diverse. (See Map 10.4.) India illustrates how cross-cultural integration can just as easily preserve diversity as promote internal unity.

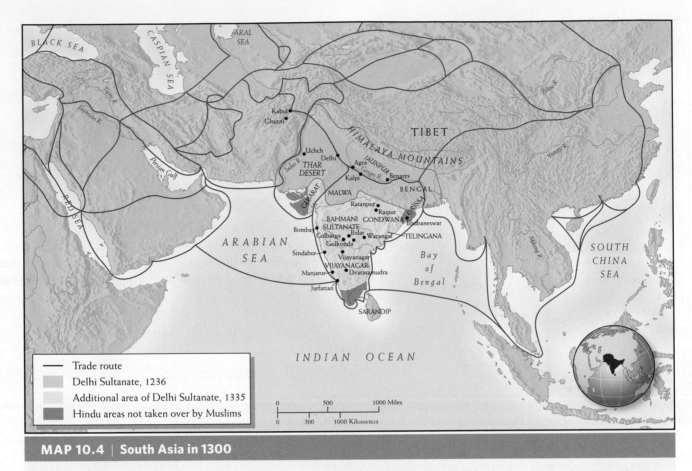

MAP 10.4 | South Asia in 1300

As the fourteenth century began, India was a blend of many cultures. Politically, the Turkish Muslim regime of the Delhi Sultanate dominated the region.

- Use the key to the map to identify the areas dominated by the Delhi Sultanate.
- How do you suppose the trade routes helped to spread the Muslims' influence in India?
- Now use the key to find the Hindu areas. Based on your reading, what factors accounted for Hinduism's continued appeal despite the Muslims' political power?

With its pivotal location along land- and sea-based routes, India became an intersection for the trade, migration, and culture of Afro-Eurasian peoples. With 80 million inhabitants in 1000 CE, it had the second-largest population in the region, not far behind China's 120 million. (See Analyzing Global Developments: Growth in the World Population to 1340.) Turks ultimately spilled into India as they had the Islamic heartlands, bringing their newfound Islamic beliefs. But the Turkish newcomers encountered an ethnic and religious mix of which they were just one part.

Before the Turks arrived, India had been splintered among rival chiefs called *rajas*. These leaders gained support from high-caste Brahmans by doling out land grants to them. Since much of the land was uncultivated, the Brahmans first built temples, then converted the indigenous hunter-gatherer peoples to the Hindu faith, and finally taught the converts how to cultivate the land. In this way the Brahmans simultaneously spread their faith and expanded the agrarian tax base for themselves and the rajas. They also repaid the rajas' support by compiling elaborate genealogies for them and endowing them with legitimizing ancestries. In return, the rajas demonstrated that they, too, were well versed in Sanskrit culture and were prepared to patronize artists and poets. Ultimately, many of the warriors and their heirs became Indian rajas.

Invasions and Consolidations

When the Turkish warlords began entering India, South Asia's rulers, the rajas, had neither the will nor the resources to resist them after centuries of fighting off invaders. The most powerful and enduring of the Turkish Muslim regimes of northern India was the **Delhi Sultanate** (1206–1526), whose rulers brought political integration but also strengthened the cultural

Hindu Temple. *When Buddhism started to decline in India, Hinduism was on the rise. Numerous Hindu temples were built, many of them adorned with ornate carvings like this small tenth-century temple in Bhubaneshwar, in eastern India.*

diversity and tolerance that were a hallmark of the Indian social order. Sultans recruited local artisans for building projects, and palaces and mosques became displays of Indian architectural tastes adopted by Turkish newcomers. But the sultans did not force their subjects to convert, so South Asia never became an Islamic-dominant region. Nor did they display much interest in the flourishing commercial life along the Indian coast, permitting these areas to develop on their own and allowing Persian Zoroastrian traders to settle around modern-day Mumbai (Bombay). Farther south, the Malabar coast became the preserve

of Arab traders. The Delhi Sultanate was a rich and powerful regime that brought political integration but did not enforce cultural homogeneity.

What Was India?

During the eleventh, twelfth, and thirteenth centuries, India became the most diverse and, in some respects, most tolerant region in Afro-Eurasia. India in this era arose as an impressive but fragile mosaic of cultures, religions, and ethnicities.

When the Turks arrived, the local Hindu population, having had much experience with foreign invaders and immigrants, assimilated these intruders as they had done earlier peoples. Before long, the newcomers thought of themselves as Indians who, however, retained their Islamic beliefs and steppe ways. They continued to wear their distinctive trousers and robes and flaunted their horse-riding skills. At the same time, the local population embraced some of their conquerors' ways, donning the tunics and trousers that characterized central Asian peoples.

Diversity and cultural mixing became most visible in the multiple languages that flourished in India. Although the sultans spoke Turkish languages, they regarded Persian literature as a high cultural achievement and made Persian their courtly and administrative language. Meanwhile, most Hindu subjects spoke local languages, followed their caste regulations, and practiced diverse forms of Hindu worship. The rulers did what Muslim rulers in Southwest Asia and the

Lodi Gardens. *The Lodi dynasty was the last dynasty of the Delhi Sultanate. Lodi Gardens, the cemetery of Lodi sultans, placed central Asian Islamic architecture in an Indian landscape, thereby creating a scene of "heaven on the earth."*

Mediterranean did with Christian and Jewish communities living in their midst: they collected the *jizya* tax and permitted communities to worship as they saw fit and to administer their own communal law.

Ultimately, Islam in India proved that it did not have to be a conquering religion to prosper. Although Buddhism had been in decline there for centuries, it, too, became part of the cultural intermixing of these centuries. As Vedic Brahmanism evolved into Hinduism (see Chapter 8), it absorbed many Buddhist doctrines and practices, such as *ahimsa* (nonkilling) and vegetarianism. The two religions became so similar that Hindus simply considered the Buddha to be one of their deities—an incarnation of the great god Vishnu. Many Buddhist moral teachings mixed with and became Hindu stories.

Once the initial disruptive effects of the Turkish invasions were absorbed, India remained a highly diverse and tolerant region during this period. Most important, it emerged as one of the four major cultural spheres, enjoying a tremendous level of integration as Turkish-Muslim rulership and their traditions and practices successfully blended into the native Hindu society, leading to a more integrated and peaceful India.

Vishnu. *In addition to the Buddha, the four-armed Vishnu has nine other avatars, some of whom are portrayed at his feet in this tenth-century sandstone sculpture.*

SONG CHINA: INSIDERS VERSUS OUTSIDERS

The preeminent world power in 1000 CE was still China, despite its recent turmoil. Once dampened, the turbulence yielded to a long era of stability and splendor that made China a regional engine of Afro-Eurasian prosperity. In 907 CE, the Tang dynasty splintered into regional kingdoms, mostly led by military generals. In 960 CE, one of these generals ended the fragmentation, reunified China, and assumed the mandate of heaven for the Song dynasty (960–1279). (See Maps 10.5 and 10.6.) Ultimately, a nomadic group, the Jurchen (ancestors of the Manchu, who would rule China from the seventeenth until the twentieth century), would bring the Song dynasty to an end, but not before Song influence had fanned out into Southeast Asia, helping to create new identities in the political systems there.

Economic Progress

China, like India and the Islamic world, participated in Afro-Eurasia's powerful long-distance trade. Chinese merchants were as energetic as their Muslim and Indian counterparts. Yet China's commercial successes could not have occurred without the country's strong agrarian base—especially its vast wheat, millet, and rice fields, which fed a population that reached 120 million. Agriculture benefited from breakthroughs in metalworking that produced stronger iron plows, which the Song harnessed to sturdy water buffalo to extend the agricultural frontier.

Manufacturing also flourished. In 1078, for example, total Song iron production reached between 75,000 and 150,000 tons, roughly the equivalent of European iron production in the early eighteenth century. The Chinese piston-driven bellows that provided forced air for furnaces were of a size unsurpassed until the nineteenth century. Also, in the early tenth century, Chinese alchemists mixed saltpeter with sulfur and charcoal to produce a product that would burn and that could be deployed on the battlefield: gunpowder. Song entrepreneurs were soon inventing a remarkable array of incendiary devices that flowed from their mastery of techniques for controlling explosions and high heat. Moreover, artisans produced increasingly light, durable, and exquisitely beautiful porcelains. Before long, their porcelain (now called "china") was the envy of all Afro-Eurasia. Also unspooling from the artisans' hands were vast amounts of clothing and handicrafts, made from the fibers grown by Song farmers. In effect, the Song Chinese oversaw the world's first manufacturing revolution, producing finished goods on a large scale for consumption far and wide.

MONEY AND INFLATION Expanding commerce transformed the role of money and its wide circulation. By now the

MAP 10.5 | East Asia in 1000

Several states emerged in East Asia between 1000 and 1300, but none were as strong as the Song dynasty in China.

- Using the key to the map, try to identify the factors that contributed to the Song state's economic dynamism.
- What external factors kept the Song dynasty from completely securing its reign?
- What factors drove the Chinese commercial revolution in this period?

Song government was annually minting nearly 2 million strings of currency, each containing 1,000 copper coins. In fact, as the economy grew, the supply of metal currency could not match the demand. One result was East Asia's thirst for gold from East Africa. At the same time, merchant guilds in northwestern Shanxi developed the first letters of exchange, called **flying cash**. These letters linked northern traders with their colleagues in the south. Before long, printed money had eclipsed coins. Even the government collected more than half its tax revenues in cash rather than grain and cloth. The government also issued more notes to pay its bills—a practice that ultimately contributed to the world's first case of runaway inflation.

New Elites

Song emperors ushered in a period of social and cultural vitality. They built on Tang institutions by expanding a central bureaucracy of scholar-officials chosen through competitive civil service examinations. Zhao Kuangyin, or Emperor Taizu (r. 960–976 CE), himself administered the final test for all who had passed the highest-level palace examination. In subsequent dynasties, the emperor was the nation's premier examiner, symbolically demanding oaths of allegiance from successful candidates. By 1100, these ranks of learned men had accumulated sufficient power to become China's new ruling elite.

MAP 10.6 | East Asia in 1200

The Song dynasty regularly dealt with "barbarian" neighbors.

- What were the major "barbarian" tribes during this period?
- Approximately what percentage of Song China was lost to the Jin in 1126?
- How did the "barbarian" tribes affect the Han Chinese identity in this period?

Expansion of the civil service examination system was crucial to a shift in power from the still powerful hereditary aristocracy to a less wealthy but more highly schooled class of scholar-officials. Consider the career of the Northern Song reformer Wang Anshi (1021–1086), who ascended to power from a commoner family outside of Hangzhou in the east. He owed his success to gaining high marks in Song state examinations—a not insignificant achievement, for in nearby Fujian Province alone, of the roughly 18,000 candidates who gathered triennially to take the provincial examination, over 90 percent failed! After gaining the emperor's ear, Wang eventually challenged the political and cultural influence of the old Tang dynasty elites from the northwest.

Song Dynasty Coin. *The Song dynasty's rapid economic development led to the use of vast amounts of metal currency, including many copper coins like this one. The hole in the center meant that the coins could be strung together in groups.*

Negotiating with Nomads on the Borderlands

As the Song flourished, nomads on the outskirts eyed the Chinese successes closely. To the north, Khitan, Tungusic, Tangut, and Jurchen nomadic societies formed their own dynasties and adopted Chinese institutions. Located within the "greater China," as defined by the Han and Tang dynasties, these non-Chinese nomads saw China proper as an object of both conquest and emulation.

In military power the Song dynasts were relatively weak. Despite their sophisticated weapons, they could not match their enemies on the steppe when the latter united against them. Steel tips improved the arrows that the Song soldiers shot from their crossbows, and flamethrowers and "crouching tiger catapults" sent incendiary bombs streaking into their enemies' ranks. But none of these breakthroughs was secret. Warrior neighbors on the steppe mastered the new arts of war more fully than did the Song dynasts themselves.

China's strength as a manufacturing powerhouse made economic diplomacy an option, so the Song relied on "gifts" and generous trade agreements with the borderlanders. For example, after losing North China to the Khitan Liao dynasty, the Song agreed to make annual payments of 100,000 ounces of silver and 200,000 bolts of silk. The treaty allowed them to live in relative peace for more than a century. Securing peace meant emptying the state coffers and then printing more paper money. The resulting inflation added economic instability to military weakness, making the Song an easy target when Jurchen invaders made their final assault.

What Was China?

Paradoxically, the increasing exchange between outsiders and insiders within China hardened the lines that divided them and gave residents of China's interior a highly developed sense of themselves as a distinctive people possessing a superior culture. Exchanges with outsiders nurtured a "Chinese" identity among those who considered themselves true insiders and referred to themselves as Han. Driven south from their ancient homeland in the eleventh century, they grew increasingly suspicious and resentful toward the outsiders living in their midst. They called these outsiders "barbarians" and treated them accordingly.

Vital in crystallizing this sense of a distinct Chinese identity was print culture. Of all Afro-Eurasian societies in 1300, the Chinese were the most advanced in their use of printing and book publishing and circulation. Moreover, their books established classical Chinese as the common language of educated classes in East Asia. The Song government used its plentiful supply of paper to print books, especially medical texts, and to distribute calendars. The private publishing industry also expanded. Printing houses throughout the country produced Confucian classics, works on history, philosophical treatises, and literature—all of which figured in the civil examinations. Buddhist publications, too, were available everywhere.

Wang Anshi. *He owed his rise from a commoner family to a powerful position as a reformer to the Song state examinations.*

Chinese and Barbarian. *After losing the north, the Han Chinese grew resentful of outsiders. They drew a dividing line between their own agrarian society and the nomadic warriors, calling them "barbarians." Such identities were not fixed, however. Chinese and so-called barbarians were mutually dependent.*

In many respects, the Song period represented China's greatest age. China's resources, its huge population base coupled with a strong agrarian economy, and its strong foreign trade and diplomatic relations made it the most wealthy among the four major cultural spheres; its common language and its transfer of power to nonhereditary Confucian scholars made it the most unified. The country's bureaucracy was the largest in the world, totaling between 200,000 and 300,000 civil servants during the Song period, of whom 20,000 were high officials. No society had larger cities or a more urbanized population. In mid-Song times, an estimated 5 percent of its people lived in cities. The capital, Kaifeng, had a population of 1 million; 30 cities varied in size from 40,000 to 100,000 or more; 60 cities had about 15,000 residents; and 400 cities, mainly county seats and smaller prefectural centers, had populations ranging between 4,000 and 5,000.

Yet in spite of its great wealth, immense population, highly developed bureaucracy, and powerful military forces, the Han Chinese never felt secure from the strong nomadic pastoralists who inhabited the western and northern frontiers. The construction of walls in the north and military outposts along the frontiers never seemed to afford complete protection. Especially when dynastic regimes weakened, China was vulnerable to invasion and conquest by these well-armed tribal confederacies. They moved south into China proper whenever the Chinese dynasty faltered and environmental conditions drove the militarily skilled nomads in search of better lives.

CHINA'S NEIGHBORS ADAPT TO CHANGE

Feeling the pull of China's economic and political gravity, cultures around China consolidated their own internal political authority and defined their own identities in order to keep from being swallowed up. At the same time, they increased their commercial transactions.

The Rise of Warriors in Japan

Japan, like China, laid many political and cultural foundations for its later development in the three centuries between 1000 and 1300. Not only did its leaders distance themselves from Chinese influences, but they also developed a strong sense of their islands' distinctive identity. Even so, the long-standing dominance of Chinese ways remained apparent at virtually every level of Japanese society and was most pronounced at the imperial court in the capital city of Heian, present-day Kyoto. (See Primary Source: The Tale of Genji.) The city itself, founded in 795 CE, was modeled after the former Tang Chinese capital city of Chang'an.

Outside Kyoto, however, a less China-centered way of life existed and began to impose itself on the center. Here, local notables, mainly military leaders and large landowners, began to challenge the imperial court for dominance. These military adventurers nevertheless elected to keep the Japanese emperors and their court at Kyoto in office even while stripping them of real power; Japan continued to have an emperor residing at the imperial city of Kyoto right down to 1868, when the Meiji restoration took place (see Chapter 17).

The emergence of these military men marked the arrival of an important new social group in Japanese society—the warriors, or samurai. In lightweight leather armor, these expert horsemen defended their private estates with remarkable long-range bowmanship and superbly crafted single-edged long steel swords, lethal for close combat in warfare. The warriors also brought an idealization of their martial ethics, with an emphasis on loyalty, self-discipline, and a simple life tied to the land, which helped to shape Japanese society until recent times.

By the beginning of the fourteenth century, Japan had multiple sources of political and cultural power: an endangered and declining aristocracy; an imperial family with prestige but little authority; powerful landowning notables based in the provinces; and a rising and increasingly ambitious class of samurai. This yielded a combustible mix of refined high culture in the capital versus a warrior ethos in the provinces. Such a mix produced social intrigue in politics and led different provincial factions to vie with one another for preeminence.

PRIMARY SOURCE

The Tale of Genji

Lacking a written language of their own, Heian aristocrats adopted classical Chinese as the official written language while continuing to speak Japanese. Men at the court took great pains to master the Chinese literary forms, but Japanese court ladies were not expected to do so. Lady Murasaki Shikibu, the author of The Tale of Genji, *hid her knowledge of Chinese, fearing that she would be criticized. In the meantime, the Japanese developed a native syllabary (a table of syllables) based on Chinese written graphs. Using this syllabary, Murasaki kept a diary in Japanese that gave vivid accounts of Heian court life. Her story— possibly the world's first novel—relates the adventures of a dashing young courtier named Genji. In the passage below, Genji evidently speaks for Murasaki in explaining why fiction can be as truthful as a work of history in capturing human life and its historical significance.*

Genji . . . smiled, and went on: "But I have a theory of my own about what this art of the novel is, and how it came into being. To begin with, it does not simply consist in the author's telling a story about the adventures of some other person. On the contrary, it happens because the storyteller's own experience of men and things, whether for good or ill—not only what he has passed through himself, but even events which he has only witnessed or been told of—has moved him to an emotion so passionate that he can no longer keep it shut up in his heart. Again and again something in his own life or in that around him will seem to the writer so important that he cannot bear to let it pass into oblivion. There must never come a time, he feels, when men do not know about it. That is my view of how this art arose.

"Clearly then, it is no part of the story-teller's craft to describe only what is good or beautiful. Sometimes, of course, virtue will be his theme, and he may then make such play with it as he will. But he is just as likely to have been struck by numerous examples of vice and folly in the world around him, and about them he has exactly the same feelings as about the pre-eminently good deeds which he encounters: they are more important and must all be garnered in. Thus anything whatsoever may become the subject of a novel, provided only that it happens in this mundane life and not in some fairyland beyond our human ken.

"The outward forms of this art will not of course be everywhere the same. At the court of China and in other foreign lands both the genius of the writers and their actual methods of composition are necessarily very different from ours; and even here in Japan the art of storytelling has in course of time undergone great changes. There will, too, always be a distinction between the lighter and the more serious forms of fiction. . . . So too, I think, may it be said that the art of fiction must not lose our allegiance because, in the pursuit of the main purpose to which I have alluded above, it sets virtue by the side of vice, or mingles wisdom with folly. Viewed in this light the novel is seen to be not, as is usually supposed, a mixture of useful truth with idle invention, but something which at every stage and in every part has a definite and serious purpose."

> **QUESTIONS FOR ANALYSIS**
>
> • According to this passage, what motivates an author to write a story (that is, fiction)?
> • Genji feels it is appropriate for a writer to address not only "what is good or beautiful" but also "vice and folly." What explanation does he give? Do you agree?

Source: Sources of Japanese Tradition, compiled by Ryūsaku Tsunoda, William Theodore de Bary, and Donald Keene (New York: Columbia University Press, 1964), vol. 1, pp. 177–79.

Southeast Asia: A Maritime Mosaic

Southeast Asia, like India, now became a crossroads of Afro-Eurasian influences. Its sparse population of probably around 10 million in 1000 CE—tiny compared with that of China and India—was not immune to the foreign influences riding the sea-lanes into the archipelago. The Malay Peninsula became home to many trading ports and stopovers for traders shuttling between India and China, because it connected the Bay of Bengal and the Indian Ocean with the South China Sea. (See Map 10.7.)

Indian influence had been prominent both on the Asian mainland and in island portions of Southeast Asia since 800 CE, but Islamic expansion into the islands after 1200 gradually superseded these influences. Only Bali and a few other islands far to the east of Malaya preserved their Brahmanic-Vedic religious

Heiji Rebellion. *This illustration from the Kamakura Shogunate (1185–1333) depicts a battle during the Heiji Rebellion, which was fought between rival subjects of the cloistered emperor Go-Shirakawa in 1159. Riding in full armor on horseback, the fighters on both sides are armed with devastating long bows.*

origins. Elsewhere in Java and Sumatra, Islam became the dominant religion. In Vietnam and northern portions of mainland Southeast Asia, Chinese cultural influences and northern schools of Mahayana Buddhism were especially prominent.

During this period, Cambodian, Burmese, and Thai peoples founded powerful mixed polities along the Mekong, Salween, Chao Phraya, and Irrawaddy River basins of the Asian mainland. Important Vedic and Buddhist kingdoms emerged here as political buffers between the strong states in China and India and brought stability and further commercial prosperity to the region.

Consider the kingdom that ruled Angkor in present-day Cambodia. With their capital in Angkor, the Khmers (889–1431) created the most powerful and wealthy empire in Southeast Asia. Countless water reservoirs enabled them to flourish on the great plain to the west of the Mekong River after the loss of eastern territories. Public works and magnificent temples dedicated to the revived Vedic gods from India went hand in hand with the earlier influence of Indian Buddhism. Eventually, the Khmer kings united adjacent kingdoms and extended Khmer influence to the Thai and Burmese states along the Chao Phraya and Irrawaddy Rivers.

Angkor Wat. *Mistaken by later European explorers as a remnant of Alexander the Great's conquests, the enormous temple complexes built by the Khmer people in Angkor borrowed their intricate layout and stupa architecture from the Brahmanist Indian temples of the time. (A stupa is a moundlike structure containing religious relics.) As the capital, Angkor was a microcosm of the world for the Khmer, who aspired to represent the macrocosm of the universe in the magnificence of Angkor's buildings and their geometric layout.*

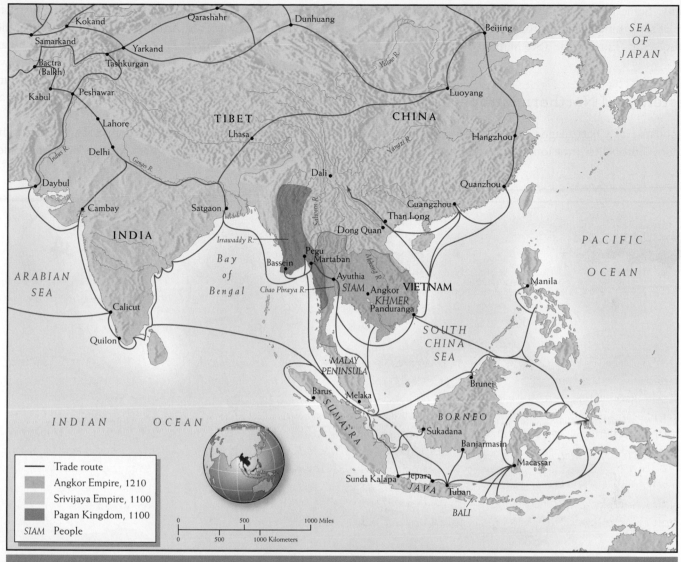

MAP 10.7 | Southeast Asia, 1000–1300

Cross-cultural influences affected Southeast Asian societies during this period.

- What makes Southeast Asia unique geographically compared with other regions of the world?
- Based on the map, why were the kingdoms of Southeast Asia exposed to so many cross-cultural influences?
- In this chapter, the term *mosaic* describes both South and Southeast Asia. Compare Map 10.4 with this map, and explain how the mosaic of Southeast Asia differed from the mosaic of India.

One of the greatest temple complexes in Angkor exemplified the Khmers' heavy borrowing from Vedic Indian architecture. Angkor aspired to represent the universe in the magnificence of its buildings. As signs of the ruler's power, the pagodas, pyramids, and terra-cotta friezes (ornamented walls) presented the life of the gods on earth. The crowning structure of the royal palace was the magnificent temple of Angkor Wat, possibly the largest religious structure ever built. In ornate detail and with great artistry, its buildings and statues represented the revival of the Hindu pantheon within the Khmer royal state.

CHRISTIAN EUROPE

Europe from 1000 to 1300 was a region of strong contrasts. Intensely localized power was balanced by a shared sense of Europe's place in the world, especially with respect to Christian identity. Some inhabitants even began to believe in the existence of something called "Europe" and increasingly referred to themselves as "Europeans." (See Map 10.8.)

Western and Northern Europe

The collapse of Charlemagne's empire had exposed much of northern Europe to invasion, principally from the Vikings, and left the peasantry with no central authority to protect them from local warlords. Armed with deadly weapons, these strongmen collected taxes, imposed forced labor, and became the unchallenged rulers of society. Within this growing warrior aristocracy, northern France led the way. The Franks (later called Frenchmen) were the trendsetters of eleventh- and twelfth-century western Europe.

The most important change was the peasantry's subjugation to these strongmen, many of whom became large landholders.

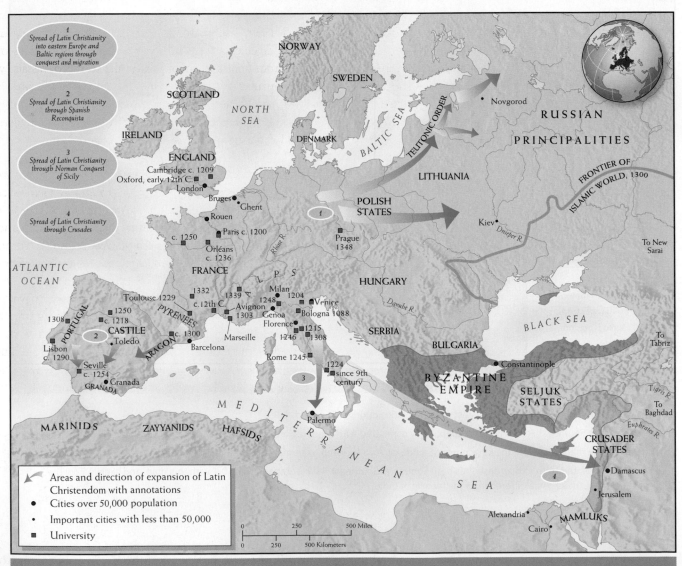

MAP 10.8 | Latin Christendom in 1300

Catholic Europe expanded geographically and integrated culturally during this era.

- According to this map, into what areas did western Christendom successfully expand?
- What factors contributed to the growth of a widespread common culture and shared ideas?
- How did long-distance trade shape the history of the region during this time?

Previously, well-to-do peasants had carried arms as "free" men. The moment the farmers lost the right to carry arms, they were no longer free. They slipped back to being mere agricultural laborers. Each peasant toiled under the authority of a landholding lord, who controlled every detail of his or her life. This was the basis of a system now called **manorialism**.

This landholding manorial class emerged around the Mediterranean basin as the Roman Empire declined in the west and the Byzantine Empire rose in the east. In both regions, important individuals in the imperial bureaucracies were granted land in payment for their service. Many turned the imperial system's large supply of slaves as well as free peasants into dependent workers serving on their estates. Estates valued self-sufficiency, and most became bipartite: the land, owned by the lord, was divided into two units. The lord held one unit, a demesne, on which the peasants had labor, tax, and other service obligations to the lord. The other consisted of small holdings farmed by peasant families for themselves. Estates also had fisheries, mills, and mineral rights. Lords constructed their homes or manors in the villages. Some were large and ornate, though the majority were modest. Many of the wealthy owners preferred to reside in large cities and turned the management of the estate over to administrators.

In lands distant from the Mediterranean, notably England, France, and Germany, manorial villages emerged out of tribal lands. These lands, originally held by chiefs, were distributed to churches and important officials. Here, too, the bipartite division of the land occurred, and here, too, though some estates were huge, nearly two-thirds of the estates were 500 acres or less.

The manorial system provided the economic and territorial foundations of this era. Political and social ties, which formed the basis of what we call **feudalism**, also bound different classes of peoples together. Feudal societies essentially had three orders: those who prayed (the clergy), those who fought (the lords), and those who toiled (the peasants). Each had obligations to the others. Lords were expected to provide protection for peasants and clerics, while clerics promoted an ethical and holy life for all. Peasants provided society's sustenance. What we might call the classic form of feudalism existed only in England, Sicily, and the Holy Land, those lands conquered by Norman warriors in the tenth century CE from their base in Normandy, France. Here, powerful landholding lords, including kings, gave some of their lands to other freemen, called vassals, in return for fealty, or loyalty, and military service. The grant of land was called a fief, and over time these lands, held by the vassals, became private estates that could be passed on to heirs. Elsewhere in Europe, feudal arrangements were not so clear-cut. The handing over of lands from nobles to subordinates, the so-called vassals, was not accompanied by formal ceremonies, the taking of oaths, and the swearing of fealty, as was the case in regions under Norman authority. Nor were the lands held by vassals always known as fiefs, and even the nobles' ownership of these lands was often disputed.

Assured of control of the peasantry, feudal lords and their vassals watched over an agrarian breakthrough—which fueled a commercial transformation that drew Europe into the rest of the global trading networks. Lordly protection and more advanced metal tools like axes and plows, combined with heavier livestock to pull plows through the root-infested sods of northern Europe, led to massive deforestation. Above this clearing activity stood castles, built by powerful lords and sometimes by strong vassals to ensure their regional autonomy. Their threatening presence also enabled lords to collect rents and tithes (shares of crops, earmarked as "donations" for the church) from the peasantry. In this blunt way, the feudal and manorial systems harnessed agrarian energy to their own needs. The population of western

The Bayeux Tapestry. *This tapestry was allegedly prepared by Queen Matilda, wife of William the Conqueror, and her ladies to celebrate the successful invasion of England in 1066. It shows the fascination of the entire "feudal" class, even women, with war. Great horses, tightly meshed chain mail, long shields, and stirrups all made such cavalry warfare possible.*

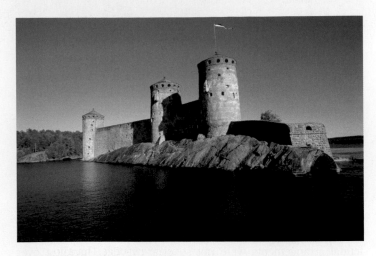

Olavinilinna Castle. *This castle in Finland was the easternmost extension of a "western" feudal style of rule through great castles. It was built at the very end of the Baltic, to keep away the Russians of Novgorod.*

Europe as a whole leaped forward, most spectacularly in the north. As a result, northern Europe, from England to Poland, ceased to be an underdeveloped "barbarian" appendage of the Mediterranean.

Eastern Europe

Nowhere did pioneering peasants develop more land than in the wide-open spaces of eastern Europe, the region's land of opportunity. Between 1100 and 1200, some 200,000 farmers emigrated from Flanders (in modern Belgium), Holland, and northern Germany to eastern frontiers. Well-watered landscapes covered with vast forests filled up what are now Poland,

the Czech Republic, Hungary, and the Baltic states. "Little Europes," whose castles, churches, and towns echoed the landscape of France, now replaced economies that had been based on gathering honey, hunting, and the slave trade. For 1,000 miles along the Baltic Sea, forest clearings dotted with new farmsteads and small towns edged inward from the coast up the river valleys.

The social structure here was a marriage of convenience between migrating peasants and local elites. The area offered the promise of freedom from the feudal lords' arbitrary justice and imposition of forced labor. Even the harsh landscape of the eastern Baltic (where the sea froze every year and impenetrable forests blocked settlers from the coast) was preferable to life in the feudal west. For their part, the elites of eastern Europe—the nobility of Poland, Bohemia, and Hungary and the princes of the Baltic—wished to live well, in the "French" style. But they could do so only if they attracted workers to their lands by offering newcomers a liberty that they had no hope of enjoying in the west.

The Russian Lands

In Russian lands, western settlers and knights met an eastern brand of Christian devotion. This world looked toward Byzantium, not Rome or western Europe. Russia was a giant borderland between the steppes of Eurasia and the booming centers of Europe. Its cities lay at the crossroads of overland trade and migration, and Kiev became one of the region's greatest cities. Standing on a bluff above the Dnieper River, it straddled newly opened trade routes. With a population exceeding 20,000, including merchants from eastern and western Europe

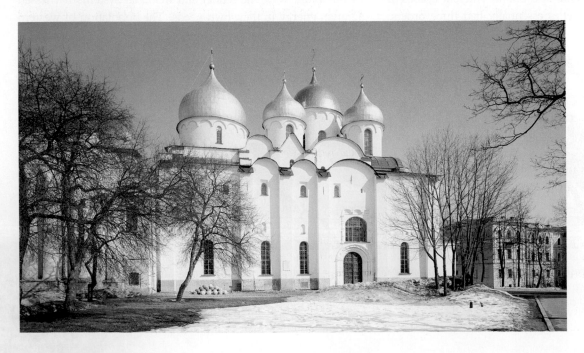

Saint Sophia Cathedral, Novgorod. *The cathedral of Novgorod (like that of Kiev) was called Hagia Sophia. It was a deliberate imitation of the Hagia Sophia of Constantinople, showing Russia's roots in a glorious Roman/Byzantine past that had nothing to do with western Europe.*

PRIMARY SOURCE

The Birch Bark Letters of Novgorod

The city of Novgorod was a vibrant trading center with a diverse population. From 1951 onward, Russian archaeologists in Novgorod have excavated almost 1,000 letters and accounts scratched on birch bark and preserved in the sodden, frequently frozen ground. Reading them, we realize how timeless people's basic concerns can be.

First, we meet the merchants. Many letters are notes by creditors of the debts owed to them by trading partners. The sums are often expressed in precious animal furs. They contain advice to relatives or to partners in other cities:

> Giorgii sends his respects to his father and mother: Sell the house and come here to Smolensk or to Kiev: for the bread is cheap there.

Then we meet neighborhood disputes:

> From Anna to Klemiata: Help me, my lord brother, in my matter with Konstantin. . . . [For I asked him,] "Why have you been so angry with my sister and her daughter. You called her a cow and her daughter a whore. And now Fedor has thrown them both out of the house."

There are even glimpses of real love. A secret marriage is planned:

> Mikiti to Ulianitza: Come to me. I love you, and you me. Ignato will act as witness.

And a poignant note from a woman was discovered in 1993:

> I have written to you three times. What is it that you hold against me, that you did not come to see me this Sunday? I regarded you as I would my own brother. Did I really offend you by that which I sent to you? If you had been pleased you would have torn yourself away from company and come to me. Write to me. If in my clumsiness I have offended you and you should spurn me, then let God be my judge. I love you.

QUESTIONS FOR ANALYSIS

- What does the range of people writing on birch bark tell us about these people?
- Think of the messages you send to friends and relatives today. Even if texting and e-mailing seem centuries distant from writing on birch bark, can you relate in any way to these ancient letter writers?

Source: A. V. Artsikhovskii and V. I. Borkovski, *Novgorodskie Gramoty na Bereste,* 11 vols. (Moscow: Izd-vo Akademii nauk SSSR, 1951–2004), document nos. 424, 531, 377, and 752.

---

and Southwest Asia, South Asia, Egypt, and North Africa, Kiev was larger than Paris—larger even than the much-diminished city of Rome.

Kiev looked south to the Black Sea and to Constantinople. Under Iaroslav the Wise (1016–1054), it became a small-scale Constantinople on the Dnieper. A stone church called St. Sophia stood (as in Constantinople) beside the imperial palace. With its distinctive "Byzantine" domes, it was a miniature Hagia Sophia (see Chapter 8). Its highest dome towered 100 feet above the floor, and its splendid mosaics depicting Byzantine saints echoed the religious art of Constantinople. But the message was political as well, for the ruler of Kiev was cast in the mold of the emperor of Constantinople. He now took the title *tsar* from the ancient Roman name given to the emperor, Caesar. From this time onward, *tsar* was the title of rulers in Russia.

The Russian form of Christianity replicated the Byzantine style of churches all along the great rivers leading to the trading cities of the north and northeast. These were not agrarian centers, but hubs of expanding long-distance trade. (See Primary Source: The Birch Bark Letters of Novgorod.) Each city became a small-scale Kiev and a smaller-scale echo of Constantinople. The Orthodox religion looked to Byzantium's Hagia Sophia rather than the Catholic faith associated with the popes in Rome. Russian Christianity remained the Christianity of a borderland— vivid oases of high culture set against the backdrop of vast forests and widely scattered settlements. Like the agricultural manors of western Europe, these Russian cities demonstrated the highly localized nature of power in Europe during this period.

What Was Christian Europe?

Christianity in this era—primarily the Roman Catholicism of the west, but also the Orthodoxy of the east—became a universalizing faith that transformed the region that was becoming known as "Europe." The Christianity of post-Roman Europe had been a religion of monks, and its most dynamic centers were great monasteries. Members of the laity were expected to revere and support their monks, nuns, and clergy, but not to imitate them. By 1200, all this had changed. The internal colonization of western Europe—the clearing of woods and founding of villages—ensured that parish churches arose in all but the wildest landscapes. Their spires were visible and their bells were audible from one valley to the next. Church graveyards were the only places where good Christians could be buried; criminals' and outlaws' bodies piled up in "heathen" graves outside the cemetery walls.

Now the clergy reached more deeply into the private lives of the laity. Marriage and divorce, previously considered family matters, became a full-time preoccupation of the church. And sin was no longer an offense that just "happened"; it was a matter that every person could do something about. Regular confession to a priest became obligatory for all Catholic, western Christians. The followers of Francis of Assisi (1182–1226) emerged as

Saint Francis of Assisi. *In this fresco by the Renaissance artist Giotto, Saint Frances of Assisi is seen renouncing his earthly wealth and embarking on a life of poverty. Saint Francis founded the order that took his name, the Franciscan Order, and promoted his principles of a life of poverty, devotion to the teachings of Jesus Christ, and concern for the poor.*

an order of preachers who brought a message of repentance. Their listeners were to weep, confess their sins to local priests, and strive to be better Christians. Franciscans instilled in the hearts of all believers a Europe-wide Catholicism based on daily remorse and daily contemplation of the sufferings of Christ and his mother, Mary. From Ireland to Riga and Budapest, Catholic Christians came to share a common piety.

UNIVERSITIES AND INTELLECTUALS Vital to the creation of Europe's Christian identity was the emergence of universities, for it was during this era that Europe acquired its first class of intellectuals. Since the late twelfth century, scholars had gathered in Paris, where they formed a *universitas*—a term borrowed from merchant communities, where it denoted a type of union. Those who belonged to the *universitas* enjoyed protection by their fellows and freedom to continue their trade. Similarly protected by their own "union," the scholars of Paris began wrestling with the new learning from Arab lands. When the bishop of Paris forbade this undertaking, they simply moved to the Left Bank of the Seine, so as to place the river between themselves and the bishop's officials, who lived around the Notre Dame Cathedral.

Those scholars were called schoolmen because of the halls—*scholae* in Latin—in which they taught. Their philosophy, scholasticism, sought to render the Christian tradition totally intelligible: God and his creation were penetrable by human reason; they made sense; so did the Bible and the traditions of the church. Teaching took the form of commentaries on the Bible and on the laws of the church (canon law). The aim was to explain every passage in the Bible so that its message could be preached with confidence. The day's teaching began with theology and the Bible—for the mind was freshest in the morning! But this community now involved rational discussions of science, astronomy, and medicine. The greatest poet of the age, the Italian Dante Alighieri (1265–1321), reflects this new expansive view of the universe. In his *Divine Comedy* (1307), he imagined a journey to heaven through hell and purgatory in which every stage—from the punishments of hell through purgatory to the fullness of joy in heaven—reflected the supreme wisdom of God, which human reason could understand and enjoy.

The scholars' ability to organize themselves gave them an advantage that their Arab contemporaries lacked. For all his genius, Ibn Rushd had to spend his life courting the favor of individual monarchs to protect him from conservative fellow Muslims, who frequently burned his books. Ironically, European scholars congregating in Paris could quietly absorb the most persuasive elements of Arabic thought, like Ibn Rushd's. Yet they endeavored to prove that Christianity was the only religion that fully met the aspirations of all rational human beings. Such was the message of many scholars, including the great intellectual Thomas Aquinas, who wrote *Summa contra Gentiles* (Summary of Christian Belief against Non-Christians) in 1264.

The Europe of 1300 was more culturally unified than in previous centuries. It was permeated by Catholicism, and its leading intellectuals extolled the virtues of Christian learning. Such a confident region was not, however, a tolerant place for heretics, Jews, or Muslims.

Christian Europe on the Move: The Crusades and Iberia

By the tenth and eleventh centuries CE, western Christianity was on the move, spreading into Scandinavia, southern Italy, the Baltic, and eastern Europe. Its ambitions to reconquer Spain and Portugal (which had been under Islamic control since the eighth century CE) demonstrated one of the effects of feudal power: the lords' self-confidence, their belief in their military capability, and their pious sense of destiny were all inflated. Besides, the wealth of the east was irresistible to those whose piety entwined with an appetite for plunder. Yet the two Christendoms formed an uneasy alliance to roll back the expanding frontiers of Islam. Europeans zealously took war outside their own borders.

CRUSADES In the late eleventh century, western Europeans launched a wave of attacks known as the Crusades. The First Crusade began in 1095, when Pope Urban II appealed to the warrior nobility of France to put their violence to good use: they should combine their role as pilgrims to Jerusalem with that of soldiers and free Jerusalem from Muslim rule. What the clergy proposed was a novel kind of war. Whereas previously war had been a dirty business and a source of sin, now the clergy told the knights that good and just wars were possible. Such wars could cancel out the sins of those who waged them.

Starting in 1097, an armed host of around 60,000 men moved all the way from northwestern Europe to Jerusalem. This was a huge crowd. But it was divided. Knights in heavy armor led, as they did in Europe. But in the eastern Mediterranean they depended on poor masses who joined the movement to help besiege cities and construct a network of castles as the Christian knights drove their frontier forward. Later Crusaders brought their wives, especially those from the upper class. As in many colonial societies away from the homeland, these women felt freer. Eleanor of Aquitaine, for example, led her own army. Also, queens were crucial in identifying with the problems of local populations. Consider the Armenian queen, Melisende (r. 1131–1152): regarded as wise and experienced in affairs of the state, she was popular with local Christians. As a result, the society of the Crusader states remained more open to women and the lower classes than in Europe. Above all, the Crusades could not have happened without the sailors and merchants of

Crusader. *Kneeling, this Crusader promises to serve God (as he would serve a feudal lord) by going to fight on a Crusade (as he would fight for any lord to whom he had sworn loyalty). The two kinds of loyalty—to God and to one's lord—were deliberately intertwined in promoting the Crusades. Both were about war. But fighting for God was unambiguously good, while fighting for a lord was not always so clear-cut.*

Italy. It was the fleets of Venice, Genoa, and Pisa that transported the later Crusaders and supplied their kingdom.

No fewer than nine crusades were fought in the two centuries that followed Urban II's call, but none ultimately created permanent Christian kingdoms in the lands they "reconquered." Only a small proportion of Crusaders remained in Southwest Asia, and those who did met their match in Muslim armies. (See Current Trends in World History: The Crusades from Dual Perspectives.) Part of the problem was that few Crusaders had any intention of becoming colonists. Only a small number remained to defend the Kingdom of Jerusalem after the First Crusade. Most knights returned home, their epic pilgrimage completed. The remaining fragile network of Crusader lordships could barely threaten the Islamic heartlands.

The Crusades from Dual Perspectives

World history promotes comparative historical study, and when two cultures come together, as they did in the European crusades, their meeting offers a unique opportunity to see how the two societies view each other, as well as providing a sense of each culture's self-identity. Such a confrontation took place during the crusades between European Christians and Muslims between 1095 and 1272 CE

In 1095, Pope Urban II called for the First Crusade with the following words:

"Oh, race of Franks, race from across the mountains, race chosen and beloved by God, as shines forth in very many of your works, set apart from all nations by the situation of your country, as well as by your Catholic faith and the honor of the Holy Church! To you our discourse is addressed, and for you our exhortation is intended. We wish you to know what a grievous cause has led us to your country, what peril, threatening you and all the faithful, has brought us."

The "grievous cause" was the occupation of the Holy City of Jerusalem by the Islamic empire. Formed within the complex relationship between the Byzantine Empire and the western Christian papacy and kingdoms of Europe, the religious motivation behind the Crusades became the subject of many literary renditions of the tumultuous events. It also generated emotionally stirring and polemical (argumentative) writing, depicting either a Muslim or Christian enemy (depending on the work's author).

Polemics are often passionate, harsh, and emotional. They also inspire and reinforce the conviction of fellow believers, with little concern for accuracy. Thus, authors of polemics in the time of the Crusades were usually too biased or too misinformed to present accurate portraits of their enemies. But occasionally, first-hand accounts in the form of chronicles and histories offer us unique glimpses into Christian-Muslim relations in the age of the Crusades.

Consider Usāmah ibn Munqidh (1095–1188), the learned ruler of the city

of Shaizar in western Syria. Skirmishes, truces, and the ransoming of prisoners were part of his daily life, and Usāmah socialized with his Frankish neighbors as much as he fought with them. He offers a dismissive opinion of his enemies. Basically, they struck him as "animals possessing the virtues of courage and fighting, but nothing else." In particular, their medical practice appalled him. More strange, the Franks allowed their wives to walk about freely and to talk to strangers unaccompanied by male guardians. How could men be at once so brave and yet so lacking in a proper, Arab sense of honor, which would lead a man to protect his women? Unlike other Muslim authors of his time, however, Usāmah does not refer to the Franks in derogatory terms such as "infidels" or "devils." In fact, he occasionally refers to some of them as his companions and writes of a Frank who called him "my brother" (Hitti, p. 16).

Christian authors had similar interests in documenting the customs of their enemies in battle. Jean de Joinville (1224/1225–1317) was a chronicler of

---

Muslim leaders, however, did not see the Frankish knights as a threat. For them, the Crusades were irrelevant. And as far as the average Muslim of the region was concerned, the Crusaders hardly mattered at all. Jerusalem and Palestine had always been fringe areas in Southwest Asia. Real prosperity and the capital cities of Muslim kingdoms lay inland, away from the coast—at Cairo, Damascus, and Baghdad. The assaults' long-term effect was to harden Muslim feelings against the Franks and the millions of nonwestern Christians who had previously lived peacefully in Egypt and Syria. Muslims viewed the Crusaders as brave but uncivilized warriors. A neighboring Muslim wrote: "The Franks possess none of the virtues of men except courage. . . . Nobody counts for them except knights." (See again Current Trends in World History: The Crusades from Dual Perspectives.) Their lack of medical knowledge shocked this observer. He noted that they would rather chop off a man's leg than administer ointments, as Muslim doctors would have advised.

IBERIA Other campaigns of Christian expansion, like the Iberian efforts to drive out the Muslims, were more successful. Beginning with the capture of Toledo in 1061 CE, the Christian kings of northern Spain slowly pushed back the Muslims. Eventually, they reached the heart of Andalusia in southern Iberia and conquered Seville, adding more than 100,000 square miles of territory to Christian Europe. Another force from northern France crossed Italy to conquer Muslim-held Sicily, ensuring Christian rule in the strategically located mid-Mediterranean island. Unlike the Crusaders' fragile foothold at the edge of Southwest Asia, these two conquests turned the tide in relations between Christian and Muslim power.

Christianity—in particular the rise of the Roman Catholic Church, the spread of universities, and the fight against the Muslims in their native and spiritual homelands—would be the force that would create the fourth cultural sphere known as medieval France. During one crusade, while in the service of the king, Joinville had occasion to note the Muslims' social behavior:

> "Whenever the Sultan was in the camp, the men of the personal Guard were quartered all round his lodging, and appointed to guard his person. At the door of the Sultan's lodging there was a little tent for the Sultan's door-keepers, and for his musicians, who had Arabian horns and drums and kettledrums; and they used to make such a din at daybreak and at nightfall that people near them could not hear one another speak, and that they could be heard plainly all through the camp. The musicians never dared sound their instruments in the daytime unless by the order of the Chief of the Guard. Thus it was, that whenever the Sultan had a proclamation to make he used to send for the Chief of the Guard, and give him the order; and then the Chief would cause all the Sultan's instruments to be sounded; and thereupon all the host would come to hear the Sultan's commands."

Although scholars regard such literary renditions with caution, they are useful for gleaning personal details that other types of works omit. The colorful accounts by authors such as Usāmah ibn Munqidh and Joinville are invaluable resources for the social history of the Crusaders.

Jeane de Joinville. *Joinville dictating his memoir of St. Louis, in which he described the Seventh Crusade.*

QUESTIONS FOR ANALYSIS

- What customs or practices of their opponents did the Muslim and Christian writers select to write about? Why?
- What aspects of the other side's customs does each writer seem to see as unusual or praiseworthy? What does that tell us about their perceptions of the strangers they encountered?
- If a historian is to use polemical written sources like this to analyze societies in the past, what can he or she say is trustworthy about them?

Explore Further

Hodgson, Natasha. *Women, Crusading and the Holy Land in Historical Narrative* (2007).

Maalouf, Amin. *The Crusades through Arab Eyes,* translated by Jon Rothschild (1984).

Peters, Edward (ed.). *The First Crusade: The Chronicle of Fulcher of Chartres and Other Source Materials* (1971).

Europe, whose peoples would become known as European, at the western end of the Afro-Eurasian landmass.

SUB-SAHARAN AFRICA COMES TOGETHER

During this period, sub-Saharan Africa's relationship to the rest of the world changed dramatically. Before 1000 CE, sub-Saharan Africa had never been a world entirely apart, but now its integration became much stronger. Africans and outsiders were determined to overcome the sea, river, and desert barriers that had blocked sub-Saharan peoples from participating in long-distance trade and intellectual exchanges (see Map 10.9). Increasingly, interior hinterlands found themselves touched by the commercial and migratory impulses emanating from the Indian Ocean and Arabian Sea transformations.

West Africa and the Mande-Speaking Peoples

Once trade routes bridged the Sahara Desert (see Chapter 9), the flow of commodities and ideas linked sub-Saharan Africa to North Africa and Southwest Asia. As the savanna region became increasingly connected to developments in Afro-Eurasia, Mande-speaking peoples emerged as the primary agents for integration within and beyond West Africa. Exploiting their expertise in commerce and political organization, the Mande edged out rivals.

The Mande, or Mandinka, homeland was a vast area, 1,000 miles wide, between the bend in the Senegal River to the west and the bend of the Niger River to the east, stretching more than 2,000 miles from the Senegal River in the north to the Bandama River in the south. This was where the kingdom of Ghana had arisen (see Chapter 9) and where Ghana's successor state—the Mandinka state of Mali, discussed shortly—emerged around 1100 CE.

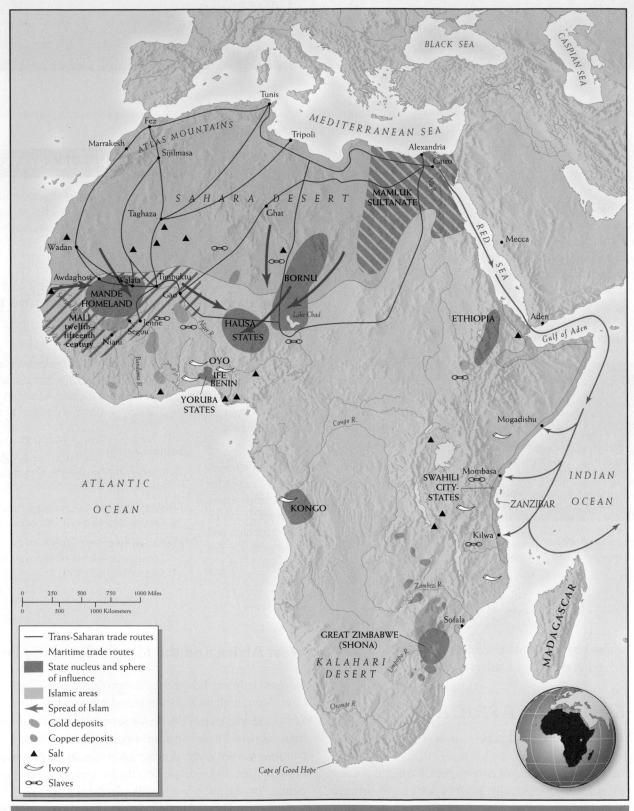

Map labels (within the image):

CASPIAN SEA

BLACK SEA

MEDITERRANEAN SEA

Tunis

Fez

Marrakesh

Tripoli

Sijilmasa

Alexandria

Cairo

ATLAS MOUNTAINS

SAHARA DESERT

MAMLUK SULTANATE

Taghaza

Ghat

Nile R.

Mecca

Wadan

RED SEA

Awdaghost

Walata

Timbuktu

BORNU

Senegal R.

MANDE HOMELAND

Gao

Lake Chad

ETHIOPIA

Aden

MALI twelfth–fifteenth century

Jenne

Segou

HAUSA STATES

Gulf of Aden

Niani

Niger R.

OYO

IFE BENIN

YORUBA STATES

Bandama R.

Congo R.

Mogadishu

ATLANTIC OCEAN

INDIAN OCEAN

SWAHILI CITY-STATES

Mombasa

ZANZIBAR

KONGO

Kilwa

MADAGASCAR

Zambezi R.

Sofala

GREAT ZIMBABWE (SHONA)

KALAHARI DESERT

Limpopo R.

Orange R.

Cape of Good Hope

Scale:
0 250 500 750 1000 Miles
0 500 1000 Kilometers

Legend:
— Trans-Saharan trade routes
— Maritime trade routes
▨ State nucleus and sphere of influence
░ Islamic areas
➤ Spread of Islam
● Gold deposits
● Copper deposits
▲ Salt
〜 Ivory
⊶ Slaves

MAP 10.9 | Sub-Saharan Africa in 1300

Increased commercial contacts influenced the religious and political dimensions of sub-Saharan Africa at this time. Compare this map with Map 9.3 (p. 329).

- Where had strong Islamic communities emerged by 1300?

- According to this map, what types of activity were affecting the Mande homeland?

- To what extent had sub-Saharan Africa "come together"?

PRIMARY SOURCE

An African Epic

The traditional story of the founding of the kingdom of Mali was passed down orally from generation to generation by griots, counselors, and other official historians to the royal family. Only in 1960 was it finally written down in French. The narrative recounts the life of Sundiata, the heroic founder of the Mali state. The following passage provides insight into the role of the narrator (the griot) in the Malian kingdom, as well as some of the qualities of good and bad rulers.

Griots know the history of kings and kingdoms and that is why they are the best counsellors of kings. Every king wants to have a singer to perpetuate his memory, for it is the griot who rescues the memories of kings from oblivion, as men have short memories.

Kings have prescribed destinies just like men, and seers who probe the future know it. They have knowledge of the future, whereas we griots are depositories of the knowledge of the past. But whoever knows the history of a country can read its future.

Other peoples use writing to record the past, but this invention has killed the faculty of memory among them. They do not feel the past any more, for writing lacks the warmth of the human voice. . . .

I, Djeli Mamoudou Kouyaté, am the result of a long tradition. For generations we have passed on the history of kings from father to son. The narrative was passed on to me without alteration and I deliver it without alteration, for I received it free from all untruth.

Listen now to the story of Sundiata, the Na'Kamma, the man who had a mission to accomplish.

At the time when Sundiata was preparing to assert his claim over the kingdom of his fathers, Soumaoro was the king of kings, the most powerful king in all the lands of the setting sun. The fortified town of Sosso was the bulwark of fetishism against the word of Allah. For a long time Soumaoro defied the whole world. Since his accession to the throne of Sosso he had defeated nine kings whose heads served him as fetishes in his macabre chamber. Their skins served as seats and he cut his footwear from human skin. Soumaoro was not like other men, for the jinn had revealed themselves to him and his power was beyond measure. So his countless sofas [soldiers] were very brave since they believed their king to be invincible. But Soumaoro was an evil demon and his reign had produced nothing but bloodshed. Nothing was taboo for him.

His greatest pleasure was publicly to flog venerable old men. He had defiled every family and everywhere in his vast empire there were villages populated by girls whom he had forcibly abducted from their families without marrying them.

QUESTIONS FOR ANALYSIS

- What are you able to understand about the function of the griot after reading this passage?
- What makes this kind of oral history reliable? What makes it unreliable?
- Soumaoro, the adversary of Sundiata, exemplified the characteristics of a bad ruler. What were they? Can you tell, indirectly, what the characteristics of a good ruler (like Sundiata) were?

Source: Sundiata: An Epic of Old Mali, compiled by D. T. Niane (Harlow, UK: Longman Group, 1965), pp. 40–41.

The Mande-speaking peoples were constantly on the go and marvelously adaptable. By the eleventh century, they were spreading their cultural, commercial, and political hegemony from the high savanna grasslands southward into the woodlands and tropical rain forests stretching to the Atlantic Ocean. Those dwelling in the rain forests organized small-scale societies led by local councils, while those in the savanna lands developed centralized forms of government under sacred kingships. These peoples believed that their kings had descended from the gods and that they enjoyed the gods' blessing.

As the Mande broadened their territory to the Atlantic coast, they gained access to tradable items that residents of the interior were eager to have—notably kola nuts and malaguetta peppers, for which the Mande exchanged iron products and manufactured textiles.

From the eleventh century to the late fifteenth century, the most vigorous businesses were those that spanned the Sahara Desert. The Mande-speaking peoples, with their far-flung commercial networks and highly dispersed populations, dominated this trade as well. Here one of the most prized commodities was salt, mined in the northern Sahel around the city of Taghaza; it was in demand on both sides of the Sahara. Another valuable commodity was gold, mined within the Mande homeland and borne by camel caravans to the far northern side of the Sahara, where traders exchanged it for various manufactures. Equally important in West African commerce were slaves, who were shipped to the settled Muslim communities of North Africa and Egypt. By 1300, the Mandinka merchants had followed the Senegal River to its outlet on the coast and then pushed their commercial frontiers farther inland and down the coast. Thus, even before European explorers and traders arrived in the mid-fifteenth century, West African peoples had created dynamic networks linking the hinterlands with coastal trading hubs.

The Empire of Mali

As booming trade spawned new political organizations, the **Mali Empire** became the Mande successor state to the kingdom of Ghana. Founded in the twelfth century, it exercised political sway over a vast area for three centuries.

The Mali Empire represented the triumph of horse warriors, and its origins are enshrined in the epic poem *The Epic of Sundiata,* which tells the story of the dynasty's founder, the legendary Sundiata. Sundiata might well have actually existed. Arab historian Ibn Khaldun referred to him by name and reported that he was "their [Mali's] greatest king" (Levtzion and Pouwels, p. 64). His triumph, which occurred in the thirteenth century, marked the victory of new cavalry forces over traditional foot soldiers. Horses—which had always existed in some parts of Africa—now became prestige objects of the savanna peoples, symbols of state power. (See Primary Source: An African Epic.)

Under the Mali Empire, commerce was in full swing. With Mande trade routes extending to the Atlantic Ocean and spanning the Sahara Desert, West Africa was no longer an isolated periphery of the central Muslim lands. Mali's most famous sovereign, Mansa Musa (r. 1312–1332), made a celebrated hajj, or pilgrimage to Mecca, in 1325–1326, traveling through Cairo and impressing crowds with the size of his retinue and his displays of wealth, especially many dazzling items made of gold.

Mansa Musa's visit to Cairo was a sensation in its time. The stopover in one of Islam's primary cities astonished the Egyptian elite and awakened much of the world to the fact that Islam had spread far below the Sahara and that a sub-Saharan state could mount such an ostentatious display of power and wealth. Mansa Musa spared no expense to impress his hosts. He sent ahead an enormous gift of 50,000 dinars (a unit of money widely used in the Islamic world at this time), and his entourage included soldiers, wives, consorts, and as many as 12,000 slaves, many wearing rich brocades woven of Persian silks. And there was gold—a lot of it. He brought immense quantities and distributed it lavishly during his three-month stay. Preceding his retinue as it crossed the desert were 500 slaves, each carrying a golden staff. The caravan also included around 100 camels, each bearing two 300-pound sacks of gold.

The Mali Empire boasted two of West Africa's largest cities. Jenne, an ancient entrepôt, was a vital assembly point for caravans laden with salt, gold, and slaves preparing for journeys west to the Atlantic coast and north over the Sahara. The city had originated as an urban settlement around 200 BCE; by 1000 CE, most substantial structures were made of brick. Around the city ran an impressive wall over 11 feet thick at its base and extending over a mile in length. More spectacular was the city of Timbuktu; founded around 1100 CE as a seasonal camp for nomads, it grew in size and importance under the patronage of various Malian kings. By the fourteenth century, it was a thriving commercial and religious center famed for its two large mosques, which are still standing. Timbuktu was also renowned for its intellectual vitality. Here, West African Muslim scholars congregated to debate the tenets of Islam and to ensure that the faithful, even when distant from the Muslim heartland, practiced their religion with no taint of pagan observances. These clerics acquired treatises on Islam from all over the world for their personal libraries, remnants of which remain to this day.

Trade between East Africa and the Indian Ocean

Africa's eastern and southern regions were also integrated into long-distance trading systems. Because of monsoon winds, East Africa was a logical end point for much of the Indian Ocean trade. Swahili peoples living along that coast became brokers for trade from the Arabian Peninsula, the Persian Gulf territories, and the western coast of India. Merchants in the city of Kilwa on the coast of present-day Tanzania brought ivory, slaves, gold, and other items from the interior and shipped them to destinations around the Indian Ocean.

West African Gold. *This 1375 picture shows the king of Mali, head of West Africa's largest empire, known for its great wealth based on supplies of gold.*

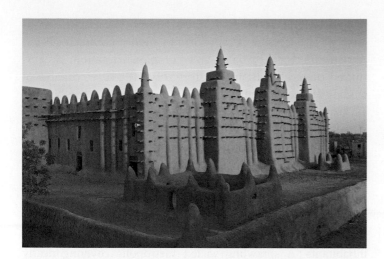

Jenne Mosque. *This fabulous mosque arose in the kingdom of Mali when that kingdom was at the height of its power. The mosque speaks to the depth and importance of Islam's roots in the Malian kingdom and well before. Jenne had originated in 200 CE and soon became an important trade city for all of West Africa, facilitating trade between West Africa and North Africa. The mosque viewed here was modernized at the beginning of the twentieth century.*

The most valued commodity being traded was gold. Shona-speaking peoples grew rich by mining the ore in the highlands between the Limpopo and Zambezi Rivers. By the year 1000 CE, the Shona had founded up to fifty small religious and political centers, each one erected from stone to display its power over the peasant villages surrounding it. Around 1100 CE, one of these centers, Great Zimbabwe, stood supreme among the Shona. Built on the fortunes made from gold, its most impressive landmark was a massive elliptical building made of stone fitted so expertly that it needed no grouting. The buildings of Great Zimbabwe probably housed the king and may also have contained smelters for melting down gold.

THE SLAVE TRADE African slaves were as valuable as African gold in shipments to the Mediterranean and Indian Ocean markets. There had been a lively trade in African slaves (mainly from Nubia) into pharaonic Egypt well before the Common Era. After Islam spread into Africa and sailing techniques improved, the slave trade across the Sahara Desert and Indian Ocean boomed. Although the Quran attempted to mitigate the severity of slavery, requiring Muslim slave owners to treat their slaves kindly and praising manumission as an act of piety, nonetheless the African slave trade flourished under Islam.

Africans became slaves during this period much as they had before: some were prisoners of war; others were considered criminals and sold into slavery as punishment. Their duties were varied. Some slaves were pressed into military service; others with seafaring skills worked as crewmen on dhows or as dockworkers. Still others, mainly women, were domestic

servants, and many became concubines of Muslim political figures and businessmen. Slaves also did forced labor on plantations, the most oppressive being the agricultural estates of lower Iraq. There, slaves endured fearsome discipline and revolted in the ninth century CE in one of the great slave wars documented in world history (the Zanj Rebellion). Yet in this era, plantation slave labor, like that which later became prominent in the Americas, was the exception, not the rule. Slaves were more prized as additions to family labor or as status symbols for their owners.

Unlike the Americas, sub-Saharan Africa no longer remained a people and a territory apart. The desert that had shielded Africans living beneath the Sahara desert was bridged, and commodities like salt, gold, and captive human beings that became slaves in North Africa and Indian Ocean countries were exchanged for textiles, horses, and other products of the north.

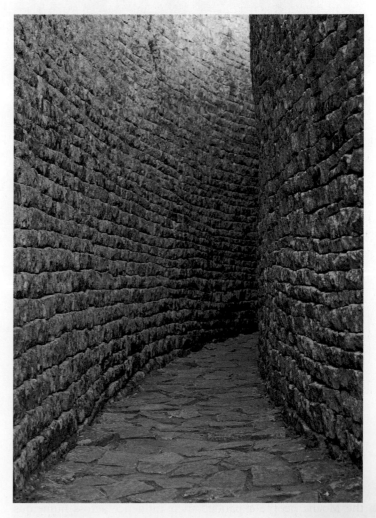

Great Zimbabwe. *These walls surrounded the city of Great Zimbabwe, which was a center of the gold trade between the East African coastal peoples and traders sailing on the Indian Ocean. Great Zimbabwe flourished during the thirteenth, fourteenth, and fifteenth centuries.*

Slave Market. *Slaves were a common commodity in the marketplaces of the Islamic world. Turkish conquests during the years from 1000 to 1300 put many prisoners on the slave market.*

THE AMERICAS EXPAND REGIONAL CONTACTS

During this period, the Americas were untouched by the connections reverberating across Afro-Eurasia. Apart from limited Viking contacts in North America (see Chapter 9), navigators still could not cross the large oceans that separated the Americas from other lands. Yet, here, too, commercial and expansionist impulses fostered closer contact among the peoples who lived there.

Andean States

Growth and prosperity in the Andean region gave rise to South America's first empire. Known as the **Chimú Empire**, it developed early in the second millennium in the fertile Moche Valley, bordering the Pacific Ocean. (See Map 10.10.) Ultimately, the Moche people expanded their influence across numerous valleys and ecological zones, from pastoral highlands to rich valley floodplains to the fecund fishing grounds of the Pacific coast. As their geographical reach grew, so did their wealth.

A THRIVING LOWLAND ECONOMY The Chimú economy was successful because it was highly commercialized. Agriculture was its base, and complex irrigation systems turned the arid coast into a string of fertile oases capable of feeding an increasingly dispersed population. Cotton became a lucrative export to distant markets along the Andes. Parades of llamas and porters lugged these commodities up and down the steep mountain chains that are the spine of South America. As in China, a well-trained bureaucracy oversaw the construction and maintenance of canals, with a hierarchy of provincial administrators watching over commercial hinterlands.

Between 850 and 900 CE, the Moche peoples founded their biggest city, Chan Chan, with a core population of 30,000 inhabitants. A sprawling walled metropolis covering nearly 10 square miles, with extensive roads circulating through neighborhoods, it boasted ten huge palaces at its center. Protected by thick walls 30 feet high, the opulent residence halls bespoke the rulers' power. Within the compound, emperors erected mortuary monuments for storing their accumulated riches: fine cloth, gold and silver objects, splendid *Spondylus* shells, and other luxury goods. Around the compound spread neighborhoods for nobles and artisans; farther out stood rows of commoners' houses. The Chimú regime, centered at Chan Chan, lasted until Incan armies invaded in the 1460s and incorporated the Pacific state into their own immense empire.

AN INVENTIVE HIGHLAND STATE The Andes also saw its first highland empires during this period. On the shores of the Lake Titicaca, the people of Tiahuanaco forged a high-altitude state. Though neither as large nor as wealthy as the Chimú Empire, its residents converted the inhospitable highlands to an environment where farmers and herders thrived. There is evidence of long-distance trade with neighbors in semitropical valleys and even signs of highlanders migrating to the lowlands to produce agrarian staples for their kin in the mountains. Dried fish and cotton came from the coast; fruits and vegetables came from lowland valleys. Trade sustained an enormous urban population of up to 115,000 people. Looming over the skyline of Tiahuanaco was an imposing pyramid of massive sandstone blocks. Its advanced engineering system conveyed water to the summit, from which an imitation rainfall coursed down the carefully carved sides—an awesome spectacle of engineering prowess in such an arid region.

Connections to the North

Additional hubs of regional trade developed farther north, showing once again that even in areas of relative geographical isolation, cultures could flourish and interact within expanding regional spheres. The Toltecs and the Cahokians are superb examples.

MAP 10.10 | Andean States

Although the Andes region of South America was isolated from Afro-Eurasian developments before 1500, it was not stagnant. Indeed, political and cultural integration brought the peoples of this region closer together.

- Where are the areas of the Chimú Empire and Tiahuanaco influence on the map?
- What kinds of ecological niches did they govern?
- According to your reading, how did each political system encourage greater cultural and economic integration?

THE TOLTECS IN MESOAMERICA By 1000 CE, Mesoamerica had seen the rise and fall of several complex societies. Caravans of porters worked the intricate roads that connected the coast of the Gulf of Mexico to the Pacific and the southern lowlands

of Central America to the arid regions of modern Texas. (See Map 10.11.) The region's heartland was the rich valley of central Mexico. Here the **Toltecs** filled the political vacuum left by the decline of Teotihuacán (see Chapter 8) and tapped into the commercial network radiating from the valley.

The Toltecs were a combination of migrant groups, refugees from the south, and farmers from the north. They settled northwest of Teotihuacán as the city waned, making their capital at Tula. They relied on a maize-based economy supplemented by beans, squash, and dog, deer, and rabbit meat. Their rulers made sure that enterprising merchants provided them with status goods such as ornamental pottery, rare shells and stones, and precious skins and feathers.

Tula was a commercial hub, a political capital, and a ceremonial center. While its layout differed from Teotihuacán's, many features revealed borrowings from other Mesoamerican peoples. Temples consisted of giant pyramids topped by colossal stone soldiers, and ball courts where subjects and conquered peoples alike played their ritual sport were found everywhere. The architecture and monumental art reflected the mixed and migratory origins of the Toltecs: a combination of Maya and Teotihuacáno influences. At its height, the Toltec capital teemed with 60,000 people, a huge metropolis by contemporary European standards (if small by Song and Abbasid Islamic standards).

THE CAHOKIANS IN NORTH AMERICA As in South America (Chan Chan of the Chimú) and Mesoamerica (Tula of the Toltecs), cities took shape at the hubs of trading networks all across North America. The largest was **Cahokia**, along the Mississippi River near modern-day East St. Louis, Illinois. A city of about 15,000, it approximated the size of London at the time. Farmers and hunters settled in the region around 600 CE, attracted by its rich soil, its woodlands for fuel and game, and its access to the

Andean States. *Left: This photo shows what remains of Chan Chan. The city covered 15 square miles and was divided into neighborhoods for nobles, artisans, and commoners, with the elites living closest to the hub of governmental and spiritual power. Right: The buildings of Tiahuanaco were made of giant, hand-hewn stones assembled without mortar. Engineers had not discovered the principle of curved arches and keystones and instead relied on massive slabs atop gateways. Gateways were important symbolic features, for they were places where people acknowledged the importance of sun and moon gods.*

trading artery of the Mississippi. Eventually, fields of maize and other crops fanned out toward the horizon. The hoe replaced the trusty digging stick, and satellite towns erected granaries to hold the increased yields.

Now Cahokia became a commercial center for regional and long-distance trade. The hinterlands produced staples for Cahokia's urban consumers, and in return Cahokia's crafts rode inland on the backs of porters and to distant markets in canoes. The city's woven fabrics and ceramics were especially desirable. In exchange, traders brought mica from the Appalachian Mountains, seashells and sharks' teeth from the Gulf of Mexico, and copper from the upper Great Lakes. Cahokia became more than an importer and exporter: it was the exchange hub for an entire regional network trading in salt, tools, pottery, woven stuffs, jewelry, and ceremonial goods.

Dominating Cahokia's urban landscape were enormous mounds (thus the Cahokians' nickname, "mound people"). These earthen monuments reveal a sophisticated design and careful maintenance: their builders applied layers of sand and clay to prevent the foundations from drying and cracking. It was from these artificial hills that the people paid homage to spiritual forces. Building this kind of infrastructure without draft animals, hydraulic tools, or even wheels was labor-intensive, so

the Cahokians recruited neighboring people to help. A palisade around the city protected the metropolis from marauders.

Ultimately, Cahokia's success led to its downfall. As woodlands fell to the axe and arable soil lost nutrients, timber and food became scarce. In contrast to the sturdy dhows of the Arabian Sea and the bulky junks of the China Sea, Cahokia's river canoes could carry only limited cargoes. Cahokia's commercial networks met their limits. When the creeks that fed its water

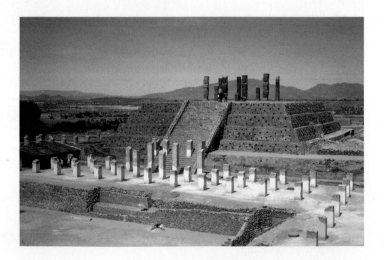

Toltec Temple. *Tula, the capital of the Toltec Empire, carried on the Mesoamerican tradition of locating ceremonial architecture at the center of the city. The Pyramid of the Morning Star cast its shadow over all other buildings. And above them stood columns of the Atlantes, carved Toltec god-warriors, the figurative pillars of the empire itself. The walls of this pyramid were likely embellished with images of snakes and skulls. The north face of the pyramid has the image of a snake devouring a human.*

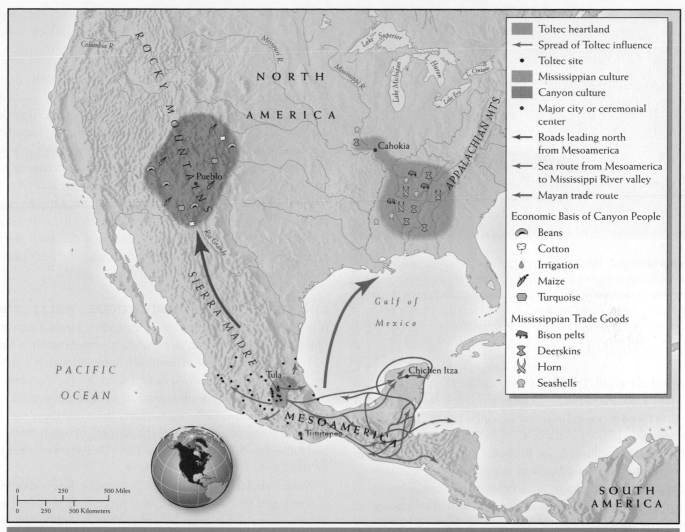

MAP 10.11 | Commercial Hubs in Mesoamerica and North America, 1000 CE

Both Cahokia and Tula were commercial hubs of vibrant regional trade networks.

- Where are Cahokia and Tula on the map?
- According to the map, what kinds of goods circulated through these cities?
- How much political influence on the surrounding region do you think each city had?

system could not keep up with demand, engineers changed their course, but to no avail. By 1350, the city was practically empty. Nevertheless, Cahokia was a remarkable center of exchange while it lasted. It represented the growing networks of trade and migration and the ability of North Americans to organize vibrant commercial societies.

Two forces contributed to a growing integration in sub-Saharan Africa and the Americas—trade and urbanization. The commodities differed: salt, gold, and slaves in as well as out of sub-Saharan Africa; and pottery, shells, textiles, and metals in the Americas. The new urban areas were Jenne, Timbuktu, and Great Zimbabwe in sub-Saharan Africa and Chan Chan,

Tula, and Cahokia in the Americas. But while Sub-Saharan Africa experienced contact with the North African, European, and Asian worlds, the Americas had to wait until the sixteenth century to be drawn into this larger community of peoples.

THE MONGOL TRANSFORMATION OF AFRO-EURASIA

The world's sea-lanes grew crowded with ships; ports buzzed with activity. Commercial networks were clearly one way to integrate the world. But just as long-distance trade connected people, so could conquerors—as we have seen throughout the

Cahokia Mounds. *This is all that is left of what was once a large city organized around temple mounds in what today is Illinois. The largest of the temples, known as Monks Mound, was likely a burial site, with four separate terraces for crowds to gather. Centuries of neglect and erosion have taken their toll on what was once the largest human-made earthen mound in North America.*

history of the world. Transformative conquerors now came from the Inner Eurasian steppes, the same place that centuries earlier had unleashed horse-riding warriors such as the Xiongnu (see Chapters 6 and 7).

Like the Xiongnu and the Kushans before them, the Mongols not only conquered but also intensified trade and cultural exchange. By consolidating a latticework of states (known as khanates) across northern and central Asia, they created an empire that straddled east and west. (See Map 10.12.) It was unstable and not as durable as other dynasties. It did not even have a shared faith; the mother of the conquering emperors Hulagu and Kubilai Khan was a devout Christian, reflecting Nestorian missionaries' (see Chapter 8) centuries-long efforts to convert the nomads. Many Europeans prayed that the entire empire would convert. But it did not; the Mongols were a religious patchwork of Afro-Eurasian belief systems. Yet they brought far-flung parts of the world together as they conquered territories much larger than their own.

Who Were the Mongols?

The Mongols were a combination of forest and prairie peoples, dwelling in Inner China in a region that today is known as Mongolia. Residing in circular, felt-covered tents, which they shared with some of their animals, they lived by hunting and livestock herding. They changed campgrounds with the seasons. Life on the steppes was such a constant struggle that only the strong survived. Their food, primarily animal products, provided high levels of protein, which built up their muscle mass and their

strength. Always on the march, their society resembled a perpetual standing army with bands of well-disciplined military units led by commanders chosen for their skill.

MILITARY SKILLS Mongol archers were uniquely skilled. Wielding heavy recurved compound bows made of sinew, wood, and horns, they were deadly accurate at over 200 yards—even at full gallop. Their small but sturdy horses, capable of withstanding extreme cold, bore saddles with high supports in front and back, enabling the warriors to maneuver at high speeds. With their feet secure in iron stirrups, the archers could rise in their saddles to aim their arrows without stopping. These expert horsemen often remained in the saddle all day and night, even sleeping while their horses continued on. Each warrior kept many horses, replacing tired mounts with fresh ones so that the armies could cover up to 70 miles per day.

KINSHIP NETWORKS AND SOCIAL ROLES Mongol tribes solidified their conquests by extending kinship networks, building an empire out of an expanding confederation of familial tribes. The tents, or households, were interrelated mostly by marriage: they were alliances sealed by the exchange of daughters. Conquering men married conquered women, and conquered men were selected to marry the conquerors' women. Chinggis Khan (the founder of the Mongol dynasty) may have had more than 500 wives, most of them daughters of tribes that he conquered or that allied with him.

Women in Mongol society were responsible for child-rearing, shearing and milking livestock, and processing pelts for clothing. But they also took part in battles. The niece of Kubilai Khan (the first official Mongol ruler of China), Khutulun, became famous for besting men in wrestling matches and claiming their horses as spoils. Although women were often bought and sold, Mongol wives had the right to own property and to divorce. Elite women even played important political roles. Consider Sorghaghtani Beki, Kubilai Khan's mother, who helped to engineer her sons' rule. Illiterate herself, she made sure that each son acquired a second language to aid in administering conquered lands. She gathered Confucian scholars to prepare Kubilai Khan to rule China. Chabi, Kubilai's senior wife, followed a similar pattern, offering patronage to Tibetan monks who set about converting the Mongol elite in China to Tibetan Buddhism.

Conquest and Empire

The Mongols' need for grazing lands contributed to their desire to conquer the splendors of distant fertile belts and rich cities. As they acquired new lands, they increasingly craved control of richer agricultural and urban areas nearby to increase their wealth and power through tribute. The Mongols depended on

Mongol Warriors. *This miniature painting is one of the illustrations for* History *by Rashid al Din, the most outstanding scholar under the Mongol regimes. Note the relatively small horses and strong bows used by the Mongol soldiers.*

settled peoples for grain and manufactured goods—including iron for tools, wagons, weapons, bridles, and stirrups—and their first expansionist forays followed caravan routes.

The expansionist thrust began in 1206 under a united cluster of tribes. A gathering of clan heads acclaimed one of those present as Chinggis (Genghis) Khan, or Supreme Ruler. Chinggis (c. 1155–1227) launched a series of conquests southward across the Great Wall of China and westward to Afghanistan, Persia, and Russia and created a series of interconnected imperial states. The Mongols even invaded Korea (Koryo) in 1231. The armies of Chinggis's son reached both the Pacific Ocean and the Adriatic Sea. His grandsons founded dynasties in China, in Persia, and on the southern Eurasian steppes. One of them, Kubilai Khan, enlisted thousands of Koryo men and ships for ill-fated invasions of Japan. Thus, a realm took shape that touched all four of Afro-Eurasia's main worlds.

Mongol raiders ultimately built a permanent empire, incorporating conquered peoples and some of their ways and also at the same time absorbing the learning and institutions of these settled societies. Their feat of unification was far more surprising and sudden than the ties developed incrementally by traders and travelers on ships. Now, Afro-Eurasian regions were connected by land and by sea in historically unparalleled ways.

MONGOLS IN CHINA In the east, Mongol forces under Chinggis Khan entered northern China at the beginning of the thirteenth century, defeating the Jin army, which was no match for the Mongols' superior cavalry, on the North China plain. But below the Yangzi River, where the climate and weather changed, the Mongol horsemen fell ill from diseases such as malaria, and their horses perished from the heat. To conquer the semitropical south, the Mongols took to boats and fought along rivers and canals. Kubilai Khan (1215–1294) seized the grandest prize of all—southern China—after 1260. His cavalry penetrated the higher plateaus of southwest China and then attacked South China's economic heartland from the west. The Southern Song army fell before his warriors brandishing the latest gunpowder-based weapons (which the Mongols had borrowed from Chinese inventors only to be used against them).

Hangzhou, the last Song capital, succumbed in 1276. Rather than see the invaders pillage the city and their emperors' tombs, the Southern Song bowed to the inevitable. Kubilai Khan's most able commander, Bayan, led his crack Mongol forces in seizing town after town, ever closer to the capital. The empress dowager tried to buy them off, proposing substantial tribute payments, but Bayan kept his eye on the prize: Hangzhou, which fell under Mongol control but survived reasonably intact. Bayan escorted the emperor and the empress dowager to Dadu (present-day Beijing), where Kubilai treated them with honor. Within three years, Song China's defeat was complete. With all of South China in their grip, the Mongols established the Yuan dynasty with a new capital at Dadu, "Great Capital."

Although it fell to Mongol control, Hangzhou was still one of the greatest cities in the world when it was visited by the Venetian traveler Marco Polo in the 1280s and by the Muslim traveler Ibn Battuta in the 1340s. Both men agreed that neither Europe nor the Islamic world had anything like it. (See Current Trends in World History: The Travels of Marco Polo and Ibn Battuta.)

BALTIC SEA

POLAND

Leignitz

Moscow

RUSSIAN
PRINCIPALITIES

Kiev

UKRAINE

Buda Pest

KHANATE OF THE GOLDEN HORDE

URAL MOUNTAINS

New Sarai

Old Sarai

Lake Balkas

ARAL
SEA

ADRIATIC SEA

BLACK SEA

CAUCASUS MTS.

CASPIAN SEA

Constantinople

BYZANTINE
EMPIRE

Tabriz

KHANATE OF TI

Samarkand

Aleppo

Damascus

MEDITERRANEAN SEA

Baghdad

Jerusalem

IL-KHANATE

PERSIA

Balkh

HINDU KUSH MTS.

Herat

AFGHANISTAN

HIMALAY

RED
SEA

ARABIA

SULTANATE
OF DELHI

INDIAN   OCEAN

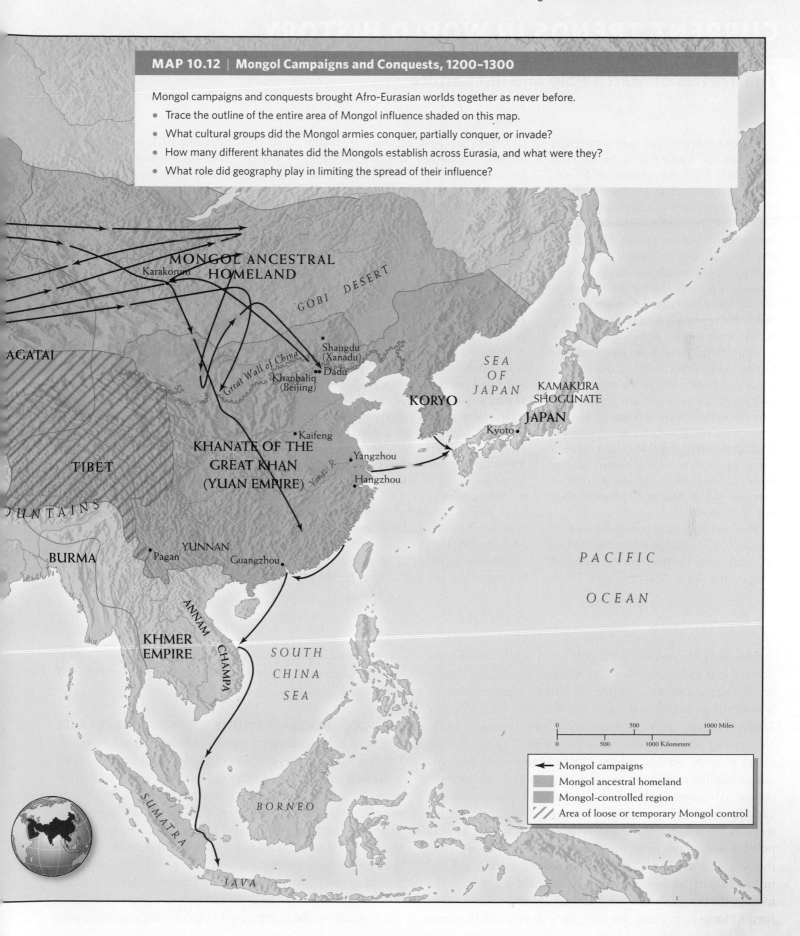

MAP 10.12 | Mongol Campaigns and Conquests, 1200–1300

Mongol campaigns and conquests brought Afro-Eurasian worlds together as never before.

• Trace the outline of the entire area of Mongol influence shaded on this map.

• What cultural groups did the Mongol armies conquer, partially conquer, or invade?

• How many different khanates did the Mongols establish across Eurasia, and what were they?

• What role did geography play in limiting the spread of their influence?

Mongol campaigns
Mongol ancestral homeland
Mongol-controlled region
Area of loose or temporary Mongol control

The Travels of Marco Polo and Ibn Battuta

Travelers are one of the most important resources for world historians because they create firsthand accounts of foreign rulers, their societies, and their cultures through their diaries, letters, and books. Recall from the start of the chapter our two Turkish Christian monks, Bar Sāwmā and Markōs, whom Kubilai Khan sent to learn more about the Muslims and Europeans prior to the Mongol invasions across the Afro-Eurasian landmass. At nearly the same time they were setting out on their travels, Marco Polo, one of the most famous European travelers, was setting out to visit China and the Mongol emperor, creating one of the most widely read travel narratives in world history. It also helped motivate the search for the most direct route to China and Southeast Asia. Only fifty years later, Ibn Battuta would travel most of the known Islamic world, leaving an invaluable portrait of much of North Africa, Southwest Asia, and South Asia.

Polo and Battuta encountered a world linked by trade routes that often had as their ultimate destination the imperial court of the Great Khan in China. These two men, as well as less celebrated travelers, observed worlds that were highly localized and yet culturally unified.

In 1271, Marco Polo (1254–1324), the son of an enterprising Venetian merchant, set out with his father and uncle on a journey to East Asia. Making their way along the fabled Silk Road across central Asia, after a three-and-a-half-year journey the Polos arrived in Xanadu, the summer capital of the Mongol Empire. There they remained for more than two decades. When they returned to Venice in 1295, fellow townsmen greeted them with astonishment, believing that the Polos had perished years before. So, too, Marco Polo's published account of his travels generated an incredulous reaction. Some of his European readers considered his tales of eastern wonders to be mere fantasy; yet others found their appetites for Asian splendor whetted by his descriptions.

A half-century after Polo began his travels, the Moroccan-born scholar Muhammad ibn Abdullah ibn Battuta (1304–1369) embarked on a journey of his own. Then just twenty-one, he vowed to visit the whole of the Islamic world without traveling the same road twice. It was an ambitious goal, for Islam's domain extended from one end of the Afro-Eurasian landmass to the other and far into Africa as well. On his journey, Ibn Battuta eventually covered some 75,000 miles. Along his way, he claimed to have met at least sixty rulers, and in his book he recorded the names of more than 2,000 persons whom he knew personally.

The writings of Marco Polo and Ibn Battuta provide a wealth of information on the well-traversed lands of Africa, Europe, and Asia. What they and other travelers observed was the extreme diversity of Afro-Eurasian peoples, reflecting numerous ethnicities, political formations, and religious faiths. In addition, they observed that the vast majority of people lived deeply localized lives, primarily seeking to obtain the basic necessities of everyday life. Yet, they were also aware that the same societies welcomed trade and cultural exchange. In fact, they wrote most eloquently about how each of the four major cultural systems of the landmass—Christian, Muslim, Indian, and

---

The Mongol conquest both north and south changed the political and social landscape. But Mongol rule did not impose rough steppe-land ways on the "civilized" urbanite Chinese. Non-Chinese outsiders—a mixed and varied group of Mongols, Tanguts, Khitan, Jurchen, Muslims, Tibetans, Persians, Turks, Nestorians, Jews, Armenians—took political control. Like earlier nomadic pastoral groups who had conquered China and established their authority over the Han Chinese, the Mongols embraced Chinese cultural and political institutions within China proper while retaining their own political and cultural ways in the original homeland. The result was a dual set of political institutions in China proper and Mongolia, such that the Mongols allowed Chinese elites considerable autonomy in local affairs while employing non-Mongol subordinates to manage the central dynastic political system and to collect taxes for the Mongols. In China, the Mongols' rule employed the same dynastic and bureaucratic institutions that previous Chinese dynasties had used, but in their steppe lands they maintained their nomadic pastoral ways.

MONGOL REVERBERATIONS IN SOUTHEAST ASIA
Southeast Asia also felt the whiplash of Kubilai Khan's conquest. Circling Song defenses in southern China, the Mongols galloped southwest and conquered states in Yunnan and in Burma. From there, in the 1270s, the armies headed directly back east into the soft underbelly of the Song state. In this sweep, portions of mainland Southeast Asia became annexed to China for the first time. Even the distant Khmer regime felt repercussions when the Mongol fleet, which grew out of the conquered Song navy, passed by on its way to attack Java (unsuccessfully) in 1293. Kubilai Khan amalgamated the conquered Chinese fleets with the remnants of the Korya navy to push his expansionism onto

Chinese—struggled to define itself. Interestingly, if Ibn Battuta and Marco Polo had been able to travel in the "unknown" worlds—the African hinterlands, the Americas, and Oceania—they would have witnessed to varying degrees similar phenomena and challenges.

QUESTIONS FOR ANALYSIS

- To what extent were travelers like Marco Polo and Ibn Battuta connecting new worlds as opposed to following routes that had already been established by others?
- What were the different incentives that impelled Marco Polo and Ibn Battuta to undertake their journeys of exploration? And what might that tell us about how and why greatly divergent worlds contact each other?
- Why were the Polos and Ibn Battuta able to undertake very long-range journeys? What enables travelers like these to function and to strengthen connections across the globe?

Marco Polo. *This medieval painting shows the caravan of Marco Polo's father and uncle crossing Asia.*

Explore Further

Battuta. *The Travels of Ibn Battuta,* translated by H. A. R. Gibb (2002).

Polo, Marco. *The Travels of Marco Polo,* edited by Manuel Komroff, translated by William Marsden (1926).

the high seas. He also used improved navigation technology to enable his ships to sail into deep waters; yet his invasions of Japan from Korea failed in 1274 and 1281. The ill-fated Javanese expedition was his last.

MONGOLS IN THE ISLAMIC WORLD In the thirteenth century, Mongol tribesmen streamed out of the steppes, crossing the whole of Asia and entering the eastern parts of Europe. Möngke Khan, a grandson of Chinggis, made clear the Mongol aspiration for world domination: he appointed his brother Kubilai to rule over China, Tibet, and the northern parts of India; and he commanded another brother, Hulagu, to conquer Iran, Syria, Egypt, Byzantium, and Armenia.

When Hulagu reached Baghdad in 1258, he encountered a feeble foe and a city that was a shadow of its former glorious self. Merely 10,000 horsemen faced his army of 200,000 soldiers, who were eager to acquire the booty of a wealthy city. Even before the battle had taken place, Baghdadi poets were composing elegies for their dead and mourning the defeat of Islam.

The slaughter was vast. Hulagu himself boasted of taking the lives of at least 200,000 people. The Mongols pursued their adversaries everywhere. They hunted them in wells, latrines, and sewers and followed them into the upper floors of buildings, killing them on rooftops until, as an Iraqi historian observed, "blood poured from the gutters into the streets. . . . The same happened in the mosques" (Lewis, pp. 82–83). In a few weeks of sheer terror, the venerable Abbasid caliphate was demolished. Hulagu's forces showed no mercy to the caliph himself, who was rolled up in a carpet and trampled to death by horses, his blood soaked up by the rug so it would leave no mark on the ground. With Baghdad crushed, the Mongol armies pushed on to Syria, slaughtering Muslims along the way.

The world experienced considerable human population growth during the first millennium of the Common Era in spite of occasional downturns, such as in Asia and Europe between 200 CE and 600 CE that were the result of climate change, movement of peoples, and the decline of the Roman and Han Empires. Overall, however, an upward trajectory occurred, though it averaged out to a mere 0.06 percent per year. For the period from 1750 to 1950, that percentage increased to a little more than 0.5 percent per year, and since 1950, the number has risen to 1.75 percent per year. Even so, as we will see in the next chapter, the major populations in the Afro-Eurasian landmass were terrified by the loss of life that accompanied the spread of the Black Death across this immense area. Since the Afro-Eurasian recovery from the Black Death, the world's population has been on a steady increase, spectacularly so in the twentieth century, the result of more abundant food supplies, more accurate knowledge of the spread of diseases and a resulting control of epidemic diseases, and a general rise in the standards of living.

QUESTIONS FOR ANALYSIS

- Why was the rate of population growth so limited in premodern times?
- Comparing the population size of the regions in 1340, what do the numbers tell us about where the largest share of wealth and power resided? How does this compare with earlier eras in the chart?
- Why was the population of the Americas in 1340 so small considering its large territorial size?
- Why were the peoples living in the Afro-Eurasian landmass so vulnerable to epidemic diseases in the fourteenth century?
- How do changes in global population relate to the developments tracked in this chapter: a maritime revolution; a more integrally connected Africa; a thriving Abbasid caliphate; and an expanding Mongol Empire?

Regional Human Population (in millions)						
Year	Asia	Europe	Africa	Americas	Oceania	World
400 BCE	97	30	17	8	1	153
1 CE	172	41	26	12	1	252
200	160	55	30	11	1	257
600	136	31	24	16	1	208
1000	154	41	39	18	1	253
1200	260	64	48	26	2	400
1340	240	88	80	32	2	442

Source: Massimo Livi-Bacci, *A Concise History of World Population* (Malden, MA: Wiley-Blackwell, 2012), p. 25.

The Collapse of Mongol Rule

In the end, the Mongol Empire reached its outer limits. In the west, the Egyptian Mamluks stemmed the advancing Mongol armies and prevented Egypt from falling into their hands. In the east, the waters of the South China Sea and the Sea of Japan foiled Mongol expansion into Java and Japan. And in the northwest, Mongol armies moved through Ukraine and went to the border of Poland. Yet they proved better at conquering than governing. They struggled to rule their vast possessions in makeshift states. Bit by bit, they yielded control to local administrators and dynasts who governed as their surrogates. There was also chronic feuding among the Mongol dynasts themselves. In China and Persia, Mongol rule collapsed in the fourteenth century. Ultimately, the Mongols would meet a deadly adversary more brutal than they were—the plague of the fourteenth century (see Chapter 11).

Mongol conquest reshaped Afro-Eurasia's social landscape. Islam would never again have a unifying authority like the caliphate or a powerful center like Baghdad. China, too, was divided and changed, but in other ways. The Mongols introduced Persian, Islamic, and Byzantine influences on China's architecture, art, science, and medicine. The Yuan policy of benign tolerance also brought elements from Christianity, Judaism, Zoroastrianism, and Islam into the Chinese mix. The Mongol thrust led to a great opening, as fine goods, traders, and technology flowed from China to the rest of the world in ensuing centuries. Finally, the Mongol conquests, somewhat like those of Alexander the Great in an earlier age (see Chapter 5), encouraged an Afro-Eurasian interconnectedness, but on a scale that the huge landmass had not known before and would not experience again for hundreds of years. Out of conquest and warfare would come centuries of trade, migration, and increasing contact between Africa, Europe, and Asia.

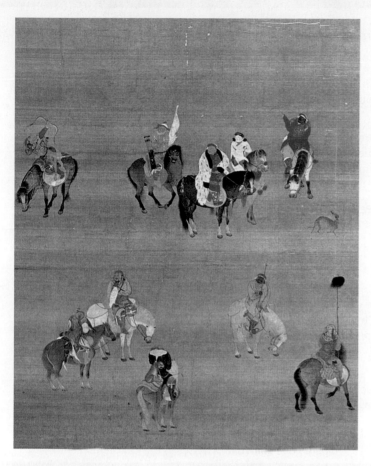

Mongols on Horseback. *Even after the Mongols became the rulers of China, the emperors remembered their steppe origin and maintained the skills of horse-riding nomads. This detail from a thirteenth/fourteenth-century silk painting shows Kubilai Khan hunting.*

CONCLUSION

Between 1000 and 1300 CE, Afro-Eurasia was forming large cultural spheres. As trade and migration spanned longer distances, these spheres prospered and became more integrated. In central Afro-Eurasia, Islam was firmly established, its merchants, scholars, and travelers acting as commercial and cultural intermediaries as they spread their universalizing faith. As seaborne trade expanded, India, too, became a commercial crossroads. Merchants in its port cities welcomed traders arriving from Arab lands to the west, from China, and from Southeast Asia. China also boomed, pouring its manufactures into trading

networks that reached throughout Eurasia and North Africa and even Sub-Saharan Africa. Christian Europe had two centers, both of which were at war with Islam. In the east, Byzantium was a formidable empire with a resplendent and unconquerable capital city, Constantinople, in many ways the pride of Christianity. In the west, the Catholic papacy had risen from the ashes of the Roman Empire and sought to extend its ecclesiastical authority over Rome's territories in western Europe.

Neither the Americas nor sub-Saharan Africa saw the same degree of integration, but trade and migration in these areas had profound effects. Certain African cultures flourished as they encountered the commercial energy of trade on the Indian Ocean. Africans' trade with one another linked coastal and interior regions in an ever more integrated world. American peoples also built cities that dominated cultural areas and thrived through trade. American cultures shared significant features: reliance on trade, maize, and the exchange of goods such as shells and precious feathers. And larger areas honored the same spiritual centers.

By 1300, trade, migration, and conflict were connecting Afro-Eurasian worlds in unprecedented ways. When Mongol armies swept into China, into Southeast Asia, and into the heart of Islam, they applied a thin coating of political integration to these widespread regions and built on existing trade links. At the same time, most people's lives remained quite local, driven by the need for subsistence and governed by spiritual and governmental representatives acting at the behest of distant authorities.

Still, locals noticed the evidence of cross-cultural exchanges everywhere—in the clothing styles of provincial elites, such as Chinese silks in Paris or Quetzal plumes in northern Mexico; in enticements to move (and forced removals) to new frontiers; in the news of faraway conquests or advancing armies. Worlds were coming together within themselves and across territorial boundaries, while remaining apart as they sought to maintain their own identity and traditions. In Afro-Eurasia especially, as the movement of goods and peoples shifted from ancient land routes to sea-lanes, these contacts were more frequent and far-reaching. Never before had the world seen so much activity connecting its parts. Nor within them had there been so much shared cultural similarity—linguistic, religious, legal, and military. By the time the Mongol Empire arose, the regions composing the globe were those that we now recognize as the cultural spheres of today's world.

After You Read This Chapter

Go to **INQUIZITIVE** to see what you know & learn what you've missed.

TRACING THE GLOBAL STORYLINES

FOCUS ON: *Foundational Cultural Spheres*

The Islamic World

- Islam undergoes a burst of expansion, prosperity, and cultural diversification but remains politically fractured.

- Arab merchants and Sufi mystics spread Islam over great distances and make it more appealing to other cultures, helping to transform Islam into a foundational world.

- Islam travels across the Sahara Desert; the powerful gold- and slave-supplying empire of Mali arises in West Africa.

China

- The Song dynasty reunites China after three centuries of fragmented rulership, reaching into the past to reestablish a sense of a "true" Chinese identity as the Han through a widespread print culture and denigration of outsiders.

- Agrarian success and advances in manufacturing—including the production of both iron and porcelain—fuel an expanding economy, complete with paper money.

India

- India remains a mosaic under the canopy of Hinduism despite cultural interconnections and increasing prosperity.

- The invasion of Turkish Muslims leads to the Delhi Sultanate, which rules over India for three centuries, strengthening cultural diversity and tolerance.

Christian Europe

- Catholicism becomes a "mass" faith and helps to create a common European cultural identity.

- Feudalism organizes the elite-peasant relationship, while manorialism forms the basis of the economy.

- Europe's growing confidence is manifest in the Crusades and the reconquering of Iberia, an effort to drive Islam out of Christian lands.

CHRONOLOGY

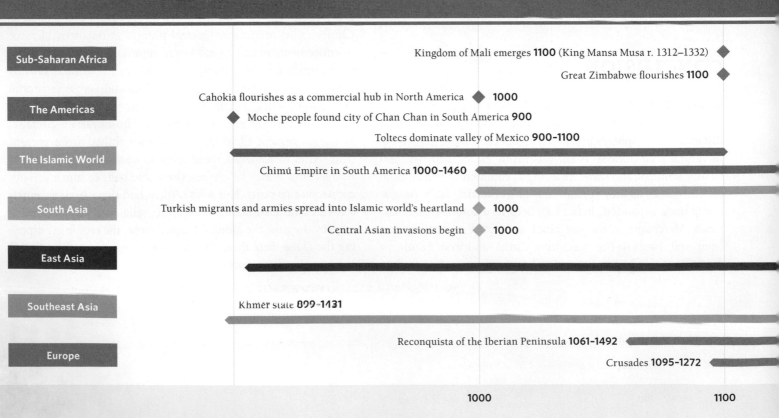

Sub-Saharan Africa

Kingdom of Mali emerges **1100** (King Mansa Musa r. 1312–1332)

Great Zimbabwe flourishes **1100**

The Americas

Cahokia flourishes as a commercial hub in North America **1000**

Moche people found city of Chan Chan in South America **900**

Toltecs dominate valley of Mexico **900–1100**

The Islamic World

Chimú Empire in South America **1000–1460**

South Asia

Turkish migrants and armies spread into Islamic world's heartland **1000**

Central Asian invasions begin **1000**

East Asia

Southeast Asia

Khmer state **899–1431**

Europe

Reconquista of the Iberian Peninsula **1061–1492**

Crusades **1095–1272**

1000　　　　　　　　　　　　　　　　　　　　　　　　　**1100**

KEY TERMS

STUDY QUESTIONS

1. **Explain** how specific technological advances, especially in ship design and navigation, facilitated the expansion of Afro-Eurasian trade. In what ways did global commercial hubs in Egypt, China, Melaka, and India reflect revolutions in maritime transportation and foster commercial contact regionwide?

2. **Analyze** the social and political forces that shaped the Islamic world, India, China, and Europe at this time. **Evaluate** the degree to which these forces integrated cultures and geographical areas.

3. **Identify** environmental and political forces that contributed to fragmentation within the Islamic world. **Describe** the cultural forces that enabled diverse Islamic communities to achieve a uniform regional identity.

4. **Discuss** the impact of Muslim Turkish invaders on India. To what extent did India remain distinct from the Islamic world in this era?

5. **Explain** how economic and manufacturing developments, coupled with political developments, cemented the power of the Song dynasty. How did Song interactions with nomads and neighbors lead to distinctive identities for both the Song and their neighbors?

6. **Compare and contrast** cultural and political developments in Korea, Japan, and Southeast Asia during this era. **Analyze** the influence of other regional cultures on these societies.

7. **Describe** how Christianity expanded its geographical reach during this era; **evaluate** the roles of manorialism and feudalism, universities, and the Crusades in contributing to Europe's identity as a fragmented yet distinctive cultural sphere.

8. **Identify** the areas of sub-Saharan Africa that were parts of the larger Afro-Eurasian world by 1300. **Explain** how contact with other regions shaped political and cultural developments in sub-Saharan Africa.

9. **Analyze** the extent to which American peoples established closer contact with each other. How extensive were these contacts compared with those in the Afro-Eurasian world? Compared with those in sub-Saharan Africa?

10. **Describe** the empire that the Mongols created in the thirteenth century. How did their policies promote greater contact among the various regions and peoples of Afro-Eurasia? **Contrast** the expansion of Hulagu into the west with that of Kubilai Khan into the east.

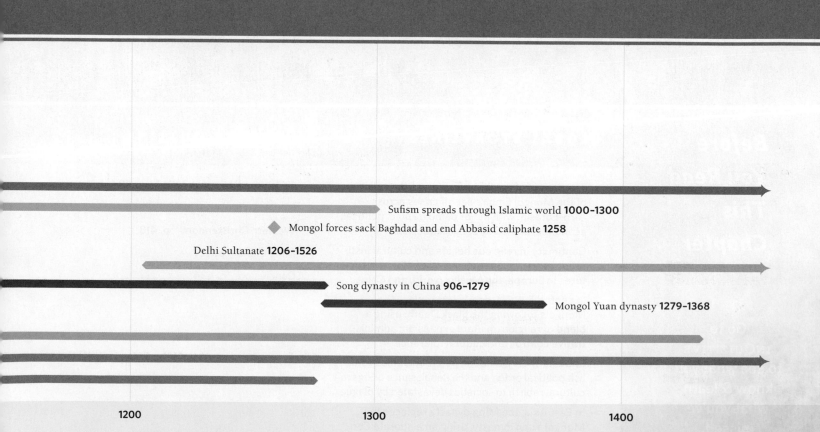

Sufism spreads through Islamic world **1000-1300**

Mongol forces sack Baghdad and end Abbasid caliphate **1258**

Delhi Sultanate **1206-1526**

Song dynasty in China **906-1279**

Mongol Yuan dynasty **1279-1368**

| 1200 | 1300 | 1400 |

Before You Read This Chapter

Go to **inQuizitive** to see what you know & learn what you've missed.

GLOBAL STORYLINES

- The spread of the Black Death and the collapse of the Mongol Empire set off crises across Afro-Eurasia, with major demographic, political, economic, and cultural consequences.
- Continuity in religious beliefs and cultural institutions accompanies changes in political structures in Europe, the Muslim world, and China.
- In central Eurasia, new rulers replace the Mongols following the Black Death, using a blend of religion, military expansion, administrative control, and cultural tolerance.
- In western Christendom, new monarchies establish political order, and the Renaissance brings a cultural rebirth to societies devastated by plague.
- In East Asia, the Ming dynasty replaces the Mongol Yuan dynasty, using an elaborate Confucian bureaucracy to oversee infrastructure and long-distance exchange.

11

Crises and Recovery in Afro-Eurasia, 1300–1500

FOCUS QUESTIONS

- What were the nature and origins of the crises that spanned Afro-Eurasia during the fourteenth century? How extensive were their effects, locally and transregionally?

- In what ways did religious belief systems maintain continuity from the fourteenth through the fifteenth centuries?

- How similar and different were the ways in which regional rulers in postplague Afro-Eurasia attempted to construct unified states? What were their greatest successes?

- How did the art and architecture of different regions reflect political realities, and what themes communicate these messages to viewers?

- In what different ways did the Iberian kingdoms, the Ottoman, Safavid, and Mughal Empires, the Ming dynasty, and European political systems extend their territory and regional influence?

When Mongol armies besieged the Genoese trading outpost of Caffa on the Black Sea in 1346, they not only damaged trading links between East Asia and the Mediterranean but also unleashed a devastating disease: the bubonic plague. Defeated Genoese merchants and soldiers withdrew, inadvertently taking the germs with them aboard their ships. By the time they arrived in Messina, Sicily, half the passengers were dead. The rest were dying. People waiting on shore for the ships' trade goods were horrified at the sight and turned the ships away. Desperately, the captains went to the next port, only to face the same fate. Despite these efforts at isolation, Europeans could not keep the plague (called the Black Death) from reaching their shores. As it spread from port to port, it eventually contaminated all of Europe, killing nearly two-thirds of the population.

This story illustrates the disruptive effects of the Mongol invasion from which the bubonic plague originated and the long-distance trade routes the Mongol Empire imposed on societies. The invasions left behind a series of khanates ruled by local warlords, rather than a centralized state. But they also ushered in an age of intensified cultural and political contact, and the channels of exchange—the land trails and sea-lanes of human voyagers—became accidental conduits for deadly microbes. These germs devastated societies far more decisively than did Mongol warfare. They were the real "murderous hordes" of world history, infecting people from every community, class, and culture. So staggering was the Black Death's toll that population densities did not recover for 200 years. Most severely affected were regions that the Mongols had brought together: settlements and commercial hubs along the old Silk Road and around the Mediterranean and South China Seas. While segments of the Indian Ocean trading world experienced death and disruption, South Asian societies, which had escaped the Mongol conquest, also escaped the great loss of life and political disruptions associated with the Black Death.

This chapter explores the ways in which Afro-Eurasian peoples restored what they thought was valuable from the old while discarding what they felt had failed them in favor of radically new institutions and ideas. The recovery had striking similarities across Afro-Eurasia. Societies reaffirmed their most deeply held and long-standing beliefs, though in a modified form. Chinese elites relied on Confucian tenets and dynastic institutions to revive their devastated communities. In the societies of India, Iran, and Turkey, new rulers turned to Islam for solace in peoples' suffering and hope for the future. Europeans also looked to their traditions. New monarchies, the forerunners of European nation-states, rose to provide leadership, while scholars looked to the Greek and Roman past for cultural and political inspiration.

Radically new political institutions and ideas appeared all across Afro-Eurasia in the aftermath of the Black Death. What historians have called the "Renaissance" captivated the European learned elite and sent its practitioners in search of the scholarship of the Greeks and Romans. They used this inspiration to produce a cultural flourishing in the arts, literature, architecture, and political and financial institutions. While recognizing the new mindsets that appeared in these centuries, this chapter also stresses continuity. Considering how grievously people suffered and how many had died, it is surprising that so much of the old—particularly religious beliefs and institutions—survived the aftermath of the Black Death. Rulers altered but did not transform inherited traditions. What was truly new and would prove enduring was a group of imperial dynasties that emerged all across Afro-Eurasia.

COLLAPSE AND CONSOLIDATION

Although the Mongol invasions overturned political systems, the plague devastated society itself. The pandemic killed millions, disrupted economies, and threw communities into chaos. Rulers could explain to their people the assaults of "barbarians," but it was much harder to make sense of an invisible enemy. Many concluded that mass death was God's wish and humankind's punishment. However, the upheaval gave ruling groups the opportunity to consolidate power by making dynastic matches through marriage, establishing new armies and taxes, and creating new systems to administer their states.

The Black Death

The spread of the **Black Death** was the fourteenth century's most significant historical development. (See Map 11.1.) Originating in Inner Asia, the disease stemmed from a combination of bubonic, pneumonic, and septicemic plague strains, and it caused a staggering loss of life. Among infected populations, death rates ranged from 25 to 65 percent.

How did the Black Death spread so far? One explanation may lie in climate changes. A cooler climate—what scholars refer to as the "Little Ice Age"—may have weakened populations and left them vulnerable to disease. In Europe, for instance, beginning around 1310, harsh winters and rainy summers shortened the growing season and ruined harvests. Here, exhausted soils no longer supplied the resources required by growing urban and rural populations, while nobles squeezed the peasantry in an effort to maintain their luxurious lifestyle. The ensuing European famine lasted from 1315 to 1322, during which time millions died of starvation or of diseases against which the malnourished population had little resistance. This climate change and famine was a factor in the Black Death that soon followed. Another climate-related factor in the spread of the plague occurred in East Asia: here, the drying up of the central Asian steppe borderlands, where bubonic plague had existed for centuries, forced rodents out of their usual dwelling places and pressed pastoral peoples, who carried the strains, to move closer to settled agricultural communities. So, it is thought, began the migration of microbes.

What spread the germs across Afro-Eurasia was the Mongols' trading network. The first outbreak in a heavily populated region occurred in the 1320s in southwestern China. From there, the disease spread through China and then took its death march along the major trade routes. The main avenue of transmission was across central Asia to the Crimea and the Black Sea and from there by ship to the Mediterranean Sea and the Italian city-states. Secondary routes were by sea: one from China to the Red Sea, and another across the Indian Ocean, through the Persian Gulf, and into the Fertile Crescent and Iraq. All routes terminated at the Italian port cities, where ships with dead and dying men aboard arrived in 1347. From there, what Europeans called the Pestilence or the Great Mortality engulfed the western end of the landmass.

The Black Death struck an expanding Afro-Eurasian population, made vulnerable because its members had no immunity to the disease and because its major realms were thoroughly dynasty (960–1279) and subsequent Mongol rule. But by 1300, hunger and scarcity began to spread as resources stretched thin. A weakened population was especially vulnerable to plague. For seventy years, the Black Death ravaged China and shattered the Mongols' claim to a mandate from heaven. In 1331, plague may have killed 90 percent of the population in Bei Zhili (modern Hebei) Province. From there it spread throughout other provinces, reaching Fujian and the coast at Shandong. By the 1350s, most of China's large cities suffered severe outbreaks.

The reign of the last Yuan Mongol rulers was a time of utter chaos. Even as the Black Death was engulfing large parts of China, bandit groups and dissident religious sects were undercutting the state's power. As in other realms devastated by the plague, popular religious movements foretold impending doom. Most prominent was the **Red Turban Movement**, which took its name from its soldiers' red headbands. This movement blended China's diverse cultural and religious traditions, including Buddhism, Daoism, and other faiths. Its leaders emphasized strict dietary restrictions, penance, and ceremonial rituals in which the sexes freely mixed, and made proclamations that the world was drawing to an end.

PLAGUE IN THE ISLAMIC WORLD The plague devastated parts of the Muslim world as well. The Black Death reached Baghdad by 1347, perhaps carried there by an Azerbaijani army that besieged the city. By the next year, the plague had overtaken Egypt, Syria, and Cyprus; one report from Tunis records the death of more than 1,000 people a day in that North African city. Animals, too, were afflicted. One Egyptian writer commented: "The country was not far from being ruined. . . . One found in the desert the bodies of savage animals with the bubos under their arms. It was the same with horses, camels, asses, and all the beasts in general, including birds, even the ostriches" (Dols, p. 156). In the eastern Mediterranean, the plague left much of the Islamic world in a state of near political and economic collapse. The great Arab historian Ibn Khaldun (1332–1406), who lost his mother and father and a number of his teachers to the Black Death in Tunis, underscored the sense of desolation: "Cities and buildings were laid waste, roads and way signs were obliterated, settlements and mansions became empty, dynasties and tribes grew weak," he wrote. "The entire world changed" (p. 67). (See Primary Source: Qalandar Dervishes in the Islamic World.)

Plague Victim. *The plague was highly contagious and after a series of grotesque symptoms quickly resulted in death. Here the physician and his helper cover their noses, most likely in attempt to block out the unbearable stench emanating from the patient's boils.*

connected through trading networks. Rodents, mainly rats, carried the plague bacilli that caused the disease. Fleas transmitted the bacilli from rodent to rodent, as well as to humans. The epidemic was terrifying, for its causes were unknown at the time. Infected victims died quickly—sometimes overnight—and in great agony, coughing up blood and oozing pus and blood from ugly black sores the size of eggs. Some European sages attributed the ravaging of their societies to an unusual alignment of Saturn, Jupiter, and Mars. Many believed that God was angry with humankind. One Florentine historian compared the plague to the biblical Flood and believed that the end of humankind was imminent. Everywhere in Afro-Eurasia peoples of all classes had no explanation for the dying and often acted in ways that would be considered reprehensible or outrageous in normal times.

PLAGUE IN CHINA China was ripe for the plague's pandemic. Its population had increased significantly under the Song

PLAGUE IN EUROPE In Europe, the Black Death first ravaged the Italian Peninsula; then it seized France, the Low Countries (present-day Netherlands, Belgium, and Luxembourg), the Holy Roman Empire, and Britain in its deathly grip. The overcrowded and unsanitary cities were particularly vulnerable. Bremen lost at least 8,000 souls, perhaps two-thirds of its population; Hamburg, another port city, at least as

SCANDINAVIA
•1349

NORTH SEA

BALTIC SEA

Novgorod

Moscow
MUSCOVY
•1351

Edinburgh
(1350)

Dublin
(1349)
BRITAIN

Oxford
(1348)

London
(1348)

Bremen
(1349)

Lübeck
(1349)
Danzig

Cologne
(1349)

Amiens
(1348)
Paris
(1348)
EUROPE

Cracow

Kiev

KHANATE OF THE
GOLDEN HORDE

Rostov
New Sarai

ARAL
SEA

Bordeaux
(1348)

Venice
(1347)

Buda
(1349)

CASPIAN
SEA

Avignon
(1347)

Genoa
(1347)
Florence
(1347)
Pisa
(1347)
Siena
(1347)

BLACK
SEA

Caffa
(1346)

Trebizond

Tabriz

Bukhara

Barcelona
(1348)

Marseille

Naples

Constantinople
(1347)

ANATOLIA

Maraghah

Silk route

Madrid

Palermo
(1347)

Messina
(1347)

Athens
(1347)

SYRIA
Aleppo
(1347)

PERSIA

IL-KHANAT

Lisbon
(1349)
SPAIN
•1348

Ceuta
Fez

Algiers
Tunis

CYPRUS

Damascus
(1347)

Baghdad
(1347)

Isfahan

Shiraz

Basra

MEDITERRANEAN   SEA

Tripoli
(1348)

Alexandria
(1347)

Jerusalem
(1347)

Hormuz

Persian Gulf

Marrakesh
(1349)

Cairo
(1347)
EGYPT

AFRICA

RED SEA

Medina

Mecca
(1348)

ARABIA

Aden
(1351)

ARABIA

Mogadishu

INDIA

ATLANTIC

OCEAN

◀	Progress of bubonic plague
—	Trade routes
•	Known areas of major outbreaks
*	Modern Chinese provincial names for regions affected by outbreak of plague

MAP 11.1 | The Spread of the Black Death

The Black Death was an Afro-Eurasian pandemic of the fourteenth century.

- What was the origin point of the Black Death?
- What were the main trade routes that allowed the Black Death to spread across Afro-Eurasia?
- Can you explain why certain parts of Afro-Eurasia were more severely affected than others?

many. The poor, sleeping in crowded quarters, were especially at risk. But master bakers, bankers, and aristocrats died too, unless they were able to flee to the relatively safer countryside in time to escape infection. No one had seen dying on such a scale. Nearly two-thirds of Europe's total population perished between 1346 and 1353.

After 1353, the epidemic subsided, having killed all those with no natural immunity and most of the original carriers of the disease, the European black rat. But the plague would return every seven years or so for the rest of the century, as well as sporadically through the entire fifteenth century, killing the young and those who had managed to escape exposure in the first epidemic. The European population continued to decline, until by 1450 many areas had only one-quarter the number of a century earlier. Indeed, it took three centuries to return to population levels that existed prior to the Black Death.

Disaster on this scale had enduring psychological, social, economic, and political effects. Many individuals turned to pleasure, even debauchery, determined to enjoy themselves before it came their turn to die. Some blamed Jews for unleashing the plague, even though Jews died in numbers equal to those of Christians. Others, believing the church had lost God's favor, sought consolidation in more individualized forms of piety, such as extreme fasting or worshipping in private chapels. The Flagellants were so sure that humanity had incurred God's wrath that they whipped themselves to atone for human sin. They also bullied communities that they visited, demanding to be housed, clothed, and fed. Characteristic of the period was a new intensity of private piety, exhibited by figures such as Catherine of Siena, who was widely admired for punishing her body to purify her soul.

The Black Death wrought devastation throughout Afro-Eurasia. The Chinese population plunged from 115 million in 1200 to 75 million or less in 1400, the result of the Mongol invasions of the thirteenth century and the disease and disorder of the fourteenth. (See Analyzing Global Developments: Population Changes in Fourteenth-Century Afro-Eurasia.) Over the course of the fourteenth century, Europe's population shrank by more than 50 percent. In the most densely settled Islamic territory—Egypt—a population that had totaled around 6 million in 1400 was cut in half.

When farmers fell ill or died with the plague, food production collapsed. Famines ensued and killed off survivors. Worse afflicted were the coastal cities, especially coastal ports. Some cities lost up to two-thirds of their populations. Refugees from urban areas fled their homes, seeking security and food in the countryside. The shortages of food led to rapidly rising prices, hoarding, work stoppages, and unrest. Political leaders added to their unpopularity by repressing the unrest. Everywhere regimes collapsed. The Mongol Empire, which had held so much of Eurasia together commercially and politically, collapsed. Thus, the way was prepared for experiments in state building, religious beliefs, and cultural achievements.

Rebuilding States

Starting in the late fourteenth century, Afro-Eurasians began the task of reconstructing both their political order and their trading networks. (By then the plague had subsided, though it continued to afflict peoples for centuries.) The rebuilding of military and civil administrations—no easy task—also required political legitimacy. Rulers needed to revive confidence in themselves and their political systems, which they did by fostering beliefs and rituals that confirmed their legitimacy and by increasing their control over subjects.

The form that power took in most places was a political institution well known to Afro-Eurasians for centuries: the **dynasty**, the hereditary ruling family that passed control from one generation to the next. Dynasties sought to establish their legitimacy in three ways. First, ruling families insisted that their power derived from a divine calling: Ming emperors in China claimed for themselves what previous dynasts had asserted—the "mandate of heaven"—while European monarchs claimed to rule by "divine right." From their base in Anatolia, Ottoman warrior-princes asserted that they now carried the banner of Islam. In these ways, ruling households affirmed that God or the heavens intended for them to hold power. The new Safavid regime on the Iranian plateau embraced a Shiite form of governance. Second, leaders squelched squabbling among potential heirs by establishing clear rules about succession to the throne. Many European states tried to standardize succession by passing titles to the eldest male heir, but in practice there were countless complications and quarrels. In the Islamic world, successors could be designated by the incumbent or elected by the community; here, too, struggles over succession were frequent. Third, ruling families elevated their power through conquest or alliance—by ordering armies to forcibly extend their domains or by marrying their royal offspring to rulers of other states or members of other elite households. Once it established legitimacy, the typical royal family would consolidate power by enacting coercive laws and punishments and sending emissaries to govern far-flung territories. It would also establish standing armies and new administrative structures to collect taxes and to oversee building projects that proclaimed royal power.

As we will see in the remainder of this chapter, the innovative state building that occurred in the wake of the plague's devastation would not have been as successful had it not drawn on older traditions. In Europe, a cultural flourishing based largely on ancient Greek and Roman models gave rise to thinkers who proposed novel views of governance. The peoples of the Islamic world held fiercely to their religion as two successor states—the

ANALYZING GLOBAL DEVELOPMENTS

Population Changes in Fourteenth-Century Afro-Eurasia

Famine, warfare, and disease led to vast population declines all across Afro-Eurasia in the fourteenth century. The Mongols were instrumental players in spreading disease across the landmass, starting in China and moving westward along land- and sea-based trading routes toward the Mediterranean World and ultimately northern Europe. (See Map 11.1.) While the effects of these destructive forces were felt across the Afro-Eurasian landmass, some states and regions were less affected than others. The population data in the table come from the best historical studies of the last forty years and are based on painstaking archival research. They serve as one of the best ways for us to gain historical insight into this tumultuous century.

QUESTIONS FOR ANALYSIS

- In what regions or cities does population loss seem to have been lower? Higher? What might account for those variations in the death rate?

- How do the losses in urban areas compare with the losses in the region where those urban areas are located? What might that comparison suggest about the impact of fourteenth-century disasters on urban versus other populations?

- Why do you think the population decline was more severe and widespread in Europe than in Asia?

- In what ways was the great loss of population in Europe and China a turning point in their histories?

Location	Earlier Population Figures	Later Population Figures	Percent Change
By Region			
Europe	80 m[a] in 1346	30 m in 1353	−60%
Asia	230 m in 1300	235 m in 1400	+2%
Islam	(regional data are not available)		
By Country			
Spain	6 m in 1346	2.5 m in 1353	−60%
Italy	10 m in 1346	4.5 m in 1363	−55%
France	18 m in 1346	7.2 m in 1353	−60%
England	6 m in 1346	2.25 m in 1353	−62.5%
China	115 m in 1200	75 m in 1400	−35%
Japan	9.75 m in 1300	12.5 m in 1400	+28%
Korea	3 m in 1300	3.5 m in 1400	+17%
India	91 m in 1300	97 m in 1400	+6.5%
By City			
London	100,000 in 1346	37,000 in 1353	−62.5%
Florence	92,000 in 1346	37,250 in 1353	−59.5%
Siena	50,000 in 1346	20,000 in 1353	−60%
Bologna	50,000 in 1346	27,500 in 1353	−45%
Cairo	500,000 in 1300	300,000 in 1400	−40%
Damascus	80,000 in 1300	50,000 in 1400	−37%

[a]m = millions

Sources: Ole J. Benedictow, *The Black Death, 1346–1353: The Complete History* (2004); Michael Dols, *The Black Death in the Middle East* (1974); Colin McEvedy and Richard Jones, *Atlas of World Population History* (1978). Ping-ti Ho, *Studies on the Population of China, 1368–1953* (1959).

Ottoman Empire and the Safavid state—absorbed numerous Turkish-speaking groups. A third Islamic state—the Mughal Empire—drew on local traditions of religious and cultural tolerance as its rulers built a new regime on the foundations of the weakened Delhi Sultanate (see Chapter 10). The Ming, having failed in their attempts to control northern Vietnam and Korea, renounced the expansionist Mongol legacy and emphasized a return to Han rulership, consolidating control of Chinese lands and concentrating on internal markets rather than overseas trade. Many of these regimes lasted for centuries, promoting political institutions and cultural values that became deeply embedded in the fabric of their societies.

ISLAMIC DYNASTIES

The devastation of the Black Death followed hard on the heels of the Mongol destruction of Islam's most important city, Baghdad (see Chapter 10), and eliminated Islam's old political order. Nonetheless, these two catastrophes prepared the way for new Islamic states to emerge. Although the Arabic-speaking peoples remained vital, still at the heart of Islam geographically, they now had to cede authority to Persian and Turkish political leaders. Persians and Turks had embraced Islam and had made their cultural, intellectual, and military influence felt well before the Mongol invasions and the Black Death. Now they became

PRIMARY SOURCE

Qalandar Dervishes in the Islamic World

The Qalandar dervish order sprang up in Damascus, Syria, and Egypt in the thirteenth century and spread rapidly throughout the Islamic world. In reaction to the period's widespread unrest, its members renounced the world and engaged in highly individualistic practices as they moved from place to place. The educated elite, however, criticized them as ignorant hypocrites living on alms obtained from gullible common folk. One of their practices was chiromancy, or palm reading. In this excerpt, Giovan Antonio Manavino, a European observer of Ottoman society, gives an obviously biased account of the Qalandars, whom he called the torlaks.

Dressed in sheepskins, the *torlaks* [Qalandars] are otherwise naked, with no headgear. Their scalps are always clean-shaven and well rubbed with oil as a precaution against the cold. They burn their temples with an old rag so that their faces will not be damaged by sweat. Illiterate and unable to do anything manly, they live like beasts, surviving on alms only. For this reason, they are to be found around taverns and public kitchens in cities. If, while roaming the countryside, they come across a well-dressed person, they try to make him one of their own, stripping him naked. Like Gypsies in Europe, they practice chiromancy, especially for women who then provide them with bread, eggs, cheese, and other foods in return for their services.

Amongst them there is usually an old man whom they revere and worship like God. When they enter a town, they gather around the best house of the town and listen in great humility to the words of this old man, who, after a spell of ecstasy, foretells the descent of a great evil upon the town. His disciples then implore him to fend off the disaster through his good services. The old man accepts the plea of his followers, though not without an initial show of reluctance, and prays to God, asking him to spare the town the imminent danger awaiting it. This time-honored trick earns them considerable sums of alms from ignorant and credulous people.

QUESTIONS FOR ANALYSIS

- Describe the way the Qalandar dervishes dressed, where they congregated, and how they obtained food. How did their lifestyle reflect the turmoil of the times?
- Why do you think the Qalandars chose individualistic practices rather than communal living?
- Why do you think Manavino is so critical of the Qalandars?

Source: Ahmet I. Karamustafa, "Dervish Groups in the Ottoman Empire, 1450–1550," from *God's Unruly Friends: Dervish Groups in the Islamic Later Middle Period, 1200–1550* (Salt Lake City: University of Utah Press, 1994), pp. 6–7.

Islam's most effective rulers. The world that they dominated occupied a vast geographical triangle. It stretched from Anatolia in the west to Khurasan in the east and to the southern apex at Baghdad.

The Ottomans, the Safavids, and the Mughals emerged as the dominant states in the Islamic world in the early sixteenth century. They exploited the rich agrarian resources of the Indian Ocean regions and the Mediterranean Sea basin, and they benefited from a brisk seaborne and overland trade. By the mid-sixteenth century, the Mughals controlled the northern Indus River valley; the Safavids occupied Persia; and the Ottomans ruled Anatolia, the Arab world, and much of southern and eastern Europe.

Despite sharing core Islamic beliefs, each empire had unique political features. The most powerful, the **Ottoman Empire**, occupied the pivotal area between Europe and Asia. The Ottomans embraced a Sunni view of Islam, while adopting traditional Byzantine ways of governance and trying new ways of integrating the diverse peoples of their expanding territories. The Safavids, though adherents of the Shiite vision of Islam, were at the same time ardently devoted to the pre-Islamic traditions of Persia (present-day Iran). Unlike the Ottomans, their rulers were not so effective at expanding beyond their Persian base. The Mughals ruled over the wealthy but divided realm that is much of today's India, Pakistan, and Bangladesh; here they carried even further the region's religious and political traditions of assimilating Islamic and pre-Islamic Indian ways. Their wealth and the decentralization of their domain made the Mughals constant targets for internal dissent and eventually for external aggression.

The Ottoman Empire

The rise of the Ottoman Empire owed as much to innovative administrative techniques and religious tolerance as to military strength. Although the Mongols considered Anatolia to be a borderland region of little economic importance, their military forays against the Anatolian Seljuk Turkish state in the late thirteenth century brought political turmoil bordering on chaos, but opened up the region to new political forces. The ultimate victors here were the Ottoman Turks. They transformed themselves from warrior bands roaming the borderlands between Islamic and Christian worlds into rulers of a settled state and, finally, into sovereigns of a far-flung, highly bureaucratic empire. (See Map 11.2.)

Many modern Western-trained historians have portrayed the early Ottoman state as a plundering regime, engaged in rape and slaughter and carrying out campaigns of massive devastation by galvanizing their zealous warriors to terrorize local populations. They did indeed have stern and disciplined warriors, known as *ghazis*, whose commitment to Islam and their leaders was boundless. Even so, what enabled the Ottoman leaders to triumph in a region of widespread disorder was their ability to form alliances with previously hostile divergent ethnic and religious communities. Their first chief, Osman (r. 1299–1326), and his son Orhan (r. 1326–1362) were Sunni Muslims but proved skilled at working with those who held different religious beliefs, such as Byzantine leaders, Kurds, Sufi dervish orders, and Shiites. By constructing eclectic political institutions possessing enormous elasticity, they succeeded in offering not merely toleration to diverse populations but opportunities to exercise power and gain wealth. Theirs was a hybrid state, which welcomed Christian supporters as fervently as Muslims. Hence, they prevailed over other Turkic competitors and transformed their small principality in northwestern Anatolia during the fourteenth century into the preeminent state in Anatolia. The principal characteristics of the early Ottoman state were inclusivity, resilience, and syncretism. Their takeover of the city of Bursa in 1404 marked an ascendancy in Anatolia that now threatened the very existence of the once powerful, now greatly weakened Byzantine Empire. Other Turkic warrior bands, which like the Ottomans lived off the land and fought for booty under charismatic military leaders, ultimately failed in their quest for power because they had little regard for other groups such as artisans, merchants, bureaucrats, and clerics, whose support was essential in the Ottoman rise.

THE CONQUEST OF CONSTANTINOPLE The empire's spectacular territorial expansion into Europe and eventually the Arab world was at heart a military affair. To recruit followers, the Ottomans promised wealth and glory to new subjects. This was an expensive undertaking, but territorial expansion generated financial and administrative rewards. Moreover, by spreading the spoils of conquest and lucrative administrative positions, rulers bought off potentially discontented subordinates. Still, without military might, the Ottomans would not have enjoyed the successes associated with the brilliant reigns of Murad II (r. 1421–1451) and his aptly named successor, Mehmed the Conqueror (r. 1451–1481).

Mehmed's most stunning triumph was the conquest of Constantinople, an ambition for Muslim rulers ever since the birth of Islam. Mehmed left no doubt that this was his primary goal. Indeed, shortly after his coronation, he vowed to capture the capital of the Byzantine Empire, a city of immense strategic and commercial importance. He exclaimed early in his reign that Constantinople was "an island in the midst of an Ottoman ocean." His desire to take the city "never left his tongue" (Faroqhi, p. 23). Mehmed knew this feat would require a large and well-armed fighting force, for the heavily fortified city had kept Muslims at bay for almost a century. First he built a fortress of his own, on the European bank of the Bosporus Strait,

The Fall of Constantinople. *The use of heavy artillery in the fifty-three-day siege of Constantinople was instrumental to the Ottoman victory. At the center of this Turkish miniature is one such cannon, possibly of Hungarian origin, which required hundreds of men and oxen to transport and secure outside the city walls.*

MAP 11.2 | The Ottoman Empire, 1300–1566

This map charts the expansion of the Ottoman state from the time of its founder, Osman, through the reign of Suleiman, the empire's most illustrious ruler.

- Identify the earliest part of the empire under Osman. Then identify all the areas of conquest under Suleiman. Against whom did the Ottomans fight between the years 1326 and 1566?
- What were the geographical limits of the empire?
- According to your reading, how did Ottoman rulers promote unity among such a diverse population?

to prevent European vessels from reaching the capital. Then, by promising his soldiers free access to booty and portraying the city's conquest as a holy cause, he amassed a huge army that outnumbered the defending force of 7,000 by more than tenfold. For forty days his troops bombarded Constantinople's massive walls with artillery that included enormous cannons built by Hungarian and Italian engineers. On May 29, 1453, Ottoman troops overwhelmed the surviving soldiers and took the ancient Roman and Christian capital of Byzantium—which Mehmed promptly renamed Istanbul.

Although Christians generally portrayed the "fall" of Constantinople as an insult and a disaster, in fact the Muslim conquest had cultural benefits for western Europe. Many Christian survivors

fled to ports in the west, bringing with them classical and Arabic manuscripts previously unknown in Europe. The well-educated, Greek-speaking émigrés generally became teachers and translators, thereby helping to revive Europeans' interest in classical antiquity and spreading knowledge of ancient Greek (which had virtually died out in medieval times). These manuscripts and teachers would play a vital role in Europe's Renaissance.

THE TOOLS OF EMPIRE BUILDING Mehmed made Istanbul the Ottoman capital, adopting Byzantine administrative practices to unify his enlarged state and incorporating many of Byzantium's powerful families into it. From Istanbul, Mehmed and his successors would continue their expansion, eventually seizing all of Greece and the Balkan region. As a result, Ottoman navies increasingly controlled sea-lanes in the eastern Mediterranean, curtailing European access to the rich ports that handled the lucrative caravan trade. By the late fifteenth century, Ottoman forces menaced another of Christendom's great capitals, Vienna, and European merchants feared that never again would they obtain the riches of Asia via the traditional overland route.

Having penetrated the heartland of Christian Byzantium, under Selim (r. 1512–1520) and Suleiman (r. 1520–1566), the Ottomans turned their expansionist designs to the Arab world. During the latter's reign, the Ottomans reached the height of their territorial expansion, with Suleiman himself leading thirteen major military campaigns and many minor engagements. An exceptional military leader, Suleiman was an equally gifted administrator. His subjects called him "the Lawgiver" and "the Magnificent" in recognition of his attention to civil bureaucratic efficiency and justice for his people. His fame spread to Europe, where he was known as "the Great Turk." Under Suleiman's administration, the Ottoman state ruled over 20 to 30 million

people. By the time Suleiman died, the Ottoman Empire bridged Europe and the Arab world. Istanbul by then was a dynamic imperial hub, dispatching bureaucrats and military men to oversee a vast domain.

Ottoman dynastic power was, however, not only military; it also rested on a firm religious foundation. The sultans combined a warrior ethos with an unwavering devotion to Islam. Describing themselves as the "shadow of God" on earth, they claimed to be caretakers for the welfare of the Islamic faith and assumed the role of protectors of the holy cities on the Arabian Peninsula and in Jerusalem after the conquests in the Arab world. They devoted substantial resources to the construction of elaborate mosques and to the support of Islamic schools throughout the empire and to extend the borders of Islam. Thus, the Islamic faith helped to unite a diverse and sprawling imperial populace, with the sultan's power fusing the sacred and the secular.

ISTANBUL AND THE TOPKAPI PALACE Istanbul reflected the splendor of this awesome empire. After the Ottoman

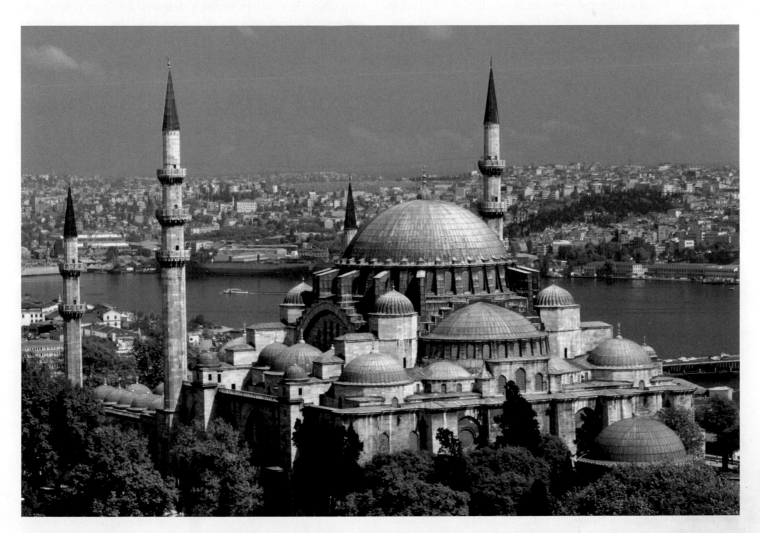

The Suleymaniye Mosque. *Built by Sultan Suleiman to crown his achievements, the Suleymaniye Mosque was designed by the architect Sinan to dominate the city. Four tall minarets called the faithful to prayer.*

conquest, the sultans' engineers rebuilt the city's crumbling walls, while their architects redesigned homes, public buildings, baths, inns, and marketplaces to display the majesty of Islam's new imperial center. To crown his achievements, Suleiman ordered the construction of the Suleymaniye Mosque, which sat opposite the Hagia Sophia. The latter, a domed Byzantine cathedral, was formerly the most sacred of Christian cathedrals, the largest house of worship in all of Christendom, but Suleiman had it turned into a mosque. Moreover, the Ottoman dynasts welcomed (indeed, forcibly transported) thousands of Muslims and non-Muslims to the city and revived Istanbul as a major trading center. Within twenty-five years of its conquest, its population more than tripled; by the end of the sixteenth century, 400,000 people regularly swarmed through its streets and knelt in its mosques, making it the world's largest city outside China.

Istanbul's **Topkapi Palace** reflected the Ottomans' view of governance, the sultans' emphasis on religion, and the continuing influence of Ottoman familial traditions—even in the administration of a far-flung empire. Laid out by Mehmed II, the palace complex reflected a vision of Istanbul as the center of the world. As a way to exalt the sultan's magnificent power, architects designed the complex so that the buildings containing the imperial household nestled behind layers of outer courtyards in a mosaic of mosques, courts, and special dwellings for the sultan's harem.

The growing importance of Topkapi Palace as the command post of the empire represented a crucial transition in the history of Ottoman rulers. Not only was the palace the place where future bureaucrats received their training; it was also the place where the chief bureaucrat, the grand vizier, carried out the day-to-day running of the empire. Whereas the early sultans had led their soldiers into battle personally and had met face-to-face with their kinsmen, the later rulers withdrew into the sanctity of the palace, venturing out only occasionally for grand ceremonies. Still, every Friday, subjects queued up outside the palace to introduce their petitions, ask for favors, and seek justice. If they were lucky, the sultans would be there to greet them—but they did so behind grated glass, issuing their decisions by tapping on the window. The palace thus projected a sense of majestic, distant wonder, a home fit for commanders of the faithful.

And Topkapi was indeed a home for the increasingly sedentary sultan and his harem. Among his most cherished quarters were those set aside for women. At first, women's influence in the Ottoman polity was slight. But as the realm consolidated, women became a powerful political force. The harem, like the rest of Ottoman society, had its own hierarchy of rank and prestige. At the bottom were slave women; at the top were the sultan's mother and his favorite consorts. As many as 10,000 to 12,000 women inhabited the palace, often in cramped quarters. Those who had the ruler's ear conspired to have him favor their own children, which made for widespread intrigue. When a sultan died, the entire retinue of women would be sent to a distant palace poignantly called the Palace of Tears, because the women who occupied it wept at the loss of the sultan and their own banishment from power.

DIVERSITY AND CONTROL The fact that the Ottoman Empire endured into the twentieth century owed much to the ruling elite's ability to gain the support and employ the talents of exceedingly diverse populations. After all, neither conquest nor conversion eliminated cultural differences in the empire's distant provinces. Thus, for example, the Ottomans' language policy was one of flexibility and tolerance. Although Ottoman

The Topkapi Palace. *A view of the inner courtyard of the seraglio, where the sultan and his harem lived.*

Turkish was the official language of administration, Arabic was the primary language of the Arab provinces, the common tongue of street life. Within the empire's European corner, the sounds and cadences of various languages continued to prevail. From the fifteenth century onward, the Ottoman Empire was more multilingual than any of its rivals.

In politics, as in language, the Ottomans showed flexibility and tolerance. The imperial bureaucracy permitted extensive regional and religious autonomy. In fact, Ottoman military cadres perfected a technique for absorbing newly conquered territories into the empire by parceling them out as revenue-producing units among loyal followers and kin. Regional appointees could collect local taxes, part of which they earmarked for Istanbul and part of which they pocketed for themselves. (This was a common administrative device for many world dynasties ruling extensive domains.)

Like other empires, the Ottoman state was always in danger of losing control over its provincial rulers. Local rulers—the group that the imperial center allowed to rule locally—found that great distances enabled them to operate independently from central authority. These local authorities kept larger amounts of tax revenues than Istanbul deemed proper. So, to clip local autonomy, the Ottomans established a corps of infantry soldiers and bureaucrats (called janissaries) who owed direct allegiance to the sultan. The system at its high point involved a conscription of Christian youths from the empire's European lands. This conscription, called the **devshirme**, required each village to hand over a certain number of males between the ages of eight and eighteen. Uprooted from their families and villages, selected for their fine physiques and good looks, these young men were converted to Islam and sent to farms to build up their bodies and learn Turkish. A select few were moved on to Topkapi Palace to learn Ottoman military, religious, and administrative techniques. Some of these men—such as the architect Sinan, who designed the Suleymaniye Mosque—later enjoyed exceptional careers in the arts and sciences. Recipients of the best education available in the Islamic world, trained in Ottoman ways, instructed in the use of modern weaponry, and shorn of all family connections, the *devshirme* recruits were prepared to serve the sultan (and the empire as a whole) rather than the interests of any particular locality or ethnic group.

Thus, the Ottomans established their legitimacy via military skills, religious backing, and a loyal bureaucracy. They artfully balanced the decentralizing tendencies of the outlying regions with the centralizing forces of the imperial capital. Relying on a careful mixture of faith, patronage, and tolerance, the sultans curried loyalty and secured political stability. Indeed, so strong and stable was the political system that the Ottoman Empire dominated the coveted and highly contested crossroads between Europe and Asia for many centuries.

The *Devshirme*. *A miniature painting from 1558 depicts the* devshirme *system of taking non-Muslim children from their families in the Balkan Peninsula as a human tribute in place of cash taxes, which the poor region could not pay. The children were educated in Ottoman Muslim ways and prepared for service in the sultan's civil and military bureaucracy.*

The Safavid Empire in Iran

The Ottoman dynasts were not the only rulers to extend Islam's political domain. In Persia, too, a new empire arose in the aftermath of the Mongols. The legitimacy of the Safavid Empire, like that of the Ottoman, rested on an Islamic foundation. But the Shiism espoused by Safavid rulers was quite different from the Sunni faith of the Ottomans, and these contrasting religious visions shaped distinct political systems.

In the western part of central Asia, the khanate of Chagatai, one of four governments created by the Mongols (see again Map 11.1), slipped into decline at the end of the thirteenth century. With no power dominating the area, the region fell into disorder, with warrior chieftains squabbling for preeminence. Adding to the volatility were various populist Islamic movements, some of which urged followers to withdraw from society or to parade around without clothing. Among the more prominent movements was a Sufi brotherhood led by Safi al-Din (1252–1334), which gained the backing of religious adherents and Turkish-speaking warrior bands. However, his successors, known as Safaviyeh or Safavids, embraced Shiism.

A RELIGIOUS SHIITE STATE The Safavid aspirants to power had their origins among Turkic Sufi groups in eastern Anatolia and Azerbaijan. The Ottoman takeover of most of Anatolia turned these regions into conflict zones between the Ottomans and the Safavids, but Ottoman power also forced the communities living there to find a new location. This they did in the Iranian plateau, rallying support from tribal groups in badly devastated parts of Persia and promising good governance. Forsaking their Sufi origins in this new land, they also steeped themselves in the separatist sacred tradition of Shiism. As a result, of the three great Islamic empires, the Safavid state became the most single-mindedly religious, persecuting those who did not follow its Shiite form of Islam. The most dynamic of Safi al-Din's successors, Ismail (r. 1501–1524), required that the call to prayer announce that there is no God but Allah, that Muhammad is His prophet, and that Ali is the successor of Muhammad. Rejecting his advisers' counsel to tolerate the Sunni creed of the majority of the city's population, Ismail made Shiism the official state religion. He offered the people a choice between conversion to Shiism or death, exclaiming at the moment of conquest that "with God's help, if the people utter one word of protest, I will draw the sword and leave not one of them alive" (Savory, p. 29). In 1502, Ismail proclaimed himself the first shah of the Safavid Empire. (*Shah* is the Persian word for king or leader, a title that many other cultures adopted as well.) Under Ismail and his successors, the Safavid shahs restored Persian sovereignty over the entire region traditionally regarded as the homeland of Persian speakers. (See Map 11.3.)

In the hands of the Safavids, Islam assumed an extreme and often militant form. The Safavids revived the traditional Persian idea that rulers were ordained by God, believing the shahs to be divinely chosen. Some Shiites even went so far as to affirm that there was no God but the shah. Moreover, Persian Shiism fostered an activist clergy who (in contrast to Sunni clerics) saw themselves as political and religious enforcers against any heretical authority. They compelled Safavid leaders to rule with a sacred purpose. Because the Safavids did not tolerate diversity, unlike the Ottomans, they never had as expansive an empire. Whatever territories they conquered, the Safavids ruled much more directly, based on central—and theocratic—authority. They also succeeded in transforming Iran, once a Sunni area, into a Shiite stronghold, a change that has endured down to the present.

MAP 11.3 | The Safavid Empire, 1500–1722

The Safavid Empire rose to prominence alongside the Ottoman state.

- Locate the area where it originated. With which empire did the Safavids fight the most battles?
- Why were most of the battles limited to the regions of Azerbaijan, Kurdistan, and Mesopotamia?
- What were the geographical and political limits on the growth of the Safavid Empire?

The Delhi Sultanate and the Early Mughal Empire

A quarter century after the Safavids seized power in Persia, another Islamic dynasty, the Mughals, emerged in South Asia. Like the Ottomans and Safavids, the Mughals created a regime destined to last for many centuries. But unlike those other empires, the Mughals did not replace a Mongol regime. Instead, they erected their state on the foundations of the old Delhi Sultanate, which had come into existence in 1206. Although spared the devastating effects of the Mongols and the Black Death, nonetheless the peoples of India had to deal with an invading nomadic force every bit as destructive as the Mongols: the warriors of Timur, or Tamerlane. His military forays crushed the Delhi Sultanate

Raid on Delhi. *Timur's swift raid on Delhi in 1398 was notable for the death and destruction it caused. This sixteenth-century miniature captures the plunder and violence.*

and opened the way for a new, even more powerful regime. (See Chapter 10 for more on the Delhi Sultanate.)

RIVALRIES, RELIGIOUS REVIVAL, AND THE FIRST MUGHAL EMPEROR A wave of religious revival followed in the wake of Timur's conquests. Bengal broke away from Delhi and soon embraced a Sufi form of mystical Islam, emphasizing personal union with God. Here, too, a special form of Hinduism, called Bhakti Hinduism, put down deep roots. Its devotees preached the doctrine of divine love. In the Punjab, previously a core area of the Delhi Sultanate, a new religion known as Sikhism came into being. Sikhism largely followed the teachings of Nanak (1469–1539). Although born a Hindu, he was inspired by Islamic ideals and called on his followers to renounce the caste system and to treat all believers as equal before God. (See Primary Source: Nanak's Teachings in India.)

Following Timur's attack, rival kingdoms and sultanates asserted their independence. The Delhi Sultanate became a mere shadow of its former self, just one of several competing powers in northern India. Out of this political chaos emerged a Turkish prince, Babur (the "Tiger"), invited in 1526 by the governor of the Punjab to restore order. A great-grandson of Timur, Babur traced his lineage to both the Turks and the Mongols (he was said to be a descendant of Chinggis Khan). For years, Babur had longed to conquer India. Massing an army of Turks and Afghans armed with matchlock cannons, he easily breached the wall of elephants put together by defenders of the sultan. Delhi fell, and the Delhi Sultanate came to an end. Babur proclaimed himself emperor and spent the next few years snuffing out the remaining resistance to his rule. (See Map 11.4.) Thus, he laid the foundation of the Mughal Empire, the third great Islamic dynasty (discussed in detail in Chapter 12).

By the sixteenth century, then, the Islamic heartland had seen the emergence of three new empires. Their differences were obvious, especially in the religious sphere. The Ottomans were Sunni Islam's most fervent champions, determined to eradicate the Shiite heresy on their border, where an equally determined Persian Safavid dynasty sought to expand the realm of Shiism. In contrast to these dynasties' sectarian religious commitments, the Mughals of India, drawing on well-established Indian traditions of religious and cultural tolerance, were open-minded toward non-Muslim believers and sectarian groups within the Muslim community. Yet, the political similarities of these imperial dynasties were equally clear-cut. Although these states did not hesitate to go to war against each other, they shared similar styles of rule. All established their legitimacy via military prowess, religious backing, and a loyal bureaucracy. This combination of spiritual and military weaponry enabled emperors, espousing Muhammad's preachings, to claim vast domains. Moreover, their religious differences did not prevent the movement of

Nanak's Teachings in India

Nanak (1469–1539), generally recognized as the founder of Sikhism, lived in northern India and participated in the religious discussions that were prominent at the time. As in western Europe and Islamic Southwest Asia, this was a period of political turmoil and intense personal introspection. The following excerpts demonstrate Nanak's views on the failings of the age and his use of Islamic and Hindu ideas to elaborate a unique spiritual perspective. Nanak stressed the unity of God, an emphasis that reflected Islamic influences. Nonetheless, his insistence on the comparative unimportance of prophets ran counter to Islam, and his belief in rebirth was strictly Hindu.

There is but one God, whose name is true, the Creator, devoid of fear and enmity, immortal, unborn, self-existent; God the great and bountiful. Repeat His Name.

Numberless are the fools appallingly blind;
Numberless are the thieves and devourers of others' property;
Numberless are those who establish their sovereignty by force;
Numberless the cutthroats and murderers;
Numberless the liars who roam about lying;
Numberless the filthy who enjoy filthy gain;
Numberless the slandered who carry loads of calumny on their heads;
Nanak thus described the degraded.
So lowly am I, I cannot even once be a sacrifice unto Thee. Whatever pleaseth Thee is good.
O Formless One, Thou art ever secure.

The Hindus have forgotten God, and are going the wrong way.

They worship according to the instruction of Narad.
They are blind and dumb, the blindest of the blind.
The ignorant fools take stones and worship them.
O Hindus, how shall the stone which itself sinketh carry you across?

What power hath caste? It is the reality that is tested.
Poison may be held in the hand, but man dieth if he eat it.
The sovereignty of the True One is known in every age. He who obeyeth God's order shall become a noble in His court.

Those who have meditated on God as the truest of the true have done real worship and are contented;
They have refrained from evil, done good deeds, and practiced honesty;

They have lived on a little corn and water, and burst the entanglements of the world.
Thou art the great Bestower; ever Thou givest gifts which increase a quarterfold.
Those who have magnified the great God have found Him.

QUESTIONS FOR ANALYSIS

• Identify all the "numberless" groups that Nanak lists. What range of social classes do they represent? How does this enumeration reflect the tumultuous times?
• What criticisms of Hindu worship does Nanak raise?
• What lines reveal his belief in rebirth?
• How does Nanak expect true believers to behave?

Source: "Nanak's Teachings in India." In William Theodore de Bary, *Sources of Indian Tradition* (New York: Columbia University Press, 1958), pp. 536–38.

goods, ideas, merchants, and scholars across political and religious boundaries—even across the most divisive boundary of all, that between Sunni Iraq and Shiite Persia.

WESTERN CHRISTENDOM

No region suffered more from the Black Death than western Christendom, and no region made a more spectacular comeback. From 1100 to 1300, Europe had enjoyed a surge in population, economic growth, and significant technological and intellectual progress, only to see these achievements halted in the fourteenth century by famine and the Black Death. Europeans responded by creating new political and cultural forms. New dynasties arose, and a cultural flourishing called the Renaissance revived Europe's connections with its Greek and Roman past and produced masterpieces in art, architecture, and other forms of thought.

Reactions and Revolts

The Black Death brought with it social and economic disorder that challenged the political order. The massive death toll and

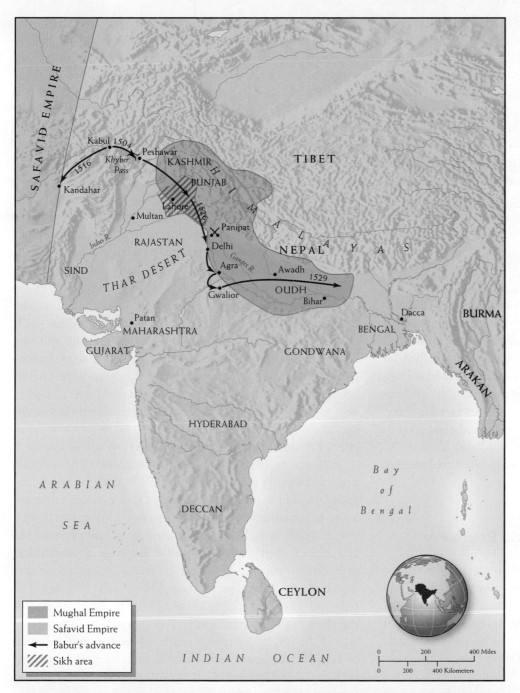

MAP 11.4 | The Mughal Empire, 1530

Compare the Mughal state with the other major Asian empires of this period, notably the Ottoman, Safavid, and Ming states (see Maps 11.2, 11.3, and 11.6).

- What geographical characteristic distinguished the Mughal state at this time from the others?
- Where in the landmass did the new state arise, and what effect do you think its place of origin had on the nature of Mughal rule?
- Based on its geographical location, to what religious traditions did the Mughals need to be sensitive?

the suddenness with which the disease struck also prompted survivors to ask questions about the major institution uniting Christendom, the Catholic Church. Even before the plague arrived, the late medieval western Church had found itself divided at the top (at one point there were three popes) and challenged from below, both by individuals critical of the extravagant lifestyles of some clergymen and by increasing demands on the clergy and church administration. Now the Black Death raised questions about God's relationship to humankind and the Catholic Church's role as God's appointed mediator on earth: Could sinful mortals ever find mercy from a vengeful God, and could an already overstretched and self-interested Church lead them to salvation? Facing challenges to its right to define religious doctrine and practices, the Church responded by demanding strict obedience to the true faith. This entailed the persecution of heretics, Jews, Muslims, homosexuals, prostitutes, and "witches." But the Church also reacted to society's suffering during this period, expanding its charitable and bureaucratic functions, providing alms to the urban poor, and registering births, deaths, and economic transactions. Its responses reassured many that God—and the church—had not abandoned true Christians and shored up the power of religious authorities.

Persecution and administration, however, cost money. Indeed, the needs as well as the extravagances of the clergy spurred certain questionable money-making tactics. One was the selling of indulgences (certificates that reduced one's time in purgatory, where souls continued the repentance that would eventually make them fit for heaven). This sort of unconventional fund-raising, and the growing gap between the church's promises and its ability to bring Christianity into people's everyday lives, more than the persecutions, eventually sparked the Protestant Reformation (see Chapter 12).

At the same time, the high death toll of the fourteenth and fifteenth centuries emboldened those who survived to seek higher wages or reductions in their feudal obligations. When landlords resisted or kings tried to impose new taxes, there were uprisings, including a 1358 peasant revolt in France that was dubbed the Jacquerie (the term derived from "Jacques Bonhomme," a name that contemptuous masters used for all peasants). Armed with only knives and staves, the peasantry went on a rampage, killing hated nobles and clergy and burning and looting all the property they could get their hands on. At issue was the peasants' insistence that they should no longer be tied to their land or have to pay for the tools they used in farming.

A better-organized uprising took place in England in 1381. Although the English Peasants' Revolt began as a protest against a tax levied to raise money for a war on France, it was also fueled by postplague labor shortages: serfs demanded the freedom to move about, and free farmworkers called for higher wages and lower rents. When landlords balked at these demands, aggrieved peasants assembled at the gates of London. The protesters demanded abolition of the feudal order, but the king ruthlessly suppressed them. Nonetheless, in both France and England, a free peasantry gradually emerged as labor shortages made it impossible to keep peasants bound to the soil.

State Building and Economic Recovery

Out of the chaos of famine, disease, and warfare, the diverse peoples of Europe found a political way forward. This path involved the formation of centralized monarchies, much as the Ottomans, Safavids, Mughals, and Ming were accomplishing in Asia. (A **monarchy** is a political system in which one individual holds supreme power and passes that power on to his or her next of kin.) Consolidation of these political systems occurred sometimes through strategic marriages but more often through warfare, both between local princely families and with local aristocratic allies and foreign mercenaries. Many of these dynasties fell as a result of civil war or conquest, but some, like the Tudors in England and the Valois in France, consolidated considerable power. In central Europe, one family, the Habsburgs, established a powerful and long-lasting dynasty. This family provided emperors for the Holy Roman Empire from 1440 to 1806. The Holy Roman Empire included territory that would later be divided into separate states such as the Netherlands, Germany, Austria, Belgium, and Croatia, and it also incorporated parts of present-day Italy, Poland, and Switzerland. Yet the Habsburg monarchs never succeeded in restoring an integrated empire to western Europe (as Chinese dynasts had done by claiming the mandate of heaven). Indeed, although hereditary monarchy was Europe's dominant form of governance, there were also a number of oligarchic republics in which a handful of wealthy and influential voters selected their leaders, a sprinkling of political systems ruled by archbishops or other clergymen, and many "free" towns, surrounded by walls and protective of their special privileges.

Those who sought to rule the emerging states faced numerous obstacles. For example, rival claimants to the throne financed private armies. Also, the clergy demanded and received privileges and often meddled in politics themselves. The church's huge landholdings and exemptions from taxation made it, too, a formidable economic powerhouse. Towns—many of which had the right to rule themselves—refused to submit to rulers' demands. And once the printing press became available in the 1460s, printers circulated anonymous pamphlets criticizing the court and the clergy. Some states had consultative bodies—such as the Estates General in France, the Cortes in Spain, and Parliament in England—in which princes formally asked representatives of their people for advice and, in the case of the English Parliament, for consent to new forms of taxation. Such bodies gave no voice to most nonaristocratic men and no representation to women. But they did allow the collective expression of grievances against high-handed policies.

If Europe in 1450 had no central government and no prospect of obtaining political unity, it also had no common language. In China, the written literary Chinese script remained a key administrative tool for the dynasts. And in the Islamic world, Arabic was the common language of faith, Persian the language of poetry, and Turkish the language of administration. But in Europe, Latin lost ground as rulers chose various regional dialects to be their official state language. For centuries afterward, Latin continued to be the language of the church and of scholarship. Poets, however, took advantage of the upgrading of vernacular languages such as Italian or English and composed sophisticated poetic masterpieces, such as Dante Alighieri's *The Divine Comedy* or, later, Edmund Spenser's *The Faerie Queen*.

Despite, or perhaps because of, Europe's political fragmentation, new economic initiatives began to take hold, as the English and Flemish competed to expand cloth production and German and Dutch merchants extended their trading networks in the North Sea. Economic recovery was swiftest in southern Europe, where trade with Southwest Asia enriched merchants and subsidized the flourishing of luxury industries, such as glass-making in Venice. Although they remained small compared with Asian cities such as Istanbul or Beijing, Europe's towns rebounded quickly from the Black Death, particularly in Italy, the Netherlands, and along the North Sea coast. (See Map 11.5.) New prosperity and the influx of Christian

Legend:
- English territories, 1420–1428
- Possessions of House of Burgundy, 1429–1453
- Holy Roman Empire
- ✳ Popular uprising
- ✕ Battle
- ← Campaigns of Henry V, 1415, 1421–1422
- ← Campaign of Joan of Arc, 1429
- Ottoman advance, 1453

MAP 11.5 | Europe, 1400–1500

Europe was a region divided by dynastic rivalries during the fifteenth century.

- Locate the most powerful regional dynasties on the map: Portugal, Castile, Aragon, France, England, and the Holy Roman Empire. Where did the heaviest fighting occur?

- Why do you think one state was the scene for so many battles?

- On the basis of this map, predict which European territories and political systems would become powerful in subsequent centuries and which would not.

exiles from Istanbul into Italian city-states such as Venice and Florence led to a cultural flowering known as the Renaissance (discussed shortly). In northern and western Europe, the process took longer. In England and France, in particular, internal feuding, regional warfare, and religious fragmentation delayed recovery for decades (see Chapter 12).

Political Consolidation and Trade in Portugal

Portugal's fortunes demonstrate how political stabilization and the emergence of a stronger state could be useful in the revival of trade. After the chaos of the fourteenth century, Spain,

England, and France followed the Portuguese example and established national monarchies. In Spain and Portugal, warfare against Muslims would help unite Christian territories, and Mediterranean trade would add valuable income to state coffers.

Through the fourteenth century, Portuguese Christians devoted themselves to fighting the Moors, who were Muslim occupants of North Africa, the western Sahara, and the Iberian Peninsula. Decisive in this struggle was the Portuguese decision to cross the Strait of Gibraltar and seize the Moorish Moroccan fortresses at Ceuta, in North Africa: their ships could now sail between the Mediterranean and the Atlantic without Muslim interference. With that threat diminished, the Portuguese perceived their neighbor, Castile (part of what is now Spain), as their chief foe. Under João I (r. 1385–1433) the Castilians were defeated, and the monarchy could seek new territories and trading opportunities in the North Atlantic and along the West African coasts. João's son Prince Henrique, known later as Henry the Navigator, further expanded the family's domain by supporting expeditions down the coast of Africa and offshore to the Atlantic islands of the Madeiras and the Azores. The west and central coasts of Africa and the islands of the North and South Atlantic, including the Cape Verde Islands, São Tomé, Principe, and Fernando Po, soon became Portuguese ports of call.

The Portuguese monarchs granted the Atlantic islands to nobles as hereditary possessions on condition that the grantees colonize them, and soon the colonizers were establishing lucrative sugar plantations. In gratitude, noble families and merchants threw their political weight behind the king. Subsequent monarchs continued to reduce local elites' authority and to ensure smooth succession for members of the royal family. This political consolidation enabled Portugal to thrive in the wake of the Black Death.

Dynasty Building and Reconquest in Spain

The road to dynasty in Spain was arduous. Medieval Spain comprised rival kingdoms that quarreled ceaselessly. Also, Spain lacked religious uniformity: Muslims, Jews, and Christians lived side by side in relative harmony, and Muslim armies still occupied strategic areas in the south. Over time, however, marriages and the formation of kinship ties among nobles and between royal lineages yielded a new political order. One by one, the major houses of the Spanish kingdoms intermarried, culminating in the fateful wedding of Isabella of Castile and Ferdinand of Aragon. Thus, Spain's two most important provinces were joined, and Spain became a state to be reckoned with.

THE UNION OF CASTILE AND ARAGON By the time Isabella and Ferdinand married in 1469, Spain was recovering from the miseries of the fourteenth century. This was more than a marriage of convenience. Castile was wealthy and populous; Aragon enjoyed an extended trading network in the Mediterranean. Together, the monarchs brought unruly nobles and distant towns under their domain. They topped off their achievements by marrying their children into other European royal families—especially the Habsburgs, central Europe's most powerful dynasty.

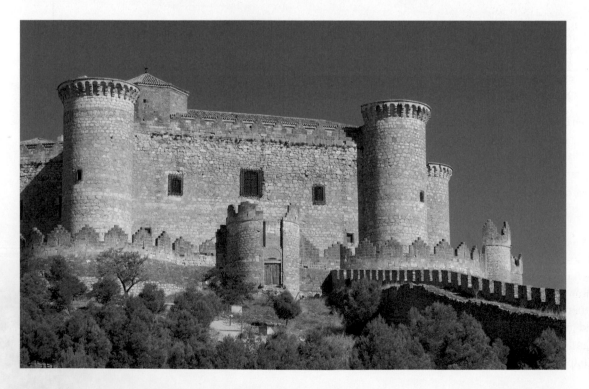

Renaissance Fortifications. *This image of Belmonte Castle in Castile, Spain, built by Don Juan de Pacheco in 1456, shows just how much money and material European nobles were willing to invest to protect their centers of power.*

The new rulers also sent Christian armies south to push Muslim forces out of the Iberian Peninsula. By the mid-fifteenth century, only Granada, a strategic lynchpin overlooking the straits between the Mediterranean and the Atlantic, remained in Muslim hands. After a long and costly siege, Christian forces captured the fortress there in January 1492. This was a victory of enormous symbolic importance, as joyous, to Christians, as the fall of Constantinople was depressing. Many people in Spain thumped their chests in pride, unaware or unconcerned that at the same time Ottoman armies were conquering large sections of southeastern Europe.

THE INQUISITION AND WESTWARD EXPLORATION
Just as the Safavid rulers had tried to stamp out all non-Shiite forms of Islam within their domains, so Isabella and Ferdinand sought to drive all non-Catholics out of Spain. Terrified by Ottoman incursions into Europe, in 1481 they launched the **Inquisition**, taking aim especially against *conversos*—converted Jews and Muslims—whom they suspected were Christians only in name. When Granada fell, the crown ordered the expulsion of all Jews from Spain; after 1499, a more tolerant attempt to convert the Moors by persuasion gave way to forced conversion—or emigration. This lack of tolerance meant that Spain, like other European states in this era, became increasingly homogenous. With fewer groups vying for influence within their territories, rulers turned their attention outward, fueling rivalries among the various European states.

Confident in the stability of their state, by late 1491 the Spanish monarchs were willing to listen to a Genoese navigator whose pleas for patronage they had previously rejected. Christopher Columbus promised them unimaginable riches that could finance their military campaigns and bankroll a crusade to liberate Jerusalem from Muslim hands. Off he sailed with a royal patent that guaranteed the monarchs a share of all he discovered. Soon the Spanish economy was reorienting itself toward the Atlantic, and Spain's merchants, missionaries, and soldiers were preparing for conquest and profiteering in what had been, just a few years before, a blank space on the map.

The Struggles of France and England and the Success of Small States

Warfare and strategic marriages allowed the Portuguese and Spanish monarchies to consolidate state power and to lay the foundations for revived commerce. But by no means were all states immediately successful. In France and England, the great age of European monarchy had yet to dawn.

When French forces finally pushed the English back across the English Channel in the Hundred Years' War (1337–1453), the French House of Valois began a slow process of consolidating royal power. Although diplomatic marriages helped the French crown expand its domain, two more centuries of royal initiatives and civil war were required to tame the powerful nobility. In England, even thirty years of civil war between the houses of Lancaster and York did not settle which one would take the throne. Both families in this War of the Roses ultimately lost out to the Tudors, who seized the throne in 1485.

Even where stable states did arise, they were fairly small compared with the Ottoman and Ming Empires. In the mid-sixteenth century, Portugal and Spain, Europe's two most expansionist states, had populations of 1 million and 9 million, respectively. England, excluding Wales, was a mere 3 million in 1550. Only France, with 17 million, had a population close to the Ottoman Empire's 20 to 30 million. And these numbers paled in comparison with Ming China's population of nearly 200 million in 1550 and Mughal India's 110 million in 1600.

But in Europe, small was advantageous. Portugal's relatively small population meant that the crown had fewer groups to instill with loyalty. Also, in the world of finance, the most successful merchants were those inhabiting the smaller Italian city-states and, a bit later, the cities of the northern Netherlands. The Florentines developed sophisticated banking techniques, created extensive networks of agents throughout Europe and the Mediterranean, and served as bankers to the popes. Venetian merchants enjoyed a unique role in the exchange of silks and spices from the eastern Mediterranean. It was in these prosperous city-states that the Renaissance began.

The Renaissance

Just as the Ming harkened back to Han Chinese traditions and the Ottomans looked to Sunni Islam to point the way forward, so European elites looked to their own traditions for guidance as they rebuilt after the devastation of the plague. They found inspiration in ancient Greek and Roman ideas. Europe's political and economic revival also included a powerful outpouring of cultural achievements, led by Italian scholars and artists and financed by bankers, churchmen, and nobles. Much later, scholars coined the word **Renaissance** ("rebirth") to characterize the expanded cultural production of the Italian city-states, France, the Low Countries, England, and the Holy Roman Empire in the period 1430–1550. What was being "reborn" was ancient Greek and Roman art and learning— knowledge that could illuminate a world of expanding horizons and support the rights of people other than clergymen or kings to exert power in it. Although the Renaissance was largely funded by popes and Christian monarchs, it broke the medieval church's monopoly on answers to the big questions and opened the way for secular forms of learning and a more human-centered understanding of the cosmos.

THE ITALIAN RENAISSANCE The Renaissance, ironically, was all about the new—new exposure, that is, to the old classical texts and ancient art and architectural forms. Although some Greek and Roman texts were known in Europe and the Islamic world, the fall of Constantinople and the invention of the printing press made others accessible to western scholars for the first time. Scholars now realized that the pre-Christian Greeks and Romans had known more: more about how to represent and care for the human body; more about geography, astronomy, and architecture; more about how to properly govern states and armies. It was no longer enough to understand Christian doctrine and to trust medieval authorities; one had to accurately retranslate the original sources, which required the learning of languages and of history. This dive backward into ancient Greece and Rome became known as **humanism**, the aspiration to know more about the human experience beyond what the Christian scriptures offered. Humanism was a powerful tool in the hands of those who knew how to use it. Several women, including the celebrated Italian humanist Laura Cereta (1469–1499), used their learning and rhetorical skills to defend the equality of male and female intellects at a time in which both the church and society as a whole believed women scholars to be freaks of nature. (See Primary Source: A Renaissance Defense of Human Equality.)

Wealthy families, powerful rulers, and the Catholic Church were the sponsors of Renaissance achievement. For example, by the 1480s, the Medici family had been patronizing art based on ancient models for three generations. The Medicis were bankers but also influential political players in Florence and

Rome. The family contributed greatly to making Florence one of the showplaces of Renaissance art and architecture as well as the center stage for early Renaissance philosophy. Cosimo de' Medici (1389–1464) funded the completion of the sumptuous duomo (cathedral) of Florence, topped by the architect Brunelleschi's masterful dome, the largest built since antiquity. Cosimo's grandson, Lorenzo the Magnificent, supported many of the great Renaissance artists, including Leonardo da Vinci, Sandro Botticelli, and Michelangelo Buonarroti.

The artists who flourished in Florence, Rome, and Venice embraced their own form of humanism. For them, the return to ancient sources meant reviving the principles of the Roman architect Vitruvius and the imitation of nude classical sculpture. Their masterpieces, like Leonardo's *Last Supper* or Michelangelo's *David*, used the technique of perspective and classical treatments of the body to give vivacity and three-dimensionality to paintings and sculptures—even religious ones. Raphael's madonnas portrayed the Virgin Mary as a beautiful individual and not just as a symbol of chastity; similarly, Michelangelo's Sistine Chapel ceiling gave Adam the beautiful body of a Greek god so that viewers could appreciate the glory of the Creation. Of course, these artists also hoped to draw attention to their own achievements, and they were not disappointed. For soon northern European princes, too, sought out both ancient artifacts and the modern artists and humanists who could bring this inspiring new style to their courts.

THE RENAISSANCE SPREADS In the sixteenth century, a series of crises on the Italian Peninsula—including the sacking

Renaissance Masterpieces. Left: *Leonardo da Vinci's* The Last Supper *depicts Christ's disciples reacting to his announcement that one of them will betray him.* Right: *Michelangelo's* David *stands over 13 feet high and was conceived as an expression of Florentine civic ideals.*

A Renaissance Defense of Human Equality

Laura Cereta (1469-1499) was fortunate to have been the daughter of well-educated parents, her father a highly placed lawyer and her mother a successful businesswoman. But it was Laura who devoted herself at a young age to obtaining a deeply human-ist education, provided at first at the convent in her home town of Brescia, Italy, and then pursued by intense self-discipline once she had become her father's assistant (at age 12) and after her early marriage (at age 15). As a young woman she became widely known among Renaissance scholars for her learning. This achievement, however, embroiled her in a controversy that had been raging for decades about whether or not intelligent women were freaks of nature. Cereta responded to this line of thought with anger and disdain.

In the following letter to a fictional corre-spondent—but meant to denounce men such as the medieval writer Boccaccio, who had ridiculed women's intellects—Cereta uses her extensive knowledge of the ancient world and her rhetorical bril-liance to denounce those who, in praising her exceptional talents, showed contempt for others of her "race." She invokes fig-ures from Near Eastern and classical antiquity to show that there have always been women who were learned and wise. Notice, too, that the pursuit of the good that Cereta recommends does not involve the church; although she was a pious Christian, Cereta here recommends that individuals pursue secular knowledge rather than devote themselves to religious duties or to prayer.

To Bibolo Semproni
January 13, 1488

Your complaints are hurting my ears, for you say publicly and quite openly that you are not only surprised but pained that I am said to show this extraordinary intel-lect of the sort one would have thought nature would give to the most learned of men—as if you had reached the conclu-sion, on the facts of the case, that a similar girl had seldom been seen among peo-ples of the world. You are wrong on both counts, Semproni, and now that you've abandoned the truth, you are going to spread information abroad that is clearly false.

. . . My cause itself is worthy; I am impelled to show what great glory that noble lineage which I carry in my own breast has won for virtue and literature—a lineage that knowledge, the bearer of hon-ors, has exalted in every age. For the pos-session of this lineage is legitimate and sure, and it has come all the way down to me from the continuance of a more enduring race.

We have read that the breast of Ethi-opian Sabba, imbued with divinity, solved the prophetic riddles of the Egyptian king Solomon. . . . The enduring fame of Inachan Isis will flourish, for she alone of the Argive goddesses revealed to the Egyptians her own alphabet for reading. But Zenobia, an Egyptian woman of noble erudition, became so learned not only in Egyptian but also in Latin and Greek lit-erature that she wrote the histories of barbarian and foreign peoples. . . . Those little Greek women Phyliasia and Las-thenia were wonderful sources of light in the world of letters and they filled me with new life because they ridiculed the students of Plato, who frequently tied themselves in knots over the snare-filled sophistries of their arguments.

All history is full of such examples. My point is that your mouth has grown foul because you keep it sealed so that no arguments can come out of it that might enable you to admit that nature imparts one freedom to all human beings equally—to learn. But the question of my exceptionality remains. And here choice alone, since it is the arbiter of charac-ters, is the distinguishing factor. For some women worry about the styling of their hair, the elegance of their clothes, and the pearls and other jewelry they wear on their fingers. Others love to say cute little things, to hide their feeling behind a mask of tranquility, to indulge in dancing, and lead pet dogs around on a leash. But those women for whom the quest for the good represents a higher value restrain their young spirits and ponder better plains. They harden their bodies with sobriety and toil, they control their tongues, they carefully monitor what they hear, they ready their minds for all-night vigils. . . . For knowledge is not given as a gift but by study. For a mind free, keen, and unyield-ing in the face of hard work always rises to the good, and desire for learning grows in depth and breadth.

Source: Laura Cereta, *Collected Letters of a Renaissance Feminist*, transcribed, translated and edited by Diana Robin (Chicago: University of Chicago Press, 1997), pp. 76-79.

QUESTIONS FOR ANALYSIS

- Why is Cereta upset that she is seen as exceptional?
- How does she counter claims that women are not equal to men in intelligence?
- What recommendations does she have for women who want to pursue "the quest for the good"?

of Rome in 1527 by troops under the control of the Holy Roman Empire—and increasing economic prosperity in other parts of Europe helped to spread Renaissance culture throughout Europe. Philip II of Spain, for example, purchased more than 1,000 paintings during his reign; Henry IV of France and his queen, Marie de' Medici, invested a fortune in renovating the Louvre, building a new royal residence at Fontainebleau, and hiring Peter Paul Rubens to paint grand canvases. Courtiers built up-to-date palaces and invited scholars to live on their estates; Dutch, German, and French merchants also patronized the arts. All wanted their sons to be educated in the humanistic manner. Some families and religious institutions offered women access to the new learning, and some men encouraged their sisters, daughters, and wives to expand their horizons. The well-educated nun Caritas Pirckheimer (1467–1532), for example, exchanged learned letters and books with male humanists in the German states. Studying Greek, Latin, and ancient rhetoric did not make the commercial elite equal to the aristocrats, or women equal to men, but this sort of education did enable some non-nobles to obtain social influence and to criticize the ruling elites.

THE REPUBLIC OF LETTERS Since political and religious powers were not united in Europe (as they were in China and the Islamic world), scholars and artists could play one side against the other or, alternatively, could suffer both clerical and political persecution. Michelangelo completed commissions for the Medicis, for the Florentine Wool Guild, and for Pope Julius II. Peter Paul Rubens painted for the courts of France, Spain, England, and the Netherlands, as well as selling paintings on the open market. These two painters, renowned for showing a great deal of flesh, frequently offended conservative church officials, but their secular patrons kept them in oils. The Dutch scholar Desiderius Erasmus was able to ridicule the church because he had the patronage of English, Dutch, and French supporters. Other scholars used their learning to defend the older elites: for example, numerous lawyers and scholars continued to work for the popes, defending the papacy.

The search for patrons and the flight from persecution, especially after the Reformation, made Europe's educated elite increasingly cosmopolitan (as it had in China and the Islamic empires). Scholars met one another in royal palaces and cultural centers such as Florence, Antwerp, and Amsterdam. Seeking specialized information or rare books, they formed what was known as "the republic of letters"—a network of correspondents who were more interested in individual knowledge or talent than in noble titles or clerical rank. In this way, the Renaissance knitted together the European elite. This did not mean, however, that a consensus emerged about who should rule.

POWER AND THE RENAISSANCE THEORIZING ABOUT WAR The Renaissance was not only an embrace of the arts and

sciences of this world, but also a vehicle that enabled the more direct study of worldly power. Close reading of the ancient histories of Sallust, Livy, and Caesar emboldened scholars to address more forthrightly the conditions under which power could be maintained or undermined. New forms of governance were invented—and older forms buttressed. The Florentines pioneered a form of civic humanism under which all citizens were to devote themselves to defending the state against tyrants and foreign invaders; according to this view, the state would reward their civic virtue by ensuring their liberty. Yet it was also a Florentine, Niccolò Machiavelli, who wrote the most famous treatise on authoritarian power, *The Prince* (1513). Machiavelli argued that political leadership was not about obeying God's rules but about mastering the amoral means of modern statecraft. Holding and exercising power were ends in themselves, he claimed; civic virtue was merely a pretense on the part of those (like the Medici family he knew so well) who simply wanted to keep the upper hand.

In his own lifetime, Machiavelli was even more renowned for his essay *The Art of War* (1521). Here, the Florentine humanist argued that Roman military tactics, including the deploying of trained, armed citizens, would make for a more trustworthy army than the use of mercenary soldiers. The enrollment of a broadly based citizenry in the defense of the state, he insisted, would also make for political stability. His advice was hardly practicable in a Europe in which monarchs put little trust in their fellow nobles and even less in their subjects, but his ideas circulated widely and would gradually catch on and inspire military reforms in the Dutch Republic and during the Thirty Years' War (see Chapter 13). And he made little of the use of artillery, although the cannon had been used in European siege warfare since at least the 1420s; the Portuguese had already mounted them on oceangoing ships and had begun to use them to blast open South Asian ports. Machiavelli's fellow humanist Niccolò Tartaglia noticed the upsurge in cannon usage and produced an important treatise on ballistics, in which mathematics was first applied to the trajectory of projectiles. But neither of these was as influential as a wave of publications devoted to proper fortification designs, written by specialized military engineers who, for the first time, advocated the construction of defenses not to be pleasing to the eye but to best absorb the force of modern cannons. Thus began a long-lasting battle between military architects seeking to construct invincible defenseworks and artillery makers seeking to destroy them.

Like artistic and early manufacturing techniques, European military technologies diffused across the continent through conflict between states. Europeans learned much by observing one another at close range, especially during the many wars that marked the fifteenth and sixteenth centuries. As princes began to orient themselves more and more to obtaining and preserving power in this world, they began to value subjects who could build sturdy fortifications or more effectively mix gunpowder (a Chinese invention in widespread use in Europe by 1400). By the sixteenth century, many had also formed what were essentially standing armies and had begun to invest heavily in improved fortifications, not only for their castles but for their cities of residence as well. But like the church's new worldly activities, these princely activities also cost a great deal of money and demanded an expansion of state operations. In orienting the elite toward both ancient ideas and this-worldly power, in this way, too, the Renaissance revolutionized both European culture and politics—even if it could not unify the states and peoples who cultivated it.

MING CHINA

Like the Europeans, the Chinese saw their stable worldview and political order crumble under the cataclysms of human and bacterial invasions. Moreover, like the Europeans, people in China had long regarded outsiders as "barbarians." Together, the Mongols and the Black Death upended the political and intellectual foundations of what had appeared to be the world's most integrated society. The Mongols brought the Yuan dynasty to power; then the plague devastated China and prepared the way for the emergence of the Ming dynasty.

Ruled by ethnically Han Chinese, the Ming dynasty defined itself against its foreign predecessors. Ming emperors sought to reinforce everything Chinese. In particular, they supported China's vast internal agricultural markets in an attempt to minimize dependence on merchants and foreign trade.

Restoring Order

In the chaotic fourteenth century, as plague and famine ravaged China and as the Mongol Yuan dynasty collapsed, only a strong military movement capable of overpowering other groups could restore order. That intervention began at the hands of a poor young man who had trained in the Red Turban Movement: Zhu Yuanzhang. He was an orphan from a peasant household in an area devastated by disease and famine and a former novice at a Buddhist monastery. At age twenty-four, Zhu joined the Red Turbans, after which he rose quickly to become a distinguished commander. Eventually, his forces defeated the Yuan and drove the Mongols from China.

It soon became clear that Zhu had a much grander design for all of China than the ambitions of most warlords. When he took the important city of Nanjing in 1356, he renamed it Yingtian ("In response to Heaven"). Buoyed by subsequent successful military campaigns, twelve years later Zhu (r. 1368–1398) proclaimed the founding of the Ming ("brilliant") dynasty. Soon thereafter, his troops met little resistance when they seized the Yuan capital of Beijing, causing the Mongol emperor to flee to his homeland in the steppe. It would, however, take Zhu almost another twenty years to reunify the entire country.

Centralization under the Ming

Zhu and successive Ming emperors had to rebuild a devastated society from the ground up. Although in the past China had experienced natural catastrophes, wars, and social dislocation,

The Forbidden City. *The Yongle Emperor relocated the capital to Beijing, where he began the construction of the Forbidden City, or imperial palace. The palace was designed to inspire awe in all who saw it.*

the plague's legacy was devastation on an unprecedented scale. It left the new rulers with the formidable challenge of rebuilding the great cities, restoring respect for ruling elites, and reconstructing the bureaucracy.

IMPERIAL GRANDEUR AND KINSHIP The rebuilding began under Zhu, the Hongwu ("expansive and martial") Emperor, whose extravagant capital at Nanjing reflected imperial grandeur. When the dynasty's third emperor, the Yongle ("perpetual happiness") Emperor, relocated the capital to Beijing, he flaunted an even more grandiose style. Construction here mobilized around 100,000 artisans and 1 million laborers. The city had three separate walled enclosures. Inside the outer city walls sprawled the imperial city; within its walls lay the palace city, the Forbidden City. Traffic within the walled sections navigated through boulevards leading to the different gates, above which imposing towers soared. The palace compound, where the imperial family resided, had more than 9,000 rooms. Anyone standing in the front courts, which measured more than 400 yards on a side and boasted marble terraces and carved railings, would gasp at the sense of awesome power. That was precisely the effect the Ming emperors wanted (just as the Ottoman sultans did in building Topkapi Palace).

Marriage and kinship buttressed the power of the Ming imperial household. The dynasty's founder married the adopted daughter of a leading Red Turban rebel (her father, according to legend, was a convicted murderer), thereby consolidating his power and eliminating a threat. Empress Ma, as she was known, became the Hongwu Emperor's principal wife and was praised for her compassion. Emerging as the kinder face of the regime, she tempered the harsh and sometimes cruel disposition of her spouse. He had numerous other consorts as well, including Korean and Mongol women, who bore him twenty-six sons and sixteen daughters (similar to, although on smaller scale than, the sultan's harem at Topkapi Palace).

BUILDING A BUREAUCRACY Faced with the challenge of reestablishing order out of turmoil, the Hongwu Emperor initially sought to rule through his many kinsmen by giving imperial princes generous stipends, command of large garrisons, and significant autonomy in running their domains. However, when the princes' power began to threaten the court, the emperor slashed their stipends, reduced their privileges, and took control of their garrisons. No longer dependent on these men, he established an imperial bureaucracy beholden only to him and to his successors. These officials won appointments through their outstanding performance on a reinstated civil service examination.

In addition, the Hongwu Emperor took other steps to install a centralized system of rule. He assigned bureaucrats to oversee the manufacture of porcelain, cotton, and silk products as well as tax collection. He reestablished the Confucian school system as a means of selecting a cadre of loyal officials (not

Chinese Irrigation. *Farmers in imperial China used sophisticated devices to extract water for irrigation, as depicted in this illustration from the Yuan Mongol period.*

PRIMARY SOURCE

The Hongwu Emperor's Proclamation

This proclamation by the founder of the Ming dynasty, the Hongwu Emperor (r. 1368–1398), reveals how he envisioned reconstructing the devastated country as his own personal project. He sought a return to austerity by denouncing the morally corrosive effect of money and material possessions, and he especially distrusted his officials. Although frustrated in his efforts, the Hongwu Emperor nonetheless set the tone for the centralization of power in the person of the emperor.

To all civil and military officials:

I have told you to refrain from evil. Doing so would enable you to bring glory to your ancestors, your wives and children, and yourselves. With your virtue, you then could assist me in my endeavors to bring good fortune and prosperity to the people. You would establish names for yourselves in Heaven and on earth, and for thousands and thousands of years, you would be praised as worthy men.

However, after assuming your posts, how many of you really followed my instructions? Those of you in charge of money and grain have stolen them yourselves; those of you in charge of criminal laws and punishments have neglected the regulations. In this way grievances are not redressed and false charges are ignored. Those with genuine grievances have nowhere to turn; even when they merely wish to state their complaints, their words never reach the higher officials. Occasionally these unjust matters come to my attention. After I discover the truth, I capture and imprison the corrupt, villainous, and oppressive officials involved. I punish them with the death penalty or forced labor or have them flogged with bamboo sticks in order to make manifest the consequences of good or evil actions. . . .

Alas, how easily money and profit can bewitch a person! With the exception of the righteous person, the true gentleman, and the sage, no one is able to avoid the temptation of money. But is it really so difficult to reject the temptation of profit? The truth is people have not really tried.

Previously, during the final years of the Yuan dynasty, there were many ambitious men competing for power who did not treasure their sons and daughters but prized jade and silk, coveted fine horses and beautiful clothes, relished drunken singing and unrestrained pleasure, and enjoyed separating people from their parents, wives, and children. I also lived in that chaotic period. How did I avoid such snares? I was able to do so because I valued my reputation and wanted to preserve my life. Therefore I did not dare to do these evil things. . . .

In order to protect my reputation and to preserve my life, I have done away with music, beautiful girls, and valuable objects. Those who love such things are usually "a success in the morning, a failure in the evening." Being aware of the fallacy of such behavior, I will not indulge such foolish fancies. It is not really that hard to do away with these tempting things.

QUESTIONS FOR ANALYSIS

- What criticisms does the Hongwu Emperor level against the Mongol Yuan, whose rule he overthrew?
- What crimes does he accuse his own officials of committing, and what punishments does he carry out?
- Why would this Chinese emperor issue a decree that focuses on defining moral behavior?

Source: Patricia Buckley Ebrey (ed.), *Chinese Civilization: A Sourcebook*, Second Edition, revised and expanded (New York: The Free Press, 1993), pp. 205–6.

unlike the Ottoman janissaries and administrators). He also set up local networks of villages to rebuild irrigation systems and to supervise reforestation projects to prevent flooding—with the astonishing result that the amount of land reclaimed nearly tripled within eight years. Historians estimate that the Hongwu Emperor's reign oversaw the planting of about 1 billion trees, including 50 million sterculia, palm, and varnish trees around Nanjing. Their products served in building a maritime expedition fleet in the early fifteenth century. For water control, 40,987 reservoirs underwent repairs or new construction.

Now the imperial palace not only projected the image of a power center; it *was* the center of power. Every official received his appointment by the emperor through the Ministry of Personnel. The Hongwu Emperor also eliminated the post of prime minister (he executed the man who held the post) and henceforth ruled directly. Ming bureaucrats literally lost their seats and had to kneel before the emperor. In one eight-day period, the Hongwu Emperor reputedly reviewed over 1,600 petitions dealing with 3,392 separate matters. The drawback, of course, was that he had to keep tabs on this immense system, and his bureaucrats were not always up to the task. Indeed, the Hongwu Emperor constantly juggled personal and impersonal forms of authority, sometimes fortifying the administration, sometimes undermining it lest it become too autonomous. In due course, he nurtured a bureaucracy far more extensive than those of the Islamic empires. The Ming thus established the most highly centralized system of government of all the monarchies of this period. (See Primary Source: The Hongwu Emperor's Proclamation.)

Religion under the Ming

Just as the Ottoman sultans projected themselves as Muslim rulers, calling themselves the shadow of God, and European monarchs claimed to rule by divine right, so the Ming emperors enhanced their legitimacy by drawing on ancient Chinese religious traditions. Citing the mandate of heaven, the emperor revised and strengthened the elaborate protocol of rites and ceremonies that had undergirded dynastic power for centuries. As well as underscoring the emperor's centrality, official rituals (such as those related to the gods of soil and grain) reinforced political and social hierarchies.

Under the guise of "community" gatherings, rites and sacrifices solidified the Ming order by portraying the rulers as the moral and spiritual benefactors of their subjects. On at least ninety occasions each year, the emperor engaged in sacrificial rites, providing symbolic communion between the human and the spiritual worlds. These lavish festivities reinforced the ruler's image as mediator between otherworldly affairs of the gods and worldly concerns of the empire's subjects. The message was clear: the gods were on the side of the Ming household.

As an example of religious rituals reinforcing hierarchies, the emperor sanctioned official cults that were either civil or military and further distinguished as great, middle, or minor as well as celestial, terrestrial, or human categories. Official cults, however, often conflicted with local faiths. In this regard, they revealed the limits of Ming centralism. Consider Dongyang, a hilly interior region. As was common in Ming China, the people of Dongyang supported Buddhist institutions. Guan Yu, a legendary martial hero killed centuries earlier, was enshrined in a local Buddhist monastery there. But he was also worshipped as part of a state cult. Herein lay the problem: the state cult and the Buddhist monastery were separate entities, and imperial law held that the demands of the state cult prevailed over those of the local monastery. So the state-appointed magistrates in Dongyang kept a watchful eye on local religious leaders, although the magistrates refrained from tampering directly in the monastery's affairs. Although the imperial government insisted that people honor their contributions to the state, Dongyang's residents delivered most of their funds to the Buddhist monks. So strong were local sentiments that even the officials siphoned revenues to the monastery.

Ming Deities. *A pantheon of deities worshipped during the Ming, demonstrating the rich religious culture of the period.*

Ming Rulership

Religious sources of political power were less essential for the Ming dynasty than for the Islamic dynasties. Conquest and defense helped establish the realm, and bureaucracy kept it functioning. The empire's large scale (see Map 11.6) required a remarkably complex administration. To many outsiders (especially Europeans, whose region was in a state of constant war), Ming stability and centralization appeared to be political wizardry.

In terms of the structures underlying Ming power, the usual dynastic dilemmas were present. The emperor wished to be seen as the special guardian of his subjects. He wanted their

MAP 11.6 | Ming China, 1500s

The Ming state was one of the largest empires at this time—and the most populous. It had a long seacoast and even longer internal borders.

- What were the two Ming capitals, and what were the three main seaport trading cities?
- According to the map, where did the Ming rulers expect the greatest threat to their security?
- From your reading, how did the Ming rulers view foreign contact and exchange during this period?

allegiance as well as their taxes and labor. But during hard times, poor farmers were reluctant to provide resources—taxes or services—to distant officials. For these reasons alone, the Hongwu Emperor preferred to entrust management of the rural world to local leaders, whom he appointed as village chiefs, village elders, or tax captains. (In fact, a popular Chinese proverb was "The mountain is high and the emperor is far away.") Within these communities, the dynasty created a social hierarchy based on age, sex, and kinship. While women's labor remained critical for the village economy, the government reinforced a

gender hierarchy by promoting women's chastity and constructing commemorative arches for widows who refrained from remarrying. The Ming thus produced a more elaborate system for classifying and controlling its subjects than did the other Afro-Eurasian dynasties. But individuals also sought to define themselves by dressing in ways that expressed their own view of their place in the social order. (See Current Trends in World History: Ming Fashion.)

The Ming Empire, like the European and Islamic states, also faced periodic unrest and rebellion. Rebels often proclaimed

Ming Fashion

Ming rulers liked to represent themselves as custodians of the "civilized" Han traditions, in contrast to the "barbarian" ways of the previous Mongol Yuan dynasty. However, from governmental practices to clothing fashions, there were visible signs everywhere that the Ming, despite their rhetoric, followed in the footsteps of the Yuan and became more and more linked to an ever-growing, interconnected world. As trade with neighboring and faraway lands continued unabated and merchants and travelers kept moving, it proved to be impossible for the Ming to keep outside influences at arm's length. At the same time, the rhetoric of a return to the Han traditions did generate moves to invoke antiquity in the realm of fashion. Status-conscious elites with newfound wealth eagerly purchased clothes in what they believed to be the ancient Han style, hoping to set themselves apart from the common people. Their flirtation with antiquity, however, often ended up being more reinvention to satisfy the surging demands of the market than a genuine return to earlier conventions.

Founder Zhu Yuanzhang set the tone of the Ming by trying to rid the country of the close-fitting tunics worn by the Mongols. He advocated instead the wearing of the reputedly Tang-style garment of earlier times. While this measure did meet with some success, the vibrant clothing sector was hardly free of its fascination with the "exotic," such as horsehair skirts from Korea for men. A rare commodity when they first arrived, probably via trade missions, by the late fifteenth century, local weavers had become so skilled in making these skirts and consumers so eager to obtain them that craftsworkers were caught stealing the tails of horses to satisfy the soaring demand for the raw materials. Indeed, undoubtedly to the chagrin of the first Ming emperor and his descendants, much of the Yuan style and even terminology in both male and female clothing persisted during the Ming era.

The retro movement in fashion, as mentioned, had more to do with the demands of a changing Ming society than with the official advocacy for restorationism. Nowhere was this more

An example of headwear used by Ming officials, reputedly following the style of earlier dynasties. The beams attached to the crown of the cap indicate the official's rank, so the cap is known as a "beamed cap."

apparent than in the myriad styles of hats for men—a convenient yet highly visible way to make a statement in social standing. Invoking the names of earlier dynasties, there were the Han cap, the Jin cap, the Tang cap, and so on. The most interesting, however, was the Chunyang hat,

their own brand of religious beliefs, just as local elites resented central authority. Outright terror helped stymie threats to central authority. In a massive wave of carnage, the Hongwu Emperor slaughtered anyone who posed a threat to his authority, from the highest of ministers to the lowliest of scribes. From 1376 to 1393, four of his purges condemned close to 100,000 subjects to execution.

Yet, despite the emperor's immense power, the Ming Empire remained undergoverned. Indeed, as the population multiplied, there were too few loyal officials to handle local affairs. By the sixteenth and early seventeenth centuries, for example, some 10,000 to 15,000 officials shouldered the responsibility of managing a population exceeding 200 million people. Nonetheless, the Hongwu Emperor bequeathed to his descendants a set of tools for ruling that drew on subjects' direct loyalty to the emperor and on the intricate workings of an extensive bureaucracy. His legacy enabled his successors to balance local sources of power with the needs of dynastic rulership.

Trade and Exploration

In the fourteenth century, China began its economic recovery from the devastation of disease and political turmoil. Gradually, political stability allowed trade to revive. Now the new dynasty's merchants reestablished China's preeminence in long-distance commercial exchange. Chinese silk and cotton textiles, as well as fine porcelains, ranked among the world's most coveted luxuries. Wealthy families from Lisbon to Kalabar loved to wash their hands in delicate Chinese bowls and to flaunt fine wardrobes made from bolts of Chinese dyed linens and smoothly spun silk. When a Chinese merchant ship sailed into port, trading partners and onlookers crowded the docks to watch the unloading of precious cargoes. Although Ming rulers' support for overseas ventures wavered and eventually declined, this period saw important developments in Chinese trade and exploration.

During the Ming period, Chinese traders based in ports such as Hangzhou, Quanzhou, and Guangzhou (Canton) were

The "paddy-field gown" for women might have had its origins in Buddhist robes.

which allegedly drew upon both Han and Tang styles in its design but had actually become a symbol of the so-called new and strange fashion that so often attracted commentary in Ming writings. In fact, it was favored by the young, who had nothing but disdain for ancient styles!

Nor was the rage for fashion reserved for men only or even for just the privileged. As one Ming writer lamented, perhaps with a hint of exaggeration: "Nowadays the very servant girls dress in silk gauze, and the singsong girls look down on brocaded silks and embroidered gowns." Respectable women, we are told, looked to the clothing and style of the courtesans of the prosperous southern region of the country for ideas and inspiration for fashion. Indeed, much of our visual knowledge of Ming womens' clothing comes from paintings likely of highly trained courtesans or those female "entertainers" ubiquitous in Ming urban centers. These paintings reveal the different and consistently evolving styles of clothing for Ming women, including the "paddy-field gown"—which might have owed its origins to Buddhist robes—that were the focus of much criticism from those who frowned on the growing penchant for the exotic, the strange, the outrageous, and the irreverent in the realm of fashion. If nothing else, this debate about clothing certainly tells us that despite the often conservative stance and policies of the Ming regime, the everyday life of many Ming subjects was a constant exercise in negotiating the multiple impacts of both the old and the new as well as the familiar and the foreign in different arenas of their rapidly changing society.

QUESTIONS FOR ANALYSIS

- Why did the elite cultivate an "ancient" Han style?
- Can you think of "retro" styles popular today? What do they say about the people who cultivate them?
- How do we know about changes in women's fashion in the Ming era? Are there any dangers in using these sources to understand the dress of all Ming women?

Explore Further

Finnane, Antonia. *Changing Clothes in China: Fashion, History, Nation* (2008).

as energetic as their Muslim counterparts in the Indian Ocean. These ports were home to prosperous merchants and the point of convergence for vast sea-lanes. Leaving the mainland ports, Chinese vessels carried precious wares to offshore islands, the Pescadores, and Taiwan. From there they sailed on to the ports of Kyūshū, the Ryūkyūs, Luzon, and maritime Southeast Asia. As entrepôts for global goods, East Asian ports flourished. Former fishing villages developed into major urban centers.

The Ming dynasty viewed overseas expansion with suspicion, however. The Hongwu Emperor feared that too much contact with the outside world would cause instability and undermine his rule. In fact, he banned private maritime commerce in 1371. But enforcement was lax, and by the late fifteenth century, maritime trade once again surged. Because much of the thriving business took place in defiance of official edicts, it led to constant friction between government officials and maritime traders. Although the Ming government ultimately agreed to issue licenses for overseas trade in the mid-sixteenth century, its policies continued to vacillate. To Ming officials, the sea represented problems of order and control rather than opportunities.

THE EXPEDITIONS OF ZHENG HE One spectacular exception to the Ming's attitude toward maritime trade was a series of officially sponsored expeditions in the early fifteenth century. It was the ambitious Yongle Emperor who took the initiative. One of his loyal followers was a Muslim whom the Ming army had captured as a boy. The youth was castrated and sent to serve at the court (as a eunuch, he could not continue his family line and so theoretically owed sole allegiance to the emperor). Given the name **Zheng He** (1371–1433), he grew up to be an important military leader. The emperor entrusted him with venturing out to trade, collect tribute, and display China's power to the world.

From 1405 to 1433, Zheng He commanded the world's greatest armada and led seven naval expeditions. His larger ships stretched 400 feet in length (Columbus's *Santa Maria* was 85 feet), carried hundreds of sailors on four tiers of decks, and

Zheng He's Ship. *A testament to centuries of experience in shipbuilding and maritime activities, the largest ship in Zheng He's armada in the early fifteenth century was about five times the length of Columbus's Santa Maria (pictured next to Zheng's ship) and had nine times the capacity in terms of tonnage. It had nine staggered masts and twelve silk sails, all designed to demonstrate the grandeur of the Ming Empire.*

maneuvered with sophisticated rudders, nine masts, and watertight compartments. The first expedition set sail with a flotilla of 62 large ships and over 200 lesser ones. All 28,000 men aboard pledged to promote Ming glory.

Zheng He and his entourage aimed to establish tributary relations with far-flung territories—from Southeast Asia to the Indian Ocean ports, to the Persian Gulf, and to the east coast of Africa. (See Map 11.7.) These expeditions did not seek territorial expansion, but rather control of trade and tribute. Zheng traded for ivory, spices, ointments, exotic woods, and even some wildlife, including giraffes, zebras, and ostriches. He also used his considerable force to intervene in local affairs, exhibiting China's might in the process. If a community refused to pay tribute, Zheng's fleet would attack it. He encouraged rulers or envoys from Southeast Asia, India, Southwest Asia, and Africa to visit his homeland. When local rulers were uncooperative, Zheng might seize them and drag them all the way to China to face the emperor, as he did the rulers of Sumatra and Ceylon.

As spectacular as they were, Zheng's accomplishments could not survive the changing tides of events at home. Although many items gathered on his voyages delighted the court, most were not the stuff of everyday commerce. The expeditions were glamorous but expensive, and in 1424, when the Yongle Emperor died, they lost their most enthusiastic patron. Moreover, by the mid-fifteenth century, there was a revival of military threats from the north. At that time, the Ming court was shocked to discover that during a tour of the frontiers, the emperor had been captured and held hostage by the Mongols. Recalling how the maritime-oriented Song dynasty had been overrun by invaders from the north (see Chapter 10), Ming officials withdrew imperial support for seagoing ventures and instead devoted their energies to overland ventures and defense. Thus, Zheng's expeditions came to a complete halt in 1433. Never again did the Ming undertake such large-scale maritime ventures, although individual merchants, of course, returned to their profitable coastal trade routes.

The Chinese decision to forgo overseas ventures after 1433 was momentous. Although China remained the wealthiest, most densely settled region of the world with the most fully developed state structure and thriving market, the empire's wariness of overseas projects deprived merchants and would-be explorers of vital support in an age when others were beginning to look outward and across the oceans.

CONCLUSION

How could all the dying and devastation that came with the Black Death not have transformed the peoples of Afro-Eurasia? Much did change, but certain underlying ideals and institutions endured. What changed were mainly the political regimes, which took the blame for the catastrophes. The Delhi Sultanate, the Abbasid Empire, and the Yuan dynasty collapsed. In contrast, universal religions and wide-ranging cultural systems persisted even though they underwent vast transformations. The Ming dynasts in China set the stage for a long tenure by claiming, as had previous rulers, the mandate of heaven and stressing China's place at the center of their universe. A strict Shiite version of Islam emerged in Iran, while a fervent form of Sunni Islam found its champion in the Ottoman Empire. In Europe, national monarchies appeared in Spain, Portugal, France, and England. Debilitated by death and disorder, the Catholic Church recovered its centrality, though some Europeans, too, began to

← Voyages of Zheng He, 1405–1433

MAP 11.7 | Voyages of Zheng He, 1405–1433

Zheng He's voyages are some of the most famous in world history. Many historians have speculated about how history might have been different if the Chinese emperors had allowed the voyages to continue.

- For how many years did Zheng's voyages last?
- How far did Zheng's voyages take him?
- Why did Chinese expeditions not have the same impact as European voyages of exploration toward the end of the fifteenth century?

satisfy their spiritual longings in ways that went beyond traditional practices.

The new states and empires had notable differences. These were evident in the ambition of a Ming warlord who established a new dynasty, the military expansionism of Turkish households bordering the Byzantine Empire, the unifying vision of Mughal rulers in northern India, and the desire of various European rulers to consolidate power. But interactions among peoples also mattered: an eagerness to reestablish and expand trade networks and a desire to convert unbelievers to "the true faith"—be it a form of Islam, a variant of Hinduism, an exclusive Christianity, or a local type of Buddhism.

The dynasties all faced similar problems. They had to establish legitimacy, ensure smooth succession, deal with religious groups, and forge working relationships with nobles, townspeople, merchants, and peasants. Yet each state developed distinctive traits as a result of political innovation, traditional ways of ruling, and borrowing from neighbors. European monarchies achieved significant internal unity, often through warfare and in the context of a cultural Renaissance. Ottoman rulers perfected techniques for ruling an ethnically and religiously diverse empire: they moved military forces swiftly, allowed local communities a degree of political and religious autonomy, and trained a

bureaucracy dedicated to the Ottoman and Sunni Islamic way of life. The Ming dynasty fashioned an imperial system based on a Confucian-trained bureaucracy and intense subordination to the emperor so that it could manage a mammoth population. The rising monarchies of Europe, the Shiite regime of the Safavids in Persia, and the Ottoman state all blazed with religious fervor and sought to eradicate or subordinate the beliefs of other groups.

The new states displayed unprecedented political and economic powers. All demonstrated military prowess, a desire for stable hierarchies and secure borders, and a drive to expand. Each legitimized its rule via dynastic marriage and succession, state-sanctioned religion, and administrative bureaucracies. Each supported vigorous commercial activity. The Islamic regimes, especially, engaged in long-distance commerce and, by conquest and conversion, extended their holdings.

For western Christendom, the Ottoman conquests were decisive. They provoked Europeans to establish commercial connections to the east, south, and west. The consequences of their new toeholds would be momentous—just as the Chinese decision to turn *away* from overseas exploration and commerce marked a turning point in world history. Both decisions were instrumental in determining which worlds would come together and which would remain apart.

After You Read This Chapter

Go to INQUIZITIVE to see what you know & learn what you've missed.

FOCUS ON: *Crisis and Recovery in Afro-Eurasia*

Collapse and Consolidation

- Bubonic plague originates in Inner Asia and afflicts people from China to Europe.

- Climate change and famine leave people vulnerable, while commerce facilitates the spread of disease.

- The plague kills 25 to 65 percent of infected populations and leaves societies in turmoil.

Islamic Dynasties

- Ottoman, Safavid, and Mughal Empires replace the Mongols.

- Ottomans overrun Constantinople and become the primary Sunni regime in the Islamic world.

- The Ottomans establish their legitimacy with military prowess, religious backing, and a loyal bureaucracy.

- Sultans manage decentralizing tendencies of outlying provinces with flexibility and tolerance, relying on religious faith, patronage, and bureaucracy.

- Safavid and Mughal regimes arise in Iran and South Asia.

Western Christendom

- New dynastic monarchies that claim to rule by divine right appear in Portugal, Spain, France, and England.

- The Inquisition takes aim against *conversos*—converted Jews and Muslims.

- A rebirth of classical learning, known as the Renaissance, originates in Italian city-states and spreads throughout western Europe.

- War making becomes more scientific, expensive, and deadly.

Ming China

- The Ming dynasty replaces the Mongol Yuan dynasty and rebuilds a strong state from the ground up, claiming a mandate from heaven.

- An elaborate, centralized bureaucracy oversees the revival of infrastructure and long-distance trade.

- The emperor and bureaucracy concentrate on developing internal markets and overland trade at the expense of overseas commerce.

CHRONOLOGY

Islamic World

Osman begins Ottoman Empire **1299**

The Black Death arrives in Baghdad **1347**

Western Christendom

Black Death reaches Italian port cities **1347**

Peasant revolts in England and France **1358–1381**

East Asia

Black Death reaches China **1320**

The Hongwu Emperor founds Ming dynasty **1368**

1300

1350

STUDY QUESTIONS

1. **Explain** how the Black Death, or bubonic plague, spread throughout Afro-Eurasia. What human activity facilitated its diffusion?

2. **Describe** the long-term consequences of bubonic plague for the Afro-Eurasian world. What were the plague's social, political, and economic ramifications in various parts of the landmass?

3. **Identify** the three main Islamic dynasties that emerged after the bubonic plague. How were they similar, and how were they different?

4. **Analyze** the ways in which the Ming dynasty centralized its power in China in the fourteenth and fifteenth centuries. What political innovations did it pursue, and what traditions did it sustain? **Compare** Chinese efforts at bureaucratic centralization with those of the Ottomans.

5. **Describe** the goals of the Ming dynasty's maritime exhibitions. Why did the government later abandon them?

6. **Compare and contrast** the ways in which regional rulers in post-plague Afro-Eurasia attempted to construct unified states. **Identify** their greatest successes.

7. **Explain** why the bubonic plague undermined the feudal order of the Catholic Church. How did regional monarchs in Europe capitalize on this development?

8. **Identify** the ways in which religious belief systems maintained continuity from the fourteenth through the fifteenth centuries.

9. **Describe** the key features of the Renaissance in Europe. How did the Renaissance spread and change?

10. **Discuss** how the art and architecture of different regions reflected the political realities of this period. **Identify** themes that communicated these messages to viewers.

11. **Analyze** the role of philosophical and religious developments—both elite movements, like humanism in Europe, and popular movements, like the Red Turban Movement in China—in politics from 1300 to 1500, and **explain** how they provided both continuity and change in each society.

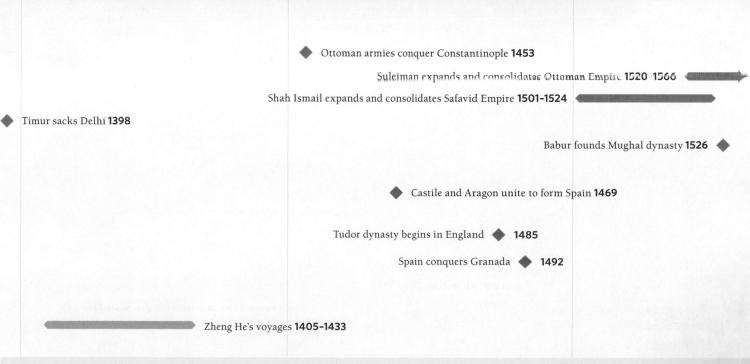

Ottoman armies conquer Constantinople **1453**

Suleiman expands and consolidates Ottoman Empire **1520–1566**

Shah Ismail expands and consolidates Safavid Empire **1501–1524**

Timur sacks Delhi **1398**

Babur founds Mughal dynasty **1526**

Castile and Aragon unite to form Spain **1469**

Tudor dynasty begins in England **1485**

Spain conquers Granada **1492**

Zheng He's voyages **1405–1433**

1400   1450   1500

FURTHER READINGS

CHAPTER 1

Alley, Richard B., and Michael L. Bender. "Greenland Ice Cores: Frozen in Time." *Scientific American* 278 (February 1998): 80–85. A study that describes the pioneering work that astronomers and climatologists have carried out in the twentieth century to enhance our knowledge of climate change and its impact on plants and animals, including human beings.

Arsuaga, Juan Luis. *The Neanderthal's Necklace: In Search of the First Thinkers*, translated by Anthony Klatt (2002). A stimulating overview of prehistory that focuses on the Neanderthals and compares them with *Homo sapiens*.

Barham, Lawrence, and Peter Mitchell. *The First Africans: African Archaeology from the Earliest Toolmakers to Most Recent Foragers* (2008). New findings on the evolution of hominins in Africa.

Barker, Graeme. *Agricultural Revolution in Prehistory: Why Did Foragers Become Farmers?* (2006). The most recent, truly global, and up-to-date study of this momentous event in world history.

Bellwood, Peter. *First Farmers: The Origins of Agricultural Societies* (2005). A state-of-the-art global history of the origins of agriculture, including recent archaeological, linguistic, and microbiological data.

Bender, Michael L. *Paleoclimate* (2013). A definitive overview of the world's climate over the entire life of our universe, written by a renowned geoclimatologist.

Bogucki, Peter. *The Origins of Human Society* (1999). An authoritative overview of prehistory.

Brooke, John L. *Climate Change and the Course of Global History: A Rough Journey* (2014). An excellent overview of the impact of climate on history, particularly useful for the hominin period and the emergence of *Homo sapiens*.

Cauvin, Jacques. *The Birth of the Gods and the Origins of Agriculture*, translated by Trevor Watkins from the original 1994 French publication (2000). An important work on the agricultural revolution of Southwest Asia and the evolution of symbolic thinking at this time.

Cavalli-Sforza, Luigi Luca. *Genes, Peoples, and Languages*, translated by Mark Selestad from the original 1996 French publication (2000). An expert's introduction to the use of gene research for revealing new information about the evolution of human beings in the distant past.

Childe, V. Gordon. *What Happened in History* (1964). A classic work by one of the pioneers in studying the early history and evolution of human beings. Though superseded in many respects, it is still an important place to start one's reading and a work of great power and emotion.

Christian, David. *Maps of Time: An Introduction to Big History* (2004). A definitive historical work on the origins of our universe and the emergence of plant and animal life, including the hominin populations. The work synthesizes discoveries since the end of World War II that have transformed our knowledge of the universe and its peopling.

Clark, J. Desmond, and Steven A. Brandt (eds.). *From Hunters to Farmers: The Causes and Consequences of Food Production in Africa* (1984). Excellent essays on the agricultural revolution.

Coon, Carleton Stevens. *The Story of Man; from the First Human to Primitive Culture and Beyond*, 2nd ed. (1962). An important early work on the evolution of humans, emphasizing the distinctiveness of "races" around the world.

Cunliffe, Barry (ed.). *The Oxford Illustrated Prehistory of Europe* (1994). The definitive work on early European history.

Ehrenberg, Margaret. *Women in Prehistory* (1989). What was the role of women in hunting and gathering societies, and how greatly were women affected by the agricultural revolution? The author offers a number of stimulating generalizations.

Ehret, Christopher. *The Civilizations of Africa: A History to 1800* (2002). Although this is a general history of Africa, the author, a linguist and an expert on early African history, offers new information and new overviews of African peoples in very ancient times.

Fagan, Brian. *People of the Earth: An Introduction to World Prehistory* (1989). An

authoritative overview of early history, widely used in classrooms.

Fage, J. D., and Roland Oliver (eds.). *The Cambridge History of Africa*, 8 vols. (1975–1984). A pioneering work of synthesis by two of the first and foremost scholars of the history of Africa. Volume 1 deals with African prehistory.

Frison, George C. *Survival by Hunting: Prehistoric Human Predators and Animal Prey* (2004). An archaeologist applies his knowledge of animal habitats, behavior, and hunting strategies to an examination of prehistoric hunting practices in the North American Great Plains and Rocky Mountains.

Gebauer, Anne Birgitte, and T. Douglas Price (eds.) *Transition to Agriculture in Prehistory* (1992). Excellent essays on the agricultural revolution, especially those written by the two editors.

Harari, Yuval Noah. *Sapiens: A Brief History of Humankind* (2015). A largely successful overview of human history from the hominins to the present.

Imbrie, John, and Katherine Palmer Imbrie. *Ice Ages and Solving the Mystery* (1979). A readable overview of the work done by geologists and climatologists on the earth's temperatures, written by two scholars who contributed to these breakthroughs.

"Inter-Group Violence among the Early Holocene Hunter-Gatherers of West Turkana, Kenya." *Nature* 529 (January 21, 2016): 394–398. Describes a spectacular discovery of the remains of hunter-gatherers who engaged in warfare.

Johnson, Donald, Lenora Johnson, and Blake Edgar. *Ancestors: In Search of Human Origins* (1999). A good overview of human evolution, with insightful essays on *Homo erectus* and *Homo sapiens*.

Jones, Steve, Robert Martin, and David Pilbeam (eds.). *The Cambridge Encyclopedia of Human Evolution* (1992). A superb guide to a wide range of subjects, crammed with up-to-date information on the most controversial and obscure topics of human evolution and early history.

Ki-Zerbo, J. (ed.). *Methodology and African Prehistory*, vol. 1 of the UNESCO *General*

History of Africa (1981). A general history of Africa, written for the most part by scholars of African descent.

Klein, Richard G., and Blake Edger. *The Dawn of Human Culture* (2002). A fine and reliable guide to the tangled history of human evolution.

Leakey, Richard. *The Origin of Humankind* (1994). A readable and exciting account of human evolution, written by the son of the pioneering archaeologists Louis and Mary Leakey, a scholar of equal stature to his parents.

Lewin, Roger. *The Origin of Modern Humans* (1993). Yet another good overview of human evolution, with useful chapters on early art and the use of symbols.

Loewe, Michael, and Edward Shaughnessy (eds.). *The Cambridge History of Ancient China: From the Origins of Civilization to 221 B.C.* (1999). A good review of the archaeology of ancient China.

Mellaart, James. *Çatal Höyük: A Neolithic Town in Anatolia* (1967). A detailed description of one of the first towns associated with the agricultural revolution in Southwest Asia.

Meredith, Martin. *Born in Africa: The Quest for Human Origins* (2011). A well-written and authoritative overview of the evolution of humankind from the earliest hominins to *Homo sapiens*.

Mithen, Steven. *The Prehistory of the Mind: The Cognitive Origins of Art and Science* (1996). A stimulating discussion of the impact of biological and cultural evolution on the cognitive structure of the human mind.

Olson, Steve. *Mapping Human History: Genes, Race, and Our Common Origins* (2003). Using the findings of genetics and attacking the racial thinking of an earlier generation of archaeologists, the author writes powerfully about the unity of all human beings.

Price, T. Douglas (ed.). *Europe's First Farmers* (2000). A discussion of the agricultural revolution in Europe.

Price, T. Douglas, and Anne Birgitte Gebauer (eds.). *Last Hunters, First Farmers: New Perspectives on the Prehistoric Transition to Agriculture* (1996). An exciting collection of essays by some of the leading scholars in the field studying the transition from hunting and gathering to settled agriculture.

Reich, David, et al. "Genome-Wide Patterns of Selection in 230 Ancient Eurasians." *Nature*, November 23, 2015, Vol. 522, published online, November 23, 2015. New DNA research on the skeletons of 230 West-Eurasians who lived between 6500 and 300 BCE shows the three waves of migrations into Europe in its distant past. These migrations came from Africa via Southwest Asia, Anatolia, and the Russian steppes.

Ruddiman, William F. *Plows, Plagues, and Petroleum: How Humans Took Control of Climate* (2005). An excellent study of how energy sources have changed over the very long run.

Sahlins, Marshall. "Notes on the Original Affluent Society." In *Man the Hunter*, edited by Richard B. Lee and Irven DeVore (1968), pp. 85–89. Sahlins coined the widely used and now famous expression "affluent society" for hunter-gatherers.

Scarre, Chris (ed.). *The Human Past: World Prehistory and the Development of Human Societies* (2005). An encyclopedia and an overview rolled up into one mammoth volume, written by leading figures in the field of early human history.

Shaw, Thurstan, Paul Sinclair, Bassey Andah, and Alex Okpoko (eds.). *The Archaeology of Africa: Food, Metals, and Towns* (1993). Research on the earliest history of human beings in Africa.

Shreeve, James. "Mystery Man." *National Geographic* 228 (October 2015): 30–57. An authoritative and up-to-date account of the extraordinary discovery of fossil remains of a hominid species, now named *Homo naledi*.

Smith, Bruce D. *The Emergence of Agriculture* (1995). How early humans domesticated wild animals and plants.

Stringer, Christopher, and Robin McKie. *African Exodus: The Origins of Modern Humanity* (1996). Detailed data on why Africa was the source of human origins and why *Homo sapiens* is a recent wanderer out of Africa.

Tattersall, Ian. *The Fossil Trail: How We Know What We Think We Know about Human Evolution* (1995). A passionately written book about early archaeological discoveries and the centrality of Africa in human evolution.

Tattersall, Ian. *The World from Beginnings to 4000 BCE* (2008). A brief up-to-date overview of humanity's early history by a leading authority.

Tattersall, Ian. *Masters of the Planet: The Search for Our Human Origins* (2012). The most recent survey of human evolution.

Van Oosterzee, Penny. *Dragon Bones: The Story of Peking Man* (2000). Describes how the late nineteenth-century unearthing of sites in China containing fossils of animals used for medicinal purposes led to the discovery of Peking Man.

Weiss, Mark L., and Alan E. Mann. *Human Biology and Behavior: An Anthropological Perspective* (1996). The authors stress the contribution that biological research has made and continues to make to unravel the mystery of human evolution.

Wrangham, Richard. *Catching Fire: How Cooking Made Us Human* (2009). The author shows how fire made it possible for humans to have a more varied and richer diet but also one that provided energy for the one organ—the brain—that consumes the most energy.

CHAPTER 2

Adams, Robert McCormick. *The Evolution of Urban Society* (1966). A classic study of the social, political, and economic processes that led to the development of the first urban civilizations.

Algaze, Guillermo. *Ancient Mesopotamia at the Dawn of Civilization* (2008). A compelling analysis of the complex environmental and social factors underlying the rise of the world's first urban culture in southern Mesopotamia.

Andrews, Carol. *Egyptian Mummies* (1998). An illustrated summary of Egyptian mummification and burial practices.

Bagley, Robert. *Ancient Sichuan: Treasures from a Lost Civilization* (2001). Describes the remarkable findings in Southwest China, particularly at Sanxingdui, which have challenged earlier accounts of the Shang dynasty's central role in the rise of early Chinese culture.

Bar-Yosef, Ofar, and Anatoly Khazanov (eds.). *Pastoralism in the Levant: Archaeological Materials in Anthropological Perspectives* (1992). Classic study of the role of nomads in the development of societies in the Levant during the Neolithic period.

Bruhns, Karen Olsen. *Ancient South America* (1994). The best basic text on pre-Columbian South American cultures.

Butzer, Karl W. *Early Hydraulic Civilization in Egypt: A Study of Cultural Ecology* (1976). The best work on how the Egyptians dealt with the Nile floods and the influence that these arrangements had on the overall organization of society.

Cunliffe, Barry. *Europe between the Oceans, 9000 BC–AD 1000* (2008). A very up-to-date and spectacularly illustrated account of early Europe.

Feng, Li. *Early China: A Social and Cultural History* (2013). An important new study on the origins of Chinese culture.

Fukuyama, Francis. *The Origins of Political Order: From Prehistoric Times to the French Revolution* (2011). A superb overview of the powerful political elements that were behind the great river-basin societies in ancient times.

Habu, Junko. *Ancient Jomon of Japan* (2004). Study of prehistoric Jomon hunter-gatherers on the Japanese archipelago that incorporates several different aspects of anthropological studies, including hunter-gatherer archaeology, settlement archaeology, and pottery analysis.

Jacobsen, Thorkild. *The Treasures of Darkness: A History of Mesopotamian Religion* (1976). Best introduction to the religious and philosophical thought of ancient Mesopotamia.

Kemp, Barry J. *Ancient Egypt: Anatomy of a Civilization* (1989). An overview of the culture of the pharaohs.

Kramer, Samuel Noah. *The Sumerians: Their History, Culture and Character* (1963). Classic study of the Sumerians and their culture by a pioneer in Sumerian studies.

Pollock, Susan. *Ancient Mesopotamia: The Eden That Never Was* (1999). An analysis of the social and economic development of Mesopotamia from the beginnings of settlement until the reign of Hammurapi.

Possehl, Gregory L. *Indus Age: The Beginnings* (1999). The second of four volumes analyzing the history of the Indus Valley civilization.

Postgate, J. N. *Early Mesopotamia: Society and Economy at the Dawn of History* (1992). A study of the economic and political development of the Sumerian civilization.

Preziosi, Donald, and L. A. Hitchcock. *Aegean Art and Architecture* (1999). One of the best general guides to the figurative and decorative art produced by the Minoans and Mycenaeans and by related early societies in the region of the Aegean.

Ratnagar, Shereen. *Understanding Harappa: Civilization in the Greater Indus Valley* (2001). Harappan site archaeological data of the last century organized into a historical narrative comprehensible to the general audience.

Ratnagar, Shereen. *Trading Encounters: From the Euphrates to the Indus in the Bronze Age,* 2nd ed. (2004). A comprehensive presentation of the evidence for the relationship between the Indus Valley and its western neighbors.

Rice, Michael. *Egypt's Legacy: The Archetypes of Western Civilization, 3000–300 BC* (1997). The author argues for the decisive influence of Egyptian culture on the whole of the Mediterranean and its later historical development.

Roaf, Michael. *Cultural Atlas of Mesopotamia and the Ancient Near East* (1990). A comprehensive compendium of the historical and cultural development of the Mesopotamian culture from the Neolithic background through the Persian Empire.

Shaw, Ian (ed.). *The Oxford History of Ancient Egypt* (2000). The most up-to-date and comprehensive account of the history of Egypt down to the Greek invasion.

Thapar, Romila. *Early India: From the Origins to AD 1300* (2002). The standard work on this period in Indian history by India's leading historian.

Thorp, Robert. *The Chinese Neolithic: Trajectories to Early States* (2005). Uses the latest archaeological evidence to describe the development of early Bronze Age cultures in North and Northwest China from about 2000 BCE.

Tignor, Robert L. *Egypt: A Short History* (2011). An overview of the history of Egypt from the rise of the pharaohs to the present.

Van de Mieroop, Marc. *The Ancient Mesopotamian City* (1997). A highly readable presentation of the earliest cities in the world.

Van de Mieroop, Marc. *A History of the Ancient Near East, ca. 3000–323 BC* (2004). An overview of the Near East in its period of historical prominence, written by an expert historian and archaeologist.

Wright, Rita P. *The Ancient Indus: Urbanism, Economy, and Society* (2010). A reconstruction of the Indus society with updated archaeological data.

CHAPTER 3

Allan, Sarah. *The Shape of the Turtle: Myth, Art and Cosmos in Early China* (1991). Explains the roles of divination and sacrifice in artistic representations of the Shang cosmology.

Allen, James P. *Middle Egyptian: An Introduction to the Language and Culture of Hieroglyphs* (2000). An introduction to the system of writing and its use in ancient Egypt.

Anthony, David W. *The Horse, the Wheel, and Language: How Bronze-Age Riders from the Eurasian Steppes Shaped the Modern World* (2007). A superb analysis of the origins and spread of the Indo-European peoples.

Arnold, Dieter. *Building in Ancient Egypt: Pharaonic Stone Masonry* (1996). Details the complex construction of monumental stone architecture in ancient Egypt.

Baines, John, and Jaromir Málek. *Atlas of Ancient Egypt* (1980). Useful compilation of information on ancient Egyptian society, religion, history, and geography.

Beal, Richard H. *The Organization of the Hittite Military* (1992). A detailed study based on textual sources of the world's first chariot-based army.

Behringer, Wolfgang. *A Cultural History of Climate* (2010). A general history of the impact of climate on many different societies.

Bell, Barbara. "The Dark Ages in Ancient History. I. The First Dark Age in Egypt," *American Journal of Archaeology,* 75 (January 1971): 1–26. An environmental analysis of the decline of the Old Kingdom and the emergence of the First Intermediate Period.

Bogucki, Peter, and Pam J. Crabtree (eds.). *Ancient Europe 8000 BC–AD 1000: Encyclopedia of the Barbarian World,* 2 vols. (2004). An indispensable handbook on the economic, social, artistic, and religious life in Europe during this period.

Bruhns, Karen Olsen. *Ancient South America* (1994). The best basic text on pre-Columbian South American cultures.

Bryant, Edwin. *The Quest for the Origins of Vedic Culture: The Indo-Aryan Migration Debate* (2001). Insight into the highly charged debate on who the Indo-European speakers were, where they originated, and where they migrated to.

Castleden, Rodney. *The Mycenaeans* (2005). One of the best current surveys of all aspects of the Mycenaean Greeks.

Chadwick, John. *The Decipherment of Linear B,* 2nd ed. (1968). Not only a retelling of the story of the decipherment of the Linear B script, but also an introduction to the actual content and function of the tablets themselves.

Cline, E. H. *Sailing the Wine-Dark Sea: International Trade and the Late Bronze Age Aegean* (1994). An excellent account of the trade and contacts between the

Aegean and other areas of the Mediterranean, Europe, and the Near East during the late Bronze Age.

Cunliffe, Barry. *Facing the Ocean: The Atlantic and Its Peoples, 8000 BC–AD 1500* (2001). An in-depth, highly useful treatment of western Europe during this period.

Cunliffe, Barry (ed.). *Prehistoric Europe: An Illustrated History* (1997). A state-of-the-art treatment of first farmers, agricultural developments, and material culture in prehistoric Europe.

Curry, Andrew. "Slaughter at the Bridge," *Science* 351 (March 25, 2016): 1384–1389. New information on a battle among hunter-gatherer warriors in northern Europe in the thirteenth century BCE.

Davis, W. V., and L. Schofield. *Egypt, the Aegean and the Levant: Interconnections in the Second Millennium BC* (1995). A discussion of the complex interactions in the eastern Mediterranean during the "international age."

Doumas, Christos. *Thera: Pompeii of the Ancient Aegean* (1983). A study of the tremendous volcanic eruption and explosion that destroyed the Minoan settlement on the island of Thera.

Drews, Robert. *Coming of the Greeks: Indo-European Conquests in the Aegean and the Near East* (1988). A good survey of the evidence for the "invasions" or "movements of peoples" that reconfigured the world of the eastern Mediterranean and Near East.

Finley, M. I. *The World of Odysseus*, 2nd rev. ed. (1977; reprint, 2002). The classic work that describes what might be recovered about the social values and behaviors of men and women in the period of the so-called Dark Ages of early Greek history.

Frankfort, Henri. *Ancient Egyptian Religion: An Interpretation* (1948; reprint, 2000). A classic study of Egyptian religion and culture during the pharaonic period.

Frayne, Douglas. *Old Babylonia Period, 2003–1595 B.C.* (1990). A standard and still useful study of this period in Babylonian history.

Jamison, Stephanie W. *Sacrificed Wife, Sacrificer's Wife: Women, Ritual, and Hospitality in Ancient India* (1996). A linguistic analysis of gender roles in Vedic literature.

Keightley, David N. *The Ancestral Landscape: Time, Space, and Community in Late Shang China, ca. 1200–1045 BC* (2000). Provides insights into the nature of royal kinship that undergirded the Shang court and its regional domains.

Kemp, Barry J. *Ancient Egypt: Anatomy of a Civilization* (2006). A definitive presentation of the history, culture, and religion of ancient Egypt.

Klein, Jacob. "The Marriage of Martu: The Urbanization of 'Barbaric' Nomads." In Meir Malul (ed.), *Mutual Influences of Peoples and Cultures in the Ancient Near East* (1996). A collection of essays written by scholars of the ancient Near East.

Kristiansen, Kristian. *Europe before History* (1998). The finest recent survey of all the major developmental phases of European prehistory.

Kuhrt, Amelie. *The Ancient Near East, c. 3000 BCE–300 CE*, 2 vols. (1995). A fundamental treatment of Egypt and Southwest Asia during these three millennia by a top scholar.

Leick, Gwendolyn (ed.). *The Babylonian World* (2007). Comprehensive presentation of the Babylonian world based on archaeology, texts, and works of art.

McIntosh, Jane. *Handbook to Life in Prehistoric Europe* (2006). Highlights the archaeological evidence that enables us to re-create the day-to-day life of different prehistoric communities in Europe.

Pines, Yuri. *The Everlasting Empire: The Political Culture of Ancient China and Its Imperial Legacy* (2012). How imperial unity became the norm in ancient China.

Preziosi, Donald, and L. A. Hitchcock. *Aegean Art and Architecture* (1999). One of the best general guides to the figurative and decorative art produced by both the Minoans and the Mycenaeans and by related early societies in the region of the Aegean.

Quirke, Stephen. *Ancient Egyptian Religion* (1992). A highly readable presentation of ancient Egyptian religion that summarizes the roles and attributions of the many Egyptian gods.

The Rigveda, the Earliest Religious Poetry of India, translated by Stephanie W. Jamison and Joel P. Bereton (2014). A new translation of the earliest literature of South Asia, correcting errors made in earlier translations.

Robins, Gay. *Women in Ancient Egypt* (1993). An interesting survey of the place of women in ancient Egyptian society.

Robins, Gay. *The Art of Ancient Egypt* (1997). The most comprehensive survey to date of the art of pharaonic Egypt.

Romer, John. *Ancient Lives: Daily Life in Egypt of the Pharaohs* (1990). A discussion of the economic and social lives of everyday ancient Egyptians.

Roth, Martha. *Law Collections from Mesopotamia and Asia Minor* (1985). An assemblage of law codes from Southwest Asia, including Hammurapi's famous legal edicts.

Sandars, N. K. *The Sea Peoples: Warriors of the Ancient Mediterranean* (1985). A readable discussion of a very complex period of Levantine history.

Simpson, William Kelly (ed.). *The Literature of Ancient Egypt: An Anthology of Stories, Instructions, and Poetry* (1972). A compilation of the most important works of literature from ancient Egypt.

Thapar, Romila. *The Past before Us: Historical Tradition of Early North India* (2013). A comprehensive evaluation of ancient Indian literature.

Thorp, Robert L. *China in the Early Bronze Age: Shang Civilization* (2005). Reviews the archaeological discoveries near Anyang, site of two capitals of the Shang kings.

Warren, Peter. *The Aegean Civilizations: From Ancient Crete to Mycenae*, 2nd ed. (1989). An excellent textual and pictorial guide to all the basic aspects of the Minoan and Mycenaean societies.

Wilson, John A. *The Culture of Ancient Egypt* (1951). A classic study of the history and culture of pharaonic Egypt.

Yadin, Yigael. *The Art of Warfare in Biblical Lands in the Light of Archaeological Discovery* (1963). A well-illustrated presentation of the machinery of war in the second and first millennia BCE.

Yoffee, Norman (ed.). *The Cambridge World History*, Vol. 3, *Early Cities in Comparative Perspective* (2014). One of nine volumes that trace world history through individual articles written by experts.

CHAPTER 4

Ahlström, Gosta W. *The History of Ancient Palestine from the Paleolithic Period to Alexander's Conquests* (1993). An excellent survey of the history of the region by a renowned expert, with good attention to the recent archaeological evidence.

Astour, Michael. "New Evidence on the Last Days of Ugarit," *American Journal of Archaeology* 69 (1965). An early and important article on the destruction of important cities in the Levant in the twelfth century BCE.

Aubet, Maria Eugenia. *The Phoenicians and the West*, 2nd ed. (2001). The basic survey of the Phoenician colonization of the western Mediterranean and Atlantic, with special attention to recent archaeological discoveries.

Behringer, Wolfgang. *A Cultural History of Climate*, translated by Patrick Camiller (2010). A summary view of the place of climate in historical change, written by an expert in historical climatology.

Benjamin, Craig (ed.). *The Cambridge World History*, Vol 4: *A World with States, Empires, and Networks, 1200 BCE–900 CE* (2015). An important overview of developments in the world, with individual chapters written by experts.

Briant, Pierre. *From Cyrus to Alexander: A History of the Persian Empire*, translated by Peter T. Daniels (2002). A complex and comprehensive history of the Persian Empire by its finest modern scholar.

Bright, John. *A History of Israel*, 4th ed. (2000). An updated version of a classic and still very useful overview of the whole history of the Israelite people down to the end of the period covered in this chapter.

Cook, John M. *The Persian Empire* (1983). An older but still useful and highly readable standard history of the Persian Empire.

Fagan, Brian. *The Long Summer: How Climate Changed Civilization* (2004). An accessible overview of the role of climate in historical change, written by one of the leading historians of ancient history and an individual who has brought together considerable evidence about climatic change and historical development.

Falkenhausen, Lothar von. *Chinese Society in the Age of Confucius (1000–250 BC): The Archaeological Evidence* (2006). A timely reassessment of early Chinese history that compares the literary texts on which it has traditionally been based with the new archaeological evidence.

Fukuyama, Francis. *The Origins of Political Order: From Prehuman Times to the French Revolution* (2011). Argues that the first real kings in Chinese history and the first real states and dynasties did not appear until the Qin and Han.

Grayson, A. Kirk. "Assyrian Civilization." In *Cambridge Ancient History*, Vol. 3, pt. 2 (1992), pp. 194–228. Examines the Assyrian and Babylonian Empires and other states of Southwest Asia from the eighth to the sixth centuries BCE.

Hornung, Erik. *Akhenaten and the Religion of Light*, translated from the German by David Lorton (1999). A brief but important biography of Egypt's most controversial pharaoh.

Hornung, Erik. *History of Ancient Egypt: An Introduction*, translated from the German by David Lorton (1999). An accessible overview of the history of ancient Egypt by a leading Egyptologist.

Isserlin, Benedikt J. *The Israelites* (1998). A well-written illustrated history of all aspects of life in the regions of the Levant inhabited by the Israelites.

Keay, John. *India: A History* (2010). A useful, readable overview of the sweep of Indian history.

Lancel, Serge. *Carthage: A History*, translated by Antonia Nevill (1997). By far the best single-volume history of the most important Phoenician colony in the Mediterranean. (The first three chapters are especially relevant to materials covered in this chapter.)

Lemche, Niels Peter. *Ancient Israel: A New History of Israelite Society* (1988). A quick, readable, and still up-to-date summary of the main phases and themes.

Lewis, Mark Edward. *Writing and Authority in Early China* (1999). A work that traces the changing uses of writing to command assent and obedience in early China.

Liverani, Mario. *The Ancient Near East: History, Society and Economy* (2014). Parts 5 and 6 are especially relevant to the materials covered in this chapter.

Liu, Guozhong. *Introduction to the Tsinghua Bamboo-Strip Manuscripts*, translated by Christopher J. Foster and William N. French (2016). An important essay on the implications of these texts for our understanding of early Western Zhou history.

Markoe, Glenn E. *Phoenicians* (2000). A thorough survey of the Phoenicians and their society as it first developed in the Levant and then expanded over the Mediterranean, with excellent illustrations of the diverse archaeological sites.

Matthews, Victor H., and Don C. Benjamin. *Social World of Ancient Israel, 1350–587 BCE* (1993). A thematic overview of the main occupational groups and social roles that characterized ancient Israelite society.

Oates, Joan, and David Oates. *Nimrud: An Assyrian Imperial City Revealed* (2001). A fine and highly readable summary of the state of our knowledge of the Neo-Assyrian Empire from the perspective of the early capital of Assurnasirpal II.

Oded, Bustenay. *Mass Deportations and Deportees in the Neo-Assyrian Empire* (1979). A detailed textual examination of the deportation strategy of the Assyrian kings.

Potts, D. T. *The Archaeology of Elam: Formation and Transformation of an Ancient Iranian State* (1999). The definitive study of the archaeology of western Iran from the Neolithic period through the Persian Empire.

Quinn, Josephine C., and Nicholas C. Vella (eds.). *The Punic Mediterranean* (2014). A valuable and readable collection of chapters on various aspects of how the Phoenician colonization of the Mediterranean led to the formation of new cultural identities.

Radner, Karen. *Ancient Assyria: A Very Short Introduction* (2015). A highly readable and up-to-date survey of all the important aspects of Assyrian government and society.

Shaughnessy, Edward L. *Sources of Western Zhou History: Inscribed Bronze Vessels* (1992). Detailed work on the historiography and interpretation of the thousands of ritual bronze vessels discovered by China's archaeologists.

Stein, Burton. *A History of India*, 2nd ed., edited by David Arnold (2010). One of the standard general histories of India, brought up to date by a leading historian of the subcontinent.

Tanner, Harold M. *China: A History* (2009). A readable and up-to-date overview of the sweep of Chinese history.

Thapar, Romila. *From Lineage to State* (1984). The only book on early India that uses religious literature historically and analyzes major lineages to reveal the transition from tribal society to state institutions.

Thapar, Romila. *The Aryan. Recasting Constructs* (2011). On the rise of the theory of an Aryan race and the beginnings of Indian history.

Tignor, Robert L. *Egypt: A Short History* (2010). A succinct treatment of the entire history of Egypt from the pharaohs to the present, with three chapters on the ancient period.

Trautmann, Thomas. *India: Brief History of a Civilization* (2011). A highly readable survey of Indian history with emphasis on its early history.

Tubb, Jonathan N. *Canaanites* (1998). The best recent survey, well illustrated, of one of the main ethnic groups dominating the culture of the Levant.

CHAPTER 5

Adams, William Y. *Nubia: Corridor to Africa* (1977). The authoritative historical overview of Nubia, the area of present-day Sudan just south of Egypt and a geographical connecting point between the Mediterranean and sub-Saharan Africa.

Allan, Sarah. *Buried Ideas: Legends of Abdication and Ideal Government in Early Chinese Bamboo-Slip Manuscripts* (2016). Four recently discovered Warring States texts challenge long-standing ideas about Chinese intellectual history.

Armstrong, Karen. *Buddha* (2001). A readable and impressive account of the life of the Buddha.

Aubet, Maria Eugenia. *The Phoenicians and the West*, 2nd ed. (2001). The basic survey of the Phoenician colonization of the western Mediterranean and Atlantic, with special attention to recent archaeological discoveries.

Barker, Graeme, and Tom Rasmussen. *The Etruscans* (1998). The most up-to-date introduction to this important pre-Roman society in the Italian peninsula, with strong emphasis on broad social and material patterns of development as indicated by the archaeological evidence.

Benjamin, Craig (ed.). *The Cambridge World History*, Vol. 4: *A World with States, Empires, and Networks, 1200 BCE–900 CE* (2015). Essays by experts on these centuries in world history. Especially important for thinking about the Axial Age is the chapter by Bjorn Wittrock, "The Axial Age in World History," pp. 101–119.

Bresson, Alain. *The Making of the Ancient Greek Economy: Institutions, Markets, and Growth in the City-States*, translated by Steven Rendall (2015). The most conceptually sophisticated and factually up-to-date account of the economic regimes of the Greek city-states.

Burkert, Walter. *Greek Religion*, translated by John Raffan (1985). The best one-volume introduction to early Greek religion, placing the Greeks in their larger Mediterranean and Near Eastern contexts.

Burns, Karen Olsen. *Ancient South America* (1994). A very useful overview of recent debates and conclusions about pre-Columbian archaeology in South America, including both the Andes and the lowland and coastal regions.

Cartledge, Paul (ed.). *The Cambridge Illustrated History of Ancient Greece* (2002). An excellent history of the Greek city-states down to the time of Alexander the Great.

Chakravarti, Uma. *The Social Dimensions of Early Buddhism* (1987). A description of the life of Buddha drawn from early Buddhist texts.

Cho-yun, Hsu. *Ancient China in Transition* (1965). An account of the political, economic, social, and intellectual changes that occurred during the Warring States period.

Coarelli, Filippo (ed.). *Etruscan Cities* (1975). A brilliantly and lavishly illustrated guide to the material remains of the Etruscans: their cities, their magnificent tombs, and their architecture, painting, sculpture, and other art.

Coe, Michael, Richard A. Diehl, David A Freidel, et al. (eds.), *The Olmec World: Ritual and Rulership* (1996). A collection of field-synthesizing articles with important illustrations, based on one of the most comprehensive exhibitions of Olmec art in the world.

Confucius. *The Analects (Lun Yü)*, translated by D. C. Lau (1979). An outstanding translation of the words of Confucius as recorded by his major disciples. Includes valuable historical material needed to provide the context for Confucius's teachings.

Eisenstadt, S. N. (ed.). *The Origins and Diversity of Axial Age Civilizations* (1986). A set of essays that develops Jaspers's concept of the Axial Age cultures.

Elman, Benjamin A., and Martin Kern (eds.). *Statecraft and Classical Learning: The Rituals of Zhou in East Asian History* (2010). Traces the long-term political rise of classical learning and state rituals in East Asia from the decline of the Eastern Zhou kingdom to the rise of later imperial dynasties in China, Japan, and Korea.

Finley, M. I., and H. W. Pleket. *The Olympic Games: The First Thousand Years* (2005). A fine description of the most famous of the Greek games; it explains how they exemplify the competitive spirit that marked many aspects of the Greek city-states.

Garlan, Yvon. *War in the Ancient World: A Social History*, translated by Janet Lloyd (1976). A discussion of the emergence of the forms of warfare, including male citizens fighting in hoplite phalanxes and the development of siege warfare, that were typical of the Greek city-states.

Garlan, Yvon. *Slavery in Ancient Greece*, translated by Janet Lloyd (1988). A treatment of the emergence, development, and institutionalization of chattel slavery in the Greek city-states.

Iliffe, John. *Africans: The History of a Continent*, 2nd ed. (2007). A first-rate scholarly survey of Africa from its beginnings, with a strong emphasis on demography.

Jaspers, Karl. *The Origin and Goal of History* (1953). The book that first developed the idea of the Axial Age.

Lancel, Serge. *Carthage: A History*, translated by Antonia Nevill (1997). By far the best single-volume history of the most important Phoenician colony in the Mediterranean.

Lewis, Mark Edward. *Sanctioned Violence in Early China* (1990). An analysis of the use of sanctioned violence as an element of statecraft from the Warring States period to the formation of the Qin and Han Empires in the second half of the first millennium BCE.

Lewis, Mark Edward. *Writing and Authority in Early China* (1999). A revisionist account of the central role of writing and persuasion in models for the invention of a Chinese world empire.

Ling, Trevor. *The Buddha: Buddhist Civilization in India and Ceylon* (1972). An overview of Buddhism in India and Ceylon.

Lloyd, G. E. R. *Early Greek Science: Thales to Aristotle* (1970). An especially clear and concise introduction to the main developments and intellectuals that marked the emergence of critical secular thinking in the early Greek world.

Lloyd, G. E. R., and Nathan Sivin. *The Way and the Word: Science and Medicine in Early China and Greece* (2002). A comprehensive rethinking of the social and political settings in ancient China and city-state Greece that contributed to the different views of science and medicine that emerged in each place.

Mote, Frederick. *Intellectual Foundations of China* (1971). An early but still useful description of the seminal figures in China's early intellectual life.

Murray, Oswyn. *Early Greece*, 2nd ed. (1993). One of the best introductions to the emergence of the Greek city-states down to the end of the Archaic Age.

Ober, Josiah. *The Rise and Fall of Classical Greece* (2015). A compelling general interpretation of the rise of the Greek city-states in the sixth and fifth centuries BCE and their subsequent demise in the fourth century.

Osborne, Robin. *Archaic and Classical Greek Art* (1998). An outstanding book that clearly explains the main innovations in Greek art, setting them in their historical context.

Osborne, Robin. *Greece in the Making, 1200–479 BC* (1999). The standard history of the whole early period of the Greek city-states characterized by an especially fine and judicious mix of archaeological data and literary sources.

Pallottino, Massimo. *The Etruscans,* rev. ed., translated by J. Cremona (1975). A fairly traditional but still classic survey of all aspects of Etruscan history and political and social institutions.

Pines, Yuri, Paul R. Goldin, and Martin Kern (eds.). *Ideology of Power and Power of Ideology in Early China* (2015). A new assessment of state ideology and political legitimation under the Eastern Zhou dynasty during the Warring States era.

Redford, Donald B. *From Slave to Pharaoh: The Black Experience of Ancient Egypt* (2004). A description of Egypt's Twenty-fifth Dynasty, which was made up of Sudanese conquerors.

Schaberg, David. *A Patterned Past: Form and Thought in Early Chinese Historiography* (2002). A comprehensive study of the intellectual content of historical anecdotes by the followers of Confucius collected around the fourth century BCE.

Schaps, David. *The Invention of Coinage and the Monetization of Ancient Greece* (2004). A new analysis that offers a broad overview of the emergence of coined money in the Near East and the eastern Mediterranean and its effects on the spread of money-based markets.

Sharma, J. P. *Republics in Ancient India, c. 1500 B.C.–500 B.C.* (1968). Relying on information from early Buddhist texts, this book first revealed that South Asia had not only monarchies but also alternative polities.

Shaw, Thurston. *Nigeria: Its Archaeology and Early History* (1978). An important introduction to the early history of Nigeria by one of that country's leading archaeologists.

Shinnie, P. L. *Ancient Nubia* (1996). An excellent account of the history of the ancient Nubians, who, we are discovering, had great influence on Egypt and on the rest of tropical Africa.

Snodgrass, Anthony. *Archaic Greece: The Age of Experiment* (1981). A good introduction to the archaeological evidence of Archaic Greece.

Taylor, Christopher, Richard Hare, and Jonathan Barnes. *Greek Philosophers* (1999). A fine, succinct, one-volume introduction to the major aspects of the three big thinkers who dominated the high period of classical Greek philosophy: Socrates, Plato, and Aristotle.

Torok, Laszlo. *Meroe: Six Studies on the Cultural Identity of an Ancient African State* (1995). A good collection of essays on the most recent work on Meroe.

Von Falkenhausen, Lothar. *Chinese Society in the Age of Confucius (100–250 BC)* (2006). The larger Chinese society under the influence of Confucian thought.

Welsby, Derek. *The Kingdom of Kush: The Napatan and Meroitic Empires* (1996). A fine book on these two important Nubian kingdoms.

CHAPTER 6

Bradley, Keith. *Slavery and Rebellion in the Roman World, 140 B.C.–70 B.C.* (1989). A description of the rise of large-scale plantation slavery in Sicily and Italy and a detailed account of the three great slave wars.

Bresson, Alain. *The Making of the Ancient Greek Economy: Markets and Growth in the City-States,* translated by Steven Rendall (2015). An up-to-date and theoretically well-informed analysis of the market economics of the Greek city-states in the Hellenistic era.

Browning, Iain. *Palmyra* (1979). A narrative of the history of the important desert city that linked eastern and western trade routes.

Casson, Lionel. *The Periplus Maris Erythraei* (1989). An introduction to a typical ancient sailing manual, this one of the Red Sea and Indian Ocean.

Casson, Lionel. *Ships and Seamanship in the Ancient World* (1995). The classic account of the ships and sailors that powered commerce and war on the high seas.

Colledge, Malcolm. *The Art of Palmyra* (1976). A well-illustrated introduction to the unusual art of Palmyra with its mixture of eastern and western elements.

Fowler, Barbara H. *The Hellenistic Aesthetic* (1989). How the artists in this new age saw and portrayed their world in new and different ways.

Green, Peter. *Alexander to Actium: The Historical Evolution of the Hellenistic Age* (1990). The best general guide to the whole period in all of its various aspects, and well illustrated.

Habicht, Christian. *Athens from Alexander to Antony,* translated by Deborah L. Schneider (1997). The authoritative account of what happened to the great city-state of Athens in this period.

Hansen, Valerie. *The Silk Road: A New History* (2012). The most recent work on the Silk Road; authoritative on the eastern terminus of this vital trade route.

Herodotus. *The Histories,* 4 volumes, translated by Tom Holland (2013). A basic work, which many scholars regard as the first world history. The translation given here was done by Brent Shaw and came from the original Greek.

Holt, Frank L. *Thundering Zeus: The Making of Hellenistic Bactria* (1999). A basic history of the most eastern of the kingdoms spawned by the conquests of Alexander the Great.

Hopkirk, Peter. *Foreign Devils on the Silk Road* (1984). A historiography of the explorations and researches on the central Asian Silk Road of the nineteenth and early twentieth centuries.

Juliano, Annette L., and Judith A. Lerner (eds.) *Nomads, Traders and Holy Men along China's Silk Road* (2003). A description of the travelers along the Silk Road in human terms, focusing on warfare, markets, and religion.

Keay, John. *India: A History* (2000). A well-written and well-researched overview of the entire history of South Asia.

Kosmin, Paul J. *The Land of the Elephant Kings: Space, Territory, and Ideology in the Seleucid Empire* (2014). The best current analysis of the relationships of Seleucid kings, both with their own subjects and, especially, with the Mauryan kingdom of India and the nomadic peoples of central Asia.

Kuzima, E. E. *The Prehistory of the Silk Road* (2008). Valuable information on the early history of the Silk Road.

Lane Fox, Robin. *Alexander the Great* (1973). Still the most readable and in many ways the sanest biography of the world conqueror.

Lewis, Naphtali. *Greeks in Ptolemaic Egypt* (1986). An account of the relationships between Greeks and Egyptians as seen through the lives of individual Greek settlers and colonists.

Liu, Xinru. *Ancient India and Ancient China* (1988). The first work to connect political and economic developments in India and China with the evolution and spread of Buddhism in the first half of the first millennium.

Liu, Xinru. *The Silk Road in World History* (2010). A study of the history of the great trade and communications route that connected the different regions of Afro-Eurasia between the third century BCE and the thirteenth century CE.

Long, Antony A. *Hellenistic Philosophy: Stoics, Epicureans, Sceptics*, 2nd ed. (1986). One of the clearest guides to the new trends in Greek philosophical thinking in the period.

Martin, Luther H. *Hellenistic Religions: An Introduction* (1987). An introduction to the principal new Hellenistic religions and cults that emerged in this period.

Mendels, Doron. *The Rise and Fall of Jewish Nationalism* (1992). A sophisticated account of the various phases of Jewish resistance in Judah to foreign domination.

Miller, James Innes. *The Spice Trade of the Roman Empire, 29 B.C. to A.D. 641* (1969). A first-rate study of the spice trade in the Roman Empire.

Pomeroy, Sarah B. *Women in Hellenistic Egypt: From Alexander to Cleopatra* (1990). A highly readable investigation of women and family in the best-documented region of the Hellenistic world.

Ray, Himanshu P. *The Wind of Change, Buddhism and the Maritime Links of Early South Asia* (1994). Ray's study of Buddhism and maritime trade stretches from the Arabian Sea to the navigations between South Asia and Southeast Asia.

Rosenfield, John. *The Dynastic Art of the Kushans* (1967). Instead of focusing on the Gandharan Buddhist art itself, Rosenfield selects sculptures of Kushan royals and those representing nomadic populations in religious shrines to display the central Asian aspect of artworks of the period.

Rostovtzeff, Michael Ivanovich. *Caravan Cities*, translated by D. and T. Talbot Rice (1932). Though published more than eight decades ago, this small volume contains accurate descriptions of the ruins of many caravan cities in modern Jordan and Syria.

Rostovtzeff, Michael Ivanovich. *The Social and Economic History of the Hellenistic World* (1941). A monumental achievement. One of the great works of history written in the twentieth century. An unsurpassed overview of all aspects of the politics and social and economic movements of the period. Despite its age, there is still nothing like it.

Schoff, Wilfred H. (ed. and trans.). *The Periplus of the Erythraean Sea* (1912). An invaluable tool for mapping the names and places from the Red Sea to Indian coastal areas during this period.

Shipley, Graham. *The Greek World after Alexander, 323–30 BC* (2000). A more up-to-date survey than Peter Green's work (above), with more emphasis on the historical detail in each period.

Thapar, Romila. *Aśoka and the Decline of the Mauryas* (1973). Using all available primary sources, including the edicts of Aśoka and Greek authors' accounts, Thapar gives the most authoritative analysis of the first (and most important) empire in Indian history.

Vainker, Shelagh. *Chinese Silk: A Cultural History* (2004). A work that traces the cultural history of silk in China from its early origins to the twentieth century and considers its relationship to the other decorative arts. The author draws on the most recent archaeological evidence to emphasize the role of silk in Chinese history, trade, religion, and literature.

Wood, Francis. *The Silk Road: Two Thousand Years in the Heart of Asia* (2004). Illustrated with drawings, manuscripts, paintings, and artifacts to trace the Silk Road to its origins as far back as Alexander the Great, with an emphasis on its importance to cultural and religious movements.

Young, Gary K. *Rome's Eastern Trade: International Commerce and Imperial Policy, 31 BC–AD 305* (2001). This study examines the taxation and profits of eastern trade from the perspective of the Roman government.

CHAPTER 7

Barbieri-Low, Anthony J., and Robin D. S. Yates. *Law, State, and Society in Early Imperial China (2 Vols): A Study with Critical Edition and Translation of the Legal Texts from Zhangjiashan Tomb No. 247* (2015). A new account of changes in Western (Former) Han dynasty law in terms of its moralization via instituting Confucianism.

Batty, Roger. *Rome and the Nomads: The Pontic-Danubian Realm in Antiquity* (2007). A comprehensive account of relations between the Roman Empire and the nomads of the western Eurasian steppelands.

Bodde, Derk. *China's First Unifier: A Study of the Ch'in Dynasty as Seen in the Life of Li Ssu (280?–208 B.C.)* (1938). A classic account of the key Legalist adviser, Li Si, who formulated the Qin policy to enhance its autocratic power.

Bowman, Alan K. *Life and Letters on the Roman Frontier: Vindolanda and Its Peoples* (1994). An introduction to the exciting discovery of writing tablets from a Roman army base in northern Britain.

Bradley, Keith. *Slavery and Society at Rome* (1994). An excellent overview of the major aspects of the slave system in the Roman Empire.

Chevallier, Raymond. *Roman Roads,* translated by N. H. Field (1976). A guide to the fundamentals of the construction, maintenance, administration, and mapping of Roman roads.

Coarelli, Fillipo (ed.). *Pompeii,* translated by Patricia Cockram (2006). A lavishly illustrated large volume that allows the reader to sense some of the wondrous wealth of the buried city of Pompeii.

Colledge, Malcolm A. R. *The Parthians* (1967). A bit dated but still a fundamental introduction to the Parthians, the major power on the eastern frontier of the Roman Empire.

Cornell, Tim. *The Beginnings of Rome: Italy and Rome from the Bronze Age to the Punic Wars, c. 2000 to 264 B.C.* (1995). The single best one-volume history of Rome through its early history to the first war with Carthage.

Cornell, Tim, and John Matthews. *Atlas of the Roman World* (1982). A history of the Roman world; much more than simply an atlas. It provides not only good maps and a gazetteer but also marvelous color illustrations and a text that guides the reader through the basics of Roman history.

Csikszentmihalyi, Mark. *Readings in Han Chinese Thought* (2006). A volume presenting a representative selection of primary sources to illustrate the growth of ideas in early imperial times; a useful introduction to the key strains of thought during this crucial period.

Dien, Albert E. "The Qin Army and Its Antecedents." In Liu Yang (ed.), *China's Terracotta Warriors: The First Emperor's Legacy* (2013). An account of the Qin army in light of its Warring States precedents.

Dixon, Suzanne. *The Roman Family* (1992). The best one-volume guide to the nature of the Roman family and family relations.

Elvin, Mark. *The Retreat of the Elephants: An Environmental History of China* (2004). A pioneering environmental history of China covering over 4,000 years of its history.

Garnsey, Peter, and Richard Saller. *The Roman Empire: Economy, Society, and Culture*, 2nd ed. (2014). A perceptive and critical introduction to three basic aspects of social life in the empire.

Giardina, Andrea (ed.). *The Romans*, translated by Lydia Cochrane (1993). Individual studies of important typical figures in Roman society, from the peasant and the bandit to the merchant and the soldier.

Goldsworthy, Adrian. *The Roman Army at War: 100 B.C.–A.D. 200* (1996). A summary history and analysis of the Roman army in action during the late Republic and early Roman Empire.

Harris, William. *Ancient Literacy* (1989). A basic survey of what is known about communication in the form of writing and books in the Roman Empire.

Hopkins, Keith. *Death and Renewal: Sociological Studies in Roman History*, vol. 2 (1983). Innovative studies in Roman history, including one of the best on gladiators and another on death and funerals.

Hopkins, Keith. *A World Full of Gods: Pagans, Jews and Christians in the Roman Empire* (1999). A somewhat unusual but interesting and provocative look at the world of religions in the Roman Empire.

Hughes, J. Donald. *Environmental Problems of the Greeks and Romans: Ecology in the Ancient Mediterranean*, 2nd ed. (2014). A much improved and expanded edition of a classic work on the environment in Greek and Roman antiquity and a state-of-the-art summary of our current knowledge.

Juliano, Annette L., and Judith A. Lerner (eds.). *Nomads, Traders and Holy Men along China's Silk Road* (2003). A description of the travelers along the Silk Road in human terms, focusing on warfare, markets, and religion.

Kern, Martin, and Michael Hunter (eds.). *The Analects. A Western Han Text?* (2013). Challenges the assumption that the Confucian *Analects* was compiled before the Han dynasty.

Knapp, Robert C. *Invisible Romans* (2011). A highly readable introduction to the lower orders of Roman imperial society: the poor, slaves, freedmen, prostitutes, gladiators, bandits, and pirates (among others).

Lewis, Mark. *The Early Chinese Empires: Qin and Han* (2007). A recent account of the rise of imperial China after the Warring States period.

Liang, Cai. *Witchcraft and the Rise of the First Confucian Empire* (2014). A new account of the rise of the Confucians at the Former (Western) Han court during the famous witchcraft trials circa 91–87 BCE.

Loewe, Michael. *The Government of the Qin and Han Empires: 221 BCE–220 CE* (2006). A useful overview of the government of the early empires of China. Topics include the structure of central government, provincial and local government, the armed forces, officials, government communications, the laws of the empire, and control of the people and the land.

Millar, Fergus. *The Emperor in the Roman World, 31 B.C.–A.D. 337* (1992). Everything you might want to know about the Roman emperor, with special emphasis on his role as the administrator of the empire.

Millar, Fergus. *The Crowd in the Late Republic* (1990). An innovative study of the democratic power of the citizens in the city of Rome itself.

Potter, David. *The Roman Empire at Bay: A.D. 180–395*, 2nd ed. (2014). A new basic text covering the later Roman Empire, including the critical transition to a Christian state.

Qian, Sima. *Records of the Grand Historian: Qin Dynasty*, 3rd ed., translated by Burton Watson (1995). The classic work of Chinese history in a readable translation. The Han dynasty's Grand Historian describes the slow rise and meteoric fall of the Qin dynasty from the point of view of the succeeding dynasty, which Sima Qian witnessed or heard of during his lifetime.

Southern, Pat. *The Roman Army: A Social and Institutional History* (2006). A guide to all aspects of the Roman army.

Vainker, Shelagh. *Chinese Silk: A Cultural History* (2004). A work that traces the cultural history of silk in China from its early origins to the twentieth century and considers its relationship to the other decorative arts. The author draws on recent archaeological evidence to emphasize the role of silk in Chinese history, trade, religion, and literature.

Wood, Francis. *The Silk Road: Two Thousand Years in the Heart of Asia* (2004). A work illustrated with drawings, manuscripts, paintings, and artifacts to trace the Silk Road to its origins as far back as Alexander the Great. The author stresses the importance of the Silk Road to cultural and religious movements.

Woolf, Greg (ed.). *The Cambridge Illustrated History of the Roman World* (2005). A good guide to various aspects of Roman history, culture, and provincial life.

Woolf, Greg. *Rome: An Empire's Story* (2012). An up-to-date narrative of the Roman empire, told according to major themes that are particularly relevant to world history.

CHAPTER 8

Bowersock, Glen W. *Empires in Collision in Late Antiquity* (2013). Brilliant, short studies of the relations between Ethiopia, Arabia, and Byzantium as a background to the origins of Islam.

Brown, Peter. *The World of Late Antiquity: From Marcus Aurelius to Muhammad, AD 150–750* (1989). A social, religious, and cultural history of the late Roman and Sasanian Empires, with illustrations and a time chart.

Brown, Peter. *The Rise of Western Christendom: Triumph and Diversity, A.D. 200–1000*, 2nd ed. (2003). The rise and spread of Christianity in Europe and Asia, with up-to-date bibliographies on all topics, maps, and time charts. Reprinted with a new introduction in 2013.

Brown, Peter. *Through the Eye of a Needle: Wealth, the Fall of Rome, and the Making of Christianity in the West, 350–550* (2012). Christianity and Roman society before and after the end of the empire.

Brown, Peter. "The Silk Road in Late Antiquity." In V. H. Maier and J. Hickman (eds.), *Reconfiguring the Silk Road* (2014). Silk Road from the perspective of its western outlets and influences.

Brown, Peter. *Treasure in Heaven: The Holy Poor in Early Christianity* (2016). On the social role of early Christian monasticism in Syria and Egypt.

Bühler, G. (trans.). *The Laws of Manu* (1886). The classic translation of one of India's most important historical, legal, and religious texts.

Canepa, Matthew P. *The Two Eyes of the Earth: Art and Ritual of Kingship between Rome and Sasanian Iran* (2009). An interesting look at how two great global powers, Rome and Iran, shared images of rulership.

Coe, Michael D. *The Maya*, 6th ed. (1999). A work by the world's most famous Mayanologist, with recent evidence, analyses, and illustrations.

Cowgill, George L. "The Central Mexican Highlands and the Rise of Teotihuacan to the Decline of Tula." In Richard Adams and Murdo Macleod (eds.), *The Cambridge History of the Native Peoples of the Americas*, Vol. 2: *Mesoamerica, Part 1* (2000). A thorough review of findings about urban states in central Mexico.

Fash, William L. *Scribes, Warriors and Kings: The City of Copan and the Ancient Maya* (2001). A fascinating and comprehensive study of one of the most elaborate of the Mayan city-kingdoms.

Fisher, Greg. *Between Empires: Arabs, Romans, and Sasanians in Late Antiquity* (2011). Arab, Roman, and Sasanian empires compared.

Fisher, Greg (ed.). *Arabs and Empires before Islam* (2015). A collection of up-to-date studies on the relationships of various Arab groups with imperial powers, especially Rome and Persia.

Fowden, Elizabeth Key. *The Barbarian Plain: Saint Sergius between Rome and Iran* (1999). The study of a major Christian shrine and its relations to Romans, Persians, and Arabs.

Fowden, Garth. *Empire to Commonwealth: The Consequences of Monotheism in Late Antiquity* (1993). A study of the relation between empire and world religions in western Asia.

Gombrich, Richard F., and Sheldon Pollack (eds.). *Clay Sanskrit Library* (2005–2006). All major works from the Gupta and post-Gupta periods, in both Sanskrit and English versions. During the Gupta period, classical Sanskrit literature reached its apex, with abundant drama, poetry, and folk stories.

Gordon, Charles. *The Age of Attila* (1960). The last century of the Roman Empire in western Europe, vividly illustrated from contemporary sources.

Haldon, John. *The Empire That Would Not Die: The Paradox of Eastern Rome's Survival* (2010). Incorporates much new climatological evidence.

Hansen, Valerie. *The Silk Road: A New History* (2012). A detailed history of the Silk Road, based largely on Chinese sources.

Harper, Prudence. *The Royal Hunter: The Art of the Sasanian Empire* (1978). The ideology of the Sasanian Empire as shown through excavated hoards of precious silverware.

Heather, Peter. *The Fall of the Roman Empire: A New History of Rome and the Barbarians* (2006). A military and political narrative based on up-to-date archaeological material.

Herrmann, Georgina. *Iranian Revival* (1977). The structure and horizons of the Sasanian Empire as revealed in its monuments.

Hillgarth, Jocelyn (ed.). *Christianity and Paganism, 350–750: The Conversion of Western Europe*, rev. ed. (1986). A collection of contemporary sources.

Holcombe, Charles. *In the Shadow of the Han: Literati Thought and Society at the Beginning of the Southern Dynasties* (1994). A clear and concise account of the evolution of thought in China after the fall of the Han dynasty in 220 CE. The book presents the rise of Buddhism and Daoism as popular religions as well as elite interest in classical learning in a time of political division and barbarian conquest in North and South China.

La Vaissière, Étienne de. *Sogdian Traders: A History*, translated by James Ward (2005). A summary of historical facts about the most important trading community and its commercial networks on the Silk Road, from the early centuries CE to its demise in the ninth century CE.

Little, Lester (ed.). *Plague and the End of Antiquity: The Pandemic of 541–750* (2008). A series of debates over the nature and impact of the first great pandemic attested in global history.

Liu, Xinru, and Lynda Norene Shaffer. *Connections across Eurasia: Transportation, Communication, and Cultural Exchanges on the Silk Roads* (2007). A survey of trade and religious activities on the Silk Road.

Lopez, Ariel G. *Shenoute of Atripe and the Uses of Poverty: Rural Patronage, Religious Conflict, and Monasticism in Late Antique Egypt* (2013). Places a leading Egyptian abbot in his full social context.

Maas, Michael. *Readings in Late Antiquity: A Source Book* (1999). Well-chosen extracts that illustrate the interrelation of Romans and non-Romans and of Christians, Jews, and pagans.

Maas, Michael. *The Age of Atilla: The Cambridge Companion to the Age of Attila* (2013). Essays on this important age in the late Antique period.

Maas, Michael (ed.). *The Cambridge Companion to the Age of Justinian* (2005). A survey of all aspects of the Eastern Roman Empire in the sixth century CE.

Moffett, Samuel. *A History of Christianity in Asia*, Vol. 1 (1993). Particularly valuable on Christians in China and India.

Munro-Hay, Stuart. *Aksum: An African Civilization of Late Antiquity* (1991). The origins of the Christian kingdom of Ethiopia.

Murdock, George P. *Africa: Its Peoples and Their History* (1959). A vital introduction to the peoples of Africa and their history.

Oliver, Roland. *The African Experience: From Olduvai Gorge to the Twenty-First Century* (1999). An important overview, written by one of the pioneering scholars of African history and one of the leading authorities on the Bantu migrations.

Payne, Richard. *A State of Mixture: Christians, Zoroastrians, and Iranian Political Culture in Late Antiquity* (2015). A new view of Christianity in Sasanian Iran.

Pourshariati, Parvaneh. *The Decline and Fall of the Sasanian Empire: The Sasanian-Parthian Confederacy and the Arab Conquest of Iran* (2008). An innovative perspective on the demise of the Sasanians and the relevance of their decline for the Arab conquest of Iran.

Pregadio, Fabrizio. *Great Clarity: Daoism and Alchemy in Early Medieval China* (2006). An examination of the religious aspects of Daoism. The book focuses on the relation of alchemy to the Daoist traditions of the third to sixth century CE and shows how alchemy was integrated into the elaborate body of doctrines and practices of Daoists at that time.

Tempels, Placide. *Bantu Philosophy* (1959). A highly influential effort to argue for the underlying cultural unity of all the Bantu peoples.

Vansina, Jan. *Paths in the Rainforests: Toward a History of Political Tradition in Equatorial Africa* (1990). The best work on Bantu history.

Walker, Joel. *The Legend of Mar Kardagh: Narrative and Christian Heroism in Late Antique Iraq* (2006). Christians and Zoroastrians in northern Iraq and in Iran.

Yarshater, Ehsan. *Encyclopedia Iranica* (1982+). This encyclopedia offers countless articles dealing with all aspects of the Sasanian Empire and religion and culture in the regions between Mesopotamia and central Asia.

Zhang, Xun, *Fian Zhuan Jiaozhu* (1985) The account of a Chinese Buddhist who traveled to India to learn more about Buddhism and to bring back to China copies of important texts. The text excerpted in this chapter was done by Xinru Liu.

Zürcher, E. *The Buddhist Conquest of China: The Spread and Adaptation of Buddhism in Early Medieval China*, 3rd ed. (2007). A reissue of the classic account of the assimilation of Buddhism in China during the medieval period, with particular focus on the religious and philosophical success of Buddhism among Chinese elites in South China.

CHAPTER 9

Ahmed, Leila. *Women and Gender in Islam* (1992). A superb overview of the relations between men and women throughout the history of Islam.

Aneirin. *Y Gododdin: Britain's Oldest Heroic Poem*, edited and translated by A. O. H. Jarman (1988). A sixth-century CE Welsh text that describes the battle of the last Britons against the invading Anglo-Saxons.

Arberry, Arthur J. (trans.), Introduction to *The Koran Interpreted: A Translation* (1986). One of the most eloquent appreciations of this classical work of religion.

Augustine. *The City of God*, translated by H. Bettenson (1976). An excellent translation of Augustine's monumental work of history, philosophy, and religion.

Berkey, Jonathan P. *The Formation of Islam: Religion and Society in the Near East, 600–1800* (2005). A recent overview of the history of Islam before the modern era. It is particularly sensitive to the influence of external elements on the history of the Muslim peoples.

Bol, Peter. *This Culture of Ours: Intellectual Transitions in T'ang and Sung China* (1994). A study tracing the transformation of the shared culture of the Chinese learned elite from the seventh to the twelfth centuries.

Bowersock, G. W. *The Throne of Adulis: Red Sea Wars on the Eve of Islam* (2013). A vital study of the kingdom of Himyar, in present-day Yemen, a center of Judaism and Christianity before the rise of Islam in the Arabian Peninsula.

Brooke, John L. *Climate Change and the Course of Global History: A Rough Journey* (2014). An overview of a changing climate and its impact on historical developments.

Brown, Peter. *The Rise of Western Christendom: Triumph and Diversity, AD 200–1000*, 2nd ed. (2003). A description of the changes in Christianity in northern Europe and the emergence of the new cultures and political structures that coincided with this development.

Bulliet, Richard W. *Conversion to Islam in the Medieval Period: An Essay in Quantitative History* (1979). A study of the rate at which the populations overrun by Arab conquerors in the seventh century CE embraced the religion of their rulers.

Bulliet, Richard W. *Cotton, Climate, and Camels in the Early Islamic State* (2009). A fascinating account of the economic development on the Iranian plateau, with an emphasis on climate.

Cook, David. *Understanding Jihad* (2005). An exploration of the meaning of Jihad, a significant Muslim concept in today's world, as understood in early Islam.

Cook, Michael. *Muhammad* (1983). A brief but careful life of the Prophet that takes full account of the prolific and often controversial preexisting scholarship.

Cook, Michael. *The Koran: A Very Short Introduction* (2000). A useful overview of Islam's holy book.

Creswell, K. A. C. *A Short Account of Early Muslim Architecture*, revised and supplemented by James W. Allan (1992). The definitive treatment of the subject.

Crone, Patricia, *The Nativist Prophets of Early Islam: Rural Revolt and Local Zoroastrianism* (2012). The rise of protest movements in Islam that led to the Abbasid takeover from the Umayyads.

Cross, S. H., and O. P. Sherbowitz-Westor (trans.). *The Russian Primary Chronicle* (1953). A vivid record of the Viking settlement of Kiev, the conversion of Kiev, and the princes of Kiev in the tenth and eleventh centuries.

Donner, Fred M. *The Early Islamic Conquests* (1981). The best account of the Arab conquests in the Persian and Byzantine Empires in the seventh century CE.

Donner, Fred M. *Muhammad and the Believers at the Origins of Islam* (2010). A richly detailed study of Muhammad's prophecy and the rise of Islam during the Umayyad period.

Duncan, John. *The Origins of the Chosŏn Dynasty* (2000). A historical account of the early Korean dynasties from 900 to 1400.

Elman, Benjamin. *Precocious China: Civil Examinations, 1400–1900* (2013). Summary of civil exams in China from medieval times.

Fage, J. D. *Ghana: A Historical Introduction* (1966). A brief but authoritative history of Ghana from earliest times to the mid-twentieth century.

Fisher, Humphrey J. *Slavery in the History of Muslim Black Africa* (2001). A general history of the relations between North Africa and black Africa, focusing on one of the most important aspects of contact—the slave trade.

Fowden, Garth. *Before and after Muhammad: The First Millennium Refocused* (2014). The author sets Islam in its larger Greek and Christianity setting, part of the work of the Late Antique scholarly community.

Graham-Campbell, James. *Cultural Atlas of the Viking World* (1994). A positioning of the Vikings against their wider background in both western and eastern Europe.

Haider, Najam. *The Origins of the Shi'a: Identity, Ritual, and Sacred Space in Eighth-Century Kufah* (2011). A definitive study on the origin of Shiism.

Hawting, G. R. *The First Dynasty of Islam: The Umayyad Caliphate, A.D. 661–750* (2000). The essential scholarly treatment of Islam's first dynasty.

Herrmann, Georgina. *Iranian Revival* (1977). The structure and horizons of the Sasanian Empire as revealed in its monuments.

Hillgarth, J. N. (ed.). *Christianity and Paganism, 350–750: The Conversion of Western Europe*, rev. ed. (1986). A collection of contemporary sources.

Hodges, Richard, and David Whitehouse. *Mohammed, Charlemagne, and the Origins of Europe* (1983). A spirited comparison of Islam and the rise of Europe.

Hodgson, Marshall G. S. *The Venture of Islam: Conscience and History in a World Civilization*, 3 vols. (1977). A magnificent history of the Islamic peoples. Its first volume, *The Classical Age of Islam*, is basic reading for anyone interested in the history of the Muslim world.

Holdsworth, May. *Women of the Tang Dynasty* (1999). An account of women's lives during the Tang dynasty.

Hourani, Albert. *History of the Arab Peoples* (2002). The best overview of Arab history.

Hoyland, Robert G. *In God's Path: The Arab Conquests and the Creation of the Islamic Empire* (2015). New work that draws on non-Arabic sources to fill in gaps in Islamic historiography.

Jones, Gwynn. *The Norse Atlantic Saga* (1986). The Viking discovery of America.

Kennedy, Hugh. *The Prophet and the Age of the Caliphate: The Islamic Near East from the Sixth to the Eleventh Century* (2004). A very good recent synthesis of the rise and spread of Islam.

Lee, Peter, et al. (eds.). *Sources of Korean Tradition,* vol. 1 (1996). A unique view of Korean history through the eyes and words of the participants or witnesses themselves, as provided in translations of official documents, letters, and policies.

Levtzion, Nehemia. *Ancient Ghana and Mali* (1980). The best introduction to the kingdoms of West Africa.

Levtzion, Nehemia, and Jay Spaulding. *Medieval West Africa: Views from Arab Scholars and Merchants* (2003). An indispensable source book on early West African history.

Levy-Rubin, Milka. *Non-Muslims in the Early Islamic Empire: From Surrender to Co-existence* (2011). The exploitation of non-Muslims in early Islam and their later conversion and rise to prominence.

Lewis, Bernard. *The Middle East: Two Thousand Years of History from the Rise of Christianity to the Present Day* (1995). A stimulating introduction to an area that has seen the emergence of three of the great world religions.

Lewis, Bernard (trans.). *Islam from the Prophet Muhammad to the Capture of Constantinople.* Vol. 2: *Religion and Society* (1974). A fine collection of original sources that portray various aspects of classical Islamic society.

Lewis, David Levering. *God's Crucible: Islam and the Making of Europe, 570–1215* (2008). An exciting and well-written overview of the high period of Islamic power and cultural attainments.

Middleton, John. *The Swahili: The Social Landscape of a Mercantile Community* (2000). An exciting synthesis of the Swahili culture of East Africa.

Miyazaki, Ichisada. *China's Examination Hell* (1981). A study of China's examination system.

Nurse, Derek, and Thomas Spear. *The Swahili: Reconstructing the History and Language of an African Society, 800–1500* (1984). A work that explores the history of the Muslim peoples who lived along the coast of East Africa.

Peters, F. E. *Muhammad and the Origins of Islam* (1994). A work that explores the early history of Islam and highlights the critical role that Muhammad played in promoting a new religion and a powerful Arab identity.

Pourshariati, Parveneh. *Decline and Fall of the Sasanian Empire* (2008). Fundamental analysis of the end of the Sasanian Empire and the reasons for the success of the Arab/Muslim invasions.

Robinson, Chase F. *The New Cambridge History of Islam,* Vol. 1: *The Formation of the Islamic World, Sixth to Eleventh Centuries* (2010). An authoritative and up-to-date six-volume overview of the history of Islam from the sixth century CE to the present.

Schirokauer, Conrad, et al. *A Brief History of Japanese Civilization,* 2nd ed. (2005). A balanced account; chapters focus on developments in art, religion, literature, and thought as well as on Japan's economic, political, and social history in medieval times.

Shoemaker, Stephen T. *The Death of a Prophet: The End of Muhammad's Life and the Beginnings of Islam* (2012). The use of non-Arabic sources to learn about Muhammad and the rise of Islam.

Smith, Julia. *Europe after Rome: A New Cultural History, 500–1000* (2005). A vivid analysis of society and culture in so-called Dark Age Europe.

Totman, Conrad. *History of Japan* (2004). A recent and readable summary of Japanese history from ancient to modern times.

Twitchett, Denis. *Financial Administration under the T'ang Dynasty* (1970). A pioneering account—based on rare Dunhuang documents that survived from medieval times in Buddhist grottoes in central Asia—of the political and economic system undergirding the Chinese imperial state.

Twitchett, Denis. *The Birth of the Chinese Meritocracy: Bureaucrats and Examinations in T'ang China* (1976). A description of the role of the written civil examinations that began during the Tang dynasty.

Whittow, Mark. *The Making of Byzantium, 600–1025* (1996). A study on the survival and revival of the Eastern Roman Empire as a major power in eastern Europe and Southwest Asia.

Wood, Ian. *The Missionary Life: Saints and the Evangelization of Europe, 400–1050* (2001). The horizons of Christians on the frontiers of Europe.

CHAPTER 10

Allsen, Thomas. *Commodity and Exchange in the Mongol Empire: A Cultural History of Islamic Textiles* (1997). A study that uses golden brocade, the textile most treasured by Mongol rulers, as a lens through which to analyze the vast commercial networks facilitated by the Mongol conquests and control.

Allsen, Thomas. *Culture and Conquest in Mongol Eurasia* (2001). A work that emphasizes the cultural and scientific exchanges that took place across Afro-Eurasia as a result of the Mongol conquest.

Bagge, Svere, Michael Gelting, and Thomas Lundkvist (eds.). *Feudalism: New Landscapes of Debate* (2011). A collection of essays on interpretations of feudalism by experts on the topic.

Bailey, Mark. *The English Manor, c. 1200–c. 1500* (2002). An important detailed study of English manorialism.

Bartlett, Robert. *The Making of Europe: Conquest, Colonization and Cultural Change, 950–1350* (1993). The modes of cultural, political, and demographic expansion of feudal Europe along its frontiers, especially in eastern Europe.

Bay, Edna G. *Wives of the Leopards: Gender, Politics, and Culture in the Kingdom of Dahomey* (1998). A work that stresses the role of women in an important West African society and dips into the early history of this area.

Beach, D. N. *Shona and Zimbabwe, 900–1850: An Outline of Shona History* (1980). A good place to start for exploring the history of Great Zimbabwe.

Bloch, Marc. *Feudal Society,* translated by L. A. Manyon (1961). The classic study of feudalism, now being criticized.

Brooks, George E. *Landlords and Strangers: Ecology, Society, and Trade in Western Africa, 1000–1630* (1993). A survey assembled from primary sources of early West African history that stresses transregional connections.

Bulliet, Richard W. *Cotton, Climate, and Camels in Early Islamic Iran* (2009). An analysis of the upswing of the Iranian plateau economy after the Muslim conquest and then its decline as a result of climate change.

Buzurg ibn Shahriyar of Ramhormuz. *The Book of the Wonders of India: Mainland, Sea and Islands,* edited and translated by G. S. P. Freeman-Greenville (1981). A collection of stories told by sailors, both true and fantastic; they help us imagine the lives of sailors of the era.

Chappell, Sally A. Kitt. *Cahokia: Mirror of the Cosmos* (2002). A thorough and vivid account of the "mound people"; it explores not just what we know of Cahokia but how we know it.

Christian, David. *A Short History of Russia, Central Asia, and Mongolia*. Vol. 1: *Inner Eurasia from Prehistory to the Mongol Empire* (1998). Essential reading for students interested in interconnections across the Afro-Eurasian landmass.

Curtin, Philip. *Cross-Cultural Trade in World History* (1984). A groundbreaking book on intercultural trade with a primary focus on Africa, especially the cross-Saharan trade and Swahili coastal trade.

Dawson, Christopher. *Mission to Asia* (1980). Accounts of China and the Mongol Empire brought back by Catholic missionaries and diplomats after 1240 CE.

Duby, Georges. *The Three Orders: Feudal Society Imagined*, translated by Arthur Goldhammer (1982). Another classic study of feudalism.

Ellenblum, Ronnie. *The Collapse of the Eastern Mediterranean: Climate Change and the Decline of the East, 950–1072* (2012). An analysis of the impact of freezing temperatures and drought on the societies of the eastern Mediterranean.

Flori, Jean. "Knightly Society." In David Luscombe and Jonathon Riley Smith (eds.), *The New Cambridge Medieval History*, Vol. 4, Part 1: *c. 1024–1198* (2004). A brilliant overview of knights in medieval times and an overview of the debate on feudalism with the author's own insightful conclusions. Other useful articles in this volume are by Susan Reynolds and by David Luscombe and Jonathon Riley Smith.

Foltz, Richard C. *Religions of the Silk Road: Overland Trade and Cultural Exchange from Antiquity to the Fifteenth Century* (1999). A study of the populations and the cities of the Silk Road as transmitters of culture across long distances.

Franklin, Simon, and Jonathan Shepherd. *The Emergence of Rus: 750–1200* (1996). The formation of medieval Russia between the Baltic and Black Seas.

Ganshof, F. L. *Feudalism*, translated by Philip Griersur (1952). Perhaps the work most often dealt with by critics of the term *feudalism*. Simple, straightforward, easily comprehended study of feudalism.

Gibb, Hamilton A. R. *Saladin: Studies in Islamic History*, edited by Yusuf Ibish (1974). A sympathetic portrait of one of Islam's leading political and military figures.

Goitein, S. D. "New Light on the Beginnings of the Karim Merchants." *Journal of the Economic and Social History of the Orient* 1 (1957): 175–184. Goitein's description of Egyptian trade.

Goitein, S. D. *Letters of Medieval Jewish Traders* (1973). The classic study of medieval Jewish trading communities based on the commercial papers deposited in the Cairo Geniza (a synagogue storeroom) during the tenth and eleventh centuries; it explores not only commercial activities but also the personal lives of the traders around the Indian Ocean basin.

Goitein, S. D. *A Mediterranean Society: An Abridgment in One Volume*, revised and edited by Jacob Lassner (1999). A portrait of the Jewish merchant community with ties across the Afro-Eurasian landmass, based largely on the documents from the Cairo Geniza (of which Goitein was the primary researcher and interpreter).

Harris, Joseph E. *The African Presence in Asia: Consequences of the East African Slave Trade* (1971). One of the few books that looks broadly at the impact of Africans and African slavery on the societies of Asia.

Hartwell, Robert. "Demographic, Political, and Social Transformations of China, 750–1550." *Harvard Journal of Asiatic Studies* 42 (1982): 365–442. A pioneering study of the demographic changes that overtook China during the Tang and Song dynasties, which are described in light of political reform movements and social changes in this crucial era.

Historical Relations across the Indian Ocean: Report and Papers of the Meeting of Experts Organized by UNESCO at Port Louis, Mauritius, from 15 to 19 July, 1974 (1980). Excellent essays on the connections of Africa with Asia across the Indian Ocean.

Hitti, Philip. *An Arab-Syrian Gentleman and Warrior in the Period of the Crusades: Memoirs of Usāmah ibn-Munqidh* (1929). The Crusaders seen through Muslim eyes.

Hodgson, Natasha. *Women, Crusading, and the Holy Land in Historical Narrative* (2007). A book dealing with the Crusades and focusing on the place of women in them.

Holt, P. M. *The Age of the Crusades: The Near East from the Eleventh Century to 1517* (1984). The Crusades period as seen from the eastern Mediterranean and through the lens of a leading British scholar of the area.

Huff, Toby E. *The Rise of Early Modern Science* (2009) A bold attempt to look at the rise of scientific work in the Islamic world, premodern China, and Europe, seeking to explain why the scientific revolution occurred in Europe rather than the Islamic world or China.

Hunter, Timothy (ed.). *The New Cambridge Medieval History*, Vol. 3: *c. 900–c. 1024* (1999). Comprehensive articles written by experts of this period.

Hymes, Robert, and Conrad Schirokauer (eds.). *Ordering the World: Approaches to State and Society in Sung Dynasty China* (1993). A collection of essays that traces the intellectual, social, and political movements that shaped the Song state and its elites.

Ibn Battuta. *The Travels of Ibn Battuta*, translated by H. A. R. Gibb (2002). A readable translation of the classic book, originally published in 1929.

Ibn Fadlan, Ahmad. *Ibn Fadlan's Journey to Russia: A Tenth Century Traveler from Baghdad to the Volga River*, translated with commentary by Richard Frye (2005). A coherent summary of the observations of an envoy who traveled from Baghdad to Russia.

Irwin, Robert. *The Middle East in the Middle Ages: The Early Mamluk Sultanate, 1250–1582* (1986). Egypt under Mamluk rule.

Jeppie, Shamil, and Souleymane Bachir Diagne (eds.). *The Meanings of Timbuktu* (2008). New materials on the ancient Muslim city of Timbuktu by scholars who have been preserving its manuscripts and writing about its historical importance.

Keay, John. *India: A History* (2000). A spirited and informative overview of the entire history of the South Asian subcontinent.

Lancaster, Lewis, Kikun Suh, and Chai-shin Yu (eds.). *Buddhism in Koryo: A Royal Religion* (1996). A description of Buddhism at its height in the Koryo period, when the religion made significant contributions to the development of Korean culture.

Levtzion, Nehemia, and Randall L. Pouwels (eds.). *The History of Islam in Africa* (2000). A useful general survey of the place of Islam in African history.

Lewis, Bernard (trans.). *Islam: From the Prophet Muhammad to the Capture of Constantinople* (1974). Vol. 2: *Religion and Society*. A fine collection of original sources that portray various aspects of classical Islamic society.

Lopez, Robert S. *The Commercial Revolution of the Middle Ages, 950–1350* (1976). An account focusing on the development around the Mediterranean of commercial practices such as the use of currency, accounting, and credit.

Lyons, Malcolm C., and D. E. P. Jackson. *Saladin: The Politics of the Holy War* (1984: reprint 2001). The fundamental revisionist work on one of the more important historical figures of the time.

Maalouf, Amin. *The Crusades through Muslim Eyes,* translated by Jon Rothschild (1984). The European Crusaders as seen by the Muslim world.

Marcus, Harold G. *A History of Ethiopia* (2002). An authoritative overview of the history of this great culture.

Mass, Jeffrey. *Yoritomo and the Founding of the First Bakufu: The Origins of Dual Government in Japan* (1999). A revisionist account of how the Kamakura military leader Minamoto Yoritomo established the "dual polity" of court and warrior government in Japan.

McDermott, Joseph. *A Social History of the Chinese Book: Books and Literati Culture in Late Imperial China* (2006). The history of the book in China since the Song dynasty, with comparisons to the book's role in other civilizations, particularly the European.

McEvitt, Christopher. *The Crusaders and the Christian World of the East: Rough Tolerance* (2008). Excellent work on the relations of religious groups in the Crusader kingdoms.

McIntosh, Roderik. *The Peoples of the Middle Niger: The Island of Gold* (1988). A historical survey of an area often omitted from other textbooks.

Moore, Jerry D. *Cultural Landscapes in the Ancient Andes: Archaeologies of Place* (2005). The most recent and up-to-date analysis of findings based on recent archaeological evidence, emphasizing the importance of local cultures and diversity in the Andes.

Mote, F. W. *Imperial China, 900–1800* (1999). Still the best general history of China, written by one of the world's leading Sinologists.

Niane, D. T. (ed.). *General History of Africa.* Vol. 4: *Africa from the Twelfth to the Sixteenth Century* (1984). The fourth volume of the UNESCO history of Africa with articles by experts on this period. The work features the scholarship of Africans.

Oliver, Roland (ed.). *From c. 1050 to c. 1600,* vol. 3 of *The Cambridge History of Africa,* edited by J. D. Fage and Roland Oliver (1977). Another general survey of African history. This volume draws heavily on the work of British scholars.

Peters, Edward. *The First Crusade* (1971). The Crusaders as seen through their own eyes.

Petry, Carl F. (ed.). *Islamic Egypt, 640–1517,* vol. 1 of *The Cambridge History of Egypt,* edited by M. W. Daly (1998). A solid overview of the history of Islamic Egypt up to the Ottoman conquest.

Polo, Marco. *The Travels of Marco Polo,* revised from Marsden's translation and edited by Manuel Komroff (1926). A solid translation of Marco Polo's famous account.

Popovic, Alexandre. *The Revolt of African Slaves in Iraq in the 3rd/9th Century,* translated by Leon King (1999). The account of a massive revolt against their slave masters by African slaves taken to labor in Iraq's mines and fields.

Reynolds, Susan. *Fiefs and Vassals: The Medieval Evidence Reinterpreted* (1994). The book that made the most determined attack on the concept of feudalism.

Sarris, Peter. "The Origins of the Manorial Economy: New Insights from Late Antiquity." *The English Historical Review* 119 (April 2004): 279–311. An original contribution on the origins of manorialism, based first on Egyptian papyri and extended to other parts of the Byzantine Empire and western Europe.

Scott, Robert. *Gothic Enterprise: A Guide to Understanding the Medieval Cathedral* (2003). The meaning and social function of religious building in medieval cities in northern Europe.

Shaffer, Lynda Norene. *Maritime Southeast Asia to 1500* (1996). A history of the peoples of the southeast fringe of the Eastern Hemisphere, up to the time that they became connected to the global commercial networks of the world.

Shimada, Izumi. "Evolution of Andean Diversity: Regional Formations (500 BCE–CE 600)." In Frank Salomon and Stuart Schwartz (eds.), *South America,* vol. 3 of *The Cambridge History of the Native Peoples of the Americas,* part 1, pp. 350–517 (1999). A splendid overview that contrasts the varieties of lowland and highland cultures.

Steinberg, David Joel, et al. *In Search of Southeast Asia: A Modern History* (1987). An account of the emergence of the modern Southeast Asian polities of Cambodia, Burma, Thailand, and Indonesia.

Tyerman, Christopher. *God's War: A New History of the Crusades* (2006). The balance of religious and nonreligious motivations in the Crusades.

Waley, Daniel. *The Italian City-Republics,* 3rd ed. (1988). The structures and culture of the new cities of medieval Italy.

Watson, Andrew. *Agricultural Innovation in the Early Islamic World: The Diffusion of Crops and Farming Techniques, 700–1100* (1983). An impressive study of the spread of new crops throughout the Muslim world.

West, Charles. *Reframing the Feudal Revolution: Political and Social Transformation between Marne and Moselle, c. 800–c. 1100* (2013). Big change seen through an intensely studied region.

Wickham, Chris. *Sleepwalking into a New World: The Emergence of Italian City Communes in the Twelfth Century* (2015). Origins of the city democracies of medieval Italy.

Williamson, Tom. *Shaping Medieval Landscapes: Settlement, Society, Environment* (2004). A study of the manorial system in England.

CHAPTER 11

Barkey, Karen. *Empire of Difference: The Ottomans in Comparative Perspective* (2008). A revisionist view of the rise and flourishing of the Ottoman Empire.

Benedictow, Ole J. *The Black Death, 1346–1351: The Complete History* (2004). An exhaustive statistical study of the mortality during the first years of the Black Death's arrival in Europe.

Bois, Guy. *The Crisis of Feudalism: Economy and Society in Eastern Normandy, c. 1300–1550* (1984). A good case study of a French region that illustrates the turmoil in fourteenth-century France.

Brook, Timothy. *Praying for Power: Buddhism and the Formation of Gentry Society in Late Ming China* (1994). An analysis of the role of a significant religious force in the political and social developments of the Ming.

Dardess, John. *A Ming Society: T'ai-ho County, Kiangsi, Fourteenth to Seventeenth Centuries* (1996). A work that covers the different changes and developments of a single locality in China through the centuries.

Dols, Michael W. *The Black Death in the Middle East* (1977). One of the few scholarly works to examine the Black Death outside Europe.

Dreyer, Edward. *Early Ming China: A Political History, 1355-1435* (1982). A useful account of the early years of the Ming dynasty.

Faroqhi, Suraiya N., and Kate Fleet (eds.). *The Cambridge History of Turkey*, Vol. 2: *The Ottoman Empire as a World Power, 1453-1603* (2013). An overview of this crucial period in Ottoman history, written by experts in the field.

Finkel, Caroline. *Osman's Dream: The Story of the Ottoman Empire, 1300-1923* (2005). The most authoritative overview of Ottoman history.

Hale, John. *The Civilization of Europe in the Renaissance* (1994). A beautifully crafted account of the politics, economics, and culture of the Renaissance period in western Europe.

He, Yuming. *Home and the World: Editing the "Glorious Ming" in Woodblock-Printed Books of the Sixteenth and Seventeenth Centuries* (2013). An insightful exploration of Ming society through a close look at its vibrant print culture and market for books.

Ho, Ping-ti. *Studies on the Population of China, 1368-1953* (1959). A useful overview of China's population from Ming times until the mid-twentieth century.

Hodgson, Marshall. *The Venture of Islam: Conscience and History in a World Civilization,* vol. 3 (1974). A good volume on the workings of the Ottoman state.

Hoffman, Philip T. *Why Did Europe Conquer the World?* (2015). Makes an interesting case for the importance of Europe's use of gunpowder technologies.

Itzkowitz, Norman. *Ottoman Empire and Islamic Tradition* (1972). Another good book on the Ottoman state.

Jackson, Peter. *The Delhi Sultanate* (1999). A meticulous, highly specialized political and military history.

Jackson, Peter, and Lawrence Lockhart (eds.). *The Cambridge History of Iran*, Vol. 6 (1986). A volume that deals with the Timurid and Safavid periods in Iran.

Jones, E. L. *The European Miracle* (1981). A provocative work on the economic and social recovery from the Black Death.

Kafadar, Cemal. *Between Two Worlds: The Construction of the Ottoman State* (1995). A thorough reconsideration of the origins of one of the world's great land empires.

Karamustafa, Ahmed. *God's Unruly Friends: Dervish Groups in the Islamic Later Middle Period, 1200-1550* (1994). A book that describes the unorthodox Islamic activities that were occurring in the Islamic world prior to and alongside the establishment of the Ottoman and Safavid Empires.

Levathes, Louise. *When China Ruled the Seas: The Treasure Fleet of the Dragon Throne, 1405-33* (1994). A book that provides a lively account of the Zheng He expeditions.

Lowry, Heath W. *The Nature of the Early Ottoman State* (2003). New perspectives on the rise of the Ottomans to prominence.

McNeill, William. *Plagues and Peoples* (1976). A pathbreaking work with a highly useful chapter on the spread of the Black Death throughout the Afro-Eurasian landmass.

Morgan, David. *Medieval Persia, 1040-1797* (1988). Contains an informative discussion of the Safavid state.

Peirce, Leslie. *The Imperial Harem: Women and Sovereignty in the Ottoman Empire* (1993). A work that describes the powerful place that imperial women had in political affairs.

Pirenne, Henri. *Economic and Social History of Medieval Europe* (1937). A classic study of the economic and social recovery from the Black Death.

Reid, James J. *Tribalism and Society in Islamic Iran, 1500-1629* (1983). A useful account of how the Mongols and other nomadic steppe peoples influenced Iran in the era when the Safavids were establishing their authority.

Savory, Roger. *Iran under the Safavids* (1980). A standard work on Safavid history and still useful.

Schäfer, Dagmar. *The Crafting of the 10,000 Things: Knowledge and Technology in Seventeenth-Century China* (2011). An innovative study of the philosophy of technology and crafts in the late Ming period with important implications for the global history of science.

Singman, Jeffrey L. (ed.). *Daily Life in Medieval Europe* (1999). An introductory description of the social and material world experienced by Europeans of different walks of life.

Tuchman, Barbara W. *A Distant Mirror: The Calamitous Fourteenth Century* (1978). A book that shows, in a vigorous way, how war, famine, and pestilence devastated Europeans in the fourteenth century.

Wittek, Paul. *The Rise of the Ottoman Empire* (1958). A work that contains vital insights on the emergence of the Ottoman state amid the political chaos in Anatolia.

CHAPTER 12

Axtell, James. *Beyond 1492: Encounters in Colonial North America* (1992). A wonderfully informed speculation about Indian reactions to Europeans.

Brady, Thomas A., et al. (eds.). *Handbook of European History 1400-1600: Late Middle Ages, Renaissance, and Reformation.* Vol. 1: *Structures and Assertions* (1996). A good synthetic survey of recent literature and historiographical debates.

Brook, Timothy. *Vermeer's Hat: The Seventeenth Century and the Dawn of the Global World* (2008). An interesting look at the connections forged across the globe through the works of a well-known European artist.

Burns, Bradford. *A History of Brazil* (1993). A comprehensive study of the long-term effects of the European colonization of Brazil.

Casale, Giancarlo. *The Ottoman Age of Exploration* (2010). The author places Ottoman exploration in a comparative context alongside European overseas expansion.

Cass, Victoria. *Dangerous Women: Warriors, Grannies, and Geishas of the Ming* (1999). An original study of Chinese female archetypes in memoirs, miscellanies, short stories, and novels.

Chaudhuri, K. N. *Trade and Civilisation in the Indian Ocean: An Economic History from the Rise of Islam to 1750* (1985). An excellent, comprehensive work that deals with the Indian Ocean economy and the appearance of European merchants there from the sixteenth century onward.

Clendinnen, Inga. *Aztecs: An Interpretation* (1991). Brilliantly reconstructs the culture of Tenochtitlán in the years before its conquest.

Cortés, Hernán. *Five Letters of Cortés to the Emperor, 1519-1526* (1991). Offers fascinating insights into the mind of the conqueror.

Crosby, Alfred W. *The Columbian Exchange: Biological and Cultural Consequences of 1492* (1972). A provocative discussion of the ecological consequences that followed the European "discovery" of the Americas.

Crosby, Alfred W. *Ecological Imperialism: The Biological Expansion of Europe, 900-1900* (1986). Another important work on the ecological consequences of European expansion.

Curtin, Philip. *Cross-Cultural Trade in World History* (1984). A work stressing the role of trade and commerce in establishing cross-cultural contacts.

Diamond, Jared. *Guns, Germs, and Steel: The Fates of Human Societies* (1997). An influential argument about the biological and technological determinants of how some societies took charge over others.

Díaz del Castillo, Bernal. *The Conquest of New Spain* (1963). The eyewitness account of a Spanish soldier who participated in the conquest of the Aztec Empire.

Faroqhi, Suraiya N. (ed.). *The Cambridge History of Turkey*, Vol. 3: *The Later Ottoman Empire, 1603-1839* (2008). Definitive articles on this important period in Ottoman history.

Faroqhi, Suraiya N., and Kate Fleet (eds.). *The Cambridge History of Turkey*, Vol. 2: *The Ottoman Empire as a World Power, 1453-1603* (2013). A collection of articles written by leading scholars of this crucial period in Ottoman history.

Febvre, Lucien. *The Problem of Unbelief in the Sixteenth Century: The Religion of Rabelais* (1982). A tour de force of intellectual history by the man who moved the study of the Reformation away from great men to the broader question of religious revival and mentalities.

Finkel, Caroline. *Osman's Dream: The History of the Ottoman Empire* (2005). A detailed and exhaustively researched history of the Ottomans from the origins of the Ottoman state at the end of the thirteen century to the dismantling of the empire after World War I.

Flynn, Dennis, and Arturo Giráldez (eds.). *Metals and Monies in an Emerging Global Economy* (1997). Contains several articles relating to silver and the Asian trade.

Frank, Andre Gunder. *ReOrient: Global Economy in the Asian Age* (1998). A reassessment of the role of Asia in the economic development of the world from around 1400 onward.

Glahn, Richard von. *The Economic History of China: From Antiquity to the Nineteenth Century* (2016). A masterful new survey of Chinese economic history.

Greenblatt, Stephen. *Marvelous Possessions: The Wonder of the New World* (1991). An insightful study of the ways in which Europe's encounters with the New World changed European culture.

Gruzinski, Serge. *The Conquest of Mexico* (1993). An important work on the conquest of Mexico.

Habib, Irfan. *The Agrarian System of Mughal India* (1963). One of the best studies on the subject.

Hall, Richard Seymour. *Empires of the Monsoon: A History of the Indian Ocean and Its Invaders* (1996). A very engaging journalistic account with fabulous details.

Hodgson, Marshall. *The Venture of Islam*, vols. 2 and 3 (1974). A magisterial work that includes the Indian subcontinent in its careful study of the political and cultural history of the whole Islamic world.

Hulme, Peter. *Colonial Encounters: Europe and the Native Caribbean, 1492-1797* (1986). Presents an interesting interpretation of the encounters of Europeans and Native Americans.

Lach, Donald F. *Asia in the Making of Europe*, 5 books in 3 vols. (1965-). Perhaps the single most comprehensive and innovative guide to the European voyages of discovery.

Las Casas, Bartolomé. *A Short Account of the Destruction of the Indies*, edited by Anthony Pagden (2004). The most famous book written about the conquest of the New World.

Lockhart, James, and Stuart Schwartz. *Early Latin America* (1983). One of the finest studies of European expansion in the late fifteenth century.

McCann, James. *Maize and Grace: Africa's Encounter with a New World Crop, 1500-2000* (2005). A significant study of how maize, a New World crop, became Africa's most widely grown grain.

Melville, Elinor G. K. *A Plague of Sheep: Environmental Consequences of the Conquest of Mexico* (1994). A history of the transformation of a valley in Mexico from the Aztec period to the era of Spanish rule.

Mignolo, Walter D. *The Darker Side of the Renaissance: Literacy, Territoriality, and Colonization* (1995). Uses literary theory and literary images to present provocative interpretations of the encounter of Europeans and Native Americans.

Ozbaran, Salih. *Ottoman Expansion toward the Indian Ocean in the 16th Century* (2009). An important treatment of the Ottoman entry into the Indian Ocean at a time when the Portuguese were also expanding there.

Pagden, Anthony. *European Encounters with the New World* (1993). A complex look at the deep and lasting imprint of the New World on its conquerors.

Phillips, William D., and Carla Rahn Phillips. *The World of Christopher Columbus* (1992). One of the finest studies of European expansion in the late fifteenth century.

Roper, Lyndal. *Martin Luther: Renegade and Prophet* (2016). A magisterial biography that demonstrates the ways in which Luther was a rebel but also a man of his time.

Russell-Wood, A. J. R. *The Portuguese Empire, 1415-1808* (1992). An important survey of early Portuguese exploration.

Salmon, W. H. *An Account of the Ottoman Conquest of Egypt in the Year A.H. 932 (A.D. 1516), Translated from the Third Volume of the Arabic Chronicle of Muhammad Ahmed Ibn Iyas, an Eyewitness of the Scenes He Describes* (1921). An evocative primary source on the Ottoman-Mamluk conflict.

Von Glahn, Richard. *Fountain of Fortune: Money and Monetary Policy in China, 1000-1700* (1996). Includes an excellent analysis of the history of silver in Ming China.

CHAPTER 13

Alam, Muzaffar. *The Crisis of Empire in Mughal North India* (1993). Represents the best of the scholarly interpretations on the subject.

Bay, Edna. *Wives of the Leopard: Gender, Politics, and Culture in the Kingdom of Dahomey* (1998). A useful treatment of gender issues in Dahomey.

Blackburn, Robin. *The Making of New World Slavery: From the Baroque to the Modern, 1492-1800* (1997). A good place to begin when studying African slavery and the Atlantic slave trade, it compares the early expansion of the plantation systems across the Atlantic and throughout the Americas.

Blanning, Tim. *The Pursuit of Glory: Europe, 1648-1815* (2007). An elegantly written and deeply insightful overview of European political history from the Thirty Years' War to the fall of Napoleon.

Bushkovitch, Paul. *Peter the Great* (2016). An updated version of a standard work, offering a concise overview of one of Russia's most celebrated and energetic rulers.

Calloway, Colin G. *One Vast Winter Count: The Native American West before Lewis and Clark* (2003). A sweeping survey of North American Indian histories prior to the nineteenth century.

Crossley, Pamela. *A Translucent Mirror: History and Identity in Qing Imperial Ideology* (1999). The author deals with the formation of identities such as "Manchu" and "Chinese" during the Qing period.

Dale, Stephen F. *The Muslim Empires of the Ottomans, Safavids, and Mughals* (2010). A comparative overview of Islam's three most powerful empires of the sixteenth and seventeenth centuries.

Eaton, Richard. *Essays on Islam and Indian History* (2000). A wide-ranging account that pays particular attention to Islam's social history in the subcontinent.

Eltis, David, and Richardson, David. *Atlas of the Transatlantic Slave Trade* (2010). This work contains the most up-to-date data on the Atlantic slave trade, the numbers transported, where the captives came from, and where they landed.

Fleischer, Cornell H. *Bureaucrat and Intellectual in the Ottoman Empire (1542-1600)* (1986). A probing study into Mustafa Ali, the Ottoman Empire's leading sixteenth-century intellectual.

Flynn, Dennis O., and Arturo Giraldez (eds.). *Metals and Money in an Emerging World Economy* (1997). A collection of articles about the place of silver in the world economy.

Forsyth, James. *A History of the Peoples of Siberia: Russia's North Asian Colony 1581-1990* (1992). A narrative overview of a violent history reminiscent of the western expansion of the United States.

Glahn, Richard von. *Fountains of Fortune: Money and Monetary Policy in China, 1000-1700* (1996). A discussion of the place of silver in the Chinese economy.

Halperin, Charles J. *Russia and the Golden Horde: The Mongol Impact on Medieval Russian History* (1985). A book on the rise of Muscovy, forebear of the Russian Empire, from within the Mongol realm.

Hämäläinen, Pekka. *The Comanche Empire* (2008). A book that inverts the conventional history of empires in North America by arguing that the Comanches were the most successful expansionist power in the middle of the continent during the eighteenth century.

Hartley, Janet. *Siberia: A History of the People* (2014). A vivid portrait of diverse conquerors—fur traders, Cossack adventurers, political criminals—of a region larger than almost all continents.

Hattox, Ralph S. *Coffee and Coffeehouses: The Origins of a Social Beverage in the Medieval Near East* (1985). This work shows how widespread and popular coffee consumption and coffeehouses were around the world.

Herzog, Tamar. *Frontiers of Possession: Spain and Portugal in Europe and the Americas* (2015). An exploration of how Spanish and Portuguese rulers carved up the New World, less by military action and diplomatic treaties and more by quarrels over land settlement and rights to trade and travel.

Huang, Ray. *1587, a Year of No Significance: The Ming Dynasty in Decline* (1981). An insightful analysis of the problems confronting the late Ming.

Lensen, George. *The Russian Push Toward Japan: Russo-Japanese Relations 1697-1875* (1959). A discussion of why and how Japan established its first border with another state and how Russia pursued its ambitions in the Pacific.

Lockhart, James. *The Nahuas after the Conquest* (1992). A landmark study of the social reorganization of Mesoamerican societies under Spanish rule.

Lovejoy, Paul. *Transformations in Slavery: A History of Slavery in Africa* (1983). An excellent discussion of African slavery.

Mathee, Rudi. *Persia in Crisis, Safavid Decline, and the Fall of Isfahan* (2012). A study of the disintegration of the Safavid state.

Mikhail, Alan. *Nature and Empire in Ottoman Egypt: An Environmental History* (2011). An important study of the impact of the environment on Egypt in the eighteenth century.

Monahan, Erika. *The Merchants of Siberia: Trade in Early Modern Eurasia* (2016). A stirring account of entrepreneurs battling the harshest imaginable conditions to establish trading networks connecting the far-flung territories north of the ancient Silk Road.

Moon, David. *The Plough That Broke the Steppes: Agriculture and Environment in Russia's Grasslands, 1700-1913* (2013). A bold incorporation of environmental aspects to retell the epic story of Russia's most numerous social group.

Nakane, Chie, and Shinzaburo Oishi (eds.). *Tokugawa Japan: The Social and Economic Antecedents of Modern Japan* (1990). First-rate essays on Japanese village society, urban life, literacy, and culture.

Nwokeji, G. Uko. *The Slave Trade and Culture in the Bight of Biafra: An African Society in the Atlantic World* (2010). A study of the Aro peoples of southeastern Nigeria and their use of their commercial powers to promote a vigorous trade with European slavers on the coast.

Pamuk, Sevket. *A Monetary History of the Ottoman Empire* (2000). A discussion of the place of silver in the Ottoman Empire.

Parker, Geoffrey. *Global Crisis: War, Climate Change, and Catastrophe in the Seventeenth Century* (2013). A comprehensive and exhaustively researched study of the effects of the Little Ice Age on the governments and societies of the entire world in the seventeenth century.

Parker, Geoffrey (ed.). *The Thirty Years' War* (1997). The standard account of the conflict and its outcomes.

Perdue, Peter C. *China Marches West: The Qing Conquest of Central Asia* (2005). This volume chronicles the expansion of the Qing Empire to its northwest, drawing comparisons to other colonial empires and their legacies.

Platonov, S. F. *Ivan the Terrible* (1986). Covers the controversies over Russia's infamous tsar.

Rawski, Evelyn. *The Last Emperors: A Social History of Qing Imperial Institutions* (1998). This volume explores the mechanisms and processes through which the Qing court negotiated its Manchu identity.

Reid, Anthony. *Charting the Shape of Early Modern Southeast Asia* (1999). A collection of articles by a leading historian of Southeast Asia.

Spence, Jonathan, and John Wills (eds.). *From Ming to Ch'ing: Conquest, Region, and Continuity in Seventeenth-Century China* (1979). Covers the various aspects of a tumultuous period of dynastic transition.

Subramanyam, Sanjay. *From the Tigris to the Ganges, Explorations in Connected History* (2012). A study that demonstrates that Afro-Eurasia in the seventeenth and eighteenth centuries contained a porous network of empires, cultures, and economies.

Subramanyam, Sanjay, and Muzaffar Alam. *Indo-Persian Travels in the Age of Discoveries, 1400–1800* (2012). A lively portrait of cultural exchanges between Persia, central Asia, and India as seen in travel literature.

Taylor, Alan. *American Colonies: The Settling of North America* (2001). Brings together British, French, and Spanish colonial histories and shows how the fortunes of each were entangled with one another and with those of diverse Native American peoples.

Thornton, John K. *Africa and Africans in the Making of the Atlantic World, 1400–1800* (1998). A wonderful discussion of how African slaves played a large role in the formation of the Atlantic world.

Thornton, John K. *The Kongolese Saint Anthony: Dona Beatriz Kimpa Vita and the Antonian Movement, 1684–1706* (1998). An excellent monograph on religious movements in the Kongo.

Toby, Ronald P. *State and Diplomacy in Early Modern Japan: Asia in the Development of the Tokugawa Bakufu* (1984). The author shows that the Japanese, far from being isolated from the outside world, engaged in vigorous and successful diplomacy.

Van Dusen, Nancy E. *Global Indios: The Indigenous Struggle for Justice in Sixteenth-Century Spain* (2015). A remarkable study of the ways that Spanish rulers enslaved Amerindians in the Americas and even exported them back to Europe.

Vilar, Pierre. *A History of Gold and Money* (1991). An excellent study of the development of the early silver and gold economies.

CHAPTER 14

Axtell, James. *The Invasion of America: The Contest of Cultures in Colonial North America* (1985). Discusses the strategies of Christian missionaries in converting the Indians, as well as the success of Indians in converting Europeans.

Babaie, Sussan. *Isfahan and Its Palaces: Statecraft, Shi'ism and the Architecture of Conviviality in Early Modern Iran* (2008). An overview of the city of Isfahan, as the capital of the Safavid state.

Barmé, Geremie R. *The Forbidden City* (2008). A concise introduction to the history of one of the most important physical emblems of Chinese imperial power.

Berlin, Ira. *Many Thousands Gone: The First Two Centuries of Slavery in North America* (1998). Surveys the development of African American culture in colonial North America.

Bleichmar, Daniela. *Visible Empire: Botanical Expeditions and Visual Culture in the Hispanic Enlightenment* (2012). A fascinating and beautifully illustrated history of creole botanical expeditions in the eighteenth century.

Brockey, Liam. *Journey to the East: The Jesuit Mission to China, 1579–1724* (2007). A detailed and definitive treatment of the Jesuits in China up to 1724, the year when Jesuit influence began to decline.

Brook, Timothy. *The Confusions of Pleasure: Commerce and Culture in Ming China* (1999). An insightful survey of Ming society.

Clunas, Craig. *Superfluous Things: Material Culture and Social Status in Early Modern China* (1991). A good account of the late Ming elite's growing passion for material things.

Collcutt, Martin, Marius Jansen, and Isao Kumakura. *A Cultural Atlas of Japan* (1988). A sweeping look at the many different forms of Japanese cultural expression over the centuries, including the flourishing urban culture of Edo.

Crèvecoeur, Hector St. John de. *Letters from an American Farmer*, reprinted from the orginal edition, with a prefatory note by W. P. Trent and an introduction by Ludwig Lewisohn (New York: Fox, Duffield, 1904). Powerful and informative letters of a French settler in the Americas in the eighteenth century.

Darnton, Robert. *The Business of the Enlightenment: A Publishing History of the Encyclopédie, 1775–1800* (1979). The classic study of Europe's first great compendium of knowledge.

Dash, Mike. *Tulipomania: The Story of the World's Most Coveted Flower and the Extraordinary Passions It Aroused* (1999). A global perspective on and lively account of the spread of the tulip around the world as a flower signifying both beauty and status.

Dikötter, Frank. *The Discourse of Race in Modern China* (1992). A good survey of Chinese discussions of race in the modern era.

Doniger, Wendy. *The Hindus: An Alternative History* (2009). A deeply scholarly yet accessibly written history of Hinduism that takes into account both texts and popular practices and contains a lively account of dissenting traditions.

Eaton, Richard. *Essays on Islam and Indian History* (2000). A wide-ranging account that pays particular attention to Islam's social history in the subcontinent.

Elman, Benjamin A. *On Their Own Terms: Science in China, 1550–1900* (2005). A study of the development of "native" Chinese science and how the process interacted with the introduction of western science to China over the course of three and a half centuries.

Eze, Emmanuel Chukwudi (ed.). *Race and the Enlightenment: A Reader* (1997). Readings examining the idea of race in the context of the Enlightenment.

Fleischer, Cornell. *Bureaucrat and Intellectual in the Ottoman Empire: The Historian Mustafa Ali (1540–1600)* (1986). Offers good insight into the world of culture and intellectual vitality in the Ottoman Empire.

Grafton, Anthony, April Shelford, and Nancy Siraisi. *New Worlds, Ancient Texts: The Power of Tradition and the Shock of Discovery* (1995). A concise discussion of the impact of the New World on European thought.

Gutierrez, Ramon. *When Jesus Came, the Corn Mothers Went Away: Marriage, Sexuality, and Power in New Mexico, 1500–1846* (1991). A provocative dissection of the spiritual dimensions of European colonialism in the Americas.

Harley, J. B., and David Woodward (eds.). *The History of Cartography.* Vol. 2, Book 2: *Cartography in the Traditional East and Southeast Asian Societies* (1994). An authoritative treatment of the subject.

Hart, Roger. *Imagined Civilizations: China, the West, and Their First Encounter* (2013). A treatment of the Jesuit mission to China as the first contact between Chinese and European cultures.

Horton, Robin. *Patterns of Thought in Africa and the West: Essays on Magic, Religion, and Science* (1993). Reflections on African patterns of thought and attitudes toward nature, which can help us understand African American religious beliefs and resistance movements.

Huff, Toby. *The Rise of Early Modern Science* (2003).

Huff, Toby. *Intellectual Curiosity and the Scientific Revolution: A Comparative Perspective* (2011). Huff's two books represent a sustained effort to deal with Europe's scientific revolution comparatively, asking the question why Europe and not China or the Islamic world.

Kai, Ho Yi. *Science in China, 1600–1900: Essays by Benjamin Elman* (2015). Elman, an expert on Chinese science, offers his latest word on China's scientific achievements in a context of Europe's transmission of science through the Jesuit mission.

Keene, Donald. *The Japanese Discovery of Europe: Honda Toshiaki and Other Discoverers, 1720–1798* (1952). A study of the ways Japan managed to incorporate knowledge from the outside world with the development of national traditions.

Ko, Dorothy. *Teachers of the Inner Chambers: Women and Culture in Seventeenth-Century China* (1994). Explores the lives of elite women in late Ming and early Qing China.

Lewis, Bernard. *Race and Color in Islam* (1979). Examines the Islamic attitude toward race and color.

Mazower, Mark. *Salonica, City of Ghosts: Christians, Muslims and Jews, 1430–1900* (2006). An overview of one of the most important cities of the Ottoman Empire.

Morgan, Philip D. *Slave Counterpoint: Black Culture in the Eighteenth-Century Chesapeake and Lowcountry* (1998). Describes the development of African American culture in colonial North America.

Munck, Thomas. *The Enlightenment: A Comparative Social History, 1721–1794* (2000). A wonderful survey, with unusual examples from the periphery, especially from Scandinavia and the Habsburg Empire.

Necipoglu, Gulru. *Architecture, Ceremonial, and Power: The Topkapi Palace in the Fifteenth and Sixteenth Centuries* (1991). A magnificently illustrated book that shows the enormous artistic talent that the Ottoman rulers poured into their imperial structure.

Needham, Joseph "Mathematics and Science in China and the West." In *Science and Civilisation in China*, Vol. 3, pp. 150–168 (1954). An important section of Needham's exhaustive multivolume treatment of Chinese science.

This section deals with what Needham considered the fundamental difference between Chinese and European science at the time of the scientific revolution, namely, Europe's mathematization of the natural world.

Needham, Joseph. *The Grand Tritation: Science and Society in East and West* (1969). Along with his three other entries here, Joseph Needham's efforts to understand Chinese science in relationship to Europe's new science.

Needham, Joseph. "The Evolution of Oecumenical Science: The Role of Europe and China." *Journal of Interdisciplinary Science* 1 (1976): 202–214. More from Needham on European and Chinese science.

Needham, Joseph. *Science in Traditional China: A Comparative Perspective* (1981). Needham's thoughts on Chinese science after the publication of his monumental *Science and Civilisation in China*.

Parker, Kenneth. *Early Modern Tales of the Orient: A Critical Anthology* (1999). A collection of travelers' accounts of the Near East.

Publishing and the Print Culture in Late Imperial China (Special Issue). *Late Imperial China* 17:1 (June 1996). A collection of important articles with a foreword by the French cultural historian Roger Chartier.

Qaisar, Ahsan Jan. *The Indian Response to European Technology, AD 1498–1707* (1998). A meticulous, scholarly work on this little-studied subject.

Rizvi, Athar Abbas. *The Wonder That Was India*. Vol. 2: *A Survey of the History and Culture of the Indian Sub-Continent from the Coming of the Muslims to the British Conquest, 1200–1700* (1987). A deeply learned work in intellectual history.

Safier, Neil. *Measuring the New World: Enlightenment Science and South America* (2008). Examines the ways in which European, and especially Parisian, surveyors set about gauging the curvature of the earth, starting in Quito, Ecuador. Along the way, they learned much more about local natural history, which flowed back to Paris to inform the Enlightenment.

Shapiro, Steven. *The Scientific Revolution* (1996). Still one of the most authoritative overviews of Europe's new science.

Sivan, Nathan. "Why the Scientific Revolution Did Not Take Place in China—or Didn't It?" The author questions the value of asking why China did not have

a scientific revolution even while arguing that the Chinese, in fact, did.

Smith, Bernard. *European Vision and the South Pacific* (1985). An excellent cultural history of Cook's voyages.

Smith, Richard J. *Chinese Maps: Images of "All under Heaven"* (1996). Provides a good introduction to the history of cartography in China.

Sorkin, David. *The Religious Enlightenment: Protestants, Jews, and Catholics from London to Vienna* (2008). Discusses a wide range of thinkers who were able to reconcile Enlightenment thought with religious belief.

Tignor, Robert L. "W. R. Bascom and the Ife Bronzes." *Africa: Journal of the International African Institute* 60, no. 3 (1990): 425–434. Explores controversies over issues of where antiquities of great artistic value like the Ife bronzes should reside.

Welch, Anthony. *Shah Abbas and the Arts of Isfahan* (1973). Describes the astonishing architectural and artistic renaissance of the city of Isfahan under the Safavid ruler Shah Abbas.

Whitfield, Peter. *The Image of the World: Twenty Centuries of World Maps* (1994). A good introduction to the history of cartography in different parts of the world.

Wilks, Ivor. *Forests of Gold: Essays on the Akan and the Kingdom of Asante* (1993). A study that focuses on the Asante's drive for wealth.

Zilfi, Madeline C. *The Politics of Piety: The Ottoman Ulema in the Post-Classical Age (1600–1800)* (1988). Explores the cultural flourishing that took place within the Islamic world in this period.

CHAPTER 15

Allen, Robert C. *The British Industrial Revolution in Global Perspective* (2009). The most recent and authoritative study of the industrial revolution in Britain and its implications around the world.

Anderson, Fred. *Crucible of War: The Seven Years' War and the Fate of Empire in British North America, 1754–1766* (2000). The best synthesis of the "great war for empire" that set the stage for the American Revolution.

Bayly, C. A. *Indian Society and the Making of the British Empire* (1998). A useful work on the early history of the British conquest of India.

Blackburn, Robin. *The Overthrow of Colonial Slavery, 1776-1848* (1988). Places the abolition of the Atlantic slave trade and colonial slavery in a large historical context.

Brown, Harold G. *Ending the French Revolution: Violence, Justice, and Repression from the Terror to Napoleon* (2007). Describes how the Directory and Napoleon imposed stability on France in the wake of the revolution.

Cambridge History of Egypt: Modern Egypt from 1517 to the End of the Twentieth Century, Vol. 2 (1998). Volume 2 contains authoritative essays on all aspects of modern Egyptian history, including the impact of the French invasion and the rule of Muhammad Ali.

Cassel, Par Kristoffer. *Grounds of Judgement: Extraterritoriality and Imperial Powers in Ninetheenth-Century China and Japan* (2012). A study of the idea and practice of extraterritoriality within the context of the triangular relationship between China, Japan, and the West.

Chaudhuri, K. N. *The Trading World of Asia and the East India Company, 1660-1760* (1978). An authoritative economic history of the East India Company's operations.

Crafts, N. F. R. *British Economic Growth during the Industrial Revolution* (1985). A pioneering study that emphasizes a long-term, more gradual process of adaptation to new institutional and social circumstances.

de Vries, Jan. *The Industrious Revolution: Consumer Behavior and the Household Economy, 1650 to the Present* (2008). A book on the lead-up to the industrial revolution, written by the leading economic historian who coined the term *industrious revolution.*

Diamond, Jared, and James A. Robinson (eds.). *Natural Experiments of History* (2010). This book consists of eight comparative studies drawn from history, archaeology, economics, economic history, geography, and political science, covering a spectrum of approaches, ranging from a nonquantitative narrative style to quantitative statistical analyses.

Doyle, William. *The Oxford History of the French Revolution* (1990). A highly detailed discussion of the course of events.

Drescher, Seymour. *Abolition: A History of Slavery and Anti-Slavery* (2009). A recent and authoritative overview of slavery and its opponents.

Elvin, Mark. *The Retreat of the Elephants: An Environmental History of China* (2004). A study of the different ways in which China's natural environment was shaped.

Fick, Carolyn E. *The Making of Haiti: The Saint Domingue Revolution from Below* (1990). Provides a detailed account of the factors that led to the great slave rebellion on the island of Haiti at the end of the eighteenth century.

Findley, Carter. *Bureaucratic Reform in the Ottoman Empire: The Sublime Porte, 1789-1922* (1980). A useful guide to Ottoman reform efforts in the nineteenth century.

Geggus, David (ed.). *The Impact of the Haitian Revolution in the Atlantic World* (2001). A lively effort to disentangle the effects of the Haitian Revolution from those of the French Revolution.

Hevia, James. *Cherishing Men from Afar: Qing Guest Ritual and the Macartney Embassy of 1793* (1995). Offers a definitive interpretation of the nature of Sino-British conflict in the Qing period.

Hobsbawm, Eric. *Nations and Nationalism since 1780* (1990). An important overview of the rise of the nation-state and nationalism around the world.

Howe, Daniel Walker. *What Hath God Wrought: The Transformation of America, 1815-1848* (2007). A Pulitzer Prize-winning interpretation of how new technologies and new ideas reshaped the economy, society, culture, and politics of the United States in the first half of the nineteenth century.

Hunt, Lynn. *Politics, Culture and Class in the French Revolution* (1984). Examines the influence of sociocultural shifts as causes and consequences of the French Revolution, emphasizing the symbols and practice of politics invented during the revolution.

Inikori, Joseph. *Africans and the Industrial Revolution in England* (2002). Demonstrates the important role that Africa and Africans played in facilitating the industrial revolution.

Isset, Christopher Mills. *State, Peasant, and Merchant in Qing Manchuria, 1644-1862* (2007). A study of the relationships between the sociopolitical structures and peasant lives in a key region during the Qing.

James, C. L. R. *The Black Jacobins: Toussaint L'Ouverture and the San Domingo Revolution* (1938). A classic chronicle of the only successful slave revolt in history, and providing a critical portrait of their leader, Toussaint L'Ouverture.

Jones, E. L. *Growth Recurring* (1988). Discusses the controversy over why the industrial revolution took place in Europe, stressing the unique ecological setting that encouraged long-term investment.

Kinsbruner, Jay. *Independence in Spanish America* (1994). A fine study of the Latin American revolutions that argues that the struggle was as much a civil war as a fight for national independence.

Landers, Jane. *Atlantic Creoles in the Age of Revolutions* (2011). A collection of fascinating and unique portraits of Atlantic world creoles who managed to move freely and purposefully through French, Spanish, and English colonies and through Indian territory in the unstable century between 1750 and 1850.

Lieven, Dominic. *Russia Against Napoleon* (2010). Explains how outnumbered Russian forces were able to defeat the massive army that Napoleon assembled for his conquest of Russia.

Mayer, Arno J. *The Furies: Violence and Terror in the French and Russian Revolutions* (2000). A stimulating and provocative essay comparing the French and Russian Revolutions.

Mokyr, Joel. *The Lever of Riches* (1990). An important study of the causes of the industrial revolution that emphasizes the role of small technological and organizational breakthroughs.

Mokyr, Joel. *Enlightened Economy: An Economic History of Britain, 1700-1850* (2009). Perspectives on the evolution of the British economy in the era that produced the industrial revolution.

Naquin, Susan, and Evelyn Rawski. *Chinese Society in the Eighteenth Century* (1987). A survey of mid-Qing society.

Neal, Larry. *The Rise of Financial Capitalism* (1990). An important study of the making of financial markets.

Nikitenko, Aleksandr. *Up from Serfdom: My Childhood and Youth in Russia, 1804-1824* (2001). One of the very few recorded life stories of a Russian serf.

Parthasarathi, Prasannan. *Why Europe Grew Rich and Asia Did Not: Global Economic Divergence, 1600-1800* (2011). A work that places the British industrial revolution in a global context, with much emphasis on India's textile manufacturing before being superseded by British manufacturers.

Pomeranz, Kenneth. *The Great Divergence: Europe, China, and the Making of the Modern World Economy* (2000). Offers explanations of why Europe and not some other place in the world, like parts of China or India, forged ahead economically in the nineteenth century.

Rudé, George. *Europe in the Eighteenth Century* (1972). Emphasizes the rise of a new class, the bourgeoisie, against the old aristocracy as a cause of the French Revolution.

Taylor, Alan. *American Revolutions: A Continental History, 1750–1804* (2016). A sweeping interpretation of the founding of the United States that places the War of Independence in a North American perspective, bringing together the diverse revolutions that transformed societies and borders across the continent.

Wong, R. Bin. *China Transformed: Historical Change and the Limits of European Experience* (2000). Draws attention to the relative autonomy of merchant capitalists in the European dynastic states in comparison with China.

Wood, Gordon S. *Empire of Liberty: A History of the Early Republic, 1789–1815* (2009). An excellent synthesis of the history of the United States in the tumultuous years between the ratification of the Constitution and the War of 1812.

Wortman, Richard. *Scenarios of Power: Myth and Ceremony in Russian Monarchy,* 2 vols. (1995–2000). Examines how dynastic Russia confronted the challenges of the revolutionary epoch.

CHAPTER 16

Anderson, David M. *Revealing Prophets: Prophets in Eastern African History* (1995). Good discussion of the prophets in eastern Africa.

Beecher, Jonathan. *The Utopian Vision of Charles Fourier* (1983). A fine biography of this important thinker.

Boyd, Jean. *The Caliph's Sister: Nana Asma'u, 1793–1865, Teacher, Poet, and Islamic Leader* (1988). A study of the most powerful female Muslim leader in the Fulani religious revolt.

Clancy-Smith, Julia. *Rebel and Saint: Muslim Notables, Populist Protest, Colonial Encounter (Algeria and Tunisia, 1800–1904)* (1994). Examines Islamic protest movements against western encroachments in North Africa.

Clogg, Richard. *A Concise History of Greece* (1997). A good introduction to the history of Greece in its European context.

Dalrymple, William. *The Last Mughal: The Fall of a Dynasty: Delhi, 1857* (2007). A deeply researched and riveting account of Delhi during the 1857 revolt.

Danziger, Raphael. *Abd al-Qadir: Resistance to the French and Internal Consolidation* (1977). Still the indispensable work on this important Algerian Muslim leader.

Dowd, Gregory E. *A Spirited Resistance: The North American Indian Struggle for Unity, 1745–1815* (1992). Emphasizes the importance of prophets like Tenskwatawa in the building of pan-Indian confederations in the era between the Seven Years' War and the War of 1812.

Earle, Rebecca. *The Return of the Native: Indians and Myth Making in Spanish America, 1810–1930* (2007). Examines how Indian resistance and the memory of struggles over sovereignty and land shaped emerging national identities, especially in Mexico and the Andes.

Guha, Ranajit. *Elementary Aspects of Peasant Insurgency in Colonial India* (1983). Not specifically on the Great Rebellion of 1857 but includes it in its pioneering "subalternist" interpretation of South Asian history.

Hamilton, Carolyn (ed.). *The Mfecane Aftermath: Reconstructive Debates in Southern African History* (1995). Debates on Shaka's *Mfecane* movement and its impact on southern Africa.

Hiskett, Mervyn. *The Sword of Truth: The Life and Times of the Shehu Usman dan Fodio* (1994). An authoritative study of the Fulani revolt in northern Nigeria.

Johnson, Douglas H. *Nuer Prophets: A History of Prophecy from the Upper Nile in the Nineteenth and Twentieth Centuries* (1994). Deals with African prophetic and charismatic movements in eastern Africa.

Keddie, Nikki. *An Islamic Response to Imperialism: Political and Religious Writings of Sayyid Jamal ad-Din "al-Afghani"* (1968). Definitive information on the Afghani's life and influence, coupled with a translation of one of his most important essays.

Laven, David, and Lucy Riall (eds.). *Napoleon's Legacy: Problems of Government in Restoration Europe* (2000). Excellent collection of essays on Restoration politics in various states.

Mukherjee, Rudrangshu. *Awadh in Revolt 1857–58* (1984). A careful case study of the Indian Rebellion.

Omer-Cooper, J. D. *The Zulu Aftermath: A Nineteenth-Century Revolution in Bantu Africa* (1966). A good place to start in studying Shaka's *Mfecane* movement, which greatly rearranged the political and ethnic makeup of southern Africa.

Ostler, Jeffrey. *The Plains Sioux and U.S. Colonialism from Lewis and Clark to Wounded Knee* (2004). Uses the lens of colonial theory to track relations between the Sioux and the United States, offering fresh insights about the Ghost Dance movement.

Peires, J. B. (ed.). *Before and After Shaka* (1981). Discusses elements in the debate over Shaka's *Mfecane* movement.

Pilbeam, Pamela. *French Socialists Before Marx: Workers, Women and the Social Question in France* (2001). Describes the development of a variety of socialist ideas in early nineteenth-century France.

Platt, Stephen R. *Autumn in the Heavenly Kingdom: China, the West, and the Epic Story of the Taiping Civil War* (2012). A study of the Taiping from a global perspective.

Reed, Nelson. *The Caste War of Yucatan* (1964). A classic narrative of the Caste War of the Yucatán.

Restall, Matthew. *The Maya World* (1997). Describes in economic and social terms the origins of the Yucatán upheaval in southern Mexico.

Ruedy, John. *Modern Algeria: The Origins and Development of a Nation* (2005). Still the best overview of the modern political history of Algeria.

Rugeley, Terry. *Rebellion Now and Forever: Mayans, Hispanics, and Caste War Violence in Yucatán, 1800–1880* (2009). Explains the combination of economic and cultural pressures that drove the Mayas in the Yucatán to revolt in the Caste War.

Spence, Jonathan. *God's Chinese Son: The Taiping Heavenly Kingdom of Hong Xiuquan* (1996). A fascinating portrayal of the Taiping through the prism of its founder.

Sperber, Jonathan. *Karl Marx: A Nineteenth-Century Life* (2013). An engaging and authoritative biography of Marx that emphasizes his role as a radical journalist.

Stedman Jones, Gareth. *Karl Marx: Greatness and Illusion* (2016). Now the authoritative biography of the founder of communism, showing Marx's own ambivalence about what he had created.

Wagner, Rudolf. *Reenacting the Heavenly Vision: The Role of Religion in the Taiping Rebellion* (1982). A brief but insightful analysis of the religious elements in the Taiping's doctrines.

White, Richard. *The Middle Ground: Indians, Empires, and Republics in the Great Lakes Region, 1650–1815* (1991). A pathbreaking exploration of intercultural relations in North America that offers a provocative interpretation of the visions of Tenskwatawa and the efforts of Tecumseh to resist the expansion of the United States.

CHAPTER 17

Berry, Sara. *Cocoa, Custom and Socio-Economic Change in Western Nigeria* (1975). Innovative study based on interviews with local farmers that suggests that farmer enterprise and microeconomic theory better explain the spectacular growth in cocoa production than grand economic theory.

Cain, P. A., and A. G. Hopkins. *British Imperialism: Innovation and Expansion, 1688–1914* (1993). An excellent discussion of British imperialism, especially British expansion into Africa.

Clark, Christopher. *Iron Kingdom: The Rise and Downfall of Prussia, 1600–1947* (2009). Includes an excellent discussion of the rise of German nationalism and Prussian power.

Cronon, William. *Nature's Metropolis: Chicago and the Great West* (1991). Makes connections between territorial expansion, industrialization, and urban development.

Davis, John. *Conflict and Control: Law and Order in Nineteenth-Century Italy* (1988). A superb study of the north-south and other rifts after Italian political unification.

Frankel, S. Herbert. *Capital Investment in Africa: Its Course and Effects* (1938). A careful study based on a mass of detailed figures and statistics on the general economic development of states in sub-Saharan Africa.

Friesen, Gerald. *The Canadian Prairies* (1984). The most comprehensive account of Canadian westward expansion.

Gluck, Carol. *Japan's Modern Myths: Ideology in the Late Meiji Period* (1985). A study of how states fashion useful historical traditions to consolidate and legitimize their rule.

Goswami, Manu. *Producing India: From Colonial Economy to National Space* (2004). An excellent study of how political economy produced the space of India, which the nationalists claimed as a national space.

Headrick, Daniel R. *The Tools of Empire: Technology and European Imperialism in the Nineteenth Century* (1981). A useful general study of the relationship between imperialism and technology.

Herbst, Jeffrey. *States and Power in Africa: Comparative Lessons in Authority and Control* (2000). An overview of the impact of colonial rule on contemporary African states.

Heyia, James I. *English Lessons: The Pedagogy of Imperialism in Nineteenth-Century China* (2003). A study of British imperialism in Qing China as a pedagogical project and a cultural endeavor.

Hill, Polly. *The Gold Coast Cocoa Farmer: A Preliminary Survey* (1965). An early but still important study of the introduction and spread of cocoa farming in the Gold Coast.

Hine, Robert V., and John Mack Faragher. *The American West: A New Interpretive History* (2000). Presents an excellent synthesis of the conquests by which the United States expanded from the Atlantic to the Pacific.

Hobsbawm, Eric J. *Nations and Nationalism since 1780: Programme, Myth, Reality* (1993). An insightful survey of the origins and development of nationalist thought throughout Europe.

Hochschild, Adam. *King Leopold's Ghost* (1998). A full-scale, eminently readable study of Europe's most egregiously destructive colonial regime in Africa.

Judson, Peter. *The Habsburg Empire: A New History* (2016). An innovative history of the relationship between "the people" and the state in a multiethnic empire.

Lieven, Dominic. *Empire: The Russian Empire and Its Rivals* (2000). A comparison of the British, Ottoman, Habsburg, and Russian Empires.

Mackenzie, John M. *Propaganda and Empire* (1984). Contains a series of useful chapters showing the importance of the empire to Britain.

Mamdani, Mahmood. *Citizen and State: Contemporary Africa and the Legacy of Late Colonialism* (1996). A survey of the impact of European colonial powers on African political systems.

McClintock, Anne. *Imperial Leather: Race, Gender and Sexuality in the Colonial Contest* (1995). A study of the imperial relationship between Victorian Britain and South Africa from the point of view of cultural studies.

McNeil, William. *Europe's Steppe Frontier: 1500–1800* (1964). An excellent study of the definitive victory of Russia's agricultural empire over grazing nomads and independent frontier people.

Mitchell, B. R. *International Historical Statistics: Africa, Asia, and Oceania, 1750–2005* (2007). This comparative volume provides data from over two centuries for all principal areas of economic and social activity in both eastern and western Europe.

Mittler, Barbara. *A Newspaper for China? Power, Identity and Change in Shanghai's News Media, 1872–1942* (2004). An analysis of how the influential foreign-managed newspaper *Shenbao* succeeded in capturing its Chinese readership in the late Qing.

Montgomery, David. *The Fall of the House of Labor: The Workplace, the State, and American Labor Activism, 1865–1925* (1987). An excellent discussion of changes in work in the late nineteenth century.

Myers, Ramon, and Mark Peattie (eds.). *The Japanese Colonial Empire, 1895–1945* (1984). A collection of essays exploring different aspects of Japanese colonialism.

Needell, Jeffrey. *A Tropical Belle Epoque: Elite Culture and Society in Turn of the Century Rio de Janeiro* (1987). Shows the strength of the Brazilian elites at the turn of the century.

Porter, Bernard. *The Absent-Minded Imperialists: What the British Really Thought about Empire* (2004). A careful discussion of the ways in which empire changed the British—and did not.

Prakash, Gyan. *Another Reason: Science and the Imagination of Modern India* (1999). A study of how science and technology transformed the British imperial governance and unified India into a geographical unity.

Prasad, Ritika. *Tracks of Change: Railways and Everyday Life in Colonial India*

(2016). A detailed analysis of how railways transformed the everyday experience of Indians under colonial rule.

Stengers, Jean. *Combien le Congo a-t-il coûté à la Belgique?* (1957). A detailed financial accounting of how much Leopold put into the Congo and how much he took out, underscoring just how ruthlessly he exploited this possession.

Topik, Steven. *The Political Economy of the Brazilian State, 1889–1930* (1987). An excellent discussion of the Brazilian state, especially of its elites.

Walker, Mack, *German Home Towns: Community, State, and the General State, 1648–1871* (1971, 1998). A brilliant, street-level analysis of the Holy Roman Empire (the First Reich) and the run-up to the German unification of 1871 (the Second Reich).

Wasserman, Mark. *Everyday Life and Politics in Nineteenth-Century Mexico* (2000). Wonderfully captures the way in which people coped with social and economic dislocation in late nineteenth-century Mexico.

Weeks, Theodore R. *Nation and State in Late Imperial Russia: Nationalism and Russification on the Western Frontier, 1863–1914* (1990). A good discussion of the Russian Empire's responses to the concept of the nation-state.

White, Richard. *Railroaded: The Transcontinentals and the Making of Modern America* (2011). A seering exposé of the corruptions and a startling critique of the economic and environmental costs associated with the expansion of railroad lines across Canada, the United States, and Mexico.

Zarrow, Peter. *After Empire: The Conceptual Transformation of the Chinese State, 1885–1924* (2012). A history of the changing ideas regarding the Chinese state that eventually led to the abandonment of monarchical rule by the Chinese people.

CHAPTER 18

Bayly, C. A. *The Birth of the Modern World, 1780–1914: Global Connections and Comparisons* (2004). A general study of the key political, economic, social, and cultural features of the modern era in world history.

Bergère, Marie-Claire. *Sun Yat-sen* (1998). Originally published in French in 1994, this is a judicious biography of the man generally known as the father of the modern Chinese nation.

Chatterjee, Partha. *The Nation and Its Fragments* (1993). One of the most important works on Indian nationalism by a leading scholar of "Subaltern Studies."

Conrad, Joseph. *Heart of Darkness* (1899). First published in a magazine in 1899, this novella contains a searing critique of King Leopold's oppressive and exploitative policies in the Congo and was part of a growing concern for the effects that European empires were having around the world, especially in Africa.

Crosby, Alfred. *Ecological Imperialism: The Biological Expansion of Europe, 900–1900* (2nd ed., 2004). A fascinating biohistory of European imperialism.

Esherick, Joseph. *The Origins of the Boxer Uprising* (1987). The definitive account of the episode.

Esherick, Joseph. "How the Qing Became China." In Joseph W. Esherick, Hasan Kayali, and Eric Van Young (eds.), *Empire to Nation: Historical Perspectives on the Making of the Modern World* (2006). A study of the processes through which the Qing Empire became the nation-state of China.

Everdell, William R. *The First Moderns: Profiles in the Origins of Twentieth-Century Thought* (1997). A rich account of the many faces of modernism, focusing particularly on science and art.

Finnane, Antonia. *Changing Clothes in China: Fashion, History, Nation* (2008). An exploration of changing Chinese identities from the perspective of clothing.

Gay, Peter. *The Cultivation of Hatred* (1994). A provocative discussion of the violent passions of the immediate pre–Great War era.

Hochschild, Adam. *King Leopold's Ghost: A Story of Greed, Terror, and Heroism in Colonial Africa* (1998). A well-written account of the violent colonial history of the Belgian Congo under King Leopold in the late nineteenth century.

Judge, Joan. *The Precious Raft of History: The Past, the West, and the Woman Question in China* (2008). An insightful exploration of the "woman question" in China at the turn of the twentieth century.

Katz, Friedrich. *The Life and Times of Pancho Villa* (1998). An exploration of the Mexican Revolution that shows how Villa's armies destroyed the forces of Díaz and his followers.

Keddie, Nikki. *An Islamic Response to Imperialism: Political and Religious Writings of Sayyid Jamal ad-Din "al-Afghani"* (1968). Definitive information on Afghani's life and influence, coupled with a translation of one of his most important essays.

Kern, Stephen. *The Culture of Time and Space 1880–1918* (1986). A useful study of the enormous changes in the experience of time and space in the age of late industrialism in Europe and America.

Kuhn, Philip. *Chinese among Others: Emigration in Modern Times* (2008). An overview of the history of Chinese migration.

McKeown, Adam. *Melancholy Order: Asian Migration and the Globalization of Borders* (2008). An examination of global migration patterns since the mid-nineteenth century and how regulations designed to restrict Asian migration to other parts of the world led to the modern regime of migration control.

Meade, Teresa. *"Civilizing" Rio: Reform and Resistance in a Brazilian City, 1889–1930* (1997). A wonderful study of cultural and class conflict in Brazil.

Moon, David. *The Plough That Broke the Steppes: Agriculture and Environment on Russia's Grasslands, 1700–1914* (2013). An excellent environmental history of the Russian steppe.

Pick, Daniel. *Faces of Degeneration: A European Disorder, c. 1848–c. 1918* (1993). A study of Europe's fear of social and biological decline, particularly focusing on France and Italy.

Pretorius, Fransjohn (ed.). *Scorched Earth* (2001). A study of the Anglo-Boer War in terms of its environmental impact.

Saler, Michael (ed.). *The Fin de Siècle World* (2014). A comprehensive anthology of essays on turn-of-the-century politics and culture across the world.

Sarkar, Sumit. *The Swadeshi Movement in Bengal* (1973). A comprehensive study of an early militant movement against British rule.

Schorske, Carl E. *Fin-de-Siècle Vienna: Politics and Culture* (1980). The classic treatment of the birth of modern ideas and political movements in turn-of-the-century Austria.

Trachtenberg, Alan. *The Incorporation of America: Culture and Society in the Gilded Age* (1982). A provocative synthesis of changes in the American economy, society, and culture in the last decades of the nineteenth century.

Wang, David Der-wei. *Fin-de-Siècle Splendor: Repressed Modernities of Late Qing Fiction, 1849–1911* (1997). A fine work that attempts to locate the "modern" within the writings of the late Qing period.

Warren, Louis. *Buffalo Bill's America: William Cody and the Wild West Show* (2005). A superb portrait of William F. Cody, the person; of Buffalo Bill, the persona Cody (and others) created; and of the popular culture his Wild West shows brought to audiences in Europe and North America.

Warwick, Peter. *Black People and the South African War, 1899–1902* (1983). An important study that reminds readers of the crucial involvement of black South Africans in this bloody conflict.

Womack, John, Jr. *Zapata and the Mexican Revolution* (1968). A major work on the Mexican Revolution that discusses peasant struggles in the state of Morelos in great detail.

CHAPTER 19

Akcam, Taner. *The Young Turks' Crime Against Humanity: The Armenian Genocide and Ethnic Cleansing in the Ottoman Empire* (2012). An exhaustive examination of the factors that impelled the Turkish authorities to carry out ethnic cleansing against the Armenians during World War I.

Aksakal, Mustafa. *The Ottoman Road to War in 1914: The Ottoman Empire and the First World War* (2008). An important study of the personalities and factors that led the Ottomans to join with Germany and Austria-Hungary during World War I, a fateful decision that ultimately spelled the end of the Ottoman Empire.

Ambedkar, B. R. *Annihilation of Caste: The Annotated Critical Edition* (1936). Ambedkar's brilliant polemic against Gandhi on caste. With a new introduction by Arundhati Roy, this work is an essential reading for an understanding of Ambedkar's thoughts.

Anderson, Scott. *Lawrence in Arabia: War, Deceit, Imperial Folly, and the Making of the Middle East* (2013). A new and authoritative biography of T. E. Lawrence, with significant new material on British policies in the Middle East as seen through the eyes of a strong pro-Arab figure.

Bloxham, Donald. *The Great Game of Genocide: Imperialism, Nationalism, and the Destruction of the Ottoman Armenians* (2005). The definitive work on the Armenian genocide, set in a wide historical context.

Bosworth, R. J. B. *Mussolini's Italy: Life under the Dictatorship, 1915–1945* (2006). An eye-opening treatment of fascism in Italy beyond Mussolini.

Brown, Judith. *Gandhi: Prisoner of Hope* (1990). A biography of Gandhi as a political activist.

Clark, Christopher. *Sleepwalkers: How Europe Went to War* (2012). A reexamination of the crucial role of Austria-Hungary in triggering the world war.

De Grazia, Victoria, and Ellen Furlough (eds.). *The Sex of Things: Gender and Consumption in Historical Perspective* (1996). Path-breaking essays on how gender affects consumption.

Dumenil, Lynn. *The Modern Temper: America in the 1920s* (1995). A general discussion of American culture in the decade after World War I.

Fainsod, Merle. *Smolensk under Soviet Rule* (1989). The most accessible and sophisticated interpretation of the Stalin revolution in the village.

Gelvin, James. *Divided Loyalties: Nationalism and Mass Politics in Syria at the Close of Empire* (1998). Offers important insights into the development of nationalism in the Arab world.

Horne, John (ed.). *State, Society, and Mobilization during the First World War* (1997). Essays on what it took to wage total war among all the belligerents.

Horne, John (ed.). *A Companion to World War I* (2010). A collection of articles written by leading scholars of World War I; the most comprehensive and up-to-date work on this war.

Johnson, G. Wesley. *The Emergence of Black Politics in Senegal* (1971). A useful examination of the stirrings of African nationalism in Senegal.

Kennedy, David M. *Freedom from Fear: The American People in Depression and War, 1929–1945* (1999). A wonderful narrative of turbulent years.

Kershaw, Ian. *Hitler*, 2 vols. (1998–2000). A masterpiece combining biography and context.

Kimble, David. *A Political History of Ghana* (1963). An excellent discussion of the beginnings of African nationalism in Ghana.

Kotkin, Stephen. *Magnetic Mountain: Stalinism as a Civilization* (1995). Recaptures the atmosphere of a time when everything seemed possible, even creating a new world.

Kotkin, Stephen. *Stalin*. Vol. 1: *Paradoxes of Power* (2014). A sweeping history of the tsarist regime, world war, Russian Revolution, civil war, and rise of Stalin.

Lambert, Nicholas A. *Planning Armageddon: British Economic Warfare and the First World War* (2012). Mines new archives to show that the British had an aggressive plan before the war to destroy Germany financially, which the British government approved and began to enact until the United States forced them to back off.

LeMahieu, D. L. *A Culture for Democracy: Mass Communication and the Cultivated Mind in Britain between the Wars* (1988). One of the great works on mass culture.

Lyttelton, Adrian. *The Seizure of Power: Fascism in Italy, 1919–1929* (1961). Still the classic account.

Marchand, Roland. *Advertising the American Dream: Making Way for Modernity, 1920–1945* (1985). An excellent discussion of the force of mass production and mass consumption.

Mazower, Mark. *Dark Continent: Europe's Twentieth Century* (1999). A wide-ranging overview of Europe's tempestuous twentieth century.

McGirr, Lisa. *The War on Alcohol: Prohibition and the Rise of the American State* (2016). Emphasizes the power of cultural reaction against modernity that brought about Prohibition and the irony that its enforcement helped to expand the power of the modern state.

McKeown, Adam. *Melancholy Order: Asian Migration and the Globalization of Border* (2008). A major study of the vast movement of peoples around the globe between the middle of the nineteenth and middle of the twentieth centuries.

Morrow, John H., Jr. *The Great War: An Imperial History* (2004). Places World War I in the context of European imperialism.

Musgrove, Charles D. *China's Contested Capital: Architecture, Ritual, and Response in Nanjing* (2013). An exploration of how the Chinese Nationalist capital of Nanjing served as a focal point for the making of a nation and a new form of mass politics.

Nottingham, John, and Carl Rosberg. *The Myth of "Mau Mau": Nationalism in Kenya* (1966). Dispels the myths in describing the roots of nationalism in Kenya.

Pedersen, Susan. *The Guardians: the League of Nations and the Crisis of Empire* (2015). Skillfully reexamines the neglected effort to regulate the colonial world under a so-called mandate system.

Rutledge, Ian. *Enemy on the Euphrates: The British Occupation of Iraq and the Great Arab Revolt, 1914-1921* (2014). An impassioned investigation of Britain's effort to take control of the oil-rich territory of Iraq and the determined resistance of the Iraqi peoples.

Strand, David. *An Unfinished Republic: Leading by Word and Deed in Modern China* (2011). A study of how the need for popular support led to a new political culture characterized by public speaking and performance in early twentieth-century China.

Suny, Ronald Gregor. *"They can Live in the Desert but Nowhere Else": A History of the Armenian Genocide* (2015). A careful, document-based analysis of the Armenian genocide.

Taylor, Jay. *The Generalissimo: Chiang Kai-shek and the Struggle for Modern China* (2009). The first serious biographical study of Chiang Kai-shek in English, although its reliance on Chiang's own diary as a source does raise some questions of historical interpretation.

Thorp, Rosemary (ed.). *Latin America in the 1930s* (1984). An important collection of essays on Latin America's response to the shakeup of the interwar years.

Tsin, Michael. *Nation, Governance, and Modernity in China: Canton, 1900-1927* (1999). An analysis of the vision and social dynamics behind the Guomindang-led revolution of the 1920s.

Vianna, Hermano. *The Mystery of Samba* (1999). Discusses the history of samba, emphasizing its African heritage as well as its persistent popular content.

Wakeman, Frederic Jr. *Policing Shanghai, 1927-1937* (1995). An excellent account of Guomindang rule in China's largest city during the Nanjing decade.

Winter, J. M. *The Experience of World War* (1988). A comprehensive presentation of the many sides of the twentieth century.

Young, Louise. *Japan's Total Empire: Manchuria and the Culture of Wartime Imperialism* (1998). An innovative case study of Japanese imperialism and mass culture with broad implications.

Zuber, Terence. *Inventing the Schlieffen Plan: German War Planning, 1871-1914* (2002). Uses new archives to demonstrate definitively that the famed Schlieffen Plan is essentially a myth, and explains how that myth was created.

CHAPTER 20

Aburish, Said K. *Nasser: The Last Arab* (2004). A recent and impressive look at Egypt's most powerful political leader in the 1950s and 1960s.

Anderson, Jon Lee. *Che Guevara: A Revolutionary Life* (1997). A sweeping study of the radicalization of Latin American nationalism.

Austin, Granville. *The Indian Constitution: Cornerstone of a Nation*, 2nd ed. (1999). A classic study of constitution making in India.

Bayly, Christopher, and Tim Harper. *Forgotten Armies: Britain's Asian Empire and the War with Japan* (2004). A brilliant social and military history of World War II as fought and lived in South and Southeast Asia.

Chatterjee, Partha. *Nationalist Thought and the Colonial World: A Derivative Discourse* (1986). An influential interpretation of the ideological and political nature of Indian nationalism and the struggle for a postcolonial nation-state.

Cook, Alexander C. (ed.). *Mao's Little Red Book: A Global History* (2014). A look at the global impact of the Chinese Cultural Revolution through the lens of the iconic "little red book" of quotations from Mao.

Crampton, R. J. *Eastern Europe in the Twentieth Century and After*, 2nd ed. (1997). A comprehensive overview covering all Soviet-bloc countries.

Dikötter, Frank. *Mao's Great Famine: The History of China's Most Devastating Catastrophe, 1958-1962* (2010). A recent detailed account of one of the greatest human-made disasters in twentieth-century history.

Dower, John W. *Embracing Defeat: Japan in the Wake of World War II* (1999). A prize-winning study of the transformation of one of the war's vanquished.

Elkins, Caroline. *Imperial Reckoning: The Untold Story of Britain's Gulag in Kenya* (2005). A Pulitzer Prize–winning study of the brutal war to suppress the nationalist uprising in Kenya in the 1950s that ultimately led to independence for that country.

Feshbach, Murray, and Alfred Friendly Jr. *Ecocide in the USSR: Health and Nation under Siege* (1992). A crucial study of ecological disasters in the Soviet Union.

Gao Yuan. *Born Red: A Chronicle of the Cultural Revolution* (1987). A gripping personal account of the Cultural Revolution by a former Red Guard.

Gordon, Andrew (ed.). *Postwar Japan as History* (1993). Essays covering a wide range of topics on postwar Japan.

Hargreaves, John D. *Decolonization in Africa* (1996). A good place to start when exploring the history of African decolonization.

Hasan, Mushirul (ed.). *India's Partition: Process, Strategy and Mobilization* (1993). A useful anthology of scholarly articles, short stories, and primary documents on the partition of India.

Iriye, Akira. *Power and Culture: The Japanese-American War, 1941-1945* (1981). A discussion that goes beyond the military confrontation in Asia.

Jackson, Kenneth T. *Crabgrass Frontier: The Suburbanization of the United States* (1985). An insightful and influential consideration of the movement of the American population from cities to suburbs.

Jalal, Ayesha. *The Sole Spokesman: Jinnah, the Muslim League and the Demand for Pakistan* (1985). A study of the high politics leading to the violent partition of British India.

Keep, John L. H. *Last of the Empires: A History of the Soviet Union 1945-1991* (1995). A detailed overview of the core of the "Second World."

Morris, Benny. *Righteous Victims: A History of the Zionist-Arab Conflict, 1881-1999* (2000). On the Arab-Israeli War of 1948.

Pantsov, Alexander V. *Mao: The Real Story*, translated by Steven I. Levine (2012). A well-researched biography of Mao.

Patterson, James T. *Grand Expectations: The United States, 1945-1974* (1996). Synthesizes the American experience in the postwar decades.

Patterson, Thomas. *Contesting Castro* (1994). The best study of the tension between the United States and Cuba. Culminating in the Cuban Revolution, it explores the deep American misunderstanding of Cuban national aspirations.

Roberts, Geoffrey. *Stalin's Wars: From World War to Cold War, 1939-1953* (2007). A reassessment of Stalin's wartime leadership that conveys the vast scale of what took place.

Ruedy, John. *Modern Algeria: The Origins and Development of a Nation* (1992). Gives the history of the Algerian nationalist movements and provides an overview of the Algerian War of Independence.

Tignor, Robert L. *W. Arthur Lewis and the Birth of Development Economics* (2006). An intellectual biography of the Nobel Prize–winning, West Indian–born economist who proposed formulas to promote the economic development of less developed societies and then sought to implement them in Africa and the West Indies.

Wiener, Douglas R. *A Little Corner of Freedom: Russian Nature Protection from Stalin to Gorbachev* (2002). A groundbreaking book about Russian environmentalism.

Zatlin, Jonathan. *The Currency of Socialism: Money and Political Culture in East Germany* (2007). A fascinating description of how the economy of East Germany did—and did not—work.

Zubkova, Elena. *Russia after the War: Hopes, Illusions, and Disappointments, 1945-1957* (1998). Uses formerly secret archives to catalogue the devastation and difficult reconstruction of one of the war's victors.

CHAPTER 21

Collier, Paul. *The Bottom Billion: Why the Poorest Countries Fail and What Can Be Done about It* (2007). Shows that despite the world's advancing prosperity, more than a billion people have been left behind in abject poverty.

Davis, Deborah (ed.). *The Consumer Revolution in Urban China* (2000). A look at the different aspects of the recent profound social transformation of urban China.

Davis, Mike. *City of Quartz: Excavating the Future in Los Angeles* (1990). Offers provocative reflections on the recent history, current condition, and possible future of Los Angeles.

Dutton, Michael. *Streetlife China* (1999). A fascinating portrayal of the survival tactics of those inhabiting the margins of society in modern China.

Eichengreen, Barry. *Globalizing Capital: A History of the International Monetary System* (1996). An insightful analysis of how international capital markets changed in the period from 1945 to 1980.

Gourevitch, Philip. *We Wish to Inform You That Tomorrow We Will Be Killed with Our Families: Stories from Rwanda* (1999). A volume that reveals the hatreds that culminated in the Rwanda genocide.

Guillermoprieto, Alma. *Looking for History: Dispatches from Latin America* (2001). A collection of articles by the most important journalist reporting on Latin American affairs.

Han, Minzhu (ed.). *Cries for Democracy: Writings and Speeches from the 1989 Chinese Democracy Movement* (1990). A collection of documents from the events leading up to the incident in Tiananmen Square on June 4, 1989.

Herbst, Jeffrey. *States and Power in Africa: Comparative Lessons in Authority and Control* (2000). Explores the political dilemmas facing modern African polities.

Honig, Emily, and Gail Hershatter. *Personal Voices: Chinese Women in the 1980's* (1988). A record of Chinese women during a period of rapid social change.

Huang, Yasheng. *Capitalism with Chinese Characteristics: Entrepreneurship and the State* (2008). A sharp, unsentimental inside look at China's market economy and its future prospects.

Kavoori, Anandam P., and Aswin Punathambekar (eds.). *Global Bollywood* (2008). A collection of essays by leading film scholars on Indian cinema on different aspects of the processes by which the Hindi film industry became Bollywood.

Klitgaard, Robert. *Tropical Gangsters* (1990). On the intimate connections between corrupt native elites and international aid agencies.

Kotkin, Stephen. *Armageddon Averted: The Soviet Collapse, 1970-2000* (2001). Places the surprise fall of the Soviet Union in the context of the great shifts in the post–World War II order.

Macekura, Stephen. *Of Limits and Growth: The Rise of Global Sustainable Development in the Twentieth Century* (2016). Explores the rise of global environmental politics in the 1970s and 1980s and the debate about resources and climate change.

Mamdani, Mahmood. *When Victims Become Killers: Colonialism, Nativism, and the Genocide in Rwanda* (2001). Discusses the genocide in Rwanda in light of the legacy of colonialism.

Mehta, Suketu. *Maximum City: Bombay Lost and Found* (2005). Examines one of the great, and contradictory, cities in the era of globalization.

Miller, Chris. *The Struggle to Save the Soviet Economy: Mikhail Gorbachev and the Collapse of the USSR* (2016). An insightful analysis of internal debates in Moscow over rival directions for the Soviet economy and the response to Chinese reforms after 1978.

Mottahedeh, Roy. *The Mantle of the Prophet: Religion and Politics in Iran,* 2nd ed. (2008). Perhaps the best book on the 1979 Iranian Revolution and its aftermath.

Nathan, Andrew, and Perry Link. *The Tiananmen Papers* (2002). An inside look at the divisions within the Chinese elite in connection with the 1989 crackdown.

Portes, Alejandro, and Rubén G. Rumbaut. *Immigrant America,* 2nd ed. (1996). A good comparative study of how immigration has transformed the United States.

Prakash, Gyan. *Mumbai Fables* (2010). A spirited account of the rise of India's most modern city, a center of intellectual, commercial, and political vitality.

Prunier, Gerald. *Africa's World War: Congo, the Rwandan Genocide, and the Making of a Continental Catastrophe* (2009). A chilling discussion of the spillover effects of the Rwandan genocide on central, eastern, and southern Africa.

Punathambekar, Aswin. *From Bombay to Bollywood: The Making of a Global Media Industry* (2013). A study of the transformation of the Indian film industry that globalizes its content and reach.

Reinhart, Carmen, and Kenneth Rogoff. *This Time Is Different: Eight Centuries of Financial Folly* (2009). Explains the latest financial crash using historical perspective.

Ruggie, John Gerard. *Just Business: Multinational Corporations and Human Rights* (2013). Shows how even big business got into human rights advocacy.

Sikkink, Kathryn. *The Justice Cascade: How Human Rights Prosecutions Are Changing World Politics* (2011). Shows how new forms of global organizing and new social norms are changing the political rules across borders.

Stein, Judith. *Pivotal Decade: How the United States Traded Factories for Finance in the Seventies* (2010). A comprehensive study of the rise of American banking and the decline of heartland industries.

Ther, Philipp. *Europe since 1989: A History* (2016). A concise account of European integration and neoliberalism since the fall of the Berlin Wall.

Van Der Wee, Hermann. *Prosperity and Upheaval: The World Economy, 1945-1980* (1986). Describes very well the transformation and problems of the world economy, particularly from the 1960s onward.

Westad, Odd Arne. *The Global Cold War: Third World Interventions and the Making of Our Times* (2007). A genuinely global perspective on the Cold War and its consequences.

Winn, Peter. *Americas: The Changing Face of Latin America and the Caribbean* (1992). A useful portrayal of Latin America since the 1970s.

EPILOGUE

Achcar, Gilbert. *Morbid Symptoms: Relapse in the Arab Uprising* (2016). An up-to-date overview of the difficulties that the proponents of the Arab Spring encountered, with long and detailed treatments of Syria and Egypt.

Christensen, Thomas J. *The China Challenges: Shaping the Choices of a Rising Power* (2015). A survey of "China's Rise" and the challenges and choices the country faces in the contemporary world.

Cleveland, William L., and Martin Bunton. *A History of the Modern Middle East*, 6th ed. (2016). The sixth edition of an important textbook that covers the whole of the Middle East from 1800 to the present.

Cooper, Frederick. *Africa in the World: Capitalism, Empire, Nation-State* (2014). An overview of Africa's place in global history, based on the most recent scholarship.

Darwall, Rupert. *The Age of Global Warming: A History* (2013). An accessible narrative about how scientists became increasingly aware of the threat of climate change and the multinational effort to reduce carbon emissions.

Deaton, Angus. *The Great Escape: Health, Wealth, and the Origins of Inequality* (2013). An examination of the heightened degree of inequality by a Nobel Prize–winning authority who emphasizes that contemporary well-to-do individuals have largely failed to help those not so fortunate to achieve their potential.

Eichengreen, Barry. *Hall of Mirrors: The Great Depression, the Great Recessions and the Uses—and Misuses—of History* (2015). A chronicle of the financial upheaval of 2008–2009, comparing the policies and mindsets of major decision makers to the choices made in the 1930s.

Esposito, John L., Tamara Sonn, and John O. Voll. *Islam and Democracy after the Arab Spring* (2016). An analysis of the prospects of democracy in Muslim countries, with case studies of Tunisia, Egypt, and Turkey, among others.

Ferguson, James. "Seeing Like an Oil Company: Space, Security, and Global Capital in Neoliberal Africa." *American Anthropologist* 107 (2005): 377–382. A critique of James Scott's book *Seeing Like a State*, and a view of the role of oil and mining companies in Africa and their failure to promote economic growth there.

Ferguson, James. *Global Shadows: Africa in the Neo-Liberal World Order* (2006). Journal articles brought together in a book by one of the leading African anthropologists. They deal with contemporary African issues and dilemmas, placed in a global context.

Ferguson, James. *Give a Man a Fish: Reflections on the New Politics of Distribution* (2015). An analysis of social welfare programs in southern Africa, involving cash payments to the poorest members of societies, and their implications for neoliberal capitalism.

Franco, Jean. *Cruel Modernity* (2013). An examination of the cultural dimensions of Latin America's experience with recent neoliberal policies and the tensions and violence of relatively stateless societies.

Gerges, Fawaz A. *ISIS: A History* (2016). One of a series of books that explores the rise of ISIS and stresses the place of violence in building a new Islamic state.

Jaffrelot, Christophe. *Saffron Modernity in India: Narendra Modi and His Experiment with Gujarat* (2014). A political history of how Narendra Modi emerged dominant in Gujarat using anti-Muslim nationalist ideology, captured the leadership of the BJP, and built a personality cult that catapulted him as a national leader.

Judis, John. *The Populist Explosion: How the Great Recession Transformed American and European Politics* (2016). A book by a journalist and political analyst that argues that the contemporary populist upsurges on both the right and left are responses to neoliberal globalization.

Lacau, Ernest. *On Populist Reason* (2007). This dense but insightful study by a political theorist offers original philosophical views on the meaning of "the people" by examining historical examples of populism.

Lee, Soo im, and Stephen-Murphy-Shigematsu. *Japan's Diversity Dilemmas: Ethnicity, Citizenship, and Education* (2006). Still an important work that examines whether Japan can assimilate foreigners, crucial for its aging workforce, or is condemned to demographic and economic decline because of its extremely low birthrate and pride in ethnic purity.

Lepore, Jill. *The Whites of Their Eyes: The Tea Party's Revolution and the Battle over American History* (2011). A history of the American far right and the Tea Party and their imagination of a nostalgic American past.

Lynch, Marc. *The New Arab Wars: Uprisings and Anarchy in the Middle East* (2016). Brings the narrative of the Arab Spring and the ambitions of its diverse proponents up to the present.

McCants, William. *The ISIS Apocalypse: The History, Strategy, and Doomsday Vision of the Islamic State* (2015). An important study of ISIS, based on a wide reading of ISIS's publications.

Milankovic, Brian. *Global Inequality: A New Approach for the Age of Globalization* (2016). Using the most up-to-date data on worldwide incomes, the author shows how the last quarter-century has yielded a convergence in global income distribution across societies and the widening of a gap within societies.

Moubayed, Sami. *Under the Black Flag: At the Frontier of the New Jihad* (2015). A study of the rise of jihadism within the Arab world, with a concentration on Syria.

Muller, Jan-Werner. *What Is Populism?* (2016). The sharpest analysis yet of the nature and prospects of populism, especially its relations to political establishments, which it condemns but on which it depends.

Owen, Roger. *The Rise and Fall of Arab Presidents for Life, with a New Afterword* (2014). A study that examines the emergence of Arab leaders who endeavored to hold on to power for as long as they lived, with insights into the actions of those who brought many of the leaders down during the Arab Spring.

Pietz, David A. *The Yellow River: The Problem of Water in Modern China* (2015). A critical look at health and environmental issues in China today, from a historical perspective through the lens of one of its major rivers.

Radelet, Steven. *Emerging Africa: How Seventeen Countries Are Leading the Way* (2010). An Afro-optimist sees many African countries enjoying economic growth and political stability, proving that Africa can also join much of the rest of the world in achieving economic and political progress.

Radelet, Steven. *The Great Surge: The Ascent of the Developing World* (2015). An overview of the extraordinary progress that many of the countries in what once was called the Third World have achieved in economic and political successes.

Reid, Michael. *Forgotten Continent: The Battle for Latin America's Soul* (2009). A journalistic account of how Latin America grappled with market openings, new democratic forces, and the search for policies to close the gap between the haves and have-nots.

Shambaugh, David. *China Goes Global: The Partial Power* (2013). An analysis of China's role in the global arena and its impact, from economics to culture.

Trenin, Dmitri. *Should We Fear Russia?* (2016). A clear-eyed view of what contemporary Russia is and is not.

Warwick, John. *Black Flags Flying: The Rise of ISIS* (2015). A detailed account of the leadership groups within ISIS and its relationship to al-Qaeda.

Weiss, Michael, and Hassan Hassan. *ISIS: Inside the Army of Terror* (2015). An account based on interviews and wide reading of western and Arabic sources on the rise of ISIS.

Wright, Lawrence. *The Looming Tower: Al-Qaeda and the Road to 9/11* (2006). A Pulitzer Prize–winning study of the origins and evolution of al-Qaeda.

Wright, Lawrence. *The Terror Years: From al-Qaeda to ISIS* (2016). Primarily a study of the decline of the power of al-Qaeda, which created an opening for the more territorially based ISIS.

GLOSSARY

Abd al-Rahman III Islamic ruler in Spain who held a countercaliphate and reigned from 912 to 961 CE.

aborigines Original, native inhabitants of a region, as opposed to invaders, colonizers, or later peoples of mixed ancestry.

absolute monarchy Form of government where one body, usually the monarch, controls the right to tax, judge, make war, and coin money. The term *enlightened absolutists* was often used to refer to state monarchies in seventeenth- and eighteenth-century Europe.

acid rain Precipitation containing large amounts of sulfur, mainly from coal-fired plants.

adaptation Ability to alter behavior and to innovate; finding new ways of doing things.

African National Congress (ANC) Multiracial organization founded in 1912 in an effort to end racial discrimination in South Africa.

African sacred kingships Institutions that marked the centralized politics of East, West, and central Africa. The inhabitants of these kingships believed that their kings were descendants of the gods.

Afrikaners Descendants of the original Dutch settlers of South Africa; often referred to as Boers.

agones Athletic contests in ancient Greece.

Ahmosis Egyptian ruler in the southern part of the country who ruled from 1550 to 1525 BCE. Ahmosis used Hyksos weaponry—horse chariots in particular—to defeat the Hyksos themselves.

Ahura Mazda Supreme god of the Persians believed to have created the world and all that is good and to have appointed earthly kings.

AIDS (acquired immunodeficiency syndrome) Virus that compromises the ability of the infected person's immune system to ward off disease. First detected in 1981, AIDS was initially stigmatized as a "gay cancer," but as it spread to heterosexuals, public awareness about it increased. In its first two decades, AIDS killed 12 million people.

Akbarnamah Mughal intellectual Abulfazl's *Book of Akbar*, which attempted to reconcile the traditional Sufi interest in the inner life within the worldly context of a great empire.

Alaric II Visigothic king who issued a simplified code of innovative imperial law.

Alexander the Great (356–323 BCE) Leader who used novel tactics and new kinds of armed forces to conquer the Persian Empire, which extended from Egypt and the Mediterranean Sea to the interior of what is now Afghanistan and as far as the Indus River valley. Alexander's conquests broke down barriers between the Mediterranean world and Southwest Asia and transferred massive amounts of wealth and power to the Mediterranean, transforming it into a more unified world of economic and cultural exchange.

Alexandria Port city in Egypt named after Alexander the Great. Alexandria was a model city in the Hellenistic world. It was built up by a multiethnic population from around the Mediterranean world.

Al-Khwarizmi Scientist and mathematician who lived from 780 to 850 CE and is known for having modified Indian digits into Arabic numerals.

Allied Powers Name given to the alliance between Britain, France, Russia, and Italy, who fought against Germany, Austria-Hungary, and the Ottoman Empire (the Central Powers) in World War I. In World War II the name was used for the alliance between Britain, France, and America, who fought against the Axis Powers (Germany, Italy, and Japan).

allomothering System by which mothers rely on other women, including their own mothers, daughters, sisters, and friends, to help in the nurturing and protection of children.

alluvium Area of land created by river deposits.

alphabet A writing system in which each character ideally represents a single sound. The first full alphabet was developed by the Phoenicians in the mid-second millenium BCE and consists of 22 letters (all of them consonants).

American Railway Union Workers' union that initiated the Pullman Strike of 1894, which led to violence and ended in the leaders' arrest.

Amnesty International Nongovernmental organization formed to defend "prisoners of conscience"—those detained for their beliefs, race, sex, ethnic origin, language, or religion.

Amorites Name that Mesopotamian urbanites called the transhumant herders from the Arabian desert. Around 2300 BCE, the Amorites, along with the Elamites, were at the center of newly formed dynasties in southern Mesopotamia.

Amun Once insignificant Egyptian god elevated to higher status by Amenemhet (1991–1962 BCE). *Amun* means "hidden" in ancient Egyptian; the name was meant to convey the god's omnipresence.

Analects Texts that include the teachings and cultural ideals of Confucius.

anarchism Belief that society should be a free association of its members, not subject to government, laws, or police.

Anatolia Now mainly the area known as modern Turkey. In the sixth millennium BCE, people from Anatolia, Greece, and the Levant took to boats and populated the Aegean. Their small villages endured almost unchanged for two millennia.

ancestral worship Religious practice in which the living honor their dead ancestors through rituals, believing that the dead intervene with their powers on behalf of the living.

Angkor Wat Magnificent Khmer Vaishnavite temple that crowned the royal palace in Angkor. It had statues representing the Hindu pantheon of gods.

Anglo-Boer War (1899–1902) War in South Africa between the British and the Afrikaners over the gold-rich Transvaal. In response to the Afrikaners' guerrilla tactics and in order to contain the local population, the British instituted the first concentration camps. Ultimately, Britain won the conflict.

animal domestication Gradual process that occurred simultaneously with or just before the domestication of plants, depending on the region.

annals Historical records. Notable annals are the cuneiform inscriptions that record successful Assyrian military campaigns.

Anti-Federalists Critics of the U.S. Constitution who sought to defend the people against the power of the federal government and insisted on a bill of rights to protect individual liberties from government intrusion.

apartheid Racial segregation policy of the Afrikaner dominated South African government. Legislated in 1948 by the Afrikaner National Party, it existed in South Africa for many years.

Arab-Israeli War of 1948–1949 Conflict between Israeli and Arab armies that arose in the wake of a UN vote to partition Palestine into Arab and Jewish territories. The war shattered the legitimacy of Arab ruling elites.

Aramaic Dialect of a Semitic language spoken in Southwest Asia; it became the lingua franca of the Persian Empire.

Aristotle (384–322 BCE) Philosopher who studied under Plato but came to different conclusions about nature and politics. Aristotle believed in collecting observations about nature and discerning patterns to ascertain how things worked.

Aryans Nomadic charioteers who spoke Indo-European languages and entered South Asia in 1500 BCE. The early Aryan settlers were herders.

Asante state State located in present-day Ghana, founded by Akan-speaking peoples at the end of the seventeenth century. It grew in power in the next century because of its access to gold and its involvement in the slave trade.

ascetic One who rejects material possessions and physical pleasures.

Asiatic Society Cultural organization founded by British Orientalists who supported native culture but still believed in colonial rule.

Aśoka Emperor of the Mauryan dynasty from 268 to 231 BCE. A great conqueror and unifier of India, he is said to have embraced Buddhism toward the end of his life.

Assur One of two cities on the upper reaches of the Tigris River that were the heart of Assyria proper (the other was Nineveh).

Aśvaghosa First known Sanskrit writer. He may have lived from 80 to 150 CE and may have composed a biography of the Buddha.

Ataturk, Mustafa Kemal (1881–1938) Ottoman army officer and military hero who helped forge the modern Turkish nation-state. He and his followers deposed the sultan, declared Turkey a republic, and constructed a European-like secular state, eliminating Islam's hold over civil and political affairs.

Atlantic system New system of trade and expansion that linked Europe, Africa, and the Americas. It emerged in the wake of European voyages across the Atlantic Ocean.

Atma Vedic term signifying the eternal self, represented by the trinity of deities.

Atman In the Upanishads, an eternal being who exists everywhere. The atman never perishes but is reborn or transmigrates into another life.

Attila Sole ruler of all Hunnish tribes from 433 to 453 CE. Harsh and much feared, he formed the first empire to oppose Rome in northern Europe.

Augustus Title meaning "Revered One," assumed in 27 BCE by the Roman ruler Octavian (63–14 BCE). This was one of many titles he assumed; others included *imperator*, *princeps*, and *caesar*.

australopithecines Hominin species that appeared 3 million years ago and, unlike other animals, walked on two legs. Their brain capacity was a little less than one-third that of a modern human's, or about the size of the brain capacity of today's African apes. Although not humans, they carried the genetic and biological material out of which modern humans would later emerge.

Austro-Hungarian Empire New configuration of the Austrian Empire in which Hungary received greater autonomy; established in 1867, it collapsed at the end of World War I.

authoritarianism Centralized and dictatorial form of government, proclaimed by its adherents to be superior to parliamentary democracy and especially effective at mobilizing the masses. This thinking was widely accepted in parts of the world during the 1930s.

Avesta Compilation of holy works transmitted orally by Zoroastrian priests for millennia and eventually recorded in the ninth century CE.

axial age Term often used to describe the pivotal period of the first millennium BCE, when radical thinkers across the "second-generation societies" of Afro-Eurasia—including the Greek philosophers of the Mediterranean, Zoroaster in Southwest Asia, Buddha in South Asia, and Confucius and Master Lao in East Asia—offered dramatically new ideas that challenged their times.

Axis Powers The three aggressor states in World War II: Germany, Japan, and Italy.

Aztec Empire Mesoamerican empire that originated with a league of three Mexica cities in 1430 and gradually expanded through the Central Valley of Mexico, uniting numerous small, independent states under a single monarch who ruled with the help of counselors, military leaders, and priests. By the late fifteenth century, the Aztec realm may have embraced 25 million people. In 1521, they were defeated by the conquistador Hernán Cortés.

baby boom Post–World War II upswing in U.S. birthrates; it reversed a century of decline.

Bactria A Hellenistic kingdom that broke away from the Seleucids around 200 BCE to establish a state in the Gandhara region of modern Pakistan, which served as a bridge between South Asia and the Mediterranean Greek world.

bactrian camel Two-humped animal domesticated in central Asia around 2500 BCE. The bactrian camel was heartier than the one-humped dromedary and became the animal of choice for the harsh and varied climates typical of Silk Road trade.

Baghdad Capital of the Islamic Empire under the Abbasid dynasty, founded in 762 CE (in modern-day Iraq). In the medieval period, it was a center of administration, scholarship, and cultural growth for what came to be known as the Golden Age of Islamic science.

Baghdad Pact (1955) Middle Eastern military alliance between countries friendly with America who were willing to align themselves with the western countries against the Soviet Union.

Balam Na Stone temple and place of pilgrimage for the Maya people of Mexico's Yucatán Peninsula.

Balfour Declaration Letter (November 2, 1917) by Lord Arthur J. Balfour, British foreign secretary, that promised a homeland for the Jews in Palestine.

Bamboo Annals Shang stories and foundation myths that were written on bamboo strips and later collected.

Bantu Language first spoken by people who lived in the southeastern area of modern Nigeria around 1000 CE.

Bantu migrations Waves of rapid population movement from West Africa into eastern and southern Africa during the first millennium CE that brought advanced agricultural practices to these regions and absorbed most of the preexisting hunting and gathering populations.

barbarian Originally a relatively neutral Greek term for non-Greek speakers, it evolved into a derogatory term used by other cultures to describe outsiders, often pastoral nomads, painting them as enemies of civilization.

barbarian invasions Violent migration of people in the late fourth and fifth centuries CE into Roman territory. These migrants had long been used as non-Roman soldiers.

basilicas Early church buildings, based on old royal audience halls.

Battle of Adwa (1896) Battle in which the Ethiopians defeated Italian colonial forces. It inspired many of Africa's later national leaders.

Battle of Wounded Knee (1890) Bloody massacre of Sioux Ghost Dancers by U.S. armed forces.

Bay of Pigs (1961) Unsuccessful invasion of Cuba by Cuban exiles supported by the U.S. government. The invaders

intended to incite an insurrection in Cuba and overthrow the communist regime of Fidel Castro.

Bedouins Nomadic pastoralists in the deserts of the Middle East.

Beer Hall Putsch (1923) Failed Nazi attempt to capture Bavarian leaders in a Munich beer hall, a prelude to a planned seizure of power in Germany. Adolf Hitler was imprisoned for a year after the incident.

Beghards (1500s) Eccentric European group whose members claimed to be in a state of grace that allowed them to do as they pleased—from adultery, free love, and nudity to murder; also called Brethren of Free Speech.

bell beaker Ancient drinking vessel, an artifact from Europe, so named because its shape resembles an inverted bell.

Berenice of Egypt Egyptian "queen" who helped rule over the Kingdom of the Nile from 320 to 280 BCE.

Beringia Prehistoric thousand-mile-long land bridge that linked Siberia and North America (which had not been populated by hominins). About 18,000 years ago, *Homo sapiens* edged into this landmass.

Berlin Airlift (1948) Supply of vital necessities to West Berlin by air transport primarily under U.S. auspices. It was initiated in response to a land and water blockade of the city instituted by the Soviet Union in the hope that the Allies would be forced to abandon West Berlin.

Berlin Wall Wall built by the communists in Berlin in 1961 to prevent citizens of East Germany from fleeing to West Germany; torn down in 1989.

bhakti Religious practice that grew out of Hinduism and emphasizes personal devotion to gods.

Bhakti Hinduism Popular form of Hinduism that emerged in the seventh century. The religion stresses devotion (*bhakti*) to God and uses vernacular languages (not Sanskrit) spoken by the common people.

big men Leaders of the extended household communities that formed village settlements in African rain forests.

big whites French plantation owners in Saint Domingue (present-day Haiti) who created one of the wealthiest slave societies.

Bilad al-Sudan Arabic for "the land of the blacks"; it consisted of the land lying south of the Sahara.

bilharzia Debilitating waterborne illness. It was widespread in Egypt, where it infected peasants who worked in the irrigation canals.

Bill of Rights First ten amendments to the U.S. Constitution; ratified in 1791.

bipedalism Walking on two legs, thereby freeing hands and arms to carry objects such as weapons and tools; one of several traits that distinguish hominins.

Black Death Great epidemic of the bubonic plague that ravaged Europe, East Asia, and North Africa in the fourteenth century, killing large numbers, including perhaps as many as 65 percent of the European population.

Black Jacobins Name employed by a West Indian historian for the rebels in Saint Domingue, including Toussaint L'Ouverture, a former slave who led the slaves of this French colony in the world's largest and most successful slave insurrection.

Black Panthers Radical African American group in the 1960s and 1970s who advocated black separatism and pan-Africanism.

black shirts Fascist troops of Mussolini's regime. The squads received money from Italian landowners to attack socialist leaders.

Black Tuesday (October 29, 1929) Historic day when the U.S. stock market crashed, plunging the United States and international trading systems into crisis and leading the world into the Great Depression.

blitzkrieg "Lightning war"; type of warfare in which the Germans, during World War II, used coordinated aerial bombing campaigns along with tanks and infantrymen in motorized vehicles.

bodhisattvas In Mahayana Buddhism, enlightened demigods who were ready to reach *nirvana* but delayed so that they might help others attain it.

Bolívar, Simón (1783–1830) Venezuelan leader who urged his followers to become "American," to overcome their local identities. He wanted the liberated countries to form a Latin American confederation, urging Peru and Bolivia to join Venezuela, Ecuador, and Colombia in the "Gran Colombia."

Bolsheviks Former members of the Russian Social Democratic Party who advocated the destruction of capitalist political and economic institutions and overthrew the Provisional Government in the second phase of the Russian Revolution of 1917. In 1918, the Bolsheviks changed their name to the Russian Communist Party.

Bonaparte, Napoleon (1769–1821) French military leader who rose to power in a postrevolutionary coup d'état, eventually proclaiming himself emperor of France. He placed security and order ahead of social reform and created a civil legal code. Napoleon expanded his empire through military action, but after his disastrous Russian campaign, the united European powers defeated him and forced him into exile. Napoleon escaped and reassumed command of his army but was later defeated at the Battle of Waterloo.

Book of the Dead Ancient Egyptian funerary text that contains drawings and paintings as well as spells describing how to prepare the jewelry and amulets that were buried with a person in preparation for the afterlife.

bourgeoisie The middle class, defined not by birth or title, but by capital and property.

Boxer Protocol Written agreement between the victors of the Boxer Uprising and the Qing Empire in 1901 that placed western troops in Beijing and required the regime to pay exorbitant damages for foreign life and property.

Boxer Uprising (1899–1900) Chinese peasant movement that opposed foreign influence, especially that of Christian missionaries; it was put down after the Boxers were defeated by an army composed mostly of the Japanese, Russians, British, French, and Americans.

Brahma One of three major deities that form a trinity in Vedic religion. Brahma signifies birth. *See also* Vishnu *and* Siva.

Brahmans Vedic priests who performed rituals and communicated with the gods. Brahmans provided guidance on how to live in balance with the forces of nature as represented by the various deities. The codification of Vedic principles into codes of law took place at the hands of the Brahmans. They memorized Vedic works and compiled commentaries on them. They also developed their own set of rules and rituals, which developed into a full-scale theology. Originally memorized and passed on orally, these may have been written down sometime after the beginning of the Common Era. Brahmanism was reborn as Hinduism sometime during the first half of the first millennium CE.

British Commonwealth of Nations Union formed in 1926 that conferred "dominion status" on Britain's white settler colonies in Canada, Australia, and New Zealand.

British East India Company *See* East India Company.

bronze Alloy of copper and tin brought into Europe from Anatolia; used to make hard-edged weapons.

brown shirts Informal name for the men who joined the Nazi SA (Sturmabteilung); they participated in mass rallies and street brawls, persecuting Jews, communists, and others who opposed the Nazis.

bubonic plague Acute infectious disease caused by a bacterium that is transmitted to humans by fleas from infected rats; sometimes referred to as the "Black Death." It ravaged Europe and parts of Africa and Asia in the fourteenth century.

Buddha (Siddhartha Gautama; 563–483 BCE) Indian ascetic who founded Buddhism.

Buddhism Major South Asian religion that aims to end human suffering through the renunciation of desire, derived from the teachings of Siddhartha Gautama, the Buddha (563–483 BCE). Buddhists believe that removing the illusion of a separate identity will lead to a state of contentment (nirvana). These beliefs challenged the traditional Brahmanic teachings of the time and provided the peoples of South Asia with an alternative to established traditions.

bullion Uncoined gold or silver.

Byzantium Modern term for the eastern Roman Empire (lasting from the fourth to the fifteenth century), centered at its "new Rome," Constantinople (founded by emperor Constantine in 324 CE on the site of a Greek city, Byzantium).

Cahokia Commercial center for regional and long-distance trade in North America. Its hinterlands produced staples for urban consumers. In return, its crafts were exported inland by porters and to North American markets in canoes. *See also* "Mound people."

calaveras Allegorical skeleton drawings by the Mexican printmaker and artist José Guadalupe Posada. The works drew on popular themes of betrayal, death, and festivity.

caliphate Institution that arose as the successor to Muhammad's leadership and became both the political and religious head of the Islamic community. Although the caliphs exercised political authority over the Muslim community and were the head of the religious community, the *umma,* they did not inherit Muhammad's prophetic powers and were not authorities in religious doctrine.

Calvin, Jean (1509–1564) A French theologian during the Protestant Reformation. Calvin developed a Christianity that emphasized moral regeneration through church teachings, laid out a doctrine of predestination, and established Calvinist dominance in Geneva, Switzerland.

Candomblé Yoruba-based religion in northern Brazil; it interwove African practices and beliefs with Christianity.

Canton system System officially established by imperial decree in 1759 that required European traders to have Chinese guild merchants act as guarantors for their good behavior and payment of fees.

caravan city Commercial hub of long-distance trade, where groups of merchants could assemble during their journeys. Several of these developed into full-fledged cities, especially in the deserts of Arabia.

caravans Companies of men who transported and traded goods along overland routes in North Africa and central Asia. Large caravans consisted of 600 to 1,000 camels and as many as 400 men.

caravansarais Inns along major trade routes that accommodated large numbers of traders, their animals, and their wares.

caravel Sailing vessel suited for nosing in and out of estuaries and navigating in waters with unpredictable currents and winds.

carrack Ship used on open bodies of water, such as the Mediterranean.

Carthage City in what is modern-day Tunisia; emblematic of the trading aspirations and activities of merchants in the Mediterranean. Pottery and other archaeological remains demonstrate that Carthaginian trading contacts were as far-flung as Italy, Greece, France, Iberia, and West Africa.

cartography Mapmaking.

caste system Hierarchical social system of organizing people and distributing labor.

Caste War of the Yucatán (1847–1901) Conflict between Maya Indians and the Mexican state over Indian autonomy and legal equality, which resulted in the Mexican takeover of the Yucatán Peninsula.

Castro, Fidel (1926–2016) Cuban communist leader whose forces overthrew Batista's corrupt regime in early January 1959. Castro became increasingly radical as he consolidated power, announcing a massive redistribution of land and the nationalization of foreign oil refineries. He declared himself a socialist and aligned himself with the Soviet Union in the wake of the 1961 CIA-backed Bay of Pigs invasion.

Çatal Hüyük Site in Anatolia discovered in 1958. It was a dense honeycomb of settlements filled with rooms whose walls were covered with paintings of wild bulls, hunters, and pregnant women. Çatal Hüyük symbolizes an early transition into urban dwelling and dates to the eighth millennium BCE.

Cathedra Bishop's seat, or throne, in a church.

Catholic Church Unifying institution for Christians in western Europe after the collapse of the Roman Empire. Rome became the spiritual capital of western Europe, and the bishops of Rome emerged as popes, the supreme head of the church, who possessed great moral authority.

Cato the Elder (234–149 BCE) Roman statesman, often seen as emblematic of the transition from a Greek to a Roman world. Cato the Elder wrote a manual for the new economy of slave plantation agriculture, invested in shipping and trading, learned Greek rhetoric, and added the genre of history to Latin literature.

caudillos South American local military chieftains.

cave drawings Images on cave walls. The subjects are most often large game, although a few are images of humans. Other elements are impressions made by hands dipped in paint and pressed on a wall or abstract symbols and shapes.

Celali revolts (1595–1610) Peasant and artisan uprisings against the Ottoman state.

Central Powers Defined in World War I as Germany, Austria-Hungary, and the Ottoman Empire.

Chan Chan City founded between 850 and 900 CE by the Moche people in what is now modern-day Peru. It had a core population of 30,000 inhabitants.

Chandra Gupta II King who reigned in South Asia from 320 to 335 CE. He shared his name with Chandragupta, the founder of the Mauryan Empire.

Chandravamsha One of two main lineages (the lunar one) of Vedic society, each with its own creation myth, ancestors, language, and rituals. Each lineage included many clans. *See* Suryavanha.

Chan Santa Cruz Separate Maya community formed as part of a crusade for spiritual salvation and the complete cultural separation of the Maya Indians; means "little holy cross."

chapatis Flat, unleavened Indian bread.

chariots Horse-driven carriages brought by the pastoral nomadic warriors from the steppes that became the favored mode of warfare and transportation for an urban aristocratic warrior class and for other men of power in agriculture-based societies. Control of chariot forces was the foundation of the new balance of power across Afro-Eurasia during the second millennium BCE.

charismatic Person who uses personal strengths or virtues, often laced with a divine aura, to command followers.

Charlemagne King of the Franks from 768 CE, king of the Lombards from 774 CE, and emperor of the Romans from 800 CE until his death in 814 CE.

chartered companies Firms that were awarded monopoly trading rights over vast areas by European monarchs (e.g., Virginia Company, Dutch East India Company).

Chartism (1834–1848) Mass democratic movement to pass the Peoples' Charter in Britain, granting male suffrage, secret ballot, equal electoral districts, and annual parliaments and absolving the requirement of property ownership for members of the parliament.

chattel slavery Form of slavery that sold people as property, the rise of which coincided with the expansion of city-states. Chattel slavery was eschewed by the Spartans, who also rejected the innovation of coin money.

Chavín A people who lived in what is now northern Peru from 1400 to 200 BCE. They were united more by culture and faith than by a unified political system.

Chernobyl Site in the Soviet Union (in Ukraine) of the 1986 meltdown of a nuclear reactor.

Chiang Kai-shek (1887–1975) Leader of the Guomindang following Sun Yat-sen's death. Chiang mobilized the Chinese masses through the New Life movement. In 1949, he lost to the communists and moved his regime to Taiwan.

Chimú Empire South America's first empire; it developed during the first century of the second millennium in the Moche Valley on the Pacific coast.

chinampas Floating gardens used by the Aztecs in the 1300s and 1400s to grow crops.

China's Sorrow Name given to the Yellow River, which, when it changed course or flooded, could cause mass death and waves of migration.

chinoiserie Chinese silks, teas, tableware, jewelry, and paper, popular among Europeans in the seventeenth and eighteenth centuries.

Christendom Entire portion of the world in which Christianity prevailed.

Christianity Religion that originated at the height of the Roman Empire and in direct confrontation with Roman imperial authority, founded by Yeshua ben Yosef (Joshua son of Joseph, known today by the Greek form of his name, Jesus), whom the Romans condemned for sedition and crucified. In the fourth century CE, Christianity was officially recognized as the Roman state religion.

Church of England Official form of Christianity established in England when Henry VIII broke with Rome during the Reformation. The English monarch, not the pope, is the head of this church.

city Highly populated concentration of economic, religious, and political power. The first cities appeared in river basins, which could produce a surplus of agriculture. The abundance of food freed most city inhabitants from the need to produce their own food, which allowed them to work in specialized professions.

city-state Political organization based on the authority of a single, large city that controls outlying territories.

Civil Rights Act (1964) U.S. legislation that banned segregation in public facilities, outlawed racial discrimination in employment, and marked an important step in correcting legal inequality.

civil rights movement Powerful movement for equal rights and the end of racial segregation in the United States that began in the 1950s with nonviolent boycotts and court victories against school segregation.

civil service examinations The world's first written civil service examination system, instituted by the Tang dynasty to recruit officials and bureaucrats. Open to most males, the exams tested a candidate's literary skills and knowledge of the Confucian classics. They helped to unite the Chinese state by making knowledge of a specific language and Confucian classics the only route to power.

Civil War, American (1861–1865) Conflict between the northern and southern states of America, leading to the abolition of slavery in the United States.

clan A social group comprising many households claiming descent from a common ancestor.

clandestine presses Small printing operations, especially in Switzerland and the Netherlands, that published banned texts in the early modern era.

closing of the frontier In 1893, responding to the recent U.S. Census, the historian Frederick Jackson Turner popularized the idea that the western frontier—so long crucial to the making of American identity—had closed. His announcement spurred many to worry that having lost the manliness and self-reliance nurtured by the hard life on the frontier, Americans would grow soft and weak.

Clovis people Early humans in America who used basic chipped blades and pointed spears in pursuing prey. They extended the hunting traditions they had learned in Afro-Eurasia, such as establishing campsites and moving with their herds. They were known as Clovis people because the arrowhead point that they used was first found by archaeologists at a site near Clovis, New Mexico.

Code of Manu Part of the handiwork of Brahman priests; a representative code of law that incorporated social sanctions and practices and provided guidance for living within the caste system.

codex Early form of book, with separate pages bound together; it replaced the scroll as the main medium for written texts. The codex emerged around 300 CE.

cognitive skills Skills such as thought, memory, problem solving, and—ultimately—language. Hominins were able to use these skills and their hands to create new adaptations, like tools that helped them obtain food and avoid predators.

Cohong Chinese merchant guild that traded with Europeans under the Qing dynasty.

coins Form of money that replaced goods, which previously had been bartered for services and other products. Originally used mainly to hire mercenary soldiers, coins became the commonplace method of payment linking buyers and producers throughout the Mediterranean.

Cold War (1945–1990) Ideological conflict in which the Soviet Union and eastern Europe opposed the United States and western Europe.

colonies Regions under the political control of another country.

colons French settler population in Algeria.

Colosseum Huge amphitheater, originally begun by Flavian and completed by Titus, which was dedicated in 80 CE. The structure is named after a colossal statue of Nero that formerly stood beside it.

Columbian exchange Movement between Afro-Eurasia and the Americas of previously unknown plants, animals, people, diseases, and products that followed in the wake of Columbus's voyages.

commanderies Provinces. Shi Huangdi (First August Emperor) divided China into commanderies (*jun*) to enable the Qin dynasty to rule the massive state effectively. The thirty-six commanderies were then subdivided into counties (*xian*).

Communist Manifesto Pamphlet published by Karl Marx and Friedrich Engels in 1848 at a time when political revolutions were sweeping Europe. It called on the workers of all nations to unite in overthrowing capitalism.

compass Navigation instrument invented by the Chinese and used to determine directions with a magnetized needle, which always points to the north cardinal direction on the compass rose.

Compromise of 1867 Agreement between the Habsburgs and the Austrian Empire's Hungarian population that gave the Hungarian lands more autonomy; the empire was now renamed the Austro-Hungarian Empire.

concession areas Territories, usually ports, where Chinese emperors allowed European merchants to trade and European people to settle.

Confucian ideals The ideals of honoring tradition, emphasizing the responsibility of the emperor, and respect for the lessons of history, promoted by Confucius, which the Han dynasty made the official doctrine of the empire by 50 BCE.

Confucianism Ethics, beliefs, and practices stipulated by the Chinese philosopher Kong Qiu, or Confucius, which served as a guide for Chinese society up to modern times.

Confucius (551–479 BCE) Influential teacher, thinker, and leader in China who developed a set of principles for ethical living. He believed that coercive laws and punishment would not be needed to maintain order in society if men following his ethics ruled. He taught his philosophy to anyone who was intelligent and willing to work, which allowed men to gain entry into the ruling class through education.

Congo Free State Large colonial state in Africa created by Leopold II, king of Belgium, during the 1880s, and ruled by him alone. After rumors of mass slaughter and enslavement, the Belgian parliament took the land and formed a Belgian colony.

Congress of Vienna (1814–1815) International conference to reorganize Europe after the downfall of Napoleon. European monarchies agreed to respect each other's borders and to cooperate in guarding against future revolutions and war.

cong tube Ritual object crafted by the Liangzhu. A cong tube was made of jade and was used in divination practices.

conquistadors Spanish military leaders who led the conquest of the New World in the sixteenth century.

Constantine Roman emperor who converted to Christianity in 312 CE. In 313 CE, he issued a proclamation that gave Christians new freedoms in the empire. He also founded Constantinople (at first called "New Rome").

Constantinople Capital city, formerly known as Byzantium, which was founded as the New Rome by Constantine the Great.

Constitutional Convention (1787) Meeting to formulate the Constitution of the United States of America.

Contra rebels Opponents of the Sandinistas in Nicaragua. They were armed and financed by the United States and other anti-communist countries (1980).

Conversion of Constantine Inspired by a dream to arm his soldiers with shields bearing Christ's name, the Emperor Constantine won a decisive battle for Rome in 312 CE. Afterward, he issued a proclamation giving privileges to Christian bishops, which began the process of spreading Christianity throughout the Roman Empire.

conversos Jewish and Muslim converts to Christianity in the Iberian Peninsula and the New World.

Coptic Form of Christianity practiced in Egypt. It was doctrinally different from Christianity elsewhere, and Coptic Christians had their own views of Christology, or the nature of Christ.

Corn Laws Laws that imposed tariffs on grain imported to Great Britain, intended to protect British farming interests. The Corn Laws were abolished in 1846 as part of a British movement in favor of free trade.

cosmology Branch of metaphysics devoted to understanding the order of the universe.

cosmopolitans The inhabitants of the multiethnic cities that thrived in the Hellenistic world, literally meaning "citizens belonging to the whole world" as opposed to a particular city-state.

Council of Nicaea Church council convened in 325 CE by Constantine and presided over by him as well. At this council, a Christian creed was articulated and made into a formula that expressed the philosophical and technical elements of Christian belief.

Counter-Reformation Movement initiated by the Catholic Church at the Council of Trent in 1545 with the aim of countering the spread of the Reformation. The Catholic Church enacted reforms to attack clerical corruption and placed a greater emphasis on individual spirituality. During this time, the Jesuits were founded to help revive the Catholic Church.

coup d'état Overthrow of the established state by a group of conspirators, usually from the military.

creation narratives Various accounts of the creation of the universe and humankind's place in it, conceived by virtually all peoples.

creed Formal statement of faith or expression of a belief system. A Christian creed, or "credo," was formulated by the Council of Nicaea in 325 CE.

creoles Persons of full-blooded European descent who were born in the Spanish American colonies.

Crimean War (1853–1856) War waged by Russia against Great Britain and France. Spurred by Russia's encroachment on Ottoman territories, the conflict revealed Russia's military weakness when Russian forces fell to British and French troops.

crossbow Innovative weapon used at the end of the Warring States period that allowed archers to shoot their enemies with accuracy, even from a distance.

Crusades Wave of attacks launched in the late eleventh century by western Europeans. The First Crusade began in 1095, when Pope Urban II appealed to the warrior nobility of France to free Jerusalem from Muslim rule. Four subsequent Crusades were fought over the next two centuries.

Cuban Missile Crisis (1962) Diplomatic standoff between the United States and the Soviet Union that was provoked by the Soviet Union's attempt to base nuclear missiles in Cuba; it brought the world close to a nuclear war.

cult Religious movement, often based on the worship of a particular god or goddess.

cultigen Organism that has diverged from its ancestors through domestication or cultivation.

cuneiform Wedge-shaped form of writing, used primarily by the Sumerian, Assyrian, and Persian Empires. By impressing these signs into wet clay with the cut end of a reed, scribes engaged in cuneiform.

Cyrus the Great Founder of the Persian Empire. This sixth-century ruler (559–529 BCE) conquered the Medes and unified the Iranian kingdoms.

Daimyo Ruling lords who commanded private armies in pre-Meiji Japan.

dan Fodio, Usman (1754–1817) Fulani Muslim cleric whose visions led him to challenge the Hausa ruling classes, whom he believed were insufficiently faithful to Islamic beliefs and practices. His ideas gained support among those who had suffered under the Hausa landlords. In 1804, his supporters and allies overthrew the Hausa in what is today northern Nigeria.

Daoism School of thought developed at the end of the Warring States period that focused on the importance of following the Dao, or the natural way of the cosmos. Daoism emphasized the need to accept the world as it was rather than trying to change it through politics or the government. Unlike Confucianism, Daoism scorned rigid rituals and social hierarchies.

Dar al-Islam Arabic for "the House of Islam"; it describes the territories ruled by Muslims and is contrasted with *Dar al-Harb*, the land of war, not yet under Islamic rule.

Darius I (521–486 BCE) Leader who put the emerging unified Persian Empire on solid footing after Cyrus's death.

Darwin, Charles (1809–1882) British scientist who became convinced that the species of organic life had evolved under the uniform pressure of the laws of natural selection, not by means of a special, one-time creation as described in the Bible.

D-Day (June 6, 1944) Day of the Allied invasion of Normandy under General Dwight Eisenhower to liberate western Europe from German occupation.

Dear Boy Nickname of an early human remain (an almost totally intact skull) discovered in 1931 by archaeologists Mary and Louis Leakey. Other objects discovered with Dear Boy demonstrated that by the time of Dear Boy, early humans had begun to fashion tools and to use them for butchering animals and possibly for hunting and killing smaller animals.

Decembrists Russian army officers who were influenced by events in revolutionary France and formed secret societies that espoused liberal governance. They were put down by Nicholas I in December 1825.

Declaration of Independence U.S. document stating the theory of government on which the United States was founded.

Declaration of the Rights of Man and Citizen (1789) French charter of liberties formulated by the National Assembly that marked the end of dynastic and aristocratic rule. The seventeen articles later became the preamble to the new constitution, which the assembly finished in 1791.

decolonization End of empire and emergence of new independent states in Asia and Africa as a result of anticolonial nationalism, the weakening of the European colonial powers in World War II, and the rise of the United States and the USSR as superpowers after the war, both of whom favored ending imperial rule.

degeneration In the later 19th century, many Europeans began to fear that Darwin had been wrong: urbanization, technology, racial hybridity, the emergence of the "modern" woman, and over-refinement were causing Europeans not to progress as a species, but to degenerate. This fear was often combined with anxieties about colonialism, homosexuality, emigration, and/or the advancement of women.

Delhi Sultanate (1206–1526) Muslim Turkish regime of northern India. The regime strengthened the cultural diversity and tolerance that were a hallmark of the Indian social order, which allowed it to bring about political integration without enforcing cultural homogeneity.

democracy The idea that people, through membership in a nation, should choose their own representatives and be governed by them.

Democritus Thinker in ancient Greece who lived from 470 to 360 BCE. He deduced the existence of the atom, postulating that there was such a thing as an indivisible particle.

demotic writing The second of two basic forms of ancient Egyptian writing. Demotic was a cursive script written with ink on papyrus, on pottery, or on other absorbent objects. It was the most common and practical form of writing in Egypt and was used for administrative record keeping and in private or pseudo-private forms like letters and works of literature. *See also* hieroglyphs.

developing world Term applied to countries collectively called the Third World during the Cold War; countries seeking to develop viable nation-states and prosperous economies.

devshirme System of taking non-Muslim children in place of taxes in order to educate them in Ottoman Muslim ways and prepare them for service in the sultan's bureaucracy.

dhamma Moral code espoused by Aśoka in the Kalinga edict, which was meant to apply to all—Buddhists, Brahmans, and Greeks alike.

***dhimma* system** Muslim law and practice that permitted followers of religions other than Islam, such as Christians, Jews, and Zoroastrians, and later Buddhists and Hindus, to choose their own religious leaders and to settle internal disputes within their religious communities as long as they accepted Islam's political dominion.

dhows Ships used by Arab seafarers. The dhow's large sails were rigged to maximize the capture of wind.

Dien Bien Phu (1954) Defining battle in the war between French colonialists and the Viet Minh that secured North Vietnam for Ho Chi Minh and his army and left the south to form its own government to be supported by France and the United States.

Din-I-llahi "House of worship" in which the Mughal emperor Akbar engaged in religious debate with Hindu, Muslim, Jain, Parsi, and Christian theologians.

Diogenes Greek philosopher who lived from 412 to 323 BCE and who espoused a doctrine of self-sufficiency and freedom from social laws and customs. He rejected cultural norms as out of tune with nature and therefore false.

Directory Temporary military committee that took over the affairs of the state of France in 1795 from the radicals and held control until the coup of Napoleon Bonaparte.

divination The interpretation of rituals used to communicate the wishes of gods or royal ancestors to foretell future events. Divination was used to legitimize royal authority and demand tribute.

Djoser Ancient Egyptian king who reigned from 2630 to 2611 BCE. He was the second king of the Third Dynasty and celebrated the Sed festival in his tomb complex at Saqqara.

domestication Bringing wild plants and animals under human control.

Dominion in the British Commonwealth Canadian promise to keep up the country's fealty to the British crown, even after its independence in 1867. It later applied to Australia and New Zealand.

Dong Zhongshu Emperor Wu's chief minister, who advocated a more powerful view of Confucius by promoting texts that focused on Confucius as a man who possessed aspects of divinity.

double-outrigger canoes Vessels used by early Austronesians to cross the Taiwan Straits and colonize islands in the Pacific. These sturdy canoes could cover over 120 miles per day.

Duma Russian parliament, first convened in 1906.

Dutch learning Broad term for European teachings that were strictly regulated by the shoguns inside Japan.

dynastic cycle Political narrative in which influential families vied for supremacy. Upon gaining power, they legitimated their authority by claiming to be the heirs of previous grand dynasts and by preserving or revitalizing the ancestors' virtuous governing ways. This continuity conferred divine support.

dynasty Hereditary ruling family that passed control from one generation to the next.

Earth Summit (1992) Meeting in Rio de Janeiro between many of the world's governments in an effort to address international environmental problems.

Eastern Front Battlefront between Berlin and Moscow during World War I and World War II.

East India Company (1600–1858) British charter company created to outperform Portuguese and Spanish traders in the Far East; in the eighteenth century, the company became, in effect, the ruler of a large part of India.

Edict of Nantes (1598) Edict issued by Henry IV to end the French Wars of Religion. The edict declared France a Catholic country but tolerated some Protestant worship. It was revoked by Louis XIV in 1685.

Egyptian Middle Kingdom Period of Egyptian history lasting from about 2040 to 1640 BCE, characterized by a consolidation of power and building activity in Upper Egypt.

Eiffel Tower Steel monument completed in 1889 for the Paris Exposition. It was twice the height of any other building at the time.

eight-legged essay Highly structured essay form with eight parts, required on Chinese civil service examinations.

Ekklesia Church or early gathering committed to leaders chosen by God and fellow believers.

Ekpe Powerful slave trade institution that organized the supply and purchase of slaves inland from the Gulf of Guinea in West Africa.

Elamites A people with their capital in the upland valley of modern Fars who became a cohesive polity that incorporated transhumant people of the Zagros Mountains. A group of Elamites who migrated south and west into Mesopotamia helped conquer the Third Dynasty of Ur in 2400 BCE.

empire Group of states or different ethnic groups under a single sovereign power.

Enabling Act (1933) Emergency legislation, enacted just after Hitler became German chancellor (prime minister), that undermined parliamentary democracy in Germany by giving the chancellor the right to dictate legislation without the approval of the Reichstag (German parliament). This legislation paved the way for Hitler's dictatorship.

enclosure A movement in which landowners took control of lands that traditionally had been common property serving local needs.

encomenderos Commanders of the labor services of the colonized peoples in Spanish America.

encomiendas Grants from European Spanish governors to *encomenderos* control the labor services of colonized people.

Endeavor Ship of Captain James Cook, whose celebrated voyages to the South Pacific in the late eighteenth century supplied Europe with information about the plants, birds, landscapes, and people of this uncharted territory.

Engels, Friedrich (1820–1895) German social and political philosopher who collaborated with Karl Marx on many publications, including *The Communist Manifesto*.

English Navigation Act of 1651 Act stipulating that only English ships could carry goods between the mother country and its colonies.

English Peasants' Revolt (1381) Uprising of serfs and free farmworkers that began as a protest against a tax levied to raise money for a war on France. The revolt was suppressed but led to the gradual emergence of a free peasantry as labor shortages made it impossible to keep peasants bound to the soil.

enlightened absolutists Seventeenth- and eighteenth-century monarchs who claimed to rule rationally and in the best interests of their subjects and who hired loyal bureaucrats to enact enlightened policies.

Enlightenment Intellectual movement in late seventeenth- and eighteenth-century Europe stressing natural laws and reason as the basis of authority.

entrepôts Trading stations at the borders between communities, which made exchange possible among many different partners. Long-distance traders could also replenish their supplies at these stations.

Epicurus (341–279 BCE) Greek philosopher who espoused emphasis on the self. He founded a school in Athens called The Garden and stressed the importance of sensation, teaching that pleasurable sensations were good and painful sensations bad. Members of his school sought to find peace and relaxation by avoiding unpleasantness or suffering.

Estates-General French quasi-parliamentary body called in 1789 to deal with the financial problems that afflicted France. It had not met since 1614.

Etruscans A dominant people on the Italian Peninsula until the fourth century BCE. The Etruscan states were part of the foundation of the Roman Empire.

eunuchs Loyal and well-paid men who were surgically castrated as youths and remained in service to the caliph or emperor. Both Abbasid and Tang rulers relied for protection on a cadre of eunuchs.

Eurasia The combined area of Europe and Asia.

European Union (EU) Western European organization that evolved out of post-1945 efforts to prevent warfare in Europe, initially by forging closer economic cooperation.

evolution Process by which the different species of the world—its plants and animals—make changes in response to their environment that enable them to survive and increase in numbers.

Exclusion Act of 1882 U.S. congressional act prohibiting nearly all immigration from China to the United States; fueled by animosity toward Chinese workers in the American West.

Ezo Present-day Hokkaido, Japan's fourth main island.

fascism Mass political movement founded by Benito Mussolini that emphasized nationalism, militarism, and the omnipotence of the state.

fascists Radical right-wing groups of disaffected citizens, often veterans of World War I, that were opposed to democracy and favored rule by a single leader. Fascist movements triumphed in Italy, Germany, Spain, Japan, and several central European countries after World War I.

Fatehpur Sikri Mughal emperor Akbar's temporary capital near Agra.

Fatimids Shiite dynasty that ruled parts of the Islamic Empire beginning in the tenth century CE. The Fatimids arose in North Africa, where they conquered Egypt and founded the city of Cairo.

February Revolution (1917) The first of two uprisings of the Russian Revolution, which led to the end of the Romanov dynasty. It ended with the forming of a Provisional Government under Alexander Kerensky.

Federal Deposit Insurance Corporation (FDIC) Organization created in 1933 to guarantee all bank deposits up to $5,000 as part of the New Deal in the United States.

Federalists Supporters of the ratification of the U.S. Constitution, which was written to replace the Articles of Confederation.

Federal Republic of Germany (1949–1990) Country formed of the areas occupied by the Allies after World War II. Also known as West Germany, this country experienced rapid demilitarization, democratization, and integration into the world economy.

Federal Reserve Act (1913) U.S. legislation that created a series of boards to monitor the supply and demand of the nation's money.

feminist movements Movements that call for equal treatment for men and women—equal pay and equal opportunities for obtaining jobs and advancement. Feminism arose mainly in Europe and in North America in the 1960s and then became global in the 1970s.

Ferangi Word taken from the Arabic word for "Franks," but referring to Europeans in general and widely used to describe the European Crusaders.

Fertile Crescent Site of the world's first agricultural revolution; an area in Southwest Asia, bounded by the Mediterranean Sea in the west and the Zagros Mountains in the east.

feudalism System instituted in medieval Europe after the collapse of the Carolingian Empire (888 CE) whereby each peasant was under the authority of a lord and typically owed him fees and/or service in exchange for protection and the right to live and work on his lands.

fiefdoms Medieval economic and political units.

First World Term invented during the Cold War to refer to western Europe and North America (also known as the "free world" or the west); Japan later joined this group. Following the principles of liberal modernism, First World states sought to organize the world on the basis of capitalism and democracy.

five pillars of Islam The five tenets, or main aspects, of Islamic practice: testification, or bearing witness, that there is no God other than God (Allah, in Arabic) and that Muhammad is the messenger of God; praying five times a day; fasting from sunup to sundown every day during Ramadan (a month on the Islamic calendar); giving alms; and making a pilgrimage to Mecca.

Five-Year Plan Soviet effort launched under Stalin in 1928 to replace the market with a state-owned and state-managed economy, to promote rapid economic development over a five-year period of time and thereby "catch and overtake" the leading capitalist countries. The First Five-Year Plan was followed by the Second Five-Year Plan (1933–1937), and so on, until the collapse of the Soviet Union in 1991. Because of the seeming Soviet economic successes, five-year plans became popular in many developing countries as a way to promote economic growth.

Flagellants European social group that came into existence during the bubonic plague in the fourteenth century. They believed that the plague was the wrath of God.

floating population Poor migrant workers in China who supplied labor under Emperor Wu.

Fluitschips Dutch shipping vessels that could carry heavy bulky cargo with relatively small crews.

flying cash Letters of exchange—early predecessors of paper cash instead of coins—first developed by guilds in the northwestern Shanxi. By the thirteenth century, paper money had eclipsed coins.

fondûqs Complexes in caravan cities that included hostels, storage houses, offices, and temples.

Forbidden City of Beijing Palace city of the Ming and Qing dynasties.

Force Publique Colonial army used to maintain order in the Belgian Congo.

During the early stages of King Leopold's rule, it was responsible for bullying local communities.

Fourierism Form of utopian socialism based on the ideas of Charles Fourier (1772–1837). Fourier envisioned communes where work was made enjoyable and systems of production and distribution were run without merchants. His ideas appealed to middle-class readers, especially women, as a higher form of Christian communalism.

free labor Wage-paying rather than slave labor.

free markets Unregulated markets.

Free Officers Movement Secret organization of Egyptian junior military officers led by Gamal Abdel Nasser that came to power in a coup d'état in 1952, forced King Faruq to abdicate, and consolidated control through dissolving the parliament, banning opposing parties, and rewriting the constitution.

free trade Domestic and international trade unencumbered by tariff barriers, quotas, and fees.

Front de Libération Nationale (FLN) Algerian anticolonial, nationalist party that waged an eight-year war against French troops, beginning in 1854, that forced nearly all of the 1 million colonists to leave.

Fulani A widespread ethnic group in West Africa, some of whose members embraced Islam and carried out religious revolts at the end of the eighteenth and the beginning of the nineteenth centuries in an effort to return to the pure Islam of the past.

fur trade Trading of animal pelts (especially beaver skins) by Indians for European goods in North America.

Gandharan art Buddhist sculptures, particularly from the northern Kushan territory, that show a high degree of Greek and Roman influences.

Gandhi, Mohandas Karamchand (Mahatma) (1869–1948) Indian leader who led a nonviolent struggle for India's independence from Britain.

garrisons Military bases, often built inside cities and often used for political purposes, such as protecting rulers, putting down domestic revolts, or enforcing colonial rule.

garrison towns Stations for soldiers originally established in strategic locations to protect territorial acquisition. Eventually, they became towns. Alexander the Great's garrison towns evolved into cities that served as centers from which Hellenistic culture was spread to his easternmost territories.

gauchos Argentine, Brazilian, and Uruguayan cowboys who wanted a decentralized federation, with autonomy for their provinces and respect for their way of life.

Gdansk shipyard Site of mass strikes in Poland that led in 1980 to the formation of the first independent trade union, Solidarity, in the communist bloc.

gendered relations A relatively recent hypothesis that gender roles emerged only with the appearance of modern humans and perhaps Neanderthals. When humans began to think imaginatively and in complex symbolic ways and give voice to their insights, perhaps around 150,000 years ago, gender categories began to crystallize.

genealogy History of the descent of a person or family from a distant ancestor.

Geneva Peace Conference (1954) International conference to restore peace in Korea and Indochina. The chief participants were the United States, the Soviet Union, Great Britain, France, the People's Republic of China, North Korea, South Korea, Vietnam, the Viet Minh party, Laos, and Cambodia. The conference resulted in the division of North and South Vietnam.

Genoa One of two Italian cities (the other was Venice) that linked Europe, Africa, and Asia as nodes of commerce in 1300 CE. Genoese ships linked the Mediterranean to the coast of Flanders through consistent routes along the Atlantic coasts of Spain, Portugal, and France.

German Democratic Republic Nation founded from the Soviet zone of occupation of Germany after World War II; also known as East Germany.

German Social Democratic Party Founded in 1875, the most powerful socialist party in Europe before 1917.

Ghana The most celebrated medieval political kingdom in West Africa and later the name of the first independent black African state.

Ghost Dance American Indian ritual performed in the nineteenth century in the hope of restoring the world to precolonial conditions.

Gilgamesh Heroic narrative written in the Babylonian dialect of Semitic Akkadian. This story and others like it were meant to circulate and unify the kingdom.

Girondins Liberal revolutionary group that supported the creation of a constitutional monarchy during the early stages of the French Revolution.

globalization Development of integrated worldwide cultural and economic structures.

globalizing empires Empires, such as the Han and the Roman, that covered immense amounts of territory, included huge, diverse populations; exerted influence beyond their own borders; and worked to integrate conquered peoples.

global warming Worldwide rising temperatures caused in large part by the release into the air of human-made carbons.

Gold Coast Name that European mariners and merchants gave to that part of West Africa from which gold was exported. This area was conquered by the British in the nineteenth century and became a British colony; upon independence, it became Ghana.

Goths One of the groups of "barbarian" migrants into Roman territory in the fourth century CE.

government schools Schools founded by the Han dynasty to provide an adequate number of officials to fill positions in the administrative bureaucracy. The Imperial University had 30,000 members by the second century BCE.

Gracchus brothers Two tribunes, the brothers Tiberius and Gaius Gracchus, who in 133 and 123–121 BCE attempted to institute land reforms that would guarantee all of Rome's poor citizens a basic amount of land that would qualify them for army service. Both men were assassinated.

Grand Canal Created in 486 BCE, a thousand-mile-long connector between the Yellow and Yangzi Rivers, linking the north and south, respectively.

grand unity Guiding political idea embraced by Qin rulers and ministers, with an eye toward joining the states of the Central Plain into one empire and centralizing administration.

"greased cartridge" controversy Controversy spawned by the rumor that cow and pig fat had been used to grease the ammunition to be used by sepoy gunners in the British army in India. Believing that this was a British attempt to defile their religion and speed their conversion to Christianity, the sepoys mutinied against their British officers and led a widespread revolt against British rule in 1857.

Great Depression Worldwide depression following the U.S. stock market crash on October 29, 1929.

great divide The division between economically developed nations and less developed nations.

Great East Asia Co-Prosperity Sphere Term used by the Japanese during the 1930s and 1940s to refer to Hong Kong, Singapore, Malaya, Burma, and other states that they seized during their run for expansion.

Great Flood One of many traditional Mesopotamian stories that were transmitted orally from one generation to another before being recorded. The Sumerian King List refers to this crucial event in Sumerian memory and identity. The Great Flood was thought to have led to Uruk's demise as punishment by the gods.

Great Game Competition for economic or political control of areas such as Turkistan, Persia (present-day Iran), and Afghanistan. The British (in India) and the Russians believed that controlling these areas was crucial to preventing their enemies' expansion.

Great League of Peace and Power Iroquois Indian alliance that united previously warring communities.

Great Leap Forward (1958–1961) Plan devised by Mao Zedong to achieve rapid agricultural and industrial growth in China. The plan failed miserably, and more than 20 million people died.

great plaza at Isfahan The center of Safavid power in the seventeenth century created by Shah Abbas (r. 1587–1629) to represent the unification of trade, government, and religion under one supreme political authority.

Great Proletarian Cultural Revolution (1966–1976) Mass mobilization of urban Chinese youth inaugurated by Mao Zedong in an attempt to reinvigorate the Chinese Revolution and to prevent the development of a bureaucratized Soviet style of communism. With this movement, Mao turned against his longtime associates in the Communist Party.

Great Trek Afrikaner migration to the interiors of Africa after the British abolished slavery in the empire in 1833.

Great War (August 1914–November 1918) Also known as World War I. A total war involving the armies of Britain, France, and Russia (the Allies) against those of Germany, Austria-Hungary, and the Ottoman Empire (the Central Powers). Italy joined the Allies in 1915, and the United States joined them in 1917, helping tip the balance in favor of the Allies, who also drew on the populations and material of their colonial possessions.

Greek Orthodoxy Enduring form of Christianity that arose in the "Roman" state inherited from Constantine and Justinian and eventually split off from the Roman Catholic Church. The Greek Orthodox capital was Constantinople, and its spiritual empire included the Russian peoples, Baltic Slavs, and peoples living in southwest Asia.

Greek philosophers "Wisdom lovers" of the ancient Greek city-states, including Socrates, Plato, Aristotle, and others, who pondered such issues as self-knowledge, political engagement and withdrawal, and the order of the world.

Greenbacks Members of the American political party of the late nineteenth century that worked to advance the interest of farmers by promoting cheap money.

griots Counselors and other officials serving royal families in African kingdoms and also in small-scale states. They were also responsible for the preservation and transmission of oral histories and repositories of knowledge.

Group Areas Act (1950) Act that divided South Africa into separate racial and tribal areas and required Africans to live in their own separate communities, including the "homelands."

guerrillas Small groups engaged in irregular fighting against larger regular forces; after the French word *guerre*.

guest workers Migrants looking for temporary employment abroad.

gulag Administrative name for the forced labor and "reeducation" camps established first by the Soviet Union and then by other Soviet-style socialist countries. Penal labor was required of both ordinary criminals (rapists, murderers, thieves) and those accused of political crimes (counterrevolution, anti-Soviet agitation).

Gulf War (1991) Armed conflict between Iraq and a coalition of thirty-two nations, including the United States, Britain, Egypt, France, and Saudi Arabia. It was started by Iraq's invasion of Kuwait, which it had long claimed, on August 2, 1990.

gunpowder Explosive powder. By 1040, the first gunpowder recipes were being written down. Over the next 200 years, Song entrepreneurs invented several incendiary devices and techniques for controlling explosions.

gunpowder empires Muslim empires of the Ottomans, Safavids, and Mughals that used cannonry and gunpowder to advance their military causes.

Guomindang Nationalist party of China, founded just before World War I by Sun Yat-sen and later led by Chiang Kai-shek.

Habsburg dynasty Powerful medieval monarchs whose hereditary lands lay along the Danube River, but whose domains also included, for a time, Spain and the Low Countries. Habsburg princes were regularly elected Holy Roman Emperors. In 1556, Charles V abdicated and divided the empire, and the Habsburgs, into a Spanish branch and an Austrian branch. In 1867, the Austrian Empire was reorganized into the Austro-Hungarian Dual Monarchy, and in 1918 it collapsed.

Hadith Sayings attributed to the Prophet Muhammad and his early converts, used to guide the behavior of Muslim peoples.

Hagia Sophia Enormous and impressive church sponsored by Justinian and built starting in 532 CE. At the time, it was the largest church in the world.

hajj Pilgrimage to Mecca; an obligation for Muslims.

Hammurapi's Code Legal code created by Hammurapi, the most famous of the Mesopotamian rulers, who reigned from 1792 to 1750 BCE. Hammurapi sought to create social order by centralizing state authority and creating a grand legal structure that embodied paternal justice. The code was quite stratified, dividing society into three classes: free men, dependent men, and slaves, each with distinct rights and responsibilities.

Han agrarian ideal Guiding principle for the free peasantry that made up the base of Han society. In this system, peasants were honored for their labors, while merchants were subjected to a range of controls, including regulations on luxury consumption, and were belittled for not engaging in physical labor.

Han Chinese Inhabitants of China proper who considered others to be outsiders. They felt that they were the only authentic Chinese.

Han Fei Chinese state minister who lived from 280 to 223 BCE; he was a proponent and follower of Xunzi.

Hangzhou City and former provincial seaport that became the political center of the Chinese people in their ongoing struggles with northern steppe nomads. It was also one of China's gateways to the rest of the world by way of the South China Sea.

Han military Like its Roman counterpart, a ruthless military machine that expanded the empire and created stable conditions that permitted the safe transit of goods by caravan. Emperor Wu heavily influenced the transformation of the military forces and reinstituted a policy that made military service compulsory.

Hannibal Great Roman general from Carthage whose campaigns in the third century BCE swept from Spain toward the Italian Peninsula. He crossed the Pyrenees and the Alps mountain ranges with war elephants. He was unable, however, to defeat the Romans in 217 BCE.

Harappa One of two cities (the other was Mohenjo Daro) that, by 2500 BCE, began to take the place of villages throughout the Indus River valley. Each city covered an area of about 250 acres and probably housed 35,000 residents.

harem Secluded women's quarters in Muslim households.

Harlem Renaissance Cultural movement in the 1920s that was based in Harlem, a part of New York City with a large African American population; also referred to as the "New Negro Movement." The movement gave voice to black novelists, poets, painters, and musicians, many of whom used their art to protest racism.

harnesses Tools made from wood, bone, bronze, and iron for steering and controlling horses. Harnesses discovered by archaeologists reveal the evolution of headgear from simple mouth bits to full bridles with headpiece, mouthpiece, and reins.

Hatshepsut Ancient Egypt's most powerful woman ruler. Hatshepsut served as regent and pharaoh for her young son, Thutmosis III, whose reign began in 1479 BCE. She remained co-regent until her death.

Haussmannization Redevelopment and beautification of urban centers; named after the city planner who modernized mid-nineteenth-century Paris.

Heian period Period from 794 to 1185 CE, during which began the pattern of regents ruling Japan in the name of the sacred emperor.

Hellenism Process by which the individuality of the cultures of the earlier Greek city-states gave way to a uniform culture that stressed the common identity of all who embraced Greek ways. This culture emphasized the common denominators of language, style, and politics to which anyone anywhere in the Afro-Eurasian world could have access.

hieroglyphs One of two basic forms of Egyptian writing that were used in conjunction throughout antiquity. Hieroglyphs are pictorial symbols; the term derives from a Greek word meaning "sacred carving"—they were employed exclusively in temple, royal, and divine contexts. *See also* demotic writing.

Hijra Tradition of Islam whereby one withdraws from one's community to create another, more holy one. The practice is based on the Prophet Muhammad's withdrawal from the city of Mecca to Medina in 622 CE.

Hinayana (Lesser Vehicle) Buddhism Form of Buddhism that accepted the divinity of Buddha himself but not of demigods, or bodhisattvas.

Hinduism A refashioning of the ancient Brahmanic Vedic religion, bringing it in accord with rural life and agrarian values. It emerged as the dominant faith in Indian society in the third century CE. Believers became vegetarians and adopted rituals of self-sacrifice. Three major deities—Brahma, Vishnu, and Siva—formed a trinity representing the three phases of the universe (birth, existence, and destruction, respectively) and the three expressions of the eternal self, or *atma*.

Hindu revivalism Movement to reconfigure traditional Hinduism to be less diverse and more amenable to producing a narrowed version of Indian tradition.

Hiroshima Japanese port devastated by an atomic bomb on August 6, 1945.

Hitler, Adolf (1889–1945) German dictator and leader of the Nazi Party who seized power in Germany after its economic collapse in the Great Depression. Hitler and his Nazi regime started World War II in Europe and systematically murdered Jews and other non-Aryan groups in the name of racial purity.

Hittites One of the five great territorial states. The Hittites campaigned throughout Anatolia, then went east to northern Syria, though they eventually faced weaknesses in their own homeland. Their heyday was marked by the reign of the king Supiliulimua (1380 to 1345 BCE), who preserved the Hittites' influence on the balance of power in the region between Mesopotamia and the Nile.

Holocaust Deliberate racial extermination of the Jews by the Nazis that claimed the lives of approximately 6 million European Jews.

Holy Roman Empire Enormous confederation of polities that encompassed much of central Europe and aspired to be the Christian successor state to the Roman Empire. It was headed by a Holy Roman Emperor, usually a Habsburg prince, selected by elite lower-level sovereigns. Despite its size, the empire never effectively centralized power.

Holy Russia Name applied to Muscovy and then to the Russian Empire by Slavic Eastern Orthodox clerics who were appalled by the Muslim conquest in 1453 of Constantinople (the capital of Byzantium and of Eastern Christianity) and who were hopeful that Russia would become the new protector of the faith.

home charges Fees India was forced to pay to Britain as its colonial master. These fees included interest on railroad loans, salaries to colonial officers, and the maintenance of imperial troops outside India.

hominins Humanlike beings who walked erect and are represented today only by modern humans.

Homo Genus that includes modern ("true") humans and species of premodern hominins.

Homo caudatus "Tailed man," believed by some European Enlightenment thinkers to be an early species of humankind.

Homo erectus Species that emerged about 1.5 million years ago and had a large brain and walked truly upright. *Homo erectus* means "standing man."

Homo habilis Species name meaning "skillful man." Toolmaking ability made *Homo habilis* the forerunners, though very distant, of modern humans.

Homo sapiens The first humans; they emerged in a small region of Africa about 200,000 years ago and migrated out of Africa about 100,000 years ago. They had bigger brains and greater dexterity than previous hominin species, whom they eventually eclipsed. *Homo sapiens* means "wise man."

horses Animals used by full-scale nomadic communities to dominate the steppe lands in western Afro-Eurasia by the second millennium BCE. Horse-riding nomads moved their large herds across immense tracts of land within zones defined by rivers, mountains, and other natural geographical features. In the arid zones of central Eurasia, the nomadic economies made horses a crucial component of survival.

Huguenots French Protestants who endured severe persecution in the sixteenth and seventeenth centuries.

humanism The Renaissance aspiration to know more about the human experience beyond what the Christian scriptures offered by reaching back into ancient Greek and Roman texts.

Hundred Days' Reform (1898) Abortive modernizing reform program of the Qing government of China.

hunting and gathering Lifestyle in which food is acquired through hunting animals, fishing, and foraging for wild berries, nuts, fruit, and grains, rather than planting crops, vines, or trees. As late as 1500, as much as 15 percent of the world's population still obtained food by this method.

Hyksos A western Semitic-speaking people whose name means "Rulers of Foreign Lands"; they overthrew the unstable Thirteenth Dynasty in Egypt around 1640 BCE. The Hyksos had mastered the art of horse chariots, and with those chariots and their superior bronze axes and composite bows (made of wood, horn, and sinew), they were able to defeat the pharaoh's foot soldiers.

Ibn Sina Persian philosopher and physician who lived from 980 to 1037 CE. He was also schooled in the Quran, geometry, literature, and Indian and Euclidian mathematics. He was known in Europe as Avicenna.

ideology Dominant set of ideas of a widespread culture or movement.

Il Duce Term designating the fascist Italian leader Benito Mussolini.

Iliad Epic Greek poem about the Trojan War attributed to Homer and completed several centuries after the events it describes. It was based on oral tales passed down for generations.

Il-khanate Mongol-founded dynasty in the thirteenth century and based in Persia.

imam Muslim religious leader among Sunni Muslims. Shiites believe that imams are the rightful successors to the Prophet Muhammad through Ali, the son-in-law of Muhammad, and accord them much greater political and religious legitimacy than the Sunnis do.

imperialism Acquisition of new territories by a state and the incorporation of those territories into a political system as subordinate colonies.

Imperial University University founded in 136 BCE by Emperor Wu. Important discoveries and advances were made here, including rational diagnoses of the body's functions, the magnetic compass, and high-quality paper. The university was a mechanism by which the Han state inculcated Confucian thought into the elite.

imperium Latin word used to express Romans' power and command over their subjects. It is the basis of the English words *empire* and *imperialism*.

Inca Empire Empire of Quecha-speaking rulers in the Andean valley of Cuzco that encompassed a population of 4 to 6 million. The Incas lacked a clear inheritance system, causing an internal split that Pizarro's forces exploited in 1533.

Indian Institutes of Technology (IIT) Institutions originally designed as engineering schools to expand knowledge and to modernize India, which produced a whole generation of pioneering computer engineers, many of whom moved to the United States.

Indian National Congress Formed in 1885, an anticolonial party deeply committed to constitutional methods, nonviolent protest, and cultural nationalism.

Indian National Muslim League Founded in 1906, an organization dedicated to advancing the political interests of Muslims in India.

Indo-Greek Fusion of Indian and Greek culture in the area under the control of the Bactrians, in the northwestern region of India, around 200 BCE.

Indu What we would today call India. It was called "Indu" by Xuanzang, a Chinese Buddhist pilgrim who visited the area in the 630s and 640s CE.

indulgences Church-sponsored fund-raising mechanism that gave certification that one's sins had been forgiven in return for money.

industrial revolution Gradual accumulation and diffusion of old and new technical knowledge that led to major economic changes in Britain at the end of the eighteenth century and spread to northwestern Europe and North America in the nineteenth century. The industrial revolution catapulted these countries ahead of the rest of the world in manufacturing and agricultural output and standard of living.

industrious revolution Interpretation of seventeenth- and eighteenth-century economic change, developed by Jan de Vries, that attributes the origins of the industrial revolution to northern European householders' decisions to work harder and longer hours to produce more for the market, enabling them to increase their income and standard of living.

innovation Creation of a new method that allows humans to make better adaptations to their environment. Toolmaking was an important innovation.

Inquisition Tribunal of the Roman Catholic Church that enforced religious orthodoxy during the Protestant Reformation.

internal and external alchemy In Daoist ritual, use of trance and meditation (internal) or chemicals and drugs (external) to cause transformations in the self.

International Monetary Fund (IMF) Agency founded in 1944 to help restore financial order in Europe and the rest of the world, to revive international trade, and to support the financial concerns of Third World governments.

invisible hand As described in Adam Smith's *The Wealth of Nations,* the idea that the operations of a free market produce economic efficiency and economic benefits for all.

iron Malleable metal found in combined forms almost everywhere in the world. It became the most important and widely used metal in world history after the Bronze Age.

Iron Curtain Term popularized by Winston Churchill after World War II to refer to the political, economic, and ideological division within Europe between western Europe, under American influence, and eastern Europe, under the domination of the Soviet Union.

irrigation The supply of water, other than through rainfall, to land and crops, often by means of water sluices and channels in river floodplains, to increase agricultural production.

Islam A religion that dates to 610 CE, when Muhammad believed God came to him in a vision. Islam ("submission"—in this case, to the will of God) requires its followers to act righteously, to submit themselves to the one and only true God, and to care for the less fortunate. Muhammad's most insistent message was the oneness of God, a belief that has remained central to the Islamic faith ever since.

Jacobins Radical French political group that came into existence during the French Revolution and executed the French king and sought to remake French culture.

Jacquerie A general term for peasant revolts, taken from the 1358 French peasant revolt against nobles and their restrictions.

jade The most important precious substance in East Asia. Jade was associated with goodness, purity, luck, and virtue and was carved into such items as ceremonial knives, blade handles, religious objects, and elaborate jewelry.

Jagat Seths Enormous trading and banking empire in eastern India.

Jainism Along with Buddhism, one of the two systems of thought developed in the seventh century BCE that set themselves up against Brahmanism. Its founder, Vardhamana Mahavira, taught that the universe obeys its own everlasting rules that no god or other supernatural being could affect. The purpose of life was to purify one's soul in order to attain a state of permanent bliss, which could be accomplished through self-denial and the avoidance of harming other creatures.

Janissaries Corps of infantry soldiers recruited as children from the Christian provinces of the Ottoman Empire and brought up with intense loyalty to Islam, the Ottoman state, and its sultan. The Ottoman sultan used these forces to clip local autonomy and to serve as his personal bodyguards.

Jati Social groups as defined by Hinduism's caste system.

Jesuits Religious order founded by Ignatius Loyola in Spain in the middle of the sixteenth century to counter the inroads of the Protestant Reformation. The Jesuits, or the Society of Jesus, were active in politics, education, and missionary work.

jihad Literally, "striving" or "struggle." This word also connotes military efforts or "striving in the way of God." It also came to mean spiritual struggles against temptation or inner demons, especially in Sufi, or mystical, usage.

Jih-pen Chinese for "Japan."

Jim Crow laws Laws that codified racial segregation and inequality in the southern part of the United States after the Civil War.

jizya Special tax that non-Muslims were forced to pay to their Islamic rulers in return for which they were given security and property and granted cultural autonomy.

jong Large oceangoing vessels, built by Southeast Asians, which plied the regional trade routes from the fifteenth century to the early sixteenth century.

Judah The southern kingdom of David, which had been an Assyrian vassal until 612 BCE, when it became a vassal of Assyria's successor, Babylon, against whom the people of Judah rebelled, resulting in the destruction of Jerusalem in the sixth century BCE.

Julius Caesar (100–44 BCE) Formidable Roman general who was also a man of letters and a great orator. He incited a civil war in 49 BCE; victorious, he seized power and began a series of populist reforms. He was assassinated by Senators who feared he was becoming a dictator in 44 BCE.

junks Trusty seafaring vessels used in the South China Seas after 1000 CE. These vessels helped make shipping by sea less dangerous.

Justinian Roman (Byzantine) emperor who ascended to the throne in 527 CE. In addition to his many building projects and military expeditions, he issued a new law code.

Kabuki Theater performance that combines song, dance, and skillful staging to dramatize conflicts between duty and passion; originated in Tokogawa, Japan.

kamikaze Japanese for "divine winds" or typhoons, such as the storm that saved Japan from a Mongol attack. The term also was used for Japanese suicide bombers during World War II.

kanun Highly detailed system of Ottoman administrative law that jurists developed to deal with matters not treated in the religious law of Islam.

Karim Loose confederation of shippers banding together to protect convoys.

karma Literally, "fate" or "action" in Confucian thought; this is a universal principle of cause and effect.

Kassites Nomads who entered Mesopotamia from the eastern Zagros Mountains and the Iranian plateau as early as 2000 BCE. They gradually integrated into Babylonian society by officiating at temples. By 1745 BCE, they had asserted order over the region, and they controlled southern Mesopotamia for the next 350 years, creating one of the territorial states.

Keynesian Revolution Economic ideas developed by British economist John Maynard Keynes during the Great Depression, wherein the state took a greater role in managing the economy, stimulating it by increasing the money supply and creating jobs. These ideas were only adopted by state policymakers after World War II.

KGB Soviet political police and spy agency, formed as the Cheka soon after the Bolshevik coup in October 1917 and known during the Stalinist period as the NKVD. The KGB grew to more than 750,000 operatives with military rank by the 1980s.

khan Ruler who was acclaimed at an assembly of elites and supposedly descended from Chinggis Khan on the male line; those not descended from Chinggis continually faced challenges to their legitimacy.

Khanate Major political unit of the vast Mongol Empire. There were four Khanates, including the Yuan Empire in China, forged by Chinggis Khan's grandson Kubilai.

Kharijites Radical sect from the early days of Islam. The Kharijites seceded from the "party of Ali" (who themselves came to be known as the Shiites) because of disagreements over succession to the role of caliph. The Kharjites were known for their strict militant piety.

Khmers A people who created the most powerful empire in Southwest Asia between the tenth and thirteenth centuries in what is modern-day Cambodia.

Khomeini, Ayatollah Ruhollah (1902–1989) Iranian religious leader who used his traditional Islamic education and his training in Muslim ethics to accuse the shah's government of gross violations of Islamic norms. He also identified the shah's ally, America, as the Great Satan. The shah fled the country in 1979; in his wake, Khomeini established a theocratic state ruled by a council of Islamic clerics.

Khufu The second pharaoh of the Fourth Dynasty in ancient Egypt (2575–2465 BCE), who constructed the Great Pyramid, the largest stone structure in the world. The pyramid is located in an area called Giza, just outside modern-day Cairo.

Khusro I Anoshirwan Sasanian emperor who reigned from 530 to 579 CE. He was a model ruler and was seen as the personification of justice.

Kiev City that became one of the greatest cities of Europe after the eleventh century. It was built to be a small-scale Constantinople on the Dnieper River.

Kikuyu Kenya's largest ethnic group; organizers of a revolt against the British in the 1950s.

King, Martin Luther, Jr. (1929–1968) Civil rights leader who borrowed his most effective weapon—the commitment to nonviolent protest and the appeal to conscience—from Gandhi.

Kingdom of Awadh One of the most prized lands for annexation and the fertile, opulent, and traditional vestige of Mughal rule in India.

Kingdom of Jerusalem A Crusader state established in Palestine in 1099 CE after the First Crusade. The kingdom lasted until 1187, when it was destroyed by Saladin.

Kizilbash Mystical, Turkish-speaking tribesmen who facilitated the Safavid rise to power.

Knossos Area in Crete where, during the second millennium BCE, a primary palace town existed.

Koine **Greek** Common form of Greek that became the international spoken and written language in the Hellenistic world. This was a simpler everyday form of the ancient Greek language.

Köprülü reforms Reforms named after two grand viziers who revitalized the Ottoman Empire in the seventeenth century through administrative and budget trimming as well as by rebuilding the military.

Korean War (1950–1953) Cold War conflict between Soviet-backed North Korea and U.S.- and UN-backed South Korea. The two sides seesawed back and forth over the same boundaries until 1953, when an armistice divided the country at roughly the same spot as at the start of the war. Nothing had been gained. Losses, however, included 33,000 Americans, at least 250,000 Chinese, and up to 3 million Koreans.

Koryo dynasty Leading dynasty of the northern-based Koryo kingdom in Korea. It is from this dynasty that the name Korea derives.

Kremlin Once synonymous with the Soviet government; refers to Moscow's walled city center.

Kshatriyas The military caste, one of the four Hindu castes, which was supposed to protect society by fighting in times of warfare and governing in times of peace.

Kubilai Khan (1215–1294) Mongol leader who seized southern China after 1260 and founded the Yuan dynasty.

Ku Klux Klan Racist organization that first emerged in the U.S. South after the Civil War and then gained national strength as a radically traditionalist movement during the 1920s.

kulak Originally a pejorative word used to designate better-off peasants, the term used in the late 1920s and early 1930s to refer to any peasant, rich or poor, perceived as an opponent of the Soviet regime; Russian for "fist."

Kumarajiva Renowned Buddhist scholar and missionary who lived from 344 to 413 CE. He was brought to China by Chinese regional forces from Kucha, modern-day Xinjiang.

Kushans Northern nomadic group that migrated into South Asia in 50 CE. They unified the tribes of the region and set up the Kushan dynasty. The Kushans' empire embraced a large and diverse territory and played a critical role in the formation of the Silk Road.

Labour Party Founded in Britain in 1900, a party that has drawn its support from workers and has espoused moderately socialist principles.

laissez-faire The concept that the economy works best when it is left alone—that is, when the state does not regulate or interfere with the workings of the market.

"Land under the Yoke of Ashur" Lands not in Assyria proper, but under its authority. The inhabitants had to make exorbitant tribute payments to the Assyrian Empire.

language families Related tongues with a common ancestral origin. Language families contain languages that diverged from one another but share grammatical features and a root vocabulary. More than a hundred language families exist.

Laozi Also known as Master Lao; perhaps a contemporary of Confucius and the person after whom Daoism is named. His thought was elaborated upon by generations of thinkers.

latifundia Broad estates that produced goods for large urban markets, including wheat, grapes, olives, cattle, and sheep.

Laws of Manu Part of the handiwork of Brahman priests; a representative code of law that incorporated social sanctions and practices and provided guidance for living within the caste system.

League of Nations Organization founded after World War I to solve international disputes through arbitration; it was dissolved in 1946, and its assets were transferred to the United Nations.

Legalism Also called Statism, a system of thought about how to live an ordered life. It was developed by Master Xun, or Xunzi (310–237 BCE). It is based on the principle that people, being inherently inclined toward evil, require authoritarian control to regulate their behavior.

Lenin, Vladimir (1870–1924) Leader of the Bolshevik Revolution in Russia and the first leader of the Soviet Union.

Liangzhu Culture spanning centuries from the fourth to the third millennium BCE that represented the last New Stone Age culture in the Yangzi River delta. One of the Ten Thousand States, it was highly stratified and is known for its jade objects.

liberalism Political and social theory that advocates representative government, individual rights, free trade, and freedom of speech and religion.

limited-liability joint-stock company Company that mobilizes capital from a large number of investors, called shareholders, who were not to be held personally liable for financial losses incurred by the company.

Linear A and B Two linear scripts first discovered on Crete in 1900. On the island of Crete and on the mainland areas of Greece, documents of the palace-centered societies were written on clay tablets in these two scripts. Linear A script, apparently written in Minoan, has not yet been deciphered. Linear B was first deciphered in the early 1950s.

"Little Europes" Urban landscapes between 1100 and 1200 CE composed of castles, churches, and towns in what are today Poland, the Czech Republic, Hungary, and the Baltic states.

Little Ice Age Period of global cooling beginning at the close of the Medieval Warm Period and lasting for centuries. The most extreme drop in temperature was in the 1600s.

Liu Bang Chinese emperor from 206 to 195 BCE. After declaring himself the prince of his home area of Han, in 202 BCE, Liu declared himself the first Han emperor.

llamas Animals similar in utility and function to camels in Afro-Eurasia. Llamas can carry heavy loads for long distances.

Long March (1934–1935) Trek of over 10,000 kilometers by Mao Zedong and his communist followers to establish a new base of operations in northwestern China.

Longshan peoples Peoples who lived in small agricultural and river-basin villages in East Asia at the end of the third millennium BCE. They set the stage for the Shang in terms of a centralized state, urban life, and a cohesive culture.

lord Privileged landowner who exercised authority over the people who lived on his land.

lost generation The 17 million former members of the Red Guard and other Chinese youth who were denied education from the late 1960s to the mid-1970s as part of the Chinese government's attempt to prevent political disruptions.

Louisiana Purchase (1803) American purchase of French territory from Napoleon, including much of the present-day United States between the Mississippi River and the Rocky Mountains.

Lucy Relatively intact skeleton of a young adult female australopithecine unearthed in the valley of the Awash River in 1974 and nicknamed Lucy. Lucy walked upright at least some of the time, and her jaw and teeth were humanlike. Until recently, Lucy was the oldest hominin skeleton ever discovered.

Luftwaffe German air force.

Luther, Martin (1483–1546) A German monk and theologian who sought to reform the Catholic Church. He believed in salvation through faith alone, the importance of reading Scripture, and the priesthood of all believers. His Ninety-Five Theses, written in 1517, enumerated the abuses by the Catholic Church and catalyzed a movement that became the Protestant Reformation.

Maastricht Treaty (1992) Treaty that formed the European Union, an integrated trading and financial bloc with its own bureaucracy and elected representatives.

Ma'at Term used in ancient Egypt to refer to stability or order, the achievement of which was the primary task of Egypt's ruling kings, the pharaohs.

Maccabees Leaders of a riot in Jerusalem in 166 BCE. The riot was a response to a Roman edict outlawing the practice of Judaism.

Madhyamika (Middle Way) Buddhism Chinese branch of Mahayana Buddhism established by Kumarajiva (344–413 CE) that used irony and paradox to show that reason is limited.

madrassas Higher schools of Muslim education that taught law, the Quran, religious sciences, and the foreign sciences.

Mahayana Buddhism School of Buddhist theology that believed that the Buddha was a deity, unlike previous groups that had considered him a wise human being.

Mahdi The "chosen one" in Islam whose appearance was supposed to foretell the end of the world and the final day of reckoning for all people.

maize A grain crop, also known as corn, that the settled agrarian communities across the Americas cultivated, along with legumes (beans) and tubers (potatoes).

Maji-Maji Revolt (early 1900s) Swahili insurrection against German colonialists, inspired by the belief that those who were anointed with specially blessed water (*maji*) would be immune to bullets. It resulted in 200,000 to 300,000 African deaths.

Mali Empire West African empire, founded by the legendary king Sundiata in the early thirteenth century and lasting until the beginning of the seventeenth century. It facilitated thriving commerce, with routes linking the Atlantic Ocean, the Sahara, and beyond.

Mamluks Military men who ruled Egypt as an independent regime from 1250 until the Ottoman conquest in 1517.

Manaus Opera House Opera house built in the interior of Brazil in a lucrative rubber-growing area at the turn of the twentieth century.

Manchukuo Japanese puppet state in Manchuria in the 1930s.

Manchus Descendants of the Jurchens, who helped the Ming army recapture Beijing in 1644 after its seizure by the outlaw Li Zicheng. The Manchus numbered around 1 million but controlled a domain that included perhaps 250 million people. Their rule lasted more than 250 years and became known as the Qing dynasty.

mandate of heaven Ideology established by Zhou dynasts to communicate the moral transfer of power. Originally a pact between the Zhou people and their supreme god, it evolved in the first century BCE into Chinese political doctrine.

Mande A people who lived in the area between the bend in the Senegal River and the bend in the Niger River east to west and from the Senegal River and Bandama River north to south. Also known as the Mandinka, their civilization emerged around 1100 CE, and their merchants were deeply involved in long-distances trade throughout the region.

Mandela, Nelson (1918–2013) Leader of the African National Congress (ANC) who was imprisoned for more than two decades by the apartheid regime in South Africa for his political beliefs. Worldwide protests led to his release in 1990. In 1994, Mandela won the presidency in South Africa's first free mass elections.

Manifest Destiny Belief that it was God's will for the American people to expand their economic and political dominion across the North American continent.

manorialism System in which the manor (a lord's home, its associated industry, and surrounding fields) served as the basic unit of economic power; an alternative to feudalism (a term primarily used to describe political and hierarchical relationships of king, lords, and peasantry) for thinking about the nature of power in western Europe, 1000–1300.

Mao Zedong (1893–1976) Chinese communist leader who rose to power during the Long March (1934). In 1949, he defeated the Nationalists and established a communist regime in China. Mao's efforts to transform China, such as the industrialization program of 1958 (known as the Great Leap Forward) and the Cultural Revolution of 1966, failed and brought great suffering to the people, but he has been credited with instilling China with a sense of purpose after decades of political and economic weakness.

maroon community Sanctuary for runaway slaves in the Americas.

Marshall Plan Economic aid package given by the United States to certain European nations after World War II in hopes of a rapid period of reconstruction and economic gain, thereby securing those countries from a communist takeover.

martyrs People executed by the Roman authorities for persisting in their Christian beliefs and refusing to submit to pagan ritual or belief.

Marx, Karl (1818–1883) German philosopher and economist who, together with Friedrich Engels, founded the first International Working Mens' Association and developed the economic and political theories we now call Marxism.

Marxism Form of scientific socialism created by Karl Marx and Friedrich Engels that was rooted in a materialist theory of history: what mattered in history was what ordinary people ate and how they lived and worked, not political events or philosophies. Marx believed that capitalism enslaved workers, and he predicted that eventually a revolution of the working classes would overthrow the capitalist order and create a classless society.

mass consumption Increased purchasing power in the early twentieth-century prosperous and mainly middle-class societies, stemming from mass production.

mass culture Distinctive form of popular culture that arose in the wake of World War I. It reflected the tastes of the working and the middle classes, who now had more time and money to spend on entertainment, and relied on new technologies, especially film and radio, which could reach an entire nation's population and consolidate their sense of being a single state.

mass production System in which factories were set up to produce huge quantities of identical products, reflecting the early twentieth-century world's demands for greater volume, faster speed, reduced cost, and standardized output.

mastaba Word meaning "bench" in Arabic; it refers to a huge flat structure identical to earlier royal tombs of ancient Egypt.

Mau Mau Revolt (1952–1957) Kenyan uprising orchestrated by a guerrilla movement of the Kikuyu peoples. This conflict forced the British to grant independence to the black majority in Kenya.

Mauryan Empire Dynasty extended by the Mauryans from 321 to 184 BCE, from the Indus Valley to the northwest areas of South Asia, in a region previously controlled by Persia. It was the first large-scale empire in South Asia and was to become the model for future Indian empires.

Mawali Non-Arab "clients" attached to Arab patrons in the early Islamic Empire. Because patronage was so much a part of the Arabian cultural system, non-Arabs who converted to Islam affiliated themselves with extended Muslim families and became clients of those groups.

Maxim gun European weapon capable of firing many bullets per second; it was used against Africans in the conquest of the continent.

Maya Civilization that ruled over large stretches of Mesoamerica, composed of a series of kingdoms, each built around ritual centers rather than cities. The Maya were not defined by a great ruler or one capital city, but by their shared religious beliefs.

McCarthyism Campaign by Republican senator Joseph McCarthy in the late 1940s and early 1950s to uncover closet communists, particularly in the State Department and in Hollywood.

Meat Inspection Act (1906) Legislation that provided for government supervision of meat-packing operations. It was part of the broader Progressive Movement dedicated to correcting the negative consequences of urbanization and industrialization in the United States.

Mecca Arabian city in which Muhammad was born. Mecca was a trading center and pilgrimage destination in the pre-Islamic and Islamic periods. Exiled in 622 CE because of resistance to his message, Muhammad returned to Mecca in 630 CE and claimed the city for Islam.

Medes Rivals of the Assyrians and the Persians. The Medes inhabited the area from the Zagros Mountains to the modern city of Tehran. Although expert horsemen and archers, they were eventually defeated by the Persians.

megaliths Literally, "great stones." The word *megalith* is used when describing a structure such as Stonehenge, a massive structure that is the result of cooperative planning and work.

megarons Large buildings found in Troy (level II) that are the predecessors of the classic Greek temple.

Meiji Empire Empire created under the leadership of Mutsuhito, emperor of Japan from 1868 until 1912. During the Meiji period, Japan became a world industrial and naval power.

Meiji Restoration Reign of the Meiji emperor, which was characterized by a new nationalist identity, economic advances, and political transformation.

Mencius Disciple of Confucius who lived from 372 to 289 BCE.

mercantilism Economic theory developed in Europe in the seventeenth century based on the idea that the world had a fixed amount of wealth, which meant that one country's wealth came at the expense of another's. Mercantilism encouraged the placing of tariffs on imports and the founding of colonies to enrich the mother countries and in this way drove European empire building.

Mercosur Free trade pact between the governments of Argentina, Brazil, Paraguay, and Uruguay.

meritocracy Rule by persons of talent.

Meroe Ancient kingdom in what is today Sudan. It flourished for nearly a thousand years, from the fifth century BCE to the fifth century CE.

mestizos Mixed-blood offspring of Spanish settlers and native Indians.

métis Mixed-blood offspring of French settlers and native Indians.

Mexican Revolution (1910) Conflict fueled by the unequal distribution of land and by disgruntled workers; it erupted when political elites split over the succession of General Porfirio Díaz after decades of his rule. The fight lasted over ten years and cost 1 million lives, but it resulted in widespread reform and a new constitution.

Mfecane movement African political revolts in the first half of the nineteenth century that were caused by the expansionist methods of King Shaka of the Zulu people.

microsocieties Small-scale communities that had little interaction with others. These communities were the norm for peoples living in the Americas and islanders in the Pacific and Aegean from 2000 to 1200 BCE.

migration Long-distance travel for the purpose of resettlement. In the case of early humans, the need to move was usually a response to an environmental shift, such as climate change during the Ice Age.

millenarian Convinced of the imminent coming of a just and ideal society.

millenarian movement Broad, popular upheaval calling for the restoration of a bygone moral age, often led by charismatic spiritual prophets.

millets Minority religious communities of the Ottoman Empire.

minaret Slender tower within a mosque from which Muslims are called to prayer.

minbar Pulpit inside a mosque from which Muslim religious speakers broadcast their message to the faithful.

Minoans A people who built a large number of elaborate, independent palace centers on Crete, at Knossos, and elsewhere around 2000 BCE. Named after the legendary King Minos, said to have ruled Crete at the time, they sailed throughout the Mediterranean and by 1600 BCE had planted colonies on many Aegean islands, which in turn became trading and mining centers.

mission civilisatrice Term French colonizers used to refer to France's form of "rationalized" colonial rule, which attempted to bring "civilization" to the "uncivilized."

mitochondrial DNA Form of DNA found outside the nucleus of cells, where it serves as cells' microscopic power packs. Examining mitochondrial DNA enables researchers to measure the genetic variation among living objects, including human beings.

Moche A people who extended their power and increased their wealth at the height of the Chimu Empire over several valleys in what is now modern-day Peru.

Model T First automobile, manufactured by the Ford Motor Company, to be priced reasonably enough to be sold to the masses.

modernism Term used to describe artistic, literary, and scientific movements of the late nineteenth and early twentieth centuries that self-consciously broke with traditional rules, practices, and forms of thought.

modernists A generation of exuberant young artists, writers, and scientists in the late nineteenth century who broke with older conventions and sought new ways of seeing and describing the world.

Mohism School of thought in ancient China, named after Mo Di, or Mozi, who lived from 479 to 438 BCE. It emphasized one's obligation to society as a whole, not just to one's immediate family or social circle.

monarchy Political system in which one individual holds supreme power and passes that power on to his or her next of kin.

monasticism Christian way of life that originated in Egypt and was practiced as early as 300 CE in the Mediterranean. The word comes from the Greek *monos*, referring to a person "living alone" without marriage or family.

monetization An economic shift from a barter-based economy to one dependent on coin.

Mongols Combination of nomadic forest and prairie peoples who lived by hunting and livestock herding and were expert horsemen. Beginning in 1206, the Mongols launched a series of conquests that brought far-flung parts of the world together under their rule. By incorporating conquered peoples and adapting some of their customs, the Mongols created an empire of four khanate states that stretched from the Pacific Ocean to the shores of the eastern Mediterranean and the southern steppes of Eurasia.

monotheism The belief in only one god.

Moors Term employed by Europeans in the medieval period to refer to Muslim occupants of North Africa, the western Sahara, and the Iberian Peninsula.

mosque Place of worship for the people of Islam.

"Mound people" Name for the people of Cahokia, since the landscape was dominated by earthen monuments in the shapes of mounds. The mounds were carefully maintained and were the loci from which Cahokians paid respect to spiritual forces. *See also* Cahokia.

Mu Chinese ruler (956–918 BCE) who put forth a formal bureaucratic system of governance, appointing officials, supervisors, and military captains to whom he was not related. He also instituted a formal legal code.

muckrakers Journalists who aimed to expose political and commercial corruption in late nineteenth- and early twentieth-century America.

muftis Experts on Muslim religious law.

Mughal Empire One of Islam's greatest regimes. Established in 1526, it was a vigorous, centralized state whose political authority encompassed most of modern-day India. During the sixteenth century, it had a population of between 100 and 150 million.

Muhammad (c. 570–632 CE) Prophet and founder of the Islamic faith. Born in Mecca in the Arabian Peninsula and orphaned when young, Muhammad lived under the protection of his uncle. His career as a prophet began around 610 CE, with his first experience of spiritual revelation.

Muhammad Ali Ruler of Egypt between 1805 and 1848. He initiated a set of modernizing reforms that sought to make Egypt competitive with the great powers.

mullahs Religious leaders in Iran who in the 1970s led a movement opposing Shah Reza Pahlavi and denounced American materialism and secularism.

multinational corporations Corporations based in many different countries that have global investment, trading, and distribution goals.

Muscovy The principality of Moscow. Originally a mixture of Slavs, Finnish tribes, Turkic speakers, and many others, Muscovy used territorial expansion and commercial networks to consolidate a powerful state and expanded to become the Russian Empire, a huge realm that spanned parts of Europe, much of northern Asia, numerous North Pacific islands, and even—for a time—a corner of North America (Alaska).

Muslim Brotherhood Egyptian organization founded in 1928 by Hassan al-Banna. It attacked liberal democracy as a cover for middle-class, business, and landowning interests and fought for a return to a purified Islam.

Muslim League National Muslim party of India.

Mussolini, Benito (1883–1945) Italian dictator and founder of the fascist movement in Italy. During World War II, he allied Italy with Germany and Japan.

Muwahhidin Term meaning "unitarians," or believers in one God, these were followers of the Wahhabi movement that emerged in the Arabian Peninsula in the eighteenth century.

Mycenaeans Mainland competitors of the Minoans; they took over Crete around 1400 BCE. Migrating to Greece from central Europe, they brought their Indo-European language, horse chariots, and metalworking skills, which they used to dominate until 1200 BCE.

Nagasaki Second Japanese city to be hit by an atomic bomb near the end of World War II.

Napoleonic Code Legal code drafted by Napoleon in 1804; it distilled different legal traditions to create one uniform law. The code confirmed the abolition of feudal privileges of all kinds and set the conditions for exercising property rights.

National Assembly of France Governing body of France that succeeded the Estates-General in 1789 during the French Revolution. It was composed of, and defined by, the delegates of the Third Estate.

National Association for the Advancement of Colored People (NAACP) Founded in 1910, the U.S. civil rights organization dedicated to ending inequality and segregation for black Americans.

nationalism The idea that members of a shared community called a "nation" should have sovereignty within the borders of their state.

National Recovery Administration (NRA) New Deal agency created in 1933 to prepare codes of fair administration and to plan for public works. It was later declared unconstitutional.

nation-state Form of political organization that derived legitimacy from its inhabitants, often referred to as citizens, who in theory, if not always in practice, shared a common language, culture, and history.

native learning Japanese movement to promote nativist intellectual traditions and the celebration of Japanese texts.

native paramountcy British form of "rationalized" colonial rule, which attempted to bring "civilization" to the "uncivilized" by proclaiming that when the interests of European settlers in Africa clashed with those of the African population, the latter should take precedence.

natural rights Belief that emerged in eighteenth-century western Europe and North America that rights fundamental to human nature are discernible to reason and should be affirmed in human-made law.

natural selection Charles Darwin's theory that populations grow faster than the food supply, creating a "struggle for existence" among species in which nature selects which individuals are "fittest" to survive and reproduce.

Nazis National Socialist German Workers Party; German organization founded after World War I and dedicated to winning workers over from socialism to nationalism. The first Nazi Party platform combined nationalism with anti-capitalism and anti-Semitism.

Neanderthals Members of an early wave of hominins from Africa who settled in western Afro-Eurasia, in an area reaching from present-day Uzbekistan and Iraq to Spain, approximately 150,000 years ago.

needle compass Chinese invention made available to navigators after 1000 CE that helped guide sailors on the high seas.

Negritos Hunter-gatherer inhabitants of the East Asian coastal islands who migrated there around 28,000 BCE but by 2000 BCE had been replaced by new migrants.

Negritude Statement of the virtues of the black identity and the validation of

African culture and the African past, even in a westernizing world. This idea was shaped by African and African American intellectuals like Senegal's first president, Léopold Sédar Senghor.

Nehemiah Jewish eunuch of the Persian court who was given permission to rebuild the fortification walls around the city of Jerusalem from 440 to 437 BCE.

Neo-Assyrian Empire Afro-Eurasian empire that dominated around 950 BCE. The Neo-Assyrians extended their control over resources and people beyond their own borders, and their empire lasted for three centuries.

neocolonialism Contemporary geopolitical policy or practice in which a politically, economically, and often militarily superior nation asserts control over a country that remains nominally sovereign.

Nestorian Christians Denomination of Christians whose beliefs about Christ differed from those of the official Byzantine church. Named after Nestorius, former bishop of Constantinople, they emphasized the human aspects of Jesus.

New Deal President Franklin Delano Roosevelt's set of government reforms enacted during the 1930s to provide jobs for the unemployed, social welfare programs for the poor, and security to the financial markets.

New Economic Policy (NEP) Enacted decrees of the Bolsheviks between 1921 and 1927 that grudgingly sanctioned private trade and private property.

New Negro Movement *See* Harlem Renaissance.

New World Term applied to the Americas that reflected the Europeans' view that anything previously unknown to them was "new," even if it had existed and supported societies long before European explorers arrived on its shores.

nirvana Literally, nonexistence; the state of complete liberation from the concerns of worldly life, as in Buddhist thought.

Noble Eightfold Path Buddhist concept of a way of life by which people may rid themselves of individual desire to achieve nirvana. The path consists of wisdom, ethical behavior, and mental discipline.

Noh drama Masked theater favored by Japanese bureaucrats and regional lords during the Tokugawa period.

Nok culture Spectacular culture that arose in the sixth century BCE in what is today Nigeria. Iron smelting occurred there around 600 BCE. Thus, the Nok people made the transition from stone to iron materials.

nomads People who move across vast distances without settling permanently in a particular place. Pastoralists, nomads, and transhumant herders introduced new forms of chariot-based warfare that transformed the Afro-Eurasian world.

nongovernmental organizations (NGOs) Term used to refer to private organizations like the Red Cross that play a large role in international affairs.

nonviolent resistance *Satyagraha*; moral and political philosophy developed by Indian National Congress leader Mohandas Gandhi and taken up by other reformers, such as Martin Luther King Jr. Gandhi believed that if Indians pursued self-reliance and self-control in a nonviolent way, the British would eventually have to leave.

North American Free Trade Agreement (NAFTA) Treaty negotiated in the early 1990s to promote free trade between Canada, the United States, and Mexico.

North Atlantic Treaty Organization (NATO) International organization set up in 1949 to provide for the defense of western European countries and the United States from the perceived Soviet threat.

Northern Wei dynasty Regime founded in 386 CE by the Tuoba, a people originally from Inner Mongolia, that lasted one and a half centuries. The rulers of this dynasty adopted many practices of the earlier Chinese Han regime. At the same time, they struggled to consolidate authority over their own nomadic people. Ultimately, several decades of intense internal conflict led to the dynasty's downfall.

Northwest Passage Long-sought marine passageway between the Atlantic and Pacific Oceans.

Oceania Collective name for the lands of Australia and New Zealand and the islands of the southwestern Pacific Ocean.

Odyssey Composed in the eighth century BCE and attributed to Homer, an epic tale of the journey of Odysseus, who traveled the Mediterranean back to his home in Ithaca after the siege of Troy.

oikos The word for "small family unit" in ancient Greece, similar to *familia* in Rome. Its structure, with men as heads of household over women and children, embodied the fundamental power structure in Greek city-states.

oligarchy Clique of privileged rulers.

Olmecs A people who emerged around 1500 BCE and lived in Mesoamerica. The name means those who "lived in the land of the rubber." Olmec society was composed of decentralized villages. Its members spoke the same language and worshipped the same gods.

Open Door Policy Policy proposed by American Secretary of State John Hay in the late nineteenth century to make sure that the United States, along with other foreign nations, would have equal access to trade with China.

Opium War (1839–1842) War fought between the British and Qing China over British trade in opium. China's loss resulted in the granting to the British the right to trade in five different ports and the ceding of Hong Kong to the British.

oracle bones Animal bones used by Shang diviners. Diviners applied intense heat to the shoulder bones of cattle or to turtle shells, which caused them to crack. The diviners would then interpret the cracks as signs from the ancestors regarding royal plans and actions.

Organization of Petroleum Exporting Countries (OPEC) International association established in 1960 to coordinate price and supply policies of oil-producing states.

Orientalism Genre of literature and painting that portrayed the nonwestern peoples of North Africa and Asia as exotic, sensuous, and economically and culturally backward with respect to Europeans.

Orientalists Western scholars who specialized in the study of the East.

Orrorin tugenensis Predecessor to hominins that first appeared 6 million years ago.

Ottoman Empire Domain that encompassed Anatolia, the Arab world, and much of southern and eastern Europe in the early sixteenth century. Ottoman leaders transformed themselves from nomadic warriors who roamed the borderlands between Islamic and Christian worlds in Anatolia into sovereigns of a vast, bureaucratic empire. The Ottomans embraced a Sunni view of Islam. They adapted traditional Byzantine governmental practices but tried new ways of integrating the diverse peoples of their empire.

Pacific War (1879–1883) War between Chile and the alliance of Bolivia and Peru.

palace Official residence of the ruler, his family, and his entourage, first appearing around 2500 BCE. Eventually, palaces became defining landmarks of city life and sources of power rivaling temples.

Palace of Versailles The palace complex, 11 miles away from the French capital of Paris, built by Louis XIV in the 1670s and 1680s to house and entertain his leading clergymen and nobles, with the hopes of diverting them from plotting against him.

Palmyra Roman trading depot in what is modern-day Syria; part of a network of trading cities that connected various regions of Afro-Eurasia.

pan movements Movements that sought to link people across state boundaries in new communities based on ethnicity or, in some cases, religion (e.g., pan-Germanism, pan-Islamism, pan-Slavism).

papacy The institution of the pope; the Catholic spiritual leader in Rome.

papal Of, relating to, or issued by a pope.

Parthians Horse-riding people who pushed southward around the middle of the second century BCE and wiped out the Greek kingdoms in Iran. They then extended their power all the way to the Mediterranean, where they ran up against the Roman Empire in Anatolia and Mesopotamia.

pastoralism Herding and breeding of sheep and goats or other animals as a primary means of subsistence.

pastoral nomads Groups of people who moved their domesticated animals from place to place to meet the animals' demanding grazing requirements. Around 3500 BCE, western Afro-Eurasia witnessed the growth and spread of pastoral nomadic communities.

paterfamilias From the Latin for "father of the family," the foundation of the Roman social order.

patria Latin, meaning "fatherland."

patrons In the Roman system of patronage, men and women of wealth and high social status who protected dependents or "clients" of a lower class.

Pax Mongolica Term that refers to the political and especially the commercial stability that the vast Mongol Empire provided for the travelers and merchants of Eurasia during the thirteenth and fourteenth centuries.

Pax Romana Latin for "Roman Peace"; refers to the period between 25 BCE and 235 CE, during which conditions in the Roman Empire were settled and peaceful.

Pax Sinica Period of peace (149–87 BCE) during which agriculture, commerce, and industry flourished in East Asia under the rule of the Han.

Peace Preservation Act (1925) Act instituted in Japan that specified up to ten years' hard labor for any member of an organization advocating a basic change in the political system or the abolition of private property.

Pearl Harbor American naval base in Hawaii on which the Japanese launched a surprise attack on December 7, 1941, bringing the United States into World War II.

Peloponnesian War War fought between 431 and 404 BCE between two of Greece's most powerful city-states, Athens and Sparta.

peninsulars Spaniards who, although born in Spain, resided in the Spanish colonial territories. They regarded themselves as superior to Spaniards born in the colonies (creoles).

Peninsular War (1808–1814) Conflict in which the Portuguese and Spanish populations, supported by the British, resisted the French invasion of the Iberian Peninsula by Napoleon.

Peoples' Charter Document calling for universal suffrage for adult males, the secret ballot, electoral districts, and annual parliamentary elections. It was signed by over 3 million British between 1839 and 1842.

periplus Book that reflected sailing knowledge; in such books captains would record landing spots and ports. The word *periplus* literally means "sailing around."

Persepolis Darius I's capital city in the highlands of Fars; a ceremonial center and expression of imperial identity as well as an important administrative hub.

Peterloo Massacre (1819) The killing of 11 and wounding of 460 following a peaceful demonstration for political reform by workers in Manchester, England.

Petra City in modern-day Jordan that was the Nabataean capital. It profited greatly by supplying provisions and water to travelers and traders. Many of its houses and shrines were cut into the rocky mountains. *Petra* means "rock."

phalanx Military formation used by Philip II of Macedonia, whereby heavily armored infantry were closely arrayed in battle formation. Term also used by Charles Fourier to describe a well-ordered utopian community.

Philip II of Macedonia Father of Alexander the Great, under whose rule Macedonia developed into a large ethnic and territorial state. After unifying Macedonia, Philip went on to conquer neighboring states but was assassinated in 336 BCE at the age of 46.

philosophes Enlightenment thinkers who applied scientific reasoning to human interaction and society.

philosophia Literally, "love of wisdom." This system of thought originally included speculation by Greek thinkers on the nature of the cosmos, the environment, and human existence. It eventually came to include thought about the nature of humans and life in society.

Phoenicians Known as the Canaanites in the Bible, an ethnic group in the Levant under Assyrian rule in the seventh century BCE; they provided ships and sailors for battles in the Mediterranean. The name *Phoenician* means "purple people," referring to the purple dye they manufactured and widely traded, along with other commercial goods and services, throughout the Mediterranean. Their major contribution was the alphabet, first introduced in the second millennium BCE, which made far-reaching communication possible.

phonemes Primary and distinctive sounds that are characteristic of human language.

piety Strong sense of religious duty and devoutness, often inspiring extraordinary actions.

plant domestication Process of growing plants, harvesting their seeds, and saving some of the seeds for planting in subsequent growing cycles, resulting in a steady food supply. This process occurred as far back as 5000 BCE, when plants began to naturally retain their seeds. Plant domestication was practiced first in the southern Levant and spread from there into the rest of Southwest Asia.

Plato (427–347 BCE) Disciple of the great philosopher Socrates; his works are the only record we have of Socrates' teaching. He was also the author of formative philosophical works on ethics and politics.

plebs In ancient Rome, term that referred to the "common people." Their interests were protected by officials called tribunes.

pochteca Archaic term for merchants of the Mexicos.

polyglot communities Societies composed of diverse linguistic and ethnic groups.

popular culture Affordable and accessible forms of art and entertainment available to people at all levels of society.

popular sovereignty The idea that the power of the state resides in the people.

Populists Members of a political movement that supported U.S. farmers in late nineteenth-century America. The term is often used generically to refer to political groups who appeal to the majority of the population.

potassium-argon dating Major dating technique based on the changing chemical structure of nonliving objects over time. It is carried out by measuring the ratio of potassium to argon, since over time potassium decays into argon. This method makes possible the dating of objects up to a million years old.

potato famine (1840s) Severe famine in Ireland that led to the rise of radical political movements and the migration of large numbers of Irish to the United States.

potter's wheel Fast wheel that enabled people to mass-produce vessels in many different shapes. This advance, invented at the city of Uruk, enabled potters to make significant technical breakthroughs.

pottery Vessels made of mud and later clay that were used for storing and transporting food. The development of pottery was a major breakthrough.

Prague Spring (1968) Popular movement that strove to create a democratic and pluralist socialism in Czechoslovakia; suppressed by Russian intervention in early 1969.

predestination Belief of many sixteenth- and seventeenth-century Protestant groups that God had foreordained the lives of individuals, including their bad and good deeds.

primitivism Western art movement of the late nineteenth and early twentieth centuries that drew upon the so-called primitive art forms of Africa, Oceania, and pre-Columbian America.

progressive reformers Members of the U.S. reform movement in the early twentieth century that aimed to eliminate political corruption, improve working conditions, and regulate the power of large industrial and financial enterprises.

proletarians Industrial wage workers.

prophets Charismatic freelance religious men of power who found themselves in opposition to the formal power of the kings, bureaucrats, and priests.

Prophet's Town Indian village in Indiana that was burned down by American forces in the early nineteenth century.

Protestantism Division of Christianity that emerged in western Europe from the Protestant Reformation.

Protestant Reformation Religious movement initiated by Martin Luther, who openly criticized the corruption in the Catholic Church and voiced his belief that Christians could speak directly to God. His doctrines gained wide support, and those who followed this new view of Christianity rejected the authority of the papacy and the Catholic clergy, broke away from the Catholic Church, and called themselves "Protestants."

Proto-Indo-European The parent of all the languages in the Indo-European family, which includes, among many others, English, German, Norwegian, Portuguese, French, Russian, Persian, Hindi, and Bengali.

Pullman Strike (1894) American Railway Union strike in response to wage cuts and firings.

Punic Wars Three wars waged between the Romans and Carthage in the third and second centuries BCE that resulted in the defeat of the Carthaginian hegemony in the western Mediterranean and demonstrated the might of the Roman military (army and navy) and the beginnings of Rome's aggressive foreign imperialism.

puppet states Governments with little power in the international arena that follow the dictates of their more powerful neighbors or patrons.

Puritans Seventeenth-century reform group of the Church of England; also known as dissenters or nonconformists.

Qadiriyya Sufi order that facilitated the spread of Islam into West Africa.

qadis Judges in the Muslim societies.

qanats Underground water channels, vital for irrigation, that were used in Persia. Little evaporation occurred when water was being moved through qanats.

Qing dynasty (1644–1911) Minority Manchu rule over China that incorporated new territories, experienced substantial population growth, and sustained significant economic growth.

Questions of King Milinda (Milindapunha) Name of a second-century BCE text espousing the teachings of Buddhism as set forth by Menander, a Yavana king. It featured a discussion between the king and a sophisticated Buddhist sage named Nagasena.

Quetzalcoatl Ancient deity and legendary ruler of Native American peoples living in Mexico.

Quran The scripture of the Islamic faith. Originally a verbal recitation, the Quran was compiled into a book soon after the death of Muhammad in the order in which we have it today. According to traditional Islamic interpretation, the Quran was revealed to Muhammad by the angel Gabriel over a period of twenty-three years.

radicalism The conviction that real change is possible only by going to the root (in Latin, *radix*) of the problem and promoting complete political and social reform. Tendencies toward radicalism can be found in every culture that develops a complex set of institutions and hierarchies, but have been found most frequently in the west since 1789.

radicals Widely used term in nineteenth-century Europe that referred to those individuals and political organizations that favored the total reconfiguration of Europe's political and/or economic systems.

radiocarbon isotope C¹⁴ Isotope contained by all living things. When organisms die, the C^{14} isotope they contain begins to decay into a stable nonradioactive element, C^{12}. The rate of decay is regular and measurable, making it possible to ascertain the date of fossils that leave organic remains for ages of up to 40,000 years.

Raj British crown's administration of India following the end of the East India Company's rule after the Great Rebellion of 1857.

raja The Sanskrit word for "king," used in South and Southeast Asia. It could also refer to the head of a family, but in South Asian city-states indicated the person who had control of land and resources.

Ramadan Ninth month of the Muslim year, during which all Muslims must fast during daylight hours.

Rape of Nanjing Attack against the Chinese in which the Japanese slaughtered at least 100,000 civilians and raped thousands of women between December 1937 and February 1938.

Rashtriya Swayamsevak Sangh (RSS) (1925) Campaign to organize Hindus as a militant, modern community in India; translated in English as "National Volunteer Organization."

Rebellion of 1857 (Great Rebellion) Indian uprising against the East India Company to bring religious purification, an egalitarian society, local and communal solidarity, and a return of a Mughal to the throne without the interference of British rule.

rebus Probably originating in Uruk, a representation that transfers meaning from the name of a thing to the sound of that name. For example, a picture of a bee can represent the sound "b." Such pictures opened the door to writing, a technology of symbols that uses marks to represent specific discrete sounds.

Reconquista Spanish reconquest of territories lost to the Islamic Empire, beginning with Toledo in 1061.

Red Guards Chinese students who were the shock troops in the early phases of Mao's Cultural Revolution in 1966–1968.

Red Lanterns Female supporters of the Chinese Boxers who rebelled against foreign intrusions in China at the turn of the twentieth century. Most were teenage girls and unmarried women, and they dressed in red garments.

Reds Bolsheviks.

Red Turban Movement Diverse religious movement in China during the fourteenth century that spread the belief that the world was drawing to an end as Mongol rule was collapsing.

Reich German word for "realm." Hitler claimed to be creating the Third German Reich (after the Holy Roman Empire and the German Empire that had lasted from 1871 to 1919).

Reichstag The German parliament.

Reign of Terror Campaign at the height of the French Revolution in the early 1790s that used violence, including systematic execution of opponents of the revolution, to purge France of its enemies and to extend the revolution beyond its borders. Radicals executed as many as 40,000 persons who were judged enemies of the state.

Renaissance Term meaning "rebirth" that historians use to characterize the expanded cultural production of European nations between 1430 and 1550. The Renaissance emphasized a break from the church-centered medieval world and a new concept of humankind as the center of the world.

republican government Government in which power and rulership rest with representatives of the people—not a king.

res publica Literally, "public thing"; this referred to the Roman republic, in which policy and rules of behavior were determined by the Senate and by popular assemblies of the citizens.

Restoration period (1815–1848) European movement after the defeat of Napoleon to restore Europe to its pre–French Revolutionary status and to quash radical movements.

Rift Valley Area of northeastern Africa where some of the most important early discoveries of human fossils were found, especially one of an intact skull that is 1.8 million years old.

river basins Areas drained by a river, including all its tributaries. River basins were rich in fertile soil, water for irrigation, and plant and animal life, which made them attractive for human habitation. Cultivators were able to produce surplus agriculture to support the first cities.

Roman army Military force of the Roman Empire. The Romans devised a military draft that could draw from a huge population. In their encounter with Hannibal, they lost up to 80,000 men in three separate encounters and still won the war.

Roman Catholicism Branch of Christianity established by 1000 CE in western Europe and led by the Roman papacy. In contrast to ancient Greek Orthodoxy, Western Catholics believed that their church was destined to expand everywhere, and they set about converting the tribes of northern Europe. Western Catholics contemptuously called the East Romans "Greeks" and condemned them for their "Byzantine" cunning.

Roman law Roman legal system, under which disputes were brought to the public courts and decisions were made by judges and sometimes by large juries. Rome's legal system featured written law and institutions for settling legal disputes.

roving bandits Large bands of dispossessed and marginalized Chinese peasants who vented their anger at tax collectors in the waning years of the Ming dynasty.

Royal Road A 1,600-mile road of the ancient Persian Empire that went from Sardis in Anatolia to Susa in Iran. It was used by messengers, traders, the army, and those taking tribute to the king.

Russification Programs to assimilate people of over 146 dialects into the Russian Empire.

S.S. (*Schutzstaffel*) Hitler's security police force.

Sack of Constantinople Rampage in 1204 by the Frankish armies on the capital city of Constantinople.

Sahel region The Arabic word for "coast," used to describe the area that borders the southern region of the Sahara Desert. This vast expanse of land, stretching from the Atlantic Ocean to the Red Sea, was significantly wetter and more temperate than the desert, especially in the upland massifs and their foothills, where villages and towns were able to emerge.

Salt March (1930) A 240-mile trek to the sea in India, led by Mohandas Gandhi, to gather salt for free, thus breaking the British colonial monopoly on salt.

Samurai Japanese warriors who made up the private armies of Japanese daimyos.

Sandinista coalition Left-leaning Nicaraguan coalition of the 1970s and 1980s.

Sanskrit cosmopolis A cultural synthesis based on Hindu spiritual beliefs and articulated in the Sanskrit language that served to culturally unify South Asia in place of a centralized empire.

Santería African-based religion, blended with Christian influences, that was first practiced by slaves in Cuba.

Sargon the Great King of Akkad, a city-state near modern Baghdad. Reigning from 2334 to 2279 BCE, Sargon helped bring the competitive era of city-states to an end and sponsored monumental works of architecture, art, and literature.

Sasanian Empire Empire that succeeded the Parthians in the mid-220s CE in Inner Eurasia. The Sasanian Empire controlled the trade crossroads of Afro-Eurasia and possessed a strong armored cavalry, which made them a powerful rival to Rome. The Sasanians were also tolerant of Judaism and Christianity, which allowed Christians to flourish.

Sati Hindu practice whereby a woman was burned to death on the pyre of her dead husband.

satrapies Provinces in the Persian Empire governed by a satrap. Each satrap was a relative or intimate associate of the king.

Satyagraha *See* nonviolent resistance.

scientific method Method of inquiry based on experimentation rather than on the acceptance of older authorities. Many of its principles were first laid out by the philosopher Sir Francis Bacon (1561–1626), who claimed that real science entailed the formulation of hypotheses that could be tested in carefully controlled experiments.

Scramble for Africa European rush to colonize parts of Africa at the end of the nineteenth century.

scribes Those who wield writing tools. From the very beginning, they were at the top of the social ladder, under the major power brokers.

Scythian ethos Warrior ethos that embodied the extremes of aggressive mounted-horse culture, c. 1000 BCE. In part the Scythian ethos was the result of the constant struggle between settlers, hunter-gatherers, and nomads on the northern frontier of Europe.

Sea Peoples Migrants from north of the Mediterranean who invaded the cities of Egypt and the Levant in the second millennium BCE. Once settled along the coast of the Levant, they became known as the Philistines and considerably disrupted the settlements of the Canaanites.

SEATO (Southeast Asia Treaty Organization) Military alliance of pro-American, anticommunist states in Southeast Asia in 1954.

second-generation societies Societies that expanded old ideas and methods by incorporating new aspects of culture and grafting them onto, or using them in combination with, established norms.

Second World Term invented during the Cold War to refer to the communist countries, as opposed to the west (or First World) and the former colonies (or Third World).

Seleucus Nikator Successor of Alexander the Great who lived from 358 to 281 BCE. He controlled Mesopotamia, Syria, Persia, and parts of the Punjab.

Self-Strengthening movement In the latter half of the nineteenth century, a movement of reformist Chinese bureaucrats that attempted to adopt western elements of learning and technological skill while retaining their core Chinese culture.

Semu Term meaning "outsiders" or non-Chinese people—Mongols, Tanguts, Khitan, Jurchen, Muslims, Tibetans, Persians, Turks, Nestorians, Jews, and Armenians—who became a new ruling elite over a Han majority population in the late thirteenth century.

sepoys Hindu and Muslim recruits of the East India Company's military force.

serfs Peasants who farmed the land and paid fees to be protected by lords under a system of rule called feudalism.

settled agriculture Application of human labor and tools to a fixed plot of land for more than one growing cycle. It entails the changeover from a hunting and gathering lifestyle to one based on agriculture, which requires staying in one place until the soil has been exhausted.

Seven Years' War (1756–1763) Worldwide war that ended when Prussia defeated Austria, establishing itself as a European power, and when Britain gained control of India and many of France's colonies through the Treaty of Paris; known in North America as the French and Indians Wars.

sexual revolution Increased freedom in sexual behavior, resulting in part from advances in contraception, notably the introduction of oral contraception in 1960, which allowed men and women to limit childbearing and to have sex with less fear of pregnancy.

shah Traditional title of Persian rulers.

shamans Certain humans whose powers supposedly enabled them to commune with the supernatural and to transform themselves wholly or partly into animals.

shamisen Three-stringed instrument, often played by Japanese geisha.

Shandingdong Man A *Homo sapiens* whose fossil remains and relics can be dated to about 18,000 years ago. His physical characteristics were close to those of modern humans, and he had a similar brain size.

Shanghai School Late nineteenth-century style of Chinese painting characterized by an emphasis on spontaneous brushwork, feeling, and the incorporation of western influences into classical Chinese pieces.

Shang state Dynasty in northeastern China that ruled from 1600 to 1045 BCE. Though not as well defined by borders as the territorial states in the southwest of Asia, it did have a ruling lineage. Four fundamental elements of the Shang state were a metal industry based on copper, pottery making, standardized architectural forms and walled towns, and divination using animal bones.

sharecropping System of farming in which tenant farmers rented land and gave over a share of their crops to the land's owners. Sometimes seen as a cheap way for the state to conduct agricultural affairs, sharecropping often resulted in the impoverishment and marginalization of the underclass.

sharia Literally, "the way"; now used to indicate the philosophy and rulings of Islamic law.

Sharpeville Massacre (1960) Massacre of sixty-nine black Africans when police fired on a rally against the recently passed laws requiring nonwhite South Africans to carry identity papers.

Shawnees Native American tribe that inhabited the Ohio Valley during the eighteenth century.

Shays's Rebellion (1786) Uprising of armed farmers that broke out when the Massachusetts state government refused to offer them economic relief.

Shi Huangdi King during the Qin era who defeated what was left of the Warring States between 230 and 221 BCE. He assumed the mandate of heaven from the Zhou and declared himself First August Emperor, to distinguish himself from other kings.

Shiism One of the two main branches of Islam, practiced in the Fatimid and Safavid Empires. Always a minority sect in the Islamic world, the interpretations of theology and politics in Shiism differ from those in Sunni Islam.

Shiites Group of supporters of Ali, Muhammad's cousin and son-in-law, who wanted him to be the first caliph and believed that members of the Prophet's family deserved to rule. The leaders of the Shiite community are known as "imams," which means "leaders."

Shinto Japan's official religion; it promoted the state and the emperor's divinity. The term means "the way of the gods."

shoguns Japanese military commanders. From 1192 to 1333, the Kamakura shoguns served as military "protectors" of the ruler in the city of Heian.

Shotoku Prince in the early Japanese Yamoto state (574–622 CE) who is credited with having introduced Buddhism to Japan.

shudras Literally, "small ones"; workers and slaves from outside the Vedic lineage.

Siddhartha Gautama Another name for the Buddha, the most prominent opponent of the Brahman way of life. He lived from 563 to 483 BCE and developed methods for overcoming life's suffering and achieving a state of grace, or nirvana.

Sikhism Islamic-inspired religion that calls on its followers to renounce the caste system and to treat all believers as equal before God.

Silicon Valley Valley between the California cities of San Francisco and San Jose, known for its innovative computer and high-technology industries.

silk Luxury textile that became a vastly popular export from China (via the Silk Road) to the cities of the Roman world.

Silk Road A series of trade routes linking China with central Asia and the Mediterranean; it extended over 5,000 miles, land and sea included, and was so named because of the quantities of silk that were traded along it. The Silk Road was a major factor in the development of cultures in China, Egypt, Persia, India, and even Europe.

Silla One of three independent Korean states that may have emerged as early as the third century BCE. These states lasted until 668 CE, when Silla took control over the entire peninsula.

Silver Islands Term used by European merchants in the sixteenth century to refer to Japan because of its substantial trade in silver with China.

Sino-Japanese War (1894–1895) Conflict over the control of Korea in which China was forced to cede the province of Taiwan to Japan.

Sipahi The Persian word for "cavalryman." *Sipahis* were expected to provide military service to the Ottoman Empire.

Siva The third of three Vedic deities, signifying destruction. *See also* Brahma *and* Vishnu.

slave plantations System whereby enslaved labor was used for the cultivation of crops to be sold for profit. Slave plantations were a crucial part of the growth of the Mediterranean economy.

small seal script Unified script that was used to the exclusion of other scripts under the Qin, with the aim of centralizing administration. Its use led to a less complicated style of clerical writing than had been in use under the Han.

social contract The idea, drawn from the works of the English writer John Locke, that all governments come into existence through agreements made between rulers and peoples; if a ruler violates those agreements, Locke argued, the people have the right to rebel.

Social Darwinism Belief that Charles Darwin's theory of evolution is applicable to humans and justifies the right of the ruling classes or countries to dominate the weak.

social hierarchies Distinctions between the privileged and the less privileged.

socialism Political ideology that calls for a classless society with collective ownership of all property.

Social Security Act (1935) New Deal act that instituted old-age pensions and insurance for the unemployed.

Socrates (469–399 BCE) Philosopher in Athens who encouraged people to reflect on ethics and morality. He stressed the importance of honor and integrity as opposed to wealth and power. Plato was his student.

Sogdians A people who lived in central Asia's commercial centers and maintained the stability and accessibility of the Silk Road. They were crucial to the interconnectedness of the Afro-Eurasian landmass.

Solidarity The communist bloc's first independent trade union, established in Poland at the Gdansk shipyard in 1980.

Song dynasty Chinese dynasty that took over the mandate of heaven for three centuries starting in 976 CE. It ruled an era of many economic and political successes but eventually lost northern China to nomadic tribes.

Song porcelain Type of ceramics perfected during the Song period that was translucent and delicate but also durable.

South African War (1899–1902) Conflict between the British and Afrikaner colonists of South Africa that resulted in bringing two Afrikaner republics under the control of the British; often called the Boer War.

Soviet bloc International alliance that included the east European countries of the Warsaw Pact as well as the Soviet Union but also came to include Cuba.

Spanish-American War (1898) War between the United States and Spain in Cuba, Puerto Rico, and the Philippines. It ended with a treaty in which the United States took over the Philippines, Guam, and Puerto Rico; Cuba won partial independence.

speciation The formation of different species.

specie Money in coin.

species Group of animals or plants possessing one or more distinctive characteristics and able to exchange genes and interbreed.

Spring and Autumn period Period between the eighth and fifth centuries BCE, during which China was ruled by the feudal system. Considered an anarchic and turbulent time, there were 148 different tributary states in this period.

Stalin, Joseph (1878–1953) Leader of the Communist Party and the Soviet Union. Stalin sought to create "socialism in one country."

St. Bartholomew's Day Massacre (1572) Roman Catholic massacre of French Protestants in Paris.

steel A metal more malleable and stronger than iron that became essential for industries like shipbuilding and railways.

stoicism Widespread philosophical movement initiated by Zeno (334–262 BCE). Zeno and his followers sought to understand the role of people in relation to the cosmos. For the Stoics, everything was grounded in nature. Being in love with nature and living a good life required being in control of one's passions and thus indifferent to pleasure or pain.

St. Patrick Former slave brought to Ireland from Briton who later became a missionary. Known as the "Apostle of Ireland," he died in 470 CE.

Strait of Malacca Seagoing gateway to Southeast and East Asia.

Strategic Defense Initiative ("Star Wars") Master plan, championed by U.S. president Ronald Reagan in the 1980s, that envisions the deployment of satellites and space missiles to protect the United States from incoming nuclear bombs.

stupa Dome monument marking the burial site of relics of the Buddha.

Suez Canal Channel completed in 1869 across the Isthmus of Suez to connect the Mediterranean Sea with the Red Sea and to lower the costs of international trade.

Sufi brotherhoods Mystics within Islam who were responsible for the expansion of Islam into many regions of the world.

Sufism Emotional and mystical form of Islam that appealed to the common people.

sultan Islamic political leader. In the Ottoman Empire, the sultan combined a warrior ethos with an unwavering devotion to Islam.

Sumerian King List Text that recounts the making of Sumerian political dynasties. Recorded around 2000 BCE, it organizes the reigns of kings by dynasty, one city at a time.

Sumerian pantheon The Sumerian gods, each of whom had a home in a particular floodplain city. In the Sumerian belief system, both gods and the natural forces they controlled had to be revered.

Sumerian temples Homes of the gods and symbols of Sumerian imperial identity. Sumerian temples also represented the gods' ability to hoard wealth at sites where people exchanged goods and services. In addition, temples distinguished the urban from the rural world.

Sunnis The majority sect of Islam, Sunnis originally supported the succession of Abu Bakr over Ali and supported the rule of consensus rather than family

lineage for the succession to the Islamic caliphate. *See also* Shiites.

Sun Yat-sen (1866–1925) Chinese revolutionary and founder of the Nationalist Party in China.

superior man In the Confucian view, a person of perfected moral character, fit to be a leader.

superpowers Label applied to the United States and the Soviet Union after World War II because of their size, their possession of the atomic bomb, and the fact that each embodied a model of civilization (capitalism or communism) applicable to the whole world.

supranational organizations International organizations such as nongovernmental organizations (NGOs), the World Bank, and the International Monetary Fund (IMF).

survival of the fittest Charles Darwin's belief that as species grow and resources become scarce, a struggle for existence arises, the outcome of which is that only the "fittest" survive.

Suryavansha The second lineage of two (the solar one) in Vedic society. *See* Chandravamsha.

Swadeshi movement Voluntary organizations in India that championed the creation of indigenous manufacturing enterprises and schools of nationalist thought in order to gain autonomy from Britain.

syndicalism A political and economic system, elaborated by the French social philosopher Georges Sorel (1847–1922), that sought to replace capitalism with a workplace organization that included unskilled laborers.

tabula rasa Term used by John Locke to describe the human mind before it begins to acquire ideas from experience; Latin for "clean slate."

Taiping Heavenly Kingdom (Heavenly Kingdom of Great Peace) Religious sect established by the Chinese prophet Hong Xiuquan in the mid-nineteenth century. Hong Xiuquan believed that he was Jesus's younger brother. The group struggled to rid the world of evil and "restore" the heavenly kingdom, imagined as a just and egalitarian order.

Taiping Rebellion Rebellion by followers of Hong Xiuquan and the Taiping Heavenly Kingdom against the Qing

government over the economic and social turmoil caused by the Opium War. Despite an army of 100,000 rebels, the rebellion was crushed.

Taj Mahal Royal palace of the Mughal Empire, built by Shah Jahan in the seventeenth century in homage to his wife, Mumtaz Mahal.

Tale of Genji Japanese work written by Lady Murasaki that gives vivid accounts of Heian court life; Japan's first novel (early eleventh century).

talking cures Psychological practice developed by Sigmund Freud whereby the symptoms of neurotic and traumatized patients would decrease after regular periods of thoughtful discussion.

Talmud Huge volumes of oral commentary on Jewish law eventually compiled in two versions, the Palestinian and the Babylonian, in the fifth and sixth centuries BCE.

Talmud of Jerusalem Codified written volumes of the traditions of Judaism, produced by the rabbis of Galilee around 400 CE.

Tang dynasty (608–907 CE) Regime that promoted a cosmopolitan culture, turning China into the hub of East Asian cultural integration, while expanding the borders of their empire. To govern such a diverse empire, the Tang established a political culture and civil service based on Confucian teachings. Candidates for the civil service were required to take examinations, the first of their kind in the world.

Tanzimat Reorganization period of the Ottoman Empire in the mid-nineteenth century. Modernizing reforms affected the military, trade, foreign relations, and civilian life.

tappers Rubber workers in Brazil, mostly either Indian or mixed-blood people.

Tarascans Mesoamerican society of the 1400s, rivals to and sometimes subjects of the Aztecs.

Tecumseh (1768–1813) Shawnee who circulated Tenskwatawa's message of Indian renaissance among Indian villages from the Great Lakes to the Gulf Coast. He preached the need for Indian unity, insisting that Indians resist any American attempts to get them to sell more land. In response, thousands of followers renounced their ties to colonial ways and prepared to combat the expansion of the United States.

tekkes Schools that taught devotional strategies and the religious knowledge that students needed to enter Sufi orders and become masters of the brotherhood.

temple Building where believers worshipped their gods and goddesses and where some peoples believed the deities had earthly residence.

Tenskwatawa (1775–1836) Shawnee prophet who urged disciples to abstain from alcohol and return to traditional customs, reducing dependence on European trade goods and severing connections to Christian missionaries. His message spread to other tribes, raising the specter of a pan-Indian confederacy.

Teotihuacán City-state in a large, mountainous valley in what is modern-day Mexico; the first major community to emerge after the Olmecs.

territorial state Political form that emerged in the river-basin cities of Mesopotamia, which was overwhelmed by the displacement of nomadic peoples. These states were kingdoms organized around charismatic rulers who headed large households; each had a defined physical border.

Third Estate The French people minus the clergy and the aristocracy; this term was popularized after 1789 and used to claim power for nonelite people during the French Revolution.

Third Reich The German state from 1933 to 1945 under Adolf Hitler.

Third World Nations of the world, mostly in Asia, Latin America, and Africa, that were not highly industrialized like First World nations or tied to the Soviet bloc (the Second World).

Thirty Years' War (1618–1648) Conflict between Protestants and Catholics in the Holy Roman Empire that escalated into a general European war.

Tiananmen Square Largest public square in the world and site of the pro-democracy movement in 1989 that resulted in the killing of as many as a thousand protesters by the Chinese army.

tiers-monde Term meaning "Third World," coined by French intellectuals to describe countries seeking a "third way" between Soviet communism and western capitalism.

Tiglath Pileser III Assyrian ruler from 745 to 728 BCE who introduced a standing army and instituted reforms that changed the administrative and social structure of the empire to make it more efficient.

Tiwanaku Another name for Tihuanaco, the first great Andean polity, on the shores of Lake Titicaca.

Tlaxcalans Mesoamerican society of the 1400s; these people were enemies of the powerful Aztec Empire.

Tokugawa shogunate Hereditary military administration founded in 1603 that ruled Japan while keeping the emperor as a figurehead; it was toppled in 1868 by reformers who felt that Japan should adopt, not reject, Western influences.

Toltecs A Mesoamerican people who, by 1000 CE, had filled the political vacuum created by the decline of the city of Teotihuacán.

tomb culture Warlike group from northeast Asia who arrived by sea in the middle of the third century CE and imposed their military and social power on southern Japan. These conquerors are known today as the "tomb culture" because of their elevated necropolises near present-day Osaka.

Topkapi Palace Political headquarters of the Ottoman Empire, located in Istanbul.

total war All-out war involving civilian populations as well as military forces, often used in reference to World War II.

transhumant herders Nomads who entered settled territories in the second millennium BCE and moved their herds seasonally when resources became scarce.

Trans-Siberian Railroad Railroad built over very difficult terrain between 1891 and 1903 and subsequently expanded. It created an overland bridge for troops, peasant settlers, and commodities to move between Europe and the Pacific.

Treaty of Brest-Litovsk (1918) Separate peace treaty between imperial Germany and the new Bolshevik regime in Russia. The treaty acknowledged the German victory on the Eastern Front and took Russia out of the war.

Treaty of Nanjing (1842) Treaty between China and Britain following the First Opium War; it called for indemnities, the opening of new ports, and the cession of Hong Kong to the British.

Treaty of Tordesillas (1494) Treaty in which the pope decreed that the non-European world would be divided into spheres of trade and missionary responsibility between Spain and Portugal.

trickle trade Also called "down the line trade," a method by which a good is passed from one village to another, as in the case of obsidian among early farming villages. The practice began around 7000 BCE.

Tripartite Pact (1940) Pact that stated that Germany, Italy, and Japan would act together in all future military ventures.

Triple Entente Alliance developed before World War I that eventually included Britain, France, and Russia.

Troy Important site founded around 3000 BCE in Anatolia, to the far west. Troy is legendary as the site of the war that was launched by the Greeks (the Achaeans) and that was recounted by Homer in the *Iliad*.

Truman Doctrine (1947) Declaration promising U.S. economic and military intervention, whenever and wherever needed, for the sake of preventing communist expansion.

Truth and Reconciliation Commission Quasi-judicial body established after the overthrow of the apartheid system in South Africa and the election of Nelson Mandela as the country's first black president in 1994. The commission was to gather evidence about crimes committed during the apartheid years. Those who showed remorse for their actions could appeal for clemency. The South African leaders believed that an airing of the grievances from this period would promote racial harmony and reconciliation. Other countries suffering from traumatic political, ethnic, and cultural events have adopted the South African experiment and established their own truth and reconciliation commissions.

truth commissions Elected officials' inquiries into human rights abuses by previous regimes. In Argentina, El Salvador, Guatemala, and South Africa, these commissions were vital for creating a new aura of legitimacy for democracies and for promising to uphold the rights of individuals.

tsar/czar Russian word derived from the Latin *Caesar* to refer to the Russian ruler of Kiev and eventually to all rulers in Russia.

Tula Toltec capital city, a commercial hub and political and ceremonial center.

Uitlanders British populations living in Afrikaner republics; they were denied voting rights and subject to other forms of discrimination in the late nineteenth century. The term means "outsiders."

ulama Arabic word that means "learned ones" or "scholars"; used for those who devoted themselves to knowledge of Islamic sciences.

Umayyads Family who founded the first dynasty in Islam. They established family rule and dynastic succession to the role of caliph. The first Umayyad caliph established Damascus as his capital and was named Mu'awiya ibn Abi Sufyan.

umma Arabic word for "community"; used to refer to the "Islamic people" or "Islamic community."

Universal Declaration of Human Rights (1948) UN declaration that laid out the rights to which all human beings are entitled.

universalizing religions Universal religions that are proselytized by energetic and charismatic missionaries, that foster a deep sense of community felt by their converts, and that are supported by powerful empires.

universal religions Religions that appeal to diverse populations, that are easily adaptable across various cultural and geographical areas, and that promote universal rules and principles to guide behavior that transcend place, time, and specific cultural practices.

universitas Term used from the end of the twelfth century to denote scholars who came together, first in Paris. The term is borrowed from the merchant communities, where it denoted the equivalent of the modern "union."

Untouchables Caste in the Indian system whose jobs, usually in the more unsanitary aspects of urban life, rendered them "ritually and spiritually" impure.

Upanishads Vedic wisdom literature collected in the first half of the first millennium BCE. It took the form of dialogues between disciples and a sage.

urban-rural divide Division between those living in cities and those living in rural areas. One of history's most durable worldwide distinctions, the urban-rural divide eventually encompassed the globe. Where cities arose, communities adopted lifestyles based on the large-scale production of goods and on specialized labor. Those living in the countryside remained close to nature, cultivating the land or tending livestock. They diversified their labor and exchanged their grains and animal products for necessities available in urban centers.

utopian socialism The most visionary of all Restoration-era movements. Utopian socialists like Charles Fourier dreamed of transforming states, workplaces, and human relations, not through bloody revolution but through the wholesale reorganization of society.

Vaishyas Householders or lesser clan members in Vedic society who worked the land and tended livestock.

Vardhamana Mahavira Advocate of Jainism who lived from 540 to 468 BCE; he emphasized interpretation of the Upanishads to govern and guide daily life.

varna Caste system established by the Vedas in 600 BCE.

vassal states Subordinate states that had to pay tribute in luxury goods, raw materials, and labor as part of a broad confederation of polities under the kings' protection.

Vedas Rhymes, hymns, and explanatory texts composed by Aryan priests; the Vedas became their most holy scripture and part of their religious rituals. The Vedas were initially passed down orally, in Sanskrit. Brahmans, priests of Vedic culture, incorporated the texts into ritual and society. The Vedas are considered the final authority of Hinduism.

Vedic people People who came from the steppes of Inner Asia around 1500 BCE and entered the fertile lowlands of the Indus River basin, gradually moving as far south as the Deccan plateau. They called themselves Aryan, which means

"respected ones," and spoke Sanskrit, an Indo-European language.

veiling Practice of modest dress, including covering the hair and much of the face, required of respectable women in the Assyrian Empire, introduced by Assyrian authorities in the thirteenth century BCE.

Venus figures Representations of the goddess of fertility drawn on the Chauvet Cave in southeastern France. Discovered in 1994, they are probably about 35,000 years old.

Versailles Conference (1919) International peace conference at the end of World War I intended to shape the future of the world after the war. Delegates decided on the principles that would shape the resultant five peace treaties, one for each of the Central Powers (the most well-known of these is the Treaty of Versailles, which forced Germany to pay reparations, admit responsibility for the war, and give up its colonies). The Soviet Union, which had already made peace with the Central Powers, was not invited to this conference.

Viet Cong Vietnamese communist group committed to overthrowing the government of South Vietnam and reunifying North and South Vietnam.

Viet Minh Group founded in 1941 by Ho Chi Minh to oppose the Japanese occupation of Indochina; it later fought the French colonial forces for independence. Also known as the Vietnamese Independent League.

Vietnam War (1955–1975) Conflict that resulted from concern over the spread of communism in Southeast Asia. The United States intervened on the side of South Vietnam in its struggle against peasant-supported Viet Cong guerrilla forces, who wanted to reunite Vietnam under a communist regime. Faced with antiwar opposition at home and ferocious resistance from the Vietnamese, American troops withdrew in 1973; the puppet South Vietnamese government collapsed two years later.

Vikings A people from Scandinavia who replaced the Franks as the dominant warrior class in northern Europe in the ninth century CE. They used their superior ships to loot other seagoing peoples and sailed up the rivers of central Russia to establish a trade route that connected

Scandinavia and the Baltic with Constantinople and Baghdad. The Vikings established settlements in Iceland and Greenland and, briefly, North America.

Vishnu The second of three Vedic deities, signifying existence. *See also* Brahma *and* Siva.

viziers Bureaucrats of the Ottoman Empire.

vodun Mixed religion of African and Christian customs practiced by slaves and free blacks in the colony of Saint Domingue.

Voting Rights Act (1965) Law that granted universal suffrage in the United States.

Wafd Nationalist party that came into existence during a rebellion in Egypt in 1919 and held power sporadically after Egypt was granted limited independence from Britain in 1922.

Wahhabism Eighteenth-century reform movement organized by Muhammad Ibn abd al-Wahhab, who preached the absolute oneness of Allah and a return to the pure Islam of Muhammad.

Wang Mang Han minister who usurped the throne in 9 CE because he believed that the Han had lost the mandate of heaven. He ruled until 23 CE.

war ethos Strong social commitment to a continuous state of war. The Roman army constantly drafted men and engaged in annual spring military campaigns. Soldiers were taught to embrace a sense of honor that did not allow them to accept defeat and, their leaders commended those who repeatedly threw themselves into battle.

War of 1812 Conflict between Britain and the United States arising from U.S. grievances over oppressive British maritime practices in the Napoleonic Wars.

War on Poverty President Lyndon Johnson's push for an increased range of social programs and increased spending on Social Security, health, education, and assistance for the disabled.

Warring States period Period extending from the fifth century BCE to 221 BCE, when the regional warring states were unified by the Qin dynasty.

Warsaw Pact (1955–1991) Military alliance between the Soviet Union and other communist states that was established in response to the creation of the NATO alliance.

Weimar Republic (1919–1933) Constitutional republic of Germany that was subverted by Hitler soon after he became chancellor.

Western Front Military front that stretched from the English Channel through Belgium and France to the Alps during World War I.

White and Blue Niles The two main branches of the Nile, rising out of central Africa and Ethiopia. They come together at the present-day capital city of Sudan, Khartoum.

White Lotus Rebellion Series of uprisings in northern China (1790–1800s) inspired by mystical beliefs in folk Buddhism and, at times, the idea of restoring the Ming dynasty.

Whites "Counterrevolutionaries" of the Bolshevik Revolution (1918–1921) who fought the Bolsheviks (the "Reds"); included former supporters of the tsar, Social Democrats, and large independent peasant armies.

White Wolf Mysterious militia leader, depicted in popular myth as a Chinese Robin Hood whose mission was to rid the country of the injustices of Yuan Shikai's government in the early years of the Chinese Republic (1910s).

wokou Supposedly Japanese pirates, many of whom were actually Chinese subjects of the Ming dynasty.

Works Progress Administration (WPA) New Deal program instituted in 1935 that put nearly 3 million people to work building roads, bridges, airports, and post offices.

World Bank International agency established in 1944 to provide economic assistance to war-torn and poor countries. Its formal title is the International Bank for Reconstruction and Development.

World War II (1939–1945) Worldwide war that began in September 1939 in Europe and pitted Britain, the United States, and the Soviet Union (the Allies) against Nazi Germany, Japan, and Italy (the Axis).

Wu or Wudi Chinese leader known as the "Martial Emperor" because of his many military campaigns during the Han dynasty. He reigned from 141 to 87 BCE.

Wu Zhao Chinese empress who lived from 626 to 706 CE. She began as a concubine in the court of Li Shimin and became the mother of his son's child. She eventually gained power equal to that of the emperor, and she named herself regent when she finagled a place for one of her own sons after their father's death.

Xiongnu The most powerful and intrusive of the nomadic peoples, originally pastoralists from the eastern part of the Asian steppe in what is modern-day Mongolia. They appeared along the frontier with China in the late Zhou dynasty and by the third century BCE had become the most powerful of all the pastoral communities in that area.

Xunzi Confucian moralist whose ideas were influential to Qin rulers. He lived from 310 to 237 BCE and believed that rational statecraft was more reliable than fickle human nature and that strict laws and severe punishments could create stability in society.

Yalta Accords Results of the meeting in February 1945 in the Crimean city of Yalta between President Roosevelt, Prime Minister Churchill, and Premier Stalin; the meeting was held to plan for the postwar order.

Yavana kings Sanskrit name for Greek rulers, derived from the Greek name for the area of western Asia Minor called Ionia, a term that then extended to anyone who spoke Greek or came from the Mediterranean.

yellow press Newspapers that seek a mass circulation by featuring sensationalist reporting.

Yellow Turbans One of several local Chinese religious movements that emerged across the empire, especially under Wang Mang's officials, who considered him a usurper. The Yellow Turbans, so called because of the yellow scarves they wore around their heads, were Daoist millenarians.

Yin City that became the capital of the Shang in 1350 BCE, ushering in a golden age.

Young Egypt Antiliberal, fascist group that gained a large following in Egypt during the 1930s.

Young Italy Nineteenth-century nationalist organization made up of young students and intellectuals, devoted to the unification and renewal of the Italian state.

Yuan dynasty Dynasty established by the Mongols after the defeat of the Song. The Yuan dynasty was strong from 1280 to 1368; its capital was at Dadu, or modern-day Beijing.

Yuan Mongols Mongol rulers of China who were overthrown by the Ming dynasty in 1368.

Yuezhi A Turkic nomadic people who roamed on pastoral lands to the west of the Xiongnu territory of central Mongolia. They had friendly relationships with the farming societies in China, but the Yuezhi detested the Xiongnu and had frequent armed clashes with them.

zaibatsu Large-scale, family-owned corporations in Japan consisting of factories, import-export businesses, and banks that dominated the Japanese economy until 1945.

zamindars Archaic tax system of the Mughal Empire, where decentralized lords collected tribute for the emperor from peasants working on their estates.

Zapatistas Group of indigenous rebels that rose up against the Mexican government in 1994 and drew inspiration from an earlier Mexican rebel, Emiliano Zapata.

Zheng King during the Qin era who defeated what was left of the Warring States between 230 and 221 BCE. He assumed the mandate of heaven from the Zhou and declared himself First August Emperor, to distinguish himself from other kings.

Zheng He (1371–1433) Ming naval leader who established tributary relations with Southeast Asia, Indian Ocean ports, the Persian Gulf, and the east coast of Africa.

Zhongguo Term originating in the ancient period and subsequently used to emphasize the central cultural and geographical location of China in the world; means "Middle Kingdom."

Zhong Shang Administrative central complex of the Shang.

ziggurat The stepped platform base of a Sumerian temple. By the end of the third millennium BCE, the elevated platform base had transformed into the stepped platform.

Zionism Movement advocating the reestablishment of a Jewish homeland in Palestine.

Zoroaster Greek name for the Persian religious reformer known as Zarathustra, thought to have been a teacher around 1000 BCE in eastern Iran and credited with having solidified the region's religious beliefs into a unified system that moved away from animistic nomadic beliefs. The main source for his teachings is a compilation called the Avesta.

Zoroastrianism Dominant religion of the Persian Empire, based on the teachings of Zoroaster.

Zulus African tribe that, under Shaka, created a ruthless warrior state in southern Africa in the early 1800s.

CREDITS

CHAPTER 1

Photo Credits Page 2: Erich Lessing/ Art Resource, NY; p. 7: Volker Steger/Science Source; p. 8: Robert Preston Photography/Alamy Stock Photo; p. 11 (left): AP Photo/Ricardo Lopez; p. 11 (right): University Of The Witwatersrand/Barcroft Media via Getty Images; p. 11 (bottom): Kenneth Garrett/National Geographic Creative; p. 12 (top): John Reader/ Science Source; p. 12 (bottom): Staffan Widstrand/Getty Images; p. 13: Pascal Goetgheluck/Science Source; p. 15: Lionel Bret/Science Source; p. 18: John Reader/Science Source; p. 20: Images of Africa Photobank/Alamy Stock Photo; p. 22 (left): French Ministry of Culture and Communication, Regional Direction for Cultural Affairs–Rhône-Alpes Region– Regional Department of Archaeology; p. 22 (right): French Ministry of Culture and Communication, Regional Direction for Cultural Affairs–Rhône-Alpes Region–Regional Department of Archaeology; p. 23: Imagno/Getty Images; p. 25: Erich Lessing/Art Resource, NY; p. 30 (left): Werner Forman/Universal Images Group/Getty Images; p. 30 (right): Universal Images Group North America LLC/DeAgostini/Alamy Stock Photo; p. 31 (top): Bruce Smith, The Emergence of Agriculture (New York: Diane Publishing Company, 1998), p. 104; p. 31 (bottom): Head of the Mayan corn god, Oaxaca, c. 500 AD (earthenware), Mayan/Private Collection/Photo © Boltin Picture Library/Bridgeman Images; p. 39: Images & Stories/ Alamy Stock Photo.

Text Credits Page 5: From *Sources of Indian Tradition 2nd Ed.*, Vol. 1: From the Beginning to 1800, edited and revised by Ainslie T. Embree, pp. 18–19. Copyright © 1988 Columbia University Press. Reprinted with permission of the publisher; p. 21: Richard B. Lee, Irven DeVore & Jill Nash, "Problems in the Study of Hunters and Gatherers," from *Man the Hunter*, pp. 3 & 5. Copyright © 1968 by Aldine Publishers. Reprinted by permission of Aldine Publishing, a division of Transaction Publishers; p. 32: Excerpt from "Popol Vuh" originally published in Adrian Recinos, *Popol Vuh: The Sacred Book of the Ancient Quiché Maya*, translated by Delia Goetz and Sylvanus G. Morley. Copyright © 1950, 1978 University of Oklahoma Press. Reprinted by permission of the publisher; p. 38: "The Milky Way," from *Mother Nature: A History of Mothers, Infants, and Natural Selection* by Sarah Blaffer Hrdy, copyright © 1999 by Sarah Blaffer Hrdy. Used by permission of Pantheon Books, an imprint of the Knopf Doubleday Publishing Group, a division of Penguin Random House LLC and by permission of Curtis Brown, Ltd.

CHAPTER 2

Photo Credits Page 42: The Trustees of the British Museum/Bridgeman Images; p. 44: © Balage Balogh/Art Resource, NY; p. 49: Granger, NYC— All rights reserved; p. 51: Peter Bull Art Studio; p. 52: Dean Conger/Getty Images; p. 53 (left): © The Trustees of the British Museum/Art Resource, NY; p. 53 (right): University of Pennsylvania Museum of Archaeology and Anthropology; p. 55: University of Pennsylvania Museum of Archaeology and Anthropology; p. 56 (top): © The Trustees of the British Museum/Art Resource, NY; p. 56 (bottom): Scala/Art Resource, NY; p. 58: National Geographic Creative/ Alamy Stock Photo; p. 61 (left): Arco Images GmbH/Alamy Stock Photo; p. 61 (right): S. VANNINI/De Agostini/Getty Images; p. 61 (bottom): Ivy Close Images/Alamy Stock Photo; p. 63 (left): Scala/Art Resource, NY; p. 63 (right): Alessandro Vannini/Corbis/ Getty Images; p. 66: robertharding/ Alamy Stock Photo; p. 68 (left): Borromeo/Art Resource, NY; p. 68 (right): © RMN-Grand Palais/Art Resource, NY; p. 70 (top): Martha Avery/Getty Images; p. 70 (bottom): HIP/Art Resource, NY; p. 71: Granger, NYC—All rights reserved; p. 75: Eric and David Hosking/Getty Images; p. 76: robertharding/Alamy Stock Photo; p. 77 (left): akg-images/ De Agostini Picture Lib./G. Dagli Orti; p. 77 (right): Album/Art Resource, NY; p. 78: Museum of Archaeology, Varna.

Text Credits Page 55: "Enmerkar and the lord of Aratta: translation," from *The Electronic Text Corpus of Sumerian Literature* (http://etcsl.orinst.ox.ac.uk/), Oxford 1998–2006. Copyright © J.A. Black, G. Cunningham, E. Robson, and G. Zólyomi 1998, 1999, 2000; J.A. Black, G. Cunningham, E. Flückiger-Hawker, E. Robson, J. Taylor, and G. Zólyomi 2001; J.A. Black, G. Cunningham, J. Ebeling, E. Robson, J. Taylor, and G. Zólyomi 2002, 2003, 2004, 2005; G. Cunningham, J. Ebeling, E. Robson, and G. Zólyomi 2006. The authors have asserted their moral rights. Reprinted by permission of Faculty of Oriental Studies, University of Oxford; p. 64: James B. Pritchard (ed.), "The Admonitions of Ipu-wer." From *Ancient Near Eastern Texts Relating to the Old Testament—Third Edition with Supplement.* © 1950, 1955, 1969, renewed 1978 by Princeton University Press. Reprinted by permission of Princeton University Press; p. 67: Shereen Ratnagar, from *Understanding Harappa: Civilization in the Greater Indus Valley* (New Delhi: Tulika Publishers, 2001), pp. 60–62. Reprinted by permission of Shereen Ratnagar; p. 73: Kwang-chih Chang, "Archaeological Evidence for Longshan Culture" from *The Archaeology of Ancient China*, 4th ed. (New Haven: Yale University Press, 1986), pp. 287–88. Copyright © 1986 Yale University Press. Reprinted by permission of Yale University Press.

CHAPTER 3

Photo Credits Page 82: Scala/Art Resource, NY; p. 85 (left): © The Trustees of the British Museum/Art Resource, NY; p. 85 (right): JTB MEDIA CREATION, Inc./Alamy Stock Photo; p. 85 (bottom): Scala/Art Resource, NY; p. 90

Coins" http://www.forumancientcoins.com/moonmoth/ancientcoins.html; p. 220: David Gurr/Corbis Documentary/Getty Images; p. 221 (left): Gift of Muneichi Nitta, 2003 © The Metropolitan Museum of Art; p. 221 (right): Purchase, Enid A. Haupt Gift, 1979 © The Metropolitan Museum of Art; p. 226: Photo by Xinru Liu; p. 228: Dagli Orti/REX/Shutterstock; p. 229: Dagli Orti/REX/Shutterstock; p. 230: Bruno Morandi/robertharding/Getty Images; p. 231: NASA/JPL.

Text Credits Page 214: Romila Thapar, from *Aśoka and the Decline of the Mauryas*, 2nd Ed., pp. 255–57. Reproduced with permission of Oxford University Press India © Oxford University Press 1997.

CHAPTER 7

Photo Credits Page 236: Erich Lessing/Art Resource, NY; p. 241 (top): Snark/Art Resource, NY; p. 241 (bottom left): © The Trustees of the British Museum/Art Resource, NY; p. 241 (bottom right): National Library of China; p. 243 (top): Terracotta Army, Qin Dynasty, 210 BC (terracotta), Chinese School, (3rd century BC)/Tomb of Qin shi Huang Di, Xianyang, China/Bridgeman Images; p. 243 (bottom): Louis Mazzatenta/National Geographic Image Collection; p. 246: Emperor Wu Ti (156–87 BC, r. 141–87 BC) welcoming a man of letters, from a history of Chinese emperors (colour on silk), Chinese School, (17th century)/Bibliotheque Nationale, Paris, France/Bridgeman Images; p. 247: © The Trustees of the British Museum/Art Resource, NY; p. 249: Model of House, Chinese. 1st century C.E., Eastern Han Dynasty (25–220 C.E.). Earthenware with unfired coloring, 52 x 33 1/2 x 27 inches (132.1 x 85.1 x 68.6 cm). The Nelson-Atkins Museum of Art, Kansas City, Missouri. Purchase: Nelson Trust, 33-521. Photograph by Jamison Miller; p. 250 (left): DEA PICTURE LIBRARY/Getty Images; p. 250 (right): Martha Avery/Corbis/Getty Images; p. 250 (bottom): Martha Avery/Corbis/Getty Images; p. 251: Erich Lessing/Art Resource, NY; p. 252 (top): Aflo Co. Ltd./Alamy Stock Photo; p. 252 (bottom): Charles K. Edmunds/National Geographic Creative; p. 254: The Art Archive/REX/Shutterstock; p. 255:

Bridgeman-Giraudon/Art Resource, NY; p. 259: Purchase, Mary Livingston Griggs and Mary Griggs Burke Foundation Gift, 2002 © The Metropolitan Museum of Art; p. 260: © Vanni Archive/Art Resource, NY; p. 261: robertharding/Alamy Stock Photo; p. 262 (top): Dagli Orti/REX/Shutterstock; p. 262 (bottom:) Atlantide Phototravel/Getty Images; p. 263 (top): Museo Arqueológico, Sevilla, Spain; p. 263 (bottom): Bridgeman-Giraudon/Art Resource, NY; p. 265 (left): Lyubov Timofeyeva/Shutterstock; p. 265 (right): Scala/Art Resource; p. 267: Andrea Pistolesi/Getty Images; p. 271: © The Trustees of the British Museum/Art Resource, NY; p. 273: Erich Lessing/Art Resource, NY.

Text Credits Page 242: "Memorial on the Burning of Books" from *Sources of Chinese Tradition 2nd Ed., Vol. 1: From Earliest Times to 1600*, edited by Wm. Theodore de Bary and Irene Bloom, pp. 209–210. Copyright © 1999 Columbia University Press. Reprinted with permission of the publisher; p. 244: Jia Yi, "Faults of the Qin," from *Sources of Chinese Tradition 2nd Ed., Vol. 1: From Earliest Times to 1600*, edited by Wm. Theodore de Bary and Irene Bloom, pp. 229–230. Copyright © 1999 Columbia University Press. Reprinted with permission of the publisher; p. 248: Dong Zhongshu, "The Responsibilities of Han Rulership," from *Sources of Chinese Tradition 2nd Ed., Vol. 1: From Earliest Times to 1600*, edited by Wm. Theodore de Bary and Irene Bloom, pp. 299–300. Copyright © 1999 Columbia University Press. Reprinted with permission of the publisher; p. 264: Julián González, "The Lex Irnitana: A New Copy of the Flavian Municipal Law", from *Journal of Roman Studies*, Vol. 76 (1986). Reprinted with permission of the Society for the Promotion of Roman Studies.

CHAPTER 8

Photo Credits Page 276: age fotostock/Alamy Stock Photo; p. 278: © RMN-Grand Palais/Art Resource, NY; p. 279 (left): Scala/Art Resource, NY; p. 279 (right): Granger, NYC—All rights reserved; p. 283 (left): The Jewish Museum, New York/Art Resource, NY; p. 283 (right): Tetra Images RF/Getty Images; p. 284: Bettmann/Getty Images; p. 286: Scala/

Art Resource, NY; p. 288: © The Egypt Exploration Society; p. 291 (left): Dagli Orti/REX/Shutterstock; p. 291 (right): Dagli Orti/REX/Shutterstock; p. 291 (bottom): Mehmet Cetin/Shutterstock; p. 293: Detail of the Roman Emperor Philip the Arab kneeling before Shapur II, Naqsh-e Rostam (photo)/Naqsh-e Rostam, Iran/© Julian Chichester/Bridgeman Images; p. 294 (top): Scala/Art Resource, NY; p. 294 (bottom): © The Trustees of the British Museum/Art Resource, NY; p. 295: British Library, London, Stein Collection; p. 296: Dean Conger/Getty Images; p. 298 (top): The Trustees of the British Museum/Art Resource, NY; p. 298 (bottom): Forman Archive/REX/Shutterstock; p. 299: bpk Bildagentur/Museum fuer Asiatische Kunst, Staatliche Museen, Berlin, Germany/Iris Papadopoulous/Art Resource, NY; p. 300: SEF/Art Resource, NY; p. 304 (left): dbimages/Alamy Stock Photo; p. 304 (right): China Images/Alamy Stock Photo; p. 305: The Collection of National Palace Museum; p. 309 (top): Dagli Orti/REX/Shutterstock; p. 309 (bottom): age fotostock/Alamy Stock Photo; p. 311: Angelo Hornak/Getty Images; p. 312 (top): Werner Forman/Art Resource, NY; p. 312 (bottom): Mayan pictograms representing the months of the year (ink) (b/w photo), French School, (20th century)/Musee de l'Homme, Paris, France/Bridgeman Images.

Text Credits Page 289: Charles H. Cosgrove, "P. Oxy 1786" from *An Ancient Christian Hymn with Musical Notation* (Tübingen, Germany: Mohr Siebeck, 2011). Notation and Greek lyrics reprinted by permission of Mohr Siebeck, Tübingen. English translation by Brent Shaw.

CHAPTER 9

Photo Credits Page 316: Patrick Ward/Corbis/VCG/Getty Images; p. 319: SUHAIB SALEM/REUTERS/Newscom; p. 321: Erich Lessing/Art Resource, NY; p. 323: Leemage/Getty Images; p. 327 (left): Vanni Archive/Corbis Documentary/Getty Images; p. 327 (right): Patrick Ward/Corbis/VCG/Getty Images; p. 328: Bettmann/Getty Images; p. 331 (left): Gary Cook/Alamy Stock Photo; p. 331 (right): Christine Osborne Pictures/Alamy Stock Photo; p. 336 (left): Nestorian subject, perhaps Palm

Sunday, mural painting from Cristano Qoco Temple, Xinjiang, China, Chinese Civilization, Tang Dynasty, late 9th century, Chinese School, (9th century)/ Dahlem Museums, Berlin/De Agostini Picture Library/Bridgeman Images; p. 336 (right): akg-images; p. 338: The Art Archive/REX/Shutterstock; p. 339 (left): Forman Archive/REX/ Shutterstock; p. 339 (right): Kurt and Rosalia Scholz/SuperStock; p. 340: Julia Waterlow/Corbis Documentary/Getty Images; p. 345: John Stevenson/Asian Art & Archaeology, Inc./CORBIS/Getty Images; p. 346 (left): © The Trustees of the British Museum/Art Resource, NY; p. 346 (right): CulturalEyes - AusGS2/ Alamy Stock Photo; p. 348 (top): Reconstruction of the Palatine Chapel of Aix-la-Chapelle (w/c on paper), French School, (20th century)/Archives Larousse, Paris, France/Bridgeman Images; p. 348 (bottom): akg-images; p. 350: CCI/REX/Shutterstock; p. 352 (left): imageBROKER/Alamy Stock Photo; p. 352 (right): robertharding/ Alamy Stock Photo; p. 353 (left): Forman Archive/REX/Shutterstock; p. 354 (right): INTERFOTO/Alamy Stock Photo.

Text Credits Page 320: Excerpts from The Qur'an, translated by Marmaduke Pickthall; revised by Jane Dammen McAuliffe. From *The Norton Anthology of World Religions: Islam*, edited by Jack Miles, et. al. Copyright © 2015 by W.W. Norton & Company, Inc. Used by permission of W.W. Norton & Company, Inc.

CHAPTER 10

Photo Credits Page 356: Ramon Manent/REX/Shutterstock; p. 358: Nik Wheeler/Corbis Documentary/ Getty Images; p. 359: Granger, NYC— All rights reserved; p. 361: Wikimedia Commons; p. 364: Peter Guttman/ Corbis Documentary/Getty Images; p. 367 (top): Keren Su/Corbis Documentary/Getty Images; p. 367 (bottom): Macduff Everton/Corbis Documentary/ Getty Images; p. 368: Rogers Fund, 1918 © The Metropolitan Museum of Art; p. 371 (top): Tom Cockrem/Lonely Planet Images/Getty Images; p. 371 (bottom): Wikimedia Commons; p. 372: Granger, NYC—All rights reserved; p. 374 (top): akg-images/Werner Forman;

p. 374 (bottom): Yann Arthus Bertrand/ Getty Images; p. 377: Erich Lessing/ Art Resource, NY; p. 378 (top): Hubert Stadler/Corbis Documentary/Getty Images; p. 378 (bottom): akg-images/ Volker Kreidler; p. 380: Mondadori Portfolio/Universal Images Group/Getty Images; p. 381: © British Library Board/ Robana/Art Resource, NY; p. 383: Snark/ Art Resource, NY; p. 386: Ramon Manent/ REX/Shutterstock; p. 387 (top): Gavin Hellier/Alamy Stock Photo; p. 387 (bottom): Kaku Suzuki/Sebun Photo/amana images RM/Getty Images; p. 388: Persian School/Getty Images; p. 390 (top): Beren Patterson/Alamy Stock Photo; p. 390 (middle): Kevin Schafer/Corbis Documentary/Getty Images; p. 390 (bottom): INTERFOTO/Alamy Stock Photo; p. 392: Michael S. Lewis/Corbis Documentary/Getty Images; p. 393: akg-images; p. 396: Bettmann/Getty Images; p. 399: Granger, NYC—All rights reserved.

Text Credits Page 362: "Writing from Alexandria after Arrival from the Muslim West," republished with the permission of Princeton University Press from *Letters of Medieval Jewish Traders*, translated by S.D. Goitein. © 1973 Princeton University Press; p. 373: "Tale of the Genji," translated by Arthur Waley. From *Sources of Japanese Tradition, Vol. 1*, compiled by Ryusaku Tsunoda, Wm. Theodore de Bary and Donald Keene, pp. 177–79. Copyright © 1958 Columbia University Press. Reprinted with permission of the publisher; p. 385: From *Sundiata: An Epic of Old Mali*, by D. T. Niane, English translation by by G.D. Pickett, pp. 40–41. Copyright © 1965 Longman Group. Originally published as *Soundjata ou l'épopée mandingue*. Copyright © 1960 Présence Africaine. Reprinted with permission of Pearson Education Limited and Présence Africaine.

CHAPTER 11

Photo Credits Page 402: Snark/Art Resource; p. 405: Sarin Images/Granger, NYC—All rights reserved; p. 411: Album/ Art Resource, NY; p. 413: robertharding/ Alamy Stock Photo; p. 414: View of the Inner Courtyard of the Seraglio, Topkapi Palace, Constantinople, engraved by Schroeder and Desmaisons, 1815

(aquatint), Melling, Anton Ignaz (1763–1831) (after)/Private Collection/The Stapleton Collection/Bridgeman Images; p. 415: A Janissary officer recruiting devsirme for Sultan Suleyman I (1495-1566), from the 'Suleymanname' (Mss Hazine. 1517 f.31v), 1558 (ink & gold leaf on vellum), Ali Amir Beg (fl. 1558)/Topkapi Palace Museum, Istanbul, Turkey/ Bridgeman Images; p. 417: Timur's defeat of Amlu Khan and the capture of Delhi. A miniature painting from a sixteenth century manuscript of the Zafarnama./ British Library, London, UK/© British Library Board. All Rights Reserved/ Bridgeman Images; p. 422: Jam World Images/Alamy Stock Photo; p. 424 (left): Images Group/REX/Shutterstock; p. 424 (right): Scala/Ministero per i Beni e le Attività culturali/Art Resource, NY; p. 427: Granger, NYC—All rights reserved; p. 428: The Art Archive/ REX/Shutterstock; p. 430: © RMN-Grand Palais/Art Resource, NY; p. 432: © RMN-Grand Palais/Art Resource, NY; p. 433: China: Detail from the painting 'Beauties in History', attributed to the Ming Dynasty artist Qiu Ying (c. 1492-1552)/Pictures from History/Bridgeman Images; p. 434: The Jan Adkins Studio.

Text Credits Page 410: Ahmet T. Karamustafa, from *God's Unruly Friends: Dervish Groups in the Islamic Later Middle Period*, pp. 6–7, © Ahmet T. Karamustafa 1994. Reprinted with the permission of University of Utah Press; p. 418: "Nanak and His Teaching," from *Sources of Indian Tradition Vol. 2*, compiled by Wm. Theodore de Bary, Stephen Hay, Royal Weiler, Andrew Yarrow, pp. 536–538. Copyright © 1958 Columbia University Press. Reprinted with permission of the publisher; p. 425: "To Bibolo Semproni" from *Laura Cereta: Collected Letters of a Renaissance Feminist*, transcribed, translated and edited by Diana Robin (Chicago: University of Chicago Press, 1997), pp. 74–79. © 1977 by The University of Chicago. Reprinted by permission of the University of Chicago Press; p. 429: "Proclamations of the Hongwu Emperor," from *Chinese Civilization: A Sourcebook, 2nd Edition* by Patricia Buckley Ebrey. Copyright © 1981 by The Free Press, a Division of Simon & Schuster, Inc. Copyright © 1993 by Patricia Buckley Ebrey. Reprinted by permission of Simon & Schuster, Inc. All rights reserved.

INDEX